WITHDRAWN
UTSA LIBRARIES

AGING AND MENTAL HEALTH

POSITIVE PSYCHOSOCIAL AND BIOMEDICAL APPROACHES

FIFTH EDITION

ROBERT N. BUTLER, M.D.
Mount Sinai School of Medicine

MYRNA I. LEWIS, M.S.W.
Mount Sinai School of Medicine

TREY SUNDERLAND, M.D.
National Institute of Mental Health

ALLYN AND BACON
Boston   London   Toronto   Sydney   Tokyo   Singapore

Editor-in-Chief, Social Sciences: Karen Hanson
Series Editor, Social Work and Family Therapy: Judy Fifer
Editorial Assistant: Mary Visco
Marketing Manager: Susan E. Brown
Editorial-Production Administrator: Donna Simons
Editorial-Production Service: Omegatype Typography, Inc.
Composition and Prepress Buyer: Linda Cox
Manufacturing Buyer: David Suspanic
Cover Administrator: Jenny Hart
Electronic Composition: Omegatype Typography, Inc.

Copyright © 1998 by Allyn & Bacon
A Viacom Company
160 Gould Street
Needham Heights, MA 02194

Internet: www.abacon.com
America Online: Keyword: College Online

Previous editions copyright 1991 by Macmillan Publishing Company, 1986 by Merrill Publishing
Company, and 1982, 1977, 1973 by C. V. Mosby Company.

All rights reserved. No part of the material protected by this copyright notice may
be reproduced or utilized in any form or by any means, electronic or mechanical,
including photocopying, recording, or by any information storage and retrieval system,
without written permission from the copyright owner.

Library of Congress Cataloging-in-Publication Data
Butler, Robert N.
    Aging and mental health : positive psychosocial and biomedical
    approaches / Robert N. Butler, Myrna I. Lewis, Trey Sunderland. —
    5th ed.
        p.   cm.
    Includes bibliographical references and index.
    ISBN 0-205-19336-6
    1. Aged—Mental health.   2. Geriatric psychiatry.   3. Aged—Mental
health services—United States.   I. Lewis, Myrna I.
    II. Sunderland, Trey.   III. Title.
RC451.4.A5B87   1998
362.2′084′6—dc21   97-30861
                                                         CIP

Printed in the United States of America

Library
University of Texas
at San Antonio

CONTENTS

APPENDIXES   415

Foreword to the Fourth Edition

I have worked with the problems of those suffering from mental illnesses for many years, ever since I first became aware of their needs while campaigning with my husband for governor. What I have learned over these years of work and study is that mental illnesses are less understood than almost any other major health problem, and that most people who experience difficulties can be helped. Many suffer needlessly. The mystery, stigma, and misconceptions that surround mental illness prevent many people in need of psychiatric help from seeking treatment. This applies doubly to our older citizens, who experience not only the stigma of mental illness, but also the stigma of old age.

I first met Dr. Robert Butler when my husband was president, and I was honorary chairperson of the President's Commission on Mental Health. At the time, Dr. Butler was director of the National Institute on Aging and helped with the Commission's Task Force on Mental Health and Aging. We worked together again with the late Senator Claude Pepper on developing hearings on aging and mental health in Congress.

While working on the mental health commission I was shocked to find that not only is there a great need for mental health personnel for the elderly, but that there are relatively few doctors in our country trained in the special needs of our older citizens. In addition, older people continue to face the problems of insufficient access to mental health services under Medicare and of high incidences of Alzheimer's disease, depression, and suicide. The need to address such problems and make more progress in these areas will become increasingly important in the years ahead.

We are living longer and longer. The statistics are eye-opening: Today some 27.4 million Americans are over 65. The elderly over 75 are one of the fastest growing segments of the U.S. population, and within that segment the fastest growing group is the 100-year-old group. This "graying of America" is expected to continue so that by the year 2020, 20% of the population will be over 65. Demographics alone tell us that increasing demands are going to be placed on the health care system by the problems of the elderly. Also, just like others of us, the chronically mentally disabled, the mentally retarded, and the developmentally disabled are living into old age. They are going to need services, too.

One of my major concerns in the areas of mental illness and aging is the associated stigma. This is where I have spent the majority of my efforts, since this is the area in which I have always thought I might be able to help. I have had some good "bully pulpits." Since we left the White House, I have continued to have a forum at the Carter Center in Atlanta. Each year, we have a conference on a major mental health issue. My focus is still stigma, and in 1989 we combined my interest in the elderly and in mental health in a symposium entitled "Mental Illness and the Elderly: Double Stigma, Double Jeopardy."

The stereotypes of mentally ill people are absolutely misleading and create an atmosphere in which persons suffering from mental illness are hesitant to let anyone know about their problems, and therefore do not seek treatment. The sad part is that stereotypes of older citizens as unhappy, lonely, ill, frail, senile, unproductive, and disoriented cause people who are approaching retirement age to believe that this is going to happen to them and that their productive and enjoyable years are over.

Those of us in the fields of aging and mental health, both lay and professional, must work together to find ways to educate people and help eliminate the stigmas associated with being mentally ill and with being elderly. Robert Butler, Myrna Lewis, and Trey Sunderland have made significant contributions to this education, not only in helping us overcome the stigmas, but in writing a seminal book on mental health and aging that has already benefited many of those who deal with older people in emotional and other crises.

This fourth edition of *Aging and Mental Health* incorporates the progress that has been made in the field since the last edition in 1986. It includes advances in the fields of neurobiology and psychopharmacology, and changes in the theory and practice of psychotherapy. The book will appeal to a wide variety of professionals involved in the care of older people and will help them understand what keeps the old well, rather than merely what makes them ill. I hope that in addition to being read by those who work with the elderly, *Aging and Mental Health* will be read by older people in general.

Jimmy and I are convinced that our later years can be the best years of our lives. It takes some involvement. It takes some adjustment. It has already taken some adjustment in our own lives. But what is life if not adjustment—to different times, to changing circumstances, to shifting health habits, and to each other?

We are deeply indebted to Dr. Butler, Ms. Lewis, and Dr. Sunderland for their contributions in making life better for our older citizens and for us all.

Rosalynn Carter

PREFACE

The fifth edition of *Aging and Mental Health* constitutes a major revision of the entire book. This new edition uses the latest demographic and epidemiological data to create an all-encompassing portrait of older people in America today, their mental health care needs, and ways to respond to those needs. The book incorporates the newest information, often technical, concerning the dementias of old age, the neurobiology of depression, and geriatric psychopharmacology. The chapters concerning the dynamics of the family and the special issues that confront our multi-ethnic and multi-racial society are organized in a manner valuable to both the scholar and the practitioner. Family caregiving has been especially emphasized. The sections on psychiatric assessment, psychological testing, and individual treatment planning have been updated, and the full range of psychosocial and biological therapies are covered as well.

A number of important developments and trends since the last edition deserve mention, because they impact on the care and well-being of older persons. The failure of governmental health reforms proposed in 1994 has contributed to the growth of managed care. Without a doubt, managed care is having a profound and not always salutary influence on the delivery of mental health services beyond that occasioned by the introduction of either health insurance coverage for mental health services or the community mental health center movement. The failure of health care reform also underscores the need for a revitalized vision of long-term health care. Private long-term care insurance initiatives have advanced only modestly and are so costly that they are accessible to only a minority of Americans.

Tax resistance has been reinforced by ideological attacks on the "welfare state," with consequent reductions in Medicare, Medicaid, and various governmental services, as well as the transfer of welfare to the states, ending it as an entitlement. Under the new welfare law, states could decide to end Medicaid coverage of older legal immigrants presently residing in nursing homes.

The 1995 White House Conference on Aging called for the preservation of Medicare and Social Security, the Older Americans Act, and other programs devoted to serving older persons. To some degree, the delegates also called for intergenerational efforts to meet the needs of other age groups, particularly children. But although older Americans constitute an important constituency and although organizations that represent them, such as the American Association of Retired Persons and the National Council of Senior Citizens, have been effective up to a point, those organizations represent only a few of the many special interest groups in America and as such pale in comparison with other powerful groups.

Despite the fact that Medicare beneficiaries are older persons and the disabled, graduate medical education funds have gone primarily to support specialty medical training and relatively little to support fellowships in geriatrics. However, in 1996 the Health Care Financing Administration extended the full Medicare direct payment for geriatric psychiatry to a fifth year of residency.

Academic and clinical geriatrics have not developed significantly in the United States. There are only two academic departments of geriatrics among 140 allopathic and osteopathic medical schools. However, about 20 of the schools have major geriatrics programs. There are also now examinations for "certificates of added qualification" in geriatrics and geriatric psychiatry administered by the Boards of Internal Medicine, Family Medicine, and Psychiatry. It is hoped that medicine, along with nursing, social work, psychology, and other allied professions, will increasingly face the training and service challenge imposed by the growing number and proportion of older people.

Research in Alzheimer's disease has progressed. Particular attention is now being paid to the role of genetics in early onset cases and to amyloid deposits. Also, apolipoprotein E4 has been discovered to be a risk factor for developing Alzheimer's. However, there has been only modest progress in the realm of therapy. The Alzheimer's Association continues to play a critical role, contributing to advocacy, research, and services that offer caregivers relief from the burdens of caring for a family member with Alzheimer's.

The Open Society Institute, funded through the financier and philanthropist George Soros, created the Project on Death in America (PDIA), which is devoted to altering the experience and culture of dying. Issues regarding dying are major concerns that need to be addressed. Death and dying are inevitably entwined in the practices of mental health providers who work with older people, who deal with both the dying and survivors. Mental health providers confront a rising rate of depression and suicide among older persons, especially old men, in response to the realization of impending death. Physician-assisted suicide is a highly emotional national issue. In the Netherlands, physician-assisted suicide has been condoned even for such highly treatable conditions as depression. To many health care providers, the increasingly casual attitude toward physician-assisted suicide is a matter of great concern. Policy makers in the United States should pay close attention to the effects such legislation has had abroad.

HOW THIS BOOK IS ORGANIZED

Mental health care of the elderly involves members of many professions and service groups working collaboratively and collegially. These include physicians, social workers, nurses, and psychologists; nurses' aides and nursing assistants; homemaker/home health aides; physical, occupational, recreational, and speech therapists; and paraprofessionals of all kinds. Mental health practitioners ideally should have a broad-based set of skills so that they can provide optimal care to the elderly. For this reason, this book offers a wide range of knowledge and skills aimed at anyone involved with mental health care of the elderly, while targeting some chapters and parts of chapters toward specific practitioners.

Chapters 1 through 4 give an overview of the elderly sociologically, demographically, and epidemiologically (in terms of mental health issues), and provide a baseline of psychologically healthy old age against which to measure illness or problems. These chapters are designed for general use by all practitioners.

Chapter 5, "Common Psychiatric Disorders," Chapter 6, "Cognitive Disorders," and Chapter 13, "Drug and Other Somatic Therapies," have a dual purpose: (1) to give nonmedical practitioners up-to-date medical and psychiatric information that will enhance their work and (2) to provide in-depth information for medical students and physicians interested in geriatric mental health care. These are the most technical and demanding chapters, particularly the drug chapter, but we hope we have presented the material clearly enough without depending on jargon, so that anyone can gain a practical sense of what is involved in these areas and can make use of such knowledge.

Chapter 7, "Special Concerns," is an eclectic chapter, drawing together a number of important themes in work with older persons—race and ethnic issues, crime, elder abuse, the special problems of older women, alcoholism, sensory problems, and sexuality.

Chapter 8, "General Treatment Principles," and Chapter 12, "Psychotherapy and Environmental Therapy," focus on the psychotherapy aspects of medical health care. It is here that we rely most heavily on our own clinical work and that of others in an ongoing effort to delineate a "psychotherapy of aging."

Chapter 9, "Diagnostic Evaluation," demonstrates more clearly than any other chapter the complexities of mental health care of the elderly—the need to consider as a whole the many aspects of each person's life in arriving at a diagnosis and treatment plan, and the need to enlist the skills of a wide variety of professional and service groups. This chapter leads inexorably to the understanding that no one profession can claim centrality; all are important at different times for different reasons and should be linked in a comprehensive package of evaluation and care.

Chapter 10, "How to Keep People at Home," and Chapter 11, "Proper Institutional Care," look at the continuum of mental health care now available, both in terms of the physical location in which care is given and the range of services that should be available at any stage of an older person's care. These chapters present the issues in the current national policy debate over long-term care—issues that should be understood by all mental health practitioners.

The appendixes have been carefully updated and expanded, and it is our intent that they will serve as convenient and useful references for a wealth of specific information related to mental health care of the elderly.

The Selected Readings at the end of each chapter represent literature particularly pertinent to each topic, both classic references as well as newer information. The endnotes provide additional reference sources.

Readers of the previous editions of this book often told us how much they enjoyed the photographs, which offered significant insights into the human condition in late life. However, those photographs were unavailable for this new edition of the text.

ACKNOWLEDGMENTS

We are exceptionally indebted to Mia Oberlink and Alexis Stern for their patience, dedication, excellent research, and editorial support in this major revision. Milagros Marrero, Morriseen Barmore, and Tomasina Wilson facilitated the work in an exemplary manner.

PART ONE

THE NATURE AND PROBLEMS OF OLD AGE

CHAPTER 1

WHO ARE THE ELDERLY?

In this chapter we will acquaint you with a general profile of the United States' older population as well as detail some specifics about the more disadvantaged minorities. Successful intervention in meeting the mental health needs of older people depends on maintaining a basic awareness of the general facts of their lives while focusing attention on the unique social, economic, and familial context of each individual.

WHO ARE THE ELDERLY?

This is a century marked by great changes and achievements for the elderly. The most spectacular is a gain of some 25 years in average life expectancy—and the century is not yet over. This gain, found throughout the industrialized world, is nearly equal to the added years of life expectancy amassed during the preceding 5,000 years of human history from the Bronze Age (3000 B.C.) until today. In the United States, the average life expectancy has grown by 28 years since the year 1900. At the founding of the American Republic

in 1776, the average life expectancy for men and women was 35. Today it is over over 75. This longevity revolution, attributed to a combination of better public sanitation and personal hygiene, improved nutrition, and general medical progress, provides the backdrop for the focus of our discussions on aging and mental health.

How do older people first come to the attention of mental health personnel? We will give a few typical examples of situations that are likely to propel older people into the hands of those who offer mental health services.

Mr. H is an 80-year-old white, middle-class male who retired two years ago. Since that time, his wife, family, and friends report that he has become increasingly depressed. His chief complaint is dizziness and chest discomfort, but upon lying down, all the symptoms disappear. He has seen approximately 20 physicians and has had dozens of examinations without any positive findings. After the psychiatrist diagnosed his problem as depression, he became angry and denied it. He maintained that if he was depressed it was because of the failure to find a reason for his symptoms—that the depression was not primary, but secondary. It was also apparent that Mr. H sustained some memory loss.

Is Mr. H suffering from depression, or does he have incipient Alzheimer's disease with accompanying depression, in part reactive to the dementia, but also possibly part of the dementia process per se? Should he return to his doctor for neuropsychological evaluation and Holter monitoring of blood pressure and other vital signs? Could circulatory disease be playing a part?

Mr. K is African American, age 66. He has come to a psychiatric hospital on his own, stating that he is depressed and has recently felt almost uncontrollable impulses to harm others. Occasionally he worries that he is being followed, that his phone may be tapped, or that his food has been tampered with. He appears in poor health and is underweight, although dressed neatly and appropriately. He lives with a 68-year-old widowed sister in two rented rooms; he was married and separated years ago and has no children. He has been employed regularly all his life in a variety of jobs, from service station attendant to cook in a hamburger shop. Two years ago he was forced to stop work because of ill health, but his sister is still employed as a housekeeper. Income is minimal. He responds to an African American female nursing assistant at the hospital with an outpouring of his feelings of anger and bewilderment but becomes strikingly passive and vague in the presence of both black and white male resident physicians.

Are Mr. K's psychiatric symptoms a result of his personality characteristics and early history? Or could a physical disease condition be affecting his personality? What part may be played by malnutrition? Is he underweight because he is either physically sick or psychologically unable to care for himself, or is it because he has almost no money for food from month to month? Is his depression an acute reaction to physical illness or a lifelong response to social conditions? Why does he speak to the nursing assistant but turn silent at the sight of doctors? Why does he seem to have so little retirement income?

Mrs. P, white, age 88, has become disoriented and wanders out on the streets at night. After neighbors called the police, a public health nurse was notified and made a home visit. Mrs. P's husband died 15 years previously, and she has been living alone in a home they purchased 50 years ago in the central part of the city. Her income is higher than that of most widows. The home is orderly but badly in need of repair. The heat has been turned off by the gas company. Mrs. P's hearing has deteriorated. She expresses a terror of intruders and has armed herself with a stick and a kitchen knife. She determinedly announces she will never leave her home.

Why is she living alone in a big house, and why has she allowed the home to deteriorate and the gas to be shut off? Is her disorientation caused by poor health, isolation resulting from hearing loss, or lack of a proper diet? Is her fear of intruders exaggerated or realistic in her neighborhood? What has she been doing with her money, since she appears to have very little food? Should she be moved forcibly to a nursing institution, or is there some way to help her remain at home?

70-year-old Mr. H is Asian American. He has contacted a private psychiatrist because he is feeling suicidal. He is well-off financially, lives with his wife, but feels increasingly upset and self-destructive. He retired as a college professor earlier in the year. His health is good but recently he has panicked because he feels his memory is failing.

Is Mr. H overreacting to a minor memory change? If so, why is this so upsetting to him? Or does he perhaps have an undiagnosed brain disease? Are suicidal thoughts rare for a man his age?

Mrs. F is a 79-year-old, Spanish-speaking woman who is progressively disoriented and confused. She becomes agitated at night and has been returned home by neighbors and police after being found confused, walking the streets. She has been incontinent of urine and feces but has no apparent neurological symptoms. Is she suffering from senile dementia of the Alzheimer type? If so, can she be cared for at home? Is the disease treatable?

Each of these older persons came to the attention of mental health personnel because of psychiatric symptoms. But evaluation of the symptoms requires an understanding of the person's entire life situation—physical status, personality, family history, racial and ethnic background, income, housing, social status, educational level. Realistic and appropriate treatment is greatly facilitated by a fairly sophisticated understanding of social, psychological, and medical phenomena. We shall therefore proceed with an overview of the social and environmental realities of older persons in order to provide a background for our later discussion of the more specific aspects of their mental health care.

WHAT AGE IS CONSIDERED "OLDER"?

Aging, of course, begins with conception. The selection of age 65 for use as the demarcation between middle and old age is an arbitrary one, patterned after social legislation of the late nineteenth and early twentieth centuries. This definition of old age has been adhered to for social purposes—as a means of determining the point of retirement or the point of eligibility for various services available to older persons. But the age of 65 has more limited relevance in describing other aspects of functioning such as general health, mental capacity, psychological or physical endurance, or creativity. Gerontologists have attempted to deal with this unreliable concept of "oldness" after 65 by dividing old age into two groups: early old age, 65 to 74 years, and advanced old age, 75 and above. But the obvious point is that age is a convenient yet frequently inaccurate indicator of a person's physical and mental status and must not be relied on too heavily for evidence about human beings.

NUMBER OF OLDER PERSONS
IN THE UNITED STATES

Total Older Population

In the United States in 1995 there were an estimated 33.5 million people age 65 and older—

about 13% of the population.[2] 18.8 million people were 65 to 74 years old, 11.1 million were 75 to 84, 3.6 million were 85 years old and older, and 1.3 million were at least 90 years of age.[3] The 75-plus and 85-plus age groups are the fastest growing age segments of the U.S. population. These statistics are of great social, economic, and medical importance because of the dramatic increase in the need for care in the 75-plus and, especially, in the 85-plus age groups. Over 40% of nursing home residents are age 85 and older, and 75% are at least age 75. In 1990, 24% of those age 85 and older lived in nursing homes.[4] The 85-plus population is expected to double in size between 1995 and 2030, and to be five times as large in 2050.[5]

The number of people age 100 and older is also growing. In 1980 there were approximately 15,000 centenarians in the United States. By 1995, the number of centenarians had grown to about 53,000. Eighty-three percent of centenarians were women, 17% were men; 85% were white, 13% were African American, 2% were other races.[6] In 1980, 80% of centenarians were widowed, 10% were married, 8% were never married, 2% were divorced or separated; 82% were American born, 18% were immigrants.[7] The Bureau of the Census estimates that there will be over 800,000 American centenarians by the year 2050.[8] In all nations—including the developing nations—there is an increase in the absolute numbers of older people because of major decreases in maternal, childhood, and infant mortality as well as in middle- and late-life mortality from heart disease and stroke. In the developed nations there is also a significant increase in the relative proportions of older versus younger persons.

The age composition of the United States is undergoing extraordinary change. In 1900 the average life expectancy was 47 years and only 4% of the population was 65 and older. The high rates of maternal, childhood, and infant mortality contributed to the low life expectancy. Social, economic, and health progress have made a vast difference. By 1991 the average life expectancy at birth was greater than 75.[9]

Between the years 2020 and 2030—when the post–World War II baby boom grows old—about 20%, or one of five, U.S. citizens could be over 65 according to current projections (Figures 1.1 and 1.2). It is important to note that so far in the twentieth century, all projections of the numbers of older people have turned out to be underestimations. This is partly because of the unprecedented drops in mortality in the middle and later years from heart disease and stroke, which have coincided with improvements in risk factors such as smoking, high blood pressure, and high blood cholesterol, as well as greater access to sophisticated medical services. A continuing 0.6% annual decline in deaths is projected by the Social Security Administration until the year 2070, for a total decline of 36% between 1996 and 2070.[10] In fact, breakthroughs in research on the prevention and treatment of cancer alone could lead to annual mortality reductions far in excess of current predictions. The other major factor in the underestimation is a drop in the birthrate, bringing it below zero population growth. In summary, with new medical discoveries, improved health care, and a persisting low birthrate, the population of older persons may increase dramatically. Researchers at the National Institute on Aging and the University of Southern California, Los Angeles, predict that by the year 2040 the number of Americans age 65 and over could reach 86.8 million and the number of elderly age 85 and over could reach 23.5 million.

This "demographic revolution" should be seen as a triumph of survivorship rather than as a cause for despair. What it means is that more and more people have the opportunity to live out a full life course.[11] This revolution or triumph will increase the median age of the population from 30 in 1980 and 34.3 in 1995, a record high, to a peak of 38.7 in 2035[12]—hardly an "aging" or "graying" soci-

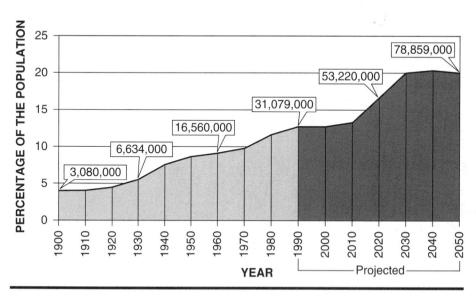

FIGURE 1.1   Percentage of U.S. population age 65 and older from 1900 to 1990, with projections for 2000 to 2050

Sources: Data for 1900 to 1990 from: U.S. Bureau of the Census (1996). *65+ in the United States. Current population reports, special studies,* Series P-23, No. 190. Washington, DC: U.S. Government Printing Office. Projections for 2000 to 2050 from: U.S. Bureau of the Census (1996). Population projections by age, sex, race and hispanic origin: 1995–2050. *Current population reports,* Series P-25, No. 1130. Washington, DC: U.S. Government Printing Office.

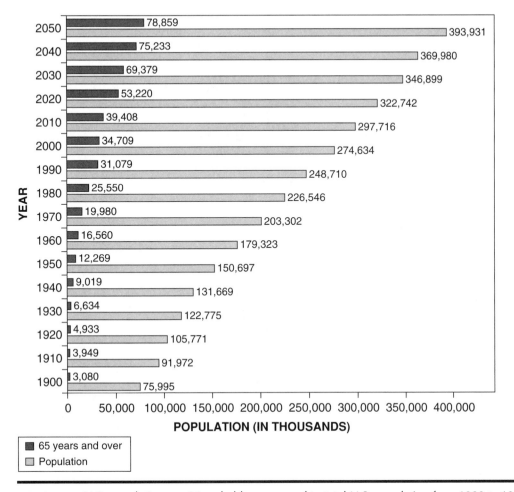

FIGURE 1.2   U.S. population age 65 and older compared to total U.S. population from 1900 to 1990, with projections for 2000 to 2050

Sources: Data for 1900 to 1990 from: U.S. Bureau of the Census (1996). 65+ in the United States. *Current population reports, special studies,* Series P-23, No. 190. Washington, DC: U.S. Government Printing Office. Projections for 2000 to 2050 from: U.S. Bureau of the Census (1996). Population projections by age, sex, race and hispanic origin: 1995–2050. *Current population reports,* Series P-25, No. 1130. Washington, DC: U.S. Government Printing Office.

ety but certainly one with a different blend of age groups and generations. The age distribution of the total population in 1995 compared to 2050 provides a clearer overall picture of our future society than either the percentage of persons over 65 or the median age (Figure 1.3).

A word should be said here about the considerable concern of policymakers and the public over what is known as the "dependency ratio"—

the income maintenance and health costs of the burgeoning older population. In truth, the proportional financial "burden" on the middle working generations has not changed much because there are also fewer children and youths for these people to support (Table 1.1). Figure 1.4 compares the actual and projected distribution of children and the elderly from 1900 to 2050. Needed, of course, is an analysis of the actual cost of care of those

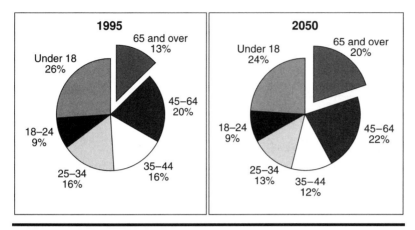

FIGURE 1.3   Age distribution of total population of the U.S. in 1995 compared to projections for the year 2050

Sources: Data for 1995 from: U.S. Bureau of the Census (February 14, 1996). *U.S. population estimates by age, sex, race, and hispanic origin: 1990–1995.* PPL-41. Washington, DC: Population Projections Branch, Population Division, U.S. Bureau of the Census. Projections for 2050 from: U.S. Bureau of the Census (1996). Population projections by age, sex, race and hispanic origin: 1995–2050. *Current population reports,* Series P-25, No. 1130. Washington, DC: U.S. Government Printing Office.

under 18 compared to that of those over 64. All sources of funding have to be considered. If one looks only at federal funding, older persons seem to receive more than young people, including children. On the other hand, the public education of children is supported primarily by local property taxes in order to reduce central governmental control of education.

Of the present older population, 8.6% were born somewhere other than in the United States. Many immigrated in their youth with the great migrations from Europe. Others came later from countries like Mexico and Cuba. Not all are citizens of the United States, not all speak English, and many still carry on the customs and cultural patterns of their mother countries in adapting to old age. This adds to the richness and uniqueness of the older population but makes the provision of services in later life more complicated.

Men versus Women

This is not only the century of increasing proportions of older people but also the century of increasing proportions of older women. A marked difference exists between the life expectancies of men and women (Table 1.2). As of 1991 in the United States, women are expected to live 6.9 years longer from birth and 3.8 years longer from age 65. Older women numbered more than 19.8 million in 1995 compared to 13.7 million men. Women outlive men every place in the world where women no longer perform backbreaking physical labor and where adequate sanitation and a reduced maternal mortality rate are present.

In 1995 there were 104.8 females per 100 males in the total U.S. population. More boy babies were born than girl babies, and males continue to outnumber females until age 30. At this point a shift occurs in the opposite direction, becoming most pronounced in the older generations. The life expectancy of a baby boy born in the United States in 1991 is 72 years and that of a baby girl is 78.9 years, almost 7 years longer. In 1991, for people who were already 65 years old, life expectancy was 17.4 additional years, again with a differential between men (15.3 years) and women (19.1 years).

TABLE 1.1   "Dependency ratio": comparison of numbers of persons under 18 and over 65 (the "dependents") to the middle generations (the "workers")

YEAR	NUMBER OF PERSONS UNDER AGE 18 PER 100 PERSONS AGE 18 TO 64	NUMBER OF PERSONS AGE 65+ PER 100 PERSONS AGE 18 TO 64	TOTAL NUMBER OF "DEPENDENTS" PER 100 "WORKERS"
Estimates			
1900	72.6	7.3	79.9
1910	65.7	7.5	73.2
1920	64.0	8.0	72.0
1930	58.6	9.1	67.7
1940	48.8	10.9	59.7
1950	51.1	13.4	64.5
1960	65.3	16.9	82.2
1970	61.1	17.6	78.7
1980	46.2	18.7	64.9
1990	41.7	20.3	62.0
Projections			
1995	42.8	20.9	63.7
2000	41.8	20.5	52.4
2010	39.0	21.2	60.2
2020	40.4	27.7	68.2
2030	43.0	35.7	78.7
2040	43.1	36.6	79.7
2050	43.9	36.0	79.9

Source: U.S. Bureau of the Census. (Feb. 1996.) Population projections of the United States by age, sex, race, and hispanic origin: 1995 to 2050. *Current population reports,* P25-1130. Washington, DC: U.S. Government Printing Office, p. 9.

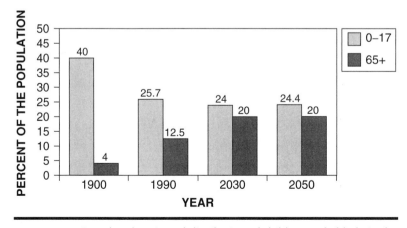

FIGURE 1.4   Actual and projected distribution of children and elderly in the population: 1900–2050

Adapted from: U.S. Bureau of the Census (1996). Population projections of the United States, by age, sex, race, and hispanic origin: 1995–2050. *Current population reports,* P25-1130. Washington DC: U.S. Government Printing Office, p. 10.

TABLE 1.2   Life expectancy at birth and age 65 by race and sex: 1900–1991

YEAR	ALL RACES[1]			WHITE			BLACK		
	BOTH SEXES	MALE	FEMALE	BOTH SEXES	MALE	FEMALE	BOTH SEXES	MALE	FEMALE
At birth									
1900[2,3]	47.3	46.3	48.3	47.6	46.6	48.7	33.0[4]	32.5[4]	33.5[4]
1950[3]	68.2	65.6	71.1	69.1	66.5	72.2	60.7	58.9	62.7
1960[3]	69.7	66.6	73.1	70.6	67.4	74.1	63.2	60.7	65.9
1970	70.8	67.1	74.7	71.7	68.0	75.6	64.1	60.0	68.3
1980	73.7	70.0	77.4	74.4	70.7	78.1	68.1	63.8	72.5
1985	74.7	71.1	78.2	75.3	71.8	78.7	69.3	65.0	73.4
1990	75.4	71.8	78.8	76.1	72.7	79.4	69.1	64.5	73.6
1991	75.5	72.0	78.9	76.3	72.9	79.6	69.3	64.6	73.8
At 65 years									
1990–1902[2,3]	11.9	11.5	12.2	*	11.5	12.2	*	10.4	11.4
1950[3]	13.9	12.8	15.0	*	12.8	15.1	13.9	12.9	14.9
1960[3]	14.3	12.8	15.8	14.4	12.9	15.9	13.9	12.7	15.1
1970	15.2	13.1	17.0	15.2	13.1	17.1	14.2	12.5	15.7
1980	16.4	14.1	18.3	16.5	14.2	18.4	15.1	13.0	16.8
1985	16.7	14.5	18.5	16.8	14.5	18.7	15.2	13.0	16.9
1990	17.2	15.1	18.9	17.3	15.2	19.1	15.4	13.2	17.2
1991	17.4	15.3	19.1	17.5	15.4	19.2	15.5	13.4	17.2

Source: National Center for Health Statistics (April, 1995). *Trends in the health of older Americans: United States, 1994.* Series 3: *Analytical and epidemiological studies* No. 30. DHHS Publication No. (PHS)95–1414. Hyattsville, MD: U.S. Dept. of Health and Human Services.

[1]Data includes races other than white and black.

[2]Death registration area only. The death registration area increased from 10 states and the District of Columbia in 1900 to the coterminous United States in 1933.

[3]Includes deaths of nonresidents of the United States.

[4]Figure is for "all other" population.

In the United States women outlive men because of the higher male mortality from arteriosclerotic heart disease, lung cancer and emphysema (associated with tobacco intake), industrial accidents and toxicity, motor vehicle and other accidents, suicide, cirrhosis of the liver (associated with alcoholism), and so forth. These account for perhaps three-quarters of the sex differential in mortality—the other one-quarter is still unclear.[13] Life-style, life stress, hormonal differences, genetic differences in immune resistance, and other possible differences between the sexes must be further studied.[14] Fears that American women will lose their capacity for long life

as they move into the labor force (the proportion of women in the labor force increased from 28% in 1950 to 58% in 1990; most were married women) have so far been unsubstantiated. For example, an eight-year study of 352 housewives, 387 working women, and 580 men involved in the Framingham Heart Study found that working women did not have a significantly higher incidence of coronary heart disease (CHD) than did housewives (7.8% versus 5.4%), and, in fact, those women working the longest period of time, for example, single women, had the lowest rate of CHD. (A factor here could be that relatively healthy women are the most likely to join the labor force, leaving less healthy women at home.) However, clerical workers with children who were married to men in blue-collar jobs had a higher risk of CHD. This suggests either that clerical work is a particularly stressful occupation, especially when combined with the demands of raising a family, or that women with personalities prone to develop stress diseases select clerical work when they become employed. Elderly women outnumber elderly men three to two. In 1995, for every 100 women age 65–69, there were only 83 men in that same age group. The ratio continues to widen with age, with only 39 men per 100 women in the 85-plus category.

African Americans[15] versus Whites

The survival pattern for the white U.S. population has always been more favorable than that of non-white populations.[15] In 1950, life expectancy at birth for whites was 8.4 years longer than that for blacks. In 1983 and 1984 the difference narrowed to 5.6 years. Unfortunately, due to higher death rates from killings, accidents, and diseases such as AIDS and tuberculosis, as well as a higher infant mortality rate, in 1991 the difference in life expectancy between blacks and whites grew to 7 years. For black men, the difference was 11.7 years (76.3 years for whites of both sexes, 64.6 years for black men). However, differences in life expectancy from age 65 are smaller. In 1991, at age 65, black men could expect to live 13.4 more years, compared to 15.4 more years for white men. Black women age 65 could expect to live 17.2 years, 2 years less than white women.[17]

The number of black older persons has risen from 1.2 million in 1960 to 2.7 million in 1995. Black older persons constituted slightly over 8% of the total black population of almost 34 million in 1995. Their lower life expectancy results, we can safely assume, from the generally lower socioeconomic status accorded to blacks in the United States.

Although they comprise almost 13% of the total population, blacks make up only 8% of the older age group. The effects of institutionalized racism fall most heavily on black men—their life expectancy in 1991 of 64.6 years was 8.3 years less than that of white men, who could expect to live 72.9 years. White and black women had life expectancies of 79.6 and 73.8 respectively, with a 5.8 year difference between them (see Table 1.2).

Black older women outlive black men to an increasing degree, as do their white counterparts. The ratio of older black men per 100 black women has decreased from 83 in 1960 to 63 in 1995, and black females made up 62% of the total black population in 1995.

The Impact of Socioeconomic Class on Survivorship

One's class definitely affects one's life expectancy. Demographic data show conclusively that an increasing life expectancy follows in the wake of increasing income and status. Professional and white-collar workers have lower mortality than blue-collar workers. In fact, the impact of social class may be even greater than is currently evident. Mortality studies are usually done by demographers and epidemiologists rather than by economists, and thus most studies fail to take note of wealth beyond yearly income. Yet such wealth enormously affects the capacity to maintain health (through greater opportunities for rest, good nutrition, recreation, emotional security, and status) and to treat illness (through greater access to the finest acute and chronic care).

MARITAL STATUS

In looking at the marital situation of older people, one fact becomes strikingly clear. Most older men are married (77% in 1994); most older women are widows (47%; See Table 1.3). One finds over five times as many widows as widowers. This imbalance of women versus men, resulting from a combination of the greater female life expectancy and the fact that most women are younger than their husbands to begin with, represents one of the most striking consequences of old age in its present form. Older men, if they survive, have greater

TABLE 1.3   Distribution of older persons by marital status, 1900 and 1994

STATUS	1994		1900	
	MEN	**WOMEN**	**MEN**	**WOMEN**
Married	77.2	42.8	67.3	34.3
Widowed	13.1	46.4	26.5	59.5
Other				
Divorced	5.0	6.0	0.5	0.3
Never married	4.7	4.3	5.8	6.0

Source: U.S. Bureau of the Census (1994). Marital Status and Living Arrangements: March 1994. *Current population reports,* P20-484. Washington DC: U.S. Government Printing Office.

options with regard to the opposite sex than women do. Chances are their wives are younger and will outlive them. But if not, a man can quite easily find a second wife. The odds are with him. There are many women from whom to choose. It is socially acceptable for a man to find a partner in either his own age group or any of the younger age groups. An older woman, however, may be looked on with suspicion if she marries or even simply dates someone much younger, although this attitude is slowly changing. In 1990, about 71,000 persons age 65 and over married in the United States. Of these 25,000 were women; 46,000 were men.

The 1987 Commonwealth Fund Commission on Elderly People Living Alone provided a close-up of the realities that older people living alone face. They experience double the poverty, tend to be persons 75 and older, are largely women, and are at higher risk of hospitalization and institutionalization. Many are overwhelmed by the situation in which they find themselves, and present government policies do not adequately address the structural problems they confront.

A larger number of older African Americans than whites do not live with their spouses. This has been attributed to the greater economic pressures on families, including unemployment and public welfare laws that have encouraged black men to leave home early in life. The shorter life expectancy of black men also is an important factor, leaving a black married woman widowed much earlier than a white married woman.

HOUSING STATUS

With Whom Do Older Persons Live?

One of the still prevalent myths about older people is that large numbers of them live in institutions: chronic disease hospitals, homes for the aged, nursing homes, mental institutions, foster homes, and so on. If one asks any group of ordinary citizens—or for that matter a group of medical, nursing, or social work students—what percentage of older people live in such settings, the answers will range all the way up to 50%. The reality is that at any one time only 5% of all older people are in such institutions.[18] This is, of course, a substantial number of people and rightly deserves serious attention. But it is important to remember that in 1994, 95% lived in the community, either by themselves (30%), with spouses (55%), with children or other relatives (12%), or with nonrelatives (2%). Again the situation differs with regard to men and women. Men, because of their shorter life expectancy, usually live with a spouse or other family members. But only slightly more than half of women do so. Women are over twice as likely to live alone or with nonrelatives. In 1994, 7.2 million older women lived alone compared with 2 million older men.[19]

In reference to the older African American population, another widely held idea bears another look. It has been frequently stated that older African Americans are more likely to live in extended families than are older whites. Yet in 1995, 31% of black people age 65 and older lived entirely alone. In addition, black men are more likely to live alone than white men (see Figure 1.5). It is true that older black persons are more likely than older white persons to be living with relatives other than their spouses: 24% of older blacks, as compared to 11% of older whites, lived with relatives. We can surmise that this is a result of economic necessity or convenience, which solidified in a cultural style of living earlier in the life cycle. Data contrasting men and women show that 63% of all older black men live with their wives but, again because of longer life expectancy, only 28% of older black women live with their husbands.[20]

Geographical Distribution

Up to the present, older people lived most frequently in central parts of cities and in rural locations. But in 1980, for the first time, a greater number of older persons lived in the suburbs (10.1

million) than in central cities (8.1 million). The Midwest and upper New England rural areas have concentrations of older people because many of the young have left the farms. Older people have the lowest migration rates of all age groups; those older persons who do migrate tend to be the most affluent. Florida has the highest proportion of elderly, with 19% of its population comprised of older residents in 1993. Over one quarter of the older people in the United States live in three states: California, New York, and Florida. Over half of the nation's aged live in nine states, adding Pennsylvania, Texas, Illinois, Ohio, New Jersey, and Michigan. In 33 states older people comprise at least 14% of the total population (see Figure 1.6). New York, California, and Florida each have more than 2 million older residents, while Illinois, Ohio, Texas, Pennsylvania, Michigan, and New Jersey each have more than 1 million older persons. The highest growth in percentage since 1980 is in Alaska, Arizona, Florida, Hawaii,

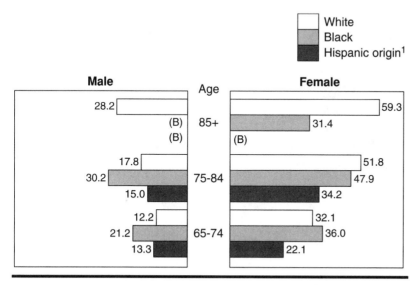

FIGURE 1.5   Percent of persons 65 years and over living alone by age, sex, race, and hispanic origin: 1993 (Civilian noninstitutional population)

Source: U.S. Bureau of the Census (1996). *65+ in the United States. Current population reports, special studies,* Series P-23, No. 190. Washington, DC: U.S. Government Printing Office.

B Base is less than 75,000.

[1]Hispanic origin may be of any race.

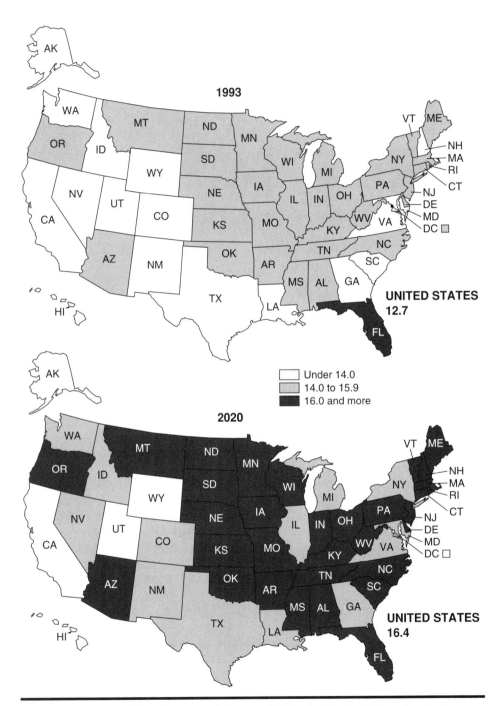

FIGURE 1.6   Percent of total state population aged 65 and older in 1993 and projections for 2020

Source: U.S. Bureau of the Census (1996). *65+ in the United States. Current population reports, special studies,* Series P-23, No. 190. Washington, DC: U.S. Government Printing Office.

Nevada, and New Mexico—with the exception of Alaska, these states have warm climates and low industrialization, which older people find appealing.[21]

Older African Americans show a somewhat different geographic distribution than older people as a whole. Over half still reside in the South, many in rural areas. But because large numbers moved to urban areas in the rural-to-urban migrations of the early 1900s, older African Americans are now also concentrated in central cities, primarily in those areas with the worst housing. Indeed, four of five older African Americans live in metropolitan areas. Many are trapped there under the dual influence of economic hardship and a continuing racism that tends to preserve the suburban areas for whites. One must add, however, that the suburbs often welcome only whites with adequate finances and acceptable credentials. Public housing and housing for older persons, the mentally ill, or white drug or alcohol abusers are fought with the same vehemence as black or integrated housing. Older African Americans increasingly share the inner city with younger African Americans and those older whites who cannot afford to leave. Recently, however, a growing number of African Americans have migrated back to the South.

Standards of Housing

It has been estimated that 10% of older persons in the United States live in inadequate housing. This is largely a result of outright poverty or marginal income. In 1994, 78% of the 20.8 million older householders owned their own homes. However, one third of these homes were purchased in early adulthood at least 30 years before, and many have become substandard.[22] The cost of maintenance, utilities (especially fuel), and property taxes has increased so that upkeep and needed improvements have become impossible for many older people on fixed incomes. The remaining one-quarter of older persons are renters, and many of these live either alone or with relatives or friends, in retirement villages, tenements, retirement hotels, low- and middle-class government-subsidized housing, or housing sponsored by unions, churches, and benevolent associations. Some older people live in public housing, which is often seen by them as a highly desirable resource in view of the wretched alternatives available.

INCOME

Extent of Poverty

Poverty, like substandard housing, is typically associated with old age. People who were poor all their lives can expect to become poorer in old age. But they are joined by a multitude of people who become poor only after becoming old (Figure 1.7). About 11.7% (almost 3.7 million) of older people were below the official poverty level in 1994.[23] The unrealistically low annual income levels of $7,108 for a single person and $8,967 for a couple, were used to demarcate that poverty level. In our opinion this is a gross underestimation of poverty. Over 26% of older people were "near poor," or had incomes of under 150% of the official poverty level in 1994. We believe this figure, based on Leon Keyserling's Deprivation Index[24], is a more realistic estimate of poverty.[25]

Of the older poor, 78% are white.[26] There are clearly many more poor whites in actual numbers than poor blacks. However, a greater proportion of the African American older persons are poor (27% of older blacks as opposed to 10% of older whites) and their poverty is more profound. Hispanic American, Native American, and certain Asian and Pacific Island American older persons are also especially disadvantaged, as are women of all ethnic and racial groups, especially women over age 85.

Older persons receive a little more than half the income of younger persons. In 1994, the median income of families headed by an older person was $18,095 as compared with $37,247 for families with heads under 65. The median income of an older person living alone or with nonrelatives in 1994 was $14,080 for men ($270 a week), and $10,572 for women ($203 a week). The median annual income for people of all ages living

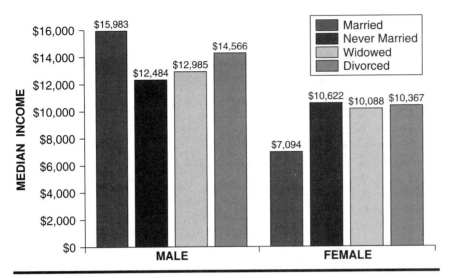

FIGURE 1.7   Median income of persons age 65 and older by sex and marital status: 1994

Source: U.S. Bureau of the Census (1994), *Current population survey,* unpublished data.

alone was $24,082 ($463 a week) for men, and $20,353 ($391 a week) for women.[27]

Without Social Security the economic picture for older people would be even more bleak. The average monthly Social Security payment to the retired worker in 1994 was $697; to the worker's wife or husband, $359; and to the worker's children, $309.[28] Almost half of older workers retire before age 65 and therefore receive "reduced benefits." Some do so out of choice, but others are forced to because of poor health or unemployment. In March 1996, over 2.1 million older people received Supplementary Security Income (SSI) benefits averaging about $263 per month.[29] However, only about 50–60% of those eligible for SSI actually receive it; many are not aware of its existence while others are reluctant to accept "welfare" because of pride or embarrassment.

Most income must go for food, shelter, and medical expenses—the essentials of existence. The lack of money has supported the myth that the aged can live on less because they do not need as much for clothing, transportation, entertainment, recreation, or education as the young. The truth is simply that older persons may not be able to af-

ford these items, which for young people are considered necessary for mental health, social status, avoidance of isolation, and personal growth.

Middle and Upper Incomes

There are, of course, middle- and upper-class older persons. Not all the old are poor. But, as we have seen, the rich "merry widow" is rare. In 1995 there were 21.4 million households headed by persons over age 65. Of these, approximately 45% had incomes in excess of $20,000 per year; 12% had incomes in excess of $50,000; and 2.7% had incomes in excess of $100,000 annually.[30]

Sources of Income

Older people earn 18% of their aggregate income from continuing employment, 18% from assets, 42% from Social Security, 19% from pensions, and 3% from other sources.[31] It is commonly believed that older persons are adequately provided for by Social Security and Medicare, but these programs have not met their needs. Many unskilled jobs, held primarily by minorities and women, were not covered by Social Security until recently. Even now, some employees (for example, many domestic workers) are not covered. Medicare, too, needs improvements. Only 45% of the health expenses of older persons are met; the rest must be paid for out of their incomes. Hearing aids, glasses, dental care, podiatry, various drugstore supplies, and, most importantly, long-term care are not covered under Medicare.

EMPLOYMENT

Employment should ideally be a matter of choice after age 65. Indeed older people do earn 18% of their income. But their ability to work is hampered by two major factors: the Social Security ceiling on earnings (which says in effect that, up to age 70, an older person is allowed only a small amount of earnings, since if more is earned, the Social Security check is reduced) and age discrimination in employment, including bias against hiring older people. (Fortunately, mandatory retirement has virtually ended in the United States as a result of the 1986 amendment to the Age Discrimination in Employment Act.) In addition, educational and technological obsolescence and the possible physical limitations of older persons combine to squeeze them out of the job market. Most of their work is concentrated in three low-earning categories: agricultural work, part-time work, and self-employment. Since 1900 the number of older men in the labor force has dropped from two-thirds to less than one-sixth (16%). The percentage of older women workers is about 8.8%.

Older African American men do not participate in the labor force as much as whites and, when they do, they earn less, do harder physical work, and are in poorer health. The proportion of older black and white women who work is about the same, but black women, like black men, earn less, usually doing domestic and service work. Retirement by choice is less of an option because African Americans' retirement benefits are often meager, in line with their previous low earnings. Indeed there may be no benefits at all. When they can no longer work, many older African Americans are simply mustered out of the labor market. They frequently must turn to SSI as the only income source available. Thus SSI programs have a disproportionate number of older blacks on their rolls, compared to whites, and it is important to understand why.

PHYSICAL AND MENTAL HEALTH

It is obvious that old people get sick more frequently than the young. Yet most move about on their own legs, and only 5.4% are confined to institutions for physical or emotional care. Most have chronic health problems of one kind or another that require more frequent visits to the doctor and more hospital stays, although the average length of stay has gone down to 8.6 days from 14 days some years ago, driven by new Medicare regulations. More periods of illness at home that result in more physical and emotional disability are experienced as well. The 1986 National Health Interview Survey Supplement on Functional Limitations found that about one-quarter (23%) of the 65-and-over population living in the community had difficulty with one or more of the seven personal care activities (activities of daily living or ADLs) inventoried, and about the same proportion (28%) had difficulty with at least one of the six home management activities (instrumental activities of daily living or IADLs). The Annual per capita expenditure for the health care of older persons in 1987 was $5,360, over four times greater than expenditures on the average person under 65 years old ($1,286). The average annual health care expenditure for those age 85 and older was $9,178. These are the latest available figures. Since 1987, health care costs have risen considerably.[32]

The mental health needs of older persons are substantial (see Chapters 5 and 6 regarding the extent of mental illness in this population). Emotional and mental illnesses escalate over the course of the life cycle. Depression in particular rises with age, and suicide attains its peak in white men in their eighties. The suicide curves of white women and black men and women rise in the middle years and then decline. Depression and hypochondriasis commonly accompany the many physical ailments of old age, which range from cardiovascular disease to arthritis and hearing loss.

EDUCATION

Although still well below that of the younger population, the educational level of the elderly has been steadily increasing. The percentage of older people who had completed high school rose from 28% in 1970 to 60% in 1993; almost 12% had a bachelor's degree or more. However, education levels vary considerably by race. In 1993, 16% of whites age 65 to 74, and 29% of whites age 75 and older never attended high school; for blacks it was approximately 38% and 61% respectively. In 1993, 63% of older whites completed high school, compared to 33% of older blacks, and 26% of older Hispanics. Only about 6% of older blacks attained a bachelor's degree or more, compared to almost 13% of older whites. Fifty-eight percent of Hispanics age 65 to 74, and 71% of Hispanics age 75 and older never attended high school.[33]

One-third of today's 17 to 21 million illiterate adults are aged 60 and over. The present elderly population has a much higher proportion of foreign-born persons who have a higher illiteracy rate and lower educational attainment than the native population.

POLITICAL POTENTIAL

The political strength of older persons is growing and is already proving to be a major force in political life. Eight states have 40% of the country's electoral votes: New York, Pennsylvania, Ohio, Illinois, Texas, California, Michigan, and Florida; all have a greater concentration of elderly residents than the national average. Over 75% of older people are registered to vote, and two-thirds vote regularly—many more than in any other age group. Older people are organizing themselves for political action and influence. Some fear a growing restlessness and militancy among the elderly

for "senior power." But evidence strongly indicates that the elderly are concerned about the welfare of all the generations. Along with the political strength of the elderly have come a new sense of self-respect and a respect from others that is not dependent on solicitude but rather on a sober recognition of the elderly's ability to have an impact on public issues.

NATIONAL AND ETHNIC IDENTIFICATION

As a consequence of the civil rights movement and the "war on poverty" of the 1960s, federal legislation focused on various racial and ethnic groups in the United States with the aim of offsetting previous and ongoing discrimination. It has been important and necessary to those who have been especially disadvantaged in our society. As we moved into the 1990s, U.S. society became even more extraordinarily diverse, multicultural, multiethnic, and multiracial with major increases in the Asian and Hispanic populations. It is important for the mental health provider or specialist to fully recognize this diversity.

Throughout the earlier parts of this chapter we presented data on the African American elderly. The following discussion includes the elderly of the other most prominent minority populations. (See Chapter 7 for mental health issues of minority elderly.)

HISPANIC OR LATINO OLDER PERSONS

Not enough is known about our second largest minority, the Hispanic population, which in fact may be the largest racial/ethnic group in the United States by the year 2000.[34] A great difficulty in talking about the so-called Hispanic American population is in simply defining that population. The various names used to describe parts or all of the group are in themselves confusing, for example, Hispanics, Chicanos, Boricuas, Mexican Americans, Latinos, Puerto Ricans, Spanish Americans, Razas, Latin Americans, "persons of Spanish origin," and "persons with Spanish surnames." Researchers and demographers have used various measures such as Spanish surname, Spanish-speaking, birthplace of the individual or of the individual's parents, Spanish-origin (self-identification of descent), and race (Indian, white [Spanish], black, or mestizo [mixture of Indian and Spanish]) to try to clarify populations under study, but no single method of "naming" has yet been generally successful. Race and class bias are built into most descriptions. We shall use "Hispanic," a term that seems more widely recognizable to the U.S. public.

The United States Hispanic population totaled almost 27 million in 1995, comprising more than 10% of the total population.[35] By the year 2000, their numbers will reach over 31 million, or over 11% of the total population.[36] Currently 5.6% of the Hispanic population is age 65 and older. Among Hispanic subgroups in the United States in 1990, Mexicans numbered 13.5 million, Puerto Ricans 2.7 million, Central and South Americans 2.3 million, Cubans 1 million, and persons from other nations numbered 2.9 million.

More than half of all Hispanics live in California or Texas. New York has 10% of the Hispanic population of the United States and Florida 7%. Illinois, Arizona, New Jersey, New Mexico, and Colorado also have sizable Hispanic populations.[37] The population of almost 27 million does not include over 3.6 million Spanish-speaking persons in Puerto Rico and the unknown number of Spanish-speaking illegal aliens now living in the United States. The 1986 Immigration Reform Act made it possible for "undocumented" and "illegal" aliens who had lived in the United States prior to January 1, 1982, to request U.S. citizenship. Nonetheless, there are still a considerable number of aliens, particularly political refugees, from Central America, specifically Honduras, Nicaragua, and El Salvador. It is difficult to estimate their number.

In addition to a lower life expectancy than that of whites, as well as poverty, poor housing, and lack of medical care and education, older Hispanics face the turmoil of drastic changes in their traditional life-styles. The young are breaking rapidly with their past, the extended family is shrinking into the nuclear family, and the aged tend to be cut adrift from their rich culture and tradition. A sense of personal privacy and pride make it difficult for older persons to ask for and accept financial or medical aid. The government's Supplementary Security Income (SSI) is not popular and often is unused. Furthermore, Spanish-speaking older persons face a language barrier and are too frequently expected to adapt to English with no instruction, rather than receiving the courtesy of translations or Spanish-speaking and Spanish-oriented services. In spite of all these problems, the number of Hispanic elderly is expected to rise dramatically, from 5.5% of the total Hispanic population in 1995 to about six and a half times larger in 2030, and over ten times larger by 2050.

NATIVE AMERICAN (AMERICAN INDIAN, ESKIMO, AND ALEUT) OLDER PERSONS

Of the 2.2 million American Indian, Eskimo, and Aleut (AIEA)[38] persons in 1995, approximately 96% were American Indians and 4% were Eskimo and Aleuts. The proportion of older persons among the Native American population has grown twice as fast as that of the African American or white elderly population, increasing by 65% between 1980 and 1990. In 1995, there were 141,000 Native Americans age 65 and older, about 6% of the total Native American population.[39] Almost half live in rural areas, a far greater proportion than any other major minority group. Approximately one-fourth of Native American elderly live on reservations or in Alaskan native villages. The majority of Native Americans are concentrated in the Southwest: Oklahoma, California, Arizona, New Mexico and Texas. Most of the remainder reside in states along the Canadian border.[40] According to the Indian Health Service, the average life expectancy at birth for Native Americans increased from only 51 years in 1940 to 71.5 years in 1987–89—still, however, over three years less than that of the general population of the United States in the same period.[41]

Native Americans are among the poorest people in the United States. In 1989, the median income for Native Americans age 60 and over was $7,109, while the median income for non-Hispanic whites age 60 and over was $11,581. Although approximately the same percentage of older Native Americans and older whites remain in the workforce, nearly twice as many older Native Americans are unemployed and actively seeking work. Older Native Americans report almost twice the level of work disability (almost 37%) as any other major minority group. Malnutrition is a constant problem. Overall, one-third of Native American elderly live below the official poverty level.[42] The traditional kinship support of the family is not feasible when the family itself has no resources. Older persons are left impoverished—particularly if their children leave to live and work elsewhere.

The medical care provided by the U.S. Public Health Service is considered less than adequate to care for the Native American population. It is said that service is provided predominately for those who manage to make it to a hospital alive, although in recent years the Public Health Service has established an outreach program. Nonetheless, older persons, along with the poor, the young, and the very sick, are at considerable risk in terms of survival on the desperate trek to the nearest medical facility.

Through all this, growing numbers of Native Americans do manage to survive to old age, imbued with a fierce sense of reverence for their land. To older Indians, Eskimos, and Aleuts the physical aspect of land is an essential element in their identity and sense of belonging—this in spite of the deprivation they experience in tenaciously holding on to that land.

Because of their physical remoteness, the Eskimo and Aleut populations in Alaska are seldom noted in discussions of American older persons. The Aleuts have a greater life expectancy than the Eskimos, perhaps because the latter live in the more demanding environments of northern Alaska and Greenland. The perilousness of the environment is demonstrated in the fact that accidents are the leading cause of death for older Alaskan natives.

ASIAN AMERICAN AND PACIFIC ISLAND AMERICAN OLDER PERSONS

In 1995, as a combined minority group, the nearly 9.3 million Asian and Pacific Islanders in the United States (primarily Chinese, Filipino, and Japanese) made up about 3.6% of the total United States population, over three times the percentage in 1980.[43] About 95% of Asian and Pacific Islanders are Asian and 5% are Pacific Islanders (mostly Hawaiian). Currently, the Chinese are the largest Asian American minority group, surpassing the Japanese, who had been the largest group since 1910.

In 1995 approximately 617,000 (6.6%) of the Asian and Pacific Islander population were age 65 and older; 36,000 (.03%) were age 85 and older.[44] Only about 7% live in rural areas. Almost two-thirds are concentrated in just two states—California and Hawaii.

Of the remainder, most live in the New York/New Jersey metropolitan area, in Illinois, or in Washington State. The ratio of women to men is somewhat lower than for the general population, reflecting pre–World War II immigration laws that prohibited women and children from accompanying men to the United States. However, only among Indonesian and Tongan (in Polynesia) older Asian and Pacific Islanders are women still in the minority. Recent Asian and Pacific Islander immigrants include many well-educated professionals; however, more Asian and Pacific Islander elderly lack formal education than do whites. Compared with the total United States population, older Asians and Pacific Islanders have the greatest proportion of those with a bachelor's degree or more, at 13% compared to 11%. Ironically, they also have the highest percentage of those with less than a ninth grade education, at 39% compared to 26%. Asians and Pacific Islanders are more likely to remain in the labor force after age 65 than whites, at 16% compared to 12%. They are also less likely to be unemployed, however this varies among nationalities.[45]

Groups within the Asian and Pacific Islander population in the United States differ significantly in language, customs, social class structure, and levels of assimilation. Of the 134,000 Chinese age 65 and older in 1990 (8% of the total Chinese American population), 98% live in cities. Nationally, 15% of older Chinese Americans had incomes below the official poverty rate in 1990. Although a larger proportion of Chinese Americans hold professional or managerial positions as compared to whites, the majority hold menial jobs.[46]

As a group, fewer older Asian and Pacific Island Americans are in poverty than the general older population. This may be, in part, because of an emphasis on familial responsibility in caring for older relatives. However, some groups of older Asian and Pacific Islanders, including Hmong (a minority group from Laos), Cambodian, Laotian, Korean, Vietnamese and Samoans, suffer from a much higher rate of poverty than the general population, as high as 47% in the case of Hmong older people.[47]

Traditional patterns of kinship and community have been damaged by the experiences of immigration and forced disruption of normal family life. Many of the older people speak little English, and can neither read nor write English or their native language, thus increasing their difficulties in an alien culture.

In 1990, 106,000 Japanese Americans, or 12.5% of the total Japanese American population were age 65 or older. Japanese Americans appear to have been able to provide their older persons with greater family support and economic security, since they were not so severely restricted from bringing their families with them when immigrating. Yet 5% of these older Japanese are poor, especially in areas outside California and Hawaii. Older Japanese men usually speak at least minimal English, but older women tend to speak only Japanese. Health surveys have found that many of these older people are physically healthy and long-lived.

Filipino Americans are the second largest Asian and Pacific Islander subgroup, with a population of over 1.4 million, yet they have only the third largest number of older people, with 104,000, or 7.4% of their population. In the 1980 Census, older Filipino men still outnumbered women, comprising 67% of the older population.[48] Most of these men were laborers recruited to work in California and Hawaii from 1910 to the 1930's. After the Tydings-McDuffie Act of 1934, Filipino immigration was restricted to only 50 people per year. Many more Filipinos were recruited during World War II, but a larger influx began after restrictions were relaxed in 1965. Many of these immigrants were older family members of Filipino American health care workers.[49] By the 1990 Census women made up 52% of the older Filipino population of the United States, but there are still a large number of single older Filipino men. Many older Filipinos are highly educated, with 16% having obtained a bachelor's degree or more, although 40% never attended high school.[50]

RURAL AND SEMIRURAL OLDER PERSONS

Although 25% of older persons lived in rural areas by 1990, only 1% actually lived on farms. The remaining 24% resided in small towns of less than 2500 people.[51] Since the 1970s, a larger proportion of elderly compared to the rest of the population have moved from urban to nonurban areas, especially areas with mild climates. Other elderly already in nonurban areas are "aging in place" where they have always lived. The benefits of rural and especially semirural life are many: fresh air and sunshine, opportunity to play and work out-of-doors, a leisurely life-style, lack of congestion, and friends and neighbors of long acquaintance. But there are also unfavorable features: transportation for older people can be especially difficult because of poor roads, lack of public transport, and the need to maintain private cars or rely on someone else. Medical facilities are often inadequate, since most health care and medical services are urban-based. Many communities are without a doctor or nurse. Income levels are low; few rural and semirural people are covered by private pension plans. Social Security, employment, savings, and welfare are the usual income sources, but Social Security benefits are lower because agricultural workers and the self-employed have only recently been covered. There is a shrinking tax base and an increasing scarcity of services and loss of family members caused by the migration of young people to cities in search of work. Semirural older persons are often left with rising property and sales taxes to maintain communities and services. A disproportionate share of the nonurban elderly live in substandard and dilapidated housing. A shortage of paid jobs hampers older people in their attempts to supplement income, and present federal programs do little to help—although nearly 40% of all older people live in nonurban areas, most federal programs primarily address the needs of urban older persons. Some progress has been made in provision of more community services.[52]

SELECTED READINGS

Aaron, H. J., Bosworth, B. P., & Butless, G. (1989). *Can America grow old? Paying for Social Security.* Washington, DC: The Brookings Institution.

American Association of Retired Persons, and Administration on Aging. (1995). *A profile of older Americans: 1995.* Washington, DC: Author.

Angel, J. L., & Hogan, D. P. (1991). The demography of minority aging populations. In The Gerontological Association of America, *Minority elders: Longevity, economics, and health, building a public policy base.* Washington, DC: The Gerontological Society of America, pp. 1–13.

Applewhite, S. R. (Ed.). (1988). *Hispanic elderly in transition: Theory, research, policy and practice.* Westport, CT: Greenwood Press.

Browne, C., & Broderick, A. (1994, May). Asian and Pacific Island Elders: Issues for social work practice and education. *Social Work, 39*(3), 252–259.

Butler, R. N. (1975). *Why survive? Being old in America.* New York: Harper & Row.

Butler, R. N. (1983, July-August). A generation at risk. When the baby boomers reach Golden Pond. *Across the Board,* 37–45.

Castex, G. M. (1994, May). Providing services to Hispanic/Latino populations: Profiles in diversity. *Social Work, 39*(3), 288–296.

Cheung, M. (1989, Sept.). Elderly Chinese living in the United States: Assimilation or adjustment? *Social Work,* 457–461.

Commonwealth Fund Commission on Elderly People Living Alone. (1987). *Old, alone, and poor.* New York: Commonwealth Fund Communications Office.

Commonwealth Fund Commission on Elderly People Living Alone. (1987). *Medicare's poor.* New York: Commonwealth Fund Communications Office.

Commonwealth Fund Commission on Elderly People Living Alone. (1989). *Poverty and poor health among elderly Hispanic Americans.* New York: Commonwealth Fund Communications Office.

Coward, R. T., & Lee, G. R. (Eds.). (1985). *The elderly in rural society: Every fourth elder.* New York: Springer.

Daniels, N. (1988). *Am I my parents' keeper? An essay on justice between the young and old.* New York: Oxford University Press.

Faulkner, A., Heisel, M. A., Holbrook, W., & Geismar, S. (1982). *When I was comin' up: An oral history of aged blacks.* Hamden, CT: Archon Books.

Gelfand, D. E. (1994). *Aging and ethnicity: Knowledge and services.* New York: Springer.

Gelfand, D. E., & Barresi, C. M. (1987). *Ethnic dimensions of aging.* New York: Springer.

Grad, Susan. (1996). *Income of the population 55 or older, 1994.* Washington, DC: U.S. Department of Health and Human Services, Social Security Administration, U.S. Government Printing Office.

Institute of Medicine. (1993). *Forecasting survival, health, and disability: Workshop summary.* Washington, DC: National Academy Press.

Jackson, J. S. (Ed.). (1988). *The Black American elderly: Research on physical and psychosocial health.* New York: Springer.

Jackson, J. S. (1995). African-American aged. In Maddox, G. L. (Ed.), *The encyclopedia of aging* (pp. 30–32). New York: Springer.

John, R., & Baldridge, D. (1996). *The National Indian Council on Aging report: Health and long-term care for Indian elders.* Washington, DC: National Indian Policy Center.

Kitagawa, E. M., & Hauser, P. M. (1973). *Differential mortality in the United States: A study in socioeconomic epidemiology.* Cambridge, MA: Harvard University Press.

Kramer, B. J. (1995). Native-American aged. In Maddox, G. L. (Ed.), *The encyclopedia of aging* (pp. 671–673). New York: Springer.

Krout, J. A. (1986). *The aged in rural America.* Westport, CT: Greenwood Press.

LaVeist, T. A. (1995). Data sources for aging research on racial and ethnic groups. *Gerontologist, 35,* 328–339.

Manson, S. M., & Callaway, D. G. (1988). Health and aging among American Indians: Issues and challenges for the biobehavioral sciences. In Manson, S. M., & Dinges, N. G. (Eds.), *Behavioral health issues among American Indians and Alaska natives.* Denver, CO: University of Colorado Health Sciences Center.

Manton, K. G., Singer, B. H., & Suzman, R. M. (1993). *Forecasting the health of elderly populations.* New York: Springer-Verlag.

Markides, K. S. (1989). Consequences of gender differentials in life expectancy for Black and Hispanic Americans. *International Journal of Aging and Human Development, 29*(2), 95–102.

Markides, K. S., & Rudkin L. (1996). Racial and ethnic diversity. In Birren, J. E. (Ed.), *Encyclopedia of gerontology* (vol. 2, pp. 371–376). San Diego, CA.: Academic Press.

National Center for Health Statistics. (1993). Health data on older Americans: United States, 1992. *Vital and Health Statistics,* Series 3, No. 30. DHHS Publication No. (PHS)93–1411. Hyattsville, MD: U.S. Department of Health and Human Services.

National Center for Health Statistics. (1995). Advance report of final marriage statistics, 1989 and 1990. *Monthly Vital Statistics Report, 43*(12), suppl. DHHS Publication No.(PHS)95–1120. Hyattsville, MD: U.S. Department of Health and Human Services.

National Center for Health Statistics. (1995). Trends in the health of older Americans: United States, 1994. *Vital and Health Statistics,* Series 3, No. 30. DHHS Publication No.(PHS)95–1414. Hyattsville, MD: U.S. Department of Health and Human Services.

Olson, L. K. (Ed.). (1994). *The graying of the world: Who will care for the frail elderly?* Binghamton, NY: The Haworth Press.

Shanas, E., & Streib, G. F. (1965). *Social structure and the family: Generational relations.* Englewood Cliffs, NJ: Prentice-Hall.

Sotomayor, M. (1995). Hispanic elderly. In Maddox, G. L. (Ed.) *The encyclopedia of aging* (pp. 458–459). New York: Springer.

U.S. Bureau of the Census. (1994). Educational attainment in the United States: March 1993 and 1992. *Current Population Reports, Population Characteristics,* Series P-20, no. 276, Washington, DC: U.S. Government Printing Office.

U.S. Bureau of the Census. (February 14, 1996). *U.S. population estimates by age, sex, race, and hispanic origin: 1990–1995.* PPL-41. Washington, DC: Population Projections Branch, Population Division, U.S. Bureau of the Census.

U.S. Bureau of the Census. (1996). 65+ in the United States. *Current Population Reports, Special Studies,* Series P-23, No. 190. Washington, DC: U.S. Government Printing Office.

U.S. Bureau of the Census. (1996). Marital status and living arrangements: March 1994. *Current Population Reports,* Series P-20, No. 484. Washington, DC: U.S. Government Printing Office.

U.S. Bureau of the Census. (1996). Population projections by age, sex, race and hispanic origin: 1995–2050. *Current Population Reports,* Series P-25, No. 1130. Washington, DC: U.S. Government Printing Office.

U.S. Department of Health and Human Services, Social Security Administration. (1996). *Income of the population 55 or older.* Washington, DC: U.S. Government Printing Office.

Waldron, I. (1985). What do we know about causes of sex differences in mortality? A review of the literature. *Population Bulletin of the United States,* no. 18.

Wykle, M., & Kaskel, B. (1991). Increasing the longevity of minority older adults through improved health status. In The Gerontological Society of America, *Minority elders: Longevity, economics and health, building a public policy base.* Washington, DC: The Gerontological Society of America.

Yeo, G., & Hikoyeda, N. (1995). Asian and Pacific Islander American elders. In Maddox, G. L. (Ed.), *The encyclopedia of aging* (pp. 80–82). New York: Springer.

Young, J. J., & Gu, N. (1995). *Demographic and socioeconomic characteristics of elderly Asian and Pacific Island Americans.* Seattle, WA: National Asian Pacific Center on Aging.

ENDNOTES_____

1. Strictly speaking, aging begins before conception. A female is born with all her ova (eggs) and they age as she ages. There are no new eggs. Because of this, there is an increased incidence of Down syndrome, causing mental retardation, in children born to older women.

2. Each day, 5,700 Americans turn 65 and 4,280 age 65 and older die. Thus, the "turnover rate," or daily gain in the 65+ population, is 1,420 (based on 1992 statistics).

3. U.S. Bureau of the Census. (February 14, 1996). *U.S. Population estimates by age, sex, race, and hispanic origin: 1990–1995.* PPL-41. Washington, DC: Population Projections Branch, Population Division, U.S. Bureau of the Census.

4. U.S. Bureau of the Census. (1996). 65+ in the United States. *Current population reports, special studies,* Series P-23, No. 190. Washington, DC: U.S. Government Printing Office.

5. U.S. Bureau of the Census. (1996). Population projections by age, sex, race and hispanic origin: 1995–2050. *Current Population Reports,* Series P-25, No. 1130. Washington, DC: U.S. Government Printing Office.

6. U.S. Bureau of the Census. (February 14, 1996). *U.S. population estimates by age, sex, race, and hispanic origin: 1990–1995.* PPL-41. Washington, DC: U.S. Bureau of the Census.

7. U.S. Bureau of the Census. (1987). America's centenarians (data from the 1980 census). *Current Population Reports,* Series P-23, No. 153. Washington, DC: U.S. Government Printing Office.

8. U.S. Bureau of the Census (1996). Population projections by age, sex, race, and hispanic origin: 1995–2050. *Current Population Reports,* Series P-25, no. 1130. Washington, DC: U.S. Government Printing Office.

9. The sharp increase in survival has had many profound social consequences; for example, when marriage was made a sacrament in the 9th century A.D., the prospect of marriage lasting into the couple's forties was small. The concepts of retirement and late-life leisure were rudimentary at best.

10. O.A.S.D.I. *1996 annual report of the board of trustees,* Baltimore, MD: Author.

11. The twentieth century has seen increased life expectancy but not increased natural or maximal life span. It is most important to distinguish between "life expectancy," the actuarial projection of probable years of life from a base year, such as birth or age 65, and "life span," the inherent, maximal length of life of a species.

12. U.S. Bureau of the Census. (1996). Population projections of the United States by age, sex, race, and Hispanic origin: 1995 to 2050. *Current Population Reports,* Series P-25, no. 1130. Washington, DC: U.S. Government Printing Office.

13. Waldron, I. (1986). What do we know about causes of sex differences in mortality? A review of the literature. *Population Bulletin of the United Nations,* No. 18-1985.

14. See Haynes, S. G., & Feinlieb, M. *Women, work and coronary heart disease: Prospective findings from the Framingham Heart Study,* paper presented at the 86th Annual Meeting of the American Psychological Association, Toronto, Canada, August 1978. For a summary on women and heart disease, see Brody, J. E. (1989, February 2). Personal health, *The New York Times,* B7. Also, see Eaker, E. D., Chesebro, J. H., Sacks, F. M., et al. (1993). Cardiovascular disease in women. *Circulation, 88,* 1999–2009.

15. Many people of African descent in the United States prefer to be called *African American.* We have decided to use this term wherever possible. However, the term *black* is used by the U.S. Bureau of the Census and other major data collecting agencies, in part because figures used include people from the Caribbean, Latin America, Africa, and many people who are not U.S. citizens and, therefore, would not consider themselves African American. Therefore we have used the term *black* in reference to any such data.

16. This is with the exception of Asian Americans of all ages, particularly Japanese and Chinese, who generally fared better than did whites in the mortality statistics. Asian Americans had the highest levels of income and education and the lowest death rates, while African Americans had the lowest income and educational levels and the highest death rates. The death rates for blacks as well as for American Indian and Alaskan natives have been particularly high in the younger and middle age groups. Deaths among black infants are more than twice as high as those among white infants. The death rate for blacks age 22 to 44 is significantly higher than that for whites of the same age, with violent causes of death—accidents and homicides—especially high.

17. National Center for Health Statistics. (1995, April). Trends in the health of older Americans, United States, 1994. Series 3. *Analytical and Epidemio-*

logical Studies, no. 30. DHHS Publication No. (PHS) 95-1414. Hyattsville, MD: U.S. Department of Health and Human Services.

18. Although only 5% of older people are in institutions at any one time, estimates are that up to 40% of all older persons will receive nursing home care at some point in their lives.

19. U.S. Bureau of the Census. (1996). Marital status and living arrangements: March 1994. *Current Population Reports,* Series P-20, no. 484. Washington, DC: U.S. Government Printing Office.

20 *Ibid.*

21. U.S. Bureau of the Census. (1996). 65+ in the United States. *Current Population Reports, Special Studies,* Series P-23, no. 190. Washington, DC: U.S. Government Printing Office.

22. American Association of Retired Persons (AARP). (1995). A Profile of Older Americans. Washington DC: Author.

23. The poverty index was adopted by a federal interagency committee in 1969. The index is based on the Agriculture Department's 1961 Economy Food Plan and reflects the different consumption requirements of families based on their size and composition, sex and age of the family head, and farm or nonfarm residence. For example, studies determined that families of three or more persons spend about a third of their income on food. As a result, the poverty level of these families was set at about three times the cost of the Economy Food Plan. "Income" refers only to money income and does not reflect nonmoney transfers such as food stamps, health benefits, and subsidized housing.

24. Butler, R. N. (1975). *Why survive? Being old in America.* New York: Harper & Row, p. 28.

25. Poverty statistics from U.S. Bureau of the Census. (1995, March). *Current Population Survey,* March Supplement. Washington, DC: U.S. Bureau of the Census.

26. A little-known example of poverty among whites is that found among the Jewish elderly. In Los Angeles alone a study found 8,000 older Jewish poor on public assistance and another 10,000 eligible who had not applied. See also the account of elderly Jews in Venice, California, by anthropologist B. Myerhoff. (1979). *Number our days.* New York: E. P. Dutton.

27. U.S. Bureau of the Census. (1995, March). *Current Population Survey,* March Supplement. Washington, DC: U.S. Bureau of the Census.

28. U.S. Department of Health and Human Services, Social Security Administration. (1995). Annual statistical supplement, 1995, to the social security bulletin.

29. U.S. Department of Health and Human Services, Social Security Administration. (1996, March). Summary Data, Social Security Record.

30. U.S. Bureau of the Census (1995, March). *Current Population Survey,* March Supplement. Washington, DC: U.S. Bureau of the Census.

31. U.S. Department of Health and Human Services, Social Security Administration. (1996). *Income of the population 55 or older.* Washington DC: U.S. Government Printing Office.

32. National Center for Health Statistics. (1993). Health data on older Americans: United States, 1992. *Vital and Health Statistics,* Series 3, No. 30. DHHS Publication No.(PHS)93–1411. Hyattsville, MD: U.S. Dept. of Health and Human Services.

33. U.S. Bureau of the Census. (1994). Educational attainment in the United States: March 1993 and 1992. *Current Population Reports, Population Characteristics,* Series P20, no. 476. Washington, DC: U.S. Government Printing Office.

34. See Castex, G. M. (1994, May). Providing services to Hispanic/Latino populations: Profiles in diversity. *Social Work, 37*(3), 288–296.
    The U.S. Bureau of the Census directly measured the "Spanish origin" (the Census Bureau term) population in the 1980 Census and the "Hispanic Origin" population in the 1990 Census, in contrast to the past when the Bureau took limited samplings of the group, using different identifiers (language, surname, national origin) in different states. Partly because of fear and distrust, some, and perhaps many, members of the Hispanic community have avoided the census taker. Thus there is probably an undercount, affecting federal funding to assist Hispanic Americans in need.

35. U.S. Bureau of the Census. (February 14, 1996). *U.S. population estimates by age, sex, race, and hispanic origin: 1990–1995.* PPL-41. Washington, DC: Population Projections Branch, Population Division, U.S. Bureau of the Census.

36. U.S. Bureau of the Census. (1996). Population projections by age, sex, race and hispanic origin: 1995–2050. *Current Population Reports,* Series P-25, No. 1130. Washington, DC: U.S. Government Printing Office.

37. U.S. Bureau of the Census. (1991). Resident population distribution for the United States, regions, and states, by race and hispanic origin: 1990. *Press release* CB91-100. Washington DC: U.S. Bureau of the Census.

38. The U.S. Bureau of the Census uses this term. Criteria include at least one-fourth Indian ancestry and registration on a recognized and approved tribal roll.

39. U.S. Bureau of the Census. (February 14, 1996). *U.S. population estimates by age, sex, race, and hispanic origin: 1990–1995*. PPL-41. Washington, DC: Population Projections Branch, Population Division, U.S. Bureau of the Census.

40. Kramer, B.J. (1995). Native-American aged. In Maddox, G. L. (Ed.), *The encyclopedia of aging* (pp. 671–673). New York: Springer.

41. John, R., & Baldridge, D. (1996). *The National Indian Council on Aging report: Health and long-term care for Indian elders*. Washington, DC: National Indian Policy Center.

42. *Ibid*.

43. U.S. Bureau of the Census. (February 14, 1996). *U.S. population estimates by age, sex, race, and hispanic origin: 1990–1995*. PPL-41. Washington, DC: Population Projections Branch, Population Division, U.S. Bureau of the Census.

44. *Ibid*.

45. Young J. J., & Gu, N. (1995). *Demographic and socio-economic characteristics of elderly Asian and Pacific Island Americans*. Seattle, WA: National Asian Pacific Center on Aging.

46. *Ibid*.

47. *Ibid*.

48. *Ibid*.

49. Yeo, G., & Hikoyeda, N. (1995). Asian and Pacific Islander American elders. In Maddox, G. L. (Ed.), *The encyclopedia of aging* (pp. 80–82). New York: Springer.

50. Young, J. J., & Gu, N. (1995). *Demographic and socio-economic characteristics of elderly Asian and Pacific Island Americans*. Seattle, WA: National Asian Pacific Center on Aging.

51. U.S. Bureau of the Census. (1990). *Social and economic characteristics, United States summary,* CP-2-1. Washington, DC: U.S. Government Printing Office.

52. Coward, R. T. & Lee, G. R. (Eds.). (1985). *The elderly in rural society: Every fourth elder*. New York: Springer Publishing Co.

CHAPTER 2

OLDER PEOPLE AND THEIR FAMILIES

Understanding the family life of older people is central to understanding the mental health issues of later life. The family—both the immediate and extended family—is the arena in which the majority of us develop our sense of others and ourselves. It is a critical force that shapes our feelings and thoughts about the very meaning and value of life, and it is a vital piece of our environment that either promotes or obstructs our mental health. In old age the quality of family life can be pivotal in determining what resources one has to draw on in times of trouble. And when that quality is good, family life can provide a unique blend of warmth and personal satisfaction that can transform the later years into a rich and gratifying stage of life. But can this be true in the United States, where the prevailing view is that the elderly are isolated and rejected by their families? We will spend a good part of this chapter refuting that negative view of family life. It is certainly true that old age itself is not highly valued by many people in the United States. A number of factors have had a negative influence on U.S. attitudes toward old age:

1. A history of mass immigration, still ongoing, mostly consisting of the young leaving the elderly behind in Europe and Asia
2. A nation founded on principles of individualism, independence, and autonomy
3. The development of technologies that demand rapid change and specialized skills
4. A general devaluation of tradition
5. Increased mobility of the population within a large continental space
6. Medical advances that have relegated most deaths to later life, producing a tendency to associate death with old age

All of these have made it difficult to embrace old age itself as a valued and contributory phase of life. But can a culture so institutionalize its negativism against old age that ties of affection and loyalty between elderly parents and their adult children are discarded? Probably not. The tenacity of kinship bonds throughout history—in spite of wars, conquest, slavery, immigration, political ideology, and cultural change—should lead one to doubt easy assumptions concerning the demise of parent–child relationships. And indeed, as we shall see in the following discussion, kinship ties have survived in the United States. Only the impact of major addictions to drugs and alcohol or the stress of mental illness, too frequently compounded by poverty, have been shown to threaten natural family relationships and loyalties, leaving older parents threatened, abused, or abandoned by their adult or adolescent children.

From the standpoint of mental health it has been established that young human beings can never function or grow in a healthy manner without reasonably warm, emotional, and interactive bonds with adults who care about them. This drive for emotional sustenance does not disappear as people reach adulthood. (A small but important piece of evidence is the common complaint of many elderly that they are not physically touched and hugged enough.) The strength of the impulse toward human closeness is all the more impressive in a country like the United States, which has not yet learned to appreciate old age itself as a valuable stage of life. In fact, survival in a productivity-focused society may make kinship support between the generations *more* necessary and meaningful, as human beings are buffeted by constant challenges, competition, and reexaminations of their worth in the outside world.

Some believe that kinship relationships may become more intense in the future because of changes in mortality and fertility patterns. Most people now survive into old age, and therefore relationships have a long time to build. In addition, because of a lower birthrate, there may be more time and inclination to invest in the adult relationships across generational lines.[1]

Serious historical studies of the U.S. family and aging have been undertaken only since 1960.[2] Before that, historians showed little interest in the family, and those studying the family showed little interest in history. By 1978 two major historical studies had been completed—*Growing Old in America,* by David H. Fischer, and *Old Age in a New Land,* by W. Andrew Achenbaum—as well as a number of articles on the history of old age. All of these have broadened our understanding of aging and the contemporary family in its historical context. However, attention now needs to be paid to the great variety of family styles, as well as racial and ethnic variations within the United States and cross-national comparisons with other countries.

FAMILY LIFE CYCLE[3]

Lowered birthrates and increased longevity have greatly lengthened the time people have in which to build their family life. A family may span three to five living generations, encompassed by a past reaching farther back than one can trace and a future stretching beyond the lives of any present family members. Each person experiences his or her individual life cycle from birth to death while at the same time participating as an integral part of a family with a collective life cycle of its own. Four-fifths of all older people have living children. (Half of these have only one or two, and half have three or more children.) But even for those who are childless, it is rare to find an older person who truly has no "family," even if it means only distant relatives. The closeness of kin in terms of blood relationships and the number of kin give no clear indication of the amount of meaningful contacts. But they do indicate the *kin potential,* implying usually an emotional tie, whether positive or negative. A person cannot easily "divorce" his blood relatives, since his or her own identity is intricately bound up with those to whom he or she is physically related. (For example, adopted children seem inevitably to yearn at various points in their lives for knowledge of their kin and may actively search for them even though their lives may be otherwise satisfactory.) A feeling of kin relatedness is probably an essential element in orienting oneself in time and space as a significant human being.

The number of people who are considered "family" by an older person may change markedly throughout a lifetime. Some older people have grown up with brothers and sisters but never married and therefore have no immediate family of children and grandchildren. Others may have expanded from a small childhood family unit to produce a large number of sons, daughters, grandchildren, and great-grandchildren with their assorted in-laws. Some older people relate closely to distant kin, and others even adopt as kin people to whom they are not related at all. One should never be deceived by statements from older people claiming they have broken off contact with a family member (for example, not speaking to a brother or sister for 30 years). Such relationships usually have as much emotional content as more directly active ones—or even more—as demonstrated by the concerted expenditure of effort to deny emotional involvement. Holding the memory of someone "in hate" can require more emotional energy than holding them "in love" or "in friendship."

The development and changing use of birth control has greatly altered the "traditional" kin family. People over 70 years of age are likely to have larger numbers of brothers and sisters (and nephews and nieces) and smaller numbers of children than the middle generation (over 50), which has fewer siblings and more offspring because of the post–World War II baby boom. The baby boom children themselves, ages 33 to 51 in 1997, will be somewhat more like their grandparents, with more siblings and fewer children of their own, than their parents.

People who are now 35 years of age or younger are the first generation to truly feel the birth-control–produced, generational "kin squeeze": Many have few or no brothers and sisters, and most will have no more than one and at the most two children. (The average number of children per mother has decreased from 3.9 in 1900 to 1.8 today.) Yet this generation is likely to have parents, grandparents, and even great-grandparents in their immediate family. For the first time, the average married couple has more parents than children.[4] The kin family is shrinking increasingly within each generation (not only will there be fewer brothers and sisters, but also fewer nephews and nieces and fewer aunts and uncles), but it is stretching out for the first time in human history over four and even five generations. This means

multiple sets of grandparents. It is fascinating to speculate on the consequences of large numbers of people from different generations interacting with one another. For one thing, it means that the greater part of one's life will be spent relating to other family members as fellow adults. China has gone furthest as a government in institutionalizing the generational "kin squeeze." If its one child policy succeeds, the 21st century will bring *only* vertical relationships in China: Except for husbands and wives, who will share the same generation, individuals will grow up with no siblings, cousins, aunts, or uncles.[5]

There is great potential for family life under the new demographic conditions. Hagestad comments, "Current patterns of longevity create new opportunities for long-lasting, complex relationships and emerging roles for the able elderly. They represent a major family and societal resource."[6]

Gutmann extends this idea as an imperative to society:

> Instead of thinking of the aged as hopeless recipients of services over which they have little control, they can begin to study the ways in which post-parental potentials can be transformed—into resources and capacities—not only for elders, but for us all.[7]

The concept of the family itself is changing—the great "classical family of western nostalgia," as Stanford University sociologist William J. Goode once called it, does not exist and probably never existed to any great degree. The so-called extended family of early America often consisted of conglomerations of nuclear family members, unmarried siblings of the nuclear couple, lodgers, hired hands, slaves, indentured servants, apprentices, and a relatively small number of older kin who managed to survive the infections, ailments, and accidents that made life so generally short and brutal. Whether older people fared any better in these households than they do today is still a matter of debate, as is the romantic urban view that the early American rural existence was a gentler way of life for older folks. Table 2.1 details the contemporary family of America.

TABLE 2.1   Family living and working arrangements

Living Arrangements

HOUSEHOLD TYPE	% OF ALL HOUSEHOLDS
Family Households	
Married couples with children under 18	25.8
Married couples without children under 18	29.0
Female householder (no spouse present) with own children under 18	7.9
Female householder (no spouse present) without own children under 18	4.9
Male householder (no spouse present) with own children under 18	1.4
Male householder (no spouse present) without own children under 18	1.6
Nonfamily Households	
Male householder, living alone	9.7
Female householder, living alone	14.6
Other nonfamily households	5.2

Working Arrangements

WORKING ARRANGEMENT TYPE	% OF ALL MARRIED COUPLES
Married couple, husband and wife in labor force	55.00
Married couple, only husband in labor force	21.95
Married couple, only wife in labor force	5.80
Married couple, neither in labor force	17.25

Source: U.S. Bureau of the Census, (1994, March). Household and Family Characteristics. *Current Population Reports,* Series P-20, no. 483.

Imagine the families of the next decades! Families will come in increasingly varied forms—single-parent families, two-paycheck couples, the blended families of divorce, and generational and intergenerational communes, to name a few. Another new pattern is the return of an adult child to the family nest after a personal setback or a need to conserve financial resources. (See Table 2.2 for definitions of families.) Betty Friedan, a founder of the latest wave of U.S. feminism who has also become interested in aging issues, has coined the phrase "the extended family of choice." This is a new definition of "family" and an additional option for those who prefer literally to choose those whom they identify as their family, whether they are related by blood and law or not. Such choice is based primarily on affection and mutual interests.

Less than 4% of American families meet the traditional concept of husband-breadwinner, housewife, and two dependent children. Some of the likely consequences of the variety in family structure will be more effective child-care as well as day-care programs for older persons who cannot be left alone and more opportunities for families to work at home, with spouses sharing in the care of the children and infirm older parents. New problems may arise. For example, it is not clear whether the less traditional family forms, such as the "extended family of choice," or communal groups will be able or willing to handle crises of illness and disability among older members.

TABLE 2.2   Definitions of families and other family-like arrangements

General definition of family   Those who consider themselves economically and emotionally related to each other by blood (consanguinity) or by marriage (conjugality).

Nuclear family   A married pair (conjugal) with dependent children and an independent household, bound to outside kin by voluntary ties of affection or duty.

Extended family   All of those related to one another by blood or marriage.

Modified and extended family   Separate households for all but very old or sick, with a complex, viable, supportive pattern of family relationships with kin. The nuclear family is part of the extended kin family. The latter is a highly integrated network of social relations and mutual assistance—vertical over generations and bilateral to other kin.

Household   A number of persons who share a residence, exchange services, and give emotional support to each other.

Social network   Those individuals with whom one interacts during the course of one's daily life.

Support system   A group of individuals who join together to give support and assistance to each other, sometimes for a specific purpose.

However, anecdotal reports suggest that such support depends on the quality of the relationships, much the same as in more traditional families.

A whole new possibility of kin networks for the old (as well as the opposite possibility of loss of kin contact) is appearing with rising divorce and remarriage rates. While 50% of all new marriages are projected to end eventually in divorce, 80% of those who divorce remarry, bringing a whole clan of step-relatives along to add to their partner's potential kin network. Two or more divorces bring even more kin potential. The popular image of step-families is usually something similar to the feud between the Hatfields and the McCoys, with each side of the family staking out its emotional territory. The reality is that many amicable and lifelong alliances form among family members who become related through first, second, or more marriages even though the marriages themselves may or may not succeed. This is especially true of women family members (mothers and daughters-in-law, sisters-in-law, nieces-in-law), who are more likely to maintain contacts with each other after divorce than male family members. Some attribute this to women's "kin-keeping" tendencies; others see it as women's shared involvement with the children in a family as mothers, grandmothers, and aunts. For the paternal grandmother, "a daughter-in-law is no longer a son's wife [due to divorce], but she is still the mother of her grandchildren."[8]

DO AMERICAN FAMILIES "ABANDON" THEIR OLDER MEMBERS?

Research Evidence

Urbanization and industrialization have led to theories about changes and/or breakdown in family structure. The nuclear family consisting of mother, father, and several children has been postulated as the most functional family unit in industrialized societies; it requires mobility, compactness, and an emotional self-sufficiency that can be built in and carried along. Older people and other extended family members are seen as failing to fit into this streamlined picture. The popular public image is that the nuclear family has closed its ranks and its heart, determined to manage on its own, while older parents and grandparents are left to fend for themselves. This may sound plausible, but it has not happened in the United States and is not likely to.

In fact, in one of the few cross-national studies of attitudes toward the elderly, a comparison of three generations of women in Japan and the United States found the following:

> It is worth noting that in Japan which is noted for her cultural tradition of "respect for the elderly," and where in fact elders are paid high regard in many aspects of social life, the attitudes toward aging and old people seem to be more negative than in the United States regardless of generation.[9]

The emerging picture of family life in the United States, as clarified by research, is one of separate households for all but the very old or sick, while at the same time maintaining a complex pattern of family relationships that are viable and supportive. As an early observer, Sussman called this the "modified and extended" family system in which the nuclear family is not isolated but is part of "an extended kin-family system, highly integrated within a network of social relationships and mutual assistance that operates along bilateral kin lines and vertically over several generations."[10]

Even earlier, Litwak defined the modified extended family in relation to what he called the "classical extended" and nuclear types:

> [It] differs from the "classical extended" family in that it does not demand geographical propinquity, occupational involvement, or nepotism, nor does it have an hierarchical authority structure. On the other hand, it differs from the isolated nuclear family structure in that it does provide significant continuing aid to the nuclear family.[11]

Aid to older persons takes the form of economic help, household services, living arrangements with families when this is imperative, and affection and companionship. Brothers, sisters, children, grandchildren, aunts, uncles—even nephews, nieces, and cousins—may be involved in the flow of mutual aid. When families do not offer help to their older members, a whole range of personal, social, and economic forces are usually at work rather than a simple attitude of neglect and abandonment.

Many studies over the years have verified the continuing existence of strong family ties in the United States and elsewhere. A 1959 World Health Organization report stated:

> Wherever careful studies have been carried out in the industrialized countries, the lasting devotion of children for their parents has been amply demonstrated. The great majority of old people are in regular contact with their children, relatives, or friends. . . . Where distance permits, the generations continue to shoulder their traditional obligations, of the elders toward their children, and the children to the aged.[12]

Townsend, in England in 1965, found that the families of institutionalized aged showed "much more evidence of genuine affection and loyalty than the reverse. . . ."[13]

Studies indicate that the majority of older people choose independent living quarters with a spouse or alone as long as this is possible and then expect to move in with family members when their health or financial situation deteriorates. Approximately three out of every ten older people in the United States currently live alone. Most of these are single, widowed, or divorced, and a large proportion are women. Many have children but prefer to live apart from them. A greater proportion of the very old (over 80) live with family members because of declining capacities. Unmarried people in frail health may live with siblings or friends.

In commenting on intergenerational ties, Shanas observed in 1980:

> While the proportion of old people who live with their children has decreased over the last 20 years, the proportion living close to children has increased substantially. In 1975, the proportion of old people living in the same household with one of their children was 18 percent. [By 1985 this proportion had declined to 13%.] Thirty-four percent of all persons over 65 with children, however, live apart from children, but within 10 minutes distance from at least one of them. As a result, in 1975, half of all people with children (52 percent) lived either in the same household with a child, or next door, down the street, or a few blocks away. Old people who live

alone are commonly considered a particularly vulnerable group among the elderly. Yet, among those old people who have children and who live alone, half are within 10 minutes distance of a child.[14]

A number of more recent studies continue to confirm the existence of active and viable family supports.[15] In New York City, Mary Mayer, Director of Research for the Department of Aging, reported in 1989 that:

> Eighty percent of the City's elderly have children and two-thirds of this group have at least one child who lives very nearby. Almost a third have a child a few hours away. Moreover, almost all elderly who have children (95 percent) are in at least weekly telephone contact with them and nearly two-thirds receive weekly visits from children.
>
> Additionally, most elderly (92 percent) say they have someone to care for them should they need help for a few days. However, if the days grow into weeks, significantly fewer (85 percent) will have someone to assist them. Not surprisingly, those living alone or without children tend to be less likely to have assistance.[16]

Shanas believes that the "myth of alienation" or the notion of families abandoning their elderly has been created and perpetuated by two groups: *professional workers* in the field of aging, who tend to see those older persons who do not have sufficient family supports, and *childless old people,* who constitute one-fifth of all older people and are likely to believe that the aged are neglected by their children. For most elderly, however, Shanas sees the family as a "safe harbor" where the elderly have a role in old age and a haven in time of need.

Evidence has begun accumulating that ethnic and racial minorities such as African Americans, Hispanic Americans, and Asian Americans make even heavier use of extended kin and friendship networks because of generally more limited economic resources and also because of ongoing cultural traditions.[17]

There is, of course, no doubt that elder neglect and abuse exist in some families, as will be discussed in Chapter 7. The "battered older person" syndrome is the most shocking form of such abuse; verbal disparagement and cruelty are more common.

Living independently from relatives can be demonstrated to be a sign of medical and economic advances rather than family neglect. Markson reports a striking decline in past years in the proportion of those elders over age 75 who are living with relatives. This is partly due to greater longevity, resulting in more married persons who are still living with their spouses. But another factor is the greater tendency of older women to live alone, probably as a result of an increased economic capacity to do so.[18]

"Filial" Economic Responsibility

Filial responsibility includes more than just law and custom, since it refers also to personal attitudes of responsibility toward parents: the ethical and emotional responses of adult children toward their mothers and fathers.[19] Historically, grown children were held totally accountable for the care of their parents under medieval church law; it was not until the Elizabethan Poor Law that the concept of community assistance was introduced. However, families were expected to do everything they could before receiving outside help. During the early part of the twentieth century, filial responsibility versus a wider societal responsibility began to be tested to a greater degree. There were greater numbers of older people, sometimes two generations of them in one family, and the preindustrial, agricultural society was disappearing. In its place came industrialization, separating wages from the ownership of the means of production. Older people no longer had the power of ownership of land, tools, and animals or the sustenance of the agricultural community; therefore they became more vulnerable economically as they aged. Their children were forced to take on more responsibility for them or look to the larger society, especially government, for assistance.

Social Security, beginning in 1935 in the United States, provided basic economic maintenance for increasing numbers of older people. Instead of individual families supporting their own older members, Social Security was predicated on the concept of intergenerational support whereby the entire middle- and younger-aged generations in the labor force support the older generation. Financial insurance for health care under Medicare and the state-federal program of welfare assistance for health care, namely Medicaid, began in 1965, supplanting earlier federal-state and local health-care financing programs for the aged. Supplementary Security Income in 1972 brought the poor aged, who had been receiving "welfare" income transfers under Old-Age Assistance, under the umbrella of the Social Security Administration.

The results of these programs are obvious. For example, a survey of 17,000 U.S. households (the Survey of Income and Program Participation [SIPP]), conducted by the Bureau of the Census in 1985 (the most recent data available), examined the number of persons who were regularly making cash payments for the support of persons not living with them in their households. (Noncash transfers such as food, clothing, or services to individuals were not included.) Of about 2.9 million adults who received financial help from someone outside their households, about one-third were older parents of adult children. (Remember that there were altogether about 29 million persons aged 65 or over.) The average support payment was $1,484 annually. This study demonstrates that financial cash support is now relatively uncommon, and when it does exist, it is usually modest. As would be expected, persons with higher incomes ($45,000 or over) were much more likely (three times more likely) to be supporting their parents financially than persons with incomes under $15,000.[20]

Older persons, age 65 or older, constitute about 7% of all adults who provide cash help to others, and 94% of these elderly are supporting other adults. In fact, old people often support other old people. About one-half of all financially dependent persons in nursing homes who received cash help from others received that help from persons—usually a noninstitutionalized spouse—who were themselves 65 years of age or over. The

other half received help from their adult children. The average amount of cash help for nursing home care was $2,886 annually.[21]

The SIPP study did not examine a major form of help in U.S. family support networks: the noncash goods and personal services given by the old to the young and by the young to the old. Examples are the caregiving (known to be substantial) of young children by older grandmothers and the caregiving of the elderly by family members, usually wives of elderly men and daughters and daughters-in-law. A major methodological problem has been both a reluctance as well as a very real difficulty in quantifying such care (classified generally as "housework") and then placing a monetary value on it. Such a methodology began to be developed by the National Center of Health Statistics, under the leadership of Dorothy Rice, for the purpose of determining costs of illness.[22] Morgan also attempted a measurement and valuation of time spent in various forms of inter-family and intra-family transfers of help, based on a 1980 Panel Study of Income Dynamics at the Survey Research Center, University of Michigan at Ann Arbor. His data indicated that affluent families are more likely to send money to needy elderly relatives, while less affluent, larger families are more likely to invite the elderly to share their home as their way of helping.[23]

Morgan's work suggests a number of other interesting points:

1. Measurements of family or individual well-being ideally must include some estimation of the value of time spent or received in the form of housework, child care, and elder care in order to accurately reflect available resources. The value of such time should be seen as part of the total real income of the family or individual, together with labor income, other taxable and nontaxable income, and cash and noncash transfer payments such as Social Security, pensions, food stamps, and so forth.

2. Overall, in family life, women are the major providers of time, while men and children are the beneficiaries; however, with time contributions to the elderly, although the providers are still likely to be women, the beneficiaries are also likely to be women, albeit elderly women. The reason lies in the fact that women outlive men.

3. Contributions of time to others often come at a real cost to the provider of that time, namely a loss of leisure, an increase in stress, a decline in health, and so on. Caregiver exhaustion and burnout can result.

4. After considering both time and money transfers between and among family members, it is clear that there is still real sharing in our society. "The growth of public transfer systems has not supplanted all of the old private altruism or extended family responsibilities." In fact, according to Morgan, "We have not 'socialized' the responsibility for dependent members of society as far as we might think; families remain responsible for most of the burden."[24]

A major new role for families is that of intermediaries and advocates for the elderly as they negotiate their way through state, federal, and local bureaucracies. However, although the Social Security Administration and other governmental agencies are necessarily providing financial support and services for older persons, some financial policies still reflect the earlier traditions of total filial or family responsibility. The "responsible relative" clause in many state welfare programs is the most obvious example. Although seldom enforced, more than half of the states still have laws that could be used to require children to provide financial help to needy parents. Such requirements, if enforced, would result in many families having to deny other family members' needs, including children, in order to finance an older person's care. Family savings could easily be completely used up in a single bout of illness, endangering the family's future. Much painful pauperization of spouses of older persons has already been brought about by the "spend-down" requirement to gain Medicaid coverage for nursing homes and home care. (See Chapters 10 and 11.)

Family responsibility laws are questionable from a civil liberties perspective because of the potential for arbitrary and capricious enforcement. But more practically, with two generations of elderly, the young-old and the old-old, present in more and more families, the younger generations simply cannot afford to be financially "responsible" relatives to all, especially when even one long-term or catastrophic illness can deplete most families' financial resources. The remaining financial burdens of care, mostly for long-term care of the elderly, should be removed from families so that they can attend to the many other emotional and personal needs of older people. Ongoing efforts to provide public or public/private financing for long-term institutional and home care is expected to eventually succeed.

One of the fears of public policymakers is that liberalization of federal benefits such as Medicare home care might lead to an abandonment of older persons by families already providing support. Thus there would be a "raid on the federal treasury" or a "woodwork effect," with families seemingly coming "out of the woodwork" to claim services and supports, withdrawing their own usual supports in the meantime. However, experiences of other nations that offer such assistance do not confirm this fear.

In Denmark, older persons are completely independent financially from their children because of the comprehensive welfare structure; yet they maintain a high degree of interaction and mutuality with their families in every other respect. Old people are not dependent on the politics of potentially emotion-laden family largess for necessary services. Instead, the interaction with family members is voluntary, based on mutual interest and emotional interdependence. In Norway, another country with no financial family-responsibility laws, even for long-term care, the continued involvement of family members, particularly women, is so obvious that it has been called "the hidden welfare state,"—a complex, family-run system of provision of an array of services and supports.[25]

Cherlin is optimistic about family relations that do not include financial responsibilities. He suggests the hypothesis that "the relations between the elderly and their adult children tend to be more emotionally satisfying—closer, warmer, more loving, and more affectionate—when neither generation is economically dependent on the other."[26] He believes this condition is more possible in the present than in our nation's past. In colonial America, the elderly controlled most of society's resources, and the relations between the generations were "correct but cold," as the middle-aged and young contended with financial dependency and the power and authority of the old.[27]

Sussman postulates that providing "back up supports," especially economic and health care assistance to care-giving kin and other caregivers, could serve to strengthen family and friendship support to the elderly, particularly among potential caregivers who are not yet giving care. These latter might move into the home-care or service-provider role if given financial assistance and supports to do so.[28]

Are Older People "Dumped" into Institutions?

The image of Americans "dumping" their elderly into nursing homes is another of the myths that confuse the realities of life in old age. (Remember that only 5% of those over the age of 65 are in nursing homes or other institutions.) There are, of course, some families who abandon their responsibilities to older family members by placing them prematurely and precipitously in institutions. More commonly, isolated older people without families may be institutionalized when they become ill or feeble, simply because there is no other place for them to go. For example, in New York City, 7% of the elderly have no living children or siblings. Friends and neighbors may provide supports to some, but these elderly are essentially without immediate family support.[29]

Most people who have families move in with their relatives when they can no longer live independently. Institutional care is reserved as the last recourse after everything else has been tried. Families will often go through unbelievable hardship before deciding on placement. The following is a letter we received from a son seeking help for his mother:

> My 84-year-old mother lives with me in my four-room apartment. Her senility has become worse and she is totally confused, unable to sit still, care for herself, or even remain continent. Three years ago I had to quit my job in order to stay home with her, as she used to wander the streets and get lost. I live on my savings; I am unmarried. I am 52 years old, still unemployed and have passed up two good jobs. I am at my wit's end. What should I do? I love the poor woman. But I cannot enjoy life at all. What is the best thing for her? And me?

Ideally, families should have a whole range of services to assist them in keeping the older person at home, including economic aid (see Chapter 10 on home care). But when the burden becomes too great, institutional care may be necessary and appropriate—and such care should be reliable, therapeutic, and reasonably priced. (Chapter 11 discusses institutional care in greater detail.)

OLDER PEOPLE AS PARENTS

Parent–child interactions in late life have focused primarily on how adult children meet the needs of their older parents (filial responsibility and filial maturity). It is curious that we have shown so little attention to the ways in which elderly parents relate to and meet the needs of their adult children. This no doubt reflects the lagging societal appreciation of the contribution of the elderly. Older parents are parents until either their own death or that of their children; many now live to see their own children grow old. One-fourth of women who were age 60 in 1980 still had living mothers.[30]

What role do these older parents play? One view is that they become "emeritus parents," with older women, especially, managing and monitoring extended families.[31] Hagestad calls such women the "ministers of the interior."[32] The female pattern of greater emphasis on interpersonal intimacy and "kin-building" would seem logically related to a major yet unacknowledged role in providing supports to younger generations. And if Gutmann is correct that men move toward greater interpersonal sensitivity and interaction in old age, they may be playing such a role as well.

Hagestad comments on how little is known about parenting over time and muses about whether "parenting styles" are stable throughout life or are subject to individual or predictable changes.[33]

GRANDPARENTHOOD, GREAT-GRANDPARENTHOOD, AND GREAT-GREAT-GRANDPARENTHOOD

Longer lives have increased the likelihood of families with three, four, or even five generations. Increased survivorship is a result of fewer women dying in childbirth, fewer children dying of childhood disease, fewer infants dying in utero or at birth, and fewer older people dying of infections. Modern medicine and improved public health measures can be thanked for these life-giving contributions. Almost one-half of all persons 65 and over with living children are members of four-generation families. A sizable number of persons over 65 years of age have one or two living parents. About one out of ten older people has a child over 65. In fact, aging parents may have their aging children living with them, rather than vice versa. It is not uncommon to see parents in their eighties caring for aging and ailing children in their sixties.

Reliable nationwide figures for the number of older people with living children and grandchildren (and those older persons with living parents) are not available. These questions have not been included in any known U.S. census survey or other large representative sampling. Such important data are necessary to evaluate the amount of potential family support an older person has available. In a national survey by Shanas, nearly three-fourths of those studied who were 80 and above were great-grandparents, as were one-fourth of those 65 to 66. These figures are increasing, with the continual improvement in life expectancy and a decreasing fertility rate.[34]

All in all, an estimated three-fourths of adults will live to be grandparents.[35] Of the four-fifths of

persons over 65 with living children, 94% are grandparents (three generations) and 46% are great-grandparents (four generations). A proportion are also great-great-grandparents (five generations). One 1986 survey estimates that overall there are 49 million U.S. grandparents, great-grandparents, and great-great-grandparents.[36] (See Table 2.3 for ages of grandparents and grand-children.) The following reveals how the chances of being a grandparent have increased dramatically:

Studies show that in 1920 only four out of five children at the age of 10 were apt to have one living grandparent whereas 50 years later 19 out of 20 were apt to. In 1920 the chance of a 10-year-old child having at least two grandparents alive was two in five. In 1970 it was three in four. The chance of a 10-year-old having at least three living grandparents has risen from one in ten to three in eight. The chance of having all four has gone from one in 90 to one in 14. (These figures pertain to white children.)[37]

The duration of grandparenthood is growing. Many will be grandparents for 30, 40, or more years, eventually adding great-grandparenthood and, possibly, great-great-grandparenthood to the repertoire of family roles. Some have suggested that there may already be more great-grandparents currently alive than there were grandparents at the turn of the century. In contrast to the growing duration of grandparenthood, grandparents have fewer grandchildren today (an average of three

TABLE 2.3 Modern grandparents

AGES OF GRANDPARENTS		WITH GRANDCHILDREN AGES	
35–44 years	6.4%	Under 1 year	22%
45–49	10.1	1–2	27
50–54	10.8	3–5	42
55–64	34.9	6–11	47
65+	37.8	12–15	30
		16–21	28
		Adults	20

Source: Meredith Corporation, 1987.

grandchildren) compared to 1900 (an average of 12 to 15 grandchildren). Grandparenthood, like many of the other aspects of late life, has received only meager research attention, primarily in the form of small pilot studies, which may or may not be generalizable to grandparents as a whole. But they do add intriguing pieces of clarifying information about a function so familiar to us.

Early psychoanalytic interpretations of grandparenthood were rather grim and villainous, reflecting patriarchal values. Ferenczi pictured the grandfather as either an imposing, authoritarian old man who frightened and challenged his grandchild or a helpless, feeble person who invited the grandchild's disparagement because he was weak and near death.[38] Ferenczi conceded that boy children may learn about death for the first time through contacts with grandfathers, but he viewed this essentially in an Oedipal context as an opportunity to learn a new way of getting rid of father.

Grandmothers likewise received stern treatment historically from scholars and practitioners (for example, Abraham, 1955). A zealous social worker defending children from the evils of grandmothers wrote an article in 1942 titled "Grandma Made Johnny Delinquent," in which the author argued that grandparents "interfering with the raising of a child" should be removed from the home. LaBarre, Jessner, and Ussery (1960) wrote in the same vein in their paper, "The Significance of Grandmothers in the Psychopathology of Children."[39]

In 1958, Rappaport warned of the possible "detrimental effect" of grandparents living in the home of their children. Such a living arrangement "infantilized the parents and created feelings of omnipotence in the grandchild if the grandparent is also weak. In addition, grotesque and bizarre character traits are apt to develop [in grandchildren] because of grandparental identification."[40]

Others were more positive. Haber wrote,

> Regarding grandparents, it is obvious that the grandparent can serve as a modulating function of significance in view of both their presence and concern and real position of objectivity and experience. They can fulfill and be fulfilled. The goal of

thoughtful involvement containing an appropriate degree of emotion by oldsters with their younger relative should be studied and encouraged.[41]

Contemporary evidence shows that grandparents, somewhat less than 10%, function as surrogate parents, and many of these have been lifesavers rather than evildoers in the lives of grandchildren.

Benedek identified the grandparent role as one available universally to most older people:

> Grandparenthood is a new lease on life because grandparents—grandmothers more intensely than grandfathers—relive the memories of the early phase of their own parenthood in observing the growth and development of their grandchildren. Grandparenthood is, however, parenthood one step removed. Relieved from the immediate stresses of motherhood and the responsibilities of fatherhood, grandparents appear to enjoy their grandchildren more than they enjoyed their own children. Their instinctual wish to survive being gratified, they project the hope of the fulfillment of their narcissistic self-image to their grandchildren. Since they do not have the responsibility for raising the child toward that unconscious goal, their love is not as burdened by doubts and anxieties as it was when their own children were young.[42]

Neugarten and Weinstein (1964) differentiated types of grandparents in their study of 70 middle-class, older couples: the formal grandparent, the "compassionate" or fun-seeker grandparent, the surrogate parent, the reservoir of family wisdom, and the distant figure who arrives only on holidays and family occasions. They found the fun-seeker and the distant figure most common of the types. It was noted that not all older people wanted the grandparent role or expressed satisfaction with it. Some felt exploited by their children (as babysitters, etc.); others expressed negative attitudes toward their own children through their grandchildren. Some joined forces with the young in secret struggles against the middle generation.

Kahana and Kahana (1970) studied grandparenthood from the grandchild's perspective (white, middle-class sample). The feelings of grandchildren depend on the amount of contact, grandparents' behavior toward them, parents' relationships with grandparents, and the child's perceptions of older people in general and grandparents in particular. Children's responses to grandparents change as the youngsters develop; very young children react to gifts, favors, and open affection, whereas slightly older ones prefer sharing activities and having mutual fun.

Some suggest that grandparents tend to feel closest to grandchildren when the children are between the ages of 3 and 12. But grandchildren also value and need their grandparents during adolescence, when rebellions against parents are common and emotional confusion is rampant. Grandparents can be a stable, accepting port in the storm, acting as counselors and confidants. Biological continuity, emotional self-fulfillment, vicarious accomplishment, teaching, and helping in various ways were some of the meaningful roles in grandparentage.

Grandparenthood now occurs in middle age as well as old age. The new longevity may produce uncertainty. The possible roles a grandparent can play are becoming more open to individual interpretation: "In a society where grandparents range from twenty-five years old to centenarians, and where grandchildren run the spectrum from infants to retirees, we should not be surprised to find that cultural images of grandparenthood harbor both variety and uncertainty."[43]

When grandparents have power and responsibility (as in the role of surrogate parents), they are likely to be more formal and perhaps authoritarian. But when removed from responsibility, they tend to be indulgent, enjoying the grandchildren but not feeling burdened. (Even the travel industry has begun to focus on doting grandparents. Organizations like Grandtravel, a division of the Ticket Counter, 6900 Wisconsin Ave., Chevy Chase, Maryland 20815 (301) 986-0790, and Vistatours' Grandparents and Grandchildren's Tours (a division of Frontier Tours) (702) 882-2100, 1923 N. Carson, Carson City, Nevada 89701, arrange special tours for grandparents and their grandchildren.) Some volunteer to be surrogate grandparents to other people's children, as in the Foster Grandparent Program. Youthful grand-

parents may avoid any element of the traditional grandparent role, preferring to be called by their first names and functioning as friends. The image of the white-haired, elderly grandpa and grandma may eventually have to be reserved for great-grandparents.

The "safety-valve" or indirect stabilizing function of grandparents is an intriguing one. Hagestad suggests that one must look beyond the *actual* contribution of the elderly to the young and examine the *potential* contributions that could be drawn on in case of illness, divorce, inflation, desertion, and other crises and emergencies. This potential may never be used, but because it is there, the younger generation may be less restrained in their life choices and feel a greater sense of personal security.[44]

Grandparenthood undoubtedly also has an impact on the mental health of grandparents themselves. The grandparent role has potential for continuing delight as well as for ongoing bitterness; for satisfaction as well as disappointment. Kivnick has attempted to formulate a model to measure the emotional impact of grandparenthood on individual grandparents as well as to suggest "self-help" mechanisms that might make the grandparent role more fulfilling.[45]

There is a growing need to look at the impact of rising divorce rates and single parent families on grandparents' roles. (Marital breakup and remarriage are not new phenomena in the United States. What is new is that these now occur largely because of divorce whereas in the past they were caused by high death rates, particularly high maternal mortality.) Nearly 28% of the nation's 67 million children under 18 years of age lived with only one of their parents in 1994. Thirty-seven percent of these children lived with a divorced parent, 18% with a separated parent, 36% with a parent who had never been married, 4% with a widowed parent, and 4% with a parent whose spouse was absent for reasons other than marital divorce.[46] About 72% of children lived with two parents: Of this group, 82% lived with both biological parents, 15% with their biological mother and stepfather, and 1% with their biological father and stepmother.[47]

There is evidence that divorce, and probably single parenthood as well, tend to intensify grandparent–grandchild relationships on the maternal side (since most children live with their mothers, and these mothers tend to remain close to their own mothers). Conversely, there is often a weakening of relations on the paternal side, unless the children's father makes successful efforts to remain positively involved, thereby increasing the likelihood that his parents' role as grandparents is welcomed by the children's mother.[48] It is clear that the quality of the grandparents' relationships with their divorcing children and in-laws is critical since it is the adult children, particularly those who have custody of the grandchildren, who act as the mediators between grandparents and grandchildren. Matthews and Sprey expand on this point, namely that to understand the impact of divorce on the grandparent role, one must understand the dynamics of the extended family relationships with each other. For example, the position of grandparents is strengthened if they control resources that are important to the parents of their grandchildren, such as a family business or property. If this is not the case, their position is less secure and they must rely on the goodwill of the middle generation in maintaining contacts with grandchildren.[49]

Since the 1970s, all states have passed laws providing some kind of protection for grandparents' rights to interact with grandchildren after divorce. In most states, grandparents can petition courts for visitation rights in case of divorce, separation, or widowhood of the adult children. The court then determines if it is in the best interest of the child to allow the grandparents to visit. The state of Illinois has gone furthest, allowing that same right of petition to grandparents when the child's parents are still married and are refusing contact with grandparents. Some states encourage mediation or family therapy to work out grandchildren contacts that are mutually agreeable to all. Groups have formed to represent grandparents.

Divorce of adult children may also pose a threat to grandparents' retirement plans specifically or to the financial or emotional well-being of the elderly generally. Family disruption of all kinds may place grandparents, especially grandmothers, in the position of rescuers. For example, the drug epidemic of crack in the Harlem community of New York City has brought many middle-aged and older grandmothers into active mothering roles for grandchildren.

OLDER MARRIED COUPLES

The "postparental" period (after the children have grown up and gone) of life for older couples has been extended because of greater longevity, generally earlier marriage, and fewer children. In 1890 the last child married an average of two years *after* the death of one of the parents; in 1950 the last child married 13 to 14 years *before* the death of one parent.[50] Most parents have completed childrearing by their late forties and early fifties, leaving them an average of 13 years alone together, or one-third of their entire married life. In 1994, 55.1% of the nation's 28.5 million persons 65 years and over were married and living with their spouses. However, the pattern of men and women is quite different. Both sexes are highly likely to marry when young. But men are more likely than women to be married throughout life. In 1994, 81% of men aged 55 to 64 were married, as were 80% of men aged 65 to 74 and 72% of men 75 and older. In striking contrast, while 69% of women aged 55 to 64 were married, only 54% of those aged 65 to 74 and 28% of those aged 75 and older were married. Most of this is due to longer life expectancy for women and thus an increased chance of widowhood.[51]

Care during illness, household management, and emotional gratification are three expectations found in older marriages. The older couple married for many years will find they have a different marriage in old age than they had in middle or early life. Each of them has been changing and experiencing life individually as well as together. They may have grown more different or more alike. Conflicts between them can intensify or dissipate as they age, with more tolerance or, on the other hand, more rigidity in their expectations of each other. Some researchers have maintained that there is a degree of deterioration in up to one-third of older marital relationships.[52] But that also means that two-thirds are doing well.

Studies of marriage in old age, particularly marital satisfaction, have been criticized on both conceptual and methodological grounds. Data have been largely cross-sectional; but longitudinal studies are enormously expensive and time-consuming.[53] Further, it is difficult to assess an adult in his or her total environment because the circumstances are much more complicated than those of a child. Many more people, life experiences, accidental happenings, stresses, losses, and accomplishments are involved, and prediction of eventual individual outcome is precarious. It requires an innocent and hopeful faith to promise in marital vows to love and honor someone "until death do us part," for in 20, 30, or 40 years the partner one married may have become quite a different human being. Men who married "sweet young things" may not accept the fact that women age just as they themselves do. Women who doted on their roles as wives and mothers may rebel at the thought of being nursemaid to an ailing and aging husband. Of course there are people who expect and accept change with dignity and constructive response, having reached maturity with relatively few personality handicaps that would impede adaptability. Environmental influences, physical and mental health, and the historical period of time in which one is living are other variables affecting marriages over a long span of time.

Divorce in old age received little attention in gerontological literature until recently, probably because late-life divorce was relatively uncommon. In the past, divorce was more easily risked in youth or middle age when resources and options were greater. Children and grandchildren served as a strong bond between marital partners. Couples who reached old age together usually adapted to each other in a way that each found supportive or at least more acceptable than the uncertain world of divorce and the disapproval of society.[54]

In 1990, about 32,000 people aged 65 and older divorced in the U.S.[55] Those 65 and older account for about 1% of all divorces in the United States in a year (remembering that the elderly are 13% of the population), and only about 6% of all persons age 65 and over are divorced. Even during the overall rapid increase of divorce during the 1970s and 1980s, late-life divorce showed little change. But the situation may begin to shift. In the future, divorce may become more common as women enter old age with greater economic resources of their own, making them less economically dependent on their husbands.[56]

Most older marriages are broken by death rather than divorce. In 1994, 33% of those over 65 were widowed, while only 6% were divorced.[57] African American and Hispanic elderly are more likely to be widowed, divorced, or separated, reflecting both a lower life expectancy and greater economic pressures. Older people can become intensely dependent on each other for intimacy, personal services, and mutual support. A major psychological blow then occurs when one partner dies. As we have said before, factors of the immediate environment are very closely related to the older person's behavior and attitudes, with significant persons being the most important of these factors. Thus, in general, divorce is more likely to occur before old age, if it is to occur at all, and older married couples seem to perceive threats to themselves emanating from outside the marital relationship as more significant than those from within. It might be said that marriage becomes a more valued human relationship by the very fact of powerful outside forces and eventual death. When so many other losses are occurring naturally, marriage may be one of the more familiar and comfortable patterns remaining.

Older marriages, although less likely to dissolve, may have problems that carry over from the past or develop as a result of current stress.

Mr. and Mrs. H had been married 40 years. They had arrived at serious disagreements and mistrust early in the marriage but had stayed together because of the children. They reached a state of truce in which there was as little contact between them as possible. Mr. H obtained employment that required him to travel about 80% of the time. For 30 years he devoted his energy and interest to his work and to impermanent, extramarital relationships. After retirement at 65, he returned to their loveless home.

He became depressed and thought often of death. Finally he developed numerous hypochondriacal symptoms, which occupied his time and energy in much the same manner as had his former job. He and Mrs. H continue to live together, each obviously unwilling to leave the other.

A common difficulty in older marriages is the disequilibrium caused by the physical or emotional illness of either spouse. Major chronic changes occurring with dementia, for example, can drastically alter the marital relationship. One partner may become the caretaker or nursemaid of the other, often with little help from elsewhere. Illnesses can drain the physical, emotional, and financial capacities of the caretaker spouse. Anger and depression may occur, and it is not unusual to find the formerly well spouse developing physical or psychiatric symptoms of his or her own.

Patterns of dominance may shift in old age, with the female assuming a more active and responsible role than formerly.[58] Many of today's older persons were brought up in a male-dominant, female-subordinate culture. But with shorter life expectancies for men and their practice of marrying women younger than themselves, they are usually older than their mates and consequently less capable physically. As early as 1960 Gold, in studying age and sex patterns of familial dominance in 24 preliterate societies, found a shift to female dominance in later life in 14 of these. She stated, "Although old women did not gain the upper hand in all societies studied, aging in no instance led to the husband's gaining in authority."[59] She suggested that husbands may be willing to accept female domination as the price of security as they age. Women, having been deprived of equal cultural status all their lives, may greatly enjoy the opportunity to exert their influence. Unfortunately their taste of greater autonomy and independence is frequently mitigated by the need to provide nursing services to husbands who become dependent and infirm more quickly. When their hus-

bands die, women's hard-won role of greater influence and control over their lives depends on a number of factors such as health, economic circumstances, and living conditions. In the future, mutuality and greater equality (for example, in sex roles and age of marriage) throughout life may produce less extreme patterns and carry over to a more consistently mutual relationship in old age.

There seems to be some interdependence between the life spans of husband and wife. In addition, a comprehensive study of 16 industrial countries' death rates back to the 1940s concludes that married people live longer than unmarried people.[60] This may be a result of selection (healthy people may select other healthy people as partners, while frailer men and women may not marry) or to the marital environment itself, which is posited as encouraging a moderate, temperate life. Suicide rates are also lower for married men and higher for divorced. Further studies will attempt to clarify why marriage is beneficial and nonmarriage, whether single or divorced, is hazardous, especially for men. In old age the mutual aid and support in a marriage may become the crucial factor in the health of each partner, just as depression and loss of support after the death of a spouse can contribute to the deterioration of the surviving partner's health, particularly for males.

For many older men, the maintenance of closeness with a spouse is the center of existence up to the very end of life. As we have seen, this is less true for women, for whom remarriage after widowhood or divorce is less likely. However, remarriage, after death or divorce of a spouse, does occur with some frequency. In 1990 some 71,000 older persons married in the United States—about 25,000 women and 46,000 men 65 years of age and over. Older males are more likely to remarry than older females for two reasons: They have a larger pool of partners from which to choose (since women outlive men), and they have a long cultural history of marrying younger women as well as their own age peers. However, although there are May–December marriages in which an older man marries a much younger woman, marriages between people of approximately the same age are more usual.

Children from an earlier marriage may or may not welcome the new union. Their negative attitudes may be voiced strongly, particularly if they believe a parent is being taken advantage of, is acting foolishly, or is endangering their inheritance; on the other hand, children may actively encourage parents to find new lives for themselves through remarriage. McKain, in an early study, found that success of late-life marriage is related to the following factors: the children encouraged the marriage, the couple knew each other a number of years before marriage, there was sufficient income, the couple pooled financial resources, and both were reasonably satisfied with their lives.[61] Common sense would lead one to believe these factors still hold true.

It is interesting to note that very few people marry for the first time in old age. The entire pool of never-marrieds is very small. For example, in 1994, some 94% of women and 92% of men in the 45–54 age group had been married at some point in their lives.[62] After age 75, only 4% of men and 5% of women had never been married.

IN-LAWS

Sooner or later almost everyone becomes an in-law. Each person who marries receives an average of six members of the spouse's family as in-laws. In the public mind, "in-law" means "trouble," especially if it happens to be a mother-in-law closely involved with her son's or daughter's life. When a mother-in-law "problem" exists, it partly stems from the cultural encouragement of competition among women from the time they are small girls for the attention of men. Added to this are the stresses facing the older woman because of her longer life span and low social status. Overinvolvement with children is another possible factor. But the entire problem is very likely exaggerated, since numbers of people manage to get along reasonably and often superbly well with in-laws, including mothers-in-law. In-laws can be supportive as well as trouble-making. Personality

factors are probably as critical as social roles in determining the quality of in-law relationships.

SIBLINGS

The siblings of older persons, particularly those older persons who are widowed or living alone, play a relatively invisible, but frequently vital role in maintaining a sense of family, connectedness, and well-being. There is little written on this subject in the field of gerontology, leading one to speculate on why such an obvious and often life-sustaining and life-enhancing set of relationships has been overlooked. Since female siblings assume the major role in tending and preserving these relationships, has their role been overlooked as insignificant or taken for granted, as has been the case in much of our recent history with housework, caregiving to children and the elderly, and other traditionally female-designated activities? Rosenthal's study of *kinkeeping* (defined as the person in an extended family who fosters family interactions and rituals) found that female siblings were most likely to play this role, usually during their 50s and 60s. The role was most likely to be assumed by a sister sibling after the illness or death of the clan mother. Thus, female siblings often play a critical role in keeping male siblings connected to the family and in providing them with supports when needed.[63]

Cicirelli comments on a number of important points surrounding sibling-ship:

1. Sibling relationships last longer than most other relationships, beginning at birth and continuing until the death of a sibling.

2. The sibling relationship can apply to step-siblings, half-siblings, and adoptive siblings, as well as biological siblings.

3. The uniqueness of sibling relationships includes not only their long duration, but also their typically egalitarian nature, their common cultural and, often, common genetic heritage, and, frequently, their common early experiences from childhood.

4. Even most of the advanced elderly currently have at least one living sibling. A 1975 national survey found eight out of ten old people had living siblings (75-year-olds came from families with an average of five children). Those who were unmarried had closer bonds with their siblings and many lived in the same house.[64]

5. Sibling contact tends to renew itself in late middle age (perhaps connected with more leisure time and with intimations of mortality) and then gradually declines with age as siblings become more infirm and contact becomes more difficult. But even then, most continue to write, talk on the phone, visit when possible, or send messages through kin.

6. Sister siblings are the closest affectionately, and brother siblings are least close.

7. Brother and sister siblings tend to become closer as they grow older.

8. Sisters do most of the tending of sibling and other family relationships. Some suggest that one reason women invest more time and energy in kinkeeping may be enlightened self-interest, namely the realization that most of them will outlive their husbands and require supports from others. (It is not uncommon for five-generation families to have three generations of widows.) But it is also clear that human relationships have a higher priority for females, whether culturally or biologically derived, from childhood on.

9. Rivalry between siblings tends to decline with age, although some rivalries manage to persist to the bitter end or reappear under stress. The more common pattern, however, is for siblings to mellow or to work actively to repair their relationships.

10. Some of the strength of the sibling bond arises from the joint sibling experience of loss of parents through death and the desire to maintain a sense of the childhood family.[65]

Rising divorce rates and similar family restructurings may make sibling relationships even more meaningful as a source of emotional support and stability in the future. On the other hand, an increase in one-child families will lessen the possibility of having a sibling. The impact of these demographic changes on what has long been a major, but seldom fully acknowledged support in old age deserves further study.

FRIENDSHIP

Friends are considered "family" by many older persons, adding to the extended support system that protects an older person in times of illness or other need. The definition of friendship differs by age, sex, class, race, and ethnicity, but most elderly appear to choose friends near their own age, based largely on shared interests, experiences, and concerns. Such friendships contribute as much or more to the physical and emotional well-being of older persons as contacts with family members.[66]

Kinship and friendship often overlap. A relative may be defined foremost as a friend rather than a relative. Friends may be considered "part of the family" and may be referred to with titles like "aunt" or "uncle." Neighbors represent a special category of friend-potential and can be important for both socializing and day-to-day help. They may be especially helpful in emergencies and sudden illness because of their close proximity.

There is general agreement that female friendships are more likely to be intimate and emotionally self-disclosing, while males are more superficial—reflecting the larger social roles of males as more emotionally reserved and even repressed. Men are more likely to turn to their spouse for emotional intimacy, thus making them exceptionally vulnerable to loss of a spouse in old age. Research is beginning to indicate that one reason for greater female longevity may be women's skills in seeking and maintaining friendships. "Network analysis" has been an effective research technique in uncovering and clarifying friendship patterns and their meaning in old age.[67]

OLDER "ISOLATES" VERSUS "DESOLATES"

Isolates, as we are defining it here, refer to individuals who have minimal or no contact with other human beings. Some people become isolated in old age because of life circumstances and would choose to live differently if they could.

Others isolate themselves by choice, often following a lifelong pattern of existence as "loners." Townsend distinguishes between "isolates" and "desolates":

> Those who are secluded from family and society, as objectively assessed on the basis of defined criteria, are the isolates. Those who have been recently deprived by death, illness or migration of someone they love—such as a husband or wife or child—are the desolates. A major conclusion of the present analysis is that though the two are connected, the underlying reason for loneliness in old age is desolation rather than isolation."68

The emotional meaning of isolation depends on whether it is a habitual life-style or whether it has come about or been exacerbated by emotional loss.

Shanas made much the same point when she commented that isolation is not synonymous with loneliness, nor is it a direct causative factor in mental illness.[69] Some older people have lived alone so long they have lost the notion of what loneliness means. Shanas found that the loneliest and most isolated people appear to be those widowed persons who have no children and live alone. On the other hand, isolation and loneliness of people are not necessarily relieved by closeness of children or frequent contact with them. In this case, isolation is a state of mind rather than actual social alienation.

Attempting to explain the fact that a greater number of single or widowed people over 65 are admitted to mental hospitals, as compared to married people, Shanas believed the blame cannot be placed on social isolation. Instead, she postulated that serious illnesses can devastate the person who is alone because there is no one to care for him or her; thus continuation in the community becomes impossible, whereas this would not be the case for someone with family or friends. Lowenthal, in tracing the connection between social isolation and mental illness in old age, found:

> Lifelong extreme isolation (or alienation) is not necessarily conducive to the development of the kinds of mental disorder that bring persons to the psychiatric ward in their old age; lifelong marginal social adjustment may be conducive to the development of such disorder; late-developing isolation is apparently linked with mental disorder but it is of no greater significance among those with psychogenic disorders than among those with organic disorders, and may be more of a consequence than a cause of mental illness in the elderly; finally, physical illness may be the critical antecedent to both the isolation and the mental illness.70

The choice to be a loner must be respected. As we have seen, people who isolate themselves are not all frail, dependent, lonely persons. We must be able to differentiate this group from those older people who truly want and need assistance in making changes in their lives. Above all, both loners and those isolated unwillingly by circumstance should have the help they require in order to maintain the kind of life most satisfactory to them.

INHERITANCE AND THE FAMILY

The issue of who gets the inheritance, if there is any, is a sensitive one for many families, and the manner in which this is handled is a good indicator of family problem solving. Some older people make their wills early and in secret. Others fully inform each child. For many people, making a will is such a painful process that it is put off and they die intestate (without a will). Children who are used to sharing with each other and who have resolved their major conflicts with parents may be able to settle an estate amicably with no ill will. But for others this is precisely the time for angry, hurt, and disappointed feelings to come to the fore, and a royal battle ensues.

The making of a will can be therapeutic for several reasons. The older person, by his or her own action, takes the potential for conflict out of the hands of the children. The estate will be handled according to the parent's own wishes. The disposing of the burden of possessions through a will can free older people and simplify their lives; many give things away even before they die. The will tells a great deal about the relations of the legator to his or her legatees (children, charitable interests, etc.). The nature of wills varies according to the stage of life of the testator. For example, if one has young children, trusts may be set up. Selection of executors and trustees is important: The executor is appointed to execute the will; the trustees are persons or agents, such as a bank, holding legal title to property in order to administer it for a beneficiary.

In some states a person may make an oral or nuncupative will; in others a holographic will—one written in the testator's own handwriting and unwitnessed—is acceptable. Older people may need to know that there are two main classes of property: real and personal. The former refers to such immovable objects as land, houses, and trees. The latter includes all other kinds of property (called legacy). If no will has been made, the property descends to lawful heirs, as legally prescribed, or to the state. Property passes into the hands of the executor who sells it and divides the proceeds among the next of kin. If a will has been made and the person dies, the will must be probated, or proved to be authentic. The executor brings the will before the court (probate or surrogate's court), and any possible heir is given the opportunity to object to the probate of the will.

It is likely that the future will bring changes in laws of inheritance, since many question the right of ownership in fee simple—that is, absolute ownership—in a complex society providing many goods and services funded through public revenues.

The use of *prenuptial agreements* is a time-honored method, in most states, of allaying the fears of children when their parents remarry in old age. Such agreements also protect older people themselves by keeping their resources intact and unavailable to anyone but designated persons. Wealthy people are inclined to use prenuptial agreements even in earlier marriages to protect family estates. With people now living longer, with more late-life marriages, and with more inherited wealth, prenuptial agreements are increasingly common. Legal consultation is necessary. The agreement customarily describes what will

not be available to the opposite spouse. Trusts can be alternatives to prenuptial agreements.

FAMILY INVOLVEMENT IN MENTAL HEALTH CARE OF OLDER PERSONS

Family Caregiving

Twelve and a half percent of elderly people live with their children or other family members—6% of all older men and 17% of older women live with children or other family members. Such arrangements generally occur when the older person has become too infirm mentally or physically or too impoverished to live alone. Since most people move in with their relatives at an advanced age, the average length of their stay is not a long one because of death or serious illness requiring hospital or nursing care. But the actual length of caregiving for any one individual can range from days to years. In most instances the pattern is one of an older mother moving in with her daughter and family. The manner in which these two women relate is often the key to success or failure of the living arrangement. Many families manage the inevitable problems of caregiving and joint households quite well. Others experience mild to severe physical and/or emotional stress and financial hardship, which can turn family caregiving into a major challenge. Genuine affection combined with a sense of ethical responsibility motivates a high proportion of children to voluntarily assist their elderly parents. Others carry out what they perceive to be their "duty," in spite of conflicting emotional feelings. Care for an aged parent can, in fact, be one way of overcoming emotional ambivalence, resolving guilt, and even building a new relatedness. Family caregiving will be discussed further in Chapter 10.

Family Therapy

By now it should be clear that most older people are *not* alienated from their families; therefore one must go further and assume that any problems, crises, and changes affecting an older person also affect his or her family. The newly forming field of family therapy, begun in the 1950s, has recognized that the problems of older people have impact on the entire kinship network. How do adult siblings work out a division of labor in caring for older parents? How does the entire family network handle change in its oldest members? Even the youngest family members will be reacting emotionally to events in the lives of their grandmother and grandfather. It is through these experiences that they learn firsthand about late life, and many of their attitudes toward older persons and their own eventual aging will be modeled after the situations and attitudes in the family circle. Family therapy involving everyone from young to old can be a way of helping to understand what is happening to the older person, clarify feelings, review and deal with old conflicts (which may be surprisingly undiluted by the passage of time), and mobilize everyone in the care and concern for the older member. (See Chapter 12 for discussion of family therapy and counseling.)

"Filial Maturity"

Blenkner has used the term "filial maturity" to describe a middle-aged developmental stage beyond the usual Freudian framework.[71] (The latter encompasses development from birth through early adulthood, with little theoretical consideration given to middle and late life.) Adults in their forties and fifties experience a "filial crisis" when it becomes evident that their parents are aging and the offspring will be called on to provide the support and comfort that older parents need. This may contrast with childhood visions of parents as powerful and nurturing individuals who assist and support their offspring, rather than vice versa. In view of the vicissitudes of early parent–child relationships, there is often unfinished developmental work to be done in freeing middle-aged adults from hostile, ambivalent, or immature parental ties that impede a healthy relationship. Maturity for the middle-aged child "involves being *depended on* and therefore being dependable insofar

as his parent is concerned," with full recognition of the parent as an individual with his or her own rights, needs, limitations, and life history. "It is often necessary to assist the child to complete his unfinished emancipation from the parent *in order that he may then be more free to help his parent.*"[72] Neurotic guilt toward parents must be differentiated from the real guilt of failure to assume filial responsibility. Neurotic guilt can lead to doing too much for parents and interfering with their independence and autonomy. A failure to address real guilt may result in the adult child doing too little for a parent. Silverstone and Hyman have emphasized the importance of determining the "right" amount of help by looking at problems realistically and by becoming aware of the feelings underlying the relationship between older parent and the adult child.[73]

Much past psychiatric and social work literature has treated the interactions between older people and their children in a negative, patronizing fashion. The term "role-reversal" has been a favored concept because it fits so comfortably with the negative stereotypes depicting the aged as dependent or regressed; the child supposedly becomes the parent to his or her own parents as they slip from self-sufficient adulthood to a state of childish dependency. But surely a more misleading interpretation of the realities of old age could not be imagined.[74] This is true even in the face of advanced dementia. Spark and Brody comment: "The behavior of a brain-damaged regressed old person may appear child-like but he is not a child. Half a century [or more] of adulthood cannot be wiped out."[75] The complexities of caring for an older person are far different than those of caring for an infant or a child, requiring specialized skills. But most importantly, the older person remains an adult, and every effort should be made to view and treat him or her as such. The presence of physical or mental impairment does not alter that reality. And remembering this simple fact can have profound effects on caregivers, care receivers, and the process of care-giving itself.

Adult children may also need help in differentiating what can't be done from what can be done. For example, the aging and eventual decline of a parent will inevitably occur and cannot be avoided, but much can be done to protect and even improve functioning and quality of life at every stage, even up to the very point of death.

Some of the more practical matters of helping the elderly can be easily learned.[76] Indeed, several rehabilitation centers and hospitals now teach families how to perform required therapies and other services. Classes for adult children can provide knowledge about aging and the illnesses frequently occurring in old age, as well as offering a

means of coping and an opportunity for sharing concerns with others. Visiting nurses and home health specialists perform a teaching function within the family (see Chapter 10). It is clear that many older people can remain at home if their problems are detected early and prompt psychiatric, social, medical, and economic resources are made available. When given adequate support, families often provide the unique blend of affection and personal services that is so essential to mental health and comfort in old age.

SELECTED READINGS

Abraham, K. (1955). Some remarks on the role of grandparents in the psychology of neuroses. In Abraham, H. (Ed.), *Selected papers: Clinical papers and essays in psychoanalysis* (vol. 2). New York: Basic Books.

Achenbaum, W. A. (1979). *Old age in the new land.* Baltimore: Johns Hopkins Press.

Adelman, R., & Butler, R. N. (1989). Elder abuse and neglect. In Kaplan, H. I., & Sadock, B. J. (Eds.), *Comprehensive textbook of psychiatry V* (Chap. 46.7a). Baltimore, MD: Williams & Wilkins.

Bass, S. A., & Caro, R. G. (1996, Spring). The economic value of grandparent assistance. *Generations, 20*(1), 29–33.

Bengtson, V. L., & Achenbaum, W. A. (1993). *The changing contract across generations.* Hawthorne, NY: Aldine de Gruyter.

Bengtson, V. L., & Hartootyan, R. (Eds.). (1994). *Intergenerational linkages: Hidden connections in American society.* New York: Springer.

Bengston, V. L., & Robertson, J. F. (Eds.). (1985). *Grandparenthood.* Beverly Hills, CA: Sage.

Bengtson, V. L., Rosenthal, C. J., & Burton, L. M. (1995). Paradoxes of families and aging at the turn of the century. In Binstock, R. H., & George, L. (Eds.), *Handbook of aging and the social sciences,* 4th ed. San Diego, CA: Academic Press.

Bengtson, V. L., Schaie, K. W., & Burton, L. M. (Eds.). (1995). *Adult intergenerational relations: Effects of societal change.* New York: Springer.

Bergeman, C. S., Plomin, R., Pedersen, N. L., McClearn, G. E., & Nesselroade, J. R. (1990, May).

Genetic and environmental influences on social support: The Swedish adoption/twin study of aging. *Journal of Gerontology, 45*(3), 101–106.

Blenkner, M. (1965). Social work and family relationships in later life with some thoughts on filial maturity. In Shanas, E. & Streib, G. F. (Eds.), *Social Structure and the family: Generational relations* (pp.46–59). Englewood Cliffs, NJ: Prentice Hall.

Blieszner, R., & Bedford, V. H. (Eds.). (1995). *Handbook of aging and the family.* Westport, CT: Greenwood.

Brody, E. (1990). *Women in the middle: Their parent-care years.* New York: Springer.

Bumagin, V. E., & Hirn, K. E. (1990). *Helping the aging family: A guide for professionals.* Glenview, IL: Scott, Foresman.

Cain, B. S. (1988, November). Divorce among elderly women: A growing social phenomenon. *Social Case Work: The Journal of Contemporary Social Work,* 563–568.

Cantor, M. H. (1993). *Growing older in New York City in the 1990's: A study of changing lifestyles, quality of life, and quality of care,* vol. 2. New York: New York Center for Policy on Aging, New York Community Trust.

Cicirelli, V. G. (1987). Siblings. In Maddox, G. L. (Ed.), *The encyclopedia of aging* (pp. 608–609). New York: Springer.

Cicirelli, V. G. (1992). Siblings as caregivers in middle and old age. In Dwyer, J. E., & Coward, R. T. (Eds.), *Gender, families, and elder care* (pp. 84–101). Newbury Park, CA: Sage Publications.

Cicirelli, V. G. (1994). Sibling relationships in cross-cultural perspective. *Journal of Marriage and the Family,* col. 56, 7–20.x

Cicirelli, V. G. (1995). Siblings. In Maddox, G. L. (Ed.), *The encyclopedia of aging* (pp. 857–859). New York: Springer.

Commonwealth Fund Commission on Elderly People Living Alone. (1987). *Old, alone, and poor.* New York: Commonwealth Fund Communications Office.

Cutler, N. E., & Devlin, S. J. (1996, Spring). A framework for understanding financial responsibilities among generations. *Generations, 20*(1), pp. 24–28.

Finley, N. J., Roberts, M. D., & Banaham, B. F. (1988). Motivators and inhibitors of attitudes of filial obligation towards aging parents. *The Gerontologist, 28,* 73–78.

Fischer, D. H. (1978). *Growing old in America.* Expanded edition. New York: Oxford University Press.

Giarrusso, R., Silverstein, M., & Bengtson, V. L. (1996, Spring). Family complexity and the grandparent role. *Generations, 20*(1), 17–23.

Gibson, R. C. (1986). Outlook for the black family. In Pifer, A. & Bronte, L. (Eds.), *Our aging society* (pp. 181–97). New York: W. W. Norton.

Gold, D. (1987). *Siblings in old age: Their relationships and roles* (monograph). Chicago: Center for Applied Gerontology.

Gutmann, D. (1987). *Reclaimed powers: Toward a new psychology of men and women in later life.* New York: Basic Books.

Gutmann, D. (1985) The parental imperative revisited: Towards a developmental psychology of adulthood and later life. In Menchem, J. A. (Ed.), *Contributions to human development.* Basel: Karger.

Hagestad, G. (1985). Continuity and connectedness. In Bengtson, V. L. & Robertson, J. F. (Eds.), *Grandparenthood* (pp. 31–48). Beverly Hills: CA: Sage.

Hagestad, G. (1986). The family: Women and grandparents as kin-keepers. In Pifer, A. & Bronte, L. (Eds.), *Our aging society* (pp. 141–160). New York: W. W. Norton.

Hamon, R. R., & Blieszner, R. (1990, May). Filial responsibility—expectations among adult child-older parents pairs. *The Journal of Gerontology, 45*(3), 110–112.

Hardgrave, T. D., & Anderson, W. T. (1992). *Finishing well: Aging and reparation in the intergenerational family.* New York: Brunner/Mazel.

Hu, Y., & Goldman, N. (1990, May). Mortality differences by marital status: An international comparison. *Demography, 27*(2), 233–250.

Jarvik, L., & Small, G. (1988). *Parentcare: A commonsense guide for adult children.* New York: Crown Publishing.

Kingson, E. R., Hirshorn, B. A., & Cornman, J. M. (1986). *The ties that bind: The interdependence of generations.* Washington, DC: Seven Locks Press.

Morris, V. (1996). *How to care for aging parents.* New York: Workman Publishing.

Parsons, T. & Bales, R. (1955). *Family, socialization and interaction process.* New York: Free Press of Glencoe.

Pillemer, K. A., & Wolf, R. S. (Eds.). (1986). *Elder abuse. Conflict in the family.* Dover, MA: Auburn House.

Pruchno, R. A., & Johnson, K. W. (1996, Spring). Research on grandparenting: Review of current studies and future needs. *Generations, 20*(1), 65–70.

Robertson, J. F. (1995). Grandparenting in an era of rapid change. In Blieszner, R., & Bedford, V. H. (Eds.), *Handbook of aging and the family.* Westport, CT: Greenwood Press.

Rossi, A. S., & Rossi, P. H. (1990). *Of human bonding: Parent–child relations across the life course.* New York: Aldine de Gruyter.

Schiff, H. S. (1996). *How did I become my parent's parent?* New York: Viking.

Schorr, A. L. (1960). *Filial responsibility in the modern American family.* Washington, DC: U.S. Department of Health, Education, and Welfare, Social Security Administration, U.S. Government Printing Office.

Shanas, E. (1980, February). Older people and their families: The new pioneers. *Journal of Marriage and the Family,* 9–15.

Shanas, E., & Streib, G. F. (1965). *Social structure of the family: Generational relations.* Englewood Cliffs, NJ: Prentice-Hall.

Townsend, P. (1957). *The family life of old people.* London: Routledge and Kegan Paul.

Troll, L. (Ed.). (1987). *Family issues in current gerontology.* New York: Springer.

Troll, L. E., & Bengtson, V. L. (1992). The oldest old in families: An intergenerational perspective. *Generations, 17,* 39–44.

U.S. Bureau of the Census. (1992). 65+ in America. *Current population reports, special studies,* Series P-23, No. 190. Washington, DC: U.S. Government Printing Office.

ENDNOTES

1. Hagestad, G. (1986). The family: Women and grandparents as kin-keepers. In Pifer, A., & Bronte, L. (Eds.), *Our aging society* (pp. 141–160). New York: W. W. Norton.

2. Elder, G. H. (1980, October). *History and the family*. Burgess Award Lecture, National Council on Family Relations, Portland, OR.

3. Models of the developmental processes of families are as important as models of individual personality development. Sociology, anthropology, psychiatry, and social work all have valuable experience in this area, which they do not often share with each other. Margaret Mead has said, "We've never adequately differentiated between a household, a biological nuclear family and whatever else people think the family really is. . . . We have no way of dealing with people who are members of a biological family but who aren't living within the nuclear family."

4. Preston, S. H. (1984, December). Children and the elderly. *U.S. Scientific American,* 44–49.

5. Hagestad, *The family,* p. 146.

6. Hagestad, G. (1987). Able elderly in the family context: Changes, chances and challenges. *The Gerontologist, 27*(4), 421.

7. Gutmann, D. L. (1985). The parental imperative revisited: Towards a developmental psychology of adulthood and later life. In Manchem, J. A. (Ed.), *Contributions to human development* (Vol. 14, pp. 31–60). Basel: Karger.

8. Johnsen, L. J., & Barer, B. M. (1987). Marital instability and the changing kinship networks of grandparents. *The Gerontologist, 27*(3), 334.

9. Maeda, D., Brody, E., Campbell, R., Okuyama, S., & Okuyama, N. (1985). *Attitudes of three generations of Japanese women toward aging and old people,* a paper presented at the XIII International Congress of Gerontology, 1985, New York.

10. Sussman, M. B. (1965). Relationships of adult children with their parents in the United States. In Shanas, E., & Streib, G. F. (Eds.), *Social structure and the family: Generational relationships.* Englewood Cliffs, NJ: Prentice-Hall.

11. Litwak, E. (1960). Extended kin relations in industrial democratic societies: Occupational mobility and extended family cohesion. *American Sociological Review, 25,* 9–21. See also Litwak, E. (1960). Geographic mobility and extended family cohesion. *American Sociological Review, 25,* 385–394.

12. World Health Organization. (1959). *Mental health problems of the aging and the aged,* Technical Report Series No. 171, Geneva: World Health Organization.

13. Townsend, P. (1965). The effects of family structure on the likelihood of admission to an institution in old age: The application of a general theory. In Shanas, E., & Streib, G. (Eds.), *Social structure and the family* (pp. 163–88). Englewood Cliffs, NJ: Prentice-Hall.

14. Shanas, E. (1980). Older people and their families: The new pioneers. *Journal of Marriage and the Family, 42*(l), 12. This three-decade-old study focuses on those four out of five noninstitutionalized older persons with living children.

15. For example, Kivett, V. R., & Atkinson, M. P. (1984). Filial expectations, associations, and helping as a function of number of children among older rural-transitional parents. *Journal of Gerontology, 39,* 499–503; Bengtson, V. L., Rosenthal, C. J., & Burton, L. M. (1995). Paradoxes of families and aging at the turn of the century. In Binstock, R. H., & George, L. (Eds.), *Handbook of aging and the social sciences.* San Diego, CA: Academic Press; Blieszner, R., & Bedford, V. H. (Eds.). (1995). *Handbook of aging and the family.* Westport, CT: Greenwood; Finley, N. J., Roberts, M. D., & Banaham, B. F. (1988). Motivators and inhibitors of attitudes of filial obligation towards aging parents. *The Gerontologist, 28,* 73–78. Rossi, A. S., & Rossi, P. H. (1990). *Of human bonding: Parent–child relations across the life course.* New York: Aldine de Gruyter.

16. Mayer, M. J. (1989). *The New York City elderly: A changing population.* Presented at Visions for the Future, a conference of the Council of Senior Centers and Services of New York City, Fordham University, June 15, 1989, pp. 6–7.

17. McAdoo, H. P. (1982). Levels of stress and family support in black families. In McCubbin, H., Cauble, A. E., & Patterson, J. (Eds.), *Family stress, coping and social supports.* Springfield, IL: Charles C. Thomas; Jackson, J. J. (1980); Gelfand, D. E. (1994). *Aging and ethnicity: Knowledge and services.* New York: Springer; Lockery, S. A. (1991, Fall/Winter). Family and social supports: Caregiving among racial and ethnic minority elders. *Generations, 15*(4), 58–62; Luckey, I. (1994, February). African American elders: The support network of generational kin. *Families in society:*

The journal of contemporary human services, 75(2), 82–89.

18. Markson, E. (1995). Marital status. In Maddox, G. L. (Ed.), *The encyclopedia of aging* (pp. 602–604). New York: Springer.

19. The classic work on the subject is that of Schorr, A. L. (1960). *Filial responsibility in the modern American family.* Washington, DC: U.S. Department of Health, Education, and Welfare, Social Security Administration, U.S. Government Printing Office.

20. U.S. Bureau of the Census. (1988). Who's helping out? Support networks among American families. *Current Population Reports,* Series P-70, No. 13. Washington, DC: U.S. Government Printing Office.

21. *Ibid.*

22. Lewis, M. I. *Economic perspectives in calculating the costs of women family members providing home elder care.* Unpublished paper, Mount Sinai School of Medicine, New York, 1990.

23. Morgan, J. N. (1984). The role of time in the measurements of transfers and economic well-being. In Moon, M. (Ed.), *Economic transfers in the United States* (pp. 199–238). Chicago: University of Chicago Press.

24. *Ibid.,* pp. 206, 214.

25. Waerness, K. (1978). The invisible welfare state: Women's work at home. *Acta Sociologica,* Supplement 1978, 193–207.

26. Cherlin, A. (1983). A sense of history: Recent research on aging and the family. In Riley, M. W., Hess, B. B., & Bond, K. B. (Eds.), *Aging in society: Selected reviews of recent research* (p. 8). Hillsdale, NJ: Lawrence Erlbaum Associates.

27. *Ibid.*

28. Sussman, M. B. (1985). The family life of old people. In Binstock, R. H., & Shanas, E. (Eds.), *Handbook of aging and the social sciences,* 2nd ed. (pp. 415–445). New York: Van Nostrand Reinhold.

29. Mayer, M. J. *The New York City elderly: A changing population.* Presented at Visions for the Future, a conference of the Council of Senior Centers and Services of New York City, Fordham University, June 15, 1989, pp. 6–7.

30. Winsborough, H. H. (1980). A demographic approach to the life cycle. In Back, K. W. (Ed.), *Life course: Integrative theories and exemplary populations.* (pp. 65–76). Boulder, CO: Westview Press.

31. Gutmann, The parental imperative revisited.

32. Hagestad, G., Able elderly in the family context.

33. Hagestad, G. O. (1984). The continuous bond: A dynamic multigenerational perspective on parent–child relations. In Perlmutter, M. (Ed.), *Minnesota Symposium on Child Psychology* (vol. 17, pp. 129–58). Hillsdale, NJ: Lawrence Erlbaum Associates.

34. Shanas, E. (1978). *A national survey of the aged.* Final report to the Administration on Aging. Washington, DC: U.S. Department of Health, Education, and Welfare.

35. Pruchno, R. A., & Johnson, K. W. (Spring, 1996). Research on grandparenting: Review of current studies and future needs. *Generations,* 65–70.

36. From a 1986 sampling by the Valley Forge Survey Co. for Meredith Corporation, the publisher of *Grandparents Magazine.*

37. *Metropolitan Life Statistical Bulletin, 52,* 8–10, 1972.

38. Ferenczi, S. (1926). The "grandfather complex." In Rickman, J. (Comp.), *Theory and technique of psychoanalysis* (pp. 323–324). London: Hogarth Press.

39. Presented at 1958 annual meeting, University of North Carolina School of Medicine, Chapel Hill.

40. Rappaport, E. A. (1958). The grandparent syndrome. *Psychoanalytic Quarterly, 27,* 518–538.

41. Haber, M. (1965). The importance of grandparents in family life. *Family Process, 4,* 228–240.

42. Benedek, T. (1970). Parenthood during the life cycle. In Anthony E. J. (Ed.), *Parenthood* (p. 201). Boston: Little, Brown.

43. Hagestad, *The family,* p. 148.

44. *Ibid.,* p. 152.

45. Kivnick, H. Q. (1982). Grandparenthood: An overview of meaning and mental health. *The Gerontologist, 22*(1), 59–66.

46. U.S. Bureau of the Census. (1994, March). Marital status and living arrangements. *Current Population Reports,* Series P-20, No. 484. Washington DC: U.S. Government Printing Office.

47. U.S. Bureau of the Census. (1992, October). Marriage, Divorce and Remarriage in the 1990's. *Current Population Reports,* Series P-20, no. 180.

48. Hagestad, G. O., Sanger, M. A., & Stierman, K. L. (1984). Parent-child relations in adulthood: The impact of divorce in middle age. In Cohen, R., Weissman, S., & Cohler, B. (Eds.), *Parenthood: Psychodynamic perspectives* (pp. 247–62). New York: Guildford Press; Fisher, E. O. (Ed.). (1982). *Impact of divorce on the extended family.* Binghamton, NY: The Haworth Press.

49. Matthews, S. H., & Sprey, J. (1984). The impact of divorce on grandparenthood: An exploratory study. *The Gerontologist, 24*(1), 41–47.

50. Glick, P. C. (1957). *American families.* New York: John Wiley.

51. U.S. Bureau of the Census. (1994, March). Marital status and living arrangements. *Current Population Reports,* Series P-20, No. 484. Washington DC: U.S. Government Printing Office.

52. Yarrow, M. R., Blank, P., Quinn, O. W., Youmans, E. G., & Stein, J. (1963). Social psychological characteristics of old age. In Birren, J. E., Butler, R. N., Greenhouse, S. W., Sokoloff, L., & Yarrow, M. R. (Eds.), *Human aging: A biological and behavioral study.* Pub. No. (PHS) 986. Washington, DC: U.S. Government Printing Office (reprinted as Pub. No. [HSM] 71–9051 1971, 1974). See also Pineo, P. C. (1968). Disenchantment in the later years of marriages. In Neugarten, B. L. (Ed.), *Middle age and aging* (pp. 258–262). Chicago: University of Chicago Press.

53. Markides, K. S. (1995). Marital satisfaction. In Maddox, G. L. (Ed.), *The encyclopedia of aging.* (pp. 601–602). New York: Springer.

54. It is noteworthy that in the NIMH study of healthy older men, there were many criticisms and complaints about wives, yet only one man reported even considering separation from his spouse, and none believed that either his marriage or his choice of a spouse was a mistake. Whether this is a tribute to the success of these marriages or an indication that such an indictment of a large segment of their lives was too painful to face is an interesting question. Generally, however, these men appeared to "tell it like it was," or at least close to like it was, about their marriages.

55. National Center for Health Statistics. (1995). Advance report of final divorce statistics, 1989 and 1990. *Monthly Vital Statistics Report, 43*(8), supplement. Hyattsville, MD: Author.

56. Cain, B. S. (1988, November). Divorce among elderly women: A growing social phenomenon. *Social Case Work: The Journal of Contemporary Social Work,* 563–568; Ulenberg, P., & Meyers, M. P. (1981). Divorce among the elderly. *The Gerontologist, 21*(3), 276–281.

57. U.S. Bureau of the Census. (1994, March). Marital status and living arrangements. *Current Population Reports,* Series P-20, No. 484. Washington DC: U.S. Government Printing Office.

58. Gutmann, D. (1987). *Reclaimed powers: Toward a new, psychology of men and women in later life.* New York: Basic Books.

59. Gold, S. (1960, Spring). Cross-cultural comparisons of role change with aging. *Student Journal of Human Development,* 11a.

60. Hu, Y., & Goldman, N. (1990, May). Mortality differences by marital status: An international comparison. *Demography, 27*(2), 233–250.

61. McKain, W. C. (1969). *Retirement marriage.* Storrs, CT: University of Connecticut, p. 168.

62. U.S. Bureau of the Census. (1994, March). Marital status and living arrangements. *Current Population Reports,* Series P-20, No. 484. Washington DC: U.S. Government Printing Office.

63. Rosenthal, C. (1985, November). Kinkeeping in the familial division of labor. *Journal of Marriage and the Family,* 965–974.

64. Shanas, E. (1979). Social myth as hypothesis: The care of the family relations of old people. *The Gerontologist, 19*(1), 3–9. Also see U.S. Bureau of the Census. (1979). Marital status and living arrangements, March 1978. *Current Population Reports,* Series P-20, No. 338, Washington, DC: U.S. Government Printing Office.

65. Cicirelli, V. G. (1987). Siblings. In Maddox, G. L. (Ed.), *The encyclopedia of aging* (pp. 608–609). New York: Springer; Cicirelli, V. G. (1985). The role of siblings as family caregivers. In Sauer, W. J., & Coward, R. T. (Eds.), *Social support networks and the care of the elderly* (pp. 93–107). New York: Springer; and Cicirelli, V. G. (1985). Sibling relationships throughout the life cycle. In L'Abate, L. (Ed.), *The handbook of family psychology and therapy* (vol. 1, pp. 177–214). Homewood, IL: Dorsey Press.

66. Chappell, N. L. (1983). Informal support networks among the elderly. *Research on Aging, 5,* 77–99.

67. Cohen, C. I., & Rajkowski, H. (1982). What's in a friend? Substantive and theoretical issues. *The Gerontologist, 22,* 261–266.

68. Townsend, P. (1968). The emergence of the four-generation family in industrial society. In Neugarten, B. L. (Ed.), *Middle age and aging: A reader in social psychology* (pp. 255–257). Chicago: University of Chicago Press.

69. Shanas, E. (1964). The older person at home—a potential isolate or participant. Reprinted from National Institute of Mental Health. In *Research utilization in aging: An exploration,* proceedings of a conference sponsored by Community Research and Services Branch, April 30–May 3, 1963. Washington, DC: U.S. Government Printing Office.

70. Lowenthal, M. F. (1968). Social isolation and mental illness in old age. In Neugarten, B. L. (Ed.), *Middle age and aging: A reader in social psychology* (p. 234). Chicago: University of Chicago Press.

71. For an excellent summary on family relationships in old age, see Blenkner, M. (1965). Social work

and family relationships in later life with some thoughts on filial maturity. In Shanas, E., & Streib, G. F. (Eds.), *Social structure and the family: Generational relations* (pp. 46–59). Englewood Cliffs, NJ: Prentice-Hall.

72. *Ibid.*, p. 50.

73. Silverstone, B., & Hyman, H. K. (1976). *You and your aging parent.* New York: Pantheon Books.

74. See series of five articles on the issue of "role reversal," presented at a symposium: Role reversal: Is it a valid concept? 41st Annual Scientific Meeting of the Gerontological Society of America, in San Francisco, November 18–22, 1988. Reprinted in *Journal of Gerontological Social Work, 15*(½), 1–38, 1990.

75. Spark, G., & Brody, E. (1972). The aged as family members. In Sager, C., & Kaplan, H. (Eds.), *Progress in group and family therapy* (p. 717). New York: Brunner Mozel.

76. Useful books for the families of older persons are Shelley, F. D. (1988). *When your parents grow old.* New York: Harper & Row; Jarvik, L., & Small, G. (1988). *Parentcare: A commonsense guide for adult children.* New York: Crown Publishing; and Morris, V. (1996) *How to care for aging parents.* New York: Workman Publishing.

HEALTHY, SUCCESSFUL OLD AGE

Old age can be an emotionally healthy and satisfying time of life with a minimum of physical and mental impairment. But what are the optimal conditions that make this possible? This chapter has been designed as an overview of healthy old age and some of its important components.

Mr. S, a 76-year-old retired businessman, is spontaneous, talkative, and in touch with reality. He has varied emotional response appropriate to the situation and no sign of psychomotor retardation. When interviewed, he spoke in a frank and integrated manner about his achievements. Although some general forgetfulness is noted on his history, there is no sign of a marked intellectual decline, and no memory impairments were found on the mental status examination.

Mr. S was born on a farm in central Europe, the oldest of ten children. He was already employed at age 9 and left home at age 13. He describes his parents as having some problems, and he states that he felt closer to his mother but attained a greater understanding of his father as years went by. At age 23 he married and emigrated to the United States. His marriage is viewed by him as an excellent one, and his wife is in good health. Mr. S has experienced a modest decrease in sexual desire and continues sex relations on a less frequent basis. His relation-

ship with children and grandchildren is satisfying, with moderate interaction. He remembers that his children's adolescent rebellions gave him a chance to look anew at his own early years.

Mr. S had made plans for his older years and continues to plan optimistically for the future. He feels concerned about death and hopes he will have a sudden death or die in his sleep. He feels some interest in religion but denies any marked change since youth. He has made out a will and has arranged for a burial site.

In viewing his aging condition, Mr. S shows a reasonable recognition of his capacities and limitations, with no obvious denial. He appears to have accepted his physical changes. He is no longer very active but takes walks and moves about the house and yard with regularity. He shows no history of lifelong psychopathology, and there is no evidence of new psychopathology as he ages. There is no psychological isolation, and it is deemed unlikely that he will have a functional breakdown in the future.

Mr. S is an example of an older person who has adapted to old age with minimal stress and a high level of morale. With old age, just as with any other age, one can learn much about pathological conditions by understanding healthy developmental processes. Unfortunately, until recently, healthy older people have rarely been the subjects of research investigation or theoretical constructs. The study of "normal" development, seldom explored beyond early adult years, must now expand to include older persons. The psychology of human development will then reach a new dimension, encompassing the entire life span.

NEGATIVE STEREOTYPE OF OLD AGE

Although many Americans still find difficulty in thinking of old age as a time of potential health and growth, an increasing number of older persons are able to lead healthy and vigorous lives. There has been some steady improvement in their lot in recent years. But those who are widowed, live alone, belong to minorities, or are very old are still vulnerable to a wide array of stresses and struggles in late life. And these vulnerable elderly continue to fuel national stereotypes of old age as a time of decrepitude and decline.

In a larger sense, Western civilization itself produces a negative view of aging. The Western concept of the life cycle is decidedly different from that of the Far East, since they derive from two opposing views of what "self" means and what life is all about. Eastern philosophy places the individual's self, life, and death *within* the process of the human experience. The personal experience blends with the universal. Life and death are familiar and intertwined. Death is characteristically seen as a welcome relief from suffering or, as in Japanese ancestor worship, a step upward in social mobility to join the revered ancestors.[1] In Buddhism, death is merely a passage to another reincarnation unless the person achieves an enlightenment that releases him or her from the eternal cycle.

In the West, death is considered to be *outside* of the process of the human experience. To be a self (a person) one must be alive, in control, and aware of what is happening. The greater and more narcissistic Western emphasis on individuality and control makes death an outrage, a tremendous affront to humans rather than the logical and necessary process of old life making way for new.

The opposite cultural views of East and West evolved to support two very different ways of life, each with its own merits; but the Western predilection for "progress," conquest over nature, and personal self-realization has produced difficult problems for older persons and for those preparing for old age. This is particularly so when the national spirit of the United States and the spirit of this period in time have emphasized and expanded the notion of measuring human worth in terms of individual productivity and power. Older people are led to see themselves as "beginning to fail" as they age, a phrase that refers as much to self-worth as it does to physical strength. Religion has been the traditional solace by promising another world wherein the self again springs to life, never to be further threatened by loss of its own integrity. Thus the consummate dream of immortality for Westerners is fulfilled by religion, yet the integration of the aging experience into their life process remains incomplete. To make matters more complicated, increasing secularization produces a frightening void around the subject of death itself, which frequently is met by avoiding and denying the thought of one's own decline and death and by forming self-protective prejudices against the old.

Medicine and the behavioral sciences have mirrored societal attitudes by presenting old age as a grim litany of physical and emotional ills. Until 1960 most of the medical, psychological, psychiatric, and social work literature on the aged was based on experience with the sick and the institutionalized, even though only 5% of older people were confined to institutions. Decline of the individual was the key concept. Fortunately, research studies that have concentrated on the healthy aged give indications of positive potential for the entire age group.

WHAT IS A HEALTHY OLD AGE?

In thinking about health, one is led to the understanding that, in addition to the general lack of interest in older persons, science and medicine have historically been more concerned with treating "what went wrong" than with clarifying the complex, interwoven elements necessary to produce and support health. Typical of this is the treating of coronary attacks after the fact rather than prescribing a preventive program of diet, exercise, protection from stress, and absence of smoking. Most of the major diseases of older people can be cited as examples of this same phenomenon. The tedious and less dramatic process of prevention requires an understanding of what supports or what interferes with healthy development throughout the course of the life cycle.

The World Health Organization in 1946 first defined health as "a state of complete physical, mental, and social well-being and not merely the absence of disease or infirmity." This, of course, represents an ideal with many possible interpretations. But the broad elements of health—physical, emotional, and social—are the framework in which one can begin to analyze what is going well in addition to what is going wrong. The attempt must be made to locate those conditions that enable humans to thrive, not merely survive.

Old age does involve unique developmental work. Childhood might be defined as a period of gathering and enlarging strength and experience, whereas a major developmental task in old age is to clarify, deepen, and find use for what one has already attained in a lifetime of learning and adapting. Older people must teach themselves to conserve their strength and resources when necessary and to adjust in the best sense to those changes and losses that occur as part of the aging experience. The ability of the older person to adapt and thrive is contingent on physical health, personality, earlier life experiences, and on the societal supports he or she receives: adequate finances, shelter, medical care, social roles, recreation, and the like. An important point to emphasize is that, as is true for children, adolescents, and the middle-aged, it is imperative that older people continue to develop and change in a flexible manner if health is to be promoted and maintained. Failure of adaptation at any age or under any circumstance can result in physical or emotional illness. Optimal growth and adaptation can occur throughout the life cycle when the individual's strengths and potentials are recognized, reinforced, and encouraged by the environment in which he or she lives.

Popular ideas of human development need revision to encompass the experience of older persons. They should not have to view themselves as "failing" or "finished" because one or another element of life is changing or declining. For example, a loss in physical health or the loss of a loved one is indeed a serious blow, but the potential for continuing adjustment and growth needs therefore to be even more carefully exploited than under less critical circumstances. In our too quick assumption that old age is a relentless downhill course, we ignore the potential of older persons for strength as well as for a richer emotional, spiritual, and even intellectual and social life than may be possible for the young. Youth must concentrate on the piece-by-piece accumulation of personality and experience. Old age, in its best sense, can mean enjoyment of something closer to the finished product—a far more mature, complex human being.

BECOMING "OLD"

To attempt to clarify and disentangle what "old" means, we must emphasize that the concern here is not with those characteristics of old people that are the result of preexistent personality factors. The kind of personality one carries into old age is a crucial factor in how one will respond to the experience of being older; personality traits produce individual ways of being old. However, we wish to deal with the more general characteristics of old age and the changes that are fairly common to the aging population as a whole in the United States.

Physical Changes

Some of the outward alterations experienced by older persons are graying of hair, loss of hair and teeth, elongation of ears and nose, losses of subcutaneous fat, particularly around the face, wrinkling of skin, fading of eyesight and hearing, postural changes, and a progressive structural decline that may result in a shortened trunk with comparatively long arms and legs. Not all of these changes happen to everyone—nor at the same rate. A person can be a "young" 90-year-old, in a physical sense, or an "old" 60-year-old. Little is known about the onset and progress of many of these changes, since they were long thought to be simply the inescapable and universal consequences of growing old. But recent research has revealed that some, or perhaps many, are results of disease states that occur with greater frequency in late life and may be treatable—either by slowing the course of the disease or by preventing it entirely. Atherosclerosis and osteoporosis are cases in point. The rate of heart disease in the United States has already shown some decline. Even cancer may someday be conquered, although not many years ago someone dying of cancer was said to be dying of "old age." Other reasons for bodily changes have been identified as results of unusual amounts of exposure to some pathogenic element—too much sun (causing skin wrinkles), cigarette smoke, and air pollution, to name a few. Genetic traits can be responsible for changes like graying hair and loss of hair. Yet in the best of all future worlds, with acute and chronic disease states identified and eliminated, undesirable genetic traits nullified, and pathogenic environmental conditions removed, a process called aging will still occur. The potential for life can be lengthened and enhanced, but the mysterious flow of human existence from birth through death will prevail. As many older people realize more calmly than the young, aging and death must be accepted as part of human experience.

The overall physical health of the body plays a critical role in determining the energies and adaptive capacities available to older people. They experience a good deal more acute and chronic disease than the younger population. Specific physical disabilities and diseases, such as cardiovascular and locomotor afflictions, are particularly debilitating, especially when they affect the integrative systems of the body—the endocrine, vascular, and central nervous systems. Severe or even mild organic brain disease can interfere markedly

with functioning. Perceptual losses of eyesight and hearing can deplete energy and cause social isolation. However, although more than four out of five older persons have one or more chronic health problems, 95% are able to live in the community. Their conditions are mild enough to enable 80% or so of older persons to get around with no outside assistance. If significant breakthroughs occur in research and treatment of diseases of the aged (heart disease, cancer, arthritis, arteriosclerosis, and acute and chronic brain syndromes), one can envision a very different kind of old age. Assuming adequate environmental supports, including proper nutrition, old age could become a time of lengthy good health with a more gentle and predictable decline. Older persons would not have to battle the ravages of disease, and a fuller measure of their physical strength could be available for other uses. Already today one can see the possibilities in those older people who are disease-free. They can cope more vigorously with the emotional and social changes specific to their age group and in so doing have the opportunity for a successful and satisfying later life.

Emotional Changes

Older people are often stereotyped as slow thinkers, forgetful, rigid, mean-tempered, irritable, dependent, and querulous. Certainly they do suffer from anxiety, grief, depression, and paranoid states that may be experienced at any age. But one must separate out the personality traits demonstrated in earlier life, realistic responses to actual loss of friends and loved ones, personal reactions to the idea of one's own aging and death, and the predictable emotional responses of human beings at any age to physical illness or social loss. The emotional aspects of aging are more fully discussed in Chapter 4.

Intellectual Changes

The effects of aging on intellectual functioning have been studied since the post–World War I era. The earliest assumptions were that intelligence declined progressively with age. The Army Alpha Test of World War I on officers and recruits 18 to 60 years of age and older seemed to confirm the idea of intellectual decline, since lower and lower test scores were found as age increased. In 1932 Miles and Miles reported much the same results with 823 subjects ranging from age 5 to 94.[2] Intelligence scores were shown to increase until age 18 and then begin a long decline. Jones and Conrad in 1933 produced similar general results with 1,191 subjects age 10 to 60, including children, parents, and grandparents.[3] In 1955 Wechsler (the Wechsler Adult Intelligence Scale [WAIS]) developed an IQ test adjusted for each age group, which artificially gave older people a boost in their otherwise declining raw test scores.

All the above studies were cross-sectional, with each subject interviewed once. This methodology produced inherent biases favoring the better educated young and reflecting historical and environmental differences between the generations. On the other hand, longitudinal studies on the same individual over a period of time were also being done, making it possible to measure actual intelligence changes over the life cycle while avoiding the pitfalls of cross-sectional research.[4] In the 1920s both Bayley and Bradway conducted longitudinal studies, still continuing today, in which they have tested and retested persons (now in later life), beginning with childhood.[5] They found IQ scores increasing until the twenties and then eventually leveling off, remaining unchanged until late in life. There was no overall decline with age. The work of Owens and others corroborated these findings.[6]

Lorge, meanwhile, tested the assumption that one aspect of intelligence—speed of reaction—may indeed decrease with age.[7] (Reaction time studies, such as those by Birren, demonstrate a loss in speed of response in the central nervous system with age.) He concluded that, generally speaking, if older persons were given enough time on tests, they functioned as accurately as younger persons. The health factor in later life has also been evaluated for its effect on intelligence and other psychometric tests. Even minimal poor health can adversely affect test scores.[8] Jarvik and others found a drop in intellectual measures in the period just before death.[9]

The distinction between "crystallized" intelligence and "fluid" intelligence, introduced by Horn and Cattell, has been a useful one.[10] Crystallized intelligence is a result of experience and tends to increase throughout life in healthy, active people. Meanwhile, fluid intelligence is determined biologically and is thought to be more subject to decline with aging.

Eisdorfer and others found that the overarousal of the autonomic nervous system during stress affected the verbal learning abilities of older people.[11] Therefore, by giving an adrenergic blocking agent to one group and a placebo to another they found fewer errors as well as lower pre-fatty acid levels (a reflection of stress).

In general, with good physical and mental health, adequate educational levels, and intellectual stimulation, it appears that there is not as great a decline in intellectual abilities with age as previously thought, especially in the 60 and 70 year age group.[12] Some abilities, such as judgment, accuracy, and general knowledge, may, in fact, increase. However, if one lives long enough there are decrements in important abilities of intelligence that are not yet readily accounted for by disease.[13] There appear to be losses in brain cells, for example, and brain cells, unlike other cells in the body, do not continue to replace themselves throughout life. Nonetheless, the significance of the cell loss, since there is a redundancy of cells, is not established. There are also changes in the nerve cell (neuron) itself, especially the dendrites, which participate in neurotransmission.[14]

Studies of intellectual function and memory decline among the aged have shown that when older persons were presented with real problems, they scored much better than when they were tested with trivial or artificial problems. Sternberg and Wagner (1986) have studied practical intelligence in the performance of real-life situations. In addition, studies of aerobically trained individuals suggest that exercise is associated with improved cognitive function.

The Seattle Longitudinal Study (Schaie) found wide individual differences in intellectual changes over time, with a large number of elderly persons showing little decline, even in their eighties. Schaie has postulated a number of factors that characterize such elderly: (1) they have no cardiovascular disease; (2) they are not poor—rather, they are at least average economically; (3) they have an active involvement in life; and (4) they describe themselves as having already been flexible in attitudes and behavior in mid-life.[15]

Social Changes

It is in the social realm of an older person's life that the most clearly age-specific patterns can presently be seen. The nature of families and societies in the course of the life cycle decrees certain conditions that can be described as "natural" for older people. They find themselves the eldest group in the population with two, three, or even four generations below them. Many have grown children and grandchildren with whom they are involved. Grandparentage becomes a new social role. The older husband and wife each face prospects of widowhood and membership in a peer group with a large proportion of widowed contemporaries. There are increasing numbers of women compared to men as they age. Many older persons are less involved than previously in work and income-related activities and thus have more time available for their own use.

Beyond these certain basic social conditions, older people experience wide variations from culture to culture. The old may be venerated or scorned, treated overly sentimentally or rejected, protected or abandoned. At times they are arbitrarily respected for great wisdom and counsel while at other times, paradoxically, they are seen as burdens that waste their society's strength and resources. Cross-cultural studies in the psychology of later life give insights concerning universal features of aging and offer opportunities for borrowing new social and cultural arrangements from each other.

The older person's relative position in any society tends to be favorably influenced by several institutional factors:

1. Ownership of property and control over the opportunities of the young
2. Command of strategic knowledge and skills
3. Strong religious and sacred traditions
4. Strong kinship and extended family bonds
5. A less product-oriented society
6. High mutual dependence and reciprocity among society members

In the United States, a split and contradictory set of roles exists for older men, since some of them remain active in government, political parties, religious affairs, and business life. They may have strong executive and administrative responsibilities. In the United States Supreme Court, 85% of all service has been supplied by men over 65. Such opportunities exist for relatively few older men, however, and this generation of older women, because of their major roles as homemakers, have far fewer positions of public power and status.

The feelings of social loss among the aged can be tremendous. Retirement and Social Security regulations put them out of the work force when many would prefer employment. Income becomes drastically reduced, in many cases to outright poverty. Thirty percent live alone and 55% live with a spouse. Children and grandchildren who live miles away may have few face-to-face contacts. It must be added, however, that outright neglect or isolation from families is *not* the norm, except when geographical distances are a factor in creating isolation. Even though they may live in separate households, which both generations may prefer, many families are deeply supportive of their older members.

Old age, then, is a multiply-determined experience that depends on an intricate balance of physical, emotional, and social forces, any one of which can upset or involve the others. An older person who is socially lonely may not eat well and therefore may develop physical symptoms of malnourishment, which in turn cloud intellectual functioning. Hearing loss can lead to a suspiciousness that irritates people and causes them to shun the person's company, leaving that person isolated. A widower, grieving the loss of his wife, may develop psychosomatic symptoms and lose his job.

We already have the knowledge and skills available to alleviate much of the suffering in old age. We know that people need to be fed and sheltered decently, they must have medical and psychiatric care, they need loving and supportive personal contacts, and, finally, they require meaningful social roles. Health is not really an elusive concept, but it does require that we make commitments *as* human beings *to* human beings, and these commitments require much energy and many resources.

HISTORICAL FACTORS IN ADAPTATION

People are shaped not only by their own personal history, family environment, and inherent personality characteristics, but also by the larger world around them. So in understanding the aged it is useful to consider those factors in local, national, and world history that may have influenced them as they grew from infancy to old age.[16]

The present 65-plus population was born around the time when Herbert Spencer's social Darwinism or "survival of the fittest" was the popular social theory. Huge fortunes were amassed by families with names like Gould, Morgan, Rockefeller, and Carnegie, while poorly paid immigrant workers provided labor. The Protestant ethic, inspired by Calvin's philosophy of success through hard work and self-sacrifice, was the dominant religious influence. The labor movement, women's suffrage, and child labor laws were evolving as protection against exploitation. Thus the nation had reached a crossroads between accepting the notion of survival of the strongest and attempting to protect everyone, including the weak.

This raw dichotomy was the earliest societal experience of the now-older population. Many of

them still feel the tug of these forces in their personal lives and insist on being independent in the face of real personal limitations. They may berate themselves for not being allowed or able to work. They may accept their difficult economic and social conditions as evidence that they are not among the elite or "fittest." The massive depression of the 1930s served to propel scores of such "rugged individualists" into reluctant acceptance of governmental intervention in their lives, but many saw such intervention as evidence of personal failure rather than overwhelming social forces. They have contended with the tumultuous concept of progress through industrialization and automation and with the technological notion of human obsolescence. All this has served to increase their sense of uncertainty about their own value if their productive capacities wane.

POPULAR MYTHS ABOUT AGING

It is a myth that chronological age determines how "old" one is. A more apt measure of actual age might be that old maxim "You're as old as you feel." Young 80-year-olds can look very different from old 80-year-olds. It is well established that large disparities often exist between physiological, psychological, chronological, and social ages. People age at such different rates that physiological indicators show a greater range from the mean in old age than in any other age group, and people may become more diverse rather than similar as they age.[17] Of course certain diseases have a leveling effect, which causes a look-alike appearance from person to person. Massive organic brain damage and the major illnesses can so damage body and brain that their victims may react and behave very much like each other. Poverty and illiteracy also tend to obscure individual uniqueness and variation.

Another widespread myth surrounding aging is the conviction that all old people are "senile." *Senility,* although not an actual medical term, is still often used by doctors and lay people alike to explain the behavior and condition of older people. Many of the reactive emotional responses of older people, such as depression, grief, and anxiety, are labeled senile and thus considered chronic, untreatable states. Senility is an especially convenient tag put on older women by doctors who do not wish to spend the time and effort necessary to diagnose and treat their complaints. The popular medical school term for older people is "crocks"; thus attitudes are formed that affect future practice. To be sure, brain damage from multi-infarct dementia and Alzheimer's disease is a realistic problem, probably causing 50% or more of cases of mental disorder in old age. But even with brain disease there can be overlays of depression, anxiety, and psychosomatic disorders that are responsive to medical and psychotherapeutic intervention.

A third myth, the *tranquility myth,* presents a strange and contradictory position, considering the general situation of older persons. This myth sets forth the sugar-coated "Grandma-baking-goodies" vision of old age as a time of idyllic serenity and tranquility when older persons enjoy the fruits of their labors. A combination of wishful thinking about their own future old age and denial of the realities that presently exist is evident in the younger generation's image of happy-go-lucky older people.

Mrs. G and her husband retired with an estate of a quarter of a million dollars. He had been a successful doctor in a Midwestern city. Dr. G was 69 when he chose to retire and his wife was four years younger. Only two years later he was dead. Their son, age 44, died of a coronary a year afterward. Mrs. G paid many of the expenses of her son's terminal illness and also helped her daughter-in-law meet the college expenses of her grandchildren. Ten years later, at 77 years of age, Mrs. G, the respected and wealthy physician's wife, was herself impoverished and enfeebled. Her money had run out.

We cite this example to illustrate how people who may have entered old age in the most favorable circumstances can nonetheless be subject to major and continuing emotional and financial crises.

There is also the *myth of unproductivity* associated with old age. It is assumed that older people can no longer produce in a job or be active socially and creatively. They are presumed to be disengaged from life, declining and disinterested. But in the absence of disease and social adversity, this does not happen. Older people tend to remain actively concerned about their personal and community relationships. Many are still employed. Numbers of others do "bootleg work" to avoid reporting their earnings, because of Social Security income ceilings.

The *myth of resistance to change* is as suspect as all the others. It is true that adult character structure is remarkably stable, but ability to change depends more on previous and lifelong personality traits than on anything inherent in old age. Often when conservatism occurs, it derives not from aging but from socioeconomic pressures. An example might be the decision of older people to vote against school loans because of the increase those loans would mean in their personal property taxes.

NEW INTERPRETATIONS OF AGING FROM RESEARCH

In attempting to gain a more realistic picture of aging, a few midcentury investigators, responding to the paucity of information in this area, began studying healthy older people. Community-resident and socially autonomous older people were examined from a wide range of research perspectives in studies beginning in the late 1950s and early 1960s. The Busse et al. (1985) and National Institute of Mental Health (NIMH) studies (Birren et al., 1963) were responsible for some of the first work, and Shock (1984) studied some 600 men longitudinally every 18 months. The NIMH undertook collaborative studies involving separate academic disciplines and medical specialties over a period of 11 years. The NIMH findings were surprisingly optimistic and in general reinforced the hypothesis that much of what has been called aging is really disease.

Decreased cerebral (brain) blood flow and oxygen consumption were found to be probable results of arteriosclerosis rather than an inevitable companion of aging. Healthy older men with an average age of 71 presented cerebral physiological and intellectual functions that compared favorably with those in a younger control group with an average age of 21. Some evidence of slowing in speed and response was found, but this correlated with environmental deprivation and depression as well as with physical decline.

Older persons were found to have the same psychiatric disorders as the young with similar genesis and structure. Adaptation and survival appeared to be associated with the individual's self-image and sense of ongoing usefulness as well as continuing good physical health. Current environmental satisfaction and support were found to be critical to psychological stability. Individuals who were "self-starters" and could structure and carry out new contacts, activities, and involvements were found to have the least disease and the longest survival rates. The interrelating between sound health and adaptability was validated by the sensitivity of psychometric test results to even

minimal disease. In general the healthy aged were characterized by flexibility, resourcefulness, and optimism, whereas manifestations of mental illness were attributed to medical illness, personality factors, and sociocultural effects rather than the aging process.

See Table 3.1 for illustrative longitudinal studies involving older people. Such studies are important to our understanding of human change over time.

PSYCHOSOCIAL THEORIES OF AGING

G. Stanley Hall was a pioneer, writing the first major American book on the psychology of old age in 1922. Since then, a variety of theories have evolved concerning the psychology of aging. The controversial "disengagement theory" in gerontology evolved from the Kansas City aging studies conducted by the University of Chicago Committee on Human Development in the late 1950s.[18] This theory postulated that older people

TABLE 3.1   Illustrative longitudinal studies involving normal older people

STUDY	YEAR BEGAN	SEX STUDIED
Berkeley/Oakland Human Development Studies (National Institute of Child and Human Development/National Institute on Aging)	1928/1932	Male and female
Adaptation to Life (Harvard Medical School)	1937	Male
Thousand Aviators (U.S. Navy)	1940	Male
Framingham Study (National Heart Lung and Blood Institute and National Eye Institute)	1950	Male and female
Duke University I and II (National Institute on Aging—supported)	1955	Male and female
National Institute of Mental Health of the National Institutes of Health	1955	Male
Baltimore Longitudinal Study (National Institute on Aging—intramural)	1958	Male and female
Langley-Porter/University of California, San Francisco (National Institute of Child and Human Development/National Institute on Aging)	1958	Male and female
Veterans Administration Normative Study	1958	Male
Gothenburg, Sweden Studies (A. Svanborg)	1971	Male and female

and society mutually withdraw from each other as part of normal aging, and that this withdrawal is characterized by psychological well-being on the part of the older person. Later the disengagement theory was modified by Havighurst et al. in a series of papers beginning in 1963, using the original Kansas City data.[19] Disengagement was redefined by them as simply a process rather than a theory of optimum aging and as only one of many possible patterns of aging. Of 88 subjects studied, all but 18 fell into the following psychological groups: (1) the integrated, who were high on most positive personality variables; (2) the "defended" group, aggressive and full of energy; (3) the passive-dependent group; and (4) the unintegrated group, low on almost all personality measures. These four categories were common to both men and women. There were two further groups of men: One group was characterized as introspective, timid, stable, and high on super-ego control but lacking in internalization of institutional values. The other group was fearful of failure and of becoming dependent on others. One group of women had feelings of inferiority and self-doubt and was overcontrolled and dissatisfied. Another group of women similarly was self-doubting but very aggressive and competitive.

Reichard et al. interviewed 87 men, 55 to 84 years of age, in California.[20] They found 64 of these subjects fit into five groups. Three of these groups were accepting of aging: (1) the mature, philosophical men, (2) the rocking chair men who seemed glad to have time to relax, and (3) the armored men who tried to keep active at all costs and used this as a defense against old age and death. The fourth group was labeled aggressive and seemed to blame others for its disappointments and frustrations. Those in the fifth group were intrapunitive (Reichard's term for self-punitive), depressed, and gloomy. Of the 87 men, 23 did not fit neatly into any of these categories.

Carp's study of residents in a home for the aging in Texas produced evidence that in a positive environment older people generally moved toward activity and informal social contacts, rather than disengagement.[21] She raised the possibility that so-called "age-related behavior" such as disengagement may be the result of the environmental conditions that so often accompany old age. Carp also observed that rigidity was not intrinsic to the aging personality. Rigid behavior could be brought on by difficult social or physical situations; but once the difficulties were alleviated, the rigidity disappeared.

Rosow (*The Social Integration of the Aged,* 1967) showed that older people who live among other older people make more friends than those who live among the young, refuting a conclusion of the disengagement theory. His sample included 1,200 older people living in three kinds of housing—one with a mix of ages, one with a number of older people, that is, "age concentrated," and one almost totally aged, that is, "age dense." Hochschild (*The Unexpected Community,* 1973) also found in her intensive study of 43 older people residing in a small apartment building that "age dense" housing arrangements expand the potential circle of friends for older people. An "exchange" theory pertaining to imbalances in social exchange and their relationship to rewards and power has been posited as an explanation for the disengaging behavior seen in some older persons.[22] Martin and Dowd, in particular, have advanced the notion that the more one values rewards, the more one loses power.[23]

Havighurst and colleagues from Holland, Italy, Germany, and the United States conducted a cross-national study of steelworkers and retired teachers in order to test and expand on the findings of the Kansas City studies.[24]

Out of all of this has come the current and prevailing view that activity rather than disengagement produces the most agreeable psychological climate for older people.[25] The "activity theory" maintains that older people should remain active as long as they possibly can. When certain activities and associations must be given up (for example, employment), substitutes should be found. The older person's personality is a key element in shaping reactions to biological and social changes—an active rather than a passive role is important for mental health and satisfaction.

Lowenthal and associates studied 216 adults at four points in their lives, beginning with high school seniors and ending with men and women about to retire.[26] They compared life-styles, adaptation, and attitudes and examined concepts such as intimacy, mutuality, and time orientation. They identified ways in which adults cope with changes and compared the socialization and response to stress and change in women versus men. Differences between the sexes were more significant than between the old and the young. The authors found that the old were no more rigid psychologically than the young and that an individual's point of view, values, and outlook depended on how well one had managed to adapt to one's particular life stage.

Neugarten and Gutmann advanced the interesting conclusion that men and women begin to reverse roles in terms of authority within the family structure somewhere in their mid-fifties.[27] Their study found men becoming more nurturing and women more aggressive and assertive. (Jung described this as the emergence of animus or the masculine component in women, and anima or the feminine component in men.)

David Gutmann's work based upon studies of several cultures, the Druze in Israel, middle-class white Americans in Kansas City, the Navajo Indians, and the Mayan Indians, found universal themes suggesting that, with aging, women characteristically become more assertive as men become more nurturant. His book *Reclaimed Powers* (1987) concludes that potentials that had been denied to men and women earlier in life are available to them in later life since they are freed from what he calls the "parental emergency."[28]

In spite of the work already done, the study of the effects of age and other elements on personality development in later life is just beginning. The more obvious problems at this point are the measurement of generational differences and the lack of adequate norms against which to measure behavior. There is growing attention to what has been called "life-span developmental psychology"—the attempt to study development as a life-long process.[29]

Alvar Svanborg's longitudinal studies of aging involved 70-year-olds in Gothenburg, Sweden. The subjects fall into one of three representative groups: (1) born in 1901–1902; (2) born in 1906–1907; and (3) born in 1911–1912. By 1988, the groups had been followed through ages 85, 79, and 72, respectively. An intervention program was added to the third cohort in order to further examine relationships between vitality and the state of health, as well as life-style or ecology. Direct evidence of age cohort differences was observed concerning longevity, cognitive function, disability, and certain medical disorders. Memory was not changed significantly at ages 70 and 75 in the healthy elderly. Perceptual speed apparently started to decline in early life. Most importantly, each successive cohort appeared healthier than the preceding one.[30]

The Framingham study, from which the coronary heart disease profile was derived, convened in 1950. Now, as the children of the original sample are under study, Framingham has become a major, multigenerational research program. It focuses upon a variety of late-life disease outcomes, including dementia and cataracts.[31]

The University of Southern California Andrus Gerontology Center longitudinal study of three-generation families in 1971 followed 2,044 individuals, including grandparents, parents, and grandchildren, representing 328 families. In 1985, the study leaders contacted the surviving 1,300 participants again to compare 1970 and 1985 results. They concluded that there was somewhat less of a perceived generation gap in 1985, compared to 1970. This trend continues in ongoing triannual surveys (1988, 1991, 1994).[32]

SOME SPECIAL CHARACTERISTICS OF OLDER PEOPLE

A number of characteristics that we have seen quite frequently in older people are connected with the unique sense of having lived a long time and having accepted the concept of life as a cycle from birth through death.

Desire to Leave a Legacy

Human beings have a need to leave something of themselves behind when they die. This legacy may be children and grandchildren, work or art, personal possessions, memories in the minds of others, even bodies or body parts for use in medical training and research. Motivations for the tendency toward legacy are generally a combination of not wanting to be forgotten, of wanting to give of one's self magnanimously to those who survive, of wishing to remain in control in some way even after death (for example, through wills), and of desiring to tidy up responsibly before death. Legacy provides a sense of continuity, giving the older person a feeling of being able to participate even after death.

The "Elder" Function

Closely connected with legacy, the "elder" function refers to the natural propensity of the old to share with the young the accumulated knowledge and experience they have collected. If unhampered and indeed encouraged, this "elder" function takes the form of counseling, guiding, and sponsoring those who are younger. It is tied to the development of an interconnectedness between the generations. It is important to a sense of self-esteem to be acknowledged by the young as an elder, to have one's life experience seen as interesting and valuable; on the other hand, it can be devastating to be shrugged off by seemingly uninterested younger people as old-fashioned and irrelevant. Not all older people, however, have a nurturant feeling toward the young. Some, because of their life experience, look on the young with envy and distrust.

Mental health personnel can learn much about how to help older people by respecting and benefiting from what the elderly have to teach. This occurs through listening to them with an open mind, reading the writings of older people, viewing their arts, hearing their music, and in general absorbing the culture created by them.

Attachment to Familiar Objects

In the very old, an increasing emotional investment in the things surrounding their daily lives—home, pets, familiar objects, heirlooms, keepsakes, photo albums, scrapbooks, old letters—may be noticed. Such objects provide a sense of continuity, aid the memory, and provide comfort, security, and satisfaction. Fear of loss of possessions at death is a frequent preoccupation. Older people generally feel better if they can decide in an orderly manner how their belongings will be distributed and cared for. Younger family members or friends should take such concerns seriously, offering their help rather than denying that the older person will someday die. Possessions may have to be painfully given up before death as a result of moves from a house to an apartment, an institution, and so on. Some institutions are now recognizing the value of encouraging people to bring some of their own familiar possessions with them.

Change in the Sense of Time

There may be a resolution of fears about time running out, with an end to time panics and to boredom, and the development of a more appropriate valuation of time. While the middle-aged begin to be concerned with the number of years they have left to live, older persons tend to experience a sense of immediacy, of here and now, of living in the moment. This could be called a sense of "presentness" or "elementality." The elemental things of life—children, friendship, nature, human touching (physical and emotional), color, shape—assume greater significance as people sort out the more important from the less important. Old age can be a time of emotional and sensory awareness and enjoyment.

Sense of the Life Cycle

Older people experience something that younger people cannot: a personal sense of the entire life cycle. We discuss this further in Chapter 8. There may be a greater interest in philosophy and religion, in enduring art or literature. For example, in Japan it is common for old men to begin to write poetry, thus giving another expression of life and its meaning. A sense of historical perspective and a capacity to summarize and comment upon one's time, as well as one's life, sometimes develop.

Creativity, Curiosity, and Surprise

Creativity does not necessarily decline with age. Many persons recognized as creative have continued their work far into old age—Cervantes, Voltaire, Goethe, Tolstoy, Picasso, Martha Graham, Georgia O'Keefe, and Marguerite Yourcenar—to name a few. It is of course easy to recognize persons of achievement who continue to be productive in late life. But less well known is the fact that *most* older people remain productive and active in the absence of disease and social problems. Many become creative for the first time in old age, and the list does not begin and end with Grandma Moses. Factors that impede or support creativity and activity must be studied.

Curiosity and an ability to be surprised are other qualities that have a strikingly adaptive quality. Such qualities are especially attractive to younger people, who take heart and hope in them for their own old age. This type of enthusiasm probably reflects lifelong personality traits and serves the individual well in old age.

Sense of Consummation or Fulfillment in Life

A feeling of satisfaction with one's life is more common than recognized but not as common as possible. It is a quality of "serenity" and "wisdom," which derives from resolution of personal conflicts, reviewing one's life and finding it acceptable and gratifying, and viewing death with equanimity. One's life does not have to be a "success" in the general sense of that word in order to result in serenity. The latter can come from a feeling of having done one's best, from having met challenge and difficulty, and sometimes from simply having survived against terrible odds.

MIDDLE AGE AND THE TRANSITION TO OLD AGE

An understanding of old age requires consideration of the transition from the middle years. Neugarten and Lowenthal have contributed much to the study of mid-life. Middle age is usually regarded as the period from age 40 to 65, during which most people are engaged in providing the livelihood for a family and finishing the rearing of children. The middle-aged are the people in command in society in terms of power, influence, norms, and decisions. They make up roughly 25% of the population and carry much responsibility for the old and the young.

Two themes that predominate in mid-life are the growing awareness of personal aging (eventual death) and the changes in life patterns that occur as the middle-aged person's children grow up, parents grow old, and new roles are assumed personally and socially. People become aware of a different sense of time; they begin to think about how long they have left to live rather than about how long they have lived. Men are aware of the possibility of their own imminent death, whereas women, who have a longer life expectancy and often are married to an older spouse, worry first about the death of the husband and later about their own aging and demise. They may consciously or unconsciously prepare for widowhood. Many women become concerned about outliving their financial resources and a good number of them actually do. (See case of Mrs. G. on page 61.)

A personal sense of death can no longer be easily denied and avoided. The death of parents leaves the middle-aged next in line. Friends and peers begin to die; unmistakable physical changes occur; one's own children reach adulthood. But the perception of death may be a matter-of-fact acceptance rather than negative fears and worries. It can lead to greater respect for and attention to one's physical health; Neugarten (1968) has called this "body monitoring": the activities undertaken to keep the body in physical condition and to care for any physical illnesses or chronic conditions that have developed. It also leads to a reassessment of one's life, a stocktaking in terms of marriage, career, personal relationships, values, and other commitments made earlier in youth, According to Neugarten, an increased "interiority" takes place. Career changes and divorces are not infrequent, and sometimes the whole way of life may be changed. Mid-life has been compared to a second adolescence—one in which people reassess, change, and strike out in new directions.

Other such periods may occur after retirement or after widowhood, when again one sees reevaluation, with new identities and directions emerging. A conception of personal death may become consciously realized. At first this can be frightening and painful, but if favorably resolved, a mature resignation frees the person from fear. (Some, of course, must maintain a denial of death because of vulnerabilities that do not allow for direct confrontation with the end of life.) Mid-life and eventually old age can then be enjoyed but with a full or at least partial awareness of the eventuality of death. Appreciations of some of the elemental things that people tend to value more highly as they age—human love and affection, insight, pleasures of the senses, nature, children, pets— are probably a result of the restructuring and reformulation of concepts of time, self, and death.

Studies thus far seem to indicate that the majority of people adjust and adapt remarkably well to the demands and problems of middle life. But difficulties do occur and are sometimes called "mid-life crises." Middle-aged people may panic and attempt to recapture youth by adopting inappropriately young dress, manners, and behavior. They may envy the young and feel inferior to them or, on the other hand, hate and disparage them. There can be an overexaggeration of body monitoring, which becomes hypochondriacal. There can be such a fear of change that people will remain in pressured or boring jobs and marriages or will leap into almost identical situations if they do decide to take action. There may be preoccupations with age and appearance and self-consciousness about how to act and relate. Depression and alcoholism tend to increase. Although the "empty nest" (when children have left home) and the menopause do not ordinarily cause serious problems for women (and indeed may bring a sense of freedom and spontaneity), both of these may become overemphasized as potential problem areas. Sexual promiscuity in order to prove youth and attractiveness may develop, as well as increased religiosity that has a hollow and desperate ring to it. Men may be haunted by a need to "succeed." All of these represent unresolved fears of aging and attempts to deny it by trying to turn back the clock. One can see fixation, rigidity, fatalism, pessimism, or overexpansiveness.

Middle age can be and is for most people the prime of life. But it can be complicated by periods of genuine crises, ranging from the superficial and reversible to the profound and more pathological. The middle-aged person who truly wants to be young again is rare, but most would like to preserve the good health and energy of youth. In its best sense mid-life can become a time of increasing sensitivity, self-awareness, use of capacities and skills to the fullest, and separation of that which is valuable from the less valuable in order to use time wisely and enjoyably. It can in this sense become a healthy preparation for the transition to old age.[33]

THE CHANGING AWARENESS OF OLD AGE

A large aged population is a new phenomenon, with older people no longer considered a rarity. Older people have become more highly visible since the nineteenth century as greater life expectancy and various social and economic conditions have unfolded the life cycle, making its stages stand out in bolder relief. At the beginning of the twentieth century, only 1 in 25 Americans was over 65; in 1995, 1 in 8 was at least 65. Each day there are over 1,000 more older Americans; each year nearly 400,000 more. By the year 2030, older people could make up one-fifth of the total population. As their numbers grow, older people have slowly begun to be of interest to U.S. sociologists and psychologists, although the medical and psychotherapeutic professions, which come most closely in contact with older people, still have not made an active enough commitment to their special concerns and problems. Politicians have begun to grasp the value of supporting programs to benefit older persons since they have become a major political constituency. Older people have begun to show a growing self-awareness and sophisticated use of public opinion and public policy. Their financial power is impressive, with people over 50 now controlling 50% of discretionary income in the United States. These facts, combined with their increasing good health and survival rates, may at last bring older people hope for a vital participation in a better future for themselves and all of us.

SELECTED READINGS

Atchley, R. C. (1991). *The social forces in later life.* Belmont, CA: Wadsworth Publishing.

Atchley, R. C. (1994). *The social forces and aging: An introduction to social gerontology.* Belmont, CA: Wadsworth Publishing.

Bates, P. B., & Brim, O. G., Jr. (Eds.). (1984) *Life span development and behavior.* Orlando, FL: Academic Press.

Bengtson, V. L., Reedy, M. N., & Gordon, C. (1985). Aging and self-conceptions: Personality pressures and social contexts. In Birren, J. E., & Schaie, K. W. (Eds.), *Handbook of the psychology of aging,* 2nd ed. (pp. 544–593). New York: Van Nostrand Reinhold.

Bengtson, V. L., & Robertson, J. F. (1985). *Grandparenthood.* Beverly Hills, CA: Sage.

Bengtson, V. L., Silverstein, M., & Giarrusso, R. (1995). Longitudinal study of generations. In Maddox, G. L. (Ed.), *The encyclopedia of aging* (pp. 582–584). New York: Springer.

Binstock, R., & George, L. K. (Eds.). (1990). *Handbook of aging and the social sciences,* 3rd ed. San Diego, CA: Academic Press.

Birren, J. E., & Bengtson, V. L. (Eds.). (1988). *Emergent theories of aging.* New York: Springer.

Birren, J. E., Butler, R. N., Greenhouse, S. W., Sokoloff, L., & Yarrow, M. R. (Eds.). (1963). *Human aging: A biological and behavioral study.* Pub. no. (PHS) 986. Washington DC: U.S. Government Printing Office. (Reprinted as Pub. no. (HSM) 71–9051, 1971, 1974).

Birren, J. E., & Shaie, K. W. (Eds.). (1991). *Handbook of the psychology of aging,* 3rd ed. San Diego: Academic Press.

Bond, L. A., Cutler, S. J., & Grams, A. E. (Eds.). (1995). *Promoting successful aging.* Thousand Oaks, CA: Sage.

Buhler, C. (1968). The general structure of the human life. In Buhler, C., & Massarik, F. (Eds.), *The course of human life: A study of goals in the human perspective.* New York: Springer.

Busse, E. W., & Maddox, G. L. (1985). *The Duke Longitudinal Studies of Normal Aging 1955–1980: An overview of history, designs, and findings.* New York: Springer.

Butler, R. N. (1989). Productive aging. In Bengtson, V. L., & Shaie, K. W. *The course of later life.* New York: Springer.

Butler, R. N. (1989). Psychosocial aspects of aging. In Kaplan, H. I., & Saddock, B. J. (Eds.), *The Comprehensive textbook of psychiatry,* 5th ed. (pp. 2014–2019). Baltimore: Williams & Wilkins.

Butler, R. N., Oberlink, M. R., & Schechter, M. (1989). *Promise of productive aging.* New York: Springer.

Costa, P. T., Jr., & McCrae, R. P. (1989). Personality continuity and the changes of adult life. In Storandt, M., & Vanden Bos, G. R. (Eds.), *The adult years: Continuity and change* (pp. 45–77). Washington, DC: American Psychological Association.

Field, D. (Guest Ed.). (1991). Special issue: Personality and aging. *Journal of Gerontology: Psychological Sciences, 46*(6).

Granick, S., & Patterson, R. (1971). *Human aging II: An eleven-year follow-up biobehavioral study.* Washington, DC: National Institute of Mental Health, Pub. no. (HSM) 71–9037.

Granick, D. (1987). *Reclaimed powers: Toward a new psychology of men and women in later life.* New York: Basic Books.

Hall, G. S. (1922). *Senescence: The last half of life.* New York: D. Appleton.

Lowenthal, M. F., & Chiriboga, D. (1972). Transition to the empty nest: Crisis, challenge, or relief? *Archives of General Psychiatry, 26,* 8–15.

McCrae, R. R., & Costa, P. T., Jr. (1984). *Emerging lives, enduring dispositions: Personality in adulthood.* Boston: Little, Brown.

Myerhoff, B. G. (1979). *Number our days.* New York: E. P. Dutton.

Neugarten, B. L. (Ed.). (1968). *Middle age and aging.* Chicago, IL: University of Chicago Press.

Palmore, E. (1970). *Normal aging: Reports from the Duke Longitudinal Study, 1955–1969.* Durham, NC: Duke University Press.

Palmore, E., Busse, E. W., Maddox, G. L., Nowlin, J. B., & Siegler, I. C. (1985) *Normal aging III.* Durham, NC: Duke University Press.

Perlmutter, M., Adams, C., Berry, J., et. al. (1987). Aging and memory. In Shaie, K. W., & Eisdorfer, C. (Eds.). *Annual Review of Gerontology and Geriatrics, 8* (pp. 57–92). New York: Springer.

Pressey, S. L., & Kuhlen, R. G. (1957). *Psychological development through the life cycle.* New York: Harper & Row.

Riley, M. W. (Ed.). (1979). *Aging from birth to death.* Boulder, CO: Westview Press.

Rosow, I. (1975). *Socialization to old age.* Berkeley, CA: University of California Press.

Rowe, J. W., & Kahn, R. L. (1987). Human aging: Usual and successful. *Science, 237,* 143–149.

Schaie, K. W. (1983). *Longitudinal studies of adult psychological development.* New York: Guilford Press.

Schaie, K. W. (1994) The course of adult intellectual development. *American Psychologist, 49,* 304–313.

Schaie, K. W. (1995). *Intellectual development in adulthood: The Seattle Longitudinal Study.* New York: Cambridge University Press.

Schaie, K. W., Campbell, R. T., Meredith, W. M., & Rawlings, S. C. (Eds.). (1988). *Methodological issues in aging research.* New York: Springer.

Shock, N. W., Greulich, R. C., Andres, R., Arenberg, D., Costa, P. T., Jr., Lakatta, E. G., & Tobin, J. D. (1984). *Normal human aging: The Baltimore Longitudinal Study of Aging.* NIH Publication No. 84–2450. Bethesda, MD: National Institutes of Health.

Thomae, H. (1976). *Patterns of aging: Findings from the Bonn Longitudinal Study of Aging.* Basel, Switzerland: S. Karger.

World Health Organization. (1946). Constitution of the World Health Organization. *Public Health Report, 61,* 1268–1277.

ENDNOTES

1. There appears to be a relative absence of fear of death. For a discussion of psychological attitudes toward death among older Japanese-Americans, see Osako, M. (1980). Aging, social isolation and kinship ties among Japanese-Americans. In *Project Report to the Administration on Aging.* (pp. 116–120). Washington, DC: The Administration on Aging.

2. Miles, C. C., & Miles, W. R. (1932). The correlation of intelligence scores and chronological age from early to late maturity. *American Journal of Psychology 44,* 44–78.

3. Jones, H. E., & Conrad, H. S. (1933). The growth and decline of intelligence. A study of a homogeneous group between the ages of ten and sixty. *Genetic Psychological Monograph 13,* 223–298.

4. Longitudinal research presents methodological problems of its own, as described by Greenhouse and Morrison (1963) and Schaie (1965, 1983). When a sample is studied over a span of time, differentiating intrinsic changes from those caused by environment becomes difficult, and it is impossible to rule out the bias of survivorship itself. See Greenhouse, S. W., & Morrison, D. F. (1963). Statistical methodology. In Birren, J. E., Butler, R. N., Greenhouse, S. W., Sokoloff, L., & Yarrow, M. R. (Eds.), *Human aging: A biological and behavioral study,* Pub No. (PHS) 986, Washington, DC: U.S. Government Printing Office (reprinted as Pub. No. [HSM] 71–9051, 1971, 1974); Schaie, K. W. (1965). A general model for the study of developmental problems. *Psychological Bulletin* 64:92–107. Baltes, P. B. (1968). Longitudinal and cross-sectional sequences in the study of age and generation effects. *Human Development 11,* 145–171, and Schaie, K. W. (1993). *Longitudinal studies of adult psychological development.* New York: Guilford Press.

5. Bayley, N., & Oden, M. H. A. B. (1955). The maintenance of intellectual ability in gifted adults. *Journal of Gerontology 10,* 91–107.

6. Owens, W. A. (1966). Age and mental abilities: A second adult follow-up. *Journal of Educational Psychology 57,* 316–25.

7. Lorge, I. (1936). The influence of the test upon the nature of mental decline as a function of age. *Journal of Educational Psychology 32,* 100–110.

8. Botwinick, J., & Birren, J. E. (1963). Mental abilities and psychomotor responses in healthy aged men. In Birren, J. E., Butler, R. N., Greenhouse, S. W., Sokoloff, L., & Yarrow, M. R. (Eds.), *Human aging: A biological and behavioral study,* Pub. No. (PHS) 986, Washington, DC: U.S. Government Printing Office (reprinted as Pub. No [HSM] 71–9051, 1971, 1974).

9. Jarvik, L. F., Eisdorfer, C., & Blum, J. E. (Eds.). (1975). *Intellectual functioning in adults.* New York: Springer Verlag.

10. Horn, J. L., & Cattell, R. B. (1966). *Age differences in primary mental ability factors. Journal of Gerontology 21,* 210–220; Craik, F. J., & Tehub, S. (Eds.). (1982). *Aging and cognitive processes.* New York: Plenum.

11. Eisdorfer, C. (1972). Autonomic changes in aging. In Gaitz, C. M. (Ed.), *Aging and the brain.* New York: Plenum Publishing.

12. Birren, J. E., & Schaie, K. W. (1985). *Handbook of the psychology of aging.* 3rd ed. New York: Van-Nostrand Reinhold; Ivnik, R. J., Malec, J. F., Smith, G. E., et al. (1992). Mayo's older Americans normative studies: WAIS-R norms for ages 59–97. *Clinical Neuropsychologist 6,* pp. 1–30.

13. Horn, J. L., & Donaldson, G. (1976). On the myth of intellectual decline in adulthood. *American Psychologist 31*(10), 701–719; Perlmutter, M., Adams, C., Berry, J., et al. Aging and memory. In Schaie, K. W., & Eisdorfer, C. (Eds.), *Annual review of Gerontology and Geriatrics* (Vol. 8, pp. 57–92). New York: Springer; Schaie, K. W. (1995). *Intellectual development in adulthood: The Seattle Longitudinal Study.* New York: Cambridge University Press; Schaie, K. W. (1994a). The course of adult

intellectual development. *American Psychologist, 49,* 304–313.

14. Scheibel, M. E., Lindsay, R. D., Tomiya, V. & Scheibel, A. B. (1975). Progressive dendritic changes in aging human cortex. *Experimental Neurology 47,* 392–403.

15. Schaie, K. W. (1995). Longitudinal Research (pp. 575–576) & Intelligence (pp. 513–514). In Maddox, G. L. (Ed.), *The encyclopedia of aging.* New York: Springer.

16. For an overview of the experience of today's older persons, it is useful to read Barbara Tuchman's *The proud tower* and Frederick Lewis Allen's *The big change.*

17. See the National Institute of Mental Health's *Human Aging* studies (Birren et al.) and the work of Heron and Chown (1967).

18. Cummings, E., & Henry, W. E. (1961). *Growing old: The process of disengagement.* New York: Basic Books.

19. Havighurst, R. J., Neugarten, B. L., & Tobin, S. S. (1968). Disengagement and patterns of aging. In Neugarten, B. L. (Ed.), *Middle age and aging.* Chicago: University of Chicago Press.

20. Reichard, S., Livson, F., & Peterson, P. G. (1962). *Aging and personality.* New York: John Wiley & Sons.

21. Carp, F. M. (1966). *A future for the aged: Victoria Plaza and its residents.* Austin: University of Texas Press.

22. Homans, G. (1961). *Social behavior: Its elementary forms.* New York: Harcourt Brace and World; and Blau, P. (1964). *Exchange and power in social life.* New York: John Wiley and Sons.

23. Martin, J. D. (1971). Power, dependence and the complaints of the elderly. A social exchange perspective. *Aging and Human Development 2,* 108–112; and Dowd, J. J. (1975). Aging as exchange: A preface to theory. *Journal of Gerontology, 30,* 584–594.

24. Havighurst, R. J. (1963). Successful aging. In Williams, R. H., Tibbitts, C., & Donahue, W. (Eds.), *Processes of aging.* New York: Atherton Press.

25. For discussions of the disengagement theory see Carp, F. M. (1968). Some components of disengagement. *Journal of Gerontology, 23,* 383–386; Hochschild, A. R. (1975). Disengagement theory: A critique and proposal. *American Sociology Review 40,* 553–569; Tallmer, M., & Kutner, B. (1970). Disengagement and morale. *The Gerontologist, 110,* 317–320; and Orbach, H. L. (1973). Disengagement—activity controversy: Underlying theoretical models of aging. *The Gerontologist, 13,* 72.

26. Lowenthal, M. F., et al. (1975). *Four stages of life: A comparative study of women and men facing transitions.* San Francisco: Jossey-Bass.

27. Neugarten, B., & Gutmann, D. (1968). Age-sex roles and personality in middle age: A thematic apperception study. In Neugarten, B. L. (Ed.), *Middle age and aging.* Chicago: University of Chicago Press.

28. Gutmann, D. (1987). *Reclaimed powers: Toward a new psychology of men and women in later life.* New York: Basic Books.

29. There have been four important books on life-span developmental psychology, all generated by West Virginia University and published in New York by Academic Press: Goulet, L. R., & Baltes, P. (Eds.), *The theory and status of lifespan research,* 1979; Nesselroade, J., & Reese, H. W. (Eds.), *Methodological issues,* 1973; Baltes, P. B., & Schaie, K. W. (Eds.), *Life-span developmental psychology: Personality and socialization,* 1973; and Datan, N., & Ginsberg, L. H. (Eds.), *Life-span developmental psychology: Normative life crises,* 1975.

30. Svanborg, A. (1977). Seventy-year-old people in Gothenburg. A population study in an industrialized Swedish city. II. General presentation of social and medical conditions. *Acta Medica Scandinavica,* Suppl. *611,* 5–37.

31. Kannel, W. B. (1987). Rethinking the good life: Forty years at Framingham. In Bernstein, E. (Ed.), *The Encyclopedia Britannica Medical and Health Annual.* Chicago: Encyclopedia Britannica, pp. 24–39.

32. Bengston, V. L., Silverstein, M., & Giarrusso, R. (1995). Longitudinal Study of generations. In Maddox, G. L. (Ed.), *The encyclopedia of aging* (2nd ed., pp. 582–584.) New York: Springer.

33. There have been two books of considerable theoretical interest about middle age, although limited only to men: Levinson, D. J., Darrow, C. M., Klein, E. B., Levinson, M. H., & McKee, B. (1978). *The seasons of a man's life.* New York: Alfred A. Knopf; and Vaillant, G. E. (1977). *Adaptation to life.* Boston: Little, Brown. There is also Rubin's book on middle-aged women: Rubin, L. S. (1979). *Women of a certain age: The midlife search for self.* New York: Harper & Row. This is an in-depth study of the psychological identity of 160 women. Rubin concludes that issues around the stages of life are not intraspsychic per se but rather directly connected with social events and trends. The future should bring increasing research attention to the middle-life period of men and women.

CHAPTER 4

COMMON EMOTIONAL PROBLEMS

COMMON EMOTIONAL REACTIONS
AS EXPRESSED IN OLD AGE
EMOTIONAL REACTIONS TO AGE-RELATED
LIFE CRISES

COMMON ADAPTIVE TECHNIQUES
OTHER DEFENSIVE BEHAVIOR
THE LIFE REVIEW

Older persons experience the same emotions as those of people of every age, but as with each age, there is a uniqueness in the character of such emotions. Both the uniqueness and the similarities bear examination if one is to clarify the distinctive nature of old age.

Loss is one of the predominant themes in characterizing the common emotional problems of older people. Losses in every aspect of late life compel many older persons to expend enormous amounts of physical and emotional energy in grieving and resolving grief, adapting to the changes that result from loss, and recovering from the stresses inherent in these processes. The psychological treatment goal is obtaining insight and restitution possibilities within the limits of the life situation and individual personality. Older people can be confronted by multiple losses, which may occur simultaneously: death of marital partner, older friends, colleagues, relatives; decline of physical health and coming to personal terms with death; loss of status, prestige, and participation in society; and, for large numbers of the older population, additional burdens of marginal living standards. Inevitable losses that can accompany aging may be aggravated by cultural devaluation and neglect. In the complex of factors affecting subjective experience, overt behavior, and level of adaptation of the older persons, any or all of the following may be significant.

Environmental or Extrinsic Factors
Personal losses or gains
- Marital partners; other loved and significant figures (friends, children)

Social forces (losses or gains)
- Status changes, prestige changes: in social groups other than family and as paterfamilias
- Socioeconomic adversities: income drop, inflation
- Unwanted retirement: arbitrary retirement policies
- Cultural devaluation of older persons: sense of uselessness, therapeutic pessimism, forced isolation, forced segregation

Intrinsic Factors
Nature of personality
- character structure (defensive and integrative mechanisms), life history, survival characteristics

Physical diseases
- disease of any organ system
- perceptual decrements
- sexual losses

- disease of integrative systems (hormonal, vascular, and central nervous systems)
- brain damage
- arteriosclerosis, senile dementia, etc.
- physical limitations (such as arthritis)

Age-specific changes (largely obscure and mysterious, but inexorable with the passage of time)
- losses of speed of processes and response
- involutionary processes
- others (heredity, survival qualities)
- changes in body size and appearance ("slipping" and "shrinkage")

Experience of bodily dissolution and approaching death (subjective passage of time)

Older people often are handicapped by their own bodies, which respond to challenge with less energy and strength than were formerly available, particularly if major illnesses have taken their toll. Emotionally, a rapid succession of losses can leave individuals with accumulated layers of unresolved grief along with fatigue and a sense of emptiness. There may be little societal support for grief and mourning as the rituals of religion and custom are increasingly questioned and discarded.

It is an odd distortion of reality when older persons are popularly depicted as weak, unassuming, gently tranquil people who passively wait out their last days. Becoming old, being old, and dying are active physical and emotional processes that test the mettle of each person. Reluctance to accord older people appropriate recognition for their strengths and capacities indicates a failure to understand what is required in being old. We have lost our naiveté about the carefree nature of childhood as we have developed our understanding of the difficult and frightening developmental work each child must do to grow up. But simplistic illusions about old age continue, with little conceptualization of the normative stages one must pass through in later life.[1] Certain dramatic events (for example, widowhood) have been more widely studied than others, but there is as yet no cohesive, reliable body of information against which to measure adjustment patterns.

COMMON EMOTIONAL REACTIONS AS EXPRESSED IN OLD AGE

Grief (Mourning)

Grief as a result of loss is a predominate factor in aging. Loss of the marital partner or other significant and loved people can be profound, particularly since it becomes more difficult in later life to find substitutes for such losses. This is illustrated in the tender and grief-stricken reference to his mother's death by St. Augustine in his *Confessions:*

> I pressed her eyes closed, and a huge wave of sorrow flooded my heart and flowed outward in tears. . . . What, then, was it which caused grievous pain within me, if not the fresh wound arising from the sudden breaking of a very sweet and cherished habit of living together? Since I was thus bereft of such great comfort from her, my soul was wounded and it was as if life which had been made one from hers and mine was torn to shreds. . . . It was a relief to weep in Thy sight about her and for her, about myself and for myself.[2]

Older persons in the United States today do not receive necessary cultural support for grief and mourning. Learning how to mourn productively and restoratively requires models in ritual and custom as well as in personal experiences with others who mourn. Lack of such support can prolong depression and leave grief unresolved. Patterns of mourning for the dead are in disarray as many time-honored customs become discarded (wearing black clothing, abstaining from social events for a period of time) and others are practiced piecemeal (religious rituals, the rallying around of friends and family). Still other patterns are recent and psychologically suspect innovations (funeral directors or morticians who "console" the family, the use of sedatives to calm nerves and deaden the feelings). Gorer remarks that, up to 1900, every society in the world had definite rules for mourners to follow.[3] This is no longer true. Our culture seems reluctant to acknowledge the pain of death and to bear the agony of experiencing it through to acceptance. Some churches and many individuals deny the existence of death, preferring to speak of it as "merely sleep" or "the beginning of life hereafter." This may reassure individuals but it does not help them resolve the pain of separation and the need to find new attachments.

In the United States people receive some support in the period of initial shock, from the time of the death to burial. But after the church services are over, the undertaker disappears with a sizable portion of the mourner's money and relatives and friends go home, taking away their casserole dishes and other gestures of help and support. But for the mourner the intense period of mourning is just beginning, and it must usually be experienced alone. Onlookers may try to divert the mourner's attention to other things. Crying may be considered indulgent and possibly harmful rather than a psychological necessity. Gorer compares our present attitudes toward death and mourning with the prudish attitudes toward sex in the past: death has become an obscenity—one should not discuss it in public, the feelings are "bad," and any indulgence in mourning must be done in secret.

Gorer goes on to point out the maladaptive behavior that results. Exaggerated depression, aimless busyness, deification of the dead person, or callous denial of others' grief as well as one's own may occur. People may become excessively preoccupied with death or violence. Since death is an unavoidable crisis inherent in the human life cycle, it is peculiar that a society can so determinedly avoid the provisions of cultural custom and ritual that could make it easier to bear.

The primary adaptive purpose of grief and mourning is to accept the reality of the loss and to begin to find ways of filling up the emptiness caused by the loss through movement toward a new style of life and new people.

Mary and Zelda were two maiden sisters who had lived together for over 45 years when Zelda suddenly died of a heart attack. Mary was devastated. Initially, friends and distant relatives who lived nearby offered both consolation and practical support in day-to-day living. But after several weeks of grieving, it was clear that Mary, who had been functioning quite independently prior to Zelda's death, could no longer manage alone. Without giving up her apartment, she was admitted to a rehabilitation facility, despite the fact that she had no physical impairment. After several weeks there, she was transferred to a low supervision nursing home where she eventually met Helen, another woman in her 60s, who was in good health but had nowhere to live and few friends in the area. Mary and Helen struck up an immediate friendship and soon moved into Mary's apartment where they now live happily and frequently entertain other friends.

Parkes, in his studies of London widows, describes the futile search for the lost love object in which the mourner is torn between the desire to recover or resurrect the dead person and the knowledge that this is irrational.[4] Studies indicate that some widowed people have hallucinations and delusions of contact with the lost spouse. These may last for years and are more likely to occur in individuals who had been happily married. The most common hallucination reported was feeling the dead spouse's presence; others thought they saw, heard, were touched by or spoken to by the spouse.

A cultural adaptation regarding grief is found in the practice of ancestor worship in Shintoism and Buddhism, where the mourner believes the presence of a departed loved one remains (to be fed, prayed to, etc.) yet in a new spirit form that does not allow direct physical contact. Thus both the reality of death and the wishful recovery of the person are provided for, in a religious belief that gives structure to the grief process.

A typical grief reaction has an almost predictable pattern of onset, regardless of age—numbness and inability to accept the loss, followed by the shock of reality as it begins to penetrate. There are physical feelings of emptiness in the pit of the stomach, weak knees, perhaps a feeling of suffocation, shortness of breath, and a tendency to deep sighing. Emotionally the person experiences great distress. As mentioned earlier, there may be a sense of unreality, including delusions and obsessive preoccupations with the image of the lost person and acting as though the deceased were still present. Generally feelings of guilt are present as well as anger and irritability, even toward friends and relatives. There is usually a disorganization of normal patterns of response, with the bereaved person wandering about aimlessly, unable to work or take social initiative. Anxiety and longing alternate with depression and despair. Insomnia, digestive disturbances, and anorexia are common. Acute grief ordinarily lasts a month or two and then begins to lessen; on the average, grief may be largely over in six to twelve months, although further loss, stress, or some reminder can reactivate it.

Exaggerated grief reactions may occur:

A 66-year-old woman was as angry and depressed over the loss of her husband 16 months after his death as she was in the immediate weeks. She had passed through the "markers" of a year—the anniversary of their marriage, Thanksgiving, Christmas, Valentine's Day, Easter, and summer vacation reminiscence. But she could not shake her oppressive depression. She was furious at her brother-in-law, who she felt would find ways to cheat her of her inheritance. She chastised her two sons for their neglect. It was only through open exploration of her anger, first with the help of her emotionally sophisticated clergyman and then with a psychiatrist, that her depression began to lift.

"Morbid" grief reactions are distortions or prolongations of typical grief. Such reactions may take the form of delay, in which the grief is delayed for days, months, or even years, and in its extreme form is generally bound up with conscious or unconscious antagonism or ambivalence toward the deceased. Inhibited grief, according to Parkes, produces minimal mourning but other symptoms develop, such as somatic illnesses, overactivity, or disturbed social interaction. Chronic grief, yet another of the morbid grief reactions, is the prolongation and intensification of normal grief over an extended or limited period of time; psychotherapy and/or medication may be indicated.

We have observed a not infrequent form of grief reaction that we call "enshrinement," in which the survivor attempts to keep things just as they were before the death of a loved one occurred. The dead person's possessions and even entire rooms may be kept intact as shrines to the person's memory. The survivor may surround himself or herself with photographs and memorabilia connected with the lost person and make regular and conscious attempts to evoke memories of the deceased. There may be frequent references to the dead person in conversation with others, as well as a deliberate avoidance of new contacts that might replace the role of the one who died. Much of this is a result of survival guilt and a misplaced fear of infidelity if one were to take an active role in getting life moving again. It can also be symptomatic of a silent and internal adult temper tantrum—a stubborn refusal to accept death.

Anticipatory grief is the process of mourning in advance, before an actual loss is sustained. This form of mourning can occur during long illnesses; for example, a wife caring for a sick husband may go through a grief reaction and may have reached some degree of acceptance before death occurs. Such grief is seen as a protective device that prepares the bereaved for the loss, but it can lead to problems if it causes loved ones to disengage themselves prematurely, leaving the dying person isolated and alone.

Interrelationships between grief and vulnerability to both physical and emotional illness have been the subject of a number of investigations. Bereavement over a loss is hypothesized to be the single most crucial factor in predicting decline or breakdown in functioning on a physical or emotional level. Research data on large numbers of surviving spouses have in fact revealed marked increases in mortality of the spouses, especially the male survivors, in the first three months of bereavement.[5] In addition, losses of health, money, possessions, employment, or social status or changes in appearance seem to be possible factors in precipitating decline or lowering resistance.

Guilt

While old age can be a time of proud reflection and happy reminiscence, it can also evoke difficult memories and a resurgence of past conflicts and regrets. Guilt feelings may play a significant role as the older person reviews life, attempting to consolidate a meaningful judgment as to the manner in which life has been lived and to prepare for death and cope with any fears of death. The sins of omission and commission for which an individual blames himself weigh even more heavily in the light of approaching death and dissolution. If expiation and atonement are to occur, they must occur now; time for procrastination begins to run out. Individuals who have held grudges for a lifetime may decide to resolve their differences. Some may undertake a variety of reparations for the past. Others become more religiously active, in the hope of gaining forgiveness. Such feelings should be dealt with seriously and not simply treated with facile reassurance. For many the resolution of guilt feelings is an essential part of final acceptance of their lives as worthwhile.

Other forms of guilt are the "death survival guilt" from outliving others, especially if chance occurrences like accidental death or homicide appear to have a role in the earlier demise of the spouse or loved one.[6] Those who survive often carry the burden of guilt and unresolved conflicts for decades, supporting the observation in Thomas Mann's *The Magic Mountain* that "a man's dying is more the survivor's affair than his own."

Loneliness

In infancy, being alone is a condition that provokes terror, anger, and disconsolation. A baby's early cries communicate the primitive drive for physical survival. But very early a new element is introduced. As the child alternately experiences the gratifying warmth and comfort of his family and the aloneness of his crib, he learns a new fear, the fear of not being able to get back to people— of being left alone. Thus there appear to be two elements in the early sense of loneliness: *aloneness,* or the fear for physical survival in a threatening, uncertain world, and *loneliness,* the fear of emotional isolation, of being locked inside oneself and unable to obtain the warmth and comfort that one has learned is available from others if one can gain it. Growth and a refinement occur as children

move outside of themselves and their isolation, not only toward other people but also toward an absorption in play, learning, work, and other creative efforts. That moment is significant when the child first learns to escape his own aloneness or consciousness of himself and becomes totally involved in a task—a moment described as an escape from loneliness, which is not dependent on the presence of another person. (Paul Tillich describes this as a distinction between loneliness and solitude.)

The developmental etiology of loneliness is significant in regard to older people, not in a simplistic sense of comparing them to children but in attempting to comprehend the special character of loneliness in old age. The primitive fears concerning physical survival and emotional isolation recede as human beings grow to adulthood and learn to provide successfully for their own physical sustenance and achieve emotional satisfactions through family, friends, and work. But with old age, the combination of harsh external forces and a diminishing self-mastery revives once again the latent threats. The old adage that we are born alone and we die alone reflects the experience that each of us encounters in the course of the life cycle. But, unlike the usual experience of children, the older person does not suffer so much from a fear of being unable to relate as from the reality of having no one to relate to. With the death of loved ones, there is a diminishing circle of significant people who are not readily replaceable. Former compensations of work may be gone. Children and grandchildren, if they exist, may live far away. The all too limited outlets of religious activities, hobbies, television, pets, and a few acquaintances, which form the daily existence of so many older persons, are not enough to satisfy emotional needs.

The American dream of self-reliance and independence can further isolate the older person within himself. At a time when increased human contact could be supportive, older people hold on to cultural notions that living alone and "doing for oneself" must be maintained. Familiarity with and determination to continue such patterns can make communal living in hospitals, nursing homes, or group homes difficult in sheerly social terms. It has been observed that older people in more group-oriented societies, such as the rural kibbutzim in Israel, can enjoy the companionship and involvement inherent in a close living situation with others without the same loss of self-esteem and sense of dependency felt by "rugged individualists." Cultures that advocate societal and group responsibility for the individual are perhaps more in sympathy with the natural needs of older people.

Depression

Depressive reactions increase in degree and frequency with old age as a corollary to the increased loss of much that is emotionally valued by the older person. Unresolved grief, guilt, loneliness, and anger are expressed in mild to severe depressions with symptomatology including insomnia, despair, lethargy, anorexia, loss of interest, and somatic complaints.

Sadness is a normal part of life and an emotion experienced frequently by the elderly. But it should not be the predominant emotion at this or any other time of life. When sadness progresses to depression with increased symptoms of tearfulness, appetite disturbances, decreased energy, decreased concentration, and increased somatic complaints, a diagnosis of major depression and psychiatric consultation should be considered[7] (see Chapters 5 and 9 for further descriptions). Interestingly, some studies have shown that the incidence of major depression may actually go down slightly with age,[8] suggesting a successful coping strategy within most elderly. Some have suggested that this strategy involves maintaining close confiding relationships well into old age.[9]

Anxiety

The sense of free-floating anxiety can intensify in older people as illness and imminent death undermine illusions of invulnerability built up as protection during a lifetime. (A very powerful anxiety is the fear of becoming a pauper.) In addition, new modes of adaptation become necessary, creating additional anxieties in the face of constant change. Notice is seldom taken of the amount of new learning an older person must undergo to adapt to the accelerating changes in body, feelings, and environment. As with any new learning, anxiety develops in proportion to the task at hand, the resources available to master it, and the chances for and consequences of failure.

Anxiety manifests itself in many forms: rigid thinking to protectively exclude external stimuli (a person may "hear" only what he wants to hear), fear of being alone, and suspiciousness to the point of paranoid states. It may also become somatized into physical illness. Frequently anxiety and its expressions are incorrectly diagnosed as "early dementia" and wrongly considered untreatable.

One type of anxiety derives from life history such as observations of older people when they themselves were children. For example, the fear that they will have the diseases of old age that as children they observed in their grandparents or in other older people is one possible ingredient in the denial or projection seen in the aged.

A 70-year-old retired chemist who had been born when his mother was 40 years old had seen her develop severe Parkinsonism and become increasingly helpless when he was 20 years old. He carried this image with him all his life, but after he retired, it became obsessional. He gradually convinced himself and his doctors that he did have the disease. If he did, it was clinically negligible.

Sense of Impotence and Helplessness

A significant reaction of older men, particularly those white men who as a group can be postulated to have once held the major power and influence in American society, is a sense of their present impotence and helplessness. The highest suicide rates occur among older white men in their eighties. The older African American man and all women, be they African American, white, or other races, are affected by loss of esteem and cultural status as they age but do not experience quite the same degree of loss of power and privilege. In fact, an interesting reversal can occur for older women within the traditional marital relationship. As their husbands decline, wives may assume more of the initiative, taking over financial management, nursing care, and household repairs; they may therefore experience more control and influence than at any previous point in their lives.

Older people may "learn" to be helpless if family, friends, and health professionals too quickly attempt to compensate for the physiological or emotional losses that may occur with age. The result is not only an acceleration of the older person's helplessness, but also the possibility of greater susceptibility to disease and disability.[10]

As a reaction to a sense of helplessness, some older persons may flaunt their positions of status and financial worth over their children and use inheritance as a way of manipulating them. King Lear was a prime example of this when he required his three daughters to publicly declare their love for him in order to collect their inheritance.[11]

Rage

Another of the emotional manifestations of old age is a sense of rage at the seemingly uncontrollable forces that confront older persons, as well as the frequent indignities and neglect of the society that once valued their productive capacities. The description of some older people as cantankerous, ornery, irritable, or querulous would be more realistically interpreted if one became sensitive to the degree of outrage older people feel, consciously or unconsciously, at viewing their situation. (Interestingly, grouchiness and pugnacity have been related to a longer life expectancy in one study.) Much of the rage is an appropriate response to inhumane treatment. Some older people, of course, rage against the inevitable nature of aging and death, at least at some point in their coming to terms with these forces, but this too would seem to be a legitimate reaction. Dylan Thomas's words, "Do not go gently into that good night," express the desire of many to be alive to the end and to die with a sense of worth and pur-

pose, if not righteous indignation at being obliged to leave life.

EMOTIONAL REACTIONS TO AGE-RELATED LIFE CRISES

Certain life crises occur in old age regardless of socioeconomic and cultural circumstances, as part of the current aging experience in the United States.

Widowhood

The loss of a spouse represents a major psychological issue. The mourning process itself occurs at the same time as the need to make practical though emotion-laden decisions about where to live, what to do about the family home and possessions, how to dispose of the spouse's personal effects, what kind of contact to maintain with the spouse's relatives, what to do about new social roles, and, in some cases, whether or not even to go on living. Although research data are not available on the progress of couples (or of individuals, for that matter) through the entire life span, one can observe the interdependence that results from years of living together. The interdependence or mutual support of *some* older couples can become symbiotic to the extent that the remaining member may die shortly after the death of the other, even though he or she has been seemingly healthy. In other cases, severe depression may occur. Studies by Helsing et al.[12] and Mellstrom et al.[13] found that increased morbidity and mortality following the death of the spouse are greater in the male than the female, possibly as a result of women's better social networks. Women are more likely to share intimate feelings, including grief, as compared to men, whose conversations and relationships among fellow men are focused more upon activities such as business and sports. However, as evidence of the resilience of most individuals, McCrae and Costa found in a ten-year follow-up of a national sample of respondents age 25 to 74 that, although those who were widowed had less income and were more likely to have been hospitalized at some point, they were no different from those who were married in terms of psychological health.[14]

There are other complications of widowhood as well. The widowed and their children may be ambivalent about the more involved roles that many grown children feel compelled to accept in relation to the remaining parent. Friends and associates tend to socially ostracize the widowed individual for varieties of reasons: pain over the reminder of the loss of a friend; anxieties and denial of their own aging; awkwardness in knowing how to comfort a grieving person; and uneasiness about accepting a single man or woman into a cultural pattern of couples. Thus widows and widowers may be forced to seek out each other's companionship or fall back on their own resources. Programs such as the widow-to-widow program, begun by Silverman in 1964, can be immensely valuable in facilitating adjustment.[15]

Marital Problems[16]

Couples who enter old age together find new situations awaiting them. There is a greater amount of close contact and free time for each other. With retirement, the older man spends most of his day at home for the first time in his adult life. Those women who spent their lives as housewives may complain of husbands being underfoot all day with nothing to do as the wives continue their accustomed routines of housework. Some men actively pursue new interests but many encounter difficulties in finding a meaningful substitute for work. Women who retire from the outside work force may experience similar adjustment problems. As one or the other becomes ill and requires nursing care, the healthy spouse is torn between the desire to provide such care for the sick person and a need to have a life of his or her own outside the sickroom.[17] These decisions and the increased physical burden in caring for a loved one can in themselves lead to psychiatric morbidity,[18] although this point is debated in the literature.[19]

Typically, because of a shorter life expectancy and a tendency to be older than his wife at the time of marriage, it is the husband who becomes ill, often chronically so, and the wife who nurses him until his death. If the illness is a long and draining one, the wife can be expected to feel some bitterness and sense of exploitation. This becomes a more serious problem when the wife denies her feelings and insists on the pretense that her husband is no burden. The husband, sensing his wife's frustrations, may react with hurt and anger, and a troubled marital relationship ensues wherein both need guidance and reassurance.

Discrepant rates of change, narcissism, fear of death, and the relationship to the children are among critical variables that are pertinent to marital problems in late life and require study.

A daughter of a 78-year-old patient wrote concerning the present relationship of her parents: "I might note here that when I was growing up, my father objected to even the words 'darned' or 'damned.' He now swears freely and will mutter 'Jesus Christ' under his breath the minute he hears mother call. He seems to feel that both her present philosophical outlook and her physical inabilities could be improved if she 'had the guts.' He bitterly resents her balkings and her standard 'I can't answer.' His answer to her frequent plea 'love me' is 'give me something to love'. . . . He is crushed by her condition. She is crushed by his cruelty and intolerance."

At times, underlying disease states may be misread by a spouse as emotional moods.

The wife of a 75-year-old patient bitterly complained of her husband's glum, depressed nature. He denied being as depressed as she insisted. He had the typical "ironed-out" facial expression of Parkinsonism, although no other manifestations of this disorder were present. A medical examination revealed that he did indeed have Parkinsonism.

Mental health personnel must be alert for danger signals between couples, collaborating when necessary with other family members and friends to protect both parties.

John B has for 40 years been a kindly and devoted husband. Since the onset of his cognitive difficulties, however, he has had a marked personality change. In addition to being increasingly withdrawn and depressed, he has also become irritable and, at times, physically abusive. The wife denies to the physician that the intermittent physical outbursts are a problem. In private, however, the daughter reports that on at least three occasions the mother has had unexplained bruises on her shoulders and arms, which she claims were the result of "accidental falls." The daughter also reports that her father, previously a pious and quiet man, is now frequently heard shouting expletives at the slightest provocation in the home and that the mother is actually quite frightened for her safety, but is too embarrassed to discuss the issue openly.

Sexual Problems

Sex relations, although tending to be diminished in frequency, are practiced by many older people; however, problems can arise physically and emotionally in relationship to aging and illness. Surgery requiring a colostomy, for example, can seriously deter sexual expression for esthetic and physical reasons. Physiological changes in females (for example, untreated atrophic vaginitis) and prostatic problems in males are some of the possible organic impediments to sexual intercourse. Other impediments may be psychological or even ethical, as evidenced by a follow-up report on the case of John B.

Within weeks of receiving treatment for his depression and agitation, John B was calmer and his wife was greatly relieved. Six months later, however, she returned with another dilemma. Despite becoming increasingly impaired cognitively, Mr. B frequently approached Mrs. B sexually. While she still very much enjoyed the encounters and occasionally initiated them herself, she always felt guilty that she was "taking advantage of him" or "giving in to animal instincts" rather than controlling herself. The

anxiety was building to the point where she found herself frequently "putting him off" and thereby avoiding sexual relations altogether.

Older people, like the young, tend to react with anxiety and depression over threats to potency and sexual fulfillment. In addition, new fears can present themselves. One of the more common worries is fear of the effects of sexual exertion on the heart or circulatory system. Studies indicate that much of this fear is unwarranted. Other problems result from spending a long life together: One partner may begin to find the other less and less sexually attractive as they age or be simply bored by the routine of the same partner over a period of years. A widow has an especially difficult situation, since chances for remarriage are so slight. Older people are inclined to follow the strict sexual customs of their youth—no sex outside of marriage—and are therefore forced into celibacy regardless of personal inclination. (We discuss sexual issues more fully in Chapter 7.)

Iatrogenicity (a physician's induction of pathological reactions) is pertinent to the discussion of sexual problems. By means that range from the injunction to "take it easy," said to the active man now suffering from a cardiac disorder, to the failure to prepare the patient who is about to have a prostatectomy or orchidectomy, to the induction of impotence as an unwanted consequence of prescribed medications, the physician may unwittingly contribute both to sexual dysfunction and to the depression that often accompanies it in older people. Practical advice about the physiology and psychology of sexuality in aging can be very valuable to older patients.[20]

Retirement

Everyone reacts to retirement, but not everyone goes through a "retirement crisis." Retirement does not mean the same thing for everybody. Although some view it as the end of their worthwhile life and think that anything beyond is downhill, others see retirement as a relief from hard work, a chance to rest, a period of enjoyment and relaxation. Still others believe that it marks the completion of their commitment to society and the beginning of their active commitment to themselves and all the things they have been waiting and wanting to do. It is not unusual to see second and even third careers occurring in late life, creative ventures beginning, and whole new personalities emerging as people discover and rediscover themselves. The emotional quality of retirement depends on the individual personality, income, health, social circumstances, and sense of worth.

Women enjoy a mixed blessing in relation to retirement. Many of the current generation of older women have never worked outside the home and therefore are not as subject as men to the psychological difficulties many individuals find with retirement. The traditional housewife's job identity is threatened in mid-life as her children leave home, but as she adjusts to caring for only herself and her husband, she has a definite pattern of work—at least until her husband dies. Even in her widowhood a woman continues to have the routines of homemaking available to her. For those women who do work outside the home, many carry the dual role of homemaker and employed worker, thus ameliorating the impact of retirement.

For men, retirement is a concern that can affect the very essence of their lives. A large number of men derive an almost singleminded identity from their work (some even becoming "workaholics"—addicted to work). Many develop no diversified interests outside their employment and are caught up in a narrow definition of who they are and what they are worth as people. Work and life become so interconnected that the loss of a job can eliminate the reason for living.

Dr. P, a 72-year-old retired surgeon, has been increasingly restless and irritable over the last six months. He retired as a cardiovascular surgeon five years ago but kept a busy consulting practice until earlier this year. His wife had wanted to travel more, and he had agreed to end his career, only to become disgruntled around the house. He was also described as "being less fun" when they traveled together on vacation with the family. When interviewed, he freely admitted that he missed his exalted position as one of the preeminent surgeons in the community. He stated that he especially missed the sense of being needed.

Men should be encouraged to take a more active part in all aspects of life—with more involvement in the care of children and home, a sharing of responsibility for financial support with the wife, more leisure time throughout life for rest and study, and active involvement in cultural and social activities. A call for male as well as female liberation is in order if men are to escape the crushing burden of overidentification with work and problems of stress, coronary disease, retirement shock, and shortened life expectancy that are associated with it.

The syndrome of the restless and depressed retired person is common indeed, but the abolition of mandatory retirement and the establishment of pre- and postretirement programs have begun to address this situation. Both common sense and research indicate that people adjust better if they can choose when and how to retire. Eventually a redefinition of work itself may bring a more satisfying retirement picture. Work, leisure, and study could be alternated throughout the life cycle instead of being parceled out according to age group.

The phenomena of both overpreparation and underpreparation for retirement can be observed. The overly prepared are those who anxiously begin to plan ahead in early middle age, with elaborate attentions to the details of their future life. Such overachievers are usually indicating that they are unhappy or insecure in their present life and are trying desperately for something better in the future. On the other extreme are those who do not even conceive of, let alone prepare for, retirement and who are sadly surprised when it catches them unaware. The most successful retirees are those who take reasonable precautions for their old age but enjoy living in the present rather than expecting some future "golden age."

Financial Worries

There is considerable financial distress among older persons, as we have emphasized earlier. Poverty and the fear of poverty do of course influence mental health. Moreover, continuing public discussion of the integrity and unfunded liability of Social Security and Medicare, as well as public and private pension systems other than Social Security, add to the worries of older people. Economic projections into the future have emphasized the declining number of workers to contribute to the support of older people. Frequently, the fact that there is also a declining number of young people for the working generation to support is not emphasized. (See Chapter 1, Table 1.1, "Dependency Ratio.")

Sensory Loss

Hearing loss is approximately seven times more prevalent for people age 65 to 74 than for people under 45 years old.[21] According to most estimates some degree of hearing loss is experienced by approximately 30% of people aged 65 to 75, and 50% of people aged 75 and older.[22] This high prevalence in the elderly is very important because hearing loss can reduce reality testing and lead to marked suspiciousness and even paranoia. The finding that this deficit is generally underreported suggests that clinicians should be vigilant in looking for evidence of hearing loss in their patients even before the problem becomes overtly symptomatic.[23]

Hearing loss causes greater social isolation than blindness, perhaps because verbal communication is so vital to human interaction. Onlookers may mistake the hard-of-hearing as mentally abnormal or "senile." There is little social sympathy—older people who are deaf are often excluded from activities and become less and less well oriented. The loud or badly articulated speech associated with hearing loss can have a negative effect on others, and the hard-of-hearing are given less consideration than the elderly blind, probably because their handicap is not so obvious to the onlooker. As a result, it is a common clinical observation that hearing loss is associated with depression.[24]

Although most old people need glasses, poor vision is not as widespread as is usually thought. While about one in eight older people are severely visually impaired,[25] many have fair to adequate visual acuity to age 90 and even beyond. Often one eye may continue to function, even if the other does not. Older persons find the possibility of cataracts, glaucoma, and other disorders frightening because of the isolating and immobilizing effects. Visual loss can cause decreasing mobility, poor orientation, and frightening visual impressions that resemble hallucinations. Reading, television, and other visual pastimes are reduced or eliminated. Social and travel plans are often restricted to accommodate visual limitations. Furthermore, older people feel more vulnerable to danger and crime when handicapped by sensory loss.

Smell also declines with age and up to 30% of people who are over 80 years have difficulty identifying common substances by smell.[26] Taste also may be affected, since taste sensations are often dependent on the ability to smell; in addition, taste buds decrease in number with age. However, recent and highly sophisticated studies of taste acuity of healthy community residents have found that, basically, the gustatory system functions reasonably well across the age span.[27] Taking advantage of the National Institute on Aging's Baltimore Longitudinal Study, Weiffenbach et al. saw the automatic decline in taste acuity over time as modest (10%). Environmental factors such as tobacco and medications are more influential in such decreases than is age. For example, 30% of those on medication experience some loss of taste.

There is also a falloff of tactile response as both perception and motor expression decline in reaction to stimuli. However, the slowing of speed and response, which at first appears to be a characteristic of old age, was found in the NIMH studies to be also related to environmental deprivation and depression.

Disease and Disability

Contrary to persistent popular belief, old age is not always accompanied by illness and sadness.

However, the chronic and acute illnesses and diseases in old age do provide the fulcrum determining the physical functioning and energy levels that are available to older people. Just as loss and grief define the critical emotional variable for the old, so illness presents the prime physical variable. The Roman adage *mens sana in corpore sano* ("a sound mind in a sound body") recognizes the interrelationships between the two. To provide a perspective on the most prominent of the chronic diseases and impairments, elderly women have higher rates than men for arthritis, diabetes, hypertension, back pain, and visual impairment. Men have higher rates of asthma, chronic arthritis, hernia, peptic ulcer, and hearing impairments. Psychometric tests, especially those sensitive to concurrent levels of depression, have proved to be unusually sensitive to even minimal disease. Physical illness frequently generates both appropriate and distorted emotional reactions, since it represents so much that is inherently frightening to human beings.

When physical illness is chronic, the incidence of psychiatric disorder increases significantly.

Mary B is a 75-year-old former school teacher with a history of chronic and painful arthritis. She retired from her position as a music instructor ten years ago, but continued her private lessons until recently. She felt she had to give up her remaining pupils because of increasing pain in her hands due to arthritis and her inability to tolerate the significant side effects of the treatment regimen. She is married and has a very supportive family locally, but was noted to display signs of increasing irritability and social withdrawal over the last few months. She sometimes keeps busy with housework and various activities with the family, but keeps to herself most of the time. Remarkably, she rarely listens to music in her home, previously a passionate hobby.

Clearly, Mrs. B was adjusting to her medical plight. To have lost her beloved teaching due to arthritis was obviously a devastating blow. She had further reason to be frustrated by the lack of tolerance to the medication side effects (often a major problem with arthritis sufferers). Her emotional reaction was a global one of disappointment. Consultation and therapy might be directed at helping her adjust to her impediments and exploring whether she could obtain continued enjoyment from music and the coaching of students in some way that would be both possible and satisfying for her.

Hospitalization and Surgery

Heart and circulatory diseases, digestive conditions, and disturbances of the nervous system are the primary causes of hospitalization after age 65. Hospitalization is drastic and dramatic proof that something is wrong or may be wrong. Fears become heightened and, since so many older persons now die in hospitals and nursing homes rather than at home, such institutions come to be viewed as places to die as well as places to regain health. There is still far too little attention paid to the emotional feelings of sick people, and this is especially the case with the aged. The emphasis on treating physical disease, the often cold and cheerless environment of hospitals, the generally efficient but overworked and impersonal medical staff, and visiting regulations that are either too lax or too rigid combine to make the older person feel isolated, unprotected, lonely, and bored. There is often little to do except watch television, a problematic pastime that becomes even more limited if hearing or sight is impaired. Occupational and recreational therapies are usually minimal. Removal from the home environment (with consequent deprivation of adequate contact with family and friends, lack of responsibility, and restriction of mental and somatic activity) encourages anxiety, irritability, disorientation, and eventual regression.

Insufficient thought has been given to the side effects of various surgical procedures. A classic example is the "black patch" syndrome, which some years ago puzzled the medical profession. Following bilateral cataract surgery when patches were placed over both eyes, certain older people became delirious and disoriented. It was observed that the syndrome did not occur when one eye was operated on at a time, leaving the sight in the other available to the patient. Finally, the conclusion was correctly drawn that the black patch reaction was simply the result of loss of contact with people and environment. Therefore, operating on one eye at a time and providing additional sensory stimuli will allow patients to maintain orientation. It seems logical that other undesirable side effects of surgery might be alleviated through just such careful thinking through of the problems.

Several organizations assist persons undergoing particular kinds of surgery. The Reach to Recovery program of the American Cancer Society is a rehabilitation program for women who have had breast surgery. The United Ostomy Association offers information and counseling to those who have had colostomies and ileostomies.[28]

Fears, Body Image Anxiety, and Chronic Pain

Since there are so many potential problems, medical and otherwise, for the elderly, it is understandable why fears may increase. Whereas the fears in the young and middle-aged are often of the accidental or avoidable tragedies of life (i.e., motor vehicle accidents, flying, lightening), the fears of the elderly often relate to threats that may not be avoidable (i.e., cancer, memory loss, financial ruin, death). Elderly people can become consumed with fears. Currently, "Alzheimer-phobia" is one such powerful fear, causing elderly and not-so-elderly patients to frequent their doctors' offices in unprecedented numbers just to get a "memory check-up."

The fear of injury in older persons is well-founded. In 1993, almost 28,000 elderly deaths were the result of accidents.[29] Approximately 800,000 older Americans are disabled by injury for at least one day a year. Burns and scalds are three times more likely to occur among older persons. Falls account for three out of four accidents in the elderly and 60 to 90% of home-related deaths. Between 15 and 50% of those who need to go to a hospital due to a fall die within a year.[30]

Although fall-related deaths increase with age, most falls do not lead to death. However, considerable morbidity results from falls. Approximately 25% of hospital admissions and 50% of nursing home admissions of the elderly are directly related to falling.

Latent fear and anxiety about death surface with illness and suffering. Feelings of helplessness and vulnerability buried deep within the individual may be resurrected in the face of implacable illness and the aging process. Hope for cures from medicines, luck, or a supreme being may diminish. Older people's sense of pride in their own body's reliability can be shaken when they experience greater susceptibility to communicable diseases, air pollution, dampness, cold weather, and exertion. Moreover, aging and disease threaten people's sense of who they are—their identities—as their bodies change "in front of their eyes." People report feelings of shock and disbelief at their mirror image, in reaction both to aging (Is that old person really me?) and to illness, which even more rapidly changes the size, shape, and appearance of the body. The line between symptom and fear often blurs as the duration and severity of chronic illness grows.

Eighty-six percent of older persons have some kind of chronic health problem requiring more visits to the doctor, added stays in the hospital, special diets, exercises, drugs, rehabilitative therapy, or additional provisions for daily life at home. With 81% of older people ambulatory, and to a substantial degree responsible for their own self-care, it is apparent that body monitoring—the need to concern oneself with the care of one's body and its functions in a more concerted way than before—is a compelling preoccupation. Bodily processes that formerly took care of themselves or required minimal attention begin to demand more and more time as people age. Some older people welcome the relief from other anxieties, which occurs as they absorb themselves in their own care. But others are annoyed, wearied, or bored by the routines imposed on them by ill health and the decline of their bodies. The composer Stravinsky, in his eighties, wrote of his irritation at having to spend so much time on his body when he wanted to write music. One can assume that his complaint is echoed by many who wish to continue active, interesting lives.

While pain is not found only in the elderly, it is certainly more common with age. Acute illnesses such as myocardial infarction and cerebrovascular accidents are now recognized as being associated with subsequent depression and anxiety, and the need for psychiatric assessment is well documented.[31] What is perhaps less well known is the degree to which depression and the other psychiatric syndromes are also associated with chronic pain.

The periodic aches and pains of rheumatism, the throbbing relentless pains of arthritis, the sharp distress of angina pectoris—these are examples of pain in some of its shapes and forms. Older persons deal with pain according to their life-style, personality, and cultural background, as well as the nature and extent of the pain. Individual pain thresholds vary from person to person and vary also in intensity at different times in the same individual. For many persons, the use of drugs offers the most consistent relief, yet drugs often produce side effects that can be particularly devitalizing or disorienting to older people—dizziness, loss of appetite, weakness, nausea, or dulling of consciousness. Drug use for pain requires careful monitoring for the best balance between freedom from pain and freedom from the side effects of the pain medication (see Chapter 13).

Dying and Death (See Chapter 12)

Preparation for death involves a condition unknown in past or present experience, for one cannot truly imagine one's own nonexistence. Yet, strangely, although fear of death is part of human experience, older people tend to fear it less than the young do and often are more concerned about the death of those they love than about their own. Many can accept personal death with equanimity. In terminal illness it may even be welcomed as a release from pain and struggle. Reactions to death are closely related to a resolution of life's experiences and problems as well as a sense of one's contributions to others. Profound religious and

philosophical convictions facilitate acceptance. The process of working through one's feelings about death begins with a growing personal awareness of the eventual end of life and the implications of this for one's remaining time alive. For some people the process begins early; for others the physical signs of aging occur before awareness is allowed to surface. Some few attempt to deny death to the very end. A resolution of feelings about death may be responsible for those elusive qualities, seen in various old people, known as "wisdom" and "serenity." The German philosopher Feurbach has written that "anticipation of death is seen as the instrument of being—of authentic existence." There are of course varying degrees and levels of acceptance; perhaps the most satisfying is that described by another philosopher, Spinoza: "The adult who sees death as completion of a pattern and who has spent life unfettered by fears, living richly and productively, can integrate and accept the thought that life will stop."

Few older persons today have the opportunity to die at home as their parents and grandparents did. More than 50% of all deaths take place in hospitals, and many in nursing homes. The process of dying is made more difficult by this shift from home to institutions, where the emphasis is on physical rather than emotional concerns. Short and inflexible visiting hours and lack of accommodations for intimate family contact encourage families and friends to withdraw from dying persons, in anticipatory grief (working out feelings of grief as though the person were already dead). Thus the aged person, who may have resolved many of his own difficult feelings about death itself, is left without human comfort and warmth as death approaches. Older people often remark that their greatest fear is of "dying alone."

There is an increasing interest in the subject of death and dying, as evidenced by a growing body of research and literature. One of the best-known reports is the Kübler-Ross book on the stages of dying, in which she suggests five more or less distinct stages or levels of experience during the actual course of dying. The first stage is *denial of death,* in which the person simply refuses to believe the evidence of his or her own approaching demise. In the second stage, denial is replaced by *anger and rage* at the injustice and unfairness of life's ending. Third, the person moves into a *bargaining stage* during which he or she tries to make a deal with God or fate in return for life (promises of being a better person, showing more concern for others, etc.). When this is seen to be futile, the person moves into a period of *depression* and preparatory grief over the loss of life and loved ones. Finally, in the last stages, a level of *acceptance* is reached—a quiet expectation of death and a lessening of interest in the outer world, including loved ones. In our experience and that of many others working with dying persons, these stages seldom occur as neatly and orderly as described here. Therefore, keeping the various stages in mind can be very useful in understanding the dying, as long as one does not depend on them too rigidly.

COMMON ADAPTIVE TECHNIQUES

Defense Mechanisms

Older persons have throughout their lifetimes acquired individual and characteristic methods of handling anxiety, aggressive impulses, resentments, and frustration. Such methods, known as *defense mechanisms,* are internal, automatic, unconscious processes whereby the personality protects itself by attempting to provide psychological stability in the midst of conflicting or overwhelming needs and stresses that are part of human existence. As people mature, new defenses may be added and old ones discarded; but others persist throughout life, taking on different tones and colorations at different stages in the life cycle. Emphasis here will be on the defense mechanisms that most often appear in old age and on nuances that are characteristic of older people.

Denial.   The denial of old age and death found in the young person's attitude of "This won't happen to me" may also occur in old age in the form of "This isn't happening to me." In one of its extreme forms, denial can manifest itself in a "Peter Pan" syndrome, with the older person pretending to be young and refusing to deal with the realities of aging. There may be a self-attribution of strength—claiming that one is still capable of everything. Not all denial is pathological. It is, in fact, a necessary and useful component for maintaining a sense of stability and equilibrium. But the usefulness of denial is eroded when it begins to seriously interfere with the developmental work of any particular age. In old age, an individual who denies that he or she is sick and refuses to take medicine or see a doctor demonstrates an example of denial that no longer accomplishes a life-protective purpose.

Denial, like other defenses, often responds to psychotherapy:

Chief complaint: *"I can't catch my breath." This is the case of a man who was always in a hurry and had eventually to stop to catch his breath.*

A 68-year-old, highly intelligent and intellectual sociologist developed a severe cough on his return from an extended and exciting journey abroad. An X-ray shadow increased the medical suspicion of malignancy. Without prior discussion and preparation, the patient was inadvertently but directly told this by a secretary arranging his admission for surgery. The operation revealed a lung abscess and the patient responded well physically both to the operative procedure and in the recovery period, with one exception: he could not catch his breath. His internist suggested an extended vacation, and later tranquilizers, and offered reassurance. After some months the doctor strongly recommended psychotherapy, as he realized the patient was becoming increasingly agitated and depressed without adequate medical explanation. The patient was extremely tense and restless. He appeared somewhat slovenly. His pants hung loose from his suspenders and his fly was partly open. In short, he gave the impression of having some organic mental disorder but he spoke clearly and well. Despite his obvious gloom, he managed some humor and clarity in giving his present and past history.

His situation was socially and personally favorable. He had a good relationship with a devoted wife. He had many good friends and professional colleagues. He was well regarded professionally. He was under no pressure to retire, and consultancies were open to him. He had a wide range of interests in addition to his professional field. His relationships with his brothers and sisters were good. With the exception of the chief complaint, his physical status was excellent. He believed his physician's report that there was no major organic disease; in other words, he was not suffering from a fear that he was being misled. But despite all of this, he was tense and depressed. Recurrent dreams included one in which "a paper was due" and another in which he was "behind in an exam." He had never taken out any life insurance. He had made no conscious admission to himself that he might age. He had made nothing of birthdays. Nor did he have a very clear concept of the natural evolution of the life cycle. He did not have any sense of stages and development of middle and later life. He had an enormous capacity for work and had kept busy all his life as though unaware of the passage of time. He had never been bored. He had great capacity for self-discipline and was not given to marked expression of either grief or anger but only to a narrow spectrum of affects, including fearfulness and pleasure. He was a kind of Peter Pan, and he and his wife eventually concluded in the course of his psychotherapeutic work that he, and in some measure she, had imagined themselves as remaining in their twenties instead of being in their late sixties. As he reviewed his life and the realities of aging and death, he became freer in his expression of more negative affect. His depression and tension improved and he remained well in a follow-up of some six months. He was no longer short of breath.

Projection.   Some older persons attempt to allay anxieties by projecting feelings outward onto someone else. They may appear suspicious and fearful, with characteristic complaints of merchants cheating them, doctors ignoring them, their children neglecting them. They often become concerned about physical safety on the streets. Much of what is termed projection may indeed be legitimate complaints and fears about situations that exist, either potentially or in actuality, and one runs the risk of denying reality by labeling them projection. But actual projection itself does occur, signifying internal stress (people with hearing losses are prime victims) and can reach paranoid proportions unless the stress is alleviated.

Fixation.   Fixation is most often associated with old age as a carryover defense from earlier life, implying that the fixation point occurred somewhere in childhood. But if one views old age as having developmental work of its own, fixation is a useful concept in describing the older person who may reach a particular level of development and be unable to go further. An example might be the person who has adapted well to living alone, without a spouse, but cannot accept in an insightful manner the need for outside help as physical strength wanes. Such a person may unconsciously want to stop the action and refuse to accept a new change.

Regression.[32]   Regression, or a return to an earlier level of adaptation, is an overused and catchall explanation for much behavior in old age. Familiar descriptions of older people as "childlike," "childish," or "in second childhood" imply a slide back to earlier developmental stages with no cognizance of a lifetime of experience that unalterably separates them from their childhood patterns of coping. A pejorative connotation is given, with the notion that older people lose their "adultness" under stress of illness and age and begin to act like children. Regression implies a disruptive, deteriorative, nonadaptive retreat in which the personality is not up to facing the stress it must overcome; the weakness is internal. But in old age much of the stress is from external sources that strain the resources of even the most healthy personalities. The use of the concept of regression to describe the attempts of older people to adapt in such situations is similar to the popular use of the term "paranoid" to describe the reactions of certain minority groups to racial discrimination. What appears to be pathological may indeed be the typical and even necessary patterns of response to stressful circumstances.

Displacement.   The function of displacement is to disguise the real source of anxiety or discomfort for a person by placing it on some other object or circumstance. For example, a person whose body is drastically undergoing change may displace the cause of his or her emotional distress by declaring that the world is going to ruin or that things are not the way they were when he or she was young.

Counterphobia. Counterphobia is the compelling and sometimes risky tendency to look danger in the face in an attempt to convince oneself that it can be overcome.[33] An older man with dizzy spells may insist on climbing a ladder to fix his own roof. Another, with a history of visual blackouts, may demand that he drive the family car just as before. A woman with heart trouble ignores her racing pulse as she continues to carry tubs of laundry from her basement. In each case the individual ignores a realistic appraisal of limitations and relies upon sheer force of will to undo the danger.

Idealization. One type of defense is the idealization of the lost object, be it person, place, lifestyle, or status. A person may, for instance, idolize a deceased mate, glorifying the past and the good old days. The purpose is often to make one's life seem meaningful and not wasted, but the result is more often to alienate those people who remain.

Jim H is a 79-year-old retired plumber of good means with a large extended family. He is in excellent physical health and has no immediate complaints himself, but is brought in for consultation by his daughters and second wife of 21 years because of his increasing irritability over the last three months. They complain that no matter what the wife does, he finds fault with her. Their recent vacation was ruined when he insisted on driving to an old family campground and staying there despite poor weather. Furthermore, he has been sexually much less attentive lately and has been criticizing how "old" his wife looks. The daughters also report that their father has been "different" lately; he has spent an inordinate amount of time reminiscing with them about their childhoods, something he rarely did until recently. They worry that he is lost in the "good

old days" and paying less attention to his grandchildren and other family duties.

On further evaluation and review with Mr. H, it became clear that he was indeed quite critical of his "new" wife. Although he has been married to her for over two decades, his children had all been raised by his first wife before her sudden death 25 years ago. As it turned out, the 50th wedding anniversary with his first wife was rapidly approaching, and he stated that no one except him seemed to be aware of that fact. Over the next several weeks, he was able to talk more openly about the pain he still felt about the sudden and unexpected loss of his first wife and the hollowness he initially felt after her death. Eventually, he was able to share these feelings with his current wife. As she had done some 25 years before, when they first met and fell in love, she consoled and comforted him through his memories of the grief. Later, in a quiet ceremony, the family as a whole did mark the 50th anniversary with a memorial dinner. Once reassured of his current wife's continuing love for him, he was able to stop comparing the idealized image of his first wife with her. His criticism of her stopped, and they went on to celebrate their own silver anniversary several years later.

Rigidity. There is little evidence that older people become more rigid in personality as they age. Rather, when rigidity is seen, it is a defense against a general sense of threat or actual crises.

OTHER DEFENSIVE BEHAVIOR

While not necessarily considered classic defense mechanisms, the following types of defensive behavior are commonly employed by older people.

Psychosomatic Complaints

Although actual data on the incidence and prevalence of psychosomatic disorder is hard to come by, there is little disagreement that exaggerated physical complaints do occur in the elderly and that they can be defensive in nature. It is rare, for instance, that a typical psychosomatic disorder has its beginnings in old age, with the exception perhaps of systemic hypertension, but psychological components of such traditional diseases of the elderly as rheumatoid arthritis and coronary artery disease are common. More common somatization reactions or episodes of hypochondriasis are also frequent in the elderly and include symptoms of back pain, stomach distress, trouble breathing, or bowel irregularities. These symptoms often herald underlying anxieties, depression, or other strongly felt emotions that are difficult to express more directly.

Selective Attention

The dulling of memory and the propensity to remember distant past events with greater clarity than events of the recent past have generally been attributed to atherosclerotic and senile brain changes in old age. However, it appears that such memory characteristics can at times have a psychological base, in that the older person may be turning away from or tuning out the painfulness of the present to dwell on a more satisfying past. The adaptive value of "forgetfulness" in dealing with vast amounts of information has also been emphasized. It may be a mechanism for sorting out the relevant from the irrelevant.

A process of "exclusion of stimuli" has been observed in older people, by which they block off the sensorium that they feel unprepared to deal with.[34] This is more often observed in people with hearing problems who, at times, seem to hear what they want to hear. This may be the only way an older person can control the amount of input impinging upon him. At the same time, however, older people have been shown to use "escapist fantasy" less often than younger subjects, suggesting that avoidance of painful stimuli is not always the motivating factor.

Exploitation of Age and Disability

Older people can use changes occurring in their lives to obtain secondary gains—that is, benefits which in and of themselves may be satisfying or desired. An example is shown by older persons who insist they must remain in a hospital or other care facility, even though they no longer need medical care, because they enjoy the extra attention and sense of importance accruing from the illness. Or an individual with a proclivity to control others may use illness or impending death to manipulate those around him. Examples are the tyrant on the sick bed who terrorizes family and friends through guilt, and the invalid who commandeers personal services from everyone through appearing totally helpless and passive. Exploitation of age and disability can also result in freedom from social expectation, with the older person not feeling bound by the social amenities and established patterns. In this sense, the defensive behavior may allow the person to try on a new identity or a new way of relating. Behavior that in youth might have been considered unacceptable or even bizarre can be viewed in old age as pleasantly idiosyncratic, or at least harmless.

An interesting form of age exploitation is what we have called the "old man" or "old woman" act. This is the older person who, even when physically and mentally sound, puts on an act of being a tottering, frail, helpless "old" person. This phenomenon can occur as early as the fifties but may be used by older people at any age to avoid responsibility toward themselves and others and to evoke sympathy. Sometimes the older person uses this act very selectively on those who are most gullible, while appearing quite sound and capable to others.

Restitution, Replacement, or Compensatory Behavior

Numerous activities may be adopted to make up for a loss. These may include practical measures such as memory pads and reminders of all kinds to compensate for poor memory. Or they can take the form of finding new persons to replace lost ones. Attempted restitution is frequently seen, in which a person tries to give back or get back that which has been lost or taken away.

Use of Activity or Busyness

General busyness, known as "working off the blues," is a defense against depression, anxiety, and other conditions that are painful or unacceptable. It involves concentrating on activity of some kind, whether productive or nonproductive, with the purpose of warding off the unwanted feelings.

Use of Groups

In part thanks to the "support group" approaches that have been developed over recent years, many individuals have survived experiences such as widowhood, chronic illness, and chronic stress much better than before. The reduction of isolation has been considerable and the adaptive techniques of strong social networks have been extremely valuable. One possible drawback, however, is that group identification, particularly if immediately following a crisis or during a continuing stress, may partially suppress an individual's expression of painful emotions. Thus a balance between group support and opportunities for individual expression appears necessary for the continuing maturation and adaptation of the older person.

Humor as an Adaptive Technique

Most people would agree that a joke, even a bad joke, can provide a welcome relief in a tense or otherwise difficult situation. Positive thinking and joking are characteristic of youth, but it is unclear how prevalent they are among the elderly. McCrae found that these defense mechanisms appeared less frequently as coping skills in his sample of older versus younger or middle-aged populations. Perhaps the development of humor should be considered a goal of both psychological maturity and, when a psychotherapeutic relationship exists, of psychotherapy itself.

Norman Cousins writes about the healing power of humor from his own experience as a patient:[35]

> Any medical student can give you a horrendous catalogue of all the terrible things that happen to the body under the impact of negative emotions: fear, hate, rage, exasperations, frustration. You learn about constriction of the blood vessels, increase in blood pressure, excess flow of hydrochloric acid, adrenal depletion, indigestion, headaches. But we

haven't yet sufficiently recognized that the body does not operate only on one wave length. It doesn't respond just to the negative emotions, it also responds to the positive emotions. It's impossible to have one without having the other. But the salutary effect is not as well understood.

The Changing Adaptive Value of Psychopathology

Related to adaptation is the changing adaptiveness found with psychopathology, which will be discussed in Chapter 9. Paranoid personality structures appear to become even less adaptive with age as the few persons in the paranoid's circle die, isolation grows, and crises occur. On the other hand, the schizoid personality structure may insulate against loss. The obsessional and compulsive personality whose fussbudget behavior may have impaired effectiveness earlier in life may adjust well to the void left by retirement or losses, through meticulous and ritualistic activities.

Insight as an Adaptive Technique

Insight, or understanding of one's motivations and behavior, is the most widely used and successful adaptation found in healthy older people. Successful adjustments to real-life conditions are not optimally possible if feelings and behavior are unconsciously motivated and therefore not subject to conscious control. Similarly, it can prove nonadaptive to be unaware of the natural course of life: what to expect, what can be changed, and what cannot. Thus insight requires not only an inner sense of oneself and motivations but also an inner knowledge of the human life cycle—a realization of life and how it changes. The older individual who has a steady comprehension of the life process from birth to death is thereby assisted in his or her efforts to decide what to oppose and what to accept, when to struggle and when to acquiesce, and, ultimately, to understand the limits of what is possible. An example is what coauthor Myrna Lewis calls "responsible dependency." This concept implies the realistic evaluation of when one begins to require help from others and an ability to accept that help with dignity and co-operativeness, rather than denying the need or abusing the opportunity to be dependent. Insight includes the willingness and ability to substitute available satisfactions for losses incurred.

Exercising rational control over one's life is a mature, effective concomitant of insight. The conscious suppression of problems ("sufficient unto the day is the evil thereof"), the mastery of feelings, the unanxious anticipation of events, seeking pleasures and avoiding pain, and sublimation of unacceptable feelings by more acceptable ones are illustrative. Moreover, deliberate altruism, the personal and social concern for others, is a sophisticated and enlightened form of self-interest.

THE LIFE REVIEW

The tendency of older persons toward self-reflection and reminiscence used to be thought of as indicating a loss of recent memory and therefore a sign of aging. However, in 1961 coauthor Robert Butler first postulated that reminiscence in the aged was part of a normal life review process brought about by realization of approaching dissolution and death.[36] It is characterized by the progressive return to consciousness of past experiences and particularly the resurgence of unresolved conflicts that can be looked at again and reintegrated. If the reintegration is successful, it can give new significance and meaning to one's life and prepare one for death by mitigating fear and anxiety.[37]

This is a process that is believed to occur universally in all persons in the final years of their lives, although they may not be totally aware of it and may in part defend themselves from realizing its presence. It is spontaneous, unselective, and seen in other age groups as well (adolescence, middle age); but the intensity and emphasis on putting one's life in order are most striking in old age. In late life, people have a particularly vivid imagination and memory for the past and can recall with sudden and remarkable clarity early life events. There is renewed ability to free associate and bring up material from the unconscious. Individuals realize that their own personal myth of invulnerability and immortality can no longer be maintained. All of this results in reassessment of life, which brings depression, acceptance, or satisfaction.[38] The life review is not synonymous with reminiscence, although it includes this activity; it is one level or type of reminiscence.

The life review can occur in a mild form through mild nostalgia, mild regret, a tendency to reminisce, story-telling, and the like. Often the person will give his life story to anyone who will listen. At other times it is conducted in silent monologue without witnesses. It is in many ways similar to the psychotherapeutic situation in which a person is reviewing his or her life in order to understand present circumstances.

As part of the life review one may experience a sense of regret that is increasingly painful. In severe forms it can yield anxiety, guilt, despair, and depression. And in extreme cases, if a person is unable to resolve problems or accept them, terror, panic, and suicide can result. The most tragic life review is that in which a person decides life was a total waste.

Some of the positive results of reviewing one's life can be a righting of old wrongs, making up with enemies, coming to acceptance of mortal life, a sense of serenity, pride in accomplishment, and a feeling of having done one's best. It gives people an opportunity to decide what to do with the time left to them and work out emotional and material legacies. People become ready but are in no hurry to die. Possibly the qualities of serenity, philosophical development, and wisdom observable in some older people reflect a state of resolution of their life conflicts. A lively capacity to live in the present is usually experienced, including the direct enjoyment of elemental pleasures such as nature, children, forms, colors, warmth, love, and humor. One may become more capable of mutuality with a comfortable acceptance of the life cycle, the universe, and the generations. Creative works may result, such as memoirs, art, and music. People may put together family albums and scrapbooks and study their genealogies.

One of the greatest difficulties for younger persons (including mental health personnel) is to listen thoughtfully to the reminiscences of older people. (See Chapter 12 for a discussion on life review therapy.) We have been taught that this nostalgia represents living in the past and a preoccupation with self and that it is generally boring, meaningless, and time-consuming. Yet as a natural healing process it represents one of the un-derlying human capacities on which all psy-chotherapy depends. The life review should be recognized as a necessary and healthy process in daily life as well as a useful tool in the mental health care of older people.

SELECTED READINGS

Ariès, P. (1982). *The hour of our death.* New York: Vintage Books.

Bartoshuk, L. M., Rifkin, B., Marks, L. E., & Bars, P. (1986). Taste and aging. *Journal of Gerontology, 41,* 51–57.

Birren J. E., Butler, R. N., Greenhouse, S. W., Sokoloff, L., & Yarrow, M. R. (1963). Summary and interpretations. In Birren, J. E., Butler, R. N., Greenhouse, S. W., Sokoloff, L., & Yarrow, M. R. (Eds.), *Human aging: A biological and behavioral study,* pub. no. (PHS) 986. Washington, DC: U.S. Government Printing Office (reprinted as pub. no. [HSM] 71–9051, 1971, 1974).

Blieszner, R., & Hilkevitch Bedford, V. (Eds.). (1995). *Handbook of aging and the family.* Westport, CT: Greenwood Press.

Butler, R. N. (1963). The life review: An interpretation of reminiscence in the aged. *Psychiatry, 26,* 65–76.

Butler, R. N., & Lewis, M. I. (1995). Late-life depression: When and how to intervene. *Geriatrics, 50*(8), 44–55.

Butler, R. N., & Lewis, M. I. (1995). *Love and sex after sixty.* New York: Ballantine.

Castillo, C. S., Schultz, S. K., & Robinson, R. G. (1995, August). Clinical correlates of early-onset and late-onset poststroke general anxiety. *American Journal of Psychiatry, 152*(6), 1174–1179.

Chappell, N. L., & Badger, M. (1989). Social isolation and well-being. *The Journal of Gerontology, 44*(5), S169–S176.

Coffey, C. E., & Cummings, J. L., with Lovell, M. L., & Pearlson, G. D. (Eds.). (1994). *Textbook of geriatric neuropsychiatry.* Washington, DC: American Psychiatric Press.

Conway, P. (1988, November). Losses and grief in old age. *Social Casework,* 541–549.

Coombs, R. H. (1991). Marital status and personal well-being: A literature review. *Family Relations, 40,* 97–102.

Coroni-Huntley, J., Brock, D. B., Ostfeld, A. M., Taylor, J. O., & Wallace, R. B. (Eds.). (1986). *Established populations for epidemiologic studies of the elderly.* Resource data book, NIH Publication no. 86–2443. Washington, DC: National Institute on Aging.

Fasey, C. N. (1990, March/April). Grief in old age: A review of the literature. *International Journal of Geriatric Psychiatry, 5*(2), 67–76.

Flint, A. J. (1994). Epidemiology and comorbidity of anxiety disorders in the elderly. *American Journal of Psychiatry, 151,* 640–649.

Glaser, B. G., & Strauss, A. C. (1965). *Awareness of dying.* Chicago: Aldine.

Goldman, N., Korenman, S., & Weinstein, R. (1994). Marital status and health among the elderly. *Office of Population Research Working Paper,* no. 94–3. Princeton, NJ: Princeton University, Office of Population Research.

Gorer, G. (1965). *Death, grief, and mourning.* New York: Doubleday.

Helsing, K. J., Szklo, M., & Comstock, G. W. (1981, August). Factors associated with mortality after widowhood. *American Journal of Public Health, 71,* 802–809.

Hollingshead, A. B., & Redlich, F. (1958). Social class and mental illness. New York: John Wiley & Sons.

Lindemann, E. (1965). Symptomatology and management of acute grief. In Parad, H. J. (Ed.), *Crisis intervention: Selected readings* (pp. 7–21). New York: Family Service Association of America.

Lopata, H. Z. (1995). Feminist perspectives on social gerontology. In Blieszner, R. & Hilkevitch Bedford, V. (Eds.), *Handbook of aging and the family* (pp. 114–131). Westport, CT: Greenwood Press.

Lopata, H. Z. (1996). *Current widowhood: Myths and realities.* Newbury Park, CA: Sage Publications.

Martin-Matthews, A. (1991). *Widowhood in later life.* Toronto, Canada: Butterworths/Harcourt Brace.

McCrae, R. R., & Costa, P. T., Jr. (1988). Psychological resilience among widowed men and women: A 10-year follow-up of a national sample. *Journal of Social Issues, 44*(3), 129–142.

Mellstrom, D., Nilsson, A., Oden, A., Rundgren, A., & Svanborg, A. (1982). Mortality among the widowed in Sweden. *Scandinavian Journal of Social Medicine, 10,* 33–41.

National Advisory Mental Health Council. (1993, October). Health care reform for Americans with severe mental illness: Report of the National Advisory Mental Health Council. *American Journal of Psychiatry, 150*(10), 1447–1465.

O'Bryant, S. L., & Hansson, R. O. (1995) Widowhood. In Blieszner, R., & Hilkevitch Bedford, V. (Eds.), *Handbook of aging and the family* (pp. 440–458). Westport, CT: Greenwood Press.

Pellman, J. (1992) Widowhood and elderly women: Exploring its relationship to community integration, hassles, stress, social support and social support seeking. *International Journal of Aging and Human Development, 35*(4), 253–264.

Perlin, S., & Butler, R. N. (1963). Psychiatric aspects of adaptation to the aging experience. In Birren, J. E., Butler, R. N., Greenhouse, S. W., Sokoloff, L., & Yarrow, M. R. *Human aging: A biological and behavioral study,* pub. no. (PHS) 986. Washington, DC: U.S. Government Printing Office. (Reprinted as pub. no. [HSM] 71–9051, 1971, 1974).

Stroebe, M. S., Stroebe, W., & Hansson, R. O. (Eds.). (1993). *Handbook of bereavement.* New York: Cambridge University Press.

Tolstoy, L. (1886). *The death of Ivan Ilych.*

Umberson, D., Wortman, C., & Kessler, R. (1992). Widowhood and depression: Explaining long-term gender differences in vulnerability. *Journal of Health and Social Behavior, 33*(1), 10–24.

Valliant, G. E. (1986). An empirical validated hierarchy of defense mechanisms. *Archives of General Psychiatry, 42,* 597–601.

Weinberg, J. (1956). Personal and social adjustment. In Anderson, J. E. (Ed.), *Psychological aspects of aging.* Washington, DC: American Psychological Association.

Weisman, A. D., & Kastenbaum, R. (1968) The psychological autopsy: A study of the terminal phase of life. *Community Mental Health Journal.* Monograph no. 4. New York: Behavioral Publications.

Wolinsky, F., & Johnson, R. (1992). Widowhood, health status, and the use of health services by older adults: A cross sectional and prospective approach. *Journal of Gerontology,* S8–S16.

ENDNOTES

1. *Senescence* is a term that has been used to describe the developmental stages of later life. It is an analogue to pubescence and adolescence; no similar term has been formulated for middle age.

2. Pusey, E. B. (trans.). (1949) *The confessions of St. Augustine* (book IX). New York: Modern Library.

3. Gorer, G. (1965). *Death, grief and mourning.* New York: Doubleday Anchor.

4. Parkes, C. M. (1970). Seeking and finding a lost object. *Social Science and Medicine, 4,* 187–201; Parkes, C. M., & Weiss, R. S. (1983). *Recovery from bereavement.* New York: Basic Books.

5. Mellstrom, D., Nilsson, A., Oden, A., Rundren, A., & Svanborg, A. (1982). Mortality among the widowed in Sweden. *Scandinavian Journal of Social Medicine, 10,* 33–41.

6. Chodoff especially has emphasized "survival guilt" as a result of concentration camp experiences. We have observed this also in older people who have outlived their peers and spouses, although, of course, many take pride in survival as well. See Chodoff, P. C. (1963). Late effects of the concentration camp syndrome. *Archives of General Psychiatry, 9,* 323–333.

7. Butler, R. N., & Lewis, M. I. (1995). Late-life depression: When and how to intervene. *Geriatrics, 50*(8), 44–55.

8. Blazer, D., Hughes, D. C., & George, L. K. (1987). The epidemiology of depression in an elderly community population. *Gerontologist, 27,* 281–287.

9. Murphy, E. (1982). Social origins of depression in old age. *British Journal of Psychiatry, 141,* 135–142.

10. Rats subjected to Jay Weiss's "yoke" electric shock paradigm dramatically demonstrate the relationship between learned helplessness and disease. See Sklar, L. S., & Anisman, H. (1979). Stress and coping factors influence tumor growth. *Science, 205,* 512–515; Visintainer, M. A., Volpicelli, J. R., & Seligman, M. E. (1982). Tumor rejection in rats after inescapable or escapable shock. *Science, 216,* 437–439.

11. Hess, N. (1987). King Lear and some anxieties of old age. *British Journal of Medical Psychology, 60,* 209–215.

12. Helsing, K. J., Szklo, M., & Comstock, G. W. (1981). Factors associated with mortality after widowhood. *American Journal of Public Health, 7,* 802–809.

13. Mellstrom et al., *Mortality among the widowed,* 33–41.

14. McCrae, R. R., & Costa, P. T. (1988). Psychological resilience among widowed men and women: A

10-year follow-up of a national sample. *Journal of Social Issues, 44*(3), 129–142.

15. Silverman, P. (1985). *Widow to widow.* New York: Springer.

16. Very little data are available on old-age marital relationships. There have been few studies of husband and wife through the life span. Therefore, we must largely theorize from clinical experience.

17. Morycz, R. K. (1985). Caregiving strain and the desire to institutionalize family members with Alzheimer's disease. *Research on Aging, 7,* 329–361.

18. Goldman, L. S., & Luchins, D. J. (1984). Depression in the spouses of demented patients. *American Journal of Psychiatry, 141,* 1467–1468; Cohen, D., & Eisdorfer, C. (1988). Depression in family members caring for a relative with Alzheimer's disease. *Journal of the American Geriatrics Society, 36,* 885–889.

19. Eagles, J. M., Beattie, J. A. G., Blackwood, G. W., Restall, D. B., & Ashcroft, G. W. (1987). The mental health of elderly couples: I. The effects of a cognitively impaired spouse. *British Journal of Psychiatry, 150,* 299–303; Eagles, J. M., Craig, A., Rawlinson, F., Restall, D. B., Beattie, J. A. G., & Besson, J. A. O. (1987). The psychological well-being of supporters of the demented elderly. *British Journal of Psychiatry, 150,* 293–298.

20. Butler, R. N., & Lewis, M. I. (1993). *Love and sex after sixty.* New York: Ballantine.

21. Corso, J. F. (1995). Hearing. In Maddox, G. L. (Ed.), *The encyclopedia of aging.* (pp. 449–452). New York: Springer.

22. Weinstein, B. E. (1994, August). Age-related hearing loss: How to screen for it, and when to intervene. *Geriatrics, 49*(8), 40–45.

23. Older people usually first notice hearing loss in the high-frequency range. This includes the consonants. To get a sense of what many older people miss, write a sentence and remove the *f*'s, *s*'s, and *th*'s.

24. Eastwood, M. R., Corbin, S. L, Reed, M., Nobbs, H., & Kedward, H. B. (1985). Acquired hearing loss and psychiatric illness: An estimate of prevalence and co-morbidity in a geriatric setting. *British Journal of Psychiatry, 147,* 552–556.

25. American Foundation for the Blind. (1996). *Fact sheet: Facts about aging and vision.* Available from: American Foundation for the Blind, 11 Penn Plaza, Suite 300, New York, N.Y. 10001. (800)232-5463.

26. Doty, R. L., Shaman, P., Applebaum, S. Z., Giberson, R., Siksorski, L., & Rosenberg, L. (1984).

Smell identification ability: Changes with age. *Science, 226,* 1441–1443.

27. Thus, Shakespeare was wrong, at least about taste, when in *As You Like It* he described old age as "sans teeth, sans eyes, sans taste, sans everything."

28. Central office—36 Executive Park Ste., Irvine, CA. 92714, with 580 local chapters.

29. National Center for Health Statistics. (1996). Advance Report of Final Mortality Statistics, 1993. *Monthly Vital Statistics Report, 44*(7), supplement. Hyattsville, MD: National Center for Health Statistics.

30. Tideiksaar, R. (1989). *Falling in old age: Its prevention and treatment.* New York: Springer.

31. Robinson, R. G., Stan, L. B., & Price, T. R. (1984). A two-year longitudinal study of mood disorder following stroke: Prevalence and duration at six months follow-up. *British Journal of Psychiatry, 14,* 256–262; Carney, R. M., Rich, M. W., Tevelde, A., Saini, J., Clark, K., & Jaffe, A. S. (1987). Major depressive disorder in coronary artery disease. *American Journal of Cardiology, 60,* 1273–1275; Castillo, C. S., Schultz, S. K., & Robinson, R. G. (1995, August). Clinical correlates of early-onset and late-onset poststroke generalized anxiety. *American Journal of Psychiatry, 152*(8), 1174–1179.

32. Originally a neurological rather than a psychological concept, constructed by English neurologist Hughlings Jackson.

33. See the original contribution of Frenichel, O. (1939). The counterphobic attitude. *International Journal of Psychoanalysis, 20,* 263.

34. Weinberg, J. (1956). Personal and social adjustment. In Anderson, J. E. (Ed.), *Psychological aspects of aging* (pp. 17–20). Washington, DC: American Psychological Association.

35. Cousins, N. (1979). *Anatomy of an illness as perceived by the patient.* New York: W. W. Norton.

36. Butler, R. N. (1961). Reawakening interest. *Nursing Homes, 10,* 8–19; and Butler, R. N. (1963). The life review: An interpretation of reminiscence in the aged. *Psychiatry, 26,* 65–76.

37. In *The Experience of Old Age: Stress, Coping, and Survival* (New York: Basic Books, 1983), authors M. Lieberman and S. Tobin confirm that reminiscence is crucial to the emotional livelihood of an older person, helping to resolve past conflicts and enabling the development of a coherent life history.

38. Coleman, P. G. (1974). Measuring reminiscence characteristics from conversation and adaptive features of old age. *International Journal of Aging and Human Development, 5,* 281–294.

CHAPTER 5

COMMON PSYCHIATRIC DISORDERS

With the publication of the *Diagnostic and Statistical Manual,* 4th Edition (DSM-IV), there has been a significant change in the approach taken with psychiatric conditions in the elderly. No longer are there distinctions made between the "organic" and "functional" disorders, as with previous editions. In fact, the term "organic mental disorder" has been eliminated entirely because of the implication that the other conditions were without an underlying organic component. Instead, the psychiatric disorders are viewed independently with attention to the current foundation of clinical research information. The diagnostic nomenclature thus reflects the separation of clinical syndromes by their defining features. This does not suggest that all subjects with the same syndrome are alike or that syndromal boundaries are mutually exclusive. Rather, these diagnostic categories are meant to be useful to communicate important characteristics of a diagnostic category, however heterogeneous that category might be. The categories are also meant to allow a foundation for further clinical research to advance the understanding of that syndrome. For the elderly, this common ground is essential as the field of geriatric psychiatry expands and considers crucial clinical research questions.

The extent of psychiatric disorders in the elderly is considerable. It has been estimated by the American Psychiatric Association that 15 to 25% of the elderly suffer from symptoms of mental illness.[1] While depression is considered the most common mental disorder, afflicting up to 20% of people 65 years and older, many other conditions are found in this age group, including anxiety, alcoholism, drug abuse, schizophrenia, and personality disorders. In addition, psychiatric symptoms are known to be prevalent in older patients suffering from conditions such as Alzheimer's disease and other chronic illnesses.

In general medical settings, it is estimated that up to 10% of acute care geriatric patients have a depressive illness and as many as 30% have clinically significant depressive symptoms,[2] but only a small minority ever receive psychiatric treatment. This is an unfortunate oversight, because the depressive syndromes of the elderly are often responsive to treatment when diagnosed properly.[3] Even in nursing homes, where more than 50% of the elderly residents are thought to be suffering from one or more psychiatric syndromes, fewer than 5% receive mental health services either through a trained specialist or an interested general practitioner.[4]

For some elderly, a psychiatric disorder may have been part of their lives for many decades. Illnesses such as bipolar disorder and schizophrenia generally manifest themselves in early adulthood and are known to have chronic courses which can certainly extend into later life. Major depressive disorder, dysthymic disorder (a milder form of depression), and delusional disorder can all have much later onsets so that an older person might be stricken for the first time after the age of 65 years. Whether these late onset syndromes are biologically distinct from the younger onset illnesses is not yet known. What is too often assumed, however, is that the psychiatric syndromes arising in later life are secondary to the problems of aging itself and thus diagnosis and treatment are often not pursued. On the other hand, while many health problems do increase in the elderly, these changes do not always give rise to psychiatric disorders and cannot be used as a blanket explanation for emotional difficulties. As with any younger patient, the new onset of a psychiatric disorder in an older patient must be evaluated and, when appropriate, treated actively.

MOOD DISORDERS IN THE ELDERLY

Perhaps the most widely diagnosed psychiatric conditions in the elderly, the mood disorders actually are made up of several distinct but overlapping entities:

1. Major Depressive Disorder
2. Bipolar Disorder
3. Dysthymic Disorder

While bipolar disorders are possibly better known, perhaps because of the often flamboyant presentations of bipolar patients, the depressive disorders are far more common. Psychotic features (gross impairment of reality testing) may be present but are not a necessary prerequisite in either condition. A psychological stress may set off the first episode of bipolar or unipolar depressive disorders, but recurrent episodes can occur apparently without a precipitating factor. For many other people, stressful events are *not* a necessary condition for the development of a mood disorder.

Major Depressive Disorder

When introducing the topic of depression, it is important to define terms. *Major depression* is a syndrome with well-defined features as described in DSM-IV.[5] The essential feature of a major depressive episode is the existence of depressed mood or a marked loss of interest or pleasure for at least two consecutive weeks. Associated symptoms include sleep disturbance, appetite and weight changes, decreased concentration, feelings of fatigue or loss of energy, psychomotor disturbances, and recurrent thoughts of death. By definition, the syndrome of depressive disorder involves a significant impairment in normal daily functioning. In order to reach criteria for a major depressive disorder, an individual must manifest at least one of the essential features and five or more of the nine symptoms listed in Table 5.1.

TABLE 5.1 Diagnostic features of a major depressive episode as listed in the American Psychiatric Association's DSM-IV manual

---

MAJOR DEPRESSIVE DISORDER: DIAGNOSTIC CRITERIA

Essential Features (1 of 2 required):
1. Depressed mood
2. Loss of interest or pleasure
Associated Symptoms (5 of 9 required):
1. Depressed mood for most of the day
2. Marked reduction in interest in daily activities
3. 5% weight loss or significant change in appetite (increase or decrease)
4. Almost daily insomnia or hypersomnia
5. Almost daily physical agitation or retardation
6. Almost daily decreased energy or fatigue
7. Almost daily feelings of worthlessness or feelings of guilt
8. Almost daily decreased concentration or decreased decisiveness
9. Frequent thoughts of death or suicide

Depression is the most common of the emotional disorders found in older people and can occur at any time in life. Depression varies all the way from transient "blues," which everyone experiences, to the extremes of psychotic withdrawal or suicide. Although epidemiologic estimates vary from study to study, the current data suggest that rates for major depression are actually lower (approximately 2%) in the elderly compared to younger adults (3–5%).[6] When using more inclusive criteria for major depressive disorder, this figure increases to approximately 6% for the elderly. Other surveys using structured interviews have reported depression prevalence rates of 19 to 31% in the elderly. In outpatient settings, significant depressive symptoms have been seen in 7 to 25% of patients surveyed.[7] These discrepancies across studies over the last twenty years regarding the rates of depression in the elderly are perplexing but may in part be explained by the higher incidence of atypical symptoms, including increased socioeconomic problems, concurrent medical illnesses, and changing epidemiologic and diagnostic techniques.[8]

Depression in the elderly is frequently considered to be much different from that seen in younger adults. This misconception is understandable since there are so many medical and psychosocial variables that change with age. Indeed, many of the medical conditions that occur with more frequency in the elderly, such as stroke, heart disease, and arthritis, can precipitate or be associated with major depression. The differential diagnosis of depression is often confounded by concurrent medical conditions, especially those which impair cognitive functioning (e.g., Alzheimer's disease or vascular dementia) and lead to diagnostic and therapeutic dilemmas (see Chapter 9 for further discussion of diagnostic evaluation). Nonetheless, the signs and symptoms of major depression in the elderly may not be as different as previously believed.

Mr. W, a 69-year-old businessman, has been severely depressed for eighteen months. He has a previous history of major depression which had generally responded to tricyclic antidepressant medications. Since the death of his wife last year, he has been in a profound depression with symptoms of tearfulness, insomnia, early morning awakening, weight loss, hopelessness, and suicidal preoccupations. Several antidepressants have been tried on an outpatient basis with only partial success, and he has recently suffered a serious downturn which has required him to temporarily take a leave of absence from his part-time job. He was admitted to the hospital when he developed the belief that his internal organs were "shutting down and rotting away," thus preventing him from eating any food. During a course of 10 unilateral (one side of the head) electroconvulsive therapy (ECT) treatments, he began to show gradual improvement and was discharged from the hospital three weeks later.

To address the question of symptom differences across age amongst depressed patients, Blazer and colleagues compared middle-aged and older inpatients.[9] Somewhat surprisingly, these two groups were remarkably similar. While the older group was more likely to suffer weight loss and symptoms of constipation and less likely to have suicidal thoughts, the two groups of patients with depression were otherwise comparable across a host of symptom profiles, family histories, and treatment responses. When studying less depressed groups of outpatients, differences between the middle-aged and those who were older did emerge[10]; the older patients reported increased physical symptoms, such as abdominal complaints, sleep disturbances, lethargy, and constipation, as well as increased thoughts of death and feelings of depression. The response to medications does not necessarily differ according to age, however, and will be discussed in Chapter 13.

When comparing groups of elderly and younger depressed subjects, Alexopoulos and colleagues[11] reported that while objective clinical ratings of depression were similar across age groups, the older subjects experienced generally lower levels of self-rated depression, anger and psychotic thoughts. Similarly, Lyness and colleagues find a general underreporting of depressive symptoms in the older subjects.[12] Since the objective measures of depression were not significantly different between the two groups, it can only be assumed that older subjects tend to underreport the severity of their symptoms. This subjective–objective dichotomy should be seriously considered when evaluating an older depressed subject, especially during an initial evaluation.

Bipolar Disorders (Manic-Depressive Illness)

Bipolar disorders are characterized as severe mood swings from depression to elation or the full or partial development of one or more manic episodes alone with a persistent elevated, expansive, or irritable mood (see the glossary at the end of this chapter for descriptions of the individual diagnostic terms). Bipolar disorders typically occur before age 30 and are apparently found equally commonly in men and women. They can persist into old age, but the typical lifelong course is not yet clearly understood.

There are two major bipolar disorders: *bipolar disorder* itself, in which there are one or more manic episodes associated with one or more major depressive episodes; and *cyclothymia,* in which there is a history of several hypomanic episodes (similar to but less severe than manic episodes) and numerous depressive episodes. A third bipolar disorder, called *bipolar disorder NOS* ("not otherwise specified") replaces the older classification of "atypical bipolar disorder" and includes what is sometimes referred to as "bipolar II"— patients who have hypomanic but not manic episodes along with major depressive episodes.

Because bipolar disorder is by definition a recurrent illness, episodes occurring in later life are generally not first attacks.[13] However, there is a slow but steady incidence of first admissions for mania in both men and women with increasing age.[14] When bipolar illness does develop for the first time in later decades, concurrent medical disorders, especially those involving the central nervous system, should be investigated.[15] The lifetime risk of death from bipolar illness is estimated to be approximately 1 to 3%.[16] It is be-

lieved that bipolar disorder is a familial illness and numerous family histories attest to this fact, but the genetics of the illness are far from being fully explained.

Mrs. Q, an 83-year-old widow, has had episodes of mania and hypomania for over 60 years. Currently, she lives with her devoted sister who helps her with her medication (lithium) and accompanies her to doctor visits at a local psychiatric clinic. Over the last several decades of widowhood, she has had more doctors take care of her than episodes of mania, and her sister carefully documents all treatment to facilitate the transition from doctor to doctor. Currently, she is well-maintained on a low dose of lithium, but she remembers the days long before the advent of lithium. During that era, she required large doses of anti-psychotic drugs and hospitalization to control her manic episodes. Before the drugs were introduced, she was forced to undergo a series of long-since abandoned psychiatric "cures" including cold wet packs, sleep therapy, and isolation, just to name a few, until her bipolar episodes subsided spontaneously. She leads a quiet life now with only occasional episodes of hyper-irritability and insomnia which are successfully treated with brief increases in her lithium level and low doses of a sedating anti-psychotic drug (i.e., chlorpromazine). She is still in full control of her faculties and can regale any interested listener with a complete history of psychiatry as it developed into the modern era of psychopharmacologic management.

Dysthymic Disorder

While considered a milder form of depression, *dysthymic disorder* can nonetheless pose a significant and chronic problem for elderly patients. Symptoms of dysthymic disorder include low self-esteem, poor concentration, difficulty with decision-making, over-eating or poor appetite, low energy, insomnia or hypersomnia (too much sleep), and feelings of hopelessness. These symptoms are generally less acute than those found in major depression, but they can interfere with day-to-day experiences and last at least two years by definition. Sadness, which can of course be a normal mood experience, is also a frequent problem in the elderly. While sadness is not formally considered a diagnostic entity in the DSM-IV, its symptoms can include frequent tearfulness, social isolation, decreased ability to take action, anhedonia (the inability to experience pleasure), and increased physical complaints. All too frequently, these symptoms are simply labeled as part of the aging process. In fact, when sadness encroaches on one's mood more often than a "normal" amount (different for each individual), then it too can be considered a pathologic symptom worthy of some therapeutic intervention.

Not all sadness and depression is reason for an older person to see a psychiatrist. While this fact may seem obvious, it is important to remember that sadness and occasional periods of depression can be a very normal reaction to the changes which come with aging. Stressors such as bereavement, retirement followed by declining socioeconomic status, and deteriorating physical health can be powerful influences on overall mood and self-esteem.[17] For most individuals, these stresses lead to some difficult times and understandable temporary changes in mood. For other older individuals, including those with a previous history of depression, these same stresses may precipitate a major depressive episode. Other more pervasive but perhaps less acute factors, such as alcohol consumption, slowly increasing physical disabilities, problems with sexual dysfunction, and personality disorders, can also play a role in the development of depression in the elderly (see Sunderland et al., 1988[18] and Chapter 7). It is, therefore, the job of the clinician to help families recognize when the depressive reaction goes beyond "normal" and would perhaps benefit from some therapeutic intervention.

The underlying cause of mood disorders in the elderly is no better understood than that in younger adults. Theories of neurotransmitter abnormalities in both the norepinepherine and serotonin system have been proposed for years,[19] and there have been suggestions of "dysregulation" of these systems,[20] but convincing biochemical and neuropathologic evidence is, for the most part, still lacking. However, the fact that these patients generally respond therapeutically to psychiatric medications certainly favors a specific biologic cause, as yet undetermined, of these conditions. Perhaps the most exciting lead in this direction is the longstanding recognition of a genetic or familial factor in the mood disorders. With the rapid evolution and expanding availability of powerful molecular biology techniques, the initial finding of an abnormality in chromosome 11 in certain families with a high prevalence for bipolar disorder[21] has been followed by a series of contrasting studies, which leaves the field quite confusing.[22] The early excitement regarding the genetic "mapping" of mood disorders for purposes of diagnostic evaluation and potential earlier therapeutic intervention has not yet been realized. In the meantime, the coexistence of depression with other medical illnesses in the elderly such as dementia of the Alzheimer type and strokes provides us with a potential human model for depression.[23] These conditions have known neuropathologic changes and may well provide clues into the pathophysiology (underlying physical causes) of depression as well as a human model for the testing of new psychopharmacologic agents.

OTHER MOOD DISORDERS IN THE ELDERLY

Medical and Psychiatric Comorbidity (Coexistent Illness) in the Elderly

Clinicians are often asked to differentiate between medical and mental health problems in the elderly. Depression is a well-recognized concomitant of many chronic medical illnesses, and the medical difficulties can certainly enter into the differential diagnosis of any elderly patient with depressive symptoms.[24] In fact, depression can occasionally be the presenting symptom for some medical conditions. With the elderly, these diagnostic criteria are sometimes confused with intercurrent medical illnesses which may interfere with a clinician's evaluation of these symptoms.

While it is obviously important not to overinterpret expected mood symptoms which are entirely related to physical ailments, the careful clinician must also be sensitive to the possibly exaggerated physical complaints with routine medical conditions. Much like a pediatrician would be attentive to a slowed weight gain in an otherwise normal, growing child as a possible sign of depression, a geriatrician should be aware of accelerated weight loss in a cancer patient as a possible sign of superimposed depression. In fact, it is estimated that 20 to 25% of individuals with certain medical conditions (i.e., cancer, cerebrovascular accidents, diabetes and myocardial infarction) will at some point develop a major depressive episode (see Table 5.2).[25]

The comorbidity of Alzheimer's disease and depression is of particular interest because of the overlapping symptoms and overlapping biology.[26] In one study of 37 depressed demented patients, for instance, the autopsy revealed evidence of degeneration in both the locus coeruleus and substantia nigra.[27] These findings are consistent with the catecholamine hypothesis of affective disorders. Similarly, Zweig and colleagues have shown a relationship between major depression and degeneration of the locus coeruleus and the dorsal raphe nuclei (serotonergic) in Alzheimer's disease.[28]

Late Onset Depression. The concept of "late onset" depression has received a great deal of attention recently. Whether the initial development of depression after the age of 60 represents a distinct biologic subtype of depression remains controversial.[29] One important issue raised by this controversy is the existence of concurrent medical illness, especially cardiovascular disease, in the elderly with depression.[30] One type of "late-onset" depression that is particularly interesting includes depressed subjects who first present with mild cognitive impairments. While the initial diagnosis is not clearly Alzheimer's disease (AD), it has been reported that up to 47% of these patients go on to develop progressive dementia within three years.[31] Other studies have reported somewhat lower rates of conversion to dementia,[32] but they all show a greater rate of AD compared with controls. Although it is still preliminary, there is also some suggestion that these older depressives are more likely to have APO E4

TABLE 5.2   Medical conditions commonly associated with depression in the elderly

CONDITION
Coronary artery disease
Hypertension, myocardial infarction, coronary artery bypass surgery, congestive heart failure
Neurologic disorders
Cerebrovascular accidents, Alzheimer's disease, Parkinson's disease, amyotrophic lateral sclerosis, multiple sclerosis, Binswanger's disease
Metabolic disturbances
Diabetes mellitus, hypothyroidism or hyperthyroidism, hypercortisolism, hyperparathyroidism, Addison's disease, autoimmune thyroiditis
Cancer
Pancreatic, breast, lung, colonic, and ovarian carcinoma; lymphoma, and undetected cerebral metastasis
Other conditions
Chronic obstructive pulmonary disease, rheumatoid arthritis, chronic pain, sexual dysfunction, renal dialysis, chronic constipation

Source: Sunderland, T., Lawlor, B. A., Molchan, S. E., & Martinez, R. A. (1988). Depressive syndromes in the elderly: Special concerns. *Psychopharmacology Bulletin* 24:567. Reprinted by permission.

alleles,[33] a known associative marker for AD (see Chapter 13 for more details). This finding is intriguing and does lend evidence to the speculation that "late-onset" depression is a biologically distinct classification. Careful prospective follow-up with large groups of late-onset depressives is now required to address this important clinical research question more directly.

Mrs. D had a history of nervousness all her life. When she experienced her menopause at age 55, she suffered a series of depressive symptoms of tiredness, irritability, forgetfulness, and frequent crying. Her physician prescribed replacement hormones which alleviated her symptoms quickly. Ten years later, at the age of 65, the symptoms of sadness, forgetfulness, and irritability returned, but this time, they did not respond to replacement hormone therapy. Subsequent antidepressant trials with amitriptyline and doxepin created acute confusional states before being discontinued. Trazodone, however, in low doses reduced the depressive symptoms for several years. Then, at age 69, Mrs. D returned for follow-up care with a history of gradual worsening of her cognitive state. On formal examination, she had bilateral slowing on her EEG, enlarged ventricles on CT scan, and neuropsychological testing indicating marked deterioration. A presumptive diagnosis of Alzheimer's disease was made at that time.

Suicide in Old Age.   Whatever the underlying epidemiology of depression, it is clear that depression is a significant factor for the elderly, because suicide rates are higher in the elderly than in any other age group.[34] In fact, suicide remains one of the 10 leading causes of death in the United States. The highest rate of suicide occurs in white men in their eighties. Older persons, representing 13% of the population, accounted for roughly 20% of reported suicides—about 6,000—in 1995.[35] Furthermore, the percentage of people who have attempted suicide previously goes down tremendously with age (51% in the young versus 20% in those over 60 years of age).[36]

In general, older depressives are much more likely to commit suicides than younger depressives. Women are more likely to attempt suicide

than men, but men are more likely to succeed when they make an attempt. The peak rate of suicide for white women occurs in middle age. However, throughout the world, suicide rates have been increasing for women, especially older women. Rates for nonwhite men and women are lower, with a peak for black men in the years 25 to 34.[37] Table 5.3 shows suicides per 100,000 population by age and sex.[38] The increased suicide rate with age is found in all countries which keep reliable statistics.

Older people use all the usual methods of killing themselves: drugs, guns, hanging, and jumping off high places. In the United States firearms and explosives are at the top of the list. Suicide may also be accomplished "subintentionally," by the slower means of not eating, not taking medicines, drinking too much, delaying treatment, and taking risks physically. This long-term process of suicidal erosion is of course not part of suicide statistics, since suicide is seen as a single act. More common in the elderly is a process of slow deterioration ("chronic suicide") where the will to live is lessened and important recurrent needs of the individual are neglected either consciously or unconsciously in a self-destructive manner. Most laws regarding commitment require specific evidence of a current and active danger to oneself or to others (rightfully

TABLE 5.3   Suicides per 100,000 population by age and sex, United States: 1995

AGE	TOTAL	MALE	FEMALE
15–24	13.3	22.5	3.7
25–34	15.4	25.6	5.2
35–44	15.2	24.1	6.5
45–54	14.6	22.8	6.7
55–64	13.3	22.0	5.3
65–74	15.8	28.7	5.4
75–84	20.7	44.8	5.5
85+	21.6	63.1	5.5
Total	11.9	19.8	4.4

Source: Unpublished data, National Center for Health Statistics, 1997.

protecting the civil liberties of people). Therefore such long, drawn-out self-destructive behavior often presents a touchy legal problem: is intervention warranted or not?

A 72-year-old man lived by himself in a small apartment in a large inner city. He was in failing health due to chronic asthma but refused to live with his son and family in the country where the air was cleaner because he did not want to be a "burden." Without clear medical precipitant, he began to slowly lose weight. He also stopped taking care of himself in the usual manner. Having previously been a fastidious man, he was now disheveled. His apartment was no longer hygienic. Despite many protestations from his family, he continued to lose weight and died alone in his apartment during a long cold winter. He was of sound mind throughout this period leading to his death.

Mary B, a 66-year-old executive, was found dead of a lethal injection two weeks after learning that she had been diagnosed with early Alzheimer's disease. She had played competitive tennis one week before the diagnosis and was active socially before her death, which was ruled a suicide by police.

Police in Blaine, Minnesota, reported that an 85-year-old man, depressed over a painful illness, arranged for his own funeral, then drove to the mortuary and shot himself in his car. Police said he telephoned the Wexler Funeral Home Sunday and inquired about the cost of cremation, telling an employee he would be over later. He wrote a note to his wife. Authorities found him dead in his car with a $300 check made out to the funeral home.

Attitudes toward Suicide.   In German, *suicide* (*Selbstmord*) means "self-murder." This etymology tells something of the motives of hatred of self or others that are present in many suicides. Freud in 1925 said that perhaps no one could find the psychic energy to kill himself unless in the first place he was thereby killing at the same time someone with whom he had identified himself. Menninger in 1938 has written that the suicide victim wishes to die, to kill, and to be killed. Indeed, suicide is three times more common than homicide. Perhaps it is emotionally less threatening to consider killing oneself than others.

Self-control is an important motivational element in suicide. Seneca said, "Against all the injuries of life, I have the refuge of death"; and Nietzsche stated, "The thought of suicide gets one successfully through many a bad night." Death itself is certain but its timing and its character are not. One can defy and control death by virtue of initiating the act of one's own death. Control also extends beyond the grave—survivors are deeply affected and a grim, unmistakable legacy of guilt, shame, and regret may be left for them to bear.

A rational or *philosophical* decision to kill oneself is undoubtedly more common in old age as people perceive themselves to be failing. Older men, especially, may decide to kill themselves rather than leave their widows penniless from the cost of a long illness. Married couples may commit double suicide or a combination of mercy killing of one and suicide of the other.

Documents left by the married couples yield a typical picture of an aging man and woman, one or both suffering from grave illness, which is never absent from their thoughts. A deeply devoted pair, childless, in modest circumstances and with few interests and friends, they are deeply absorbed in their own small world. Prolonged insomnia speeds the decisive act. "We are at the end of our rope" is a phrase which repeatedly occurs. Here is a typical situation. A 56-year-old ex-miner, with impaired vision and an injured leg, underwent an operation for cancer of the bowel. The operation was not successful and he was confined to his bed with frequent, violent attacks of pain. His wife was disabled by Parkinson's disease and had been partly paralyzed for 15 years.[39]

A sacrificial romantic quality can be present in the double suicide pacts of lovers, old or young, as noted below:

In death pacts between lovers we meet the age-old belief, found in myth and history, that two people who die together are united forever beyond the grave. This belief is also encountered in the German Romantic Period. In Japan it is known as shinju. It is but a step from such a belief towards symbolization of the grave as a bridal bed.[40]

Mental health personnel should take suicide threats of older persons seriously. Persons attempting suicide are more likely to fail if below age 35 and to succeed if over 50. It is most rare for an attempt by anyone over 65 to fail. Men are more successful than women. (For indicators of suicide risk, see Chapter 9.) It has been suggested in the research literature that a "lenient" or generally accepting attitude toward suicide or assisted suicide is in itself a risk factor for suicide. While elderly subjects polled showed a lower overall rate of leniency toward suicide compared with younger adults, there was an association between a lenient response and risk factors for suicide (i.e., alcoholism, depression, hopelessness and recent losses).[41] This suggests that clinicians should inquire about individuals' attitudes towards suicide and perhaps use that information, if "lenient" attitudes are discovered, as an avenue for exploration of possible underlying risk factors for suicidal behavior.

Reducing the frequency of depression and providing for its effective treatment when present are the major ways of reducing suicide in old age. One must be especially alert with people whose depressions seem to have lifted. They may be gathering enough energy to commit the suicide they had contemplated earlier. When there is evidence of suicidal preoccupations, one must schedule extra time and additional sessions. It is important to openly discuss the subject rather than, ostrichlike, hope it will go away. Ongoing studies of Conwell and associates have supported the observation that the majority of elderly suicides occur in first episode depressions of mild-to-moderate severity.[42] The obvious suggestion of this work is that appropriate but aggressive intervention with pharmacologic and behavioral treatment might well be effective in preventing suicide among the elderly subjects. This tells us that outreach services are imperative to reach depressed people who may have withdrawn and become isolated. If suicide is seen as a reasonable alternative (i.e., "leniency" in attitude) and the underlying factors associated with suicidal behavior are present (i.e., depression, hopelessness, recent stressors, etc.), then the clinical situation should be viewed as a psychiatric emergency and treated aggressively. Perhaps the French novelist and essayist, Albert Camus, was correct when he saw suicide as submission and stated, "there is only one truly serious philosophical problem and that is suicide."[43]

SCHIZOPHRENIA AND PARANOID DISORDERS

It is generally believed that *schizophrenia* is a disorder of youth. In fact, until the introduction of DSM IIIR in 1987, one of the criteria for the diagnosis of schizophrenia was the onset of illness prior to age 45. With the advent of DSM-IV in 1994, there is no age specification, and there is an acceptance of later onset schizophrenia, especially in women. In the elderly, schizophrenia is more likely to include paranoid delusions and hallucinations while negative or disorganized symptoms are less common. The overall lifetime prevalence of schizophrenia is still estimated to be 0.5 to 1% of the population, with first degree relatives having about ten times greater risk of developing the illness than the overall population.[44]

By definition, schizophrenia is a severe psychiatric disorder marked by disturbances of thinking, mood, and behavior. Thought disorder is the primary feature of the illness and characteristic features include hallucinations, delusions, and poor reality testing. Typically, the disturbance has been going on continuously for at least six months and is associated with a decline in work productivity, social relationships, and self-care. In the active phase of schizophrenia, there must be at least one month with two of the following symptoms:

- Delusions
- Hallucinations
- Disorganized speech

- Grossly disorganized or catatonic behavior
- Negative symptoms

Many older people have developed types of schizophrenia in earlier years and carried them into old age.[45] These persons are often called "chronic schizophrenics." One sees persons with schizophrenia who have been hospitalized as long as 50 or 60 years; many never received treatment and were simply "stored" out of sight in hospitals, beyond the mainstream of medicine and psychiatry. Originally, it was assumed that all early-onset chronic schizophrenics suffered a uniformly downhill course over time. Recent longitudinal studies have called that assumption into question, as it appears that chronic schizophrenia may well have a more variable outcome, with some patients remaining quite stable over time. The following is an example of a chronic schizophrenic patient hospitalized for 40 years:

Mr. M is 67 years of age. The diagnosis in his case was schizophrenic reaction, chronic undifferentiated type, of moderate severity, with onset at approximately 21 years of age. He was also diagnosed as showing a moderate depressive reaction for the past two years. Mr. M was first hospitalized about 40 years ago and in the last six months has been moved to a foster care home where he now lives with a long-despised brother. He has only minimal impairment of his recent memory and his level of intellectual functioning has not declined. His impairments of judgment and abstraction are interpreted as psychogenic and not organic. Psychiatric symptoms include hypochondriacal ideas, suspiciousness, depressive trend, illusions, obsessions, compulsions, phobias, nightmares, sexual maladaptation (he claims he never had sexual intercourse), and psychosomatic symptoms. There is a history of auditory hallucinations.

Over the last six months, Mr. M has become increasingly nervous and depressed. Although he sees himself as trapped in a home with a despised brother and deserted by the death of sisters, he holds out the hope that he "may find the answer" to a better life for himself. His defense is to continue to be future-oriented. In addition to his personality characteristics it seems clear that there was little basic understanding of the environmental stresses on Mr. M at the time of his breakdown and little treatment given, beyond minimal care. But 40 years later he is still hoping for a cure and a better future. One could say either that he is denying reality or that in spite of everything he has refused to give up.

While American researchers have generally limited their study of schizophrenia to younger subjects, European investigators have recognized the existence of late-onset schizophrenia.[46] Paraphrenia was first introduced by Kraepelin near the turn of the century[47] and furthered by Sir Martin Roth[48] and others.[49] More recent study of late-onset schizophrenia in several American research centers has revealed that these patients are mostly women, have a high prevalence of visual or auditory impairment, are less likely to demonstrate a marked thought disorder, and have a predominance of paranoid symptoms.[50]

Mrs. Q is a 75-year-old former professional dancer who lives alone in her large home in New England. She has been widowed for 15 years but has managed quite well on her husband's pension and modest income from a rental property. Her daughter, who lives in the same city and visits her frequently, has become increasingly concerned about the mental state of her mother over the last few months. While there has never before been any need for psychiatric help, she arranged for a psychiatric consultation in the home. During the visit, it became immediately clear that Mrs. Q has been cloistered in her home for quite some time. There are multiple locks on all the entrances to the house, all the shades are drawn, and the pictures hanging on the wall are each covered with aluminum foil. Mrs Q is convinced that the neighbors are involved in a plot to overthrow the government and that they are spying on her. The aluminum foil is "strategically placed" to avoid microwave monitoring of her activities in the home. Mrs. Q is calm when she describes these beliefs and is knowledgeable about the current affairs in her community as reported in the daily news. She speaks coherently and articulately. For instance, she rationally explains away the lack of alarm in the world around her by pointing out that the news media is being manipulated by the anarchists. Before bidding goodbye to the psychiatrist, who she thought was a member of the underground resistance movement, she offers advice on how to better fortify the defenses in his part of town.

Clinical Presentation of Schizophrenia

Clinically, the schizophrenic disorders are still subdivided into five types in the DSM-IV manual: catatonic, disorganized, paranoid, undifferentiated, and residual. These differentiations are made primarily based on the clinical picture and are not yet known to have tremendous prognostic or treatment validity. As with all major disorders, however, it is important to carefully differentiate schizophrenia from other diagnoses, especially organic mental disorders in elderly subjects. It is not uncommon, for instance, for Alzheimer's disease or drug intoxication to first present with symptoms identical to those found in schizophrenia.[51] Other risk factors for the onset of late-life schizophrenia include premorbid (pre-existing) personality abnormalities, physical illness, social stresses, and possible genetic factors.[52]

Delusional (Paranoid) Disorder is defined as the persistence of pseudo-logical delusions that are not due to other medical or organic causes. The age of onset is generally much later than in schizophrenia, and it is not uncommon for the first symptom to appear after the age of 65. Behavioral symptoms can be associated with a delusional disorder but are not usually prominent. Premorbid personality factors have often been associated with the onset of late-life paranoid disorder.[53] Perhaps more crucial is the association between various forms of motor and sensory impairment, particularly hearing loss, and the development of paranoid ideation or thought processes.[54] The subtypes of delusional disorders include: (1) Erotomanic, (2) Grandiose, (3) Somatic, (4) Persecutory, (5) Jealous, and (6) Unspecified. Little is known about the familial pattern of the delusional disorders in the elderly. While the prevalence for the overall population is estimated to be low (about 3%), it is generally accepted that these conditions are found more commonly in the elderly with "mild schizophrenic symptoms" being found in as many as 6.7% of the noninstitutionalized elderly.[55]

Biology of Schizophrenia and the Delusional Disorders

The search for a single gene to explain the biology of schizophrenia has been frustrated by the difficulties in defining a single phenotype (clinical presentation) for the syndrome. Furthermore, there has been a discouraging series of non-replicated genetic findings in the scientific literature.[56] While many researchers continue to search for a single gene, the general consensus is that the illness probably involves a complex inheritance pattern with polygenic factors. This genetic heterogeneity would help explain the wide variability in clinical presentations in this patient population and the fact that three different chromosomes (6, 8, and 22) have now been linked to the illness.[57] Although there are still no specific genes which have been directly associated with schizophrenia, several of the known genes for the brain dopamine receptor subtypes have been excluded by linkage analysis.[58]

Other biological markers have previously been investigated in the older schizophrenics and in delusional disorders. For example, studies of CT scans have revealed that late-onset schizophrenics have significantly larger ventricle-to-brain ratios (i.e., greater cortical atrophy) than age-matched controls, much like early-onset schizophrenics.[59] Findings in these radiologic studies have been supported by a 6% overall decrease in brain size seen at autopsy compared to elderly depressives; the most striking area of relative decrease is in the temporal lobes.[60] Comparison of cerebrospinal fluid (CSF) metabolites between Alzheimer and schizophrenic patients revealed a relative decrease in the schizophrenics for the dopamine metabolite, homovanillic acid (HVA), and the serotonin metabolite, 5-hydroxyindoleacetic acid (5-HIAA); there was no relationship in the schizophrenic group with either age or cognitive function and the levels of these metabolites.[61] In postmortem studies, relationships in schizophrenics have been found between CSF concentrations of HVA and the norepinephrine metabolite, 3-methoxy-4-hydroxyphenylglycol (MHPG) with antemortem measures of depressed mood.[62] An association was also found in this study between brain dopamine and MHPG content in the nucleus accumbens and antemortem cognitive functioning. Finally, autopsy studies have also revealed selective decreases in the B-form of the monoamine oxidase enzyme in selected brain areas of older schizophrenics with primarily negative symptoms.[63] Other biologic variables include the significant over-representation of women among the late-onset schizophrenics and the increased likelihood of developing tardive dyskinesia.[64] Nonetheless, the combined power of all these results has not yet led to a clear picture of the biology of the schizophrenic illnesses.

Psychosocial Factors and Prognosis

Social isolation and increasing loneliness is thought to play a role in late-onset schizophrenia. Most studies have revealed the older schizophrenic patients to have more often been unmarried, have fewer surviving children, live alone, and belong to a lower socioeconomic class than nonschizophrenics.[65] As noted previously, sensorimotor impairment, particularly hearing impairments and mild cognitive decline are frequently associated with the late-onset schizophrenias and paranoid delusions.

The clinical course and prognosis of late-onset schizophrenia is usually noted to be chronic and poor.[66] Many patients, often due to their general lack of social supports, are relegated to institutional living. On the other hand, many, and perhaps most, people with paranoid disorders go through life outside hospitals. They may be relatively harmless to others but are unable to experience intimacy and full psychological growth. They are seen as cranks, eccentrics, hard to get along with, touchy, angry. They are avoided, and what few human and other attachments they may have in life increasingly disappear with advancing age. Following is an example of the growing late-life isolation of a person suffering from a paranoid disorder.

Dr. J, a 72-year-old man, was diagnosed as having paranoid personality with obsessive features, chronic, severe, and of lifelong duration. His second diagnosis was depressive reaction, moderate, and of two or three years' duration. He compensated well in a suitable, supportive, and structured environment. He was a dentist in semiretirement who was irritable, suspicious, depressed, and anxious. He was extremely intelligent and integrated very well during interviews. He was paranoid, belligerent, and self-centered; yet it was remarkable how he could put aside his belligerence and tell of his delusions. He was in semiretirement because of a failing practice and not of his own choice. He applied for room in an old age home because he felt he was at the end of his rope. He saw his situation as resulting from the imperfections of the world and other people but at other times described his life adjustment as poor and said he hated himself.

He was born in Poland, came to the United States at 20, was unusually attached to his mother, and had "nothing in common" with his siblings. His father died when Dr. J was 12. He rebelled against education and did not enter dental school until he was 32. He married at 37 against his own desires, out of fear of an implied breach of promise suit, and was divorced 4 years later. He never considered remarriage. Marriage was his first and only sexual experience. He practiced dentistry in a poor neighborhood and had no close personal relationships. He distrusted others and thought that only his alertness saved him from being exploited by them. As Dr. J grew older, his isolation became more complete and he developed an angry depression through which he despised himself and the world. He seemed unable to experience pleasure.

As Dr. J illustrates, such a person may paradoxically get along in the community by being isolated. No one bothers with him and he bothers no one. But eventually a problem will emerge in which the person no longer can care for himself and must obtain help in some way. This is frequently the paranoid person's path to the mental hospital or, as in Dr. J's case, to an old age home.

Sometimes the paranoid symptoms may be very discrete or circumscribed. An older woman in her late seventies may seem free of major psychopathological symptoms, but at nighttime she thinks that the neighbor above is purposely taking a cane and pounding on the ceiling or that fumes are being sent out from the radiator in the bathroom. However, study may uncover the fact that this is a discrete, circumscribed delusion related to fears, say, of being alone at night or lacking visual orientation in the dark. Such symptoms are, characteristically, isolated and may not influence everyday activities.

A shared psychotic disorder (formerly known as *folie à deux*) is a mental disorder in which two persons who are intimately associated with each other develop the same delusions. One person is dominant. The submissive partner may be more shaky in his or her beliefs and when separated from the stronger personality may give up the delusional system. It is more frequent among people with similar backgrounds, such as siblings, parents, and children, but it can develop among unrelated (nonconsanguineous) persons, including husband and wife. Misperception may attain paranoid proportions.

The frightened voice of a woman begged me (R.N.B.) on the phone to see her and her mother because (and she lowered her voice) "mother wants to move again." Otherwise "they" will get her.

At the appointed hour a woman of 42 and of faded attractiveness arrives, with a frail, sharp-faced woman of 70. In the office they insist on my seeing them together, not separately. They describe the harassment they have received from two men living below. They mention the possibility that some wires are used to listen to them, perhaps in connection with their TV set or toaster. The older woman reveals excellent intellectual functioning, but she states that a man in the apartment above is shooting rays at her body, including "indecent places." He wants to kill her and she is powerless. He brings pains to her hands and knees, scorches parts of her body, and "stuns my consciousness." She refuses to see doctors, considers medications "harmful," and denies any illnesses (despite the obvious malnutrition, manifestation of probable hypovitaminosis, arthritic changes, and a Meniere-like syndrome). She also insists that she has aged very little. Her unmarried daughter, deeply conflicted, nearly "be-

lieves" there are men responsible. Such quasi folies à deux are not rare.

The older paranoid person can be dangerous. Paranoid rage and murderousness do occur.

A slight, 89-year-old man who needed a cane to walk killed his daughter, a librarian, with a hatchet. "I wanted to see her die before I do," he said. The body of the daughter, 57, was found in her bed with deep wounds in her head and body. Her father, who notified police by telephone that he had slain his daughter, was booked on a murder charge. "The devil prompted me to do this," he told police.

However, such extreme behavior is the exception. In general, the following rule of thumb can be followed in evaluating paranoid disorders: "Show me one truly paranoid person and I will show you ten who are truly persecuted." Much of what appears to be paranoid behavior is a reaction to extraordinary and unbearable stress—physical, emotional and environmental. Studies are now investigating the relative importance of selective psychosocial stresses on these late-onset conditions. See Chapter 13 for a discussion of the drug treatment of late-onset schizophrenia and the delusional disorders.

ANXIETY DISORDERS

While anxiety itself is part of everyday life, commonly associated with many physical illnesses, and may affect up to 10% of the population over age 65 at any one time,[67] the actual prevalence of specific anxiety disorders is reported to be reduced in the older populations.[68] A. J. Flint conducted a meta analysis of literature from 1970 through 1994 to explore the epidemiology of anxiety disorders and common comorbidities in older persons. Flint found that the prevalence rates of all anxiety disorders, phobic disorders, and generalized anxiety disorders in the elderly varied. Rates for panic disorders and obsessive compulsive disorders were more consistent. Anxiety disorders are less common in older persons than younger persons, but as many as 18.6% of those over age 65 suffer from them.[69] Still, anxiety disorders remain one of the most common psychiatric conditions in the elderly.[70] This group of psychiatric conditions includes *panic disorder* with or without *agoraphobia, social phobia, simple phobia,* and *generalized anxiety disorder.* Each of these conditions is distinguished by the precipitant, the time course, and accompanying behaviors of the predominant anxiety.[71] With the anxiety disorders, anxiety is experienced directly by a person rather than controlled unconsciously by conversion, denial, or other psychological defense mechanisms. Although the overall condition may be less common in the elderly, these disorders can nonetheless appear for the first time in old age or represent an increase in a previous history of anxiety. They may take the form of a nameless dread and sense of threat when no obvious danger is present, or they may be an exaggerated response to real trouble and danger. Also, like people of all ages, older people may be struggling to curb unconscious and unacceptable impulses, aggressive or sexual. Finally, anxiety symptoms may portend some oncoming physical disease or condition that is beginning to unfold. While not considered identical illnesses, there is a great deal of clinical, epidemiologic, biologic, and treatment response overlap between panic disorder and major depression.[72]

Mrs. C is a 69-year-old retired secretary who had 25 years of work experience after raising her family of three boys and one girl. She lost one boy in battle during the Vietnam war. She has a history of mild claustrophobia throughout her life, but the only time she required psychiatric treatment was after the death of her son when she received antianxiety agents to help her sleep for several weeks only. She is now widowed for five years and living on a modest pension. Mrs. C has a broad social support system and appeared to be doing quite well when suddenly she developed an intense fear of tunnels. At one point, she actually stopped her car in the middle of a tunnel and ran out, leaving her car to tie up traffic for hours. She stated that she "panicked" in the tunnel while experiencing an intense shortness of breath, a rapid heart beat, and a strong sense of dying. Her ability to get out and about town was severely impaired when Mrs. C's fear was extended to

include bridges as well as tunnels. Mrs. C's daughter soon took her to see a local psychiatrist. After several months of weekly sessions and a course of low-dose imipramine, Mrs. C was able to drive again without experiencing panic attacks near bridges or tunnels. She now recognized that these attacks were associated with thoughts of her husband and son, and she was beginning to review in therapy the intense sadness those losses had caused her.

Understanding the biology of the anxiety disorders has been difficult, in part because of the diagnostic uncertainties reflected by the rapidly changing nomenclatures. Nonetheless, great technical strides have been made in recent years with animal, pharmacologic, and brain mapping studies.[73] Theories have emerged with conflicting data to support the central role of the noradrenergic and serotonergic neurotransmitter systems in anxiety and obsessive compulsive disorders, but definitive conclusions as to the exact mechanisms of the disorders are currently far from reached.

Obsessive Compulsive Disorder is also classified as an anxiety disorder because of the distress caused by the recurrent obsessions and compulsions. When these intrusive thoughts and impulses are resisted, for instance, the individual suffers a marked increase in inner tension which can lead to significant disruption in the normal work or personal life. Common examples of these obsessions include thoughts of contamination, sexuality, violence, or danger. While compulsions do not always accompany obsessions, they frequently include idiosyncratic rituals of washing, touching, pacing, and checking which can appear unusual and be time-consuming and distressing. As with most anxiety disorders, the incidence of obsessive compulsive disorder is thought to decrease with age.[74] Interestingly, the incidence of anxiety as a comorbid condition with depression is no less frequent in older depressives than younger depressives.[75]

SOMATOFORM DISORDERS

The somatoform disorders exhibit physical symptoms that suggest a physical disorder, but on examination they appear to be psychologically rather than physically caused. These disorders include *conversion disorder,* an example of which is the person who cannot move an arm or leg although there is no physical reason for the impairment. Only the special senses or the voluntary nervous system are involved. The mechanism for causing this is unconscious, thus keeping the underlying conflict hidden ("primary gain") as opposed to the conscious manipulations of the malingerer who is well aware of the subterfuge. The autonomic nervous system is not usually involved in the conversion disorders and thus provides diagnostic differentiation from the psychophysiological (psychosomatic) disorders. In older people with this tendency, symptoms or illnesses may be exaggerated, and in this way a "secondary gain" is achieved in the form of extra attention and help and the avoidance of a noxious stimulus.

Hypochondriasis, another somatoform disorder, is an overconcern with one's physical and emotional health, accompanied by various bodily complaints for which there is no physical basis. However, this does not mean that the complaints are "imaginary." They have an emotional basis that requires treatment. Hypochondriasis is commonly associated with depressive feelings, but it may stand alone. It has many meanings, one of which may be a symbolization of the older person's sense of defectiveness and deterioration (see self-drawings, Chapter 9, p. 252). It may be a means of communication and interaction with others—family members, doctors, nurses, social workers. It can be used to displace anxiety from areas of greater concern. It can include identification with a deceased loved one who had similar symptoms. And it can serve as punishment for guilt, as an inhibition of impulses, and as an aid in the desire to control others.

There is much overlap between depression and hypochondriasis. Most depressive individuals show some hypochondriacal preoccupations, and hypochondriasis has a gloomy and depressive mood associated with it. But whereas a basically depressed person will withdraw and not seek help,

the hypochondriac sees his or her problems as physical and goes frequently to the doctor, thus at least relieving the isolation. Even if the symptom cannot be eliminated, a service is being provided. Patients with hypochondriasis should be listened to and accepted. Of course, special difficulties arise if hypochondriasis is connected with a real organic condition. Then, diagnosis and treatment may be difficult. Because of the steep rise in organic conditions found in the elderly, great care must be taken before ascribing any consistent complaint arising in the elderly as hypochondriacal.[76] A case of a brain tumor first presenting as anxiety attacks in a 69-year-old woman with no previous history of such attacks is a powerful reminder of the importance of careful differential diagnosis in the elderly.[77]

Psychotherapy can be helpful, as demonstrated in the following case example:

Mr. B visited to ask our help for a pruritic scalp condition on his essentially bald head; he "incidentally" told us of the recent death of his wife. He could not get himself to say Kaddish, the mourner's prayer in his Jewish faith. The scalp condition was similar in shape to the rim of a skull cap, worn by men in the synogogue. After his already infected lesions were treated medically, short-term psychotherapy focused on his wife and the question of saying Kaddish. Months later, he reported having said the prayer and having a "clear" scalp. (He also reported newly growing hair!)

DISSOCIATIVE DISORDERS

Dissociative disorders are seen when the integration of an older person's consciousness, identity, memory or perception of the environment is suddenly and temporarily altered, resulting in fugue states, stupor, amnesia, and confusion. Sleep walking or night wandering is sometimes included in this category when there is no physical basis for such behavior. Psychotic features may also be present. Little epidemiologic information is available to estimate how common these conditions are in the elderly relative to younger adults.

SEXUAL AND GENDER IDENTITY DISORDERS

We discuss some of these disorders in Chapter 6, but sexual exhibitionism is a specific paraphilia that is often associated in the public's mind with older men and will be dealt with here. Simply put, sexual exhibitionism in older people is overestimated and overstated. Most studies have shown that such sexual pathology is related to young adulthood. Sensationalism in court cases concerning children who have been "molested" by older people has been misleading in many instances. The sexual element may have been less significant than the loneliness of the older person, who may have no children or grandchildren. Some older men have fantasies of rejuvenation in contact with young children,[78] rather than any direct sexual preoccupation. By all means, children must be protected from any exploitation that may occur. But the older person needs sympathetic understanding rather than punishment, and efforts should be made to provide that which is lacking in their lives. In some cases, total misinterpretation occurs. We have known of older people who were supposedly molesting younger children and have been arrested for exhibitionism; actually they were confused, needed to urinate, and found the most convenient spot. Where the charge is warranted, then indeed, the act is strictly punishable under the law and should be pursued. In today's environment, however, with its frequent accusations and fears of abuse, the presumption of innocence must be protected, especially with those who are easily confused.

PERSONALITY DISORDERS

There are ten recognized personality disorders in DSM-IV,[79] and they are designated as encoding patterns of inner experience and behavior that are markedly different from the expectations of the person's surrounding culture. Personality traits become personality disorders only when they are so inflexible and maladaptive that they cause serious problems for an individual. Personality disorders are coded separately from the other disorders in the DSM-IV classification, in part to avoid overlooking them. In this broad group of disorders we see defects in personality development that are of lifelong nature. There is little sense of anxiety or distress associated with them. Maladaptive patterns of behavior are deeply ingrained and may actually become less evident with increasing age.

Certain personality disorders serve different adaptive functions, depending on the stage in the life cycle. This phenomenon, the changing adaptive nature of psychopathology, was observed in the early NIMH studies by Perlin and Butler. For example, a so-called schizotypal personality may function somewhat better in old age. Such an individual tends to be insulated against the experiences of life and therefore may feel relatively more comfortable with some of the loneliness and difficulties of old age. On the other hand, he or she may become even more of a recluse with almost no human contact. The person with a paranoid personality has perhaps the most problems in later life, as the individual loses what few friends and relationships he or she has and becomes increasingly isolated.[80] The inadequate, dependent person may welcome and enjoy the opportunity for greater dependence in old age and the freedom from work responsibilities. Obsessive compulsiveness can become useful in scrupulous caretaking of oneself and in keeping busy with many details; in fact, this type of individual can create a whole life for himself by "taking care" of things—possessions, spouse, grandchildren, bodily ailments, and personal finances.

Mr. H has been retired for three years. His obsessions and compulsions are useful mechanisms in filling the vacuum of a forced retirement. "My home is always in order," says Mr. H, as he putters around the house, arranging everything according to strict schedule in a careful, meticulous manner. He is thrifty and even hoarding of his possessions, not to mention his feelings.

He takes care of his health with religious fervor and follows the doctor's orders precisely. He has arranged for two grave sites (one in St. Louis and one in Florida) so he can be well taken care of in case he dies, whether at home or on vacation. He has checked actuarial tables to predict his death at age 88, leaving no stone unturned.

From a therapeutic perspective, it is important to realize the possible adaptive qualities of personalities. A dependent personality can be fostered by the therapist to help activate an individual psychologically. Persons with obsessions may be encouraged to make constructive use of ritual. The therapist can help a person with a histrionic personality keep alive their dramatic qualities and, at times, their childlike expectations. The antisocial criminal activities of an antisocial personality are rare in late life. Violent crimes are seldom committed, although embezzlement and other less violent crimes do occur. Old "sociopaths" do fade away, it seems. Thus geriatric delinquency is not a problem to rouse one's keen interest.

HOW IMPORTANT IS DIAGNOSTIC CLASSIFICATION?

Throughout this chapter, we have emphasized the importance of the diagnostic nomenclature. Still, we must acknowledge the primitive status of our scientific understanding in this area. Unlike many of the organic brain disorders (see Chapter 6), we do not have known lesions and specific pathologic verification available to us at autopsy for these conditions. At present, most of the psychiatric disorders in the elderly are therefore defined operationally, based on clinical symptoms and, quite often, retrospectively, after response to drug treatment (see Chapter 13). Therefore, we must be cautious in our assumptions that each of these disorders is a homogeneous entity with its own biology. Most likely, many of these conditions will be interrelated genetically and biochemically (i.e., panic disorder and major depression) with much overlap in both young and older groups. Research studies with experimental diagnostic approaches such as genetic markers, brain imaging tests (i.e., PET, functional MRI, and SPECT scans), pharmacologic challenge tests, and peripheral cell markers may eventually be helpful in differentiat-

ing these conditions as well as distinguishing the effects of aging on the expression of psychiatric disorders. (See Chapter 9 for further discussion of diagnostic approaches.)

DIAGNOSTIC NOMENCLATURE

We are including abbreviated outlines of the American Psychiatric Association's *Diagnostic and Statistical Manual of Mental Disorders* (DSM-IV) in the following glossary.[81] Earlier versions of this nomenclature left much to be desired in diagnosing conditions of older persons, particularly in the case of acute and chronic brain disorders. Fortunately, the 1980 DSM-III and 1987 DSM-IIIR represent some improvements in the classification of the mental disorders of older persons. The DSM-IV features much more specific diagnostic criteria, an expanded description of disorders, and a multilevel or multiaxial approach to evaluation that takes into consideration the following five axes:

1. Clinical Syndromes
2. Developmental and Personality Disorders
3. Physical Disorders and Conditions
4. Severity of Psychosocial Stressors
5. Global Assessment of Functioning

Assessment of the older person's functioning is critical. For example, an older person who is diagnosed as having severe brain damage (by sophisticated psychiatric examination and psychological test scores) may function quite well in a supportive milieu. Another person may have minimal brain damage but have no economic, personal, and social supports and thus have more trouble functioning—not because of any inherently serious mental condition, but because he or she has no environmental supports. Thus, diagnosis and treatment, as well as prevention, must go beyond the traditional psychiatric diagnostic evaluation in the elderly to include the *context* in which symptoms develop and the assets and resources of the individual.

We might add here that the use of insurance forms requiring a therapist to state the diagnosis of a patient creates a sticky, ethical problem. The patient's interest may be compromised if a diagnosis is given that can be later used irresponsibly. We have no assurances about the confidentiality of insurance records; and they do get lost, misplaced, and confused with other patients' records. On the other hand, a vague, general diagnosis can make the whole matter of insurance information irrelevant, especially when data are collected from these sources on the "mental illness" of policyholders. Nonetheless, many practitioners choose to protect their patients as much as possible. Diagnoses such as schizophrenia or personality disorder may be downplayed. The nomenclature more commonly used includes such designations as anxiety, depression, and other terms that are less revealing.

Glossary of Psychiatric Nomenclature as Applied to the Elderly

Mania.   Most people think of mania as a high-flying period of joyous mood unbridled by normal restraints. In fact, the essential feature of mania is a distinct period of abnormal and persistently elevated, expansive, or irritable mood that is sufficient to cause disruption in work or social settings. Associated symptoms of mania include grandiosity, racing thoughts, distractibility, decreased need for sleep, increased physical agitation and activity, persistent talkativeness, and excessive involvement in pleasurable but potentially harmful activities. The important clarification is that mania is not always associated with an elated or elevated mood. In fact, an "irritable" mania is fairly common in the elderly and has led to the use of the terms of "dysphoric mania" or "mixed manic state" to describe the contrasting moods found in manic patients. *Hypomania* is essentially a milder form of the above without the marked impairments in occupational and social functioning that often lead to hospitalization for manic subjects. In addition, hypomania is never associated with the delusions that can sometimes accompany mania. For the elderly, it is especially important to realize that manic symptoms may change with age

and course of illness. It is not uncommon for a typical elderly manic patient to be quite different from a younger patient, that is, showing agitation rather than euphoria.

Anxiety.   As with depression, the discussion of anxiety requires a careful definition of terms. Symptoms of anxiety can range from a simple nervousness before an important event to a sense of having a heart seizure during a panic attack. These symptoms each represent anxiety but reflect the tremendous range included under one classification. One of the common behaviors associated with anxiety is avoidance, so it is not surprising that *phobias* are the most prevalent of the anxiety disorders, especially in the older age groups. These phobias represent a persistent fear of a certain stimuli (i.e., shopping, snakes, closed spaces, etc.). Approaching those stimuli is generally associated with an anticipatory anxiety response including increased heart rate, feeling sweaty, a sense of panic, and difficulty breathing. *Panic attacks* are more distinct, with intense periods of fear and discomfort. The associated symptoms are more severe than those mentioned for phobia and may include a sense of choking, chest pain, dizziness, shortness of breath, nausea, trembling, and a fear of dying or going crazy. These attacks often come out of the blue and are usually followed by a period of persistent fear of a return of the symptoms. *Obsessions* and *compulsions* can also be symptoms of anxiety. Obsessions are intrusive and senseless thoughts or impulses which are persistent and irrepressible. (Compulsions are repetitive behaviors performed in response to an obsession, and designed to neutralize some dreaded event or situation, for example, repeatedly checking the gas stove in the kitchen, continuously checking to see that the doors are locked, or repetitive washing of the hands.) Any attempt to change the regular routine of a compulsion is generally met with increasing tension and anxiety. *Fear* is differentiated from anxiety by the degree of awareness of the fact that one is afraid. In the elderly, when fear of death and loss is quite real, the associated anxiety or nervousness is often internalized and unconscious. The source of nervousness may not always be so obvious as in a simple phobia or an obsessive-compulsive ritual, and the anxiety may be focused on physical symptoms or the fear of having a disease (hypochondriasis) rather than the more common manifestations (rapid heart beat, shortness of breath, increased sweating, etc.).

Psychosis.   This term involves major distortions in reality testing. It does not apply to minor impairments in reality testing or perception. For example, a depressed woman who believes that her life is "over" because her husband has died is not necessarily psychotic, but a woman who feels she must kill herself to join her dead husband in the afterlife may be delusionally depressed. *Psychosis* is a general term which can describe many different behaviors. Hallucinations are perhaps the best known of the psychotic symptoms and can be defined as a sensory perception of sights, sounds, and so forth that are not actually present. These perceptions seem very real to the individual. Hallucinations can take the form of any of the five senses, but most commonly they are auditory (sounds) or visual (sights). With the decreasing hearing capacities of increasing age, auditory hallucinations are particularly common in the elderly. Hallucinations should be distinguished from *illusions,* where the incoming stimuli are misinterpreted or misperceived by the individual. *Delusions* are false personal beliefs firmly held despite the external reality and the repeated attempts by others to show evidence and obvious proof to the contrary. Delusions are often subdivided by their content for more specific psychiatric classification (i.e., persecutory, grandiose, somatic, bizarre, ideas of reference, nihilistic, and jealous). It is important to differentiate mental delusions from religious beliefs or strong personal convictions, although they may look very similar to someone who is not familiar with an individual's cultural environment.

Paranoid ideation (thought processes) involves suspiciousness or the sense of being treated unfairly. Typical examples of paranoia are thoughts of continued harassment or persecution by an outside, often malicious, source. Paranoia may also be associated with isolation from others and a sense of being easily slighted by others. Paranoid individuals are ofter quick to react with anger and may question, without obvious reason, the fidelity of a spouse or loyalty of friends. Excessive paranoid ideation can develop into the more firmly held paranoid delusions. When a person's behavior is so disturbed that individual hallucinations, delusions, or paranoid ideation do not show themselves, the general term *psychotic* may be appropriate. A wildly manic patient with incoherent speech or a delirious alcoholic in acute withdrawal from alcohol may both be psychotic despite obviously different underlying causes of their behavior.

Agitation and *psychomotor retardation* are bodily manifestations of underlying problems. Excessive physical movements that are generally repetitive, nonproductive, and associated with inner tension are described as *agitation.* This symptom can be relatively mild, as demonstrated in the lower leg restlessness (i.e., mild akasthisia) sometimes caused by neuroleptic medications (major tranquilizers or anti-psychotic drugs), or quite severe and requiring physical restraints, as seen in patients with acute alcohol withdrawal (i.e., delirium tremens). Associated behaviors can include shouting, complaining, throwing objects, pacing, and sleep-wake cycle disturbances. The source of the agitation is often unknown to the patient and can reflect mental disturbances ranging from anxiety to severe depression to psychosis. *Psychomotor retardation* is the generalized and visible slowing of physical responsiveness, including self-initiated movements, speech, and even facial reactions. While such motor retardation is often associated with depression, it can also be secondary to physical problems (i.e., Parkinsonism or stroke), drug intoxication or withdrawal, and other organic conditions (i.e., Alzheimer's disease).

Grief Reactions.   While mourning can be a natural part of life at any age, it is particularly important in the elderly. Issues of death and dying are often central to an older person's life and learning to deal with these challenges can be a major concern. Acute grief reactions can frequently mimic a full depression syndrome, at least temporarily. Symptoms of grief include sleep disturbance, appetite disturbance, thoughts of death, increased guilt feelings, impairment in daily functioning, and a sense of worthlessness. The reactions can occur immediately after the loss of the loved one or several months later; the duration of "normal" grief reaction symptoms are quite variable from person to person and can differ in each cultural group. Generally, if grief reactions are severely interfering with normal day-to-day functioning or persist beyond six months, then the reaction may be considered

abnormal and professional attention may be warranted. Careful differentiation and eventual treatment is important because there is a marked increase in both psychiatric morbidity and overall mortality associated with prolonged or pathologic grief reactions (see Chapter 14 for a more detailed discussion).

The elderly are also susceptible to other losses, such as physical and mental impairments, which can in turn be associated with grief reactions. Symptoms of chronic complaining, tearfulness, feelings of self-pity, and irritability are not uncommon in these cases. Conversely, psychosomatic complaints and intense worries about memory loss (i.e., "Alzheimer's Phobia") are increasingly common symptoms for those elderly unable to express their grief in other ways.

SELECTED READINGS

Alexopoulos, G. S., Young, R. C., Meyers, B. S., Abrams, R. C., & Shamoian, C. A. (1988). Late-onset depression. *Psychiatric Clinics of North America, 11,* 109–115.

American Psychiatric Association (1987). *Diagnostic and statistical manual of mental disorders,* Revised 3rd Edition. Washington, DC: American Psychiatric Association.

American Psychiatric Association (1994). *DSM-IV diagnostic and statistical manual of mental disorders,* Fourth Edition. Washington, DC, American Psychiatric Association.

Arean, P. A., Perri, M. G., Nezu, A. M., et. al. (1993). Comparative effectiveness of social problem-solving therapy and reminiscence therapy as treatments for depression in older adults. *Journal of Consulting and Clinical Psychiatry, 61,* 1003–1010.

Baldwin, R. C. (1994). Is there a distinct subtype of major depression in the elderly? *Journal of Psychopharmacology, 8*(3), 177–184.

Baughman, O. L. (1989). Diagnosis and management of anxiety in the older patient: The role of azapirones. *Advances in Therapy, 6*(6), 269–286.

Berkman, L. F., Berkman, C. S., Kasl, S., Freeman, D. H., Leo, L., Ostfeld, A. M., Cornoni-Huntley, J., & Brody, J. A. (1986). Depressive symptoms in relation to physical health and functioning in the elderly. *American Journal of Epidemiology, 124,* 372–388.

Blazer, D., Bachar, J. R., & Hughes, D. C. (1987). Major depression with melancholia: A comparison of middle-aged and elderly adults. *Journal of the American Geriatrics Society, 35,* 927–932.

Blazer, D., George, L., & Landerman, R. (1986). The phenomenology of late life depression. In Bebbington, P. E. & Jacoby, R. (Eds.), *Psychiatric disorders in the elderly.* (pp. 143–152). London: Mental Health Foundation.

Blazer, D., George, L. K., & Hughes, D. (1988). Schizophrenic symptoms in an elderly community population. In Brody, J. A., Maddox, G. L. (Eds.), *Epidemiology and aging: An international perspective* (pp. 134–149). New York: Springer.

Blazer, D., Hughes, D. C., & George, L. K. (1987). The epidemiology of depression in an elderly community population. *Gerontologist, 27,* 281–287.

Bohm, C., Robinson, D. S., Gammans, R. E., Shrotriya, R. C., Alms, D. R., Leroy, A., & Placchi, M. (1990). Buspirone therapy in anxious elderly patients: A controlled clinical trial. *Journal of Clinical Psychopharmacology, 10,* 47S–51S.

Borson, S., Barnes, R. A., Kukull, W. A., Okimoto, J. T., Veith, R. C., Inui, T. S., Carter, W., & Raskind, M. A. (1986). Symptomatic depression in elderly medical outpatients. I. Prevalence, demography, and health service utilization. *Journal of the American Geriatrics Society, 34,* 341–347.

Breslau, L. & Haug, M. (Eds.). (1983). *Depression and aging: Causes, care and consequences,* New York: Springer.

Bridge, T. P., Kleinman, J. E., Soldo, B. J., & Karoum, F. (1987). Central catecholamines, cognitive impairment, and affective state in elderly schizophrenics and controls. *Biological Psychiatry, 22,* 139–147.

Bridge, T. P., & Wyatt, R. J. (1980). Paraphrenia: Paranoid states of late life: I. European research. *Journal of the American Geriatrics Society, 27,* 193–200.

Brown, R., Colter, N., Corsellis, J. A. N., Crow, T. J., Frith, C. D, Jagoe, R., Johnstone, E. C., & Marsh, L. (1986). Postmortem evidence of structural brain changes in schizophrenia. *Archives of General Psychiatry, 43,* 36–42.

Burns, B. J., Wagner, D. R., Taube, J. E., Magaziner, J., Pernutt, T. & Landerman, L. R. (1993). Mental health service use by the elderly in nursing homes. *American Journal of Public Health, 83,* 331–337.

Caligiuri, M. P., Lohr, J. B., Panton, D., & Harris, J. (1993). Extrapyramidal motor abnormalities associated with late-life psychosis. *Schizophrenia Bulletin 19*(4), 747–754.

Carney, S. S., Rich, C. L., Burke, P. A., & Fowler, R. C. (1994). Suicide over 60: the San Diego Study. *Journal of the American Geriatrics Society, 42,* 174–180.

Chen, W. J., Faraone, S. V. & Tsuang, M. T. (1992). Linkage studies of schizophrenia: a simulation study of statistical power. *Genetic Epidemiology, 9,* 123–139.

Christenson, R., & Blazer, D. (1984). Epidemiology of persecutory ideation in an elderly population in the community. *American Journal of Psychiatry, 141,* 1088–1091.

Clayton, P. J. (1981). The epidemiology of bipolar affective disorder. *Comprehensive Psychiatry, 22,* 31–43.

Conwell, Y. (1994). Suicide in elderly patients. In Schneider, L. S., Reynolds, C. F., Lebowitz, B. D., & Friedhoff, A. J. (Eds.) *Diagnosis and treatment of depression in late life* (pp. 397–418). Washington, DC: American Psychiatric Press.

Conwell, Y., Olsen, K., & Caine, E. D. (1990). Completed suicide at age 50 and over. *Journal of the American Geriatrics Society, 38,* 640–644.

Copeland, J. R. M., Davidson, I. A., Dewey, M. E., et al. (1992). Alzheimer's disease, other dementias, depression and pseudodementia: prevalence, incidence and three-year outcome in Liverpool. *British Journal of Psychiatry, 161,* 230–239.

Costa, P. T., McCrae, R. R., & Norris, A. H. (1981). Personal adjustment to aging: Longitudinal prediction from neuroticism and extroversion. *Journal of Gerontology, 36,* 78–85.

Craig, T. J., & Bregman, Z. (1988). Late onset schizophrenia-like illness. *Journal of the American Geriatrics Society, 36,* 104–107.

De Leo, D., Carollo, G., & Buono, M. D. (1995). Lower suicide rates associated with a tele-help/tele-check service for the elderly at home. *American Journal of Psychiatry, 152,* 632–634.

Denmark, J. S. (1985). A study of 250 patients referred to a department of psychiatry for the deaf. *British Journal of Psychiatry, 146,* 282–286.

Duberstein, P. R., Conwell, Y., Cox, C., Podgorski, C. A., Glazer, R. S., & Caine, E. D. (1995). Attitudes toward self-determined death: A survey of primary care physicians. *Journal of the American Geriatrics Society, 43,* 395–400.

Eagles, J. M., & Whalley, L. J. (1985). Ageing and affective disorders: The age of first onset of affective disorders in Scotland, 1969–1978. *British Journal of Psychiatry, 147,* 180–187.

Eastwood, M. R., Corbin, S. L., Reed, M., Nobbs, H., & Kedward, H. B. (1985). Acquired hearing loss and psychiatric illness: An estimate of prevalence and co-morbidity in a geriatric setting. *British Journal of Psychiatry, 147,* 552–556.

Egeland, J. A., Gerhard, D. S., Pauls, D. L., Sussex, J. M., Kidd, K. K., Allen, C. R., Hostetter, A. M., & Housman, D. E. (1987). Bipolar affective disorders linked to DNA markers on chromosome 11. *Nature, 325,* 783–787.

Finch, E. L. J., Ramsay, R. & Katona, C. L. E. Depression and physical illness in the elderly. *Clinics in Geriatric Medicine, 8,* 275–287.

Freimer N. B., Reus, V. I., Escamilla, M. A., McInnes,L. A., Spesny, M., Leon, P., Service, S. K., Smith, L. B., Silva, S., Rohas, E., Gallegos, A., Meza, L., Fournier, E., Bahorloo, S., Blankenship, K., Tyler, D. J., Batki, S., Vinogradov, S., Weissenback, J., Barondes, S. H., & Sandkuijl, L. A. (1996). Genetic mapping using haplotype, association and linkage methods suggests a locus for severe bipolar disorder (BPI) at 18q22-q23. *Nature Genetics, 12,* 436–441.

George, L. K., Blazer, D. G., Winfield-Laird, I., Leaf, P. J., & Fischbach, R. L. (1988). Psychiatric disorders and mental health service use in later life: Evidence from the epidemiologic catchment area program. In Brody, J. A., Maddox, G. L. (Eds.), *Epidemiology and aging: An interna-*

tional perspective (pp. 189–219). New York: Springer.

Gershanik, O. S. (1994). Drug-induced Parkinsonism in the aged: Recognition and prevention. *Drugs and Aging, 5*(2), 127–132.

Ghadirian, A. M., Gauthier, S., & Bertrand, S. (1986). Anxiety attacks in a patient with a right temporal lobe meningioma. *Journal of Clinical Psychiatry, 47*, 270–271.

Glesia, G. L., & Ban, A. N. (1970). Psychosis and other manifestations of levodopa therapy. *Archives of Neurology, 23*, 193–200.

Greenwald, B. S., & Kramer-Ginsberg, E. (1988). Age at onset in geriatric depression: Relationship to clinical variables. *Journal of Affective Disorders, 15*, 61–68.

Gurland, B. J. (1994). The range of quality of life: Relevance to the treatment of depression in elderly patients. In Schneider, L. S., Reynolds, C. F., Lebowitz, B. D., & Friedhoff, A. J. (Eds.), *Diagnoses and treatment of depression in late life* (pp. 61–80). Washington, DC: American Psychiatric Press.

Gurland, B. J., Dean, L., Cross, P., & Golden, R. (1980). The epidemiology of depression and dementia in the elderly: The use of multiple indicators of these conditions. In Cole, J. O., & Barrett, J. E. (Eds.), *Psychopathology of the aged* (pp. 37–62). New York: Raven Press.

Hanninen, T., Hallikainen, M., Koivisto, K., Helkala, E. L., Reinikainen, K. J., Soininen, H., Mykkanen, L., Laakso, M., Pyorala, K., & Riekkinen, P. J. (1995). A follow-up study of age-associated memory impairment: Neuropsychological predictors of dementia. *Journal of the American Geriatrics Society, 43*, 1007–1015.

Hendrie, H. C., Callahan, C. M., Levitt, E. E., Hui, S. L., Musick, B., Austrom, M. G., Nurnberger, J. I. Jr., & Tierney, W. M. (1995). Prevalence rates of major depressive disorders: The effects of varying the diagnostic criteria in an older primary care population. *American Journal of Geriatrics Psychiatry, 3*, 119–131.

Holden, N. L. (1987). Late paraphrenia or the paraphrenias? A descriptive study with a 10-year follow-up. *British Journal of Psychiatry, 150*, 635–639.

Hunter, R. C. A., & Cleghorn, R. A. (1982). Psychosomatic disorders in the elderly. *Canadian Journal of Psychiatry, 27*, 362–365.

Jamison, K. R. (1979). Manic-depressive illness in the elderly. In Kaplan, O. J. (Ed.), *Psychopathology of aging* (pp. 79–95). New York: Academic Press.

Jenike, M. A. (1989). *Geriatric psychiatry and psychopharmacology: A clinical approach.* Boca Raton, FL: CRC Press.

Jeste, D. V., Harris, M. J., Pearlson, G. D., Rabins, P., Lesser, I., Miller, B., Coles, C., & Yassa, B. (1988). Late-onset schizophrenia: Studying clinical validity. *Psychiatric Clinics of North America, 11*, 1–13.

Jeste, D. V., Lacro, J. P., Gilbert, P. L., Kline, J., & Kline, N. (1993). Treatment of late-life schizophrenia with neuroleptics. *Schizophrenia Bulletin 18*(4), 817–830.

Kalish, S. C., Bohn, R. L., Mogun, H., Glynn, R. J., Gurwitz, J. H., & Avorn, J. (1995). Antipsychotic prescribing patterns and the treatment of extrapyramidal symptoms in older people. *Journal of the American Geriatrics Society, 43*, 967–973.

Katon, W. & Schulberg, H. C. (1992). Epidemiology of depression in primary care. Special section: Developing guidelines for treating depressive disorder in the primary care setting. *General Hospital Psychiatry, 14*, 237–247.

Katz, I. R., & Alexopoulos, G. S. (1996, Fall). Consensus update conference: Diagnosis and treatment of late-life depression, proceedings of the Geriatric Psychiatry Alliance—January 20, 1996. *The American Journal of Geriatric Psychiatry, 4*(4), supplement 1.

Kay, D. W. K. (1963). Late paraphrenia and its bearing on the etiology of schizophrenia. *Acta Psychiatrica Scandinavica, 39*, 159–169, 1963.

Kay, D. W. K., & Roth, M. (1961). Environmental and hereditary factors in the schizophrenias of old age ("late paraphrenia") and their bearing on the general problem of causation in schizophrenia. *Journal of Mental Science, 107*, 649–686.

Kendler, K. S., & Diehl, S. R. (1993). The genetics of schizophrenia: A current, genetic-epidemiologic perspective. *Schizophrenia Bulletin, 19*, 261–285.

Kendler, K. S., & Walsh, D. (1995). Gender and schizophrenia: Results of an epidemiologically based family study. *British Journal of Psychiatry, 167*, 184–192.

Klerman, G. L., Lavori, P. W., Rice, J., Reich, T., Endicott, J., Andreasen, N. C., Keller, M. B., & Hirschfeld, R. M. A. (1985). Birth-cohort trends in rates of major depressive disorder among relatives of patients with affective disorder. *Archives of General Psychiatry, 42*, 689–693.

Kraepelin, E. (1900). Psychiatrie. In *Ein Lehrbuch fur Studierende und Artzte* (pp. 1909–1915). Leipzig: Barth.

Kral, V. A., & Emory, O. B. (1989). Long-term follow-up of depressive pseudodementia of the aged. *Canadian Journal of Psychiatry, 34,* 445–446.

Krishnan K. R. R., Tupler, L. A., Richie, J. C., Mc-Donald, W. M., Knight, D. L., Nemeroff, C. B., & Carroll, B. J. (1996). Apolipoprotein E-4 frequency in geriatric depression. *Biological Psychiatry, 40,* 69–71.

Lebowitz, B. D., Martinez, R. A., Niederehe, G., Pearson, J. L., et al. (1995). Treatment of depression in late-life. *Psychopharmacology, 31*(1), 185–202.

Lipsey, J. R., Robinson, R. G., Pearlson, G. D., Rao, K., & Price, T. R. (1984). Nortriptyline treatment of post-stroke depression: A double-blind study. *Lancet, I,* 297–300.

Lyness, J. M., Cox, C., Curry, J., Conwell, Y., King, D. A., & Caine, E. D. (1995). Older age and the underreporting of depressive symptoms. *Journal of the American Geriatrics Society, 43,* 216–221.

Manton, K. G., Blazer, D. G., & Woodbury, M. A. (1987). Suicide in middle age and later life: Sex and race specific life table and cohort analyses. *Journal of Gerontology, 42,* 219–227.

Markovitz, P. J. (1993). Treatment of anxiety in the elderly. *Journal of Clinical Psychiatry, 54*(Suppl. 5), 64–68.

Murphy, E., & Brown, G. W. (1980). Life events, psychiatric disturbance and physical illness. *British Journal of Psychiatry, 136,* 326–338.

Naguib, M., McGuffin, P., Levy, R., Festenstein, H., & Alonso, A. (1987). Genetic markers in late paraphrenia: A study of HLA antigens. *British Journal of Psychiatry, 150,* 124–127.

National Institutes of Health Consensus Development Conference. (1991, November 4–5). Diagnosis and treatment of depression in late life. Reprinted from: *NIH Consensus Development Conference Consensus Statement,* vol. 9, no. 3. Bethesda, MD: NIH.

National Institutes of Health, Office of the Medical Applications of Research. (1992). Consensus Development Panel on Late Life: Diagnosis and treatment of depression in late life. *Journal of the American Medical Association (JAMA), 268,* 1010–1024.

Norquist, G., Wells, K. B., Rogers, W. H., Davis, L. M., Kahn, K., & Brook, R. (1995). Quality of care for depressed elderly patients hospitalized in the speciality units of general medical wards. *Archives of General Psychiatry, 52,* 695–701.

Owen, F., Crow, T. J., Frith, C. D., Johnson, J. A., Johnstone, E. C., Lofthouse, R., Owens, D. G. C., & Poulter, M. (1987). Selective decreases in MAO-B activity in post-mortem brains from schizophrenic patients with type II syndrome. *British Journal of Psychiatry, 151,* 514–519.

Parnetti, L., Gottfries, J., Karlsson, I., Langstrom, G., Gottfries, C.-G., & Svennerholm, L. (1987). Monoamines and their metabolites in cerebrospinal fluid of patients with senile dementia of Alzheimer type using high performance liquid chromatography and gas chromatography-mass spectrometry. *Acta Psychiatrica Scandinavica, 75,* 542–548.

Pauls, D. L., Ott, O., Paul, S. M., Allen, C. R., Fann, C. S. J., Carulli, J. P., Falls. K. M., Southillier, C. A., Gravius, T. C., Keith, T. P., Egeland, J. A., & Ginns, E. I. (1995). Linkage analyses of chromosome 18 markers do not identify a major susceptibility locus for bipolar affective disorder in the older order Amish. *American Journal of Human Genetics, 57,* 636–643.

Pearlson, G., & Rabins, P. (1988). The late-onset psychoses: Possible risk factors. *Psychiatric Clinics of North America, 11,* 15–32.

Pekkarinen, P., Terwilliger, J. Bredbacka, P., Lonnqvist, J. & Peltonen, L. (1995). Evidence of a predisposing locus to bipolar disorder on Xq24-q27.1 in an extended Finnish pedigree. *Genome Research, 5,* 105–115.

Pickar, D. (1995). Prospects for pharmacotherapy of schizophrenia. *Lancet, 345,* 557–562.

Post, M. (1966). *Persistent persecutory states of the elderly.* Oxford: Pergamon Press.

Post, R. M., Ballenger, J. C., & Goodwin, F. K. (1984). Cerebrospinal fluid studies of neurotransmitter function in manic and depressive illness. In Post, R. M., & Ballenger, J. C. (Eds.), *Neurobiology of Mood Disorders* (pp. 685–717). Baltimore: Williams and Wilkins.

Rabins, P., Pearlson, G., Jayaram, G., Steele, C., & Tune, L. (1987). Increased ventricle-to-brain ratio in late-onset schizophrenia. *American Journal of Psychiatry, 144,* 1216–1218.

Rabins, P. V., Harvis, K., & Koven, S. (1985). High fatality rates of late-life depression associated with cardiovascular disease. *Journal of Affective Disorders, 9,* 165–167.

Reding, M., Haycox, J., Blass, J. (1985). Depression in patients referred to a dementia clinic: A three-year prospective study. *Archives of Neurology, 42,* 894–896.

Retterstol, N. (1968). Paranoid psychoses: The stability of nosological categories illustrated by a personal follow-up investigation. *British Journal of Psychiatry, 114,* 553–562.

Rich, C. L., Young, D., & Fowler, R. C. (1986). San Diego suicide study. *Archives of General Psychiatry 43,* 577–582.

Richelson, E. (1994). The pharmacology of antidepressants at the synapse: Focus on newer compounds. *Journal of Clinical Psychiatry, 55*(9, Suppl. A), 34–39.

Robinson, R. G., Lipsey, J. R., Bolla-Wilson, K., Bolduc, P. L., Pearlson, G. D., Rao, K., & Price, T. R. (1985). Mood disorders in left-handed stroke patients. *American Journal of Psychiatry, 142,* 1424–1429.

Robinson, R. G., Starr, L. B., Kubos, K. L., & Price, T. R. (1983). A two-year longitudinal study of post-stroke mood disorders: Findings during the initial evaluation. *Stroke, 14,* 736–741.

Rodin, G., & Voshart, K. (1986). Depression in the medically ill: An overview. *American Journal of Psychiatry, 143,* 696–705.

Roose, S. P., Glassman, A. H., Attia, E., & Woodring, R. (1994). Comparative efficacy of selective serotonin reuptake inhibitors and tricyclics in the treatment of melancholia. *American Journal of Psychiatry, 151,* 1735–1739.

Roth, M. (1955). The natural history of mental disorders in old age. *Journal of Mental Science, 101,* 281–295.

Roth, M. (1987). Late paraphrenia: Phenomenology and etiological factors and their bearing upon problems of the schizophrenia family of disorders. In Miller, N. E., & Cohen, G. D. (Eds.), *Schizophrenia, paranoia and schizophreniform disorders in later life* (pp. 217–234). New York: Guilford Press.

Rovner, B. W., German, P S., L. J., et al. (1991). Depression and mortality in nursing homes. *Journal of the American Medical Association, 265,* 993–996.

Ruegg, R. G., Zisook, S., Swerdlow, N. R. (1988). Depression in the aged: An overview. *Psychiatric Clinics of North America, 11,* 83–99.

Schildkrant, J. J. (1965). The catecholamine hypothesis of affective disorders: A review of supporting evidence. *American Journal of Psychiatry, 122,* 509–522.

Schneider, L. S., Reynolds, C. F., Lebowitz, B., & Friedhoff, A. (Eds.). (1994). *Diagnosis and treatment of depression in late life: Results of the NIH consensus development conference.* Washington, DC: American Psychiatric Press.

Seidlitz, L., Duberstein, P. R., Cox, C., & Conwell, Y. (1995). Attitudes of older people toward suicide and assisted suicide: An analysis of Gallop poll findings. *Journal of the American Geriatrics Society, 43,* 993–998.

Sheikh, J. I. (1996). Anxiety disorders. In Sadavoy, J., Lazarus, L. W., Jarvik, L. F. & Grossberg, G. T. (Eds.), *Comprehensive Review of Geriatric Psychiatry II,* Second Edition (pp. 615–636). Washington, DC: American Psychiatric Press.

Shulman, K., Post, F. (1980). Bipolar affective disorder in old age. *British Journal of Psychiatry, 136,* 26–32.

Siever, L. J., & Davis, K. L. (1985). Overview: toward a dysregulation hypothesis of depression. *American Journal of Psychiatry, 142,* 1017–1031.

Stern, T. A., & Tesar, G. E. (1988). Anxiety and the cardiovascular system. *Mount Sinai Journal of Medicine, 55,* 230–239.

Straub, R. E., MacLean, C. J., O'Neill, A. O., Burke, J., Murphy, B., Duke, F., Shinkwin, R., Webb, B. T., Zhang, J., Walsh, D. & Kendler, K. S. (1995). A potential vulnerability locus for schizophrenia on chromosome 6p24–22: Evidence for genetic heterogeneity. *Nature Genetics, 11,* 287–293.

Sunderland, T., Cohen, R. M., Molchan, S., Lawlor, B. A., Mellow, A. M., Newhouse, P. A., Tariot, P. N., Mueller, E. A., & Murphy, D. L. (1994). High-dose selegiline in treatment-resistant older depressive patients. *Archives of General Psychiatry, 51,* 607–615.

Sunderland, T., Lawlor, B. A., Molchan, S. E., & Martinez, R. A. (1988). Depressive syndromes in the elderly: Special concerns. *Psychopharmacology Bulletin, 24,* 567–576.

Sunderland, T., Little, J., Cantillon, M., Bahro, M., & Molchan, S. (1994). Pharmacologic treatment of depression in elderly neuropsychiatric patients. In Langer, S. Z., Brunello, N., Racagni, G., & Mendlewicz, J. (Eds.), *Critical issues in the treatment of affective disorders* (pp. 52–57). Basel, Switzerland: S. Karger AG, Int. Acad. Biomed. Drug Res., Vol. 9.

Sunderland, T., Molchan, S. E., & Zubenko, G. S. (1995). Biological markers in Alzheimer's disease. In Bloom, F. E. & Kupfer, D. J. (Eds.), *Psychopharmacology: The fourth generation of progress* (pp. 1389–1399). New York: Raven Press.

Tran-Johnson, T. K., Krull, A. J., & Jeste, D. V. (1992). Late life schizophrenia and its treatment: Pharmacologic issues in older schizophrenic patients. *Clinics of Geriatric Medicine, 8*(2), 401–410.

Veith, R. C., Raskind, M. A. (1988). The neurobiology of aging: Does it predispose to depression? *Neurobiology of Aging, 9,* 101–117.

Watt, J. A. G. (1985). The relationship of paranoid state to schizophrenia. *American Journal of Psychiatry, 142,* 1456–1458.

Weissman, M. M., & Myers, J. K. (1978). Affective disorders in a U.S. urban community. *Archives of General Psychiatry, 35,* 1304–1311.

Wells, K. B., & Burnam, M. A. (1991). Caring for depression in America: Lessons from early findings of the medical outcomes study. *Psychiatric Medicine, 9,* 503–519.

Woods, R. T., & Britton, P. G. (1985). *Clinical psychology with the elderly.* Rockville, MD: Aspen Publications.

Yassa, R., Nair, V., & Schwartz, G. (1986). Early versus late onset psychosis and tardive dyskinesia. *Biological Psychiatry, 21,* 1291–1297.

Zisook, S., Shuchter, S. R., Sledge, P. A., et. al. (1994). The spectrum of depressive phenomena after spousal bereavememt. *Journal of Clinical Psychiatry, 55,* 29–36.

Zubenko, G. S., Moossy, J., & Kopp, U. (1990). Neurochemical correlates of major depression in primary dementia. *Archives of Neurology, 47,* 209–214.

ENDNOTES

1. American Psychiatric Association. (1994). *DSM-IV diagnostic and statistical manual of mental disorders,* Fourth Edition. Washington, DC: American Psychiatric Association.

2. Finch, E. L. J., Ramsay, R., & Katona, C. L. E. (1992). Depression and physical illness in the elderly. *Clinics of Geriatric Medicine, 8,* 275–287.

3. Katon, W., & Schulberg, H. C. (1992). Epidemiology of depression in primary care. Special section: developing guidelines for treating depressive disorder in the primary care setting. *General Hospital Psychiatry, 14,* 237–247.

4. Burns, B. J., Wagner, D. R., Taube, J. E., Magaziner, J., Pernutt, T., & Landerman, L. R. (1993). Mental health service use by the elderly in nursing homes. *American Journal of Public Health, 83,* 331–337.

5. American Psychiatric Association. (1994). *DSM-IV diagnostic and statistical manual of mental disorders,* Fourth Edition. Washington, DC: American Psychiatric Association.

6. Lyness, J. M., Cox, C., Curry, J., Conwell, Y., King, D. A., & Caine, E. D. (1995). Older age and the underreporting of depressive symptoms. *Journal of the American Geriatrics Society, 43,* 216–221; Hendrie, H. C., Callahan, C. M., Levitt, E. E., Hui, S. L., Musick, B., Austrom, M. G., Nurnberger, J. I. Jr., & Tierney, W. M. (1995). Prevalence rates of major depressive disorders: The effects of varying the diagnostic criteria in an older primary care population. *American Journal of Geriatric Psychiatry, 3,* 119–131; Klerman, G. L., Lavori, P. W., Rice, J., Reich, T., Endicott, J., Andreasen, N. C., Keller, M. B., & Hirschfield, R. M. A. (1985). Birth-cohort trends in rates of major depressive disorder among relatives of pa-

tients with affective disorder. *Archives of General Psychiatry 42,* 689–693; and Blazer, D., Hughes, D.C., & George, L. K. (1987). The epidemiology of depression in an elderly community population. *Gerontologist, 27,* 281–287.

7. Hendrie, H. C., Callahan, C. M., Levitt, E. E., Hui, S. L., Musick, B., Austrom, M. G., Nurnberger, J. I. Jr., & Tierney, W. M. (1995). Prevalence rates of major depressive disorders: The effects of varying the diagnostic criteria in an older primary care population. *American Journal of Geriatric Psychiatry, 3,* 119–131.

8. Lebowitz, B. D., Martinez, R. A., Niederehe, G., Pearson, J. L., et al. (1995). Treatment of depression in late-life. *Psychopharmacology, 31*(1), 185–202; Baldwin, R. C. (1994). Is there a distinct subtype of major depression in the elderly? *Journal of Psychopharmacology, 8*(3), 177–184; Ruegg, R. G., Zisook, S., & Swerdlow, N. R. (1988). Depression in the aged: An overview. *Psychiatric Clinics of North America, 11,* 83–99.

9. Blazer, D., Bachar, J. R., & Hughes, D. C. (1987). Major depression with melancholia: A comparison of middle-aged and elderly adults. *Journal of the American Geriatrics Society, 35,* 927–932.

10. Blazer, D., George, L., & Landerman, R. (1986). The phenomenology of late life depression. In Bebbington, P. E., & Jacoby, R. (Eds.), *Psychiatric disorders in the elderly.* London: Mental Health Foundation; Blazer, D., Bachar, J. R., & Hughes, D. C. (1987). Major depression with melancholia: A comparison of middle-aged and elderly adults. *Journal of the American Geriatrics Society, 35,* 927–932.

11. Alexopoulos, G. S., Meyers, B. S., Young, R. C., Chester, J., Feder, M., & Einhorn, A. (1995). Anx-

iety in geriatric depression: Effects of age and cognitive impairment. *American Journal of Geriatric Psychiatry, 3,* 108–118.

12. Lyness, J. M., Cox, C., Curry, J., Conwell, Y., King, D. A., & Caine, E. D. (1995). Older age and the underreporting of depressive symptoms. *Journal of the American Geriatrics Society, 43,* 216–221.

13. Jamison, K. R. (1979). Manic-depressive illness in the elderly. In Kaplan, O. J. (Ed.), *Psychopathology of aging.* New York: Academic Press, pp. 79–95.

14. Eagles, J. M., & Whalley, L. J. (1985). Ageing and affective disorders: The age of first onset of affective disorders in Scotland, 1969–1978. *British Journal of Psychiatry, 147,* 180–187.

15. Shulman, K., & Post, F. (1980). Bipolar affective disorder in old age. *British Journal of Psychiatry, 136,* 26–32.

16. Clayton, P. J. (1981). The epidemiology of bipolar affective disorder. *Comprehensive Psychiatry, 22,* 31–43; and Weissman, M. M., & Myers, J. K. (1978). Affective disorders in a U.S. urban community. *Archives of General Psychiatry 35,* 1304–1311.

17. Lebowitz, B. D., Martinez, R. A., Niederehe, G., Pearson, J. L., et al. (1995). Treatment of depression in late-life. *Psychopharmacology, 31*(1), 185–202; Murphy, E., & Brown, G. W. (1980). Life events, psychiatric disturbance and physical illness. *British Journal of Psychiatry, 136,* 326–338; and Woods, R. T., & Britton, P. G. (1985). *Clinical psychology with the elderly.* Rockville, MD: Aspen Publications.

18. Sunderland, T., Lawlor, B. A., Molchan, S. E., & Martinez, R. A. (1988). Depressive syndromes in the elderly: Special concerns. *Psychopharmacology Bulletin, 24,* 567–576.

19. Schildkrant, J. J. (1965). The catecholamine hypothesis of affective disorders: A review of supporting evidence. *American Journal of Psychiatry, 122,* 509–522; Post, R. M., Ballenger, J. C., & Goodwin, F. K. (1984). Cerebrospinal fluid studies of neurotransmitter function in manic and depressive illness. In Post, R. M., & Ballenger, J. C. (Eds.), *Neurobiology of mood disorders* (pp. 685–717). Baltimore: Williams and Wilkins; and Veith, R. C., & Raskind, M. A. (1988). The neurobiology of aging: Does it predispose to depression? *Neurobiology of Aging, 9,* 101–117.

20. Siever, L. J., & Davis, K. L. (1985). Overview: toward a dysregulation hypothesis of depression. *American Journal of Psychiatry, 142,* 1017–1031.

21. Egeland, J. A., Gerhard, D. S., Pauls, D. L., Sussex, J. M., Kidd, K. K., Allen, C. R., Hostetter, A. M., & Housman, D. E. (1987). Bipolar affective

disorders linked to DNA markers on chromosome 11. *Nature, 325,* 783–787.

22. Freimer N. B., Reus, V. I., Escamilla, M. A., McInnes, L. A., Spesny, M., Leon, P., Service, S. K., Smith, L. B., Silva, S., Rohas, E., Gallegos, A., Meza, L., Fournier, E., Bahorloo, S., Blankenship, K., Tyler, D. J., Batki, S., Vinogradov, S., Weissenback, J., Barondes, S. H., & Sandkuijl, L. A. (1996). Genetic mapping using haplotype, association and linkage methods suggests a locus for severe bipolar disorder (BPI) at 18q22–q23. *Nature Genetics, 12,* 436–441; Pauls, D. L., Ott, O., Paul, S. M., Allen, C. R., Fann, C. S. J., Carulli, J. P., Falls. K. M., Southhillier, C. A., Gravius, T. C., Keith, T. P., Egeland, J. A., & Ginns, E. I. (1995). Linkage analyses of chromosome 18 markers do not identify a major susceptibility locus for bipolar affective disorder in the older order Amish. *American Journal of Human Genetics, 57,* 636–643; and Pekkarinen, P., Terwilliger, J. Bredbacka, P., Lonnqvist, J., & Peltonen, L. (1995). Evidence of a predisposing locus to bipolar disorder on Xq24–q27.1 in an extended Finnish pedigree. *Genome Research, 5,* 105–115.

23. Robinson, R. G., Starr, L. B., Kubos, K. L., & Price, T. R. (1983). A two-year longitudinal study of post-stroke mood disorders: Findings during the initial evaluation. *Stroke, 14,* 736–741; Robinson, R. G., Lipsey, J. R., Bolla-Wilson, K., Bolduc, P. L., Pearlson, G. D., Rao, K., & Price, T. R. (1985). Mood disorders in left-handed stroke patients. *American Journal of Psychiatry, 142,* 1424–1429; Reding, M., Haycox, J., & Blass, J. (1985) Depression in patients referred to a dementia clinic: A three-year prospective study. *Archives of Neurology, 42,* 894–896; and Lipsey, J. R., Robinson, R. G., Pearlson, G. D., Rao, K., & Price, T. R. (1984). Nortriptyline treatment of post-stroke depression: A double-blind study. *Lancet 1,* 297–300.

24. Baldwin, R. C. (1994). Is there a distinct subtype of major depression in the elderly? *Journal of Psychopharmacology, 8*(3), 177–184; Rodin, G., & Voshart, K. (1986). Depression in the medically ill: An over-view. *American Journal of Psychiatry, 143,* 696–705; Berkman, L. F., Berkman, C. S., Kasl, S., Freeman, D. H., Leo, L., Ostfeld, A. M., Cornoni-Huntley, J., & Brody, J. A. (1986). Depressive symptoms in relation to physical health and functioning in the elderly. *American Journal of Epidemiology, 124,* 372–388; and Sunderland, T., Lawlor, B. A., Molchan, S. E., & Martinez, R. A. (1988). Depressive syndromes in the elderly: Spe-

cial concerns. *Psychopharmacology Bulletin, 24,* 567–576.

25. American Psychiatric Association. (1994). *DSM-IV Diagnostic and Statistical Manual of Mental Disorders,* Fourth Edition. Washington, DC: American Psychiatric Association.

26. Sunderland, T., Molchan, S. E., & Zubenko, G. S. (1995). Biological markers in Alzheimer's disease. In Bloom, F. E., & Kupfer, D. J. (Eds.), *Psychopharmacology: The fourth generation of progress.* New York: Raven Press, pp. 1389–1399.

27. Zubenko, G. S., Moossy J., & Kopp, U. (1990). Neurochemical correlates of major depression in primary dementia. *Archives of Neurology, 47,* 209–214.

28. Zweig, R. M., Ross, C. A., Hedreen, J. C., Steele, C., Cardillo, J. E., Whitehouse, P. J., Folstein, M. F., & Price, D. L. (1988). The neuropathology of aminergic nuclei in Alzheimer's disease. *Annals of Neurology, 24,* 233–242.

29. Alexopoulos, G. S., Young, R. C., Meyers, B. S., Abrams, R. C., & Shamoian, C. A. (1988). Late-onset depression. *Psychiatric Clinics of North America, 11,* 109–115; and Greenwald, B. S., & Kramer-Ginsberg, E. (1988). Age at onset in geriatric depression: Relationship to clinical variables. *Journal of Affective Disorders, 15,* 61–68.

30. Rabins, P. V., Harvis, K., & Koven, S. (1985). High fatality rates of late-life depression associated with cardiovascular disease. *Journal of Affective Disorders, 9,* 165–167.

31. Baldwin, R. C. (1994). Is there a distinct subtype of major depression in the elderly? *Journal of Psychopharmacology, 8*(3), 177–184; Reding, M., Haycox, J., & Blass, J. (1985). Depression in patients referred to a dementia clinic: A three-year prospective study. *Archives of Neurology, 42,* 894–896.

32. Baldwin, R. C. (1994). Is there a distinct subtype of major depression in the elderly? *Journal of Psychopharmacology, 8*(3), 177–184; Kral, V. A., & Emory, O. B. (1989). Long-term follow-up of depressive pseudodementia of the aged. *Canadian Journal of Psychiatry, 34,* 445–446; and Copeland, J. R. M., Davidson, I. A., Dewey, M. E., et al. (1992). Alzheimer's disease, other dementias, depression and pseudodementia: prevalence, incidence and three-year outcome in Liverpool. *British Journal of Psychiatry, 161,* 230–239.

33. Krishnan K. R. R., Tupler, L. A., Richie, J. C., McDonald, W. M., Knight, D. L., Nemeroff, C. B. & Carroll, B. J. (1996). Apolipoprotein E-4 frequency in geriatric depression. *Biological Psychiatry, 40,* 69–71.

34. Carney, S. S., Rich, C. L., Burke, P. A., & Fowler, R. C. (1994). Suicide over 60: the San Diego Study. *Journal of the American Geriatrics Society, 42,* 174–180; Rich, C. L., Young, D., & Fowler, R. C. (1986). San Diego suicide study. *Archives of General Psychiatry, 43,* 577–582; and Manton, K. G., Blazer, D. G., & Woodbury, M. A. (1987). Suicide in middle age and later life: Sex and race specific life table and cohort analyses. *Journal of Gerontology, 42,* 219–227.

35. The actual rate of suicide is underreported because of shame and guilt. Some religious groups such as Catholics and Orthodox Jews have denied burial rites to persons who committed suicide. It is also underestimated because of deception to protect life insurance benefits.

36. Carney, S. S., Rich, C. L., Burke, P. A., & Fowler, R. C. (1994). Suicide over 60: the San Diego Study. *Journal of American Geriatrics Society, 42,* 174–180.

37. Conwell, Y., Olsen, K., & Caine, E. D. (1990). Completed suicide at age 50 and over. *Journal of the American Geriatric Society, 38,* 640–644.

38. For national suicide rates, see U.S. Bureau of the Census (1987). *Statistical abstract of the United States: 1988,* 108th edition. Washington, DC: U.S. Government Printing Office; and Rich, C. L., Young, D., & Fowler, R. C. (1986). San Diego suicide study. *Archives of General Psychiatry, 43,* 577–582.

39. From Cohen, J. (1964). Forms of suicide and their significance, *Triangle, 6,* 280–286.

40. *Ibid.*

41. Seidlitz, L., Duberstein, P. R., Cox, C., & Conwell, Y. (1995). Attitudes of older people toward suicide and assisted suicide: An analysis of Gallop poll findings. *Journal of the American Geriatrics Society, 43,* 993–998.

42. Lyness, J. M., Cox, C., Curry, J., Conwell, Y., King, D. A., & Caine, E. D. (1995). Older age and the underreporting of depressive symptoms. *Journal of the American Geriatrics Society, 43,* 216–221; Conwell, Y., Olsen, K., & Caine, E. D. (1990). Completed suicide at age 50 and over. *Journal of the American Geriatrics Society, 38,* 640–644.

43. Camus, A. (1959). *The myth of Sisyphus.* New York: Vintage Books.

44. Tran-Johnson, T. K., Krull, A. J., Jeste, D. V. (1992). Late life schizophrenia and its treatment: Pharmacologic issues in older schizophrenic patients. *Clinics in Geriatric Medicine, 8*(2), 401–410.

45. For an investigation of changes over time in the manifestations of schizophrenia, including the the-

ory that schizophrenic illness "burns out" as one ages, see Lawton, M. P. (1972). Schizophrenia 45 years later. *Journal of the Genetic Psychology, 121,* 133–143.

46. Bridge, T. P., & Wyatt, R. J. (1980). Paraphrenia: Paranoid states of late life: I. European research. *Journal of the American Geriatrics Society, 27,* 193–200.

47. Kraepelin, E. (1900). Psychiatrie. In *Ein Lehrbuch fur Studierende und Artzte* (pp. 1909–1915). Leipzig: Barth.

48. Roth, M. (1955). The natural history of mental disorders in old age. *Journal of Mental Science, 101,* 281–295.

49. Bridge, & Wyatt, R. I., (1980).

50. Tran-Johnson, T. K., Krull, A. J., & Jeste, D. V. (1992). Late life schizophrenia and its treatment: Pharmacologic issues in older schizophrenic patients. *Clinics in Geriatric Medicine, 8*(2), 401–410; Eastwood, M. R., Corbin, S. L., Reed, M., Nobbs, H., & Kedward, H. B. (1985). Acquired hearing loss and psychiatric illness: An estimate of prevalence and co-morbidity in a geriatric setting. *British Journal of Psychiatry, 147,* 552–556; Jeste, D. V., Harris, M. J., Pearlson, G. D., Rabins, P., Lesser, I., Miller, B., Coles, C., & Yassa, B. (1988). Late-onset schizophrenia: Studying clinical validity. *Psychiatric Clinics of North America, 11,* 1–13; and Pearlson, G., & Rabins, P. (1988). The late-onset psychoses: Possible risk factors. *Psychiatric Clinics of North America, 11,* 15–32.

51. Christenson, R., & Blazer, D. (1984). Epidemiology of persecutory ideation in an elderly population in the community. *American Journal of Psychiatry, 141,* 1088–1091.

52. Pearlson, G., Rabins, P. (1988). The late-onset psychoses: Possible risk factors. *Psychiatric Clinics of North America, 11,* 15–32.

53. Kay, D. W. K., & Roth, M. (1961). Environmental and hereditary factors in the schizophrenias of old age ("late paraphrenia") and their bearing on the general problem of causation in schizophrenia. *Journal of Mental Science, 107,* 649–686; Post, M. (1966). *Persistent persecutory states of the elderly.* Oxford: Pergamon Press; and Retterstol, N. (1968). Paranoid psychoses: The stability of nosological categories illustrated by a personal follow-up investigation. *British Journal of Psychiatry, 114,* 553–562.

54. Caligiuri, M. P., Lohr, J. B., Panton, D., & Harris, J. (1993). Extrapyramidal motor abnormalities associated with late-life psychosis. *Schizophrenia Bulletin, 19*(4), 747–754; Denmark, J. S. (1985). A study of 250 patients referred to a department of psychiatry for the deaf. *British Journal of Psychiatry, 146,* 282–286; Eastwood, et al. (1985); Post (1966); and Watt, J. A. G. (1985). The relationship of paranoid state to schizophrenia. *American Journal of Psychiatry, 142,* 1456–1458.

55. Blazer, D., George, L. K., & Hughes, D. (1988). Schizophrenic symptoms in an elderly community population. In Brody, J. A., & Maddox, G. L. (Eds.), *Epidemiology and aging: An international perspective* (pp. 134–149). New York: Springer.

56. Kendler, K. S., & Walsh, D. (1995). Gender and schizophrenia: results of an epidemiologically based family study. *British Journal of Psychiatry, 167,* 184–192; Chen, W. J., Faraone, S. V., & Tsuang, M. T. (1992). Linkage studies of schizophrenia: A simulation study of statistical power. *Genetic Epidemiology, 9,* 123–139; Kendler, K. S., & Diehl, S. R. (1993). The genetics of schizophrenia: A current, genetic-epidemiologic perspective. *Schizophrenia Bulletin, 19,* 261–285.

57. Straub, R. E., MacLean, C. J., O'Neill, A. O., Burke, J., Murphy, B., Duke, F., Shinkwin, R., Webb, B. T., Zhang, J., Walsh, D., & Kendler, K. S. (1995). A potential vulnerability locus for schizophrenia on chromosome 6p24-22: evidence for genetic heterogeneity. *Nature Genetics, 11,* 287–293; Pulver, A. E., et al. (1994). Follow-up of a report of a potential linkage for schizophrenia on chromosome 22q12–q13.1: Part 2. *American Journal of Medical Genetics, 54,* 44–50.

58. Su, Y. et al. (1993). Exclusion of linkage between schizophrenia and the D2 dopamine receptor gene region of chromosome 11q in 112 Irish multiplex families. *Archives of General Psychiatry, 50,* 205–211.

59. Rabins, P., Pearlson, G., Jayaram, G., Steele, C., & Tune, L. (1987). Increased ventricle-to-brain ratio in late-onset schizophrenia. *American Journal of Psychiatry, 144,* 1216–1218.

60. Brown, R., Colter, N., Corsellis, J. A. N., Crow, T. J., Frith, C. D, Jagoe, R., Johnstone, E. C., & Marsh, L. (1986) Postmortem evidence of structural brain changes in schizophrenia. *Archives of General Psychiatry, 43,* 36–42.

61. Parnetti, L., Gottfries, J., Karlsson, I., Langstrom, G., Gottfries, C.-G., & Svennerholm, L. (1987). Monoamines and their metabolites in cerebrospinal fluid of patients with senile dementia of Alzheimer type using high performance liquid chromatography and gas chromatography-mass spectrometry. *Acta Psychiatrica Scandinavica, 75,* 542–548.

62. Bridge, T. P., Kleinman, J. E., Soldo, B. J., & Karoum, F. (1987). Central catecholamines, cognitive impairment, and affective state in elderly schizophrenics and controls. *Biological Psychiatry, 22,* 139–147.

63. Owen, F., Crow, T. J., Frith, C. D., Johnson, J. A., Johnstone, E. C., Lofthouse, R., Owens, D. G. C., & Poulter, M. (1987). Selective decreases in MAO-B activity in post-mortem brains from schizophrenic patients with type II syndrome. *British Journal of Psychiatry, 151,* 514–519.

64. Pearlson & Rabins (1988); Roth (1955); Roth (1987); and Yassa, R., Nair, V., & Schwartz, G. (1986). Early versus late onset psychosis and tardive dyskinesia. *Biological Psychiatry, 21,* 1291–1297.

65. Jeste, D. V., Harris, M. J., Pearlson, G. D., Rabins, P., Lesser, I., Miller, B., Coles, C., & Yassa, B. (1988). Late-onset schizophrenia: Studying clinical validity. *Psychiatric Clinics of North America, 11,* 1–13.

66. Post (1966); and Jeste, et. al. (1988).

67. Markovitz, P. J. (1993). Treatment of anxiety in the elderly. *Journal of Clinical Psychiatry, 54* (Suppl.5), 64–68.

68. Stern, T. A., & Tesar, G. E. (1988). Anxiety and the cardiovascular system. *Mount Sinai Journal of Medicine, 55,* 230–239; and George, L. K., Blazer, D. G., Winfield-Laird, I., Leaf, P. J., & Fischbach, R. L. (1988). Psychiatric disorders and mental health service use in later life: Evidence from the epidemiologic catchment area program. In Brody, J. A., & Maddox, G. L. (Eds.). *Epidemiology and aging: An international perspective* (pp. 189–219). New York: Springer.

69. Flint, A. J. (1994, May). Epidemiology and Co-morbidity of Anxiety Disorders in the Elderly. *American Journal of Psychiatry, 151*(5), pp. 640–649.

70. Sheikh, J. I. (1996). Anxiety Disorders. In Sadavoy, J., Lazarus, L. W., Jarvik, L. F., & Grossberg, G. T. (Eds.), *Comprehensive review of geriatric psychiatry II,* Second Edition (pp. 615–636). Washington, DC: American Psychiatric Press.

71. The landmark National Comorbidity Survey, conducted from 1990 to 1992, found that 3.5% of adults had panic disorder at some time in their lives. Unfortunately, this survey of 8,000 Americans covered ages 15 to 54 only. [Kessler, R. C., et. al. (1994, January). Lifetime and 12-month prevalence of DSM-III-R psychiatric disorders in the United States. *Archives of General Psychiatry, 51,*

8–19.] Another major survey, the National Institute of Mental Health's Epidemiologic Catchment Area Study, for which 20,000 adults of all ages were interviewed in the 1980s, found that fewer than one percent of people age 65 and older had panic disorder in their lives. [Robins, L. N., Regier, D. A. (Eds.) (1991). *Psychiatric disorders in America: The epidemiologic catchment area study.* New York: The Free Press.] This low figure is due in part to the fact that the disorder usually occurs in young adulthood, and to the relatively strict definition of panic disorder, which requires the incidence of at least three intense attacks in any three-week period and at least one occurring with no obvious phobic stimulus. As many as 10% of Americans, however, have had panic attacks at some time in their lives.

72. Stern, T. A., & Tesar, G. E. (1988). Anxiety and the cardiovascular system. *Mount Sinai Journal of Medicine, 55,* 230–239.

73. Salzman, C., Schneider, L. S., & Alexopoulos, G. S. (1995). Pharmacological treatment of depression in late life. In Bloom, F. E., & Kupfer, D. J. (Eds.). *Psychopharmacology: The fourth generation of progress* (pp. 1471–1477). New York: Raven Press; Sunderland, T., Lawlor, B. A., Martinez, R. A., & Molchan, S. E. (1991). Anxiety in the elderly: Neurobiological and clinical interface. In Salzman, C., & Lebowitz, B. (Eds.), *Anxiety in the elderly: Treatment and research* (pp. 105–129). New York: Springer.

74. George, L. K., Blazer, D. G., Winfield-Laird, I., Leaf, P. J., & Fischbach, R. L. (1988). Psychiatric disorders and mental health service use in later life: Evidence from the epidemiologic catchment area program. In Brody, J. A., & Maddox, G. L. (Eds.). *Epidemiology and aging: An international perspective* (pp. 189–219). New York: Springer.

75. Alexopoulos, G. S., Meyers, B. S., Young, R. C., Chester, J., Feder, M., & Einhorn, A. (1995). Anxiety in geriatric depression: Effects of age and cognitive impairment. *American Journal of Geriartics Psychiatry, 3,* 108–118.

76. Gershanik, O. S. (1994). Drug-induced Parkinsonism in the aged: Recognition and prevention. *Drugs Aging, 5*(2), 127–132; Hunter, R. C. A., & Cleghorn, R. A. (1982). Psychosomatic disorders in the elderly. *Canadian Journal of Psychiatry, 27,* 362–365.

77. Ghadirian, A. M., Gauthier, S., & Bertrand, S. (1986). Anxiety attacks in a patient with a right temporal lobe meningioma. *Journal of Clinical Psychiatry, 47,* 270–271.

78. This idea is of a standard Biblical conception. The elderly King David, for example, was advised to "lay" with young girls.

79. American Psychiatric Association. (1994). *DSM-IV diagnostic and statistical manual of mental disorders.* Fourth Edition. Washington, DC: American Psychiatric Association.

80. Occasionally a *folie à deux* (as defined earlier on page 106) may result, involving the older person and someone close to him or her. One kind of "eccentricity" is observed when a mother and daughter, two brothers, or two sisters become recluses, living in a house that ages as they do—or, more precisely, deteriorates. It is usually the health department that becomes alerted for purposes of cleanup or eviction. Electricity may be off, plumbing and toilets may not function, there may have been small fires, human feces may be found on the bathroom floor, cat litter may be evident, window screens may be rusting, the house may need painting and repairs, the garden may be overgrown.

81. Notes on the history and evolution of the DSM's are included in Chapter 6, p. 152, note 3.

## CHAPTER 6

COGNITIVE DISORDERS

DELIRIUM, DEMENTIA, AND OTHER
COGNITIVE DISORDERS
CHANGES IN NOMENCLATURE
DELIRIUM

DEMENTIA
POSSIBLE REVERSIBLE CAUSES
OF COGNITIVE IMPAIRMENT
SUMMARY

Once neglected by American medicine, the dementias and other cognitive disorders are now one of the most intensely studied syndromes in all of medicine. Perhaps because of the epidemiologic imperative, researchers and clinicians alike are turning their attention to the cognitive disorders of the elderly, and the pace of scientific advance is frenetic. While no cures are yet available, the first FDA-approved medication for the specific treatment of Alzheimer's disease is now available, and many more pharmacotherapies are in the "pipeline" of drug development. The field is moving ahead furiously, with both clinical and basic science advances shedding light on a previously quiescent corner of medicine and psychiatry.

DELIRIUM, DEMENTIA, AND OTHER COGNITIVE DISORDERS

It is estimated that up to five million Americans suffer from some form of cognitive decline.[1] The most common causes of cognitive impairment are dementia and delirium with specific amnestic syndromes and other cognitive disorders far less prevalent (see Table 6.1). While each of these conditions can present with memory failure, they often manifest themselves with different presentations and usually reflect divergent underlying pathologies. As a result, recognizing and under-

standing the differences between these cognitive conditions is vitally important in the clinical classification and care of patients.

Delirium is characterized by a potentially reversible alteration in one's state of consciousness accompanied by a change in cognition. Although most diagnosticians associate delirium with a typically rapid (over hours) change in consciousness, this is not always the case. In the elderly, chronic medication side effects may slowly (over days) lead to a subacute delirium sometimes referred to as a confusional state. Behavioral disturbances are commonly associated with delirium as well, but they generally recede when the underlying metabolic disturbance is reversed.

Dementia, on the other hand, is generally a slowly progressive and irreversible condition best characterized by multiple cognitive impairments

TABLE 6.1 Four classes of cognitive disorders outlined in the American Psychiatric Association's Diagnostic and Statistical Manual, IVth edition[2]

1. Dementia
2. Delirium
3. Amnestic Disorder
4. Cognitive Disorder Not Otherwise Specified

including memory difficulties. The underlying organic pathology with dementia is presumably localized or widespread permanent brain damage. In contrast to delirium, the etiology of dementia is not readily detectable, and the diagnosis is therefore commonly one of exclusion after an extensive evaluation.

Amnestic disorders are quite rare and are defined as isolated memory conditions without other cognitive impairments. Patients may have selective or broad new learning deficits or free recall difficulties in the absence of changes in consciousness or progressive dementia. In other words, amnestic disorders are not diagnosed in conjunction with delirium or dementia. However, there may be broad behavioral and vocational complications associated with the memory deficits, as the amnestic disorder may be quite disruptive of normal functioning.

Dementia, delirium, and amnestic syndromes can occur at any age in the life cycle, but they are far more common at both ends of the age spectrum and are most prevalent in the elderly. The course of illness depends on the underlying cause and may be quite variable, even within the same diagnostic category. While "acuteness" was in the past associated with "reversibility," and "chronic" was synonymous with "irreversibility," such pairing of concepts has not been demonstrated to be clinically accurate.

The prognosis of specific memory disorders is largely dependent on the underlying etiology. For instance, intoxication and withdrawal reactions are usually directly related to the offending agents and are generally of limited duration if properly managed. On the other hand, any disorder causing structural damage in the brain itself (i.e., vascular dementia) is likely to cause permanent impairment. But even when damage is permanent, many of the emotional and physical symptoms can be treated, resulting in support and actual improvement of functioning.

Psychological or behavioral changes frequently accompany the organic mental syndromes in the older person. These changes may include the onset of paranoia, decreased control over sexual or aggressive impulses, shifts in personality traits, or other emotional disturbances such as increased irritability, mood lability, social withdrawal, apathy, and overt depression. It is often difficult to determine whether these changes are caused by direct damage to the brain or by the person's emotional reaction to cognitive and other psychological changes secondary to the brain disorder. A course of treatment, both physical and psychological, often helps to clarify the diagnosis, although diagnostic "fine tuning" in this area may be impossible with our present state of knowledge (see Chapter 13 for more details).

CHANGES IN NOMENCLATURE

In the ever-evolving world of diagnostic nomenclature, perhaps the best approach to the complex subject of organic mental disorders would be a brief historical review of the classification systems. Before the twentieth century, the organic brain disorders of late life were grouped together in a category known as *organic senile dementia.* But at the turn of the century, neuropathologists examining the brain in autopsies began separating arteriosclerotic conditions from senile dementia, and both of these from neurosyphilis. Kraepelin, in emphasizing clinical description and symptomatology, described five signs of an organic brain disorder: (1) simple dementia, (2) delirium, (3) paranoid states, (4) depressed and agitated types, and (5) presbyophrenic types; but these subdivisions did not differentiate between the mental conditions themselves and the affective reactions to, and in connection with, such mental changes. In the 1950s, Roth devised a more sophisticated classification by dividing all the disorders of old age into (1) affective psychoses, (2) senile psychoses, (3) arteriosclerotic psychoses, (4) delirious states, and (5) late paraphrenia.[2] The American Psychiatric Association's *Diagnostic and Statistical Manual of Mental Disorders* (DSM) and its revisions constructed new diagnostic terminology.[3] DSM-I (1952) presented the acute and chronic brain disorders, with qualifying psychotic, neurotic, and behavioral reactions; DSM-II (1968) reversed the emphasis by describing psychotic and nonpsychotic disorders, with a single introductory remark distinguishing acute from chronic conditions. DSM-III (1980) did not divide the "organic mental disorders" into psychotic/nonpsychotic or acute/chronic forms. Instead, the DSM-III classification contained seven descriptive organic brain syndromes[4] and used the concepts of acuteness and chronicity to refer to mode of onset and duration of a disorder rather than reversibility or irreversibility of the disorder.

DSM-IIIR (1987) continued the important differentiation between a syndrome (cause unknown) and disorder (cause is known and an associated medical diagnosis is listed). Six major categories of organic mental syndromes and disorders remained, including (1) delirium and dementia, (2) amnestic syndrome and organic hallucinosis, (3) organic delusional syndrome, (4) organic personality syndrome, (5) intoxication and withdrawal and (6) organic mental syndrome not otherwise specified.

DSM-IV (1994) has come a long way in clarifying the nomenclature. The term "organic mental disorder" (formerly the title of this chapter) is no longer used because it incorrectly implied that the other mental disorders (i.e., mood disorders and schizophrenia) did not have a biologic basis. Rather, DSM-IV establishes four major classes of cognitive disorders (see Table 6.1) and then subdivides them according to underlying etiology. For instance, dementia is broadly defined as a syndrome with multiple cognitive deficits including an impairment in memory; dementia of the Alzheimer type and vascular dementia are therefore considered specific members of this class.

This classification system is meant to help clarify the confusion surrounding the multiple terms used historically to describe demented subjects. Reviewing any older textbook or medical charts, it would be easy to be quickly mired in terms such as "chronic brain syndrome," "organic brain syndrome," "senility," "presenile dementia," or even the more recent "primary degenerative dementia." Many of these terms were used to describe what we now know as dementia of the Alzheimer type, the most prevalent form of dementia in the elderly. For years, the more general terms were used interchangeably without reference to clear diagnostic classifications. In an odd turnabout over recent years, the specific diagnosis of dementia of the Alzheimer type has become much more prominent as researchers, clinicians, and the public turned their attention to the tragedies associated with this illness. As a result, the diagnosis of Alzheimer's disease is often employed more generally even when the underlying cause of the dementia is unknown or, worse yet, directly related to some other cause of dementia such as cerebrovascular disease. According to the DSM-IV classification, the general term should simply be "dementia" with specific diagnosis of dementia of the Alzheimer type as the most common subclassification.

DELIRIUM

Delirium is a fluctuating clinical state characterized by disturbances of attention, cognition, arousal, mood, and self-awareness. Delirium usually develops over a short period of time, but it can develop more insidiously, particularly when superimposed on a preexistent chronic intellectual impairment. However, since "acute brain syndrome" has been a traditional term for delirium, some clarification is warranted. "Acute" carries with it the notion of rapid onset, dramatic symptoms, and short duration—none of which is reliably present in the delirium of older people. Delirium may evolve slowly, especially if it results from systemic illness or metabolic imbalance. The term "reversible" is perhaps a more useful description; reversibility of the clinical course, even if not the cause of the brain pathology, remains the one consistent characteristic, especially if the diagnosis and treatment are applied promptly and accurately. Left untreated, however, most patients with delirium have a poor prognosis, including premature death, prolonged hospitalization, and extended symptom duration.

TABLE 6.2   Different classifications of delirium in the elderly*

1. Delirium due to general medical conditions
2. Delirium due to substance abuse
3. Delirium due to substance withdrawal
4. Delirium due to multiple etiologies
5. Delirium not otherwise specified

*See International Classification of Diseases, 10th Revision, Clinical Modification (ICD-10-CM) in the appendix for a listing of specific conditions and their associated codes.

Delirium in its more subtle forms remains a frequently undiagnosed illness. In hospitalized medical patients, it is estimated that up to 30% of the elderly show evidence of delirium. Given that the elderly may already be receiving multiple medications or have underlying cognitive changes, they are particularly prone to delirium, especially considering the added stress of hospitalization.[5]

Symptoms of Delirium

Two of the most prominent signs of delirium are the impairments in attention and disorientation. Evidence of distracted, slowed, and disorganized thinking is usually obvious, and cognitive status should be monitored carefully.[6] There is generally a fluctuating level of awareness, which may vary from mild confusion all the way to stupor or active delirium. Hallucinations may be present, particularly of the visual rather than auditory type. The person typically is disoriented or mistaking one person for another; other intellectual functions can also be impaired. Speech may be incoherent and confusion regarding day-to-day procedures or individual roles is common. Remote as well as recent memory is markedly impaired. Behaviorally, restlessness, a dazed expression, or aggressiveness may be present, and the person can appear frightened either by the disorientation or as a result of the vivid visual hallucinations. Delusions of persecution may be present. A predominant feature of delirium is disturbance of the sleep-wake cycle. Anxiety and lack of cooperativeness are other symptoms. Disturbances tend to fluctuate unpredictably in the course of a day, but the impairments are often most severe at night. There may be occasional lucid intervals. (See Table 6.3.)

While neurologic signs are inconsistent, the EEG often reveals a generalized slowing of background activity or an increase in fast activity. Signs of heightened autonomic activity (i.e., tachycardia, sweating, flushed face, dilated pupils, and elevated blood pressure) are frequent, depending on the underlying etiology of the delirium. If an infection is the suspected cause of delirium, then an examination of the cerebrospinal fluid is required to determine the underlying infectious agent. Drug screens may be helpful if the suspected cause is an exogenously administered agent.

Causes of Delirium

There are a myriad of possible causes of delirium. Most organic causes of delirium can be classified

TABLE 6.3   Contrasting clinical presentations of delirium and dementia

DELIRIUM	DEMENTIA
Rapid onset	Usually insidious onset
Marked attentional disturbance	Memory systems impaired
Confusion prominent	Consciousness intact
Fluctuating clinical course	Slower, progressive course
Agitation & behavioral symptoms	Subtle behavioral symptoms
Potentially reversible	Usually irreversible

as *metabolic, structural,* or *infectious* disturbances. For the proper diagnosis, obtaining a detailed history from an observer (family, friend,
acquaintance) is essential, since the patient is unlikely to be able to supply it. Onset of the illness
should be documented, with an account of preexistent disorders. Exposure to toxic substances
should be carefully checked. Some of the most
common causes include acute strokes or transient
ischemic attacks, drug intoxication or withdrawal,
exacerbations of a underlying medical illness, and
postoperative stress. It should be noted, however,
that nonorganic ("functional") causes of delirium
such as psychotic depression, mania, and schizophrenia must also be considered. These functional
causes of delirium are usually preceded by a history of psychiatric disturbances. (See Chapter 9
for a staged approach to the diagnosis of these conditions and a comprehensive tabulation of causes.)

Course of Illness and Treatment of Delirium

Delirium has a relatively brief duration, usually
less than a week. One consequence of failure to
identify and treat delirium is death from the underlying and undiagnosed cause; another is that
the disorder may shift to a more stable dementia,
and the older person then becomes a chronic patient, often in a long-term institutional care facility or nursing home. Currently, even with proper
diagnosis and treatment, a high immediate death
rate during delirium is common (an estimated
40% die, either from exhaustion or from accompanying physical illness); but of those who survive the immediate crisis, a fast recovery and
discharge from the hospital are also common. The
person who survives the crisis has a good chance
of returning to the community. It appears that
much delirium can result in complete recovery, although little follow-up work has been done on
older recovered patients to determine whether
their health is maintained. Other causes of delirium are only partially reversible, especially when
there is an underlying chronic disorder.

The specific treatment for delirium is always
dictated by the proper identification of the underlying etiology. When the diagnosis is rapidly established and managed appropriately, many of the
symptoms of delirium are reversible, especially
with respect to the infections, drug withdrawal, or
iatrogenic causes. Nonetheless, several general
principles for the treatment of delirious patients
apply. First, under the guidance of a physician or
trained nurse, a *carefully-controlled environment*
should be maintained to ensure a physically secure surrounding as much as possible. The physical restlessness, disorientation, or hallucinations
of a delirious patient can lead to agitated wandering and precipitate a needless fall, seriously exacerbating the already complicated situation. A
good rule of thumb is to *simplify the environment*
to moderate the stimuli as much as possible. The
use of bed rails when available, reduced noise levels, soft lighting, night lights, limited visiting
hours, and consistent caregivers are all helpful
suggestions. Second, *brief but continued reassur-
ances* can be important to the patient, especially
in the brief periods of near-lucidity that punctuate
the fluctuating course of the disorder. The acute
medical setting can be very upsetting, even to the
intellectually intact patient, so frequent explanations to patient and family are essential when
dealing with a delirious patient. Third, the *nutritional and fluid status* of the patient should be rig-
orously observed. Because delirious patients often
ignore their own needs and have often failed to do
so for several days, metabolic imbalances may
further complicate the clinical picture, even if they
are not directly involved in the underlying pathology. With the superimposed agitation and confusion, it is easy to overlook the basics, but they are
particularly important in the elderly delirious patient. Finally, while drugs are often the underlying
cause of delirium and should generally be avoided
if at all possible some behaviors, such as physical
agitation, hallucinations, severe anxiety, or profound insomnia, do require pharmacologic intervention. When psychiatric medications are
contemplated, those with the least anticholinergic
properties are recommended. As always in the elderly, the lowest possible dose should be employed for the shortest possible time. Doses of

haloperidol as low as 0.25 mg/day can be of help in managing delirium in the elderly (see Chapter 13 for general guidelines regarding the use of psychiatric medications).

DEMENTIA

General Observations

It is estimated that between 2 and 5% of the population over the age of 65 has some form of dementia. The incidence of dementia is strongly associated with age, so the estimates go up markedly as the age group gets older. For instance, as many as 10% of 75-year-olds may have evidence of dementia and the figure goes to 20% for those over 85.[7] Dementia of the Alzheimer type is by far the most common, but the diagnosis is uncertain clinically and remains one of exclusion. Other causes, though less frequent, are plentiful (see Table 6.4) and must be considered carefully in any initial diagnostic evaluation, especially since some of the causes are associated with potentially meaningful treatments.

Symptoms of Dementia

The hallmark of any dementia is the abnormality of short and long-term memory. There can also be associated changes in judgment, intellectual abilities, activities of daily living, and in some cases,

personality. The onset and course of dementia depends on the underlying cause and varies considerably from one cause to the next. Whereas dementia is usually considered to be irreversible, it is important to point out that as used in the DSM-IV, "dementia" is a descriptive term which is based on a series of clinical symptoms (see Table 6.5). A specific dementia may be irreversible and progressive, stable, or partly reversible depending on the cause and resultant treatment.

Memory.   Memory changes are one of the most obvious and noticeable symptoms of dementia, since memory so intimately affects interpersonal relationships with family and friends. Everyone has seen the older person whose memory for past events is clear although he or she is unable to remember who came to visit today or what happened in the news yesterday. Dementia represents a more profound and pervasive loss of memory. It is a common notion that recent memory is more vulnerable to the deteriorative process in the brain, with memories from the past remaining intact longer. This conjures up a picture of a brain filing system for memory storage, which protects its contents proportionate to the time elapsed since filing. Studies of the brain have not confirmed any such occurrence, nor are there reliable tests for remote memory that enable us to judge how accurate past reminiscences are. A more

TABLE 6.4   Selected causes of non-Alzheimer dementia

STRUCTURAL	METABOLIC	INFECTIOUS
Vascular dementia	Hypothyroidism	Tuberculosis
Parkinson's disease	Hypercalcemia	Creutzfeldt-Jacob
Lewy Body dementia	Chronic ETOH	Viral encephalitis
Pick's disease	Nutritional deficits	Neurosyphilis
Head trauma	Pernicious anemia	HIV-related dementia
Cerebellar degeneration	Folic acid deficiency	Gerstmann-Straussler
Korsakoff's dementia	Hepatic encephalopathy	
Brain tumor	Uremic encephalopathy	
Huntington's chorea	Bromide intoxication	
PSP, ALS, NPH	Respiratory encephalopathy	

TABLE 6.5   Five common signs in dementia

1. **Impairment of memory.**   This is an essential feature of dementia and may involve the initial registration of stimuli in the mind, the retention of the memory that was registered or the ability to recall the memory voluntarily.
2. **Multiple disturbances of cognition.**   Dementia involves more than just memory problems. Other cognitive functions impaired may include comprehension, language skills, calculation, general fund of information and the ability to learn.
3. **Impairment of executive function.**   Comprehension and the ability to think abstractly and formulate decisions and actions must be checked. Inappropriate choices may be defended vehemently, and memory problems in general may be denied entirely.
4. **Disorientation.**   Orientation for time, place, and person depend on the capacities for attention, perception and memory. Time is often the first sphere to be impaired, place is next, and the identities of others and of oneself are usually the last sphere to be affected.
5. **Behavioral changes.**   Excessive emotional responses, blunting of feeling and response, and shallowness and inappropriate affect can be demonstrated. Emotional symptoms may be prominent throughout or variable during the course of the illness.

---

relevant explanation for recent memory loss is the postulation that brain damage interferes with registration of incoming stimuli and affects the ability for retention and recall. In this event, an experience that ordinarily would become a memory registers either inaccurately or not at all.

Attentional Deficits

I feel very often that Henry is simply not receiving new knowledge, that he does not retain the facts and experiences he does receive, that he is not registering visual experience. . . . On a recent trip he tried to follow the instructions of tour guides ("on your left you see . . . ,") but would look straight ahead or turn to the left long after the scene had passed.

An added factor in memory loss is the possibility of emotional influence on recall capacities. Older people may need to deny, to disremember, or to distort that which is overwhelming or too painful to face; depression and preoccupation with problems may not be noticed yet can interfere with learning and memory.

Anxiety and Denial

Judge G has been experiencing slow, progressive, organic changes but is only slightly aware of them.

He cannot face up to the degree and the implications of what is happening to him. He seems to live in a state of constant fear, inadequate to even small demands on him, forgetting everything, missing trains, and becoming confused about schedules or well-rehearsed plans. I am never sure whether the confirmation of his fears that he will do everything badly is a true mental disability or a self-fulfilling prophecy.

In some cases, the deficits are not obvious, and the clinician must think carefully whether the changes are age-related or due to an underlying dementia.

Normal versus Pathological Memory Changes

Mrs. J, a hearty, good-natured woman of 83, compensated for her waning memory in a variety of ways. She made lists of things to remember, she tied letters to be mailed to the doorknob so she would see them when she went out, and she attached her wallet and keys onto her belt or slip strap. She asked friends to call and remind her of appointments, and she made deliberate efforts to read and talk about the daily newspaper "to keep my brain active."

Is this early Alzheimer's disease or simply a normal variant of aging?

Age-Related Cognitive Decline

V. A. Kral first introduced the term *benign senescent forgetfulness* to describe the "inability of the subject to recall relatively unimportant data and parts of an experience (e.g., a name, a place, or a date). . . ." Since then, this concept has undergone numerous metamorphoses, including "age-associated memory impairment"[8] and most recently "age-related memory decline." The disorder appears to occur equally in males and females and may represent the "normal" decline of physiologic aging. However, whether there is a relationship between this form of memory impairment and eventual dementia is not yet determined. Only time and careful documentation of the progression of memory difficulties will help establish a clinical diagnosis of dementia and distinguish it from the normal memory loss associated with aging.

Disorientation is a more easily and accurately tested symptom. Disorientation about time (the day, the hour, the year) is the first major confusion to occur as a result of dementia. Loss of sense of place (where am I, what is this place, what country am I in?) is likely to follow and, last, the person loses the ability to recognize other people and eventually cannot remember who he or she is. One sees this in individuals who do not recognize themselves in the mirror, do not know their own names or the names of loved ones, and so on.

Disorientation

Six months later, Henry is now disoriented as to date and time. He is frequently confused in new surroundings . . . Last week he shocked several women when he wandered into the ladies' bathroom by mistake in the local shopping mall. He is also having increasing difficulties assisting his wife at the grocery store. Instead of dividing the shopping list in two and going down the aisles separately, he now requests simply to push the cart and accompany his wife while she manages the shopping on her own. When they happen upon friends in the store, Henry smiles politely but rarely initiates a conversation.

People react to threats to their intellectual capacities in highly individualized ways, and this is most true in the beginning phases of decline. A conspicuous feature is often the presence of a successful social facade in which everything looks normal until one begins to examine responses more carefully. Friends and relatives gradually notice small differences in physical, mental, and emotional functioning.

Other areas of higher cortical function are also impaired in dementia including *language, judgment, motor function,* and *attention.* It is worthy of note that the language disorder (*aphasia*) of dementia often differs depending on the underlying pathology. For instance, in vascular dementia, the aphasia most commonly occurs when the stroke involves known speech centers of the brain such as Broca's area. Patients with Alzheimer's disease, on the other hand, rarely display discrete aphasias without evidence of other intellectual impairments. Whereas language difficulties and geographic disorientation may be readily apparent to family and friends early in the course of illness, *errors in judgment* are often more difficult to discern.

Errors in Judgment

Ray C, a 62-year-old engineer, has experienced increasing difficulties at work with the complexities of the turbine engines for which he is responsible. He writes himself complete lists of the details and procedures of his daily routines but tells no one of his difficulties despite the inherent dangers of the job. In addition, Ray has recently been called by his local stock broker. Over the next few months, without any discussions with his wife or family, he drastically changed his formerly conservative investment strategy and traded risky securities, ultimately losing a large portion of his life savings before his increasing dementia was finally diagnosed and his financial matters were taken over by his wife.

While this clinical example may represent a sad extreme of the judgment errors displayed by patients with dementia, it is not all that uncommon.

Behavioral changes can occur at any time during the course of dementia. While drastic alterations in the person's underlying personality are relatively rare, there can be the behavioral manifestations including agitation, anxiety, depression, irritability, sleep disorder, and apathy. These changes can occur suddenly or develop gradually depending on the underlying pathology. In fact, it has been estimated that up to 50% of dementia patients suffer from depression at some point in their illness. Paranoid delusions and hallucinations can also be present. Some researchers report up to 70% of patients with dementia develop symptoms of psychosis within seven years of getting the diagnosis.[9] In some cases, the behavioral symptoms can actually precede the medical diagnosis of dementia.

Depression as Presenting Symptom

Lee M, a 70-year-old housewife, had growing problems in managing her home and has become more withdrawn socially. She would neglect to adequately stock the house with normal amounts of food and spent much of the day sitting alone. Her husband has taken on many of the responsibilities and is worried that his wife is depressed. After a visit to a local psychiatrist, she was started on a trial of antidepressant medication. The first medicine, a highly anticholinergic antidepressant, caused Lee to become severely agitated and confused, so it was discontinued. A subsequent medication indeed helped with the symptoms of social withdrawal and apathy. She was noted to be more active and appeared more alert, but she still had some mild memory difficulties. Over the next few months, Lee's memory difficulties and time disorientation became increasingly obvious and a clinical diagnosis of progressive dementia was soon established.

Physiological correlates of dementia are entirely dependent on the underlying cause of the illness. In the dementia associated with Parkinson's disease, for instance, patients often display various extrapyramidal motor symptoms (signs and symptoms of neurological disturbances) characteristic of the illness, in addition to the intellectual impairments. With vascular dementia, there may be focal neurologic symptoms (in one particular limb or muscle group) consistent with the areas of cerebral damage. Dementia of the Alzheimer's

type, on the other hand, may be diagnosed without evidence of any concurrent physiologic or motor abnormality. As the illness progresses, however, there may be associated sleep disorders, physical restlessness, incontinence, and even seizures on occasion. It is worth noting that opthalmologic problems are often suspected in the mild-to-moderately affected dementia patient because of increasing visuospatial difficulties related to the improper interpretation of visual stimuli by the brain.

Visuospatial Abnormalities

Mr. B is a 62-year-old truck driver who initially complained of trouble reading his maps while on long routes. He recently had become lost several times on a cross-country trip he had made repeatedly without difficulty over the last 10 years. When questioned, he also admitted to having increasing problems reading the morning paper. He said he just could not focus as well as in the past and that his glasses were 10 to 15 years old. On exam, however, his doctor noted that his visual acuity was unchanged. Mr. B later admitted that he was having trouble keeping a proper tally of receipts on the long trips; the "figures just never seemed to come out right anymore."

While it is always wise to investigate physical complaints, especially those with potential treatments, such as hearing and vision problems, these complaints can sometimes be seen as evidence of more generalized cognitive difficulties. For obvious reasons, it is often more acceptable for the patient to recognize a physical problem such as increased visual impairments than to admit to increasing intellectual difficulties and the possibility of an incipient dementia.

Progression of Dementia

Eventually, a leveling effect takes place as impairment increases, and in the final stages—"end-stage dementia"—the effect is one of "look alike" or sameness in response as vital basic capacities drop away. People may become completely mute or inattentive. There is also less immediate individuality of reaction when damage is sudden and massive (as with cerebrovascular accidents) rather than gradual.

When there is a clear progression in the illness over time, the general diagnosis of dementia becomes more apparent. Even so, the exact diagnosis frequently is not known until autopsy verification of the neuropathologic changes which distinguish one dementia from another.

Dementia of the Alzheimer Type

When Alois Alzheimer first described the case of a 51-year-old woman, the incidence of progressive dementia was rare at any age. Over the past century, there has been an astounding change in numbers of patients with the illness that now bears Alzheimer's name. It is currently estimated that 2.5 to 4 million individuals in the United States suffer from Alzheimer's disease. While the name used to describe this illness has frequently changed (i.e., senility, organic brain disease, presenile dementia, primary degenerative dementia, probable Alzheimer's disease and dementia of the Alzheimer type), the disease progression has remained consistent, and the total numbers of people afflicted has climbed steadily as the older population has increased and diagnostic accuracy has improved.

What is perhaps even more disturbing is that given the rapidly aging population in this country combined with the fact that our risk of getting dementia increases by approximately 1% with each year after the age of 65, there may be as many as seven to nine million victims of Alzheimer's disease by the year 2025. (At current costs and routine expenditures for the care of such patients, that would mean an estimated increase in annual expenses in this country from $100 billion to approximately $200 billion over the next several decades.) The disorder occurs more frequently in women that men, probably because of their longer life expectancy. And while accurate figures are not available for all parts of the world, it does appear that the incidence of dementia is similar throughout.

Diagnosis of Dementia of the Alzheimer Type. Since dementia of the Alzheimer type is a diagnosis of exclusion, there are no specific, clinically-acceptable diagnostic markers as of yet. Rather, the clinical diagnosis still relies on satisfying the inclusion criteria of the syndrome and falling outside the diagnostic categories of any other major illness related to cognitive impairment. In practice, dementia of the Alzheimer type makes up the vast majority of dementia cases and even represents the clinical diagnosis in 70% of cases presenting with memory disorder.[10] Even without reliable physiologic or radiologic tools, the clinical tools of medical evaluation and cognitive testing provide clinicians with an enviable rate of 80 to 90% accuracy in making a diagnosis that is later verified by autopsy criteria (see Table 6.6).[11]

Brain Pathology. More than ninety years after the original report of neurofibrillary tangles and senile plaques, such changes remain the characteristic neuropathologic findings of Alzheimer's disease. While clinical diagnostic criteria are becoming increasingly sophisticated, definitive diagnosis always awaits either autopsy or biopsy verification. The plaques and tangles are best visualized with special silver staining techniques and are found throughout the neocortex, especially in the hippocampus, frontal, parietal, and temporal lobes. The plaques are usually composed of a ß-amyloid core surrounded by a collection of dendritic processes, glial cells, and other degenerating cell parts. The neurofibrillary tangles are made up of highly insoluble paired helical filaments and microtubule-associated proteins.[12] Current research is focusing on how the large amyloid precursor protein (APP) is metabolized to create abnormal collections of the smaller ß-amyloid protein and whether the ß-amyloid itself is neurotrophic (promoting growth of brain cells) at low, physiologic concentrations or neurotoxic (causing destruction of brain cells) at higher concentrations. One outgrowth of this research has been an intensive search for measurable levels of ß-amyloid in peripheral tissues such as cerebrospinal fluid (CSF). First characterized by Seubert and

TABLE 6.6 Pathologic diagnoses given to patients diagnosed as having dementia antemortem

PATHOLOGIC DIAGNOSIS	TOTAL	(%)
Alzheimer's disease (AD)	88	45%
AD plus other	29	15%
AD plus cerebrovascular disease	25	13%
Other causes:	23	12%
Lewy Body dementia	13	7%
Cerebrovascular disease	9	5%
AD plus Parkinson's disease	8	4%
Parkinson's disease	1	0%
TOTALS	196	100%

Source: Modified from Victoroff, J., Mack, W. J., Lyness, S. A., and Chui, H. C. (1995, Oct.) Multicenter clinicopathological correlation in dementia. *American Journal of Psychiatry, 152*(10): 1476–1484. Copyright 1995, the American Psychiatric Association. Reprinted by permission.

colleagues,[13] ß-amyloid, specifically the ß-amyloid-42 that is found to predominate the extracellular amyloid plaques in Alzheimer brains, has now been documented to be reduced in the CSF of Alzheimer patients versus controls.[14] Previously, others had shown that the soluble APP, the precursor to ß-amyloid, was also reduced in the CSF of Alzheimer patients.[15] This finding suggests a reduced central clearance of ß-amyloid-42, which may in time support the suggestion that ß-amyloid-42 is preferentially deposited in the brains of subjects with Alzheimer's disease, leading to neuronal toxicity and the brain pathology associated with plaques.

Another known pathologic hallmark of Alzheimer's disease is the presence of abnormal *tau* (a structural protein important in brain cells) in neurofibrillary tangles in the brain. While tau is a constitutitive microtubule protein found in a normal human brain, it is hyperphosphorylated in Alzheimer brains to generate the abnormal paired helical filaments (PHF) that make up neurofibrillary tangles.[16] This so-called *PHF-tau* is known to be hyperphosphorylated at several serine-threonine sites compared to the normal tau molecule, and CSF measures of tau have been shown to be elevated in Alzheimer CSF compared to controls.[17] Interestingly, the phosphorylation of tau

has also been connected to the biologic effects of the ß-amyloid precursor protein, at least in the laboratory, suggesting these two mechanisms of neurotoxicity may be related in the clinical disease.[18] In the meantime, both CSF assays are being developed for potential commercial applications as diagnostic measures in the evaluation of dementia patients.

Genetics of Dementia of the Alzheimer Type. As research groups around the world focus on the etiology and genetics of AD, it is now generally accepted that the inheritance pattern for this disease or family of diseases is complex. Four different chromosomes, each with multiple loci, have been identified that confer inherited susceptibility to dementia of the Alzheimer type. For instance, multiple mutations in the gene for ß-amyloid precursor protein (APP) on chromosome 21 were initially found in a small number of the families with autosomal dominant, early-onset illness. A larger percentage of the early-onset, autosomal dominant families were found to have an inherited abnormality at the AD3 locus of chromosome 14. Subsequent research has revealed two specific gene mutations (S182 and STM2) on chromosomes 4 and 1, respectively, and these genes have now been renamed SP1 and

SP2 to simplify the nomenclature. Finally, the E4 allele of the apolipoprotein E gene (Chromosome 14) has been shown to be associated with a large proportion of late-onset, sporadic cases of Alzheimers's disease.[19]

It has long been suggested that AD is a multifaceted syndrome, and the discovery of four different genetic loci may further support this speculation. At the very least, the inheritance pattern is complicated and may instead represent a myriad of illnesses or susceptibility markers for disease if properly stimulated by as of yet unknown environmental factors. Until the direct connection between inherited abnormal genes and pathophysiology is made, however, the search continues. In the meantime, clinicians will soon have to deal with the question of genetic testing in suspected AD patients or family members at risk for developing the illness. Since the risk conferred by each marker and the time course associated with that factor is currently unknown, genetic counseling is difficult. Prospective studies with at-risk groups are needed to study the time course and likelihood of disease development as well as the interaction of various risk factors; these studies are now ongoing.

Pathology of Dementia of the Alzheimer Type.

The three characteristic pathologic changes in the brains of subjects with AD are *cell loss, extracellular amyloid plaques* and *neurofibrillary tangles.* While each of these findings can be seen in normal brain tissue, it is the extent of devastation in AD brains that leads to the diagnosis and, in turn, the clinical symptoms associated with the illness. As a result, the pathologic criteria for the diagnosis of AD are age-adjusted such that a small number of plaques and tangles are diagnostic for a 45-year-old whereas many more amyloid plaques per high power field are necessary to establish the diagnosis in persons over the age of 75.[20]

The amount of cell loss in the brains of AD patients is quite significant. Up to 40% of brain mass is lost by the time of death in end-stage AD, making the pathologic diagnosis straightforward in a typical case. The cell loss is most often characterized by the decrease in cholinergic cells and their constituent markers such as the enzyme choline acetyl transferase.[21] Specifically, the nucleus basalis of Meynert (a small cholinergic nucleus in the basal forebrain) is usually devastated by the illness.[22] However, it should be pointed out that many other neurotransmitters (e.g., serotonin, norepinephrine and dopamine) and peptides (e.g., somatostatin) are also effected by the pathology of AD.[23] The cholinergic system may be the first, but it is certainly not the only system affected by the neuronal destruction.

On a cellular level, the ß-amyloid protein has been targeted as the most likely source of toxicity in AD, and much research has focused on the biologic function of this peptide and possible mechanism(s) of its neuronal toxicity.[24] Similarly, the function of tau, a basic building block of microtubules, has been intensively examined as it is abnormally phosphorylated in AD brains, leading to the neurofibrillary tangles characteristic of the illness.

Apolipoprotein E is known primarily for its importance in cholesterol transport in the body, but it has also been found to be associated with AD. One of the alleles, APO E4 is found more often in AD patients, while APO E2 may actually confer some protection against the illness. The fact that APO E4 binds strongly to ß-amyloid is now being investigated as a possible link to the pathophysiology of the illness.[25] Clinically, APO E4 has been found to be associated with parietal hypometabolism in cerebral glucose utilization on positron emission tomography (PET) scans both in relatives of AD patients and cognitively normal subjects who are homozygous for the E4 allele.[26] Individuals with mild cognitive impairments who do not meet criteria for dementia are also more likely to have the E4 alleles and subsequently go on to develop AD.[27]

Another suspect in the search for a pathophysiologic explanation of AD is the neuroimmune system. While few would argue a primary role for the neuroimmune system, there is growing evidence of an inflammatory response in AD which may exacerbate the process. Specifically, there are activated microglia and complement proteins in the brains of AD subjects over controls. Furthermore, there is an inverse relationship between treatment with anti-inflammatory therapies and the incidence of AD in various retrospective studies.[28] Perhaps the initiation of an inflammatory response following ß-amyloid-induced neuronal toxicity leads to a prolonged "bystander lysis" cascade and further neuronal destruction.[29]

Many other hypotheses relating to the pathophysiology of AD have been proffered in the past. Some of these theories include aluminum toxicity, slow viruses, accelerated aging and environmental toxins, but none have yet gathered the scientific weight of the aforementioned group of ß-amyloid, hyperphosphorylated tau and the secondary inflammatory response. While many researchers still assume some environmental co-conspirators in the development of AD, none have yet been convincingly elucidated, and exploratory research continues.

Subtypes of Alzheimer's Disease.   As of yet, there are no specific biologic markers by which we can separate Alzheimer's disease into subtypes. Previous attempts to distinguish subgroupings of Alzheimer's patients by age of onset, family history, or clinical symptoms have generally failed to reveal pathologically or biologically distinct entities. Such efforts continue, however, in search of a subtype in the hopes of finding a group of dementia patients more responsive to the available treatments. One recent clinical subclassification involves the presence or absence of behavioral symptoms such as depression.[30]

Lee M, the 70-year-old housewife previously misdiagnosed as having depression, was now appropriately recognized as suffering from "probable Alzheimer's disease." Her husband took over more and more of her household chores as the intellectual deficits increased. In addition, she was less inclined to socialize when friends visited and rarely accompanied her husband on his outings to town. She appeared less interested in her usual activities at home and showed few signs of pleasure, even when her grandchildren visited. During most days, she sat alone on the porch and stared aimlessly at passing

cars. After several months of this behavior, her husband again took her to a local psychiatrist for evaluation. This time, a diagnosis of dementia with secondary depression was made, and several clinical steps were taken to help alleviate her symptoms. First, a structured set of outside-the-home activities was established including regular visits to a local senior citizen facility which specialized in treating elders with cognitive difficulties. Second, a list of simple "chores" was posted for Mrs. M to carry out during the day (e.g. make bed, get paper in the morning, help feed the cat, etc.). These chores were adjusted according to her level of functioning and were maintained with the occasional help of her husband. Third, the local psychiatrist prescribed a low dose of an antidepressant with few anticholinergic side effects. While this combined regimen did not alter the slow progression of Mrs. D's memory impairments, she was more active and clearly took more enjoyment in her surroundings over the next several months.

Clinical Symptoms.   The symptoms of dementia of the Alzheimer's type are much as described earlier for dementia generally (p. 129). It is rare for a family or physician to miss the clinical presentation of Alzheimer's disease once it has reached the moderate stage where daily functions are definitely impaired. In the very early stages patients themselves are often able to "cover up" and even deny their problems without too much difficulty. In fact, the older person may pass from normal old age, with its "age-related memory loss," to dementia with no abrupt changes. (This "slippery slope" explanation is in no way meant to link the onset of dementia with the process of normal aging. Instead, the normal memory changes of aging may sometimes act as camouflage for the prodromal pathological symptoms of Alzheimer's disease, thereby obscuring the diagnosis initially.) Friends, coworkers, and relatives may notice gradual, small differences in physical, emotional, and mental functioning. If the diagnosis is not obvious, it is best to document the deficits with clinical, medical, and neuropsychological testing, if available, so that on follow-up any deterioration can be detected and quantified.

This insidious but progressive deterioration over time is characteristic of Alzheimer's disease. Perhaps as a result of the considerable publicity given to Alzheimer's disease over the last decade, it is not uncommon for cognitively intact older individuals to complain bitterly of Alzheimer-like symptoms, often with much associated anxiety and fear. While some degree of age-related memory impairment probably does exist in a certain percentage of those individuals and should be properly assessed, "Alzheimer phobia" has become an increasing diagnostic problem for many physicians and memory clinics evaluating large groups of patients. In the absence of reliable diagnostic markers, the only course of action with such individuals is careful clinical follow-up with neuropsychologic testing when appropriate.

Course of Illness. People do not die of Alzheimer's disease *per se.* (Note: There is a move within the medical profession to list AD in the death certificate so that future generations will have documentation of the illness. Still, it is rarely the actual cause of death.) Rather, they eventually succumb to other natural causes or to illnesses associated with the decreasing self-care and self-awareness characteristic of late-stage Alzheimer's disease. Thus, they die *with* Alzheimer's disease. The life expectancy of Alzheimer patients depends on two major factors. First, how early is the diagnosis established? With the increased attention surrounding Alzheimer's disease, many more individuals are coming to medical attention sooner than they would have a decade ago; thus, the diagnosis is being made earlier in the course of the illness. Second, the duration of illness in the later stages is very much dependent on the type of medical supervision provided. Because there is usually a lack of self-awareness and proper personal hygiene in these patients, infections are common. Vigilant supervision and treatment of urinary tract infections, skin lesions, poor nutritional intake, and aspiration pneumonias can make a large difference in survival. With earlier diagnosis and careful attention to medical treatment, the life expectancy can be much longer than the four to eight years cited in many textbooks. Definite life expectancies are not known, but a more likely estimate is from 8 to 18 years.[31] How long it takes to progress from one stage of Alzheimer's disease to another (i.e., mild to moderate to severe) is currently under study at multiple research centers.

Treatment of Alzheimer's Disease. When reviewing treatments for dementia of the Alzheimer type, one must consider two separate approaches: research and clinical. While there are some overlaps between the two approaches, there are many differences. Physicians and consumers must be very careful to distinguish between the two, especially as the underlying population is cognitively impaired and therefore vulnerable from the perspective of informed consent.

Research treatments are advancing at a rapid pace. No longer are the treatment options only involving the cholinergic replacement hypothesis. Although currently the only FDA-approved medication for AD is tacrine (Cognex), a cholinesterase inhibitor that augments the naturally occurring acetylcholine that remains in the brains of AD patients, many other medications are now being tested in research clinics around the country. In fact, there are presently over 20 medications in various stages of FDA-approved review, compared to only a handful a few years ago. These research medications range from tacrine-like, which may have fewer side effects, to nicotine-like drugs, specific muscarinic agonists, metabolic enhancers, and agents designed to impede the build-up of ß-amyloid in the brains of AD patients. As this research progresses, several groups are continuing to attempt overlapping treatments to search for synergistic combinations of these individual agents.[32] Furthermore, other therapeutic tactics are being investigated, most notably the anti-inflammatory approach where drugs are being used in an attempt to slow the body's immune response to the neuronal destruction presumably initiated by ß-amyloid toxicity.[33] To stop the neuronal toxicity before it crosses the clinical threshold, agents are also being developed to retard the buildup of ß-amyloid in the brain. This line of therapeutic drug development has been greatly aided by the introduction of a mouse model expressing excessive amyloid precursor protein[34] that opens the way for potential prophylactic drug treatment trials in the future.

The current clinical treatment of Alzheimer's patients is primarily supportive in nature. In the absence of a therapeutic agent that has real promise concerning the slowing or reversal of the cognitive impairments of the illness, the clinician is forced to treat the secondary symptoms. The treatment of associated medical illnesses has already been discussed and can make a difference in the extension of life expectancy. As for the possible "reversibility" of some dementia symptoms, actual treatment is the only reliable way to judge the reversibility of symptoms. We also wish to emphasize that advanced dementia is not necessarily the fixed condition it first appears to be. Orientation, for example, may be improved by providing direct instruction and supplying orientation aids such as lights, signs, colors, and sounds as well as clocks and calendars. Chronicity is often used as an excuse for not doing anything when there may be many treatment techniques that could comfort, support, and even greatly increase the functioning of brain-damaged individuals.

Since behavioral symptoms such as agitation, depression, sleep disorder, paranoia, and apathy are common, pharmacologic treatment with the neuroleptics, antidepressants, benzodiazepines, and other medications can prove of great value. As with all elderly subjects, and especially with Alzheimer patients who appear to be even more sensitive to the anticholinergic effects of these medications, caution must be observed to use these drugs at the lowest dose and for the shortest duration possible.

As for nonpharmacologic interventions, much can be done for the patient by suitably adjusting the environment. Structuring of a medically and socially prosthetic milieu, whether at home or in an institution, is important. Simplification, order, the balancing of care and self-care, moderation of excessive stimuli, the provision of recreational and occupational therapy, and the utilization of objects, personnel, and techniques to preserve orientation are among general procedures of value. Music therapy is a desirable approach because it does not require as much discrete intellectual attention as does drama or reading therapy. Home care services oriented toward patients with AD or other dementias can be excellent when available.

Supportive individual and/or group psychotherapy for the patient and his or her family is often advisable. Psychotherapy is most effective when heavily oriented toward affect, the experiencing of warmth, and enhanced self-esteem. Smiles, hugs, hand-holding, and a warm, supportive manner are communications to which even the most severely demented person may respond. Much repetition and little "new material" distinguish the psychotherapeutic process in treating dementia.

Cognitive therapy approaches have also been attempted with demented individuals in the early stages of their illness with some success.[35] Sensitivity to the level of mental and emotional functioning is crucial. We learned of one older man who refused to be bathed unless he was wearing his cap. A sensitive nurse learned that he was remembering from his past a caution by his mother that he would catch a cold if his head was wet. The nurse wisely let the man wear his cap in the bathtub—a form of security that comforted him in the often frightening world of mental confusion.

Family education and involvement are of great help to the older person with Alzheimer's disease or other dementias. Studies of spouses and other caregivers of AD victims have revealed that the level of depression in the nonaffected family member is also higher than would be expected in the general population. Support groups for these family members have demonstrated that increased awareness and guidance can be of great benefit both to the family members and the care of the dementia patient.

The Alzheimer's Association, founded in 1979 and based in Chicago, is a national federation of chapters from cities and towns across the country. Its goals include (1) public and professional education on dementia, (2) the building of family support groups for families with one or more members suffering from dementia, and (3) the fostering of research on dementia. The local chapters are an immense resource to those families with a loved one suffering from dementia. Chapters in areas throughout the country can be located by calling (800) 272-3900.

Vascular Dementia

Formerly called "multiinfarct dementia," *vascular dementia* is a chronic disorder that often shows an uneven and erratic downward progression, as compared to the more steady decline seen in dementia of the Alzheimer type. The disorder is associated with damage to the cerebral blood vessels through arteriosclerosis (a term that includes both *arteriosclerosis*—a hardening of the vessel wall, and *atherosclerosis*—a narrowing and closing of the vessel itself), but the exact relationship between dementia and cerebrovascular disease is difficult to assess.[36] As a result, the clinical differentiation between vascular dementia and dementia of the Alzheimer type is frequently difficult, especially as each condition is relatively common and can occur independently in the same patient.

Vascular dementia is found in middle and later life because it is a progressive disease that may remain asymptomatic until that point. Age of onset is generally between 50 and 70 years, and it is usually associated with concurrent hypertension. Although less common than Alzheimer's dementia, vascular dementia can account for up to 20% of unselected dementia cases in autopsy surveys.[37] Vascular dementia can be characterized as showing progressive cognitive decline, often with stepwise deterioration associated with new vascular incidents. The intellectual and behavioral functions affected are related to the specific areas of the brain involved in the vascular accidents. Previous attempts to separate Alzheimer's disease and vascular dementia have led to a list of 13 criteria developed by Hachinski and colleagues.[38] Follow-up clinicopathologic study has suggested that eight of the original criteria for the "Ischemic

Score" are valid (see Table 6.7). The presence of four or more of these factors is highly suggestive of vascular dementia.

Brain Pathology. The brain typically shows areas of softening with complete deterioration of cerebral tissue over a circumscribed, limited area. The damaged area may be anemic or hemorrhagic, resulting from the inadequate blood supply caused by blocked vessels. Multiple pockets of brain degeneration or "lacunes" of varying size may be visualized throughout the brain by MRI, with lesions often appearing in both grey and white matter structures, including nuclei and other subcortical areas. While individual lacunes have been described at autopsy in patients without any known cognitive impairment during life, it is believed that the accumulated effect of multiple cortical and subcortical infarcts leads to the clinical presentation of vascular dementia.

Clinical Symptoms. Early symptoms are dizziness, headaches, decreased physical and mental vigor, and vague physical complaints. Onset can be gradual or sudden, with over 50% of cases occurring acutely in the form of a sudden attack of confusion or delirium. Cases with slower onset can look much like senile dementia. There is usually a gradual intellectual loss, and impairment of memory tends to be spotty rather than complete. A person may be unable to remember anything one minute and regain total capacity the next. There may be a certain loss of insight and judgment, again in a spotty sense. Subtypes of the

TABLE 6.7 Summary of Hachinski's Ischemia criteria

1. Abrupt onset
2. Step-wise deterioration
3. Somatic complaints
4. Emotional incontinence
5. History of presence of hypertension
6. History of cerebrovascular accidents
7. Focal neurologic symptoms
8. Focal neurologic signs

illness include dementia with delirium, depression, or uncomplicated. The course is up and down rather than progressively downhill. (Note the "lucid interval" in forensic psychiatry; see Chapter 9.) The person may hallucinate and become delirious, indicating the insufficiency of cerebral circulation. Focal neurological abnormalities are often present, along with *dysarthria* (speech disturbance) and an abnormal gait with short steps. The limbs may be spastic and the reflexes brisk.

Causes of Vascular Dementia. The causes of arteriosclerosis are still unclear, although many explanations have been offered. Lipid dysfunction, heredity, diet (especially cholesterol), smoking, environmental pollution, lack of exercise, and other elements have been held contributory. Hypertension still appears to be the most common risk factor for the development of vascular dementia, and as such, men are reported to develop this condition more than women.[39] The type of vascular dementia can be classified according to the location of the predominant lesions (i.e., basal ganglia, subcortical white matter, or cortical grey matter) and size of the vessels involved in the damaged area (i.e., small, medium, or large arteries).

Course of Illness and Treatment in Vascular Dementia. With dementia due to cerebrovascular disease there is great diversity from person to person, even within the same person at different times, although the onset is often abrupt. An acute cerebrovascular accident causing confusion or clouding of the mental state can lead quickly to a fatal outcome or may produce an organic condition lasting as long as 10 to 15 years. The average survival of those admitted to a mental hospital has been estimated in the past to be three to four years. Vascular dementia is also common amongst those with severe vascular disease. Many die soon after the onset of the dementia symptoms, but those who survive may experience a subsidence of the problem, with varying amounts of intellectual impairment.

Early treatment of hypertension and vascular disease may prevent further progression. However, if new attacks follow, each does additional damage in a classic stepwise temporal pattern. Often the person's physical condition is worse than that seen in dementia of the Alzheimer type because of the neurological or cardiac problem; many are bedridden, at least during acute stages. Death, when it occurs, is usually from cerebrovascular accidents, arteriosclerotic heart disease, or pneumonia.

In treatment there is a greater need for special medical care because of the critical physical involvement in vascular dementia.[40] If and when remission occurs, the person is at greater risk for significant depression that can in some cases respond to pharmacologic treatment.[41] In addition, these patients can often benefit from psychotherapy, physical therapy, recreation, and all the usual therapeutic supports and services. Physical capacities are often a greater problem than intellectual capacities, although intellectual damage can be profound after massive or repeated cardiac attacks or strokes.

Binswanger's disease, another variant of cerebrovascular disease, is a slowly progressing dementia and subcortical demyelination, apparently resulting from arteriosclerosis of small arteries supplying the white matter. Generally, it occurs in persons between the ages of 50 and 65, and evidence of focal cerebral disease is always present. Diagnosis is impossible until autopsy.

Parkinson's Dementia

The exact prevalence of dementia in Parkinson's patients is not known, but estimates vary from 20% to 60%.[42] The dementia is more likely found in older subjects with more advanced motor disease. The cognitive impairments of Parkinson's disease have previously been characterized as evidence of "subcortical dementia" to denote the primary involvement of subcortical brain areas without the significant number of grey matter plaques and tangles usually associated with Alzheimer's disease.[43] The clinical changes most often observed include forgetfulness, a slowing of thought processes, altered personality, and an impaired ability to manipulate acquired knowledge.[44] While the overt motor findings of Parkinson's patients can often clearly differentiate them from the other dementias, the neuropsychological pattern is more confusing.[45] Concurrent medication, especially those with anticholinergic potency, can also pose a threat to clinical differentiation as patients with idiopathic (unknown cause) Parkinson's and Alzheimer's disease have both been shown to be especially sensitive to drug-induced confusion.[46] Furthermore, recent evidence has suggested a great deal of biochemical and neuropathologic overlap between the two conditions, which may help explain the clinical similarities often noted.[47]

The pathophysiology of Parkinson's dementia is unknown, but bilateral atrophy in frontal and temporal lobes is reported along with the characteristic pigmentation loss in the basal ganglia. There are also neurofibrillary changes in the cerebral cortex and brain stem similar to those seen in dementia of the Alzheimer type. While environmental factors may account for some of the Parkinson's syndrome, dementia is more commonly seen in Parkinson's patients without known exposure to exotic toxins. One toxin, MPTP, has been implicated in the neurodegenerative process of Parkinson's disease. Discovered during a series of studies with addicts who had mysteriously developed severe Parkinsonism while still quite young, MPTP has now provided an important animal and human model for the study of this condition and is already generating potential therapeutic candidates such as the neurotrophic gangliosides.[48]

Another line of research has focused on the Parkinsonism-dementia complex of Guam that is particularly common among the Chamorro population of the Mariana islands.[49] Parkinson's disease occurs in males two or three times more frequently than in females and accounts for some 7% of deaths among adult Chamorros. Recent investigation has revealed that the extensive brain damage in these patients may be related to the seed of the neurotoxic plant, Cycus Circinalis, which was a traditional source of food and medi-

cine for the Chamorro people before World War II.[50] The pathologic findings in this condition are similar to those found in dementia of the Alzheimer type; however, senile plaques are not generally present.

Korsakoff's Syndrome

Korsakoff's syndrome is a neurologic disorder distinguished by a profound short term memory failure. Distinct from the acute thiamine deficiency characteristic of the Wernicke-Korsakoff syndrome, the Korsakoff syndrome can develop despite an adequate nutritional intake and is associated with a chronic dementia that is resistant to treatment.[51] The primary offending agent in this syndrome is, of course, alcohol, but the principal presenting symptom is a dense amnesia for recent events. Other areas of cognition, including judgment and the ability to carry out previously learned skills, are generally much less affected by the progressive illness. This pattern of intellectual change and history of marked alcohol abuse usually allows for straightforward clinical differentiation from other major dementia syndromes.

Neuropathologically, Korsakoff's syndrome is associated with small lesions in the brain area surrounding the collections of ventricular fluids. While these changes are quite different from those found in Alzheimer, stroke, and Parkinson's dementia patients, there are some similarities suggested by reports of abnormalities of neurotransmitter metabolites in the cerebrospinal fluid of Korsakoff patients.[52] Progression of the dementia is usually halted by the cessation of drinking, but restorative therapy is currently limited to experimental studies with the various agents designed to augment endogenous neurotransmitter function.[53]

Pick's Disease

Pick's disease is a less common disorder but is clinically very similar to Alzheimer's and differentiation may be impossible until autopsy reveals the distinctive pathologic brain condition. There is usually an earlier onset (in the fourth decade), although it may occur also after age 65. General behavior is most often a lack of initiative rather than the overactivity frequently seen with the Alzheimer patient. Symptomatology includes early selective impairment of mental functioning with the memory reasonably intact except for new material. Focal signs begin to appear at a later stage (aphasia, apraxia, etc.), and eventually, the person sinks into a vegetative existence before death. The Kluver-Bucy syndrome, characterized by emotional blunting, visual agnosias, hypersexuality, and hyperorality (e.g., sucking and smacking of lips with associated food foraging) may be found early in the course of Pick's disease. The cause is unknown, but genetic factors appear relevant. The prognosis is always fatal, with survival from 2 to 15 years. The course of Pick's disease is steadily progressive, and treatment of secondary symptoms is all that can be done presently. Pathologically, the brain shows distinctive "Pick bodies" with a clear-cut and circumscribed rather than global atrophy, concentrating on the anterior portions of the frontal and temporal lobes of the brain.

Normal Pressure Hydrocephalus

Normal pressure hydrocephalus is an uncommon but treatable dementia. First described by Hakim and Adams in the 1960s, it is marked by three major symptoms—dementia, gait difficulty or apraxia, and incontinence of urine.[54] It is associated with gradual enlargement of ventricles while cerebrospinal fluid pressure remains normal. The cause is thought to be an obstruction to the absorption of spinal fluid, and the syndrome may follow a subarachnoid hemorrhage, meningitis, or previous head trauma. There is no evidence of cortical atrophy or of air over the surface of the brain when tested by a computer-assisted tomography of the head. For years, treatment consisted of shunting the cerebrospinal fluid from the ventricular space to the peritoneal space, the atrium of the heart, or the pleural cavity.[55] These surgical techniques are still in practice and retrospective studies indicate that up to 75% of patients improve at some point after the operation.[56] How-

ever, the differential diagnostic criteria for normal pressure hydrocephalus, specific surgical indications, and prognostic indicators for a successful surgical outcome remain unproved and have led some to reexamine the clinical criteria for the surgical therapeutic approach.[57]

Huntington's Disease (HD)

Huntington's disease is a hereditary disease (a single autosomal dominant gene on the short arm of chromosome 4) that usually begins in middle age but can occur in children and octogenarians. It progresses inexorably to death some 10 to 20 years following inception. Early clumsiness becomes the incessant, uncontrollable, twisting, choreiform movements associated with progressive dementia and behavioral problems.[58] The cognitive impairments of Huntington's disease are characterized by a loss of finely detailed memories as well as decreased skills in organizing and sequencing higher cortical functions and are usually distinguishable from the abnormalities seen in dementia of the Alzheimer type. Interestingly, the average performances on generalized intelligence testing does not show profound change in the early stages of Huntington's disease.[59] Biochemically, increases in dopamine activity and brain levels of various neuropeptides have been reported compared to normal controls and other psychiatric populations.[60] Neuropathologically, Huntington's disease is associated with a loss of small neurons in the striatum (a motor control center) of the brain as well as severe atrophy ("shrinkage") and gliosis (scar tissue in the brain) resulting in ventricular enlargement in the area of the caudate (another motor control center). There have been occasional reports of the coexistence of Alzheimer's disease and Huntington's disease in individual patients, but this phenomenon is considered very rare.[61]

While genetic techniques may allow us to diagnose Huntington's disease long before the clinical symptoms become apparent, even before birth, there currently is no therapeutic agent available that has proven effective in the treatment of the underlying cause of this disorder. Because of the profound psychological impact of early diagnostic markers, it is recommended that genetic counseling be performed at centers with experience with Huntington's disease patients and their families.

Creutzfeldt-Jakob Disease (CJD)

Creutzfeldt-Jakob disease is a rare progressive neurological and dementing disorder (also called *spongiform encephalopathy*) caused by "slow viruses" or prions. It is estimated that 200 Americans die annually of CJD; internationally, there is one death from CJD per million people annually. The syndrome commonly begins in the fifth or sixth decade of life. The dementia and general decline associated with CJD is usually more rapidly progressive than that of Alzheimer's disease, and death may occur within 9 to 12 months. Myoclonus, seizures, motor findings, and gross EEG abnormalities frequently develop along with a rapidly progressive dementia. Behavioral syndromes, including anxiety, mood changes, sleep disorder, fatigue and difficulty concentrating, can precede the onset of dementia. Diagnosis is usually made on the basis of the rapid clinical course but is only confirmed by pathologic findings at biopsy or autopsy.

Dementia Associated with Down Syndrome

Down syndrome is the most prevalent cause of mental retardation, accounting for 10 to 20% of all patients. Because of the increased mortality associated with Down Syndrome and other forms of mental retardation, the percentage of older retarded persons is low compared to the population at large. While diagnostic differentiation between dementia of the Alzheimer's type and the dementia of Down syndrome would never present a clinical dilemma, the clinical overlap between these two syndromes includes the occurrence of seizures or electroencephalographic changes, focal neurologic signs, and personality changes in many but not all Down syndrome patients over the age of 30 years. Anatomically, there are also pathologic similarities between the plaques and neurofibrillary tangles of Alzheimer's disease and Down syndrome documented for over 50 years.[62] Researchers have also demonstrated a decrease in cholinergic cells in the nucleus basalis of Meynert like that associated with Alzheimer's disease.[63] The fact that chromosome 21 is duplicated in 96% of cases with Down syndrome and is also the site of amyloid precursor protein mutations in at least some of the familial Alzheimer's disease (FAD) pedigrees makes this line of comparative research particularly interesting.[64]

POSSIBLE REVERSIBLE CAUSES OF COGNITIVE IMPAIRMENT

Because reversibility may be possible in both dementia and delirium, we have organized a list of some of the most prevalent reversible causes of these two mental impairments. (See Chapter 9 for a more comprehensive list of reversible disorders leading to delirium and dementia or both.)

Pseudodementia

The dementia associated with depression, especially depression in the elderly, is perhaps the most important of all the reversible dementias. Since antidepressant medications are currently available for this condition (see Chapter 13 for details), careful diagnostic differentiation and pharmacologic treatment is essential; yet, surveys of general dementia clinics consistently reveal a large percentage of depressed patients misdiagnosed as demented. Part of this diagnostic dilemma can be explained by the high degree of clinical overlap between these two conditions. Twenty to 50% of Alzheimer patients will, at some point in the illness, demonstrate symptoms of depression, such as social withdrawal, guilt feelings, somatic complaints, crying, weight loss, and insomnia.

Hypoxia

Congestive heart failure refers to decompensation resulting from the heart's declining capacity to pump blood. Thus oxygen, sugar, and necessary nutrients are undersupplied to the brain; a conservatively estimated 13% of acute myocardial infarctions come to medical attention primarily as confusional states. Acute myocardial infarctions can also be associated with reversible deliriums as well as postoperative coronary bypass patients. These patients are frequently found to be disoriented or delirious by the staffs of intensive care units but differ significantly from demented patients in that the course of their delirium is normally short-lived and responsive to acute treatment. Pulmonary disease such as Chronic Obstructive Pulmonary Disease (COPD) can also lead to a chronic reduction of oxygen supply to the brain and result in mental deterioration.

Malnutrition and Anemia

A large proportion of the older population of the United States is undernourished, although this is vehemently denied by some medical and lay people. Older people develop reversible brain syndromes associated with avitaminosis, pellagra,[65] and metabolic disorders. Malnourishment in older persons has both social and economic associations. Poverty forces many to go hungry, while social isolation and depression from living alone can result in persons' simply not eating regularly or well enough to maintain proper nutrition. Older people may have problems in getting to stores for shopping, especially when physical infirmities are present. Appetites may decline as a result of depression, anxiety, or illness, and the loss of teeth can interfere with eating solid foods. Therefore, even middle-class and upper-class older persons may be surprisingly malnourished.

Infection

Infection may not provoke the same level of effective bodily protection as in the young (fever, increase in blood white cell count, etc.). With infection comes fatigue and sometimes dehydration, which leave the individual vulnerable to mental confusion. Of particular concern is the acute worsening of demented patients with an oc-

cult (undetected) infection, such as that found with a silent urinary tract infection. While the underlying dementia cannot be reversed even with adequate medical attention, the precipitous decline can often be averted or reversed if the infection is treated.

Drugs and Other Toxic Substances

One of the major clues that Alzheimer's disease was related to the cholinergic system came from drug studies. When the cholinergic blocking agent scopolamine was administered to young volunteers, for instance, a temporary memory impairment was created.[66] More recently, it has been learned that older subjects in general and Alzheimer patients in particular are even more sensitive to the effects of this anticholinergic agent.[67] This discovery takes on clinical significance in light of the fact that many of the therapeutic drugs such as the antidepressant medications have marked anticholinergic properties and potentially strong antimemory effects, suggesting extreme caution when prescribing these drugs in the elderly.

With increasing use of drugs of all kinds in the medical and psychiatric management of older people, drug reactions are a significant cause of reversible disorders.[68] Attempted suicide through use of drugs or toxic materials is another factor. In addition to the above mentioned difficulties with antidepressants, barbiturates, tranquilizers, bromides, thiocyanates, gases, and hormones are not unmixed blessings; for example, both reversible and irreversible organic brain disorders can occur with use of the cortisone series. Tranquilizers may cause damage if prescribed too long; steroids can affect mood, with manic or depressive manifestations. Older people who are undernourished or who have markedly reduced kidney function or arteriosclerosis may show greater negative response to even small amounts of drugs. The pathologic brain conditions resulting from medications ordered by doctors are termed "iatrogenic" disorders, meaning they have resulted paradoxically from medical treatment itself and not from any usual physical dysfunction. Diuretics (such as the thiazides) may lead to dehydration and mental confusion. Levodopa (antiparkinsonian) and indomethacin (antiarthritic) may cause psychotic behavior.

Older people may also have exaggerated drug reactions that do not reach acute confusional proportions; examples are agitation from barbiturates or depression from tranquilizers. Such reactions can increase if the person is not clear about the side effects of various drugs and adds his or her own fears to the clinical picture. Thus tranquilized persons may become extremely depressed if they fear loss of physical powers and are not aware that this is a transitory reaction to a medication. Doctors and medical personnel owe each person an exact description of what to expect from drugs, so unnecessary emotional complications can be avoided.

Head Trauma

For people over age 65, 72% of all deaths from falls and 30% of all pedestrian fatalities are a result of head trauma. Older people are more subject than younger ones to brain injuries in any type of accident, even minor ones. Nonfatal head injuries may leave the older person severely disabled (for example, by the subdural hematomas that occur after falls resulting from weakness, lack of coordination, or alcoholism). Tumor growths (neoplasms) and brain surgery are other traumas that can impair brain functioning. Head trauma can result in delirium followed by an irreversible disorder; for example, a head injury may lead to concussion or coma, traumatic delirium, and then Korsakoff's syndrome with confabulation and fabrication.

Alcohol

Alcoholism is more common in old age than is generally recognized. Alcohol, as a central nervous system depressant, impairs intellectual functioning. Intoxication at any age results in a reversible brain syndrome. Chronic alcoholism can lead to more serious permanent cognitive

changes as described in the section on Korsakoff's syndrome (see page 141). More commonly, alcohol contributes to the clinical picture of dementia by exacerbating an underlying chronic brain syndrome or exaggerating the memory-impairing effects of other medications. Therefore, a thorough history regarding alcohol use is essential when diagnosing any elderly subject with complaints of memory problems.

Other Causes

Diabetic acidosis, liver failure, dehydration, uremia, emphysema, hypothyroidism (myxedema), brain tumors, general surgery, blindfolding during eye surgery, drastic environmental changes, and bereavements are some of the other common causes of reversible delirium or other acute exacerbations of an underlying dementia. Another cause is hypercalcemia caused by metastatic carcinoma of lung or breast, primary hyperparathyroidism, multiple myeloma, or Paget's disease. Nonketotic hyperosmolarity syndrome, in which hyperglycemia and confusion occur without any ketosis, is not an uncommon cause of reversible brain syndrome.[69] Older persons show much the same reactions as younger people to exhaustion, vitamin deficiencies, and general disease—but they are likely to be more vulnerable. In general, studies have reported that elderly patients with any underlying brain damage are more prone to the transient and reversible cognitive disorders caused by concurrent medical, social, or environmental perturbations.[70]

SUMMARY

While dementia of the Alzheimer type is by far the most common form of progressive cognitive decline, it still accounts for only 60% of the autopsy-verified cases of dementia. Many other syndromes must be considered when first evaluating a patient with progressive memory decline. Furthermore, the clinical presentations of Alzheimer and non-Alzheimer patients are sufficiently variable that great care should be taken when diagnosing and treating such patients. As more reliable diagnostic markers, including genetic tests, become available, and the pathologic mechanisms are better elucidated for each of the dementias, rapid progress should follow in the development of therapeutic and prophylactic interventions. In the meantime, many of the associated behavioral symptoms are treatable conditions and should be aggressively managed to preserve the individual's level of functioning for as long as possible (see Chapter 13 for specific medication recommendations).

A glossary of neurological deficits[71] commonly found in demented patients, especially those with vascular dementia, would include the following:

acalculia   Loss of a previously possessed facility with arithmetic calculation.

agnosia   Inability to recognize objects presented by way of one or more sensory modalities that cannot be explained by a defect in elementary sensation or a reduced level of consciousness or alertness.

agraphia   Loss of a previously possessed facility for writing.

anosognosia   The apparent unawareness of or failure to recognize one's own functional defect, for example, hemiplegia, hemianopia.

aphasia   Loss of a previously possessed facility of language comprehension or production that cannot be explained by sensory or motor defects or diffuse cerebral dysfunction.

anomic or *amnestic aphasia*   Loss of the ability to name objects.

Broca's aphasia   Loss of the ability to produce spoken and (usually) written language with comprehension retained.

Wernicke's aphasia   Loss of the ability to comprehend language, coupled with the production of inappropriate language.

apraxia   Loss of a previously possessed ability to perform skilled motor acts that cannot be explained by weakness, abnormal muscle tone, or elementary incoordination.

constructional apraxia   An acquired difficulty in drawing two-dimensional objects or forms or in producing or copying three-dimensional arrangements of forms or shapes.

confabulation   Fabrication of stories in response to questions about situations or events that are not recalled.

dysarthria   Difficulty in speech production as a result of incoordination of speech apparatus.

perseveration   Tendency to emit the same verbal or motor response again and again to varied stimuli.

SELECTED READINGS

Adolfsson, R., Gottfries, C. G., Oreland, L., et al. (1978). Reduced levels of catecholamines in brain and increased activity of MAO in platelets in Alzheimer's Disease. In Katzman, R., Terry, R. D., & Bick, K. L. (Eds), *Aging,* (vol. 17, pp. 447–481). New York: Raven Press.

Adolfsson, R., Gottfries, C. G., Ross, B. E., & Winblad, B. (1979). Changes in the brain catecholamines of patients with dementia of the Alzheimer type. *British Journal of Psychiatry, 135,* 216–223.

Aisen, P. S., & Davis, K. L. (1994). Inflammatory mechanisms in Alzheimer's disease: Implications for therapy. *American Journal of Psychiatry, 151,* 1105–1113.

Albert, M. L. (1978). Subcortical dementia. In Katzman, R., Terry, R. D., & Bick, K. L. (Eds.), *Alzheimer's disease: Senile dementia and related disorders* (pp. 173–180). New York: Raven Press.

American Psychiatric Association. (1994). *DSM-IV diagnostic and statistical manual of mental disorders.* Fourth Edition. Washington, DC: American Psychiatric Association.

Anderson, M. (1986). Normal pressure hydrocephalus. *British Medical Journal, 293,* 837–838.

Arai, H., Terjima, M., Miura, M., Higuchi, S., Muramatsu, T., Seiki, H., Takase, S., Clark, C. M., Lee, V. M. Y., Trojanowski, J. Q., & Sasaki, H. (1995). Tau in cerebrospinal fluid: A potential diagnostic marker in Alzheimer's disease. *Annals of Neurology, 38,* 649–652.

Barclay, L. L., Zemcov, A., Blass, J. P., & Sansone, J. (1985). Survival in Alzheimer's disease and vascular dementias. *Neurology, 35,* 834–840.

Bierer, L. M., Haroutunian, V., Gabriel, S., Knott, P. J., Carlin, L. S., Purohit, D. P., Perl, D. P., Schmeidler, J., Kanof, P., & Davis, K. L. (1995). Neurochemical correlates of dementia severity in Alzheimer's disease: Relative importance of the cholinergic deficits. *Journal of Neurochemistry, 64,* 749–760.

Braekhus, A., Laake, K., & Engedal, K. (1995). A low, "normal" score on the mini-mental state examination predicts development of dementia after three years. *Journal of the American Geriatrics Society, 43,* 656–661.

Breitner, J. C. S., Gau, B. A., Welsh, K. A., Plassman, B. L., McDonald, W. M., Helms, M. J., & Anthony, J. C. (1994). Inverse association of anti-inflammatory treatments and Alzheimer's disease: Initial results of a co-twin control study. *Neurology, 44,* 227–232.

Brown, P., Cathala, F., Sadowsky, D., & Gajdusek, D. C. (1979). Creutzfeldt-Jakob disease in France: II. Clinical characteristics of 124 consecutive verified cases during the decade 1968–1977. *Annals of Neurology, 6,* 430–437.

Cabelos, R., Nordberg, A., Caamano, J., Franco-Maside, A., Fernandez-Novoa, L., Gomez, M. J., Alvarex, X. A., Takeda, M., Prous, J., Nishimura, T., & Winblad, B. (1994). Molecular strategies for the first generations of antidementia drugs (I). Tacrine and related compounds. *Drugs of Today, 30*(4), 295–337.

Caine, E. D., Hunt, R. D., Weingartner, H., & Ebert, M. H. (1978). Huntington's dementia. *Archives of General Psychiatry, 35,* 377–384.

Caine, E. D., & Shoulson, I. (1983). Psychiatric syndromes in Huntington's disease. *American Journal of Psychiatry, 140,* 728–733.

Casanova, M. F., Walker, L. C., Whitehouse, P. J., & Price, D. L. (1985). Abnormalities of the nucleus basalis in Down's syndrome. *Annals of Neurology, 18,* 310–313.

Chapman, J., Bachar, O., Korczyn, A. D., Wertman, E., & Michaelson, D. M. (1988). Antibodies to cholinergic neurons in Alzheimer's disease. *Journal of Neurochemistry, 51,* 479–485.

Chan-Palay, V., & Asan, E. (1989). Alterations in catecholamine neurons of the locus coeruleus in senile dementia of the Alzheimer type and in Parkinson's disease with and without dementia and depression. *The Journal of Comparative Neurology, 287,* 373–392.

Chen, Y. C., Stern, Y., Sano, M., & Mayeux, R. (1991). Cumulative risks of developing extrapyramidal signs, psychosis, or myoclonus in the course of Alzheimer's disease. *Archives of Neurology, 48,* 1141–1143.

Chui, H. C., Mortimer, J. A., Slager, U., Zarow, C., Bondareff, W., & Webster, D. D. (1986). Pathologic correlates of dementia in Parkinson's disease. *Archives of Neurology, 43,* 991–995.

Collins, M. A. (1982). A possible neurochemical mechanism for brain and nerve damage associated with chronic alcoholism. *Trends in Pharmacological Sciences, 3,* 373–375.

Coleman, L. M., Fowler, L. L., & Williams, M. E. (1995). Use of unproven therapies by people with Alzheimer's disease. *Journal of the American Geriatrics Society, 43,* 747–750.

Corder, E. H., Saunders, A. M., Strittmatter, W. J., Schmechel, D. E., Gaskell, P. C., Small, G. W., Roses, A. D., Haines, J. L., & Pericak-Vance, M. A. (1993). Gene dose of apolipoprotein Etype 4 allele and the risk of Alzheimer's disease in late onset families. *Science, 261,* 921–923.

Crook, T. H., & Larrabee, G. J. (1988). Age associated memory impairment: diagnostic criteria and treatment strategies. *Psychopharmacology Bulletin, 24,* 509–514.

Cummings, J., Benson, D. F., & LoVerme, S. (1980). Reversible dementia. *Journal of the American Medical Association, 243,* 2434–2439.

Cummings, J. L., & Benson, F. (1984). Subcortical dementia: Review of an emerging concept. *Archives of Neurology, 41,* 874–879.

Dalton, A. J., & Crapper-McLachlan, D. R. (1986). Clinical expression of Alzheimer's disease in Down's syndrome. *Psychiatric Clinics of North America, 9,* 659–670.

Davies, P., & Mahoney, A. J. (1976). Selective loss of central cholinergic neurons in Alzheimer's disease. *Lancet, 2,* 1403–1405.

DeSmet, Y., Ruberg, M., Serdaru, M., Dubois, B., Lhermitte, F., & Agid, Y. (1982). Confusion, dementia and anticholinergics in Parkinson's disease. *Journal of Neurology, Neurosurgery and Psychiatry, 45,* 1161–1164.

Dikmen, S., Reitan, R. M., & Temkin, N. R. (1983). Neuropsychological recovery in head injury. *Archives of Neurology, 40,* 333–338.

Drachman, D. A., & Leavitt, J. (1974). Human memory and the cholinergic system. *Archives of Neurology, 30,* 113–121.

Dubois, B., Danze, F., Pillor, B., Cusimano, G., Lhermitte, F., & Agid, Y. (1987). Cholinergic-dependent cognitive deficits in Parkinson's disease. *Annals of Neurology, 22,* 26–30.

Eisdorfer, C., & Cohen, D. (1981). Management of the patient and family coping with dementing illness. *The Journal of Family Practice, 12*(5), 831–837.

Farlow, M., Ghetti, B., Benson, M. D., Farrow, J. S., VanNostrand, W. E., & Wagner, S. L. (1992). Low cerebrospinal-fluid concentrations of soluble amyloid ß-protein precursor in hereditary Alzheimer's disease. *Lancet, 340,* 453–454.

Feinberg, T., & Goodman, B. (1984). Affective illness, dementia, and pseudodementia. *Journal of Clinical Psychiatry, 45,* 99–103.

Forstl, H., Levy, R., Burns, A., Luthert, P., & Cairns, N. (1994). Disproportionate loss of noradrenergic and cholinergic neurons as cause of depression in Alzheimer's disease: a hypothesis. *Pharmacopsychiatry, 27,* 11–15.

Games, D., Adams, D., Alessandrini, R., Barbour, R., Berthelette, P., Blackwell, C., Carr, T., Clemens, J., Donaldson, T., Gillespie, F., Guido, T., Hagopian, S., Johnson-Wood, EK., Khan, K., Lee, M., Leibowitz, P., Lieberburg, I., Little, S., Masliah, EE., McConlogue, L., Montoya-Zavala, M., Mucke, L., Paganini, L., Penniman, E., Power, M., Schenk, D., Seubert, P., Snyder, B., Soriano, F., Tan, Hua., Vitale, J., Wadsworth, S., Wolozin, B., & Zhao, J. (1995). Development of neuropathology similar to Alzheimer's disease in transgenic mice overexpressing the 717V-F ß-amyloid precursor protein. *Nature, 373,* 523–528.

Geldmacher, D. S., & Whitehouse, P. J. (1996). Evaluation of dementia. *The New England Journal of Medicine, 335*(5), 330–336.

Goldstein, K. (1942). *Aftereffects of brain injuries in war and their evaluation and treatment.* New York: Grune & Stratton.

Glenner, G. G., & Wong, C. W. (1984). Alzheimer's disease: Initial report of the purification and characterization of a novel cerebrovascular amyloid protein. *Biochemical and Biophysical Research Communications, 120,* 885–890.

Greenberg, S. M., Koo, E. H., Selkoe, D. J., Qiu, W. Q., & Kosik, K. S. (1994). Secreted ß-amyloid precursor protein stimulates mitogen-activated protien kinase and enhances tau phosphorylation. *Proceedings of the National Academy of Sciences of the United States of America, 91,* 7104–7108.

Gusella, J. F., Wexler, N. S., Conneally, P. M., Naylor, S. L., Anderson, M. A., Tanzi, R. E., Watkins, P. C., Ottina, K., Wallace, M. R., Sakaguchi, A. Y., Young, A. B., Shoulson, I., Bonilla, E., & Martin, J. B. (1983). A polymorphic DNA marker genetically linked to Huntington's disease. *Nature, 306,* 234–238.

Hachinski, V. C., Iliff, L. D., Phil, M., Zilhka, E., Du Boulay, G. H., McAllister, V. L., Marshall, J., Russell, R. W. R., & Symon, L. (1975). Cerebral blood flow in dementia. *Archives of Neurology, 32,* 632–637.

Hardy, J. A., Mann, D. M. A., Wester, P., & Winblad, B. (1986). An integrative hypothesis concerning the pathogenesis and progression of Alzheimer's disease. *Neurobiology of Aging, 7,* 489–502.

Heston, L., Mastri, A., Anderson, E., White, J. (1981). Dementia of the Alzheimer type: Clinical genetics, natural history, and associated conditions. *Archives of General Psychiatry, 38,* 1085–1090.

Heyman, A., Wilkinson, W., Hurwitz, B., Schmechel, D., Sigmon, A. H., Weinberg, T., Helms, M. J., & Swift, M. (1983). Alzheimer's disease: Genetic aspects and associated clinical disorders. *Annals of Neurology, 14,* 507–515.

Jacobs, D. M., Sano, M., Dooneief, G., Marder, K., Bell, K. L., & Stern, Y. (1995). Neuropsychological detection and characterization of preclinical Alzheimer's disease. *Neurology, 45,* 957–962.

Jarvik, L. F., & Winograd, C. H. (Eds.), (1988). *Treatments for the Alzheimer patient: the long haul.* New York: Springer.

Jellinger, K. (1976). Neuropathological aspects of dementias resulting from abnormal blood and cerebrospinal fluid dynamics. *Acta Neurologica Belgica, 76,* 83–102.

Judd, B. W., Meyer, J. S., Rogers, R. L., Gandhi, S., Tanahashi, N., Mortel, K. F., & Tawaklna, T. (1986). Cognitive performance correlates with cerebrovascular impairments in multi-infarct dementia. *Journal of the American Geriatrics Society, 34,* 355–360.

Kosik, K. S., Joachim, C. L., & Selkoe, D. J. (1986). Microtubule-associated protein tau is a major antigenic component of paired helical filaments in Alzheimer disease. *Proceedings of the National Academy of Sciences of the United States of America, 83,* 4044–4048.

Leverenz, J., & Sumi, S. M. (1986). Parkinson's disease in patients with Alzheimer's disease. *Archives of Neurology, 43,* 662–664.

Levy, R., & Howard, R. (Eds.). (1995). *Developments of dementia and functional disorders in the elderly.* Stroud, Petersfield, and Hampshire, UK: Wrightson Biomedical.

Lieberman, A., Dziatolowski, M., Kuppersmith, M., Serby, M., Goodgold, A., Korein, J., & Goldstein,

M. (1979). Dementia in Parkinson's disease. *Annals of Neurology, 6,* 355–359.

Lipowski, Z. J. (1983). Transient cognitive disorders (delirium, acute confusional states) in the elderly. *American Journal of Psychiatry* 140, 1426–1436.

Lipsey, J. R., Robinson, R. G., Pearlson, G. D., Rao, K., Price, T. R. (1984). Nortriptyline treatment of post-stroke depression: A double-blind study. *Lancet I,* 297–300.

Liston, E. H., & La Rue, A. (1983). Clinical differentiation of primary degenerative and multi-infarct dementia: A critical review of the evidence. Part II: Pathological studies. *Biological Psychiatry, 18,* 1467–1484.

Manuelidis, E. E., de Figueiredo, J. M., Kim, J. H., Fritch, W. W., & Manuelidis, L. (1988). Transmission studies from blood of Alzheimer disease patients and healthy relatives. *Proceedings of the National Academy of Sciences of the United States of America, 85,* 4898–4901.

Marin, D. B., & Davis, K. L. (1995). Experimental therapeutics. In Bloom, F. E., & Kupfer, D. J. (Eds.), *Psychopharmacology: The fourth generation of progress* (pp. 1417–1426). New York: Raven Press.

Mas, J.-L., Bousser, M.-G., Lacombe, C., & Agar, N. (1985). Hyperlipidemic dementia. *Neurology, 35,* 1385–1387.

Masur, D. M., Sliwinski, M., Lipton, R. B., Blau, A. D., & Crystal, H. A. (1994). Neuropsychological prediction of dementia in the absence of dementia in healthy elderly persons. *Neurology, 44,* 1427–1432.

Matsuo, E. S., Shin, R. W., Billingsley, M. L., deVoorde, A. V., O'Connor, M., Trojanowski, J. Q., & Lee, V. M. Y. (1994). Biopsy-derived adult human brain tau is phosphorylated at many of the same sites as Alzheimer's disease paired helical filament tau. *Neuron, 13,* 989–1002.

McEntee, W. J., Mair, R. G., & Langlais, P. J. (1984). Neurochemical pathology in Korsakoff's psychosis: Implications for other cognitive disorders. *Neurology, 34,* 648–652.

McGeer, P. L., & Rogers, J. (1992). Medical hypothesis: antiinflammatory agents as a therapeutic approach to Alzheimer's disease. *Neurology, 42,* 447–449.

Mohs, R. C. (1995). Neuropsychological assessment of patients with Alzheimer's disease. In Bloom, F. E., & Kupfer, D. J. (Eds.), *Psychopharmacology: The fourth generation of progress* (pp. 1377–1388). New York: Raven Press.

Molchan, S. E., Hill, J. L., Martinez, R. A., Lawlor, B. A., Mellow, A. M., Rubinow, D. R., Bissette, G., Nemeroff, C. B., & Sunderland, T. (1993). CSF Somatostatin in Alzheimer's disease and major depression: Relationship to hypothalamic-pituitary-adrenal axis and clinical measures. *Psychoneuroendocrinology, 18,* 509–519.

Molchan, S. E., Martinez, R. A., Hill, J. L., Weingartner, H. J., Thompson, K., Vitiello, B., & Sunderland, T. (1992). Increased cognitive sensitivity to scopolamine with age and a perspective on the scopolamine model. *Brain Research Reviews, 17,* 215–226.

Mortimer, J. A., Christensen, K. J., & Webster, D. D. (1985). Parkinsonian dementia. In Frederiks, J. A. M. (Ed.), *Handbook of clinical neurology. Vol. 2. Neurobehavioral disorders* (pp. 371–384). Amsterdam: Elsevier Science Publishers.

Mortimer, J. A., French, L. R., Hutton, J. T., & Schuman, L. M. (1985). Head injury as a risk factor for Alzheimer's disease. *Neurology, 35,* 264–267.

Motter, R., Vigo-Pelfrey, C., Kholodenko, D., Barbour, Johnson-Wood, K. Galasko, D., Chang, L., Miller, B., Clarke, C., Green, R., Olson, P. Southwick P., Wolfert, R., Munroe, B., Lieberburg, I., Seubert, P., & Schenk, D. (1995). Reduction of amyloid beta peptide[42] in the CSF of Alzheimer's patients. *Annals of Neurology, 38,* 643–648.

Mulrow, C. D., Feussner, J. R., Williams, B. C., & Vokaty, K. A. (1987). The value of clinical findings in the detection of normal pressure hydrocephalus. *Journal of Gerontology, 42,* 277–279.

Nemeroff, C. B., Youngblood, W. W., Manberg, P. J., Prange, A. J., & Kizer, J. S. (1983). Regional brain concentrations of neuropeptides in Huntington's chorea and schizophrenia. *Science, 221,* 972–975.

Nitsch, R. M., Slack, B. E., Wurtman, R. J., & Growdon, J. H. (1992). Release of Alzheimer amyloid precursor derivatives stimulated by activation of muscarinic acetylcholine receptors. *Science, 258,* 304–307.

Nordberg, A. (1993). Effect of long-term treatment with tacrine (THA) in Alzheimer's disease as visualized by PET. *Acta Neurologica Scandinavica Supplementum, 149,* 62–65.

Oakley, F., Sunderland, T., Hill, J. L., Phillips, S. L., Makehon, R., & Ebner, J. (1991). The daily activities questionnaire: A functional assessment for people with Alzheimer's disease. *Physical & Occupational Therapy in Geriatrics, 10*(2), 67–81.

O'Donnell, V. M., Pitts, W. M., & Fann, W. E. (1986). Noradrenergic and cholinergic agents in Korsakoff's syndrome. *Clinical Neuropharmacology, 9,* 65–70.

Palmer, A. M., Wilcock, G. K., Esiri, M. M., Francis, P. T., & Bowen, D. M. (1987). Monoaminergic innervation of the frontal and temporal lobes in Alzheimer's disease. *Brain Research, 401,* 231–238.

Petersen, R. C., Mokri, B., & Laws, E. R. (1985). Surgical treatment of idiopathic hydrocephalus in elderly patients. *Neurology, 35,* 307–311.

Petersen, R. C., Smith, G. E., Ivnik, R. J., Tangalos, E. G., Schaid, D. J., Thibodeau, S. N., Kokmen, E., Waring, S. C., & Kurland, L. T. (1995). Apolipoprotein E status as a predictor of the development of Alzheimer's disease in memory-impaired individual. *Journal of the American Medical Association, 273,* 1274–1278.

Post, S. J. (1995). *The moral challenge of Alzheimer disease.* Baltimore, MD: Johns Hopkins University Press.

Reding, M. J., Orto, L. A., Winter, S. W., Fortuna, I. M., Di Ponte, P., & McDowell, F. H. (1986). Antidepressant therapy after stroke. *Archives of Neurology, 43,* 763–765.

Reiman, E. M., Caselli, R. J., Lang, S. Y., Chen, K., Bandy, D., Minoshima, S., Thibodeau, S. N., & Osborne, D. (1996). Preclinical evidence of Alzheimer's disease in persons homozygous for the E4 allele for apolopoprotein E. *New England Journal of Medicine, 334,* 752–758.

Reyes, M. G., & Gibbons, S. (1985). Dementia of the Alzheimer's type and Huntington's disease. *Neurology, 35,* 273–277.

Rosen, W. G., Terry, R. D., Fuld, P. A., Katzman, R., & Peck, A. (1980). Pathological verification of ischemic score in differentiation of dementias. *Annals of Neurology, 7,* 486–488.

Sahakian, B. J., & Coull, J. T. (1993). Tetrahydroaminoacridine (THA) in Alzheimer's disease: An assessment of attentional and mnemonic function using CANTAB. *Acta Neurologica Scandinavica, Supplementum 149,* 29–35.

Salmon, D. P., Thal, L. J., Butters, N., & Heindel, W. C. (1990). Longitudinal evaluation of dementia of the Alzheimer type: A comparison of three standardized mental status examinations. *Neurology, 40,* 1225–1230.

Schaie, K. W. (1996). Normal cognitive development in adulthood. In Fillit, H., & Butler, R. N. *Cognitive decline: Strategies for prevention* (pp. 9–21). London: Greenwich Medical Media Limited.

Schlageter, N. L., Carson, R. E., & Rapoport, S. I. (1987). Examination of blood-brain barrier permeability in dementia of the Alzheimer type with [68Ga]EDTA and positron emission tomography. *Journal of Cerebral Blood Flow and Metabolism, 7,* 1–8.

Schneider, J. S., Pope, A., Simpson, K., Taggart, J., Smith, M. G., & DiStefano, L. (1992). Recovery from experimental Parkinsonism in primates with Gm1 ganglioside treatment. *Science, 256,* 843–846.

Schweber, M. (1985). A possible unitary genetic hypothesis for Alzheimer's disease and Down Syndrome. *Annals of the New York Academy of Sciences, 450,* 213–238.

Seubert, P., Vigo-Pelfrey, C., Esch, F., Lee, M., Dovey, H., Davis, D., Sinha, S., Schlossmacher, M., Whaley, J., Swindlehurst, C., McCormack, R., Wolfert, R., Selkoe, D., Leiberburg, I., & Schenk, D. (1992). Isolation and quantification of soluble Alzheimer's ß-peptide from biological fluids. *Nature, 359,* 325–327.

Sherrington, R., Rogaev, E. I., Liang, Y., Rogaeva, E. A., Levesque, G., Ikeda, M., Chi, H., Li, G., Holman, K., Tsuda, T., Mar, L., Foncin, J. F., Bruni, A. C., Montesi, M. P., Sorbi, S., Tainero, I., Pinessi, L., Nee, L., Chumakov, I., Pollen, D., Brookes, A., Sanseau, P., Polinsky, R. J., Wasco, W., DaSilva, H. A. R., Haines, J. L., Pericak-Vance, M. A., Tanzi, R. E., Roses, A. D., Fraser, P. E., Rommens, J. M., & St. George-Hyslop, P. H. (1995). Cloning of gene bearing missense mutations in early-onset familial Alzheimer's disease. *Nature, 375,* 754–760.

Small, G. W., Mazziotta, J. C., Collinis, M. T., Baxter, L. R., Phelps, M. E., Mandekern, M. A., Kaplan, A., La Rue, A., Adamson, C. F., Chang, L., Guze, B. H., Corder, E. H., Saunders, A. M., Haines, J. L., Pericak-Vance, M. A., & Poses, A. D. (1995). Apolipoprotein E type 4 allele and cerebral glucose metabolism in relatives at risk of familial Alzheimer disease. *Journal of the American Medical Association, 273,* 942–947.

Spencer, P. S., Nunn, P. B., Hugon, J., Ludolph, A. C., Ross, S. M., Roy, D. N., & Robertson, R. C. (1987). Guam amyotrophic lateral sclerosis—Parkinsonism—dementia linked to a plant excitant neurotoxin. *Science, 237,* 517–522.

St. George-Hyslop, P. H., Tanzi, R. E., Polinsky, R. J., Neve, R. L., Pollen, D., Drachman, D., Growdon, J., Cupples, L. A., Nee, L., Myers, R. H., O'Sullivan, D., Watkins, P. C., Amos, J. A., Deutsch, C. K., Bodfish, J. W., Kinsbourne, M., Feldman, R. G., Bruni, A., Amaducci, L., Foncin, J.-F., & Gusella,

J. F. (1987). Absence of duplication of chromosome 21 genes in familial and sporadic Alzheimer's disease. *Science, 238,* 664–666.

Stern, M. B., Gur, R. C., Saykin, A. J., & Hurtig, H. I. (1986). Dementia of Parkinson's disease and Alzheimer's disease: Is there a difference. *Journal of the American Geriatrics Society, 34,* 475–478.

Stern, Y., Gurland, B., Tatemichi, T. K., Tang, M. X., Wilder, D., & Mayeux, R. (1994). Influence of education and occupation on the incidence of Alzheimer's disease. *Journal of the American Medical Association, 271,* 1004–1010.

Strittmatter, W. J., Saunders, A. M., Schmechel, D., Pericak-Vance, M., Enghild, J., Salvesen, G. S., & Roses, A. D. (1993). Apolipoprotein E: high-avidity binding to ß-amyloid and increased frequency of type 4 allele in late-onset familial Alzheimer disease. *Proceedings of the National Academy of Sciences of the United States of America, 90,* 1977–1981.

Sunderland, T., Esposito, G., Molchan, S. E., Coppola, R., Jones, D. W., Gorey, J., Little, EJ. T., Bahro, M., & Weinberger, D. R. (1995). Differential cholinergic regulation in Alzheimer's patients compared to controls following chronic blockade with scopolamine: A SPECT study. *Psychopharmacology, 121,* 231–241.

Sunderland, T., Molchan, S., Lawlor, B., Martinez, R., Mellow, A., Martinson, H., Putnam, EK., & LaLonde, F. (1992). A strategy of "combination chemotherapy" in Alzheimer's disease: Rationale and preliminary results with physostigmine plus deprenyl. *International Psychogeriatrics, 4,* 291–309.

Sunderland, T., Molchan, S. E., & Zubenko, G. S. (1995). Biological markers in Alzheimer's disease. In Bloom, F. E., & Kupfer, D. J. (Eds.), *Psychopharmacology: The fourth generation of progress* (pp. 1389–1399). New York: Raven Press.

Sunderland, T., Tariot, P. N., Cohen, R. M., Weingartner, H., Mueller, E. A., & Murphy, D. L. (1987). Anticholinergic sensitivity in patients with dementia of the Alzheimer type and age-matched controls: A dose-response study. *Archives of General Psychiatry, 44,* 418–426.

Tanzi, R. E. (1995). A promising animal model of Alzheimer's disease. *New England Journal of Medicine, 332*(22), 1512–1513.

Teri, L., McCurry, S. M., Edland, S. D., Kukull, W. A., & Larson, E. B. (1995). Cognitive decline in Alzheimer's disease: A longitudinal investigation of risk factors for accelerated decline. *Gerontology: Medical Sciences 1,* M49–M55.

Thal, L. (1988). Dementia: Characteristics of a referral population and factors associated with progression. *Neurology, 38,* 1083–1090.

Thompson, T. L., Filley, C. M., Mitchell, W. D., Culig, K. M., LoVerde, M., & Byyny, R. L. (1990). Lack of efficacy of hydergine in patients with Alzheimer's disease. *New England Journal of Medicine, 323*(7), 445–448.

Van Nostrand, W. E., Wagner, S. L., Shankle, W. R., Farrow, J. S., Dick, M., Rozemuller, J. M., Kuiper, M. A., Wolters, E. C., Zimmerman, J., Cotman, C. W., & Cunningham, D. D. (1992). Decreased levels of soluble amyloid ß-protein precursor in cerebrospinal fluid of live Alzheimer disease patients. *Proceedings of the National Academy of Sciences of the United States of America, 89,* 2551–2555.

Victoroff, J., Mack, W. J., Lyness, S. A. & Chui, H. C. (1995). Multicenter clinicopathological correlations in dementia. *American Journal of Psychiatry, 152,* 1476–1484.

Vigo-Pelfrey, C., Seubert, P., Barbour, R., Blomquist, C., , Lee, M., Lee, D., Coria, F., Chang, L., Miller, B., Lieberburg, I., & Schenk, D. (1995). Elevation in microtubule-associated protein tau in the cerebrospinal fluid of patients with Alzheimer's disease. *Neurology, 45,* 788–792.

Whitehouse, P. J., Price, D. L., Struble, R. G., Clark, A. W., Coyle, J. T., DeLong, M. R. (1982). Alzheimer's disease and senile dementia: loss of neurons in the basal forebrain. *Science 215,* 1237–1239.

Yankner, B. A., & Mesulam, M. M. (1991). ß-amyloid and the pathogenesis of Alzheimer's disease. *New England Journal of Medicine, 325*(26), 1849–1857.

Zubenko, G. S., Moossy, J., & Kopp, U. (1990). Neurochemical correlates of major depression in primary dementia. *Archives of Neurology, 47,* 209–214.

Zubenko, G. S., Moossy, J., Martinez, J., Rao, G., Classen, D., Rosen, J., & Kopp, U. (1991). Neuropathologic and neurochemical correlates of psychosis in primary dementia. *Archives of Neurology, 48,* 619–624.

Zweig, R. M., Ross, C. A., Hedreen, J. C., Steele, C., Cardillo, J. E., Whitehouse, P. J., Folstein, M. F., & Price, D. L. (1988). The neuropathology of aminergic nuclei in Alzheimer's disease. *Annals of Neurology, 24,* 233–242.

ENDNOTES

1. Mohs, R. C. (1995). Neuropsychological assessment of patients with Alzheimer's disease. In Bloom, F. E., & Kupfer, D. J. (Eds.), *Psychopharmacology: The fourth generation of progress* (pp. 1377–1388). New York: Raven Press.

2. Paraphrenia is a diagnosis used by some investigators to apply to paranoid-hallucinative disturbances in late life. Others deny the existence of the late-life schizophrenia implied in this description.

3. We will include here a few words on the evolution of the DSMs since the changes in the five editions have been confusing to many. The American Psychiatric Association adopted an official classification of mental disorders for the United States in 1952, called the Diagnostic and Statistical Manual of Mental Disorders (DSM-I, 1952). The primary concern for this classification was to facilitate communication. The DSM-I represented a series of compromises with a conglomeration of different conceptual approaches to the area of psychopathology. Psychiatry next became concerned with differences in nomenclature across national boundaries. The second edition of the DSM (DSM-II, 1968) was formed in conjunction with the World Health Organization, and the result was intended to form the basis for international communication. Because the two editions of the DSM were designed primarily for communication purposes, their scientific quality left much to be desired. Studies concluded that the reliability of these systems was mediocre. In DSM-III (1980) the emphasis was put on enhancing the scientific value of the new classification, studying it through field trials at approximately 125 different institutions in the United States. Categories within the DSM-III are accompanied by detailed descriptions with explicit diagnostic rules. The DSM-III R was issued in order to incorporate data from new studies that revealed inconsistencies with some diagnostic criteria of DSM-III. DSM-IV was released in 1994 to further clarify the diagnostic nomenclature for clinical diagnoses based on an empirical foundation and to facilitate the communication between clinicians and researchers.

4. The organic brain syndromes are (1) delirium, (2) dementia, (3) amnestic syndrome, (4) organic hallucinosis, (5) organic personality syndrome, (6) organic delusional syndrome, (7) organic affective syndrome.

5. Lipowski, Z. J. (1983). Transient cognitive disorders (delirium, acute confusional states) in the elderly. *American Journal of Psychiatry, 140,* 1426–1436.

6. Christensen, K. J., Bettin, K. M., Jilk, K. M, Weldon, D. T., & Mach, J. R. (1996). Neuropsychological test for monitoring delirium severity in elderly patients. *American Journal of Geriatric Psychiatry, 4,* 69–76.

7. Sunderland, T., Molchan, S. E., & Zubenko, G. S. (1995). Biological markers in Alzheimer's disease. In Bloom, F. E., & Kupfer, D. J. (Eds.), *Psychopharmacology: The fourth generation of progress* (pp. 1389–1399). New York: Raven Press.

8. Crook, T. H., & Larrabee, G. J. (1988). Age associated memory impairment: Diagnostic criteria and treatment strategies. *Psychopharmacology Bulletin, 24,* 509–514.

9. Chen, Y. C., Stern, Y., Sano, M., & Mayeux, R. (1991). Cumulative risks of developing extrapyramidal signs, psychosis, or myoclonus in the course of Alzheimer's disease. *Archives of Neurology, 48,* 1141–1143.

10. Thal, L. (1988). Dementia: characteristics of a referral population and factors associated with progression. *Neurology, 38,* 1083–1090.

11. Victoroff, J., Mack, W. J., Lyness, S. A., & Chui, H. C. (1995). Multicenter clinicopathological correlations in dementia. *American Journal of Psychiatry, 152,* 1476–1484.

12. Kosik, K. S., Joachim, C. L., & Selkoe, D. J. (1986). Microtubule-associated protein tau is a major antigenic component of paired helical filaments in Alzheimer disease. *Proceedings of the National Academy of Sciences of the United States of America, 83,* 4044–4048.

13. Seubert, P., Vigo-Pelfrey, C., Esch, F., Lee, M., Dovey, H., Davis, D., Sinha, S., Schlossmacher, M., Whaley, J., Swindlehurst, C., McCormack, R., Wolfert, R., Selkoe, D., Leiberburg, I., & Schenk, D. (1992). Isolation and quantification of soluble Alzheimer's ß-peptide from biological fluids. *Nature, 359,* 325–327.

14. Motter, R., Vigo-Pelfrey, C., Kholodenko, D., Barbour, Johnson-Wood, K., Galasko, D., Chang, L., Miller, B., Clarke, C., Green, R., Olson, P., Southwick P., Wolfert, R., Munroe, B., Lieberburg, I., Seubert, P., & Schenk, D. (1995). Reduction of amyloid beta peptide[42] in the CSF of Alzheimer's patients. *Annals of Neurology, 38,* 643–648.

15. Van Nostrand, W. E., Wagner, S. L., Shankle, W. R., Farrow, J. S., Dick, M., Rozemuller, J. M.,

Kuiper, M. A., Wolters, E. C., Zimmerman, J., Cotman, C. W., & Cunningham, D. D. (1992). Decreased levels of soluble amyloid ß-protein precursor in cerebrospinal fluid of live Alzheimer disease patients. *Proceedings of the National Academy of Sciences of the United States of America, 89*, 2551–2555.

16. Matsuo, E. S., Shin, R. W., Billingsley, M. L., deVoorde, A. V., O'Connor, M., Trojanowski, J. Q., & Lee, V. M. Y. (1994). Biopsy-derived adult human brain tau is phosphorylated at many of the same sites as Alzheimer's disease paired helical filament tau. *Neuron, 13*, 989–1002.

17. Motter, R., Vigo-Pelfrey, C., Kholodenko, D., Barbour, Johnson-Wood, K. Galasko, D., Chang, L., Miller, B., Clarke, C., Green, R., Olson, P. Southwick P., Wolfert, R., Munroe, B., Lieberburg, I., Seubert, P., & Schenk, D. (1995). Reduction of amyloid beta peptide42 in the CSF of Alzheimer's patients. *Annals of Neurology, 38*, 643–648; Vigo-Pelfrey, C., Seubert, P., Barbour, R., Blomquist, C., Lee, M., Lee, D., Coria, F., Chang, L., Miller, B., Lieberburg, I., & Schenk, D. (1995). Elevation in microtubule-associated protein tau in the cerebrospinal fluid of patients with Alzheimer's disease. *Neurology, 45*, 788–792.

18. Greenberg, S. M., Koo, E. H., Selkoe, D. J., Qiu, W. Q., & Kosik, K. S. (1994). Secreted ß-amyloid precursor protein stimulates mitogen-activated protien kinase and enhances tau phosphorylation. *Proceedings of the National Academy of Sciences of the United States of America, 91*, 7104–7108.

19. Sherrington, R., Rogaev, E. I., Liang, Y., Rogaeva, E. A., Levesque, G., Ikeda, M., Chi, H., Li, G., Holman, K., Tsuda, T., Mar, L., Foncin, J. F., Bruni, A. C., Montesi, M. P., Sorbi, S., Tainero, I., Pinessi, L., Nee, L., Chumakov, I., Pollen, D., Brookes, A., Sanseau, P., Polinsky, R. J., Wasco, W., DaSilva, H. A. R., Haines, J. L., Pericak-Vance, M. A., Tanzi, R. E., Roses, A. D., Fraser, P. E., Rommens, J. M., & St. George-Hyslop, P. H. (1995). Cloning of a gene bearing missense mutations in early-onset familial Alzheimer's disease. *Nature, 375*, 754–760.

20. Mirra S. S., Heyman, A., McKeel, D., Sumi, S. M., Crain, B. J., Brownlee, L. M., Vogel, F. S., Hushes, J. P., van Belle, G., Berg, L. and participating CERAD neuropathologists (1991). The consortium to establish a registry for Alzheimer's Disease (CERAD). Part II. Standardization of the neuropathologic assessment of Alzheimer's disease. *Neurology, 41*, 479–486; McKhann, G., Drachman, D., Folstein, M., Datzman, R., Price, D., & Stadlan, E. M. (1984). Clinical diagnosis of Alzheimer's disease: report of the NINCDS-ADRDA Word Group under the auspices of the Department of Health and Human Services Task Force on Alzheimer's Disease. *Neurology, 34*, 86–101.

21. Davies, P., & Mahoney, A. J. (1976). Selective loss of central cholinergic neurons in Alzheimer's disease. *Lancet, 2*, 1403–1405.

22. Whitehouse, P. J., Price, D. L., Struble, R. G., Clark, A. W., Coyle, J. T., & DeLong, M. R. (1982). Alzheimer's disease and senile dementia: loss of neurons in the basal forebrain. *Science, 215*, 1237–1239.

23. Chan-Palay, V., & Asan, E. (1989). Alterations in catecholamine neurons of the locus coeruleus in senile dementia of the Alzheimer type and in Parkinson's disease with and without dementia and depression. *The Journal of Comparative Neurology, 287*, 373–392; Palmer, A. M., Wilcock, G. K., Esiri, M. M., Francis, P. T., & Bowen, D. M. (1987). Monoaminergic innervation of the frontal and temporal lobes in Alzheimer's disease. *Brain Research, 401*, 231–238; Zubenko, G. S., Moossy, J., Martinez, J., Rao, G., Classen, D., Rosen, J., & Kopp, U. (1991). Neuropathologic and neurochemical correlates of psychosis in primary dementia. *Archives of Neurology, 48*, 619–624; Zweig, R. M., Ross, C. A., Hedreen, J. C., Steele, C., Cardillo, J. E., Whitehouse, P. J., Folstein, M. F., & Price, D. L. (1988). The neuropathology of aminergic nuclei in Alzheimer's disease. *Annuals of Neurology, 24*, 233–242.

24. Yankner, B. A., & Mesulam, M. M. (1991). ß-amyloid and the pathogenesis of Alzheimer's disease. *New England Journal of Medicine, 325*(26), 1849–1857; Tanzi, R. E. (1995). A promising animal model of Alzheimer's disease. *New England Journal of Medicine, 332*(22), 1512–1513; Greenberg, S. M., Koo, E. H., Selkoe, D. J., Qiu, W. Q., Kosik, K. S. (1994). Secreted ß-amyloid precursor protein stimulates mitogen-activated protien kinase and enhances tau phosphorylation. *Proceedings of the National Academy of Sciences of the United States of America, 91*, 7104–7108.

25. Strittmatter, W. J., Saunders, A. M., Schmechel, D., Pericak-Vance, M., Enghild, J., Salvesen, G. S., Roses, A. D. (1993). Apolipoprotein E: high-avidity binding to ß-amyloid and increased frequency of type 4 allele in late-onset familial Alzheimer disease. *Proceedings of the National Academy of Sciences of the United States of America, 90*, 1977–1981; Corder, E. H., Saunders, A. M.,

Strittmatter, W. J., Schmechel, D. E., Gaskell, P. C., Small, G. W., Roses, A. D., Haines, J. L., & Pericak-Vance, M. A. (1993). Gene dose of apolipoprotein Etype 4 allele and the risk of Alzheimer's disease in late onset families. *Science, 261,* 921–923; Petersen, R. C., Smith, G. E., Ivnik, R. J., Tangalos, E. G., Schaid, D. J., Thibodeau, S. N., Kokmen, E., Waring, S. C., & Kurland, L. T. (1995). Apolipoprotein E status as a predictor of the development of Alzheimer's disease in memory-impaired individual. *Journal of the American Medical Association, 273,* 1274–1278.

26. Reiman, E. M., Caselli, R. J., Lang, S. Y., Chen, K., Bandy, D., Minoshima, S., Thibodeau, S. N., & Osborne, D. (1996). Preclinical evidence of Alzheimer's disease in persons homozygous for the E4 allele for apolopoprotein E. *New England Journal of Medicine, 334,* 752–758; Small, G. W., Mazziotta, J. C., Collins, M. T., Baxter, L. R., Phelps, M. E., Mandelkern, M. A., Kaplan, A., LaRue, A., Adamson, C. F., Chang, L., Guze, B. H., Corder, E. H., Saunders, A. M., Haines, J. L., Pericak-Vance, M. A., & Roses, A. D. (1995). Apolipoprotein E type 4 allele and cerebral glucose metabolism in relatives at risk for familial Alzheimer disease. *Journal of the American Medical Association, 273,* 942–947.

27. Petersen, R. C., Smith, G. E., Ivnik, R. J., Tangalos, E. G., Schaid, D. J., Thibodeau, S. N., Kokmen, E., Waring, S. C., & Kurland, L. T. (1995). Apolipoprotein E status as a predictor of the development of Alzheimer's disease in memory-impaired individuals. *Journal of the American Medical Association, 273,* 1274–1278.

28. Breitner, J. C. S., Gau, B. A., Welsh, K. A., Plassman, B. L., McDonald, W. M., Helms, M. J., & Anthony, J. C. (1994). Inverse association of antiinflammatory treatments and Alzheimer's disease: Initial results of a co-twin control study. *Neurology, 44,* 227–232; McGeer, P. L., & Rogers, J. (1992). Medical hypothesis: Antiinflammatory agents as a therapeutic approach to Alzheimer's disease. *Neurology, 42,* 447–449.

29. McGeer, P. L., & Rogers, J. (1992). Medical hypothesis: Antiinflammatory agents as a therapeutic approach to Alzheimer's disease. *Neurology, 42,* 447–449.

30. Feinberg, T., & Goodman, B. (1984). Affective illness, dementia, and pseudodementia. *Journal of Clinical Psychiatry, 45,* 99–103.

31. Barclay, L. L., Zemcov, A., Blass, J. P., & Sansone, J. (1985). Survival in Alzheimer's disease and vascular dementias. *Neurology, 35,* 834–840.

32. Sunderland, T., Molchan, S., Lawlor, B., Martinez, R., Mellow, A., Martinson, H., Putnam, EK., & LaLonde, F. (1992). A strategy of "combination chemotherapy" in Alzheimer's disease: Rationale and preliminary results with physostigmine plus deprenyl. *International Psychogeriatrics, 4,* 291–309; Marin, D. B., & Davis, K. L. (1995). Experimental therapeutics. In Bloom, F. E., & Kupfer, D. J. (Eds.), *Psychopharmacology: The fourth generation of progress* (pp. 1417–1426). New York: Raven Press.

33. McGeer, P. L., & Rogers, J. (1992). Medical hypothesis: Antiinflammatory agents as a therapeutic approach to Alzheimer's disease. *Neurology 42,* 447–449; Aisen, P. S., & Davis, K. L. (1994). Inflammatory mechanisms in Alzheimer's disease: Implications for therapy. *American Journal of Psychiatry, 151,* 1105–1113.

34. Games, D., Adams, D., Alessandrini, R., Barbour, R., Berthelette, P., Blackwell, C., Carr, ET., Clemens, J., Donaldson, T., Gillespie, F., Guido, T., Hagopian, S., Johnson-Wood, EK., Khan, K., Lee, M., Leibowitz, P., Lieberburg, I., Little, S., Masliah, EE., McConlogue, L., Montoya-Zavala, M., Mucke, L., Paganini, L., Penniman, E., Power, M., Schenk, D., Seubert, P., Snyder, B., Soriano, F., Tan, Hua., Vitale, J., Wadsworth, S., Wolozin, B., & Zhao, J. (1995). Development of neuropathology similar to Alzheimer's disease in transgenic mice overexpressing the 717V-F ß-amyloid precursor protein. *Nature, 373,* 523–528; Teri, L., McCurry, S. M., Edland, S. D., Kukull, W. A., & Larson, E. B. (1995). Cognitive decline in Alzheimer's disease: A longitudinal investigation of risk factors for accelerated decline. *Geraotoloty: Medical Sciences, 1,* M49–M55.

35. Teri, L., McCurry, S. M., Edland, S. D., Kukull, W. A., & Larson, E. B. (1995). Cognitive decline in Alzheimer's disease: a longitudinal investigation of risk factors for accelerated decline. *Geraotoloty: Medical Sciences, 1,* M49–M55.

36. Liston, E. H., & La Rue, A. (1983). Clinical differentiation of primary degenerative and multi-infarct dementia: A critical review of the evidence. Part II: Pathological studies. *Biological Psychiatry, 18,* 1467–1484.

37. Judd, B. W., Meyer, J. S., Rogers, R. L., Gandhi, S., Tanahashi, N., Mortel, K. F., & Tawaklna, T. (1986). Cognitive performance correlates with cerebrovascular impairments in multi-infarct dementia. *Journal of the American Geriatrics Society, 34,* 355–360; Jellinger, K. (1976). Neuropathological aspects of dementias resulting from abnormal

blood and cerebrospinal fluid dynamics. *Acta Neurologica Belgica, 76,* 83–102.

38. Hachinski, V. C., Iliff, L. D., Phil, M., Zilhka, E., Du Boulay, G. H., McAllister, V. L., Marshall, J., Russell, R. W. R., & Symon, L. (1975). Cerebral blood flow in dementia. *Archives of Neurology, 32,* 632–637.

39. Judd, B. W., Meyer, J. S., Rogers, R. L., Gandhi, S., Tanahashi, N., Mortel, K. F., & Tawaklna, T. (1986). Cognitive performance correlates with cerebrovascular impairments in multi-infarct dementia. *Journal of the American Geriatrics Society, 34,* 355–360.

40. In an occasional case, surgical treatment (endarterectomy or angioplasty) is indicated in instances
of occlusive disease of the extracranial cerebrovascular supply, particularly in early and incomplete obstructions.

41. Reding, M. J., Orto, L. A., Winter, S. W., Fortuna, I. M., Di Ponte, P., & McDowell, F. H. (1986). Antidepressant therapy after stroke. *Archives of Neurology, 43,* 763–765; and Lipsey, J. R., Robinson, R. G., Pearlson, G. D., Rao, K., & Price, T. R. (1984). Nortriptyline treatment of post-stroke depression: A double-blind study. *Lancet, 1,* 297–300.

42. Lieberman, A., Dziatolowski, M., Kuppersmith, M., Serby, M., Goodgold, A., Korein, J., & Goldstein, M. (1979). Dementia in Parkinson's disease. *Annals of Neurology, 6,* 355–359; Mortimer, J. A., Christensen, K. J., & Webster, D. D. (1985). Parkinsonian dementia. In Frederiks, J. A. M. (Ed.), *Handbook of clinical neurology. Vol. 2. Neurobehavioral disorders* (pp. 371– 384). Amsterdam: Elsevier Science Publishers.

43. Albert, M. L. (1978). Subcortical dementia. In Katzman, R., Terry, R. D., & Bick, K. L. (Eds.), *Alzheimer's disease: Senile dementia and related disorders* (pp. 173–180). New York: Raven Press.

44. Cummings, J. L., & Benson, F. (1984). Subcortical dementia: Review of an emerging concept. *Archives of Neurology, 41,* 874–879.

45. Stern, M. B., Gur, R. C., Saykin, A. J., & Hurtig, H. I. (1986). Dementia of Parkinson's disease and Alzheimer's disease: Is there a difference? *Journal of the American Geriatrics Society, 34,* 475–478.

46. DeSmet, Y., Ruberg, M., Serdaru, M., Dubois, B., Lhermitte, F., & Agid, Y. (1982). Confusion, dementia and anticholinergics in Parkinson's disease. *Journal of Neurology, Neurosurgery and Psychiatry, 45,* 1161–1164; Sunderland, T., Tariot, P. N., Cohen, R. M., Weingartner, H., Mueller, E. A., &

Murphy, D. L. (1987). Anticholinergic sensitivity in patients with dementia of the Alzheimer type and age-matched controls: A dose-response study. *Archives of General Psychiatry, 44,* 418–426.

47. Chui, H. C., Mortimer, J. A., Slager, U., Zarow, C., Bondareff, W., & Webster, D. D. (1986). Pathologic correlates of dementia in Parkinson's disease. *Archives of Neurology, 43,* 991–995; and Leverenz, J., & Sumi, S. M. (1986). Parkinson's disease in patients with Alzheimer's disease. *Archives of Neurology, 43,* 662–664.

48. Schneider, J. S., Pope, A., Simpson, K., Taggart, J., Smith, M. G., & DiStefano, L. (1992). Recovery from experimental Parkinsonism in primates with Gm1 ganglioside treatment. *Science, 256,* 843–846.

49. Hirano, A., Kurland, L. T., Krooth, R. S., & Lassell, S. (1961). Parkinsonism-dementia complex on Guam, II. Pathological features, *Brain, 84,* 662–679.

50. Spencer, P. S., Nunn, P. B., Hugon, J., Ludolph, A. C., Ross, S. M., Roy, D. N., & Robertson, R. C. (1987). Guam amyotrophic lateral sclerosis—Parkinsonism—dementia linked to a plant excitant neurotoxin. *Science, 237,* 517–522.

51. O'Donnell, V. M., Pitts, W. M., & Fann, W. E. (1986). Noradrenergic and cholinergic agents in Korsakoff's syndrome. *Clinical Neuropharmacology, 9,* 65–70.

52. McEntee, W. J., Mair, R. G., & Langlais, P. J. (1984). Neurochemical pathology in Korsakoff's psychosis: Implications for other cognitive disorders. *Neurology, 34,* 648–652.

53. O'Donnell, et. al. (1986).

54. Hakim, S., & Adams, R. D. (1965). The special clinical problem of symptomatic hydrocephalus with normal cerebrospinal fluid pressure: Observations on cerebrospinal fluid hydrodynamics. *Journal of the Neurological Sciences, 2,* 307–327.

55. Adams, R. D., Fisher, C. M., Hakim, S., Ojemann, R. G., & Sweet, W. H. (1965). Symptomatic occult hydrocephalus with "normal" cerebrospinal fluid pressure: a treatable syndrome. *New England Journal of Medicine, 273,* 117–126.

56. Petersen, R. C., Mokri, B., & Laws, E. R. (1985). Surgical treatment of idiopathic hydrocephalus in elderly patients. *Neurology, 35,* 307–311.

57. Anderson, M. (1986). Normal pressure hydrocephalus. *British Medical Journal, 293,* 837–838; Mulrow, C. D., Feussner, J. R., Williams, B. C., & Vokaty, K. A. (1987). The value of clinical findings in the detection of normal pressure hydrocephalus. *Journal of Gerontology, 42,* 277–279.

58. Caine, E. D., & Shoulson, I. (1983). Psychiatric syndromes in Huntington's disease. *American Journal of Psychiatry, 140,* 728–733.

59. Caine, E. D., Hunt, R. D., Weingartner, H., & Ebert, M. H. (1978). Huntington's dementia. *Archives of General Psychiatry, 35,* 377–384.

60. Nemeroff, C. B., Youngblood, W. W., Manberg, P. J., Prange, A. J., & Kizer, J. S. (1983). Regional brain concentrations of neuropeptides in Huntington's chorea and schizophrenia. *Science, 221,* 972–975.

61. Reyes, M. G., & Gibbons, S. (1985). Dementia of the Alzheimer's type and Huntington's disease. *Neurology, 35,* 273–277.

62. Dalton, A. J., & Crapper-McLachlan, D. R. (1986). Clinical expression of Alzheimer's disease in Down's syndrome. *Psychiatric Clinics of North America, 9,* 659–670.

63. Casanova, M. F., Walker, L. C., Whitehouse, P. J., & Price, D. L. (1985). Abnormalities of the nucleus basalis in Down's syndrome. *Annals of Neurology, 18,* 310–313.

64. St. George-Hyslop, et al. (1987).

65. Pellagra is a disease characterized by mental, neurological, cutaneous, mucous membrane, and gastrointestinal symptoms. It is caused by a severe deficiency of niacin (nicotinic acid) or its amide (niacinamide) along with their amino acid precursor, tryptophan. As late as 1945, H. A. Meyersburg reported cases of brain syndrome from pellagra in older people in his work (See Meyersburg, H. A. [1945]. Senile psychosis and pellagra: A report of two cases, *New England Journal of Medicine, 233,* 173–176).

66. Drachman, D. A., & Leavitt, J. (1974). Human memory and the cholinergic system. *Archives of Neurology, 30,* 113–121.

67. Sunderland, T., Tariot, P. N., Cohen, R. M., Weingartner, H., Mueller, E. A., & Murphy, D. L. (1987). Anticholinergic sensitivity in patients with dementia of the Alzheimer type and age-matched controls: A dose-response study. *Archives of General Psychiatry, 44,* 418–426.

68. Lipowski, Z. J. (1983). Transient cognitive disorders (delirium, acute confusional states) in the elderly. *American Journal Psychiatry, 140,* 1426–1436.

69. Cummings, J., Benson, D. F., & LoVerme, S. (1980). Reversible dementia. *Journal of the American Medical Association, 243,* 2434–2439.

70. Lipowski, et al. (1983).

71. Modified from American Psychiatric Association (1988). *A psychiatric glossary,* Sixth edition. Washington, DC: American Psychiatric Association.

SPECIAL CONCERNS: RACE AND ETHNICITY, OLDER WOMEN AND GENDER ISSUES, CRIME, ALCOHOLISM, DEAFNESS, BLINDNESS, AND SEXUALITY

THE IMPACT OF RACE AND ETHNICITY
ON MENTAL HEALTH CARE

OLDER WOMEN AND GENDER ISSUES

CRIMES AGAINST THE ELDERLY

ALCOHOLISM

HEARING IMPAIRMENT

VISUAL IMPAIRMENT

SEXUALITY IN OLD AGE

How do race and ethnicity affect the lives of older people? Are older women at greater risk in old age because they are female? Do alcoholics live long enough to become old? Are there "geriatric criminals"? Are older people interested in and capable of sexuality? In this chapter we consider some of the important human issues that are part of old age.

THE IMPACT OF RACE AND ETHNICITY ON MENTAL HEALTH CARE[1]

Older people are a multiracial and multicultural group. Many are immigrants from other countries. Others, namely older African Americans, had ancestors who were brought to the United States by force. In 1995 more than 4.8 million, or almost 15% of the older population, were members of a minority group. Minority groups are generally defined as those who have suffered subordination and discrimination as a result of race or ethnicity, especially African Americans, Hispanics, Native Americans, and Asian and Pacific Island Americans. Other ethnic groups have also been or are still subject to prejudice—Poles, Greeks, Arabs,

and Jews, among others. Of the 33.5 million people aged 65 and older in 1995, 89.6% were white; 8.1% were black; 4.5% of Hispanic origin (this category is not exclusive, that is the Census Bureau has included people of Hispanic origin in other groups as well, especially the white and black groups); 1.8% Asian and Pacific Islanders; and 0.4% American Indian, Eskimo, and Aleut.[2] By 2050, 33% of the older population is likely to be non-white or Hispanic.[3]

A nation as diverse as the United States would greatly benefit from transcultural studies of the older persons within its own borders. Different cultural and ethnic groups have different conceptions of the life cycle and different attitudes toward use of formal as well as family help; each has been treated somewhat differently by the majority culture. Research on the minority elderly has become active since the 1960s, with most attention focused on African Americans and, to a lesser extent, Hispanics, particularly Southwest Mexican Americans. Since the 1980s, other minority groups have begun to receive attention as well. National ethnic organizations began forming in the 1970s, stimulated by the absence of focus on minority elderly in the initial planning phase of the 1971 White House Conference on Aging. The National Caucus and Center on the Black Aged was begun and funded in 1972 by the Administration on Aging. This was followed by the National Indian Council on Aging in 1976, the Asociacion Nacional Por Personas Mayores in 1975, the National Hispanic Council on Aging in 1978, and the National Pacific/Asian Resource Center on Aging in 1979. All of these organizations received support from the Administration on Aging and have been active in advocacy, promotion of research and training in minority aging, and creation of public and professional awareness of ethnic and minority aging. Each national group held its own mini Conference at the 1981 White House Conference on Aging. Individual states have been slower to develop their own state-level responses to minority aging, although such development is likely to occur in the future. Certain religious groups, such as Jews and Mormons, have formal associations and provide an array of special services to their own and other elderly.

Two major and distinctly separate issues are evident regarding minority older people. First are the unique cultural elements found in each minority group. These have bearing on the lives of the group's older members. Second are the effects on older persons of living as minority members in a majority culture. We would like to touch on both of these issues, even though most available research centers around vital statistics and the social and economic effects of various racial and ethnic groups' experience as minorities rather than the cultural life of individual groups. Much more needs to be done to recognize the varied and distinctive lifestyles within and between the various cultural groups in the United States. Jackson has called such studies *ethnogerontology,* namely "the study of the causes and the consequences of race, national origin, and culture on individual and population aging."[4] In the strictest sense, all Americans are ethnics. Our present focus on the more disadvantaged ethnic minorities is understand-

able. However, it is expected that study will broaden to include European and other ethnic groups as well, particularly Germans, Scandinavians, English, Polish, Irish, and Italians. Ethnic variety should be preserved, protected, and used as an important consideration in physical and mental health diagnosis and treatment.

In Chapter 1 we presented some of the general facts and figures of minority old age in America. This chapter deals with the direct and indirect effects of race and ethnicity on the mental health needs and care of older people.

Mental Health Care for Minority Elderly

In comparison with the overall population, older persons are underserved by the mental health system, with minority elderly the most severely underserved. Indifference and neglect, as well as overt and covert racial prejudice and discrimination, are operating to produce this unenviable inequity.

African American Elderly

A current debate surrounding African American aging is whether elderly blacks face a "double jeopardy," namely a wider disparity between blacks and whites than existed earlier, due to the combined effects of age and race. Two major factors have influenced scholars to question the validity of this debate. The first is the fact that income disparity between blacks and whites is actually less in old age than earlier, and the second is that in very late old age some studies have shown that blacks have a longer life expectancy than whites. However, both of these issues are complex, uncertain, and controversial. Retirement income tends to represent a dramatic drop for many whites, with less of a drop for blacks, reflecting earlier income disparities. Also wealth, as represented by income and resources outside of pensions and governmental subsidies, is higher for whites but is not counted in income figures. As for longer life expectancy, the so-called advantage of blacks, if true, seems a direct result of a disadvantage of greater mortality earlier in life, leaving the strongest to survive into old age.

Two of the most obvious effects of discrimination have been the overrepresentation of African American elderly on Supplemental Security Income and their shorter life expectancies at birth. Whites often have Social Security and private pensions, while many jobs open to blacks were never covered or only relatively recently have been covered by Social Security. And since blacks, especially men, are more likely to die at a younger age, they may never become eligible for retirement benefits even if they have accumulated them.

Outpatient Mental Health Care.   It is a widely acknowledged fact that most mental health professionals, products of white middle-class America, are unable to bridge the cultural chasm between themselves and poverty-stricken black people in the context of mental health work. Diagnosis and treatment are based on traditional psychiatric concepts of mental health and mental disorder. These in turn hinge on white middle-class norms and values. Effective mental health workers must be able not only to identify with the culture of their clients, but also to distinguish between the effects of societal pathology and individual psychopathology.

In a classic analysis of black–white relations, psychoanalyst Franz Fanon wrote that any study of the psychology of a black person must include (1) a psychoanalytic interpretation of the actual life experience of the black man and woman and (2) a psychoanalytic interpretation of the Negro myth as it has been formulated by whites.[5] Grier and Cobbs made similar points.[6] A body of theory and treatment techniques designed especially for the African American population has been slow in emerging. Dr. William A. Reid emphasizes that too many mental health workers arbitrarily assign individual responsibility for misfortune rather than considering social factors.[7]

Outpatient mental health care for the African American aged has been inadequate in general. Hospital emergency rooms give minimal attention to psychiatric problems, particularly if a minority patient is both old and poor. Day hospitals and day-care center accommodations are rare. These services receive little priority in municipal and county hospital budgets, and private sponsorship is difficult to obtain.

Institutional Care.   The African American family has been the subject of wide speculation, but until relatively recently, only minimal rigorous study. Two extreme views have persisted. The first is the idealistic position that most older blacks are cared for by loving, extended family networks. The second and opposite view is that poverty-stricken black elderly have been abandoned as a result of the disorganization and disintegration of the family. The reality falls somewhere in between, with families doing their best as long as they can, depending on their circumstances. Cultural institutions, such as African American churches, continue to be stabilizing forces and resources in the mental health care of the elderly, providing many older persons with social participation, prestige, and power.

A long-held view is that the African American community does not readily seek admission of its older people for institutional care. Some studies suggest that in black families the older person is more respected and considered less of a burden than in white families. Some have postulated that a wider range of behavior is tolerated in minority communities. But others believe that the tendency to avoid or delay institutionalization represents a basic distrust of institutions because of previous life experiences. What is readily apparent to all is the lack of institutional facilities for the older African American. Families simply have few places to turn to for institutional help with their elderly.

Many African American elderly simply cannot afford nursing home care, a particular problem in states with weak Medicaid provisions. African American-owned facilities having difficulty in meeting health, fire, and building standards may be closed rather than given assistance and encouragement.

The integration of public psychiatric hospitals has occurred relatively recently in most cases. St.

Elizabeth's Hospital in Washington, DC, one of the well-known hospitals in the nation, was segregated until 1955; the hospitals in North Carolina were segregated until 1966. Segregated black hospitals were underfinanced and consequently in worse condition than the already inadequate white hospitals. With integration and the sharing of facilities, blacks fared somewhat better than before in terms of physical accommodations, but it is doubtful that their medical or psychiatric treatment has improved, since custodial care rather than active treatment is still customary.

Lifelong attitudes and conditioning often persist in old age, even after mental impairment occurs. In one integrated hospital, an aged white woman with strong racial prejudices managed, in spite of brain damage and incoherence, consistently to call African American staff members, including her psychiatrist, "niggers." One can occasionally see older African American patients waiting on white patients by performing personal services, while the whites give orders. There may be rebellion among older African Americans; in one case an elderly African American man spent his last years giving verbal vent to his murderous feelings toward whites. His anger had been stored up for a lifetime, released only when his demented mental state caused him to lose both caution and control. Older African Americans may share a belief that African American health professionals are inferior. It is not unusual in an integrated institution for them to prefer white health care personnel. Conversely, other African American elderly feel more comfortable if their care is given by persons of their own race.

The specific psychological and cultural implications of African American old age are a growing subject of investigation. There are differences between rural and urban dwellers, Northerners and Southerners, upper- and middle-income citizens versus those with lower incomes, as well as the various age groups and professions. For example, the concept of retirement may be meaningless for those black elderly who are ineligible for adequate pensions and cannot afford to stop work. Thus "retirement crisis" does not apply to people who are in a "survival crisis." On the other hand, those who receive some form of stable pension, however small, may find old age more secure than an earlier life of sporadic, low-paying jobs in the labor market.[8] The task of future research is to capture the differences as well as the similarities within minority groups themselves.

Hispanic (or Latino) Elderly

Racial discrimination has had many of the same social and economic effects on the Hispanic elderly as on the African American elderly. Both groups are disproportionately poor and poorly served by mental health systems. The reasons for this underutilization of services by the Hispanic population is a complex combination of the following factors: discrimination, linguistic and cultural differences, lack of outreach, discriminatory policies of health agencies, discrimination due to immigration status, and factors due to class and level of education.

Hispanics are a very heterogeneous group, with origins in 26 nations, according to federal definition. The largest groups are of Mexican origin and ancestry in the southwest, Puerto Ricans in New York City and Cubans in Florida. Other growing populations come from the Dominican Republic, Columbia, Ecuador, El Salvador, and other Central and South American countries.

Hispanics are not culturally or linguistically heterogeneous. Although the majority of Hispanics are Roman Catholic, there are a growing number of Protestants and many Hispanics of other faiths, including traditional indigenous cultures. There are also differences in customs and beliefs between and within regions. Inability to speak English is a common difficulty among Hispanics; however, many Hispanics speak English only, and many do not speak Spanish as a first language, or at all. Other languages spoken by Hispanics are other European languages, such as Portuguese, Native American languages, such as Quechua, Mayan, Aymara and Guarani, and Creole languages, such as Garifuna, spoken in coastal Honduras.[9]

The accuracy and scope of health statistics are extremely inadequate with regard to the Hispanic population in the United States. The Hispanic population seems to have an average life expectancy near that of the non-Hispanic white population, despite a weaker socio-economic profile. This may be due to extreme inaccuracies in reporting on death certificates, thought to be greater than for African Americans. A major factor may be selective immigration (recent research indicates that immigrants from any group are healthier than non-immigrants), and the long life expectancy of economically advantaged groups, such as Cuban Americans. Similarly, older Hispanics have low rates of heart disease and major cancers. The reasons for this are also uncertain. Older Hispanics, however do have death rates of double the non-Hispanic white population from diabetes, chronic liver disease and cirrhosis, and high rates of mortality for these diseases. In addition, older Hispanics need more help with activities of daily living (ADLs) and instrumental activities of daily living (IADLs) than non-Hispanic whites.[10]

A 1988 Commonwealth Commission national survey of the three largest groups of elderly Hispanics—Mexican Americans, Puerto Ricans, and Cubans—found the following:

- Four in ten Hispanic elderly do not speak English.
- Three out of four have an eighth-grade education or less, twice the proportion of all elderly.
- Nearly one-third live with children, siblings, or others; many are unable to afford living alone.
- The poverty rate of elderly Hispanics is nearly twice that of all elderly (22% compared to 12%). The average Hispanic older person lives on less than $104 per week.
- Many are not eligible for Social Security or private pensions. Seventy-seven percent receive Social Security, compared to 92% of all elderly, and 19% receive private pensions, compared to 45% of all elderly.
- The Hispanic elderly are more dependent on Supplemental Security Income (SSI) and Med-

icaid. However, 55% of those elderly Hispanics who are eligible for SSI do not receive it. Of those eligible, 26% were not aware of SSI or their eligibility.
- They have greater physical handicaps and a greater need for long-term care services than do elderly people in general.
- They rely heavily on their families for long-term and other care.
- Elderly Mexican Americans have the highest rate of poverty among Hispanic subgroups, while elderly Puerto Ricans report the worst health status.
- The majority of elderly Mexican Americans were born in the United States (58%) while 98% of both Cuban and Puerto Rican elderly were born in Cuba or Puerto Rico.[11]

Torres-Gil has outlined the special challenge the elderly Hispanics present, now and in future years.[12]

Native American Elderly

The 116,153 Native Americans age 65 or older in 1990 represents the smallest elderly minority group in the United States. Native Americans have the youngest median age of the principal minority groups in the U.S.—16.8 years—and the smallest percentage of adults living to age 65—only 5.4%.[13]

As members of approximately 500 nations, tribes, bands, or Alaskan native villages, Native Americans are extremely diverse culturally and linguistically. Native Americans are the most rural of the major minority populations. However, partly as the result of government policy encouraging resettlement and as an attempt to escape poverty on the reservations, Native Americans have become increasingly urban. While 59% of all Native Americans, including elders, live in urban areas, 22% live on the 314 reservations and land trusts.[14] The increasing urbanization of Native Americans can not only create a sense of alienation for elders, but puts them out of reach of the Indian Health Service and tribal services. On the other hand, integration with the larger community has its advantages.

28.5% of Native Americans age 60 and older lived with incomes below the official poverty level in 1990, compared to only 9.8% of non-Hispanic whites aged 60 and older. 58.5% of Native Americans age 60 or older lived with incomes of only twice the poverty level or less, compared to 31.6% of older whites. 38% of rural Native Americans age 65 and older lived in poverty. In addition, 30% of Native American elders in rural areas had no vehicle available, 31% had no telephone, and 24% spoke English poorly.[15]

Health research about Native American older people is highly inadequate. However, a landmark study by National Indian Council on Aging (1981) found that at age 45 reservation-dwelling Native Americans had the health characteristics of the average American at age 65, and urban-dwelling Native Americans had these characteristics at age 55. Lowered age eligibility for services is now available through Title VI of the Older Americans Act, but only on reservations.

Native American older people have less heart disease and cancer than the general population, because they do not live long enough on average to develop them. However, they do have the poorest five-year survival rate for cancer of the major minority groups. They also have high death rates for pneumonia and influenza, diabetes mellitus, accidents, chronic liver disease, cirrhosis and other alcohol related deaths, and septicemia.[16] They also suffer from high rates of gallbladder disease and hypertension.

Although the Indian Health Service has made great progress in treating infectious and acute disease, a 1996 National Indian Council on Aging report criticized it for not attending to the health needs of older Native Americans. The Indian Health Service does not recruit geriatricians, provide geriatric training, or provide long-term care of any kind. Despite recent statements of a commitment to improve services for older people, little progress has been made, and the Indian Health Service continues to contend that it is not mandated to provide long-term care. Some tribes, particularly those with gaming or gambling revenue, have been able to sponsor long-term care facilities, but these facilities are inadequate, and no other federal agency has assumed responsibility. The few Native American nursing homes in existence are operating at full capacity.

It is important for providers of geriatric care for Native Americans to be culturally sensitive. For example, in the two nursing homes of the Navajo Nation, the largest reservation-based Native American nation, the majority of residents speak the Navajo language and eat traditional food. Respect is paid to Navajo cultural practices, such as bathing in sweat baths, sleeping on sheepskins or mattresses stacked on the floor, religious practices, visitation of clan members, and practices regarding death, such as not speaking about the dead.[17]

Ho has attempted to delineate shared characteristics of Native Americans as well as to acknowledge the tremendous tribal diversity.[18] Strong extended family ties and multiple household systems provide an interdependent family framework. In order to survive, the elderly have had to adopt skills related to the dominant white culture while trying to preserve their own rich traditions. All of this has taken place in the midst of fast-paced social change and the often insensitive attempts on the part of federal and state governments to identify and meet their needs.

Asian American and Pacific Island American Older Persons

Asian and Pacific Island Americans are an extremely diverse group, often with little in common due to vast differences in language, class, culture, religion and history. The largest groups of Asian Americans are Chinese (with 134,000 people age 65 and older in 1990), Filipino (with 104,000 older people), and Japanese (with 106,000 older people). Other Asian American populations are Korean, Asian Indian, Vietnamese, Cambodian, Laotian, Hmong (a tribal minority from Laos), Thai, Pakistani, and Indonesian. Only 5% of the total Asian Pacific Island American Population are Pacific Island American. The majority of Pacific

Island Americans are Hawaiian and Samoan. Others are Tongan or other Polynesian, Micronesian (includes Guam), and Melanesian (from Fiji).[19]

Although many generalizations are made about them, there are vast differences in the social and economic status of different Asian and Pacific Island Americans. Older Asian and Pacific Island Americans are more likely to be in the labor force than the general population and less likely to be unemployed, but the figures differ greatly among groups. The poverty rates for older Japanese, Filipino, and Asian Indian Americans are among the lowest in the United States, but the poverty rates for Southeast Asian older people (Hmong, Cambodian, Laotian, and Vietnamese) are among the highest—as high as 47% in the case of Hmong elders. Compared with other ethnic groups in the United States, older Asian and Pacific Island Americans have both the highest proportion of their people with less than a ninth grade education and the highest proportion of those with a bachelor's degree or more, and these statistics vary greatly among nationalities. Asian and Pacific Island Americans have almost equal numbers of older people who are native born, naturalized, or not U.S. citizens. A higher percentage (58%) of older Asian and Pacific Island Americans have limited English proficiency than all other major ethnic groups.[20]

Health statistics about Asian and Pacific Island Americans are problematic, and are often weighted towards the more healthy Asian groups. Chinese and Japanese have longer life expectancies then white Americans, but some subgroups, such as Southeast Asian immigrants and Native Hawaiians generally have poorer health. Asian and Pacific Island Americans in general have high rates of tuberculosis, hepatitis, anemia, hypertension, multiinfarct dementia, and osteoporosis.

Studies suggest that Asian Americans have higher rates of mental health problems than whites in the United States. The suicide rate for older Chinese American women, for example, is ten time that for older white women. This problem is compounded by low rates of mental health service use by older Asian Pacific Island Americans, possibly due to a distrust of government, belief in non-Western models of medicine, and barriers such as class, language, lack of sensitivity among providers to cultural differences, and prejudice, such as a still pervasive belief in the stereotype of the "problem-free" Asian.[21]

Service providers should be sensitive to different cultural and religious beliefs, such as filial respect, among many Asian and Pacific Island Americans, and efforts should be made, in many cases, to incorporate family, kinship groups, or other cultural organizations into care. Specific historical backgrounds should also be considered. There may be attitudinal differences between refugees (including those who may suffer from depression or Post-Traumatic Stress Disorder, those who were colonized, such as Native Hawaiians, or Japanese who were interned during World War II and who may distrust government services), and those who emigrated by choice. The degree to which the individual is assimilated into the new culture and whether he or she is an immigrant are also important factors to take into account.[22]

The traditional role of family supports has been weakened by immigration patterns. Chinese men were prohibited through the Chinese Exclusion Act of 1882 from bringing their wives and children with them, and they were forbidden to intermarry in America.[23]

Others chose to come alone as young men, hoping to make money quickly and then return to live in China. War and the subsequent Communist takeover prohibited their return. As a result, in most areas with Chinese American populations there have been large groups of single males without families.

American immigration policies changed after 1970, making it possible for the immigration of Chinese family groups. A new group of older Chinese are beginning to emerge as a result of the liberalization of immigration laws that permitted the reunion of long-separated families, including parents and other older relatives of U.S. citizens. This group appears to have a larger proportion of older women than men. Added to these are the increasing numbers of persons who were born in the United States and are now growing older, again a higher proportion of whom are women. Older Chinese Americans tend to prefer to live in ethnic communities rather than with their children in outlying areas. Many elderly are quite isolated from American culture. Younger Chinese Americans are much more acculturated and many have intermarried outside the Chinese community.

Early immigration of Filipinos produced an imbalance of males similar to that of the Chinese. Some came to the United States as farm laborers; others came because they were awarded U.S. citizenship as veterans of the U.S. armed forces after World War II. Most had no families here, and many lost contact with their relatives in the Philippines. A more recent wave of immigration came in the early 1970s because of political problems in the Philippines. This wave doubled the size of the Filipino population in California alone and many of these later immigrants arrived in families. In recent years, a number of elderly persons also have immigrated to the United States to join children, many of whom came as health care workers, who were already here.

Early Japanese immigration policies in the United States were not so devastating and dehumanizing as those of other Asians. Women and children were allowed to accompany men, and this has had a profound effect on the lives of present-day older persons. Family structure is much more stable and supportive. Japanese older people were able to weather the World War II internment in relocation centers with the loss of jobs and their roles in U.S. society primarily because their children carried on for them. Many of the children have become highly educated and successful while retaining patterns of loyalty to their parents.[24]

The widespread belief that respect for older persons is culturally stronger in Asian societies needs to be reevaluated from the viewpoint of economic and social class as well as immigration effects. Tradition, of course, has a powerful effect on shaping an individual's attitudes, but economic and social circumstances either support or undermine such traditions. For example, the American-

ization of younger Asian Americans has partially eroded the traditional role of, and respect for, the elderly.

What Can Be Done to Improve Mental Health Care for Minority-Group Older Persons?

1. Income maintenance, especially for the minority elderly who are more likely to experience poverty, is a prime requirement for improving the mental health and the mental health care of older members of minority groups. Supplemental Security Income should be raised to provide an adequate standard of living, ideally to some level above rather than below the poverty line. Efforts must be made to resolve the inequities in Social Security that arise from lower life expectancies in certain ethnic groups. Pension plans should become portable from one place of employment to another. Hiring and wage discrimination in the labor market, based on age or ethnicity, must be continuously monitored and addressed.

2. Minority professionals and older minority elderly themselves should be in key decision-making and advisory positions in any actions affecting older minority persons as a group.

3. Mental health staffs should reflect the racial and ethnic composition they serve. Training in the mental health field should be widely available for minority-group members.

4. Nonminority personnel should have special training and, ideally, supervisory monitoring by minority-group or ethnically sensitive professionals if they work with minority clientele.

5. Research from the minority perspective should be funded and encouraged. Problems pertinent to the minority aged need emphasis. The quality of minority aging research must be improved.[25]

6. More alternative methods of care must be made available—home-care services, nursing homes and homes for the aged, psychiatric hospitalization outside of state hospitals, day care, and day hospitals. Techniques of individual and group psychotherapy relevant to minority needs should be developed. Meals-on-Wheels could supply ethnic foods, and food stamps should be usable in ethnic groceries. Recreation and leisure therapy should be aimed at cultural interests. Information systems, service workers, legal assistance, and psychiatric therapy should all be provided on a bilingual basis for older persons who do not speak English.

The On Lok Senior Health Service in San Francisco began in 1972 as a rather rare example of the provision of ethnic-related services. On Lok is a day treatment center for frail older persons in San Francisco's Chinatown/North Beach area and serves those who would otherwise be placed in nursing homes or intermediate care facilities. Participants are of Chinese, Filipino, Hispanic, Italian, and other European ethnic backgrounds and often do not speak English. They receive medical evaluation; primary physician care; medical services such as podiatry, dentistry, optometry, and audiology; occupational, physical, and reality therapy; diet counseling; recreation; transportation; home-care services; "meals-on-wheels"; day health care services; sheltered/supervised apartments; brief nursing home care; and hospital placement when needed. Staff members at On Lok must be able to speak at least one of the languages spoken by participants, in addition to English. Programs are geared to the ethnic cultures; for example, Chinese as well as American food is served.[26]

Federal legislation passed in 1986 authorized national demonstration projects by nonprofit organizations nationwide for the replication of the On Lok model. By 1996 there were 27 such replications called Programs for All-Inclusive Care for the Elderly (PACE). The programs operate under dual capitation payments (Medicare and Medicaid) and are designed to keep members out of costly nursing homes.

Numbers of therapists and theorists are beginning to devise specific forms and styles of psychotherapy to reach the minority elderly. Ho's work (1987) is an example of important efforts to address mental health care of the four major ethnic groups (African Americans, Native Americans, Hispanics, and Asian Pacific Island Americans) from a cultural context. He uses a family systems approach, with the objective of supplementing already-existing family therapy theories by (1) identifying a "culturally relevant theoretical framework"; (2) providing an overview of the political, social, and economic problems that each minority family faces, along with the unique culturally derived strengths and weaknesses such families carry; (3) clarifying the cultural values and changing family patterns of each ethnic group; and (4) providing specific mental health practitioner guidelines on work with ethnic families, including single-parent families.[27] Ho recognizes the dangers of cultural stereotypes inherent in this approach; nonetheless he believes that such stereotyping can be mitigated by individuating each family within the context of a larger understanding of the possible impact of culture and ethnicity.

An example of his perspective can be found in a description of work with Hispanic families: "Many Hispanic Americans are gradually acculturated to the middle-class mainstream society, but a vast majority of them are still struggling with basic survival needs. . . . These families need more than feeling good about themselves and other family members; they need the basic necessities to survive. Hence the role of a therapist extends beyond the psychologically oriented healer role [and] . . . may consist of roles as cultural broker, mediator, educator and advocate."[28]

Boyd-Franklin has focused on therapy with the African American family, bringing together past and current research and cultural knowledge on the subject.[29] A major purpose is to provide mental health therapists with the clinical tools necessary to work effectively with black families. The author stresses that the issue of racism and, for many black families, poverty, must be part of the treatment process and that a multisystems approach is generally preferable.

Kim and Kim (1989) have made beginning attempts to develop a curriculum for training mental health professionals for work with Asian American elderly.[30] Die and Seelback have focused on elderly Vietnamese.[31] Ho provides insights into therapy with Native Americans.[32]

OLDER WOMEN AND GENDER ISSUES

In the United States, 17 million women were age 65 years or older in 1995. This constitutes 7.6% of the total population, 14.8% of all women, and 59.3% of the older population.[33] Sexism and ageism are the twin prejudices directed against them. Many have experienced sex discrimination all their lives, but age discrimination begins only after they have lost their youth and accelerates as they age. The end result is a greater rate of poverty and social unacceptability than for men, combined ironically with a longer life span. The cultural denigration of the older woman is taught to children at an early age through fairy tales that depict old hags, evil crones, scary old witches, and nasty biddies of all kinds. Negative mother-in-law stories abound. Doctors and medical students often call the very oldest female patients "crocks." Unmarried aunts may be scorned as "old maids." Even grandma can become a family nuisance as she outlives grandpa and experiences and expresses the emotional and physical facts of aging. Thus the message comes across that a woman is valuable for bearing and rearing children and perhaps to nurse her husband in his dotage and often through his terminal illness, but after that it is clearly useless and even burdensome to have her around. The mistreatment of older women is a national shame that has yet to be fully challenged even by older women themselves.

Low Visibility of the Older Woman

Except for unusual events, such as the passage of the Social Security Act in 1935, one of the tendencies of the U.S. social and political system is to attempt to resolve social problems piecemeal and intermittently. The most stubborn problems tend to persist under this approach. The economic and social conditions of the poor, now mostly women and children, and a number of our ethnic and racial minorities, are periodically "discov-ered" with great alarm and then allowed to sink back into oblivion and neglect. Older women living alone seldom even receive the benefit of occasional public scrutiny. It is assumed that they have shared equally with men in the progress made since 1935 in establishing nominal economic security in old age. We shall be examining that assumption in the following pages.

Profile of the Older Woman

What is the life of an *average* older woman like? In many cases it means being widowed and living alone, on a low or poverty-level income, often in substandard housing, with inadequate medical care and little chance of employment to supplement resources.

Income. A small proportion of older women are well-off financially, and some few have inherited enormous wealth. At the other end of the spectrum are those women who have been poor all their lives and can expect even greater poverty in old age. But in between these two groups is a multitude of women who have lived comfortably throughout their lives and first experience poverty after they are old and widowed: They are the newly poor. Poverty is not reserved for women alone, since older men, too, are often in dire financial condition. Yet whenever poverty is found, it is generally more profound and of greater consequence for women.

According to the official poverty index in 1992, 71.3% of all of the older poor were women, most of them widows living alone. Of women aged 75 and older, 41.7% had incomes below or only slightly above the poverty level. Only 22% of women received income from private pensions in 1992, with an average benefit of $5,432 a year, compared to 49% of men, who received an average benefit of $10,131 per year.[34]

Due to less pay for equal work compared to men, discontinuous outside work experience (often due to care-giving for children and older persons), and built-in inequities in the Social Security system, women still receive less in Social

Security benefits than do men. In 1994, the average monthly Social Security benefit was $601 for women, compared to $785 for men. Social Security benefits for women workers in general averaged 77% of the amount for men. African American women received an average of only $476 monthly in Social Security benefits in 1994.[35]

One of several common paths to poverty in old age is to become a displaced homemaker in midlife. Displaced homemakers are women—10.5 million over the age of 65 in 1990—who have lost their primary source of income due to separation, divorce, or widowhood.[36] Compounding their precarious financial state, in 1989, 12% of such women (2.8 million) between the ages of 45 and 64 had no health insurance.[37]

In the current generation, even women with sufficient income may encounter problems; many of them have not learned to handle money on their own behalf. This generation of women has been encouraged to turn its money over to others to manage—to bank representatives, guardians, lawyers, adult children—and those women who do take care of their own finances are often untrained and ill-prepared to make sound decisions. Even women who are well above average in income, job level, education, and years of experience may know little about investments or how to increase capital. Money management for older women tends to be a passive activity in which they prefer the false security of savings, cash, and annuities over a sounder investment program that requires an understanding of economics and finance. Courses in finance designed especially for women are fortunately beginning to reverse this trend.

Employment. Over 1.5 million, or 8.5%, of women 65 years of age or older are employed, often out of necessity.[38] Although there has been a decrease in work among men age 55 and older, older women's work involvement has remained steady or has slightly increased. Many never worked outside their homes until their children left home. Others who were employed all their lives usually earned much less than men of comparable talent, training, and initiative. Women workers of all ages earned 75 cents for every dollar earned by men in 1995.[39] All of this has resulted in lower Social Security and private retirement benefits and, combined with a longer life span for women, produces lower income that must be stretched over a greater number of years.

Employers are reluctant to hire older women because of stereotyped attitudes that they are not adaptable to today's jobs and technology; older women are seen as cantankerous, unattractive, overly emotional, and unreliable because of health problems. Yet corporate studies indicate that they make exceptionally good employees, with lower turnover, less absenteeism and equal productivity compared to younger women. Further, a majority of companies report that health insurance costs for older women workers are no greater than those for younger women workers.[40]

Social Security poses a peculiar problem regarding equity for women. It was devised in 1935 with the traditional family in mind, namely a working husband and an economically dependent housewife. However, today two-thirds of women are in the paid work force and only 20% are full-time homemakers. As more women have moved into the workplace, Social Security benefits continue to favor the wife at home. For example, two-earner couples often end up with lower benefits than one-earner couples with the wife at home. The concept of "marital earnings sharing" has been proposed as a solution to this inequity. This would mean that every couple would split their combined earnings in half, with each receiving equal Social Security credit. However, this would immediately require modification and supplementation in order to prevent loss of benefits for certain categories of recipients. Another solution, to give housewives Social Security credits for their unpaid work, has not yet produced a viable method of placing a value on such services and is considered more unworkable than the marital-earnings-sharing plan.

In other areas, such as the disability protection of Social Security, it is the housewife who is disadvantaged. If she is a disabled widow, she faces a stricter disability standard than a disabled employed woman and will receive the lowest Social Security benefit of any recipient group, with an average payment even lower than the maximum Supplementary Security Income (SSI) benefit for the very poor who are unqualified for Social Security. If she becomes disabled or dies while her husband is still alive, the loss of her unpaid but very real services is not covered by Social Security at all.

Social Security also penalizes women who take time out from employment for care-giving of children, the elderly, and the disabled in their families. Women average 11.5 years out of the work force compared to 1.3 years for men. These lost years are factored as zeros into the wage record for Social Security of 35 required years of work and have a large effect in reducing benefit levels. Alternative solutions proposed for this problem are (1) to simply leave out the "zero" years for caregivers and base the benefit on the remaining years, or (2) to provide Social Security credits for care-giving.

Divorced women must have been married ten years in order to receive their ex-husband's Social Security. Yet most divorces occur before 10 years of marriage, and such women are left without benefits if they themselves are not in the work force. Even if they do qualify for benefits as divorced wives, the spousal benefit is so low that women will be in poverty if they have no other source of income.

It is important to continue to amend Social Security to meet the needs of modern older women. Currently Social Security's weaknesses and incongruities are most noticeable in cases of two-earner families, care-giving, divorce, early retirement, and long life, all of which affect women disproportionately. In 1994 Social Security was the only source of income for 22% of unmarried older women, compared to 19% of unmarried older men.[41]

Social Security has proven to be the most effective of all antipoverty programs for the aged, compared to cash welfare programs, tax programs, and others. Approximately 50% of retirees would be below the poverty level if it were not for Social Security.[42] Its next challenge is to target the poverty of older women living alone.

Marriage. The average American woman born today can anticipate about 10 years of widowhood. Of the 18 million older women, 46.9% are widows and an additional 6% are divorced. Approximately 4.3% of older women have never been married.[43] Thus almost 60% of older women are on their own, an interesting fact when one remembers that they, more than any younger group, were raised from childhood to consider themselves dependent on men.

Why so many widows? Women outlive men their own age and also tend to marry men who are an average of about 2.5 years older than themselves. The difference in life expectancy from birth has been occurring from the turn of the century, if not before. Males born in 1920 could expect to live 53.6 years and females a year longer, but by 1991 a 6.9 year spread was evident, with a life expectancy at birth of 72 for men and 78.9 for women.[44]

Older men have a tremendous advantage over older women when it comes to marriage. Because they tend to marry younger women who will outlive them, they are much less likely to be widowed. More than that, they can count on a fairly healthy spouse to nurse them as they age. Should the wife die prematurely, they have usually plentiful options for remarriage. At ages 65 through 69 when men number 4.5 million, the over 5.4 million women already outnumber men by almost one million and the odds improve as men get older.[45] In remarrying, men can bypass their own age group altogether and marry women from 65 all the way down to girls in their twenties or teens. One can readily see what is happening to older women in all of this; their chances for remarriage are small, and only about 27,000 remarried in 1990. To exacerbate the situation, it is still less socially acceptable for older women than for older men to date or marry persons much younger than themselves.

Motherhood.   Many contemporary older women are childless. The cohort (generation) of women born between 1905 and 1909, now in their late 80s, is a low-fertility cohort, since these women produced fewer children than any recorded group of American women before or after. At the height of its childbearing years, this group was confronted with the worst economic depression in U.S. history, with 25%—one of every four workers—unemployed. Many couples felt they could not support a large or even moderately sized family. About 20% of the women had no children, another 22% had only one, and another 20% two. The long-term result is that about 25% currently have no living children. (Nearly 30% of African American women in this age group are childless.) They are, however, likely to have brothers and sisters (and therefore nieces and nephews), because their own mothers had large families. Thus there may be extended family support for some of the childless.

Interestingly, the women born between 1925 and 1930, now in their 70s, were the high-fertility, post–World War II cohort. Only about 10% never had a child, and the "ideal" was four children. While many will face divorce or will become widowed because of the male–female differential life expectancy, most will have children.

Living Arrangements.   In 1994, 9.3 million elderly lived alone and, of these, 78% or 7.2 million were women. Currently, 40% of all older women live alone, 41% live with husbands, 17% with relatives, and 2% with nonrelatives.[46] Many women have never lived alone until old age.

Physical Health.   Major differences exist between the health condition of men and women in later life:

- Men have higher death rates than do women at all ages.
- In old age, women have more numerous, but less life-threatening health problems; older men's illnesses are less numerous, but more serious.

- Hospitalization rates are higher for older men (reflecting the more serious nature of their illnesses); women use more outpatient care and medications (reflecting a pattern of more frequent, but also milder, illnesses).

In summary, older women have higher rates of illness than men, but lower death rates. Verbrugge postulates five possible reasons for these differences:

1. Biological risk factors due to genetic and reproductive differences between men and women
2. Acquired risk factors, due to different social and environmental circumstances between men and women
3. Illness behavior: gender differences in response to illness
4. Health reporting: gender differences in talking about and reporting illness
5. Past history of illness behavior that has an impact on new health responses.[47]

Medicare insurance, with its strength in the area of hospital coverage and its weakness in home care and nursing home care, better fits the profiles of older men's illness than older women's. Women make up 75 to 80% of nursing home residents, yet Medicare makes very little contribution toward nursing home costs. Many women are forced to spend their resources down to the poverty level in order to be eligible for highly variable state-funded Medicaid help with such costs. The same can be said for home care. In addition, Medicare does not cover routine physical examinations, drugs, hearing aids, and eyeglasses, all of which are of importance to women because of the chronicity and multiplicity of their health problems. One view of reforms is to strengthen and adjust Medicare to better meet women's needs, but many others believe that only a comprehensive national health insurance program will provide the insurance coverage needed by older women.

Mental Health.   Both older men and older women are heavily stereotyped in psychological theory as "old" people. As a further problem, sex differences are by and large invisible in theories about aging, and the old are viewed as gender-neutral. For example, psychoanalytic theory, with its view of very different psychosexual stages for boys and girls, does not carry this analysis into old age. Much of what is described as old age (with the exception of Jungian theory, see Chapter 12) is simply a description of the adaptation of the elderly to the stages in late life, such as retirement, widowhood or widowerhood, decline of health, and confrontation with death.

Gutmann's field studies challenge the gender-neutrality view of old age. He postulates that each sex has repressed a portion of its psychological potential early in childhood—males tend to repress nurturing characteristics while females repress assertive capacities. This allows children to survive and thrive in cultures that reward males for competitiveness and females for cooperativeness. However, in later life, each sex begins to reclaim its lost birthright, with males allowing their more nurturing qualities to develop and females their assertiveness. Gutmann's studies have suggested that this occurs in many different cultures and, perhaps, universally.[48]

Common sense, it would seem, should lead to examination of the gender-neutral view of the psychology of late life. Whether by nature (genetics) or nurture (the environment in which we grow up), women and men have differences which, in turn, produce differences in adjustment to the common stages and occurrences of later life.

Education and Research Efforts on Older Women

The major textbooks on geriatric medicine pay scant attention to the medical implications of females living longer than males. Nor do they attach much import to the question of whether women age differently than men, even at the same ages. The "unisex" quality of current geriatric medical literature represents a lag in recognizing the clinical implications of the differences between males and females.

Clinical and basic research efforts have long been biased against women in general and older women in particular. In a 1990 study by the U.S. General Accounting Office, the National Institutes of Health—the major research institutes in the United States—failed to implement their own 1987 policy requiring researchers to include women in federally funded studies. This failure extended also to preliminary research studies on animals, especially rats. Females, both human and animal, were routinely excluded from many studies because of the view that their hormonal cycles cause complications for researchers. In addition, they might become pregnant, further complicating research efforts. But as U.S. Representative Olympia Snow has wryly observed, "women have been bearing children for quite some time now, and are likely to continue doing so in the future. Medical research, rather than ignoring that fact as an inconvenience, should work to accommodate it."[49] It might be emphasized that older women have neither menstrual cycles nor pregnancies, yet the rate of inclusion of women in studies does not rise with age, strengthening the view that bias rather than sound judgment is operating.

One of the most important studies of aging, the Baltimore Longitudinal Study of Aging, examined men for over 20 years, before beginning to include women in 1978. The National Institute of Mental Health's landmark work on healthy aging, published in 1963, involved only men.[50] Certain processes common to all women as they age remain mysterious; for example, there is no agreement yet on the basic physiology of the menopausal hot flash. On a more urgent level, the breast cancer death rates in the United States have not significantly improved. Breast cancer mortality has remained about the same since 1950, with only a modest decline of 4.7% between 1989 and 1992.[51] In response to criticism regarding research on women's problems and the use of women as research subjects, the National Institutes of Health created an Office of Research on Women's Health to coordinate and accelerate women's health studies. A major nationwide study, the Women's Health Initiative, is now underway, focusing on a variety of health conditions experienced by women after the menopause.

Certain health conditions can be singled out as immediate targets for major new or expanded research efforts because of their impact on so many older women and because of current controversy surrounding treatment—Alzheimer's disease, breast cancer, uterine cancer, hypertension, stroke, osteoporosis (brittle bones), diabetes, arthritis, and urinary incontinence are some of the most apparent. Nearly half of the over 500,000 people who die of heart attacks in the United States each year are women. Further research around the use of estrogens, hysterectomies, and mastectomies is indicated. As already mentioned, the menopause and post-menopausal period require greater understanding. Occupational health hazards for women, both in the home and in the outside workplace, warrant further examination. Better understanding and prevention of hypothermia (dangerously low body temperature) and heat stroke are important, especially for the frail elderly.

What's Good about Being an Older Woman?

We have detailed some of the difficulties of older women. But there is more. Many older women have learned much about the mechanisms of sex and age discrimination and have a great deal to teach the young. Their experiences give us guidelines for combating prejudice and supporting older women in their efforts to find a satisfying life.

In terms of personal expression, older women today have both realized accomplishments and unexplored potential. In addition to their increasingly good records of health and longevity, they do not have to struggle with the conflicts between mothering and careers, which, even with a resolution of child care issues, often trouble younger women. They are in the interesting position of being the only adult females who are truly free of the demands of child responsibility (unless they are responsible for their grandchildren or other children) and, in many cases, marital responsibil-

ity. The idea of dependency on a male is deeply ingrained in white and in many minority cultures, but many older women do not conform to this stereotype, and, indeed, live independent and satisfying lives.

Older women who demonstrate successful aging give younger women confidence in the knowledge that a rich life can await them as they age. A considerable number of older women have forged unique positions for themselves in terms of identity, personal achievement, and even financial and political power. They need to be given greater visibility. Within the extended family, women are often the oldest and most influential members, frequently serving as the kin-keepers who provide contact and cohesion for others (Chapter 2).

Politically, the older woman is in an advantageous position that is likely to improve. With a voting strength of over 18 million, almost 75% of whom are registered voters and most of whom vote regularly,[52] they represent a major and fast-growing constituency that already could elect their own congresspersons in those states where they reside in high proportions. They have the available time and energy to lobby, campaign, and promote candidates, since over 90% are not employed. There is reason to suppose that women as candidates for the presidency and as additional appointees to the Supreme Court will come from this age group, since older people historically have often filled these positions.

In spite of widespread poverty for many women, there are tremendous sums of money in the hands of widows and female heirs. More women might be encouraged to take on their own financial management instead of entrusting it to male husband-surrogates. Women of wealth could exert much greater influence in economic, social, and other spheres than they now do. As an example, they could provide resources for solving the problems faced by women in later life.

Advocacy groups specifically for older women are beginning to form. The Older Women's League (OWL) was begun in 1978 by Tish Sommers and Laurie Shields and became a national organization in 1980. By 1996, OWL had 11,000 members and 62 chartered chapters in 30 states. Tish Sommers had earlier organized programs for "displaced homemakers," a phrase she coined for women who become displaced and economically vulnerable in mid-life through divorce, separation, or widowhood.

CRIMES AGAINST THE ELDERLY

According to crime statistics, the actual incidence of crime against persons over age 65 is lower than the incidence against other age groups. National crime surveys show that except for personal larceny such as purse-snatching and picking pockets, older persons have the lowest victimization rates of any age group in all types of crime.[53] However, the quality of the data must be questioned. Much crime against the elderly goes unreported. The elderly may be too feeble or too fearful to contact authorities. They may fear retaliation from their attackers, especially if the perpetrator lives in their neighborhood or, more frightening, is a member of their own household and family. Moreover, many older people live in fear—especially in cities—and often stay indoors to an unnatural degree, triple-locking their doors and thereby protecting themselves from crime by virtual self-imprisonment in their own homes. Thus, what appears to be a lower incidence of crime against the elderly compared to other age groups may be largely due to older people's extraordinary measures to protect themselves and to their reluctance to report crime when it occurs.

The District of Columbia Report to the 1971 White House Conference on Aging, subtitled "Metropolitan Police Contact with the Elderly,"[54] is among the few documents of even relatively recent date that show the degree to which crimes are committed against older persons. Project Assist co-director Phyllis Brostoff pointed to

> a large group of old people (over 60) . . . a depressed underclass . . . who are particularly vulnerable to crime, easy victims of street robbery, unable to move out of high-crime neighborhoods . . . and likely to have no other community resource to turn to other than the police if trouble occurs. . . .

Police reports often do not indicate the age of victims. However, the incidence of crime recorded against older persons indicates that crimes occur primarily where large numbers of older people are concentrated. Public housing complexes are a prime target. Bus and subway stops, basement laundry rooms in apartment buildings, dark halls, back doors, elevators, and short-cuts (paths and passageways hidden from view) can all be dangerous places for older people. Mailboxes in unguarded apartment vestibules are the province of thieves who know when Social Security and welfare checks arrive. Food stamps are a frequently stolen item. The disabilities of old age—deafness, slowness, blindness, spotty memory—make older people especially vulnerable.

In the Project Assist report, about 90% of crimes against older persons were robberies and 8% were assaults. Most robberies take place on the streets rather than at home. The methods used are purse-snatching, intimidation, and strong-arming. The amount of money stolen is often small, and little is ever recovered. Stolen checks and food stamps are recoverable, but the delay can mean having no food or rent money when it is needed. Many of the very poorest aged have no phone on which to notify police of crime. Crimes committed by relatives or landlords against older people rarely are prosecuted because they are not taken seriously.

Naturally, the primary responsibility of the police is law enforcement, and their focus is on prevention of crime and apprehension of criminals. When older people present social problems, the police are often the first neighborhood public service personnel who are called on for help. Many are uneasy, unwilling, or unable to provide social services, but will arrange for referral of social problems to appropriate agencies, especially if they have a responsive agency they can easily call. Social agencies serving the elderly could work more closely with the police than they now do. The police can be excellent sources of information about the location of older people who are isolated or vulnerable, including those with chronic brain syndromes who wander from home, older alcoholics who collapse on the street or become obstreperous, elder abuse victims, and acute brain syndrome victims who require emergency care.

A safe environment (versus one of fear and genuine danger) is crucial to the mental health of older people. In addition to referral mechanisms for a variety of social services, many steps could be taken to better protect older people from crime. Escort services could be arranged by volunteer groups; dead-bolt locks could be provided for the older person's residence. The federal government now arranges to send checks directly to banks free of charge for those persons who would prefer this, thus reducing the theft of checks. Special low-cost checking account service might encourage people not to carry cash but to establish credit and to pay by check whenever possible. If it were generally known that older people no longer dealt in cash, the incentive for criminal attack would be markedly reduced. Vertical policing throughout all the floors in high-rise buildings should be done by police on the beat or by volunteers. Police could perform security audits of buildings to spot crime hazards. Tenants themselves could guard mailrooms at the beginning of each month to protect against check thefts. An older woman might carry an old empty purse or an older man a wallet with a few dollars as decoys to give up under attack. Elderly people also need protection against fraud and deceit (for example, medical quackery, religious exploitation, and consumer fraud) that prey on their vulnerabilities.

Elder Abuse

Butler described the "battered old person syndrome"[55] (known in England as "granny-bashing" or "gran-slamming"), now more commonly called "elder abuse." Battering and abuse take place within the home or family circle, perpetrated by relatives or acquaintances or home-service workers, or in institutions where the elderly reside. Elder abuse is a problem that has existed throughout the history of family and institutional life, but it has only recently been defined as a social problem and is still rather poorly understood. Research

on elder abuse first began in the 1970s and focused national attention on the issue.

A growing literature has been accumulating since research began.[56] Pillemer and Finkelhor's random sample survey of 2,000 older Bostonians (1988) remains the only community based study on elder abuse. The study found that 3.2% of those surveyed had experienced some form of abuse or neglect since they had reached age 65.[57] National estimates of the prevalence of elder abuse range from 4% to 10%, but are unreliable. In response to 1992 amendments to the Older Americans Act, the Administration on Aging commissioned the formation of the National Center on Elder Abuse, which is conducting the first national elder abuse incidence study, scheduled for completion in the summer of 1997.[58]

The Definition of Elder Abuse has fluctuated over the past 20 years. However, five basic types of elder abuse are:

1. *Physical abuse:* The infliction of physical pain or injury (e.g., slap, cut, burn)
2. *Psychological abuse:* The infliction of mental anguish (e.g., name calling, intimidation, threats)
3. *Financial abuse:* The illegal or improper exploitation and/or use of resources
4. *Active neglect:* Refusal or failure to fulfill a caretaking obligation, *including* a conscious and intentional attempt to inflict physical or emotional stress on the elder (e.g., deliberate abandonment or deliberate denial of food or health-related services)
5. *Passive neglect:* Refusal or failure to fulfill a caretaking obligation, *excluding* a conscious and intentional attempt to inflict physical or emotional distress on the elder (e.g., nonprovision of food or services because of inadequate knowledge or own infirmity)[59]

In a 1988 overview on elder abuse for the House and Senate Committees on Aging, the following points were emphasized:

1. There is no reliable evidence that the incidence of elder abuse is rising. Such abuse has

always existed. What is new is our recent national interest and focus on the issue.

2. According to several well-done studies, as many as a million elderly people have been victims of abuse at some point. However, this is substantially lower than the frequently quoted statistic that 4% of the elderly are abused each year, although the difficulty of case detection is acknowledged. A national incidence and prevalence study of elder abuse should be done to obtain a more reliable picture of the nature and extent of abuse.

3. Abuse of the elderly is a serious matter, involving physical as well as psychological and behavioral damage.

4. Abuse by a spouse is the most prevalent form of abuse, followed by abuse from an adult child.

5. Much abuse appears to be related to chronic psychological and/or physical conditions on the part of caregivers, such as developmental disabilities, mental illness, and alcoholism. Caregiver stress is less of a factor in elder abuse than deviance and the resultant dependency, often financial as well as emotional, of family abusers on their victims.

6. Mandatory elder abuse reporting laws may at times do more harm than good, especially when they are not coupled with a program of services. Such laws, which typically require physicians and other health providers to report suspected cases of elder abuse, remove decision making from the hands of the elderly and lead in many cases to institutionalization. Few states offer adequate services to explore remedies for the situation in the older person's own home. On the other hand, health care personnel may be the only link the older person has with the outside world, and mandatory reporting is an attempt to capitalize on this link.

7. A program of comprehensive and coordinated services to victims and their families is the best solution to elder abuse. Some examples are home-care services, consciousness-raising and support groups for both victims and abusers, greater police involvement and response to family violence involving the elderly, with possible use of arrest as a deterrent, direct help to abusers for their own personal problems, and a system of referral of elders and their families to community services such as case managers and elder abuse programs.[60]

Pillemer also points out the need for more well-constructed research, especially on the risk factors for elder abuse and on the effectiveness of various kinds of services in response to these risk factors. Breckman and Adelman (1988) have constructed a list of risk factors. The presence of one or more of these factors indicates increased risk for mistreatment.

- *Family member psychopathology:* Presence of mental illness, mental retardation, dementia, or drug or alcohol abuse
- *Transgenerational violence:* Family history of violence
- *Dependency:* Patient or family member dependent on the other for housing, finances, emotional support, or care-giving
- *Isolation:* Patient does not have the opportunities to relate with people or pursue activities and interests in a manner he or she chooses
- *Stress:* Recent occurrence of stressful life events such as loss of a job, moving, or death of a significant other
- *Living arrangements:* Patient and family member live together[61]

Crime Committed by the Elderly

Older people commit very little crime; they have the lowest arrest rates in every category of crime, and most arrests involve minor offenses, often alcohol-related.[62] The older man or woman who is convicted of a major crime such as homicide usually warrants front page news coverage as a curiosity.

However, many older people are in prisons for crimes committed earlier in life and the proportion of older prisoners is growing. This mirrors the growing number of elderly in the general population as well as longer sentencing that has decreased the possibility of parole.

A national survey conducted by Edith E. Flynn, of Northwestern University, found that the percentage of inmates age 55 and older has doubled in the last ten years, to 6% of the total inmate population of 1.2 million.[63] Specially designated prisons for the elderly have been forecast as the wave of the future in U.S. corrections. Already a few states such as North and South Carolina and Florida have begun to create such facilities. But most of the nation's current elderly prisoners still serve their time in the general prison population. The majority are male, reflecting a generation in which serious crime was predominately a male activity. Often called "Old Joes," these men place special demands on the prison system because of health-care problems and special needs typical of the elderly. The cost of incarcerating older prisoners has been estimated at up to three times the costs for younger inmates. State prisons are especially hard hit financially since inmates are not eligible for the usual federal benefits that include Medicare, veteran's benefits, or Social Security. Most states find that taxpayers balk at the thought of providing expensive medical procedures like heart bypass surgery and CAT scans as well as recreational and social programs suitable for the elderly. Meanwhile, even basic chronic disease and disability care is placing a strain on state prison budgets.

Some have suggested that age itself is a rehabilitator and that many older prisoners could be released, especially those serving long sentences for crimes committed many years ago. Prisons report that violent behavior tends to drop precipitously with age. Studies on the relationship between crime and age indicate that efforts at prevention directed at young offenders are more effective than the continued incarceration of the old. But others argue that releasing an elderly inmate, especially after a long incarceration, is itself a form of cruel and unusual punishment, depriving that person of familiar routines, physical security and guaranteed health care. Especially with frail elderly parolees, major social, financial, and health supports would be needed to assist them in adjusting to the outside world.

ALCOHOLISM[64]

Estimates of the number of older Americans who are problem drinkers vary widely. One source says that the prevalence of alcohol abuse in older people ranges from 2 to 5% for men and about 1% for women—lower figures than for younger age groups. Another source, however, says that 10% of the elderly have drinking problems, the same as the population as a whole. Still others say that 10% is a low estimate. There are a number of reasons for these wide-ranging estimates. For example, problem drinking is often a hidden condition in later life because most older problem drinkers are retired and can retreat to their homes while drinking. Standard measures for the diagnosis of alcoholism may not apply as well to older people as they do to younger age groups. Furthermore, physicians may be reluctant to make a diagnosis of alcoholism in their older patients because they believe it is too late in their patients' lives to do anything about it. Whatever the case, a number of sources say that alcoholism in the elderly will become more widespread in the next half century when the number of older people increases substantially with the aging of the baby boomers. It is estimated that between a third and a half of older people with an alcohol problem developed the problem late in life, perhaps due to the stresses so common in late life, such as illness, loss of a loved one, depression, and so on.

Response to alcohol changes with age. After drinking alcohol, older people have higher blood alcohol levels than younger people and become more prone to its toxic effects. Family members, even health professionals, may attribute memory loss, unsteady gait, confusion, disorientation, falls, and hostility to old age, when they are really a function of alcohol. In addition, the addiction to alcohol may not be recognized by the older alcoholic and his or her family if drinking has continued steadily but quietly over the years. When physical illness strikes, the alcohol may interact adversely with medication, confusing the clinical picture. Addiction may also become apparent when the older person is placed in an institutional setting like a hospital, where alcohol is not available. The older person then goes into withdrawal; if unrecognized, severe symptoms may follow.

The National Council on Alcoholism has issued a set of criteria to diagnose the "disease" of alcoholism.[65] Alcoholism is defined as a condition resulting from excessive ingestion of or idiosyncratic reaction to alcohol. A *problem drinker* is one who drinks enough to cause problems for him- or herself and society.[66] Acute alcoholism is a state of acute intoxication with temporary and reversible mental and bodily effects. *Dipsomania* refers to periodic or "binge" drinking. *Chronic* alcoholism is the fact and consequence of habitual use.

The major criteria that constitute alcoholism include the following:

1. Drinking a fifth of whiskey a day, or its equivalent in wine or beer, for a 180-pound person[67]
2. Alcoholic "blackouts"
3. Withdrawal syndrome—gross tremor, hallucinosis, convulsions, or delirium tremens (DTs)
4. Blood alcohol level above 150 mg/100 ml without seeming intoxicated
5. Continued drinking despite medical advice or family or job problems clearly caused by drinking

Minor criteria include such signs as gulping drinks, frequent car accidents, surreptitious drinking, repeated "going on the wagon," and drinking to relieve anger, fatigue, or depression.

Thus major criteria are symptoms that represent conclusive evidence of physiological or psychological dependence, while minor ones are symptoms usually associated with, but not specific to, alcoholism. (For diagnostic clues for the clinical presentation of alcoholism in old age, see Table 7.1.)

Alcoholism is a leading health problem in the United States.[68] Most deaths directly caused by alcoholism are a result of cirrhosis of the liver. A substantial portion of highway and home acci-

TABLE 7.1 Diagnostic clues for the clinical presentation of alcoholism in old age

1. Insomnia
2. Impotence
3. Problems with control of gout
4. Rapid onset of confusional state
5. Uncontrollable hypertension
6. Unexplained falls/bruises
7. Excessive sleepiness
8. Flushed face
9. Bloated appearance

dents are the result of drinking. It is estimated that alcoholism shortens life expectancy by 10 to 12 years. It may cause heart disease of several kinds and can damage the brain. It may lead to chronic impotence in men by damaging the central nervous system and upsetting hormonal balance. (Transient impotence from excessive drinking may also occur but is reversible.)

Alcohol is a central nervous system depressant substitute that adds to impairments that may already exist as a result of various forms of dementia. It is not, as many believe, a stimulant except as it indirectly inhibits cortical control (higher intellectual functions are associated with the cerebral cortex) and thereby releases emotional reactions. With inhibition of cortical control and impairment of intellectual functions comes failure in judgment, which adds to existing impairments resulting from cerebral atherosclerosis and senile brain disease. Alcohol can affect muscular coordination and bodily equilibrium, causing falls and accidents, including fire setting.

Opinions abound as to what causes alcoholism. Some believe it is genetically determined; others see it as a learned adaptation to psychological stresses. It may be secondary to depression, for example, or it may be an inability to tolerate frustration. Still others view alcoholism as a reflection of social conditions, such as poverty, or an outgrowth of the encouragement of drinking by various cultures.

Studies at the National Institute on Aging have shown that alcohol more severely impairs older subjects (55 to 80 years) than younger (20 to 54 years) on a number of important behavioral measures, including reaction time and delayed recognition (memory). Aging does not significantly influence alcohol metabolism but does impair physiological tolerance to alcohol. The older subjects not only were more severely impaired immediately after drinking but also recovered significantly more slowly.

Chronic alcoholism usually involves poor nutrition primarily caused by vitamin and protein deficiencies and liver dysfunction. In addition to a general deterioration of the personality, one may see delirium tremens followed by Korsakoff's psychosis.[69] Confabulations or fabrications of memory and inability to retain new information (retention defect) are the latter's most striking symptoms. Short-term memory loss (amnesia) and disorientation are present.

Wernicke's encephalopathy may also occur with chronic alcoholism. It is characterized by mental changes such as delirium, apathy, and/or Korsakoff's syndrome, ataxia, and eye signs (for example, motor palsies and nystagmus). Thiamine deficiency is the major cause, and prompt intravenous administration may be lifesaving.

The alcoholic amnestic syndrome (a loss of memory for events occurring during a drinking session, probably caused by bilateral damage to the hippocampal and limbic systems of the brain) has led some to postulate an "alcoholic dementia"—with mental and personal deterioration. However, the latter clear up on cessation of drinking and the provision of care. Only the amnestic syndrome remains. Therefore, the evidence for a dementia associated with alcoholic damage of the central nervous system is not very convincing.

Alcoholism in old age is of two types in terms of duration: early onset and late-life onset (although there is current debate about whether the latter is significant in terms of actual numbers of persons involved). Early onset alcoholism used to result in death of middle-aged persons, but because of antibiotics, better nutritional care, and hospital management, many alcoholics now live to grow old. Late-life onset alcoholism may ap-

pear as a self-medicating mechanism in reaction to grief, depression, loneliness, boredom, or pain. A grief-stricken widow who drinks to lessen her sorrow is an example of this. A more familiar pattern is a lifelong habit of controlled drinking that becomes more pronounced and uncontrolled as life stresses increase.

One sees a high proportion of alcoholism among older patients, mostly men, in veterans' hospitals and domiciliaries. It has been suggested that war experiences and exposure to the cultural drinking patterns of the armed services play a causative role, not to mention the special discount liquor stores run by the military in the United States and around the world.

One also sees many older men and women among the homeless derelicts who sleep on sidewalks, doorsteps, park benches, subway trains, and train stations.[70] However, the stereotype of the "Bowery bum" applies to only about 5% of alcoholics in the United States. The Salvation Army and other religious groups provide free care, food, and lodging. Dorothy Day's exemplary work in her Bowery mission concentrated on the homeless alcoholic. Canter and Koretzky emphasize the importance of a comprehensive after-care program, including halfway houses and counseling, for all older alcoholics and especially the homeless.[71]

Alcoholism in nursing homes and homes for the aging is another problem. Family members may bring alcohol to the patient directly or in a disguised bottle. (Old Listerine bottles are favorites for this use. Cough syrups containing alcohol are also common, innocuous-looking disguises.) In some nursing homes, older alcoholics are able to bribe staff members to get them drinks. Alcoholics Anonymous has become involved in some nursing homes with good results.

Treatment of chronic alcoholism usually consists of detoxification or "drying out," supplemented by vitamins, meals, rest, and medical care. There can be many associated physical problems. A full physical examination should be done, checking for such conditions as diabetes, pancreatitis, tuberculosis, peripheral neuropathy, and subdural hematomas. A mental status examination is indicated (ideally after two or three weeks abstinence) if cognitive problems are apparent.

Many alcoholics who are poor or isolated from their families come to medical attention through police. The middle- or upper-income alcoholic is often hospitalized under a disguised diagnosis, for example, malnutrition or gastritis, in order to avoid the stigma of alcoholism.[72]

Disulfiram (Antabuse) is a drug used to maintain sobriety while a person undergoes supportive or psychotherapeutic treatment. If taken as prescribed on a regular basis, it produces highly unpleasant symptoms whenever a person drinks, including pounding of the heart, nausea, vomiting, and shortness of breath (the result of acetaldehyde production). Side effects in the usual dose range of 0.25 gm daily include fatigue, reduced libido, and reduced potency. Toxic psychoses can occur at higher doses. In a patient over 60 it is of utmost importance to evaluate his or her cardiovascular status, since myocardial and coronary diseases are definite contraindications. Diabetes mellitus, cerebral damage, kidney disease, hypothyroidism, and hepatic cirrhosis or insufficiency all require extreme caution because of possible accidental reactions. Disulfiram may also affect the metabolism of other drugs. It should either be administered by a responsible family member or by a local emergency room, rather than self-administered by the patient.

Tranquilizers and sedatives mixed with alcohol can be life threatening. Many doctors believe that such drugs should only be given on an inpatient basis when alcohol is involved.

Alcoholics Anonymous (AA) has an impressive record of helping alcoholics achieve sobriety.[73] This organization, founded in 1935 by two men—one a stockbroker, the other a practicing surgeon—today has nearly 1.8 million members in over 89,000 groups around the world. Based on the simple proposition that recovered alcoholics can collectively reach out and help a fellow sufferer, AA has been called "an ever-expanding chain reaction of liberation."[74] AA also has a program for spouses and other relatives of alcoholics (Al Anon) and one for teenagers whose parents drink (Alateen). Because of the magnitude of drinking problems among older people, it would be useful to have AA programs set up especially for them—perhaps called Ala-elder. Their adult children and their grandchildren should also be involved where possible, since families tend to be more negative and unsupportive to the older person who drinks heavily.

The Hanley-Hazelden Center in West Palm Beach, Florida, is one of the nation's few treatment centers that has a special unit for elderly alcoholics. The Hazelden method is based on the idea that alcoholism is a disease and that abstinence is the only cure. Individual and group therapy is facilitated by a multidisciplinary team including a clergyman, a psychologist, a physician, and a chemical dependency counselor.

Nursing homes and other institutions should develop treatment programs. Group therapy (alone or with supportive psychotherapy and family counseling), is another useful approach. Recreation therapy and pastoral counseling may be helpful. Labor-management programs to treat problem drinking among employees have been successful because of the powerful added incentive of avoiding the loss of one's job. In general, however, alcoholism is extremely difficult to control. Determination and patience on the part of both the alcoholic and doctor, therapist, or other health practitioner are crucial. It may be necessary to start over again and again; the treatment of alcoholism is usually long-term or lifelong. Family and other social supports are immensely important.

For other referrals to treatment centers contact the National Council on Alcoholism and Drug Dependence, Inc. National Headquarters, 12 W. 21st St., 8th Floor, New York, NY, 10010, or call (800)NCA-CALL.

HEARING IMPAIRMENT[75]

Perceptual impairments, especially hearing loss, are of great import to older people. As the third most commonly reported chronic condition among older adults, hearing loss is more common than vision loss, although both increase with age. Over thirty percent of persons 65 years and older reported having hearing impairments. Hearing impairments rise gradually with age and then increase sharply over the age of 60. About 23% of individuals age 65 to 74 (30% of men and 17.5% of women) reported some problem in hearing, as did 32.7% of those age 75 to 84 (39.9% of men and 28.2% of women). This is compared to 48.4% of those 85 years and older (58.3% of men and 44.3% of women) with self-reported hearing loss.[76] About 13% of those 65 years and over and living in the community reported deafness in one or both ears. This was over 3 million of a total of 26 million elderly. Eight percent, or about 2 million, elderly reported using hearing aids. In earlier studies, the National Health Examination Survey of 1961–1962 studied pure tone audiometric measurements at six different frequencies in persons 18 to 79 years of age. Nearly 30% of persons age 65 to 74 and almost half of those age 75 to 79 showed hearing loss for speech alone, as compared to 10% in the general population. In the older age group 450,000 people were profoundly deaf and totally isolated from any sound. The National Health and Nutrition Examination Survey (HANES I) of 1971, which also included audiometric testing, found slightly lower percentages of hearing loss. However, in the 1977 Health Interview Survey, hearing impairment in those age 65 and over was again in the 30% range.[77] These surveys provide general estimates of the prevalence of hearing loss. In all, about 35% of those over 65 have hearing problems. (None of the studies addresses the type or cause of hearing loss.)

Hearing loss is more common among older men than older women; contrary to general belief, the Framingham study suggests that it is unlikely that a greater rate of exposure to noise in the workplace for males is the reason for male preponderance in hearing loss;[78] yet the actual cause or causes for the difference have not been found. Interestingly, intensive hearing loss is more common among older women than among older men, for reasons yet unclear.

In the late years one may experience nerve as well as conduction deafness. Conduction deafness is caused by middle or external ear pathologic conditions (sound waves are blocked before they reach the inner ear), whereas nerve deafness results from interruption of the auditory nerve pathway. Nerve deafness is much more serious since it implies damage to the nerve that carries impulses to the brain or damage to the brain itself.

Another source of hearing impairment involves the cochlea, a spiral tube of the inner ear, which resembles a small shell. The cochlea contains about 20,000 hair cells at birth. These gradually die off and cannot be replaced. Loss of these ganglion cells is called *presbycusis* and is believed to be associated with the aging of the body and/or brain. Presbycusis is the most common auditory disorder.[79] The central nervous system also is very important in hearing loss because it is the analyzing mechanism for sounds. Older people may be able to hear sounds but not understand them. Immigrants who have learned a second language appear to have special difficulty with their second language in this respect as they age.

Diseases like Meniere's syndrome may be characterized by hearing loss and are often treatable. It is also important not to overlook simple impacted wax (cerumen) in the ear as a cause of reduced hearing, although wax secretion probably diminishes with age. Infections, diabetes, cancer, chronic cardiovascular disease, and many other conditions can also cause ear problems; thus referral to the ear-nose-and-throat specialist is always indicated. Special measures may be necessary to differentiate hearing loss from cognitive impairment in older persons who are severely disabled by conditions such as stroke.

Medicines can have a cumulative effect leading to hearing loss. Extensive use of aspirin, antibiotics such as the aminoglycosides, certain common diuretics, anti-tumor agents, and other medications have a known ototoxicity (literally meaning "ear poisoning"), as do some drugs whose effects on hearing remain unknown. Many of the 38% of the older population who have arthritis consume large enough quantities of aspirin to affect their hearing. The increases in hypertension and heart failure with age signify a heightened probability of diuretic use and thus the danger of hearing loss. The possible effects on hearing must be taken into consideration when prescribing any drugs in large quantities or over a long term.

The hearing impairment occurring during aging is noted first in the higher sound frequencies and begins to be observed after age 50. This does not in itself interfere with normal speech, but the person may miss the songs of birds, a distant telephone ring, or the ticking of a watch. A person with no hearing defect can hear a whispered message at 20 feet in a reasonably quiet room. When a whisper cannot be heard at three feet, the person already has a moderate hearing loss and probably has difficulty with ordinary conversation. This is especially true if the speaker talks rapidly or there is background noise. If a conversational voice cannot be heard one foot away, the person has severe hearing loss. Obviously the loss is profound if the person cannot hear a loud shout with the mouth to the ear. Generally, it is easier for older people to hear hard consonants than soft ones, and there are often problems involving consonants such as *p* as in *pay, s* as in *sam, th* as in *then, t* as in *to, k* as in *keep, h* as in *house, sh* as in *shoe,* or *ch* as in *church.* Older persons simply may not hear any of these sounds or hear only some of them.

Noise pollution is increasingly a factor in hearing loss. The decibel level of the environment can become great enough to permanently damage the tiny hairs in the inner ear. (The decibel, named after Alexander Graham Bell, is the smallest difference in loudness the human ear can detect.) For example, violinists tend to develop slight deafness in the left ear. Many experts predict and are beginning to find hearing loss in young people who listen to loud music at high decibel levels. The increasing noise of city life portends hearing problems for the population in general. Studies of the Mabaans of Sudan, a tribe so isolated that they do not even use drums, show very clearly how lack of noise protects hearing, for they live with a background noise of 40 decibels and experience very little hearing damage. Hospitals themselves have a high decibel level in spite of their "Quiet, please" signs. Following are examples of noises and their decibel levels:

Normal breathing	10 decibels
Leaves rustling in the breeze	20 decibels
Whisper	30 decibels
Quiet restaurant	50 decibels
Normal speech	60 decibels
Busy traffic	70 decibels
Niagara Falls	90 decibels
Subway	100 decibels
Pneumatic riveter	130 decibels
Jet takeoff (discomfort)	140 decibels

The phenomenon of increased reaction time associated with decreased auditory acuity in the presence of depression warrants investigation,[80] as well as the association of mild hearing losses in the aged with diminished performance on verbal tests of intellectual ability.[81]

A comprehensive evaluation of hearing loss is essential. It is estimated that the majority of older persons wait 5 to 10 years after the beginning of their hearing loss to seek medical evaluation and treatment.[82] Careful early diagnosis is critical in salvaging what otherwise might be lost and in restoring as much function as is recoverable.

Hearing loss in older patients in mental hospitals and nursing homes is likely to be neglected. The attitude may be that it hardly matters. Yet institutions should ideally be places where verbal communication is both necessary and rewarding to patients. The results of careful diagnosis and treatment can be favorable even in a large population of institutionalized patients.

Most of the elderly with hearing problems first consult their primary care physician. He or she will refer the patient for an audiologic evaluation. Once a diagnosis has been established and the extent of hearing loss is known, audiologic rehabilitation may be called for. This includes (1) hearing aid fitting and orientation when appropriate; (2) personal and family counseling regarding strategies for aging with hearing loss; (3) speech reading instruction (teaching the person to watch face, body, and situation cues to understand another person better); and (4) referral to self-help groups.

A variety of devices may be helpful; for example, Assistive Listening Devices (ALDs) are remote microphones that bring sound from the source directly to a person's ears. One example is an infrared listening device for the television, which will eliminate room noise interference and allow for greater volume control. ALDs are also available for speech, telephones, and theatrical events. The two million older Americans who use hearing aids may choose from over one thousand different available models. Generally the stereophonic or binaural aids, which bring sound to both ears, are better than monaural aids, which bring sound to only one ear. Digitally programmable hearing aids are now available, which are effective but extremely costly ($1,500 to $3,000). Hearing aids, long associated with a dismal record of usefulness and even outright fraud, are now regulated under the Medical Devices Amendments to the Food, Drug, and Cosmetic Act and may be sold only to people who have had a medical evaluation of their hearing loss unless the examination is specifically waived by the purchaser. The evaluation must have taken place within six months of the purchase of the hearing aid. It must be remembered that not all hearing loss can be improved with a hearing aid. Cochlear implants may be recommended for certain types of hearing loss.

Hard-of-hearing individuals may also take courses in lip-reading at schools such as the Institute of Lifetime Learning of the American Association of Retired Persons—National Retired Teachers Association. The American Speech-Language-Hearing Association (ASHA), 10801 Rockville Pike, Rockville, MD 20852, can answer questions about hearing loss in the elderly and hearing aids, and provide a list of certified audiologists and speech-language pathologists in each state. Self-Help for Hard-of-Hearing People (SHHH), 7910 Woodmont Ave., Suite 1200, Bethesda, MD 20814, is a national organization that provides educational programs, self-help programs, publications, and gives referrals to local chapters.[83]

Depression and paranoid ideation are the most common severe emotional consequences of hearing loss:

> When a person becomes deaf through disease . . . not knowing what his fellow men are saying he becomes doubtful of auditory memories and images; he misinterprets auditory sense impressions which have been distorted by disease, and incorporates tinnitus caused by such disease into his world of inner phantasy. He projects his inner feelings of inferiority caused by his deafness onto his environment and develops ideas of reference. Systematization soon follows, with active delusions of persecution. If the personality is sufficiently unstable a psychotic illness results.[84]

In Chapter 5 we discuss the relationship between hearing loss and depression. Hard-of-hearing individuals are often mistakenly thought to be retarded or mentally ill. The dramatic story of Ludwig von Beethoven notwithstanding, the hearing impaired receive less interest and empathy than the visually impaired and are more subject to depression, demoralization, and even at times psychotic symptomatology. Hearing defects create irritation in others because they interfere so markedly with communication. The loud, badly articulated speech of the hard-of-hearing person and the need to shout and speak slowly make simple conversations frustrating. Wearing a hearing aid can result in a person feeling self-conscious and stereotyped as handicapped. Those with hearing problems may find themselves isolated in a crowd or at a large dinner party because the background noise exacerbates the hearing loss. Many persons with hearing problems worry about the embarrassment that might follow from missing or misunderstanding a comment in the conversation. Much of this is a reaction to the tendency of others to be impatient and insensitive to a person with a deficit.

Those with hearing deficits can often benefit from individual and group therapy and self-help groups. A sense of active help and the elimination of isolation are key components in the care of those with perceptual deficits. Therapy should initially be directed at expressing the underlying anger, grief, and sadness about having a sensory deficit in the first place, but should soon be focused on how the individual can improvise and move on to other accomplishments. Learning from and supporting others with similar deficits can be a major restorative.

A major unresolved problem with hearing loss is the lack of adequate third-party insurance reimbursement. This is a critical reason why so many elderly delay going for help with a hearing problem. Hearing aids range in price from $500 to $3,000 or more for a digital hearing aid. Medicare will reimburse for audiologic services to diagnose and evaluate hearing loss for medical or surgical treatment. However, it will *not* pay for hearing aid evaluation or consultation, nor will it pay for the hearing aid itself or any other assistive listening device. Medicaid coverage for hearing aids varies from state to state. A few private health plans provide some coverage for hearing aids, but such plans are relatively rare.

VISUAL IMPAIRMENT[85]

Vision loss is among the most frequently reported disabilities affecting older people. An estimated 4.1 million older Americans are blind or severely visually impaired. *Visual impairment* is defined as decreased visual ability that impacts on daily activities. *Severe visual impairment* is defined as the inability to read newspaper print, even with corrective lenses.[86] Five percent of people aged 65 to 74 are unable to read newsprint. The percentages are higher for older age groups: 16% at age 75 to 84 and 27% at age 85 and older are unable to read newsprint. Nearly one-half of nursing home residents aged 65 and older report some problem with vision.[87]

The four most common causes of visual impairment in people over 65 years are macular degeneration, cataracts (lens opacities), glaucoma, and diabetic retinopathy. *Macular degeneration* affects a vital part of the retina and leads to a loss of central vision, leaving peripheral vision intact. *Glaucoma* involves increased tension within and hardening of the eyeball as a result of increased

fluid. There are two basic types: acute congestive (narrow angle) and chronic (wide angle). The latter is the most common form of the disease. *Diabetic retinopathy* is a deterioration of the retina caused by chronic diabetes. Nearly half of the legally blind population is 65 years of age or older. (In legal blindness, central visual acuity does not exceed 20/200 in either eye with corrective lenses, or the visual field is less than an angle of 20 degrees.)

Much vision loss is avoidable either through prevention or treatment of the disability, especially cataracts and glaucoma. Glaucoma screening tests, for example, are an age-specific preventive health care measure recommended for persons over 40 years of age. Damage may be done to the optic nerve, with loss of vision, if glaucoma is not detected quickly enough.

Nonmedical members of mental health teams should learn the common physical symptoms of eye problems in order to avoid placing a psychiatric label on a physical process and also to increase empathy and understanding. For instance, if a person reports colored halos around lights, this could be one of the classic prodromal symptoms of glaucoma and not an illusion caused by psychological processes. Such knowledge can result in quicker referral for diagnosis and treatment.

Nearly 95% of elderly use glasses. About 50% of the oldest old, including those who wear glasses, describe some difficulty visually. Deterioration of close vision is common with aging. Nearly all older people who wear glasses do so because of presbyopia or "elder's eyes"—a loss of visual accommodation occurring after middle age, caused by diminished elasticity of the crystalline lens. Except for presbyopia, about 80% of older people have reasonably good sight until age 90 and beyond. In many cases at least one eye functions well, even though the other may lose vision.

There may be an increased slowness in visually adapting to darkness; for this reason, proper lighting is especially important, including night lights. Many older persons report visual difficulty related to glare. Night driving may need to be curtailed or, at least, the person may need to avoid looking directly at oncoming headlights while driving at night.

Psychologically, older persons greatly fear going blind and, consequently, tend to overestimate the possibilities of it happening. But actual vision impairment can be devastating, both in terms of psychological isolation and physical immobilization. With many people vision loss is gradual, and they are able slowly to compensate and adjust. A sudden loss of vision or a loss occurring when the person is feeble and unable to muster resources is usually the most difficult. The social restrictions and resultant sense of isolation for the blind or visually-impaired individual is generally greater than with the hearing-impaired. The public tends to stigmatize and stereotype those with vision problems more than those with hearing problems, probably because the handicap is more visible. Individual and group psychotherapy, as well as support groups for those with vision problems, can be highly effective in facilitating adjustment.

Rehabilitative solutions are becoming more varied and accessible.[88] A variety of low vision lenses, lights, and other optic assistive devices may help. Traditional rehabilitative and assistive efforts such as the teaching of Braille to totally blind individuals and the provision of large-type newspapers (for example, *The New York Times* and the *Reader's Digest*) and cookbooks for visually impaired individuals are still widely used today. The Library of Congress operates the Talking Books Program, which provides free tape players and record players, along with a large selection of books that have been read and recorded onto cassettes or phonograph records. In addition, many new technological devices have been developed. Hand-held magnifiers, some with light attachments, as well as concave mirrors and telescopic lenses permanently attached to the upper part of eyeglasses may be used to supplement low vision. Electronic devices that can translate print to voice output are getting better and more sophisticated. A variety of computers, calendars, thermometers, clocks, and rheostats also have voice capacity, using synthesized speech.

Volunteer readers should be available, as well as books or records on tape, stocked by public libraries.[89] Radio reading services and closed circuit television with lenses to enlarge the image on a cathode ray tube to aid in reading are available. A wide-angle mobility light (WAMO) can help persons with retinitis pigmentosa or other problems with night vision. Seeing-eye dogs and walking canes can assist those with severe visual problems.

Total blindness in both eyes, a relatively rare phenomena, even among the very old, requires special rehabilitation efforts that include (1) training the other senses; (2) training in skills and the use of assistive devices; (3) individual psychotherapy; and (4) group supports, including self-help groups. Family members or close friends should be included in training as well.[90]

The Directory of Services for Blind and Visually Impaired Persons in the U.S., 24th edition, is an exhaustive compendium of services, programs, self-help groups for specific sight disorders, and so forth around the country. It is available from the American Foundation for the Blind, 11 Pennsylvania Plaza, Suite 300, New York, NY 10001, (800) 232-3044.[91]

SEXUALITY IN OLD AGE

Societal Attitudes

Many people, young and old, are astonished at the idea of human beings making love in their seventies, eighties, and even beyond.[92] It is assumed that (1) older people do not have sexual desires, (2) they could not make love even if they did want to, (3) they are too fragile physically and it might hurt them, (4) they are physically unattractive and therefore sexually undesirable, and (5) anyway, the whole notion is shameful and decidedly perverse. There may also be anxieties on the part of adult children related to oedipal connections with their parents. (Many of us remain convinced that *our* parents were not interested in sex.) Yet, in work with older people it is clear that sex is a major concern in late life. Fear about loss of sexual prowess is a common preoccupation for the older man and can reach devastating proportions. Older women will often describe sexual desires, but many regard such feelings as undignified, if not depraved. Some older persons can freely accept their interest in sex, but their children and grandchildren may disapprove and make them feel guilty.

Older persons become the butt of jokes. Older men are frequently ridiculed as impotent or as "dirty old men." (A bumper sticker protesting this idea reads "I'm not a dirty old man. I'm a sexy senior citizen.") Older women fare even worse in the public eye. They are the neuters of our culture, who have mysteriously metamorphosed into sexual oblivion once they reach the age of 50 and beyond.

Homes for the aged, nursing homes, and mental institutions all add to the impression that older persons are sexless. There are seldom serious and dignified provisions for privacy; in fact, there seems to be an agreement that the aged must be prevented from having any sexual contacts. They are often rigidly segregated, men from women, with no visiting in each other's rooms. Conjugal visits with spouses are seldom provided for. Even husbands and wives living in the same institution may not be allowed to live or sleep together. Nursing staffs become anxious and upset when older persons, understandably, resort to masturbation. The problem is often no less difficult for older people who live with their children or in other people's homes. Federal regulations issued on June 1, 1978, provide some right to privacy in institutions, but only for married couples, and only in nursing homes that participate in federal Medicare and Medicaid programs.

The fear of death is another factor affecting sexuality. There are many symbolic associations between sexual activity and death—as in the French word for orgasm, *petit mort* or "little death." Fears of the occurrence of heart attacks or strokes during the course of sex may lead couples to acquire twin beds, separate bedrooms, and a habit of abstinence that may or may not be justified medically. Currents of anxiety, depression, and hostility can accompany these fears as sexuality is inhibited.

Female longevity creates another baffling situation. Since 4.3% of older women have never been married, many others are widowed, often relatively early, and still others have husbands who are older than they and perhaps in poor health, there are many women without partners. What alternatives do they have? Compared to men, women as a group do not yet have the same cultural freedoms to socialize with younger members of the opposite sex. There are not enough older men available. Extramarital affairs are difficult for many to reconcile religiously or morally. Masturbation, although increasing in old age, is still frequently considered shameful or harmful. Thus women legitimately complain that they do not have suitable sexual expression or even information that is relevant to sexual needs in late life. Solutions include the eventual equalizing of the life expectancies of men and women through knowledge obtained from research, the equalizing of sex roles to give women the same opportunities as men, the encouragement of dating and relationships with younger men, the provision of accurate information about the benefits of masturbation, and the development of more lenient attitudes toward the homosexuality that already exists.[93]

Homosexuality as a life-style has both advantages and disadvantages in the later years. The stereotype of the aging homosexual is that of a lonely, bitter, isolated person. The reality, according to studies in this area, is much more complex and includes many close, satisfying relationships that have lasted 40 years or more.[94] Kimmel's study in the late 1970s of 14 aging gay men, ages 55 to 81, found older gays were used to taking care of themselves, with fewer role disruptions than older men with wives and families. On the negative side, gay men experienced both age and sexual-orientation discrimination, and the combination contributed to a tendency among older gay couples to withdraw from society. Lesbian women have a particular advantage as they reach mid-life and beyond, since partners who are their own age will have the same life expectancy, and in later life they move into a world that becomes increasingly female with each decade.

Bereavement, disablement, problems of inheritance and other legal issues, and ageism within the gay community itself can obviously all become problems for older gays. A program called Senior Action in a Gay Environment (SAGE), developed by the gay community in New York to offer free social services to older gay men and women, has become a model of supportive services to the gay community nationwide.

Specific sexual issues for male homosexuals and, increasingly, for the public at large, result from the AIDS epidemic beginning in the early 1980s. Although the majority of AIDS cases to date have been homosexual or bisexual men, AIDS treatment centers are beginning to find more women with AIDS. In addition, the number of AIDS patients over the age of 60 is rising. Early detection and treatment with drugs such as AZT and protease inhibitors can now prolong lives and improve the quality of life. More importantly, prevention of the disease through the practice of safe sex, including the routine use of condoms, the avoidance of exchange of body fluids (semen, blood, and possibly saliva), and testing of potential partners for the AIDS virus can save lives. Most cities have centers and services that can offer testing, information, support, and direct help in treating and preventing AIDS. The U.S. Public Health Service and most state health departments now provide information and referral services.

Research Findings

The data that have been accumulating on the sexuality of older persons have generally supported the view that sexual capacity has been underestimated except where illness or lack of a sexual partner is a factor. Kinsey can be considered the pioneer in modern studies of sexuality in older people. The aged constituted only a small part of his sample, but his findings were useful in beginning to demolish the notion of termination of sexuality in late life. It was found that most men at age 60 were sexually capable physically and

that there was little evidence of sexual decline in women even late in life.

Masters and Johnson's contributions included direct clinical observations of sexual performance as well as interviews. The Duke Longitudinal Study examined 250 people between ages 60 and 94 every three years (Palmore, 1970). Interestingly, these studies found that about 15% of older persons actually increased their patterns of sexual activity and interest as they aged. The Baltimore Longitudinal Study studied the sexuality of older men over a period of years.

Studies by Brecher (1984) as well as by Starr and Weiner (1981) queried the elderly directly about sexual behavior and feelings. Both found a high degree of interest in sexuality and continued sexual activity when a partner was available. Many older persons reported that sex was as satisfying or even more satisfying in later years.

Physical Characteristics of Sex in Old Age

Older Men. Changes that occur with aging are often misinterpreted as evidence that older men are becoming impotent. "From a psychosexual point of view, the male over age 50 has to contend with one of the great fallacies of our culture. Every man in this age group is arbitrarily identified by both public and professional alike as sexually impaired."[95]

There are certain sexual changes associated with chronological aging. The older man ordinarily takes longer to obtain an erection and to achieve ejaculation. Manual stimulation of the penis may be necessary in the initial phase of lovemaking. But as Masters and Johnson point out, "one of the advantages of the aging process with specific reference to sexual functioning is that, generally speaking, control of ejaculatory demand in the 50–75 year age group is far better than in the 20–40 year age group."[96] Translated, this means that many older men can maintain a sexual erection and make love longer before coming to orgasm. This can be a decided advantage for female partners. There is also the advantage of lovemaking experience gained throughout a lifetime.

Older men will notice a reduction in the volume of seminal fluid, which explains the decrease in the pressure to ejaculate. Orgasm begins to be experienced in a shorter one-stage period, as compared to two stages in earlier life, but it remains pleasurable. There is, after age 50, a physiologically extended refractory period, meaning that the capacity for erection following ejaculation cannot be regained as quickly as in younger men. It may be 12 to 24 hours before sex is again possible. Couples who are aware of this may want to delay ejaculation in order to make love for a longer period of time. The penis will become flaccid more promptly after ejaculation; this is natural and not a sign of impairment.

A vital point to remember is that the older man does not lose his facility for erection as he ages unless physical illness or emotional anxiety interferes. For example, laboratory studies at Mount Sinai Hospital in New York City found that most men over 60 had penile erections with their sexual dreaming, including one who was 96. Many men over 60 are satisfied with one or two ejaculations a week or less. But others enjoy sex and satisfy a partner more frequently than that. The amount of sexual activity tends to reflect patterns established earlier in life. A consistent pattern of sexual expression also helps to maintain sexuality.

Older men are usually able to continue some form of physical sexual response until their seventies, eighties, and beyond. If they lose interest or become impotent, there can be a number of factors involved: boredom, fatigue, overeating, excessive drinking, medical and psychiatric disabilities (impotence can be one of the first signs of depression), and fear of failure. The last is common and often based on misinformation about what is normative in old age. Among physical causes of erectile dysfunction are atherosclerotic, cardiorespiratory, endocrine, genitourinary, hematological, neurological, and infectious disorders. Frequently, perineal prostatectomy and occasionally suprapubic and urethral prostatectomy can be factors. Drugs may also be responsible. Tranquilizers, antidepressants, and certain antihypertensive drugs, as well as alcohol have all been reported as inducing impotence. Papaverine, phentolamine, and/or prostaglandin E-1 are effective intracavernous pharmacotherapeutic agents. External vacuum devices are also widely used and effective.

In cases of intractable physical impotence caused by disease, injury, or in rare cases, by psychological factors which do not respond to other forms of treatment, surgical penile implants or prosthesis may be useful. Careful evaluation of both partners in a relationship is necessary to select appropriate candidates for implants. More often, erectile problems are not intractable and respond to medical treatments as well as various psychotherapies, including group, individual, couples, and sexual therapies.

Older Women.   Biologically, the older woman experiences little sexual impairment as she ages. If she is in reasonably good health, she can expect to continue sex activities until late in life, assuming she has maintained a frame of mind that encourages this and has a sexual partner with whom to enjoy it. Menopause, also called "change of life" or "climacteric," occurs with the cessation of menstruation, usually between the ages of 45 and 50. Certain myths have surrounded menopause, including a fear of insanity, the ending of sexual desire and attractiveness, and the myths of inevitable depression, adverse physical symptoms, and defeminization. These have been disputed by research observations of the female climacteric. About 60% of women experience no remarkable physical or emotional symptoms with menopause, and many of those who do have minimal to moderate physical complaints. A small percentage have severe problems requiring a variety of medical and other interventions. Adverse psychological reactions such as depression occur for some, but these are not inevitable, and in fact often reflect a pattern of depression beginning earlier in life, unconnected to the menopause. Psychotherapy and various forms of group supports can provide relief. In severe cases, drug therapies may be successful.

The physiological situation of older women during and after menopause requires review. They commonly suffer from the effects of gradual steroid insufficiency, which causes a thinning of the vaginal walls. Cracking, bleeding, and pain (dyspareunia) during sexual intercourse can result. There may be vaginal burning and itching (estrogen-deficient vaginitis). The urethra and bladder can become more subject to irritation as they are less cushioned by the atrophied vaginal walls, and there can be burning or frequency of urination after sexual contact. The loss of sex steroids may also reduce the length and diameter of the vagina and may shrink the major labia. Estrogen replacement therapy can substantially reduce menopausal symptoms such as vaginal atrophy and dryness. The natural estrogen complex (conjugated estrogens, USP) has been in use for more than 40 years. It is inexpensive and can be helpful against osteoporosis (chronic backache, compression fractures, and "dowager's hump"), estrogen-deficient vaginitis, pruritus, and other aggravating symptoms. Studies of hormone replacement therapy published in 1975 and 1976 showed a somewhat increased risk of endometrial cancer, especially if estrogen was taken for more than one year. Since that time, new guidelines for use include smaller and shorter-term dosages, often combined with another female hormone, progestin (as a protection against endometrial cancer), and a greater clarity about contraindications. However, because of continuing concern about estrogen and breast cancer, long-term use of hormone replacement therapy remains controversial. On the positive side, recent studies have found that women on estrogen therapy were less at risk for the development of heart disease, osteoporosis, and other late life conditions. Possible benefits and risks must be carefully weighed for each patient. The National Heart, Lung, and Blood Institute conducted a double-blind, placebo-controlled, clinical trial in post-menopausal women of unopposed estrogen (estrogen alone) and estrogen/progestational agent combinations (called PEPI). This study supports the value of hormone replacement therapy. Further large-scale studies of the menopause are underway under the auspices of the National Institutes of Health's Women's Health Initiative.

Vaginal secretions that lubricate the vagina may decrease with age. But this does not seem to occur in women who maintain sexual stimulation on a regular basis once or twice a week from youth on, whether through self-stimulation or with a partner. As with men, a consistent pattern of sexual activity is beneficial to women in maintaining their sexual capacities. Muscle tone affecting the "grip" of the vagina on the penis during intercourse can be improved through special exercises (Kegel) designed originally for other gynecological problems.

Sex and Chronic Physical Conditions

The realization that people with chronic illnesses have sexual interests may be unexpected and even unwelcomed. It complicates the medical picture for doctors. The well spouse may not know how to respond. Yet patients may live for years with the help of medical treatment and want as normal a life as possible, including sex. Most current studies of sex concentrate on healthy populations rather than including people with disabling conditions. Sexual activity may be both therapeutic and preventive medicine. There is some evidence, for example, that sexual activity helps arthritis, probably because of adrenal gland production of cortisone. The sexual act is itself a form of physical activity, helping people stay in good physical condition. It can help to reduce both physical and psychological tensions.

Cerebrovascular accidents and coronary attacks can cause much concern, especially if patients and doctors do not discuss if and when sex can be safely resumed. The oxygen cost in sexual intercourse is equivalent to that in climbing a flight or two of stairs or walking briskly at a rate of two miles an hour. The heart rate ranges from 90 to 150 beats a minute, with an average of 120 beats—about the level for light to moderate physical effort. There is not yet a conclusive mass of data regarding sudden death during sex, but it probably occurs much less often than patients fear and somewhat more than the reported incidence (because of reluctance to report accurately). A conservative estimate is that less than 1% of sudden coronary deaths occur during intercourse. Potency may be affected psychologically because heart disease is not only frightening but also tends to undermine confidence in physical capacities. One could easily argue that the anxiety caused by restricting sex may be greater for some people than the actual physical risk from participating in it. A program of physical conditioning under a doctor's care is necessary in preparing for the safe resumption of sexual activities.

Diabetes mellitus is common in old age and causes impotence two to five times as often as in the general population, although sex interest and desire may persist. Impotence from poorly controlled diabetes usually disappears when control is established. But the adequately controlled diabetic man who develops impotence usually has a more permanent problem. The effects of diabetes on the sexuality of women have not yet been well studied, but current research suggests that sexuality is affected far less by diabetes in women than in men.

Pelvic surgery must be carefully planned to avoid unnecessary sexual impairment. Of men who have had prostatectomies, 70% remain potent. Three types of prostatectomy are performed:

1. *Transurethral resection of the prostate (TURP).* A thin, hollow, fiber-optic tube is inserted in the penis, an electric loop is maneuvered through the tube, and the gland is removed. The tissue sometimes grows back; therefore TURP is indicated chiefly when the prostate is not too enlarged, and for men over seventy.

2. *Perineal.* An incision is made between the scrotum and anus, removing most of the prostate. This procedure is used in the surgical treatment of cancer of the prostate.

3. *Suprapubic or retropubic.* The incision is made through the abdomen and is performed when the gland is very enlarged.

After a prostatectomy the semen is deposited in the bladder rather than ejaculated, resulting in "dry ejaculations." However, some semen may still pass through the penis or the prostate may regrow; therefore, a prostectomy is not a reliable form of birth control. Potency is rarely affected with the TURP and suprapubic approaches, and some men even have increased potency. Impotence may occur for psychological reasons. Nonpsychological, physical impotence is most often associated with the perineal approach.

In general, hysterectomies, with or without oophorectomy, do not produce long-term change in sexual desire or performance in women, although some women are especially sensitive to the loss of sexual sensations from the cervix and womb and may need to learn to focus more on clitoral stimulation and sensation. Women may experience a physiologically induced emotional lability and instability for a period of time, although this usually clears without medical treatment. Other psychological reactions include the fear of sexual impairment, fear of loss of sexual desire, and fear of becoming sexually unattractive. Like men, women tend to react emotionally to any subtractive surgery, especially if it is a major subtraction like hysterectomy. Mastectomies, ileostomies, and colostomies are other common surgical procedures that can lead to sexual concern and possible problems. The provision of information, counseling, and individual and group psychotherapies and support can all be immensely helpful in resolving psychological issues.

Peyronie's disease can interfere with sexual performance in men unless it responds to treatment or regresses spontaneously. The symptoms are an upward bowing of the penis, with a shift angled to the right or left. Hard tumors in the corpora cavernosa cause the symptoms, but the cause of these tumors is unknown. Intercourse may be difficult and painful or completely impossible. A variety of treatments may be used and the disease itself may regress in about four years. This disease has been thought to be rare, but judging from our own clinical experience, we suspect it is more common than is believed.

Mental Health Treatment Considerations

Sex, self-esteem, and self-image are closely related. A task of the mental health specialist is to help older people deal with their personal feelings, fears, and possible misunderstandings about sex in old age as well as to recognize and support the special developmental qualities of sex and intimacy that can occur in the later years. One of these special qualities we call "the second language of sex"—a growing capacity, seen in many emotionally healthy older persons, to develop intimacy and communication in a love relationship to new levels.[97] The capacity for sexual intercourse is only one of the measures of a successful relationship. Other forms of stimulation and arousal can be equally important. But perhaps most important is the quality of the emotional interaction between partners. If sexual activity and potency decline while interest remains high, the therapist and patient must consider whether improvement is possible in any or all of the areas—including physical capacity, other forms of stimulation that do not rely on erectile ability, and the emotional relationship itself. Physical examinations, medical treatments, marital counseling, individual and group psychotherapy, sex counseling and support groups may be indicated and can be successful.[98]

Masters and Johnson, in treating older people in their clinic, reported a higher incidence of referrals of men with sexual dysfunction than women, probably because of the need for erectile capacity in male sexuality. They reported a higher failure rate with their older patients, which they attributed to the length of time the problem existed and not the ages of the patients. Nonetheless, there was a more than 50% success rate even when the problem may have existed 25 years or longer.

> The fact that innumerable men and women have not been sexually effective before reaching their late fifties or early sixties is no reason to condemn them to continuing sexual dysfunction as they live out the rest of their life-span. The disinclination of the medical and behavioral professions to treat the aging

population for sexual dysfunction has been a major disservice perpetrated by those professions upon the general problem.[99]

Sex education for older people is important. Normal age changes need to be understood so that neither men nor women mistake such changes for loss of sexuality. Techniques of sexual activities especially pertinent to old age should be clarified. (For example, sex in the morning may be preferable for those older persons who fatigue easily.) The importance of masturbation when sexual partners are unavailable should be emphasized for those who do not find its practice personally upsetting. As discussed earlier, masturbation helps preserve potency in men and sexual functioning in women, releases tensions, stimulates sexual appetite, and contributes to general well-being. It must always be remembered that the current generation of older people was brought up to believe that masturbation is harmful physically and mentally. Such cultural and historic viewpoints cannot be lightly dismissed, but people may be responsive to new information.

Another cultural element is seen in the reluctance of some older women to go to a doctor for help with gynecological problems. Women with even advanced carcinoma of the vulva may delay asking for medical care. Some older women tolerate general prolapse of the uterus for long periods of time, and it is not unusual to find infection and edema from such untreated conditions. Women may need encouragement in accepting examinations on a regular basis.

Regular physical examinations, proper medical treatment, and adequate diet and exercise all help to preserve sexual capacities. As Masters and Johnson have so encouragingly reported, the two major requirements for enjoyable sexual activity until late in life are reasonably good health and an interested and interesting partner.

SELECTED READINGS

Abrams, R. C., & Alexopoulos, G. S. (1987). Substance abuse in the elderly: Alcohol and prescription drugs. *Hospital and Community Psychiatry, 38,* 1285–1287.

Adelman, R. D., & Butler, R. N. (1989). Elder abuse and neglect. In Kaplan, H. I., & Saddock, B. J. (Eds.), *Comprehensive textbook of psychiatry,* 5th ed. (pp. 2053–2056). Baltimore, MD: Williams & Wilkins.

Ade-Ridder, L. (1990). Sexuality and marital qualities among older married couples. In Brubaker, T. H. (Ed.), *Family relationships in later life,* 2nd ed. (pp. 29–48). Newbury Park, CA: Sage Publications.

Administration on Aging. (1996). Opening the door on elder abuse (special issue.) *Aging, 367.*

American Foundation for the Blind. (1993). *The directory of services for blind and visually impaired persons in the U.S.,* 24th ed. New York: Author.

Allers, C. (1990). AIDS and the older adult. *The gerontologist, 30,* 405–407.

Almvig, C. (1982). *The invisible minority: Aging and lesbianism.* Utica, NY: Institute of Gerontology.

American Association of Retired Persons. (1993). *A report on hearing aids: User perspectives and concerns.* Washington, DC: Author.

American Association of Retired Persons, Minority Affairs. (1995). *A portrait of older minorities.* Washington, DC: Author.

American Association of Retired Persons, Women's Initiative. (1994). *Facts about older women: Income and poverty.* Washington, DC: Author.

Anderson Jr., W. B. (1995). Eye: Clinical issues. In Maddox, G. L. (Ed.) *The Encyclopedia of aging* (pp. 354–357). New York: Springer.

Aravanis, S. C., Adelman, R. D., Breckman, R., et. al. (1993). *Diagnostic and treatment guidelines on elder abuse and neglect.* Chicago: American Medical Association.

Axin, J. (1989). Women and aging: Issues of adequacy and equity. *Journal of Women and Aging, 1*(3), 339–362.

Bandler, J. (1989, July). Family protection and women's issues in social security. *Social Work,* 307–311.

Barker, J. C. (1994). Recognizing cultural differences: Health-care providers and elderly patients. *Gerontology and Geriatrics Education, 15*(1), 9–21.

Barresi, C. M., & Stull, D. E. (Eds.) (1993). *Ethnic elderly and long-term care.* New York: Springer.

Bennett, G., & Kingston, P. (1993). *Elder abuse, concepts theories and interventions.* London: Chapman & Hall.

Beresford, T. P., & Gomberg, E. S. L. (1995). *Alcohol and aging.* New York: Oxford University Press.

Berger, R. M. (1982). *Gay and gray: The older homosexual.* Urbana, IL: University of Illinois Press.

Bienenfeld, D. (1987). Alcoholism in the elderly. *American Family Physician, 36*(2), 163–196.

Birren, J. E., Butler, R. N., Greenhouse, S. W., Sokoloff, L., & Yarrow, M. R. (1963). *Human aging: A biological and biobehavioral study.* U.S. Public Health Service pub. no. 986. Washington, DC: U.S. Government Printing Office. (Reprinted 1971, 1974).

Blazer, D. G. (1995). Alcohol abuse and dependence. In Abrams, W. B., Beers, M. H., & Berkow, R. (Eds.), *The Merck manual of geriatrics,* 2nd ed. (pp. 1245–1248). Whitehouse Station, NJ: Merck & Co.

Blendon, R. J., Aiken, L. H., Freeman, H. E., & Corey, M. A. (1989). Access to medical care for black and white Americans, a matter of continuing concern. *Journal of the American Medical Association, 261,* 278–281.

Breckman, R., & Adelman, R. (1989). *Helping victims of elder mistreatment.* Newbury Park, CA: Sage Publications.

Brink, T. L. (Ed.). (1994). *The forgotten aged: Ethnic, psychiatric, and societal minorities.* Binghamton, NY: The Haworth Press.

Brink, T. L. (Ed.). (1992). Hispanic aged mental health. Binghamton, NY: The Haworth Press.

Brody, E. M. (1990). *Women in the middle: Their parent care years.* New York: Springer.

Browne, C., & Broderick, A. (1994, May). Asian and Pacific Island Elders: Issues for social work practice and education. *Social Work, 39*(3), 252–259.

Browne, C., Fong, R., & Mokuau, N. (1994). The mental health of Asian and Pacific Island elders: Implications for research and mental health administration. *Journal of Mental Health Administration, 21*(1), 52–59.

Burr, J. A., & Mutchler, J. E. (1993). Nativity, acculturation, and economic status: Explanations of Asian American living arrangements in later life. *Journal of Gerontology: Social Sciences, 48,* S55–S63.

Butler, R. N. (1975). *Why survive? Being old in America.* New York: Harper & Row.

Butler, R. N., & Lewis, M. I. (1993). *Love and sex after sixty,* revised ed. New York: Ballantine.

Canter, W. A., & Koretzky, M. B. (1989). Treatment of geriatric alcoholism. *Clinical Gerontologist, 9*(1), 67–69.

Carter, T. (1994, Sept.). Age related vision changes: A primary care guide. *Geriatrics, 49*(9), 37–45.

Castex, G. M. (1994, May). Providing services to Hispanic/Latino populations: Profiles in diversity. *Social Work, 39*(3), 288–296.

Chaneles, L. M., & Burnett, C. (1989). *Older offenders: Current trends.* Binghamton, New York: The Haworth Press.

Chatters, L. M. (1990). The family life of older black adults. *Journal of Health and Social Policy, 1,* 45–53.

Chatters, L. M., & Taylor, R. J. (1989, July). Life problems and coping strategies of older black adults. *Social Work,* 313–319.

Chen, Y. (1993). Improving the economic security of minority persons as they enter old age. In *Minority elders: Longevity, economics, and health.* Washington, DC: Gerontological Society of America.

Chung, M. (1989, September). Elderly Chinese living in the United States: Assimilation or adjustment. *Social Work,* 457–461.

Coke, M., & Twaite, J. A. (1995). The black elderly: Satisfaction and quality of later life. Binghamton, NY: The Haworth Press.

Comfort, A. (1978). *Sexual consequences of disability.* Philadelphia: George F. Stickley.

Commonwealth Fund Commission on Elderly People Living Alone. (1993). *The unfinished agenda: Improving the well-being of elderly people living alone.* New York: The Commonwealth Fund.

Commonwealth Fund Commission on Elderly People Living Alone. (1989, September). *Poverty and poor health among elderly Hispanic Americans.* New York: The Commonwealth Fund.

Congressional Caucus for Women's Issues. (1990, June 29). Women excluded from federally funded research, study finds. *Update, 10*(5), 1, 13.

Corso, J. F. (1995). Auditory perception. In Maddox, G. L. (Ed.), *The encyclopedia of aging* (pp. 95–97). New York: Springer.

Corso, J. F. (1995). Hearing. In Maddox, G. L. (Ed.) *The encyclopedia of aging* (pp. 449–452). New York: Springer.

Covey, H. C., & Menard, S. (1987). Trends in arrests among the elderly. *The Gerontologist, 27,* 666–672.

Cutler, S. J. (1995). Crime (against and by the elderly). In Maddox, G. L. (Ed.), *The encyclopedia of aging* (pp. 243–244). New York: Springer.

Daly, A, Jennings, J., Beckett, J. O., & Leashore, B. R. (1995, March). Effective coping strategies of African Americans. *Social Work, 40*(2), 240–248.

Daniels, R. S., Baumhover, L. A., & Clark-Daniels, C. L. (1989). Physicians' Mandatory Reporting of Elder Abuse. *The Gerontologist, 29*(3), 321–327.

Dodson, J. E. (Ed.). (1983). *Strengths of black families—An afrocentric educational manual: Toward a non-deficit perspective in services to families and children.* Nashville, TN: University of Tennessee, School of Social Work.

Douglas, K. C., & Fujimoto, D. (1995). Asian Pacific Elders: Implications for health care providers. *Ethnogeriatrics, 11,* 69–83.

Dowd, J. J., & Bengtson, V. L. (1978). Aging in minority populations: An examination of the double jeopardy hypothesis. *Journal of Gerontology, 33*(3), 427–436.

Dufour, M. C., Archer, L., & Gordis, E. (1992). Alcohol and the elderly. *Clinics in Geriatric Medicine,* 6(127).

Eastman, M. (1994). Old age abuse: A new perspective (2nd ed.) London: Chapman & Hall.

Fanon, F. (1967). *Black skin, white masks.* New York: Grove Press.

Feldman, M. D., Fillit, H., & McCormick, W. C. (1994). AIDS in the older patient. *Patient Care, 28,* 61–71.

Fillit, H., Fruchtman, S., Sell, L., & Rosen, N. (1989). AIDS and the elderly: A case and its implications. *Geriatrics, 44,* 65–70.

Flynn, E. E. (1996). Crime and age. In Birren, J. E. (Ed.), *Encyclopedia of gerontology* (vol. 1, pp. 353–359). San Diego, CA: Academic Press.

Fulmer, T. T., & O'Malley, T. A. (1987). *Inadequate care of the elderly.* New York: Springer.

Fulop, G., Reinhardt, J., Strain, J. J., Paris, B., Miller, M., & Fillet, H. (1993). Identification of alcoholism and depression in a geriatric medicine outpatient clinic. *Journal of the American Geriatrics Society, 41,* 737–741.

Garner, J. D., & Young, A. A. (Eds.). (1994). *Women and healthy aging: Living productively in spite of it all.* Binghamton, NY: The Haworth Press.

Gelfand, D. E. (1994). *Aging and ethnicity: Knowledge and services.* New York: Springer.

Gibson, R. C., & Jackson, J. S. (1992). The black oldest old: Health functioning and informal support. In Suzman, R., Willis, D., & Manton, K. (Eds.), *The oldest old* (pp. 129–147). New York: Oxford University Press.

Gomberg, E. S. L. (1996). Alcohol and drugs. In Birren, J. E. (Ed.), *Encyclopedia of gerontology* (vol. 1, pp. 93–101). San Diego, CA.: Academic Press.

Goodman, H. (1985, Spring/Summer). Serving the elderly blind: A generic approach. *Journal of Gerontological Social Work, 8*(3/4), 153–168.

Gordon-Salant, S. (1995). Hearing. In Birren, J. E. (Ed.), *Encyclopedia of gerontology* (vol. 2, pp. 643–653). San Diego, CA.: Academic Press.

Grad, S. (1996). *Income of the population 55 or older, 1994.* Washington, DC: U.S. Department of Health and Human Services, Social Security Administration, U.S. Government Printing Office.

Gran, L., & Susser, I. (1989). *Women in the later years: Health, social, and cultural perspectives.* Binghamton, NY: The Haworth Press.

Graham, K., Saunders, S. J., Flower, M. C., Timney, C. B., White-Campbell, M., & Pietropaolo, A. Z. (1994). *Addiction treatment for older adults: Eval-*

uation of an innovative client-centered approach. Binghamton, NY: The Haworth Press.

Greenwald, M. (1984). The Sage model for serving older lesbians and gay men. In *Homosexuality and Social Work* (p. 53–61). Binghamton, NY: The Haworth Press.

Guam, J. K., & Whitford, G. S. (1992). Adaptation and age-related expectations of older gay and lesbian adults. *The Gerontologist, 32*(3), 367–374.

Gulya, A. J. (1995) Ear disorders. In Abrams, W. B., Beers, M. H., & Berkow, R. (Eds.), *The Merck manual of geriatrics,* 2nd ed. (pp. 1315–1342). Whitehouse Station, NJ: Merck & Co.

Gutmann, D. (1987). *Reclaimed powers: Toward a new psychology of men and women in later life.* New York: Basic Books.

Harper, M. S. (Ed.). (1990). *Minority aging: Essential curricula content for selected health and allied health professionals.* (DHHS Publication no. HRS P-DV-90–4). Washington, DC: U.S. Government Printing Office.

Hartman, A. (1990). Aging is a feminist issue. *Social Work, 35*(5), 387–388.

Haug, M. R., Ford, A. B., & Sheafor, M. (Eds.). (1985). *The physical and mental health of aged women.* New York: Springer.

Haynes, C. L. (Ed.). (1993). *Women in midlife: Planning for tomorrow.* Binghamton, NY: The Haworth Press.

Hazzard, W. R. (1985). The sex differential in longevity. In Andres, R. Biermen, E. L., & Hazzard, W. R. (Eds.), *The principles of geriatric medicine* (pp. 72–81). New York: McGraw-Hill.

Herzog, A. R., Holden, K. C., & Seltzor, M. M. (Eds.). (1989). *Health and economic status of older women.* Amityville, NY: Baywood.

Ho, M. K. (1987). *Family therapy with ethnic minorities.* Newbury Park, CA: Sage Publications.

Indian Health Service (1995). *Trends in Indian health.* Washington, DC: U.S. Department of Health and Human Services, Indian Health Service.

Jackson, J. S. (1995). African American aged. In Maddox, G. L. (Ed.), *The encyclopedia of aging* (pp. 30–32). New York: Springer.

Jackson, J. S., Albright, J., Miles, T. P., Miranda, M. R., Nunez, C., Stanford, E. P., Yee, B. W. K., Yee, D. L., & Yeo, G. (Eds.). (1994). *Minority elders: Five goals toward building a public policy base.* Washington, DC: The Gerontological Society of America.

Jackson, J. S., Chatters, L. M., & Taylor, R. J. (1993). *Aging in black America.* Newbury Park, CA: Sage Publications.

Jackson, J. S., & Kalavar, J. (1994). Equity and distributive justice across age cohorts: A life-course family perspective. In Cohen, L. (Ed.), *Justice across generations: What does it mean?* Washington, DC: American Association of Retired Persons.

John, R. (1995). *American Indian and Alaska Native elders: An assessment of their current status and provision of services.* Rockville, MD: Indian Health Service.

John, R. (1991). *Defining and meeting the needs of Native American elders.* Final Report of the Administration on Aging Grant # 90AR0117/01 (11 volumes). National Technical Information Service, series PB91174284.

John, R., & Baldridge, D. (1996). *The National Indian Council on Aging Report: Health and long-term care for Indian elders.* Washington, DC: National Indian Policy Center.

Johnson, T. F. (Ed.). (1995). *Elder mistreatment: Ethical issues, dilemmas, and decisions.* Binghamton, NY: The Haworth Press.

Jones, F. C. (1973, January). The lofty role of the black grandmother. *The Crisis,* 19–21.

Kelly, J. (1977). The aging male homosexual: Myth and reality. *The Gerontologist, 17*(4), 328–331.

Kimmel, D. C. (1992). The families of older gay men and lesbians. *Generations, 16–17*(3), 37–38.

Kimmel, D., Raphael, S., Catalano, D. J., & Robinson, M. (1984). Older lesbians and gay men. In *Sourcebook on lesbian/gay healthcare.* San Francisco, CA: National Gay Health Education Foundation.

Kinsey, A. C., Pomeroy, W. B., Martin, C. R., & Gebhard, P. H. (1948). *Sexual behavior in the human male.* Philadelphia: W. B. Saunders.

Kinsey, A. C., Pomeroy, W. B., Martin, C. R., & Gebhard, P. H. (1953). *Sexual behavior in the human female.* Philadelphia: W. B. Saunders.

Kleinschmidt, J. J. (1996). An orientation to vision loss program: Meeting the needs of newly visually impaired older adults. *The Gerontologist, 36*(4), 534–538.

Kosberg, J. I., & Garcia, J. L. (1995). *Elder abuse: International and cross-cultural perspectives.* Binghamton, NY: The Haworth Press.

Kramer, B. J. (1995). Native-American aged. In Maddox, G. L. (Ed.), *The encyclopedia of aging* (pp. 671–673). New York: Springer.

Krause, N. (1993). Race differences in life satisfaction among aged men and women. *Journal of Gerontology: Social Sciences, 48,* S235–S244.

Kunitz, S. J., & Levy, J. E. (1991). *Navajo aging.* Tucson, AZ: The University of Arizona Press.

Kupfer, C. (1995). Ophthalmologic disorders. In Abrams, W. B., Beers, M. H., & Berkow, R. (Eds.), *The Merck manual of geriatrics,* 2nd ed. (pp. 1289–1314). Whitehouse Station, NJ: Merck & Co.

Lachs, M. S., & Pillemer, K. (1995). Abuse and neglect of elderly persons. *New England Journal of Medicine, 332,* 437–443.

Lazzari, M. M., Ford, H. R., & Haughey, K. J. (1996, March). Making a difference: Women of action in the community. *Social Work, 41*(2), 197–205.

Lee, J. A. (Ed.). (1991). *Gay midlife and maturity.* Binghamton, NY: The Haworth Press.

Lee, M. H. M., & Itoh, M. (1995). Rehabilitation: Self-help devices. In Abrams, W. B., Beers, M. H., & Berkow, R. (Eds.), *The Merck manual of geriatrics,* 2nd ed. (pp. 376–77). Whitehouse Station, NJ: Merck & Co.

Leighton, D. A. (1985). Special senses—aging of the eye. In *Textbook of Geriatric Medicine and Gerontology,* 3rd ed. (Ch. 21). Edinburgh: Churchill Livingstone.

Levin, J. S., & Taylor, R. J. (1993). Gender and age differences in religiosity among black Americans. *The Gerontologist, 33,* 16–23.

Lewis, M. I. (1985). Older women and health: An overview. In Golub, S., & Freedman, R. J. (Eds.), *Health needs of women as they age.* NY: The Haworth Press.

Lewis, M. I., & Butler, R. N. (1972). Why is women's lib ignoring old women? *International Journal of Aging and Human Development, 3*(3), 223–231.

Lieber, C. S. (1995). Medical disorders of alcoholism. *New England Journal of Medicine, 333,* 1058–1065.

Linet, O. I., & Ogrinc, F. G. (1996, April 4). Efficacy and safety of intracavernosal alprostadil in men with erectile dysfunction. *New England Journal of Medicine, 334*(14), 873–877.

Logan, S. M. L., Freeman, E. M., & McRoy, R. G. (1990). *Social work practice with black families.* New York: Longman.

Lopez, C., & Aguilera, E. (1991). *On the sidelines: Hispanic elderly and the continuum of care.* Washington, DC: National Council of La Raza.

Luckey, I. (1994, Feb.). African American elders: The support network of generational kin. *Families in Society: The Journal of Contemporary Human Services, 75*(2), 82–89.

Lum, O. M. (1995). Health status of Asians and Pacific Islanders. *Ethnogeriatrics, 11,* 53–67.

Maddox, G. L. (1995). Alcohol use. In Maddox, G. L. (Ed.), *The encyclopedia of aging* (pp. 53–54). New York: Springer.

Markides, K. S. (1994). Gender and ethnic diversity on aging. In Mannheimer, (Ed.), *Older Americans' almanac.* Detroit: Gale Research.

Markides, K. S., & Black, S. A. (1996). Race, ethnicity and aging: The impact of inequality. In Binstock, R. H., & George, L. K. (Eds.), *The handbook of aging and the social sciences,* 4th ed. San Diego: Academic Press.

Markides, K. S, & Mindel, C. H. (1987). *Aging and ethnicity.* Newbury Park, CA: Sage Publications.

Markides, K. S., & Rudkin L. (1996). Racial and ethnic diversity. In Birren, J. E. (Ed.), *Encyclopedia of gerontology* (vol. 2, pp. 371–376). San Diego, CA: Academic Press.

Martin, E. P., & Martin, M. (1983). The black extended family. In Dodson, J. E. (Ed.), *Strengths of black families—An afrocentric educational manual: Toward a non-deficit perspective in services to families and children* (pp. 160–167). Nashville, TN: University of Tennessee, School of Social Work.

Masters, W. H., & Johnson, V. E. (1966). *Human sexual response.* Boston: Little, Brown.

Masters, W. H., & Johnson, V. E. (1970). Human sexual inadequacy. London: J. & A. Churchill.

McDonald, L. (1996). Abuse and neglect of elders. In Birren, J. E. (Ed.), *Encyclopedia of gerontology* (vol. 1, pp. 1–10). San Diego, CA: Academic Press.

McGoldrick, M., Peonce, J., & Giordano, J. (Eds.). (1982). *Ethnicity and family therapy.* New York: Guilford Press.

Mercer, S. O. (1996, March). Navajo elderly people in a reservation nursing home: Admission predictors and culture care practices. *Social Work, 41*(2), 181–189.

Minkler, M., & Stone, R. (1985). The feminization of poverty and older women. *Gerontologist, 25*(4), 351–357.

Money, J. (1988). *Gay, straight, and in between.* New York: Oxford University Press.

Mooradian, A. D., & Greiff, V. (1990). Sexuality in older women. *Archives of Internal Medicine, 150,* 1033–1038.

Morioka-Douglas, N., & Yeo, G. (1990). *Aging and health: Asian/Pacific Island American elderly.* Stanford, CA: Stanford Geriatric Education Center.

Moscicki, E. K., Elkins, E. F., Baum, H. M., & McNamara, P. M. (1985). Hearing loss in the elderly: An epidemeology of the Framingham Heart Study Cohort. *Ear and Hearing, 6*(4), 184–190.

Mount Sinai/Victim Services Agency Elder Abuse Project. (1988). *Elder mistreatment guidelines for health care professionals: Detection, assessment and intervention.* New York: Mt. Sinai Medical Center.

Mui, A. C. (1996, November). Depression among elderly Chinese immigrants: An exploratory study. *Social Work, 41*(6), 633–645.

Muller, C. F. (1990). *Health care and gender.* New York: Russell Sage.

National Center for Health Statistics. (1995). Trends in the health of older Americans: United States, 1994. *Vital and Health Statistics,* Series 3, No. 30. DHHS Publication No.(PHS)95–1414. Hyattsville, MD: U.S. Deparment of Health and Human Services.

National Center for Health Statistics. (1995). Advance report of final marriage statistics, 1989 and 1990. *Monthly Vital Statistics Report, 43*(12), supplement. DHHS Publication No.(PHS)95–1120. Hyattsville, MD: U.S. Department of Health and Human Services.

National Institutes of Health. (1992, Dec. 7–9). *Impotence consensus development conference statement.* Bethesda, MD: National Institutes of Health.

Newman, E. S., Newman, D. J., & Gerwirtz, M. (Eds.). (1984). *Elderly criminals.* Boston: Oelgeschlanger, Gunn & Harin.

Ory, M. G., & Warner, H. R. (Eds.). (1990). *Gender, health and longevity: Multidisciplinary perspectives.* New York: Springer.

Padgett, D. K. (Ed.). (1995). *Handbook on ethnicity, aging, and mental health.* Westport, CT: Greenwood Press.

Palmore, E. (1970). *Normal aging: Reports from the Duke Longitudinal Study, 1955–69.* Durham, NC: Duke University Press.

Parris, B. E., Meier, D. E., Goldstein, T., & Fein, E. D. (1995, April). Elder abuse and neglect: How to recognize warning signs and intervene. *Geriatrics, 50*(4), 47–51.

Perry, C. M., & Johnson, C. L. (1994). Families and support networks among African American oldest-old. *International Journal of Aging and Human Development, 38*(1), 41–50.

Pinderhughes, E. B. (1982). Family functioning of black Americans. *Social Work, 27,* 91–96.

Ponterotto, J. G., Casas, J, Suuzuki, L. A., & Alexander, C. M. (Eds.). (1995). *Handbook of multicultural counseling.* Thousand Oaks, CA: Sage Publications.

Preston, S. H., Elo, I. T., Rosenwaike, I., & Hill, M. (1996, May). African-American mortality at older ages: Results of a matching study. *Demography, 33*(2), 193–209.

Quinn, M. J., & Tomita, S. K. (1986). *Elder abuse and neglect: Causes, diagnosis and intervention.* New York: Springer.

Ramirez de Arellano, A. B. (1994). The elderly. In Molina, C. W., & Aguirre-Molina, M. (Eds.), *Latino health in the U.S.: A growing challenge.* Washington, DC: American Public Health Association.

Ripich, D. (Ed.). (1991). *Handbook of geriatric communication disorders.* Austin, TX: Pro-Ed.

Riley, M. W., Ory, M., & Zablotsky, D. (Eds.). (1990). *AIDS in an aging society: What we need to know.* New York: Springer.

Roberts, J. C. (1995). Eye: Structure and function. In Maddox, G. L. (Ed.), *The encyclopedia of aging* (pp. 357–359). New York: Springer.

Robertson, N. (1988). *Getting better: Inside Alcoholics Anonymous.* New York: William, Morrow and Co.

Robinson, J. B. (1989, July). Clinical treatment of black families: Issues and strategies. *Social Work,* 323–329.

Rosenthal, E. (Ed.). (1990). *Women, aging and ageism.* Binghamton NY: The Haworth Press.

Rosenzweig, R., & Fillit, H. (1992). Probable heterosexual transmission of AIDS in an aged woman. *Journal of the American Geriatrics Society, 40,* 1261–1264.

Scannapieco, M., & Jackson, S. (1996, March). Kinship care: The African American response to family preservation. *Social Work, 41*(2), 190–196.

Schiavi, R. C., Schreiner-Engel, P., Mandeli, J., Schanzer, H., & Cohen, E. (1990). Healthy aging and male sexual function. *American Journal of Psychiatry, 147*(6), 766–771.

Scialfa, C. T., & Kline, D. W. (1996). Vision. In Birren, J. E. (Ed.), *Encyclopedia of gerontology* (vol. 2, pp. 605–612). San Diego, CA: Academic Press.

Schiff, S. M. (1988, Summer). Treatment approaches for older alcoholics. *Generations,* 41–45.

Shanas, E., & Sussman, M. B. (1977). *Family, bureaucracy and the elderly.* Durham, NC: Duke University Press.

Silverstein, M., & Waite, L. J. (1993). Are blacks more likely than whites to receive and provide social support in middle and old age? Yes, no, and maybe so. *Journal of Gerontology: Social Sciences, 48,* S212–S222.

Social Security Administration, U.S. Department of Health and Human Services (1995). *Annual statistical supplement to the social security bulletin.*

Washington, DC: U.S. Government Printing Office.

Sotomayor, M. (1995). Hispanic elderly. In Maddox, G. L. (Ed.), *The encyclopedia of aging* (pp. 458–459). New York: Springer.

Stanford, E. P., Paddecord, K. M., & Lockery, S. A. (1990). Variations among the elderly in black, hispanic, and white families. In Brubaker, T. H. (Ed.), *Family relationships in later life* (pp. 212–241). Newbury Park, CA: Sage Publications.

Stanford, E. P., & Torres-Gil, F. M. (Eds.). (1991, Fall/Winter). Diversity: New approaches to ethnic minority aging. (Special Issue). *Generations, 15*(4).

Steffensmeier, D. J. (1987). The invention of the "new" senior citizen criminal: An analysis of crime trends of elderly males and elderly females, 1964–1984. *Research on Aging, 9,* 281–311.

Steinmetz, S. K. (1990). Elder abuse: Myth and reality. In Brubaker, T. H. (Ed.) *Family relationships in later life* (pp. 193–212). Newbury Park, CA: Sage Publications.

Stetten, D. (1981, August 20). Coping with blindness. *New England Journal of Medicine, 305,* 458–460.

Stock, R. W. (1996, April 18) Alcohol lures the old. *The New York Times,* C1–C2.

Taylor, R. J., & Chatters, L. M. (1991). Extended family networks of older black adults. *Journals of Gerontology, 46,* S210–S217.

Thompson, E. H. (Ed.). (1994). *Older men's lives.* Thousand Oaks, CA.: Sage Publications.

U.S. Bureau of the Census. (1996). 65+ in the United States. *Current Population Reports, Special Studies,* Series P-23, No. 190. Washington, DC: U.S. Government Printing Office.

U.S. Bureau of the Census. (1995). Population profile of the United States: 1995. *Current Population Reports,* Series P-23, No. 189. Washington, DC: U.S. Government Printing Office.

U.S. Bureau of the Census. (February 14, 1996). *U.S. population estimates by age, sex, race, and hispanic origin: 1990–1995.* PPL-41. Washington, DC: Population Projections Branch, Population Division, U.S. Bureau of the Census.

U.S. Bureau of the Census (1996). Marital status and living arrangements: March 1994, *Current Population Reports,* Series P-20, No. 484. Washington, DC: U.S. Government Printing Office.

U.S. House of Representatives Select Committee on Aging. (1989). *The quality of life for older women: Older women living alone.* Comm. pub. no. 100–693. Washington, DC: U.S. Government Printing Office.

Verbrugge, L. (1995). Sex differences in health. In Maddox, G. L. (Ed.), *The encyclopedia of aging* (pp. 850–854). New York: Springer.

Vestal, R. E. (1985). Clinical parmacology. In Andres, R., Bieman, E. L., & Hazzard, W. R. (Eds.), *Principles of geriatric medicine* (pp. 424–443). New York: McGraw-Hill.

Vestal, R. E., McGuire, E., Tobin, J. Andres, R., Norris, M., & Mesey, E. (1977). Aging and alcohol metabolism. *Clinical Pharmacology and Therapeutics, 21*(3), 343–354.

Wake, W. (1988). *Considering the special issues of older lesbians and gay men.* Unpublished paper. Available from author: Send a SASE to William Wake, BSN, P.O. Box 1782, Old Chelsea Station, New York, NY 10011.

Watson, W. H. (1991, Fall/Winter). Ethnicity, crime, & aging: Factors and adaptation. *Generations, 25*(4), 53–57.

Weber, N. D. (Ed.). (1992). *Vision and aging: Issues in social work practice.* Binghamton, NY: The Haworth Press.

Weinberg, A. D., & Wei, J. Y. (1995). *The early recognition of elder abuse.* Bayside, NY: American Medical Publishing Co.

Weinstein, B. E. (1994, August). Age related hearing loss: How to screen for it, and when to intervene. *Geriatrics, 49*(8), 40–45.

Wieland, D., Benton, D., Kramer, B. J., & Dawson, G. D. (Eds.). (1994). *Cultural diversity and geriatric care: Challenges to the health care professions.* Binghamton, NY: The Haworth Press.

Wilcott, J. F. (1991). *Aging and the auditory system: Anatomy, physiology and phychophysics.* San Diego, CA: Singular Publishing Group.

Wolf, R. S. (1992). Victimization of the elderly: Elder abuse and neglect. *Reviews in Clinical Gerontology, 2,* 269–276.

Wolf, R. S. (1994). What's new in elder abuse programming? Four bright ideas. *Gerontologist, 34*(1), 126–129.

Wolf, R. S. (1994, March). Elder abuse: A family tragedy. *Ageing International,* 60–64.

Wolf, R. S., & Pillemer, K. (1989). *Helping elderly victims: The reality of elder abuse.* New York: Columbia University Press.

Women Work! (1994). *Women work, poverty persists: A status report on displaced homemakers & single mothers in the United States.* Washington, DC: Women Work! The National Network for Women's Employment.

Wood, W. G. (1995). Alcoholism. In Maddox, G. L. (Ed.), *The encyclopedia of aging* (pp. 51–53). New York: Springer.

Yeo, G. (1995). Ethical considerations in Asian and Pacific Island elders. *Ethnogeriatrics, 11,* 139–152.

Yeo, G., & Hikoyeda, N. (1995). Asian and Pacific Islander American elders. In Maddox, G. L. (Ed.), *The encyclopedia of aging* (pp. 80–82). New York: Springer.

Young, J. J., & Gu, N. (1995). *Demographic and socio-economic characteristics of elderly Asian and Pacific Island Americans.* Seattle, WA: National Asian Pacific Center on Aging.

ENDNOTES

1. References on ethnic minority elderly can be found in the selected readings at the end of this chapter.
2. U.S. Bureau of the Census. (1996, February 14). *U.S. population estimates by age, sex, race, and hispanic origin: 1990–1995.* PPL-41. Washington, DC: Population Projections Branch, Population Division, U.S. Bureau of the Census.
3. U.S. Bureau of the Census. (1996, July). Population profile of the United States: 1995. *Current Population Reports,* series P-23, no. 189. Washington DC: U.S. Government Printing Office.
4. Jackson, J. J. (1985). Race, national origin, ethnicity, and aging. In Binstock, R. H., & Shanas, E. (Eds.), *Handbook of aging and the social sciences,* 2nd ed. (pp. 264–303). New York: Van Nostrand Reinhold.
5. Fanon, F. (1967). *Black skin, white masks.* New York: Grove Press.
6. Grier, W. H., & Cobbs, P. M. (1968). *Black rage.* New York: Basic Books.
7. Dr. William A. Reid, personal communication, 1972.
8. Jackson, J. S., & Gibson, R. C. (1985). Work and retirement among the black elderly. In Blau, Z. (Ed.), *Current perspectives on aging and the life cycle.* New York: JAI Press.
9. Castex, G. M. (1994, May) Providing services to Hispanic/Latino populations: Profiles in diversity. *Social Work, 39,* 288–296.
10. Markides, K. S., & Rudkin, L. (1996). Racial and ethnic diversity. In Birren, J. E. (Ed.), *Encyclopedia of gerontology* (vol. 2, pp. 371–376). San Diego, CA: Academic Press; Sotomayor, M. (1995). Hispanic elderly. In Maddox, G. L. (Ed.), *The encyclopedia of aging* (pp. 458–459). New York: Springer.
11. Commonwealth Fund Commission on Elderly People Living Alone. (1989, September). *Poverty and poor health among elderly Hispanic Americans.* New York: The Commonwealth Fund.
12. Torres-Gil, F. (1986). Hispanics: A special challenge. In Pifer, A., & Bronte, L. (Eds.), *Our aging society* (pp. 219–242). New York: W.W. Norton.
13. Kramer, B. J. (1995). Native-American aged. In Maddox, G. L. (Ed.), *The encyclopedia of aging* (pp. 671–673). New York: Springer.
14. *Ibid.*
15. John, R., & Baldridge, D. (1996). *The National Indian Council on Aging report: Health and long-term care for Indian elders.* Washington, DC: National Indian Policy Center.
16. Indian Health Service. (1995). *Trends in Indian health: 1995.* Rockville, MD: S. Department of Health and Human Services, Indian Health Service.
17. Mercer, S. O. (1996, March). Navajo elderly people in a reservation nursing home: Admission predictors and culture care practices. *Social Work, 41*(2), 181–189.
18. Ho, M. K. (1987). *Family therapy with ethnic minorities.* Newbury Park, CA: Sage Publications.
19. Young, J., & Gu, N. (1995). *Demographic and socio-economic characteristics of elderly Asian and Pacific Island Americans.* Seattle, WA: National Asian Pacific Center on Aging.
20. *Ibid.*
21. Browne, C., & Broderick, A. (1994, May). Asian Pacific Island elders: Issues for social work practice and education. *Social Work, 39*(3), 252–259.
22. *Ibid,*
23. From 1848 to 1882, over 100,000 Chinese men, as compared to 9,000 Chinese women, immigrated mostly to California and the Rocky Mountain states where they mined gold (they made up 25% of California's gold miners), worked on the railroad (helping to complete the first transcontinental railroad by 1869), and were employed in forestry. The Chinese Exclusion Act of 1882, which also disenfranchised Chinese immigrants and barred them from certain jobs, had as its most long-lasting effect the barring of wives and children from joining their men. By 1943 when the law was repealed, the ratio of males to females in New York's Chinatown was an incredible 17:1

(historical data from Tanzer, A. *The American experience of Chinatown's elderly,* unpublished paper, 1980).

24. The *Issei* (Japanese who were born and raised in Japan before immigrating to the United States) were discriminated against before World War II and placed in internment camps during the war. Despite adversities the *Issei* encouraged and supported the education of their children, the *Nisei,* the majority of whom now have professional and technical occupations.

25. Jackson, J. S. (1989). Race, ethnicity and psychological theory and research. *Journal of Gerontology: Psychological Sciences, 44*(1), 1–2; Gibson, R. G. (1989). Minority aging research: Opportunity and challenge. *Journal of Gerontology: Social Sciences, 44*(1), 2–3.

26. Yee, D. L. (1981, July–August). On Lok senior health services: Community-based long-term care. *Aging, 319–320,* 26–30.

27. Ho, M. K. (1987). *Family therapy with ethnic minorities.* Newbury Park, CA: Sage Publications.

28. *Ibid,* 177.

29. Boyd-Franklin, N. (1989). *Black families in therapy: A multi-system approach.* New York: The Guilford Press.

30. Kim, P. K., & Kim, J. (1989). Curriculum development for social work with Asian-American elderly. *Gerontology and Geriatrics Education, 10*(2), 89–98.

31. Die, A. H., & Seelback, W. C. (1988). Problems, sources of assistance and knowledge of services among elderly Vietnamese immigrants. *The Gerontologist, 28*(4), 448–452.

32. Ho, *Family therapy,* 69–112.

33. U.S. Bureau of the Census (February 14, 1996). *U.S. population estimates by age, sex, race, and hispanic origin: 1990–1995.* PPL-41. Washington, DC: Population Projections Branch, Population Division, U.S. Bureau of the Census.

34. AARP Women's Initiative. (1994). *Facts about older women: Income and poverty.* Washington, DC: American Association of Retired Persons.

35. Annual Statistical Supplement, 1995, to the Social Security Bulletin. Table no. 5.A3. Washington, DC: Social Security Administration.

36. Women Work! (1994). *Women work, poverty persists: A status report on displaced homemakers & single mothers in the United States.* Washington, DC: Women Work! The National Network for Women's Employment.

37. National Congress of Working Women of Wider Opportunities for Women. (1989). *Women, work*

and age: An overview. Washington, DC: Wider Opportunities for Women.

38. U.S. Bureau of Labor Statistics, Current Population Survey, 1995 Annual Averages.

39. U.S. Bureau of the Census, March 1995, Current Population Survey.

40. National Congress of Working Women of Wider Opportunities for Women. (1989). *Women, work and age: An overview.* Washington, DC: Wider Opportunities for Women.

41. Social Security Administration. (1996, January). *Income of the population 55 or older, 1994.* Washington, DC: U.S. Government Printing Office.

42. *Ibid.*

43. U.S. Bureau of the Census (1996). Marital status and living arrangements: March 1994. *Current Population Reports,* Series P-20, No. 484. Washington, DC: U.S. Government Printing Office.

44. National Center for Health Statistics. (1995). Trends in the health of older Americans, 1994. *Monthly Vital Statistics Report, 43*(12), supplement. Hyattsville, MD: U.S. Department of Health and Human Services.

45. U.S. Bureau of the Census. (1996, February 14). *U.S. population estimates by age, sex, race, and hispanic origin: 1990–1995.* PPL-41. Washington, DC: Population Projections Branch, Population Division, U.S. Bureau of the Census.

46. U.S. Bureau of the Census (1996). Marital status and living arrangements: March 1994. *Current Population Reports,* Series P-20, No. 484. Washington, DC: U.S. Government Printing Office.

47. Verbrugge, L. (1995). Sex differences in health. In Maddox, G. L. (Ed.), *The encyclopedia of aging* (pp. 850–854). New York: Springer.

48. Gutmann, D. (1987). *Reclaimed powers: Toward a new psychology of men and women in later life.* New York: Basic Books.

49. Congressional Caucus for Women's Issues. (1990, June 29). Women excluded from federally-funded research, study finds. *Update, 10*(5), 1, 13.

50. Birren, J. E., Butler, R. N., Greenhouse, S. W., Sokoloff, L., & Yarrow, M. R. (1963). *Human aging: A biological and behavioral study.* U.S. Public Health Service Pub. No. 986. Washington, DC: U.S. Government Printing Office. (Reprinted 1971, 1974).

51. American Cancer Society. *Breast cancer facts & figures 1996.* New York: Author.

52. U.S. Bureau of the Census, November 1994 Current Population Survey, PPL-23.

53. See summary of data by Cutler, S. J. (1995). Crime (against and by the elderly) in Maddox, G. L. (Ed.),

The encyclopedia of aging (pp. 243–244). New York: Springer.

54. Brostoff, P., Brown, R., & Butler, R. N. (1972). The public interest: Report no. 6: Beating up on the elderly: Police, social work, crime. *Aging and Human Development, 3,* 319–322.

55. Butler, R. N. (1975). *Why survive? Being old in America.* New York: Harper & Row.

56. The following references on elder abuse are especially useful: Administration on Aging. (1996). Opening the door on elder abuse (special issue.) *Aging, 367;* Breckman, R., & Adelman, R. (1989). *Helping victims of elder mistreatment.* Newbury Park, CA: Sage Publications; Fulmer, T. T., & O'-Malley, T. A. (1987). *Inadequate care of the elderly.* New York: Springer; Parris, B. E., Meier, D. E., Goldstein, T., & Fein, E. D. (1995, April). Elder abuse and neglect: How to recognize warning signs and intervene. *Geriatrics, 50*(4), 47–51; Quinn, M. J., & Tomita, S. K. (1986). *Elder abuse and neglect: Causes, diagnosis and intervention.* New York: Springer; Wolf, R. S., & Pillemer, K. (1989). *Helping elderly victims: The reality of elder abuse.* New York: Columbia University Press.

57. Pillemer, K. A., & Finkelhor, D. (1988). The prevalence of elder abuse: A random sample survey. *The Gerontologist, 24,* 51–57.

58. National Center on Elder Abuse, American Public Welfare Association, 810 First Street, NE, Suite 500, Washington, DC 20002. Information can also be obtained from the National Clearinghouse on Elder Abuse and Neglect (CANE), University of Delaware, (302) 831-3235.

59. Wolf, R. S., & Pillemer, K. A. (1989). *Helping elderly victims.* New York: Columbia University Press.

60. Pillemer, K. A. (1988). Maltreatment of the elderly at home and in institutions: Extent, risk factors, and policy recommendations. In *Legislative agendas for an aging society: 1988 and beyond.* Proceedings of a Congressional Forum, House Select Committee on Aging (Pub. Nbr. 100664) and Senate Special Committee on Aging (Pub. Nbr. 100-J), Washington, DC: U.S. Government Printing Office.

61. Breckman, R., & Adelman, R. (1988). *Strategies for helping victims of elder mistreatment.* Newbury Park, CA: Sage Publications.

62. See: Covey, H. C., & Menard, S. (1987). Trends in arrests among the elderly. *The Gerontologist, 27,* 666–672; Cutler, S. J. (1995). Crime (against and by the elderly). In Maddox, G. L. (Ed.), *Encyclopedia of aging* (pp. 243–244). New York: Springer; Flynn, E. E. (1996). Crime and age. In Birren, J. E. (Ed.), *Encyclopedia of gerontology* (vol. 1, pp. 353–359). San Diego, CA: Academic Press; Steffensmeier, D. J. (1987). The invention of the "new" senior citizen criminal: An analysis of crime trends of elderly males and elderly females, 1964–1984. *Research on Aging, 9,* 281–311; Watson, W. H. (1991. Fall/Winter). Ethnicity, crime, & aging: Factors and adaptation. *Generations, 25*(4), 53–57.

63. Stock, R. W. (1996, January 18) Inside prison, too, a population is aging. *The New York Times,* p. C8.

64. Gomberg, E. S. L. (1996). Alcohol and drugs. In Birren, J. E. (Ed.), *Encyclopedia of gerontology* (vol. 1, pp. 93–101). San Diego, CA: Academic Press; Stock, R. W. (1996, April 18). Alcohol lures the old. *The New York Times,* C1–C2; Wood, W. G. (1995). Alcoholism. In Maddox, G. L. (Ed.), *Encyclopedia of aging* (pp. 51–53). New York: Springer.

65. During the 1950s, the World Health Organization and the American Medical Association declared alcoholism a disease. This, of course, raised the issue of whether personal responsibility (self-control) plays a role in addiction. For example, drug addiction is still treated as a crime rather than as a public health problem similar to alcoholism. There is great question as to the conceptual validity and the therapeutic wisdom of regarding alcoholism solely as a disease. A balance must be struck between that which the individual can control and that which is beyond his or her control.

66. As defined by the U.S. Department of Health and Human Services' National Institute on Alcohol Abuse and Alcoholism (NIAAA).

67. Beers and wines have a relatively higher concentration of various kinds of solids, which account for slower absorption. The alcohol in whiskey, brandy, vodka, and gin is absorbed more rapidly.

68. Federal Agencies concerned with alcoholism (and drug abuse) are: (1) Substance Abuse and Mental Health Services Administration (SAMHSA), a government agency within the U.S. Department of Health and Human Services responsible for administering federal grant programs to advance and support research, training, and service programs in the areas of alcoholism, drug abuse, and mental health. Within SAMHSA are the Center for Substance Abuse Prevention, the Center for Substance Abuse Treatment, and the Center for Mental Health

Services; (2) National Institute of Alcohol Abuse and Alcoholism, an institute within the National Institutes of Health; and (3) National Institute on Drug Abuse, also within the National Institute of Health.

69. Delirium tremens is an acute and sometimes fatal brain disorder (in 10% to 15% of untreated patients) caused by withdrawal or relative withdrawal from alcohol, usually developing in 24 to 96 hours. A history of excessive and unusually prolonged intake is present, and the symptoms of the syndrome include fever, tremors, ataxia, and sometimes convulsions, frightening illusions, delusions, and hallucinations. The condition is often accompanied by nutritional deficiencies. It is a medical emergency.

70. For the moving account of an older man's life as an alcoholic, see Straus, R. (1974). *Escape from custody: A study of alcoholism and institutional dependency as reflected in the life record of a homeless man.* New York: Harper & Row.

71. Canter, W. A., & Koretzky, M. B. (1989). Treatment of geriatric alcoholics. *Clinical Gerontologist, 9*(l), 67–69.

72. The American Hospital Association claims that 25% to 30% of all adult medicosurgical patients in metropolitan hospitals, regardless of diagnosis, have been found to be suffering from alcoholism.

73. Most towns and cities have an AA listing in the telephone book. If not, information may be obtained by writing to AA World Services Inc., 475 Riverside Dr., New York, NY 10115. There are no dues or fees for membership.

74. Robertson, N. (1988). *Getting better: Inside Alcoholics Anonymous.* New York: William Morrow.

75. Corso, J. F. (1995). Auditory perception. In Maddox, G. L. (Ed.), *Encyclopedia of aging* (pp. 95–97). New York: Springer; Gordon-Salant, S. (1995). Hearing. In Birren, J. E. (Ed.), *Encyclopedia of gerontology* (vol. 2, pp. 643–653). San Diego, CA: Academic Press; Gulya, A. J. (1995) Ear disorders. In Abrams, W. B., Beers, M. H., & Berkow, R. (Eds.), *The Merck manual of geriatrics,* 2nd ed. (pp. 1315–1342). Whitehouse Station, NJ: Merck & Co.; and Weinstein, B. E. (1994, August). Age related hearing loss: How to screen for it, and when to intervene. *Geriatrics, 49*(8), 40–45.

76. National Center of Health Statistics, Havik, R. J. (1996, September 19). Aging in the eighties: Impaired senses for sound and light in persons age 65 years and over. Preliminary data from the supplement in aging for the *National Health Interview Survey.* United States, January–June 1987, Ad-

vance Data from Vital and Health Statistics. No. 125, DHHS Pub. No. (PHS) 86–1250. Hyattsville, MD: Public Health Service.

77. Kovar, M. G. (1977). Elderly people: The population 65 years and over. In Department of Health, Education and Welfare, National Center for Health Statistics. *Health, United States 1976–1977.* Pub No. (HRA) 77–1232, Washington, DC: U.S. Government Printing Office.

78. Moscicki, E. K., Elkins, E. F., Baum, H. M., & McNamara, P. M. (1985). Hearing loss in the elderly: An epidemiology of the Framingham Heart Study cohort. *Ear and Hearing, 6*(4), 184–190.

79. Corso, J. F. (1995). Hearing. In Maddox, G. L. (Ed.), *The encyclopedia of aging* (pp. 499–552). New York: Springer.

80. Birren, J. E., Butler, R. N., Greenhouse, S. W., Sokoloff, L., & Yarrow, M. R. (1963). Interdisciplinary relationships: Interrelations of physiological, psychological, and psychiatric findings in healthy elderly men. In Birren, J. E., Butler, R. N., Greenhouse, S. W., Sokoloff, L., & Yarrow, M. R. (Eds.), *Human aging: A biological and behavioral study.* Pub. No. (PHS) 986. Washington, DC: U.S. Government Printing Office (reprinted as Pub. No. [HSM] 71–9051, 1971, 1974).

81. Gennis, V., Garry, P. J., Haaland, K. Y., Yeo, R. A., & Goodwin, J. S. (1991, November). Hearing and cognition in the elderly. New findings and a review of the literature. *Archives of Internal Medicine, 151*(11), 2259–2264.

82. Weinstein, B. E. (1994, August). Age related hearing loss: How to screen for it, and when to intervene. *Geriatrics, 49*(8), 40–45.

83. Information is also available from: National Information Center on Deafness (NICD), Gallaudet University, 800 Florida Ave. NE, Washington, DC 20002; National Institute on Deafness and Other Communication Disorders (NICD), National Institutes of Health, 31 Center Dr., MSC 2320, Bethesda, MD 20892; American Academy of Otolaryngology—Head and Neck Surgery, Inc. (AAO-HNS), One Prince St., Alexandria VA 22314; and the American Tinnitus Association, P.O. Box 5, Portland, OR 97207.

84. From Houston, F., & Royse, A. B. (1954). Relationship between deafness and psychotic illness. *The Journal of Mental Science, 100,* 990–993; see also Cooper, A. F., Kay, D. W. K., Curry, A. R., Garside, R. F., & Roth, M. (1974). Hearing loss in paranoid and affective psychoses of the elderly. *Lancet ii,* 851–854.

85. Kupfer, C. (1995). Opthamologic disorders. In Abrams, W. B., Beer, M. H., & Berkow, R. (Eds.), *The Merck manual of geriatrics,* 2nd ed. (pp. 1289–1314). Whitehouse Station, NJ: Merck & Co.

86. American Foundation for the Blind. (1996). *Facts about aging and vision.* Available from American Foundation for the Blind, M. C. Migel Library and Information Center, 11 Penn Plaza, Suite 300, New York, NY 10001.

87. Carter, T. (1994, September). Age related visual changes: A primary care guide. *Geriatrics, 49*(9), 37–45.

88. For a highly readable and useful personal description of learning about visual aids, see Stetten, D. (1981, August 20). Coping with blindness. *Sounding Board, New England Journal of Medicine, 305,* 458–460.

89. For more information on talking books and other library services, contact the National Library Service for the Blind and Visually Handicapped. 1291 Taylor St. NW, Washington, DC 20542, (800) 424-8567.

90. Lee, M. S., & Itoh, M. (1995). Rehabilitation: Section on "self-help devices in the home." In Abrams, W. B., Beer, M. H., & Berkow, R. (Eds.), *The Merck manual of geriatrics,* 2nd ed. (pp. 376–377). Whitehouse Station, NJ: Merck & Co.

91. For additional information and services contact: The National Eye Institute (NIE) of the National Institute of Health (NIH), 900 Rockville Pike, Building 31, Room 6A32, Bethesda, MD 20892-3655; The American Optometric Association, 243 North Lindbergh Blvd., St. Louis, MO 63141; The Lighthouse National Center for Vision and Aging, 111 E. 59th St., New York, NY 10022; The National Association for the Visually Handicapped, 22 W. 21st St. New York, NY 10010; The National Eye Care Project of the American Academy of Ophthalmology (AAO), P.O. Box 6988, San Francisco, CA 94120 (A helpline provides referrals for disadvantaged older people to free eyecare and information. Call (800)222-EYES); The National Society to Prevent Blindness, 500 E. Remington Rd., Schaumberg, IL 60173; and The Vision Foundation, 818 Auburn St., Watertown, MA 02172.

92. Butler, R. N., & Lewis, M. I. (1993). *Love and sex after sixty,* revised ed. New York: Ballantine.

93. Homosexuality per se was eliminated as a mental disorder by the American Psychiatric Association in DSM-II (1973). Thus homosexuality itself can no longer be medically labeled psychopathological; only when it is "egodystonic" (the individual does not accept being a homosexual), causing severe distress or disability, is it deemed a mental disorder.

94. A number of references on homosexuality and aging are included in the Selected Readings for this chapter.

95. Masters, W. H., & Johnson, V. E. (1970). *Human sexual inadequacy.* London: J. & A. Churchill, 316, 318.

96. *Ibid.*

97. Butler, R. N., & Lewis, M. I. (1993). *Love and sex After sixty,* revised ed. New York: Ballantine, 276–288.

98. As an example, a bachelor participating in the NIMH Human Aging Studies undertook intensive psychotherapy four times a week at age 65 and married for the first time. Another example is the English sexologist Havelock Ellis, who overcame lifelong impotence in his old age with the help of a loving and responsive woman (Calder-Marshall, A. [1959]. *The sage of sex: A life of Havelock Ellis.* New York: G. P. Putnam's Sons.)

99. From Masters, W. H., & Johnson, V. E. *Human sexual inadequacy.*

PART TWO

EVALUATION, TREATMENT, AND PREVENTION

CHAPTER 8

GENERAL TREATMENT PRINCIPLES

We are writing the treatment section of this book on two levels: one describing what we consider to be appropriate and ideal mental health care of older people and the other dealing with contemporary realities, far from ideal. Our aim is to keep in sight the direction for improvements, while also advising mental health personnel, older people themselves, and anyone involved in their welfare on how to make the best of what is now available.

There has been a steady growth in theory and practice in the mental health treatment of older persons, emphasizing the importance of active, restorative, and rehabilitative possibilities. Most important, the potentiality of reversibility has been demonstrated, both in the functional disorders and in some of the organic disorders, particularly delirium.

Prevention, comprehensive evaluations, and genuine therapeutic efforts have begun to be accepted as worthwhile activities on behalf of older persons.

CHANGES IN PERSPECTIVES TOWARD MENTAL HEALTH TREATMENT OF OLDER PERSONS

The body of theory surrounding mental health treatment of the elderly has slowly evolved from more general theory about human behavior. Beginning with psychiatry at the turn of the century, theories about abnormal behavior had a detached quality—observing and cataloging exterior behavior. Later, dominated by Freudian thinking, the focus moved to the inner life of humans—probing subjective experience and internalized modes of adaptation. Since World War II, psychiatry has moved out somewhat (but only *somewhat*) into the community—examining the influences of institutions and environmental conditions on human behavior, inner experience, and adaptations. This is reflected in the American Psychiatric Association's 1980 *Diagnostic and Statistical Manual* and its later revisions, which require consideration of social stresses as part of a psychiatric diagnosis. Biological psychiatry has made significant advances that have resulted in useful psychoactive medications. Recently some attention has been given to the inherent changes of the individual as he or she progresses through the life cycle. Thus, in about 90 years, psychiatry has looked at people's outward behavior, their inner life, their environment, their biology, and finally their passage through their finite existence—the life cycle. This includes a new interest in understanding old age.

American psychotherapist Carl R. Rogers's concept of humanistic psychology—emphasizing a person's own capacity for life-long growth and development rather than dwelling largely on the past—has been helpful in work with the elderly. Rogers and other founders of humanistic psychology, such as Abraham Maslow and Rollo May, have been called the "Third Force in Psychology" in order to distinguish their work from two other prominent schools of thought, psychoanalysis and behaviorism. Today their client-centered approach is widely used among therapists and counselors.

Cognitive psychotherapy, originally formulated by Aaron Beck, emphasizes finding solutions to definable, reality-based problems by means of interpretation, explanation, and practical information. It has been found to be especially useful with well-motivated, depressed older people who have few or no physically based mental impairments.

Other forms of psychotherapy include psychoanalysis and psychoanalytic psychotherapy, behavior therapy, hypnosis, group psychotherapy, psychodrama, family therapy, couples therapy, and brief or crisis therapy, all of which can be useful in work with older persons. These will be described more fully in Chapter 12.

There are also ongoing, exciting recent developments occurring in the neurosciences that are ultimately likely to make great contributions to understanding human behavior and to the treatment of mental disorders. Examples are the catecholamine hypothesis of the origins of affective disorders like depression (see Chapter 5) and the new understandings of the genetics and neurochemistry of Alzheimer's disease.

The Special Relevance of Life-Cycle Theory

A major direction in developing a psychology of old age has resulted in what has been called "life-cycle" theory. Social, biological, medical, and other changes have led to longer life and increased visibility of the stages of the life cycle. As a result, attention has begun to turn to the inherent psychological changes of the individual as he or she progresses through the life cycle. A science, or perhaps more humbly, a perspective and body of knowledge of the life cycle, is being born.

Improved public health and medical care have prolonged life in both the formerly dangerous years of infancy and the often frail years of late life. The middle years of life stand as a fulcrum and largely support the two ends of the life cycle—childhood and old age. This is true for individuals, when parents are responsible both for their children and for their own parents; it is true also in society, where middle-aged people hold the power, make the decisions, and produce the goods. We do not yet know to what extent normative, modal features of the life cycle account for the varying patterns of change and adaptation we see. A few investigators like Matilda White Riley have been engaged in disentangling the features of the successive phases of the life cycle from the contributions of such influences as social change, medical disease, and historical variation.[1] Butler (1968) introduced the term "average expectable life cycle" as a counterpart to Heinz Hartman's concept "average expectable environment"[2] to bring focus to the notion that there are average, normative experiences against which to measure individual patterns. If, for example, we see correlations of conservative behavior with age, are these a result of the conditions of youth carried forward in time, or are they intrinsic to aging? If we observe preoccupation with bowel function in aged persons, is it a result of the popular lore relating health with bowel function that was prevalent at the turn of the century or a consequence of the inherent character of old age? Are the declines in memory associated with aging to be interpreted as a consequence of brain disease, educational obsolescence, social anomie, depression, or the mysterious, inevitable, irreversible process called *aging?*

There is not yet a sufficiently sensitive methodology to weigh the relative significance of the many elements that are involved in the production of changes in people and adaptation to those changes. We believe the life cycle itself—the changes inherent in the rhythm of a life from birth to death—makes profound contributions to the variability. The study of human development has tended in the past to stop with adolescence. Recently social scientists have begun to study the psychology of mid-life. Persons involved in fact gathering and theoretical formulations now need to build up a head of steam and plunge through middle age to old age instead of losing interest after surveying the "achievement" of adulthood. Contemporary personality and developmental theories need enlargement and expansion to provide a full account of human nature. Such an effort would give further direction to the treatment of older people.

In clinical work and reflections, Butler speaks of the development of an *individual inner sense of the life cycle,* which is neither the same as the average expectable life cycle nor the same as a personal sense of identity, although it is related to both. It is a subjective feel for the life cycle as a whole—its rhythm, its variability, and the relation of this to the individual's sense of self. This inner sense seems to be a necessary personal achievement in order for individuals to orient themselves wherever they happen to be in the life cycle. It becomes particularly important as people age and begin to comprehend their own eventual end.

In adolescents, the middle-aged, and older persons, such a personal sense of the cycle of human life is a necessary adaptive mechanism. Understanding the kinds of changes to be expected and facing the reality and inevitability of these changes, including death itself, is important to individual security. A sense of the life cycle gives people the opportunity to prepare themselves, to plan and order their lives in more meaningful ways, and perhaps more important, to be assured that they are not alone in their experiences. All former and future generations and all of their fellow living human beings share many of the same basic realities. The understanding of this is part of what humans long for when they speak of searching for the meaning of life through religion or a personal philosophy of life. An inner sense of the life cycle—often unspoken—produces a profound

awareness of change and evolution—birth, maturation, aging, and death—and therefore a profound but nonmorbid realization of the precious and limited quantity of life. For older people it is not the same as "feeling old"; it is instead a deep understanding of what it means to be human.

One sees all kinds of people struggling for greater sensibility about life but, for various reasons, not being able to face what is there. There are adolescents who can comprehend the notion of suicide (perhaps because in killing oneself, one has active control over one's death) but cannot imagine death in old age or even that they themselves will grow old. Middle-aged persons often develop anxiety symptoms about aging and try to turn the clock back to youth by dressing and acting young. Even in old age, one sees Peter Pans—those who have never grown up to face their own age and the fact of death.

In our own work, we have seen what an inner sense of the life cycle can mean in old age. It can portend adaptation to inevitable changes in the best manner possible; or its absence can guarantee maladaptation, wherein the older person reacts with terror, dependency, and prolonged grief to personal change. The following case examples are illustrative.

A handsome, warm, and magnetic 78-year-old former politician, who had received many public awards, called for a psychiatric consultation, his voice full of despair. He had always been healthy and unusually vigorous until the previous summer, at which time he developed glaucoma. Shortly thereafter he began to notice weakness of his left arm. By means of a myelogram, electromyelographic studies, and other tests, it was determined that the patient had anterior horn cell disease.

He had been an unusually healthy man all his life, extremely vigorous, and very proud of his sexual prowess and attractiveness. He had been married three times and had had many private affairs.

However, until his recent problems, he had never taken seriously the fact that he could become old. Moreover, his much younger brother was suffering from severe chronic brain disorder and was residing in a nursing home; this fact began to preoccupy him.

Our patient remained somewhat busy in public life but had recently given up his last private love affair. During a warm and somewhat grief-stricken lunch together, the two quoted Ecclesiastes to each other: "Everything in its season. . . ."

Yet he never prepared for old age. He never thought about old age when he was younger; in fact he gave it little thought until his glaucoma. On the rare occasions when he did, he would say to himself, "Why shouldn't I live to be 100?" Whenever he, again rarely, thought about death, he wished for, and he thought that he would have, a quick sudden death. He had turned aside suggestions that he write his memoirs.

Now he felt helpless. His sense of omnipotence was under sudden siege and near collapse. He became extremely hypochondriacal. He not only went to physicians from a whole range of specialties but sought out possible quacks.

In summary, he had not experienced aging or the diseases associated with aging gradually. All was precipitous, with no stepwise intimations of mortality!

Although he had five children, he was not in any sense strongly involved with them, which suggests that he had not grown into or fulfilled the life-cycle task of parenthood.

Once engaged in psychotherapy, he became very much dependent on the therapist. Although the psychotherapist was obviously doing nothing "material," he believed the therapist was the only physician who was "doing anything" for him—in spite of the fact that the others had offered drugs and had conducted a variety of tests. Emphasis in psychotherapy was on consideration of the unfolding of the life cycle and on renunciation and restitution; that is, on grieving and accepting things as they were and finding other avenues for personal pleasure and development—particularly those pertinent to later life such as teaching, counseling, and leaving "traces." It was eventually necessary to reduce the number of sessions to help him resolve his dependency. He improved, but any lengthy separations from the therapist created setbacks, and he continued regular contacts as a way of maintaining his equilibrium.

In 1965 an 87-year-old former schoolteacher sustained a stroke from which she recovered except for a residual right hemiplegia. There was no aphasia. She had always been an extremely independent person, and she was quite agitated and depressed over what had happened to her. Unlike the previous patient, however, she did not respond with helplessness. She was a very courageous fighter, pulling herself up and down stairs for dinner each day. This was still true five years later at age 92. The therapist continued seeing her, although the agitated depression had gone. They seemed unable to give each other up. They would meet approximately once monthly, usually on Saturday afternoon, at which time at her insistence they would have a fine sherry or Madeira together. There were occasions when she would put herself to bed and seem to be failing. However, nothing would be amiss on physical examination, and it became clear that these episodes were related to the thought on her part that maybe she was just about to die. In view of her advanced age, this was not such an irrational idea. Then, after several days in bed, she would awaken to the realization that she was neither dead nor dying and would be back up functioning again.

At other times the therapist would simply tell her she was all right, whereupon she would agree and resume life. These episodes were characterized psychologically by great preoccupation with leaving things and with what the recipients would do with the objects of her legacy. It was very important to her that she not be falsely reassured about death but that respectful attention be given to her ideas about dying, death, burial, and the objects of her legacy—religious items, pictures of her parents, favorite old books, and so on. Unlike the previous patient, she had always had a sound sense of the evolving process of life, the life cycle. But her advancing age—or diseases—narrowed the opportunities in which she could express her personality. Thus she had to rely more and more on verbal or bodily expression of needs (rather than action). She had responsiveness in abundance from her daughter as well as from her therapist. She continued to do quite well.

In attempting to understand an individual's life cycle, it is useful to identify events that typically characterize a life. One way to approach this is to examine rites of passage or cultural observances of biological and social changes. Christenings, confirmations or bar mitzvahs, marriages, and burials are the most obvious, but there are countless others, all adding structure and meaning to lives. They lend predictability and help to ease the individual's movement from one stage to the next. Such rites help us to "know the score"; offer social supports from time of birth and early development; confirm our religious, sexual, occupational, and social identity; consecrate marriages as well as provide for their dissolution; and offer models for dealing with happiness and fulfillment as well as with failure, grief, loss, and eventual death. However, rites of passage, as with all other cultural institutions, are often out of tune with human needs as history unfolds. It is necessary to understand the nature of the particular life cycle in order to judge the validity of the rites of passage associated with it. Rites of passage undergo constant revision—and when the revision is delayed, complicated, incomplete, or aborted, humans flounder and suffer from the lack of a meaningful structure. An example in the present is the problem in handling grief that has resulted from increasing secularization and the loss of religious supports. Older people, and especially their children, often do not know what to do with grief. Should they cry, maintain a stoic front, deny it, become angry, or something else? For many there is no longer a structured and supportive mourning period. Some mourners pretend the loss never happened; others wait silently, hoping grief will go away. Yet we know theoretically what "grief work" is and what could be done to help find the best possible psychological resolution to loss. It remains for such knowledge to become part of popular psychology. People who no longer belong to an institutionalized religion must learn to do for themselves some of the work they formerly left up to the church or synagogue.

Other parts of the life cycle are changing as a result of alterations in biology and changes in the life span. Changes occur so quickly that people may be left bewildered. The bewilderment is greatest in those for whom the change is greatest. Small children born today have never experienced anything but accelerating change, and it has been

suggested that change itself is an accepted way of life for them. But for the present generation of older people who remember a more slowly moving past, the contrast with the present can be horrifying, disconcerting, and disorienting, particularly if the older person feels or is in some way personally victimized by change.

New rites of passage are needed to support new developments. Recent and still-growing controls of the events of the life cycle bear comment. Flexibility of classic rites is needed to cope with birth control, liberalized abortion, genetic manipulation, sex prediction before birth—all of which could (and already do) allow considerable control over the occurrence and timing of birth and quality of children. The arrival of menstruation for girls has moved ahead thirty-six months in the last hundred years. The rite of marriage (which first became a sacrament in the ninth century A.D., when people seldom lived longer than 40 years) is being influenced by trial marriages, the ability to control births, and the notion of divorce by consent. The event of death is subject to greater control. Organ transplants, new thoughts about criteria for death (as a result of medical discoveries), interest in passive and active euthanasia—all produce legal, ethical, and medical considerations that will become part of the evolving rites surrounding death.

One feature of present life—retirement—has almost no formal rites of passage and no precedent historically. The institution of retirement is barely 100 years old and is a consequence of the lengthening of the life span for vast numbers of people. Many will spend 20 years or more in retirement. Similar demographic changes are occurring in other countries, some of which are responding more positively than we have. Our present lack of structured and meaningful rites for retirement has led to anomic nonparticipation of many people in American life.

Because of medical progress since the turn of the century, people are now free from many of the previously fixed biological states that have long controlled the culturally defined rites of passage. What such freedom means for the future is hard to fathom. But we do know that both present and future generations of older people need to have a secure place for themselves in a society that makes sense to them. Good mental health is not possible in chaos and meaninglessness.

OBSTACLES TO TREATMENT IN OLD AGE

Ageism and Countertransference

We have described the many negative attitudes toward older people by coining the general term *ageism*—the prejudices and stereotypes that are applied to older people sheerly on the basis of their age.[3] (Another term, *gerontophobia,* refers to a more rare "unreasonable fear and/or constant hatred of older people, whereas ageism is a much more comprehensive and useful concept.")[4] Ageism, like racism and sexism, is a way of pigeonholing people and not allowing them to be individuals with unique ways of living their lives. Prejudice toward older people begins in childhood[5] and is an attempt by younger generations to shield themselves from the fact of their own eventual aging and death and to avoid having to deal with the social and economic problems of increasing numbers of older people. It provides a rationalization for pushing older people out of the job market without devoting much thought to what will happen to them when they are no longer allowed to work. (Relatively recent U.S. retirement laws have ended mandatory retirement in the public and private sectors and are a powerful counterforce to this trend, but most other countries still maintain a fixed retirement age.) Ageism is the sacrifice of older people for the sake of "productivity" and the youth image that the working world feels compelled to project. A terrible awakening comes when these younger people themselves grow old and suddenly find that they are the victims of attitudes they once held against others.

Countertransference in the classic sense occurs when mental health personnel find themselves perceiving and reacting to older persons in ways that are inappropriate and reminiscent of previous patterns of relating to parents, siblings, and other key childhood figures. Love and protectiveness may vie with hate and revenge. Ageism takes this a step further. Mental health personnel not only have to deal with leftover feelings from their personal pasts, which may interfere with their perceptions of older persons, but they must also be aware of a multitude of negative cultural attitudes toward older persons, which pervade social institutions as well as individual psyches.

The Group for the Advancement of Psychiatry report, "The Aged and Community Mental Health," in 1971 listed some of the major reasons for negative staff attitudes toward treating older persons.[6] This list still holds true. Some items no doubt represent universal, timeless feelings about old age. Others are more culturally or historically specific to a particular time and place. These attitudes are the following:

1. The aged stimulate the therapist's fears about his or her own old age.
2. They arouse the therapist's conflicts about his or her relationship with parental figures.
3. The therapist believes he or she has nothing useful to offer older people because he or she believes they cannot change their behavior or that their problems are all due to untreatable organic brain diseases.
4. The therapist believes that his or her psychodynamic skills will be wasted when working with the aged, since they are near death and not really deserving of attention (similar to the triage system of the military, in which the sickest receive the least attention because they are least likely to recover).
5. The patient might die while in treatment, which could challenge the therapist's sense of importance.
6. The therapist's colleagues may be contemptuous of his or her efforts on behalf of aged patients. (One often hears the remark that gerontologists or geriatric specialists have a morbid preoccupation with death; their interest in older persons is therefore "sick" or suspect.)

Another factor in ageism and negative countertransference is what appears to be a human propensity for hostility toward the handicapped. There is often an unconscious overidentification with older people, especially those who are physically handicapped: They are thought of as defective, crippled, powerless, or castrated. Excessive sentimentality, sympathy, avoidance, or hostility may result. It is estimated that some 300 million people in the world have highly visible deformities. These cause emotional problems—in part because of the attitudes of society. In certain primitive cultures such "cripples" (and, we might add, old people) were often put to death. This "final solution" is not so obvious in present societies, but attitudes remain surprisingly similar.

Some people have described the treatment they have received as handicapped patients. An American writer, Eric Hodgins, in his book *Episode: Report on the Accident inside My Skull*[7] tells of his own doctor, an old friend of many years, who talked to others about him in the hospital room after his stroke as though Hodgins were no longer an aware human being. Hodgins's superb account is useful reading for all who work with patients of any age.

Publications in the field of mental health have long contained evidence of ageism. A respected and well-known clinical psychiatric textbook, as late as 1977, read:

> A dislike of change, a reduction in ambition and activity, a tendency to become constricted and self-centered in interests, an increased difficulty in comprehension, an increase in time and effort in adapting to new circumstances, a lessened sympathy for new ideas and views and a tendency to reminiscence and repetition are scarcely signs of senile dementia, yet they pass imperceptibly into mental destitution and personality regression. Many elderly people have little capacity to express warm and spontaneous feelings toward others. . . .
>
> The patient resents what he considers as interference by younger persons and may complain that he is being neglected. Some show a hostile but anxious and fearful dependence. Natural affections become blunted and may turn to hatred. A certain tendency to isolation occurs.[8]

There are half-truths in this statement in the case of persons with dementia. But more obvious is the pessimistic, patronizing view of old age, tempered only slightly by hints that some of the changes might be psychological reactions to loss and stress. Anyone reading such material was confirmed in his or her negative attitudes.

Reactions of Older Persons against Treatment

Force, deceit, or any other measure taken by mental health personnel "for the older person's own good," when it is against the wishes of that older person, cannot be justified morally or legally, except in those cases in which the person is a clear and present danger to the life of himself or others. Older people may resist mental health intervention in their lives for many reasons: desire for independence, fear of change, suspiciousness based on past experiences, realistic appraisal of the inadequacies of most "helping" programs for older persons, clumsy, insensitive, or patronizing intervention techniques on the part of mental health staff, and so forth. Many times older people will tenaciously hold on to what little they have rather than risk the unknown. They may prefer to live in their own homes despite crime, dilapidation, and isolation. They may resist medical examinations, surgery, and medications. Some have been known to keep guns to use on themselves or others if someone comes to take them to a nursing home— a fate feared by many as worse than death. Pride and desire for self-reliance, as well as depression and mental confusion, must be considered as factors in resistance.

One approaches the resistance of older persons just as one would the resistances of any age group—by gradual development of trust, provision of information, and a commitment to self-determination and civil rights. Members of the clergy can often be helpful in talking through problems and decisions, as can family members, neighbors, and friends. Whenever possible, the older person must be closely involved in any decision making about him- or herself. Action, rather than just verbalization by mental health staff, can bring satisfying results. An example is the case of an older, New York woman with mild intellectual impairment who refused to move out of her condemned apartment. No amount of talking could convince her. Finally a staff member offered to physically help her move and stay with her the first night. The old woman accepted. Her fears had been met with an appropriate response.

Another problem affecting treatment is the low self-esteem of some older people who have incorporated the negative cultural view of themselves. This reaction of the victims of discrimination has been called "self-hatred" and takes the form of depression, with passive giving up or active self-denigration. These elderly look at themselves as so many younger people see them and thus do not like what they see. Open discussions about ageism can help such people reexamine their self-views, particularly if at the same time they begin to experience new acceptance on the part of people around them. Age-integrated group therapy is especially useful in this regard.

Lack of Knowledge

We simply do not know enough about old age, especially about healthy old age. Most clinical experience and studies have been of the sick and institutionalized aged. Generally, older persons are not admitted to research and training centers. And most research experience has been limited to brief periods of contact—to short-term evaluation rather than to treatment.

One major consequence of this limitation is the lack of the more enduring, intensive relationship of treatment personnel and patients, which can be an important source of data about the older person as well as a check on one's evaluation of him or her. Indeed, referral for mental health treatment is not only relatively uncommon in the community, but when it does occur, it is usually late in the course of illness, again affecting the accumulation of basic knowledge for evaluation, as

well as decreasing the likelihood of therapeutic success.

Financial and Bureaucratic Impediments

Mental health care is expensive, especially when private psychiatrists, other psychotherapists, private-duty nurses, and private hospitalization are involved. Such care is far beyond the budget of most older people. Public care is occasionally adequate and at times exemplary, but usually it is a far cry from satisfactory. Until adoption of a comprehensive medical insurance plan for all U.S. citizens, the major method of obtaining care for older persons will continue to be the Medicare system. Medicare now covers only about 40% of the average older person's health expenses. The deductibles (that which the patients pay) are just that—deductions from the care of the aged. Older people often simply do not purchase the excluded items (including dentures, eyeglasses, outpatient drugs, physical examinations) because they cannot afford them. Unfortunately, the out-of-pocket proportion of the cost of medical care has actually risen for older people since the introduction of Medicare because of increases in physician's fees, hospital costs, long-term care, and other services that Medicare does not cover, as well as the general inflationary spiral. There is also no proof that the deductible features of Medicare deter unnecessary use of health services. Instead, the exclusions may actually increase the government's bill by discouraging preventive and early rehabilitative care and rewarding hospitalization. For example, some older people, with their doctor's collaboration, have themselves checked into a hospital simply to obtain a physical examination (basing it on some physical complaint) because routine physical examinations are not covered by Medicare on an outpatient basis.

Medical coverage for psychiatric disorders is unrealistically limited and was inserted in the Medicare legislation as a kind of afterthought. (The initial diagnostic work-up and medical management of psychotropic drugs are reimbursed at the usual 80% Medicare rate). There is a 190-day lifetime limit on treatment in mental hospitals; and the patient must pay approximately 50% of allowed charges for outpatient therapy given by a physician and, as of July 1990, by a psychologist or a social worker.

For the currently limited but growing numbers of older people in health maintenance organizations, patterns of coverage for mental health care are still uncertain.

Nursing homes unfortunately have gotten into the business of providing "care" for psychiatric patients; yet they are not in any sense of the word psychiatric institutions. The conditions for eligibility for extended care under the Medicare program are both inadequate and inadequately applied. As a result, tens of thousands of older patients, including those with psychiatric problems, are receiving no more than routine custodial care.

Many nursing home facilities are substandard. The frequent occurrence of fires in nursing homes is one consequence. Too often a nursing home can be defined as a place with few nurses and few of the characteristics of home. Social and restorative services hardly exist in many homes, and activity programs usually receive more advertising than implementation. It is rare for psychiatric or social work services to ever play a part in the nursing home program. Most commercial nursing homes as well as many voluntary homes do not provide a social work staff. In addition, nursing home care is not primarily funded by Medicare, but rather by Medicaid and public assistance. Medicaid pays about 42% of nursing home care. Medicare pays only 2%. Patients themselves pay 51%, and private health insurance picks up the remaining 5%.

New federal legislation, applied as of January 1, 1989, states, in effect, that nursing homes cannot care for patients who suffer from active psychiatric disorders or mental retardation. Some therefore began refusing admission to people seeking care solely because they are retarded or mentally ill, although states have varied in the speed with which they adopted these new federal regulations. However, from the perspective of this legislation, Alzheimer's disease is not considered to be an active psychiatric disease, and, therefore, Alzheimer's patients continue to be accepted in nursing homes.

Centralized information and referral services for provision of mental health care are lacking. Bureaucratic confusion abounds. The stress and frustration older people go through to collect Medicare and private health insurance must be experienced to be believed. We present a case that is not atypical in our work.

We attempted to assist one of our clients who was having difficulty collecting payments for psychotherapy. Medicare was sending payments in different amounts for the same service and the same fee, and Mrs. K wanted to know why. In addition, her supplementary major medical insurance with Blue Cross-Blue Shield was refusing to pay for psychiatric services even though the insurance agent handling the policy assured us our client was covered.

In a five-month period we made multiple calls to Medicare (Mrs. K had already spoken to eight different people in the Medicare office during the previous six months), asking for an explanation and a list of allowable charges. We were told that a computer was faulty, and an audit was being done.

Five months later Mrs. K received a notice that she had been overpaid $60 and that she must pay it back. There was still no explanation or list of allowable charges. Mrs. K refused to believe anything any longer and decided to ignore the $60, feeling sure another mistake had been made.

During the same five months we were told twice by Blue Cross-Blue Shield that Mrs. K was eligible for psychiatric services and three times that she was not. We were twice asked to resubmit everything (previous material had been lost, couldn't be transferred from one part of BC-BS to another, etc.). After five months of work on our part, Mrs. K still had not been paid. Like the carrot on a stick, there was a constant promise of resolution—"in a month or six weeks."

We checked with Mrs. K ten months after our first contact. She had finally been paid by BC-BS. She had never paid Medicare the $60 and was never billed for it. She continued to receive different payments from Medicare for the same service and said, "but I don't question it anymore—as long as I get *something back." Medicare never sent a list of allowable charges, and BC-BS said they could not furnish her with a list of covered services or allowable charges for people who also had Medicare, because "each case is considered separately."*

When an older person with anxiety, anger, and frustration about public and private health insurance programs comes to the attention of mental health personnel, the following are possibilities to consider before simply deciding that the person is "acting dependent" or that he or she "can't cope":

1. It is often difficult to reach the proper insurance or government official by phone.
2. Clients are shifted from one person to another person and tend to give up before they reach the "right" person.
3. Phone calls are often not returned; neither are messages received. Materials that are promised may not be sent.
4. Conflicting information may be given. Many health insurance employees do not know their own office procedures or the specifics of the programs they serve.
5. Records seem, routinely, to get lost. Then the client must begin all over again.
6. There may be no explanation about payments or inconsistent payments, especially in Medicare.
7. When a mix-up occurs, clients often hear an insurance representative say, "It's out of my hands" (in the computer, another office, etc.); there is seldom any avenue to retrieve it promptly.
8. Even when insurance or government personnel are pleasant and interested, they often give the impression of being helpless in straightening out problems efficiently. Thus the older person is made to feel guilty about complaining or causing a fuss.

As we mentioned in Chapter 2, one of the new, major, time-consuming functions emerging for middle-aged offspring is helping their older parents deal with and untangle bureaucratic red tape in order to collect the benefits to which they are entitled. To assist older persons and their relatives in general, federal and state agencies should work toward

1. Centralizing or unifying offices in each locality to which older people must go for assistance under various federal and state programs.
2. Developing a common application form for various programs.
3. Arriving at uniform definitions.
4. Unifying and simplifying procedures for determining eligibility and recertification of eligibility under various programs (for example, as of October 1, 1990, physicians are required to submit Medicare claims for their patients).
5. Unifying hearing and appellate procedures for various benefit programs.

PROGRESS TOWARD DEVELOPING PROFESSIONAL INTEREST AND SKILLS IN PROVIDING MENTAL HEALTH CARE TO THE ELDERLY

Psychiatrists and Other Physicians

In the mental health field, ageism has become professionalized—often to the point where it is not recognized. In some of the earliest investigations on this subject, Gibson noted in 1970 that psychiatrists were pessimistic about the treatability of older persons.[9] In reviewing the records of 138 patients over 65 who were admitted to a private hospital during a three-year period, it was found that the prognosis was considered poor in 80% of the patients; yet 60% were discharged as improved to their homes within 90 days. Even earlier, Gallagher et al. in 1965 found age correlating with therapeutic pessimism.[10] Of patients between 15 and 29 years of age, 66.7% received psychotherapy; of patients who were 30 to 39, 38.5% did; and of those 40 to 65, only 15.4% did.

A study of 179 psychiatrists, published in 1980, corroborates findings from earlier studies. The study indicates that

1. Psychiatrists regarded older patients as less ideal to work with than younger patients with identical symptoms.

2. The prognosis for older persons was considered poorer than that for young persons, even though the data (admittedly limited) on the prognosis of older persons do not support this conclusion.

3. Psychiatrists were much less likely to use psychotherapy, especially with older depressed women, than they were with younger persons. Instead they gave drugs, with the implication that psychotherapy would not be worthwhile.[11]

A 1987 study of primary care settings by German et al. found that despite the prevalence of emotional and psychiatric problems in the older generation, physicians in general practice are less likely to diagnose mental disorders among older persons than they are in younger persons. There is a tendency to confuse certain symptoms with general signs of aging; diagnostic mistakes also occur due to confusion over drug side effects.[12] In an accompanying editorial, Glass termed this tendency to attribute psychiatric symptoms either to changes expected to come with age or to concomitant physical disorders "a subtle form of ageism on the part of some primary care providers."[13] Interestingly, one early study found that older psychiatrists who see a higher proportion of older patients, advocate more comprehensive treatment and find older patients more interesting and gratifying.[14]

The American Geriatrics Society has pointed out that community surveys suggest that 1% or fewer of the elderly receive psychiatric care. More specifically, only 4% of community mental health center patients are over age 65; fewer than 4% of patients seen by private practitioners are elderly; and less than 1.5% of all community-based mental health care goes to the older population.[15] German et al. note that the elderly's limited use of mental health specialty care is also influenced by the stigma the elderly themselves attach to mental illness, namely that it denotes a morally weak person and may result in becoming an outcast.[16]

Although the 1980 Mendenhall psychotherapy study reports that the average psychiatrist spends only 5.3% total patient time on patients over 65,[17]

over 2,000 psychiatrists now identify themselves as having a primary interest in older patients (the extent of their knowledge or ability to work with older persons is unknown). The recent development of geriatric psychiatry (Great Britain's comparable development is called "psychogeriatrics") is evident in Sanford Finkel's organization of the American Association for Geriatric Psychiatry (AAGP) in 1978.[18] More than 400 physicians joined the AAGP in its first year, and by 1996 membership had increased to 1,400.

Many believe that geriatric psychiatry probably should not become a practice specialty in and of itself since all psychiatrists may have older people as patients and all of them will need to know the principles of geriatric psychiatry. From this point of view, the major goal for geriatric psychiatry should be academic, to train the teachers and researchers whose responsibility it is to train future generations of psychiatrists.

Leaders in the field of geriatric psychiatry have begun to emerge. In addition to contributing to the development of treatment approaches, Berezin, Busse, Eisdorfer, Gaitz, Gitelson, Goldfarb, Greenleigh, Grotjahn, Pfeiffer, Rothschild, Simon, Thompson, and Weinberg are among the U.S. psychiatrists whose work has stimulated research into the psychopathology and psychodynamics of aging.

Liaison psychiatry has also become important, particularly in hospitalized populations of older people, because it addresses the interpersonal, psychological, and psychosocial needs of patients whose illnesses are primarily nonpsychiatric. Together with the medical-surgical physicians and nonphysician staff, the liaison psychiatrist attempts to augment the diagnosis, treatment, and management of the patient. Although consultation usually consists of a brief intervention by a liaison team with a biophysical approach to illness, it sometimes leads to a recommendation for more in-depth psychotherapy.

Major labor needs exist in both the present and the future for both psychiatry and primary care medicine.[19] In 1979 the American Psychiatric Association showed a commitment to aging by establishing a Council on Aging. The American Board of Medical Specialties, based on the recommendations of the American Boards of Psychiatry and Neurology (ABPN) agreed to give examinations beginning in 1991 to those interested in receiving a Certificate of Added Qualification in Geriatric Psychiatry, following the American Board of Internal Medicine and the American Academy of Family Practice's development of a certificate of competence in geriatrics. (Applications for the ABPN examination can be obtained by calling 847-945-7900. The Beeson Report of the Institute of Medicine, *Aging and Medical Education,* was an important catalyst toward high-quality geriatric medicine, along with the National Institute on Aging's Geriatric Medicine Academic Awards, open to departments of internal medicine, family medicine, and psychiatry.[20]

On the whole, however, psychiatry as a practice specialty has not kept pace with the theoretical aspects of the discipline. Private psychotherapy, analytic practice, and psychopharmacology remain psychiatry's main preoccupations, with little active participation in the broader field of community psychiatry. Meanwhile, other disciplines have become more involved than ever in mental health work. Nurses, social workers, psychologists, pastoral counselors, paraprofessionals, and members of still-forming specialties are doing much of the work traditionally thought of as psychiatry in the past. Financial reimbursement by insurance companies and government programs of mental health services to the elderly do not yet adequately reflect this new reality. Psychologists and social workers are becoming increasingly recognized as independent vendors of mental health services.

Psychologists

The American Psychological Association's task force on training and aging updated a report on graduate education in August 1985.[21] Those U.S. and Canadian universities with psychology-related doctoral programs as listed in the American Psychological Association's publication *Graduate Study in Psychology for 1983–1984* were queried. Of these, 303 academic units responded. About 21%, 65 units, provided a specialization in adult development and aging. Another 76, or about 33%, were without specialization, but had at least one full-time faculty member with a primary interest in adult development and aging and had at least one course in this area. Thus, apparently 46% of the academic units have no faculty, courses, or programs related to aging.

As of July 1990, under Public Law 101–231, psychologists became reimbursable as independent vendors for their mental health services to the elderly (Medicare Part B outpatient mental health benefits). They also have pressed for the right to prescribe medication and to admit patients to psychiatric hospitals on their own, rather than under the supervision of psychiatrists. These rights, especially for prescribing medications, have been questioned by many and are currently under review in numerous jurisdictions.

Nurses

Nurses have, of course, always taken care of older people, and those in the nursing field have been showing increasing interest in such care.[22] Nurses who have taken leadership with regard to aging are Faye G. Abdullah, Doris Alford, Sister Rose Therese Bahr, Anna M. Brock, Myrtle I. Brown, Sister Erika Bunke, Irene M. Burnside, Sally Busck, Barbara Davis, Priscilla Ebersole, May Futrel, Laurie M. Gunter, Barbara W. Hansen, Jacqueline Heppler, Lois Knowles, Mathy Mezey, Helen Monea, Dorothy Moses, Maxine Patrick, Valencia Prock, Joan Quinn, Sister Marilyn Schwab, Doris Schwartz, Eldonna Shields, Edna M. Stilwell, Virginia Stone, Mary O. Wolanin, and May Wykie. Nurses are usually the first medical contact older people have (67% of RNs work in acute care hospitals and 6% in nursing homes; the rest are in clinics, private doctors' offices, and public health programs, with a few in private practice).[23] Therefore their training, skills, and sensitivity are crucial in creating positive and effective health care for the old. Because of their pioneering work as a profession in the field of aging, we have compiled a historical summary of their activity (Table 8.1). In the 1970s nurses began moving away from primary emphasis on a medical model to a nursing model, emphasizing health and prevention of illness as well as care during illness (rising out of the tradition of the public health nurse). At the same time they began to move away from their previous focus on institutionalized older persons to care in other settings, such as home care. Leadership in teaching nurses to work with other professions in a multidisciplinary approach to the problems of old age became a focus of the nursing profession.

Certification as a geriatric nurse recognizes the registered nurse who practices in a health care setting or performs health care functions where the primary responsibility is the care of the aged, where actions are focused on a particular patient in a case management style, and where there is personal responsibility and accountability to the patient for the outcome of such actions. Only those who are in the clinical practice of nursing qualify for such certification. Consultants, researchers, administrators, and educators are eligible to seek certification if they are also in clinical practice and can meet the criteria as specified.[24] As of October, 1995, the American Nurses' Credentialing Center listed 11,081 certified gerontologic nurses and 1,941 certified gerontologic nurse practitioners.

There are now a number of nursing schools that offer gerontological courses at the undergraduate and graduate levels. Duke University was the first to offer a master's degree in gerontological nursing, under the direction of Dr. Virginia Stone. Several schools have geriatric nurse practitioner programs,[25] but lack of interest and resistance against work with older persons remains.

Unfortunately, the broadening role of nurses—for example, as nurse practitioners—combined with modest pay, low status, and often difficult working conditions (largely because it has been a "female" profession) continue. There are increasing needs for nursing in certain areas, notably AIDS, drug addiction, and Alzheimer's disease.

Furthermore, cutbacks in federal funds for nursing research in the 1980s and early 1990s hamper the discovery of new techniques for caring for older persons on the most practical levels of care. However, the new National Institute for Nursing Research at the National Institutes of Health, in collaboration with the National Institute on Aging, contributes new knowledge for the care of older persons.

Social Workers

Social workers provide the majority of mental health care to persons of all ages in the United States, and in rural areas they are often the sole providers of services. Clinical social workers are recognized in federal law as autonomous providers of mental health care under CHAMPUS (Civilian Health and Medical Benefits Program of the Uniformed Services), FEHBP (Federal Employee Health Benefits Program), and in risk-sharing HMOs (Health Maintenance Organizations) funded through Medicare. Under the FEHBP program, private insurance carriers, including Aetna, Blue Cross/Blue Shield, Prudential, Mutual of Omaha, Harvard Community Health Plan, Kaiser Permanente, and the Health Insurance Plan of Greater New York, reimburse clinical social workers for treatment of federal employees, retirees, and their dependents. In addition, all states legally regulate social workers in an effort to ensure standards of qualification and demonstrated competence and many require licensing. With regard to specific mental health care of the elderly, a law authorizing direct reimbursement of clinical social work and psychological services under Medicare Part B outpatient mental health benefits took effect July 1990. Qualified social workers no longer have to work under the supervision of a physician for the purposes of psychotherapy.

Geriatric social work has been consistently described by social policy analysts and forecasters as a field with significant growth potential. Yet the profession has been slow in responding to the growing numbers of older persons and their need

TABLE 8.1   The pioneering involvement of the nursing profession in work with older persons

1943–1948—Two articles appeared in *American Journal of Nursing,* giving geriatric nursing direction and value and viewing geriatric nursing as a potential speciality.

1950—First nursing textbook for care of the elderly published (Newton, K. [1950]. *Geriatric nursing.* St. Louis: C. V. Mosby).

1950 on—Nursing literature about nursing and the aged proliferated.

1955—American Nurses' Foundation established to promote nursing research, much of which has been concerned with care of the aged.

1958—American Nursing Association (ANA) became first health profession to support health insurance for elderly (culminated in Medicare in 1965).

1959—ANA testified before U.S. Senate Subcommittee on Aging about low standards of care in nursing homes and also recommended expansion of home care programs.

1960—ANA adopted statement on standards for nursing care in nursing homes.

1961—ANA formed conference group for geriatric nurses, which met for first time in 1962 (70 nurses).

1966—Conference group became one of five clinical divisions in the ANA.

1966—A professional publication, *Geriatric Nursing,* appeared (discontinued in 1968).

1970—ANA published its standards of geriatric nursing practice. These were revised in 1976 (see *Standards: Gerontological nursing practice,* 1976, American Nurses' Association, 2420 Pershing Rd., Kansas City, Mo. 64108). These were designed for all areas of nursing practice, not just for "gerontological nurses."

1972—ANA committee formed to develop program to certify nurses for work with the aging. First group of nurses (74) was certified in 1974. In 1980 there were over 280 such nurses. (Nurses must be RNs. Training is nine months to one year, offered by at least nine nursing programs around the United States.)

1973—National project of continuing education on geriatric nursing started.

1974—Geriatric nurse practitioner programs were being developed.[†]

1974 on—Department of Health, Education, and Welfare made grants to nursing schools to develop curricula on aging. By 1976, 9% of nursing schools had required courses in gerontological nursing.

1974 on—Nursing textbooks on aging began to appear.

1975—Membership in ANA gerontological (formerly geriatric) group rose to 30,000.

1975—ANA published *Nursing and Long-Term Care: Toward Quality Care for the Aging,* report from the American Nurses' Association, Committee on Skilled Nursing Care, prepared for the Subcommittee on Long-Term Care of the U.S. Senate Committee on Aging.

1975—*Journal of Gerontological Nursing* appeared.

1975—Nurses' Training Act gave special emphasis to work with older persons.

1980—Four doctoral nursing programs had either an individualized program or a major in gerontological nursing. Twenty-three universities had master's degree nursing programs with specialization in geriatric/gerontological nursing.[‡] About 100 baccaulaureate nursing programs included specific focus on geriatrics.

1985—Creation of the National Center for Nursing Research at the National Institutes of Health. (The National Institute on Aging collaborates with the center.) It is now a national institute.

Source: Adapted from Reif, S. D., & Hoffman, T. Have nurses made a difference: A historical perspective, paper presented at a conference for gerontological nurses entitled *Nurses Make a Difference,* St. Paul, Minn., Oct. 6, 1977; Brimmer, P. F. (1979). Past, present and future in gerontological nursing research, *Journal of Gerontological Nursing* 5(6):27–31; and Martinson, I. M. *Gerontological nursing,* presentation to the National Institute on Aging, Bethesda, Md., Oct. 1980. Reprinted by permission.

[†]*Guidelines for the preparation of geriatric nurse practitioners* and *Guidelines for short term continuing education programs preparing the geriatric nurse practitioner,* 1974, American Nurses' Association, 2420 Pershing Rd., Kansas City, MO 64108.

[‡]See Brower, T. H. (1977). A study of graduate programs in gerontological nursing, *Journal of Gerontological Nursing* 3(6):40–46, for a more complete account of graduate programs.

for services. In particular, there are few social workers trained to work clinically with the mental health problems of the old.

Two extraordinary social workers, Harry Hopkins and Wilbur Cohen, set the stage for Social Security and other welfare entitlements affecting the elderly and others. Other leaders in the field of gerontological social work include Walter M. Beattie, Jr., Marie L. Blank, Margaret Blenkner, Elaine M. Brody, Helen Turner Burr, James J. Burr, Rose Dobrof, Rebecca Eckstein, Monseignor Charles Fahey, Roberta R. Greene, Bernice Harper, Theodore Isenstadt, Hobart C. Jackson, Rosalie Kane, Wilma Klein, Ruth Knee, Virginia Lehmann, Inabel Lindsay, Helen Lokshin, Louis Lowy, Jean M. Maxwell, Robert Morris, Helen Padula, William Posner, Ollie A. Randall, Herbert Shore, Barbara Silverstone, Barbara Soloman, Cleo Tavani, Sheldon S. Tobin, Edna Wasser, Ruth Webber, and Ellen Winston.

A 1986 report on social work services for the aged by Roberta Greene of the National Association of Social Workers summarizes the situation for geriatric social work generally:[26]

• In 1986 an estimated 18 to 21% of the 103,000 members of the National Association of Social Workers (NASW), holding either Master's or Bachelor's degrees in social work, worked with the elderly either full- or part-time. One-third to one-half of these worked in hospitals. (Figures do not exist for geriatric social workers who are not members of NASW. Overall, in 1985, 438,000 persons were filling jobs with the title of "social worker." Not all have master's or bachelor's degrees in social work, and a good number have no social work training whatsoever).

• Of 6,302 *hospitals* in 1984, 83% had a social work department. The need for social workers has grown because of Medicare's introduction of a new method of reimbursement, popularly known as the "DRGs" (Diagnostic Related Groups), which pays a specific amount per diagnostic category. This has meant that social workers often play a critical role in discharge planning in order that patients can be moved out of hospitals as quickly as possible. A Medicare requirement that adequate discharge planning for the elderly must be provided has reinforced the importance of sound discharge planning, including provision of long-term home or institutional care. Unfortunately, pressure for focus on discharge often does not allow adequate attention to mental health care.

• Social work is a major provider of outpatient psychiatric clinic services; nearly 11,000 of 28,000 professional staff in *community mental health centers* and major *outpatient facilities* in 1985 were social workers. However, services for the elderly in such centers are minor since a disproportionately small portion of the clientele is elderly.

• Social workers work in the nearly 800 *Area Agencies on Aging,* which are beginning to provide more direct services for the elderly.

• *Family service agencies* are underused by the elderly. In 1985, about one-half of the 228 Family Service Agencies reported that older persons represented only 3% of their clients.

• The nation's 23,000 *nursing homes* reported few full-time or part-time social workers (not all professionally trained). The institutionalized aged have been a particularly underserviced or totally unserved population. However, effective October 1990, as part of the Omnibus Reconciliation Act of 1987, skilled nursing facilities with more than 120 beds must have at least one social worker with at least a Bachelor's degree in social work or the equivalent.

• Three thousand social workers are employed by the Veterans' Administration. In 1990 one in four veterans was 65 years of age or older. By the year 2000, it will be one in three. Because of the large numbers of young men in service in World War II, 63% of the entire U.S. male population over age 65 will be veterans in the year 2000. Thus *veterans' hospitals* and other facilities already are and will continue to be significant employers of geriatric social workers until the population of veterans thins out.

In 1988 the National Association of Social Workers created a subcommittee on aging as part of its Commission on Family and Primary Associations in order to help improve awareness of the increasing demand for social workers in the field of gerontology. A major recommendation of the subcommittee was to begin collecting data on the size, characteristics, and trends of aging services within the profession, as well as developing a vehicle for conducting labor force studies and a clearinghouse for research data on aging.

From 1983 to 1985, the Council on Social Work Education, with funds from the Administration on Aging, sponsored several projects on improving social work education in work with the aging. The purpose was to integrate gerontology into social work curricula and to develop a model curriculum for gerontological specialization at the graduate level.[27] Robert Schneider and Nancy Kropf coedited a curriculum series in gerontology for bachelor of social work programs,[28] and Roberta Greene of the National Association of Social Workers completed a continuing education curriculum for social workers already in the field of aging.[29]

Training in the field of aging has improved slowly, but is still unavailable in many social work programs. A 1988 survey found that out of 100 master's of social work programs that responded, only 34% offered a concentration in aging and an additional 33% offered at least one course in aging. Out of 372 bachelor's of social work programs that responded, only 9% offered a concentration in aging and an additional 11% offered at least one course in aging.[30] In addition, most full-time faculty in these programs have no formal training in gerontology. The conclusion to be drawn here is that schools are relying on outside lecturers and on-the-job training of faculty to present the gerontological programs.

Counselors

A valuable, expanding resource of capable counselors can be found in other areas. Within the American Counseling Association[31] are various counselors: mental health, school, employment, and so forth. Counselors work in a variety of settings, including community mental health centers, as professionals, and paraprofessionals. Standards-setting, state licensure, and third-party reimbursement are current issues confronting counselors. The AACD had a two-year cooperative agreement with the Administration on Aging to support the National Project on Counseling Older People. Through this project, various service providers who work with older persons—social service aides to administrators and attorneys—were to be provided continuing education in basic gerontological counseling skills.

Paraprofessionals

Paraprofessionals are also known as "new professionals," "nonprofessionals," "lay therapists," "community workers," "community aides," "indigenous workers," and even, condescendingly, "subprofessionals." The abundance of names points to the vagueness of the concept and the disagreement about roles. We prefer the term "paraprofessional" because its Greek roots mean "along side of" professionals, implying a working together rather than working "beneath" other staff members. Paraprofessionals should and will play increasingly more important roles in evaluation and treatment of older persons.

Paraprofessionals such as home health workers are often paid minimum wages and ironically, though health providers themselves, often receive no fringe benefits, including health insurance. Like nurses' aides, these workers are often hired off the street and are frequently young immigrants with language and culture different from their clientele. They usually lack pre-service training and are not given in-service training, let alone a career path to follow. All this is disadvantageous both to home health workers and patients. Training and supervision are crucial to growth and utilization of inherent skills. Reasonable and uniform standards of performance ensure better treatment capabilities.

In the future, various new careers are likely to evolve—one example, a "personal care worker" who would be trained to absorb a variety of functions now distributed among members of many occupations, from home health aide to home-maker to occupational therapy assistant. This would avoid the jurisdictional disputes that now arise, as shown by the homemaker who will not or cannot change a cancer dressing, the home health aide who will not clean the kitchen, and so on.

Community Mental Health Workers

Community mental health centers failed to become a major resource for the elderly. Only half of the 600 centers existing in the 1980s had services designed especially for the elderly and only 4 to 5% of all clientele at these centers were age 65 or older. Some of the reasons for low usage were (1) community mental health centers were often not easily physically accessible to the elderly, (2) few staff members had specific training in work with the elderly, (3) most did not coordinate their work with the available health and social services for the elderly, for example, Area Agencies on Aging.[32] However, those centers that did have specialized programs with trained staff and coordination with area services reported a significantly higher utilization rate by the elderly.[33] (See Chapter 10)

STAFF CONSIDERATIONS

What Kind of People Work with Older Persons?

It has been suggested that few mental health personnel actively choose to work with older people and that most of them fall into the work by chance. Professionals tend to deny having an original, personal attraction to the field, preferring to say they have responded to a "need" in society or to an intellectual curiosity about aging. Directors of institutions for older people will state that most of their employees developed interests and satisfactions after beginning their work. We suggest that these may be subtle denials, concealing a reluctance to admit an interest in old age—a reluctance fostered by the societal devaluation of the aged and by the often heard professional opinion that an interest in

aging represents a morbid preoccupation with decline and death. Naturally chance plays a part in determining career opportunities. But conscious or unconscious personal factors are as important in choosing and remaining in the field of aging as they are in any other human decisions. We offer the following as a number of possible emotional motivations for working professionally with older people.

1. Particularly warm relationships in childhood with grandparents, who then leave their grandchildren a legacy of natural sympathy and interest in older people

2. Early dependence on grandparents (i.e., the "grandmother's children" who were not reared by their own parents) or on older persons (i.e., children of parents who were already older than average when they had children or children of a young mother and a much older father)

3. Death or painful illness of an important older person when a child is young and extremely impressionable (Studies of physicians, for example, have shown that a significant number experienced an early death of a loved person. Medicine then became a way of gaining power over death and the helpless feelings of childhood.)

4. Unconscious counterphobic attempt to conquer fears of aging and death

5. Conscious attempt to prepare for old age, especially if the models of parents or grandparents are unacceptable (A 58-year-old social worker interested in working professionally in the field of the aging joined one of our age-integrated therapy groups to prepare, as she said, for old age. She was terrified at seeing herself become more and more like her mother, whom she viewed as a bitter, disillusioned old woman. She felt helpless in the grip of the model her mother presented her.)

6. Personal sense of inferiority that causes identification with older people, who are culturally defined as inferior

7. Guilt and subsequent reaction formation for feelings of fear and revulsion toward the aged

8. Admiration for and identification with someone working in the field of aging

The importance of determining one's personal motivation is obvious. A mental health specialist must know from where he or she is starting emotionally, in order to help others more effectively.

STAFF TRAINING

General therapeutic principles should be applicable in all settings—private offices, community mental health centers, hospital wards, service agencies—where older people are seen in a mental health context. Intrapsychic phenomena, mechanisms of defense, developmental theory, the structure of grief, and the dynamics of dependency are some of the key areas of knowledge. Everyone, including the paraprofessionals, should have a working knowledge of this material. Even difficult concepts can be presented in inservice training in a clear, simplified, but accurate manner.[34]

Mental health personnel working as a team can teach each other from their collective backgrounds. Anyone with special training or skills should, ideally, share such knowledge openly rather than retaining it as secret prerogatives. Psychiatrists, psychologists, and nurses have particular bodies of information to teach others, but they need to learn much more about social, economic, and cultural considerations and thus will have to be students as well. Social workers can use increased skills and knowledge in understanding and recognizing medical symptoms and in sharpening diagnostic skills. Paraprofessionals are usually weak on formal knowledge of psychopathology and psychodynamics but may be exceedingly sensitive about environmental conditions and cultural factors. A successfully working team will eventually end up sharing a mutual body of knowledge, with the final product being qualitatively more useful than the sum of its parts. Individual disciplines can maintain their individual skills while at the same time gaining from and adding to a larger whole. The danger, of course, lies in the competition and power struggles that seem to arise naturally under such circumstances. These reactions should be anticipated and a plan

of action agreed on before they occur. There is no reason why human beings who have chosen a career of helping others should not be able to help themselves in working peacefully and constructively with their colleagues. Much is known theoretically about group behavior. It remains for us to apply it in our dealings with each other as mental health practitioners.

In working specifically with the aged, it is safe to assume that all staff members will have some attitudes toward older people that are unclear untrue, and even prejudicial. Major tasks in staff training are to clear up uncertainty and misinformation and to make personnel aware of negative countertransference and ageist feelings. Sometimes this can be accomplished by simply providing accurate information. At other times it may require sensitivity training of a sort that brings a staff member's feelings to his awareness and invites and stimulates him to reexamine them. Supervisory sessions, both group and individual, are useful. For the sake of learning, it is wise to see many kinds of older people in many different settings and circumstances. It is also desirable to have had work experiences with persons from all age groups—a life-cycle view is helpful.

In-service training, planning, and problem-solving programs are ways of wrestling with staff conflicts and antagonisms when they arise, providing a forum for resolving countertransference, setting policy and programs, and planning formal and informal learning experiences. Outside teachers and consultants can be used to avoid inbreedings of ideas and outlook. Staff members generally rebel at the thought of extensive outside reading, which should be kept at a minimum and carefully selected for clarity and direct usefulness.[35]

Ideally, research should be built into any ongoing program. Any unusual observations of the older person or his or her family, responses to drugs, or other pertinent information should be recorded in observation books kept available for that purpose, as well as in the person's individual records. Such a practice can result in serendipitous findings that would otherwise be lost and may add to an accumulating body of general knowledge about older people. Another form of research is a routine, periodic reevaluation of the program or service itself. Both of these research methods can be uncomplicated, do-it-yourself ways of learning more and of revitalizing services. Cooperative and more sophisticated research can be arranged among various similar institutions or services in an area. Grants can be obtained for applied research studying delivery systems. The National Institute of Mental Health in Rockville, Maryland, can be contacted for ideas and support.

TREATMENT POINTS TO REMEMBER

What's in a Name?

What we call someone often defines how we will treat him or, at least, how we view him. What should an older person be called? Some of the names one hears are *aged, elderly, senior citizen, retiree, gramps, granny, old biddy, old fogy, old gal,* or simply *old.* If the older person comes for mental health care, is he or she a patient? A client? A "health consumer"? In our experience, people prefer the simplest and most dignified title. *Older person* can be used for anyone from a 60-year-old to a 90-year-old. *Elderly* is accepted in advanced old age—the seventies and eighties. *Aged,* to some, has implications of decrepitude and is not as favored. We have used the terms *older person* most frequently and *elderly* less often and have referred to the older person as *patient* only when it was confusing not to do so. *Patient* implies a limited role in relationship to a doctor or therapist, and we are interested in presenting the older person as a whole. Viewing someone as a patient encourages his or her self-evaluation as dependent and inferior.

In contacts with older persons, it is important to address them respectfully as Mr. or Mrs. unless they specifically ask to be called by their first names. Young students, interns, and trainees are especially tempted to use first names brashly, either through habit or as an attempt to overcome feelings of intimidation. Older people may find this insulting. African Americans and other mi-

nority elderly may be especially sensitive. The presumptuous use of first names or nicknames implies a careless, thoughtless, even contemptuous attitude toward the feelings of older people, who grew up at a time when this was a demeaning and disrespectful gesture. In the case of the African American elderly, they have too long been known only as "James" while the white person was "Mr."

There is also the habit, especially rampant in medical schools, of students and interns to refer to older patients as *gomers* (meaning get out of my emergency room!), *turkeys, gorks, dirtballs, trolls,* and the apparent all-time favorite, *crocks.* Students are too often socialized into being impatient and bored with the old, as well as resentful and fatalistic about the physical and mental deterioration found in many of the older people they see. Medical schools must begin to offer sensitivity training as well as more formal geriatric education in the early years of medical school to counter these tendencies.

Who Decides?

Treatment is a collaboration among older people, their families, and mental health personnel. Decisions should be mutually agreed on unless physical or mental incapacity prevents this. Some treatment personnel use contracts between the patients and themselves, stating specific goals of treatment, as well as the cost and length of sessions, measures for renegotiation after a stipulated period, and provisions for cancellation.

Need for Full Attention to Physical Complaints

It is very important emotionally for the older person to feel that everything possible is being done medically, even when there is really little that can be done. To exhaust the limits of the possible is very reassuring. The arthritic pain, the hypertensive flare-up, the constipation, nerves, irritable colon syndrome, unsightly varicose veins, stress incontinence, estrogen-deficient vaginitis, urinary tract infections, dry and itchy skin, gout,

Parkinsonism, osteoporosis, cold extremities, painful calves, fatigue, edema, irregular pulse, headaches, dizziness, shortness of breath, and confusion are all common complaints that must be treated with seriousness and competence. Often, side effects from the treatments must also be treated. For instance, magnesium-aluminum hydroxide helps alleviate gastric distress associated with prolonged salicylate therapy for arthritis.

It is extraordinarily painful for a human being to be sold short, to be considered unreachable, beyond help, having received the "maximum benefits" of physical therapy and other treatment. Imagine the sense of numbing despair. It is equally true, of course, that action for the sake of action can be a pointless charade. Therefore, to avoid premature dismissal or pointless continued care, a continuing collaboration is necessary with objective assessment, including assessment of the person's morale. Treatment should never be discontinued in a vacuum, without explanation from the professional and some acceptance from the patient. To do so is to risk depression and despair.

Because Medicare does not cover physical checkups, mental health personnel often do not have ready access to knowledge concerning the patient's physical condition and must necessarily be alert to signs of physical illness. For example, early signs of peripheral vascular disease (arteriosclerosis obliterans) such as mild calf pain, loss of hair on toes, slow or unusual toenail growth, cold sensitivity, and shiny skin may be presented as part of an older person's complaint and should be investigated medically.

As an additional consideration, older people often have a dilemma with regard to their family doctor. Usually the doctor is older than the patient. As the patient gets older that is often disadvantageous. It would be ageist to recommend against the older, experienced doctor; but the potential reality of retirement, disability, or death of such a physician must not be overlooked. One direction to take is to build a parallel relationship with a younger colleague of the doctor. Membership in a group practice is another solution.

Psychoanalytic Theory as It Applies to Older People

Psychoanalytic theory provides a valuable means of viewing old age. The ego, the id, the superego, and the ego ideal are useful constructs. In the presence of brain damage, impulses may overrun inhibitions; that is, the id may overpower the superego and the ego, executive functions having been damaged. Incomplete fulfillment of an individual's ego ideal occupies an important part of the content of the life review in both the brain-damaged and the unaffected individuals. In the person not brain-damaged, considerations pertinent to ego psychology indicate the continuing capacity of the older ego to grow and the superego to become more flexible. The notion of the weakening of the id or libido (vitality) with age is reminiscent of Aristotle's observation contained in the *Rhetoric* that older persons love and hate less strongly. We do not yet know enough about outer influences on ego structure or even the id to be certain how intrinsic any observed weakening of the id or ego may be.

The full range of transference possibilities can be seen in older persons as with any age group. One may see role reversal, with the older person taking the role of parent to the therapist. Coercive, dominating, or patronizing behavior may occur. For older people who manifest helplessness, the therapist may be imbued with magical powers.

How to Estimate Treatability

When in doubt, treat judiciously and see if improvement occurs. This is, of course, obvious with respect to brain disorders like delirium but should also be applied elsewhere. Improvements can occur in people who are considered hopeless. Overt behavior is too often taken as innate rather than adaptive. On the other hand, patients with apparently positive treatment possibilities may not respond well at all because of hidden, underlying processes. Treatment should be used to both rule in and rule out a diagnosis and should not be separated from evaluation.

When Not to Argue

Older people often have long-standing personal habits which may at first glance appear idiosyncratic, old-fashioned, useless, or even an interference with mental or physical health care. But take another look. Such habits frequently provide an important sense of identity, security, and comfort, especially under stress. Examples are strong food preferences, sleep rituals, and use of laxatives or other self-prescribed medications. The older and more frail the person, the more important it is not to disturb personal habits unless they present a major threat to health and well-being.

Arguing or cajoling the elderly into a shift of long-standing behavior is usually counterproductive and may be outright cruel or harmful in its impact. Health professionals faced with what may seem to be "egocentricities" of the elderly are well advised to graciously yield the right-of-way unless there is clear reason for not doing so. The elderly should be granted the luxury of their special demands, especially when they are under stress. To do so communicates respect, caring, acknowledgment of individual differences and a desire to respond to personal needs. For some of the most frail, it can mean the difference between maintaining psychic balance or being toppled into confusion and alienation.

Use of Nonverbal Communication

Because of the greater likelihood of physical impairments, nonverbal communication can facilitate treatment and in some cases become a dominant part of the relationship. Persons who are hard-of-hearing need to be able to see the lips of the person talking to them in order to "read" them. We all do this to some degree, but the hard-of-hearing often need special training. It may be necessary to speak very close to the ear, and it is important to learn if one ear is better than the other. Eye contact also is useful in relating; one can learn to "read" the eyes of a stroke victim or of someone with throat problems or certain forms of aphasia. Older people seem to be very alert and responsive to the tone and inflection of an interviewer's voice—able to judge rather accurately the personality behind the voice. Touch or tactile communication becomes extremely important. There is often a desire to be literally "in touch" with the person speaking. People who are very sick may respond more to holding hands than to talking. Shared tears of happiness or sadness on the part of both mental health personnel and older people are common and can be therapeutic. When the older person is physically unable to talk, interviews can be carried out via intuition: The therapist surmises what is on the older person's mind and verbalizes it for him; then the person signals in some way (a smile, nod, frown) if he is being understood. Affection from an older person should be accepted graciously and warmly—and returned—when appropriate. A kiss on the cheek, an embrace, or a pat on the hand for the therapist may become part of the ritual of therapy.

Patience is needed for those struggling to speak. We never shall forget the 75-year-old woman who had had a stroke and was attempting to express her feelings about her suffering. She struggled mightily for a number of minutes, but the words just would not come. Finally everything fell momentarily into place and she shouted "Shit" to the heavens, with a triumphant voice and a gleam in her eye—summing up her feelings succinctly. We and she alike considered it a therapeutic victory.

"Listening" as a Form of Therapy

Listening is an important ingredient in therapy with older persons. Some older people have a great need to talk, and their talking should not be dismissed as a bore or garrulousness. Reminiscence has meaning for the life review that occurs in nearly all people. Feelings of guilt that result from such reminiscing should not be treated as irrational, to be patched up by patronizing reassurance. Guilt is as real in old age as in any other age and must be dealt with therapeutically.

Race and Culture—Language Differences

In Chapter 7 and elsewhere we emphasize the importance of racial, cultural, and ethnic backgrounds in diagnosis and treatment. We wish to add here the problems of language differences, whether these be regional dialect, slang or accent differences, or use of a totally different language—such as Chinese, German, or Spanish. Members of minority groups should be employed in every level of mental health care. Bilingual interpreters having skill in slang or dialect interpretation, as well as actual dual language ability, should be used to train staff, provide direct interpretation, and help older members of minority groups obtain needed services. In addition, hospitals and services that hire foreign personnel, including doctors, have a responsibility to train them adequately in English or provide interpreters. Older persons should not have to bear the burden of treatment personnel's language handicaps.

Myth of Termination of Treatment

Older persons need the opportunity for continuing support and easy availability of services, even when a particular problem has been resolved. Traditional psychiatric and social work has as a goal the eventual termination of mental health care, and there is a considerable literature on countertransference and the problem of termination of treatment. With older people it may be necessary and totally appropriate to continue treatment and care, varying it according to changing conditions until a quite different termination—death.

Three Directions to Move in Treatment

Older people need a *restitution capacity,* the ability to compensate for and recover from deeply felt losses. They also need the *opportunity for growth and renewal,* which represent the opposite of obsolescence and stagnation. This can be defined as the effective striving toward discovery and utilization of innate potential. It can mean a rediscovery or even a first discovery of the self. Jung has written of individuation as one of the tasks of late life. Consequent to a successful psychotherapeutic process (or occurring naturally in a private life review) one may see either the emergence of a qualitatively different personality or a renewal.

> I for one have never touched bottom in self, nor even struck against the surface, the outlines, the boundaries of the self. On the contrary, I feel the self as an energy only which expands and contracts—Bernard Berenson at 83

And, finally, older people require *perspective,* the ability to see themselves and their lives as a whole rather than fixating on any particular aspect. This is the ability to perceive one's place in the world, free from distortion, extending to both the outer and the inner world. It is the sense of "putting one's house in order." Inherent in perspective is a time framework that includes both past and future. It is longitudinal rather than merely situational. The end result is to make acceptable sense out of one's life.

We discuss other treatment directions in later chapters: what to do when that which is "possible" becomes limited; the psychotherapy surrounding death, loss, and their emotional trappings; and advocacy—including the therapist as advocate.

RIGHT TO TREATMENT

The right to treatment is more than a moral obligation—it is now a legal right and requirement. The Age Discrimination Act of 1975 mandates against discrimination toward older persons in the delivery of mental health services. Mental health personnel have too long had the unjustified luxury of deciding whether to offer services or being able to weigh the wisdom of expending resources. Enforcement of the Age Discrimination Act could significantly reduce discrimination in mental health services to the elderly.

SELECTED READINGS

Aaron, H., & Schwartz, W. B. (1990). Rationing health care: The choices before us. *Science, 247,* 418–422.

AGS Public Policy Committee. (1993). *American Geriatrics Society position statement: Mental health and the elderly.* New York: American Geriatrics Society.

American Nurses Association, Council on Gerontological Nursing. (1987). *Standards and scope of gerontological nursing practice.* Kansas City, MO: American Nurses Association.

Ansello, E. F. (1976). Ageism and picture books. *Interracial Books for Children Bulletin, 7,* 4–10.

Ansello, E. F. (1977). Age and ageism in children's first literature. *Educational Gerontology, 2,* 255–274.

Aries, P. (1962). *Centuries of childhood: A social history of family life* (translated by R. Baldick). New York: Alfred A. Knopf.

Barusch, A. S., Greene, R. R., & Connelly, J. R. (1990). *Strategies for increasing gerontology content in social work education.* Washington, DC: Association for Gerontology in Higher Education.

Bazelon, D. (1975). Lake vs. Cameron. In Allen, R. C., Ferster, E., & Rubin, J. G. (Eds.), *Readings in law and psychiatry.* Baltimore, MD: John Hopkins University Press.

Beck, A. T. (1976). *Cognitive therapy and the emotional disorders.* New York: International Universities Press.

Birnbaum, M. (1965). Some comments on the right to treatment. *Archives of General Psychiatry, 13,* 33–45.

Butler, R. N. (1988). A U.S. view—Life after cost containment: Perspectives on meeting the health care needs of older people. In Binns, T. B., & Firth, M. (Eds.), *Health care provision under financial constraint.* Royal Society of Medicine International Congress and Symposium Series No. 115, Royal Society of Medicine Services.

Butler, R. N. (1989, May). Dispelling ageism: The cross-cutting intervention. In Riley, M. W., & Riley, J. W., Jr. (Eds.), The quality of aging: Strategies for interventions. *Annals of the American Academy of Political and Social Science, 503,* 163–175.

Butler, R. N. (1990). A disease called ageism (editorial). *Journal of the American Geriatrics Society, 38,* 178–180.

Butler, R. N. (1990). Perspectives on psychogeriatrics: Message to the 21st century. *International Psychogeriatrics, 2*(1), 9–12.

Committee on Leadership for Academic Geriatric Medicine. (1987). Report of the Institute of Medicine: Academic geriatrics for the year 2000. *Journal of the American Geriatrics Society, 35,* 773–791.

Erikson, E. H., Erikson, J. M., & Kivnick, H. Q. (1987). *Vital involvement in old age.* New York: W. W. Norton.

Frankl, V. (1963). *Man's search for meaning* (original, 1959). New York: Washington Square Press.

Fries, J. F. (1984). The compression of morbidity: Miscellaneous comments about a theme. *The Gerontologist, 24,* 354–359.

Fulop, G., Reinhardt, J., Strain, J., Paris, B., Miller, M., & Fillit, H. (1993). Identification and depression in a geriatric medicine outpatient clinic. *Journal of the American Geriatrics Society, 41,* 737–741.

Green, R. R., Barusch, A. S., & Connelly, J. R. (1990). *Social work and gerontology: Status report.* Washington, DC: Association for Gerontology in Higher Education.

Gruman, G. J. (1978). Cultural origins of present-day "age-ism": The modernization of the life cycle. In Spicker, S. F., Woodward, K. M., & VanTassel, D. D. (Eds.), *Aging and the elderly: Human perspectives in gerontology.* Atlantic Highlands, NJ: Humanities Press.

Hartman. H. (1985). *Ego psychology and the problem of adaptation.* New York: International Universities Press.

Hodgins, E. (1985). *Episode: Report on the accident inside my skull.* New York: Atheneum Press.

Hollingshead, A. B., & Redlich, F. C. (1958). *Social class and mental illness.* New York: John Wiley & Sons.

Holosko, M. J., & Feit, M. D. (Eds.) (1995). *Social work practice with the elderly,* 2nd edition. Canadian Scholars' Press.

Jung, C. G. (1933). The stages of life. In *Modern man in search of a soul* (pp. 109–131). New York: Harcourt, Brace and World.

Levin, S., & Kahana, R. (Eds.). (1967). *Psychodynamic studies on aging: Creativity, reminiscing and dying.* New York: International University Press.

Lieber, C. S. (1995). Medical disorders of alcoholism. *New England Journal of Medicine, 333,* 1058–1065.

Maslow, A. (1971). *The farther reaches of human nature.* New York: Viking Press.

Mellor, M. J., & Solomon, R. (Eds.). (1992). *Geriatric social work education.* Binghamton, NY: The Haworth Press.

Meyer, C. H. (1986). *Social work with the aging.* Washington, DC: National Association of Social Workers (NASW) Press.

Palmore, E. (1972). Gerontophobia Versus Ageism. *The Gerontologist, 12*, 213.

Parham, I. A. (1993). *Gerontological social work: An annotated bibliography.* Westport, CT: Greenwood.

Paulin, J. E., & Walter, C. A. (1992). Retention plans and job satisfaction of gerontological social workers. *Journal of Gerontological Social Work, 19*(1), 99–114.

Peterson, D. A. (1990). Personnel to serve the aging in the field of social work: Implications for educating professionals. *Social Work, 35*(5), 412–415.

Reed, C. C., Beall, S. C., & Baumhover, L. A. (1992). Gerontological education for students in nursing and social work: Knowledge attitudes, and perceived barriers. *Educational Gerontology, 18*(6), 625–636.

Rich, T. A., Connelly, J. R., & Douglas, B. (1994). *Standards and guidelines for gerontology programs.* Washington, DC: Association for Gerontology in Higher Education.

Riley, M. W. (1980). *Aging from birth to death and social change.* Paper presented for a session on New Frontiers in Science. San Francisco, CA: American Association for the Advancement of Science.

Rogers, C. R. (1980). *A way of being.* Boston: Houghton Mifflin.

Rowe, J. W., Grossman, E., Enriqueta, B., & the Institute of Medicine Committee on Leadership for Academic Geriatric Medicine. (1987, May 28). American geriatrics for the year 2000. *New England Journal of Medicine, 316*, 1425–1428.

Schell, E. (1993). The origins of geriatric nursing: The chronically ill elderly in almshouses and nursing homes, 1900–1950. *Nursing History Review, 1*, 203–216.

Swanson, E. A., & Tripp-Reimer, T. (Eds.). (1996). *Advances in gerontological nursing. Volume 1: Issues for the 21st century.* New York: Springer.

Widner, S., & Zeichner, A. (1991). Alcohol abuse in the elderly: Review of epidemiology, research, and treatment. *Clinical Gerontologist, 11*(1), 3–18.

ENDNOTES

1. Riley, M. W. (1980). *Aging from birth to death and social change.* Paper prepared for a session on New Frontiers in Science, American Association for the Advancement of Science, San Francisco.

2. Hartman, H. (1985). *Ego psychology and the problem of adaptation.* New York: International Universities Press.

3. First described by Butler, R. N. (1969). The effects of medical and health progress on the social and economic aspects of the life cycle. *Industrial Gerontology, 1*, 1–9; see also Butler, R. N. (1990). A disease called ageism. *Journal of the American Geriatric Association, 38*, 178–180.

4. Palmore, E. (1972). Gerontophobia versus ageism. *The Gerontologist, 12*, 213.

5. Ansello, E. F. (1976). Ageism and picture books. *Interracial Books for Children Bulletin, 7*, 4–10; and Ansello, E. F. (1977). Age and ageism in children's first literature. *Educational Gerontology, 2*, 255–274.

6. Group for the Advancement of Psychiatry, Committee on Aging. (1971, November). *The aged and community mental health: A guide to program development.* (vol. 8, series no. 81). New York: Brunner-Mazel.

7. Hodgins, E. (1964). *Episode: Report on the accident inside my skull.* New York: Atheneum Press.

8. From Noyes, A., & Kolb, L. (1977). *Modern clinical psychiatry,* 9th ed. Philadelphia: W. B. Saunders, 289.

9. Gibson, R. W. (1970). Medicare and the psychiatric patient. *Psychiatric Opinion, 7*, 17–22.

10. Gallagher, E. B., Sharaf, M. R., & Levinson, D. (1965). The influence of patient and therapist in determining the use of psychotherapy in a hospital setting. *Psychiatry, 28*, 297–310.

11. Ford, C. V., & Sbordone, R. J. (1980). Attitudes of psychiatrists toward elderly patients. *American Journal of Psychiatry, 137*, 571–575.

12. German, P. S., Shapiro, S., Skinner, E. A., VonKorff, M., Klein, L. E., Turner, R. W., Teitelbaum, M. L., Burka, J. B., & Burns, B. J. (1987, January 23/30). Detection and management of mental health problems of older patients by primary care providers. *Journal of the American Medical Association, 257*, 489–493.

13. Glass, R. M. (1987, January 23/30). Psychiatric megatrends and the elderly. *Journal of the American Medical Association, 257*, 527–528.

14. See Garetz, F. K. (1975). The psychiatrist's involvement with aged patients. *American Journal of Psychiatry, 132*, 63–65.

15. AGS Public Policy Committee. (1993). *American Geriatrics Society position statement: Mental*

health and the elderly. New York: American Geriatrics Society.

16. Garetz (1975).

17. University of Southern California, Division of Research in Medical Education. (1978). *Psychiatry practice study report.* Los Angeles: University of Southern California.

18. The American Association for Geriatric Psychiatry (AAGP) publishes a booklet listing its membership. It can be obtained by writing the AAGP, 7910 Woodmont Ave., Bethesda, MD, 20814.

19. Kane, R., Solomon, D., Beck, J., Keelor, F., & Kane, R. (1980). The future need for geriatric manpower in the United States. *New England Journal of Medicine, 302,* 1327–1332.

20. For a valuable assessment of these areas, see Committee on Leadership for Academic Geriatric Medicine. (1987). Report of the Institute of Medicine: Academic geriatrics for the year 2000. *Journal of the American Geriatric Society, 35,* 773–791.

21. Educational Committee of Division 20 (Adult Development and Aging), Washington, D.C., August 1985, American Psychological Association (APA). In 1996, the APA had a membership of 142,000 psychologists, with divisions in 49 subfields of psychology.

22. For example, see Irene M. Burnside's excellent book: *Nursing and the aged,* 3rd ed. New York: McGraw-Hill, 1988.

23. There were an estimated 2.2 million RNs in 1992, and 83% of these (1.8 million) were in active practice. See the U.S. Dept. of Health & Human Services, U.S. Public Health Service, HRSA. (1992, March). *The Registered Nurse Population: Findings from the National Sample of Registered Nurses.*

24. Geriatric nursing was the first nursing area to give certification exams. In addition, certification of clinical specialists began in October 1989. Candidates who achieve a passing score on the examination must submit additional documentation on their practice, reference vouchers, and evidence of continuing education. Case studies, clinical research, or a pilot project complete the requirements. Information on certification can be obtained from the American Nurses' Credentialing Center 600 Maryland Ave, SW, Suite 100W, Washington, DC 20024, (800) 274-4262.

25. See Standards of geriatric nursing practice (Appendix A) and Guidelines for short-term continuing education programs preparing the geriatric nurse practitioner (Appendix B). In Burnside, I. M.

(1988). *Nursing and the aged,* 3rd ed. New York: McGraw-Hill.

26. Greene, R. (1986). The growing need for social work services for the aged in 2020. In Vourlekis, B., & Leukefeld, C. (Eds.), *Making our case: A resource book of selected materials for social workers in health care.* Silver Spring, MD: The National Association of Social Workers.

27. The assessment, *The Current Status of Gerontology in Graduate Social Work Education,* and a four-volume work, *The CSWE Series in Gerontology,* are available from the Council on Social Work Education, 1600 Duke Street, Suite 300, Alexandria, VA 22314-3421.

28. Schneider, R., & Kropf, N. (Eds.). (1989). *Integrating gerontology into the BSW curriculum* (Vol. 1) and *Essential knowledge and skills for baccalaureate social work students in gerontology* (Vol. 2). Joint publication of the Council on Social Work Education, Washington, DC, and Virginia Commonwealth University School of Social Work, Richmond, VA.

29. Greene, R. (1988, April). *Continuing education for gerontological careers.* Washington, DC: Council on Social Work Education (1744 R St.).

30. Lubben, J. E., Damon-Rodriguez, J., & Beck, J. C. (1992). A National Survey of Aging Curriculum in Schools of Social Work. In Mellor, M. J., & Solomon, R. (Eds.), *Geriatric social work education.* Binghamton, NY: The Haworth Press.

31. American Counseling Association, 5999 Stevenson Ave., Alexandria, VA 22304, (800) 347-6647. (Note especially the division called the American Mental Health Counselors Association.)

32. Light, E., Lebowitz, B. D., & Bailey, F. (1986). CMHCs and elderly services: An analysis of direct and indirect services and service delivery sites. *Community Mental Health Journal, 22,* 294–302.

33. Lebowitz, B. D. (1988, July). Correlates of success in community mental health programs for the elderly. *Hospital and Community Psychiatry, 39*(7), 721–722.

34. For example, for general interviewing principles presented simply and clearly, we recommend Garret, A. (1982). *Interviewing—Its principles and methods* (3rd ed. revised by E. P. Zuki & M. Mangold). New York: Family Service Association of America.

35. For a beginning look at possible teaching materials, see references at the end of each chapter, as well as lists of films and fiction in Appendix E at the end of the book.

## CHAPTER 9

DIAGNOSTIC EVALUATION:
HOW TO DO A WORKUP

THE PURPOSE OF DIAGNOSTIC EVALUATION
THE ROLE OF GERIATRIC ASSESSMENT
HOW COMPREHENSIVE SHOULD
AN EVALUATION BE?

CONDITIONS FOR A GOOD EVALUATION
A BASIC EVALUATION

This chapter brings us to the core of mental health care of the elderly, namely the need to establish a sound treatment plan based on a comprehensive diagnostic evaluation of each older individual who is in need of such care.

THE PURPOSE OF
DIAGNOSTIC EVALUATION

In its simplest sense, the mental health diagnostic evaluation is a method of looking at the problems of older people, arriving at decisions that are as accurate as possible as to what is wrong, and concluding what can be done to try to alleviate or eliminate these problems. The older person, together with mental health personnel, tries to discover whether the problems are *intrinsic* (i.e., originating from long-term personality traits or emotional reactions to personal situations) and/or *extrinsic* (i.e., secondary to environmental or social causes); whether there are physical components; and whether the problems represent a new, first-time experience, an old experience with new implications, or something new superimposed on already existing difficulties. Gathering together and assessing the many factors that affect the emotional life of an older person is the process by which such evaluation is carried out. Evaluators

use historical data from the person's past; current medical, psychiatric, and social examinations; and their own personal interactions with the individual to get a many-sided and, one hopes, coherent picture of what is happening.

THE ROLE OF GERIATRIC ASSESSMENT

Much of what will be described in this chapter for the elderly in general is gradually becoming formalized, especially for the very frail elderly, under the concept of comprehensive *geriatric assessment* (GA), defined in 1988 by the National Institutes of Health Consensus Development Conference in Geriatric Assessment as:

> a multidisciplinary evaluation in which the multiple problems of older persons are uncovered, described, and explained, if possible, and in which the resources and strengths of the person are catalogued, need for services assessed, and a coordinated care plan developed to focus interventions on the person's problems.[1]

Studies of the frail elderly are beginning to document the benefits of comprehensive assessment. Such benefits include improved diagnostic accuracy, more appropriate choice of living location, improved functional and mental status, reduced medications, decreasing use of nursing homes and acute care services, prolonged survival, and more appropriate use of health care services with generally reduced health care costs.[2]

Geriatric assessment, in this more formal sense, usually involves a multidisciplinary team of professionals working together on the assessment, a distinct set of criteria for evaluating the elderly in settings that range from inpatient and outpatient to at-home locations, and three levels of intensity of assessment—brief, intermediate, or comprehensive—based on patient needs. In the remainder of this chapter, we shall broaden these concepts to include assessment of all the elderly seeking mental health care.

HOW COMPREHENSIVE SHOULD AN EVALUATION BE?

We recognize the range of opinion regarding the length, style, and content of an evaluation and the methods by which it should be conducted. A number of variations can be justified on the basis of the treatment method and setting under consideration as well as the individual's specific request for help. For example, an older person wanting only brief assistance in dealing with feelings about retirement may not require the same workup as the person needing evaluation for placement in a nursing home. But in general we believe that a comprehensive evaluation has much to recommend it. There is an astounding lack of uniformity in what happens when an older person meets with mental health practitioners or institutional facilities. There may be a failure to gather even routine information. An individual may or may not get treatment, which may or may not be based on a solid evaluation and recommendation. Busy agencies and personnel with limited resources plead that their hands are tied. Yet even the shoddiest medical facility or the busiest family doctor would not be able to deal quite as cursorily with patients if they presented physical (rather than emotional) complaints—at least some minimal workup would be done.

Court suits have been instituted claiming the "right to treatment" for persons requiring mental health care, particularly in the case of the poor. Such suits have been helpful in forcing more meaningful standards of treatment. The older person not only has a right to expect treatment, as opposed to custodial care or no care, but also to expect that it be based on a thorough evaluation.

The following categories of treatment encompass the major services to older persons in terms of evaluation:

- Emergency-crisis intervention
- Evaluation for brief services
- Evaluation for extended, comprehensive services
- Evaluation for referral elsewhere (for example, a mental health evaluation for referral to a psychiatric hospital or nursing home)
- Evaluation for legal purposes (psychiatric commitment, guardianship, etc.)

In all these categories a complete evaluation is indicated for optimal and often time-saving intervention. An emergency, of course, requires attention to the immediate crisis, but with older people a crisis often points to underlying problems and requires extended periods of recovery. Thus, an evaluation can be begun as soon as the emergency subsides. The evaluation should ideally fulfill a *preventive, screening* function as well as a diagnostic one.

As with all ages, the problem first presented by older persons is often not their major or only difficulty. They may be reluctant to reveal intimate matters or be fearful of appearing demanding and complaining. They may sometimes deny actual problems or be totally unaware of their presence. The interviewer, as with any age group, must be alert to any clues and must gently and sensitively help older persons provide as full a picture of their situation as possible. But with the elderly (as discussed in the previous chapter), the interviewer may have less patience than with younger subjects and, consequently, may fail to do this properly. (See Chapter 8 for staff training techniques.)

On the basis of the evaluation, decisions must be made as to reasonable, reachable treatment goals: Can the problem at hand be reversed or merely ameliorated? Should treatment be aimed at total recovery, partial restitution, maintaining the status quo, or—of equal importance—supporting the person during some inevitable decline? Is environmental change indicated? Would direct medical treatment be useful? Or, does the individual need psychotherapy?

The issue of the availability of personal, hospital, and community resources is an ever-present and often frustrating factor in working with and planning for the care of older people. It is, of course, necessary to know what resources are available for treatment purposes: the older person's own emotional and physical capabilities, the supports in his or her family and social structure, and the kind of services and support available in the community. Then, there is the problem of access to needed services. For example, it is increasingly evident that older people make good use of individual psychotherapy; yet it is seldom offered, even when they can afford to pay. In some cases such services are not available for any age group, and older persons are excluded along with everyone else. However, in many instances, a service may be offered to the general public but older people find themselves put at the bottom of the waiting list or totally denied access to what is theoretically available. This is an example of *institutionalized ageism*— discrimination on the basis of age. All too many mental health personnel, because of training and background, assume that certain services are not applicable for older people and thereby deny treatment possibilities. We hope that Part Two of this book will help to overcome the pessimism that has prevailed regarding rehabilitation and treatment in the later years and especially in very old age.

CONDITIONS FOR A GOOD EVALUATION

Once the goals of the evaluation are set and the available resources are known, the mental health professional is ready to proceed with the actual evaluation of the older person. Whether in the person's home, a clinic, hospital room, or private office, the evaluation should build on the following ten principles:

1. Purpose
2. Rapport
3. Authorization and consent
4. Confidentiality
5. Setting
6. Time
7. Extent and structure of evaluation
8. Impressions and feedback
9. Documentation and information sharing
10. Follow-up visit

Purpose

An explanation of the purpose of the evaluation lays out the guidelines for the work between mental health personnel and the elderly. Older persons must understand precisely why they are seeing a mental health specialist and what they can expect during and as a result of the evaluation. They also have the right to know who is interviewing or examining them (a psychiatrist, a social worker, a visiting nurse, etc.). And, finally, they deserve an intelligible explanation, in lay person's language, of the desired result of the evaluation.

Rapport

It is a standard mental health principle that the first contact for evaluation is also the first therapeutic treatment hour; the two cannot be separated. Unfortunately, for many older people it may be the first and last time they will have a structured opportunity to talk about their problems and feelings. As discussed more fully in Chapter 8, the older person needs to sense certain things in order to feel comfortable about revealing him- or herself. The individual must perceive that (1) the interviewer is not repulsed or frightened by the physical or mental changes in old age but can accept these changes as a matter of fact and can see through them to the person inside, (2) the interviewer knows what he or she is talking about when dealing with old age (the psychological aspect of being old), (3) the interviewer understands the social problems of old age, having a broad and accurate knowledge of conditions as they exist for the majority of older persons, and (4) the interviewer has the professional skills and empathy that will inspire older people to trust him or her with their confidence, in the expectation that help will follow.

Authorization and Consent

The obtaining of authorization and consent must be high on the list of principles for a thorough geriatric evaluation. Ethical and legal protections for both older people and for health care professionals are provided by obtaining informed consent for an evaluation. But there are other motivations as well. Mental health evaluations can be thwarted before they begin simply because the older person was either unaware of the impending interview or was even vehemently opposed to it. Patients need to be clear about what is being proposed and must give their consent whenever their mental or physical health status makes this possible. Even severely demented older persons should be given the opportunity to understand, however dimly, why another health care worker has entered their world. A brief introduction to the worker and to the evaluation process almost always helps orient and prepare them for the tasks ahead.

Confidentiality and Privileged Communication

Confidentiality is a critical element in gaining an accurate history and in establishing and maintaining rapport. *Privilege* is the legal right of the person to privacy of communication. With the advent of the team concept, using paraprofessionals and peer review, the legal situation has not yet been clarified. In most states a patient can sue the physician who does not preserve privileged communication, but what about the nurse, the social worker, the nursing assistant, and others? The increase in insurance forms and computer use complicates the picture. It is essential that practitioners recognize the seriousness of protecting the client's privacy. For instance, a designing relative may be trying to get possession of an older person's house and attempt to gain information toward that end from mental health personnel. It is well known that the privacy of the poor who are served in community mental health centers, public clinics, and the like is less protected than that of the privately paying person. Legal suits may help curb such practices.

It is always helpful to spell out confidentiality in detail. A few of the typical questions elderly persons may have include the following: Who will be informed about the results of the evaluation? What will be written in the record? Who will have access to that information? What will my family hear about this? Will I be seen by students as well? Time given to carefully answering these and any other related questions is well spent in terms of improved patient understanding and comfort.

Setting

All persons should be interviewed wherever possible in dignified, private surroundings—not on the run, in public hallways and open clinic areas. The office should not present barriers to successful and safe evaluation of the older person. Lighting should be sufficient (remembering that age-related yellowing of the eye lens blocks two-thirds of the light that used to reach the retina), and back lighting behind the interviewer should be avoided because the older person may have difficulty seeing the interviewer's face.

Time

Older persons, especially the frail elderly, can be more easily overcome by the challenges of tests and measurements; therefore, one must proceed carefully and cautiously in order not to upset their physical and mental equilibrium. They should be given more time when there is evidence of intellectual slowing, whether this be caused by depression or organic changes. Interviews and examinations should be unhurried and relaxed. Instructions of any kind should be written out after they have been given verbally. When organicity, severe depression, or paranoid reactions are suspected, there must be several sessions, preferably at different times of day, to take into account variation in general and cerebral circulation. Early morning confusion—before the older person has shaken off sleep—can be mistaken as chronic, fixed disorientation. There is also a "sundown syndrome"—the increased disorientation and agitation at night resulting from loss of visual orientation when daylight is gone or electric lights are turned off. If this is organically based, it has been called "senile nocturnal agitation."

Special Conditions

The Hard-of-Hearing.   When hearing loss is a problem, interviews should take place in settings with minimal background noise. Presbycusis, one common hearing disorder in old age, produces hearing loss and selectively impairs high tones and consonant perception. Accordingly, if the voice is to be raised, it should be kept at low pitch and consonants should be especially clearly articulated. The interviewer should feel free to ask directly about the hearing loss. This will be seen by most older people as a sign of sensitivity and concern. If one ear is better than the other for an older person, the interviewer should sit near and speak into that ear. The voice volume should be constant and distinct, with no trailing off at the end of a sentence. The expression on the patient's face should be noted to be certain that he or she is hearing and understanding. Many older people read lips to augment their hearing; it is difficult for them if the interviewer's face is not turned toward them or his or her mouth is covered. Beards and mustaches can be a problem for lip-readers.

Persons with Stroke.   Just as with the hard-of-hearing, the interviewer should sit on the "good" side of the stroke patient, since there may be damage to hearing and vision on the other side. When the patient has difficulty speaking (aphasia), the interviewer should allow him or her to struggle to speak. The word should be supplied only when absolutely necessary. The person should be reassured that the interviewer wants him or her to try

to talk. If words won't come, the person can try to write on a large pad or a blackboard. When asking questions, the interviewer should phrase them so the patient can respond yes or no or shake his or her head. Above all, it should *not* be assumed that the patient's intelligence has been affected. Stroke victims frequently complain that people routinely treat them as though they are intellectually impaired.

Recognizing the Goldstein Catastrophic Reaction.[3]   The *Goldstein catastrophic reaction* describes the tendency of brain-damaged persons to become flooded with anxiety and irritability when confronted with a task they cannot handle. Weinberg's "exclusion of stimuli" may have a similar basis.[4] Any examination may provoke this reaction and thus complicate or delay findings. The careful, skilled interviewer can alleviate unnecessary stress by being sensitive to the reaction of the person. (It is also, of course, important to note the presence of this reaction in diagnosing brain damage.)

When talking to a brain-damaged older person, an interviewer should be sure to get the person's attention, speak slowly with good light on the interviewer's face, and use short, meaningful sentences with appropriate gestures. If the answer seems to be inappropriate, the interviewer may try rephrasing the question in several different ways. For example, "Did you take your pill?" might be varied by saying, "What medicine have you taken today?" The purpose of all of this (and the interviewer can develop other techniques through trial and error) is to try to tap into the remaining intellectual capacity of the older person through any device that works with that individual. Only careful observation will tell if the interviewer is succeeding.

Extent and Structure of Evaluation

A brief preview of actual procedures the older person will encounter in the course of a mental health evaluation is usually helpful both in orientation and enlisting cooperation. This is in addition to the description of the overall purpose of the evaluation described earlier. It is all too common for an interviewer to assume incorrectly that the patient already knows the procedures to be followed or that the person requesting the evaluation has previously explained the routine. In any case, neither scenario generally is accompanied by accurate information, particularly in relation to mental health evaluations, because very few patients really know what goes into such an evaluation and because routines vary so much from one setting to the next.

It is also important to provide details about logistics of the evaluation. For example, several visits may be required, and in some cases, other individuals are involved (i.e., personnel to administer psychometric testing). Whenever possible, such logistics of scheduling should include the involvement of patients in planning, giving them some opportunity for a sense of control (i.e., when follow-up testing will be done, whether the patient would rather be tested in the room or in a clinic setting, etc.). While such control may seem trivial to the interviewer or may be tightly truncated by a busy schedule, any flexibility offered to the older person may be welcomed. Finally, the issue of billing is often overlooked in detailing the structure of an evaluation. Since financial concerns are so frequently a part of an elderly person's worries, it is well worth beginning to discuss the subject as soon as possible, providing assistance in planning how bills will be paid.

Impressions and Feedback

One of the greatest fears of older patients as they are being evaluated by mental health personnel is that they will be thought "crazy" or otherwise seriously disturbed. After all, someone did request a mental health evaluation. That fear can frequently be allayed with simple feedback, especially of positive findings, during the evaluation. Not only does this feedback humanize the evaluation process, but it also allows the patient to relax and thereby discuss issues more freely than might otherwise have been likely. When the evaluation

is drawing to an end, a summary review of the information gathered (even just repeating the clinical history in capsule form to verify the factual content) and a brief outline of some preliminary impressions, being careful to focus on strengths as well as problems, is usually welcomed by the patient. Further study or conference with other mental health personnel may be necessary before the final recommendations can be offered, but in the meantime, a sense of the possible outcomes once more helps to focus the patient and allay persistent fears about the process.

Documentation and Information Sharing

In the case of evaluation requests from other health or social service providers, once all the sources of information have been gathered and the data generated during an evaluation have been discussed with appropriate colleagues, it is time for delivering the formal evaluation results to the original requester. While written forms are usually required and are often the principal means of communication between consultants, direct contact in person or at least by telephone is also highly recommended. This time-consuming procedure may seem burdensome but it ensures immediate transmission of the consultation to the appropriate source, thereby avoiding the frequent delayed impact of mail services and notes left in medical charts. Further, it encourages discussion between health personnel, once more personalizing the process for the patient and increasing the likelihood of a successful outcome.

Follow-Up Visit

A brief follow-up visit with the interviewer is often valuable, if only to inform the patient that the evaluation has been completed and the recommendations are ready. Depending on the situation, this visit may be expanded to include a detailed review of the findings, a large family meeting, or even a continued relationship in ongoing therapy. If and when the family is to be involved in the follow-up process, it is usually wise to first meet with the patient alone and preview the findings. This enables the patient to digest the results privately and to once again give consent before intimate details or test results are discussed with others.

A BASIC EVALUATION

A basic mental health evaluation should include a core collection of material: (1) basic personal information, (2) medical assessment, (3) psychiatric assessment, (4) sociocultural assessment with the older person including his or her relatives and, if possible, on-the-spot evaluation of the home environment where indicated. In addition, any number of special evaluations (for example, special medical tests or nutritional evaluation) may be deemed valuable in arriving at a clear understanding of the older person.

Basic Personal Information

The question of how to collect background information or histories for use in mental health evaluations has always been a controversial and confusing one. This is largely because mental health, as we define it today, encompasses every aspect of a person's life, and the task of collecting and assimilating so much information boggles the mind. Add to this the need to take a longitudinal life cycle view, as in the evaluations of older people, and the problem grows. In an era of specialization, medical doctors have tended to limit themselves to the body and its ills, traditional psychiatrists to "inner" problems (although this is hopefully becoming less true—the trend is toward a more comprehensive biomedical and psychosocial approach), traditional social service workers to "outer" difficulties, and members of the clergy to spiritual life. However, mental health personnel, who can be from any of these professions and more, must familiarize themselves with the whole picture in order to prescribe and carry out sound treatment. Collection of basic background information should be done in a manner that ensures

comprehensiveness without being rigid. The goal is a high-quality evaluation, whether it takes place in a private hospital, a public clinic, a doctor's office, or a nursing home.

In its most complete form, personal history taking should be flexible in format, transferable to other professionals (with appropriate permission), and psychologically organizing for both the patient and the clinician alike. In addition, this body of information can provide a rich source of knowledge about older people for research purposes, as there are still tremendous gaps in our understanding of old age. As a result of our own work experiences in various hospitals, welfare departments, community mental health clinics, nursing homes, research, and private practice, we (RNB and MIL) have devised a method of collecting data that combines an adaptable format with a thorough content. (See the Personal Mental Health Data Form in Appendix G.) This form can be compiled either piecemeal or all at once, and at any time during contact with a patient. For example, when seeing a person in crisis, one must deal with the immediate situation and may not be able to obtain much background data until the crisis subsides. When we know we will be seeing a person over a period of time, we generally fill out the form with the older person ourselves in an unhurried manner as the data accumulate. However, in a period of crisis or shortage of time, a relative may complete the form, either at home or in the office. (Material, of course, is not as rich as when the patient is directly involved.)

In other cases, it is appropriate and even highly therapeutic for the patient to fill out the form alone. Patients report that filling out the form is a life review process that is helpful to them in evaluating themselves and planning for the future. We would generally not recommend this for patients with obvious severe organic brain disorders, poor eyesight, or severe hand tremors or for those who would become frustrated without help. It can, on the other hand, be extremely useful for hard-of-hearing patients, with whom interviewing is difficult, and for those who pride themselves on their independence.

We also ask patients who are entering group therapy to fill out the form themselves if they are being seen by us in only one individual, pregroup session.

A completed personal history form is like a baseline electrocardiogram: It indicates the person's present situation and provides a standard against which to measure changes in the future. It is often not accurate to think in terms of eventual "discharge from treatment" for older people in the same way as for the young. Since many will need various kinds of service the rest of their lives, it saves time to collect adequate information right from the start. Mental health personnel need to review their own thinking and attitudes about the quality of evaluation given to older people. A sloppy, haphazard approach can be rationalized neither as time-saving nor as humane care.

Another means of assessment is the Older Americans Resources and Services (OARS) methodology, produced under the direction of Dr. Eric Pfeiffer at Duke University. OARS's objectives are to develop models for mental health care, social services, and multidimensional techniques for evaluating the functional status of older people.[5] Also see the discussion on the Patient Appraisal and Care Evaluation (PACE) instrument in Chapter 11.

Several other geriatric assessment instruments have been developed over the last few years including the Comprehensive Assessment and Referral Evaluation (CARE),[6] the Association of Gerontopsychiatry System,[7] and the Cambridge Mental Disorders of the Elderly Examination (CAMDEX).[8] Each of these evaluations provides personal data forms and instructions for semi-structured interviews with elderly patients and their families, which in turn could lead to improved history taking, concurrent medical diagnoses, and careful differentiation of psychosocial problems. With the CAMDEX, in particular, the procedure has been well accepted by the older patients interviewed and found to have high interrater reliability among professionals. Reliability is an important issue when such a scale is used for research purposes.

Medical Assessment

While the focus of a mental health evaluation is usually on psychiatric symptoms, it is not uncommon in the elderly that these symptoms are secondary to underlying medical problems. With respect to depression alone, the list of medical conditions and drugs associated with depressive symptoms in the elderly is impressive. Frequently, these medical conditions are either not diagnosed adequately or the association with depression is not recognized. Therefore, it is the responsibility of the mental health professional to make these connections, and the most essential starting point is the medical evaluation.

Much has been written about medical evaluation of the elderly.[9] Of greatest importance is the routine medical history and physical. The greatest clues regarding concurrent medical problems arise here. The diagnosis is then confirmed by the laboratory evaluation. While esoteric tests are sometimes required, a basic laboratory screening is often all that is needed. As part of a standard laboratory evaluation, patients should undergo the following:

- Complete Blood Count (Hematocrit, Hemoglobin, Mean Corpuscular Volume, White Blood Count, and Platelet Count)
- Erythrocyte Sedimentation Rate
- Chemistry Profile (Serum Sodium, Potassium, Bicarbonate)
- Fasting Blood Sugar
- Thyroid Profile (Thyroxine, T3 Resin Uptake, and TSH)
- Liver Function Tests (LDH, SGOT, and Bilirubin)
- Serum Phosphorous and Magnesium
- VDRL
- B_{12} and Folate Level
- Serum Cholesterol and Triglycerides
- Chest X-Ray
- Electrocardiogram (EKG)
- Urinalysis
- Stool for Occult Blood
- Visual and Hearing Screening
- EEG and CT Scan (when indicated)

How recently these tests should have been completed depends on the condition being considered and the rate of change with the individual patient. In any case, it is imperative that the mental health professional be certain that these basic medical checkpoints have not been overlooked. Otherwise, the mental health assessment that follows can be seriously flawed due to an undiagnosed medical problem.

A thorough physical examination is mandatory. Even more than with younger adults, a thorough neurologic evaluation should be included in this examination.[10] In addition to a medical history, recent reports from the patient's family doctor or other involved physicians are also invaluable. The latter reports are often obtained verbally by phone but should be summarized in written form in the patient's record. It must be known what drugs are being taken, for what condition, for how long, and what, if any, have been the side effects, especially adverse reactions.

Hearing tests, a visual examination with a check of eyeglasses, and a dental examination are obviously important for older people. Nutrition and sleeping habits must be noted. Because of widespread poverty among older persons, sometimes combined with the physical incapacity to care for themselves, many suffer from malnutrition in subtle or gross forms.[11] Malnutrition and dehydration therefore are among the major medical problems to recognize. Dehydration without malnutrition is also common. Subtle changes in nutrition and exercise programs can, in fact, affect both mood and cognition, even in the otherwise healthy elderly.[12] The interviewer should also be familiar with changes over time in touch, pain sensitivity, and other functions.[13]

Optional and Research Testing. Electroencephalography (EEG or brain wave test) is the process of making a graphic record of the electrical activity of the brain. For the purposes of clinical evaluation and study, EEG waves are subdivided into four basic forms (delta, theta, alpha, and beta) according to the frequency of the waves. Some EEG slowing, particularly in the

alpha rhythm, is commonly seen in normal elderly subjects when compared to young normals. Women may show less delta and more beta than men, and there are some suggestions that these changes are not always symmetrical across the brain surface.[14] More commonly, EEG or the newer computerized "mapping" EEG techniques have been employed to differentiate normal populations from organically impaired individuals, especially those with Alzheimer's disease where decreases in alpha activity and increases in delta activity are well documented.[15] It should be pointed out, however, that while this technique is usually effective in differentiating groups of Alzheimer patients from groups of normal or depressed patients, it is not especially accurate with individual patients because of the large variation between subjects. In fact, there is even some recent controversy as to whether the EEG changes progress during the course of Alzheimer's disease.[16]

Introduced in 1973, computerized axial tomography (CT) is a technique for evaluating brain pathology. It is based on two principles: (1) tomography, that is, radiological serial sectioning, and (2) computerization, that is, the rapid integration of thousands of pictures via computer. A narrow beam of x-rays passes through the head rapidly in a series of thin "slices," hitting radiation detectors that feed signals into a high-speed computer. The technique is noninvasive (unlike the injection of radioactive isotopes for x-ray purposes) and uses no more radiation than is required for a traditional x-ray film of the skull. X-ray films are only two-dimensional and thus flat, as compared to the multidimensionality of a CT scan. This technique has essentially replaced the higher risk and unpleasantness of pneumoencephalography, in which air is injected into the central nervous system. It also has greatly reduced the need for angiography, isotope scanning, and some exploratory surgery. Numerous CT studies over the past decade have revealed a generalized reduction in brain size with increasing age. These age-related changes are noted either in the overall brain volume or in the ventricular size, and they are found to be markedly exaggerated in patients with Alzheimer's disease,[17] though as with the EEG, the technique is diagnostic only when differentiating groups of patients.

Magnetic resonance imaging (MRI) is a relatively new procedure which also allows cross-sectional views of the brain but without the ionizing radiation required for CT and other brain-imaging techniques. The MRI is based on the principle that atomic nuclei have an angular momentum associated with their spin, which creates a small magnetic field. The technique is quite complex but essentially relies on the measurement of relaxation times (labeled T1- or T2- "weighted") following radio-frequency excitation of magnetized tissues.[18] While the clinical advantages of MRI over CT and other noninvasive procedures are still being debated and studied, it is already clear that MRI has many applications for diagnosing brain disorders in the elderly.[19]

Since the original introduction of the nitrous oxide method by Kety and Schmidt in 1948, there has been continued interest in the measurement of cerebral blood flow and its relationship to intellectual functioning. More recently, the xenon inhalation technique has allowed safer and repeated testing of subjects with group differentiation of elderly patients with multi-infarct dementia, Pick's disease, and Alzheimer's disease.[20]

With positron emission tomography (PET) scanning, another level of brain imaging can be obtained. This technique is built on the discovery by Sokoloff that the glucose analog, 2-deoxy-glucose could be radiolabelled and taken up into brain cells much like glucose. When trace amounts of radioactive 2-deoxy-glucose is injected into a patient and is absorbed by the brain cells, these isotopes soon emit positively charged particles called positrons, which collide with negatively charged electrons normally present in the cells. Each collision produces high-energy particles called photons, whose speed and path are recorded in the PET scan. A computer processes the information in color on a screen, showing biochemical activity in the living brain. Thus, with computerized tomography, one can see structure (anatomy and pathology), but with positron emission transverse tomography one can study function and metabolism.

Using the 2-deoxy-glucose PET approach, changes in cortical glucose metabolism have been documented in Alzheimer's disease and multi-infarct patients compared to controls.[21] In addition, asymmetries in cortical measurements of Alzheimer patients have supported the clinical observations of diagnostic heterogeneity and have led to theories of metabolic uncoupling in various brain regions.[22] Further PET studies with more specific brain markers such as neurotransmitter receptor labels will certainly greatly add to our knowledge of central nervous system function in the elderly.[23]

With single photon emission computerized tomography (SPECT) scans, yet another related imaging technique, the methodology is now available to study specific brain chemical systems such as the important cholinergic system in living Alzheimer's disease patients.[24] As with all of these brain-imaging techniques, however, we must be cautious. These methodologies are primarily research tools that are not even clinically available in most cases, and they must first be proven to be of further diagnostic value before eventually becoming part of the standard clinical evaluation.

Summary of Medical Assessment.   In its best form, the medical evaluation should be comprehensive, multiphasic, continued at regular intervals, and when feasible, computerized. It is hoped there will soon be a baseline body of quality data available through automated technology and telemetry (to send information quickly, long distance) to aid in diagnosis. Heart disease, diabetes, glaucoma, emphysema, and cancer are particular foci. Indeed, after age 45 there should be regular medical checkups for the healthy and more frequent ones for the ill. Unfortunately, Medicare does not cover routine checkups, making it difficult for older persons to take advantage of the early detection and prevention possible through regular physical examinations.

Another difficulty for older people is lack of knowledge about health, medicine, and their own bodies. For obvious reasons they know less than later generations will know. Physicians have not been the major source of health education that they could be for older people. Often they are reluctant to impart information—saying it takes too much time, there is no good purpose to it, and so on—while older persons remain unenlightened as to what is being done to them. Many, for example, are given medication without knowing what it is for or what the side effects may be. Numerous other examples could be given of medical care administered in a manner that produces needless anxiety and emotional anguish.

Besides the usual diagnostic benefits, medical evaluation has two particularly important functions for the older patient. First, the examination is essential for the detection and early treatment of reversible delirium. These syndromes must be diagnosed early or they can become complicated, losing their reversibility. Second, the medical examination helps to "rule in" the functional disorders by ruling out physical causes. Thus mental health personnel may begin to suspect the possibility of a functional disorder (depression, paranoid states, etc.) and are more inclined to explore psychogenic processes.

Psychiatric Assessment

Who Does a Psychiatric Assessment? Psychiatrists are by no means the only people qualified to do psychiatric evaluations. In community mental health centers, psychiatric hospitals, and elsewhere, a team of people from many disciplines may arrive at a joint evaluation. In addition, well-trained paraprofessionals can learn to assess the psychiatric condition of patients. With inadequate psychiatric coverage in most public and many private facilities, such skills can and should be learned by others. Responsible supervision and competent training can ensure quality care, regardless of the primary discipline. The introduction in recent years of more structured diagnostic

interview instruments such as the Diagnostic Interview Schedule (DIS),[25] the Schedule for Affective Disorder and Schizophrenia (SADS),[26] and the Structured Clinical Interview for DSM-IIIR (SCID)[27] allow the broader use of clinical skills for both patient care and research purposes.

What Constitutes a "Diagnosis"? A psychiatric diagnosis is not simply a matter of psychiatric nomenclature that an evaluator, by the process of elimination, plucks out of the American Psychiatric Association's *Diagnostic and Statistical Manual.* One must know the psychological strength of persons (for example, their defenses and personality assets); their physical capabilities; and the familial, social, and cultural climate and structure of their lives. The direct and immediate environmental influence on people's lives is finally receiving its due share of importance along with the more traditional emphasis on early developmental and constitutional factors of personality. It is vital also to recognize the vast implications of prejudice in its institutional and personal forms as they affect the lives of African American, Asian American, American Indian, Latino, and other minority and ethnic elderly. (See Chapters 1 and 7.) The serious mental disorders and the emotional reactions seen in old age are multicausal.

A problem may not only have many causes; it may itself be multiple, that is, a combination of many problems, as is often the case with the diagnosis of dementia with superimposed delirium. Another serious and frequent oversight is the failure to recognize the emotional component or overlay to physical illness of the body or brain. Mental health personnel must search for possible combinations of problems where some may be less obvious than others but no less damaging. Thus, diagnosis is best viewed as a continuing, dynamic assessment, particularly in the case of older persons. Old age, indeed life at any age, is more similar to a motion picture than a still photograph; it is constantly changing. Because of this ongoing, altering process, evaluation, too, must be continuous, with treatment intervention varied accordingly.

Some Principles of Psychiatric Assessment.
The traditional psychiatric assessment derives from the medical model; it can be an unimaginative, tedious, rigid procedure of limited usefulness in mental health care of the elderly unless attention is given also to psychodynamics and socioeconomics. A completed personal data form such as we have described can provide background and direction for the psychiatric interview. But the psychiatric perspective itself is also essential. One must be ever alert, perhaps more for older people than any other age group, to the possible presence of reversible delirium and functional disorders, both of which can be treated if properly diagnosed. A psychiatric look at the everyday crises of living, too, can be valuable. Much that is swept under the rug as old age, or even viewed as reaction to environmental stress, may have a psychiatric component that rightly deserves clarification and treatment.

In conducting a psychiatric examination, it is obviously not wise to be bound to a rigid routine. Rather, one must continue to build skill in observation, perception, and intuition (for hypothesis making), while at the same time taking a comprehensive approach. The degree of comprehensiveness—the width and depth—of the study will vary according to time pressures, purposes, motivation, and unfortunately, the patient's economic status and ability to pay.

Without reviewing all the general techniques of psychiatric examination, those components of the examination that are found to be especially pertinent to older people will be stressed. For instance, the appearance and general behavior of the person can offer significant clues: Does she walk like an "old" person, or does her walk belie her age? Does he dye his hair and pretend to be youthful? Is there a peculiar gait (for instance, the distinctive Parkinsonian "march," the *marche à petits pas* with its characteristic short shuffling steps, the patient leaning forward so that the gait is propulsive, the arms not swinging)? Does she look blank-faced (indicating organicity or depression)? An ironed-out, masklike face may point to Parkinsonism. Is he slow-moving in speech and action, distractable, flighty, incoherent, or irrelevant? Does she speak *sotto voce,* quietly, while looking about suspiciously (possible paranoid feature)? Is the appearance one of premature age and debilitation (there may be a basic physical process or illness underlying the psychiatric symptomatology)? One must also be aware of behavior that might be inappropriate for younger people but is "normal" in old age—a good example is the fact that an older person may arrive an hour or more early for an interview. This should not instantly be given the label "obsessive-compulsive." Older people often are highly time-conscious and want to compensate for any unavoidable delays along the way that may be hard for them to cope with; thus they tend to overcompensate by starting very early.

The Psychiatric Examination.   The psychiatric examination generally begins with questions about what brought the person for evaluation and possible treatment—what is the chief problem or complaint. The history of the problem in the person's own words is next. Family and chronological life histories follow. Careful questioning is necessary to discover how the older person feels about his family: Does he see himself as a burden? Is he angry at them? Do they indicate annoyance with him? At every step, care must be taken to watch the nonverbal communications and revelations of the unconscious. The interviewer should try to record important aspects of the person's description in his or her own exact words, not only for any later medico-legal reasons but also for later reflection on psychodynamics.

The examiner must also be especially alert for "new" and "peculiar" behavior—keeping in mind the immediacy of the life situation as well as the life history. Immediate precipitants are crucial in old age when change, loss, and deprivation are so powerful in their effects. Certain symptoms in old age practically guarantee medical and/or psychiatric problems. Persons with organic brain disorders and severe depressions may survive—even function well—in the community, and then suddenly a change in their lot can make the underlying pathologic condition more visible. Wandering at night, evident confusion, and incontinence are examples of problems that are usually organic in nature—all of which can, however, be behavioral in origin. Wandering, for instance, may have as its psychogenic root the need to escape. Incontinence may be an expression of anger. Whatever the psychological underpinnings, these symptoms may have behavioral or pharmacologic interventions if properly evaluated and diagnosed.

The alert facade or appearance and normal-looking social habits can be deceptive, masking the presence of severe brain damage. Korsakoff's syndrome and the dementias are conditions in which an observer can be misled by first impressions of mental capacity.

Two sisters were admitted to the National Institute of Neurological Diseases and Blindness for studies of familial essential hypercholesterolemia and general research studies. One was 57, the other 55. They were anxious, depressed, fearful, restless, and perplexed. Verbal productivity was somewhat decreased. There was slurring of speech as well as delay in responses and little spontaneity of thinking. They had difficulty finding words, they were distractable. In these patients, there was perseveration of ideas, but not of words.

In spite of all of this, they appeared outwardly intact. Their personal habits and conduct were fine. The successful social facade, however, fell away drastically when tested in the mental status examination. They knew all the "right things" to say. They just didn't know such simple facts as what day it was.

Intellectual deficiency, memory loss, acalculia, inability to abstract proverbs, and impaired judgment were present. Both began to show signs of illness in their early fifties. Their courses were insidious and progressive. There was a family history of Alzheimer's disease. Four of five siblings showed signs of mental decline. Our studies showed evidence of reduced cerebral blood flow and oxygen consumption. Autopsies later confirmed the diagnosis of Alzheimer's disease.

The Search for a Psychological Baseline against Which to Measure "Illness"

Studies of Community-Resident "Healthy" Older Persons.

If we are to recognize what is problematic for an older person, we must first be able to recognize what is emotionally healthy behavior. Busse's group (Palmore, 1970) and the NIMH group (Birren et al., 1963) are among those who have evaluated healthy community-dwelling older persons. In the NIMH studies, begun in 1955, physical and emotional health was a criterion in selection for study. Part of the purpose in such work was to obtain a baseline for evaluating older people that consisted of a composite of the statistical norm (the average) and the healthy (the ideal). A longitudinal view of the life cycle is necessary and, indeed, has begun to receive attention. Senescence as a developmental stage or process in the course of the life cycle has a psychology of its own, which thus far has only been crudely delineated.

Evaluation of the Effects of Lifelong Personality.

The list given here, resulting from the NIMH studies of the healthy elderly, indicates the contribution of some aspects of lifelong personality to the psychological nature of older people.

1. Adaptive qualities for later life
   a. Candor, ease of relationships, independence, affirmation, positive self-concept, sense of usefulness
   b. Defense mechanisms: insight, denial, use of activity
2. Maladaptive qualities for later life
   a. Paranoid isolation
3. Maladaptive in early life—adaptive in later life
   a. Obsessive-compulsive features
   b. Schizoid mechanisms
   c. Dependent personality

Both adaptive and maladaptive features are brought by the person into old age. We must caution observers, however, that only through a careful knowledge of life history can differentiation be made between those qualities possessed by the individual throughout life and those that first came into being in old age through a reorganization of personality. For example, the Swedish film *Wild Strawberries* reflects the potential of an older man, set in his ways, to make rather basic changes in his personality late in life.

Lifelong personality traits that are useful in old age include a sense of self-esteem, candor, ability to relate easily with others, independence and self-motivation, and a sense of usefulness. Measures of ego strength (the ego's function as the moderating and reality-testing component of the personality) enable judgments to be made regarding the capacity to cope and adjust. Some defense mechanisms (by which the ego copes) are more useful than others. Naturally, insight is a valuable aid in alleviating anxiety and guilt by realistically appraising the changed circumstances of life and body. Denial can be beneficial if it does not interfere with needed medical or emotional care and if it facilitates relationships and activities. Older people who use appropriate activity, ranging from the creative to merely "keeping busy" in order to counteract fear or depression, also have a defense that is an asset. Less adaptive are the counterphobic defenses, wherein some older people undertake excessive and dangerous activities in order to prove their continued prowess, youthfulness, and fearlessness.

In judging the adaptations of older persons, it is vital to remember that they commonly deal with more stresses (in actual number, frequency, and profundity) than any other age group. Thus evaluation of restitutive attempts must be viewed with this in mind. Sometimes maintenance of the status quo may be all that is possible; indeed, this may be a triumph under some circumstances. A pride in present accomplishments, no matter how small, is appropriate.

Paranoid personality features have a particular maladaptiveness in old age, since so much happens to reinforce the notion that the problems are all "out there." In addition, hearing and other sensory losses increase the inability to deal with threatening forces and compound the isolation of the person with paranoid tendencies. A defensive use of perceptual loss, such as "hearing what one wants to hear," may be present. Tendencies to use age, disease, or impairment as a defense (by acting more helpless than is warranted) are common problems. Personality characteristics of rigidity, despair, depression, and the whole range of psychopathological reactions can further hamper adaptation to old age.

As we state in Chapter 5, certain psychopathology can become increasingly adaptive as people age. Obsessional maneuvers fill the emptiness of retirement; schizoid detachment apparently insulates against loss; dependency can result in a welcoming of greater care and help from others.

Diagnostic Attention to the Inner Experience of Old Age.   Aside from the complex of reality factors and the influences of the individual personality, there are inner reactions to old age that seem to be part of the developmental work of late life. One of these inner processes, the life review, appears to be a universal occurrence. (See Chapters 5 and 12.) The life review takes place through reminiscence accompanied by feelings of nostalgia, regret, and pleasure. Complications that can occur are extreme emotional pain, despair, guilt, obsessive rumination, panic, and suicide. A resolution or working through of the life review may bring atonement, serenity, constructive reorganization, and creativity.

The Holmes Social Adjustment Rating Scale (Table 9.1) provides a constructive approach to evaluating the impact of various life events on persons of all ages, moderated, of course, by the individual character of the person.

Problems Commonly Misdiagnosed or Overlooked.   We have listed a series of conditions more fully described in Chapter 6 that require special diagnostic attention from physicians conducting medical/psychiatric assessments as well as other mental health personnel involved in evaluation of the elderly. These conditions, summarized here and commonly overlooked, are often

TABLE 9.1   The social readjustment rating scale

LIFE EVENT	MEAN VALUE	LIFE EVENT	MEAN VALUE
1. Death of spouse	100	23. Son or daughter leaving home	29
2. Divorce	73	24. Trouble with in-laws	29
3. Marital separation	65	25. Outstanding personal achievement	28
4. Jail term	63		
5. Death of close family member	63	26. Wife begin or stop work	26
6. Personal injury or illness	53	27. Begin or end school	26
7. Marriage	50	28. Change in living conditions	25
8. Fired at work	47	29. Revision of personal habits	24
9. Marital reconciliation	45		
10. Retirement	45	30. Trouble with boss	23
11. Change in health of family member	44	31. Change in work hours or conditions	20
12. Pregnancy	40	32. Change in residence	20
13. Sex difficulties	39	33. Change in schools	20
14. Gain of new family member	39	34. Change in recreation	19
15. Business readjustment	39	35. Change in church activities	19
16. Change in financial state	38	36. Change in social activities	18
17. Death of close friend	37	37. Mortgage or loan less than $10,000	17
18. Change to different line of work	36		
19. Change in number of arguments with spouse	35	38. Change in sleeping habits	16
		39. Change in number of family get-togethers	15
20. Mortgage or loan over $10,000	31	40. Change in eating habits	15
21. Foreclosure of mortgage or loan	30	41. Vacation	13
		42. Christmas	12
22. Change in responsibilities at work	29	43. Minor violations of the law	11

Source: Holmes, T. H., & Rahe, R. H. (1967). The social readjustment scale, *Journal of Psychosomatic Research, 11,* 213. Reprinted by permission of Pergamon Press. See the article for complete wording of items.

recoverable and treatable. Table 9.2 lists reversible causes of mental impairment. Look especially for the following:

1. Delirium
   a. Alone
   b. Superimposed on dementia
2. Depressive reactions simulating organic brain disorders
3. Paranoid states without organic brain disease
   a. Generalized

   b. Circumscribed
   c. Chronic paranoid state with superimposed, reversible crises
4. Subdural hematomas leading to confusional states
5. Drug reactions
6. Suicide risk factors

Delirium.   Delirium usually develops quickly, is typically fluctuating in severity, and can be caused by a large number of possible reversible organic

TABLE 9.2   Reversible causes of mental impairment

CAUSE	DEMENTIA	DELIRIUM	EITHER OR BOTH
Therapeutic drug intoxication			Yes
Depression	Yes		
Metabolic			
a. Azotemia or renal failure (dehydration, diuretics, obstruction, hypokalemia)			Yes
b. Hyponatremia (diuretics, excess antidiuretic hormone, salt wasting, intravenous fluids)			Yes
c. Hypernatremia (dehydration, intravenous saline)		Yes	
d. Volume depletion (diuretics, bleeding, inadequate fluids)			Yes
e. Acid-base disturbance		Yes	
f. Hypoglycemia (insulin, oral hypoglycemics, starvation)			Yes
g. Hyperglycemia (diabetic ketoacidosis, or hyperosmolar coma)		Yes	
h. Hepatic failure			Yes
i. Hypothyroidism			Yes
j. Hyperthyroidism (especially apathetic)			Yes
k. Hypercalcemia			Yes
l. Cushing's syndrome	Yes		
m. Hypopituitarism			Yes
Infection, fever, or both			
a. Viral			Yes
b. Bacterial			
Pneumonia, Pyelonephritis, Cholecystitis, Diverticulitis		Yes	
Tuberculosis			Yes
Endocarditis			Yes
Cardiovascular			
a. Acute myocardial infarct		Yes	
b. Congestive heart failure			Yes
c. Arrhythmia			Yes
d. Vascular occlusion			Yes
e. Pulmonary embolus		Yes	
Brain disorders			
a. Vascular insufficiency			
Transient ischemia		Yes	
Stroke			Yes
b. Trauma			
Subdural hematoma			Yes
Concussion/contusion		Yes	
Intracerebral hemorrhage		Yes	
Epidural hematoma		Yes	
c. Infection			
Acute meningitis (pyogenic, viral)		Yes	
Chronic meningitis (tuberculous, fungal)			Yes
Neurosyphilis			Yes

(continued)

TABLE 9.2 *(Continued)*

CAUSE	DEMENTIA	DELIRIUM	EITHER OR BOTH
Subdural empyema			Yes
Brain abscess			Yes
d. Tumors			
Metastatic to brain			Yes
Primary in brain			Yes
e. Normal pressure hydrocephalus	Yes		
Pain			
a. Fecal impaction			Yes
b. Urinary retention		Yes	
c. Fracture		Yes	
d. Surgical abdomen		Yes	
Sensory deprivation states such as blindness or deafness			Yes
Hospitalization			
a. Anesthesia or surgery			Yes
b. Environmental change and isolation			Yes
Alcohol toxic reactions			
a. Lifelong alcoholism	Yes		
b. Alcoholism new in old age			Yes
c. Decreased tolerance with age producing increasing intoxication			Yes
d. Acute hallucinosis		Yes	
e. Delirium tremens		Yes	
Anemia			Yes
Tumor—systemic effects of nonmetastatic malignant neoplasm			Yes
Chronic lung disease with hypoxia or hypercapnia			Yes
Deficiencies of nutrients such as vitamin B_{12}, folic acid, or niacin	Yes		
Accidental hypothermia		Yes	
Chemical intoxications			
a. Heavy metals such as arsenic, lead, or mercury			Yes
b. Consciousness-altering agents			Yes
c. Carbon monoxide			Yes

Source: NIA Task Force. (1980). Senility reconsidered; treatment possibilities for mental impairment in the elderly, *Journal of the American Medical Association,* 244(3), 261–262.

conditions such as drug intoxication or metabolic and infectious disorders. Emergency diagnosis and treatment is imperative in every situation in order to achieve the highest possible rate of reversal and avoid the permanent damage that can result if the condition is allowed to fulminate.

Depressive Reactions Simulating Organic Brain Disorders.   Depressions may be masked as organic states. Observe the content of thought and the sense of interpersonal responsibilities. Listen for feelings of worthlessness. Look for specific events or stimuli that may have precipitated the feelings of depression. Many depressive episodes in old age are realistic responses to loss. When this is the case, there may be a relief of symptoms when actual loss or threat is relieved, compensated for, or replaced; this is not so with purely organic disorders. It must not be forgotten, however, that depression and organic brain disorder can coexist. The following letter from the relative of an older woman to a therapist is an example of the kind of evidence often presented:

In order to help you [the therapist] with your evaluation of her problems, I [her relative] thought it best to let you know what I have observed in her behavior, attitude, appearance, and general demeanor the last six months. She puts clothes on backwards, inside out, sometimes leaving night clothes underneath street clothes, and shoes on the wrong feet. She has lost interest in books, television, letter writing. When in my home she follows me constantly. When she can't find me, she goes all over house and garden looking for me and calling my name. She is extremely restless no matter what the situation—she cannot wait for anything, which is one reason we were an hour early for your appointment. When she is in her own apartment and not having dinner in the communal dining room, she is on the phone dialing me every 10 minutes for hours on end. If my husband and I are out, she then dials my friends until our return. She has a habit of making loud "sighs" in my presence and says aloud, "I don't know what I'm going to do." At this time she has made no effort to make new friends at the residential home for older people where she now lives although outwardly she is an extremely friendly and gregarious person.

The diagnosis was that of organic brain disorder with a concurrent depression.

Paranoid States without Organic Brain Disorder. Look for ideas of ruin and for delusions of noxious fumes, delusions of marital infidelity, and the like. Note isolated evidences of projection as well as comprehensive delusional systems. Be aware of the possibility of *folie à deux,* in which paranoid delusions may be shared by two people—most often mother and daughter, two sisters, or husband and wife. Check for hearing loss, which is associated with suspiciousness and paranoid states.

Subdural Hematomas Leading to Confusional States. Falls and fractures are common in old age. Persons over 65 account for over 70% of all fatal falls and 30% of all pedestrian fatalities. Subdural hematomas are collections of blood between the dura mater (the hard outer membrane over the brain) and the skull. They may be clinically silent. Again, a careful history may elicit a story of head injury (although the person may not remember falling because of memory loss), concussion, perhaps coma, delirium, or a syndrome (Korsakoff's) marked by fabrication and confabulation. Papilledema (swollen optic nerve head) and possibly headaches are more common in younger persons. Mental symptoms such as somnolence (sleepiness), confusion, memory loss, and hemiparesis (paralysis on one side) are more common in older persons. The hematomas of older persons are thicker than those in younger persons. This may be because of the decreasing weight of the brain that occurs with age, thereby increasing the space between the brain and the skull and making room for the hematoma to expand without increasing intracranial pressure. Subdural hematomas, as well as brain tumors, hypertension, and extracerebral vascular occlusion or narrowing, can often be successfully treated—provided they are discovered via CT scan and other diagnostic measures.

Drug Reactions. The wide use of drugs among the elderly, from tranquilizers to anti-depressants, has increased the potential for negative drug reactions. Drugs may make a differential diagnosis between functional and organic disorders exceedingly difficult, and discontinuation of the medications during an evaluation period may be required. A fuller discussion of drug reactions can be found in Chapter 13.

Suicide Risk Factors. Older people account for approximately one-fourth of all reported suicides. Therefore, a mental health evaluation should give serious consideration to behavior that might indicate self-destructive tendencies. More than any other therapeutic intervention available to mental health professionals, accurate diagnosis of suicidal intentions can directly save a life.

Although suicide in old age has already been discussed at some length in Chapter 5, we wish to list here (not necessarily in order of frequency or importance) some of the major diagnostic risk factors for suicide in old age:

- Depression (with no anger outlet)
- Withdrawal
- Bereavement (especially within first year after loss)
- Isolation: widowed; single
- Expectation of death from some cause
- Less organization and complexity of behavior than previously
- Induced helplessness
- Institutionalization
- Physical illness
- Alcoholism
- Desire and rational decision to protect survivors from financial disaster
- Philosophical decision: no more pleasure or purpose
- Meaninglessness of life
- Decreased self-regard
- Organic mental deterioration
- Changes in sleep patterns: severe nightmares
- White males (a higher rate of suicide than in any other group)

A threat to commit suicide is relatively uncommon in the elderly; they tend to simply kill themselves. Nonetheless, one must be alert for indirect or veiled threats or previous suicide attempts. Self-destruction can be abrupt or drawn out over long periods of time (not eating, not taking medication, alcoholism, delay in seeking treatment, excessive risk taking).

Mental Status, Memory, and Psychological Tests

The mental status examination should not be conducted in the absence of a thorough appreciation of what the patient is feeling and thinking. Be certain the patient can hear you and explain that you are going to ask about feelings, thinking, and cognition. Because of their variability, these functions must be appraised with delicacy. Although there have been advances in recent years in psychiatric techniques for rating or measuring the psychological functioning, mental status, and symptoms of older persons, much work remains to be done. Neuropsychology is making a great contribution. The differentiation of age-related behavior from lifelong behavior (as well as disease-determined, culturally deprived, and other behavior) must be borne in mind.

A number of brief screening instruments for cognitive impairment are available. Folstein's Mini Mental Status Examination[28] or MMSE (Tables 9.3 and 9.4) is probably the most widely used instrument in both clinical and research settings because of its ease of administration, although it does have significant limitations. For example, orientation is not necessarily a sensitive indicator of mental dysfunction. Visual and auditory deficits (as well as aphasia) may lead to misdiagnosis. The Mattis Dementia Rating Scale[29] is also a very good screening instrument, which more systematically examines a variety of cognitive skills. The Blessed[30] mental status exam developed in Great Britain is less frequently used today, but if used, gives a quick but crude impression of mental capacities. Rarely used now, the Mental Status Questionnaire[31] of Kahn and colleagues (Tables 9.5 and 9.6) is also available. It is presented here only so readers will know of this historic first step in the development of more effective measurements.

Central nervous system functioning is too complex to be left to a "simple test" except as a crude screening device. As valuable as brief mental status exams may be when screening large populations or when monitoring the potential effects of medications in geriatric patients, a more detailed exam is often indicated. No self-respecting cardiologist would use a mini cardiac status to evaluate a serious heart problem. Just as a malfunctioning heart requires a comprehensive exam, so too does the malfunctioning brain—the most complex part of the human body and the wellspring of personal and social adaptation. If, for example, a first meeting with an older patient brings

TABLE 9.3   "Mini-mental state"

MAXIMUM SCORE	SCORE	
		Orientation
5	(_____)	What is the (year) (season) (date) (day) (month)?
5	(_____)	Where are we (state) (county) (town) (hospital) (floor)?
		Registration
3	(_____)	Name 3 objects: 1 second to say each. Then ask the patient all 3 after you have said them. Give 1 point for each correct answer. Then repeat them until he learns all 3. Count trials and record. □ Trials
		Attention and calculation
5	(_____)	Serial 7's. 1 point for each correct. Stop after 5 answers. Alternatively spell "world" backwards.
		Recall
3	(_____)	Ask for the 3 objects repeated above. Give 1 point for each correct.
		Language
9	(_____)	Name a pencil, and watch (2 points). Repeat the following "No ifs, ands or buts." (1 point) Follow a 3-stage command: "Take a paper in your right hand, fold it in half, and put it on the floor." (3 points) Read and obey the following: Close your eyes (1 point) Write a sentence (1 point) Copy design (1 point)
_____		TOTAL SCORE Assess level of consciousness along a continuum

Alert	Drowsy	Stupor	Coma

Source: Folstein, M. F., Folstein, S. E., & McHugh, P. R. (1975). "Mini-Mental State," a practical method for grading the cognitive state of patients for the clinician. *Journal of Psychiatric Research, 12,* 189–98. Copyright 1975, Pergamon Press. Reprinted by permission.

up questions of intellectual decline, it is important to refer for a detailed examination of neuropsychological abilities, including attention, memory, language, abstraction, judgment, orientation to time, place, and person, and other elements of mental functioning such as visual and spatial skills and calculations. Such an exam not only provides an opportunity to diagnose Alzheimer's Disease, multiinfarct dementia or other less obvious reasons for cognitive change,[32] but also gives a baseline for later comparisons.

By now a variety of normed and well-validated neuropsychological tests exists for diagnosing older people. Verbal learning tests such as the California Verbal Learning Test[33] are among the most sensitive memory tests available. The revised Wechsler Memory Scale[34] allows evaluation of both verbal and visual memory. Visual memory can also be tested with the Benton Visual Retention Test.[35] Language functions can be tested by the naming of objects, repeating of a phrase, reading and writing samples, and ability to follow oral

TABLE 9.4 Instructions for administration of "Mini-Mental State" examination

Orientation

1. Ask for the date. Then ask specifically for parts omitted, e.g., "Can you also tell me what season it is?" One point for each correct.
2. Ask in turn "Can you tell me the name of this hospital?" (town, county, etc.) One point for each correct.

Registration

Ask the patient if you may test his memory. Then say the names of 3 unrelated objects, clearly and slowly, about 1 second for each. After you have said all 3, ask him to repeat them. This first repetition determines his score (0–3) but keep saying them until he can repeat all 3, up to 6 trials. If he does not eventually learn all 3, recall cannot be meaningfully tested.

Attention and calculation

Ask the patient to begin with 100 and count backwards by 7. Stop after 5 subtractions (93, 86, 79, 72, 65). Score the total number of correct answers.

If the patient cannot or will not perform this task, ask him to spell the word "world" backwards. The score is the number of letters in correct order, e.g., dlrow = 5, dlorw = 3.

Recall

Ask the patient if he can recall the 3 words you previously asked him to remember. Score 0–3.

Language

Naming: Show the patient a wrist watch and ask him what it is. Repeat for pencil. Score 0–2.

Repetition: Ask the patient to repeat the sentence after you. Allow only one trial. Score 0 or 1.

3-stage command: Give the patient a piece of plain blank paper and repeat the command. Score 1 point for each part correctly executed.

Reading: On a blank piece of paper print the sentence "Close your eyes," in letters large enough for the patient to see clearly. Ask him to read it and do what it says. Score 1 point only if he actually closes his eyes.

Writing: Give the patient a blank piece of paper and ask him to write a sentence for you. Do not dictate a sentence, it is to be written spontaneously. It must contain a subject and verb and be sensible. Correct grammar and punctuation are not necessary.

Copying: On a clean piece of paper, draw intersecting pentagons, each side about 1 inch, and ask him to copy it exactly as it is. All 10 angles must be present and 2 must intersect to score 1 point. Tremor and rotation are ignored.

Estimate the patient's level of sensorium along a continuum, from alert on the left to coma on the right.

Source: Folstein, M. F., Folstein, S. E., & McHugh, P. R. (1975). "Mini-Mental State," a practical method for grading the cognitive state of patients for the clinician. *Journal of Psychiatric Research,* *12,* 189–98. Copyright 1975, Pergamon Press. Reprinted by permission.

commands. Subtests of the revised Wechsler Adult Intelligence Scale (WAIS)[36] can be used to examine attention, conceptualization, and visual and spatial skills. The neuropsychological examination may take about two hours depending upon the patient. It almost always is associated with another 45 minutes of interviewing to take the history from the point of view of both the patient and family. With the rise of managed care there is pressure to reduce referral for neuropsychological testing, as there is for any specialty testing. But the argument can be justifiably made that a neuropsychological assessment will save money as a result of improved management due to early detection, and by minimizing non-compliance with treatment plans.

When do you refer the patient to the neuropsychologist for a more comprehensive examination?

1. For early detection of dementia.
2. When you are not quite clear about the differential diagnosis (e.g., Alzheimer's vs. brain tumor, Parkinson's disease, etc.)
3. Differentiation from or recognition of concurrent depression.
4. Need to treat the emotional and social context.
5. Help the patient overcome the denial of deficits. It is also helpful to the family, which may need to see the data to help them confront the deficits in the older person. This may lead to less anger at the patient by the family who now understands the deficits better.
6. At times it is important to monitor the disorder in a longitudinal fashion by repeat testing.

When would you not refer a patient to a neuropsychologist, or delay neuropsychological testing?

1. When the individual is barely testable because of too much deterioration. The only reason for some testing at this stage might be to assist the family in management.
2. When the patient is clearly severely depressed so as to require immediate inpatient or outpatient treatment. He/she should still be tested later to determine if dementia is also present.

TABLE 9.5   Mental Status Questionnaire

MENTAL STATUS QUESTIONNAIRE—"SPECIAL TEN"
1. Where are we now?
2. Where is this place (located)?
3. What is today's date—day of month?
4. What month is it?
5. What year is it?
6. How old are you?
7. What is your birthday?
8. What year were you born?
9. Who is President of the United States?
10. Who was President before him?

Source: Modified from Kahn, R. L., Goldfarb, A. I., & Pollack, M. (1964). The evaluation of geriatric patients following treatment. In Hoch, P. H., Zubin, J., (Eds.), *Evaluation of psychiatric treatment.* New York: Grune & Stratton. Reprinted by permission.

TABLE 9.6   Rating of mental functional impairment by Mental Status Questionnaire

NO. OF ERRORS	PRESUMED MENTAL STATUS
0–2	Chronic brain syndrome absent or mild
3–8	Chronic brain syndrome moderate
9–10	Chronic brain syndrome severe
Nontestable	Chronic brain syndrome severe*

Source: Modified from Kahn, R. L., Goldfarb, A. I., & Pollack, M. (1964). The evaluation of geriatric patients following treatment. In Hoch, P. H., Zubin, J., (Eds.), *Evaluation of psychiatric treatment.* New York: Grune & Stratton. Reprinted by permission.

*In the noncooperative person without deafness or insuperable language barriers.

Candor is important in discussing the results of testing with the patient and family, since it helps them to prepare for the future. For example, it is difficult to send the patient to an Alzheimer's Disease Association support group without some explanation. It is very rare that a patient would become acutely depressed or suicidal because he/she was told frankly the findings of neuropsychological testing.

The Raven Progressive Matrices, utilizing geometric figures, is presumably culture-free, but there is some debate on this issue. Another popular test is the Kent E-G-Y,[37] a 10-item, quick-screening test for intelligence. Some people, such as Goldfarb, find M. Bender's Double Simultaneous Tactual Stimulation (Face-Hand) Test[38] of value in the important differential diagnosis between organicity and depression. The Face-Hand Test (Table 9.7) is also of value in attempting to determine the degree of brain damage. The failure to properly report touch on the back of the hands is a valid and reliable suggestion of brain damage or senile brain disease. The errors made are failure to report the touch at all (extinction), displacement of the hand touch to another part of the person's body, and exosmesthesia (the touch somewhere "out there" or "over there"). The number of errors

TABLE 9.7   Order of stimulation used in Face-Hand Test

1. Right cheek—left hand
2. Left cheek—right hand
3. Right cheek—right hand
4. Left cheek—left hand
5. Right cheek—left cheek
6. Right hand—left hand
7. Right cheek—left hand
8. Left cheek—right hand
9. Right cheek—right hand
10. Left cheek—left hand

Source: Modified from Bender, M. B., Fink, M., & Green, M. (1951). Patterns in perception in simultaneous tests of the face and hand, *Archives of Neurology and Psychiatry* 66:355–62.

is recorded for the test done with the eyes closed and then for the test repeated with the eyes open.

On a more subjective level, projective tests elicit spontaneous and personal responses to a vague stimuli, thus giving valuable psychological insight into the person being tested. The Rorschach Inkblot Test is a series of 10 cards, each containing a different inkblot to which the patient associates whatever thoughts may come to mind.[39] This provides information on the formal organization of the personality and some of its unconscious features. The Thematic Apperception Test (TAT) stimuli are more suggestive but still unspecific. The test consists of 20 pictures to each of which the patient associates a story. The Sentence Completion Test is a group of unfinished sentences that the patient is asked to complete with the first thought that comes to mind.

Although we do not necessarily believe that psychological tests must be done in every case, they can be most useful when indicated. When there is uncertainty about the differential diagnosis of organic brain damage versus depression, such tests can be invaluable; but one should not forget that the patient with an organic problem can still be depressed. A patient with chronic organic brain disorder generally produces lower test scores than one with acute brain disorder; however, at the height of the acute reversible crisis (for

example, delirium), the patient is likely to be untestable.

The Life Satisfaction Measure of Neugarten et al. isolates five components of an individual's positive life satisfaction:[40] (1) taking pleasure from the round of activities that constitutes everyday life, (2) regarding life as meaningful and accepting resolutely that which life has been, (3) feeling success in achieving major goals, (4) holding a positive image of self, and (5) maintaining happy and optimistic attitudes and moods. Lawton's Morale Scale was specially designed to assess morale of the aged.[41] This scale determines self-perceptions of mood, adjustment, and well-being. The Minnesota Multiphasic Personality Inventory (MMPI) assesses personality structure and diagnostic classification through a paper and pencil inventory. Of the nine dimensions of the personality that are measured, the aged do not appear to deviate from other age groups except in the D scale, which measures depression.

Multiple scales measure mood in adult populations.[42] Unfortunately, very few mood scales are designed specifically for the elderly or organically impaired.[43] Since memory impairments are so commonly associated with depression in the elderly,[44] the clinician must carefully review whether subjective self-ratings versus objective measures are the appropriate tests for individual subjects.[45]

Diagnostic Use of Mirror and Self-Drawings. Any technique that is useful in eliciting rich, spontaneous information and response from older people can become part of the diagnostic repertoire. Such techniques may be discovered by accident. Clinical experiences by the author (RNB) of observing certain older people communicating with their mirror images led to investigation of self- and body concepts through the experimental use of the mirror and self-drawings. These techniques were introduced as cues for a collaborative self-exploration with the older person as an *active* participant—how does he view himself now, how did he in the past, and what does he see in his future?

Mirror.   To help illustrate the psychological significance of an individual's mirror image, let us quote from a Tolstoy short story, *The Death of Ivan Ilych* (1886).

> And Ivan Ilych began to wash. With pauses for rest, he washed his hands and then his face, cleaned his teeth, brushed his hair, and looked in the glass. He was terrified by what he saw, especially the limp way in which his hair clung to his pallid forehead. While his shirt was being changed he knew that he would be still more frightened at the sight of his body, so he avoided looking at it.

Asking an older person to look into a mirror and tell about what is seen is an exceptionally excellent way of acquiring data about body images and reactions to changes with age. The mirror is a powerful trigger or cue to thoughts and observations about self and changes in self. The clinician often obtains much richer data in less time than by elaborate verbal questioning about physical, personality, and other changes. The range of reactions may be accounted for by (1) reality factors in appearance, (2) personality factors, whether lifelong or in reaction to old age, and (3) organic factors. The following outline provides details:

1. Reality factors in appearance
   a. Skin-wrinkling; pigmentation; flabbiness; leathering
   b. Bodily movements—slowing
      (1) Physical impairments
      (2) Arthritis
      (3) Palsies—tremors
   c. Facial changes—palsies; wrinkling
   d. Hair—balding; graying
   e. Eyes—opacities of the lens
   f. Teeth—absence; discoloration
   g. Cartilage growth—ears; nose
   h. Chest—increased diameter; breathing rate
   i. Abdomen—protuberance
   j. Weight—loss; shrunken
2. Personality factors
   a. Lifelong
      (1) Focal emphasis on (cathexis of) parts versus whole—for example, nose; profile versus frontal view; sexual organ
      (2) Character—narcissism, self-hate, etc.
      (3) Identity—crisis

      (4) Mood-depression, hypomania, etc.
   b. Old age
      (1) Fear, anxiety, and/or tension over aging and death
      (2) Denial of aging changes
3. Organic factors
   a. Perceptual factors
      (1) Vision affected (can be defensive; cf., exclusion of stimuli—Weinberg)
   b. Organic factors
      (1) Organic brain damage: "Not me"
      (2) Disorientation for person

As is known, cartilage continues to grow in old age, so the ears and nose may consequently become more prominent, but these changes are not mentioned as often as wrinkling, sagging around the eyes, hair loss, and general appearance of "oldness." On the other hand, most healthy older people find it difficult to see themselves as having essentially changed. Of course, much turns on the term "essentially." It appears that they are in effect recognizable to themselves, and in their own minds they have not drastically altered in their character and nature in the course of time; their identity has remained solid. A sudden and rapid deterioration and change of appearance can cause an identity crisis or reaction, even in otherwise healthy people. Adjustment and acceptance are much easier when physical change comes slowly. A clue to shaky identity or difficulty in adapting to changes can be seen in people who reject their mirror image.

> *A middle-aged woman who expressed a profound fear of aging could not accept her mirror image as herself. She regarded the image as something foreign and experienced her "real" self as being on the inside of her body, feeling and reacting, while people responded to her "foreign" outside image in a way that was unacceptable to her.*

Personality factors before the mirror can be strikingly obvious. People exhibiting defensive preoccupation with themselves (narcissism) are pleased and attracted by their image, whereas those who are ashamed and guilty shun the mirror, reject their images, become anxious. A focal emphasis on or cathexis of a particular body part (for example, the nose) is observed and provides diagnostic clues. Usually a part rather than the whole is seen by the older person. Other common reactions are fear, shudders, suddenly occurring thoughts about aging and approaching death, or, conversely, a denial of aging changes and denial of fear of death.

Organic factors can affect the mirror reactions. Persons with organic brain damage may insist the image is "not me" or illustrate vividly a "disorientation for person" by not recognizing the person in the mirror. Perceptual impairments of vision can be actual or defensive in nature, the latter recalling Weinberg's concept of exclusion of stimuli, in which the person blocks out images that are too painful.

Self-Drawings.   Some classic examples of the emotion-laden quality of self-drawings are the variety of self-portraits done by well-known artists (many using their mirror image). A museum exhibit displayed such portraits with expressions ranging from pleased and serene to displeased and tortured. Goya made his self-portrait defiantly ugly and troubled, not bothering to idealize himself or impress his audience. Cézanne dressed himself in overalls and a lumpy, battered hat, beneath which he seemed to be shy and retiring. The self-portrait of Dürer was exquisitely and lovingly drawn.

Self-drawings by patients are revealing, whether done in front of the mirror or by themselves. The technique is to focus the person directly on himself. Self-drawings of older persons with and without the mirror often suggest a self-view of dissolution, sometimes bizarre; they do not appear, as some have said, similar to the drawings of children. The illustrations in Figure 9.1 show examples of self-drawings of normal older men.

Barring severe hand tremors or profound visual problems that would affect expression, drawing provides other clues to the feelings of older people. Things to look for in drawings are the size of the image and placement of figures on the page, amount and kind of detail, underemphasis or overemphasis of a body part, omissions, facial expressions, activity or inactivity of the figure, and the general emotional quality of the picture.

"Draw Your Insides."   "Draw your insides" is an interesting device because of the preoccupation of so many older people with their bodily ailments and changes. One can get clues about the emotional impact of such changes by observing the older person's response in this kind of drawing. Shown in Figure 9.2 is the figure provided for male subjects. A female figure should be provided for women.

Items most commonly drawn are intestines, heart, lungs, and stomach. Placement and size of these organs in the drawing can give indications of their meaning emotionally. In experimental tests, 20% of inner body parts were drawn as protruding out from the body or as completely outside, suggesting possible mental confusion and organicity.

Since comparative data for other age groups or various diagnostic entities are not available, no concise inferences can be drawn from findings; indeed, anatomical knowledge may be limited in the older population simply because many of them did not receive as much educational emphasis on biology and health as more recent generations have. But the draw-your-insides procedure, along with mirror reactions and self-drawing, produces rich emotional data without being unduly threatening. In the same way, reviews of family photo albums and scrapbooks can provide stimulation and diagnostic clues, while often giving immense pleasure to the older person in the process.

Personality.   One of the major advances in personality psychology in recent years has been the widespread recognition that most personality traits familiar to laypersons and conceived by personality theorists can be described in terms of five basic dimensions or factors (the Five Factor Model or FFM).[46] The Revised NEO Personality Inventory (NEO-PI-R)[47] is a 240-item questionnaire designed to measure the five factors as well as some of the more specific traits that define them. For example, the broad *Agreeableness versus Antagonism* factor includes scales measuring

SUBJECT 16

In front of mirror ▶

Subject 16.   *This 76-year-old retired merchant's counterphobic activity helped him to ward off depressive symptoms. Although emphasizing his physical well-being, his self-drawing suggests incompleteness. Character trait disorder.* Subject 20.   *This 78-year-old retired clerk has recurrent nightmares related to death. He describes himself as a "silent worrier." No psychiatric diagnosis.*

SUBJECT 20

In front of mirror ▶

● **Placement of original drawings on paper**

SUBJECT 19

In front of mirror ▶

◀ Draw a person ▶

Subject 19.   *This 75-year-old physically healthy man did not have diagnosable psychopathology. He first drew a female figure in the "draw-a-person" test; his second draw-a-person figure is essentially the same as his self-drawings.*

(continued)

FIGURE 9.1   Self-drawings of normal older men.
(*Source:* Butler, R. N. (1963). *Geriatrics, 18,* 220–232. Reprinted by permission.)

FIGURE 9.1 Continued

Subject 27. *This 71-year-old professional man was diagnosed obsessional-compulsive reaction. His narcissism was demonstrated in his pleasure before the mirror. Subject 12. This 75-year-old man with obvious artistic talent drew an actual likeness of himself in the mirror. No psychiatric diagnosis was made.*

SUBJECT 27

SUBJECT 12

In front of mirror ▶

In front of mirror ▶

SUBJECT 35

SUBJECT 39

◀ In front of mirror

◀ In front of mirror

Subject 35. *This 79-year-old retired businessman appeared happy, youthful, and alert. He had no psychiatric diagnosis, yet his self-drawings were surprising. A suprapubic prostalectomy had been performed for an obstruction twenty-three years before, after which he was sexually inactive. Subject 39. At 73 years of age, this man returned to work after retirement, which he found to be a "drudgery." His self-drawing became more orderly in front of the mirror.*

FIGURE 9.2 Figure given to a male patient when he is asked to draw his insides.

trust, straightforwardness, altruism, compliance, modesty, and tender-mindedness. Each item in the NEO-PI-R is answered on a five-point scale from "strongly disagree" to "strongly agree." The instrument has a sixth-grade reading level and usually takes 30 to 40 minutes to complete. It can be administered in groups or individually, by computer, or orally. A Spanish version is available for assessing Hispanic Americans.

The NEO-PI-R is one of the few personality inventories developed and validated on adult samples spanning the entire age range. Research comparing self reports with peer and spouse ratings has demonstrated that both the first-person and third-person versions of the instrument yield valid scores.[48] The NEO-PI-R has been used in research on personality change in dementia,[49] predictors of caregiver burden,[50] correlates of psychological well-being,[51] psychotherapy outcome,[52] and stress and coping in aging men and women.[53]

Socioeconomic Assessment

Work at the NIMH and elsewhere has documented effects of the social support system on the older person's psychological and behavioral attitudes.[54] "As the environment showed qualities of deprivation or displacement of the person (in loss of intimate persons, loss of income, in cultural displacement), the attitudes and behaviors of the aged showed more deteriorative qualities. Losses of significant persons were especially associated with deteriorative functioning,"[55] and further, "findings of this study lead to the suspicion that psychological reactions to the loss of friends and other environmental supports may amplify if not initiate changes in the older nervous system and thereby the rest of the organism."[56]

Having intimate friends in whom one can confide is very important. It must be recognized, however, that social isolation per se is not always causative of emotional and mental reactions in old age. Persons who have lived isolated lives throughout the years—"loners"—are not necessarily more susceptible to the occurrence of late-life psychopathology. It is those persons who become isolated relatively late in life, through no choice of their own, who have the most difficulties.

A socioeconomic evaluation should include general background information concerning details of family structure, housing, work or retirement, friendship patterns, economic circumstances, social roles, activities, and interests. (See examples in the personal mental health data form in Appendix G.) Interviews with the older person and members of his or her family can provide valuable insight into the contribution of social factors to the patient's problem and into potential assets that can aid and support treatment. An assessment should include the amount and quality of love and affection that exist between the family and the older person.

The evaluation of the family itself is crucial, since the genesis, precipitation, and maintenance of disorders may derive from a family context. The older person may be expressing what is really a familywide pathology in which he or she is the scapegoat or the victim of ancient angers. Sometimes the "problem" of the older person is the means by which a son or daughter seeks treatment when unable to ask for it directly. A skilled evaluator may be able to detect this phenomenon and help the younger family members obtain treatment themselves. In other situations the older person may exploit the family; for example, the domineering parent who becomes even more tyrannical in old age by playing on guilt feelings of children toward the aging and decline of a parent. A prideful overemphasis on independence and a manipulation of others through passivity are other patterns of behavior in older persons that can cause family conflict. Older people must not routinely be judged helpless or fragile. Indeed, a fair number of them wield substantial influence over family and friends.

In working with the total family, it is imperative to share evaluation findings as openly as possible with all members, guided by permission from the older person and by judgment as to the effects of such sharing. Family therapy involving the older person may be indicated—couples' therapy with the patient and spouse can be beneficial even in marriages that have been difficult for years or have deteriorated. At times, the family approach is used as a rationale to exclude the older patient (usually the result of counter-transference problems on the part of treatment personnel).

There is no point seeing the patient—you know his memory is gone. He feels rejected—I find it more useful to see the son and daughter-in-law.

One must recognize the vast implications of race and racism in the lives of older African Americans, Asian Americans, Native Americans, Latinos, and members of other groups. A knowledge of cultural patterns and traditions and the discriminatory practices and prejudices experienced in a lifetime are fundamental parts of a thorough evaluation. This applies also to ethnic origins, since so many older persons are immigrants. However, a note of caution is warranted here: At times, race or ethnic origin may be used to rationalize another form of prejudice. For example, the older African American can be denied psychiatric care because his or her problems are viewed as social or racial, while intrapsychic problems remain unnoticed. People in every culture develop internalized emotional difficulties that are not necessarily directly attributable to the social condition and that require treatment.

Treatment should ideally be planned to coincide with those cultural elements that are familiar and valued by the older person. An elderly African American man in a nursing home might prefer "soul food," whereas a Norwegian immigrant could long for "lute-fisk." Patient comfort, satisfaction, and dignity are important in a positive treatment program.

Not least among the steps in an adequate evaluation is determining the patient's health care coverage and economic circumstances. Pending the introduction of a truly comprehensive national health insurance, it is usually necessary to appraise the patient's "ability to pay" for treatment, although this notion of personal financial responsibility is generally obsolete, given the realities of escalating costs and, for older persons, the denial of adequate income programs and job opportunities. Third-party medical payments include Medicare and Medicaid (Table 9.8). Insurance to supplement Medicare may also be available. A routine check should be made to determine whether the older person is a member of one of the national organizations that sell such supplementary insurance. The National Council of Senior Citizens and the American Association of Retired Persons offer policies, as do the so-called

TABLE 9.8   Government health programs

HEALTH INSURANCE FOR THE AGED—HOSPITAL INSURANCE
(Popular name: Medicare—Part A)

This program provides hospital insurance protection for covered services to any person 65 or over who is entitled to Social Security or Railroad Retirement benefits. A dependent spouse 65 or over is also entitled to Medicare, based on the worker's record. The covered protection in each benefit period includes hospital inpatient care, posthospital extended care, hospice care (210 days), and home health visits by nurses or other health workers from a participating home health agency. It does not include doctors' services.

Under Social Security, workers, their employers, and self-employed people pay a contribution based on earnings during their working years. At age 65, the portion of their contribution that has gone into a special Hospital Insurance Trust Fund guarantees that workers will have help in paying hospital bills.

HEALTH INSURANCE FOR THE AGED—SUPPLEMENTARY MEDICAL INSURANCE
(Popular name: Medicare—Part B)

Social Security's medical insurance program helps pay for doctor bills, outpatient hospital services, medical supplies and services, home health services, outpatient physical therapy, and other health care services.

Medical insurance is not financed through payroll deductions and is not based on earnings or period of work. As a voluntary supplemental extension of Medicare's hospital insurance protection, it helps pay for many of the costs of illness not covered by hospital insurance.

MEDICAL ASSISTANCE PROGRAM
(Popular name: Medicaid Title XIX)

This program provides grants to states to administer medical assistance programs that benefit (1) the needy—all Supplemental Security Income recipients and public assistance families with dependent children—and those who would qualify for that assistance under federal regulations, (2) at a state's option, the medically needy—people in the four groups mentioned above who have enough income or resources for daily needs but not for medical expenses, and (3) all children under 21 whose parents cannot afford medical care.

State plans must include at least five basic services for the needy, and a similar or less extensive program for the medically needy. Family planning services may be included in both.

---

nonprofit Blue Cross–Blue Shield plans and the commercial insurance carriers. One must be on the lookout against fly-by-night, fraudulent Medicare supplements that have been sold to older people. A check of the additional income resources listed on a personal mental health data form (see Appendix G) and information about average living expenses will help to complete the financial assessment.

Older people, like others, may be sensitive to questions about finances, fearing that they will be billed unjustly for treatment or simply resenting an intrusion into their privacy. Some are ashamed to admit their meager incomes and out of pride

may refuse to accept financial benefits to which they are entitled. Every effort should be made to help them exploit all possible outside resources in order to protect their own incomes during treatment.

Medicare coverage may be expanded and will probably be incorporated within a national health insurance plan. In the meantime, actual coverage is limited to about 40% of the health bill of older persons. It is important to note that only Medicare Part A is an entitlement, paid for from a portion of the payroll tax on workers. Part B is voluntary, not automatic. Enrollees who opt for Part B pay a monthly premium ($42.50 in 1996), usually deducted from their Social Security check. Approximately 5% of those who are eligible decide not to opt for Part B, primarily because they cannot afford it. Confusion and ambivalence may be present. Some are opposed ideologically to the concept of Social Security; others mistakenly believe Medicare automatically covers all costs; and still others just do not understand it.

In 1989, the controversial Catastrophic Coverage Act was enacted and then repealed. Although it attempted to revamp and expand Medicare and close a few of the gaps in coverage, it still failed to cover the greatest single source of catastrophic costs: long-term custodial care, which accounts for 90% of nursing home care. A major criticism of the act, leading to its repeal, was that, rather than everyone's payroll taxes being increased, the elderly themselves paid for the new benefits.

The Medicare Catastrophic Coverage Repeal Act did maintain a small portion of these "new" benefits: protection from impoverishment for spouses of nursing home patients, coverage for Papanicolaou smears, and state Medicaid buy-in of Part B, which covers Medicare premiums and co-payments for those below the official poverty level. But for the most part, Medicare looks like it did before 1989.

Congress also initiated physician payment reform in 1989, partly sparked by the continuing annual 16% increase in fees over the previous decade. The new plan limits the amount patients can be charged above the Medicare-approved fees. It also establishes a budget methodology and limit on total Medicare spending for physician services. Moreover, as of October 1, 1990, physicians have been required to bill Medicare for all services they provide. This is helpful, of course, for those patients who find it difficult to complete the often incomprehensible claim forms. Perhaps most important is a revised fee schedule, which places more emphasis on primary and preventive care through enhancement of evaluation and management payment than on surgical, diagnostic, and treatment procedures. Moreover, doctors practicing in inner cities and rural areas receive a 10% bonus. The resource-based relative value

scale (RBRVS), as the reforms are called, does not, however, reflect the complexity of care for the frail elderly. It is necessary to address at least two additional reforms: (1) appropriate reimbursement for the extraordinary time required for care of the elderly under RBRVS; and (2) the explicit establishment of a geriatric assessment code.[57]

One of the financial resources for the chronically mentally ill patient is Social Security disability. It provides coverage for nonworkers and workers forced to retire by injuries or health infirmities before they have reached age 65. Those signed up as disabled are automatically eligible for Medicare Part A (hospitalization benefits); if impoverished, they also are eligible for Part B (doctors' benefits) through Medicaid. All of these programs can help support patients, but only if there have been adequate services to get them registered. Mental health personnel often lack systematic training in the ever-changing and complicated system of available benefits.

Managed Care

With the revolutionary changes in the health care system in the 1990's, there have been cuts in the growth of Medicare and Medicaid expenditures, a growing importance in market forces, and an increase in the number of health maintenance organizations (HMOs) and the number of people enrolled in them. By 1996 approximately 10% of Medicare beneficiaries were enrolled in managed care organizations nationally. In some sections of the country, the percentage is much higher. In San Diego County, California, for example, some 30% of Medicare beneficiaries were signed up in managed care plans. By federal arrangement, health maintenance organizations (HMOs) receive 95% of the usual Medicare fee on a capitated basis. However, where possible, HMOs market to the "young-old" (those aged 65 to 75) and try to avoid enrolling frail older persons. Eventually, however, the companies will experience "aging in" of the currently young-old enrollees, and costs will rise. HMOs have emerged that provide various services along a continuum of needed care, from home care, sub-acute care, community care, and rehabilitation, and some companies have been trying to achieve integrated care that sews together all these services in a seamless fashion. By and large, however, there have been great difficulties in coordinating mental health and medical care services in managed care plans partially due to the practice of "carving out," or subcontracting, mental health services. With respect to the geriatric, psychiatric patient it has been argued that "managed care" has really become "managed cost."

On-the-Spot Home Evaluation.   Outreach services such as home visiting by mental health personnel are still insufficient in the United States. The physician, the psychiatrist, the psychologist, the social worker, the nurse, and the paraprofessional all should make use of home visiting to keep in touch with the realities of life of older persons from various backgrounds—urban, suburban or rural. Measures of activities of daily living (ADL) in various settings are valuable.[58]

To see how older people of all socioeconomic classes live is a first-rate diagnostic tool. Extreme privation is not unusual. For example:

The old man lived in an unpainted, roach-infested, windowless closet, sleeping on a urine-smelling mattress that could not be fully extended because of the small size of the closet.

With 95% of older persons residing in the community, a home evaluation is a logical way to get a sense of the day-to-day existence of the patient. One looks for pets (companionship), a calendar (to what month is it turned?), a clock (is it running and set properly?), odors (gas leaks, spoiled food, signs of incontinence), food supply (is the person eating regularly and adequately?), mementoes (what does the person consider important?), family pictures, temperature of house (potential accidental hypothermia resulting from a cold home), and medication cabinet and night stand (to see what and how prescription and nonprescription drugs are being taken). The safety

and security of the home, the ability of the person to get around the house, and the presence of others can be assayed. (It is not uncommon to find an older person caring for someone who may be even sicker than he or she.) A realistic evaluation of the fear of crime and financial and physical limitations to transportation can be made.

The older person's community resources should be included in the evaluative process, both to determine what the community has to offer and to engage community services in ongoing evaluations of patients. A homemaker working in a patient's home may be able to furnish a picture of the person's day-to-day life. Visiting nurses, workers in Meals-on-Wheels programs, occupational therapists, and others can offer their particular viewpoints. See Chapter 10 for a fuller discussion of community services and contributions to the mental health care of the at-home elderly.

Legal Issues

Forensic (legal) psychiatry is a field of psychiatry concerned with legal issues, hearings, and trials, including insanity pleas, commitment procedures, theories, and laws dealing with criminal responsibility, guardianship, conservatorship, confidentiality, competence to stand trial, and the legal definition of "insanity."

Questions of competency and informed consent with the elderly have received increasing attention in the legal system in recent years.[59] Medical doctors, especially psychiatrists, may be called on to evaluate an older person's need for involuntary commitment to an institution or to ascertain aspects of competency (contractual or testamentary capacity). Human beings have a fundamental right to make their own decisions, enter into contracts, vote, make a will, and refuse medical or psychiatric treatment. Each of these decisions represents the individual's control over his or her own life, with the understanding that the consequences may be unfortunate as well as fortunate, folly as well as wisdom. Limitations of such rights or freedom ideally come about only when illnesses invalidate the capacity to make choices or, in the case of legal commitment, when the older person is a danger to him- or herself or to others, physically, or is in clear and present need of immediate care or treatment. Older people also need protection when they are vulnerable to exploitation by others.

In examining an older person for forensic (legal) purposes, the examiner should spell out that fact in detail. The person needs to know that he or she can be represented by an attorney and that statements to the examiner will *not* be protected either by privilege (the legal concept) or by confidentiality (the relationship). What is the test of incompetency? "Understanding" is the crucial criterion: The person must have sufficient mental capacity to *understand* the nature and effect of the *particular* transaction in question. The psychiatric diagnosis is not considered in courts of law to be as important as judgment. Commitment to a mental hospital for psychiatric reasons is not necessarily equivalent to incompetency.

Contractual capacity (the ability to make contracts) is related to the degree of judgment required—selling a major business is a complex situation that may require a greater degree of judgment than selling a car. One problem sometimes emerging in contractual cases is that in which an older person's judgment may, indeed, be adversely affected by mental or physical disorders, but this fact is unknown to the other party in the contract.

A 69-year-old woman was profoundly depressed but outwardly cheerful. She sold her $75,000 home for $55,000. It was a bona fide sale, so there was no later recourse.

The concept of the "lucid interval" is a vague and difficult one, implying the capacity to exercise sound judgment at one time and not another. The multicausal aspects of the emotional and mental disorders of old age indicate the possibility of such intervals. For example, a person with cerebral vascular insufficiency may do well until severe emotional stress (for example, death of a spouse) compromises the equilibrium; after a period of time, he or she may again stabilize and be considered "lucid." An evaluator must be extremely thorough in examining the older person for such a possibility.

Testamentary capacity (the ability to make a will) requires that the testator (person who makes the will) be "of sound mind and memory," knowing the condition of the estate, his obligations, and the import of the provisions of the will. The psychiatric examiner must consider whether the older person is unduly suggestible or under "undue influence" from others. Severe depression and paranoid states, as well as organic brain disorders, may affect the capacity to write a will; however, diagnosis of psychosis, adjudication of guardianship, or commitment per se does not invalidate a will. Extreme age, mental sluggishness, and defective memory do not render a testator incapable of making a will if he is able to recall to mind his property. Alcoholism, addictions, and unusual beliefs (for example, spiritualism) do not by themselves invalidate wills. When there is any doubt of testamentary capacity or when a contesting of the will is anticipated, it is wise of the testator to arrange for a comprehensive medical and psychiatric evaluation while he or she is alive, with a careful and complete report filed before death. It may also be wise to audiotape or videotape the testator with his or her attorney present. With the help of this technology, not only is the will clearly spelled out, but aspects of the will that are likely to be disputed can be explained. By so doing, further grief and turmoil, as in the following example, can be prevented for the family.

An 87-year-old man married his nurse and rewrote his will. Other members of the family challenged his mental soundness and pushed for a postmortem examination of his brain, resulting in bitterness and anguish for everyone concerned.

Guardianship, the appointment of a committee for a person or the person's estate, should be solely for the person's benefit and protection. The test is whether the person can or cannot protect himself or arrange his own affairs. Emotional disability, as well as intellectual impairment, is important. (Guilt or feelings of worthlessness may lead a person to give everything away.) Injudicious management and improvidence are difficult to evaluate and are not precisely correlated with intellectual debility. Laws are unclear on many points, and there is an all-or-nothing quality, whereas a continuum or scale of impairment would be more appropriate. It is here that the current use of a durable power of attorney (whereby an individual assigns someone the right to manage the individual's affairs if and when he or she becomes significantly impaired, such as through a dementing process) may well play an increasing role in the future. Certain disabilities are not considered at all by the law—visual and auditory impairments, loss of speech, and others.

Poor people are disadvantaged because of the legal costs of conservatorships;[60] since few states provide for public guardianship (the poor man's conservatorship), estates are easily eroded. The poorly educated and the uninformed are not protected, and the Roman injunction *caveat emptor* ("let the buyer beware") holds sway to a greater degree in old age than ever before.

In 1989 the Social Security Administration estimated that it appointed third-party representatives for 4.7 million beneficiaries unable to manage their own financial affairs due to mental illness, homelessness, or drug addiction. Unfortunately, a small percentage of these incompetent beneficiaries are believed to be defrauded by their representatives, whose job is to receive the benefit checks and pay the beneficiaries' living expenses.

Involuntary commitment is examined more thoroughly in Chapter 11, but we wish to discuss here the question of court cases for mental patients and older people in general. In what passes for kindness, it is often argued that court appearances are too disturbing for the older patient. Even when a hospitalized person decides to call for a jury trial, the hospital psychiatrist may back away and discharge the patient first. We believe there are serious faults with these attitudes. They

conceal from the public, from the person involved, and from the psychiatrist and mental health personnel the realities of legal processes and of property and personal rights. Patients often learn from the painful court proceedings; it becomes clear what the situation really is, and the process can have therapeutic effects. Our traditional overestimation of the fragility of patients and, indeed, our paternalism and infantilization can deny people their rights and the opportunity for self-expression.

Court appearances may also assist mental health personnel in sharpening up their diagnostic thinking. A few embarrassing moments under cross-examination in a court of law can be a humbling experience and worth hours of postgraduate training or review. Psychiatrists and other staff who complain of wasting time in court might be well-advised to keep eyes and ears open, taking the occasion to learn something more about the human condition as it unfolds in a courtroom.

The adversary system does have its cruelties, and one might argue for dispassionate commissions wherein commitment, competency, and contractual and testamentary capacities are evaluated. We would support the use of independent commissions comprised of physicians, mental health personnel, and lawyers but subject to administrative and judicial reviews. Hearings must include patients, well-represented by counsel. The amount of time provided must be adequate, not just a token. We also believe, along with others, that the various capacities under consideration (contractual, testamentary, etc.) should be considered separately and in their special contexts, rather than under a global concept called "competence."

In summary, the legal issues surrounding the protection of the elderly and their families are leading to the gradual evolution of a comprehensive system of law and precedent. Several excellent books by Strauss et al. (1990) and Regan (1990) are useful for the elderly and their families, as well as for mental health personnel in surveying these developments. But much remains to be done to make certain that the rights and privileges of each older person are safeguarded at the same time that actions are taken legally to provide supports and protections when the older person is no longer capable of self care. All of this effort must be balanced with protection of the needs and rights of family members and of the community at large.

SELECTED READINGS

Albert, M. S., & Moss, M. B. (Eds.). (1988). *Geriatric Neuropsychology.* New York: Guilford Press.

American Association for Geriatric Psychiatry. (1988). *Essentials for geriatric psychiatry, a guide for health professionals.* Lazarus, L. W., Jarvik, L. F., Foster, J. R., Lieff, J. D., & Mershon, S. R. (Eds.). New York: Springer.

Ames, L. B., Metraux, R. W., Rodell, J. L., & Walker, R. N. (1974). *Rorschach responses in old age.* New York: Brunner/Mazel.

Anthony, K., Procter, A. W., Silverman, A. M., & Murphy, E. (1987). Mood and behavior problems following the relocation of elderly patients with mental illness. *Age and Ageing, 16,* 355–365.

Applegate, W. B., Blass, J. P., & Williams, T. F. (1990, April 26). Instruments for the functional assessment of older patients. *The New England Journal of Medicine, 322*(17), 1207–1214.

Bender, L. (1938). *A visual-motor gestalt test and its clinical use.* Research Monograph No. 3. New York: American Orthopsychiatric Association.

Bender, M. B., Fink, M., & Green, M. (1951). Patterns in perception in simultaneous tests of the face and hand. *Archives of Neurology and Psychiatry, 66,* 355–362.

Benton, A. (1974). *Revised visual retention test,* 4th ed. New York: Harcourt-Brace, Jovanovich.

Birren, J. E., Butler, R. N., Greenhouse, S. W., Sokoloff, L., & Yarrow, M. R. (Eds.). (1963). *Human aging: A biological and biobehavioral study.* Pub. no. (PHS) 986. Washington, DC: U.S. Government Printing Office. (Reprinted as Pub. No. [HSM] 71–9051, 1971, 1974).

Blessed, G., Tomlinson, B. E., & Roth, M. (1968). The association between quantitative measures of dementia and of senile change in the cerebral grey matter of elderly subjects. *British Journal of Psychiatry, 114,* 797–811.

Busse, E. W. (Ed.). (1996). *APA textbook of geriatric psychiatry,* 2nd ed. Washington, DC: American Psychiatric Association Press.

Butler, R. N. (1963). The facade of chronological age. *American Journal of Psychiatry, 119,* 721–728.

Butler, R. N. (1963). The life review: An interpretation of reminiscence in the aged. *Psychiatry, 26,* 65–76.

Butler, R. N. (1963). Self-drawings of normal older men. *Geriatrics, 18,* 220–232.

Butler, R. N., & Hyer, K. (1989). Reimbursement reform for the frail elderly. *Journal of the American Geriatrics Society, 37,* 1097–1098.

Coblenz, J. M., Mattis, S., Zingesser, L. H., Kasoff, S. S., Wisniewski, H. M., & Katzman, R. (1973, November). Presenile dementia: Clinical Aspects and Evaluation of Cerebrospinal Fluid Dynamics. *Archives of Neurology, 29*(5), 299–308.

Costa, P. T., Jr., & McCrae, R. R. (1992). *Revised NEO Personality Inventory (NEO-PR-R) and NEO Five-Factor Inventory (NEO-FFI) Professional Manual.* Odessa, FL: Psychological Assessment Resource.

Costa, P. T., Jr., & McCrae, R. R. (1992). Trait Personality Comes of Age. In Sonderegger, T. B. (Ed.), *Nebraska symposium on motivation: Psychology and aging* (pp. 169–204). Lincoln, NE: University of Nebraska Press.

Costa, P. T., Jr., Somerfield, M. R., & McCrae, R. R. (1995). Personality and coping: A reconceptualization. In Zeidner, M., & Endler, N. S. (Eds.), *Handbook of coping.* New York: John Wiley & Sons.

Crook, T., Bartus, R. T., Ferris, S. H., Whitehouse, P., Cohen, G. D., & Gershon, S. (1986). Age associated memory impairment: Proposed diagnostic criteria and measures of clinical change. Report of a National Institute of Mental Health work group. *Developmental Neuropsychology, 2,* 261–276.

Daniels, N. (1988). *Am I my parents' keeper? An essay on justice between the young and the old.* New York: Oxford University Press.

Delis, D. C., Kramer, J. H., Kaplan, E., & Ober, B. A. (1987). *California verbal learning test (Adult version).* San Antonio, TX: Psychological Corp., Harcourt-Brace, Jovanovich.

Delp, H. A. (1953). Correlations between the Kent E-G-Y and the Wechsler Batteries. *Journal of Clinical Psychology, 9,* 73–75.

Digman, J. M. (1990). Personality structure: Emergence of the five-factor model. *Annual Review of Psychology, 41,* 417–440.

Duara, R., Grady, C., Haxby, J., Sundaram, M., Cutler, N. R., Heston, L., Moore, A., Schlageter, N., Larson, S., & Rapoport, S. I. (1986). Positron emission tomography in Alzheimer's Disease. *Neurology, 36,* 879–887.

Dubler, N. N. (1995). Legal issues. In Abrams, W. B., Beers, M. H., & Berkow, R. (Eds.), *The Merck manual of geriatrics,* 2nd ed. (pp. 1379–1392). Whitehouse Station, NJ: Merck & Co.

Folstein, M. F., Folstein, S. E., & McHugh, P. R. (1975). "Mini-mental state," a practical method for grading the cognitive state of patients for the clinician. *Journal of Psychiatric Research, 12,* 189–198.

Goldfarb, A. I. (1964). The evaluation of geriatric patients following treatment. In Hoch, P. H., & Zubin, J. (Eds.), *Evaluation of psychiatric treatment* (pp. 271–308). New York: Grune & Stratton.

Goldstein, K. (1942). *Aftereffects of brain injuries in war and their evaluation and treatment.* New York: Grune & Stratton, 71–73, 77–78, 93.

Goldstein, K., & Scheerer, M. (1941). Abstract and concrete behavior. *Psychological Monograph, 53*(2), 239.

Gottleib, G. L. (1995). Financial issues in geriatric psychiatry. In Kaplan, H. I., & Sadock, B. J. (Eds.), *Comprehensive textbook of psychiatry/IV* (vol. 2, pp. 2656–2661). Baltimore, MD: Williams and Wilkins.

Gurland, B. J., & Wilder, D. E. (1984). The CARE interview revisited: Development of an efficient systematic clinical assessment. *Journal of Gerontology, 39,* 129–137.

Hachinski, V. C., Iliff, L. D., Zilhka, E., Du Boulay, G. H., McAllister, V. L., Marshall, J., Russell, R. W. R., & Symon, L. (1975). Cerebral bloodflow in dementia. *Archives of Neurology, 32,* 632–637.

Holmes, T. H., & Rahe, R. H. (1967). The social readjustment rating scale. *Journal of Psychosomatic Research, 11,* 213–218.

Hooker, K., Frazier, L. D., & Monohan, D. J. (1994). Personality and coping among caregivers of spouses with dementia. *The Gerontologist, 34,* 386–392.

Jutagir, R. (1993). Geropsychology and neuropsychological testing: Role in evaluation and treatment of patients with dementia. *The Mount Sinai Journal of Medicine, 60,* 528–531.

Kane, R. A., Kane, R. L., & Rubenstein, L. Z. (1989). Comprehensive assessment of the elderly patient. In

Petersen, M. D., & White, D. L. (Eds.). *Health care of the elderly* (pp. 475–519). Beverly Hills, CA: Sage Publications.

Katz, I. R., & Alexopoulos, G. S. (Eds.). (1996, Fall). Consensus update conference: Diagnosis and treatment of late-life depression, proceedings of the Geriatric Psychiatry Alliance—January 20, 1996. *The American Journal of Geriatric Psychiatry, 4*(4), supplement 1.

Katz, S., Downs, T. D., Cash, H., & Grotz, R. C. (1970). Progress and development of the index of ADL. *The Gerontologist, 10,* 20–30.

Kent, G. H. (1946). *Kent E-G-Y test: Series of emergency scales. Manual.* New York: The Psychological Corporation.

Kramer, A. M. (1995, April 13). Health care for elderly persons—Myths and realities. *New England Journal of Medicine, 332*(15), 1027–1029.

Lachs, M. S., Feinstein, A. R., Cooney, L. M., Drickamer, M. A., Marottoli, R. A., Pannill, F. C., & Tinetti, M. E. (1990, May 1). A simple procedure for general screening for functional disability in elderly patients. *Annals of Internal Medicine, 112*(9), 699–706.

Lawton, P. (1975). The Philadelphia Geriatric Center Morale Scale: A revision. *Journal of Gerontology, 30,* 85–88.

Lebowitz, B. D., & Gottlieb, G. L. (1995). Clinical research in the managed care environment. *American Journal of Geriatric Psychiatry, 3,* 21–25.

Lubitz, J., Beebe, J., & Baker, C. (1995, April 13). Longevity and Medicare expenditures. *New England Journal of Medicine, 332*(15), 999–1003.

McCrae, R. R., & Costa, P. T., Jr. (1991). Adding *Liebe und Arbeit:* The full five-factor model and well-being. *Personality and Social Psychology Bulletin, 17,* 227–232.

McKhann, G., Drachman, D., Folstein, M., Katzman, R., Price, D., & Stadlan, E. M. (1984). Clinical diagnosis of Alzheimer's Disease: Report of the NINCDS-ADRDA work group under the auspices of the Department of Health and Human Services Task Force on Alzheimer's Disease. *Neurology, 34,* 939–944.

Monk, A. (Ed.). (1990). *Health care of the aged.* Binghamton, NY: The Haworth Press.

Moon, M. (1996). *Medicare now and in the future,* 2nd ed. Washington, DC: The Urban Institute Press.

Miller, T. (1991). The psychotherapeutic utility of the five-factor model of personality: A clinician's experience. *Journal of Personality Assessment, 57,* 415–443.

National Institute on Aging Task Force. (1980). Senility reconsidered: Treatment possibilities for mental impairment in the elderly. *Journal of the American Medical Association, 244–263.*

National Institute of Mental Health. (1979). *The diagnostic interview schedule.* Washington, DC: Center for Epidemiologic Studies, National Institute of Mental Health.

National Institutes of Health. (1988). National Institutes of Health consensus development statement: Geriatric assessment methods for clinical decision-making. *Journal of the American Geriatric Society, 36,* 342–347.

National Institutes of Health Consensus Development Conference. (1991, November 4–5). Diagnosis and treatment of depression in late life. Reprinted from: *NIH Consensus Development Conference Consensus Statement, 9,*(3). Bethesda, MD: NIH.

National Institutes of Health, Office of the Medical Applications of Research. (1992). Consensus development panel on late life: Diagnosis and treatment of depression in late life. *Journal of the American Medical Association, 268,* 1018–1024.

Neugarten, B. L., Havighurst, R. J., & Tobin, S. S. (1961). The measurement of life satisfaction. *Journal of Gerontology, 16,* 134–143.

Palmore, E. (1970). *Normal aging: Reports from the Duke Longitudinal Study, 1955–1969.* Durham, NC: Duke University Press.

Pfeiffer, E. (1975). A short portable mental status questionnaire for the assessment of organic brain deficit in elderly patients. *Journal of the American Geriatrics Society, 23,* 433–441.

Rapoport, S. I., Horwitz, B., Haxby, J. V., & Grady, C. L. (1986). Alzheimer's Disease: Metabolic uncoupling of associative brain regions. *Canadian Journal of Neurological Sciences, 13,* 540–545.

Regan, J. (1990). *The aged client and the law.* New York: Columbia University Press.

Rosen, W. G., Mohs, R. C., & Davis, K. L. (1984). A new rating scale for Alzheimer's Disease. *American Journal of Psychiatry, 141,* 1356–1364.

Rubenstein, L. Z., Campbell, L. J., & Kane, R. L. (Eds.). (1987). Geriatric assessment [Special issue]. *Clinical Geriatric Medicine, 3*(1).

Rubenstein, L. Z., Josephson, K. R., Wieland, G. D., Pietruszka, F., Tretton, C., Strome, S., Cole, K. D., & Campbell, L. J. (1987). Geriatric assessment on a subacute hospital ward. *Clinical Geriatric Medicine, 3*(1), 131–143.

Schoenfeld, B., & Tuzil, T. J. (1979). Conservatorship: A move towards more personalized protective services. *Journal of Gerontology and Social Work, 1,* 225–234.

Sheikh, J. I., & Yesavage, J. A. (1986). Geriatric depression scale (GDS): Recent evidence and development of a shorter version. In Brink, T. L. (Ed.), *Clinical gerontology* (pp. 165–173). Binghamton, NY: The Haworth Press.

Shore, J. H., Breakey, W., & Arvidson, B. (1981). Morbidity and mortality in the commitment process. *Archives of General Psychiatry, 38,* 930–934.

Siegler, I. C., Dawson, D. V., & Welsh, K. A. (1994). Caregiver ratings of personality change in Alzheimer's Disease patients: A replication. *Psychology and Aging, 9,* 464–466.

Spitzer, R. L., Williams, J. B. W., Gibbon, M., & First, M. B. (1988). *Structured clinical interview for DSM-IIIR: Patient version (SCID-P, 6/1/88).* New York: Biometrics Research Department, New York Psychiatric Institute.

Strauss, P., Wolf, R., & Shilling, D. (1990). *Aging and the law.* Chicago: Commerce Clearing House.

Sunderland, T., Alterman, I. S., Yount, D., Hill, J. L., Tariot, P. N., Newhouse, P. A., Mueller, E. A., Mellow, A. M., & Cohen, R. M. (1988). A new scale for the assessment of depressed mood in demented patients. *American Journal of Psychiatry, 145,* 955–959.

Wechsler, D. (1955). *WASI Manual: Wechsler Adult Intelligence Scale.* New York: The Psychological Corporation.

Wechsler, D. (1981). *Wechsler Adult Intelligence Scale* (Revised). San Antonio, TX: Psychological Corporation, Harcourt-Brace, Jovanovich.

Wechsler, D. (1987). *Wechsler Memory Scale* (Revised). San Antonio, TX: Psychological Corporation, Harcourt-Brace, Jovanovich.

Weinberg, J. (1956) Personal and social adjustment. In Anderson, J. E. (Ed.), *Psychological aspects of aging* (pp. 17–20). Washington, DC: American Psychological Association.

Williams, M. E. (1990, May 1). Why screen for functional disability in elderly persons? *Annals of Internal Medicine, 112*(9), 369.

Yesavage, J. A. (1986). The use of self-rating depression scales in the elderly. In Poon, L. W. (Ed.), *Handbook for clinical memory assessment* (pp. 213–217). Washington, DC: American Psychological Association.

Yesavage, J. A., Brink, T. L., Rose, T. L., Lum, O., Huang, V., Adey, M., & Leirer, V. O. (1983). Development and validation of a geriatric depression screening scale: A preliminary report. *Journal of Psychiatric Research, 17,* 37–49.

ENDNOTES_____

1. National Institutes of Health. (1988). National Institutes of Health consensus development statement: Geriatric assessment methods for clinical decision-making. *Journal of the American Geriatrics Society, 36,* 342–347.

2. Kane, R. A., Kane, R. L., & Rubenstein, L. Z. (1989). Comprehensive assessment of the elderly patient. In Petersen, M. D., & White, D. L. (Eds.), *Health care of the elderly.* Beverly Hills: Sage Publications; Rubenstein, L. Z., Campbell, L. J., & Kane, R. L. (Eds.). (1987). Geriatric assessment. *Clinical Geriatric Medicine, 3*(l); and Rubenstein, L. Z., Josephson, K. R., Wieland, G. D., Pietruszka, F., Tretton, C., Strome, S., Cole, K. D., & Campbell, L. J. (1987). Geriatric assessment on a subacute hospital ward. *Clinical Geriatric Medicine, 3*(l), 131–143.

3. Goldstein, K. (1942). *Aftereffects of brain injuries in war and their evaluation and treatment.* New York: Grune & Stratton, pp. 71–73, 77–78, 93.

4. Weinberg, J. (1956). Personal and social adjustment. In Anderson, J. E. (Ed.), *Psychological aspects of aging.* Washington, DC: American Psychological Association.

5. Pfeiffer, E. (Ed.). (1975). Multidimensional functional assessment: The OARS methodology. Durham, NC: Duke University Press, Center for the Study of Aging and Human Development.

6. Gurland, B., Kuriansky, J., Sharpe, L., Simon, R., Stiller, P., & Birkett, P. (1977). The Comprehensive Assessment and Referral Evaluation (CARE): Rationale, development and reliability. *International Journal of Aging and Human Development, 8,* 9–42; Golden, R. R., Teresi, J. A., & Guriand, B. J. (1982–1983). Detection of dementia and depression cases with the comprehensive assessment and referral evaluation interview schedule. *International Journal of Aging and Human Development, 16,* 241–254.

7. Kanowski, S., Kruger, H., & Kuhl, K. P. (1985). The AGP system: Assessment of symptoms in psychogeriatric patients. In Traber, J., & Gispen, W. H. (Eds.). *Senile dementia of the Alzheimer type* (pp. 44–59). Berlin: Springer-Verlag.

8. Roth, M., Tym, E., Mountjoy, C. Q., Huppert, F. A., Hendrie, H., Verma, S., & Goddard, R. (1986). CAMDEX: A standardized instrument for the diagnosis of mental disorder in the elderly with special reference to the early detection of dementia. *British Journal of Psychiatry, 149,* 698–709.

9. Kennie, D. C. (1983). Good health care for the aged. *Journal of the American Medical Association, 249,* 770–773; Fisk, A. A. (1983). Comprehensive health care for the elderly. *Journal of the American Medical Association, 249,* 230–236; Larson, E. B., Reifler, B. V., Sumi, S. M., Canfield, C. G., & Chinn, N. M. (1985). Diagnostic evaluation of 200 elderly outpatients with suspected dementia. *Journal of Gerontology, 40,* 536–543.

10. Granacher, R. P. (1981). The neurologic examination in geriatric psychiatry. *Psychosomatics, 22,* 485–499.

11. One should not overlook the possibility of pellagra in the workup. The complete syndrome of this vitamin deficiency disease may not be present. One can look for redness of the mouth and tongue (more obvious in acute cases), skin changes, and—of special interest to mental health personnel—evidence of intellectual changes in a chronic brain disorder.

12. Goodwin, J. S., Goodwin, J. M., & Garry, P. J. (1983). Association between nutritional status and cognitive functioning in a healthy elderly population. *Journal of the American Medical Association, 249,* 2917–2921; Wurtman, R. J. (1984). The ultimate head waiter: How the brain controls diet. *Technology Review,* July, 42–51.

13. Kenshalo, D. W. (1977). Age change in touch, vibration, temperature, kinesthesis, and pain sensitivity. In Birren, J. E., & Schaie, K. W. (Eds.), *Handbook of the physiology of aging,* New York: Van Nostrand Reinhold.

14. Torres, F., Faora, A., Loewenson, R., & Johnson, E. (1983). The encephalogram of elderly subjects revisited. *Electroencephalography and Clinical Neurophysiology, 56,* 391–398; Duffy, F. H., Albert, M. S., McAnulty, G., & Garvey, A. J. (1984). Age-related differences in brain electrical activity of healthy subjects. *Annals of Neurology, 16,* 430–438; Giaquinto, S., & Nolte, G. (1986). The EEG in the normal elderly: A contribution to the interpretation of aging and dementia. *Electroencephalography and Clinical Neurophysiology, 63,* 540–546.

15. Celesia, G. G. (1986). EEG and event-related potentials in aging and dementia. *Journal of Clinical Neurophysiology, 3,* 99–111; Brenner, R. P., Ulrich, R. F., Spiker, D. G., Sclabassi, R. J., Reynolds, C. F., Marin, R. S., & Boller, F. (1986). Computerized EEG spectral analysis in elderly normal, demented and depressed subjects. *Electroencephalography and Clinical Neurophysiology, 64,* 483–492; and

Leuchter, A. F., Spar, J. E., Walter, D. O., & Weiner, H. (1987). Electroencephalographic spectra and coherence in the diagnosis of Alzheimer's-type and multi-infarct dementia. *Archives of General Psychiatry, 44,* 993–998.

16. Rae-Grant, A. D., Blume, W. T., Lau, K., Fisman, M., Hachinski, V., & Merskey, H. (1986). The EEG in Alzheimer-type dementia: Lack of progression with sequential studies. *Canadian Journal of Neurological Sciences, 13,* 407–409.

17. McGeer, P. L. (1986). Brain imaging in Alzheimer's disease. *British Medical Bulletin, 42,* 24–28.

18. Kramer, D. M. (1984). Basic principles of magnetic resonance imaging. *Radiologic Clinics of North America, 22,* 765–778.

19. Agee, O. F. (1988). MRI vs. CT for diagnosing brain disorders in the elderly. *Geriatrics, 43,* 25–38.

20. Hachinski, V. C., Iliff, L. D., Zilhka, E., Du Boulay, G. H., McAllister, V. L., Marshall, J., Russell, R. W. R., & Symon, L. (1975). Cerebral blood flow in dementia, *Archives of Neurology, 32,* 632–637; Ingvar, D. H., Brun, A., Hagberg, B., & Gustafson, L. (1978). Regional cerebral blood flow in the dominant hemisphere in confirmed cases of Alzheimer's disease, Pick's disease, and multi-infarct dementia: Relationship to clinical symptomatology and neuropathological findings. In Katzman, R., Terry, R. D., & Bick, K. L. (Eds.), *Alzheimer's disease: Senile dementia and related disorders* (pp. 203–211). New York: Raven; and Deutsch, G., & Tweedy, J. R. (1987). Cerebral blood flow in severity-matched Alzheimer and multi-infarct patients. *Neurology, 37,* 431–438.

21. Foster, N. L., Chase, T. N., Mansi, L., Brooks, R., Fedio, P., Patronas, N. J., & Di Chiro, G. (1984). Cortical abnormalities in Alzheimer's disease. *Annals of Neurology, 16,* 649–654; Kuhl, D. E., Metter, E. J., & Riege, W. H. (1985). Patterns of cerebral glucose utilization in depression, multiple infarct dementia, and Alzheimer's disease. *Research Publications/Association for Research in Nervous and Mental Disease, 63,* 211–226; Duara, R., Grady, C., Haxby, J., Sundaram, M., Cutler, N. R., Heston, L., Moore, A., Schlageter, N., Larson, S., & Rapoport, S. I. (1986). Positron emission tomography in Alzheimer's disease. *Neurology, 36,* 879–887.

22. Rapoport, S. I., Horwitz, B., Haxby, J. V., & Grady, C. L. (1986). Alzheimer's disease: Metabolic uncoupling of associative brain regions. *Canadian Journal of Neurological Sciences, 13,* 540–545.

23. Mayberg, H. S., Robinson, R. G., Wong, D. F., Parikh, R., Bolduc, P., Starkstein, S. E., Price, T., Dannals, R. F., Links, J. M., Wilson, A. A., Ravert, H. T., & Wagner, H. N. (1988). PET imaging of cortical S_2 serotonin receptors after stroke: Lateralized changes and relationship to depression. *American Journal of Psychiatry, 145,* 937–943.

24. Holman, B. L., Gibson, R. E., Hill, T. C., Eckelman, W. C., Albert, M., & Reba, R. C. (1985). Muscarinic acetylcholine receptors in Alzheimer's disease: In vivo imaging with iodine 123-labeled 3-quinuclidinyl-4-iodobenzilate and emission tomography. *Journal of the American Medical Association, 254,* 3063–3066.

25. National Institute of Mental Health. (1979). *The diagnostic interview schedule.* Washington, DC: Center for Epidemiologic Studies, National Institute of Mental Health.

26. Spitzer, R. L., & Endicott, J. (1978). *NIMH Clinical Research Branch collaborative program on the psychobiology of depression: Schedule for affective disorders and schizophrenia (SADS).* New York: Biometrics Division, New York State Psychiatric Institute.

27. Spitzer, R. L., Williams, J. B. W., Gibbon, M., & First, M. B. (1988). *Structured clinical interview for DSM-IIIR: Patient version (SCID-P, 6/1/88).* New York: Biometrics Research Department, New York State Psychiatric Institute.

28. Folstein, M. F., Folstein, S. E., & McHugh, P. R. (1975). Mini-mental state, a practical method for grading the cognitive state of patients for the clinician. *Journal of Psychiatric Research, 12,* 189–198.

29. Coblenz, J. M., Mattis, S., Zingesser, L. H., Kasoff, S. S., Wisniewski, H. M., & Katzman, R. (1973, Nov.). Presenile dementia: Clinical aspects and evaluation of cerebrospinal fluid dynamics. *Archives of Neurology, 29*(5), 299–308.

30. Blessed, G., Tomlinson, B. E., & Roth, M. (1968). The association between quantitative measures of dementia and of senile changes in the cerebral grey matter of elderly patients. *British Journal of Psychology, 114,* 809.

31. Kahn, R. L., Goldfarb, A. I., & Pollack, M. (1964). The evaluation of geriatric patients following treatment. In Hoch, P. H. & Zubin, J. (Eds.), *Evaluation of psychiatric treatment.* New York: Grune & Stratton.

32. Jutagir, R. (1993) Geropsychology and neuropsychological testing: Role in evaluation and treatment of patients with dementia. *The Mount Sinai Journal of Medicine, 60,* 528–531.

33. Delis, D. C., Kramer, J. H., Kaplan, E., & Ober, B. A. (1987). *California verbal learning test (adult version)*. San Antonio, TX: Psychological Corp., Harcourt,-Brace, Jovanovich.

34. Wechsler, D. (1987). *Wechsler memory scale (revised)*. San Antonio, TX: Psychological Corp., Harcourt-Brace, Jovanovich.

35. Benton, A. (1974). *Revised visual retention test* (4th ed.). New York: Harcourt-Brace, Jovanovich.

36. Wechsler, D. (1981). *Wechsler adult intelligence scale* (revised). New York: Harcourt-Brace, Jovanovich.

37. Kent, G. H. (1946). *Kent E-G-Y test: Series of emergency scales. Manual.* New York: The Psychological Corporation. See Delp, H. A. (1953). Correlations between the Kent E-G-Y and the Wechsler batteries. *Journal of Clinical Psychology, 9,* 73–75.

38. Bender, M. B., Fink, M., & Green, M. (1951). Patterns in perception in simultaneous tests of the face and hand. *Archives of Neurology and Psychiatry, 66,* 355–362.

39. Ames, L. B., Metraux, R. W., Rodell, J. L., & Walker, R. N. (1974). *Rorschach responses in old age.* New York: Brunner/Mazel.

40. Neugarten, B. L., Havighurst, R. J., & Tobin, S. S. (1961). The measurement of life satisfaction. *Journal of Gerontology, 16,* 134–143.

41. Lawton, P. (1975). The Philadelphia Geriatric Center morale scale: A revision. *Journal of Gerontology, 30,* 85–88.

42. Kearns, N. P., Cruickshank, C. A., McGuigan, K. J., Riley, S. A., Shaw, S. P., & Snaith, R. P. (1982). A comparison of depression rating scales. *British Journal of Psychiatry, 141,* 45–49.

43. Yesavage, J. A., Brink, T. L., Rose, T. L., Lum, O., Huang, V., Adey, M., & Leirer, V. O. (1983). Development and validation of a geriatric depression screening scale: A preliminary report. *Journal of Psychiatric Research, 17,* 37–49; and Sunderland, T., Alterman, I. S., Yount, D., Hill, J. L., Tariot, P. N., Newhouse, P. A., Mueller, E. A., Mellow, A. M., & Cohen, R. M. (1988). A new scale for the assessment of depressed mood in demented patients. *American Journal of Psychiatry, 145,* 955–959.

44. Plotkin, D. A., Mintz, J., & Jarvik, L. F. (1985). Subjective memory complaints in geriatric depression. *American Journal of Psychiatry, 142,* 1103–1105.

45. Yesavage, J. A. (1986). The use of self-rating depression scales in the elderly. In Poon, L. W. (Ed.). *Handbook for clinical memory assessment*

(pp. 213–217). Washington, DC: American Psychological Association.

46. Digman, J. M. (1990). Personality structure: Emergence of the five-factor model. *Annual Review of Psychology, 41,* 417–440.

47. Costa, P. T., Jr. & McCrae, R. R. (1992a). *Revised NEO Personality Inventory (NEO-PI-R) and NEO Five-Factor Inventory (NEO-FFI) Professional Manual.* Odessa, FL: Psychological Assessment Resource.

48. Costa P. T., Jr. & McCrae, R. R. (1992b). Trait psychology comes of age. In Sonderegger, T. B. (Ed.), *Nebraska symposium on motivation: Psychology and aging* (pp. 169–204). Lincoln, NE: University of Nebraska Press.

49. Siegler, I. C., Dawson, D. V., & Welsh, K. A. (1994). Caregiver ratings of personality change in Alzheimer's disease patients: A replication. *Psychology and Aging, 9,* 464–466.

50. Hooker, K., Frazier, L. D., & Monahan, D. J. (1994). Personality and coping among caregivers of spouses with dementia. *The Gerontologist, 34,* 386–392.

51. McCrae, R. R. & Costa, P. T., Jr. (1991). Adding *Liebe und Arbeit:* The full five-factor model and well-being. *Personality and Social Psychology Bulletin, 17,* 227–232.

52. Miller, T. (1991). The psychotherapeutic utility of the five-factor model of personality: A clinician's experience. *Journal of Personality Assessment, 57,* 415–443.

53. Costa, P. T., Jr., Somerfield, M. R., & McCrae, R. R. (1995). Personality and coping: A reconceptualization. In Zeidner, M. & Endler, N. S. (Eds.) *Handbook of Coping.* New York: John Wiley & Sons.

54. Birren, J. E., Butler, R. N., Greenhouse, S. W., Sokoloff, L., & Yarrow, M. R., (Eds.) (1963). *Human aging: A biological and behavioral study.* Pub. No. (PHS) 986. Washington, DC: U.S. Government Printing Office (reprinted as Pub. No. [HSM]71–9051, 1971, 1974); Hiatt, L. G. (1985). Understanding the physical environment. *Pride Institute Journal of Long-Term Home Health Care, 4,* 12–22; and Anthony, K., Procter, A. W., Silverman, A. M., & Murphy, E. (1987). Mood and behavior problems following the relocation of elderly patients with mental illness. *Age and Aging, 16,* 355–365.

55. Birren et al., *Human aging,* 31.

56. *Ibid.,* 316.

57. Butler, R. N., & Hyer, R. N. (1989). Reimbursement reform for the frail elderly. Editorial, *Journal of the American Geriatrics Society, 37,* 1097–1098.

58. Katz, S., Downs, T. D., Cash, H., & Grotz, R. C. (1970). Progress and development of the index of ADL. *The Gerontologist, 10,* 20–30; and Clark, G. S. (1984). Functional assessment in the elderly. In Williams, T. F. (Ed.), *Rehabilitation in the aging* (pp. 111–124). New York: Raven Press.

59. Shore, J. H., Breakey, W., & Arvidson, B. (1981). Morbidity and mortality in the commitment process. *Archives of General Psychiatry, 38,* 930–934; Pecora, A. K. (1982, April). Medical treatment of mentally disabled adults: Limitation on the spouse's right to consent. *Maryland State Medical Journal, 54–55;* and Drane, J. F. (1984). Competency to give an informed consent: A model for making clinical assessments. *Journal of the American Medical Association, 252,* 925–927.

60. See discussion of role of social service as conservator and New York State's Conservatorship Law of 1973 in Schoenfeld, B., & Tuzil, T. J. (1979). Conservatorship: A move towards more personalized protective services. *Journal of Gerontology and Social Work, 1,* 225–234

CHAPTER 10

HOW TO KEEP PEOPLE AT HOME

Home care is the term used for the professional or personal services provided to older persons on a recurring or continuing basis at home as treatment of chronic physical or mental impairment. The term *long-term care* has often been used primarily in connection with institutionalization but, in fact, it also covers care in the older person's home or any other location. Furthermore, home care involves more than just care for chronic impairments. For example, an older person may have an acute episode of illness or disability, or a time-limited recuperation after acute hospitalization that can be managed at home. This chapter will focus on both acute and long-term care in the home. In the next chapter, we concentrate on care in institutions.

WHO NEEDS HOME CARE?

According to a Commonwealth Fund Commission study of community-dwelling elderly, impairment among the elderly is distributed as follows: Of a total of 30.8 million elderly in 1989, 77% (23.8 million) have no impairment, 13% (3.9 million) are moderately impaired, and 5% (1.6 million) are

severely impaired. Another 5% (1.5 million) of the elderly are impaired enough to be in nursing homes. The salient point for our home-care discussion is that 18% of all elderly, or 5.5 million persons, are moderately to severely impaired and remain in homes in the community. (Figure 10.1.)

The most dependent of the home-dwelling elderly are obviously those with severe impairment. Of the 1.6 million severely impaired elderly living in the community, 22% have both severe physical and cognitive impairment, 32% have severe cognitive impairment only, and 46% have severe physical impairment only. (Figure 10.2.)

What kinds of activities do impaired older persons need help with at home? The activities of daily living (ADLs) are the basic tasks of everyday life, such as eating, bathing, toileting, and moving in and out of chairs and bed. A number of different ADL measurements have evolved to estimate both the incidence and prevalence of disability generally as well as to aid in the evaluation of an individual's need for help.[1] The figures we have used in this chapter are based on the 1982 National Long Term Care Survey. Table 10.1 shows the

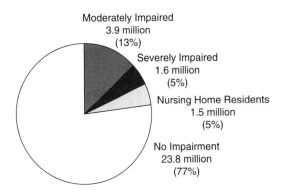

Total = 30.8 million persons

FIGURE 10.1   Distribution of elderly population by impairment, 1989

Source: The Commonwealth Fund Commission on Elderly People Living Alone. (1989). *The estimated costs of a proposed home care program* (Background Paper Series No. 16). New York: The Commonwealth Fund. Reprinted by permission.

specific activities of daily living most needed by three separate groups of persons with different levels of impairment. Of the cited impairments, the most frequent limitation was difficulty in walking.

Some 44% of persons who are most impaired in ADLs have cognitive impairment that is contributing to or causing disability. Cognitive impairment is also present in less ADL-impaired people, though it plays a smaller role. (Figure 10.3.)

LIVING ALONE

A significant proportion of the elderly live alone at home. In 1993 32.5%, or about 10 million people age 65 or older, lived independently of other family members. A small number of these (2.3%) lived with nonrelatives. The remainder, 30.2% of the elderly lived alone. 55% of the elderly were married and living with their spouses, while 12.5% lived with other relatives. Older women, mostly widowed, represented the vast majority of those living alone.[2]

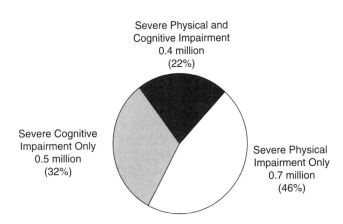

Total = 1.6 million persons

Severe Physical Impairment: human assistance with two or more ADLs

Severe Cognitive Impairment: five or more errors on SPMSQ or reported senile

FIGURE 10.2   Distribution of the severely impaired community-dwelling elderly population, 1989

Source: The Commonwealth Fund Commission on Elderly People Living Alone. (1989). *The estimated costs of a proposed home care program* (Background Paper Series No. 16). New York: The Commonwealth Fund. Reprinted by permission.

TABLE 10.1   Functional limitations of persons aged 65 and over by age, and living arrangement: 1991 (in thousands)

	AGED 65+			AGED 85+
	TOTAL	**LIVING ALONE**	**LIVING WITH OTHERS**	
Total Population	30,748	9,634	21,214	2,430
Percent with difficulty*				
Walking	14.3	18.1	12.6	34.9
Getting outside	15.9	20.7	13.8	44.8
Bathing or showering	9.4	11.2	8.7	30.6
Transferring**	9.0	10.9	8.2	21.9
Dressing	5.8	6.3	5.6	16.1
Using toilet	4.2	4.8	3.9	14.2
Eating	2.1	2.2	2.0	4.1
Preparing meals	8.6	9.1	8.4	27.6
Managing money	7.1	8.4	6.5	26.2
Using the telephone	7.1	7.1	7.1	21.4
Doing light housework	11.4	13.6	10.4	30.8
Percent of total receiving help*				
Walking	5.9	4.9	6.4	16.8
Getting outside	13.2	17.2	11.4	42.3
Bathing or showering	5.9	5.0	6.3	20.9
Transferring**	3.9	2.7	4.5	11.0
Dressing	3.9	2.7	4.4	11.1
Using toilet	2.6	1.9	2.9	7.8
Eating	1.1	0.8	1.2	2.5
Preparing meals	7.5	7.0	7.8	25.4
Managing money	6.4	7.4	5.9	24.6
Doing light housework	8.9	9.6	8.7	27.3

Source: U.S. Bureau of the Census (1996). 65+ in the United States. *Current Population Reports,* Special Studies, Series P-23, no. 190. Washington, DC: U.S. Government Printing Office.

*Difficulty due to a physical or mental health condition

**Getting in or out from a bed or chair

***Receiving help with the specified difficulty

Many of the eight million elderly living alone were not at all disabled, in poor health, suffering from lack of medical care, or lacking family or companionship. Seventy percent had children, and many of these lived near at least one child, saw their children regularly, and spoke frequently with them by phone. Many also have networks of social contacts from long years of living in the same location or from moving to retirement communities with active social programs. But almost 30% had no living children, and an additional 19% had only one child. Thus, this group represents a particularly vulnerable population when illness or disability strikes, since family members provide most home-care supports.[3]

To illustrate the importance of families, of all those living alone, most felt they had someone to help them for a few days if they needed care. Sixty-nine percent would turn to their families, and 17% had someone else. But 14% had no one. If the need

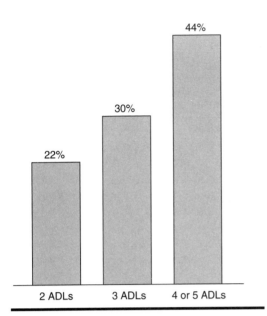

FIGURE 10.3   Percent of ADL impaired community-dwelling elderly persons with cognitive impairment, 1989

Source: The Commonwealth Fund Commission on Elderly People Living Alone. (1989). *The estimated costs of a proposed home care program* (Background Paper Series No. 16). New York: The Commonwealth Fund. Reprinted by permission.

for care lasted a few weeks or more, 67% could still rely on their families, but 24% said they had no one to care for them. Only 10% could turn to others outside of their families for lengthy care.[4]

The functional capacity of those living alone provides a framework for assessing the need for home-care services. According to the 1984 National Health Interview Survey, 60% of those living alone had no limitations in their usual activities, 17% had some outside limitations but could perform their usual activities, 16% were limited in some way in their usual daily activities, and 8% were unable to perform their usual daily activities.[5]

HOW IMPORTANT IS "HOME"?

Home is extraordinarily significant to many older persons. It is part of their identity, a place where things are familiar and relatively unchanging, and a place to maintain a sense of autonomy and con-

trol. Some insist on remaining at home regardless of the cost to their emotional and physical health and personal security. Such tenaciousness can be attributed to a desire for freedom and independence; a fear of loss of contact with familiar and loved people, places, and things; a fear of dying, because of the reputation of hospitals and nursing homes as places "where old people go to die"; and a trepidation about change and the unknown, which frightens people of all ages. In this nation of homeowners, where about 70% of older people own their homes, the idea of a home of one's own is deeply ingrained; communal or institutional living is often viewed as a loss of personal liberty and dignity.

The notion of home can refer to many things, from the four walls surrounding a person, to the neighborhood in which one's house is located, or to the possessions that make one feel at home. The meaning of the word *home* may include other individuals living with a person, as well as neighbors, pets, and plants. It can either be a place where one has lived a good part of one's life or a new place, as when older people move into a retirement community or leave the farm for a home in town. Thus the concept of home is unique to each individual.

Home can also be a euphemism. In our eagerness to recognize the importance of the feeling of home, we must not overlook those older people who dislike their living conditions, who have never felt "at home" where they are, and who are eager to move somewhere else—even to an institution. They may live in a dilapidated rooming house in a bare room with a lone light bulb suspended from the ceiling, in a boarding house with skimpy meals, in a cheap "retirement hotel" where the bath is shared with drug addicts, alcoholics, or street drifters.

Some older people are themselves homeless. They sleep on park benches or in subways, bus and train stations, bowery missions, doorways. Since the 1980s, such homelessness has become a major public issue. According to the National Coalition for the Homeless, estimates of the number of homeless in the United States are extremely inaccurate and tend to be low. One study, conducted by Bruce Link of Columbia University, examined the number of people who were homeless over a period of time to estimate that between 4.95 million and 9.32 million people experienced homelessness at some time during the second half of the 1980s. Another study conducted by the Urban Institute put the number of homeless people of all ages in the United States at between 500,000 and 600,000, using a "point in time count" during one week in 1988. The survey found 20% had been "deinstitutionalized," that is, removed from mental hospitals. Many of these are older persons.[6]

Alternatively, home may be fine physically but miserable emotionally because of family circumstances. An in-law problem may result when an older person moves in with a married son or daughter:

One 69-year-old woman was living with her son and daughter-in-law. The mother and daughter-in-law had never gotten along and couldn't tolerate talking to each other. The mother was discouraged from participating in housework. She therefore would remain in her pajamas all day, watching television. When her son was due home, she would dress, put on her makeup, and become warm and friendly. She and her daughter-in-law vied for his attentions. The mother complained that she was not invited to help the family and was considered a burden. The daughter-in-law stated that the mother expected total care. The son, caught in the middle between the two women in his life, finally asked his mother to leave.

Many situations with an older parent in the home fortunately work out much more satisfactorily. But one must avoid falling prey to one's own slogans, such as "keep people in their own homes," when this may be totally inappropriate and even cruel.

The periodic cry of reformers, "return institutional patients to the community," also needs to be examined with careful skepticism. What kind of community? What kind of home will be involved? Successful adjustment and adaptation is no more ensured in the community than anywhere else. Each decision concerning home care versus institutional care must be based on the older person's needs, but both alternatives should be as attractive

and as therapeutic as possible. In general, care centered around the home offers the best treatment location except when people are physically dangerous to themselves or others, or require inpatient medical treatment. But it is beneficial only when the home is an adequate place to begin with or can be made adequate by selected interventions and community supports.

ADVANTAGES OF HOME CARE

One of the obvious advantages of home care is that most older people prefer it. Care at home offers better morale and security as long as proper services are given to provide comfort, support, and direct treatment of physical and emotional ills. Relatives and service personnel, such as homemakers and home health aides, can often give more individualized care than nursing staffs in institutions. Families tend to become intimately involved in treatment. Familiar surroundings are reassuring, and the older person does not have to be separated from family members, friends, possessions, and pets. Earlier intervention is possible, since it is not necessary to wait until hospitalization to begin treatment, and hospital beds can be saved for those who are more critically ill. Older people who are very ill or who are not ambulatory are not forced to leave home and travel to get treatment. Physicians, nurses, social workers, and members of all other disciplines involved in home care become more familiar with community resources, learn to use them more fully, and act as monitors and advocates who note services not presently available. Older people and their families can receive not only medical and psychiatric home care but also social and economic help.

The older person and the people in his or her life have a different perception of illness and treatment in the process of home care. Instead of being whisked off to the hospital or an institution, people remain where their care can be observed and participated in. It becomes evident to family members and older people themselves that mental or physical illness can be lived with as long as the stress on caregivers does not become too great. Life does not have to stop or become totally disrupted, and rehabilitation and recovery may be seen occurring even in a proportion of the very old and sick.

It should also be mentioned that home care is a growing consumer market that is creating many new jobs and a whole new service industry. It will eventually open up the mental health professions to an influx of new personnel and new ideas. Some day, home services (and nursing homes themselves) may be operated as social or public utilities, well regulated and run in the public interest. New professions, having a broader base of skills than is now seen, may evolve.

THE INITIAL REQUEST FOR MENTAL HEALTH EVALUATION

Requests for mental health care services may come from a variety of referral sources that include the following:

- Self-referral
- Family
- Friends and neighbors
- Members of the clergy
- Physicians—often internists
- Visiting nurse service
- Welfare department
- Community agencies
- Police

The more isolated the older person, the more likely it is that his or her difficulties will remain unnoticed until an emergency occurs and the police are called. Health inspectors, shopkeepers, and service workers such as meter readers, mail carriers, and hotel and apartment clerks may be the link that connects the isolated older person with the police after something obviously begins to go wrong.

FACTORS TO CONSIDER REGARDING HOME CARE

The decision to provide treatment in the home is influenced by the older person's self-care capacities, by the environmental resources the older person has, by the care-giving situation, including family and friends, and by the services and choices of care available in the community.

Activities of Daily Living

In terms of the individual older person, one must know if he or she is physically and mentally capable of self-care, either alone or with assistance. A diagnosis of an older person's physical or mental condition has proven to be a poor predicator of the use of home care. Therefore, researchers and health practitioners have turned to assessment of the actual *functioning* of the older person in his or her environment. The list below gives the most important of the functional skills needed for living at home, particularly if the person is alone part or all of the time.

- Orientation to time, place, person
- Cooking and feeding
- Bathing
- Dressing
- Grooming
- Toileting
- Continence
- Transferring from bed to chair
- Standing and walking
- Climbing stairs
- Fire and accident security
- Shopping
- Money management
- Ability to follow instructions (for example, medication)
- Ability to seek assistance when needed
- Social participation

As discussed earlier in this chapter, measurements of the capacity for performing the ADLs have evolved, making it possible to obtain a comprehensive picture of what a person can or cannot do. The Interagency Forum on Aging-Related Statistics (1989) provides a useful analysis of the various ADL measures and their applications in 11 recent national surveys.[7] Increasingly, ADL dependency measures are used to determine whether an individual qualifies for certain benefits and services, including home-care services. They have also been found to be significant predictors of admission to a nursing home, use of home care, use of hospital services, living arrangements, overall Medicare and Medicaid expenditures, insurance coverage, and mortality.

The most frequently used measure of functional ability is the Katz Activities of Daily Living Scale, which covers bathing, dressing, transferring, toileting continence, and eating.[8] Other scales are available as well. In addition, measures have been developed to help capture an even wider range of activities necessary for independent community living. Called the "instrumental activities of daily living" (IADLs), these measures address the capacity to handle personal finances, meal preparation, shopping, traveling, doing housework, using the telephone, and taking medications.[9]

Resource Assessment

Assessment of the adequacy of an older person's resources is another consideration. How adequate are transportation, socializing opportunities, quick availability of emergency medical care, neighborhood safety, financial security? Can the rent or mortgage and the utilities, repair costs, and property taxes be paid? Does the older person have the inner resources to manage on his or her own? Are there interests and activities? Personal relationships? Sexual outlets when desired? Religious and spiritual supports?

Assessment of Family and Other Informal Caregivers

One must also consider those people with whom the older person will be living or on whom they will be relying. Does home include other family members, roomers, or companions? Is it possible to feel at home in someone else's home, perhaps with sons or daughters? Can sharing and intergenerational living work in the average family? Or would the older person be more content in a communal arrangement with other elderly persons or with an intergenerational mix of people? Relatives

or friends with whom an older person lives may not be willing or able to care for the person at home when illness or disabilities increase. Sometimes there are no comfortable or easy solutions as the needs of the elders clash with those of younger family members. However, in many situations, families will make every sacrifice to keep an older person at home and may, in fact, need help in reconsidering whether this is the wisest course of action. In other cases families need support and opportunity for respite if they do decide on home care.

Eighty to ninety percent of home care of the sick or frail elderly is provided by families, and 70 to 80% of that family care is by women. In a nationally representative probability sample of informal caregivers of elderly who are dependent in ADLs, 71.5% of 2.2 million caregivers in the United States were women, with an average age of 57.3 years. Of all caregivers, 23% were wives; 29% were daughters; 20% were other females; 13% were husbands; 8.5% were sons; and 7% were other males. (Note: The figure of 2.2 million caregivers is an underestimate of informal care-giving, since much family assistance is given to older people who need assistance but are not yet frail or sick enough for the ADL categories.) Many caregivers (31.5%) were in vulnerable economic circumstances due to poverty or near-poverty, produced or compounded by the costs of care-giving. Fewer than 10% purchased services to assist them in their work. About 9% of all caregivers had left the labor force to care for a relative or friend, and of the one million caregivers still in the work force, one-fifth cut back on hours, nearly 30% rearranged their schedules, and almost 19% took time off without pay. Wife and daughter caregivers were more likely than husband and son caregivers to take any of these measures.[10]

Looking at aging from the point of view of the caregivers of the elderly, most of whom, as we see, are female, is an emerging public policy issue. In the past, most of the literature on care of the elderly focused on the elderly themselves—their medical and social needs, their financial capacity to pay for care, their preferences and predilections regarding care—as well as the services in place or proposed for the future. In recent years attention has begun to broaden to include concern for the needs of caregivers—the physical burdens that the care of the elderly imposes, the emotional stresses common to care-giving, the financial costs to the caregiver, and the services that would need to be provided if care-giving were to become a more viable, and when possible, a more positive, enriching experience for all concerned.

What happens as the "women in the middle" (ages 40 to 55) become employed in the paid work force in increasing numbers? Brody sees a caregiving shift toward the "young-old" women, ages 55 to 74, who become responsible for the care of the old-old—those over 75. However, even young-old women are themselves increasingly in the paid work-force.

Women over age 50 are in danger of becoming a new high-risk group for "burnout" or stress because of their many roles: wife and possibly caregiver to the husband when he is ill, out-of-home worker, parent, grandparent, and caregiver to parents or the husband's parents.[11] A number of studies point to the fact that a substantial subgroup of caregivers have competing family and employment demands in addition to care-giving roles.[12] This is true of many of the daughter-caregivers as well as a number of the wife-caregivers, who may also be responsible for the care of children at home and/or work in the outside labor force. One-quarter of care-giving daughters and one-third of other care-giving females had children under the age of 18 in their households. A 1984 report on care-giving by the National Association of State Units on Aging found "the role conflict among working/caregiving women is complex. The multiple roles assumed include employee, parent, spouse, filial caregiver and, sometimes, grandparent. The combination of multiple roles and value conflicts makes the working/caregiving woman a high risk health group.[13]

Measurements of caregiver strain are being developed. Examples are Robinson's *Caregiver Strain Questionnaire* and Zarit, Reaver, and Bach-Peterson's *The Burden Interview.*[14]

The 1979 Health, Education, and Welfare Task Force on Implementation of the Report to the President from the President's Commission on Mental Health pointed out that women, one-half of whom are in the work force, cannot be expected to shoulder the entire burden of care-giving to the young, old, and sick. The report recommended that government at local, state, and federal levels continue to develop formal support systems to supplement the informal supports provided by women.

Major gaps exist on many questions concerning caregivers. Measurements of all forms of stress on caregivers are crude and inconclusive. There is little documentation, pro or con, regarding the "woodwork effect"—namely the widespread fear that providing more resources to families will cause them to "come out of the woodwork" and overburden the system of supports. Nor is there yet enough research-based clarity about the worry that families will withdraw supports to the elderly if they are available elsewhere. There is little accurate information beyond demographic evidence about the actual wishes and needs of both caregivers and care recipients. Little is known about the viability of service exchanges and bartering of care services. And finally, there is still relatively little acceptance and understanding of the economic value of the care-giving services that women provide and of the fact that if they can no longer manage the burden, the alternatives will neither be inexpensive nor uncomplicated.[15]

The literature on the subject of the cost-effectiveness and cost-benefit of institutional versus home-based eldercare has been summarized by Weissert et al. (1988).[16] Long a topic of conjecture, home care was first thought to be a less expensive form of care for the frail and disabled elderly. But a look at the literature reveals that home- and community-based care, together with the services that support them, actually raise overall health-care service costs. Nor does home care produce a marked improvement in health status of the elderly or in delaying institutionalization. What it does produce is an improved degree of satisfaction and contentment among the elderly. But what happens to the caregivers? Studies of the economic and social costs to caregivers would help clarify this question and reveal what price caregivers are paying for the enhanced contentment of the elderly.[17] Such information would improve policy decisions about provision of support and respite to caregivers if home care continues to be seen as a desirable and important part of a comprehensive program of care for the elderly.

While it is true that home care is more expensive than institutional care if it is provided on a 24-hour-per-day basis, it is important to recognize that home care (and community care) should be and is provided in "dosage" form in accord with need, for example, severity of the condition (as measured by ADLs) and the character of the patient (degree of cooperativeness). Thus, home care is not all-or-nothing. There should be a "trigger" or "circuit-breaker" mechanism that is set off when the costs of care in the community attain 75% of institutional care costs. It is then time for reassessment and, depending upon the results, possible decision time for institutional admission. (From our perspective, the residual 25% is a crude measure of the caregiver strain or burden "cost," not usually measured.)

Availability of Home Health Services—What *Really* Exists and What *Ideally* Should Exist

Any truly serious national effort to keep people in their own homes requires provision for direct home delivery of health, including mental health, services. The middle class as well as the poor suffer from the unavailability of such services. Home care should be available to the chronically ill, to those recuperating from hospitalization, to those who may be acutely ill but can be treated outside a hospital, and finally to all those older people who simply need some help here and there to fill in the gaps left by various losses or declining functions. The U.S. health care system is gradu-

ally incorporating home care into the overall system of health care. For example, U.S. hospitals have become well aware of the need for home care; in 1988, 35% had home-care departments, compared to only 6.5% in 1976. We will describe the services we believe are essential if home care is to be a comprehensive approach to the treatment and prevention of mental illness. Evaluations, treatment plans, and coordination of care by some responsible person or group are, of course, essential. (Such services, known as *geriatric assessment* and *case management* or *care coordination* will be discussed shortly.)

Home care is not a radical new idea, but rather a return to some of the sound principles of the past, strengthened by newer medical and psychiatric understanding and techniques. In the past the family doctor, by means of the house call, took care of physical problems for the homebound elderly, while members of the clergy attended to spiritual and emotional matters, buttressed by neighbors and nearby family members. However, doctors and the clergy moved away from home visits, and crime, especially in urban areas, frightened away other health service providers who had formerly performed direct community work. Now only two major groups routinely make house calls: public health nurses and social workers. Much to their credit, members of these professions—usually women—continue working unarmed and often alone in high crime areas where the poor and many urban older persons reside. Fortunately, some physicians, psychiatrists, and related professionals are becoming interested and involved once again in community work, particularly through community mental health centers and outreach programs. Paraprofessionals of all kinds entered the home-care field with the community mental health movement. But overall, nurses and social workers are the most prominent professional home-health workers, and they are likely to be the central coordinating figures in any plans for provision of home care.

Services for older people include basic maintenance services, supportive services, remedial and restorative services, and life-enrichment services. The outline here summarizes the range of services that should be part of a repertoire of home care.

Geriatric assessment

Case management/Care coordination

Mental health intake, screening, and evaluation

Mental health care

Physician's services

Nursing services

Homemaker-home health aides

Physical therapy

Occupational therapy

Speech therapy

Inhalation therapy

Dental care

Nutrition service (Meals-on-Wheels, group dining, food distribution programs)

Health education, including self-care and prevention of illness

Laundry service

Social services

Information and referral

Financial support

Legal services

Personal needs (transportation, telephone reassurance, letter writing services, bill-paying services, grooming, shopping, companions, friendly visitors, pets)

Family "respite" services

Caregiver training

Night sitters (for short-term illnesses)

Home safety and other preventive services

Chore services (handyman) or home maintenance repairs

Recreation (community center, senior center)

Employment and volunteer work (VISTA, Senior Aides, SCORE, Peace Corps, Foster Grandparent, Green Thumb, etc.)

Education (home library service, reader services, academic courses)

Religious support (clerical or pastoral counseling, "practical" ecumenism)

Police assistance

Outpatient care in clinics, community mental health centers, day hospitals, day-care centers

Alzheimer's service centers

Multipurpose senior centers

Protective services

Screening before hospital admission

Many communities will not have all or even most of these resources. Some can be created at little or no cost by volunteer groups; others can be lobbied for in state legislatures. Pressure can be put on professional groups and voluntary agencies to make their services available or to create new services.

Coverage under Medicare and the private insurance programs for older people encourages hospitalization rather than home care. The very poor may be able to obtain home-care services through Medicaid, the state welfare program (some states like New York are much more adequate than others), but self-supporting middle-class people tend not to be able to afford such services. Free care or care based on the ability to pay is sporadically available through charitable agencies and United Way organizations. There has been an increase of limited home-care support under Medicare in the 1980s, particularly after implementation of DRGs.

Six current sources of financial support for home health care services are included in the following list.

1. *Medicare.* Medicare can pay for home health visits only if all of the following four conditions are met: (1) the care needed includes intermittent skilled nursing care, physical therapy, or speech therapy; (2) the person is confined to his or her home; (3) a doctor determines that home health care is needed and sets up a home health plan; and (4) the home health agency providing services is participating in Medicare.

2. *Medicaid.* Medicaid payments depend on what individual states allow. New York state offers particularly comprehensive Medicaid coverage for home care. Overall, however, less than 3% of the

$15 billion in Federal Medicaid expenditures went to home care in 1990. A much higher proportion was used for skilled nursing home care.

3. *Social Services.* Under Title XX (SSA), state funds are available for social services.

4. *Older Americans Act.* Under Title III (OAA), payments are made to states for distribution to local branches of Area Agencies on Aging (AAA). Title VII also provides monies for home-based services.

5. *Veterans Administration.* The VA provides aid and assistance grants for purchase of home health services to families caring for disabled veterans. The VA also furnishes these services directly, usually through a VA hospital.

6. *Internal Revenue Service.* The IRS provides for an exemption under the income tax law for families purchasing medically prescribed home health care for a dependent parent.

The organization and delivery of comprehensive geriatrics to Medicare-only and Medicare-Medicaid beneficiaries are being tested in four social and health maintenance organizations (SHMOs) with about 15,000 enrollees. SHMOs unify health and social services under the direct financial management of a provider of services who carries the risk. The SHMO adds long-term care benefits to the hospital and medical benefits ordinarily provided by health maintenance organizations under capitation arrangements. The SHMO participant pays a monthly premium for a specified dollar amount of home care and nursing services; hospital and medical services are covered entirely by payments from Medicare and Medicaid. The SHMO may add preventive and other benefits as savings allow in the provision of regular Medicare services. Like health maintenance organizations (HMOs), the SHMOs are considered a prepaid health care alternative to the standard fee-for-service Medicare coverage. The four SHMOs are:

- Kaiser Permanente, Portland, OR: *Medicare Plus II*
- Metropolitan Jewish Geriatric Center, Brooklyn, NY: *Elderplan*
- Ebenezer Society–Group Health Inc., Minneapolis, MN: *Seniors Plus*
- Senior Care Action Network, Long Beach, CA: *SCAN Health Plan (SHP)*

USE OF THE HOME FOR SCREENING AND EVALUATION

Ideally, older people would be kept at home even after a request or referral for mental health services is made. Part or all of the evaluation could be done at home, except for technical (usually medical) examinations that require a specific setting. Even when most of an evaluation must be carried out elsewhere, it is important that a direct evaluation of the person's home situation be made.

In planning a program of home care, one must be clear about the objectives, whether rehabilitation, maintenance of the status quo, or support during decline and eventual death. Older people themselves should voice their opinions about the kind of mental health and physical care they want. Change is the most constant factor in the treatment of older persons. Treatment must be constantly evaluated for its appropriateness and be altered whenever circumstances change in the direction of either improved functioning or greater illness. It can be as harmful to overtreat someone who is struggling to recover as it is to undertreat someone who truly needs help. Dependency and loss of functioning can result if people of any age are overprotected and coddled when they do not need it. Deterioration and complications can result when care is not adequate.

After an evaluation of the specific nature of a person's problem has been completed (Chapter 9 describes the process of evaluation in detail), a mutually agreeable decision must be made among family members, the older person, and mental health personnel as to the nature and location of treatment. Does mental health care include such diverse services as provision of adequate income, homemakers, or even podiatry (foot treatment)? A comprehensive, broad concept of care includes whatever has to be done. The goal is to attempt to preserve any aspects of the older person's life that contribute to his or her physical and emotional well-being.

THE ROLE OF GERIATRIC ASSESSMENT AND CARE COORDINATION

Geriatric assessment is a multidisciplinary team approach, used far less in the United States than in various other countries, that employs combinations of physicians, nurses, social workers, psychologists, and others in an evaluation of an elderly patient by his or her capacity to function rather than by assessment of specific body organs, body systems, and diseases. Such an evaluation discovers and explains the older person's multiple problems, resources, strengths, and need for services. Once this is done, a coordinated care plan is developed, focusing on possible interventions. In addition, the geriatric assessment may identify problem areas requiring more detailed evaluation by other medical and nonmedical professionals such as clinical psychologists, dentists, nutritionists, or podiatrists.

This assessment process alerts mental health staff to an elderly person's true ability to function independently in the community. It also informs them about certain nonmedical needs of the patient, such as Medicaid eligibility, respite care for their caregivers, and Meals-on-Wheels.

Many inpatient studies have shown how effective this interdisciplinary approach can be. The Veterans Administration Hospital, for example, has seen reduced hospital stays, reduced readmissions, and lower mortality and morbidity rates. Team-oriented outpatient assessment was found to facilitate the delivery of high-quality care to the elderly and even possibly to decrease health care costs by supporting the elderly's functional capacity.[18]

A number of recent efforts have been made to establish methods for comprehensive evaluation of older persons prior to admission into any program—institutional or noninstitutional—with the ultimate goal of helping to keep them at home. In contrast to other societies, the United States has been slow in developing such a technique. For example, 75% of Australian elderly have access to geriatric assessment, compared to perhaps 10% of U.S. elderly.

Case management is another relatively new concept in the care of older persons. (In our experience, many older people don't like the term *case management.* They do not wish to think of themselves as "cases," nor do they like to be "managed." A better term might be *service coordination* or, when both coordination and psychotherapy are combined, as is often the case with social workers, *care coordination* might describe the role.) To obtain all the needed services for a client, a care coordinator acts as the link between client and affordable health and social service providers, such as home health care agencies or adult day-care centers. Care coordinators can be social workers, nurses, psychologists, or other geriatric specialists. A care coordinator conducts a comprehensive needs assessment, develops an overall care plan, coordinates and monitors the delivery of services, and frequently does reassessments. The hallmark of care coordination is "to hold one person responsible for overcoming fragmentation in the service delivery system." Social work care coordination also adds a clinical, social case-work or counseling approach for dealing with emotional problems surrounding illness and disability.[19] (Roberta Greene provides a comprehensive discussion of care coordination from a social work perspective.[20])

One governmental study, the Long-Term Channeling Demonstration program, attempted to document the value of assessment and care coordination.[21] Although no savings were demonstrated, the results indicated that there was a higher degree of life satisfaction for patients and families with care coordination and an integration of services. Over the past 10 years, approximately 600 for-profit care coordination agencies have developed. They essentially act as surrogates for children or other relatives who may lack the skills, time, geographic proximity, or emotional capacity to provide the services an older person needs.

One especially troublesome situation adult children confront is handling the needs of parents or other relatives in a distant location. Aging Network Services, one of the country's leading care-coordination referral services, has ties to 250 private-practice geriatric social workers nationwide who find suitable paraprofessionals for the elderly and are also available for future consultation.[22]

As an example of care coordination, the "Living at Home Program" took place at 20 sites throughout the United States from 1986 to 1989 and was supported by 39 foundations, including the Commonwealth Fund (of which Dr. Robert N. Butler was the advisory committee chairman) and the Pew Memorial Trust. The program explored ways to help people remain at home for as long as possible. Hoping to make a significant improvement in the quality of life for a substantial number of older people, the program provided each elderly person with a broad range of services. These were coordinated through a care coordinator skilled both in understanding the unique needs of each elderly individual, and in securing the necessary services. What differentiated this program is that the care coordinator developed, orchestrated, assessed, and ensured the satisfactory provision of each individually tailored set of services (medical, financial, legal, and social) from *multiple* participating agencies, including volunteer services, not just a single agency. Many of the original 20 sites in the program are continuing to operate under new funding provided by a variety of sources, giving hope to the idea that through care coordination, many existing community programs can be well utilized.

Private care coordination can be expensive and, unfortunately, is not covered by Medicare, Medicaid, or private insurance. The first assessment (including a home visit, a meeting with the physician and relatives, and a written care plan) ranges from $100 to $300 in 1996; continuing consultation can cost anywhere from $40 to $150 an hour. Religious charities, hospitals, and other nonprofit organizations also provide care-coordination services, usually at a lower cost; however, staffers tend to have

more than twice the number of elderly in their caseloads.

Since care coordination is generally unregulated, one should check credentials and references carefully when looking into such services. At minimum, care coordinators should have a master's degree in either social work or another human-services area, as well as geriatric experience.[23]

HOME DELIVERY OF SERVICES

All the services mentioned in this chapter are considered by us as part of mental health care. In addition, the specific services of psychiatrists, social workers, and all other members of mental health teams should be routinely available in people's homes. The two major types of psychiatric outreach care are emergency care (usually for persons making suicide threats and attempts or for those wandering in the streets as a result of brain damage or functional psychosis) and ongoing therapy for those who find it difficult to leave home. Evaluations for mental health services as well as screening for institutional admissions can be done in homes.[24] Screening should, of course, emphasize keeping people out of institutions, when appropriate, by use of community and home care. Mental health services are discussed more fully in Chapter 12. With outreach services one sees many people who would never appear at clinics and would only be seen in hospitals as a result of an emergency. A discussion of specific home delivery of health, mental health, and social support services follows.

Physicians' Services

Physicians should be on call for emergency home visits on a 24-hour basis and for ongoing medical evaluation and management of patients. Contact may vary from brief intensive care to weekly or monthly medical supervision and treatment. Laboratory services can also be provided. Specimens—blood, urine, feces, and so on—can be obtained from the person at home and analyzed in the laboratory. Electrocardiograms and other selected studies can be made in the home.

There are two major problems standing in the way of home medical care: doctors' reluctance to make house calls and a lack of financial resources that might make it possible to overcome this reluctance by offering incentives. In most cases doctors believe they can treat a patient better in an office or in a hospital emergency room and that the house calls take too much time. "It is rare that a house call is justified" is a common viewpoint. But doctors who do make house calls provide an enormous sense of security for the older person who may be worried about health or unable to leave home for care of aggravating but noncritical illnesses.

Mrs. H, a woman of 85 years, lives in a public housing project with her daughter's family. She is confined to her second-floor room because of arthritis and a disabled hip. She seldom sees a doctor because her son-in-law has a heart condition that prohibits him from carrying her down the stairs. In addition, her daughter must take off a day's work to transport her in the family car. Mrs. H does not want to put an extra burden on them, so she seldom mentions her aches and pains. She wept with disbelief and happiness at the sight of the physician from the neighborhood community mental health service who came to see her in her room.

Doctors are not well-distributed geographically. Some areas—especially poor urban areas and many rural areas—typically have few doctors and other health personnel. In Washington, D.C., a predominantly African American city, 90% of doctors are located west of Rock Creek Park, which essentially divides white (west) from black Washington, where some 60% of the African American population lives.

Specialization by doctors is another problem for older people. Older people frequently look in vain for a "family doctor." Although there has been insufficient congressional emphasis on geriatrics, in the 1970s congressional legislation aimed at encouraging doctors to enter family practice. Geriatric medicine has not been recognized as a practice specialty in the United States, although 40% of internists' patients are older people with whom they spend 60% of their time. In spite of the fact that older people are medically underserved, a 1980 report by the Graduate Medical Education National Advisory Committee (GMENAC), concerned about a possible oversupply of physicians, failed to consider the impact of the growing number of older people and the consequent growing need for geriatricians. Others have recognized that physicians in nearly all specialties need special training in geriatric medicine, in addition to their regular training; this would open up a whole new area of expertise as well as a new clientele.[25]

Although there has been insufficient congressional emphasis on geriatrics, in 1986 Congress established the Institute of Medicine Committee, which investigated the supply and demand for academic geriatricians. In addition, they evaluated potential strategies for bringing academic training capacity to needed levels.[26] In 1988, for the first time, the American Board of Internal Medicine and the American Academy of Family Practice gave examinations for added competence in geriatrics. The American Board of Neurology and Psychiatry also agreed to offer examinations for special competence in geriatric psychiatry. Postgraduate training (fellowships) in geriatrics must include geriatric psychiatry, especially psychopathology, mental status testing, and psychopharmacology.

Nursing Services

The services included under home nursing care are those of *registered nurses* (RNs), whose two specialties pertinent to older persons are public health nursing and psychiatric nursing; *licensed practical nurses* (LPNs); and *home health aides.* Registered nurses are qualified to assess patients, develop a care plan, and carry out skilled nursing functions. LPNs and home health aides are supervised by registered nurses.

We shall attempt to clarify the work of each of these groups as they care for older persons. *Public health nurses* are RNs, and sometimes LPNs, who work for tax-supported city or county health departments. They visit families in their homes, provide direct nursing care, give health guidance, participate in communicable disease control programs, and staff public health clinics. They may give emergency care as well as care for acute and chronic illness. Public health nurses can instruct people in the use of community health and social resources and make authorized investigations of convalescent homes, nursing homes, and other institutions. Referrals usually come from public health clinics or city and county hospitals as well as other public agencies. There is a heavy concentration of poor and inner-city people as clientele. Services are free of charge to those eligible.

The over 400 Visiting Nurse Associations are among the 15,000 home care agencies throughout the country. They are freestanding, nonprofit organizations governed by a community board of directors, or divisions of large national nonprofit organizations such as the United Way. Part of their mission is to take care of everyone regardless of their ability to pay. They are financed by tax-deductible contributions and earnings. Like the large proprietary national home care chains, they offer a full range of home care services and categories of employees. During this time of significant change in the industry, many Visiting Nurse Associations are being bought up by hospital-based systems. For example, Michigan used to have twelve Visiting Nurse Associations—now there are only two.

Visiting nurses provide almost the same services as public health nurses but tend to have smaller caseloads and can devote more time to individual patients. Public health nurses may each have several hundred patients as well as responsibilities in clinics and schools. In some communities, visiting nurses and public health nurses have merged their staffs and functions, while in others they work separately. Both groups wear similar blue uniforms, and community familiarity with these uniforms gives them protection as they work in high crime neighborhoods. Visiting nurses try to go into such areas unless deemed extremely unsafe. Escorts are often hired and if night visits are required, security personnel ac-

company them. Public health nurses are accompanied by other health care workers whenever safety is in question.

Visiting nurses do more direct home nursing, while public health nurses carry an added responsibility for preventive and community work. Referrals to visiting nurses come from private doctors and private hospitals and are initiated by patients themselves or their families or are made by overloaded public health nurses. Visiting nurses care for both poor and middle-class patients. Older people are required to pay a fee adjustable to their income or may be eligible for free service through one of the organizations contracting with the VNA and the third-party payments of Medicare and Medicaid.

Licensed practical nurses work under the supervision of RNs and perform many of the same nursing skills. *Home health aides* also provide simple nursing care, which will be discussed later. For those who can afford very expensive services, a number of agencies supply *private duty RNs, LPNs,* and *nurses aides* for up to 24-hour total nursing care.[27]

Home nursing services enable older people to leave hospitals sooner and keep them at home longer before institutionalization. Some of the common ailments for which persons are treated are strokes, cerebrovascular accidents, arthritis, cancer, hip fractures, paraplegia, and minimal to moderate dementia. Teaching a procedure, such as self-administration of insulin for diabetes, is another nursing function. Family members can be taught to do a variety of tasks, including physical therapy. Helping the patient with problems of incontinence, bedsores, care of teeth and mouth, bathing and skin care, grooming, and feeding are other tasks of nursing personnel. Home nurses are also trained to look at the patient's family from a life-cycle perspective: If there are grandchildren, are they immunized? Is the daughter-in-law (for example) receiving prenatal care if she is pregnant? What can be done about the son's chest pains? All this is in addition to the original reason for the visit, which was to serve the older patient.

Social Work Services

Earlier we discussed the multiple roles of social workers as community workers, members of geriatric assessment teams, care coordinators, hospital discharge planners, agency intake workers and caseworkers, and the like.[28] They also are responsible for much of the planning and coordination of the social services to be described next.

Home Health Aides and Homemakers/Home Care Aides

The responsibilities of home health aides can differ from state to state, depending on nurse practice laws. Nurses delegate to home health aides, so the nurse's license covers the home health aides working under her supervision. Home health aides are defined as those who provide physical care to patients at home. They work under a medically supervised plan of care to assist the client and family with household management and personal care such as bathing, dressing, and toileting. They can help with assistive devices and respond to appropriate client instructions consistent with their training. In addition, they can assist with nonsterile wound care, self-administered medications, simple procedures, and prescribed exercises.

Homemakers, or *home care aides,* as the National Association for Home Care has renamed them, are defined as those who provide housekeeping services. They assist with environmental services such as laundry, cleaning, shopping, and meal preparation in order to maintain a safe, sanitary, and healthy home environment.

Home health aide services are covered by Medicare, whereas homemaker services generally are not covered, unless they are directly related to required and approved medical care. The home health care benefit under Medicare Part A includes intermittent skilled nursing care, home health aide services, physical therapy, speech therapy, and occupational therapy. While there are no deductibles, co-insurance payments, or limits on the number of visits under the home health care

benefit, only 80% of the approved cost of durable medical equipment is covered.

Home health aides and homemakers/home care aides are always employed by an agency, organization, or administrative unit which selects, trains, and supervises them. Olsten Kimberly Quality Care and Interim Health Care are examples of such agencies. Referrals to home care agencies may be obtained from physicians, nurses, social workers, and health institutions. According to the National Association of Home Care, in 1995 there were approximately 17,561 home care agencies in the U.S. Of these, 8,747 are Medicare-certified home care agencies, 1,795 are Medicare-certified hospices, and 7,019 are home health agencies, home care aide organizations, and hospices that do not participate in Medicare.[29] For Medicare-certified agencies, there are 12 federal conditions of participation, which include aide training requirements. If the government cites an agency for violating one of these 12 conditions, the agency can lose its ability to train home health aides. Private agencies have no government regulations, but they can choose to be approved by the Community Health Accreditation Program (CHAP) of the Joint Commission on Accreditation of Healthcare Organizations (JCAHO).

According to Cindy Stonerock, editor of the *Home Health Aide Digest,* hospital-based and proprietary agencies are growing faster than any other type of agency. Proprietary agencies now comprise 40% and hospital-based agencies about one-quarter of all certified agencies. One-third of home care agencies are located in six states: California, Florida, Illinois, New York, Pennsylvania, and Texas.

Payment sources for home care include private insurance, Medicare, Medicaid, Older Americans Act, Social Services Block Grants, Workers Compensation, the Veterans Administration, health maintenance organizations, CHAMPUS, social services organizations, and private payments. Some agencies offer a sliding scale so a family need pay only what it can afford.

The U.S. Department of Labor indicates that positions for homemakers/home care aides will increase from 179,000 in 1994 to 391,000 in 2005. Positions for home health aides are expected to rise from 420,000 in 1994 to 848,000 in 2005. Despite these upward trends, many communities across the nation are without home health aide and home-maker services. Furthermore, home-care workers are too often undertrained and underpaid, according to the Home Care Aide Association of America. Minimal wages, a lack of health benefits, and limited options for career path development contribute to high turnover rates among home-care workers even as the demands for home-care services keep growing.

Physical, Massage, Occupational, and Speech Therapies

Occupational, physical, and speech therapies are partly reimbursable under Medicare, but severe restrictions limit their use. Thus patients may receive a great deal of rehabilitative work in hospitals following bone and joint diseases and strokes, but the investment is lost because home-care follow-up is not given. Massage therapy is seldom reimbursed.

Physical Therapy. Physical therapy is a critical piece of both rehabilitation and prevention of decline in older persons. Many persons with neuro-musculoskeletal problems can benefit from an individually prescribed program of physical therapy. Common problems are paralysis, weakness or pain affecting the musculoskeletal system, cardiovascular accidents, arthritis, degenerative brain conditions, and trauma. Stroke patients and fracture patients of all kinds, especially, should be seen as soon as possible by a physical therapist to increase the possibility of recovery. Patients debilitated after long bouts of illness are also prime candidates for physical therapy.

The physical therapist should be responsible for providing and teaching the use of any equipment and appliances necessary for rehabilitation, in addition to the actual provision of therapy. Physical exercise on a daily basis should be introduced, following an appropriate medical evaluation, if the older person does not exercise regularly. Two kinds of exercise are usually indicated: one to keep the body and its muscles and joints limber and the other to increase the endurance and capacity of the cardiovascular system.

Physical therapists are licensed in every state, and their services are generally available in all hospitals, rehabilitation centers, nursing homes, home-care agencies, and physical therapy private practice offices.[30]

Massage Therapy. As an adjunct to physical therapy, massage, one of the oldest forms of healing, is beneficial in later life. In China, it has been used since the Han dynasty, about 200 B.C., for relief of pain and chills, and Hippocrates recognized its positive effect on muscles and joints. Massage may hasten and improve the convalescent periods after illness or surgery. It may be used to enhance vitality, relax muscle tension, improve circulation, reduce edema and induration, and stretch adhesions from surgery. It is especially beneficial for bed-ridden patients, since it helps maintain circulation and muscle tone. Massage has psychological value in providing "touching" from one person to another, conveying essential feelings of caring and belonging. We believe that the healing and comforting quality of touch may make massage the physiological equivalent to psychotherapy. It can be taught to spouses and other family members of the older person.

The United States is the only developed country that does not consider massage an official part of its health care system. In fact, it is also the only country in the world where people mistake the word "massage" as synonymous with illicit sexual activity. Fortunately, this image is being replaced with a more positive one. Membership in the American Massage Therapy Association has increased five-fold between 1985 and 1996, from 5,000 to 25,000. In addition, the number of AMTA-accredited schools grew from 32 approved schools (actual accrediting began in the 1990s) to 65 in the same 11 year period.

Since only 25 states require that massage therapists be licensed, it is important that consumers check the credentials of any therapist they may be considering, namely whether and where the therapist attended school and the number of hours of instruction received. If the school is registered with the American Massage Therapy Association, 820 Davis St., Suite 100, Evanston, IL 60201-4444, (773) 761-2682, it is a good indicator that the therapist is legitimate; not all schools are registered with the AMTA, but those that are must require a minimum of 500 hours of instruction. Basic training must be in Swedish massage, which involves heavy strokes toward the heart. However, many massage therapists also incorporate acupressure, or *shiatsu* (pressure massage on acupuncture points) and reflexology (massage of acupuncture points on the foot) with basic Swedish techniques. The Feldenkrais method of body therapy includes gentle manipulation of the limbs with the aim of realignment of the skeletal system. The Alexander method focuses on alignment of the head, neck, and shoulders. More controversial techniques include polarity therapy (described as a "balancing of energy systems") and Rolfing (a probing, "deep tissue" treatment to purge long-held emotional tensions).

Occupational Therapy.   Occupational therapy (O.T.) is often stereotyped as "arts and crafts" or is considered infantilizing or paternalistic. This is unfortunate. Properly prescribed O.T. is of great value in maintaining or restoring self-mastery. According to the Occupational Therapy Association, occupational therapy is concerned with a person's ability and capacity to perform tasks of daily living that enable the person to be productive and maintain a satisfying life. Through the use of activities, selected according to the patient's abilities and health needs, the occupational therapist evaluates the individual's capacities related to psychological and social functioning, motor and sensory integrative functioning, and cognitive and performance abilities. Occupational therapists seek to teach, restore, and maintain the occupational performance skills, behaviors, and attitudes crucial to independent and healthy functioning. Home and daily family role demands,

work and play needs, and social or community factors that impede or contribute to health form the primary perspective of occupational therapy practice.

At its best, O.T. is geared toward helping the individual improve functioning in any way possible, as defined by the person, the family, and the therapist. This can be done through any form of therapeutic activity that encourages self-expression and use of those resources available to the individual. For example, one occupational therapist used the "life review" concept in her O.T. group program to encourage older people to examine their lives in a constructive way.[31]

Speech Therapy.   Many speech-language disorders accompany medical conditions, such as Parkinson's disease and Alzheimer's disease, commonly found in older persons. Since communication impairment can interfere with an older person's daily functioning, independence, and self-maintenance, and possibly lead to decreased interactions with others, making the older person feel isolated, the assistance of a speech therapist (or speech-language pathologist) may become necessary. Speech therapists are trained to diagnose speech, language, and swallowing disorders and provide appropriate treatment, including, when necessary, instruction in how to use speech aids and prosthetic speech devices. It is generally recommended that physicians refer patients directly in order to make certain that a qualified speech-language pathologist is chosen and that services will be reimbursable under government and private insurance plans.[32]

Dental Services

"Visiting dentists" are available in some areas and should be provided for all older people who find it difficult to leave their homes. Dental hygienists may also be willing to make home or nursing home visits. Dentistry is not covered by Medicare, even though it is a critical element of nutrition and general health.

Nutrition Services

Food stamps, governmental supplemental food programs, Meals-on-Wheels, group dining, and homemaker/home health aides who shop for and prepare food are some of the means of combating the hunger and malnutrition found in many older people. The best medical prescription for countless older persons would be a prescription for proper food rather than drugs. Reversible (and ultimately irreversible) brain syndromes can result from malnutrition. It is imperative to examine for evidences of malnutrition and hypovitaminosis even in the affluent, whose eating habits may be poor. Low-income older persons must scrimp on food. Psychological conditions—loneliness, depression, apathy, confusion—can induce malnutrition, which in turn furthers these symptoms. Physical disabilities can keep people from shopping and cooking.

Congress first passed legislation in 1972 for a national program for one nutritiously planned hot meal a day, five days a week, to people over 60 years of age. The meals are served in the form of group dining in schools, churches, synagogues, and community centers and are also delivered to people's homes. The federal government provided 90% matching money, with state and local governments or private nonprofit organizations providing the remaining 10%. Although the measure emphasized that the projects be located in low-income areas, having a low income is not a requirement and there is no eligibility test. According to the Administration on Aging, in 1994 under Title III 127 million meals were served to 2.3 million older persons at congregate facilities, and 113 million meals were delivered to 877,000 home-bound older persons. Under Title VI, which applies to Native American populations, 1.3 million meals were served to 41,000 people in congregate facilities, and 1.5 million meals were delivered to home-bound older Native Americans.

The Food Stamp Act was passed by Congress in 1964 to provide food for needy families. The program is part of the department of Agriculture. Low-income people purchase stamps at less than face value and redeem them for food in standard food stores. Of the more than 20 million registered in 1994, only about 7% were aged 60 and over; however, 16% of food stamp households have at least one member aged 60 and over. This difference is due to the typically small size of elderly households (74% were single person households), and their relatively higher income in comparison to other food-stamp recipient households of equal size.[33] Food stamps can also be used for Meals-on-Wheels, but not for group dining.

Nutritionists are available to consult with referring health care personnel, patients, and families about general food needs, special diets, food preparation, food shopping, and the like. A trained nutritionist can be located through local dietetic associations (in the phone directory) or by calling the national headquarters of the American Dietetic Association ([800] 621-6469). The designation of *licensed dietitian* (LD) means the person has met state standards. For states without licensing, the *registered dietitian* (RD) is the nearest equivalent. A qualified nutritionist should be able to perform a nutritional assessment that includes physical measurements, dietary analysis, the ordering of appropriate laboratory tests, a treatment plan, diet prescription, and follow-up. Since malnutrition among the elderly can be caused by unnecessary or poorly understood dietary restrictions, follow-up visits are especially important.[34]

Social Services

Social services are services that are not strictly medical or psychiatric, but instead represent economic and social supports. In the past, social service has been synonymous with social work, but this is no longer true. Many other professions have become involved: members of the clergy, police officers, nurses, government officials, volunteers, paraprofessionals, and physicians who are actively working in the community. In home care, however, it is still most often the social worker who works together with nursing personnel to coordinate a program designed for an individual.

Many homemaker/home health aide services are administered by professional social workers. Over 60% of certified home health agencies offer social services.

Information and Referral.   How does the older person find out about social services? Some cities have information and referral services especially for the elderly. If not, local or state commissions or advisory committees on aging may be helpful. Social services, human resources, or welfare departments (the names vary in municipalities and states) usually have information numbers to call. The same is true of local health and welfare councils and local mental health associations. Social Security district and branch offices can provide information. Family Service agencies are another resource.[35]

Some of the agencies and institutions furnishing direct social service to older people are welfare offices, voluntary agencies (the Hearing Aid Society, Societies for the Blind, etc.), public health departments, including community mental health centers, hospitals (both medical and psychiatric), visiting nurse services, nursing homes, employment offices, departments of vocational rehabilitation, religious organizations, and the police.

Financial Support.   Regardless of potential benefits of home care, one must be realistic about whether a person can survive financially. All sources for financial support must be explored for the older person at home, including free or low-cost services and any pensions or financial assistance for which he or she might be eligible. It is not unusual to find older people who do not know they are eligible for Medicare, Medicaid, Supplemental Security Income, Veterans benefits, and even Social Security benefits. Federal tax laws no longer allow a double income tax exemption for people over 65 years of age and two double exemptions for a married couple. For the blind, an exemption is allowable.

For homeowners, it is important to understand the upkeep and property tax situation. Many older homeowners face financial crises and may be forced to sell their homes. (Those seniors who own their own homes may consider a home equity conversion loan, which allows them to use the equity they have built up in their homes to help them pay for long-term care.) Older renters often experience substantial rent increases, partly necessitated by property tax increases. Energy costs in the late 1970s and early 1980s spiraled, and many older persons were forced to cut back on heat, air conditioning, light, and other energy expenses. One effect was an increase in accidental hypothermia—lowering of body temperature to such an extent that coma and even death can result. Older people are particularly susceptible to temperature changes because their bodies no longer regulate temperature as well as they did in the past.[36]

For the very poor, welfare is usually the last resort. Supplemental Security Income (SSI) is not enough for decent subsistence, and 50% or more of especially poor older persons do not receive SSI. They may not be eligible (SSI is a state-federal program), or they may not be registered even if they are eligible. Money for food must often be sacrificed for medical care and medical supplies as well as other crucial living expenses. Clothing is not a part of many welfare budgets; neither are household articles and furniture.

Personal Needs (Companions, Pets, Telephones, Shopping, Transportation, Grooming, etc.). Older persons may need live-in or part-time companions, help with shopping and transportation, instructions or direct help with grooming (home visits from beauticians and barbers can do wonders for mental health), and appliances and aides to support or compensate for various disabilities (special handles near toilet and tub, wheelchairs, wide door frames, etc.).

A telephone can mean a longer life. The National Innovations Center of London, England, reported in 1972 that people without a phone had significantly higher mortality. In increasing numbers of urban, suburban, and rural areas, telephone reassurance services have been established under the auspices of private and public agencies. Volunteers often work the phones and check to see if older people living alone are all right. "Hot lines" are for emergencies. "Warm lines" are to offer comfort and support. Special telephones are available for the hard-of-hearing. "Memory" telephones allow a phone to be programmed with a dozen or so most-used phone numbers so an older person can simply push one button per call rather than dialing seven digits.

Given the state of loneliness and isolation affecting significant numbers of older people, pets can contribute directly to mental wellbeing.[37] Dogs and cats are the most favored pets, in that order. For the older person, a dog may have the added advantage of providing some protection. Size, the need for exercise, and economy are three key points in selection. A large dog requires a daily walk and eats a great deal. On the other hand, a small dog like a poodle can be expensive to maintain because of necessary grooming every six weeks to avoid skin problems, sore feet, and eye problems. Poodles and certain other dogs have the advantage of not shedding, helpful to allergic persons and to housekeeping. One can acquire a dog from the Humane Society or an animal shelter free or at a modest cost, depending on locale. A female dog is usually more tractable. The bark of a dog may fend off an intruder. In England one can get house insurance at lower premiums if one owns a dog, and in the United States a dog is tax deductible if obtained *after* a robbery. Although the majority of older persons are homeowners, and can make independent decisions regarding their desire for pets, older persons in rental housing may be limited as to the size and type of pet they can have, and many landlords forbid pet ownership altogether.

Cats are easier to train than dogs and cost less to maintain. Birds bring pleasure to many older people. Canaries, finches, and parakeets are especially popular. Perhaps the easiest, least expensive, and least time-consuming pets to care for are fish. Plants sometimes fulfill the role of pets in the lives of many older people.

Experimental programs like "Pets on Wheels" bring pets to nursing homes during the day through the use of volunteers. The A.S.P.C.A. in New York City has a program of placing homeless pets with older persons who want pets. A new idea is the provision of "pet day care" by elderly persons at home who will care for working families' pets during the day for a small fee. *Pets and the Elderly* is a "how to" book extolling the positive effects of pets.[38]

Family Respite Services. Although home care may be the treatment of choice for most older persons, it can place such a strain on other family members in the household that care is undermined and the family's own mental health compromised. Any program of care must therefore consider regular social supports to the families themselves.

"Respite" services (more available in England than here) are a great relief to families and can make it possible for the generations to live together under even stressful circumstances. Such respite includes sending someone to care for the older person at home so the family can take holidays, weekends, and vacations by themselves. At times of particular stress, or when the older person needs more attention, it should be possible to admit the individual briefly to an institution to give the family a chance to rest and recover. This also helps to acquaint the older person with institutional life and reduces the symbolic and real associations of institutions as places of no return. Day and night sitters should be available when the family wants to go out or when the older person requires inordinate attention at night, exhausting family members. Home appliances and aids—wheelchairs, special handles and bars to assist walking, or anything else that alleviates undue dependency or physical stress on the family—can make care easier. The availability of psychiatric, medical, and social assistance on an emergency or routine basis can provide significant relief to a family.

Caregiver Training and Support. Caregiver support groups and training programs (such as employee assistance programs in corporations and nonprofit institutions) have begun to help families cope with the often-present stress resulting from caregiving. Such groups and programs are designed to teach care-giving techniques that not only ease caregivers' anxieties and mental and physical strain, but also benefit the care recipients. (See Corporate Sector Efforts, at the end of this chapter). An updated state-by-state listing of more than 750 self-help groups in 49 states, called *Caregiver Support Groups in America,* is available from the National Council on Aging.[39] Hospitals have begun to provide information, training, and support to both employees and families of patients.[40] The National Alzheimer's Disease Association has one of the most advanced programs for supporting and educating caregivers through its nationwide network of groups and programs for families. Research directions for treatment of Alzheimer's disease and family stress have been developed under the direction of the National Institute of Mental Health in 1989.[41]

We learned of several unique caregiver techniques used in a Japanese day treatment center for Alzheimer's patients[42]: The first involved use of one-way mirrors in order that Japanese family members could observe their elderly relative interact in the center. This was found to be very reassuring to families as they frequently saw their older family member showing more responsiveness than was seen at home. It also allowed them to compare notes with center staff about home versus center behavior. The second technique was a "patient notebook" in which the family wrote observations during the patient's evening hours at home and the center staff wrote comments in the same notebook during the day. This process of writing notes back and forth to each other greatly enhanced communication between family and staff and provided valuable information and a sense of collegial support for both.

Home Safety.   Accidents both in and out of the home are an area of legitimate concern. Studies show that 30 to 60% of individuals age 65 and over will experience at least one fall in a given year.[43] Among older people, accidents are the seventh leading cause of death, claiming 27,784 victims in 1993. Although they make up only 13% of the population, in 1993 30.7% of all accidental deaths happened to people age 65 and older.[44] Accidents that do not result in death can have permanent physical and emotional repercussions and may end the older person's independence of movement. A fall may so seriously undermine self-confidence that mobility is curtailed.

Falls lead as the cause of accidental injuries and deaths.[45] There is a dramatic upsurge of falls for those over 75. To get an idea of the impact of falls leading to hospitalization and nursing home admissions, consider the following:

1. People over 60 make up almost one-fourth of all hospital admissions for injuries due to falls.
2. Even more significantly, the group just described is responsible for over 80% of all hospital stays for falls. Older people also require longer periods to recover than younger people.
3. Forty percent of all older people admitted to hospitals with hip fractures die within one year; another 25% have mobility limitations.
4. Hip fractures alone are responsible for the admission of 4.4% of all nursing home residents.
5. Another 3.6% of nursing home admissions are the result of bone fractures other than hip fractures.
6. Repeated falls or immobility account for up to one-third of all nursing home admissions.
7. The median length of stay in a nursing home for a hip fracture is 85 days. One-third of hip fracture patients stay six months or more. About one-fourth never leave until their death.

Most falls occur in the home. Losses in muscle strength and coordination (often resulting from failure to actively maintain physical conditioning), sense of balance, and speed of reaction are factors. Reduced blood flow and oxygen to the brain can result in dizziness and faintness. Older people should beware of abrupt moves of the head because of changes in the balancing mechanism of the inner ear. Some people suffer "drop attacks"—sudden and unexpected falls without loss of consciousness but with loss of muscle power of body and legs. Drugs, especially sedatives and tranquilizers, may confuse and slow response. For example, phenothiazine medications may cause falls following a drop in blood pressure when standing up (postural hypotension). See Chapter 13 for further details.

The home should be made as safe as possible. Staircases are especially dangerous at the top and bottom steps. Steps should be highly visible and have good illumination, nonskid treads, and handrails. Slippery floor coverings should be eliminated. Linoleum, small mats, and sliding rugs are offenders. Nonskid floor waxes, wall-to-wall carpets or rubber-backed rugs, and tacking are wise. Corrugated shoe soles help. Nonskid mats and grab rails should be used in bathtubs and near toilets and beds. One must also be alert to the disorientation that can follow a move to a new residence.

A 73-year-old carpenter moved to Florida after living in his home for 36 years. He was accustomed to turning to the left from his bedroom door to enter the bathroom. Needing to urinate, he had to get up several times a night. In his new home a stairway was to the left. Several nights after moving, he fell down the stairs and fractured his hip.

Burns, cuts, and poisonings are other hazards. Especially dangerous practices like smoking in bed should be stopped. Room heaters and heating pads must be carefully controlled. Fires can occur when a person is cooking while wearing long sleeves or bed clothes. Medicine bottles must be read with caution; it is recommended that they be read *twice* before medicine is taken and *once* afterward to make certain the medication is correct *and* is being taken at the correct time.

The number of drivers age 65 and older has doubled in the last twenty years to about 13 million. By the year 2020 it is expected to double again.[46] Approximately two-thirds of those 65 and older are licensed to drive, accounting for 12% of all licensed drivers. Interestingly, because they drive less these older drivers have lower accident rates per person than younger drivers. However, both normal physiological changes associated with aging—losses of visual and auditory acuity, slower reflexes, poor night vision, and arthritic limitations on neck movements—as well as diseases that commonly affect the elderly can affect the ability to drive a car.

The loss of an older person's driver's license and the capacity to drive is often a very touching and powerfully disturbing experience—a blow to self-esteem as well as mobility. It represents not only a major life change for someone who has driven, but a real loss of control. Reuben et al. suggest that the elderly be given a functional assessment based on the skills necessary for driving, conducted either by a simulated or actual road test.[47] A National Research Council study also stresses functional assessment to ensure public safety, but using such an evaluation for all age groups, not for just the elderly. Age alone is a poor predictor of any individual's performance and certainly not sufficient to restrict older drivers' licenses. In addition, in keeping with the reality of an aging society, we must alter the signs and the physical dynamics of streets and highways, such as curves and timing of traffic light changes.

Friendly Visiting and Outside Contact. The world must be brought inside to the bed-ridden and the homebound. Many voluntary organizations, including the Salvation Army, provide friendly visitors programs, through which visits are made to isolated individuals. Studies indicate that such visiting has a positive effect on the mental health of those who must stay in bed or in their homes. Frequent contacts with family, friends, and neighbors help keep emotions responsive and minds interested. Television (including the use of video cassettes), radio, phonographs, and newspapers can be rich sources of enjoyment. Older people have been known to sacrifice food to pay for television repairs because television is so important to them. Some people leave their television on all day ("like a friend in the house") or sleep with it on at night. Large screens are a visual help, and volume can be adjusted for hearing difficulties. Television and radio offer recreation, education, and religious services. One man described watching television as rather like sitting on the park bench and watching the world go by, a continuous nonstop show. Another spoke of the sense of having world events at his fingertips; he had two sets, one on top of the other, which he watched simultaneously. People call or write to broadcasting stations, avidly follow their favorite newscasters and masters of ceremonies, and participate in audience talk and game shows.

Recreation, Education, and Employment. The most broadly accepted definition of therapeutic recreation describes it as a process that utilizes recreation services for purposive intervention in some physical, emotional, or social behavior to bring about a desired change in that behavior and to promote the growth and development of the individual. Recreation specialists use recreation as a medium to assist disabled people to change certain physical, emotional, or social characteristics so they may live their leisure life-styles as well and as independently as possible.[47] Treatment settings include acute care hospitals, physical rehabilitation centers, prisons, skilled care facilities, mental health centers, and the community.[48]

For those who can leave their homes, senior centers and community centers may offer a variety of possibilities. Increasing numbers of senior centers no longer simply supply recreation; they now also provide a range of social and health services.[49] A number of centers offer some kind of health education in addition to direct medical services, which include professional clinics, screening programs, immunizations, and physical examinations. They may have activities a few hours each week or may be open all day, five days a week. Shows, parties, music, beauty salon appointments, handicrafts, candle making, cooking, flower arranging, trips, discussion groups (also group therapy), games, television watching, walks, group shopping trips, and special programs for the blind are some of the activities in a well-functioning center. Some centers even offer vacations.

Continuing their education is an interest expressed by many older people. Some communities offer home library services. Inexpensive or free correspondence courses should be offered by high schools and colleges, and older people could be encouraged to enroll in regular academic classes if scholarships and low fees were possible. For example, Vartan Gregorian as president of Brown University suggested that graduates be allowed to return to Brown, free of charge, to take courses throughout their lives. Elementary and junior and senior high schools located in communities where older people live could remain open after the regular class day and provide recreation, education, and food service.

Colleges could furnish curricula especially designed for older people; some are already doing this. In the summer of 1975, five New Hampshire colleges, in a small pilot project, opened their campuses to "hostelers" of retirement age. The result was the Elderhostel program, now found at about 2,000 colleges, universities, and other institutions which offer their classrooms, dormitories, and staff for week-long programs to people age 55 and older.[51] Older people can take a wide variety of courses, live in dormitories on campus, and generally enjoy student life at reasonable costs during the off-seasons of vacation time and summers. In 1981, the first foreign programs were offered—16 in Great Britain and four in Scandinavia—arranged in connection with partner organizations abroad. Today the Elderhostel program has expanded to over 70 different countries. In 1995, 295,000 older persons took courses through the program.

The New School for Social Research's program called the Institute for Retired Professionals of New York City draws professionals and community leaders into study programs that are administered and taught by older persons.

About one-third of the 3,000 colleges and universities in the United States (a 10% increase since 1970) are now offering some kind of continuing education aimed at those over 25. The returning adult is welcomed at a time when college enrollments of younger students are slipping. Many of the returnees are middle-aged women reentering the job market. But increasingly, as it has become clear how eager older people are to continue their education, schools have begun to encourage elderly students as well. The American Association of State Colleges and Universities sees universities developing into "three-tiered" institutions, serving the traditional student, the middle-aged student, and retirees.

In their book, *You Are Never Too Old to Learn,* Cross and Florio report on a survey taken by the Academy for Educational Development.[52] Program directors at several hundred colleges and universities with large numbers of older students were asked to identify the most popular subjects with these students. The nine most popular subjects were history, psychology, health, foreign languages, literature, painting, creative writing, religion, and needlework. Philosophy, preretirement planning, and physical fitness were tied for tenth place.[53]

Employment and volunteer work allow older persons to supplement their incomes and involve them in absorbing activities that benefit them and the community. In Bethesda, Maryland, the Over 60 Counseling and Employment Service of the Montgomery County Federation of Women's Clubs, Inc. developed a program that provides job opportunities for older men and women—acting as companions for other older persons, caring for children, doing yard work and carpentry, and so on. Other scattered programs have trained unskilled older persons as family aides. The Retired Senior Volunteer Program (RSVP),[54] the Foster Grandparents Program and the Senior Companions Program are now divisions of the National Senior Service Corps which, together with AmeriCorps*VISTA (Volunteers in Service to America), forms the federally funded Corporation for National Service. Senior Aids, Service Corps of Retired Executives Association (SCORE), The Peace Corps, Green Thumb, Mature-Temps, and other employment and volunteer programs are also designed for, or accommodate, older persons.

Those with handicaps must be given every opportunity to take part in such activities. Section 504 of the 1973 Rehabilitation Act states:

No otherwise qualified handicapped individual in the United States . . . shall, solely by reason of his handicap, be excluded from the participation in, be denied the benefits of, or be subjected to discrimination under any program or activity receiving Federal financial assistance.

The purpose of the Act was to ensure that federally funded programs and activities were accessible to handicapped persons. The objectives are to ensure equal opportunity, equal access, and equally effective services and treatment for handicapped individuals.

In 1990, the Americans with Disabilities Act was passed, extending the above concept throughout the public and private sectors; even businesses or agencies that do not receive federal funds are required to comply. Called the most sweeping civil rights act in two decades, the bill bars employment discrimination against people with physical or mental disabilities, requires access to public buildings, telephone service, mass transportation, and government services for the millions of Americans with disabilities.

Religious Support

Members of the clergy of all faiths are involved in the care of older people. Some concentrate only on spiritual aspects, while increasing numbers of others become directly involved in social services, counseling, and other secular activities. Many older people are deeply religious, and members of the clergy can become an integral part in planning and providing for their care. The clergy has traditionally formed one of the few professional disciplines whose members are specifically trained to care for the dying. Home visiting with the sick and infirm is also common practice, and members of the clergy are an important source of referral to other health professionals for medical and psychiatric problems.

Religious groups have for centuries given special attention to older people. Some of the best, as well as worst, examples of homes for the aged and old-age-oriented community activities can be found under their auspices. But the need to maintain doctrinal differences has led to fragmentation of services. Each denomination builds its own little island of concern, isolated from everything else. A "practical ecumenism" could allow churches and synagogues to protect their identities yet pool their resources in a planned effort to help older persons.[55] For example, buying necessary supplies together for homes for the aged could sharply cut costs. Pooling skilled personnel would increase the range of services each home could give. Cooperative planning of vital community programs such as Meals-on-Wheels[56] and friendly visitors could reach many more people, with the churches of all denominations acting as neighborhood bases for all older persons, regardless of denomination. A national church program including all denominations could register all eligible older people for health programs, coordinate food programs, provide friendly visitors and telephone reassurance, set up information and referral services nationally, help coordinate home-care programs, and much more. Members of the clergy could receive special training for work with older persons. Religious groups should use their power and influence for improvement of older people's economic and social conditions.

Home Hospice Services

Home hospice care has become an important part of the hospice movement in the United States. Patients are considered for such care during the last days of their lives if no treatment will significantly alter the disease, and the desire is to make the patient as comfortable as possible at home. In 1982 financing for hospice care was included under Title 18 of the Social Security Act. Home nursing, psychological counseling, nutritional evaluation, home support services, and a number of other services may be available, as well as bereavement counseling for family members. Usually home care is monitored by a home health care team connected with a hospital. The patient may be readmitted to the hospital for the last 24 to 36 hours of life. Both patients and their families generally agree that such care enhances the quality of life remaining, compared to more traditional hospital care.

New Housing Arrangements

Although the vast majority of older persons continue to live in private single family houses or apartments, many must seek alternatives when independent living becomes difficult or undesirable. In addition, federal rent subsidies and support of new housing has fallen dramatically, making independent living more difficult for those on fixed incomes. Fortunately, the available continuum of alternatives to nursing homes is exploding. Assisted living and other types of supportive and alternative housing are expanding, largely as a result of private market forces.

Assisted Living. *Assisted living* is generally defined as a residential program that also provides or arranges supportive and recreational services including meals and health care, in addition to around-the-clock monitoring and assistance for those who need help with activities of daily living (ADLs). This broad definition includes a variety of programs that fall between individual homes and institutional programs, such as nursing programs, under a variety of names, due partly to individual state regulations and definitions.

Programs that offer assisted living are not new; however, this option has become more popular with the recognition of the fact that many older people need help with activities of daily living, but do not need skilled nursing care and therefore can maintain a higher level of independence. Also, pressure to diminish Medicaid expenditures on nursing facilities has increased support of assisted living programs, which are primarily paid for privately. Oregon, by using Medicaid to fund services and Supplemental Security Income to cover housing costs, has implemented a model program that makes assisted living available to low-income people who would otherwise be in nursing homes at a much higher cost.

The philosophy of assisted living also implies service that is, according to the American Association of Homes and Services for the Aged, "consumer-driven, flexible, individualized and maximizes consumer independence and dignity."[57] It is also implied that the atmosphere in assisted living facilities will be "home-like."[58] The degree to which independence and comfort is maintained, however, varies by facility and state.

Although there are no reliable figures on the assisted living industry, 1993 estimates published by the Assisted Living Facilities Association of America suggest that 30,000 to 40,000 facilities serve approximately one million older people.[59]

Congregate Housing.   Congregate housing programs are residential facilities where older people live in their own private apartments and services are provided, such as meals (often one a day), transportation, housekeeping, and health clinics. Often residents can receive some help with activities of daily living. However, unlike assisted living facilities, 24-hour-a-day assistance is not provided.

A number of states have developed programs to promote congregate housing by setting standards and licensing, by funding services at housing locations, and by making loans and grants available to build new housing. In the early 1990s the federal government promoted congregate housing by providing funding for service coordinators and services at a variety of government supported housing projects. However, in 1996 this program was eliminated due to budgetary pressures. Still, congregate housing is a cost-effective alternative for many low-income older people.

Shared Living Concept or Home Sharing.   The shared living concept centers around a living arrangement where two or more unrelated adults share a home or apartment, usually to save money. In addition, shared housing can bring companionship, increase safety, and minimize household chores. This arrangement has been particularly popular among older people who, in many cases, share dwellings with middle-aged or younger people. There are two types of shared housing. Match-ups, where homeowners share their home with a border or roommate who pays rent, are by far the most common. Group-shared residences are cooperative arrangements where two or more people share a home or apartment. The popularity of shared housing has increased rapidly. The U.S. Census reported that in 1980 670,000 older people were sharing homes, 35% more than a decade earlier. As of the 1990 census, almost 970,000 people age 45 and older lived as roommates, with an additional 1,215,900 living as unmarried partners.[60] The number of programs nationwide that match prospective home sharers rose from 50 in 1981 to over 350 in 1996.

Shared housing can also lower costs to communities and consumers. A shared home is for many an alternative to institutionalization. The National Shared Housing Resource Network (NSHRN) in Baltimore, Maryland,[61] an information clearinghouse founded by Maggie Kuhn, who also founded the Gray Panthers, estimates that the cost to the average home-sharing program to place one person ranges from $500 to $2,000, whereas a unit of public housing can cost more than $70,000. Prospective home sharers pay only a small fee to apply to a program, and an additional fee if a match is found. In shared housing arrangements, rents are often lower than market price. Homeowners who share their homes may use the extra income to maintain their residences or to buy services such as home health care, allowing them to remain independent.

Many states provide some funds for shared housing, but the government needs to play a larger role. For example, older homeowners are often dissuaded from participating in home sharing because they risk having their assistance checks (e.g., food stamps, Supplemental Security Income, rental assistance) reduced due to an increase in their total household income. The sharing of public housing units has been allowed since 1978, with rents based on individual incomes, and with individual leases.

Continuing Care Retirement Communities.
Continuing care retirement communities (CCRCs) offer a broad spectrum of housing options and social, health care, and personal services, ranging from independent living to 24-hour nursing care. Entry fees are required for many, in addition to a monthly fee for specific services. Agreements are either made for a specific period or for the rest of the resident's life. Most such housing is too expensive for more than a small proportion of the older population.

In 1996, the American Association of Homes and Services for the Aging (AAHSA) noted that approximately 350,000 residents were living in 1,100 CCRCs throughout the United States. The average age of residents in CCRCs is 81, 75% of residents are women, and 70% are single.[62] Approximately 98% of CCRCs are still sponsored by religious groups or other nonprofit organizations. However, the private sector has recently entered the industry. The Marriott Corporation is currently developing over 150 CCRCs. Thirty-seven states regulate financial aspects of CCRCs and all states regulate the health care they provide, yet there are vast differences in the quality of services provided.[63] The Continuing Care Accreditation Commission, sponsored by AAHSA, is the only accrediting body for CCRCs. As of July, 1996, under 200 CCRCs were accredited.[64]

Others. A variety of boarding homes, retirement hotels, and other facilities, which offer a variety of services and a somewhat protected environment, can be found here and there. So-called "granny flats" or "echo flats" are small units that can be attached to larger structures, such as adult children's homes, and are used to house older family members.

OUTPATIENT CARE

Outpatient services (or ambulatory care) is the term for care given to people who live in the community rather than in institutions. This care is provided by hospital outpatient clinics, neighborhood health and mental health centers, family agencies, day hospitals, and adult day-care centers. Outpatient services may be given in or outside of the home, either by bringing the person to the services or taking the services to the person. Since we have already described home care, this section emphasizes the facilities where people can go for outpatient care rather than having it brought to them.

Under Medicare, coverage of psychotherapy is unlimited in terms of length of care, but it is subject to review. Clinical psychologists now receive the same scheduled fee allowances from Medicare Part B as physicians, and clinical social workers are reimbursed at 75% of that rate. Spurred in part by the Senate's passage of the Domenici-Welstone mental illness parity provision in 1995, which requires many large insurance providers to offer equal lifetime and annual payment limits for mental and physical health care, a push for increased parity between physical and mental services is underway. Currently Medicare enrollees must pay a 50% co-payment for psychological services. In the near future, however, Medicare is expected to offer the same coverage of 80% for both psychological and physical care services.

Hospital emergency rooms are the major 24-hour facilities available for medical and psychiatric emergencies. In addition, hospitals generally offer *outpatient medical clinic care;* some have *outpatient psychiatric clinics* as well. Currently only 2% of patients in outpatient psychiatric clinics are over 60 years of age. Few of the clinics offer the services necessary for older people, especially psychotherapy. In an effort to offer integrated and comprehensive services, the Phyllis and Lee Coffey Outpatient Geriatrics Clinic of the Department of Geriatrics of Mount Sinai Medical Center provides full services (including psychiatric) to nearly 1,000 patients with an average age of 80 who have multiple, complex, and interacting acute and chronic psychosocial and physical conditions.

Community mental health centers (CMHCs) represent another potential, but unrealized, resource for older persons. In 1961, proposals regarding the establishment of community mental health centers were made and published by the

Joint Commission on Mental Illness and Health. The Federal Community Mental Health Centers Program was enacted by Congress in 1963 and amended in 1965, 1967, and 1975. The community mental health center was required to offer a minimum of five services, four of which were direct clinical activities: inpatient care, outpatient care, partial hospitalization (such as day care), and around-the-clock emergency service. The fifth required program element was community education and consultation services oriented toward prevention. In addition, Public Law 94-63, the Public Health Service Act of 1975, required that the community mental health centers provide "a program of specialized services for the mental health of the elderly, including a full range of diagnostic, treatment, liaison, and follow-up services." Community mental health centers were responsible for specific catchment areas, but certain of the center programs (such as those for children, older persons, and drug addicts) served several catchment areas.

The passage of the 1980 Mental Health Systems Act was aimed at correcting the many inadequacies found in the Community Mental Health Center Program by the 1979 President's Commission on Mental Illness, chaired by Rosalynn Carter. The act was designed to improve the delivery of mental health care in the United States, addressing such issues as the needs of the chronically mentally ill to cope in the community and prevention and improvements in state mental health systems. Although it was never adequately funded by Congress, the act contained the following potentially valuable features:

1. More community care will be provided for those who have been underserved by the current CMHC program—namely, the old, the young and adolescent, the chronically mentally ill, and certain racial and ethnic minorities. Projects can be specifically targeted for these groups.

2. All federal funding for community care must go through the states, which will act as service coordinators and program evaluators. There will be no direct federal funding to local communities as in the 1963 CMHC Act. The purpose is to return authority to the states and avoid a two-tiered federal-state system of authorization and review.

3. However, none of the money authorized can go to state hospitals. All of it must go to community-based care; thus, states are being required to commit themselves to community care of chronic-care patients if they want federal funds. This Act was supported by block grants under the Reagan administration. Thus, there is no targeting on a national basis.

Community Mental Health Centers have been adversely affected by the change in the law that led to block grants going to the states. States can elect to use their funds in a variety of ways including combining them with Medicaid to contract with private providers. Such contracts are part of the general privatization movement and make questionable the future of public mental health at both the state and federal level. The Veteran's Administration has designated patients for "behavioral health care" or total care for the chronic mentally ill. Therefore, individuals with psychiatric disorders also have their physical problems managed, all on a capitated basis. The effectiveness of this approach remains to be proven.

Both public and private agencies participated in the establishment of community mental health centers. It should be pointed out that whatever the nature of its sponsorship, the typical community mental health center was supported through a combination of public and private funds. Public monies met 75% of the total operating costs of typical centers during the first year of operation. Private funds derived from varying combinations of patient payments, third-party payments made in behalf of patients, and voluntary contributions.

By 1987 some 700 centers were operating. However, mental health service needs of older persons frequently were unmet.[65] Older people made up only 4% to 5% of community mental health center clientele.[66] The centers were never adequately funded, housed, and staffed. No standards existed. Inservice training and personnel development lagged. Racism and stereotypes about "the poor" were negative influences.

Day hospitals for patients with psychiatric problems enable persons to come to the hospital for any indicated treatment during the day and return home at night. This provides a degree of care intermediate between outpatient therapy and total institutional care. It is particularly useful for former mental hospital patients and persons with significant organic mental impairment. In this way families obtain substantial support in keeping an older person at home. Nursing and old age homes should offer similar partial care. One of the greatest problems with day hospital programs is the need for transportation, particularly in rural areas. In England, ambulances are used to transport people. Taxis (paid for by Medicaid in some states), volunteers' cars, and staff cars may be used. An ideal day hospital service has a staff-to-client ratio not exceeding one-to-eight and should offer medical care, individual and group psychotherapy, drug therapy, occupational and physical therapy, entertainment, education, a library, a store, beauty and barber shops, free lunches, baths, some form of patient government, and plenty of opportunities for congenial socializing. Day hospitals can ease the return of former mental hospital patients to community life and monitor the physical condition and reactions to medications of all patients. Relatives, friends, and community volunteers should have free access to these facilities.

Day-care centers offer day care in a nonhospital setting (often in a YMCA or a church) but provide many of the same social and recreational services as day hospitals.[67] *Adult day-care centers* serve those who are not strong enough to stay home alone, yet do not need constant care. In 1970, only a dozen or so adult day-care centers existed in the United States; by 1996, about 3,000 such centers served more than 60,000 people. Basically, there are two types of centers: those focused on medical needs and those focused on social needs.

The first recreational day center for the aged, the William Hodson Community, was set up in 1944 as part of New York City's Department of Public Welfare.[68] This center emphasized self-government, poetry, music, drama, woodwork, painting, birthday parties, discussion groups, counseling, and an added fillip in the form of country vacations. Various other groups now offer similar programs. Depending upon location and services offered, the National Council on the Aging described the average daily cost of adult day care in 1996 as ranging from $30 to $125. Medical centers may exceed $80 a day, while transportation may run another $7 a day. Yet these costs are lower than the average $100 daily cost of nursing home care or the $15 to $30 per hour charge for private nursing care. Unfortunately, Medicare Part A does not cover adult day care. Medicare Part B does cover outpatient medical and therapeutic services at day-care centers if the centers are Medicare approved vendors.

Families seeking day care for an older person should visit a center first, for although 42 states have set up quality standards for such centers, fewer than half require licensing. A search for adult day-care centers can begin by contacting the area Agency on Aging or a local health or social services department.[69]

MULTIPURPOSE SENIOR CENTERS

Former Congressman John Brademas (D-Ind.) introduced legislation in December 1971 to authorize construction of multipurpose senior citizen community centers. A revolving fund was to be established to ensure mortgages for such centers. The National Council on Aging estimates that 2,000 to 2,500 centers existed in 1990. The senior center movement illustrates the continuing debate over the development of comprehensive versus categorical programs: whether the services needed by older people should be assured within comprehensive programs for people of all ages or be provided in specialized ways. Philosophically, socially, and psychologically, integration of services for all age groups is the more desirable. Experience demonstrates, however, that older people get lost in the shuffle, and fall through the cracks.

Until there is a change in the cultural sensibility so that older persons are not ignored, it is necessary to press for special, highly visible programs aimed specifically at the elderly.

Multipurpose senior centers can provide a range of services beyond the walls of their facilities. Social workers and aides (paraprofessionals, who are sometimes called "geriatric aides") and friendly visitors may visit the homes of clients. Residential homes may be organized. Group shopping trips by bus, for check-cashing as well as shopping, may be chaperoned. Little House in Menlo Park, California, has been a pioneer example of a multipurpose senior center since 1949.

PROTECTIVE SERVICES

Protective services is the name for a group of services given to persons who are so mentally deteriorated or disturbed as to be unable to manage their affairs in their own best interest and who have no responsible relatives or friends able and willing to act on their behalf. Social work, legal, medical, psychiatric, nursing, homemaking, and home health aide services may be provided. Small amounts of cash may be available for use in certain situations.

Federal legislation was enacted to permit state welfare offices to set up protective service programs, for which the federal government covers 75% of the cost.[70] Adult protective services programs have been developing more rapidly since the passage in 1974 of Title XX of the Social Security Act. The Omnibus Reconciliation Act of 1981 amended provisions of Title XX; it also created the Social Services Block Grant Program, through which adult protective services are federally funded. Federal guidelines, however, are broad, allowing states freedom in shaping their policies and program directions.[71] Every state has an organized program of service and intervention.

Protective services clients often need assistance because of some mental condition such as paranoid ideas, organic brain syndrome, overwhelming anxiety, or severe personality disorder. Most of these clients are best helped by social

workers and nurses who are generalists in the sense that they handle their clients' problems with the support of medical, legal, and psychiatric consultations and can call on homemakers, visiting nurses, and paraprofessionals for help. A typical case illustrates the importance of such services to mental health.

A mildly confused older woman developed paranoid ideas about the gas company, which resulted in her not paying her bills for several months. She was threatened with having the gas turned off, which would leave her without heat in midwinter. Had she been without help, her gas probably would have been turned off; after a while police and medical help would have been called for, and her eventual transfer (probably in a very deteriorated condition) to an inpatient psychiatric ward would have been necessary. With protective services, the crisis with the gas company was averted. A casework aide, under the supervision of a social worker, was able to gain the woman's confidence enough to convince her to pay the gas bill. Since she had no money for an immediate payment, protective services made a partial payment of the bill and arranged with the gas company for the woman to pay the rest later. Continuing contact with the protective service worker enabled the woman to continue living in her own home. A homemaker was also provided for a few hours a week. All these helpers used psychiatric consultants to help them react appropriately to the client's psychiatric condition.

The protective service and the community mental health approaches are closely related in that both provide a variety of services to meet a person's needs while the person remains in his or her home, thus utilizing less-than-total-care institutions whenever it is in the person's best interest. The older person is seen not just as having a certain illness but in the context of psychological, social, physical, and economic conditions. Also, psychiatric needs may be met without requiring the person to accept the idea that he or she is a "mental patient."

In 1962 the Social Security Administration made a grant to the Benjamin Rose Institute of Cleveland, one of the few agencies providing extensive protective services to older people, for a research and demonstration project. It is important to note that the early work of Margaret Blenkner, director of this research, continues to be relevant to our understanding of the possible danger of intervening too quickly or too globally with protective services.[72] Any reduction in the autonomy of elderly people must be done with great care and caution.

No figure has been established for how many people need protective services. The number who have mental impairment is substantial, and this applies to people in institutions as well as in the community. Early studies showed that about 50% of institutionalized populations had mental impairment.[73] Later studies suggest that one-sixth of the noninstitutionalized elderly population— three million people—has some degree of mental impairment. Even if these figures include unrecognized or simulated depression, rather than organic impairment, for practical purposes this describes a vulnerable population. Some of the earliest studies concerning "certifiable" persons in the community estimated that 5% need protective services.[74] Less stringent later studies have estimated up to 16%, although studies are not strictly comparable because of varied criteria.

In Blenkner's approach, social casework was the core service and the directive was "do, or get others to do, whatever is necessary to meet the needs of the situation." Rapport, trust, mutual respect between the elderly and health personnel are necessary. Gradualism (nonprecipitous, careful intervention) is a guiding concept; it is not necessary or even desirable to think in terms of completing a case, except as nature dictates through death. The following are some principles crucial to protective services.

1. Entrust client or patient with decision-making power.
2. Establish trust and rapport; before all else, do not violate that trust.
3. Use gradualism—do things nonprecipitously and carefully.
4. Do not kill with kindness.
5. Work with assets.
6. Respect resistance.
7. Do not move people if it can be avoided and if it is against their will.

Blenkner's intriguing work found that the protected group as compared to the control group had higher rates of institutionalization and death. This was attributed to hopelessness (we would add helplessness) engendered by things being done for people. Members of the protected group were institutionalized earlier than they would otherwise have been and "contrary to intent . . . [protective intervention] did not . . . prove protective of the older person although it did relieve collaterals and community agents." It is essential that studies be designed to confirm or refute the Benjamin Rose studies. In the meantime, "We should . . . question our present prescriptions and strategies of treatment. Is our dosage too strong, our intervention too overwhelming, our takeover too final?"[75]

In a 1985 literature review, Zhorowsky concludes that social work must take a renewed look at protective services. The protective services literature has focused on the individual person unable to manage his or her own affairs. But this definition has begun to be broadened to include protection of the older person from neglect or abuse by others, thereby moving protective services into major new areas. Zhorowsky also describes the relatively new protective service laws in many states that give designated social workers broad powers of intervention even when an older person or caretaker is resistant. The need to balance older people's well-being with that of their civil rights and their need for autonomy represents a delicate social work practice issue that is still problematic.[76]

MODELS OF MULTIPLE SERVICE PROGRAMS

New York State's Nursing Home without Walls Program (also known as the Lombardi Program, named after its originator, New York State Senator Tarky Lombardi), established in 1977, is a viable alternative to institutional care, both providing and coordinating the delivery of nursing-home level services to the chronically ill and disabled so they may be cared for at home. A comprehensive range of health, social, and environmental services is tailored to patients' individual needs and managed on a 24-hour, seven-day-a-week basis. Care is provided by approved hospitals, residential health care facilities, and certified home health agencies and is available to any patient determined medically eligible for placement in a skilled or intermediate care nursing facility and who can be appropriately maintained at home. NHWW has allowed families to remain together and has provided care in a more personalized and compassionate manner. Many patients already hospitalized have been able to return home; at-risk community residents have avoided further deterioration; some patients have been rehabilitated. At the same time that it helps meet the increasing need for long-term care, NHWW helps contain the high costs to public and private payers. Patient care costs are approximately half of what institutional facilities charge for comparable care. Lombardi services cannot cost over 75% (or in some cases 100%) of the average cost of care in a residential health care facility.

The Minneapolis Age and Opportunity Center (MAO) is a comprehensive program of health and social services founded by its president, Daphne Krause, in 1969.[77] It is a nonprofit organization governed by seniors. The purpose of MAO is to give older frail and younger handicapped people an alternative form of care, with direct home-care network services. The goal is independence. Services include daily meal deliveries; homemaker and home health aide services (including bathing, housework, and laundry); transportation to medical services, counseling; special health counseling; legal services; employment services; nursing services; once-a-day telephone reassurance; and a "food closet" for emergency or supplementary food. Contacts between the old and young are encouraged. A free clinic was opened in 1973, sponsored by Abbott-Northwestern Hospital, with Medicare accepted as full payment for fees.

This clinic offers preventive medical services, diagnosis and treatment services, emergency service, counseling service on health matters, and inpatient service where needed. The hospital provides health care personnel and equipment, and MAO supplies volunteers and professionals for the wide range of services described earlier. Funding for MAO has been provided by Medicare, county welfare, private donations, and other sources.

The Council for the Jewish Elderly (CJE) of Chicago is a social agency with transportation, outreach, and homemaker services, Meals-on-Wheels, storefront area service centers, a senior work center, apartments, and liaisons with two hospitals. Another program with a more distinct ethnic orientation is that of the On Lok Senior Health Center for older Chinese, Filipinos, and Italians.

CORPORATE SECTOR EFFORTS

Corporate sector efforts have focused on the caregiving aspects of home care. Private sector employers are beginning to provide special benefits to employee caregivers, partly to attract women into the work force and partly to protect the existing work force from work/home conflicts arising from the growing demand for family elder care. Studies indicate that 20 to 25% of a typical employer's work force is providing some form of elder care for either a parent, a grandparent, or a spouse.[78]

Employee benefits for long-term care include long-term care insurance and caregiver assistance programs, both direct and indirect.[79] Indirect caregiver benefits are potentially beneficial to all employees. They include flex-time, personal leave policies, job sharing, employee assistance programs, and dependent care reimbursement (or flexible spending) accounts. Direct programs focus especially on employees providing elder care. They include information programs, referral programs to helpful resources, direct service programs of group support and individual counseling, occasional programs to provide access to adult day-care programs for older relatives, and subsidies for respite care.

In 1989, Ford Motor Company became the first major U.S. company to introduce an employer-financed long-term-care health plan covering both home and institutional care. Some other companies, such as Proctor and Gamble, offer employees the opportunity to purchase long-term-care insurance at special group rates. Travelers Life Insurance Company offers an array of elder care benefits under a flexible benefit program called Family Care (which also includes child care). The three basic components are financial assistance, time off, and information on referral services.

The Washington Business Group on Health and the U.S. Administration on Aging have sponsored efforts by business coalitions and government aging units in eight states to collaborate on programs for older adults and their caregivers.

A 1989 New York Business Group on Health study explored 37 companies' responses to the needs of employees who provide elder care. The study found that employers are becoming aware of the need for changes in personnel policies (flexible work schedules, leaves of absences, and so forth), financial benefits, caregiver informa-

tion, caregiver support, and support to community agencies providing caregiver services.[80]

THE PEPPER COMMISSION

The Pepper Commission, officially the U.S. Bipartisan Commission on Comprehensive Health Care (established by the Medicare Catastrophic Coverage Act), issued recommendations to Congress in 1990. Its key recommendations have not been enacted into law. Support for home and community-based care for the severely disabled of all ages would be greatly increased under the Commission's plan. All those who need assistance with three or more personal activities of daily living (i.e., eating, bathing, toileting, dressing, and transferring) or who have severe cognitive impairment due to developmental disabilities or Alzheimer's disease or a related disorder would be eligible for care. Care coordinators would determine the amount and mix of services needed, including home health care, personal care, homemaker chore services, adult day care, and respite care. Beneficiaries would pay 20% of the costs. The rest would be provided by the federal government. Special subsidies would be available for those who were unable to pay the co-insurance of 20%.[81]

SELECTED READINGS

American Association of Homes and Services for the Aging, Public Affairs. (1996). *Assisted living: Background.* Washington, DC: Author.

American Association of Homes and Services for the Aging, Public Affairs. (1996). *Continuing care retirement communities: Background.* Washington, DC: Author.

American Association of Retired Persons. (1990). *Home health care benefits covered by Medicare: A chart book.* Washington, DC: Author.

Ayers, R. E. (1990, February). The physical therapist's role in geriatric care. *Geriatrics, 45*(2), 83–84.

Barer, B. M. (1992). The relationship between homebound older people and their home care workers, or "the pas de deux" of home care. *Journal of Gerontological Social Work, 19,* 129–147.

Barer, B. M., & Johnson, C. L. (1990). A critique of the caregiving literature. *The Gerontologist, 30*(1), 26–29.

Barker, W. H. B. (1987). *Adding life to years: Organized geriatrics services in Great Britain and implications for the United States.* Baltimore: Johns Hopkins University Press.

Bass, D. M., & Bowman, K. (1990). The transition from caregiving to bereavement: The relationship of care-related strain and adjustment to death. *The Gerontologist, 30*(1), 35–42.

Berkman, L. F. (1986). Social networks, support, and health: Taking the next steps forward. *American Journal of Epidemiology, 123,* 559–562.

Blenkner, M., Bloom, M., Wasser, E., & Nielsen, M. (1971). Protective services for old people: Findings from the Benjamin Rose Institute Study. *Social Casework, 24,* 483–522.

Branch, L. G., & Stuart, N. E. (1984). A five-year history of targeting home care services to prevent institutionalization. *The Gerontologist, 24,* 387–391.

Brickel, C. M. (1986). Pet-facilitated therapies: A review of the literature and clinical implementation considerations. In Brink, T. L. (Ed.), *Clinical gerontology: A guide to assessment and intervention* (pp. 307–332). Binghamton, NY: The Haworth Press.

Brickner, P. W., Lechich, A. J., Lipsman, R., & Scharer, L. K. (1987). Long-term health care: Providing a spectrum of services to the aged. New York: Basic Books.

Brody, E. M. (1985). *Mental and physical health practices of older people: A guide for health professionals.* New York: Springer.

Brody, E. M. (1990). *Women in the middle: Their parent-care years.* New York: Springer.

Buchwalter, K. C., Smith, M., Zenenbergen, P., & Russell, D. (1991). Mental health services of the rural elderly outreach program. *The Gerontologist, 31,* 408–412.

Carcango, G. J., & Kempes, P. (1988). The evaluation of the national long-term care demonstration 1. An overview of the channeling demonstration and its evaluation. *Health Services Research, 23*(1), 1–22.

Chalfie, D. (1995). *The real Golden Girls: The prevalence and policy treatment of midlife and older people living in nontraditional households.* Washington, DC: American Association of Retired Persons, Women's Initiative.

Clark, L. W. (1990, February). Specialists for the communicatively impaired. *Geriatrics, 45*(2), 72–75.

Clemmer, E. (1995, February). Assisted living and its implications for long-term care. *AARP Public Policy Institute Issue Brief, 20.* Washington DC: American Association of Retired Persons.

Commonwealth Fund Commission on Elderly People Living Alone. (1989, May). *Help at home: Long term care assistance for impaired elderly people.* Baltimore, MD: Commonwealth Fund Commission on Elderly People Living Alone. Available from Center on Elderly People Living Alone, Public Policy Institute of AARP, 1909 K Street N. W., Washington, DC 20049.

Commonwealth Fund Commission on Elderly People Living Alone. (1987, November 20). *Medicare's poor.* Baltimore, MD: Author. Available from Center on Elderly People Living Alone, Public Policy

Institute of AARP, 1909 K Street N. W., Washington, DC 20049.

Council on Scientific Affairs. (1990, March 2). Home care in the 1990's. *Journal of the American Medical Association, 263*(9), 1241–1244.

Cusak, O., & Smith, E. (1984). *Pets and the elderly.* Binghamton, NY: The Haworth Press.

Eliopoulos, C. (1990). *Caring for the elderly in diverse care settings.* Philadelphia: J. B. Lippincott.

Fishman, P. (1990, February). A physician's guide to locating a qualified nutritionist. *Geriatrics, 45*(2), 61–65.

Flattan, K., Wilhite, B., & Reyes-Watson, E. (1987). *Recreation activities for the elderly.* New York: Springer.

Gallo, J. J., Reichel, W., & Anderson, L. (1988). *Handbook of geriatric assessment.* Rockville, MD: Aspen Publishers.

Greene, R. R. (1990). Case management: An arena for social work practices. In Vourlekis, B., & Greene, R. (Eds.), *Social Work Case Management.* New York: Aldine de Gruyter.

Gulyas, R. A. (1995, October). *AAHSA's position on assisted living.* Washington, DC: American Association of Homes and Services for the Aging.

Hamlet, E., & Read, S. (1990). Caregiver education and support group: A hospital based group experience. *Journal of Gerontological Social Work, 15*(½), 75–88.

Health Care Financing Administration. (1996). *Your Medicare handbook 1996.* Baltimore, MD: Health Care Financing Administration, U.S. Department of Health and Human Services.

Hunter College/Mount Sinai Geriatric Education Center (GEC), Levenson, D. (Ed.). (1990). Getting the job done: Helping hands in geriatric primary care. A Mount Sinai special series. *Geriatrics, 45*(2), 58–84.

Interagency Forum on Aging-Related Statistics. (1989, October). *Measuring the activities of daily living among the elderly: A guide to national surveys.* Prepared by Wiener, J. M., & Hanley, R. J., The Brookings Institution. Federal Forum: Final Report.

Kane, R. A., & Kane, R. L. (1987). *Long-term care.* New York: Springer.

Katz, S., & Stroud, M. W. (1989). Functional assessment in geriatrics, a review of progress and directions. *Journal of the American Geriatrics Society, 37,* 267–271.

Lachs, M. S., Feinstein, A. R., Cooney, L. M., Jr., Drickamer, M. A., Marottoli, R. A., Pannill, F. C., & Tinetti, M. E. (1990). A simple procedure for general screening for functional disability in elderly patients. *Annals of Internal Medicine, 112,* 699–706.

Lewin/IFC & Brookings Institution. (1989). *The estimated cost of a proposed home health care program.* Report prepared for the Commonwealth Fund Commission on Elderly People Living Alone. Background Paper Series no. 16.

Liebenson, D. S. (Ed.). (1990). *The case management resource guide.* Irvine, CA: Center for Consumer Health Care Information.

Maki, B. E., & Fernie, G. R. (1996). Accidents: falls. In Birren, J. E. (Ed.), *Encyclopedia of gerontology* (vol. 1, pp. 11–18). San Diego, CA: Academic Press.

Monk, A. (Ed.). (1990). *Handbook of gerontological services,* 2nd ed. New York: Columbia University Press.

Morrison, I. Bennet, R., Frisch, S., & Gurland, B. (Eds.). (1986). *Continuing care retirement communities.* Binghamton, NY: Haworth Press.

National Association for Home Care. (1995). *Basic statistics about home care, 1995.* Washington, DC: National Association for Home Care.

National Center for Health Statistics. (1986). Aging in the eighties, age 65 years and over and living alone, Contacts with family friends and neighbors. *Advance Data from Vital and Health Statistics.* No. 116, DHHS Pub. No. (PHS) 86–1250. Hyattsville, MD: Public Health Service.

National Center for Health Statistics. (1987). Aging in the eighties, functional limitation of individuals age 65 and over. *Advance Data from Vital and Health Statistics.* No. 133, DHHS Pub. No. (PHS) 87–1250. Hyattsville, MD: Public Health Service.

National Center for Health Statistics. (1988). Aging in the eighties, people living alone—Two years later. *Advance Data from Vital and Health Statistics.* No. 149, DHHS Pub. No. (PHS) 82–1250. Hyattsville, MD: Public Health Service.

National Center for Health Statistics. (1993). Health data on older Americans: United States, 1992. *Vital and Health Statistics,* Series 3, No. 30. DHHS Publication No. (PHS) 93–1411. Hyattsville, MD: U.S. Department of Health and Human Services.

National Center for Health Statistics. (1995). Trends in the health of older Americans: United States, 1994. *Vital and Health Statistics,* Series 3, No. 30. DHHS Publication No. (PHS) 95–1414. Hyattsville, MD: U.S. Department of Health and Human Services.

National Council on the Aging. (1990). *Caregiver support groups in America.* Washington, DC: National Council on the Aging.

National Long Term Care Survey. (1982). Funded by the Health Care Financing Administration and the Office of the Assistant Secretary for Planning and Evaluation, U.S. Department of Health and Human Services.

New York Business Group on Health. (1989, February). *Assisting employee caregivers: Employers' "eldercare" programs.* New York: New York Business Group on Health.

New York State Senate Health Committee. (1988, December). *Nursing homes without walls program—a decade of quality care at home for New York's aged and disabled.* Albany, NY: New York State Senate.

Regan, J. J. (1990). *The aged client and the law.* New York: Columbia University Press.

Reuben, D. B., Silliman, R. A., & Traines, M. (1988). The aging driver: Medicine, policy and ethics. *Journal of the American Geriatrics Society, 36,* 1135–1142.

Rubenstein, L. Z., & Kaiser, F. E. (1989). *Home care service needs for the frail elderly population.* Report prepared for the Commonwealth Fund Commission on Elderly People Living Alone. Background Paper Series no. 18.

Sheehan, S. (1983, November 28). A reporter at large: Kate Quinton, part 2. *The New Yorker,* pp. 56, 104.

Snyder, M., Egan, E., & Burns, K. R. (1995, March/April). Efficacy of hand massage in decreasing agitation behaviors associated with care activities in persons with dementia. *Geriatric Nursing,* 60–63.

Solomon, D., Chairman. (1988). National Institutes of Health Consensus Development Conference Statement: Geriatric assessment methods for clinical decision making. *Journal of the American Geriatrics Society, 36,* 342–347.

Somers, A. R. (1995). Continuing care retirement community. In Maddox, G. L. (Ed.), *The encyclopedia of aging* (pp. 224–227). New York: Springer.

Sommers, T., & Shields, L. (1987). *Women take care.* Gainesville, FL: Triad.

Spector, W. D., Katz, S., Murphy, J. B., & Fulton, J. P. (1987). The hierarchical relationship between activities of daily living and instrumental activities of daily living. *Journal of Chronic Diseases, 40*(6), 481–489.

Strauss, P. J., Wolf, R., & Shilling, D. (1990). *Aging and the law.* Chicago: Commerce Clearing House.

Streib, G., Folts, E., & Hilker, M. (1984) *Old homes—New families: Shared living for the elderly.* New York: Columbia University Press.

Transportation Research Board. (1988). *Transportation in an aging society: Improving mobility and safety for older persons,* vol. 1. (Special Report 218). Washington, DC: National Research Council.

Tully, C. T., & Jacobson, S. (1994). The homeless elderly: America's forgotten population. *Journal of Gerontological Social Work, 22*(¾), 61–81.

U.S. Bipartisan Commission on Comprehensive Health Care (The Pepper Commission). (1990, March, 2). *Recommendations to the Congress.* Washington, DC: U.S. Government Printing Office.

U.S. Bureau of the Census (1996). 65+ in the United States. *Current Population Reports, Special Studies,* Series P-23, No. 190. Washington, DC: U.S. Government Printing Office.

U.S. Bureau of the Census (1996). Marital status and living arrangements: March 1994. *Current Popula-*tion *Reports,* Series P-20, No. 484. Washington, DC: U.S. Government Printing Office.

U.S. Senate Special Committee on Aging. (1971). *Mental health care and the elderly: Shortcomings in public policy.* Washington, DC: U.S. Government Printing Office.

U.S. Senate Special Committee on Aging. (1972). *Home health services in the United States.* Washington, DC: U.S. Government Printing Office.

U.S. Senate Special Committee on Aging. (1989). *Developments in aging: 1988* (Report 101–4, vol. 1). Washington, DC: U.S. Government Printing Office.

Weissert, W. G., Cready, C. M., & Pawelak, J. E. (1988). The past and future of home- and community-based long-term care. *The Milbank Quarterly, 66*(2), 309–369.

ENDNOTES

1. ADL disability rates are much "softer" measures than, for example, mortality rates, because of the different methods of measurement involved. However, ADL estimates can differ for good reasons and there is no "right" estimate. See Interagency Forum on Aging-Related Statistics. (1989, October). *Measuring the activities of daily living among the elderly: A guide to national surveys, final report.* Prepared by J. M. Wiener & R. J. Hanley, The Brookings Institution.

2. Data excludes older persons in institutions. See U.S. Bureau of the Census. (1996). Marital status and living arrangements: March, 1994. *Current Population Reports,* Series P-20, no. 484. Washington, DC: U.S. Government Printing Office.

3. National Center for Health Statistics, M. G. Kovar. (1986, May 9). Aging in the eighties: age 65 years and over and living alone, contacts with family, friends and neighbors. *Advance Data from Vital and Health Statistics.* No. 116, DHHS Pub. No. (PHS) 86–1250. Hyattsville, MD: Public Health Service.

4. *Ibid.*

5. *Ibid.*

6. Homelessness Information Exchange, National Coalition for the Homeless. (1994, September). *How many people are homeless in the U.S.?, 1994.* Available from the National Coalition for the Homeless. 1612 K St. NW, #1004, Washington, DC 20006.

7. Interagency Forum on Aging-Related Statistics. (1989, October). *Measuring the activities of daily living among the elderly: A guide to national surveys.* Prepared by J. M. Weiner, & R. J. Hanley. Washington, DC: The Brookings Institution, October.

8. Katz, S., Ford, A., Moskowitz, R. W., Jackson, B. A., & Joffe, M. W. (1963, September 21). Studies of illness in the aged. *Journal of the American Medical Association, 185*(12), 914–919.

9. Lawton, M. P., & Brody, E. (1969). Assessment of older people: Self-maintaining and instrumental activities of daily living. *Gerontologist, 9,* 179–186.

10. Stone, R., Cafferata, G. L., & Sangl, J. (1986). *Caregivers of the frail elderly: A national profile.* National Center for Health Services Research, Public Health Services, U.S. Department of Health and Human Services. Rockville, MD: National Center for Health Services Research.

11. Brody, E. M. (1985). Parent care as a normative stress. *The Gerontologist, 25,* 19–29.

12. Bianchi, S. M., & Spain, D. (1986). *American women in transition: The population of the United States in the 1980s.* A Census Monograph Series. New York: Russell Sage Foundation; Sommers, T., & Shields, L. (with contributing authors). (1987). *Women take care.* Gainesville: Triad Publishing; and Stone, R., Cafferata, G. L., & Sangl, J. (1987). Caregivers of the frail elderly: A national profile. *The Gerontologist, 27*(5), 616–626.

13. National Association of State Units on Aging. (1984, June). *A synthesis of issues and findings on primary care-givers: Support systems.* Report prepared by NASUA for the Office of Human

Development Services. Washington, DC: Department of Health and Human Services.

14. See Zarit, S., Reever, K., & Bach-Peterson, J. (1980). The burden interview. *The Gerontologist, 20*(6), 651; and Robinson, B. (1983). The caregiver strain questionnaire. *Journal of Gerontology, 38*(3), 334.

15. Lewis, M. L. (1989). *Economic perspectives on calculating the costs of women family members providing home eldercare.* Unpublished paper. New York: Mount Sinai Medical Center.

16. Weissert, W. G., Cready, C. M., & Pawelak, J. E. (1988). The past and future of home- and community-based long-term care. *The Milbank Quarterly, 66*(2), 309–369; and Wissert, W. G. (1985, Summer). The cost-effectiveness trap. *Generations,* 47–50.

17. Pannger, L. (1983, June). *The forgotten costs of informal long-term care.* Report contract no. HHS-100–80–0158. Washington, DC: Department of Health and Human Services.

18. See Rubenstein, L. Z., Wieland, G. D., English, P., Josephson, K., Sayre, J., & Abrass, I. B. (1984). The Sepulveda VA Geriatric Evaluation Unit: Data on four-year outcomes and predictors of improved patient outcomes. *Journal of the American Geriatrics Society, 32,* 503–512; and Rubenstein, L. Z., Josephson, K., Wieland, G. D., English, P., Sayre, J., & Kane, R. L. (1984). Effectiveness of a geriatric evaluation unit. *New England Journal of Medicine, 311,* 1664–1670.

19. Greene, R. R. (1990). Case management: An arena for social work practice. In Vourlekis, B., & Greene, R. (Eds.), *Social case management.* New York: Aldine de Gryter.

20. *Ibid.*

21. See *Long-term care for the 80's: Channeling demonstrations and other initiatives.* Hearing before the Subcommittee on Health and Long-Term Care of the Select Committee on Aging. U.S. House of Representatives. 96th Congress, February 27, 1980. Committee Publication No. 96–234.

22. Aging Network Services is located at 4400 East West Highway, Suite 907, Bethesda, MD 20814, (301) 657-4329.

23. For referrals to private care coordinators, contact the National Association of Professional Geriatric Care Managers, 1604 N. Country Club Road, Tucson, AZ 85716, (602) 881-8008. The association will provide up to three referrals in your area over the phone or will send a list of local care coordinators upon request. Children of Aging Parents, 1609 Woodbourne Rd., Suite 302A, Levittown, PA 19057, (215) 945-6900, also provides referrals to private care coordinators, as well as information on nursing homes, assisted living facilities, and support groups.

24. Arne Querido's famous Amsterdam psychiatric emergency service sent teams to the homes of persons in crises. The San Francisco Geriatrics Screening Project and the Baltimore City Health Department Geriatric Evaluation Service are illustrative of the pioneering screening programs in the United States that stressed home visits.

25. Kane, R., Solomon, D., Beck, J., Keeler, E., & Kane, R. (1980). The future need for geriatric manpower in the United States. *New England Journal of Medicine, 302,*(24), 1327–1332.

26. See Committee on Leadership for Academic Geriatric Medicine. (1987). Report of the Institute of Medicine: Academic geriatrics for the year 2000, *Journal of the American Geriatrics Society, 35,* 773–791.

27. For information on home health-care agencies providing RN, LPN, and home health aide services, contact: The National Association of Home Care, (292) 547-7424, Visiting Nurse Associations of America, (303) 753-0218; Joint Commission on Accreditation of Healthcare Organizations, (708) 916-5600; or the American Association of Retired Persons, (202) 434-2277.

28. Greene, R. (1986). *Social work with the aged and their families.* Hawthorne, NY: Aldine de Gruyter.

29. National Association for Home Care. (1995). *Basic statistics about home care 1995.* Washington, DC: National Association for Home Care.

30. Ayers, R. E. (1990). The physical therapist's role in geriatric care. *Geriatrics, 45*(2), 83–84.

31. Kiemat, J. M. (1979). The use of life review activity with confused nursing home residents. *American Journal of Occupational Therapy, 33,* 306–310. For a general overview of occupational therapy, see Lewis, S. C. (1983). *Providing for the older adult: A gerontological handbook.* Thorofare, NJ: Charles B. Slack.

32. Clark, L. W. (1990, February). Specialists for the communicatively impaired. *Geriatrics, 45*(2), 72–75.

33. Smolkin, S., Stravrianos, M., & Burton, J. (1996, August 29). *Characteristics of food stamp households: Summer 1994.* Alexandria, VA: U.S. Department of Agriculture, Food and Consumer Service, Office of Analysis and Evaluation.

34. Fishman, P. (1990, February). A physician's guide to locating a qualified nutritionist. *Geriatrics, 45*(2), 61–65.

35. For information contact Family Service America, 700 West Lake Park Dr., Milwaukee, WI 53224.

36. Besdine, R. W. (1979). Accidental hypothermia: The body's energy crisis. *Geriatrics, 34,* 51–59; Butler, R. N. (1977, April 5). *Energy and aging: The impact of rising energy costs on older Americans.* Testimony before the U.S. Senate Special Committee on Aging; and U.S. Department of Health, Education and Welfare, National Institute on Aging. (1978). *A winter hazard for the old: Accidental hypothermia.* Pub. No. (NIH) 78–1646.

37. See Bustad, L. R. (1980). *Animals, aging and the aged.* Minneapolis: University of Minnesota Press. See also Schmall, V. L., & Pratt, C. (1985–1986). Elders and pets. *Generations, 10*(4), 44–45.

38. Cusak, O., & Smith, E. (1984). *Pets and the elderly.* Binghamton, NY: The Haworth Press.

39. Order from NCOA Publications, Department 5087, Washington, DC 20061-5087. (202) 479-1200.

40. Hamlet, E., & Read, S. (1990). Caregiver education and support group: A hospital based group experience. *Journal of Gerontological Social Work, 15*(½), 75–88. (Also provides a review of the literature on caregiver support and education.)

41. Light, E., & Lebowitz, B. (1989). *Alzheimer's disease treatment and family stress: Directions for research.* U.S. Department of Health and Human Services, National Institute of Mental Health. DHHS Publication No. (ADM) 89–1564.

42. Personal communication, Kazuo Hasegawa, Chairman, Department of Psychiatry, St. Marianna University, Kowasaki, Japan.

43. Maki, B. E., & Fernie, G. R. (1996). Accidents: falls. In Birren, J. E. (Ed.), *Encyclopedia of gerontology* (vol. 1, pp. 11–18). San Diego, CA: Academic Press.

44. National Center for Health Statistics. (1996). Advance report of final mortality statistics, 1993. *Monthly Vital Statistics Report, 44*(7), supplement. Hyattsville, MD: National Center for Health Statistics.

45. See Tideiksaar, Rein. (1988). *Falling in old age: Its prevention and treatment.* New York: Springer.

46. Stock, R. W. (1996, July 13). Reducing the risks for older drivers. *The New York Times,* C1, C10.

47. Reuben, D. B., Silliman, R. A., & Traines, M. (1988). The aging driver: Medicine, policy, and ethics. *Journal of American Geriatrics Society, 36,* 1135–1142.

48. To be eligible for registration as a therapeutic recreation specialist, it is necessary to be certified by the National Council for Therapeutic Recreation Certification, P.O. Box 479, Thiells, N.Y. 10984, (914) 947-4346.

49. See Flatton, K., Wilhite, B., & Reyes-Watson, E. (1987). *Recreation activities for the elderly.* New York: Springer.

50. Senior centers are sponsored by churches, synagogues, clubs, and nonprofit corporations. Financial support derives from private donations and from local, state, and federal governments.

51. Elderhostel publishes three catalogs: Summer, Fall–Winter, and Spring. Contact Elderhostel, National Office, 75 Federal St., 3rd Fl., Boston, MA 02110-1914. (617) 426-7788.

52. Cross, W., & Florio, C. (1978). *You are never too old to learn.* New York: Academy for Educational Development.

53. For further information on education programs for older persons, contact the AARP, 1909 K St., N.W., Washington, DC 20049, or the Institute of Retired Professionals, The New School, 66 W. 12th St., New York, NY 10011. For a free directory of accredited schools that offer home-study courses, write to the Distance Education and Training Council, 1601 18th St., N.W., Washington, DC 20009.

54. RSVP evolved out of the project SERVE. See Sainer, J. S., & Zander, M. L. (1971). *SERVE: Older volunteers in community service: A new role and a new resource.* New York: Community Service Society.

55. Butler, R. N. (1970). Toward practical ecumenism. *Bulletin of the American Protestant Hospital Association, 34,* 6–12. See also (1970, July). Hospital Progress. *Journal of the Catholic Hospital Association.*

56. An early effort at the coordination of 11 separately sponsored church and community programs serving over 1,300 older recipients is described by McLaughlin, C. B. (1973). Meals on Wheels reach Baltimore's elderly. *Food and Nutrition, 3,* 204.

57. American Association of Homes and Services for the Aging, Public Affairs. (1996). *AAHSA assisted living: Background.* Washington, DC: American Association of Homes and Services for the Aging.

58. Clemmer, E. (1995, February). Assisted living and its implications for long-term care. *AARP Public Policy Institute Issue Brief,* no. 20. Washington DC: American Association of Retired Persons.

59. *Ibid.*

60. Chalfie, D. (1995). *The real Golden Girls: The prevalence and policy treatment of midlife and older people living in nontraditional households.* Washington, DC: American Association of Retired Persons, Women's Initiative.

61. The National Shared Housing Resource Network (NSHRN), 321 East 25th St., Baltimore, MD 21218. For more information contact Alternative Living for Aging (ALA), 937 North Fairfax, West Hollywood, CA 90046, which operates five Cooperative Apartment Communities for older people and offers a free roommate matching service.

62. American Association of Homes and Services for the Aging, Public Affairs. (1996). *Continuing care retirement communities: Background.* Washington, DC: American Association of Homes and Services for the Aging.

63. Somers, A. R. (1995). Continuing care retirement community. In Maddox, G. L. (Ed.), *The Encyclopedia of aging* (pp. 224–227). New York: Springer.

64. American Association of Homes and Services for the Aging, Public Affairs. (1996). *Continuing care retirement communities: Background.* Washington, DC: American Association of Homes and Services for the Aging.

65. Light, E., Lebowitz, B. D., & Bailey, F. (1986). CMHCs and elderly services: An analysis of direct and indirect services and service delivery sites. *Community Mental Health Journal, 22,* 294–302.

66. "The area of mental health services represents one of the most glaring examples of discrimination on the basis of age," according to the U.S. Commission on Civil Rights. (1979). *The age discrimination study.* Washington, DC: U.S. Government Printing Office, p. 6.

67. Matlack, D. R. (1975). The case for geriatric day hospitals. *The Gerontologist, 15,* 109–113.

68. Kubie, S. H., & Landau, G. (1953). *Group work with the aged.* New York: International Universities Press.

69. Also see Helen MacLean, (1987). *Caring for your parents: A source book of options and solutions for both generations.* New York: Doubleday.

70. 1962 Public Welfare Amendment to the Social Security Act. Among pioneering books on protective services is that of Lehmann, V., & Mathiasen, G. (Eds.). (1963). *Guardianship and protective services for older people.* Albany, NY: National Council on Aging Press. More recent references include Regan, J. J. (1990). *The aged client and the law.* New York: Columbia Universities Press; and Strauss, P. J., Wolf, R., & Shilling, D. (1990). *Aging and the law.* Chicago: Commerce Clearing House.

71. In a 1982 national study of protective services, Burr discovered large differences among states in policies, costs, program emphases, methods, procedures, and service standards. See Burr, J. J. (1982). *Protective services for adults.* DHHS Publication No. (OHDS) 82–20505. Washington, DC: U.S. Administration on Aging, Office of Human Development Services.

72. Blenkner, M., Bloom, M., Wasser, E., & Nielsen, M. (1971). Protective services for old people: Findings from the Benjamin Rose Institute study. *Social Casework, 52,* 483–522.

73. Goldfarb, A. I. (1962). Prevalence of psychiatric disorders in metropolitan old age and nursing homes. *Journal American Geriatric Society, 10,* 78–84. See also U.S. Department of Health, Education and Welfare, National Center for Health Statistics. (1965). *Characteristics of residents in institutions for the aged and chronically ill, United States, April-June 1963.* Pub. No. (PHS) 100, Series 12, No. 2. Washington, DC: U.S. Government Printing Office.

74. New York State Department of Mental Hygiene, Mental Health Research Unit. (1960). *A mental health survey of older people.* Albany, NY: New York State Hospital Press.

75. Blenkner et al., pp. 483–522.

76. Zhorowsky, E. (1985). Developments in protective services: A challenge for social workers. *Journal of Gerontological Social Work, 8*(¾), 71–83.

77. Minneapolis Age and Opportunity Center, Inc. (MAO), 1801 Nicollet Ave., Minneapolis, MN 55403. See also One city's controversial plan to give seniors a fair shake on health, *American Medical News,* September 9, 1974.

78. Mercer Meidinger Hansen, W. M. (1989, July). Eldercare. *The Bulletin,* No. 151.

79. Mercer Meidinger Hansen, W. M. *Long term care: The newest employee benefit.* 1211 Avenue of the Americas, New York, NY 10036.

80. New York Business Group on Health. (1989, February). *Assisting employee caregivers: Employers' "eldercare" programs.* 622 Third Avenue, 34th Floor, New York, NY 10017-6763.

81. The U.S. Bipartisan Commission on Comprehensive Health Care (The Pepper Commission). (1990, March 2). *Recommendations to the Congress.* Washington, DC: U.S. Government Printing Office.

CHAPTER 11

PROPER INSTITUTIONAL CARE

We discuss institutional care of all sorts in this chapter, but our discussion is dominated by the overriding issue of nursing home care. Nursing home use has nearly doubled since the introduction of Medicare and Medicaid in 1966. Although only approximately 5% of the older population resides in nursing homes at any given time, the risk of institutionalization increases with age. The percentage of the population who were in nursing homes in 1990 was 6% for those aged 75 to 84 and 24% for those aged 85 and older. The nursing home population, over 1.5 million in 1995, is expected to continue to grow. However, this growth will be less than previously estimated due primarily to the boom in home health care services and utilization.

Our definition of *institutional care* includes any care (medical, nursing, psychiatric, or social) given to older people *not* residing in their own homes or the homes of family and friends. Although efforts should be directed toward helping the mentally or physically ill older person remain independent and in his or her own home, there are many situations in which it is simply not possible or advisable to do so. If active outpatient treatment fails, short- or long-term institutional care is required. Present means of financing care, the inadequacy of many facilities and services, and deficiencies in number and training of personnel

are among the obstacles to the provision of the spectrum of services and facilities needed to dovetail with the wide range of psychiatric, nursing, medical, and social needs of older people. Once again, as in other chapters, we describe what is currently available, balancing this against what would be ideal. Emergency shelter, acute and chronic hospitalization (both medical and psychiatric), nursing homes, homes for the aged, and residential (for example, foster care) homes are the basic forms of institutional care utilized by the older population. We examine what each of these has to offer, both in kind and in quality of service.

THE DECISION TO INSTITUTIONALIZE AN OLDER PERSON

The unfavorable reputation of U.S. institutions for the elderly combines with the natural reluctance of older people to leave their homes and communities; and the result is active or passive (and often justifiable) resistance to admission. As an extreme example, one older woman came to our attention because she kept an arsenal of guns at home to use on herself or others if someone came to take her to a nursing home or psychiatric hospital. Increased morbidity, disorientation, and mortality have been associated with the movement of people to institutions, since the aged are particularly vulnerable to the stress of sudden change. Thus the decision to institutionalize must be made conservatively and with care to fully prepare and cushion the individual against the inevitable shock.[1]

THE DIFFERENT KINDS OF SHORT- AND LONG-TERM INSTITUTIONAL CARE

Emergency Care and Emergency Shelter

Many older people remain in their homes until an acute psychiatric or medical crisis occurs, necessitating emergency care. Emergency rooms of hospitals have become the primary mode of providing initial care; this means, of course, that the patient must transport him- or herself, be transported by another person, or must obtain the services of an ambulance. Fire departments, police, and rescue squads may provide ambulance services, depending on the particular community, with fire departments the most commonly involved. Psychiatric emergencies are regulated differently from locale to locale, and in a number of communities only the police can legally transport such a patient.

Ambulance service staffs can range from untrained volunteers to paramedics with modern, mobile intensive care units (MICU), which transmit physiological data from the field to the hospital through telemetry. Financing of emergency transport can be a problem; for example, Medicare does not cover ambulance services.

Emergency medicine or "emergentology" is now a medical specialty and is undergoing reform. Improvements in reduction of disabilities in all age groups have resulted. But age prejudice still exists, even in emergency rooms, and private and public hospitals frequently respond less favorably to older persons than they do to younger persons. Medical and psychiatric decisions about older persons are still too often made by avoidance, by taking minimal responsibility, and by failing to consult with the patient, his or her family, and often the family doctor. Some voluntary hospitals

continue the ethically dubious practice of dropping the Medicare patient on the doorsteps of the municipal hospital.

Physicians, police, judges, and other community agents as well as families are frequently at a loss to know where to take an older person for emergency care, especially if they need a comprehensive examination or cannot be returned to their homes. Although this does not yet exist in hospitals, emergency shelter admission of the elderly should be made available in all hospitals— to allow, at the very least, for a period of decision making. Not only would the brief admission be useful to effect a proper workup, but also to begin therapy. Changes could be seen that might alter the original diagnostic impression and individual treatment program. For crisis intervention in all age groups, the availability of hospitalization for several days in a unit attached to the emergency room of the hospital would be a step forward in evolving comprehensive social, medical, nursing, and psychiatric care in general hospitals. Complete diagnostic evaluations and a therapeutic trial ideally should precede any admission to long-term mental hospitals or nursing home facilities. This would require a team approach with medical, nursing, mental health, and social evaluations.

The Department of Geriatrics at the Mount Sinai School of Medicine in New York City has developed a 16-bed geriatric evaluation and treatment unit that provides acute geriatric inpatient hospital care. It includes a comprehensive multidisciplinary health care assessment by geriatricians, nurses, psychiatrists, geriatric social workers, and consulting geriatric specialists in neurology, nutrition, pharmacology, psychology, rehabilitation, and ethics. Meetings and case conferences are held with family caregivers. The aim of the geriatric unit is to restore function and preserve a reasonable quality of life whenever possible.

Psychiatric Hospitalization

Acute Psychiatric Hospitalization. The term *acute psychiatric hospitalization* usually applies to hospital stays lasting from a few days to some weeks, during which diagnosis and treatment take place simultaneously. Transient confusional states (reversible brain syndromes) and functional disorders can respond to acute care, sometimes with dramatically positive results.

Psychiatric units in profit-making or in voluntary general hospitals usually provide short-term psychiatric care independent of age; in other words, when an older person is able to pay, he or she is more likely to receive the same degree of care as that given to younger people. If it is believed (either correctly or mistakenly) that the person is suffering from dementia, he or she will at least receive decent care until transfer elsewhere is arranged. Private psychiatric hospitals also do effective work in the acute hospitalization of older persons. In addition, the in-service units of community mental health centers (usually public hospitals), as well as municipal, county, and state hospitals, provide this service with varying degrees of quality. Pre-admission screening units, whether in the community (see Chapter 10) or in general or state psychiatric hospitals, should be alert to the disorders that can respond to acute hospitalization.

During acute hospitalization it is important to maintain orientation—through unrestricted visiting hours, personal belongings, and family liaison. Home pressures, unattended pets and plants, and mail (especially Social Security, pension, and Supplemental Security Income checks) may need attention from hospital social service workers or community agencies that provide home-care services.

Through the Diagnostic Related Groups system (DRGs), created by the 1982 Tax Equity and Fiscal Responsibility Act, a patient's diagnosis determines the fixed number of days a hospital will be reimbursed for the patient's stay. Although DRGs were initially developed for psychiatry, patients admitted to psychiatric hospitals and psychiatric units of general hospitals have been exempt from DRGs. However, any other setting that admits a psychiatric patient for whatever reason (e.g., no psychiatric hospital/unit in the area) must apply for patients to be exempt. If the hospital fails to do so, the patients are then subject to DRG rules.

It is important to note that 50% of patients discharged with a psychiatric diagnosis are affected by DRGs; in other words, these patients were in settings other than psychiatric hospitals or general hospitals with psychiatric units—settings that did not apply for DRG exemption.

Chronic Psychiatric Hospitalization. Schizophrenia and organic brain damage are the major reasons for more permanent psychiatric hospitalization. Persons with chronic physical conditions (for example, stroke victims) may be admitted to nursing homes and, at times, to chronic disease and geriatric hospitals, even though many such persons have accompanying or previously existing mental problems.

Of the 83,502 residents of state and county mental hospitals in 1992, 12,784 (15.3%) were age 65 and over. In addition, 2,832 residents of private mental hospitals and 2,655 residents in psychiatric units of Veterans Administration (VA) hospitals were 65 and over. Males of all ages outnumber females of all ages in mental hospitals overall. The sex ratio is about equal in private mental hospitals and 163 males to 100 females in state and county hospitals. (Sex ratios for those over 65 were not readily available.) The VA hospital population is almost exclusively male.

The Veterans Health Administration (VHA) in the Department of Veterans Affairs provides medical and health services to a predominately male population that includes the oldest veterans, those who served in World Wars I and II and the Korean Conflict. In recent years special programs have been developed for the increasing female veteran population, including the elderly. There are 173 VA medical centers, 37 VA domiciliaries (31 of which have special programs for homeless veterans), 131 VA nursing homes, and 399 outpatient clinics. Recently, the VHA has been reorganized into 22 Veterans Integrated Service Networks (VISNs). Each VISN includes the full range of inpatient, outpatient, and extended care services. For many years, veterans had de facto unrestricted access to VA medical care. In an effort to contain costs, that access has been curtailed by eligibility requirements such as financial means testing for veterans who do not have service-related disabilities, or are not former POWs (prisoners of war), or World War I pension recipients. In 1996, major eligibility reform for VA services was authorized by Congress.[2]

VA's interest in providing continuous care for older veterans began in the 1970s. Because of the aging of World War II and Korean Conflict veterans, approximately two out of every three males over age 65 in the United States will be veterans by the year 2000. Currently the 65 and older veteran population (8.5 million) comprises over one-third of the total veteran population (26.3 million). Thus, most of the nation's older men will be eligible for various veterans' benefits.[3]

By 1994, the VA was providing comprehensive geriatric and management services in 133 of its facilities. That same year the VA was providing nursing home care for 34,000 veterans on a daily basis; 27% were in over 3,000 community nursing homes under contract with the VA, 38% were in the VA's own nursing homes, and 35% were in state veterans nursing homes. Another 17,000 veterans received services on any given day in VA and State veteran domiciliaries, adult day care centers, hospices, and respite programs, or were provided home-based primary care, and homemaker/home health aide services. An additional 10,000 veterans were in community residential care arranged by the VA. In 1995, the VHA's Under Secretary for Health, Kenneth Kizer, M.D., published the "Vision for Change," which was the blueprint for the major reorganization and culture change occurring in the VA. In restating the mission of the VA, Dr. Kizer identified a number of special emphasis programs that would continue to be supported in the "new" VA. These programs include VA's Geriatric Research, Education, and Clinical Centers (GRECCs), Geriatric Evaluation and Management (GEM) programs, home-based primary care, community-based long-term care, and nursing home care, as well as special mental health and rehabilitation programs. Thus the VA's commitment to the care of older veterans that started in the 1970s continues as a major strength of the system.[4]

When Is Psychiatric Hospitalization Indicated?
The need for medical care in an institution is fairly apparent and is based on a physician's recommendation. However, it has not been possible to construct strict criteria for voluntary admission and involuntary commitment to state and private psychiatric hospitals; the criteria for nursing homes and homes for the aged are even more nebulous and indefinite.

Earlier, Lowenthal identified five factors that still influence the decision to place older, mentally ill persons in a hospital—some of which are relevant also for other chronic care facilities.[5]

1. Disturbances in thinking and feeling, such as delusions or depressions
2. Physical illness
3. Potentially harmful behavior such as confusion or unmanageability
4. Harmful behavior such as actual violence to others or refusing necessary medical care
5. Environmental factors such as the unavailability or incapacity of a responsible person to care for the patient

It is immediately clear that adequate social supports such as home-care services could prevent the institutionalization of a portion of the older persons described here. Medical hospitalization would be more appropriate for others, and a differentiation should be made between long-term and short-term or intermittent needs for care. The following outline illustrates an effort to build criteria for psychiatric hospitalization of older persons.[6]

1. Clearly appropriate for admission to a psychiatric unit in a general hospital or a psychiatric hospital itself:
   - Those with functional psychoses and without significant physical illness or disability, for whom outpatient treatment is not feasible. For example: patients receiving psy-

chiatric treatment in the community who require brief periods of protection from the consequences of their behavior during episodes of acute disturbance or depression (for example, suicidal or homicidal tendencies, spending sprees, refusal to eat); or chronically mentally ill patients who need protection and management, as well as treatment, during prolonged periods of disruptive or disorganized behavior and who require regular and frequent attendance of a physician

- Alcoholics without significant physical illness or disability who, following detoxification, need a period of inpatient treatment for their alcoholism
- Those with severe organic brain disorders whose usual behavior, intractable to medication, is too disturbing to be managed at home or in a nursing home or home for the aged. For example, the physically aggressive patient, the fire setter, the eloper, or the person otherwise dangerous to himself or others when physically able to carry out his potentially destructive behavior

2. Clearly inappropriate for admission
- Those with delirium, symptomatic of a grave physical illness, requiring urgent admission to a general hospital
- Those who are moribund or comatose
- Those with major medical problems and minor mental symptoms. For example, patients who become mildly confused or disturbed as a result of or in conjunction with recent head injury, cardiovascular disease, diabetes, metabolic disturbance, terminal malignancy, and so on (Psychiatric consultation might be utilized, if required, rather than psychiatric hospital admission.)
- Those with inconsequential lapses of memory and mild disorientation as a result of organic brain disorders, who are more effectively treated or managed in their own homes or, if necessary, in a foster home, a home for the aged, and so on (A state psychiatric hospital has little to offer and, in

view of the large wards in most state hospitals, may aggravate the patient's confusion.)
- Those who need only adequate living accommodations, with economic or other social support services

As a footnote to the preceding discussion, it is important to remember that self-destructive or suicidal behavior in older persons may be a slow process associated with prolonged and intense grief, loneliness, and progressive organic disease and may manifest itself in malnutrition, failure to take medicine, and other forms of deteriorating self-care.

Advisability of Voluntary Admission. Wherever possible, the older person—like a person of any age—should participate fully in all decisions regarding him- or herself, including those of institutionalization. The family, of course, should also be closely involved. Making the decision to admit a person to a nursing home, a home for the aged, or a hospital can be extremely difficult, since all these facilities are so often disliked and feared by both older persons and their families.

Moving Trauma. The vulnerability of the aged to death or illness as a result of changing their living arrangements ("transfer mortality") is a serious cause for concern. In a study of 639 elderly, one-half of whom had died, had become physically impaired, or had psychologically deteriorated one year after they had moved, Lieberman and Tobin found that moving is traumatic, regardless of whether the move is to a better or to a worse environment.[7] The older persons in their study who left a rigid, institutionalized setting for a less structured one did not fare substantially better than those who did just the opposite. Shanas's description some 30 years ago of reaction to being moved is still hauntingly true for many:

> Almost all older people view the move to a home for the aged, or to a nursing home with fear and hostility. . . . All old people—without exception—believe that the move to an institution is the prelude to death. . . . [The old person] sees the move to an institution as a decisive change in living

arrangements, the last change he will experience before he dies. . . . Finally, no matter what the extenuating circumstances, the older person who has children interprets the move to an institution as rejection by his children.[8]

Lieberman's early studies showed that a year or more of preparation may be necessary to increase survival during the first six months in an institution, even when the institution is adequate.[9]

Considerable change should be made regarding the concept of institutional care, preparation of older people and their families, and length of stay for residents in such a facility. Many people could be admitted much later if they were given more support at home. In addition, there should always be an expectation and actual possibility of discharge and return home after response to treatment and changes in the person's condition and circumstances.

Involuntary Commitment to State and Private Psychiatric Facilities.   Admission to a psychiatric institution should ideally be voluntary, but some circumstances may require commitment against a person's wishes. Extreme civil libertarians urge that legal involuntary commitment to psychiatric hospitals be done away with (but, strangely, have not commented on the de facto assignment of older people into nursing homes and related facilities—with few of the protections afforded in connection with admission to psychiatric hospitals). Others insist that people who are a danger to themselves or a threat to others need the protection of commitment to an appropriate institution. In fact, for a time, a trend arose which made these the only legal grounds for involuntary commitment. Legal procedures are currently not uniform from state to state, but in general the legal justification for action is (1) imminent physical danger to self, (2) imminent physical danger to others, or (3) a clear and present need of immediate care or treatment.

During the 1960s and 1970s, lawyers had been effective in bringing about stringent limitations on involuntary commitment of the mentally ill. This has resulted in unforeseen consequences. For example, the homeless mentally ill cannot be treated against their wishes unless they are suicidal or represent a danger to others. Psychiatrists and others have begun to press for legislation to loosen up the commitment criteria. Laws have been passed that aim at preventing a worsening of existent mental illness and reducing the physical harm that mental deterioration might bring. These changes are in keeping with a model law devised by the American Psychiatric Association in 1983, drafted under the strong influence of Allen Stone, a psychiatrist and lawyer at Harvard University.

There has also been an effort to create an "outpatient commitment" procedure whereby persons would be required to seek treatment during the day but could go home at night. Although this may fulfill the concept of the "least restrictive alternative" to psychiatric hospitalization, the outpatient commitment is not commonly used at present.

There are those, including lawyers and psychiatrists, who contend that it is possible to maintain both civil liberties and treatment. A special study group of the American Bar Association issued 50 specific recommendations in 1986 to accomplish both.

Doctors are the only practitioners who are allowed to perform commitment proceedings. Since a large percentage of the U.S. population has no access to a psychiatrist, the family physician is, by default, pressed into service in times of psychiatric emergency. Many doctors fear signing commitment papers because of possible malpractice suits. The following are some safeguards that can protect both the older person and his or her doctor.

1. Know and observe laws regarding involuntary commitment. Get to know the local judge or court clerk available for assistance and advice. Examine the patient within the legal time limit before signing papers.

2. Avoid shortcuts in examination (see discussion of the legal examination in Chapter 9). If the patient is on sedatives, give him or her time to recover from the medication's effects before being examined. If the person is comatose, decide if this is medically or psychiatrically caused. If psychiatric, re-examine at a later time, as the condition may clear up.

3. Remember that taking the word of relatives is always risky.

4. Avoid personal conflict of interest. The physician should have no personal stake in the outcome of a psychiatric examination, especially in the form of obligations, favors, or promises that involve others, including relatives.

5. Avoid use of force (for example, injections, electroconvulsive treatment).

6. Avoid illegal transportation. Most states rule that only a police officer can transport someone against his or her will. In some jurisdictions where liability insurance is lacking or inadequate, the police themselves fear legal action.

7. Avoid institutions that are unfamiliar. Get to know all local facilities.

8. Avoid acting alone when consultation is available.

The informal, nonprotesting admission or emergency admission procedure is helpful when the person is too confused to comprehend what is happening.

Deinstitutionalization. State and county mental hospitals have been the center of long-standing controversy. When the American social reformer Dorothea Lynde Dix (1802–1887) began her efforts, there were practically no hospitals for the mentally ill. The first American asylum for mental patients was established in Williamsburg, Virginia, in 1773, and it was the only facility of its kind for 50 years. Toward the mid-nineteenth century, the belief grew that the mentally and emotionally ill could be helped and that the state owed them help. Dix pressed the idea of hospital care. A state-by-state system of hospitals was established, which now has come increasingly under criticism because of the quality of care and the basic concepts of treatment that it represents. Recent years have seen vigorous efforts to move patients out of these facilities. With cries of "bring the patient back to the community," states rushed headlong into a course of dismantling the mental hospital system before establishing valid alternatives.

Since 1940, even before the introduction of tranquilizing drugs, mental hospital populations began a downward slope as attempts were made to shorten hospital stays. In the 1950s and 1960s, lower rates of admission began to be encouraged, along with shorter hospitalizations. From the 1960s on, the emphasis was on transferring the older patients out of hospitals wholesale. This was officially called "deinstitutionalization." Unofficially it was known as "dumping." The reason often given was that it was "better" for people; but the real impetus was a fiscal policy in which the states could save money by shifting costs of care to the Federal Supplementary Income (SSI) program and Medicaid. The controversial 1972 legislation regarding "intermediate care facilities" led to further transferring of older mental patients. As the saying goes, "The patient goes where the money flows."

In the meantime, in the 37-year period from 1955 to 1992 the population of state and county mental hospitals dropped from 600,000 to about 80,000 patients. In addition, length of stay became much shorter, usually less than 30 days. As a consequence, an individual is more likely to have a series of short stays rather than one long one. Admission rates for the elderly have a special character. Although the elderly currently make up about 16% of the total mental hospital inpatient population, the rate of new admissions is very low. For example, only 8.7% of all admissions in 1986 were over age 65. And because of these low admissions, the elderly patients are highly selected for exhibiting severe psychiatric symptoms. As a consequence of this selection, few elderly ever leave, largely because their behavior problems are so severe that management outside a hospital would be difficult.

Older patients were increasingly pushed from already inadequate mental institutions into other inadequate custodial facilities, known euphemistically as "the community." The result has been growing numbers of former state and county hospital patients in difficulty in the community, including a proportion who are among the homeless. According to a 1986 review of the literature, the homeless fall into four overlapping categories: (1) street people; (2) people with chronic alcoholism; (3) people with chronic mental illness; and (4) situationally homeless people.[10] The chronically mentally ill are estimated to be 20 to 30% of the homeless in large cities such as New York, Chicago, and others.

Another major effect of deinstitutionalization has been the transfer of many elderly from mental hospitals to nursing homes. Studies indicate that about 40% of the elderly with chronic mental illness who were deinstitutionalized were eventually reinstitutionalized into nursing homes.[11] Of all current nursing home residents, 8 to 10% were previously patients in state mental hospitals or long-term-care hospitals. Consequently, nursing homes have become the major location for the care of the chronically mentally ill elderly, and perhaps up to 88% of nursing home residents have diagnosable mental conditions. Many have serious behavioral problems. The most common conditions are Alzheimer's disease or multi-infarct dementia, and chronic or reactive depressions, with behavioral patterns that include confusion, depression, wandering, disorientation, agitation, withdrawal, lethargy, frustration, stress reaction, dependency, apathy, guilt, irritability, rise and fall of self-esteem, persistent talk of a wish to die, and paranoid delusions.

The 1980 Mental Health Systems Act (see Chapter 10) was one effort to help overcome some of the negative consequences of deinstitutionalization of mental patients and enable more of such persons to live in the community. Unfortunately, it was never funded, and responsibility for care was given over to the states through the mechanism of block grants.

In a new development, a federal law (an amendment to federal budget legislation of 1987) that took effect in January 1989 required that mentally ill and retarded persons in nursing homes who require active treatment be transferred to settings such as community-based centers like halfway houses and group homes. The object of the legislation was to remove mentally ill individuals from nursing homes unless they had Alzheimer's disease or required round-the-clock nonpsychiatric nursing care.

Nursing homes that did not transfer residents into alternative care settings when needed were faced with cutoffs of all payments from Medicare and Medicaid. States were to be forced to provide services in other settings. Critics of the law questioned whether all of the states would be able to afford such facilities and programs. Many worried that the chronically mentally ill would be forced back into state hospitals or into boarding homes. A number of states filed suits to delay or modify implementation of the law and the outcomes are pending.

Foster Care, Personal Care Homes, and Boarding Care

Foster care originated as foster parent programs for children; efforts to encourage families to take in older people who are unrelated to them have never been very successful. Foster care has therefore become a euphemism and really describes, in many areas, an underfinanced, unregulated, unprofessional series of homes operated for profit. Since states have sought to reduce state mental hospital rolls, many older people—usually long-term and predominately schizophrenic patients—have been transferred, often indiscriminately, into foster care, intermediate care, and other so-called nursing homes, as well as boarding homes of various types. Finding locations for community residential facilities is difficult because of state and local zoning legislation and regulations. Often such facilities are forced into high-density, commercial, transient, and low-income areas.

Personal care homes are another variation on the theme of small group homes for the elderly. They are found in different areas of the country and their definitions and regulations differ from area to area.

The passive, non-troublemaking elderly are most likely to be chosen for these residences, since foster care and personal care homes will take only tractable persons who have minimal nursing needs. The approximately 68,000 board-and-care facilities (also called *rest homes, shelter care facilities, domiciliaries,* and *adult congregate care facilities*) in the United States provide over one million elderly, retarded, or mentally handicapped residents with shelter, food, and modest help in day-to-day living.[12] Facilities range in size from two or three residents to several hundred. The average payment through Supplemental Security Income to such homes is hardly enough to provide decent food and the basic amenities, let alone medical, nursing, psychiatric, and social care.

Boarding homes and foster care homes are often not covered by safety codes because they fall into a residential rather than an institutional category. Safety and fire inspections are notoriously negligent. No official government data exist as to how many licensed board-and-care homes are substandard nor how many people live in them. According to a General Accounting Office report, a 1987 industry survey identified about 563,000 board-and-care beds in 41,000 licensed homes serving the elderly, the mentally ill, and the retarded. It is clear that many substandard nursing homes have converted into board-and-care homes, bringing their substandard conditions with them. States regulate these homes, and in many states licensing and regulating are haphazard. Although federal laws have been enacted asking states to certify that those facilities with numerous welfare residents meet certain standards, rigorous state inspections, which would help guarantee the effectiveness of such laws, are lacking.

Nursing Homes

Nursing homes fall into three classes: proprietary or commercial nursing homes, voluntary nonprofit nursing homes (frequently called homes for the aging), and government facilities. Most of the some 16,700 nursing homes, almost 70%, are commercial, while only about 1,400 (8.2%) are government facilities. The remainder are voluntary, nonprofit homes. Because of general confusion over the term *nursing home,* we shall use it here to refer to the commercial homes. The next section, "Voluntary Nonprofit Homes for the Aging," will cover the nonprofit nursing homes.

As of 1995, approximately 1.5 million older people lived in nursing homes in the United States, and these homes have received considerable adverse attention from legislators, the press, and the general public. We wish to emphasize that there are a number of fine commercial or proprietary nursing homes that give good care to older persons, and we would hope to encourage and support their efforts. However, a significant number of homes have major deficiencies, including sanitation and fire safety problems. We will be pointing out a number of such problems in order to present the reader with a picture of what remains to be accomplished in upgrading patient care. We also provide a brief description of some of the reasons why nursing homes are commercial.

Categories of Nursing Homes. Commercial nursing homes are, of course, available to people who can afford to pay for their own care. However, because costs of care have risen so precipitously to over $30,000 per year on the national average, a number of financing mechanisms have been created to assist the majority of people who could not otherwise afford care. Many problems continue to exist;[13] for example, middle-income people may have too much income to be eligible for assistance but not enough to pay for care by themselves.

From 1965 to 1989 there were two major types of long-term care institutions for the aged that were subsidized by the federal government through Medicare and Medicaid (Titles 18 and 19, respectively, of the Social Security Act). These were known as skilled nursing facilities (SNF) and intermediate care facilities (ICF). These categories were often referred to as *levels of care.* Entire sets of standards and reimbursement systems were based on these levels of care. *Skilled nursing care* referred to those services that must be performed under the supervision of professional or registered nurses. *Intermediate care* was "more than room and board, but less than skilled nursing." These terms were very unclear to the public as well as to health professionals, Congress, and the press. There is a tendency to use the term *nursing home* to cover everything described here. The degree of confusion involved in applying the definitions of skilled nursing and intermediate care can be observed in reviewing the percentages of patients classified into the two levels in different states. In New York state, approximately 80% of patients were in skilled nursing, while in New Mexico and Iowa only 15% were classified in this category. Because reimbursement for skilled nursing care was higher than for intermediate care, some states simply transformed (often without much change) ICFs into questionable SNFs. Another problem was the tendency of some nursing home operators to collude with doctors to have most people designated as SNF clients.

Originally SNFs themselves were divided into two categories, (ECFs) extended care facilities (Medicare) and (SNFs) skilled nursing care facilities (Medicaid). The 1972 Social Security Amendments created a single definition and set of standards for ECFs and SNFs; thus the category, skilled nursing facility, was introduced.

A major change in these classifications occurred in amendments to the Social Security Act in 1987 as part of the Omnibus Budget Reconciliation Act (OBRA) of 1987 (Public Law 100–203). The law mandated that the federal nursing home payment/reimbursement programs would offer only one level of facility, titled a nursing facility. Numerous states have obtained waivers from HCFA to support other types of institutional and home-based services for Medicaid recipients.

Number of Nursing Home Beds Available. There were approximately 16,000 nursing homes certified by Medicare and/or Medicaid, with almost 1.8 million beds, in 1995.[14] In addition, there were perhaps one thousand or more uncertified facilities.

Financing of Nursing Homes. In discussing nursing home care, it is important to clarify a few points about the commercial nursing home industry. The United States is one of the few countries in the world where care of sick older persons has become big business, run primarily for commercial gain. The number of nursing homes has proliferated since 1965.

As mentioned earlier, the nursing home industry consists of approximately 16,700 homes with almost 1.8 million beds. (Note: There are differing counts of the number of nursing homes.) About 70% of the homes are profit-making, some owned by large chains with publicly sold stock. Others have nonprofit sponsors such as churches and community organizations. A total of over $72 billion was spent on nursing home care in 1994. Medicaid paid over 47% of all nursing home care; Medicare paid 8.2%; and private funding, mainly out-of-pocket spending, amounted to 42.1% of the total nursing home bill. For 1995 of 13,122 Medicare certified facilities, 27% were nonprofit, 67% were proprietary, and 6% were government controlled.[15]

There are now more than twice the number of nursing homes than existed in 1960. This growth began partly in response to the increasing demand for beds as the aging population increased and was accelerated by the passage of Medicare and Medicaid. Guaranteed payments to nursing homes convinced investors that it was a no-lose proposition. By 1969, Wall Street considered nursing homes a glamour industry. Investments came from real estate developers, the insurance industry, used-car businesses, and others outside the health field. Even physicians, despite obvious conflict of interests, invest in and own nursing homes.

According to the National Center for Health Statistics, slightly over one-half of the United States' nearly 1.8 million nursing home beds are controlled by profit-making corporate chains that operate five or more homes each. The top 20 chains run one-third of the industry and are buying out more and more of the smaller owners. The major reasons for this phenomenon are the following:

1. With inflation and a squeeze in healthcare dollars, chains can outdo small owners by buying in volume, centralizing accounting, and sharing specialists' services. As one executive said, "We can McDonaldize."

2. Chains can buy the sophisticated management necessary to streamline compliance with federal, state, and local standards that often overlap. Small operators are swamped by the paperwork. The chains hire specialists to handle it.

3. Many large firms look at nursing homes as a real estate investment.

4. Corporations can write off a failing or foundering nursing home as a tax loss.

5. There is money to be made (but by 1987 there were less profits and even losses in the industry).

It should also be mentioned that chains own more than half of the nation's private psychiatric hospitals.

Conditions in Nursing Homes. There are, as we have said, some excellent homes in which emphasis is on meeting patients' needs in every way possible within financial limits. But many homes are cheerless and depressing. Others are stylized, motellike, and antiseptic—patients sit in numb silence with dejected faces or pace endlessly down hallways. According to a 1996 report by the U.S. Department of Health and Human Services, about one quarter of all nursing homes (commercial and noncommercial) that received Medicare and Medicaid funds had deficiencies in storing or serving food under sanitary conditions. About one quarter did not conduct comprehensive assessments of residents or develop comprehensive care plans. Almost one fifth were not free of accident hazards and 15% were deficient in the areas of housekeeping and maintenance.[16] Personal abuse of patients by the staff can easily occur when older people are ill, vulnerable, and unable to defend themselves, and the staff may be untrained, unmotivated, improperly supervised and subject to extremely high job turnover. Many nursing home administrators have had no specific training directly related to their work, although this is changing. There is a shortage of physician services, skilled nursing care, dental care, social services, and psychiatric care. Patients often are overmedicated and deprived of any responsibility or decision making on their own behalf.

The Omnibus Budget Reconciliation Act of 1987 (OBRA 1987) and subsequent implementing regulations strengthen requirements to address many of these past problems. All nurses' aides must complete a training program and pass a competency evaluation. Reasonable background checks must be made when hiring nurses' aides and aides who have been convicted of abusing or neglecting a resident must have their name put on a state nurses' aide registry and are not allowed to work in a nursing home. Overmedication with antipsychotics and psychoactive drugs has been addressed by a prohibition of the use of "chemical restraints" except when necessary to treat medical symptoms, and the requirements of physician services, dental care, and social services have been strengthened. A number of nursing homes have opted to reduce or eliminate the use of physical restraints on residents. Several recent research studies have shown that injuries actually decline when physical restraints are removed and that the rate of hip fracture did not change.[17]

Nursing Home Standards. Individual nursing homes are subject to state and/or federal standards, depending on their financing, but the federal government gives enforcement functions to the states. Yet even those states that have receivership laws, civil financial penalties, and the authority to withhold placements in inadequate facilities have not been altogether effective in providing quality care or in preventing facilities from violating regulations.[18] Homes that do not meet standards are often allowed to remain "temporarily" open, with the explanation given that patients would have no other place to go.

In 1981 the Reagan administration proposed deregulation of the nursing home industry. After pressure from the National Citizens Coalition for Nursing Home Reform (NCCNHR), the public at large, and Congress, the administration backed down. Congress mandated a two-year study by the Institute of Medicine of the National Academy of Sciences, resulting in a 1986 report, *Improving the*

Quality of Care in Nursing Homes. This report urged the federal government to improve the regulation of nursing homes.

Consequently, in 1987, legislation was passed, affecting all aspects of long-term care, from mandating services and standards to deciding payment eligibility. The Health Care Financing Administration (HCFA) promulgated revisions of the Conditions of Participation for skilled nursing facilities and recommended that they also apply to intermediate care facilities, bringing an end to the differences in standards for these two types of facilities. Under provisions of the nursing home reform law of 1987 Congress mandated nursing home reforms that focused not just on health and fire safety, but on the "quality of life." Nursing facilities can no longer employ any nurse's aide for more than three months unless a training and competency evaluation program has been successfully completed. Facilities must provide continuous licensed nursing care seven days a week, with RNs on duty at least 8 hours a day (although the law provides for a waiver system that will allow nursing facilities to operate without professional nursing under certain circumstances). At least one social worker must be available for each facility with more than 120 beds. Physician visits are required every 30 days for the first 90 days of care and every 60 days after that. An independent consultant outside the facility must annually review the appropriateness of the drug program for each resident receiving drugs. Rehabilitative services such as physical therapy and occupational therapy must be provided to every resident when the plan of care requires these services.

In addition, states are responsible for ensuring that applicants seeking admission to a nursing home receive preadmission screening for known or suspected mental illness or retardation and be assessed relative to their needs for active treatment for any mental disability. If such treatment is found to be necessary, referral must be made to a facility which provides such services. Estimates based on the 1987 National Medical Expenditures Survey found 31% of nursing home residents (about 475,000) with a primary or secondary di-

agnosis of mental illness, excluding those with a primary diagnosis of dementia. When dementia is included in estimates, up to 88% of all nursing home residents exhibit mental health problems.[19]

A nursing home may voluntarily apply for accreditation by the Joint Commission on Accreditation of Healthcare Organizations (JCAHO). Accreditation by JCAHO does not negate the need for federal certification to be eligible to receive Medicare and/or Medicaid funding. According to JCAHO, its certificate of accreditation means that certain basic standards have been met. The Joint Commission has standards for and conducts surveys of long-term care organizations, including subacute programs and dementia special care units. The standards are developed by health professionals and relate to all aspects of a facility's operation, including organization and administration; fire safety and construction; nursing, dietetic, and pharmaceutical services; medical/health records; and social, environmental, and other essential services. Further standards require that a facility continuously evaluate the quality of the care and the services it provides.

Dissatisfaction has long been expressed about the certification process for long-term care facilities. Although regulations had been established for the proper conduct of such facilities for reimbursement purposes, most reimbursements rely on the determination of whether a facility is *capable* of providing the needed service, not on whether it has actually delivered such a service. There had been no systematic way to identify whether the patient was receiving a service or making the progress that he or she should. In other words, survey and certification only evaluated paper compliance, not the quality of care rendered. Deficiencies continued to exist. Many nursing homes continued to operate as usual, ignoring regulations that were designed to implement the nursing home law. The 1987 nursing home reform legislation (OBRA) and the implementing regulations published by HCFA were designed to address these very real problems. The regulations and survey process now focus on individual residents, their quality of life, the care they receive, and the outcomes of that care. In addition, new enforcement regulations provide for a menu of remedies that are alternatives to termination of a nursing home from the Medicare and Medicaid programs. These alternative remedies are designed to encourage nursing homes to quickly correct their deficiencies and to maintain that correction on a continuing basis.

Consumer groups such as the National Citizens Coalition for Nursing Home Reform urge that family members request a copy of their relative's plan of care and monitor its implementation. Complaints should be brought to the attention of nursing home staff and, if necessary, to the office of the long-term-care ombudsman located in every state office on aging. Complaints may also be filed with state nursing home certification agencies.

Patient Characteristics. Nursing home residents tend to be very old (36% are 85 and older), female (72%), and white (88%). The median length of stay is 1.7 years (Table 11.1). However, not everyone who enters a nursing home becomes a "resident," staying for an extended period of time. "Short-stay" patients are admitted for recuperative or terminal care of specific ailments. In 1984–1985 the median length of stay for discharged short-stay patients was 82 days; those discharged alive had a median length stay of 70 days,

compared to those who died, who had a median stay of 163 days. Almost half of all live nursing home discharges went to general or short-stay hospitals; 2.4% went to VA hospitals. See Table 11.2 for the primary medical diagnosis at the time of admission for nursing home residents.

The numbers of people in nursing homes who suffer from psychiatric disorders have been variously estimated. As we have emphasized previously, persons with chronic physical disorders generally have psychiatric symptoms. Added to these patients are the numbers of people who have been transferred from psychiatric hospitals. As described earlier, it is rare for psychiatric care to be available. Nursing homes tend to select persons with the kinds of psychiatric symptoms that cause the least problems. Suicidal, boisterous, or hostile persons are likely to be rejected, along with those who wander off, smoke in bed, or are addicted to drugs or alcohol. The tractable, depressed, withdrawn persons are more acceptable, as well as those with incontinence and definite nursing needs.

The Ongoing Nursing Home Debate. The number of skilled nursing facilities that specialize in providing care for Alzheimer's and Huntington's disease patients is increasing. In addition, a new specialty facility has emerged—the AIDS skilled nursing facility. Much controversy has surrounded this concept and, as a result, few facilities have been designated thus far.

The latest round in the continuing national debate over nursing homes is worth noting. Some insist that too many people are in nursing homes. In 1980, Vladeck's controversial book, *Unloving Care: The Nursing Home Tragedy,* advocated phasing out the worst one-third of the nation's nursing homes and using the savings to expand special housing and home-based services for older people.[20] At that time, Vladeck divided the nursing home population into three categories:

1. Those who are fatally ill or recuperating from acute illnesses who would be better off in a hospital extended care facility where they could

TABLE 11.1 Length of stay of nursing home residents, 1985

DISTRIBUTION OF LENGTH OF STAY	PERCENTAGE OF RESIDENTS
Less than 3 months	13.0
3–6 months	9.5
6–12 months	14.0
1–3 years	31.5
3–plus years	32.0

Median length of stay: 614 days or 1.7 years

Source: U.S. Department of Health and Human Services, National Center for Health Statistics, Washington, DC: Series 13, No. 97, 1989.

TABLE 11.2   Number and percent distribution of nursing home residents by primary
diagnosis at admission and at time of survey: United States, 1985

	AT ADMISSION		AT TIME OF SURVEY	
PRIMARY DIAGNOSIS	**NUMBER OF RESIDENTS**	**PERCENT DISTRIBUTION**	**NUMBER OF RESIDENTS**	**PERCENT DISTRIBUTION**
All categories	1,491,400	100.0	1,491,400	100.0
1. Infectious and parasitic diseases	7,600	.5	5,900	.4
2. Neoplasms	35,000	2.3	35,000	2.3
Malignant neoplasms	30,600	2.1	31,900	2.1
3. Endocrine, nutritional, metabolic, and immunity disorders	83,200	5.6	81,600	5.5
Diabetes mellitus	59,400	4.0	66,000	4.4
4. Diseases of the blood and blood-forming organs	8,500	.6	10,000	.7
Anemias	7,200	.5	8,000	.5
5. Mental disorders	306,800	20.6	330,600	22.2
Senile dementia and other organic psychotic conditions	43,800	2.9	49,300	3.3
Other psychoses	80,400	5.4	81,400	5.5
Neurotic and personality disorders	9,300	.6	10,900	.7
Specific non-psychotic mental disorders due to organic brain damage	111,300	7.5	133,400	8.9
Mental retardation	36,400	2.4	34,900	2.3
Other mental disorders	25,600	1.7	20,700	1.4
6. Diseases of the nervous system and sense organs	142,100	9.5	157,300	10.5
Alzheimer's disease* and other specified and unspecified degeneration of the brain	39,800	2.7	45,800	3.1
Parkinson's disease	31,400	2.1	33,200	2.2
Multiple sclerosis	8,200	.6	9,600	.6
Blindness	*	*	5,900	.4
7. Diseases of the circulatory system	468,600	31.4	486,500	32.6
Essential hypertension	50,900	3.4	49,900	3.3
Heart disease	207,900	13.9	234,100	15.7
Coronary atherosclerosis	80,900	5.4	100,400	6.7
Other ischemic heart disease	19,000	1.3	16,500	1.1
Congestive heart failure	45,000	3.0	46,900	3.1
Other heart disease	63,000	4.2	70,300	4.7
Cerebrovascular disease	165,400	11.1	153,700	10.3
Atherosclerosis	28,500	1.9	33,700	2.3
8. Diseases of the respiratory system	57,300	3.8	51,300	3.4
Pneumonia, all forms	12,400	.8	*	*
Chronic obstructive pulmonary disease and allied conditions	36,000	2.4	39,600	2.7
9. Diseases of the digestive system	35,100	2.4	33,900	2.3

TABLE 11.2   *(Continued)*

PRIMARY DIAGNOSIS	AT ADMISSION		AT TIME OF SURVEY	
	NUMBER OF RESIDENTS	PERCENT DISTRIBUTION	NUMBER OF RESIDENTS	PERCENT DISTRIBUTION
10. Diseases of the genito-urinary system	26,900	1.8	25,800	1.7
Urinary tract infection, N.E.C.	12,300	.8	11,000	.7
12. Diseases of the skin and subcutaneous tissue	13,900	.9	11,300	.8
13. Diseases of the musculo-skeletal system and connective tissue	91,600	6.1	94,700	6.3
Rheumatoid arthritis, osteoarthritis and allied disorders, except spine	33,700	2.3	36,300	2.4
Other arthritis or rheumatism	21,300	1.4	25,500	1.7
Osteoporosis	8,100	.5	8,100	.5
14. Congenital anomalies	5,800	.4	6,400	.4
16. Symptoms, signs and ill-defined conditions	57,100	3.8	59,700	4.0
Senility without psychoses	15,600	1.0	18,100	1.2
17. Injury and poisoning	96,300	6.5	52,400	3.5
Fracture of neck or femur	50,800	3.4	26,600	1.8
Other fractures	30,800	2.1	15,900	1.1
Supplementary classifications	20,000	1.3	16,900	1.1
Persons with potential health hazards related to personal and family history	9,400	.6	9,200	.6
Persons with a condition influencing their health status	8,800	.6	6,700	.5
Unknown	35,600	2.4	31,900	2.1

NOTE: N-E-C. = Not elsewhere classified. Figures may not add to totals because of rounding.

Modified from: U.S. Department of Health and Human Services (1989, Jan.). (Number and percent distribution of nursing home residents by primary diagnosis at admission and at time of survey: United States, 1985). The National Nursing Home Survey: 1985 Summary for the United States. Series 13, No. 97. DHHS Publication No. (PHS) 89-1758. Hyattsville, Md.: National Center for Health Statistics, p. 31.

*AUTHOR'S NOTE: The very low figures for the rate of Alzheimer's disease in nursing homes most probably reflects the fact that Alzheimer's disease is not usually the primary medical diagnosis. However, it is estimated that at least 50% of nursing home residents suffer from some form of dementia.

get the medical attention they need. The majority of these persons die soon after admission to a nursing home (the average stay is six months).

2. Patients with physical disabilities who are in nursing homes because they have no one at home to care for them. Although chronically ill, these patients could live, with support, outside the nursing home in, for example, congregate housing where housekeeping services, meals, medical services, and so on would be available.

3. Patients who need round-the-clock custodial care. Vladeck believes that nursing homes are necessary for this group, and that only they should be in institutions.

On the other hand, Dunlop and others question whether a significantly reduced rate of institutionalization in nursing homes is feasible.[21] Those older persons with family members who are available to care for them are generally very severely impaired by the time they enter a nursing home. This is because family members tend to help the older person remain at home as long and sometimes much longer than is reasonable. Housekeeping, personal care, and errands are common forms of assistance given by families. When chronic and extensive nursing care becomes necessary, most families turn to nursing homes. In the last stages of illness, it is doubtful whether families could manage home care, even with increased nursing and medical supports. The situation becomes more complicated when we remember what is happening to the family and to American women. (See Chapters 2 and 10 for discussion of caregivers.) More and more middle-aged and even older women, the traditional caregivers to the old, are going to work outside the home. Mobility of family members often produces geographic separations. The size of the family itself is thinning out because of a lowered birth rate. And the increased life expectancy is bringing more four- and five-generation families, with a host of older people for the middle-aged and younger family members to be responsible for. A single-minded focus on increased home care would increase the burden for family members by enabling more of the aged to remain home in a chronically ill condition.

Although generally healthier as a group than patients with families, those nursing home patients with no family on whom to rely would frequently have to have some form of protected living (like congregate housing) as an alternative to a nursing home. This becomes an enormously expensive proposition requiring a whole new set of structures or the remodeling of older structures. Although this might be desirable for older persons, it would not necessarily reduce the cost of long-term care and could conceivably increase it.

Furthermore, unless an entirely new approach were taken, these new "quasi-institutions" might prove to be little improvement over the present facilities where most such older people now live.

All in all, many persons knowledgeable in the field of nursing homes in the United States believe that, at most, 10% of nursing home patients could live on their own in the community with home health or other supports. But this has to be balanced with the thought that perhaps that same number of persons are now existing in the community under unacceptable circumstances and really should be in institutions. Sophisticated epidemiological studies are needed to determine the facts.

By 1989, older persons admitted to nursing homes were considered sicker than in the past. This is because, under the Tax Equity and Fiscal Responsibility Act of 1982, the DRG-driven shortening of hospital stays has led to pressures on the nursing homes (as well as on home care) to meet the needs of frail older persons who are discharged from hospitals before they have fully recovered. Nursing homes have had to become more "medicalized" to care for an increasingly sicker population. They have also begun to transfer patients to acute hospitals more frequently than in the past. An additional issue is that in many parts of the country, there has been a constraint upon the creation or expansion of nursing home beds, while at the same time the older population (especially the 85-plus group) continues to grow.

Selecting a Nursing Home.[22]   Mental health personnel should be thoroughly familiar with any nursing homes to which they refer older people and their families. Initially, personnel should determine whether the home is state-licensed, whether it is certified to participate in government financial assistance programs, whether the administrator is state-licensed, and whether the home provides services such as physical therapy, social work, and specially prescribed diets. Visits to the nursing home in question are useful in order to talk to staff, observe the home and its operations, and view the patients firsthand. Families can contact local agencies (usually local ombudsman programs, public health departments, and voluntary and family agencies) and physicians who may be able to give an idea of the quality of individual homes. Health and welfare councils and mental health associations may provide help in selection. Proper placement must, of course, be based on a comprehensive evaluation of the older person's condition and needs.

Voluntary Nonprofit Homes for the Aging

Homes for the aging are voluntary, nonprofit institutions, usually sponsored by religious organizations, fraternal groups, and other nonprofit agencies. Nonprofit facilities include senior rental apartments, many with supportive services; assisted living facilities; continuing care retirement communities; and nursing homes. Many progressive changes have been made as homes for the aging move away from the limited historic connotation of "old age homes."

While different denominations sponsor their own homes, the people living in them are of varying faiths. Religious, fraternal, and trust homes ordinarily exclude the overtly mentally ill, the severely mentally impaired, and the acutely or notably physically ill. Federal law requires nursing home residents to be given mental health evaluation as well as physical assessments. If an individual's mental health needs cannot be met in the nursing home, the home cannot admit that person.

Since the 1977 Medicare-Medicaid fraud and abuse act, it has been a federal crime to coerce contributions from residents or family members as a condition of admission to or continued stay in a nursing home. Many nonprofit senior housing facilities admit only low-income residents. Assisted living facilities (sometimes called *personal care* or *board and care homes*) serve low-income as well as middle-income elderly. Because most states set their Medicaid payment rates at less than nursing homes' costs, nursing homes often do try to maintain a mix of private pay and Medicaid residents, but this is not a matter of discrimination based on wealth; it is a matter of economic survival. Even nonprofit continuing care retirement communities, whose fees not everyone can afford, subsidize the care of residents who become unable to pay or outlive their resources.

In the past, when illnesses developed after patients were admitted to a home, the patients would probably be transferred to a municipal, county, or state facility because most homes for the aging had insufficient services and personnel to provide the necessary care. Now, due to Medicare policy and the trend toward managed care, hospitals tend to discharge elderly patients home or to long-term care facilities much earlier than they used to. In many cases, today's nonprofit health care facilities can provide more complex nursing and medical care. In addition, nonprofit senior housing facilities increasingly are combining residential services with support services, so residents can get the assistance they need as they "age in place" without having to move prematurely to other care facilities. For example, senior housing may include meals, transportation, social services, counseling, and telephone reassurance. Assisted living, which bridges the gap between independent living and nursing home care, may include assistance with meals, bathing, dressing, eating, medications, housekeeping, and so on. Continuing Care Retirement Communities offer residents long-term care contracts that provide housing, services, nursing, and health care, along with recreational and educational activities.

Many older persons can live in a home for the aging or a nursing home rather than a state hospital if such facilities offer therapeutic programs and can draw on personnel usually found in a hospital. How can all these services be offered? The Philadelphia Geriatric Center has included all the combinations suggested above in one city block: a hospital, the Home for the Jewish Aged (which was the parent institution), two residential apartment buildings, a research institute, and several small-unit, intermediate boarding facilities. A day-care center for older persons exists in another part of the city.

Other homes for the aging have moved beyond their physical structure into the community. Social services, Meals-on-Wheels, and day-care centers are developing in some areas. "Drop-in" centers with recreational services, arts, and crafts may occasionally be found, along with sheltered workshops.

An outstanding long-term care facility is the Jewish Home and Hospital for Aged in New York, founded in 1870. It is the largest nonprofit institution for the care of the aged in New York City, with many programs in teaching (The Frederic D. Zeman Center for Instruction) and research. Over 1,600 individuals are cared for through an integrated group of facilities. The aged in the community are served by a day-care center and geriatric outreach program. Its two main centers provide nursing facilities for all nursing home care needs, depending on patient condition. A middle-income housing project has 320 residents.

Leslie S. Libow, Vice Chairman of the Department of Geriatrics and Adult Development of Mount Sinai Medical Center as well as Chief of Medical Services at the Jewish Home and Hospital for Aged, has continued his pioneering work both in geriatric medical education and in developing the body of knowledge of geriatric medicine at the Jewish Home and Hospital for Aged.

Other institutions of special note, some of which approximate the campus-type of environment, are the Hebrew Home for the Aged (Bronx, New York), the Carmelite Homes (the Mary Manning Walsh Home of New York City and St. Joseph's Manor of Trumbull, Connecticut), the Isabella Home Geriatric Center in New York City, the Avery Convalescent Center in Hartford, Connecticut, the Philadelphia Geriatric Center, Golden Acres (the Jewish Home for the Aged) of Dallas, Texas, the Samarkand of Santa Barbara, California, Lincoln Lutheran of Racine, Wisconsin, Loretto Geriatric Center of Syracuse, New York, Asbury Methodist Village of Gaithersburg, Maryland, the Hebrew Rehabilitation Center for the Aged of Boston, and the Wesley Homes of Atlanta, Georgia.

About 2,500 of the American Association of Homes and Services for the Aging's member organizations are involved in providing home- and community-based services such as home health care, adult day care, or respite care. Over one hundred of these organizations provide only these services. New York's "Nursing Home Without Walls" was sponsored by State Senator Tarky Lombardi.[23] (See Chapter 10 for a description of the Lombardi program.)

FINANCING INSTITUTIONAL CARE

Personal and economic costs of mental disorders, especially the dementias, are staggering. Patients and their families pay half of the nation's long-term care bill, that is, some 36 billion dollars in 1994. In the same year, Medicare paid for about 8.2% of the total nursing home bill of $72 billion. Medicaid paid for 47%, and 42% was paid for privately, mostly through out-of-pocket spending.[24] Spending per capita for the nation's 1.6 nursing home residents averages over $30,000 a year, and the more expensive homes can cost over $60,000 or more a year. This is a drastic increase from the $8,250 figure in 1955. Some families pay another $1,000 a month to obtain a 24-hour private duty nurse in the nursing home. Private psychiatric hospitals often cost $500 to $1,000 a day, including ancillary expenses.

People past the age of 65 have a 40 to 50% chance of spending some time, however brief, in a nursing home. Nonetheless, by the year 2000, 40% of those needing long-term care in or out of an institution will be under 65, since long-term care is a need throughout the life course. It is now becoming clear that long-term care should be universal and funded on an intergenerational basis.

Historically, the care and treatment of the mentally ill have been left to the individual states. The first federal assistance was offered to the states in the National Mental Health Act of 1946. Part of the Medicaid legislation with significance for mental health was sponsored by Senator Russell Long in 1965. It permits federal financial assistance for persons in the group age 65 and over who are patients in institutions for mental diseases. It is a companion piece to the Title XVIII

(Medicare) legislation, which provides specifically for those older persons with acute brain disorders and other mental illnesses who can be expected to respond to relatively brief but intensive treatment in mental hospitals.[25] The Long Amendment also makes provisions for the very many aged who are suffering from chronic disorders, either organic or functional, and who need long-term continued care in state mental health facilities. In expressing the intent of the amendment, the Senate Committee on Finance stated that it

> wishes to insure that the additional Federal funds to be made available to the States under the provisions of the bill will assist the overall improvement of mental health services in the State. State and local funds now being used for institutional care of the aged will be released as a result of the bill, but there is a great need for increased professional services in hospitals and for development of alternate methods of care outside the hospitals. To accomplish this, States may have to reallocate their expenditures for mental health to promote new methods of treatment and care. The committee bill provides that the States will receive additional federal funds only to the extent that a showing is made to the satisfaction of the Secretary that total expenditures of the States or [their] political subdivisions from their own funds for mental health services are increased.[26]

However, millions of dollars in Medicaid payments have not resulted in better programs or higher medical standards. In most states, monies designated by law for the improvement of the care of older mental patients in state hospitals go into the state general revenue fund and are seldom seen by the hospitals.

About two-thirds of all 244 state hospitals have been certified for the Medicare program. Certification came either from the Joint Commission on Accreditation of Health Care Organization or from the Social Security Administration. Certified hospitals must maintain comprehensive clinical records and must have sufficient staff to carry out "active" and "intensive" psychiatric treatment. The point of these special rules is to avoid custodial care. The Medicare regulations are spelled out in the Social Security Administration booklet

Health Insurance for the Aged: Conditions of Participation for Hospitals.

Private long-term care insurance is limited, covering less than 5% of all home and institutional care. More than 1,000 private long-term care policies were in effect in the United States in 1988, but they were of uncertain value and extremely expensive.[27] A policy's value depends on such factors as (1) the daily benefit provided in dollars; (2) the cost-of-care annual adjustment that is provided; (3) whether the premium remains level or whether it may be increased; (4) whether renewability for life is guaranteed; (5) maximum benefit period offered; (6) waiting period requirement; (7) type of institutional care provided; (8) rules regarding previous hospitalization; and (9) the nature and extent of the homecare benefit.

A current attempt to reduce costs and improve quality of care is the Social Health Maintenance Organization (SHMO), a prepaid, managed approach to acute and long-term care for the elderly population (see Chapter 10). Under this system, one provider takes responsibility for a full range of services under a fixed budget. Once elderly persons voluntarily enroll, they receive all covered services through SHMO providers. The operation is similar to the medical model health maintenance organization (HMO).

FAMILY REACTION TO INSTITUTIONALIZATION

Families often need help in dealing with their feelings about an older family member's admission to an institution. In one poignant example, we worked with a very conscientious 70-year-old man who was taking care of his 92-year-old mother and his 67-year-old wife, both of whom had severe dementia. He refused institutionalization for either of them and was devoting all of his waking hours to the very difficult task of managing their care by himself in his home. Nursing and social service departments in institutions are especially important in maintaining liaison with relatives. Many family members are extremely ambivalent, both because of the generally negative reputation of institutional care and because of their own feelings of failing or abandoning the person. After placing a relative in a nursing home, some experience a sense of relief about which they later feel guilty. Families who care (as opposed to those who reject the older person—a much less common category) often experience a grief reaction on admission as though the person had already died. This "death" may be more traumatic than the actual death of the older person later on. In some cases family members may actually stop visiting the person because of inability to tolerate their own grief and ambivalence. Some institutional care now has the built-in expectation and real possibility of home visits, which helps prevent families from cutting themselves off emotionally. Families need to be advised that some of the very supportive things they can do for an older person are to visit frequently, take the person on outings and weekend visits home if possible, become involved with the institution by getting to know the staff and administrative personnel, and provide the extra amenities and attention that only a family can give.

The actual day of admission of an older person may be handled insensitively in many institutions. The older person is simply "deposited" without any transition or preparation. This shock approach can result in increased risk of illness and even death; certainly it is questionable psychologically. Flexibility and individualization should be the rule; some persons indeed respond best to a firm, quick (but humane) admission, while many others need to take their time, to absorb things slowly with a good deal of support. The inauguration of day programs, preliminary admissions for weekends, and provisions for family or friends to sleep in the institution (nearby or even in the same room) when the older person is anxious and frightened can soften the suddenness and harshness of admission. Family and friends should be allowed and encouraged to serve as volunteers in institutional activities, from socializing to performing simple services for residents. Children and grandchildren should be given access to older relatives. In general, there should be much more fluidity between the institution and the community.

Group and individual therapy with families can be useful in helping to resolve long-term family conflicts and short-term reactions to institutionalization. See Chapter 12 for further discussion of therapy. For families with Alzheimer's victims who require intense family home care/day care or who will eventually need nursing home care, the Alzheimer's Association has become a major source of information and general support. With its more than 200 affiliated chapters throughout the United States, the Alzheimer's Association can be especially helpful for families scattered across the country. The network of family support groups for caregivers remains the backbone of this organization.[28]

OTHER FACTORS IN INSTITUTIONAL CARE

Right to Treatment

A second legal concept beyond the question of involuntary admission discussed earlier is the "right to treatment."[29] It is difficult to balance the right to freedom with the right to treatment. A federal district court for Alabama ruled in 1972 that patients committed involuntarily to a mental hospital through noncriminal procedures have a constitutional right to "adequate and effective treatment." The court further found that Alabama was failing to provide adequate treatment to the several thousand patients who had been civilly committed to Bryce Hospital in Tuscaloosa. The ruling was made as a result of a class action suit initiated by guardians of patients at Bryce and by certain hospital employees. It was stated that the Constitution requires adequate and effective treatment, because without it the hospital is transformed into a penitentiary where an individual could be held indefinitely without conviction for any offense. The court ordered a report from the hospital within 90 days that was to include a precise definition of the mission and functions of the hospital and a specific plan to deliver adequate treatment to patients.[30]

U.S. District Court Judge Frank M. Johnson, Jr., established three major aspects of an adequate treatment program: (1) a humane physical and psychological environment, (2) staffing adequate in numbers and training to provide treatment, and (3) an individual treatment plan for each patient.

In reviewing Alabama's mental health and retardation facilities in 1979, seven years after the *Wyatt* v. *Stickney* case, Judge Johnson found they still "failed to achieve substantial compliance" with the standards he set down in 1972. He had the institutions placed in receivership and issued two orders aimed at achieving full compliance within 18 months in the class action case, now on its fourth name, *Wyatt* v. *Ireland.*

In 1986, after 17 years of stalemate and legal proceedings, the state and the original patient complainants finally agreed on a settlement aimed at moving Alabama's mental health bureaucracy from "an almost exclusive reliance on institutions to a balanced system of institutional and community care." The centerpiece of the consent decree was the creation of an unusual five-member committee of independent experts, with each side appointing two members and the fifth member being a director of patient advocacy. The committee has since released its first report (1990) and has shown impressive movement toward its goals of developing community services, successfully convincing the legislature of a need for funds, implementing patient assessment procedures, helping the state achieve accreditation (through the Joint Commission on the Accreditation of Health Organizations) for its hospitals, and establishing quality assurance and patient advocacy programs. However, the committee admits that it is still too early to report on the ultimate success of its efforts to improve treatment and community alternatives for the mentally ill and retarded.[31]

The focus has also turned to other states with conditions as deplorable as in Alabama. Litigation for patients' rights has become more sophisticated and complex; for example, how does a hospital give legally required treatment to patients if they refuse treatment and are supported by law in their refusal?

Individual Treatment Plans

The right to treatment must involve an individual treatment plan for each patient.

> The need for an individual treatment plan cannot be over-emphasized. Without such a plan, there can be no evidence that the hospital has singled out the patient for treatment as an individual with his own unique problems.[32]

Preliminary diagnostic formulation and individualized treatment plans should be accomplished within 12 to 14 hours of admission to any kind of hospital or institution. Reception units or special psychogeriatric units in hospitals should be available for brief hospitalizations, perhaps for three to five days up to three to six weeks, to facilitate proper diagnosis and, in the cases of reversible brain syndromes (like delirium and some dementia) and functional disorders, definitive immediate treatment. The staff should avoid a mental "set" regarding treatability or length of hospitalization. Experience has emphasized that treatment trials constitute a major part of evaluation; for example, considerable time should be given to make certain that a seemingly fixed and permanent organic brain disorder is not a refractory depression or caused by a reversible underlying physical condition.

Periodic and comprehensive reevaluation is important. All residents must be formally assessed concerning their needs on an annual basis. Patients who arrive with one condition may develop others during their stay. Changes in psychiatric symptoms are often caused by physical changes that the patient may be unable to report.

Other Patient Rights and Privileges

The many and pervasive aspects of authoritarianism seen in hospitals and institutions are facets of infantilization and often serve the needs of the providers rather than those served. The goal should be the fewest restrictive conditions necessary to achieve the purposes of institutionalization. Patients' rights must be preserved in very specific ways.

A Hospital Patient's Bill of Rights

The American Hospital Association has devised the following patient's bill of rights:[33]

1. To expect considerate and respectful care
2. To obtain from his or her physician complete current information concerning his or her diagnosis, treatment, and prognosis, in terms he or she can understand
3. To obtain from his or her physician information necessary for informed consent before any procedure or treatment is begun; to obtain information on significant alternatives; and to know the name of the person responsible for the treatment
4. To refuse treatment to the extent permitted by law and to be informed of the medical consequences of refusal
5. To have every consideration of his or her privacy concerning his or her own medical care; persons not directly involved in his or her care must have the patient's permission to be present at case discussion, consultation, examination, and treatment
6. To expect confidentiality of all communications and records pertaining to him or her
7. To expect that within its capacity a hospital make reasonable response to his or her request for service and not transfer him or her to another institution without explanation
8. To obtain information about any relationship of his or her hospital to other health services that concern his or her care and about the existence of any professional relationships among individuals who are treating him or her
9. To be advised if the hospital proposes to engage in human experimentation affecting his or her care and to refuse to participate in such research
10. To expect reasonable continuity of care, including postdischarge follow-up
11. To examine and receive an explanation of his or her bill no matter who pays it
12. To know what hospital rules and regulations apply to his or her conduct as a patient

Resident Rights in Nursing Facilities

The following are requirements that an institution must meet in order to qualify to participate as a nursing facility in the Medicaid and Medicare program.[34] [As mentioned earlier, *nursing facility* in the Medicaid program replaced the terms *skilled nursing facility* (SNF) and *intermediate care facility* (ICF).]

Resident rights include a right to a dignified existence, self-determination, and communication with and access to persons and services inside and outside the facility. A facility must protect and promote the rights of each resident, including each of the following rights:

1. Exercise of rights
   a. The resident has the right to exercise his or her rights as a resident of the facility and as a citizen or resident of the United States.
   b. The resident has the right to be free of interference, coercion, discrimination, or reprisal from the facility in exercising his or her rights.
   c. In the case of a resident adjudged incompetent under the laws of a State by a court of competent jurisdiction, the rights of the resident are exercised by the person appointed under State law to act on the resident's behalf.
2. Notice of rights and services
   a. The facility must inform the resident both orally and in writing in a language that the resident understands of his or her rights and all rules and regulations governing resident conduct and responsibilities during the stay in the facility. Such notification must be made prior to or upon admission and during the resident's stay. Receipt of such information, and any amendments to it, must be acknowledged in writing.
   b. The resident has the right to inspect and purchase photocopies of all records pertaining to the resident, upon written request and 48 hours notice to the facility.
   c. The resident has the right to be fully informed in language that he or she can un-

derstand of his or her total health status, including but not limited to, his or her medical condition.

d. The resident has the right to refuse treatment and to refuse to participate in experimental research; and

e. The facility must:

i. Inform each resident who is entitled to Medicaid benefits, in writing, at the time of admission to the nursing facility or when the resident becomes eligible for Medicaid, of:

(a) The items and services that are included in nursing facility services under the State plan and for which the resident may not be charged;

(b) Those other items and services that the facility offers and for which the resident may be charged, and the amount of charges for those services; and

ii. Inform each resident when changes are made regarding items and services.

f. The facility must inform each resident before or at the time of admission and periodically during the resident's stay of services available in the facility and of charges for those services, including any charges for services not covered under Medicare or by the facility's per diem rate.

g. The facility must furnish a written description of legal rights which includes a description of the manner of protecting personal funds and a statement that the resident may file a complaint with the State survey and certification agency concerning resident abuse, neglect, and misappropriation of resident property in the facility.

h. The facility must inform each resident of the name, specialty, and way of contacting the physician responsible for his or her care.

i. Effective October 1, 1990, the facility must prominently display written information and provide to residents and potential residents oral and written information about how to apply for and use Medicare and Medicaid benefits and how to receive refunds for previous payments covered by such benefits.

j. Notification of changes

i. Except in a medical emergency or when a resident is incompetent, a facility must consult with the resident immediately and notify the resident's physician, and, if known, the resident's legal representative or interested family member within 24 hours when there is:

(a) An accident involving the resident which results in injury;

(b) A significant change in the resident's physical, mental, or psychosocial status;

(c) A need to alter treatment significantly; or

(d) A decision to transfer or discharge the resident from the facility.

ii. The facility must also promptly notify the resident and, if known, the resident's legal representative or interested family member when there is:

(a) A change in room or roommate assignment.

(b) A change in resident rights under Federal or State law or regulations.

iii. The facility must record and periodically update the address and phone number of the resident's legal representative or interested family member.

3. Protection of resident funds

a. The resident has the right to manage his or her financial affairs and the facility may not require residents to deposit their personal funds with the facility.

In addition to provisions for residents' rights, the 1987 reform law calls for, among other things, unannounced inspection of nursing homes, more and a wider range of penalties and, happily, requirements for training of nurses' aides. In addition, it requires that the home guarantee residents a choice of physicians and that there be a written plan of care for each patient. Specifically, the law states that a nursing facility must provide services and activities to attain or maintain the highest practicable physical, mental, and psychosocial well-being of each resident in accordance with a written plan of cure that is based on the "resident assessment."

The *resident assessment* is a requirement that all nursing facilities, beginning October 1, 1990, must conduct an assessment of the medical, nursing, and psychosocial needs of each resident at least once a year. This assessment is to be based on a "Minimum Data Set" that has been developed by the Secretary of the Department of Health and Human Services, and is to be compiled initially in the first 14 days after admission to a facility. Revisions are to be made quarterly, with a full review annually. The resident assessment is coordinated by a registered nurse with the participation of at least one physician, as well as other health care professionals. The assessment covers a broad spectrum of needs, including assessment of cognitive impairment. It also assesses "customary and daily routines" of each resident, in order to attempt to accommodate individual preferences in food, bedtime, personal hygiene, and so forth.

Each facility must also create a quality assessment and assurance committee consisting of the director of nursing, a physician, and at least three other staff members.

Commitment or voluntary admission to a mental hospital or a move to a nursing home should not per se abrogate the right to manage affairs, to sign contracts, to hold professional, occupational, or vehicle operator's licenses, to marry or obtain a divorce, to register and vote, and to make a will. Direct access to legal counsel is also mandatory.[35] Patients should not be placed incommunicado. Visitation (including small children) and telephone communications should be permitted on a 24-hour basis except when there are clear indications that such communications and visitations promote disturbances in the patient that are untherapeutic and harmful at a *particular* time. Any limit on such contact must be periodically reviewed, and renewal or continuation must not be automatic. This should require a physician's decision, and the physician must not have any ownership ties with the facility, in order not to prejudice his or her judgment.

Patients must have the unrestricted right to receive sealed mail except when responsible staff personnel can clearly defend restriction on the basis of an individualized patient plan. Again, periodic review must occur. The physician must bear ultimate responsibility since only the patient's mental or physical condition could warrant such a restriction on rights and privileges.

Privacy and space to move are other rights. Privacy is obviously qualitative as well as quantitative, and the availability of time alone each day should be made. There must be a minimum of 100 square feet of floor space in one-patient rooms. No multipatient room should exceed four persons. There must be a minimum of 80 square feet of floor space per patient, with soundproofing, screens or curtains, and at least one toilet, lavatory, shower, or tub for each six persons. Each patient bed should have an electronic signal system to call to the staff for help. A comfortable, attractive day room area (40 square feet per patient) with reading lamps, tables, chairs, and recreational facilities is considered necessary, and a dining room should include 10 square feet per patient.

Husbands and wives who both are institutionalized should have the option to live together in an institution if they so desire. If problems arise or separation becomes necessary, skilled counseling should be available to them to avoid estrangement and feelings of desertion. When only one partner is institutionalized, arrangements for conjugal visits should be possible.

Food, abundantly and attractively served, is another patient right, unless medically restricted. The diet must, at minimum, provide the recommended daily dietary allowance developed by the National Academy of Science. Opportunities for snack times (including raiding an icebox), and ordering or even preparing certain favorite foods are psychologically beneficial.

The money available to the older person (including Supplemental Security Income and Social Security checks as well as private funds) must be safeguarded.

Persons should not be stripped of their clothing and made into "patients" with shoddy institutional apparel. Patients have the right to wear their own clothes and have their own possessions with them unless this is legitimately considered dangerous. Personal possessions and clothing help to maintain orientation, self-respect, and identity. Personnel are advised also to avoid calling persons by their first or "pet" names, as this too implies loss of dignity and infantilization. Further, patients should not be on "display" for the amusement of others.

On an institutional visit we were introduced by the chief nurse to an 87-year-old woman. The nurse, who, of course, insisted on being referred to as Mrs. L by the patients, said, "Jane, sing your song for the visitors." "Jane," who had formerly been a teacher of some repute, obediently belted out a popular song. Such callous disregard for patient dignity is perhaps not common, but it does occur all too frequently.

And finally, unless they give permission, patients should not be objects of observation for visiting doctors, students, families, and so forth. Those who are capable of consent should be asked if they would be willing to talk to visitors. All persons should have access to members of the clergy and religious services of their choice.

Community advocates for institutionalized older persons should be given free access to nursing homes, hospitals, and other long-term care facilities. A National Citizens' Coalition for Nursing Home Reform was organized for the following purposes:

1. To operate exclusively for charitable and educational purposes
2. To coordinate the efforts and resources of member organizations and individuals to improve the long-term care system and quality of life for nursing home residents

3. To provide resources and information relative to nursing home reform to members and the general public
4. To solicit sources of funding to finance the Coalition's activities
5. To develop and implement nursing home advocacy training programs
6. To study nursing home issues and report and make recommendations to members and the public at large

As of October, 1990, the Coalition had 315 member organizations in 42 states, a large increase from its 72 groups in 24 states just eight years earlier.

Physical Environment

The environment of hospitals, nursing homes, and other institutions is beginning to change. Efforts are being made to design esthetic and prosthetic environments that help compensate for mental and physical losses. The Retirement Research Foundation, in conjunction with the American Association of Homes for the Aging, has funded a clearing-house on environmental design of nursing homes. In progressive institutions, wandering patients who would have in the past been physically restrained now may have the possibility of orienting themselves through the use of color coding, the buddy system, and adequate staff. Maximum security atmospheres can be reduced by such devices as attractive wooden fences, gates, and even shrubbery rather than iron bars or locked doors. (Few geriatric patients break out of institutions! Most merely need something to discourage confused wandering.)

Protection from accidents and fires needs to be improved, and all institutions should be subject to the Life Safety Code of the National Fire Protection Association. New regulations have improved fire safety in nursing homes, but boarding houses remain hazardous. Air-conditioning in summer and control of temperature and humidity in winter are crucial, since older people cannot withstand extreme atmospheric conditions. In hospitals and nursing homes that are not air-conditioned, excessive numbers of older people die during heat waves.

With the advent of plastic and electronic devices that may be under either direct or remote control, much can be done to make up for deficiencies in ambulation, audition, vision, and general stimulation. Safety devices such as handrails, grab bars, call buttons, and nonslip floors are essential. Calendars, large clocks (set to the *correct* time!), and mirrors are useful orientation devices. The general environment should be reasonably calm but alive with stimuli, lest the capacity to react to the environment atrophy. Good illumination is necessary. Colorful decorations and plants and flowers enhance pleasure. Beauty parlors, barber shops, and canteens add variety. (Easy access to cosmeticians, hairdressers, masseuses, and masseurs does wonders for patient morale.) Music should be available but not, because of the Goldstein catastrophic reaction (Chapter 9), constantly blaring. Outdoor activities such as gardening and perhaps caring for pets in mini-zoos on institutional grounds can be extremely therapeutic.

Physician's Care

Among patients' rights is the right to adequate medical care from a physician. Only 13% of the 20,000 nursing homes surveyed by the National Center for Health Statistics had a full-time equivalent physician on the premises in 1985. Under the 1987 nursing home reform law, each nursing facility must designate a physician to serve as medical director to be responsible for implementing resident care policies and coordinating medical care. All institutions should have physicians with central responsibility and commensurate authority to override private doctors of individual patients if necessary. These physicians should plan the general medical program (routine tests, dental care, immunizations), conduct regular rounds, prescribe medications, respond to emergencies, and be available for consultations with families. Physicians must be clear that they are not there for the convenience of the institution but rather for the well-being of residents. (For example, prescribing excessive medication may relieve the staff but make "zombies" out of patients.) Physicians themselves should be under the review of all staff members to guard against careless or insensitive treatment.

Teaching/Research Nursing Homes

The National Institute on Aging supports model teaching/research nursing homes at selected academic medical centers to focus on research, education, and service all at once.[36] (Ultimately, of course, it would be ideal if each of the 126 medical schools would have a teaching/research nursing home nearby as part of its program. A number have already developed affiliations.) Teaching/research nursing homes offer the unique opportunity to study disease processes in older people. Because many older people are sent to nursing homes rather than general hospitals or mental hospitals, physicians and other health care personnel in training can observe and study a number of conditions not routinely treated, at least for any great length of time, at hospitals. A major example is senile dementia of the Alzheimer type. Teaching/research nursing homes also encourage study of the effects of nutrition, drugs, exercise, and social interaction on disease; the investigation of better methods of diagnosis and treatment; the analysis of the best methods of delivering services of all kinds to nursing home residents; the training of medical, nursing, social work, psychology, and other health professions' students; and the provision of continuing education for all mental health professionals involved in the care of the aged.

Nursing Care

The role of the registered nurse in administration and in direct care in institutions is absolutely central. A registered nurse's leadership is likely to determine the quality of all aspects of care, including medical care. Supervision and on-the-job teaching of registered and practical nurses and aides are essential.

Nursing of the older patient requires flexibility, good humor without ridicule, and respect without distancing. Wolanin & Phillips (1981) have described nursing staff reactions to incontinence, difficult self-feeding, obscene language, and other unpleasant behaviors. Basic individualized knowledge of the patient is crucial and in keeping with our stress on comprehensive evaluation. The list below notes problems frequently confronted by nursing staffs and presented to medical and psychiatric consultants when they are called in to nursing homes and homes for the aged.

1. Depression among older patients
2. Confusion or other symptoms of delirium or dementia
3. Paranoia
4. Noisiness
5. Restlessness or wandering
6. Combativeness
7. Inappropriate dependency on staff
8. Persistent talk of a wish to die
9. Incontinence
10. Families who are justifiably critical or demanding of the institution

Bed rest can be dangerous, replicating all the untoward effects of chronic, debilitating illnesses: cardiovascular, respiratory, metabolic, and neuromuscular changes. To illustrate, with decreased respiration can come hypostatic pneumonia, and with immobility, a decrease in strength of muscles and weakening of bones (osteoporosis), with the risk of falls and fractures. People should be ambulated quickly, even after surgery.

Bedsores (also called decubiti, trophic ulcers, or pressure sores) can develop quickly, especially in bedridden, debilitated older persons. Such sores occur at pressure points—the bony areas of elbows, hips, and heels, and the buttocks—and are the result of reduced blood supply caused by the body's weight. Persons who are not turned in bed, who are malnourished or anemic (vitamin C deficiency and low protein intake are most dangerous), or who have been allowed to lie in urine until the skin macerates may develop infections in the sores. These infections are indolent, causing little

or no physical pain. Care should include ambulation, rotation of the patient, cleanliness and dryness, avoidance of oversedation, and checking of pressure points for early signs of redness. Physiotherapy through overhead trapeze and activity as well as active and passive exercises, including massage, are indicated. Paraplegic patients may need to be placed in frames that turn (Stryker frames). Indwelling catheters may be necessary to control urinary incontinence. Foam rubber, air mattresses and water beds, pillows, and sheepskin sheets are useful. When an ulcer has developed, it should be cleaned (debridement). Trypsin, an enzymatic digestive agent, along with topical antibiotics (for example, neomycin) is appropriate. Oral zinc therapy is controversial.

Incontinence refers to the inability to control bladder or bowel. Fifteen percent of men over 65 and 35% of women over 65 suffer from urinary incontinence. It has been estimated that one-third to one-half of older nursing home residents have this problem. In fact, it is a major reason for nursing home admission, costing facilities as much as $1 billion a year. The condition may be permanent as a result of severe injury, central nervous system disease, chronic infections, and so on. At other times it is temporary and reversible, related to anxiety, pain, hostility, and inadequate attention. It is important to overcome the idea that urinary incontinence is untreatable and that it is a normal function of aging. To some degree it is a function of bladder shrinkage and weakened muscles. Even persons with organic brain damage may be able to improve control. A careful evaluation and correct assessment as to cause must be made, and a plan for treatment built and kept. Emotional aspects should be dealt with through psychotherapy and staff involvement.

The incontinent patient with no permanent physical damage can often be retrained. In urinary incontinence one begins by giving the patient the bedpan or urinal on a regular schedule to develop a habit (for example, every two hours or on rising, after eating, and before bedtime). Bernard Engel's pioneering work on biofeedback at the National Institute on Aging's Baltimore Longitudinal Study has helped create retraining schedules for strengthening muscles and controlling the bladder and valves that shut off urination. In bowel retraining, proper timing is also of the essence. Timed food intake helps. Passive exercises for the bedridden (bending the knees and pressing the thighs against the abdomen) can sometimes stimulate the urge to defecate. Walking and other efforts to improve muscle tone help. Adult gauze diapers and underpads should be used and frequently changed until control improves.

Sometimes surgery may improve or cure incontinence by repositioning a fallen bladder or removing an obstruction. Surgical implantation of an artificial sphincter muscle to replace the tiny ring-like muscle that closes off the end of the neck of the bladder can also be helpful.[37]

Nursing Staff Problems.   Nursing staff morale and dedication are an exceptionally crucial consideration. Decent care for all patients, rich or poor, depends on the goodwill and skill of all levels of staff; yet, much of the time the poor working conditions, low pay, low status, and lack of in-service and outside training for nursing and other personnel have been ignored. Like many other groups providing human services (police, fire fighters, teachers, government workers), nursing personnel are under public pressure not to strike, for the obvious reason—the welfare of patients. Nonetheless, there are three large health care unions: the American Federation of State, County, and Municipal Employees (AFSCME), Service Employees International, and the National Union of Hospital and Health Care Employees (formerly Local 1199). All are affiliates of the AFL-CIO. They organize and undertake collective bargaining efforts in hospitals, nursing homes, and other facilities. The American Nurses' Association and the National Federation of Licensed Practical Nurses are not unions, strictly speaking, but they operate like unions to some degree. There is also the National Conference of Physicians' Unions. (Important to unionization issues, too, are the U.S. Senate Committee on Labor and Public Welfare and, of course, the Federal Mediation and Conciliation Service.)

Some have recommended that the minimum nursing staff-to-patient ratios in long-term care facilities should be 1 registered nurse per 30 residents per shift with an additional 1 nursing staff member per 7 residents per day shift, 1 nursing staff member per 12 residents per evening shift, and 1 nursing staff member per 20 residents per night shift. As a result of the 1987 nursing home reform law, efforts are under way to determine optimal staffing patterns. Obviously, there is a greater need for more staff where there are more total care patients. See Table 11.3 for a description of personnel in various care settings.

Perhaps 80% to 90% of care of institutionalized older persons is provided by nursing aides, assistants, and orderlies. Training for these groups of personnel varied in the past, ranging from no training at all to 160 hours of training in rare cases. The 1987 nursing home reform law requires that nursing homes provide a competency evaluation program for all nurses' aides. All nurses' aides must now receive a minimum of 75 hours of training, including training in caring for the cognitively impaired.

Traditionally, much of the administrative and training responsibility has rested on the registered nurse—who is usually overworked and underrewarded. It is estimated that staff turnover in institutions for the elderly is a fantastic 75% per year! Part of the solution to the problem of high turnover is preservice and in-service training and staff development, including teaching staff to relate to patients, to give psychological counseling, and to learn to do group therapy. All staff should be encouraged and expected to participate in case conferences and decisions about patient or resident care. Technical nursing skills, such as dealing with stroke problems and bowel and bladder retraining, need to be constantly reviewed and updated.

Patient Restraint

It is estimated that over one-half million persons in nursing homes and hospitals have been regularly tied to their beds and chairs. Devices include chest, wrist or ankle ties; belts; mitts; harnesses; sheets; full body suits; side rails; locked doors;

TABLE 11.3 Number and rate per 100 beds of full-time equivalent employees of nursing homes, by facility ownership, certification and bed size

FACILITY CHARACTERISTIC

OCCUPATIONAL CATEGORY		TOTAL	OWNERSHIP			CERTIFICATION				BED SIZE			
			PROPRIETARY	VOLUNTARY NONPROFIT	GOVERNMENT AND OTHER	CERTIFIED BY MEDICARE AND MEDICAID	CERTIFIED BY MEDICARE ONLY	CERTIFIED BY MEDICAID ONLY	NOT CERTIFIED	LESS THAN 50 BEDS	50-99 BEDS	100-199 BEDS	200 BEDS OR MORE
All Full-Time Equivalent Employees	Number	1,333,300	823,000	383,100	127,200	1,055,900	52,800	191,600	33,000	73,000	320,500	674,500	265,300
	Rate per 100 beds	75.3	71.5	81.8	84.2	76.6	88.5	68.4	62.8	83.7	74.5	74.7	75.6
Administrative, Medical and Therapeutic Staff	Number	20,100	13,600	4,900	1,600	15,000	1,900	2,800	400	4,700	5,200	8,400	1,800
	Rate per 100 beds	1.1	1.2	1	1.1	1.1	3.2	1	0.8	5.4	1.2	0.9	0.5
Nursing Total	Number	913,500	574,100	254,300	85,100	727,900	35,800	127,500	22,300	49,600	221,400	468,500	174,000
	Rate per 100 beds	51.6	49.8	54.3	56.3	52.8	60	45.5	42.4	56.8	51.4	51.9	49.6
Registered Nurse	Total	129,700	78,000	38,300	13,300	105,800	7,400	13,600	3,000	10,700	29,200	63,700	26,100
	Rate per 100 beds	7.3	6.8	8.2	9	7.7	12.4	4.8	5.7	12.3	6.8	7.1	7.4
Licensed Practical Nurse	Total	185,700	118,300	51,500	15,900	149,600	7,000	24,300	4,800	11,100	43,000	96,500	35,100
	Rate per 100 beds	10.5	10.3	11	10.5	10.9	11.7	8.7	9.1	12.8	10	10.7	10
Nurses Aide and Orderly	Total	600,500	379,500	164,700	56,300	473,900	21,100	90,400	15,100	29,000	148,800	310,100	112,700
	Rate per 100 beds	33.9	32.9	35.2	37.3	34.4	35.4	32.3	28.7	33.3	34.6	34.4	32.1
All Other Staff	Total	399,700	235,300	123,900	40,500	313,000	15,100	61,300	10,300	18,700	93,900	197,600	89,500
	Rate per 100 beds	22.6	20.4	26.5	26.8	22.7	25.3	21.9	19.6	21.4	21.8	21.9	25.5

Source: National Center for Health Statistics. (1997, January 23). An Overview of Nursing Homes and Their Current Residents: Data From the 1995 National Nursing Home Survey. Advance Data From Vital and Health Statistics, no. 280. Bethesda, MD: National Center for Health Statistics.

and the geriatric chair, which has a lock-tray table. Chemical restraints include sedatives, psychotropic drugs, and antihistamines. Haldol, a psychoactive drug, is the medication most frequently used in nursing homes. Those with dementia and extreme frailty are most likely to be restrained. Such restraint may have continued for months, with both physical and psychological effects. The loss of a sense of autonomy and mastery is perhaps the most disturbing fact of all.

The 1987 nursing home reform law requires facilities to provide as many alternatives to restraint as possible. Each resident is to be free from chemical and physical restraints used for punishment, involuntary seclusion, discipline, or staff convenience. Psycho-pharmacologic drugs can be administered only on order of a physician and as a part of the written plan of care. Such drugs may be used only to eliminate or modify the symptom for which they are prescribed and only if, at least annually, an independent external consultant reviews the appropriateness of the drug plan of each resident. Reducing the present use of drugs and restraints will depend on sensitization and education of nursing home employees to be realized through specific educational programs.[38]

Medical and Psychiatric Experimentation

The Ten Commandments of Medical Research Involving Human Subjects, as employed by the National Institutes of Health, should be in effect. No experimental research on older patients is permissible without express and informed consent, given after consultation with legal counsel. The volunteer should be made fully aware of the risks and benefits of the experiment and his or her right to terminate the experiment at any time. Similarly, any unusual, hazardous, or experimental treatment procedures, such as new drugs or lobotomy, must be introduced only after express and informed consent and consultation on the patient's part with legal counsel. The National Institute on Aging conducted a workshop on human protection in research, which formulated some of the early thinking on this issue.[39]

Institutional Neurosis

Institutional neurosis can occur in hospitals, nursing homes, prisons, or anywhere that persons are removed from society and live in a rigid, isolated community. It can also develop in the person's own home if he or she is isolated. The symptoms are erosion of personality, overdependence, and expressionless face, automatic behavior, and loss of interest in the outside world. Many of the immediate and long-term effects of military or concentration camp imprisonment apply also to isolated institutions for older persons.

Age, Sex, and "Clinical State" Segregation

Federal regulations issued June 1, 1978, require the right to privacy in nursing homes.[40] According to the 1987 reform law, each resident has the right to personal privacy and confidentiality. Gender segregation is a very questionable practice. It is illegal to rule out heterosexual (or homosexual) activities with spouses or other consenting adults, including other patients, as long as no clear physical or psychological danger is present. One of the authors, Dr. Robert N. Butler, established one of the first psychiatric units for older patients, at Chestnut Lodge in 1958–1959, which did not segregate patients by gender and allowed freedom and privacy for sexual activities. The results were a more relaxed patient population and a greater respect for patients' adulthood. Older people should also not be scolded for masturbation. Masturbation is a normal sexual outlet, and staff members in institutions may need help in overcoming their own anxieties about patients' use of this outlet. Conjugal visits with spouses should be encouraged.

There is a question about the wisdom of age-segregated treatment facilities. It is argued that when older persons are placed in age-integrated wards of hospitals, they receive less staff attention and may be injured by young, aggressive patients. (Assaults can be minimized if personnel is adequate.) On the other hand, restriction to an age-segregated unit can result in monotony and difficulties in recruiting and retaining well-trained, dedicated staff. Some studies have indicated that older persons show greater improvement in age-integrated facilities.

Segregation can also occur based on clinical status. Severely impaired older persons often do better in separate facilities that can offer specialized treatment programs not needed by healthier patients. Research can also take place more easily in these circumstances. But the designation of a floor or a section of an institution as the "senile floor" or "senile wing" can lead to much anxiety in healthier patients. ("Will I be moved to the senile wing?" "Does this mean I am losing my mind?") Integration of the severely impaired with the less impaired has some benefits of its own. For example, the healthier patients can benefit from giving help to the more impaired through a "buddy system." As would be expected, for some patients, such integration has a depressing effect. A choice would be ideal, with fluid connections between units to comply with the inclination of patients.

Reality-Orientation, Remotivation, and Rehabilitation Programs

Reality Orientation.   *Reality orientation* is a specific set of techniques for helping cognitively impaired or withdrawn older persons remain as oriented and as communicative as their capabilities permit.[41] James C. Folsom first organized a reality orientation program in Winter Veterans Administration Hospital in Topeka, Kansas, in 1958. The bulk of the work was done by the nursing assistants, who spent the most time with the patients.

In a typical reality orientation program, the most severely demented are presented with simple, straightforward information on a regular basis by those who are caring for them. For example, an aide might describe step-by-step exactly what she is doing as she dresses the patient.

Less severely impaired patients have formal classes in which the instructor presents basic personal and current information over and over to each patient, beginning with the patient's name, where he or she is, and the date. Only when he or she has relearned these basic facts is the patient presented with other facts such as age, home town, and former occupation. Patients are encouraged to verbalize. Caregivers are also trained to use such techniques in the home setting.

Studies of the outcome of such work have been inconclusive. Gains appear to be small and of short duration.[42] There is also a risk of infantilization. Nonetheless, reality orientation offers a method and a philosophy of treatment that makes a sincere and humane attempt to meet the patient at his or her own level and prevent decline resulting from lack of opportunity to learn and to be stimulated by close human contacts. In truth, reality orientation may be of unrecognized value to staff because it offers them hope and a defined approach to patients who might otherwise be experienced as unreachable and hopeless.

Remotivation.   Remotivation has been used as a means of reaching the large number of long-term, chronic patients residing in large mental hospitals who do not seem to want to move toward improvement or discharge. It has also been applied in nursing homes.

The remotivation technique consists essentially of the following five steps, which the psychiatric aide uses with small groups of 10 to 15 patients:

1. *The climate of acceptance*—establishing a warm, friendly relationship in the group
2. *A bridge to reality*—reading of simple poetry, current events, and so on
3. *Sharing the world*—development of the topic, introduced above, through planned objective questions, use of props, and so on
4. *An appreciation of work in the world*—designed to stimulate patients to think about work in relation to themselves
5. *The climate of appreciation*—expression of enjoyment at getting together, and so on

Remotivation must be followed by activities leading toward rehabilitation, such as occupational and recreational therapy, and finally, vocational and social rehabilitation.

The Veterans Administration Hospital in St. Cloud, Minnesota, began a program in 1972 in which sixth-grade students served as remotivation therapists for older institutionalized veterans. The students and patients were brought together twice a week for 45-minute periods for 11 weeks at a time. The students were carefully prepared and supervised. Patients were prepared by the staff for separation from the children at the end of the program (although many children kept contact through letters and gifts). Patients demonstrated significant gains in self-awareness and self-esteem during the program but, as with reality orientation, they appeared to lose gains if continued involvement with therapists was not offered.

Rehabilitation. Under federal regulations issued in January 1989, nursing homes must provide rehabilitative services to every resident. Psychiatric hospital and nursing home programs will benefit immeasurably from the routine availability of rehabilitation as a medical specialty (physiatrics), one of the significant developments of twentieth century health care. An important model is the Institute of Rehabilitation Medicine in New York (part of New York University's Medical Center), founded and directed by Dr. Howard Rusk since 1948. The blind, deaf, retarded, hemiplegic, paraplegic, and those suffering from Parkinson's disease—in short, anyone with losses in their neurosensory and physical functions—can benefit from rehabilitative programs. We review physical, occupational and speech therapies in Chapter 10.

The National Institute on Disability and Rehabilitation Research, inspired by former senator Thomas Eagleton, was given the task by Congress to report on research on the handicapped, including the elderly handicapped, being carried out by government agencies. For example, some of the institutes within the National Institutes of Health are developing various prosthetic and rehabilitative devices that may be useful for older people. This is a field where both the development of new technology and the reengineering of devices originally designed for other purposes (as in the NASA space program) are occurring.

Daily exercise should be part of routine physical care in every institution. Each patient should participate, including the bedridden, as long as exercise is geared to physical capacity. Psychological well-being is often improved as an added benefit when exercise is encouraged. Morning exercises to music are becoming a regular part of the treatment programs in some nursing homes, homes for the aged, and other institutions.

The President's Council on Physical Fitness and Sports provides free of charge a number of publications that encourage both younger and older people to exercise. Their fitness book entitled *Pep Up Your Life* is designed for people in senior centers, nursing homes, clubs, and other places where older people are concentrated. Exercises are designed to be done while sitting, standing, or confined to a wheelchair or bed. Individual exercise planning guides in *Pep Up Your Life* help older people keep track of their personal fitness programs.

Dance therapy expands on the idea of exercise by encouraging emotional and psychological expression. Dance is an expressive medium for self-recognition, communication, release of tension, and socialization.

Bibliotherapy is a term used to refer to the healing that lies in the written word. Some institutions are beginning to use circulating libraries as an adjunct to treatment programs rather than simply as a recreational pastime. Audio/video therapy—VCRs, tape recordings, phonographs, and compact discs—provides the elderly with important pleasure and stimulation.

Work Therapy and Sheltered Workshops

"Work therapy" is appropriate only as a truly therapeutic activity and not as compulsory and uncompensated housekeeping and maintenance chores that save the institution money. Patients may volunteer to do work for the institution but should be compensated, at the very least, in accordance with the minimum wage laws. Patients who are physically able should, however, make their own beds, dress themselves, and perform other acts ordinarily encompassed under the rubric of self-care.

The handicapped, including the aged, may participate in *sheltered workshops.* The sheltered workshop is a work-oriented rehabilitation facility with controlled working environment and individualized vocational goals. It utilizes work experiences and related services for assisting handicapped persons to progress toward normal living and productive vocational status.

This kind of shop gives an opportunity to make a modest amount of money, as well as providing activity and promoting pride. Because industries pay on a piece basis, it is economically feasible for them. Packaging, stuffing, stapling, tag stringing, and various types of simple repetitive assembling are examples of activities.

Patient or Resident Government

The 1987 nursing home reform law greatly strengthens the residents' voice in the nursing home. The nursing home survey process under the new law requires direct interviews with nursing home residents concerning their impressions of their care. Survey teams must also meet with residents who are members of resident councils (if they exist) in separate interviews.

There are many legitimate complaints—about food, lack of entertainment, nursing care—legitimate not only because in too many instances the complaints are valid, but also because of the deep frustration and grief associated with institutionalization and the understandable need to ventilate feelings. Therefore, patient government or resident councils, joint patient-staff conferences, and the presence of older people on the boards of trustees of hospitals and homes for the aging should be standard. Older people living in the community would do well to be their own ombudsmen and monitor the conditions and treatment in institutions in which they might some day reside.

Volunteers

With careful selection, a loyal, conscientious group of volunteers can be assembled who are a valuable adjunct to staff and contribute to the quality of the institution. The Red Cross Gray Ladies are an example of a well-trained volunteer group. Some nursing homes are wary of volunteers—fearful perhaps that their weaknesses will be exposed to the public with volunteers moving in and out at will. Others, however, welcome volunteers and use the opportunity to make them an effective component of their programs.

Research

It is imperative that research be built into institutions. Research should be of two kinds: studies concerned with enhancing the understanding of old age and chronic illness (for example, a study of senile dementia) and studies dealing with improvement in services (for example, a study of group therapy). Fortunately, nurses are beginning to be trained in research methods. Rarely is research done in either nonprofit or commercial homes. The Philadelphia Geriatric Center and the Jewish Home and Hospital for Aged (New York) are examples of voluntary institutions that have developed fine research programs.

Major Associations of Nursing Homes and Homes for the Aging

American Association of Homes and Services for the Aging, 901 E St., N.W., Suite 500, Washington, DC 20004-2037.

Membership—represents nonprofit, community-sponsored housing, homes for the aging, and health care and services-providing organizations serving older persons. Homes are sponsored by religious, fraternal, labor, civic, and county organizations.

Size—over one million older persons are served by 5,000 AAHSA member organizations.

American Health Care Association, 1201 L Street, N.W., Washington, DC 20005.

Membership—a federation of state associations of commercial homes in 50 states. 2,023 nonprofit homes also belong, usually small homes with about 60 beds. This is a nonprofit organization.

Size—11,805 facilities, with 1.2 million beds, belong.

National Citizens Coalition for Nursing Home Reform, 1424 16th Street, N.W., Suite L2, Washington, D.C. 20036-2211

Membership—a national nonprofit membership organization to improve the long-term care system and the quality of life for nursing home residents.

Size—296 organizations are members, as well as individuals.

Note: Some 750 homes, like the Mennonite homes, do not belong to any national organization, nor do they participate in Medicaid or Medicare.

SELECTED READINGS

American Nurses' Association. (1970). Standards for geriatric nursing practice. *American Journal of Nursing, 70*(9), 1894–1897.

American Association of Retired Persons. *Pep up your life: A fitness book for seniors.* Washington, DC: Author.

Avorn, J., Dreyer, P., Connelly, K., & Soumerai, S. B. (1989). Use of psychoactive medication and the quality of care in rest homes: Findings and policy implications of a statewide study. *New England Journal of Medicine, 4,* 227–232.

Ball, R. M. (with Bethell, T. N.). (1989). *Because we're all in this together: The case for a national long-term insurance policy.* Washington, DC: Families USA Foundation.

Birkett, P. (1991). *Psychiatry in the nursing home.* Binghamton, NY: The Haworth Press.

Borson, S., Liptzin, B., Nininger, J., & Rabins, P. V. (1989). *Nursing homes and the mentally ill elderly: A report of the task force on nursing homes and the mentally ill elderly.* Washington, DC: The American Psychiatric Association.

Borup, J. H. (1983–84). Transfer trauma. *Generations, 8*(3), 17–22.

Brink, T. L. (Ed.). (1990). *Mental health in the nursing home.* Binghamton, NY: The Haworth Press.

Brody, E. M., Dempsey, N. P., & Pruchno, R. A. (1990, April). Mental health of sons and daughters of the institutionalized aged. *The Gerontologist, 30*(2), 212–219.

Butler, R. N. (1980). Protection of elderly research subjects. *Clinical Research, 28,* 33–35.

Butler, R. N. (1981). The teaching nursing home. *Journal of the American Medical Association, 245*(14), 1435–1437.

Cohn, V. (1990, June 5). Finding the right nursing home. *The Washington Post,* Health Section, 12–15.

The Commonwealth Fund (1996). *Nursing home restraints program review.* New York: The Commonwealth Fund, One East 75th Street, New York, NY 10021-1276.

Consumer Reports. (1995, August). Nursing homes: When a loved one needs care. *Consumer Reports,* 518–28.

Emerson Lombardo, N. B., Fogel, B. S., Robinson, G. K., & Weiss, H. P. (1996, August). *Achieving mental health of nursing home residents: Overcoming barriers to mental health care.* Boston, MA: Hebrew Rehabilitation Center for Aged (1200 Centre St., Boston, MA 02131-1097).

Ennis, B., & Siegel, L. (1973). *The rights of mental patients: The basic ACLU guide to a mental patient's rights.* New York: Richard W. Baron.

Evans, L. R., & Strumph, N. E. (1989). Tying down the elderly: A review of the literature on physical restraint. *Journal of the American Geriatrics Society, 37,* 65–74.

Gleason-Wynn, P. E. (1995) Addressing the educational needs of nursing home social workers. *Gerontology & Geriatrics Education, 16*(2), 31–36.

Greene, R. R., Vourlekis, B. S., Gelfand, D. E., & Lewis, J. S. (1992). Current realities: Practice and education needs of social workers in nursing homes. In Mellor, M. J., & Solomon, R. (Eds.), *Geriatric social work education* (pp. 39–54). Binghamton, NY: The Haworth Press,

Halpern, C. (1969). A practicing lawyer views the right to treatment. *Georgetown Law Journal, 57,* 782–817.

Institute of Medicine. (1982). *Improving the quality in nursing homes.* Washington, DC: National Academy Press.

Kane, R. A., & Kane, R. L. (1987). *Long-term care: Principles, programs, and policies.* New York: Springer.

Katz, P. R., & Calkins, E. (Eds.). (1989). *Principles and practice of nursing home care.* New York: Springer.

Knapp, M., Bahr, Sr., R., & Strumpf, N. (1987). *Standards and scope of gerontologic nursing practice.* Kansas City, MO: American Nurses Association.

Lee, J. L., Cody, M., Cruize, M. J., Munroe, D. J., & Sullivan, T. J. (1990). Career counseling for nurses in skilled nursing facilities. *Gerontology and Geriatric Education, 10*(4), 23–36.

Liu, K. L., Doty, P., & Menton, K. (1990). Medicaid spendown in nursing homes. *The Gerontologist, 30*(1), 7–15.

Lowenthal, M. F. (1964). *Lives in distress.* New York: Basic Books.

Mathew, L., Sloan, P., Kilby, M., & Flood, R. (1988, March–April). What's different about a special care unit for dementia patients? A comparative study. *The American Journal of Alzheimer's Care and Related Disorders and Research,* 16–23.

McCoy, J. L., & Conley, R. W. (1990). Surveying board and care homes: Issues and data collection problems. *The Gerontologist, 30*(2), 147–53.

Mezey, M., Lynaugh, J., & Cartier, M. (1989). *Nursing homes and nursing care: Lessons from the teaching nursing homes.* New York: Springer.

Moss, F., & Halamandaris, V. (1977). *Too old, too sick, too bad: Nursing homes in America.* Germantown, MD: Aspen Systems.

National Association of Social Workers. (1993). *NASW clinical indicators for social work and psychological services in nursing homes.* Washington, DC: National Association of Social Workers.

National Center for Health Statistics. (1997, January 23). An overview of nursing homes and their current residents: Data from the 1995 National Nursing Home Survey. *Advance Data from Vital and Health Statistics,* no. 280. Bethesda, MD: National Center for Health Statistics.

National Center for Health Statistics. (1989). *The National Nursing Home Survey: 1985 summary for the United States.* DHHS Pub. No. PHS 89–1758. Washington, DC: U.S. Government Printing Office.

National Institute on Aging. (1978). *Protection of elderly research subjects.* Pub. no. (NIH) 79–180. Washington, DC: U.S. Government Printing Office.

New York State Senate Health Committee (T. Lombardi, Jr. Chairman). (1988, December). *Nursing home without walls program: A decade of quality care at home for New York's aged and disabled.* Albany, NY: New York State Senate.

Pillemer, K., & Moore, D. W. (1989). Abuse of patients in nursing homes: Findings from a survey of staff. *The Gerontologist, 29*(3), 314–319.

Psychiatric News. (1990, May 4). Alabama's mental health system on the road to recovery 20 years after Wyatt decision. *Psychiatric News,* 4 ff.

Quam, J. K., & Whitford, G. S. (1992). Educational needs of nursing home social workers at the baccalaureate level. In Mellor, M. J., & Solomon, R. (Eds.), *Geriatric social work education* (pp. 143–156). Binghamton, NY: The Haworth Press.

Rivlin, A. M., & Wiener, J. M. (1988). *Caring for the disabled elderly: Who will pay?* Washington, DC: The Brookings Institution.

Rovner, B. W., & Rabins, P. V. (1985). Mental illness among nursing home patients. *Hospital and Community Psychiatry, 36,* 119–20, 128.

Russell, L. B., & Manning, C. L. (1989). The effect of perspective on medicare expenditures. *The New England Journal of Medicine, 7,* 439–444.

Sager, M. A., Easterling, D. V., Kindig, D. A., & Anderson, O. W. (1989). Changes in the location of death after passage of Medicare's prospective payment system: A national study. *The New England Journal of Medicine, 7,* 433–439.

Select Committee on Aging, U.S. House of Representatives. (1989). *Board and care homes in America: A national tragedy.* Comm. pub. no. 101–711. Washington, DC: U.S. Government Printing Office.

Shaughnessy, P. W., & Kramer, A. M. (1990, January 4). The increased needs of patients in nursing homes and patients receiving home health care. *The New England Journal of Medicine, 322*(1), 21–27.

Vladeck, B. C. (1980). *Unloving care: The nursing home tragedy.* New York: The Twentieth Century Fund.

Vourlekis, B. S., Gelfand, D. E., & Green, R. R. (1992). Psychological needs and care in nursing homes: Comparison of views of social workers and administrators. *The Gerontologist, 32*(1), 113–119.

Weber, G. H., & McCall, G. J. (1987). *The nursing assistant's casebook of elder care.* New York: Springer.

ENDNOTES

1. To provide an understanding of the impact of institutional care on people, Erving Goffman's powerful essay, "On the Characteristics of Total Institutions" (1957), should be required reading, along with Stanton and Schwartz's classic study, "The Mental Hospital" (1956).

2. Personal communication, Marsha Goodwin, Director, Geriatrics and Grants Management, Office of Geriatrics and Extended Care, Veterans Health Administration, Department of Veterans Affairs, Washington, DC.

3. *Ibid.*

4. *Ibid.*

5. Lowenthal, M. F. (1964). *Lives in distress.* New York: Basic Books.

6. This outline (somewhat paraphrased) illustrates the effort of one state (Maryland) to establish guidelines (developed when Helen Padula was Coordinator, Services to the Aged, Maryland). Maryland was influenced by a preceding New York state effort. We emphasize that this is merely a guideline and should not be used in a rigid, immutable manner.

7. Lieberman, M. A., & Tobin, S. (1983). *The experience of old age: Stress, coping and survival.* New York: Basic Books. This book explores the psychological life of the elderly. Also see Borup, J. H. (1983–1984). Transfer trauma. *Generations, 8*(3), 17–22.

8. Shanas, E. (1962). *The health of older people: A social survey.* Cambridge, MA: Harvard University Press.

9. Lieberman, M. A. (1968). Psychological effects of institutionalization. *Journal of Gerontology, 23,* 343–353.

10. Fischer, J., & Breakley, W. R. (1986). Homelessness and mental health: An overview. *International Journal of Mental Health, 14,* 6–41.

11. Johnson, C. L., & Grant, L. A. (1985). *The nursing home in American society.* Baltimore, MD: Johns Hopkins University Press.

12. Select Committee on Aging, House of Representatives. (1989). *Board and care homes in America: A national tragedy.* Comm. Pub No. 101–711, Washington, DC: U.S. Government Printing Office; and Stone, R., Newcomber, R. J., & Saunders, M. (1982). *Descriptive analysis of board and care policy trends in 50 states.* San Francisco, CA: University of California, Aging Health Policy Center.

13. For a thorough review of nursing home practices, see *Consumer Reports,* August, 1995, 518–528. "Judging by the dozens of nursing homes we visited . . . and by the results of thousands of inspection reports we reviewed," the magazine says, "facilities range from inadequate to scandalous, and the good ones are hard to find."

14. National Center for Health Statistics. (1997, January 23). An overview of nursing homes and their current residents: Data from the 1995 National Nursing Home Survey. *Advance Data From Vital and Health Statistics,* no. 280. Hyattsville, MD: National Center for Health Statistics.

15. Health Care Financing Administration. (1996, Spring). *Health care financing review, 16*(3). Washington, DC: Health Care Financing Administration.

16. Health Care Financing Administration, U.S. Department of Health and Human Services. (1996, Sept. 5). OSCAR (On-line Survey, Certification, and Reporting system).

17. The Commonwealth Fund. (1996). *Nursing home restraints program review.* New York: The Commonwealth Fund, One East 75th Street, New York, NY 10021-1276.

18. For information on safety in long-term care institutions see *Standards for health care facilities,* National Fire Protection Association, Batterymarch Park, Quincy, MA 02169; and *Managing the environment of care for long-term care,* Joint Commission for Accreditation of Healthcare Organizations, 1 Renaissance Blvd., Oakbrook Terrace, IL 60181

19. Emerson Lombardo, N. B., Fogel, B. S., Robinson, G. K., & Weiss, H. P. (1996, August). Achieving mental health of nursing home residents: Overcoming

   barriers to mental health care. Boston: Hebrew Rehabilitation Center for Aged (1200 Centre St., Boston, MA 02121-1097)

20. Vladeck, B. C. (1980). *Unloving care: The nursing home tragedy.* New York: The Twentieth Century Fund.

21. Dunlop, B. B. (1980). Expanded home-based care for the impaired elderly: Solution or pipe dream? *American Journal of Public Health, 70*(5), 514–519.

22. Cohn, V. (1990, June 5). Finding the right nursing home. *Washington Post* (Health Section).

23. New York State Senate Health Committee (T. Lombardi, Jr., Chairman) (1988, December). *Nursing home without walls program: A decade of quality care at home for New York's aged and disabled.* Albany, NY: New York State Senate.

24. Health Care Financing Administration. (Spring, 1996). *Health care financing review, 17*(3). Washington, DC: Health Care Financing Administration.

25. Theoretically, the Medicaid legislation is supposed to cover the medically indigent of all ages, not all of whom are on welfare.

26. From U.S. Senate Committee on Finance. (1965). *Social Security Amendments of 1965: Report to accompany H. R. 6675, June 30, 1965.* Washington, DC: U.S. Government Printing Office, p. 149.

27. *Consumer Reports:* Who can afford a nursing home? May 1988.

28. Contact the Alzheimer's Disease and Related Disorders Association, Inc., 919 N. Michigan Ave., Suite 100, Chicago, IL, 60611-1676, (800) 621-0379.

29. We are indebted here to the work of Charles Halpern and his brief in the *Wyatt* v. *Stickney* case in Alabama concerning the right to treatment (Amici's proposed standards for adequate treatment, January 21, 1972).

30. (*Wyatt* v. *Stickney,* U.S. Court for Middle Dist. of Ala., Northern Div., Action No. 3195-N.) The Supreme Court, in handing down its unanimous decision in the landmark case of *Donaldson* v. *O'-Connor* in 1976, avoided the broad issue of "right to treatment" in favor of a more narrow judgment that a state cannot constitutionally confine a nondangerous mentally ill person who is capable of surviving safely on his or her own.

31. *Psychiatric News:* Alabama's mental health system on road to recovery 20 years after Wyatt Decision. May 4, 1990, 4 ff.

32. Bazelon, Judge D. (1969). Implementing the right to treatment. *University of Chicago Law Review,* 742, 746.

33. Modified from the statement affirmed Nov. 17, 1972 by the Board of Trustees of the American Hospital Association, The Association's most recent "Patient's Bill of Rights" is from 1975. It is expected to be revised in the near future.

34. *Federal Register 54*(21), February 2, 1989.

35. Ennis, B., & Siegel, L. (1973). *The rights of mental patients: The basic ACLU guide to a mental patient's rights.* New York: Richard W. Baron.

36. The concept of academic (teaching/research) nursing is developed in Butler, R. N. (1980). *The impact of Alzheimer's disease on the nation's elderly,* testimony before the U.S. Senate Subcommittee on Aging and the Subcommittee on Labor/HEW Appropriation, July 15, 1980; and in Butler, R. N. (1981). The teaching nursing home.

Journal of the American Medical Association, 245(14), 1435–1437.

37. The DeSimon Foundation of Wilmett, Illinois, advocates research and provides support through patient groups: 1-800-23-SIMON.

38. The October 1985 issue of *Quarterly,* the journal of the Canadian Long-Term Care Association, describes the development of practical and humane alternate solutions to the use of restraints—for example, in cases of "wanderers." Carter and T. Franklin Williams have helped bring national attention to the issue of restraints. The Williamses have reported that, contrary to popular belief, there have been no successful law suits against nursing homes because they failed to use restraints. A current research study, "The Epidemiology and Demonstration Project on Restraint Use," which is funded by the Commonwealth Fund and is being conducted at New York City's Jewish Home and Hospital for the Aged, is a further step toward the achievement of restraint-free environments in U.S. institutions.

39. National Institute on Aging. (1978). *Protection of elderly research subjects.* Pub. No. (NIH) 79–180. Washington, DC: U.S. Government Printing Office. For a summary paper on the subject, see Butler, R. N. (1980). Protection of elderly research subjects. *Clinical Research, 28,* 33–35.

40. See Health Standards and Quality Bureau, Office of Standards and Certification, Health Care Financing Administration, Baltimore, MD.

41. Taulbee, L., & Folsom, J. C. (1966). Reality orientation for geriatric patients. *Hospital and Community Psychiatry, 17,* 133–135.

42. Reisberg, B. (1987). Reality orientation. In Maddox, G. (Ed.), *The encyclopedia of aging* (pp. 558–559). New York: Springer.

CHAPTER 12

PSYCHOTHERAPY
AND ENVIRONMENTAL THERAPY

INDIVIDUAL PSYCHOTHERAPY

GROUP THERAPY

INTERGENERATIONAL FAMILY THERAPY
AND COUPLES THERAPY

BEHAVIORAL THERAPIES

ENVIRONMENTAL THERAPY

In this chapter we discuss the common modalities of psychotherapy—individual, group, family—and consider environmental therapy, under which we include age awareness and acceptance, federal policies to aid older persons, social roles, location and mobilization of resources, registration drives, self-help and self-care, employment and productive aging, advocacy, legal and consultative services, and encouragement of political activity on the part of older people.

We considered the roles of the mental health specialists and the team concept in Chapter 8. All forms of environmental therapy and psychotherapy can be provided by the mental health team as a functioning unit (in varied combinations of mental health specialists, together with the elderly and their family members) or by individual specialists from all of the disciplines.

INDIVIDUAL PSYCHOTHERAPY

Individual psychotherapy is *least* available to older people compared to other age groups, and yet it should be a vital part of the repertoire of treatment in later life. Older persons need the opportunity to talk and to have a listener. They need the therapist's support in their efforts to "seize the

day" and build a "life" during the remaining time available.[1]

Therapists in private practice have minimal contact with older persons. Public clinics also report low rates of contact of any kind, but especially little in the way of psychotherapeutic work. Psychiatrists, social workers, psychologists, and other members of mental health teams do not see many older people; when they do, the purposes are usually diagnostic and the effort is "disposition."

Old age is the period in life with the greatest number of profound crises, often occurring in multiples and with high frequency. The critical psychological events in this age group are the familiar human emotional reactions to death and grief, diseases, and disabilities. Depression and anxiety escalate, defensive behavior is seen, earlier personality components may reappear in exaggerated forms, and newly formed functional states are frequently noted. These conditions require psychotherapeutic efforts, in-depth as well as supportive.

The designation of older people as "good" or "poor" candidates for psychotherapy should be questioned, especially the implication that a number of people should not be offered treatment because they cannot "use" it. We wonder how this judgment can be made before treatment has begun. Some older people who meet all the criteria for "good" candidates fail to find therapy helpful, whereas "poor" candidates may show unexpected response and results. The test of objectivity is the willingness to give adequate trials to *all* persons without allowing our theories, prejudices, and fears to interfere. Theories, in any case, can be masterful camouflages. For example, Freud was preoccupied with death and pessimistic about old age. His work reflects his avoidance of the issues of late life and his decision to explain the human personality only in terms of the early years. Ironically, we would barely know of him had he died before the age of 40, since his finest work was done in the latter half of his life.

We submit, on the grounds of clinical experience, that many older persons, if not severely brain-damaged, are very receptive to psychotherapy and can in no way be considered poor candidates. They often exhibit a strong drive to resolve problems, to put their lives in order, and to find satisfactions and the opportunity for a "second chance." Their capacity to change has been demonstrated in many instances; the fact that older people spontaneously begin reviewing their lives in a way similar to psychotherapy (the concept of the "life review") is indicative of the manner in which this process is part of the natural course of late life. Even the brain-damaged elderly can gain from psychotherapy as Goldfarb, among others, demonstrated early on.[2]

Any evidence pointing toward older people as untreatable is usually to be found in the minds of therapists rather than in empirical studies. Powerful forces of countertransference and cultural prejudice are at work, including personal fear and despair over aging and death. Therapeutic pessimism and nihilism are inappropriate, invalid, and inhumane. Older people, like the young, can gain from insight and understanding, from objectivity and empathy. Biology is not destiny in old age any more than in youth. Personal history and cultural influences are of profound importance and form a background against which change at any age can occur through education and insight.

Theoretical Considerations

Freud and the vast majority of his followers ruled out psychoanalysis for older persons without ever testing its usefulness. Abraham raised some objections to this general negativism, reporting on five persons he called "old" who were in their fifties.[3] He and Jelliffe stated the "age of the neurosis" is more important than the age of the patient.[4] Grotjahn reported on analytic work with a 71-year-old client with "senile brain disease."[5] Wayne, Meerloo, Gitelson, Alexander, Atkin, and Kaufman were among those who first described some limited psychotherapeutic efforts with older people. In spite of early pessimism, psychoanalytic concepts have proved useful in work with the elderly (see Chapter 8).

Jung's concept of stages of development are readily applicable to the elderly condition. It is interesting that two-thirds of Jung's practice was made up of middle-aged and older persons, whereas Freud's private practice was composed of younger patients. These differences may help to account for variations in theoretical emphases, with Freud's therapy concentrating on youth and sex, while Jung emphasized individuation and creativity.

Goldfarb, Busse, Linden, Weinberg, Butler, and others have devoted substantial amounts of their public and private psychiatric clinical work to older people. Goldfarb's "brief therapy" and Linden's work with group therapy became the best known of these early efforts in therapy.[6]

Carl R. Rogers, Abraham Maslow, and Rollo May contributed to the development of the so-called "Third Force" in psychology, distinguishing it from psychoanalysis and behaviorism. (See Chapter 8.) Rogers's client-centered therapy, which referred to adopting an empathic attitude toward patients, emphasized the individual's capacity for life-long growth and development and the importance of an unconditional, positive relationship between client and therapist. In contrast to psychoanalysis, Rogers believed therapy should not dwell on the past, nor should it be built on a medical model of diagnosis and cure. Rather, it should focus on self-actualization as the main motivational force in therapy. Rogers called his perspective "humanistic psychology,"[7] and his emphasis on this approach when working with groups helped develop the "encounter group," the concept of group-centered leadership and a model for the facilitation of learning in educational settings.

Existential therapists have demonstrated little interest in old age. Yet, because of the tendency of older people to review their lives, to seek meaning and to deal with death, there is an obvious existential component to any therapeutic work with them. We have found ideas of Buber[8] (the importance of relationships with others) and Frankl[9] (the possibilities within the confines of the "death camp") to be particularly useful for older people.

Mainstream psychotherapy, in general, has become more eclectic—utilizing the best of varying theories. Especially valuable has been the emergence of cognitive therapy (Aaron Beck) which assumes that depression is based on distorted thinking and unrealistically negative views that patients have about themselves, the world, and the future. The task of the therapy is to reevaluate and correct the thinking.

An allied form of therapy, interpersonal psychotherapy, developed by Gerald Klerman and Myrna Weissman, assumes that depression is something that happens to the individual and requires treatment. Interpersonal psychotherapy focuses on interpersonal and social functioning, and improvement must be made there before the depression will be alleviated. The National Institute of Mental Health study on 250 depressed patients (aged 21 to 60), conducted at the University of Pittsburgh, University of Oklahoma, and George Washington University, found that cognitive behavioral therapy and interpersonal psychotherapy achieved results comparable to a standard antidepressant drug, Imipramine.[10] (Because of its careful and useful design, the study

was described by psychiatrist Jerome Frank, in his introduction to the 1986 annual meeting of the American Psychiatric Association as "the standard against which all other psychotherapy research will be assessed.")

All forms of psychotherapy—from "uncovering" to "supportive" to "reeducative" and from Freudian to Jungian to Rogerian—can contribute to a better understanding of the psychology and psychotherapy of old age. In addition a less "purist" attitude on the part of therapists toward the use of psychoactive medications has led to a more appropriate use of such medications as an adjunct to "talking" therapy. Further integration and eclectic utilization of all contemporary personality theories and practices, including the life-cycle perspective of human life along with the use of medication when appropriate, are needed. The complexities of late life require complex therapy.

> We cannot live the afternoon of life according to the program of life's morning, for what was great in the morning will be little at evening, and what in the morning was true, will at evening have become a lie. I have given psychological treatment to too many people of advancing years, and have looked too often into the secret chambers of their souls, not to be moved by this fundamental truth.[11]

Some Personal Experiences with Older People in Psychotherapy

It is quite amazing that the question most frequently asked by professionals and lay persons alike is whether older people can make use of any psychotherapy that goes beyond support and simple guidance. This implies a quite naive assumption that old age brings an inevitable, implacable, and global loss of mental and emotional faculties. The examples in history, philosophy, literature, music, theology, and every other field of human activity ought to be enough to make us stand in awe of the intellectual, spiritual, emotional, and creative capacities of our elders. They have been and are often our most richly endowed leaders, mentors, and teachers.

Although we have conducted psychotherapy with older persons in a wide assortment of settings and have referred to this work throughout the book, we present here seven brief examples from the recent private practice of author Myrna Lewis to give some of the personal flavor and variety of work with older people:

A married couple in their seventies came for sex counseling. After a number of months of therapy, they wished to work on their sexual concerns more intensively and contacted Masters and Johnson's clinic. They were accepted as patients, flew to St. Louis, and took the intensive 2-week treatment program (paid for with part of their savings). Medical tests also showed the man to have a physical potency problem involving vascular difficulties. They are pursuing treatment for this condition, as well as their relationship problems. Although the final results of all of their efforts are still not clear, they remain determined to try whatever possibly can improve their sex life, since both of them had enjoyed it so much in the past.

A woman in her early sixties, unmarried, with a dependent, childlike demeanor, wished to become more "mature" and less anxious and dependent. During the course of therapy she found a new job where she functioned in a more adult manner, began to move out of her passive habits socially by helping to organize groups for single older persons, and eventually reestablished a former romantic relationship with a man whom she had known for 20 years. She is now involved in developing that relationship with the help of psychotherapy.

A male homosexual couple (one man in his late sixties and one in his late fifties) requested help in resolving problems in their relationship. After having lived together for 15 years, they eventually decided, during the course of therapy, to live in separate homes and have other intimacies but to continue their close friendship and support of one another. The older man, whose health had been deteriorat-

ing, continued to receive help with his disabilities from the younger one.

A middle-aged brother and sister resolved their differences with one another in helping an aged and mentally and physically infirm mother accept a move to a nursing home. The older woman refused to join them in family therapy but was able to communicate her wishes through her children to the therapist so effectively that a solution was found that was acceptable to her as well as to them.

An 80-year-old man was referred by his doctor for depression over his heart problems. However when given the opportunity to talk confidentially, the man revealed the depression centered around his guilt at conducting a long-term affair with a middle-aged housekeeper living in his home while his wife remained unaware of the nature of this relationship. After much soul-searching he concluded that he wished to continue the affair, since his wife, as he put it, was glad to be rid of his requests for sex and affection and seemed totally involved with her many activities. He still phones for an appointment now and then to talk over his concerns about the future of the younger woman when he dies and his own feelings about his eventual death and that of his wife.

A retired married couple in their sixties wished to come to a decision about remaining married. Unable to talk civilly with each other even in the therapist's presence, they are each engaged in writing long essays in between therapy sessions about their anger, hopes, disappointments, and memories of their marriage. These are exchanged with each other and form the basis of a beginning analysis of the problems. Meanwhile, they are being helped by the therapist to learn the elementary tactics of fair fighting and problem solving.

A woman in her middle seventies came, wanting to resolve her lifelong depression and difficulty in relating to people. She felt she was "unable to love."

Through careful and often painful intensive psychotherapy aimed at insight, and after several years of treatment, she began to be able to successfully counter her tendency to avoid intimacy by drawing on her understanding of her childhood relationship with a cold, intellectual mother. In her fascination with this process she also became involved in various church groups aimed at enriching emotional responses, and she eventually moved from participant to training as a group leader, teaching others to lead such support groups. She still uses individual psychotherapy to help recognize when she is starting to withdraw and to deal with her disappointment when she does so.

It seems obvious from our own and others' case examples that we can safely lay to rest the question of the ability of older people to use psychotherapy and concentrate on the more relevant questions about the kind, length, and combinations of therapies that are most useful for the issues of later life.

Common Themes in Psychotherapy with Older Persons

New Starts and Second Chances. Older people often express a wish to undo some of the patterns of their life, to unritualize behavior and give some newness to their experiences. These people speak of the monotony or dryness of their experiences, a kind of "salt losing its savor" feeling. This should be met not just with feeble efforts to regain what has been lost but with attempts to build new interests and new possibilities.

Death in Disguise. Some older people have resolved their personal feelings about death. Others manage to deny death without serious emotional consequences. But a number of older people need help, first in recognizing the source of their anxieties and fears (death) and then in reaching some degree of accommodation with the inevitable. Therapists must be able to recognize disguised fears of death in patients (and in themselves—often a reason for avoiding working with the elderly). For example, one man spoke of "running

toward that man and then I saw him and I slowed down to a walk." He was referring to death. In his attempts to revitalize his life, the spectre of death presented him with an ominous impediment that he had to face before therapy (and life) could continue in the direction he wanted to go.

Keen Awareness of Time. There is an obvious concern with time when it is clear that the remaining days are running short. Younger therapists often have great difficulty understanding what it means *not* to think in terms of a future. We must take our cues from older people who have faced this issue squarely; the development of a sense of immediacy, of the here-and-now, of presentness—all aid in the evolution of a sense of enjoyment and tranquility, which we have called *elementality.*

Grief and Restitution. Psychotherapy in old age must deal with grief, with losses of loved ones, and with dysfunctioning of one's own body and its parts. It might be said, "Where depression is, let grief be." If grief is denied outlet, it is possible that depression may occur. Insulation or denial of grief is not the sole cause of depression, of course, since ambivalence toward the deceased (that is, anger and conflict) complicates the usual course of grief. A task of therapy is to help open up the grief process. For example, widows or widowers should be encouraged to discuss whether they felt they did all that could be done. Efforts at restitution are crucial. One of the most important goals in therapy is helping the older person find a secure confidant, a person with whom he or she can speak intimately, either in the family or in the person's circle of friends and acquaintances.

Guilt and Atonement.

We have left undone those things which we ought to have done; and we have done those things which we ought not to have done.

The 51st Psalm opens with "Miserere, mei Deus" (Have mercy on me, O God). The cry for mercy, indeed for clemency, in the face of death must be heard. Although the therapist does not often have it within his or her power to "grant" mercy or bring full alleviation of the distress, he or she can listen, really listen, bear witness, be able, as it were, to attest to the realities of the life described, and thus help give meaning and validity to that life. Reality must be central. If there were simple alignments between our drives, our moral strictures, and the workings of the world, if Freud were dead wrong, we could move merrily along. If aging and disability did not exist; if lives were not filled up with malevolence, acts of violence, and real wrongs done to others and oneself, then we could simply reassure the older people who are sick with guilt. But psychotherapy in old age is a therapy of atonement as well as of restitution. One cannot deny cruel and thoughtless acts, falsely reassuring that all is irrational Freudian guilt. Facing genuine guilt as well as the attrition of the person's physical and emotional world is what makes psychotherapy with the aging an intellectually and emotionally powerful experience. The therapist cannot win out against death, but he or she can win out for life, for a sense of the real, for the kind of growth that truly matters, dealing as it does with the evaluation of ways to love—and hate—with the meanings of human conduct, with an appreciation of human nature and the succession of the generations. And after learning to face guilt unflinchingly and honestly, reconciliation may be possible with spouses, siblings, children, and friends.

Autonomy versus Identity.   Identity, while an important concept, has been found to be difficult to study in various age groups. In our clinical experience, autonomy should be separated from identity as a concept. The so-called identity crisis of the adolescent is as much a problem of establishing freedom and achieving responsibility and self-sufficiency (autonomy) as it is one of identity ("self-sameness"), if not more so. Erikson deals with only one side of this issue.

> The term identity expresses . . . mutual relation in that it connotes both a persistent sameness within

oneself (self-sameness) and a persistent sharing of some kind of essential character with others.[12]

In old age most healthy people find themselves essentially the same as they have always been (as in data, for instance, from interviews before the mirror, Chapter 9). If significant medical and psychiatric problems emerge, such as major bodily changes and emotional difficulties like depression, the sense of self may go through rapid reevaluation. But again the problem of autonomy, not identity, is the most critical. The older person wonders, "Can I survive independently without being a burden?" It is true, of course, that if one's identity is closely bound to autonomy, the two merge, as it were, together. The person, for instance, whose identity has been that of a dependent person may find it easier to accept illness and institutionalization than the so-called independent, autonomous person whose identity has been structured accordingly. The latter may suffer more in dependent situations despite a "sound" identity by usual standards. Yet it appears to us that, in general, autonomy is a more decisive determinant of human behavior than identity—at all ages.

The eleven-year study at the National Institute of Mental Health from 1955 to 1966 showed that persons with goals and organization in their lives lived longer. The importance of mastery and control over one's life are summarized by Rodin.[13]

With respect to the life review, identity and autonomy are equally important.[14] But here again we find our experiences at variance with Erikson, but for a different reason. We find that older persons often wish to escape their identities and try something new, The fatalistic acceptance proposed by Erikson in his bipolar view of ego identity versus despair is not universal, as seen in those elderly who long for change and renewal—a shedding of their old skins for a new chance at life or a new glimpse of themselves.

Need for Assertion.   A sense of helplessness tends to occur especially when one is ill or severely incapacitated in any way. During such bouts of illness, there is seldom adequate opportunity to be assertive in a way that alleviates this feeling. A bedridden person, for example, may finally resort to purposefully urinating in bed to express angry feelings. We have known a number of people who have refused to take baths, sending what seems to be a direct, angry message to their families or caregivers. Others may become dictatorial to nursing staff or family and friends. Persons caring for the ill or handicapped must assist them in finding ways to assert themselves in a positive manner that brings at least a measure of the self-esteem necessary for human dignity.

Self-mastery and control and their relationship to health become more important in old age. Studies such as those conducted by the National Institute of Health show that restrictions in control have detrimental effects on the health of older people. At times, however, greater control over activities and health may produce negative physical and psychological results, such as stress, worry, and self-blame.[15] There may be a point of diminishing returns, beyond which the older person becomes overwhelmed by too much responsibility. This is a psychological "overload," not unlike the Goldstein catastrophic reaction described in Chapter 9.

Therapeutic Issues

Am I a "Patient"?   Insight into one's condition—that is, agreement that one has a psychiatric condition—is held by many to be a crucial prognostic indicator. On the other hand, humiliating labeling as a "patient" and all too willing acceptance of the "sick role" are questionable too. We believe it is important that appraisal be flexible and individualized. For some, a useful agreement can be made with the older person to collaborate in an effort to deal with an "illness" or "emotional problem." For other older persons it seems more functionally useful to see that they receive necessary mental health services without having to identify with the patient role.

A Vigilant Search for Signs of Health.   Training in the mental health professions tends to emphasize pathology. However, with older people, as with all ages, it is as critical to identify and encourage areas of health as it is to clarify problems. Many beautifully "diagnosed" persons never reach their full potential in treatment because the therapist fails to recognize and utilize their strengths and assets in the therapeutic process. Vigilance in searching out signs of health may be rewarded with faster treatment progress and a more satisfactory outcome.

Significance of Certain Illusions.   The therapist must not in any way be destructive of the processes of illusion and denial needed by older people. One must discuss the fact of death, the facts of loss, and the problems of grief, but this must always be in the context of possibilities, restitution, and resolution. The same principle applies in work with persons of all ages; one must work compassionately and carefully to understand and encourage a realistic lowering of defenses rather than attacking them overtly. Too much harsh or painful reality implanted too quickly can lead to overwhelming panic or emotional devastation.

The Question of "Cures."   In the strictly biomedical realm, we have come to expect genuine "cures" through the use of such agents as antibiotics and surgical interventions. However, in the emotional or psychological domain, we recognize that "cure" is a continuing and never fully completed process.

Jung wrote,

> The serious problems in life are never fully solved. If ever they should appear to be so, it is a sure sign that something has been lost. The meaning and purpose of a problem seems to lie not in its solution but in our working at it incessantly.[16]

The struggle, the need for change, and the opportunity for change—the really profound problems, the deeper intricacies of human existence—are never completed or cured; yet, they are subject to alteration up to the point of death.

The Value of Listening. It is imperative to listen attentively, to bear witness, to heed the telltale echoes of the past, to pick up the flatness of speech where distant feelings have died, to observe outbursts of unresolved issues in lives, and to empathize with the irreconcilable, even when the older patient is garrulous, continually reminiscing, importunate, and querulous, the fact is that talk is necessary and listening by another mandatory. One must also listen to and interpret silences.

The American Association of Retired People (AARP) has designed a manual to help train volunteer visitors in the art of listening to and reminiscing with homebound or institutionalized older persons.[17] Such "listeners" are trained to visit the older person and encourage reminiscence for both therapeutic and recreational purposes.

The Possible Worth of Just One Therapeutic Session. In the best of therapy, each session must involve active work, thinking through, building hypotheses, and persistently searching out ways to assist the person. This is especially true for the older person for whom there may be only one session available (because of impending death, physical weaknesses, or lack of access to the therapist). When this is the case, much can be done in a short time.

Jungian analyst Florida Scott-Maxwell, who herself was in her eighties when she wrote these words, commented:

A farmer's wife came and told a tragic story where nothing could be done, but her compassion and strength made it possible to continue. As usual with these cases, I asked if she would care to come again; she looked a little surprised, and said, "There is no need, I've told you everything." She had only wanted to confide in someone she respected, in case there was more she could do, and not to be so alone in her hard life. . . . One visit was enough for her.[18]

The brief amount of time must be measured in terms of the quality of the experience rather than the quantity.

Telephone Psychotherapy. Because of the financial and physical limitations of older people, the therapist should be very flexible about the use of the telephone in conducting psychotherapy.

> *One 75-year-old man, with a history of heart attacks and continuing angina, would talk by phone when he could not travel. Even then he might have to interrupt his sessions to place a nitroglycerin tablet under his tongue. He never took obvious "advantage" of the situation and attended about 90% of his sessions in person.*

Telephone outreach therapy is especially valuable for the homebound older person. (Unfortunately, about one-third of older people do not have telephones, reminding us again of the poverty of old age.) It is also an excellent method for giving support and reassurance to an insecure or unstable person who may need something less than a regularly scheduled office appointment. In addition, volunteers can be used to provide telephone answering services at crisis centers and in telephone reassurance programs. Some elderly (for example, those with chronic schizophrenia) may need the distancing that a telephone provides, while at the same time achieving some degree of verbal closeness. The telephone can also be a substitute for face-to-face sessions during periods of bad weather when many elderly are reluctant to travel. Fees for prearranged phone calls may be charged when such phone sessions serve as alternatives for face-to-face psychotherapy sessions.

Self-Confrontation and the Use of Memory Aids. Still and motion pictures of the individual as well as audio and video tape recordings have been used in research and in clinical practice for various age groups and diagnostic categories. In our own work, we have used photo albums, the mirror, and the tape recorder in helping older persons come "face to face" with themselves. The need for self-definition in the life review and the problem of memory argue for the value to the patient of being able to take tape recordings and video tapes home, for instance, for further listening and reflection. A major goal of such self-confrontational processes is to encourage an active participation in the therapeutic process, rather than a passive, dependent position.

Memory aids serve a further purpose. Providing direct instructions, for instance, written or taped, for medication schedules and for the statement of general treatment principles or specifics may be useful for the older patient, so long as this is not done in a manner that is disrespectful of the person's own view of his or her capacities for memory.

Life Review Therapy.   Life review therapy is a more structured and purposive concept than simple reminiscence or recalling the past.[19] (See also Chapter 4 for a description of the life review concept.) It includes the taking of an extensive autobiography from the older person and from other family members as indicated. Such memoirs can also be preserved by means of tape recordings or video tapes. The use of family albums, scrapbooks, and other memorabilia, the searching out of genealogies, and pilgrimages back to places of import all evoke crucial memories, responses, and understanding in patients. A summation of one's life work by some means is useful. For those who have children, a summary of feelings about parenting is important. The goals and consequences of these steps include a reexamination of one's life that may result in expiation of guilt, the resolution of intrapsychic conflicts, the reconciliation of family relationships, the transmission of knowledge and values to those who follow, and the renewal of ideals of citizenship and the responsibility for creating a meaningful life. Lieberman and Tobin have confirmed that reminiscence is crucial to the emotional livelihood of an elder person, helping to resolve past conflicts and enabling the development of a coherent life history.[20]

The life review can also be conducted as part of group activity.[21] Groups of all kinds—nursing home residents, senior center participants,[22] social groups, therapy groups—can use the life review to help older persons reconstruct and reevaluate their lives.[23] The concept of life review has been bolstered by an increasing interest in the United States in finding one's ethnic "roots." In fact, a significant part of tourism relates to people tracing their heritage. The United States has people from no fewer than 134 backgrounds. Fifty million, or 22% of the population, claim English lineage, and 49 million trace their lineage to Germany. The next most numerous are, respectively, Irish, African American, French, Italian, Scottish, Polish, Mexican, and American Indian. Handbooks for composing a personal autobiography are being published to aid nonprofessional writers in exploring and describing their history and lives.[24] These accounts form a valuable first-person historical source for use by families, sociologists, cultural historians, and others, in addition to providing therapeutic benefits and satisfaction for the older person.

Attempts are rapidly being made to more clearly conceptualize reminiscence and the life review and test their impact on older persons. A sample list of recent articles that discuss this popular subject appears at the end of this chapter (Selected Readings in Reminiscence).

The Validity of the Life Review.   Although the concept of life review has become entrenched in both the literature and practice of gerontology, nursing, social work, and to some degree psychology and psychiatry, aspects of the life review have been called into question, and many questions remain unanswered. For example, how does one determine whether memories have a factual basis or are defensive distortions? How effective or even possible is external verification of memories? Studies show, for example, that even mothers' memories of the timing of the most simple events in their children's development, such as toilet training, are not always recalled with accuracy. What are the interconnections between emotions and memories? Personal myths emerge from childhood and may be held throughout life, affecting one's self-image and most certainly influencing reminiscences. How do self-representations change over time? What are the connections between memories and identity or self-definition? What is more important, that which we remember or that which we forget, or both? How do we confirm some findings that people regret most the things that they failed to do rather than what they did do?

The life review helps both to uncover and stabilize one's past selfhood. Tolstoy at 81 said, "I remember very vividly that I am conscious of myself in exactly the same way now, at 81, as I was conscious of myself, my 'I,' at five or six years of age. Consciousness is immovable. Due to this alone there is a movement which we call 'time.' If time moves on, then there must be something that stands still, the consciousness of my 'I' stands still."[25] This is a common feeling, substantiated by extensive work at the National Institute on Aging's Baltimore Longitudinal Study of Aging.

There have been some careful studies that demonstrated the effect of life review on some dependent variables, such as depression and life satisfaction. It is true that much work still needs to be done to effectively operationalize outcome measures. But how does one "measure" meaning in life, guilt and expiation, redemption, and reconciliation?

Is the life review a universal occurrence? Studies report that between 49% and 84.1% of older persons have reviewed their lives or are currently reviewing them. Of course, this does not preclude the possibility that all persons might eventually do so. One study showed that those closer to death showed significantly less reminiscence activity and significantly less introspection when compared with matched controls, but this could be consistent with the original theoretical formulation that suggested post-review serenity or ataraxia. Subjects in these studies were not always followed through to the time of death. Some individuals may only review their lives on their death bed. A further complication is the difficulty of de-

termining if the life review has already occurred since the process is not always a conscious one. The life review often occurs over a considerable period of time and only after a significant relationship has been established either with a mental health professional or a trained empathic listener.

One study reported asking questions such as, "Some people review and evaluate their past in order to get an overall picture of their life. This is called a life review. Have you reviewed or are you currently reviewing your life?" This question does not always give access to the life review, and it might not be immediately answerable by all individuals. Such a literal, objective, or conscious approach also contrasts with the context of intensive psychotherapy and intensive research interviews that led to the original formulation. This formulation assumed the existence of the unconscious, the division of the mind in psychoanalytic theory that contains memories or repressed desires, not subject to conscious perception or control but often affecting conscious thought and behavior.

Professionals in nursing, social work, occupational therapy, physical therapy, arts and music therapy, psychology, medicine, and psychiatry have advocated reminiscence and life review as ways to help patients achieve self-esteem. The life review may aid people to resolve conflicts in their lives. Part of the therapeutic value of life review therapy for older persons may be the simple fact that someone is listening to them and that approaching death, affording them little time, is a potent incentive for positive change, such as improvement in mood, increased self-esteem, and so forth.

Life Review and New Directions in Psychiatry. What will happen now that psychiatrists have moved further away from psychodynamics and the inner life to the use of psychoactive medications in their practices? Perhaps more people will feel good and healthier quicker. Painful feelings will be assuaged. But were medications utilized in the context of ongoing psychotherapy, self-understanding might also grow. There need not be a dichotomy here, for both psychoactive medications, such as antidepressants, and psychotherapy should be concurrent and reinforcing.

What about the fact that relatively few gerontologists and psychologists have spent significant amounts of time being with and listening to older people? We will lose opportunities to better understand the inner life if we depend upon drugs alone and if psychologists and gerontologists do not explore human personalities in depth. We do not know how lasting either psychopharmacological or psychotherapeutic approaches are, but it is hard to believe a pill gets to the bottom of genuine guilt due to acts of commission or omission. Is there no place for some measure of human suffering? Is there not also a time for celebration when painful issues are successfully resolved?

The life review concept has contributed to a better understanding of late-life and end-of-life development as well as development across the life span. It has helped demonstrate the therapeutic value of reminiscence for older people and helped eliminate prejudice against those who reminisce. But people and their life stories are more complex than any presently available methods for their study allow. Therefore we must encourage further study of life-span developmental psychology.

It has been suggested that the life review might possibly not be universal or even exclusively precipitated by approaching death. Yet it is remarkably common among older people, and the prospect of death is one of its most common triggers. Only in old age with the proximity of death can one truly experience a personal sense of the entire life cycle. That makes old age a unique state of life and makes the review of life at that time equally unique.

Psychotherapy and the Process of Dying

Psychotherapy.   The fundamental issues in life and, consequently, in psychotherapy—love, guilt and atonement, separation and integration—can be dealt with to the very end of life. It is imperative to encourage the life review and thus aid in the resolution of old as well as recent conflicts.

Each person should have the opportunity to live as fully as possible up to the moment of death. It is unthinking and cruel, as long as they have a "present" existence, to write off as untreatable people who have no dependable "future."

The two major fears of older people with whom we have worked are (1) fear of pain, indignity, loneliness, and depersonalization during dying and the possibility of dying alone; and (2) worry about burdening survivors with the expenses of dying and burial. These fears must be addressed in any work with those who are dying.

In her work Elisabeth Kübler-Ross delineated five psychological stages that occur during the process of dying, as well as providing a therapeutic approach to assist persons with terminal illnesses. As we discussed in Chapter 4, many investigators and clinicians, eventually including Kübler-Ross herself, found the stage theory too rigid and arbitrary in describing what really happens when a person is dying. The reality is more like a jumble of conflicting or alternating reactions running the gamut from denial to acceptance, with a tremendous variation affected by age, sex, race, ethnic group, social setting, and personality. Kübler-Ross's work has brought tremendous attention, sympathy, and interest to the process of dying. Her pioneering work has been expanded on by others in the effort to help the dying in a more humane and psychologically sound manner.

The Hospice Movement.   Dr. Cicely Saunders's innovations in the care of the dying have evoked widespread interest. The modern hospice concept began in 1843 when Catholic widows in Lyons, France, established a hospice for poor women with incurable cancer.[26] In 1967, Saunders opened St. Christopher's Hospice in London for patients in the final stages of fatal disease.

> A modern hospice was planned, built, and staffed under the guidance of Dr. Cicely Saunders to enable patients who are in the last stages of their illness to have a peaceful and above all a tranquil closure to life and to be supportive to the patients' relatives and friends in their bereavement. "Contrary to com-

mon belief, patients in the proper atmosphere, and helped by modern medicine and nursing, can be maintained in an alert and peaceful frame of mind to the last. . . ."[27]

Family and friends are actively involved in care; a homelike atmosphere is encouraged with flowers, colors, and even visiting pets; and the patient often goes back and forth between hospice and home. Saunders's ideas are now providing a model for a number of hospices and hospice-service programs in the United States. Care is offered on the basis of what is most humane and comforting at each point in the dying person's life.

The National Cancer Institute, the National Institute on Aging, the National Institute on Mental Health, the Administration on Aging, and the Veterans Administration, among other federal agencies, have supported various studies and demonstrations of hospice care.[28]

Hospice concepts ideally should become automatic components of standard health care for the dying in any location, rather than requiring new buildings and new systems of reimbursement. (See Home Hospice Care in Chapter 10.) The concepts and practices central to the care of the dying are:

1. Providing physical care for the dying person, easing pain and other discomforts, giving emotional support, and assisting people to put their lives in order through use of the life review and other psychological therapies.
2. Helping people to die in their home when possible, since this is the preferred location for most people.
3. Helping support the surviving loved ones who are at risk for morbidity and mortality.
4. Educating health and social care providers and the public.

Permitting Death (The "Right to Die").   There are medico-legal considerations that go beyond psychotherapeutic efforts with the dying. Advances in technology through artificial support of circulation, respiration, and nutrition have made it possible to preserve life in persons who in the past would have died earlier.

Euthanasia, a Greek term that means a painless, good death, has become a highly emotional subject. Distinction is usually made between "passive euthanasia" and "active euthanasia" (or "mercy killing"). With passive euthanasia, a physician withdraws or refuses life-support therapy, thereby allowing a terminally-ill patient to die without medical intervention, except for pain medication and other measures solely for provision of comfort. The patient has the right to consent or refuse care. Family involvement occurs with the patient's permission.

In cases of patients too infirm or comatose to express their wishes, documents known as "advance directives" may have been signed in advance. "Living wills" and durable powers of attorney for health care decisions are examples.[29] All states now recognize the right of a patient to provide informed consent via a living will or other document. In some states, oral directives given to relatives or friends may carry legal weight.

When a patient is mentally or physically incompetent and has provided no advance directives, the situation becomes infinitely more complicated. Courts and legislatures are in the process of developing specific legal standards for decision-making. For example, the Supreme Courts of a number of states, along with a number of lower courts, have recently permitted removal of feeding tubes from comatose, severely incapacitated patients. The Council on Judicial and Ethical Affairs of the American Medical Association in 1986 stated that under certain circumstances the withholding of food and fluids from the comatose is not unethical.

On the other hand, "active euthanasia," namely the active intervention of another person to end the life of a terminally-ill person, is illegal in every country of the world, with the exception of certain specific cases in the Netherlands.

It is currently fashionable to regard medical technology as cruel when it is used to keep patients alive who are otherwise near death. At times this argument is valid. But it is extremely easy to go one step further and regard the use of such technology as wasteful when it is used on older people. The powerful devaluation of the old is thereby given new credibility under the guise of "death with dignity." Each patient is different and should receive individual consideration. Medical procedures that may be an unnecessary ordeal for some (for example, major surgery for a close-to-death cancer patient) may be life-prolonging and life-enhancing for others (like surgery to increase mobility for a cancer patient who still has some time to live).

The mental health specialist can help by individual or collective discussions and fact-finding with all the pertinent participants in the decision-making. The true feelings of the patient, if he or she is conscious at all, must be ascertained as clearly as possible. One must check to see if the individual's personal affairs are in order and if appropriate arrangements have been made in the interest of the individual and his or her family. The patient may wish to live only long enough to complete certain personal and tax arrangements. Some persons or their families may want to sustain life, for example, until after a granddaughter is born, or a favored grandson has married. The family should not be put into the difficult position of finally deciding, for the doctor has the ultimate responsibility, with or without legal directives, as deemed appropriate to the case. But the decision must derive from hard data in the context of careful moral and legal considerations. The following example illustrates what can begin to happen if the patient's rights are not carefully monitored:

A 78-year-old man's relative obtained a court order terminating his life-sustaining kidney dialysis treatments, claiming he was "mentally incompetent." The judgment was based on his lack of coherent response to them. Yet the old man was fully conscious and told nurses and a doctor that he did not wish to die. A Massachusetts appeals court judge reversed the lower court decision and ordered the resumption of treatment for the man.

Trepidation still exists around the issue of passive euthanasia. Many fear a "slippery slope" possibly leading to withdrawal of treatment not only from the terminally ill but eventually from the mentally retarded and physically handicapped. Some religious leaders view passive euthanasia as unacceptable tampering with death. Many families are worried that it is at times impossible to predict death, for example for those who may recover from comas. Some see death itself as such an insult and tragedy that any compliance with it is inhumane. Others believe that the medical profession should focus solely on the prolongation of life and should not be allowed to participate in withdrawal of treatment or nutrients. Thus, the debate over the "right to die with dignity" continues, in the attempt to be both humane *and* scrupulous about human rights.

Dr. Jack Kevorkian of Michigan became a major agent provocateur advocating physician-assisted suicide such as occurs in the Netherlands. The state of Oregon passed a law in support of physician-assisted suicide. The Hemlock Society, developed by Derek Humphrey, has also led to increased consideration of end-of-life decisions. One reason for the public attention to Kevorkian and the Hemlock Society is the failure of the medical and nursing professions and American health care institutions to develop effective palliative and end-of-life care. People need not suffer needlessly at the end of life. It is probable that once effective palliative and end-of-life medicine and nursing are developed in the United States, the call for physician-assisted suicide will diminish. The Open Society Institute (supported by financier and philanthropist George Soros) developed the Project on Death in America which is contributing to the transformation of the culture and experience of dying in America.

Helping Survivors with Funeral Arrangements. It is generally accepted that the American funeral system, with the "good funeral" and its obsequies, is outrageously expensive and offers little in the way of meaningful psychological support to mourners. Families are vulnerable to entrenched customs, the dubious approaches of some funeral directors, and the sense that they must "do right by" the deceased. The shock and grief of death are rapidly surcharged with guilt. In 1995, the average American funeral cost about $4,600[30] not including cemetery costs which can be from about $1,500 for a mausoleum to about $3,500 for a plot. Questionable practices of the funeral industry have included:

1. Inadequate presentation of lower cost alternatives, such as cremation and the use of services of memorial societies.

2. Misinformation regarding embalming. (Embalming will not prevent decomposition.) Undertakers embalm without first obtaining survivors' permission. Only some states require embalming and only under certain circumstances, yet the public is led to believe it is required.

3. Lack of availability of price information to the public and consequent reduction in competition within the "funeral industry."

4. Claims of airtight and watertight caskets that lead consumers to believe these features help prevent decomposition of the body.

In 1984, the Federal Trade Commission adopted new regulations, known as "the funeral rule," which was revised in 1994.[31] Under the funeral rule, funeral directors are required to: (1) disclose the costs of all goods and services, either with an itemized price list for in-person inquiries or over the telephone; and (2) make it easier for consumers to purchase individual items rather than predetermined packages of services.

Nonprofit memorial societies offer simple, dignified, and economical funeral arrangements. They tend to make life easier for survivors and give the deceased some control over his or her own demise. These societies are nonprofit organizations, democratically controlled by the members.[32] They are usually initiated by a church or a ministerial association and occasionally are organized by labor, civic, or educational groups. Most have modest lifetime membership fees and a small records charge at the time of death. The first society was created in Seattle, Washington, in 1939; they now exist in many cities in the United States and Canada.

Memorial services can offer valid "psychotherapy" for survivors. "In a funeral the center of attention is the dead body; the emphasis is on death. In a memorial service, the center of concern is the personality of the individual who has died . . . "[33] An honest appraisal of the deceased—with both liabilities and assets—can help the survivors work through their own complicated feelings, sometimes cast in an excessive idealization that may actually prolong grief.

In addition to earth burial and cremation, bequeathal to a medical school provides a valuable service and reduces expense.[34] Only the Orthodox Jewish faith objects to bequeathal of one's body or of organs for transplant. With changing religious attitudes and the desire to spare survivors soaring funeral costs, more bodies are now donated than are needed by medical schools in some parts of the country. Some people—status conscious to the end—want to leave their bodies to prestige schools like Harvard.

Support for the Surviving Spouse or Significant Others. The surviving partner faces practical as well as emotional problems associated with, the loss of a mate: relationships with in-laws and children, financial matters, government benefits, and unwanted callers who read the death announcement in the papers. Some decisions, such as selling one's home and moving to a new location, are best delayed until part of the mourning period is past and the survivor has greater perspective and energy at hand.

The preliminary process of adjusting to the loss of a partner is often an emotional journey of a year or longer. In a sense one never "gets over" a significant loss in one's life. Frequently one year or more of anniversaries—birthdays, Thanksgiving, the Christmas season, the Fourth of July, and all the others—must be experienced nostalgically and sadly before one is ready once again to take up life wholeheartedly. The oldest and youngest survivors may need an even longer period to adjust. Consolation is difficult and, indeed, may not be accepted at all. In therapy the task is to open up grief, uncover any complicating anger, help the person face the loss, develop new relationships, and find activities and meaning.

A comfortable standard of living (so often absent) helps in the struggle against apathy and isolation. Because of social and cultural attitudes that have prevented previous experience with finances, some widowed women may need considerable help, not only in obtaining, but also in managing finances. (See Chapter 7.) The widower may also have special problems. He may be totally unprepared to cook for himself, sew on buttons, and handle other household chores. He will need concrete assistance in learning how to do things for himself.

Socially, surviving spouses (especially women) may have a difficult time of it. They are often left out by old and good friends, since they are now "fifth wheels." If widows are attractive, others' wives may shun them; if they are dreary and mournful, everyone may stay away. Self-pity and outrage at one's fate are futile, and action of a constructive sort must be encouraged to get the person back into contact with understanding, but not patronizing, people.

Post-Cana is a Catholic lay association for widows and widowers set up to assist survivors with not only practical matters, but also with spiritual needs. The Widow-to-Widow program, originally established by Phyllis Silverman in the Boston area as an experimental mental health program of preventive intervention, is directed at new widows and staffed by other widows. It is based on the premise that the best helper of a widow at the time of grief is another widow. Silverman wrote, "Since statistics indicate a higher risk of emotional and psychiatric disturbances among younger widowed women than is to be expected from the population at large, this program was established to find ways of reaching those women (all recently widowed and under the age of 60) to determine what services would ease their distress and grief and, thereby, lessen the possibility of their developing a psychiatric disorder."[35] The idea proved promising and has been set up in various communities, applying the concept to men as well as to women, and to people of all ages.

Silverman makes the point that supportive programs such as the Widow-to-Widow are valuable for preventive purposes. Mental health agencies should offer these services as well because, as Silverman notes:

> Most mental health agencies serve those suffering from a defined psychiatric disorder, such as depression, rather than those in need of preventive services as they pass through a life crisis. This may be because most people suffering from the "hazard of living" that occurs with the death of a spouse do not consult with such agencies unless a prior contact has been established.[36]

Alcoholics Anonymous (for survivors who develop or who have had drinking problems) and Parents Without Partners are also self-help organizations that have been very useful. It is important, however, to have professional skills on hand without at the same time downplaying or interfering with the "natural" talents of the nonprofessionals. Voluntarism, however valuable, must not be used as a substitute for necessary professional services.

Professional concern is also developing for bereaved partners in nontraditional relationships, for example homosexual persons who lose a partner. The AIDS epidemic has heightened awareness of the significance of such loss for both young and older partners.[37]

GROUP THERAPY

Group Experience for Older People

Silver introduced group therapy with dementia patients in 1950.[38] He found a party atmosphere important—with milk, cookies, and music as a focus for patients with severe memory and attention deficits. However, Linden was the first, in 1953, to describe an organized program of group therapy.[39] Goldfarb, also, used the group approach in his work in assisting new residents of nursing homes with orientation.[40] Ebersole found that the use of group reminiscence was helpful to older persons in working through pain and disappointment from the past.[41] Lowy described group work with the frail elderly.[42] Klein et al. reported that community-resident older persons belonging to groups were eager to learn from and share experiences with each other and their group leaders as soon as they had gotten over initial distrust and suspicion.[43] Steuer et al. compared cognitive-behavioral and psychodynamic group psychotherapy in treatment of geriatric depression over a nine-month period.[44]

Group therapy is a very valuable procedure that should be widely used in all institutions (nursing homes, hospitals, etc.) and outpatient services. It utilizes psychotherapeutic principles and techniques from individual psychotherapy as well as techniques directly derived from group process. Yalom describes 10 curative factors potentially present in group therapy: (1) Imparting of information, (2) instillation of hope, (3) universality, (4) altruism, (5) corrective recapitulation of the primary family group, (6) development of socializing techniques, (7) imitative behavior, (8) interpersonal behavior, (9) group cohesiveness, (10) catharsis.[45]

Group therapy has been more widely used in work with older persons in and out of institutions than is generally realized or reflected in professional and scientific literature. This is partly a function of necessity, an outgrowth of the disinterest of many therapists in individual therapy with older people. But group therapy also has its own unique value in providing support, insight, and a variety of other benefits. It is also more economical than one-to-one therapy. Volunteers as well as administrators, aides, social workers, psychologists, and psychiatrists have been trained to varying degrees of competence to conduct group therapy. Nurses probably conduct more group work with older persons than do other professionals because they are already greatly involved in physical care and thus have more direct contact.[46]

Usually sociability, emotional catharsis, and perhaps insight are the main objectives of group therapy. But in institutional settings where the "management" of behavior can become a major consideration, the tendency for providers of services to control rather than help resolve the disturbed and upset feelings and actions of their patients must be questioned. Fortunately, the use of group therapy to achieve understanding and emotional support rather than simply control can result in less temptation to use chemical and physical restraints for difficult behavior.[47] Group therapy can also be useful among staff members of institutions and agencies to help them work through their negative and often unconscious attitudes toward old age.

Social agencies, community and day centers, and "golden age" or senior citizens groups offer group psychotherapy to community-resident elderly. (The overall utilization rate of golden age or senior citizens centers and clubs by the elderly is relatively low, and such activities probably attract the more gregarious older people.) The goal of these groups is usually the personal growth and emotional satisfaction of participating members through positive social experiences. Group workers also develop recreational, cultural, social, and educational group activities in the larger community.

Group therapy has been used to focus on preretirement and retirement problems. However, in general, governmental and private preretirement programs deal less adequately with the psychological and interpersonal aspects of retirement, and more adequately with financial planning and other tangible matters.

As with group therapy in general, the role of the leader in a group of older persons may range from active to passive, and may include questioning, explaining, teaching, protecting, reassuring, and confronting, as well as simply listening. Many consider the central role to be one of serving as a catalyst for emotional interchange while providing protection for individuals and the group from excessively destructive anger and disruptive anxiety among group members.

Not all groups need leaders.

In the city of Washington, one author, Dr. Robert N. Butler, founded a group for older professionals and executives, with two intents: to provide an activist, advocacy group on behalf of older persons and to provide a setting for mutual mental and emotional interchange. In effect, it became a "leaderless" group.

It never had a professional paid leader and, having begun in 1965, it lasted about twenty years, until illness, disability, and death finally decimated its members.

Groups must have momentum and vitality to maintain continuity and reduce absences and drop-outs. Selection of members is critical. Heterogeneity (aged-integrated groups) has unique advantages, one of which is to help reduce a sense of isolation of the older person from the larger world, Indeed, such group members may forget the factor of age. Groups of one's age peers have virtues of their own, including a sense of sharing a life stage together. Topics in groups composed largely of older people tend to be illness, death, loneliness, and family conflict; age-integrated groups are more likely to deal with the whole range of the life cycle, enabling older members to review and renew their own experiences and values.

Group therapy should be available for the families of older people. Getzel describes the rationale for caregiver groups, along with certain of the major issues that arise as part of the group process.[48] (Family care of the elderly is discussed further in Chapters 2 and 10.) When an older person is admitted to an institution, for example, family members often experience profound conflicts. In one sense, they are already experiencing the death of their older relative and the first grief reaction (the later actual death and subsequent grief reactions may actually have less impact). Work with relatives helps ameliorate guilt and grief and builds liaison for visitation, home stays, and discharge when possible.

Group therapy has a unique applicability and is a powerful instrument in and of itself: it should not be viewed as secondary and less valuable than individual psychotherapy. Individual and group therapy may be usefully combined in work with the same person. The person may need the opportunity for reviewing his or her life on an individual basis and for preparing for the impending encounter with death, while at the same time gaining much from the continuing human inter-change and the range of emotions—love to hate—that a well-functioning group can provide. Some persons benefit from participating in more than one group. One such man, in his late years, found what he called his "rap sessions" in two separate groups eye-opening because of the differences in the way he was seen by each group.

"Age-Integrated, Life-Crisis" Group Therapy[49]

In the early 1970s, two of the authors, Robert N. Butler and Myrna I. Lewis, conducted and studied four age-integrated life-crisis groups (eight to ten members each) with one contrasting middle-aged group. We experimented with age integration (age range from 15 years to 80 and above), in the belief that age segregation leaves very little opportunity for the rich exchange of feelings, experience, and support possible among generations. "Life crisis" refers to the near-normal to pathological reactions to adolescence, education, married or single life, divorce, parenthood, work and retirement, widowhood, illness, and impending death. Such groups are concerned not only with the intrinsic psychiatric disorders but also with preventive and remedial treatment of people as they pass through the usual vicissitudes of the life cycle. Criteria for membership in our groups included absence of active psychosis and presence of a life crisis (acute, subacute, or chronic). Reactions to life crises followed traditional diagnostic categories, of course, including depression, anxiety states, hysterical reactions, obsessive-compulsive and passive-aggressive reactions, hypochondriasis, alcoholism, and mild drug use. Groups were balanced for age, sex, and personality dynamics. They met once a week for an hour and a half. We found it useful to have a male and a female co-therapist from different disciplines to provide both a psychodynamic and a sociological orientation for each group, as well as opportunities for transference. Individual membership in a group averaged about two years, and new group members were asked to commit themselves to a minimum of three months' participation.

The life-cycle crisis approach to group therapy need be neither strictly encounter nor strictly psychoanalytic. Rather it can be equally concerned with the interaction among and between group members, as determined by reality and the past histories of each member, and with the individual problems of each member. The goals are the amelioration of suffering, the overcoming of disability, and the opportunity for new experiences of intimacy and self-fulfillment. Expression of both anger and positive feelings should be encouraged—not for a mere defusing of feeling but as a step toward constructive resolution of problems and a positive life experience.

Our group patients often continued in individual psychotherapy with their referring therapist. When this was not feasible, individual therapy was encouraged along with group therapy, either with one of the co-therapists or someone else through referral. However, absence of such therapy did not preclude participation in groups.

Regarding older persons, some of the phenomena we observed included (1) pseudo "senility," (2) a "Peter Pan" syndrome (refusal to grow up), and (3) leadership being preempted by the middle-aged, with neglect or "mascoting" of elderly and young (necessitating therapeutic intervention). Unique contributions of older persons included models for growing older, solutions for loss and grief, creative use of reminiscence, historic empathy, and a sense of the entire life cycle. Possibilities for psychological growth continued to the end of life, as illustrated by case notes on a 70-year-old woman in one of our groups:

Repeated hospital admission for psychiatric depression. Living in retirement village. No genuine financial worries but not wealthy. Episodes characterized by increasing depression, hopelessness, remorse, insomnia, and anorexia (no appetite). Attributes her illness to worry over daughter, who is subject to manic-depressive disease and hospitalizations.

Gives impression of quiet older lady who moves and talks little, nearly mute. Face looks grief-stricken and full of worry. Hand-wringing. No signs of organic failure. Slow but appropriate answers.

Denies active suicidal thought but wishes she were dead.

In life-crisis group it emerges that she believes in hereditary and physiological basis for emotional illnesses—and hence blames self for daughter's troubles. Also describes for first time an affair with a married man, conducted at 67 after death of her own husband. She feels unfaithful, disloyal.

During the year, she has become increasingly bright-eyed and alert, listening with interest to the sexual experiences of younger group members and eliciting their views of her own life. Group members focus on helping her deal with guilt over her affair and her notions of total responsibility for her daughter's problems.

INTERGENERATIONAL FAMILY THERAPY AND COUPLES THERAPY

Although family therapy for parents and their dependent or young adult children has become an accepted form of treatment for emotional dysfunction and distress, intergenerational family therapy which includes older persons with their adult children, grandchildren, and even great-grandchildren, is just developing. The lengthening life expectancy that has occurred since the turn of the century has produced many such social lags, as society struggles to catch up with the new longevity. The family should be involved in any work with an older person, unless circumstances dictate otherwise, There are, of course, some older persons who have no living children—but often they have other close relatives or friends who constitute their "family." There should always be clarification as to who constitutes the "patient." Is it an individual or the family as a unit? Sometimes the older person is brought in by a son or daughter, and it is quickly apparent that it is the adult child who needs individual help. But more commonly, the entire family is affected by changes occurring with any one individual member. Issues in family therapy include the need for decisions about the older person, family feelings of guilt and abandonment, ancient but still active family conflicts, and the need to provide continuing care of and involvement with the older member. The therapist may decide to see the entire extended family together—not only those living in the household but also those living separately.

Intergenerational family therapy models began to develop in the 1980s. Greene provides an assessment and treatment framework for work with the elderly and their families and describes an intergenerational approach that integrates a concern with the older person's functioning together with an assessment of the family system in which it takes place.[50] Bumagin and Hirn also approach treatment of the elderly in the context of the multigenerational family.[51] Eyde and Rich describe families as critical partners in both diagnosis and treatment, including their ability to supply information as "silent, unknowing biographers" of family history and to watch for "complex and subtle changes associated with normal or pathological aging" in their older family members.[52] Silverstone and Burack-Weiss focus on work with the frail elderly and their families and emphasize the need to assess the capacity to function rather than looking solely at disease and aging processes per se.[53]

In one of the rare articles on psychotherapy with older people by a private practice psychiatrist, Finkel examines family therapy as well as older forms of treatment.[54] He describes the cycle of trouble that can begin in a family when an older person experiences serious losses of some kind. The cycle can take on much of the predictability of a Rube Goldberg contraption once it gets moving. The parent suffers a loss and turns to his or her family for increased support. Frequently, stirred up feelings of sadness, frustration, and anger are present in the parent, awaiting a sympathetic ear. The family initially offers its help generously but soon begins to feel exhausted by the extra demands. Both parent and adult children struggle with their new roles toward each other. Meanwhile the adult children are carrying additional burdens of their own, specific to middle age—seeing children through college and out into the world, coping with beginning bodily changes and ailments, and carrying major responsibility in

the working world, the family, and community life. The older person begins to feel he or she is a burden. The adult children feel inadequate and ambivalent about the task of doing enough for the older person. Frustrations turn into anger and criticism. The older person may end up feeling rejected, humiliated, and intensely sad. The adult child, seeing this, experiences guilt and remorse. Often there is a brief period of "making up" and reaffirming the old parent–child bond, followed by a repeat of the entire cycle. Family therapy can do much to bring understanding and resolution into this cycle.

Older married couples may also need counseling concerning marital problems, including interpersonal conflicts, confrontations with serious illness and approaching death, and concerns about children and grandchildren. Getzel describes work with the elderly couple in crisis, as well as the changing needs of couples who have remained together for a lifetime.[55] Remarried couples may need help with premarital counseling, marital adjustment, and family reaction to the remarriage.

Systems theory (the concept that a couple or a family interact within a family "system" in which individuals and the larger family group influence each other in a complex and interdependent manner) has provided important techniques for couples and family therapy.[56] A major goal is to analyze and eliminate miscommunications and improve interaction and interdependence.

BEHAVIORAL THERAPIES

Behavioral Modification and Therapy

Lindsley in 1964,[57] developed a theoretical prospectus for the application of operant conditioning (pioneered by B. F. Skinner[58]) to the older institutionalized person. On the whole, older populations, inpatient or outpatient, have not been studied and treated according to either "behavioral modification" or "behavioral therapy."[59] The former is the practical application of operant conditioning and includes, for example, the use of token economy (reinforcing behavior by reward). Behavioral therapy, pioneered by Pavlov, Wolpe, and Skinner, includes aversion techniques (the use of noxious stimuli, desensitization, and reinforcement). Newer techniques include over-correction, habit reversal, anxiety management training, modeling, and social skills training. Many of these could be useful with the elderly. For example, assertiveness training may be valuable for older people having difficulty expressing their needs explicitly.

Biofeedback

Biofeedback, one form of behavioral therapy, refers to techniques that use electronic monitoring devices to teach patients to control selected aspects of their behavior by providing them with continuous biological information about the impact of a variety of their actions. These techniques have been applied therapeutically to a number of conditions that afflict older people, including headaches, backaches, and general anxiety. Work at the National Institute on Aging has resulted in successful application of biofeedback in the reduction of hypertension as well as fecal incontinence with young subjects but not with older subjects. Johnson and Garton have been able to retrain muscles in hemiplegia through the same techniques.[60]

Zeichner and Boczkowski (1986) present a review of recent studies reporting on biofeedback with the elderly as well as an appraisal of its usefulness. They conclude that results are unclear; biofeedback may be effective for only a select group of elderly who are able to master the self-control skills required.

Memory Training

Recent studies indicate that there may be three major kinds of memory: *episodic* for specific events; *semantic* for knowledge and facts; and *implicit* for skills exercised automatically, like speaking grammatically or riding a bike. Seman-

tic and implicit memory have not been shown to decline with age. Declines in episodic memory ("Where did I just put my keys?") show up in most people in their 70s. But researchers are beginning to believe that retirement or changes in use of mental faculties in later life may be a major factor. The mind may be reacting to lack of use and discipline by failing to respond as well as it once did. The aging process no doubt plays a role as well, with studies suggesting a degeneration of the frontal lobes of the brain. But memory strategies may allow people to compensate for memory deterioration, particularly by learning to focus on what is happening without distortions.[61]

Cognitive training for the mildly memory-impaired focuses on training the elderly to use mnemonic (memory) devices in an effort to improve recall of names, faces, lists, and other memory categories. Yesavage finds that the elderly show enormous variability of response and that the old-old subjects have much greater difficulty in learning complex mnemonics than the young-old. He describes the use of pre-training to deal with age-related deficits that appear to be interfering with capacity for both learning and memory. Pilot studies suggest that pre-training as well as lengthened mnemonic training may have a positive effect on old-old learning capacity.[62]

ENVIRONMENTAL THERAPY

We are using the term "environmental therapy" to encompass the development of age awareness, federal policies to aid older persons, social participation,[63] mobilization of community resources, self-care, self-help, and even registration drives, job placement, direct advocacy, legal and consultative services, and political organization, each of which will be discussed later. The courage of many older people in the community is striking, since they must struggle against a system marked by fragmentation, and, frequently, indifference. Self-respect and dignity in old age obviously do not follow from felt and actual powerlessness. Consequently, we regard self-assertion in all the forms just mentioned, including political activism, as supportive of mental health.

Age Awareness and Acceptance

In order to confront the realistic opportunities, challenges, and difficulties of late life, older people must first recognize their age, accept it, and even take pride in it. Second, they must recognize themselves in others of their age, empathize with common experiences, and realize "we are all in this thing together" in spite of economic differences, cultural or social backgrounds, or social status. A significant number of older people refuse to identify with people their own age or with the issues that arise with age. The well-to-do are especially prone to this, thinking of themselves as separate and apart from the poverty-stricken elderly all around them. Yet unless they are extremely wealthy, they too can be devastated financially by just one major illness or period of adversity. And they may be equally susceptible to the emotional devastations of illness and loss. When one is old, there is really no fail-safe way for any social group to escape the effects of a culture that has not yet learned to support and cherish its elderly. The most effective defense is a united challenge that combines practical, direct action with psychological support—both from others and to and from each other.

Federal Policies to Aid Older Persons

Age Discrimination Act.   Age discrimination in programs receiving federal financial support is prohibited by the Age Discrimination Act of 1975. (This act is distinctly different from the Age Discrimination in Employment Act of 1976, which will be discussed later in this chapter.) Yet older people are still often denied access to programs that are not "age-categorical" (that is, programs where age is a specific eligibility criterion). The U.S. Civil Rights Commission, then chaired by activist Arthur S. Flemming, issued a report in 1978 showing age discrimination in 10 of the major social programs of the federal government,

especially in community mental health programs, legal services, and employment training programs. Claims of age discrimination can be brought before the Federal Mediation and Conciliation Service. However the regulations accompanying the Age Discrimination Act have several serious weaknesses: Although the legislative history confirms that Congress was mainly concerned about discrimination against the elderly, the regulations do not specifically emphasize older persons. Federal, state, and local laws have been exempted from the impact of the act.

Older Americans Act.   In 1965 Congress passed the Older Americans Act (OAA), creating the Administration on Aging (AOA). The Administration on Aging, located in the U.S. Department of Health and Human Services, is the only federal agency devoted exclusively to the concerns and potential of all older Americans. AOA's primary goal, as envisioned by the Older Americans Act, are to: (1) support a national network of state and area agencies on aging; (2) develop and oversee a comprehensive and coordinated system of support services and opportunities to meet the social and human service needs of the elderly; and (3) serve as a visible advocate on behalf of older persons.

With further amendments to the act, AOA has grown to become the major federal agency in advocacy and services to the aged. Under Title III State and Community Programs, the AOA works closely with its nationwide network on aging composed of regional offices, state units on aging (also referred to as state agencies on aging) and area agencies on aging to plan, coordinate, and develop community-level systems of services that meet the needs of older persons and their caregivers.

As first enacted, the OAA authorized funding under Title III to support a state agency on aging in each state. AOA awards funds to the 57 state agencies on aging, which are located in every state and territory. Most states are divided into planning and service areas (PSAs) so that programs can be effectively developed and targeted to the needs of the elderly in particular areas. Nationwide some

670 area agencies on aging (AAAs) receive funds from their respective state agencies on aging to plan, develop, coordinate, and arrange for services in each PSA. AAA's in turn contract with public or private groups to provide services, such as home-delivered meals; transportation, home-health and homemaker services, visiting and tele-phone reassurance, legal services, multi-purpose senior centers, outreach, and information and re-ferral services. There are some 27,000 service provider agencies nationwide. In some cases, the AAA may act as the service provider, if no local contractor is available. As an illustration of how this funding process works, state agencies on aging received a total of $800 million Title III funds during fiscal year 1994. These funds were made available to the states on a formula basis upon approval of state plans by the AOA regional offices. States then allocated funds to the area agencies on aging, based on approved area plans, to pay up to 85 percent of the costs of supportive services, senior centers, and nutrition services. The AOA also supports research and training grants to improve quality of life and services for older persons.[64]

The OAA has been amended over the years. The 1987 amendments to the OAA included the establishment within the Administration on Aging of an Office for Native Hawaiian Pro-grams. This office has the responsibility for eval-uating the adequacy of the services provided by Title III to the aforementioned elderly popula-tions and to make recommendations to the Com-missioner on ways the service delivery system can be improved. The 1992 amendments included funds granted to organizations such as commu-nity-based agencies, senior centers, and medical institutions to increase public understanding of how healthy lifestyle choices throughout life re-duce the risk of chronic health conditions in later years. Title VII, the Vulnerable Elder Rights Pro-tection Title, was created by the 1992 amend-ments to OAA. This Title encourages state agencies to concentrate their advocacy efforts on issues affecting those older people who are the most socially and economically vulnerable.

Title VII brings together and strengthens four ex-isting advocacy programs—the Long-Term Care Ombudsman Program; Programs for the Preven-tion of Abuse, Neglect and Exploitation; State Elder Rights and Legal Assistance Development Programs; and Insurance/Benefits Outreach, Coun-seling, and Assistance Programs—and calls for their coordination and linkage within each state. In addition, Title VII calls on state agencies to take a holistic approach to elder rights advocacy by coordinating the four programs and fostering collaboration among programs and other advo-cates in each state to address issues of the high-est priority for the most vulnerable elders.[65]

The OAA is up for reauthorization in 1997. One proposed bill retains all seven titles of the act and reauthorizes it for three years. Another pro-posed bill, however, eliminates some broad social policy objectives that have been the foundation of the act for over 30 years. It also removes priority services, including legal assistance, for low-income, minority, and other vulnerable elders. This represents a serious threat to efforts to pro-tect older Americans.

Mobilization of Community Resources

In previous chapters we stress the role of mental health workers in effectively representing the in-terests of their patients. Older persons should also be encouraged and helped to utilize the social ser-vice system (for example, registration drives). So-cial and family agencies could play leading roles in elder advocacy in helping the elderly deal with other voluntary agencies as well as institutions of government. For instance, family agencies have at times been important community voices in en-couraging community mental health centers (CMHCs) to provide outreach care for older pa-tients.

Community workers can help develop net-works of care within the community. Community support systems are especially valuable for the older person who has no available family. Friends, neighborhood storekeepers, druggists, and others have all been involved by mental health staff in looking out for the older person. This must be done, of course, with two perspectives in mind: the privacy of the person must not be compromised, and the network must be used for strengthening the status of the person rather than undermining it through patronization or infantilization. An analysis of a person's social supports, or "network" is part of a good mental health treatment plan. The availability of support has been found to be more important in adaption to stress than the kind and amount of stress encountered.

Organized sources of information and referral, especially clearinghouses, should be created in district Social Security offices, voluntary agencies, state commissions on aging, and the like.

In the remainder of this chapter, we focus on specific ways to mobilize the community through efforts made by the mental health worker or directly by the older person.

Registration Drives.   Registration drives are among important efforts that mental health workers can initiate or support. Cloward and Piven helped generate the idea of registering all eligible recipients for various income and service programs so they could, in fact, benefit from whatever the programs were offering.[66] George Wiley expanded on this thought with the National Welfare Rights Organization, which later became a nationwide movement of welfare recipients. The operations Medicare Alert and FIND (Friendless, Isolated, Needy, Disabled) were outreach programs for older persons. The first registered older people for Medicare Part B (for doctors' coverage); the second resulted in the study "The Golden Years: A Tarnished Myth" done by the National Council on the Aging, demonstrating the enormous needs and poverty of older persons. Workers in specific cities have set up outreach programs designed to put the low-income elderly in touch with the benefits to which they are entitled under existing state and federal legislation.

The Commonwealth Fund Commission on Elderly People Living Alone, composed of national leaders and experts in health policy and aging,

conducted research on the Supplemental Security Income (SSI) Program and demonstrated methods of conducting successful SSI outreach activities on the local level.[67] It concluded that current participation rates in the SSI program are inadequate. Together with the AARP, the Commission has designed, tested, and evaluated effective approaches to increase SSI enrollment. In 1989, the Commissioner of Social Security, Gwendolyn S. King, initiated an effort to enroll many of the estimated one to two million poor people who are eligible for but not on SSI.

Self-Help and Self-Care.   The burgeoning self-care, self-help movement in the United States— estimated at 200,000 individual groups belonging to some 400 major groups—promises great, if still not well-defined, potential for older people. *Self-care* refers to actions performed by individuals for their own or their families' health and well-being and the well-being of others; *self-help* is used when groups of people who share a common interest or condition join together to offer one another mutual interchange and support. In essence, the health consumer is taking a more active role in maintaining or improving his or her physical and mental health, sometimes taking over tasks otherwise performed by health care providers and sometimes augmenting such work.

Several social factors have joined to make self-care and self-help popular:

1. A demand for better health care by the consumer movement
2. The rising cost of health care
3. A maldistribution of professional health care
4. The residual from the counterculture movement of the 1960s urging greater self-reliance for individuals

The four steps in self-care are as follows:

1. Self-knowledge (health education)
2. Body monitoring—maintaining healthful habits and detecting health problems in early stages
3. Self-treatment—learning first aid, simple home treatments, and use of a variety of med-

ical tools, such as blood pressure cuffs and simple home treatments

4. Learning when to seek professional help

A few attempts have been made to design self-care programs specifically for older persons. An early example is Sehnert's "Activated Patient" program for Medicare recipients in Reston, Virginia.[68] Many self-care concepts are pertinent to old age, from learning to take one's own blood pressure to improvements in diet and exercise.

Self-help groups usually spring up voluntarily around an issue of shared concern. Examples of self-help groups that are especially relevant for older people are Widow Outreach Programs, the Alzheimer's Association, Emphysema Anonymous, the American Cancer Society, the Arthritis Foundation, Make Today Count (for the terminally ill), the Gray Panthers, Reach to Recovery (for breast cancer patients), Recovery, Inc. (The Association of Nervous and Former Mental Patients), stroke clubs like Opus (Organization of People Undaunted by Stroke, Inc.), the American Diabetes Association, women's consciousness-raising groups, the Parkinson's Disease Foundation, the United Ostomy Association, and the American Heart Association. The National Institute on Aging has prepared a booklet describing and listing major self-help groups of particular value for the elderly.[69]

Many self-help groups and self-care concepts have been enthusiastically supported by health care providers. Other providers have been less positive, fearing encroachment in professional territory, predicting consumers would "go too far" in self-care, or simply doubting the effectiveness of the self-care, self-help movement. Serious studies of the impact of the movement have not yet been done. But the "soft indicators" of client satisfaction show that many find this new health movement satisfying and useful, as judged by their continuing voluntary participation.

Volunteer work is perhaps more highly developed in the United States than anywhere else in the world. The Salvation Army alone depends on the work of 1.2 million volunteers. A 1988 Independent Sector survey by the Gallup Organization found that 45% of all respondents volunteered time and averaged 4.7 hours each per week. Volunteering reached its highest level from ages 65 to 74, with an average of 6.0 hours per week for that age group. (Table 12.1.)

Older persons volunteer for hundreds of organizations, including wide-ranging service organizations like the Red Cross, advocacy groups like the American Association of Retired Persons, and special focus organizations like the Service Corps of Retired Executives Association (SCORE) in which retired men and women counsel people running or starting small businesses.

Those who want help in beginning to volunteer can consult the white pages in the telephone book under Volunteer Center, Voluntary Action Center, or Volunteer Bureau. Specific groups can be found in the yellow pages under "Social Service Organizations."

Employment and Productive Aging. Why do many older people seek or desire employment? Some need money because Social Security or pension checks just will not stretch far enough.[70] Some want to get out of the house to occupy their time. Many want the "meaningfulness" of work. So long as work and money have such profound financial, social, personal, and ethical significance, it is illusory to deny their importance to health, both physical and mental. Some older people are told to do volunteer work—advice that is indeed helpful to some but naive in instances where economic survival or a personal preference for paid employment is at issue.

Job placement for older persons requires vocational evaluation and counseling as critical first steps. The U.S. Employment Service (USES) has been very disappointing in its feeble efforts to place older workers, but pressure should nonetheless be placed on USES and its various offices. There are Federal Job Information Centers in various cities that give advice and information on federal job opportunities. The Women's Bureau in the Department of Labor has taken some interest in the job plight of older women and can offer

TABLE 12.1 Who volunteers

WHO VOLUNTEERS (BY AGE)		
	PERCENT WHO VOLUNTEER	**AVERAGE VOLUNTEER HOURS PER WEEK**
Ages 25–34	44.6%	4.0 hours/week
Ages 35–44	53.9%	5.3 hours
Ages 45–54	47.5%	5.8 hours
Ages 55–64	47.1%	4.7 hours
Ages 65–74	40.0%	6.0 hours
Ages 75 and over	28.6%	4.4 hours
WHO VOLUNTEERS (BY CATEGORY)		
Women	46.7%	4.7 hours
Men	43.8%	4.8 hours
Self-employed, full-time	59.1%	4.7 hours
Self-employed, part-time	59.0%	6.4 hours
Other employed, full-time	46.4%	4.4 hours
Other employed, part-time	52.9%	5.7 hours
Not employed	38.0%	4.7 hours

Source: Adapted from Hodgkinson, V. A., Weitzman, M. S., & The Gallup Organization. (1988). *Giving and volunteering in the United States.* Washington, DC: INDEPENDENT SECTOR.

advice. Various communities offer privately sponsored, nonprofit, over-60 employment and counseling services and agencies. In some there are 40-plus clubs for finding employment after age 40. For the handicapped and elderly, sheltered workshops may be available. (See Chapter 11.) In Appendix C we have outlined various governmental employment and volunteer programs to which older people can apply, some of which are specifically designed for the low-income elderly.

The Senior Opportunities Services (SOS) program of the Office of Economic Opportunity is intended to identify and meet the needs of persons over 60 with projects that serve or employ older persons predominately. The various projects include community action programs to provide employment opportunities, home health services, assistance in the Food Stamp plan, and outreach and referral services. As much as possible, these activities are staffed by older citizens, paid or volunteer. Office of Economic Opportunity Senior Aides and Senior Community Service Aides are engaged in such activities as homemaker and health assistance, nutrition, institutional care, home repair, child care, and social service administration.

Green Thumb, which involves beautification by planting, and Green Light, which employs aides in libraries, schools, and day-care centers, are federal employment programs for older people. Table 12.2 lists other jobs for older persons that could be developed to meet needs that exist in many communities.

Older workers should not feel forced to "think young" or "act young." Their accumulated work skills and experiences have a unique value. Nor should they feel compelled to misrepresent their age for any purpose, including employment. Age

TABLE 12.2   Job options for older people in meeting community needs

Transportation
Station information aides
Bus drivers
Van drivers
Pool arrangers
Improved route sign advisors
Service assistance locators

Cultural activities
Performers and artists
Programmers
Trainers
Sales and promotion workers
Facilities maintenance workers
Fund raising counselors and assistants
Audience development specialists
Arts conservators and technicians
Resource and information assistants

Employment
Job finders
Trainers
Job developers
Career and job counselors

Non-profit activities
Fund raising/membership counselors
Bookkeepers and accountants
Government regulations and compliance
   counselors
Coordinators of volunteers
Incorporation advisors

Environment
Counselors on pesticide and safety
Extended sanitation and special clean-up
   workers
Monitors
Materials recycling aides
Environmental impact analysts

Employee relations
Mediation, arbitration, and conciliation
   specialists (both employee/management
   and employer/employee relations)

Neighborhood
Guards and monitors
Clean-up aides
Repair workers for substandard housing
Energy conservation advisors and
   workers
Mediators, conciliators, and
   arbitrators
Fire and safety inspectors
Pest control workers
Translators and communicators

Health
Hospital technicians and aides
Home health care providers and aides
Rehabilitation technicians and aides
Medical equipment operators

Education
Discipline aides
Tutors and resource specialists
Class administration aides
Library workers
Career and other counselors
Special population education
   programmers and advisors
Fund raisers
Special skill enrichment advisors and
   aides
Financial aid advisors

Special services to dependent persons
Companions
Nutrition advisors
Form fillers
Eligibility & assistance advisors
Readers & communicators
Recreation advisors and workers
Meal providers and/or feeding helpers
Day care providers
Home health care aides
Rehabilitation technicians & helpers
Representative payees & guardians
Homemakers
Shopping assistance helpers

Source: National Committee on Careers for Older Americans. (1979). *Older Americans: An un-tapped resource.* New York: Academy for Educational Development. Reprinted by permission.

discrimination in employment is directly related to unemployment in later life. The Age Discrimination in Employment Act of 1976[71] is administered by the Department of Labor, Wage and Hour Administration, in 350 offices throughout the nation. (See listings in the telephone directory.) The act prohibits discrimination on the basis of age in hiring, job retention, compensation, and other terms, conditions, and privileges of employment. it originally applied only to those workers between 40 and 65 years of age; however, amendments in 1978 raised the protected age limit for workers in the private sector to 70 years of age and eliminated the upper age limit entirely for most federal employees. In 1986 mandatory retirement was virtually ended in the United States. Nonetheless, typical ways in which employers avoid hiring the older person are to declare that the person is "overqualified," "unskilled," less needful of a job as compared to the young, and less reliable and flexible.[72]

Advocacy. Advocacy includes use of all means at our disposal, from direct action to moral persuasion, to effectively represent the needs and grievances of older people. The contributions of Saul Alinsky and Ralph Nader should be known to the mental health worker. Class-action cases are essential, for instance, to compel better treatment in state mental hospitals and other governmental facilities.[73] Legal and protective services, private conservatorships, and public guardianships are essential—not only to protect older people but also to advance causes such as better housing and administrative and judicial reviews regarding Social Security and Medicare claims. Contemporary grievance mechanisms are being overhauled and improved following court cases. Contractual and testamentary rights must be protected, especially for the frail elderly. Tenant rights have become increasingly important. Neighborhood legal services, Legal Aid societies, public defenders, and public-interest law firms can be of help to those who cannot afford a private attorney.

Nursing home deficiencies must not be covered up by local, state, or federal governments.

The Freedom of Information Act can be used to compel the Social Security Administration to reveal the names of specific institutions with their particular deficiencies.

There already are existing advocates for older people. Some churches have lay commissions and special ministries to the aging. Cities and states have advisory committees and commissions. Massachusetts created the first cabinet-level Department of Elder Affairs in 1971 to oversee all programs for older persons. The department has authority over such functions as Supplemental Security Income, Disability Assistance, and the provision of a program for income maintenance (formerly functions of the Welfare Department); licensing and inspection of nursing homes, rest homes, and similar facilities for the elderly (formerly the responsibility of the Department of Public Health); and construction and administration of housing and transportation services for older persons (previously vested in the Department of Community Affairs).

The Swedish concept of ombudsman has been adopted in some situations in the United States. An *ombudsman* is a mediator who protects the rights of individual citizens and works with governmental agencies to ensure fair representation. We believe older persons themselves should take ombudsman-type leadership. There are countless ways in which they can counter the myths and prejudices against old age. For example, they should make unannounced visits to nursing homes. When they do not wish to retire, they should be willing to challenge the pressure to leave their jobs.

We have also long urged the formation of a national federation of friends and relatives of nursing home residents rather than depending solely on the establishment of federal, state, and local standards, regulations, and enforcement. The Friends and Relatives of Nursing Home Patients, Inc., a consumer group in Oregon organized principally by Ruth Shepherd in 1972, is an example of a local group whose objective is to have as a member of the organization one family member or friend who is financially or legally responsible for each resident of a nursing home. The development of the National Citizens Coalition for Nursing Home Reform (under the outstanding leadership of Elma Holder) is a move toward monitoring and improving nursing homes on a national basis.[74]

Legal Services. Congress has defined "legal services" in Section 302(4) of the Older American's Act as "legal advice and representation by an attorney (including, to the extent feasible, counseling or other appropriate assistance by a paralegal or law student under the supervision of an attorney) and includes counseling or representation by a non-lawyer where permitted by law, to older individuals with economic or social needs." Amendments to OAA in 1972 specifically included legal services for funding under Title III of the Act through state and area agencies on aging. Over 120 legal services for the elderly projects now exist nationwide, many funded under Title III. Others are financed by Title XX of the Social Security Act, the Housing and Community Development Act, revenue sharing, funds resulting from filing fee legislation, United Way, or private foundations.

The American Bar Association in 1978 created the 15-member interdisciplinary Commission on Legal Problems of the Elderly.[75] Its initial priorities were four: the delivery of legal services to older persons, age discrimination, simplification and coordination of administrative procedures and regulations affecting the elderly, and the rights of persons subject to the process of institutionalization. The 1988 American Civil Liberties Union's guide to older persons' rights is a comprehensive guide for older persons, their families, their lawyers, and members of nonlaw professions, such as social workers and nurses. It incorporates the latest changes in the Social Security Act, the Internal Revenue Code, and the Pension Reform Law.[76]

Consumer Fraud and Quackery. Consumer fraud and quackery are serious legal problems because older people are especially vulnerable.[77] Many have chronic ailments that seem never to get better. Hard-earned savings may be lost to ex-ploitative medical fakers, land salespeople, hearing aid salespeople, and others.

The human desire for magic cures and salvation runs deep. In late life, additional factors, ranging from brain damage to grief, add to the vulnerability. Public consumer education is not sufficient. Direct advice and discussion by the various service professions and vocations—mental health workers to physicians—carry considerable weight. But legislation, more than we presently have, is necessary, and its strict enforcement is mandatory. An example of such legislation is the Interstate Land Sales Full Disclosure Act.

Credit Discrimination. The Equal Credit Opportunity Act Amendment of 1976 prohibits discrimination in credit transactions, making it unlawful for a creditor to discriminate against any credit applicant on the basis of "race, color, religion, national origin, sex or marital status, or age (provided the applicant has the capacity to contract)."[78]

Consultative Services. Generally speaking, consultants to institutions and agencies provide evaluation and recommendations concerning the institution itself, its staff, or those it serves. The following list further delineates this general observation and offers some models of consultation.

1. *Administrative consultation.* The center consultant meets with the home administrator, usually to discuss staff problems, but sometimes family or financial problems. The focus is on organization and decision-making.

2. *Staff (milieu) consultation.* The center consultant meets with staff groups to discuss and interpret the psychological importance of events in the nursing home that affect staff and patient group behavior.

3. *Client-centered case consultation.* The center consultant discusses a specific case with a staff group or individual. Focus is on the patient.

4. *Consultee-centered consultation.* The focus of discussion is the patient, but the center consultant keeps the staff members' counter-transference in mind during the discussion.

5. *Didactic meetings.* These allow for an organized presentation of basic psychological principles. Many staff have a keen interest in such learning.[79]

Consultative services should be standard to agencies, homes, and religious and other organizations. The following list includes the major users of consultation regarding the problems of older people.

1. Nursing homes
2. Homes for the aged
3. Nonpsychiatrist physicians
4. General hospital inpatient and outpatient sections
5. Boarding homes, public housing for the aged, and similar residential concentrations
6. Public assistance departments, including their sections for protective service for older persons
7. Members of the clergy
8. Senior citizen centers
9. Industry and government
10. Homemaker and home health aide agencies
11. Visiting nurses and public health nurses
12. Planning bodies, such as model cities boards, senior citizen councils, commissions on aging, housing authorities

The Politics of Age.   The beginning rumblings of "politics of age" stirred controversy along with some early study and political attention.[80] Binstock (1983) wrote of the weaknesses of using older age as a political rallying point. Others saw an old-age-focused political effort as positive and inevitable. Talk of a "backlash" by the younger generation, begun already in the late 1970s, escalated into public debate in the 1980s.[81]

The severe cutback of services resulting from the $750 billion tax cut initiated by the Reagan Administration has provoked steady criticism that Social Security and Medicare provide entitlements for older people while denying them for the young. Newspapers' distortion of figures concerning a rise in the elderly's median income as more than that of any other group has led to the emergence of the "new ageism."[82] This dangerous viewpoint envies the elderly for their economic progress, yet resents the poor elderly for being tax burdens and the nonpoor elderly for making Social Security so expensive. As a result, groups, such as the Americans for Generational Equity (AGE), promote Social Security displacement, and former U.S. Secretary of Commerce Peter Peterson strongly opposes Social Security. In 1983, former Colorado Governor Richard Lamm suggested an old-age-based rationing of health care. Daniel Callahan has expounded on this suggestion, seeing the elderly as "a new social threat . . . that could ultimately (and perhaps already) do great harm."[83]

Fortunately, others have counteracted such views. For example, long-term care was an important ingredient on the national agenda in the 1988 presidential campaign, due in large part to the combined successful efforts of AARP, the Villers Foundation, and the Older Women's League. Their "Long-Term-Care '88" Campaign advocated a universal long-term care financing program based on social insurance that would cover all segments of the population, including severely impaired children and all other groups not currently eligible for Medicare/OASDI. The benefit structure was balanced wisely with home care, community care, and nursing home care. Its emphasis on tailoring to individual needs, flexibility, and innovation was particularly congenial to a patient-oriented philosophy.

Several states have an annual governor's conference on aging (for example, Indiana, North Carolina, and Ohio), and others have special days for older people (for example, "Older Vermonters' Day"). Florida, Michigan, Georgia, Missouri, Utah, West Virginia, and other states have what has been called "silver-haired legislatures"— quasi-official groups of older citizens who meet and draft legislation that is then passed on to the state legislators.

Having a sense of power and political participation is therapeutic for the elderly; the active achievement of objectives may not always be successful, but the process itself can be a source of satisfaction and increased self-esteem. Older people are beginning to be more active politically and may soon vote more consistently as a power block (they constitute 17% of the vote). The National Council of Senior Citizens and the American Association of Retired Persons (the two largest organizations for older people) have lobbied for more favorable Social Security benefits, Medicare, housing, and other areas of concern. The Gray Panthers are a much smaller but more activist group. In addition to their many other advocate activities, the Gray Panthers publish "The Network," an issue-oriented quarterly newspaper covering health care and other age-related topics.[84]

SELECTED READINGS

Aries, P. (1981). *The hour of our death.* New York: Knopf.

Bass, D. M., & Bowman, K. (1990). The transition from caregiving to bereavement: The relationship of care-related strain and adjustment to death. *The Gerontologist, 30*(1), 35–42.

Beck, A. T. (1976). *Cognitive therapy and the emotional disorders.* New York: International Universities Press.

Berezin, M. A., & Cath, S. H. (Eds.) (1965). *Geriatric psychiatry: Grief loss and emotional disorders in the aging process.* New York: International Universities Press.

Berger, R. M. (1995). *Gay and gray: The older homosexual man,* 2nd ed. Binghamton, NY: The Haworth Press.

Binstock, R. H. (1983). The aged and scapegoat. *The Gerontologist, 23,* 136–143.

Birren, J. E., & Hedlund, B. (1987). Contributions of autobiography to developmental psychology. In Eisenberg, N. (Ed.), *Contemporary topics in developmental psychology* (pp. 394–415). New York: John Wiley & Sons.

Brink, T. L. (Ed.). (1990). Mental health in the nursing home. *Clinical Gerontologist, 9*(¾), special issue.

Bumagin, U. E., & Hirn, K. E. (1990). *Helping the aging family: A guide for professionals.* Glenview, IL: Scott, Foresman.

Burnside, I. M. (Ed.). (1986). *Working with the elderly: Group process and techniques,* 2nd ed. Boston, MA: Jones and Bartlett.

Butler, R. N., Burt, R., Foley, K. M., Morris, J., & Morrison, R. S. (1996, June). A peaceful death: How to manage pain and provide quality care. A roundtable discussion: Part 2. *Geriatrics, 51*(6), 32–5, 39–40, 42.

Butler, R. N., Burt, R., Foley, K. M., Morris, J., & Morrison, R. S. (1996, May). Palliative medicine: Providing care when cure is not possible. A roundtable discussion: Part 2. *Geriatrics, 51*(5), 33–6, 42–4.

Butler, R. N., & Gleason, H. P. (Eds.). (1985). *Productive aging: Enhancing vitality in later life.* New York: Springer.

Butler, R. N., Oberlink, M. R., & Schechter, M. (1989). *The promise of productive aging.* New York: Springer.

Byock, I. (1997). *Dying well: The prospect for growth at the end of life.* New York: Riverhead Books.

Cancer Pain Relief and Palliative Care, WHO Expert Committee. (1990). Technical Report, Series 804. Geneva, Switzerland: World Health Organization.

Cantor, M., & Little, V. (1985). Aging and social care. In Binstock, R. H., & Shanas, E. (Eds.), *Handbook of aging and the social sciences* (pp. 745–781). New York: Van Nostrand Reinhold.

Cassell, C., & Omenn, G. S. (Eds.). (1995, September). Caring for patients at the end of life. *Western Journal of Medicine,* no. 163.

Colen, B. D. (1987). *The essential guide to a living will.* New York: Pharos Books.

Collins, C., & Ogle, K. (1994). Patterns of predeath service use by dementia patients with a family caregiver. *Journal of the American Geriatric Society, 42,* 719–722.

Council on Scientific Affairs and Council on Ethical and Judicial Affairs. (1990). Persistent vegetative state and the decision to withdraw or withhold life support. *Journal of the American Medical Association, 263*(3), 426–430.

Daniels, N. (1988). *Am I my parents keeper? An essay on justice between the young and the old.* New York: Oxford University Press.

Dodson, J. E. (Ed.). (1983). *Strengths of black families—An afrocentric educational manual: Toward a non-deficit perspective in services to families and children.* Nashville, TN: University of Tennessee School of Social Work.

Emanuel, E. J., & Emanuel, L. L. (1994). The economics of dying: The illusion of cost savings at the end of life. *The New England Journal of Medicine, 330*(8), 540–544.

Emanuel, E. J., Weinberg, D. S., Gonin, R., et. al. (1993). How well is the Patient Self-Determination Act working? An early assessment. *American Journal of Medicine, 95*(6), 619–628.

Erikson, E. H., Erikson, J. M., & Kivnick, H. Q. (1987). *Vital involvement in old age.* New York: W. W. Norton.

Estes, C. L. (1979). *The aging enterprise: A critical examination of social policies and serviced for the aged.* San Francisco, CA: Jossey-Bass.

Evans, R. L., & Juarequy, B. M. (1982). Phone therapy outreach for blind elderly. *The Gerontologist, 22,* 32–35.

Ferrell, B. A. (1991). Pain management in elderly people. *Journal of the American Geriatric Society, 39,* 64–73.

Finkel, S. I. (1980). Experiences of a private practice psychiatrist working with the elderly in the community. *International Journal of Mental Health, 8,* 147–172.

Finkel, S. I. (1990). Group psychotherapy with older people. *Hospital and Community Psychiatry, 41*(11), 1189–1191.

Finkel, S. I. (1995). Postscript: Research directions for treatment of depression. *International Psychogeriatrics, 7,* 139–140.

Finkel, S. I., & Rogers, S. (1992). The clinical collaboration of a psychiatrist and a geriatric care manager. *Journal of Case Management, 1*(2), 49–52.

Foley, K. M. (1995, September). Pain relief into practice: Rhetoric without reform (editorial). *Journal of Clinical Oncology, 13*(9), 2149–2151.

Foundation for Aging Policy in the 90's. (1990, February). *The 1987 Older Americans Act Amendments. Hearings before the Subcommittee on Human Services of the Select Committee on Aging, House of Representatives.* Washington, DC: U.S. Government Printing Office.

Getzel, G. S. (1983). Group work with kin and friends caring for the elderly. In Saul, S. (Ed.), *Group work with the frail elderly.* Binghamton, NY: The Haworth Press.

Getzel, G. S., & Mellor, J. M. (Eds.). (1985). Gerontological social work practices in the community. *Journal of Gerontological Social Work, 8*(¾), special issue.

Goldfarb, A. (1971). Group therapy with the old and aged. In Kaplan, H., & Saddock, B. (Eds.), *Comprehensive group psychotherapy* (pp. 623–642). Baltimore, MD: Williams and Wilkins.

Goleman, D. (1990, March 27). Studies offer fresh clues to memory. *The New York Times,* 1, 8.

Gorer, G. (1965). *Death, grief and mourning in contemporary Britain.* London: Cresset Press.

Gottlieb, G. L. (1995). Financial issues in geriatric psychiatry. In Kaplan, H. I. & Sadock, B. J. (Eds.), *Comprehensive textbook of psychiatry/IV* (vol. 2, pp. 2656–2661). Baltimore, MD: Williams and Wilkins.

Greene, R. R. (1986). *Social work with the aged and their families.* New York: Aldine de Gruyter.

Greene, R. (1989). A life systems approach to understanding parent–child relationships in aging families. In Hughston, G. A., Christopherson, V. A., & Bonjean, M. J. (Eds.). *Aging and family therapy: Practitioner perspectives on Golden Pond.* Binghamton, NY: The Haworth Press.

Hancock, B. L. (1990). *Social work with older people.* Englewood Cliffs, NJ: Prentice-Hall.

Hughston, G. A., Christopherson, V. A., & Bonjean, M. J. (Eds.). (1989). *Aging and family therapy: Practitioner perspectives on Golden Pond.* Binghamton, NY: The Haworth Press.

Jung, C. G. (1933). The stages of life. In Jung, C. G. *Modern man in search of a soul.* New York: Harcourt, Brace and World.

Kaminsky, M. (Ed.). (1984). *The uses of reminiscence: New ways of working with older adults.* Binghamton, NY: The Haworth Press.

Kaufman, S. R. (1987). *The ageless self: Sources of meaning in late life.* Madison, WI: University of Wisconsin Press.

Klerman, G. L., Weissman, M. W., Rounsaville, B. J., & Chevron, E. S. (1984). *Interpersonal psychotherapy of depression.* New York: Basic Books.

Knight, B. (1996). *Psychotherapy with older adults,* 2nd ed. Thousand Oaks, CA: Sage Publications.

Kübler-Ross, E. (1974). *Questions and answers on death and dying.* New York: Macmillan.

Lawton, M. P. (1983). Environment and other determinants of well-being in older people. *The Gerontologist, 23,* 349–357.

Lerner, M. (1990). *Wrestling with the angel: A memoir of my triumph over illness.* New York: W. W. Norton.

Logan, S. M. L., Freeman, E. M., & McRoy, R. G. (1990). *Social work practice with black families.* New York: Longman.

Lowy, L. (1985). *Social work with the aging.* New York: Longman.

MacLennon, B., Saul, S., & Weiner, M. M. (Eds.). (1988). *Group therapies for the elderly.* Madison, CT: International Universities Press.

Massie, M. J., & Holland, J. C. (1990). Depression and the cancer patient. *Journal of Clinical Psychiatry, 51,* 12–17.

Muller, M. T., van der Wal, G., van Eijk, J. Th. M., et. al. (1994). Voluntary active euthanasia and assisted suicide in Dutch nursing homes: Are the requirements for prudent practice properly met? *Journal of the American Geriatric Society, 42,* 624–629.

Munsterberg, H. (1983). *The crown of life: Artistic creativity in old age.* San Diego, CA: Harcourt Brace Jovanovich.

The National Institute on Community-Based Long-Term Care. (1988). *Care management standards: Guidelines for practice.* Washington, DC: The National Council on Aging.

Nemiroff, R. A., & Colarusso, C. A. (1985). *The race against time: Psychotherapy and psychoanalysis in the second half of life.* New York and London: Plenum Press.

Pinderhughes, E. B. (1982). Family functioning of Afro-Americans. *Social Work, 27,* 91–96.

Quam, J. K. (Ed.). (1996). *Social services for older gay men and lesbians.* Binghamton, NY: The Haworth Press.

Rechtschaffen, A. (1959). Psychotherapy with geriatric patients: A review of the literature. *Journal of Gerontology, 14,* 73–84.

Rodin, J. (1986, September 19) Aging and health: Effects of the sense of control. *Science, 233*(4770), 1271–1276.

Saunders, C. (1959). *Care of the dying.* London: Macmillan.

Schulz, J. H. (1995). *The economics of aging,* 6th ed. Westport, CT: Auburn House.

Sheppard, H. (1989). The new ageism and the "intergenerational tension" issue. *Journal of Foundation Nationale de Gerontologie.* Tampa, FL: International Exchange Center on Gerontology, University of South Florida.

Silverman, P. (1985). *Widow to widow.* New York: Springer.

SUPPORT Principal Investigators. (1995, Nov. 22/29). A controlled trial to improve care for seriously ill hospitalized patients: The Study to Understand Prognoses and Preferences for Outcomes and Risks of Treatments (SUPPORT). *The Journal of the American Medical Association, 274*(20), 1591–1598.

Teno, J., Murphy, D., Lynn, J., et. al. (1994). Prognosis-based futility guidelines: Does anyone win? *Journal of the American Geriatrics Society, 42,* 1–6.

Tolstoy, L. (1969). *The death of Ivan Illych and other stories.* New York: The New American Library of World Literature.

Toseland, R. W. (1990). *Group work with older adults.* New York: New York University Press.

Toseland, R. W., Rossiter, C. M., Peak, T., & Smith, G. C. (1990). Comparative effectiveness of individual and group interventions to support family caregivers. *Social Work, 35*(3), 209–217.

U.S. House of Representatives, Select Committee on Aging. (1988, March 2). Mental health and aging. Hearing before the Select Committee on Aging, U.S. House of Representatives. Washington, DC: U.S. Government Printing Office.

U.S. House of Representatives, Select Committee on Aging and Subcommittee on Human Services. (1989, August 3). Mental health in nursing homes: Barriers and solutions. Joint hearing before the Subcommittee on Human Services and the Select Committee on Aging, U.S. House of Representatives. Washington, DC: U.S. Government Printing Office.

Weinbach, R. W. (1989). Sudden death and the secret survivor: Helping those who grieve alone. *Social Work, 34*(1), 57–60.

Weiner, M. B., Brok, A. J., & Snadowsky, A. M. (1987). *Working with the aged: Practical approaches in the institution and community,* 2nd ed. Norwalk, CT: Appleton-Century-Crofts.

West, R. L. (1985). *Memory fitness over forty.* Gainsville, FL: Triad.

West, R. L. (1989). Planning practical memory training for the aged. In Poon, L. W., Rubin, D. C., & Wilson, B. A. (Eds.), *Everyday cognition in adulthood and later life.* Cambridge: Cambridge University Press.

Wilson, B. A. (1988). *Rehabilitation of memory*. New York: Guilford Publications.

Yalom, I. D. (1985). *The theory and practice of group psychotherapy,* 3rd ed. New York: Basic Books.

Yesavage, J. A. (1990). *Age-associated memory impairment: Conceptual background and treatment approaches.* Presented at the 1990 Sandoz Lectures in Gerontology, March 28–30, 1990.

SELECTED READINGS IN REMINISCENCE AND LIFE REVIEW

American Association of Retired Persons. (1992). *The power of memories: Creative uses of reminiscence.* Washington, DC: Author.

Birren, J. E., & Deutchman, D. E. (1991). *Guiding autobiography groups for older adults: Exploring the fabric of life.* Baltimore, MD: John Hopkins University Press.

Birren, J. E., & Hedlund, B. (1987). Contributions of autobiography to developmental psychology. In Eisenburg, N. (Ed.), *Contemporary topics in developmental psychology* (pp. 394–415). New York: John Wiley & Sons.

Black, G., & Haight, B. K. (1992). Integrality as a holistic framework for the life-review process. *Holistic Nurse Practitioner, 7*(1), 7–15.

Boggs, D, & Leptak, J. (1991). Life review among senior citizens as a product of drama. *Educational Gerontology, 17,* 239–246.

Bruner, J. (1987). Life as narrative. *Social Research, 54,* 11–32.

Burnside, I. (1993). Themes in reminiscence groups with older women. *International Journal of Aging and Human Development, 37,* 177–189.

Burnside, I, & Haight, B. K. (1994). Protocols for reminiscence and life review. *Nurse Practitioner, 19,* 55–61.

Butler, R. N. (1963). The life review: An interpretation of reminiscence in the aged. *Psychiatry, 26,* 65–76.

Chance, S. (1988). The psychological functions of genealogy in the aged. *Journal of Geriatric Psychiatry and Neurology, 1*(4), 113–115.

Colemen. P. (1991). Ageing and life history: The meaning of reminiscence in late life. *Sociological Review (Monograph), 37,* 120–143.

David, D. (1990). Reminiscence, adaptation, and social context in old age. *International Journal of Aging and Human Development, 30,* 175–188.

DeGenova, M. (1991). Elderly life review therapy: A Bowen approach. *American Journal of Family Therapy, 19,* 160–166.

Disch, R. (Ed.). (1988). Twenty-five years of the life review [Special issue]. *Journal of Gerontological Social Work, 12*(¾).

Fishman, S. (1992) Relationships among older adult's life review, ego integrity, and death anxiety. *International Psychogeriatrics, 4,* 267–277.

Freeman, M. (1993). *Rewriting the self: History, memory, narrative.* London: Routledge.

Freud, A. (1936). *Das Ich und die Abwehrmechanismen.* London: Imago.

Galassie, F. (1991). A life-review workshop for gay and lesbian elders. *Journal of Gerontological Social Work, 16,* 75–86.

Haight, B. K., & Webster, J. D. (Eds.). (1995). *The art and science of reminiscing: Theory, research, methods, and applications.* Washington, DC: Taylor and Francis.

Hargave, T. D., & Anderson, W. T. (1992). *Finishing well: Aging and reparation in the intergenerational family.* New York: Brunner/Mazel.

Lewis, M. I., & Butler, R. N. (1974). Life review therapy: Putting memories to work in individual and group psychotherapy. *Geriatrics, 29,* 165–169, 172–172.

Merriam, S. B. (1993). Butler's life review: How universal is it? *International Journal of Aging and Human Development, 37*(3), 163–175.

Rubin, D. C., Wetzler, S. E., & Nebes, R. B. (1989). Autobiographical memory across the life span. In Rubin, D. C. (Ed.), *Autobiographical Memory.* Cambridge: Cambridge University Press.

Ruth, J. E. & Birren, J. E. (1995). Personality and aging: Modes of coping and the meaning of stress. In Kruse, A., & Schmitz-Scherzer (Eds.), *Psychologie des Lebenslaufs.* Festschrift Hans Thomae. Darmstadt: Steinkopf Verlag.

Staudinger, U. M. (1989). *The study of the life review: An approach to the investigation of intellectual development across the life span.* Berlin: Max-Planck-Institut fur Bildungsforschung.

Staudinger, U. M. et al. (1992). Wisdom-related knowledge in a life review task: Age differences and the role of professional specialization. *Psychology and Aging, 7*(2), 271–281.

Webster, J. D. (1993). Construction and validation of the reminiscence functions scale. *Journal of Gerontology, 48,* 256–252.

Wholohan, D. (1992). The value of reminiscence in hospice care. *American Journal of Hospice and Palliative Care, 9,* 272–279.

Zuniga, M. (1989). Mexican-American elderly and reminiscence interventions. *Journal of Gerontological Social Work, 14*(¾), 61–73.

ENDNOTES

1. See "The Shameless Old Lady" (listed in Appendix E), based on a play by Bertolt Brecht in which an elderly widow makes the most of the last 18 months of her life.

2. For example, see Dodgen, J. C., & Ransom, J. A. (1967). Psychotherapy of a sexagenarian. *Diseases of the Nervous System, 28,* 680–683. Also see Goldfarb, A. I. (1971). Group therapy with the old and aged. In Kaplan, H. I., & Saddock, B. J. (Eds.), *Comprehensive group psychotherapy.* Baltimore: Williams & Wilkins; and Goldfarb, A. I. (1955). Psychotherapy of aged persons; IV. One aspect of the therapeutic situation with aged patients. *Psychoanalytic Review, 42,* 100–187.

3. Abraham, K. (1927). The applicability of psychoanalytic treatment to patients at an advanced age. In *Selected papers of Karl Abraham, M. D.* (pp. 312–317). London: Hogarth Press.

4. Jelliffe, S. E. (1925). The old age factor in psychoanalytic therapy. *Medical Journal and Record, 121,* 7–12.

5. Grotjahn, M. (1940). Psychoanalytic investigation of a 71-year-old man with senile dementia. *Psychoanalytic Quarterly, 9,* 80–97.

6. Goldfarb emphasized the dependent relationships of older patients, comparing them with early parent–child relationships. The physician assumes the role of parent figure pressed on him by the patient. Thus sometimes the therapist will be seen as a scapegoat and sometimes as the omnipotent helper. See Goldfarb, A. I. (1971).

7. See Rogers, C. R. (1951). *Client-centered therapy* and (1961). *On becoming a person.* Boston: Houghton-Mifflin.

8. Buber, M. (1957). The William Alanson White memorial lectures, fourth series. *Psychiatry, 20,* 95–129.

9. Frankl, V. (1963). From death camp to existentialism. In *Man's search for meaning.* New York: Washington Square Press.

10. See *Archives of General Psychiatry, 42,* 305–316, March 1985 and *46,* 971–82, November 1989.

11. Jung, C. G. (1933). *Modern man in search of a soul.* New York: Harcourt, Brace and World.

12. Erikson, E. H. (1959). The problem of ego identity. In *Identity and the life cycle, Psychological Issues, 1,* 101–164.

13. Rodin, J. (1986). Aging and health: Effects of the sense of control. *Science, 233,*(4770), 1271–1276.

14. The University of Chicago Committee on Human Development pursued studies of reminiscence. See Gorney, J. E. (1968). *Experiencing and age: Patterns of reminiscence among the elderly,* unpublished Ph.D. dissertation; Falk, J. M. (1969). *The organization of remembered life experience in old age: Its relation to subsequent adaptive capacity and to age,* unpublished Ph.D. dissertation; and Havighurst, R. J., & Glasser, R. (1972). An exploratory study of reminiscence. *Journal of Gerontology, 27,* 245–253.

15. Rodin, J. (1986).

16. Jung, C. G. (1933).

17. For further information on how to obtain the training guide *Reminiscence: Finding Meaning in Memories,* contact the Social Outreach and Support Section, Program Department, AARP, 1909 K St., N.W., Washington, DC 20049.

18. Scott-Maxwell, F. (1968). *The measure of my days.* New York: Alfred A. Knopf.

19. Lewis, M. I., & Butler, R. N. (1974). Life review therapy: Putting memories to work in individual and group psychotherapy. *Geriatrics, 29,* 165–169, 172–173; and Merriam, S. (1980). The concept and function of the reminiscence: A review of the research. *The Gerontologist, 20*(5), 604–609.

20. Lieberman M. A., & Tobin, S. S. (1983). *The experience of old age: Stress, coping and survival.* New York: Basic Books.

21. "Reminiscence group therapy has been found to be most useful in maintaining socialization and establishing group cohesiveness" (p. 965) in Katzman, R. (1986). Alzheimer's disease. *New England Journal of Medicine, 314,* 964–973.

22. For an example of reminiscence in a senior center, see the article "Senior Citizens Produce Book of Remembrances," *The Chronicle* (Milford, Delaware), June 25, 1980. The article describes a book, *The Times We Remember,* produced by residents of the local senior center.

23. Dietsche, L. M. (1979). Facilitating the life review through group reminiscence. *Journal of Gerontological Nursing, 5,* 43–46.

24. Hendricks, L. (1979). *Personal life history. Writing for older adults. A handbook for teaching personal life history classes,* Leon County School Board, Tallahassee, FL; and Daniel, L. (1980). *How to write your own life story: A step by step guide for the non-professional writer.* Chicago: Chicago Review Press.

25. Tolstoy, L. (1960). *Last diaries* (translated by L. Stilman) New York: Putnam-Capricorn, 43.

26. In the Middle Ages, hospices were run by monks for anyone who needed help: the poor, the sick and dying, or travelers and pilgrims going to the Holy Land during the Crusades.

27. From "St. Christopher's Hospice" (editorial), *London Nursing Times,* July 29, 1967. See also Saunders, C. (1959). *Care of the dying.* London: Macmillan.

28. To locate hospice programs contact the Hospice Helpline at (800)658–8898 or the National Hospice Organization, 1901 N. Moore St., Suite 901, Arlington, VA 22209.

29. For a copy of the Living Will or other advance-directive documents, write Choice in Dying, 100 Varick St., New York, New York 10014.

30. Funeral price information from the National Funeral Directors Association (NFDA) *1996 General Price List Survey.* Breakdown available from: National Funeral Directors Association, P. O. Box 27641, Milwaukee, WI 53227–0641.

31. For a copy, contact: Public Reference, Federal Trade Commission, 6th and Pennsylvania Ave. NW, Room 130, Washington, DC 20580.

32. For more information, contact Funeral and Memorial Societies of America, Inc.(FAMSA) P. O. Box 10, Hinesburg, VT 05461.

33. Morgan, E. (1980). *A manual of death education and simple burial,* 9th ed., Washington, DC: Continental Association of Funeral and Memorial Societies. (1828 L St. N.W., Washington, D.C. 20036)

34. Eye and temporal bone banks and the National Kidney Foundation also give the person a sense of valued legacy. Usually only the corneas of older people are acceptable, however. A Uniform Anatomical Gift Act or its equivalent now exists in every state and in most Canadian provinces. A Uniform Donor's Card filled out and signed by the donor and two witnesses (three in Florida) constitutes a legal document. [See Department of Health, Education and Welfare. (1979). *How to donate the body and its organs for transplantation.* Washington, DC: Medical Education and Research, Pub. No (NIH) 77–776.] An individual now has final say over the disposition of his or her body, but if a family strongly objects, most institutions will not go against their wishes. France, England, and West Germany have adopted the "Universal Donor Principle," whereby anyone who dies anywhere in these countries is available as a donor of organs or tissues provided he or she has not previously specified otherwise. When the problem of transplantation rejection is fully solved, the opportunities to help others through donation of body parts will increase significantly.

35. Silverman, P. R. (1970). The widow-to-widow program. *Archives of the Foundation of Thanatology, 2,* 134.

36. *Ibid,* 134.

37. Weinbach, R. W. (1989). Sudden death and secret survivors: Helping those who grieve alone. *Social Work, 34*(l), 57–60.

38. Silver, A. (1950). Group psychotherapy with senile psychiatric patients. *Geriatrics, 5,* 147–150.

39. Linden, M. E. (1953). Group psychotherapy with institutionalized senile women: Study in gerontology in human relations. *International Journal of Group Psychotherapy, 3,* 150–151.

40. Goldfarb, A. I. (1955). Psychotherapy of aged persons, IV. One aspect of the therapeutic situation with aged patients, *Psychoanalytic Review, 42,* 100–187.

41. Ebersole, P. P. (1976). Reminiscing and group psychotherapy with the aging. In Burnside, I. M. (Ed.), *Nursing and the aged* (ch. 12). New York: McGraw-Hill.

42. Lowy, L. (1983). Social group work with vulnerable older persons: A theoretical perspective. *Social Work with Groups, 5*(2), 21–32.

43. Klein, W. H., LeShan, E. J., & Furman, S. S. (1965). *Promoting mental health of older people through group methods.* New York: Mental Health Materials Center.

44. Steuer, J. L., Mintz, J., Hammen, C. L., Hill, M. A., Jarvik, L. F., McCarley, T., Motoike, P., & Rosen, R. (1984). Cognitive–behavioral and psychodynamic group psychotherapy in treatment of geriatric depression. *Journal of Consulting and Clinical Psychology, 52*(2), 180–189.

45. Yalom, I. D. (1985). *The theory and practice of group psychotherapy,* 3rd ed. New York: Basic Books.

46. See Burnside, I. M. (1988). *Nursing and the aged,* 3rd ed. New York: McGraw-Hill; Burnside, I. M. (Ed.), (1986). *Working with the elderly: Group process and techniques,* 2nd ed. Boston: Jones and Bartlett; Blake, D. (1980). Group work with the institutionalized elderly. In Burnside, I. M. (Ed.), *Psychosocial nursing care of the aged,* 2nd ed. New York: McGraw-Hill; Burnside, I. M. (1970). Group work with the aged: Selected literature. *The Gerontologist, 10,* 241–246; and Ebersole, P. (1975). From despair to integrity through reminiscing with the aged. In *A.N.A. clinical sessions.* New York: Appleton-Century-Crofts.

47. Cohen, S. Z., & Hammerman, J. (1974). Social work with groups. In Brody, E., and contributors. *A social work guide for long-term care facilities* (pp. 123–135). Rockville, MD: National Institute of Mental Health.

48. Getzel, G. (1983). Group work with kin and friends caring for the elderly. In Saul, S. (Ed.), *Group work with the frail elderly.* Binghamton, NY: The Haworth Press.

49. Lewis, M. I., & Butler, R. N. (1974). Life review therapy: Putting memories to work in individual and group psychotherapy. *Geriatrics, 29,* 165–169, 172–73. Also in Burnside, I. M. (Ed.). (1986). *Working with the elderly: Group process and techniques,* 2nd ed. (pp. 50–59). Boston: Jones and Bartlett.

50. Greene, R. (1986). *Social work with the aged and their families.* New York: Aldine de Gruyter.

51. Bumagin, V. E., & Hirn, K. F. (1990). *Helping the aging family.* Glenview, IL: Scott, Foresman.

52. Eyde, D. R., & Rich, J. (1983). *Psychological distress in aging: A family management model.* Rockville, MD: Aspen Publications, 45.

53. Silverstone, B., & Burack-Weiss, A. (1983). *Social work practice with the frail elderly and their families.* Springfield, IL: Charles C. Thomas.

54. Finkel, S. I. (1980). Experiences of a private-practice psychiatrist working with the elderly in the community. *International Journal of Mental Health, 8,* 147–172. (Dr. Finkel helped build the American Association for Geriatric Psychiatry.)

55. Getzel, G. (1982). Helping elderly couples in crisis. *Social Casework, 63*(9), 515–521.

56. Greene, R. (1989). A life systems approach to understanding parent–child relationships in aging families. In Hughston, G. A., Christopherson, V. A., & Bonjean, M. J. (Eds.), *Aging and family therapy: Practitioner perspectives on Golden Pond.* Binghamton, NY: The Haworth Press; Freeman, D, S. (1981). *Techniques of family therapy.* New York: Jason Aronson.

57. Lindsley, O. R. (1964). Geriatric behavior prosthetics. In Kastenbaum, R. (Ed.), *New thoughts on old age* (pp. 41–60). New York: Springer.

58. B. F. Skinner's book, *Enjoy old age* (New York: Norton, 1983), provides practical guidance for people growing older. His ideas have been questioned by many, but the approach is interesting to evaluate, given its distinguished author and his life-long interest in adaptation.

59. For illustrative studies, see Hoyer, W. J., Mishara, B. L., & Riekel, R. G. (1975). Problem behaviors as operants: Applications with elderly individuals. *The Gerontologist, 15,* 452–456; Preston, C. E. (1973). Behavior modification: A therapeutic approach to aging and death. *Postgraduate Medicine, 54,* 64–68; and Lisk, N., Howe, M. W., & Pinkstone, E. M. (1975). Behavioral group work in a home for the aged. *Social Work, 20*(6), 454–463.

60. Johnson, H. E., & Garton, W. H. (1973). Muscle reeducation in hemiplegia by use of electromyographic device. *Archives of Physical Medicine and Rehabilitation, 54,* 320–323.

61. Goleman, D. (1990, March 27). Studies offer fresh clues to memory. *The New York Times,* 1, 8.

62. Yesavage, J. A. (1990). *Age-associated memory impairment: Conceptual background and treatment approaches,* presented at the 1990 Sandoz Lectures in Gerontology, March 28–30, 1990.

63. Cavan's early study, now often overlooked, with its sizable sample of 2,988 subjects demonstrated the vast importance of social factors to adjustment. See Cavan, R. S. (1952). Personal adjustment in old age. In Lansing, A. H. (Ed.), *Cowdry's problems of aging,* 3rd ed. Baltimore: Williams & Wilkins.

64. Greenberg, S. (1995, July 30). Title III—State and Community Programs. *The Administration on Aging and the Aging Network.* Administration On Aging Web Site, http://www.aoa.dhhs.gov/aoa.

65. Greenberg, S. (1995, July 30). Title VII—Vulnerable Elder Rights Protection Activities. *The Administration on Aging and the Aging Network.* Administration On Aging Web Site, http://www.aoa.dhhs.gov/aoa.

66. Cloward and Piven argued in 1966 (Cloward, R. A., & Piven, F. F. [1966]. The weight of the poor. . . . a strategy to end poverty, *The Nation, 202,* 510–517) that "adding all eligible persons to the welfare rolls would generate a financial crisis of

such magnitude that the federal government would be pressured to respond with a plan for a guaranteed annual income." An Advisory Council on Public Welfare the same year suggested, as had others, a "national floor under assistance payments" and federal, rather than state, responsibility for public welfare program studies and financing (Advisory Council on Public Welfare. [1966]. *Having the power we have the duty.* Report to the Secretary of Health, Education and Welfare, Washington, DC: U.S. Government Printing Office). This became one of the historical steps in the development of Supplemental Security Income.

67. See The Commonwealth Fund Commission on Elderly People Living Alone. (1988). *Strategies to increase participation in the supplemental security income program: Follow-up study of poor elderly people.* Baltimore, MD: The Commonwealth Fund.

68. Sehnert, K., Awkward, B., & Lesage, D. (1976, March). *The senior citizen as an "activated patient,"* mimeographed book prepared for the Office of Assistant Secretary for Planning and Education, U.S. Public Health Service, Department of Health, Education and Welfare.

69. See also: Wright, B. (1994). *Self help among the elderly: Formal and informal support systems.* New York: Garland Publishers; and Donovan, J. (1994). *The self help directory: A sourcebook for self-help groups in the United States and Canada.* New York: Facts on File. To find out if a self-help organization is operating in a particular area, the following clearinghouses can be contacted: The National Self-Help Clearinghouse, 25 W. 43rd St., Room 620, New York, NY 10036, and The Self-Help Center, Division of MHAI, 150 N. Wacker Dr., Suite 900, Chicago, IL 60606.

70. Self-employment is often "bootleg" work (typing, babysitting, housecleaning, handyman services), which is not reported as income so as to avoid imperiling Social Security pensions.

71. Age Discrimination Act 29 U.S.C. (United States Code) 621 et seq.

72. For the pioneering references, see The National Council on the Aging. (1961, May). *Utilization of older professional and scientific workers;* Shock, N. W. (1947). Older people and their potentialities for gainful employment. *Journal of Gerontology, 2,* 92–102; and McFarland, R. A. (1943, Summer).

The older worker in industry. *Harvard Business Review, 505–510.*

73. See, for example, the classic legal case for better mental hospital care, *Wyatt* v. *Stickney,* Alabama, 1971–1972.

74. See Horn, L., & Griesel, E. (1977). *Nursing homes: A citizen's action guide. How to organize, plan and achieve nursing home reform in your community.* Boston: Beacon Press.

75. Commission on Legal Problems of the Elderly, American Bar Association, 1800 M St., N.W., Washington, DC 20036.

76. Legal Council for the Elderly Staff & Brown, R. N. (1988). *The rights of older persons: The basic ACLU guide to an older person's rights.* Carbondale, IL: Southern Illinois University Press.

77. See Butler, R. N. (1968). Why are older consumers so susceptible? *Geriatrics, 23,* 83–88.

78. P. L. 92–239 amending 15 U.S.C. (United States Code) 1691 et seq.

79. From Group for the Advancement of Psychiatry. (1971, November). *The aged and community mental health: A guide to program development, 8*(81). Formulated by the Committee on Aging.

80. A few studies appeared already in the 1970s. One relates to the question of the alleged development of greater conservatism with age (Rule, W.I.B. [1977]. Political alienation and voting attitudes among the elderly generation. *The Gerontologist, 17*[5], 400–404). Another discusses the question of why minority group elderly have a lower rate of political activity (Torres-Gill, F., & Becerra, F. M. [1977]. The political behavior of the Mexican-American elderly. *The Gerontologist, 17*[51], 392–399).

81. Ragan, P. (1977). Another look at the politicizing of old age: Can we expect a backlash effect? *Urban and Social Change Review, 10*(2), 6–13.

82. Sheppard, H. (1989). The new ageism and the "intergenerational tension" issue. *Journal of Fondation Nationale de Gerontologie.* Tampa, FL: International Exchange Center on Gerontology, University of South Florida.

83. Callahan, D. (1987). *Setting limits: Medical goals in an aging society.* New York: Simon and Schuster.

84. For a subscription to the Gray Panthers' newspaper or information on any of their other printed materials, contact the Gray Panthers, P. O. Box 21477, Washington, DC 20009-9477.

DRUG AND OTHER SOMATIC THERAPIES

Although older people make up 13% of the population, they consume about 35 to 40% of all medications prescribed in the United States, amounting to $12.7 to $14.3 billion of expenditures (approximately $245 to $475 per person).[1] The single largest out-of-pocket health care expense for older persons is the payment for out-of-hospital drugs. Twenty-five percent of those over 65 are discharged from hospitals with prescriptions for six or more drugs, compared to approximately 3% for younger cohorts.[2] Our challenge in this chapter is to better understand what constitutes appropriate treatment for older persons, particularly since they receive such a disproportionately larger share of prescribed medication.

Medical and nursing education does not yet focus adequately on pharmacology and clinical pharmacy as it relates to old age. Research studies too infrequently exclude the old in their observations, and there has been a delay by the U.S. government in issuing guidelines for the pharmaceutical industry on including elderly persons in premarketing clinical tests. We still know precious little about the changes in absorption, distribution, metabolism, and excretion of medications (called *pharmacokinetics*), and the actions and changes in drug sensitivity (*pharmacodynamics*) that occur with aging—an exciting and

important area for research with obviously practical application.[3] And while it has been known for centuries that there are increased drug side effects in the elderly,[4] it is only more recently that adverse reactions have been studied in relation to age. For example, it has been estimated that adverse drug reactions occur in 15 to 25% of elderly patients as compared to 3 to 9% for younger adults.[5]

There is considerable evidence to support the view that we have an "overmedicated society." Much concern, of course, is voiced about use of drugs in the youth culture and about barbiturate, tranquilizer, and alcohol consumption among the middle-aged. But old age has its own drug problems, resulting from high usage of tranquilizers, antidepressants, sedatives, hypnotics, and multiple over-the-counter drugs. To some degree these medications may reflect the greater anxiety, depression, and insomnia perceived in older people. But they also point to the anxiety of doctors and other health personnel, their impatience with older people (to whom they would often rather give a pill than listen), and their own need for instant gratification (treatment results). Unfortunately, drugs reinforce some of the general slowing observed in older people, aggravate a sense of aging and depression, and can contribute to or directly cause acute and chronic brain syndromes. For these reasons, we are once again reminded of the important need to prescribe and supervise these medications carefully.

GENERAL PRINCIPLES IN DRUG TREATMENT WITH THE ELDERLY

The ancient rule of medicine, *primun non nocere* (first do no harm), applies particularly to prescribing medication for older persons. Drugs should be used *only* when necessary and with as few medications used simultaneously as possible. The average older person is already taking several medications (called *polypharmacy*) at any one time, and additional drugs greatly increase the likelihood of drug interactions.[6] Nonetheless, additional medications for behavioral disorders are frequently needed for the elderly, and skills in geriatric psychopharmacology are an essential part of any general practicioner's daily interaction with patients.[7] To help in planning appropriate drug treatment for elderly patients, some guiding principles should be kept in mind.

The Medical Model: Who's the Patient?

It is not uncommon for an older person to be accompanied to a doctor's consulting room by a spouse or younger member of the family. In most circumstances, this situation is perfectly acceptable to both parties, and the diagnostic evaluation and therapy can proceed unencumbered. With the suggestion of a new medication, however, disagreements within the family can occur. Previously unexpressed conflicts and subtle pressures sometimes become manifest at this point, and the clinician is faced with the problem of identifying the most reasonable course of action. A close alliance with the patient, in addition to the "contact" person in the family, can of course be helpful, but the decisions about therapy must remain within the control of the patient him- or herself whenever possible, in order for the proposed treatment to be successfully carried out.

Exceptions might be when mental confusion or physical illness interferes with the patient's judgment.

Diagnostic Accuracy: What's the Problem?

While the insistence on diagnostic accuracy may seem an obvious point, it remains a fact that many more psychiatric medications are prescribed than there are psychiatric conditions. For instance, it is currently believed that about two-thirds of all nursing home patients receive psychotropic drugs, yet only about 20% have psychiatric diagnoses beyond dementia.[8] Insufficient staffing is perhaps the primary reason for overmedicating older persons into more manageable quietude. Other reasons are the possible concealment of a psychiatric diagnosis to get an older person admitted into a nursing home, the failure of the doctors who service nursing homes to keep apprised of the dangers of overmedication, and the fact that some states use Medicaid to pay for drugs but not for careful psychiatric diagnosis and forms of treatment other than drugs.

Drug administration in institutions is marked by special problems of its own.

1. Much medication is prescribed by doctors over the phone, based only on symptoms described by nursing personnel. Errors in diagnosis are therefore common, as well as a tendency to prescribe based on the needs of the institution rather than simply in the patient's best interest.

2. Errors in drug administration occur because medication is often given by untrained or poorly trained aides and orderlies.

3. The possibilities for errors in drug administration are compounded by the number of medications (an average of five to seven) each patient receives at once, often in varying combinations of multiple daily doses.

4. Staff shortages lead to less physical exercise for patients, more use of physical restraints, overuse of catheters, lack of sufficiently individualized diet, less personalized warmth and support, and an unstimulating environment. These problems result in a higher incidence of urinary tract infections, respiratory and circulatory disorders leading to pneumonia and bedsores, and a rise in mental depression and agitation, to name just a few conditions. All of these are eventually treated with drugs when they might have been prevented in the first place. Thus, with the institutionalized and the office-based patients, the physician should carefully reconsider the clinical picture before adding yet another medication (see Chapter 9 for a review of diagnostic evaluations).

Polypharmacy: "Do They Really Need That Extra Medicine?"

With the elderly, multiple medications and general polypharmacy should be considered the rule. It is estimated that Medicare patients receive an *average* of 10 medications in acute care hospitals.[9] The average nursing home patient reportedly receives over nine medications.[10] Furthermore, it is estimated that 70% of the elderly use over-the-counter drugs as opposed to only 10% in the general population.[11]

Older persons experience three times as many adverse reactions as younger persons. The possible adverse interactions of one drug with another should be anticipated and avoided.[12] Before prescribing any drugs for institutionalized or non-institutionalized patients, the physician should ask to see all his or her present medications, including over-the-counter medications and old, empty bottles. The patient should be asked if he or she tends to "self-medicate" and, if so, how much and for what purpose. The physician should also check with the patient's other doctors to learn if previously prescribed drugs should still be taken. Medications should be introduced one at a time when possible in order to monitor their individual effects. The dosage schedule should be kept simple and easily understandable. All medication orders should have automatic discontinuation dates; renewal requires valuable reassessment and averts prolonged, inappropriate, harmful, and useless administration of drugs.

Drug Compliance: "Are They Really Taking Their Medicine?"

Since the prescription medication offered by a physician to a patient is so important, it is short-sighted to limit the prescription process to the exchange of a piece of paper reserved for the closing seconds of an office visit. And yet, that scenario is all too common in busy medical practices. Telephone call-ins of prescriptions to a local pharmacy, hospital ward, or nursing home for the beginning of a new pharmacologic regimen can also be a problem if the doctor has not taken the time to explain the drug and how to take it.

There are many reasons for poor medication compliance: time restrictions, poor instructions, psychological concerns surrounding the question of control and autonomy, or simply forgetfulness and confusion on the part of the older person. Open discussion of these issues are frequently avoided because physicians too often assume compliance will occur automatically.

Mary is an 81-year-old widow who came to the office with her daughter for evaluation of a persistent depression. Her clinical presentation was a classic repeat of an earlier episode which had responded to imipramine, and her physician had appropriately prescribed low doses of the same medication. Three weeks later, the symptoms persisted, and Mary's blood level showed no detectable imipramine. When asked why she was not taking the medication as prescribed, Mary retorted: "Well, since the doctor talked to my daughter the whole time and gave her the slip, I figured she was supposed to take the pills, not me." Somewhat embarrassed, the physician apologized for his mistake. Once he properly addressed his primary patient and reviewed the treatment plan with her directly, she fully complied with the regimen and responded therapeutically as expected.

In addition to the psychological factors involved in taking medications, simply reviewing the details of the drug regimen can be of great value. It is exceedingly valuable for patients when doctors fill out a written sheet on each new drug prescribed so the older person can refer to it later (see Figure 13.1).

Some straightforward aides useful in compliance are the use of pill packs, automatic timers (i.e., digital clocks with buzzers preset for medication times), and clearly labeled signs in the bathroom to function as a reminder. The pharmacist should be instructed to package drugs in easy-to-open containers for older persons. It would also be useful if drug companies routinely used some special device in packaging drugs for older people, as they do with the clever calendar dispensers of the "pill," which aid younger women in remembering to take contraceptives. Such an aid is invaluable in coping with the memory problems of late life. Older patients should be warned not to take medicines in the dark or to keep them on the

Medication: _____

Who prescribed it: _____

Date: _____

For what: _____

Dosage: _____

Schedule: _____

Duration: _____

What to avoid:

   Other drugs: _____

   Alcohol: _____

   Food: _____

Use of machinery: _____

   Driving: _____

   Other: _____

Minor side effects that often occur and what to do about them: _____

_____

_____

_____

_____

Major side effects that can occur and require a call to the doctor: _____

_____

_____

FIGURE 13.1 Sample medication sheet

bedside table (there are exceptions, of course, such as nitroglycerine), since sleepiness can cause errors in judgment.

Older people may have impairments that interfere with hearing and/or understanding the doctor's orders regarding drugs, seeing labels well enough to take the correct medicine and the correct dose, or having a steady enough hand to handle fluids, tiny pills, or "child-proof" (and thus more difficult to open) drug bottles. When specifically requested, it is possible in many pharmacies to get medicine bottles that are not child proof for those elderly who would otherwise have trouble opening the bottles. Impairment of intellect (especially with senile dementia) may cause errors in judgment or lapses in memory with regard to drugs. Consequently the older person's capacity for the self-administration of drugs needs to be evaluated as carefully as his or her medical need for drugs. When forgetfulness or confusion is a frequent issue, supervision of drug taking should be arranged with relatives, friends, or neighbors. It has been estimated that half of all older people who take drugs do not take them as prescribed, and one fourth make errors serious enough to create drug-induced illnesses. It is therefore not surprising that older people comprise about half of all hospital admissions for drug intoxication.

Side Effects: "When Should I Call the Doctor?"

One of the important reasons for informing older people about the drugs they are taking is to help them distinguish side effects from other bodily changes. As we mentioned previously, we have found that older people may misinterpret the retarding effects of the tranquilizers as signs of aging. Doctors remain all too secretive in preparing patients for drug effects, partly because they fear the development of symptoms in suggestible persons. Many also simply do not wish to take the time. It is archaic to assume that "what the patient doesn't know won't hurt him," because often it does. Full disclosure is now imperative for both medical and legal reasons. Patients of

course have the legal right to refuse medications or medical procedures. One must help patients overcome fears of medications while simultaneously encouraging them to respect effects and dangers.

Drug side effects occur in the elderly as often as seven times more frequently than in younger adults.[13] The potential dangers, complications, and side effects should be carefully and fully explained to patients—both the annoying symptoms like dryness of the mouth and the dangerous symptoms such as hypotension (low blood pressure and possible fainting) and extrapyramidal symptoms (parkinsonism). Psychiatric drugs can affect sexuality in varying manner and degree from individual to individual, especially after the age of 50. When sexual problems occur, the doctor may be able to change to another drug. Each medication will have its own "profile" of likely and rare side effects. In addition, each medication will have its own time course of clinical and therapeutic effects. This last point is extremely important because psychiatric medications generally have a delayed onset of therapeutic effects. Unfortunately, the side effects usually occur immediately, so the physician is often in the position of trying to convince the patient to tolerate the side effects long enough to reap the benefits.

The *sedating effects* of a number of medications used in persons over 65 can cause serious problems. Older people who are experiencing a physical slowing of speed and coordination find these features exacerbated by a number of drugs. Some persons react with fear and depression, thinking they are failing fast or even dying. Reassurance is imperative.

The side effects can, of course, outweigh the potential benefits. Educated decision making before the initiation of medication therapy is not the only critical point. It is also important to know when to stop a medication trial (i.e., onset of tardive dyskinesia). If the patient is well informed about the predictable hazards, has easy access to medical backup for information and support from the doctor's office, and has the feeling that the trial can be abandoned if the side effects become too

TABLE 13.1   Selected factors affecting drug response with age

1. Absorption
   Stomach Transit Time
   Hydrochloric acid
2. Distribution
   Proteins in blood
   Body Composition (lean body mass, fat)
   Tissue sensitivity
   Receptors
3. Metabolism
   Liver enzymes
4. Excretion
   Kidney blood flow
   Glomerular filtration rate
5. Multiple drug use (polypharmacy)
6. Overdose (purposive or accidental)
7. Patient Compliance (omission, commission)
8. Physician failure to give complete instructions

difficult, then the "team approach" to medication management has a greater chance of ultimate success. By making side effects more predictable and controllable, one can often minimize the fear surrounding these reactions and thereby avoid the premature cessation of a drug trial.

Drug Metabolism: "Less is Usually Better!"

Older people have qualitative and quantitative differences from younger people in absorption, distribution, metabolism, and excretion of drugs. (See Table 13.1 for factors affecting drug response with age.) In general, drug effects are determined by dosage, absorption (quality and rate), distribution in the body (dependent on factors of body composition such as body fluid, organ blood flow, and cardiac output), hepatic metabolism and renal excretion, nutritional status, and personal habits (for example, smoking and alcohol intake). While the absorption rate in the older person may be slower for some drugs, the total amount of drug absorbed in the bowel by passive diffusion may be the same. Combined with the near universal slowing of liver and kidney clearance of the drugs, the expected time

course and duration of drug effects are often altered. This *pharmacokinetic* (excretion of medications) model of altered drug metabolism in the elderly is well outlined in many pharmacologic texts. What is still not well understood is the possible changing of *pharmacodynamics* (the actions and changes in drug sensitivity) in the elderly patient. Drug sensitivity is generally assumed to be increased in the older patient.[14]

Perhaps the simplest principle of pharmacologic management in the elderly is that less drug is usually more effective. In fact, some have suggested that the elderly generally need doses only 30 to 50% as large as those used in younger adults.[15] Drug metabolism in the elderly is a major factor in their drug use, since the liver may have reduced blood flow and thus the rate of drug detoxification may be slowed. Moreover, older people generally have a lower general metabolism rate, causing prolonged drug action or creating exaggerated drug reactions. Kidney impairment can also affect excretion of the drug. The older population also has a relatively greater accumulation of drugs in body fat as compared to younger people; therefore drug effects may be prolonged.

Drug Costs: "How Much Can I Afford?"

One should always think of cost in prescribing drugs for older persons, especially since Medicare does not cover out-of-hospital prescription drug costs. Out-of-pocket health care costs for the elderly have skyrocketed over 90% to $2519 per year since 1987 with prescription drugs making up at least 10% of that burden.[16] It is estimated that the elderly spend $13 to $14 billion per year (an average of $483 per person) on prescription drugs, and the majority of those payments are out-of-pocket. While there has been an increased trend for third-party payers (private insurance and Medicaid) to cover the cost of some drugs, the elderly are less likely to be covered in a voluntary insurance market. Within the elderly population, there is also a huge variance between the young elderly (65 to 69 years) and the oldest elderly (85+ years) who generally spend much more, up to

30% of their family income, in out-of-pocket health care expenses. This is a particularly vexing problem among the poor elderly whose family incomes have grown at only a fraction of the rate of growth for medical expenses, including prescriptions.[17]

Jim B is a 74-year-old retired clerk. He lives on a government pension and has been widowed for six years. After two years of increasing depression, he was referred by his long-time internist to a psychiatrist for evaluation of a major depression. After the initial consultation, the psychiatrist prescribed one of the new serotonergic reuptake inhibitor antidepressants. Mr. B responded partially to a dose of one pill a day, and after two months, the psychiatrist increased the prescription to two pills a day. Three months later, there was no improvement, and the physician called the pharmacy to increase the regimen further to three pills a day as Mr. B was suffering no side effects. To the psychiatrist's surprise, the pharmacist reported that the patient still had two refills left on his prescription, suggesting that he had never increased his dose beyond one pill a day. On further discussion, the patient was embarrassed to admit that he "couldn't afford" the increased expense which would have taken the bill to over $100 per month.

While it is well known that brand name drugs can be four to five times more expensive than their generic counterparts, evidence exists that many older people will not accept a low-priced generic substitute for a brand name just on a pharmacist's advice. Most want their doctor's approval first. Of use are lists of generic drugs such as can be found in the index of Long's *The Essential Guide to Prescription Drugs*. Discount drugs can be obtained by way of the National Council of Senior Citizens,[18] the American Association of Retired Persons,[19] and other organizations. Insurance plans which allow for bulk (i.e., three month) purchase of medications for a one-time reduced fee are also now available.

Unfortunately, not all psychiatric medications are available generically to the elderly. In this situation, the physician and patient must make a cost-benefit decision together. Occasionally, the drug manufacturers offer reduced fee or even free medication for individuals in need (this can be arranged by the physician contacting the manufacturer and filling out the appropriate forms with the patient). More often, the physician must consider other alternatives, including using less expensive generic medications (which may have more side effects) or using a lower dose of the more expensive medication in hopes that it will provide adequate coverage. In any case, the financial impact of psychotropic prescriptions should be considered with all patients, especially those on fixed incomes without medication insurance plans.

SPECIFIC DRUG TREATMENTS

The decision to use a medication in psychiatric treatment is a major therapeutic step with any patient, no matter how compelling the indication. Whereas medical patients often come to their doctors expecting that the prescription of a pill may help them improve, psychiatric patients frequently see the initiation of medication as a failure in their "talking" therapy. Perhaps fostered by years of psychoanalytic resistance to the use of medications in many therapeutic situations, these drugs are too often viewed as "crutches" which may "suppress" the target symptom but not address the underlying psychological mechanism involved. Empirically, however, these medications can work when appropriately prescribed. And while the symptom suppression can be debated endlessly from a psychological perspective, the fact remains that the medications can be an important adjunctive treatment in a therapeutic regimen. What is perhaps more important than any ideological argument between professionals is to understand the patient's life history, psychological defenses, and attitude toward medications before considering their use so as to maximize their utility in the overall treatment scheme. There is no substitute for accurate differential diagnosis and careful preparation of the patient for the potential risks and benefits of medications.

Treatment of Depression in the Elderly

When considering pharmacologic treatments for depressed elderly subjects, several important facts should be recognized immediately. First, there is a general paucity of direct knowledge of these medications in the elderly population; most of the studies with these drugs have been conducted in younger adults. There are only a few dozen placebo-controlled, double-blind antidepressant research trials with the elderly. Second, many of these published "geriatric" studies have focused on the "young-old" subjects with average ages of 60 to 70 years; therefore, the information available about people over the age of 80 is even more scarce. Third, the Food and Drug Administration (FDA) has never required drug companies to compare their products in younger versus older people formally, so we often know very little about how these drugs react in older people until they are released by the FDA and tried by clinicians. What we do know is that drugs generally have longer elimination half-lives as reflected by higher plasma levels in the elderly[20] and that this should always be kept in mind when prescribing for the elderly. Finally, the environments of depressed geriatric patients vary tremendously (i.e., home, hospital, medical clinic, nursing home, etc.), and it is not well known how these different settings might affect the therapeutic response in the elderly or how the medications might interact with other therapies, such as psychotherapy.

With all these limitations in the knowledge base, it is perhaps amazing that antidepressant medications are indeed frequently administered to the elderly. In fact, they are generally used with great success, and the geriatric database is now expanding rapidly as more investigators publish clinical trials. For purposes of review, we will consider three major pharmacologic approaches to the treatment of depression in the elderly: serotonergic reuptake blockers, traditional cyclic antidepressants and monoamine oxidase inhibitors (Table 13.2). In severe cases of depression with psychosis, neuroleptics are frequently employed as well, and those medications will be discussed in the Psychosis section.

Age itself may be a predictive variable in determining the clinical outcome of patients with antidepressants. In one study, the older patients were found to respond less well to pharmacologic treatment.[21] Other studies have shown that if left untreated for over two years, geriatric depression is more often refractory to any therapy.[22] Thus, it becomes important in the elderly to diagnose depression and initiate antidepressant therapy without undue delays.

Serotonin Reuptake Inhibitors. Since the introduction of fluoxetine (Prozac) to the American market in 1989, there has been a substantial shift in the prescribing practices for the therapy of depression in this country. Additional drugs in this class include sertraline (Zoloft), paroxetine (Paxil), and citalopram (available in Europe). Primarily due to the more limited side effect profile of these drugs compared to previous generations of antidepressants, they are generally more acceptable to patients. However, this class of medications still has many side effects, including anxiety, agitation, insomnia or sedation, nausea and sexual dysfunction.[23] Because of the prolonged elimination half-lives of most of these medications, doses for the elderly are usually reduced from those prescribed for younger subjects. Unfortunately, blood levels of these drugs have not been positively correlated with therapeutic responses, so outpatient monitoring of blood levels is not helpful.[24]

Cyclic Antidepressants. There are a tremendous variety of cyclic compounds available today as clinical antidepressants. The choices are no longer limited to the two original antidepressants, amitriptyline (Elavil) and imipramine (Tofranil). Rather, the selection ranges from the metabolite drugs such as nortriptyline and desipramine to the "second generation" drugs such as trazodone, maprotaline and buproprion. Large-scale reviews have documented the efficacy of these agents, but

TABLE 13.2 Pharmacologic agents frequently used to treat depression in the elderly

DRUGS AVAILABLE	DOSE (MG/DAY)	COMMENTS
Serotonin Reuptake Inhibitors		
Fluoxetine	10–40	• Not anticholinergic • Long drug half-life • Sexual side effects
Sertraline	50–150	• Not anticholinergic • Shorter drug half-life • Sexual side effects
Paroxetine	10–40	• Fairly anticholinergic • Sexual side effects
Heterocyclic Antidepressants		
Amitriptyline Imipramine Doxepine	25–150	• Highly anticholinergic • Sedating • Can lower blood pressure
Nortriptyline	10–125	• Less anticholinergic • Therapeutic window
Desipramine	25–125	• Less anticholinergic • Can be activating
Trazodone	50–200	• Not anticholinergic • Sedating • Can lower blood pressure
Monoamine Oxidase Inhibitors		
Phenelzine	15–45	• Not anticholinergic • Special diet required • Can lower blood pressure
Tranylcypromine	10–30	• Special diet required • Can be activating • Can lower blood pressure

no single drug has emerged as the "drug of choice" for the treatment of geriatric depression.[25]

Several variables have been suggested that may help predict the response of patients to antidepressants. Jarvik and colleagues originally noted, for instance, that pretreatment orthostatic hypotension (lowering of blood pressure on standing) is associated with improvement following treatment with imipramine or doxepin;[26] unfortunately, imipramine itself may cause undue ortho-static blood pressure changes and be a cause for discontinuing the medication before therapeutic effects are achieved.[27] Nortriptyline, on the other hand, is associated with less orthostatic changes during treatment and furthermore has the advantage of producing dose-related blood levels even in the elderly which may be predictive of therapeutic efficacy, as in younger adults.[28] Because the elderly are generally more sensitive to the cognitive effects of anticholinergic medications,[29] the antidepressant medications can also be differentiated along their anticholinergic potency (see Table 13.2). The clinician is forced to choose amongst the large list of drugs based on the clinical state of the patient and the side effect profile of the individual drug (Table 13.3).

Researchers have reported that from 7 to 35% of older depressives suffer from antidepressant-related confusional episodes as compared to less than 1% in younger adults.[30] While the overall clinical improvement associated with adequate antidepressant treatment often outweighs the deleterious anticholinergic effect on memory, it does seem reasonable to avoid the drugs with the highest anticholinergic potency in the elderly if possible. Other troublesome anticholinergic side effects include dry mouth, constipation (already a problem with many elderly), urinary hesitancy, and tremor. Trazodone, one of the heterocyclic antidepressants, may be a particularly interesting

TABLE 13.3   Relative anticholinergic potency of antidepressant medications

ANTIDEPRESSANT	POTENCY*
Amitriptyline	1
Clomipramine	2.1
Doxepine	4.7
Imipramine	5.1
Paroxetine	6.0
Nortriptyline	8.4
Desipramine	11.2
Maprotiline	31.1
Sertraline	50.9
Amoxapine	56.0
Fluoxetine	112
Buproprion	>1000
Trazodone	>1000
Venlafaxine	>1000

Source: Modified from Richelson, E. (1994): The pharmacology of antidepressants at the synapse: Focus on newer compounds. *Journal of Clinical Psychiatry, 55*(Suppl. A), 34–39. Copyright 1994, Physicians Postgraduate Press. Reprinted by permission.

*Lower number suggests higher potency at muscarinic receptor.

drug in this context. It has the lowest anticholinergic profile of all the cyclic antidepressants and has been shown to have a positive therapeutic effect in agitated aggressive patients. Although there are other side effects associated with trazodone, such as marked sedation, lowering of blood pressure, and priapism (painful sustained penile erections) in young males, it may well have a role in depressed or agitated elderly patients with evidence of cognitive decline.[31]

Monoamine Oxidase Inhibitors.   It has been widely recognized for over 30 years that monoamine oxidase inhibitors (MAOIs) are effective antidepressants. Nonetheless, they have seen limited use in the elderly, with less than a dozen careful studies reported in the geriatric literature.[32] The hesitancy to prescribe MAOIs is most likely related to two potential problems with the medications:

1. MAOIs can interact with the naturally-occurring food substance tyramine (found in pickled herring, aged cheddar, Chianti wine, smoked or pickled meats and other foods) and with a large number of drugs to produce malignant hypertension (a life threatening elevation in blood pressure).

2. Postural hypotension is frequently associated with MAOI use and can pose particularly difficult management problems in the elderly who often already have blood pressure difficulties.

With the explosion in use of the serotonic reuptake inhibitors, the MAOIs are now prescribed even less frequently. However, these drugs (i.e., phenelzine 15–90 mg/day, tranylcypromine 10–60 mg/day, and isocarboxazide 20–60 mg/day) have each been shown to produce clinical improvement in older patients with major depression and mixed anxiety-depression syndromes when used carefully.[33] In fact, Georgotas and colleagues have reported that 65% of elderly depressives were responsive to phenelzine, a figure comparable to that with the more commonly prescribed cyclic antidepressants, and the positive outcome was related to the degree of MAO inhibition in the blood.[34] Other reports have suggested that MAOI response is related to pretreatment platelet MAO levels and that baseline MAO levels may indeed increase with age in both brain and platelets.[35]

In all studies of MAOI effectiveness, a positive therapeutic outcome has been contingent on the appropriate education and supervision of patients to insure proper dietary and drug-interaction precautions (see Table 13.4 for details).[36]

With the introduction in Europe of the selective MAOIs, specifically the MAO-B selective inhibitor, selegiline, the dreaded "cheese effect" (so named because of the large tyramine content in many cheeses) was thought to be eliminated. Indeed, at low doses, it appears that selegiline is relatively free of the dangerous hypertensive interaction with tyramine and, presumably, other stimulant agents as well. Unfortunately, at the higher doses probably required for antidepressant therapeutic efficacy, the MAO-B selectivity is ap-

parently less, and the hypertensive reaction is once again present.[37] Since many elderly patients either live in a controlled, supervised setting or are perfectly willing to eliminate Chianti wine, aged cheeses, and the other tyramine-containing foods from their diets, the MAOIs can be an important and effective treatment option for the elderly patient with major depression or atypical anxiety-depression syndromes, particularly those with treatment-resistant depression.[38]

Treatment of Psychosis in the Elderly

The neuroleptics are most commonly prescribed for the treatment of agitated behavior or severely disturbed thinking.[39] However, neuroleptics are not the only medications which can be used for the treatment of agitation and psychosis in the elderly. In recent years, antiseizure medications

TABLE 13.4 Dietary and medication precautions when taking Monoamine Oxidase Inhibitors (MAOIs)

FOODS TO BE AVOIDED	EXAMPLES
Aged, unpasteurized cheeses	Cheddar, Bleu, Camembert, Swiss
Smoked fish, poultry, or meat	Herring, sausage, corned beef
Yeast extracts	Marmite, brewer's yeast
Red wine	Chianti, burgundy, sherry
Bean curd	Soy sauce, fava beans
Cured meat, poultry or fish	Chicken or beef liver, game, pate
Miscellaneous	Shrimp paste, soups, protein extracts, figs, overripe avocados

MEDICATIONS TO BE AVOIDED	EXAMPLES
Stimulants	Amphetamine, cocaine, weight-reducing agents
Decongestants	Cold tablets, nose sprays, asthma or cough medications (Ephedrine, Phenylepherine or Phenylpropanolamine)
Antihypertensives	Reserpine, Methyldopa, Guanethidine
Narcotics	Merperidine (Demerol)
Other antidepressants	Imipramine, Desipramine, Clomipramine
Miscellaneous	L-Dopa, Dopamine, L-Tryptophan

Source: Murphy, D. L., Sunderland, T., Cohen, R. M. (1984). Monoamine oxidase-inhibiting antidepressants: A clinical update. *Psychiatric Clinics of North America, 7,* 549–562. Reprinted by permission.

have been suggested for use in these populations, and preliminary studies are encouraging.[40] Other possible treatments include sedating antidepressant agents such as trazodone. Comparisons are now ongoing in an attempt to offer alternatives to the neuroleptics. The conditions which can produce these disturbances are multiple and include:

1. Chronic Schizophrenia or Late-Onset Delusional Disorder
2. Agitated or Delusional Depression
3. Brief Reactive Psychosis
4. Psychosis associated with a Chronic Organic Syndrome
5. Agitation associated with Intoxication or Delirium

While each condition may benefit from the careful use of medications, the etiologies of these disturbed behaviors are obviously quite different. As a result, side effects and dosing requirements may also vary tremendously across conditions.

Typical Neuroleptics. The two major classes of typical neuroleptics are the phenothiazines (i.e., chlorpromazine and thioridazine) and the butyrophenones (i.e., haloperidol). An emerging class of neuroleptics with a different profile of side effects is termed the *atypical* neuroleptics (i.e., clozapine). As with the antidepressants, the neuroleptics are often differentiated on the basis of their side effect profile. In general, the phenothiazines tend to be quite sedating and are associated with a lowering of blood pressure.[41] The butyrophenones, on the other hand, cause less sedation and reduction of blood pressure but are more frequently associated with extrapyramidal side effects (i.e., Parkinsonian symptoms of muscular rigidity and mask-like faces). Haloperidol is usually prescribed in much lower doses than the phenothiazines and is therefore called a "high potency" drug.

Over 60 studies of neuroleptic treatment of agitation in the elderly have been reported. In a recent review, Salzman stated that 60 to 70% of the more than 5000 patients with a variety of underlying disorders showed "good to excellent" responses with the neuroleptics. No individual drug demonstrated clear superiority to the others, although as a group, these medications were more effective than other types of medication such as the benzodiazepines.[42] Similar conclusions have also been reached in a recent review of the use of neuroleptics in published studies with over 1200 demented subjects; the symptoms most likely to respond to neuroleptics were agitation, hyperactivity, hallucinations, and hostility.[43] However, it must be emphasized that the neuroleptic side effects can be problematic in the elderly. In some cases, agitated behavior can even be exacerbated with neuroleptic treatment, so the dosing and monitoring of drug treatment must be performed conservatively with specific time-limited goals in mind.[44]

The general rule of thumb for clinical administration of the neuroleptics is the same as with each class of drug in this chapter: "Start low and go slow." For the high potency neuroleptic, haloperidol, a dose of 0.25 mg is often perfectly adequate when given one to three times a day. Higher doses may be necessary but only after failing with a lower dose. Total daily doses above 10 mg are unusual. If chronic doses are needed, they should be reduced once the patient is stabilized so as to minimize the total drug exposure. If the agitation is severe, then a phenothiazine such as chlorpromazine may be indicated. Once again, doses much smaller than those generally used in younger populations (i.e., 10 to 50 mg per day) may be adequate with the older patients. Because a lowering of blood pressure is so common with this agent, vigilance should be maintained to avoid the disastrous effects of serious falls resulting from sudden orthostatic changes. Another likely disadvantage of this class of neuroleptics is the increased anticholinergic potency. A worsening of cognitive functioning is possible, especially in the demented subjects who are known to be more sensitive to anticholinergic drugs.[45] The longer-acting depot neuroleptics (i.e., fluphenazine enanthate, 5 mg/two weeks) have also been tested in older patients with "late paraphrenia" and shown to be superior to oral haloperidol (6 mg/day), perhaps due to the increased compliance with the depot (long-acting, injectable drug dosage) product and the use of a lower dose regimen.[46]

The most worrisome side effect of chronic neuroleptic use is that of tardive dyskinesia (TD), the syndrome of involuntary movements of the tongue, mouth, face, and neck. While TD is usually associated with a long exposure to neuroleptics, it can occur as rapidly as one month after starting a neuroleptic drug. In fact, when elderly psychiatric inpatients of mixed diagnostic backgrounds were carefully evaluated for signs of abnormal movements, 49% showed evidence of TD while 51% revealed some parkinsonism; in this study, the average length of neuroleptic exposure in the TD group was less than 11 months.[47] The incidence of TD in late-onset psychosis is thought to be even higher than that of the early-onset group.[48] The greatest risk appears to be within the first two years of therapy. For bipolar patients treated with neuroleptics, there is increased risk for TD in those patients who show poorer baseline cognitive functioning, fewer depressive episodes, and less overall exposure to lithium.[49] Those with prior organic pathology or evidence of cognitive dysfunction may therefore be at greater risk for the development of TD, so particular caution should be used when prescribing neuroleptics in these populations. There is currently no effective pharmacologic treatment for tardive dyskinesia in the elderly.

Atypical Neuroleptics.   Over the last few years, several "atypical" neuroleptics have been introduced for use in the treatment of psychosis. The major advantage of these agents (i.e., clozapine, resperidol and olanzepine) is that they are generally low risk for extrapyramidal symptoms (EPS) and tardive dyskinesia; however, they do come with their own side effects. Clozapine, for instance, is highly anticholinergic and carries a risk of agranulocytosis. As a result, frequent blood tests are a required part of any clozapine monitoring regimen. Furthermore, clozapine can precipitate seizures or orthostatic hypotension. Resperidone, another new atypical neuroleptic, is

also associated with a lower risk of EPS and TD, at least at doses less than 6 mg a day, but it too can produce orthostatic hypotension. When used at low doses (0.25 mg to 2 mg a day), respiridone is generally safe. Olanzepine appears to be similarly safe from the perspective of EPS risks, but it may be associated with increased risk of weight gain. While these drugs may be more effective with fewer side effects in younger adults, large scale comparison studies in the geriatric population are still needed to assure that this safety profile extends across the age continuum.

Antianxiety Agents in the Elderly

Because the symptoms of anxiety and insomnia are so common in the elderly, the benzodiazepines are frequently prescribed. In the past, up to one third of the elderly patients in medical hospitals were given one of the benzodiazepines,[50] leading to the claim that these drugs were over prescribed in this population. Nonetheless, the benzodiazepines are proven to be effective and relatively safe in the treatment of anxiety, especially when properly fitted to the symptom profile of the individual patient.[51]

There are many age-related changes in response to the benzodiazepines, and these changes are primarily due to the pharmacokinetic alterations in metabolism. Agents which require complicated metabolic transformation to active metabolites (i.e., diazepam, chlordiazepoxide, desmethyldiazepam, florazepam, clorazepate, and prazepam) tend to have an extended duration of action in the elderly and lead to an accumulation of side effects.[52] As much as a ten-fold increase in plasma half-lives has been demonstrated with the benzodiazepines undergoing oxidative metabolism versus those with conjugated metabolism; this effect is more obvious in males than females.[53]

While diazepam and chlordiazepoxide are perhaps the oldest and best known of the benzodiazepines, their relatively long half-lives make them generally less desirable for elderly patients. Oxazepam (10 to 50 mg/day), a short-acting agent with no active metabolites, may be preferable in this population because it does not accumulate in the system. Lorazepam (0.5 to 2 mg/day), a somewhat longer-acting benzodiazepine, is another choice for the elderly because of its uncomplicated metabolic pathway, but it has frequently been associated with specific memory impairments. Flurazepam is one of the longer-acting benzodiazepines with a half-life of up to 72 hours in the elderly. Because of the potential for substantial accumulation and increased side effects, its use should probably be avoided in the aged.[54] Alprazolam is an intermediate-acting drug which has the advantage of having both anxiolytic and antidepressant effects; in the elderly, it has been used safely in divided doses of 0.5 to 4 mg/day with encouraging results.[55] Alprazolam has also been utilized with some benefit in combination with neuroleptics in treatment of young schizophrenics,[56] so there may be additional advantages of this agent with older schizophrenics as well.

Buspirone, a novel anxiolytic with serotonergic agonist activity, has quickly found a place in the treatment of anxiety in the elderly. Generally well tolerated, buspirone has been shown to have similar effectiveness but fewer side effects compared to the benzodiazepines for the treatment of generalized anxiety. Side effects in up to 30% of patients include stomach complaints, dizziness, headache, and occasional sleep disturbance.[57] With the elderly, 20 mg/day in divided doses was associated with decreased anxiety. Of note is that buspirone has had mixed results when studied in patients with cognitive impairments.[58] Other agents which may be considered for the treatment of anxiety in the elderly include beta-blockers, antidepressants, antihistamines and even neuroleptics under certain circumstances.[59]

Lithium

Lithium has been an effective agent in the treatment of patients of all ages with manic-depressive illness. Among older persons, one encounters hypomanic states that often respond to lithium in much smaller doses than would ordinarily be anticipated. Older patients should be kept at somewhat lower maintenance levels (0.6 to 0.7 mEq/L) than younger patients and should be monitored with routine physical examinations, EKGs, blood chemistry tests, and evaluation of kidney and thyroid functions. Older people must be monitored more closely than younger persons. For example, if one doctor prescribes lithium and another diuretics, without collaboration between them, the patient may have dangerous elevation in his or her serum lithium level. Hypomanic states and bipolar depressions are most susceptible to lithium therapy, and improvement can be dramatic. Evidence for the treatment of depressive states is less impressive, except in cases of cyclic depressions treated over time.[60]

Lithium is entirely eliminated from the body by the kidney. Because of the general pharmacokinetic changes with age and the small margin between the therapeutic and toxic doses of lithium, one must be vary careful when prescribing the drug to the elderly. Average doses of approximately 400 mg/day with peak serum levels of 0.8 mmol/liter have been sufficient to achieve good clinical results.[61] With older people on low-sodium diets or diuretics, the need for caution is increased; potentially neurotoxic levels above 1.2 mmol/liter should be avoided in the elderly.[62]

Lithium intoxication can cause permanent neurologic damage; thus, continuous monitoring and patient education (for example, informing patients of early side effects) is critical. This is true even when treatment with lithium salts has previously been well tolerated. Clinical signs of toxicity include diarrhea, vomiting, tremor, mild ataxia, drowsiness, thirst, polyuria (increased urination), muscular weakness, slurred speech, and confusion. The tremor and polyuria may persist for a time after reduction of the dose. It has been suggested that the elderly show earlier evidence of confusion and neuromuscular irritability when becoming lithium toxic and that the course of toxicity can be more severe and unpredictable than with younger patients. Up to 13% of geriatric patients show some toxicity on maintenance lithium therapy during an 18 month follow-up period. As with younger patients, frequent (i.e., every six months) monitoring of the thyroid status should be maintained to avoid the side effect of hypothyroidism. Other regular monitoring should include routine physical examinations, EKGs, blood chemistries, and kidney function tests.

Psychostimulants

The use of central nervous system stimulants with the elderly remains a controversial area. Despite the scarcity of careful, placebo-controlled studies revealing definite improvement in depressed elderly, dextroamphetamine is still frequently used, and many physicians are convinced of anecdotal successes. Side effects include insomnia, poor appetite, weight loss, excitement, paranoia, and palpitations; the drug can also become habit forming. When given to the elderly, doses usually range from 5 to 30 mg/day.[63] Methylphenidate, another mild stimulant, has been used previously in conjunction with psychotherapy[64] and more recently with dementia patients showing varying degrees of depression or apathy.[65] These studies have each claimed modest success with 10 to 30 mg/day of methylphenidate, leading others to call for a reconsideration of the use of psychostimulants, especially in patients with concurrent medical illness.[66] At present, these medications should probably be reserved for those patients who cannot tolerate traditional antidepressant treatment or for whom other approaches have already been exhausted.

Other Medications

In certain psychiatric conditions, combination therapy is indicated and often practiced. Perhaps the best known example is that of co-prescribing neuroleptics with lithium in acute mania. While some problems have been noted with the specific combination of haloperidol and lithium, these combinations are usually quite effective in the most severe psychotic manias. Once the acute mania is under control, however, the neuroleptic can be withdrawn and the patient stabilized on lithium alone. A subsequent combination of lithium with an antidepressant is often required for those bipolar patients with post-manic or post-psychotic depressions. As might be expected, caution must be exercised in each case to monitor blood levels of the respective drugs on a regular basis.

Delusional depression is another well-known condition which often requires combined treatment with an antidepressant plus a neuroleptic or the use of ECT and an antidepressant, at least for the period where the patient is psychotic.[67] Nondelusional but otherwise treatment-resistant depression has also been treated with combination approaches including tricyclic "augmentation" with cytomel (25 to 50 mcg/day) or lithium (300 to 600 mg/day). Interestingly, these combinations are both characterized by a rapid response when the cytomel or lithium is added to a stabilized tricyclic regimen; benefit is often seen within 24 to 48 hours. While these combinations have not been studied extensively in the elderly, there is reason to believe that they might be equally effective if all the usual thyroid and lithium precautions are taken. Another possibility includes the addition of estrogen to ongoing antidepressant therapy, and anecdotal reports of improvement in elderly postmenopausal females suggest that menopause-related mood disorders deserve further investigation.[68]

Medications borrowed from the practice of general internal medicine are sometimes of help in psychiatry and are currently the focus of much research. These drugs include the antiseizure medication, carbamazepine, which has already proven successful in acute and prophylactic treatment of lithium-resistant mania and is now being tested in elderly agitated demented patients.[69] Because of the potential for a hemolytic anemia, however, this drug must be monitored carefully with frequent complete blood counts and carbamezepine blood levels and should only be prescribed by physicians familiar with its use.

Beta-blockers have also been reported to be of help in treating the peripheral manifestations of anxiety. However, the beta-blocker most frequently used, propranolol, has also been shown to induce depressive symptoms, concentration difficulties, and reversible confusional states.[70] Oxprenolol, a beta-blocker which has not been associated with depression, is another alternative which may be safer in the elderly because of its tendency to cause less slowing of the heart. As with all beta-blockers, oxprenolol should not be used with patients with asthma, bronchitis, or diabetes. Finally, while the beta-blockers have been reported to be of value in treating agitated, aggressive behavior in organically impaired patients, there are currently no careful studies of these drugs in demented elderly patients.

Cerebral vasodilators, cerebral stimulants, hormones, and anticoagulants are among other classes of drugs that have been recommended and sold for depressed, "senile," or deteriorated older people. They are of little clinical use and may be dangerous in some instances. Vitamins are useful when there are deficiencies. Hypovitaminosis must be carefully evaluated. Victims of pellagra should receive 500 mg of nicotinic acid orally up to three times daily, as necessary. For older people, a basic vitamin-mineral combination may be given to offset effects of the processing of foods, poor dietary habits, and low appetite related to loneliness and grief.

**DRUG TREATMENTS
FOR SLEEP DISORDERS**

Five million elderly people in the United States have a severe sleep disorder. About one half of all elderly complain of sleep problems.[71] And although the elderly represent 12% of the population, they consume 40% of the prescribed sedative-hypnotics in the U.S..[72] Since the experience of sleeping is so subjective, the reports of actual sleep time, quality of sleep, and complaints of insomnia are often quite variable in the elderly. Certain sleep changes are common in later life and should not be confused with insomnia. In general, older people sleep less long and less deeply and awaken more easily than earlier in their lives. They have a greater tendency to waken throughout the night and to experience less "dreaming

sleep" (stage 4 or rapid eye movement (REM) sleep). Deep sleep (called delta sleep), the period of dreamless oblivion, lessens and may vanish in old age.[73]

The evaluation of sleep in the elderly must be done carefully and systematically because of the variable patterns of sleep in this age group. For the most part, the average amount of bed rest needed by an individual remains from seven to nine hours a day and does not change dramatically over the adult life cycle, as is commonly thought. It is also clear that concurrent medical and psychological problems influence the pattern of sleep in the elderly. For these reasons, the complete 24-hour sleep-wake cycle of the elderly individual must be examined whenever assessing complaints of insomnia. Many older persons retire early because of fatigue, waken at three or four o'clock in the morning, and then fear they have insomnia, when they may, in fact, have had an adequate six to seven hours or more of sleep.

Physiological causes of insomnia include Alzheimer's disease, nocturnal myoclonus (leg twitching), nocturnal cardiac arrhythmias, nocturnal shortness of breath from congestive heart failure, and the discomfort of arthritis. Insomnia can be produced or exacerbated by an institutional environment such as nursing homes or hospitals where the patient has little control over the lights or the timing of medications or meals. Many elderly are awakened at night by the need to go to the bathroom.

Persons with sleep difficulties related to psychological problems may fear sleep itself. In sleep, their defenses against anxiety (including fear of death), anger, and other emotions are more relaxed. The activities that protect them from anxiety during the day are gone. Psychotherapy can help in clarifying and resolving the basis for insomnia.

What may seem like a need for less sleep may therefore be the result of illness, anxiety, depression, or simply the need for more exercise and activity during the day. For example, early morning awakening is more common among the inactive who go to bed early and take catnaps (sometimes leading to serious day-night sleep reversal). This is not to say that a daily nap is not valuable; if not too long or too frequent, naps may relax the person and thus contribute to better sleep at night. Unlike in younger people, early morning awakening in the elderly is not necessarily a sign of depression, especially if there are daytime naps.

Nonpharmacologic treatment approaches for insomnia include the establishment of simple rituals that are followed regularly—perhaps warm baths, a well-made bed, bed boards for support, back massage, eye shields to stop the light, bedtime reading or soft music, or any other comfort mechanisms that suggest protection and relaxation. Patients should be encouraged to avoid excessive daytime napping, particularly the after-dinner snooze, and to have a regular schedule of activities for each day. Daily exercise and avoidance of caffeine-containing beverages like coffee and cola, especially in the afternoon and evening, is also important. There should be no heavy meals after 7:00 P.M., and the emphasis for the evening should be on relaxation when approaching the regular hour of sleep. If insomnia does occur, patients should be encouraged to get out of bed rather than tossing and turning. The psychological association with bed should be sleep, not insomnia. When insomnia becomes a chronic problem, sleep clinics may be useful in evaluating severe causes of insomnia. A list of members of the American Sleep Disorders Association may be obtained from the national office of the American Sleep Disorders Association, 1610 14th St. N.W., Suite 300, Rochester, Minnesota 55901.

There are many alternative drug treatments for insomnia (Table 13.5). While the benzodiazepines remain by far the most prescribed treatment for insomnia, other medications include chloral hydrate, barbiturates, antihistamines, and propanediols (i.e., meprobamate). Triazolam (Halcion), although a short-acting benzodiazepine, has been criticized as contributing to memory impairment, delirium, and daytime anxiety. Of the alternative treatments, the naturally-occurring amino acid L-tryptophan (500 mg to 2,000 mg at bedtime) was probably considered the safest until the problems with eosinophilic myalgias surfaced.[74]

Antihistamines are frequently suggested but must be used cautiously in the elderly because of their anticholinergic side effects. Barbiturates and meprobamate should probably be avoided altogether in the elderly because of their abuse potential and profound suppressive effects on rapid eye movement (REM) sleep. Chloral hydrate, often overlooked in the age of the benzodiazepines, is still quite effective for occasional use in the elderly at doses of 250 mg to 1000 mg at bedtime, but it can irritate the stomach lining and

TABLE 13.5   Alternative drug treatments for insomnia

MEDICATIONS	DOSE RANGE (MG/DAY)	PROS AND CONS
Serotonin Reuptake Inhibitors		
Chloral Hydrate	250–1000	• Rapidly effective • Stomach irritation possible
Diphendydramine	10–25	• Available without prescription • Relatively mild • Possible confusion
Oxazepam	5–15	• Short-acting for early insomnia • Occasional paradoxical effect • Daytime drowsiness uncommon
Diazepam	0.5–2.0	• Longer-acting for late insomnia • Daytime "hangover" common

has also been associated with confusion in geriatric patients.[75]

Wine has been widely recommended in geriatric medicine and in convalescent care. It is the world's oldest treatment for insomnia. Galen, the great Greek physician, called wine "the nurse of old age." Among the dessert wines, two to three ounces of port is useful for sleep. One must beware, however, of the unfortunate potentiating or synergistic action of alcohol on other sedatives. Many commonly prescribed drugs have altered therapeutic and/or adverse medical effects when taken with alcohol. These drugs include not only benzodiazepines, hypnotics, narcotics, antidepressants, and neuroleptics but also certain antihistamines, analgesics, anticoagulants, and antiinfective agents. In fact, alcohol use in combination with other drugs accounts for approximately 20% of the total number of accidental or suicidal deaths per year that are drug-related. Mental confusion and poor coordination can combine with alcohol to increase the risk of falling, particularly since tolerance for alcohol can decrease with increasing age. In addition, alcohol adversely influences sexual potency. Finally, anyone with alcoholic tendencies should not be encouraged to drink.

Over-the-counter drugs sold as sleep aids or sedatives, like Sominex, Nytal, and Sleep-Eze, are of questionable value, containing unsafe levels of antihistamines developed for the treatment of allergies. They may also contain scopolamine in levels for sleep inducement that can cause outbursts of uncontrolled behavior and a variety of adverse physical effects. Bromides have been used in the past in over-the-counter medications and are considered unsafe.

DRUG TREATMENT OF PAIN

Chronic pain, a physical, psychological, and social state, is conveniently defined as pain that has persisted six months or longer. It is distinguished from acute pain, which is nature's warning system. The discovery of opiate-binding sites (receptors) and endorphins (morphine-like substances) in the brain during the 1970s has moved forward fundamental research in both pain and neurobiology. The emergence of multiple pain clinics throughout the country to help deal with the complex problem of chronic pain has also been welcome. At such clinics, various therapies—acupuncture, transcutaneous electrical stimulation, exercise, psychotherapy, family counseling, and hypnosis—are applied rather than pharmacological approaches alone, which, like surgical interventions, have been disappointing in isolation. Experimental efforts to lessen pain include insertion of electrodes into the patient's brain to stimulate the secretion of enkephalins or endorphins, the brain's own "opiates." Nerve blocks, neurosurgery, and new drugs are other techniques. For older people, and especially those who are in the last days of life, it is important to provide effective, prompt relief of pain and any other discomforts without excessive preoccupation with the potentiality of addiction. Nonetheless, the search for an effective non-addictive analgesic continues.

In addition to suffering, pain brings with it anxiety and, frequently, depression. Chronic malignant pain often requires strong analgesics and certainly consistent emotional and physical support and comfort. Both chronic malignant and benign pain sufferers may also find relief through the use of psychotropic drugs—especially the benzodiazepines and other antianxiety drugs, the phenothiazines, and the antidepressants.

The wise management of chronic pain requires an understanding not only of the effects of pain itself but of the psychological conditioning that can result from the way pain is handled by the patient and by medical personnel. If the patient receives medication only when pain becomes pronounced, he or she begins to learn that only the presence of intense pain will bring relief. If a physician sees the patient only when the pain is prominent, then attention from the doctor becomes a reward for experiencing pain. To avoid such learned behavior, and to "decondition" those who have already learned it, many have recommended the increased availability of pain medication for individual patients.

Patient-controlled analgesia (PCA) has grown in popularity with physicians and patients alike over the past ten years. PCA is a pain relief program in which patients control their own pain by taking medication when they need it. Safeguards such as preset limits or timed intervals are built into PCA programs to avoid accidental or deliberate overdose. However, not all pain killers can be self-administered and not all elderly are able to handle self-medication. The decision to use PCA must be based on the nature of the pain and the needs and abilities of the patient. When used appropriately, PCA can produce a high degree of patient satisfaction and an individually calibrated mechanism for dealing with varying levels of pain.

ELECTROCONVULSIVE THERAPY

Despite being documented as an effective treatment for elderly depressives, electroconvulsive therapy (ECT) is generally underutilized by the elderly.[76] One of the major criticisms and problems with ECT is its well-documented negative effect on memory. Because of the cognitive dysfunction associated with ECT, attempts have been made to reduce the impairments by employing unilateral rather than bilateral convulsive treatment,[77] minimizing the amount of concurrent medications (especially anticholinergic medications such as atropine), and even varying the wave form used in the ECT stimulus.[78] While these efforts have been somewhat successful, there remain quantifiable memory impairments after a course of ECT, especially in geriatric patients.[79] Although some patients, particularly those suffering from "pseudodementia," actually report an improvement in memory,[80] the majority of elderly patients demonstrate cognitive impairments as a side effect of the treatment. Compared to the overall dysfunction associated with severe depression, however, the relative clinical significance of these memory difficulties has been questioned.[81] Nonetheless, the issue of whether and when to use ECT is hotly debated by many, including former patients and professionals within psychiatry itself, such that it is still reserved for

specific situations, often only after multiple pharmacologic treatment failures. Currently, there are three major indications for ECT:

1. Life threatening suicidal depression
2. Antidepressant-resistant depression
3. Medical contraindications to antidepressant medications

Additional indications include delusional depressions, prolonged refusal to eat, and other self-destructive behaviors.

In the presence of truly serious suicidal risk, it may not be advisable to wait out drug trials. After comprehensive evaluation with full patient consent and under careful conditions, including the use of appropriate preshock sedation and muscle relaxants (such as succinylcholine chloride), ECT can be quite effective against the severe depressions of old age that can lead to suicide risk. ECT can often bring about prompt relief with a limited series of four to eight treatments. In these conditions, even a history of cerebrovascular accidents and/or myocardial infarctions is not a contraindication per se. Effects on memory should be assessed at baseline and during treatment, and the number of treatments should be minimal.[82]

Age alone should not be considered a barrier to the use of ECT. In fact, a case report of a 94-year-old woman improving after receiving ECT noted that the patient's daughter "lamented the fact that ECT had been deemed to be contraindicated 15 years earlier on the grounds of advanced age."[83]

Since 1938 when Ugo Cerletti and Lucino Bini first introduced ECT, there has been controversy surrounding its use. Fear and distaste of ECT are commonplace and understandable among patients since it can be an intimidating, if often effective, treatment. Unfortunately, patients who have received ECT often hesitate and resist returning to the doctor even years later if once again they develop serious depression. Some states have passed laws strengthening the patients' right to refuse treatments like ECT; but regardless of law, patients must fully understand the treatment offered and be given the right to accept or refuse it.

Biology of ECT

With the original observation that schizophrenia rarely occurred in epileptics, it was hypothesized that inducing seizures might have an antipsychotic effect. Subsequent experimentation led to the conclusion that either chemically or electrically-induced seizures had an antidepressant effect, but the exact mechanism of that improvement has not yet been discerned. It is clear that the seizure is the key element in the treatment, for simulated ECT is not effective and the presence or absence of anesthesia does not alter outcome. Even the dreaded amnestic effect is not correlated with the antidepressant effect. Current theories about ECT's mechanism of action involve various neurotransmitter systems, especially the serotonergic and noradrenergic systems, neuroendocrine effects on the hypothalamic axis, and the release of peptides (small proteins in the brain which can act as neurotransmitters). Interestingly, ECT produces a biochemical pattern in human spinal fluid and animal experiments which is somewhat different than that found with cyclic antidepressants. Future studies will involve much greater exploration of those biochemical mechanisms, particularly as they effect the cholinergic system. Another intriguing approach will be the study of regional brain changes following ECT with the various neuroimaging techniques.[84]

MENTAL HEALTH THERAPIST'S INVOLVEMENT IN DRUG THERAPY

The mental health therapist's own attitudes toward the use of drugs may influence the effects of drugs on older people. If the therapist is philosophically against drugs (feeling that people should resolve issues for themselves) or is anxious about their side effects and potential complications, he or she is likely to convey these concerns to the older person, even when not stating them explicitly. Ideally, the therapist would be open enough to appreciate the value of drugs that are judiciously employed. There are people who need the *immediate* support of the magical/real expectations of medicine and the "medicine man" (the power of the physician as well as the actual, chemically active drug effects). One rational way of reconciling negative feelings about drugs with occasions when people need them is to note that therapy is a *process,* an experience over time. At various points, drugs might maintain working men or women on their jobs or help parents with their parenthood. But in most therapeutic efforts, drugs should be only part of the total treatment effort, although a very important part in many instances.

However, even if the therapist is totally opposed to drugs, he or she should not deny the patient their usefulness but should collaborate with a physician who will evaluate the usefulness of drugs in situations where they have been found to be helpful for others. Having separate "talking" and "drug" therapists may provoke some divided reactions in the person being treated, with manipulations in some instances, but such behavior can become a part of the treatment process.

Nonphysician mental health personnel should know what drugs an older person is taking, whether for physical or mental conditions. The *Physicians' Desk Reference,* although not ideal, is a source of information about the side effects and complications of all drugs. Long's excellent *The Essential Guide to Prescription Drugs* provides a wealth of information. The *Merck Manual* also may be useful. *The United States Pharmacopoeia* is the Medicare-designated compendium. Psychoactive drugs are classified into five categories (schedules) under the Controlled Substances Act of 1970.

All mental health personnel should be familiar with prescriptions and know how to interpret them for their patients if necessary. Nurses especially may be called on to prepare prescriptions for the signature of the physician in some circumstances.

Some of the common prescription terms are listed below:

Weights (amounts are usually expressed in milligrams, grams, or grains):

milligram   One thousandth of a gram, roughly equivalent to 1/65th grain. It is usually abbreviated mg.

gram   Unit of weight in the metric system. It is usually abbreviated g, gm, or Gm. It is equivalent to about 15.43 gr.

grain   Unit of weight in the avoirdupois system. It is usually abbreviated gr. It is equivalent to 1/480 ounce and to 0.065 gm.

ounce   One twelfth of a pound avoirdupois and equivalent to 31.1 gm. The abbreviation for ounce is oz.

teaspoonful   four to five milliliters (ml).

Note: The metric system is preferred and the old English system is slowly being phased out.

Latin abbreviations:

Rx   "Recipe."

Sig.   To write. It means the directions for taking the drugs.

b.i.d.   *Bis in die,* two times a day.

t.i.d.   *Ter in die,* three times a day.

q.i.d.   *Quater in die,* four times a day.

a.c.   *Antecibum,* before meals.

p.c.   *Post cibum,* after meals.

h.s.   *Hora somni,* before sleep.

p.r.n.   *Pro re nata,* according to circumstances, rather than routine schedule.

s.o.s.   *Si opus sit,* if necessary, if occasion requires.

Rep.   Repeat.

q.h.   *Quaque hora,* every hour.

q.2h.   *Quaque secunda hora,* every second hour, etc.

FUTURE DIRECTIONS IN DRUG AND SOMATIC THERAPIES

The introduction of the serotonin reuptake inhibitors to our treatment arsenal has had a major impact on the field of psychopharmacology over the last few years, but we are a long way from understanding how these drugs and other psychopharmacologic agents really work when given chronically. Despite the massive amount of empiric data that have accumulated over the last 20 years as to the efficacy of the psychotropic medications, our knowledge is still primitive. Labeling drugs as "dopamine blockers"(neuroleptics), "reuptake blockers" (antidepressants), "membrane stabilizers" (lithium), or "anxiolytics" (benzodiazepines) perhaps describes the acute effects of these drugs but gives very little information as to the underlying chronic mechanisms of action. Our knowledge of the workings of ECT is not much further beyond recognizing the importance of generalized seizure activity. In fact, despite similar clinical effects, it appears that ECT and conventional antidepressant drug therapies may have quite different biochemical profiles, further confusing the biology of depression for the moment. In the future, a great deal of work will be focused on the mechanism of action of the various classes of medications, particularly now that more selective and specific agents with different acute biochemical effects are available. Within geriatrics, the comparison of populations with different organic pathologies but similar clinical symptoms (i.e., depression with coexistent cognitive difficulties vs. dementia with depression) may help us better understand the underlying mechanism of depression and test the differential responses to specific medications in these populations.

Another major horizon in drug therapy is the changing responsivity seen with age. While pharmacokinetic changes can explain some of the increased sensitivity generally seen with age, phamacodynamic changes are still poorly understood for the most part and deserve much further study. Finally, the newly emerging field of pharmacogenetics, the study of inherited factors in the interindividual diversity of drug response, may well become increasingly important.[85] Not only could advances in molecular biology and pharmacogenetics help us better understand drug mechanisms at the receptor level, but eventually, the field may lead us to the pharmacologic regulation of phenotypic gene expression. For late-onset conditions, such as delusional syndromes and Alzheimer's disease, a regulatory drug that was effective in altering the phenotypic expression of a gene would have very powerful implications and constitute a major therapeutic advance.

SELECTED READINGS

Ahronheim, J. C. (1992). *Handbook of prescribing medications for geriatric patients.* Boston: Little, Brown and Co.

Alexopoulos, G. S. (1995). Methodology of treatment studies in geriatric depression. *American Journal of Geriatric Psychiatry, 3,* pp. 280–289.

Alexopoulos, G. S., Meyers, B. S., Young, R. C., Chester, J., Feder, M., & Einhorn, A. (1995). Anxiety in geriatric depression: Effects of age and cognitive impairment. *American Journal of Geriatric Psychiatry, 3,* pp. 108–118.

Avorn, J., Soumerai, S. B., Everitt, D. E., Ross-Degnan, D., Beere, M. H., Sherman, D., Salem-Schatz, S. R. & Fields, D. (1992). A randomized trial of a program to reduce the use of psychoactive drugs in nursing homes. *New England Journal of Medicine, 327,* pp. 68–173.

Billig, N., Cohen-Mansfield, J., & Lipson, S. (1991). Pharmacologic treatment of agitation in a nursing home. *Journal of the American Geriatrics Society, 39,* pp. 1002–1005.

Bloom, H. & Shlom, E. A. (1993). *Drug prescribing in the elderly.* New York: Raven Press.

Branconnier, R. J., & Cole, J. O. (1980). The therapeutic role of methylphenidate in senile organic brain syndrome. In Cole, J. O., & Barrett, J. (Eds.), *Psychopathology in the aged.* New York: Raven Press, pp. 183–195.

Bressler, R., & Katz, M. D. (Eds.) (1993). *Geriatric pharmacology.* New York: McGraw-Hill.

Bridge, T. P., Soldo, B. J., Phelps, B. H., Wise, C. D., Francak, M. J., & Wyatt, R. J. (1985). Platelet monoamine oxidase activity: Demographic characteristics contribute to enzyme activity variability. *Journal of Gerontology, 40,* pp. 23–28.

Cadieux, R. J. (1993). Geriatric psychopharmacology: A primary care challenge. *Geriatric Psychopharmocology, 93,* pp. 281–301.

Callahan, C. M., Hendrie, H. C., Dittus, R. S., Brater, D.C., Hui, S. L., & Tierney, W. M. (1994). Improving treatment of late life depression in primary care: A randomized clinical trial. *Journal of the American Geriatrics Society, 42,* pp. 839–846.

Chiarello, R. J., & Cole, J. O. (1987). Psychostimulants: A reconsideration. *Archives of General Psychiatry, 44,* pp. 286–295.

Clauw, D. J., Nashel, D. L., Umhau, A., & Katz, P. (1990). Tryptophan-associated eosinophilic connective tissue disease: A new clinical entity? *Journal of the American Medical Association, 263,* pp. 1502–1506.

Cohen, B. M., & Zubenko, G. S. (1985). Relevance of genetic variability to clinical psychopharmacology. *Psychopharmacology Bulletin, 21,* pp. 641–650.

Colenda, C. C. (1988). Buspirone in the treatment of agitated demented patients. *Lancet, ii,* pp. 411–412.

Cooper, J. W. (1996). Probable adverse drug reaction in a rural geriatric nursing home population: A four-year study. *Journal of the American Geriatrics Society, 44,* pp. 194–197.

Cooper, J. W. (1991). *Drug-related problems in geriatric nursing home patients.* New York: Pharmaceutical Products Press.

Copeland, J. R. M., Davidson, I. A., Dewey, M. E., et al. (1992). Alzheimer's disease, other dementias, depression and pseudodementia: prevalence, incidence and three-year outcome in Liverpool. *British Journal of Psychiatry, 161,* pp. 230–239.

Daly, M. P., Lamy, P. P., & Richardson, J. P. (1994). Avoiding polypharmacy and iatrogenesis in the nursing home. *Maryland Medical Journal, 43,* pp. 1139–1144.

Devanand, D. P., Verma, A. K., Tirumalasetti, F., & Sackeim, H. A. (1991). Absence of cognitive impairment after more than 100 lifetime ECT treatments. *American Journal of Psychiatry, 148,* pp. 929–932.

Dubovsky, S. L. (1994). Geriatric neuropsychopharmacology. In Coffey, C. E., & Cummings, J. L. (Eds.), *Textbook of geriatric psychiatry.* Washington, DC: American Psychiatric Press, pp. 595–631.

Feighner, J. P., Boyer, W. F., Meredith, C. H., & Hendrickson, G. (1988). An overview of fluoxetine in geriatric depression. *British Journal of Psychiatry, 153* (3 Suppl.), pp. 105–108.

Gaspar, D., & Samarasinghe, L. A. (1982). ECT in psychogeriatric practice: A study of risk factors, indications and outcome. *Comprehensive Psychiatry, 23,* pp. 170–175.

Georgotas, A., Friedman, E., McCarthy, M., Mann, J., Krakowski, M., Siegel, R., & Ferris, S. (1983). Resistant geriatric depressions and therapeutic response to monoamine oxidase inhibitors. *Biological Psychiatry, 18,* pp. 195–205.

Georgotas, A., McCue, R. E., Friedman, E., & Cooper, T. (1987). Prediction of response to nortriptyline and phenelzine by platelet MAO activity. *American Journal of Psychiatry, 144,* pp. 338–340.

Gillin, J. C., Duncan, W. C., Murphy, D. L., Post, R. M., Wehr, T. A., Goodwin, F. K., Wyatt, R. J., & Bunney, W. E. (1981). Age-related changes in sleep in depressed and normal subjects. *Psychiatry Research, 4,* pp. 73–78.

Grammans, R. E., Stringfellow, J. C., Hvizdos, A. J., et al. (1992). Use of buspirone in patients with generalized anxiety disorder and coexisting depressive symptoms: a meta-analysis of eight randomized controlled studies. *Neuropsychobiology, 25,* pp. 193–201.

Greenblatt, D. J., Sellers, E. M., & Shader, R. I. (1982). Drug disposition in old age. *New England Journal of Medicine, 306,* pp. 1081–1088.

Hardy, B. G., Shulman, K. I., MacKenzie, S. E., Kutcher, S. P., & Silverberg, J. D. (1987). Pharmacokinetics of lithium in the elderly. *Journal of Clinical Psychopharmacology, 7*(3), pp. 153–158.

Horwitz, G. J., Tariot, P. N., Mead, K., & Cox, C. (1995). Discontinuation of antipsychotics in nursing home patients with dementia. *American Journal of Geriatric Psychiatry, 3,* pp. 290–299.

Jansen, J. H. M., & Andrews, J. S. (1994). The effects of serotonergic drugs on short-term spatial memory in rats. *Journal of Psychopharmacology, 8*(3), pp. 157–163.

Jarvik, L. F., Read, S. L., Mintz, J., Neshkes, R. E., Kane, J. M., Cole, K., Sarantakos, S., Howard, A., & Borenstein, M. (1983). Pretreatment orthostatic hypotension in geriatric depression: Predictor of response to imipramine and doxepin. *Journal of Clinical Psychopharmacology, 3,* pp. 368–372.

Jeste, D. V., Caligiuri, M. P., Paulsen, J. S., Heaton, R. K., Lacro, J. P., Harris, J., Bailey, A., Fell, R. L., & McAdams, L. A. (1995). Risk of tardive dyskinesia in older patients. *Archives of General Psychiatry, 52,* pp. 756–765.

Jeste, D. V., Paulsen, J. S., & Harris, M. J. (1995). Late-onset schizophrenia and other related psychoses. In

Bloom, F. E., & Kupfer, D. J. (Eds.), *Psychopharmacology: The fourth generation of progress.* Raven Press, Ltd., New York, pp. 1437–1446.

Kane, J. M., Cole, K., Sarantakos, S., Howard, A., & Borenstein, M. (1983). Safety and efficacy of bupropion in elderly patients: Preliminary observations. *Journal of Clinical Psychiatry, 44,* pp. 134–136.

Kaufman, M. W., Cassem, N. H., Murray, G. B., & Jenike, M. (1984). Use of psychostimulants in medically ill patients with neurological disease and major depression. *Canadian Journal of Psychiatry, 29,* pp. 46–49.

Kupfer, D. J., & Reynolds III, C. F. (1997). Management of insomnia. *The New England Journal of Medicine, 336,* pp. 341–346.

Lane, R., Baldwin, D., & Preskorn, S. (1995). The SSRI's: Advantages, disadvantages, and differences. *Journal of Psychopharmacology, 9*(2)(Suppl.), pp. 167–178.

Lawlor, B. A., Radcliffe, J., Molchan, S. E., Martinez, R. A., Hill, J. L., & Sunderland, T. (1994). A pilot placebo-controlled study of trazodone and buspirone in Alzheimer's disease. *International Journal of Geriatric Psychiatry, 9,* pp. 55–59.

Lebowitz, B. D., Martinez, R. A., Niederehe, G., Pearson, J. L., et al. (1995). Treatment of depression in late-life. *Psychopharmacology, 31*(1), pp. 185–202, 1995.

Lerer, B. (1986). ECT: Possible mechanisms of action. *Psychopharmacology, 22,* pp. 472–487.

Long, S. H. (1994). *Prescription drug coverage and the elderly: Issues and options.* Washington, DC: Public Policy Institute, AARP, p.2.

Markovitz, P. J. (1993). Treatment of anxiety in the elderly. *Journal of Clinical Psychiatry, 54*(Suppl. 5), pp. 64–68, 1993.

McCall, W. V., Farah, B. A., Reboussin, D., & Colenda, C. (1995). Comparison of the efficacy of titriated, moderate-dose and fixed, high-dose right unilateral ECT in elderly patients. *American Journal of Geriatric Psychiatry, 3,* pp. 317–324.

McKeith, I., Fairbairn, A., Perry R., Thompson, P., & Perry, E. (1992). Neuroleptic sensitivity in patients with senile dementia of Lewy body type. *British Medical Journal, 305,* pp. 673–678.

Molchan, S. E., Martinez, R. A., Hill, J. L., Weingartner, H. J., Thompson, K., Vitiello, B., & Sunderland, T. (1992). Increased cognitive sensitivity to scopolamine with age and a perspective on the scopolamine model. *Brain Research Review, 17,* pp. 215–226.

Moran, M. G., Thompson, T. L., & Nies, A. S. (1988). Sleep disorders in the elderly. *American Journal of Psychiatry, 145,* pp. 1369–1377.

Murphy, D. L., Sunderland, T., & Cohen, R. M. (1984). Monoamine oxidase-inhibiting antidepressants: A clinical update. *Psychiatric Clinics of North America, 7,* pp. 549–562.

Myers-Robfogel, M. W., & Bosmann, H. B. (1984). Clinical pharmacology in the aged: Aspects of pharmacokinetics and drug sensitivity. In Williams, T. F. (Ed.), *Rehabilitation in the aging.* New York: Raven Press, pp. 23–39.

Napoliello, M. J. (1986). An interim multicentre report on 677 anxious geriatric out-patients treated with buspirone. *British Journal of Clinical Practice, 40,* pp. 71–73.

Nelson, J. P., & Rosenberg, D. R. (1991). ECT treatment of demented elderly patients with major depression: a retrospective study of efficacy and safety. *Convulsive Therapy, 7,* pp. 157–165.

Neshkes, R. E., Gerner, R., Jarvik, L. F., Mintz, J., Joseph, J., Linde, S., Aldrich, J., Conolly, M. E., Rosen, R., & Hill, M. (1985). Orthostatic effect of imipramine and doxepin in depressed geriatric out-patients. *Journal of Clinical Psychopharmacology, 5,* pp. 102–106.

O'Connor, C. (1985). Electroshock. *The Washington Post Magazine,* December 1, pp. 12–22.

O'Shea, B., Lynch, T., Falvey, J., & O'Mahoney, G. (1987). Electroconvulsive therapy and cognitive improvement in a very elderly depressed patient. *British Journal of Psychiatry, 150,* pp. 255–257.

Oreland, L., & Gottfries, C.-G. (1986). Brain and brain monoamine oxidase in aging and in dementia of Alzheimer's type. *Progress in Neuro-Psychopharmacology and Biological Psychiatry, 10,* pp. 533–540.

Ouslander, J. (1981). Drug prescribing for the elderly. *Western Journal of Medicine, 135,* pp. 455–462.

Pettinati, H. M., & Bonner, K. M. (1984). Cognitive functioning in depressed geriatric patients with a history of ECT. *American Journal of Psychiatry, 141,* pp. 49–52.

Phanjoo, A. L., & Link, C. (1990). Remoxipride versus thioridazine in elderly psychotic patients. *Acta Psychiatrica Scandinavica, 82*(Suppl. 358), pp. 181–185.

Philpot, M., & Puranik, A. (1994). Psychotropic drugs, aging, and community care. *Drugs and Aging, 5,* pp. 235–241.

Pickett, P., Masand, P., & Murray, G. B. (1990). Psychostimulant treatment of geriatric depressive disorders secondary to medical illness. *Journal of Geriatric Psychiatry and Neurology, 3,* pp. 146–151.

Pitt, B. (1985). The chemotherapy of affective disorders in the elderly. In Dewhurst, W. G., & Baker, G. B. (Eds.), *Pharmacotherapy of affective disorders.* Beckenham: Croon Helm Ltd., pp. 584–616.

Pitts, W. M., Fann, W. E., Sajadi, C., & Snyder, S. (1983). Alprazolam in older depressed inpatients. *Journal of Clinical Psychiatry, 44,* pp. 213–215.

Raskind, M. A. (1993). Geriatric psychopharmacology: Management of late-life depression and the noncognitive behavioral disturbances of Alzheimer's disease. *Psychiatric Clinics of North America, 16,* pp. 815–827.

Ray, W. A., Taylor, J. A., Meador, K. G., Lichtenstein, M. J., Griffin, M. R., et al. (1993). Reducing antipsychotic drug use in nursing homes. *Archives of Internal Medicine, 153,* pp. 713–721.

Reynolds, C. F., Frank, E., Perel, J. M., et al. (1992). Combined pharmacotherapy and psychotherapy in the acute and continuation treatment of elderly patients with recurrent major depression: A preliminary report. *American Journal of Psychiatry, 149*(12), pp. 1687–1692.

Richelson, E. (1994). The pharmacology of antidepressants at the synapse: Focus on newer compounds. *Journal of Clinical Psychiatry, 55*(Suppl. A), pp. 34–39.

Rockwell, E., Lam, R. W., & Zisook, S. (1988). Antidepressant drug studies in the elderly. *Psychiatric Clinics of North America, 11,* pp. 215–233.

Rosenthal, N. E., Sack, D. A., Carpenter, C. J., Parry, B. L., Mendelson, W. B., & Wehr, T. A. (1985). Antidepressant effects of light in seasonal affective disorder. *American Journal of Psychiatry, 142,* pp. 163–170.

Salzman, C., Schneider, L. S., & Alexopoulos, G. S. (1995). Pharmacological treatment of depression in late life. In Bloom, F. E., & Kupfer, D. J. (Eds.), *Psychopharmacology: The fourth generation of progress.* Raven Press, Ltd., New York, pp. 1471–1477.

Salzman, C. (1987). Treatment of the elderly agitated patient. *Journal of Clinical Psychiatry, 48,* pp. S19–S22.

Salzman, C. (Ed.) (1992). *Clinical geriatric psychopharmacology,* 2nd ed. Baltimore, MD: Williams and Wilkins.

Samuels, S. C., & Katz, I. (1994). Neuroleptic medication in elderly people. *Current Opinion in Psychiatry, 7,* pp. 358–363.

Sandborn, W. D., Bendfeldt, F., & Handy, R. (1995). Valproic acid for physically aggressive behavior in geriatric patients. *American Journal of Geriatric Psychiatry, 3,* pp. 239–242.

Schmidt, P. J., & Rubinow, D. R. (1991). Menopause-related affective disorders: A justification for further study. *American Journal of Psychiatry, 148,* pp. 844–852.

Schmucker, D. L. (1985). Aging and drug disposition: An update. *Pharmacological Reviews, 37,* pp. 133–148.

Selma, T. P., Palla, K., Poddig, B., & Brauner, D. J. (1994). Effect of the omnibus reconciliation act of 1987 on antipsychotic prescribing in nursing home residents. *Journal of the American Geriatrics Society, 42,* pp. 648–652.

Shaw, S. M., & Opit, L. J. (1976). Need for supervision in the elderly receiving long-term prescription medications. *British Medical Journal, 1,* pp. 505–507.

Shomoian, C. A. (Ed.) (1992). *Psychopharmacological treatment complications in the elderly.* Washington, DC: American Psychiatric Press.

Shulman, K. I., MacKenzie, S., & Hardy, B. (1987). The clinical use of lithium carbonate in old age: A review. *Progress in Neuro-Psychopharmacology and Biological Psychiatry, 11,* pp. 159–164.

Simpson, P. M., & Foster, D. (1986). Improvement in organically disturbed behavior with trazodone treatment. *Journal of Clinical Psychiatry, 47,* pp. 191–193.

Smith, R. E., & Helms, P. M. (1982). Adverse effects of lithium therapy in the acutely ill elderly patients. *Journal of Clinical Psychiatry, 43,* pp. 94–99.

Solomon, F., White, C. C., Parron, D.C., & Mendelson, W. B. (1979). Sleeping pills, insomnia and medical practice, *New England Journal of Medicine, 300,* pp. 803–808.

Squire, L. R. (1984). ECT and memory dysfunction. In Lerer, B., Weiner, R. D., & Belmacker, R. H. (Eds.), *Basic mechanisms of ECT.* London: John Libby, pp. 156–163.

Squire, L. R., & Zouzounis, J. A. (1986). ECT and memory: Brief pulse versus sine wave. *American Journal of Psychiatry, 143,* pp. 596–601.

Sunderland, T., Lawlor, B. A., Martinez, R. A., & Molchan, S. E. (1991). Anxiety in the elderly: Neurobiological and clinical interface. In Salzman, C., & Lebowitz, B. (Eds.), *Anxiety in the elderly: Treatment and research.* New York, Springer, pp. 105–129.

Sunderland, T., Mueller, E. A., Cohen, R. M., Jimerson, D.C., Pickar, D., & Murphy, D. L. (1985). Tyramine pressor sensitivity changes during deprenyl treatment. *Psychopharmacology, 86,* pp. 432–437.

Sunderland, T., & Silver, M. A. (1988). Neuroleptics in the treatment of dementia. *International Journal of Geriatric Psychiatry, 3,* pp. 79–88.

Sunderland, T., Cohen, R. M., Molchan, S., Lawlor, B. A., Mellow, A. M., Newhouse, P. A., Tariot, P. N., Mueller, E. A., & Murphy, D. L. (1994). High dose selegiline in treatment-resistant older depressives. *Archives of General Psychiatry, 51,* pp. 607–615.

Sunderland, T., Tariot, P. N., Cohen, R. M., Weingartner, H., Mueller, E. A., & Murphy, D. L. (1987). Anticholinergic sensitivity in patients with dementia of the Alzheimer type and age-matched controls: A dose-response study. *Archives of General Psychiatry, 44,* pp. 418–426.

Tariot, P. N., Frederiksen, K., Erb, R., Leibovici, A., Podgorski, C. A., Asnis, J., & Cox, C. (1995). Lack of Carbamazepine toxicity in frail nursing home patients: A controlled study. *Journal of the American Geriatrics Society, 43,* pp. 1026–1929.

Thapa, P. B., Gideon, P., Fought, R. L., & Ray, W. A. (1995). Psychotropic drugs and the risk of recurrent falls in ambulatory nursing home residents. *American Journal of Epidemiology, 142,* pp. 202–211.

Thayssen, P., Bjerre, M., Kragh-Sorensen, P., Moller, M., Petersen, O. L., Kristensen, C. B., Gram, L. F. (1981). Cardiovascular effects of imipramine and nortriptyline in elderly patients. *Psychopharmacology, 74,* pp. 360–364.

Thompson, T. L., Moran, M. G., & Nies, A. S. (1983). Psychotropic drug use in the elderly (Part I). *New England Journal of Medicine, 308,* pp. 134–138.

Thompson, T. L., Moran, M. G., & Nies, A. S. (1983). Psychotropic drug use in the elderly (Part II). *New England Journal of Medicine, 308,* pp. 194–199.

Toenniessen, L. M., Casey, D. E., & McFarland, B. H. (1985). Tardive dyskinesia in the aged: Duration of treatment relationships. *Archives of General Psychiatry, 42,* pp. 278–284.

Veith, R. C., & Raskind, M. A. (1988). The neurobiology of aging: Does it predispose to depression? *Neurobiology of Aging, 9,* pp. 101–117.

Von Moltke, L. L., Greenblatt, D. J., Harmatz, J. S., & Shader, R. I. (1995). Psychotropic drug metabolism in old age. In Bloom, F. E., & Kupfer, D. J. (Eds.), *Psychopharmacology: The fourth generation of progress.* New York: Raven Press, pp. 1461–1469.

Waddington, J. L., & Youssef, H. A. (1988). Tardive dyskinesia in bipolar affective disorder: Aging, cognitive dysfunction, course of illness, and exposure to neuroleptics and lithium. *American Journal of Psychiatry, 145,* pp. 613–616.

Wayne, G. J. (1980). Electroconvulsive treatment in the elderly. *Journal of the National Association of Private Psychiatric Hospitals, 11,* pp. 25–27.

Williamson, J., & Chopin, J. (1980). Adverse reactions to prescribed drugs in the elderly: A multicenter investigation. *Age and Ageing, 9,* pp. 73–80.

Withering, W. (1785). *An account of foxglove, and some of its medical uses: With practical remarks on dropsy, and other diseases.* London: G. G. J. and J. Robinson, 1785.

Wolkowitz, O. M., Breier, A., Doran, A., Kelsoe, J., Lucas, P., Paul, S. M., & Pickar, D. (1988). Alprazolam augmentation of the antipsychotic effects of fluphenazine in schizophrenic patients. *Archives of General Psychiatry, 45,* pp. 664–671.

Wragg, R. E., & Jeste, D. V. (1988). Neuroleptics and alternative treatments: Management of behavioral symptoms and psychosis in Alzheimer's disease and related conditions. *Psychiatric Clinics of North America, 11,* pp. 195–213.

Yassa, R., Nair, V., & Schwartz, G. (1986). Early versus late onset psychosis and tardive dyskinesia. *Biological Psychiatry, 21,* pp. 1291–1297.

Zohar, J., Shapira, B., Oppenheim, G., Ayd, F. J., & Belmaker, R. H. (1985). Addition of estrogen to imipramine in female-resistant depressives. *Psychopharmacology Bulletin, 21,* pp. 705–710.

ENDNOTES

1. Long, S. H. (1994). *Prescription drug coverage and the elderly: Issues and options.* Washington, DC: Public Policy Institute, AARP, p. 2, April, 1994.

2. Salzman, C., Schneider, L. S., & Alexopoulos, G. S. (1995). Pharmacological treatment of depression in late life. In Bloom, F. E., & Kupfer, D. J. (Eds.), *Psychopharmacology: The fourth generation of progress.* New York: Raven Press, pp. 1471–1477; Myers-Robfogel, M. W., & Bosmann, H. B. (1984). Clinical pharmacology in the aged: Aspects of pharmacokinetics and drug sensitivity. In Williams, T. F. (Ed.), *Rehabilitation in the aging.* New York: Raven Press, pp. 23–39.

3. Von Moltke, L. L., Greenblatt, D. J., Harmatz, J. S., & Shader, R. I. (1995). Psychotropic drug metabolism in old age. In Bloom, F. E., & Kupfer, D. J. (Eds.), *Psychopharmacology: The fourth generation of progress* New York: Raven Press, pp. 1461–1469; and Dubovsky, S. L. (1994). Geriatric neuropsychopharmacology. In Coffey, C. E., & Cummings, J. L. (Eds.), *Textbook of geriatric psychiatry.* Washington, DC: American Psychiatric Press, pp. 595–631.

4. Withering, W. (1785). *An account of foxglove, and some of its medical uses: With practical remarks on dropsy, and other diseases.* London: G. G. J. and J. Robinson.

5. Philpot, M., & Puranik, A. (1994). Psychotropic drugs, aging and community care. *Drugs and Aging, 5,* pp. 235–241; Von Moltke, L. L., Greenblatt, D. J., Harmatz, J. S., & Shader, R. I. (1995). Psychotropic drug metabolism in old age. In Bloom, F. E., & Kupfer, D. J. (Eds.), *Psychopharmacology: The fourth generation of progress.* New York: Raven Press, pp. 1461–1469; Dubovsky, S. L. (1994). Geriatric neuropsychopharmacology. In Coffey, C. E., & Cummings, J. L. (Eds.), *Textbook of geriatric psychiatry.* Washington, DC: American Psychiatric Press, pp. 595–631.

6. Von Moltke, L. L., Greenblatt, D. J., Harmatz, J. S., & Shader, R. I. (1995). Psychotropic drug metabolism in old age. In Bloom, F. E., & Kupfer, D. J. (Eds.), *Psychopharmacology: The fourth generation of progress.* New York: Raven Press, pp. 1461–1469; Daly, M. P., Lamy, P. P., & Richardson, J. P. (1994). Avoiding polypharmacy and iatrogenesis in the nursing home. *Maryland Medical Journal, 43,* pp. 1139–144.

7. Cadieux, R. J. (1993). Geriatric psychopharmacology: A primary care challenge. *Geriatric Psychopharmacology, 93,* pp. 281–301.

8. Horwitz, G. J., Tariot, P. N., Mead, K., & Cox, C. (1995). Discontinuation of antipsychotics in nursing home patients with dementia. *American Journal of Geriatric Psychiatry, 3,* pp. 290–299; Selma, T. P., Palla, K., Poddig, B., & Brauner, D. J. (1994). Effect of the omnibus reconciliation act 1987 on antipsychotic prescribing in nursing home residents. *Journal of the American Geriatrics Society, 42,* pp. 648–652; Von Moltke, L. L., Greenblatt, D. J., Harmatz, J. S., Shader, R. I. (1995). Psychotropic drug metabolism in old age. In Bloom, F. E., & Kupfer, D. J. (Eds.), *Psychopharmacology: The fourth generation of progress.* New York: Raven Press, pp. 1461–1469.

9. Dubovsky, S. L. (1994). Geriatric neuropsychopharmacology. In Coffey, C. E., & Cummings, J. L. (Eds.), *Textbook of geriatric psychiatry.* Washington, DC: American Psychiatric Press, pp. 595–631; Ouslander, J. (1981). Drug prescribing for the elderly. *Western Journal of Medicine, 135,* pp. 455–462.

10. Avorn, J., Soumerai, S. B., Everitt, D. E., Ross-Degnan, D., Beere, M. H., Sherman, D., Salem-Schatz, S. R., & Fields, D. (1992). A randomized trial of a program to reduce the use of psychoactive drugs in nursing homes. *New England Journal of Medicine, 327,* pp. 68–173.

11. Philpot, M., & Puranik, A. (1994). Psychotropic drugs, aging and community care. *Drugs and Aging, 5,* pp. 235–241; Thompson, T. L., Moran, M. G., & Nies, A. S. (1983). Psychotropic drug use in the elderly (Part I). *New England Journal of Medicine, 308,* pp. 134–138; Thompson, T. L., Moran, M. G., & Nies, A. S. (1983). Psychotropic drug use in the elderly (Part II). *New England Journal of Medicine, 308,* pp. 194–199.

12. Cooper, J. W. (1996). Probable adverse drug reaction in a rural geriatric nursing home population: A four-year study. *Journal of the American Geriatrics Society, 44,* pp. 194–197; Long, J. W. (1989). *The essential guide to prescription drugs; what you need to know for safe drug use,* 2nd ed. New York: Harper & Row.

13. Dubovsky, S. L. (1994). Geriatric neuropsychopharmacology. In Coffey, C. E., & Cummings, J. L. (Eds.), *Textbook of geriatric psychiatry.* Washington, DC: American Psychiatric Press, pp. 595–631.

14. Salzman, C., Schneider, L. S., & Alexopoulos, G. S. In Bloom, F. E., & Kupfer, D. J. (Eds.), *Psychopharmacology: The fourth generation of progress.* New York: Raven Press, pp. 1471–1477; Molchan, S. E., Martinez, R. A., Hill, J. L., Weingartner, H. J., Thompson, K., Vitiello, B., & Sunderland, T. (1992). Increased cognitive sensitivity to scopolamine with age and a perspective on the scopolamine model. *Brain Research Review, 17,* pp. 215–226; Myers-Robfogel, M. W., Bosmann, H. B. (1984). Clinical pharmacology in the aged: Aspects of pharmacokinetics and drug sensitivity. In Williams, T. F. (Ed.), *Rehabilitation in the aging.* New York: Raven Press, pp. 23–39.

15. Ray, W. A., Taylor, J. A., Meador, K. G., Lichtenstein, M. J., Griffin, M. R., et al. (1993). Reducing antipsychotic drug use in nursing homes. *Archives of Internal Medicine, 153,* pp. 713–721; Salzman, C., Schneider, L. S., & Alexopoulos, G. S. (1995). Pharmacological treatment of depression in late life. *Psychopharmacology: The fourth generation of progress.* New York: Raven Press, pp. 1471–1477; Dubovsky, S. L. (1994). Geriatric neuropsychopharmacology. In Coffey, C. E., & Cummings, J. L. (Eds.), *Textbook of geriatric psychiatry.* Washington, DC: American Psychiatric Press, pp. 595–631.

16. Long, S. H. (1994). *Prescription drug coverage and the elderly: Issues and options.* Washington, DC: Public Policy Institute, AARP, p. 2.

17. AARP Public Policy Institute. (1995). *Coming up short: Increasing out-of-pocket health spending by older Americans.* Report #9507, Washington, DC: Public Policy Institute, AARP.

18. Pastors Pharmacy, 136 S. York Rd., Hatboro, Pa. 19040.

19. 1909 K. St., N. W., Washington, D.C. 20049.

20. Von Moltke, L. L., Greenblatt, D. J., Harmatz, J. S., & Shader, R. I. (1995). Psychotropic drug metabolism in old age. In Bloom, F. E., & Kupfer, D. J. (Eds.), *Psychopharmacology: The fourth generation of progress.* New York: Raven Press, pp. 1461–1469.

21. Rockwell, E., Lam, R. W., & Zisook, S. (1988). Antidepressant drug studies in the elderly. *Psychiatric Clinics of North America, 11,* pp. 215–233.

22. Raskind, M. A. (1993). Geriatric psychopharmacology: Management of late-life depression and the noncognitive behavioral disturbances of Alzheimer's disease. *Psychiatric Clinics of North America, 16,* pp. 815–827.

23. *Ibid.*

24. Lebowitz, B. D., Martinez, R. A., Niederehe, G., Pearson, J. L., et al. (1995). Treatment of depression in late-life. *Psychopharmacology, 31*(1), pp. 185–202; Feighner, J. P., Boyer, W. F., Meredith, C. H., Hendrickson, G. (1988). An overview of fluoxetine in geriatric depression. *British Journal of Psychiatry., 153*(3 Suppl), pp. 105–108; Salzman, C., Schneider, L. S., & Alexopoulos, G. S. (1995). Pharmacological treatment of depression in late life. In Bloom, F. E., & Kupfer, D. J. (Eds.), *Psychopharmacology: The fourth generation of progress.* New York: Raven Press, pp. 1471–1477.

25. For a review, see Raskind, M. A. (1993). Geriatric psychopharmacology: Management of late-life depression and the noncognitive behavioral disturbances of Alzheimer's disease. *Psychiatric Clinics of North America, 16,* pp. 815–827; and Salzman, C., Schneider, L. S., & Alexopoulos, G. S. (1995).

Pharmacological treatment of depression in late life. In Bloom, F. E., & Kupfer, D. J. (Eds.), *Psychopharmacology: The fourth generation of progress.* New York: Raven Press, pp. 1471–1477.

26. Jarvik, L. F., Read, S. L., Mintz, J., Neshkes, R. E., Kane, J. M., Cole, K., Sarantakos, S., Howard, A., & Borenstein, M. (1983). Pretreatment orthostatic hypotension in geriatric depression: Predictor of response to imipramine and doxepin. *Journal of Clinical Psychopharmacology, 3,* pp. 368–372.

27. Neshkes, R. E., Gerner, R., Jarvik, L. F., Mintz, J., Joseph, J., Linde, S., Aldrich, J., Conolly, M. E., Rosen, R., & Hill, M. (1985). Orthostatic effect of imipramine and doxepin in depressed geriatric outpatients. *Journal of Clinical Psychopharmacology, 5,* pp. 102–106; Salzman, C., Schneider, L. S., & Alexopoulos, G. S. (1995). Pharmacological treatment of depression in late life. In Bloom, F. E., & Kupfer, D. J. (Eds.), *Psychopharmacology: The fourth generation of progress.* New York: Raven Press, pp. 1471–1477.

28. Salzman, C., Schneider, L. S., & Alexopoulos, G. S. (1995). Pharmacological treatment of depression in late life. In Bloom, F. E., & Kupfer, D. J. (Eds.), *Psychopharmacology: The fourth generation of progress.* New York: Raven Press, pp. 1471–1477.

29. McKeith, I., Fairbairn, A., Perry R., Thompson, P., & Perry, E. (1992). Neuroleptic sensitivity in patients with senile dementia of Lewy body type. *British Medical Journal, 305,* pp. 673–678; Molchan, S. E., Martinez, R. A., Hill, J. L., Weingartner, H. J., Thompson, K., Vitiello, B., & Sunderland, T. (1992). Increased cognitive sensitivity to scopolamine with age and a perspective on the scopolamine model. *Brain Research Review, 17,* pp. 215–226; Sunderland, T., Tariot, P. N., Cohen, R. M., Weingartner, H., Mueller, E. A., & Murphy, D. L. (1987). Anticholinergic sensitivity in patients with dementia of the Alzheimer type and age-matched controls: A dose-response study. *Archives of General Psychiatry, 44,* pp. 418–426.

30. Meyers, B. S., & Mei-Tal, V. (1983). Psychiatric reactions during tricyclic treatment of the elderly reconsidered. *Journal of Clinical Psychopharmacology, 3,* pp. 2–6.

31. Lawlor, B. A., Radcliffe, J., Molchan, S. E., Martinez, R. A., Hill, J. L., & Sunderland, T. (1994). A pilot placebo-controlled study of trazodone and buspirone in Alzheimer's disease. *International Journal of Geriatric Psychiatry, 9,* pp. 55–59; Simpson, P. M., & Foster, D. (1986). Improvement in organically disturbed behavior with trazodone treatment. *Journal of Clinical Psychiatry, 47,* pp. 191–193.

32. For review see Sunderland, T., Cohen, R. M., Molchan, S., Lawlor, B. A., Mellow, A. M., Newhouse, P. A., Tariot, P. N., Mueller, E. A., & Murphy, D. L. (1994). High-dose selegiline in treatment-resistant older depressive patients. *Archives of General Psychiatry, 51,* pp. 607–615; Rockwell, E., Lam, R. W., & Zisook, S., *op. cit.,* 1988.

33. Pitts, W. M., Fann, W. E., Sajadi, C., & Snyder, S. (1983). Alprazolam in older depressed inpatients. *Journal of Clinical Psychiatry, 44,* pp. 213–215; and Gerner, R. H., *op. cit.,* 1985.

34. Georgotas, A., Friedman, E., McCarthy, M., Mann, J., Krakowski, M., Siegel, R., & Ferris, S. (1983). Resistant geriatric depressions and therapeutic response to monoamine oxidase inhibitors. *Biological Psychiatry, 18,* pp. 195–205.

35. Oreland, L., & Gottfries, C.-G. (1986). Brain and brain monoamine oxidase in aging and in dementia of Alzheimer's type. *Progress in Neuro-Psychopharmacology and Biological Psychiatry, 10,* pp. 533–540; Bridge, T. P., Soldo, B. J., Phelps, B. H., Wise, C. D., Francak, M. J., & Wyatt, R. J. (1985). Platelet monoamine oxidase activity: Demographic characteristics contribute to enzyme activity variability. *Journal of Gerontology, 40,* pp. 23–28; and Georgotas, A., Friedman, E., McCarthy, M., Mann, J., Krakowski, M., Siegel, R., & Ferris, S. (1983). Resistant geriatric depressions and therapeutic response to monoamine oxidase inhibitors. *Biological Psychiatry, 18,* pp. 195–205.

36. Murphy, D. L., Sunderland, T., & Cohen, R. M. (1984). Monoamine oxidase-inhibiting antidepressants: A clinical update. *Psychiatric Clinics of North America, 7,* pp. 549–562.

37. Sunderland, T., Mueller, E. A., Cohen, R. M., Jimerson, D.C., Pickar, D., & Murphy, D. L. (1985). Tyramine pressor sensitivity changes during deprenyl treatment. *Psychopharmacology, 86,* pp. 432–437.

38. Sunderland, T., Cohen, R. M., Molchan, S., Lawlor, B. A., Mellow, A. M., Newhouse, P. A., Tariot, P. N., Mueller, E. A., & Murphy, D. L. (1994). High dose selegiline in treatment-resistant older depressives. *Archives of General Psychiatry, 51,* pp. 607–615.

39. Avorn, J., Soumerai, S. B., Everitt, D. E., Ross-Degnan, D., Beere, M. H., Sherman, D., Salem-Schatz, S. R., & Fields, D. (1992). A randomized trial of a

program to reduce the use of psychoactive drugs in nursing homes. *New England Journal of Medicine, 327,* pp. 168–173; Billig, N., Cohen-Mansfield, J., & Lipson, S. (1991). Pharmacologic treatment of agitation in a nursing home. *Journal of the American Geriatrics Society, 39,* pp. 1002–1005.

40. Tariot, P. N., Frederiksen, K., Erb, R., Leibovici, A., Podgorski, C. A., Asnis, J., & Cox, C. (1995). Lack of Carbamazepine toxicity in frail nursing home patients: a controlled study. *Journal of the American Geriatrics Society, 43,* pp. 1026–1929.

41. Thapa, P. B., Gideon, P., Fought, R. L., Ray, W. A. (1995). Psychotropic drugs and the risk of recurent falls in ambulatory nursing home residents. *American Journal of Epidemiology, 142,* pp. 202–211. Accidental, spontaneous, or hidden hypothermia is one of the winter hazards of age. Risk factors include the phenothiazines, tricyclic antidepressants, diseases that diminish physical activity and thus decrease heat production such as dementia and Parkinsonism, and increased heat loss such as alcohol-induced vasodilation.

42. Samuels, S. C., & Katz, I. (1994). Neuroleptic medication in elderly people. *Current Opinion in Psychiatry, 7,* pp. 358–363; Raskind, M. A. (1993). Geriatric psychopharmacology: Management of late-life depression and the noncognitive behavioral disturbances of Alzheimer's disease. *Psychiatric Clinics of North America, 16,* pp. 815–827; Salzman, C. (1987). Treatment of the elderly agitated patient. *Journal of Clinical Psychiatry, 48,* pp. S19–S22.

43. Sunderland, T., & Silver, M. A. (1988). Neuroleptics in the treatment of dementia. *International Journal of Geriatric Psychiatry, 3,* pp. 79–88.

44. Jeste, D. V., Paulsen, J. S., & Harris, M. J. (1995). Late-onset schizophrenia and other related psychoses. In Bloom, F. E., & Kupfer, D. J. (Eds.), *Psychopharmacology: The fourth generation of progress.* New York: Raven Press, pp. 1437–1446; Wragg, R. E., & Jeste, D. V. (1988). Neuroleptics and alternative treatments: Management of behavioral symptoms and psychosis in Alzheimer's disease and related conditions. *Psychiatric Clinics of North America, 11,* pp. 195–213.

45. Gerrard, J., Chen, V., & Dowd, B. (1995). The impact of the 1987 Federal guidelines on the use of psychotropic drugs in Minnesota nursing homes. *American Journal of Public Health, 85,* pp. 771–776; McKeith, I., Fairbairn, A., Perry, R., Thompson, P., & Perry, E. (1992). Neuroleptic sensitivity in patients with senile dementia of Lewy

body type. *British Medical Journal, 305,* pp. 673–678; Sunderland, T., et al., 1987, *op. cit.*

46. Raskind, M. A. (1993). Geriatric psychopharmacology: Management of late-life depression and the noncognitive behavioral disturbances of Alzheimer's disease. *Psychiatric Clinics of North America, 16,* pp. 815–827.

47. Toenniessen, L. M., Casey, D. E., & McFarland, B. H. (1985). Tardive dyskinesia in the aged: Duration of treatment relationships. *Archives of General Psychiatry, 42,* pp. 278–284.

48. Jeste, D. V., Caligiuri, M. P., Paulsen, J. S., Heaton, R. K., Lacro, J. P., Harris, J., Bailey, A., Fell, R. L., & McAdams, L. A. (1995). Risk of tardive dyskinesia in older patients. *Archives of General Psychiatry, 52,* pp. 756–765; Yassa, R., Nair, V., & Schwartz, G. (1986). Early versus late onset psychosis and tardive dyskinesia. *Biological Psychiatry, 21,* pp. 1291–1297.

49. Waddington, J. L., & Youssef, H. A. (1988). Tardive dyskinesia in bipolar affective disorder: Aging, cognitive dysfunction, course of illness, and exposure to neuroleptics and lithium. *American Journal of Psychiatry, 145,* pp. 613–616.

50. Shaw, S. M., & Opit, L. J. (1976). Need for supervision in the elderly receiving long-term prescription medications. *British Medical Journal, 1,* pp. 505–507.

51. Grammans, R. E., Stringfellow, J. C., Hvizdos, A. J., et al. (1992). Use of buspirone in patients with generalized anxiety disorder and coexisting depressive symptoms: a meta-analysis of eight randomized controlled studies. *Neuropsychobiology, 25,* pp. 193–201.

52. Von Moltke, L. L., Greenblatt, D. J., Harmatz, J. S., & Shader, R. I. (1995). Psychotropic drug metabolism in old age. In Bloom, F. E., & Kupfer, D. J. (Eds.), *Psychopharmacology: The fourth generation of progress.* New York: Raven Press, pp. 1461–1469.

53. *Ibid.*

54. Greenblatt, D. J., Sellers, E. M., & Shader, R. I. (1982). Drug disposition in old age. *New England Journal of Medicine, 306,* pp. 1081–1088.

55. Pitts, W. M., et al., *op. cit.,* 1983.

56. Wolkowitz, O. M., Breier, A., Doran, A., Kelsoe, J., Lucas, P., Paul, S. M., & Pickar, D. (1988). Alprazolam augmentation of the antipsychotic effects of fluphenazine in schizophrenic patients. *Archives of General Psychiatry, 45,* pp. 664–671.

57. Napoliello, M. J. (1986). An interim multicentre report on 677 anxious geriatric out-patients treated

with buspirone. *British Journal of Clinical Practice, 40,* pp. 71–73.

58. Lawlor, B. A., Radcliffe, J., Molchan, S. E., Martinez, R. A., Hill, J. L., & Sunderland, T. (1994). A pilot placebo-controlled study of trazodone and buspirone in Alzheimer's disease. *International Journal of Geriatric Psychiatry, 9,* pp. 55–59; Colenda, C. C. (1988). Buspirone in the treatment of agitated demented patients. *Lancet, ii,* pp. 411–412.

59. Markovitz, P. J. (1993). Treatment of anxiety in the elderly. *Journal of Clinical Psychiatry, 54*(Suppl.5), pp. 64–68.

60. Shulman, K. I., MacKenzie, S., & Hardy, B. (1987). The clinical use of lithium carbonate in old age: A review. *Progress in Neuro-psychopharmacology and Biological Psychiatry, 11,* pp. 159–164.

61. Dubovsky, S. L. (1994). Geriatric neuropsychopharmacology. In Coffey, C. E., & Cummings, J. L. (Eds.), *Textbook of geriatric psychiatry.* Washington, DC: American Psychiatric Press, pp. 595–631.

62. Smith, R. E., & Helms, P. M. (1982). Adverse effects of lithium therapy in the acutely ill elderly patients. *Journal of Clinical Psychiatry, 43,* pp. 94–99.

63. Kaufman, M. W., Cassem, N. H., Murray, G. B., & Jenike, M. (1984). Use of psychostimulants in medically ill patients with neurological disease and major depression. *Canadian Journal of Psychiatry, 29,* pp. 46–49.

64. Jacobsen, A. (1958). The use of ritalin in psychotherapy of depressions of the aged. *Psychiatry Quarterly, 32,* pp. 474–483.

65. Katan, W., & Raskind, M. (1980). Treatment of depression in the mentally ill elderly with methylplenidate. *American Journal of Psychiatry, 137,* pp. 963–965; Branconnier, R. J., & Cole, J. O. (1980). The therapeutic role of methylphenidate in senile organic brain syndrome. In Cole, J. O., & Barrett, J. (Eds.), *Psychopathology in the aged.* New York: Raven Press, pp. 183–195.

66. Frierson, R. L., Wey, J. J., & Tabler, J. B. (1990). Psychostimulants for depression in the medically ill. Pickett, P., Masand, P., & Murray, G. B. Psychostimulant treatment of geriatric depressive disorders secondary to medical illness. *Journal of Geriatric Psychiatry and Neurology, 3,* pp. 146–151; Chiarello, R. J., & Cole, J. O. (1987). Psychostimulants: A reconsideration. *Archives of General Psychiatry, 44,* pp. 286–295.

67. McCall, W. V., Farah, B. A., Reboussin, D., & Colenda, C. (1995). Comparison of the efficacy of titriated, moderate-dose and fixed, high-dose right unilateral ECT in elderly patients. *American Journal of Geriatric Psychiatry, 3,* pp. 317–324; Dubovsky, S. L. (1994). Geriatric neuropsychopharmacology. In Coffey, C. E., Cummings, J. L. (Eds.), *Textbook of geriatric psychiatry.* Washington, DC: American Psychiatric Press, pp. 595–631.

68. Schmidt, P. J., & Rubinow, D. R. (1991). Menopause-related affective disorders: a justification for further study. *American Journal of Psychiatry, 148,* pp. 844–852; Zohar, J., Shapira, B., Oppenheim, G., Ayd, F. J., & Belmaker, R. H. (1985). Addition of estrogen to imipramine in female-resistant depressives. *Psychopharmacology Bulletin, 21,* pp. 705–710.

69. Tariot, P. N., Frederiksen, K., Erb, R., Leibovici, A., Podgorski, C. A., Asnis, J., & Cox, C. (1995). Lack of Carbamazepine toxicity in frail nursing home patients: A controlled study. *Journal of the American Geriatrics Society, 43,* pp. 1026–1929.

70. Dubovsky, S. L. (1994). Geriatric neuropsychopharmacology. In Coffey, C. E., & Cummings, J. L. (Eds.), *Textbook of geriatric psychiatry.* Washington, DC: American Psychiatric Press, pp. 595–631.

71. For more information, contact: The National Sleep Foundation, 1367 Connecticut Ave. NW, Suite 200, Washington, DC 20036; American Sleep Apnea Association, 2025 Pennsylvania Ave. NW, Suite 905, Washington, DC 20006; or Restless Legs Syndrome Foundation, Dept. A., P. O. Box 7050, Rochester, MN 55903–7050. Also see: Klinkenborg, V. (1997, January 5). Awakening to Sleep. *The New York Times Magazine,* pp. 26–31, 41, 48, 51, 55–56.

72. Moran, M. G., Thompson, T. L., & Nies, A. S. (1988). Sleep disorders in the elderly. *American Journal of Psychiatry, 145,* pp. 1369–1377.

73. Reynolds, C. F., Dew, M. A., Monk, T. H. & Hoch, C. C. (1994). Sleep disorders in late life: A biopsychosocial model for understanding pathogenesis and intervention. In Coffey, C. E., Cummings, J. L. (Eds.), *Textbook of geriatric psychiatry.* Washington, DC: American Psychiatric Press, pp. 325–331; Gillin, J. C., Duncan, W. C., Murphy, D. L., Post, R. M., Wehr, T. A., Goodwin, F. K., Wyatt, R. J., & Bunney, W. E. (1981). Age-related changes in sleep in depressed and normal subjects. *Psychiatry Research, 4,* pp. 73–78.

74. Clauw, D. J., Nashel, D. L., Umhau, A., & Katz, P. (1990). Tryptophan-associated eosinophilic connective tissue disease: a new clinical entity? *Jour-*

nal of the American Medical Association, 263, pp. 1502–1506.

75. Shader, R. I., & Greenblatt, D. J. (1982). Management of anxiety in the elderly: The balance between therapeutic and adverse effects. *Journal of Clinical Psychiatry, 43,* pp. 8–18.

76. McCall, W. V., Farah, B. A., Reboussin, D., & Colenda, C. (1995). Comparison of the efficacy of titriated, moderate-dose and fixed, high-dose right unilateral ECT in elderly patients. *American Journal of Geriatric Psychiatry, 3,* pp. 317–324.

77. McCall, W. V., Farah, B. A., Reboussin, D., & Colenda, C. (1995). Comparison of the efficacy of titriated, moderate-dose and fixed, high-dose right unilateral ECT in elderly patients. *American Journal of Geriatric Psychiatry, 3,* pp. 317–324.

78. Squire, L. R. (1984). ECT and memory dysfunction. In Lerer, B., Weiner, R. D., & Belmacker, R. H. (Eds.), *Basic mechanisms of ECT.* London: John Libby, pp. 156–163; Squire, L. R., & Zouzounis, J. A. (1986). ECT and memory: Brief pulse versus sine wave. *American Journal of Psychiatry, 143,* pp. 596–601.

79. Nelson, J. P., & Rosenberg, D. R. (1991). ECT treatment of demented elderly patients with major depression: a retrospective study of efficacy and safety. *Convulsive Therapy, 7,* pp. 157–165; Pettinati, H. M., & Bonner, K. M. (1984). Cognitive functioning in depressed geriatric patients with a history of ECT. *American Journal of Psychiatry, 141,* pp. 49–52.

80. O'Shea, B., Lynch, T., Falvey, J., & O'Mahoney, G. (1987). Electroconvulsive therapy and cognitive improvement in a very elderly depressed patient. *British Journal of Psychiatry, 150,* pp. 255–257.

81. McCall, W. V., Farah, B. A., Reboussin, D., & Colenda, C. (1995). Comparison of the efficacy of titriated, moderate-dose and fixed, high-dose right unilateral ECT in elderly patients. *American Journal of Geriatric Psychiatry, 3,* pp. 317–324; Gaspar, D., & Samarasinghe, L. A. (1982). ECT in psychogeriatric practice: A study of risk factors, indications, and outcome. *Comprehensive Psychiatry, 23,* pp. 170–175.

82. The possible persistence of memory loss after ECT remains controversial. See Devanand, D. P., Verma, A. K., Tirumalasetti, F. & Sackeim, H. A. (1991). Absence of cognitive impairment after more than 100 lifetime ECT treatments. *American Journal of Psychiatry, 148,* pp. 929–932.

83. O'Shea, et. al., *op. cit.,* 1987.

84. Lerer, B. (1986). ECT: Possible mechanisms of action. *Psychopharmacology, 22,* pp. 472–487.

85. Dubovsky, S. L. (1994). Geriatric neuropsychopharmacology. In Coffey, C. E., & Cummings, J. L. (Eds.), *Textbook of geriatric psychiatry.* Washington, DC: American Psychiatric Press, pp. 595–631; Cohen, B. M., & Zubenko, G. S. (1985). Relevance of genetic variability to clinical psychopharmacology. *Psychopharmacology Bulletin, 21,* pp. 641–650.

APPENDIXES

SOURCES OF GERONTOLOGICAL LITERATURE

GENERAL BOOKS

MEDICAL, PSYCHOLOGY, SOCIAL WORK, AND NURSING BOOKS

PERIODICALS

PAMPHLETS, BULLETINS, AND REPORTS

GENERAL BOOKS

Annual review of gerontology and geriatrics. (1980, and all subsequent years). New York: Springer.

Binstock, R. H., & George, L. K. (Eds.) (1995). *Handbook of aging and the social sciences,* 4th ed. Orlando, FL: Academic Press.

Birren, J. E. (Ed.). (1996). *Encyclopedia of gerontology.* San Diego, CA: Academic Press.

Birren, J. E. (Ed.) (1985). *Handbook of aging,* three vols., 2nd ed. New York: Van Nostrand Reinhold

Birren, J. E., Sloane, R. B., & Cohen, G. D. (Eds.). (1992). *Handbook of mental health and aging,* 2nd ed. San Diego, CA: Academic Press.

Birren, J. E., & Schaie, K. W. (Eds.) (1996). *Handbook of the psychology of aging,* 4th ed. Orlando, FL: Academic Press.

Busse, E. W., & Blazer, D. G. (Eds.) (1995). *The American psychiatric press textbook of geriatric psychiatry.* Washington, DC: American Psychiatric Association.

Ferraro, K. F. (1990). *Gerontology: Perspectives and issues.* New York: Springer.

Harris, D. K. (1988). *Dictionary of gerontology.* New York: Greenwood Press.

Hayflick, L. (1994). *How and why we age.* New York: Ballantine Books.

Kastenbaum, R. (Ed.) (1993). *The encyclopedia of adult development.* Phoenix, AZ: Oryx Press.

Maddox, G. L. (Ed.) (1995). *The encyclopedia of aging,* 2nd ed. New York: Springer.

Magai, C., & McFadden, S. H. (Eds.). (1996). *Handbook of emotion, adult development and aging.* Orlando, FL: Academic Press.

McKee, P. (Ed.) (1982). *Philosophical foundations of gerontology.* New York: Human Sciences Press.

McKee, P., & Kauppinen, H. (1987). *The art of aging.* New York: Insight Books.

National Institutes of Health. (1986). *Established populations for epidemiologic studies of the elderly: Research data book.* Baltimore, MD: National Institute on Aging.

Ricklefs, R. E., & Finch, C. E. (1996). *Aging: A natural history.* New York: W. H. Freeman.

Riley, M. W., & Foner, A. (Eds.) (1968, 1969, 1972). *Aging and society: Vol. 1, An inventory of research findings; Vol. 2, Aging and the professions; Vol. 3, A sociology of age stratification.* New York: Russell Sage Foundation.

Schneider, E. L., & Rowe, J. L. (Eds.) (1996). *Handbook of the biology of aging,* 4th ed. Orlando, FL: Academic Press.

Shock, N. W. (1951, 1957, 1963). *A classified bibliography of gerontology and geriatrics: Vol. 1, 1900–1948; Vol. 2, 1948–1955; Vol. 3, 1956–1961.* Stanford, CA: Stanford University Press. [Also see: Shock, N. W. (Published quarterly through 1980). Index to current periodical literature. *Journal of Gerontology.*]

Turner, J. S. (Ed.). (1996). *Encyclopedia of relationships across the lifespan.* Westport, CT: Greenwood Press.

MEDICAL, PSYCHOLOGY, SOCIAL WORK, AND NURSING BOOKS

Abrams, W. B., Beers, M. H., & Berkow, R. (Eds.) (1995). *The Merck manual of geriatrics,* 2nd ed.. Whitehouse Station, NJ: Merck.

Albert, M. S., & Moss, M. B. (Eds.) (1988). *Geriatric neuropsychology.* New York: Guilford Press.

American Psychiatric Association. (1994). *Diagnostic and statistical manual of mental disorders: DSM-IV,* 4th Ed. Washington, DC: American Psychiatric Association.

American Psychiatric Association. (1994). *Diagnostic criteria from DSM-IV.* Washington, DC: American Psychiatric Association.

Bienefeld, D. (1990). *Verwoerdt's clinical geropsychiatry,* 3rd. ed. Baltimore, MD: Williams & Wilkins.

Blazer, D. (1993). *Depression in late life,* 2nd. ed. St. Louis, MO: Mosby Year-Book.

Breckman, R., & Adelman, R. (1988). *Strategies for helping victims of elder mistreatment.* Thousand Oaks, CA: Sage.

Brocklehurst, J. C. (Ed.) (1992). *Textbook of geriatric medicine and gerontology,* 4th ed. New York: Churchill Livingstone.

Burnside, I. M. (1988). *Nursing and the aged: A self care approach,* 3rd ed. New York: McGraw Hill.

Burnside, I., & Schmidt, M. G. (1994). *Working with older adults: Group process.* Boston: Jones & Bartlett.

Calkins, E., Ford, A. B., & Katz, P. R. (Eds.) (1992). *Practice of geriatrics,* 2nd ed. Philadelphia: Saunders.

Cassel, C. K., et. al. (Eds.) (1996). *Geriatric medicine,* 3rd. ed. New York: Springer-Verlag.

Coffey, C. E., & Cummings, J. L. (Eds.) (1994). *Textbook of geriatric psychiatry.* Washington, DC: American Psychiatric Press.

Hazzard, W. R., Andres, R., Bierman, E. L., & Blass, J. P. (Eds.) (1994). *Principles of geriatric medicine and gerontology,* 3rd ed. New York: McGraw Hill.

Institute of Medicine, Committee for a National Research Agenda on Aging Staff. (1991). *Extending life, enhancing life: A national research agenda on aging.* Washington, DC: National Academy Press.

Jenike, M. A. (1989). *Geriatric Psychiatry and Psychopharmacology.* Chicago, IL: Mosby Year-Book.

Kane, R. L., Ouslander, J. G., & Abrass, I. B. (1994). *Essentials of clinical geriatrics.* New York: McGraw Hill.

Kent, B., & Butler, R. N. (Eds.) (1987). *Human aging research: Concepts and techniques.* New York: Lippincott-Raven.

Lazarus, L. W., Jarvik, L. F., Foster, J. R., Lieff, J. D., & Mershon, S. R. (Eds.) (1988). *Essentials of geriatric psychiatry: A guide for health professionals.* New York: Springer.

National Council on the Aging. (1990). *Caregiver support groups in America.* Washington, DC: National Council on the Aging, Department 5087.

Perlmutter, M., & Hall, E. (1992). *Adult development and aging,* 2nd ed.. New York: John Wiley & Sons.

Rowe, J. W., & Besdine, R. W. (1988). *Geriatric medicine,* 2nd ed. Boston: Little, Brown.

Salzman, C. (1992). Clinical Geriatric Psychopharmacology, 2nd ed. Baltimore, MD: Williams & Wilkins.

Shock, N. W., Greulick, R. C., Andres, R., Arenberg, D., Costa, Jr., P. T., Lakatta, E. G., & Tobin, J. D. (1984). *Normal human aging: The Baltimore longitudinal study of aging.* Washington, DC: U.S. Government Printing Office.

Turner, F. J. (Ed.) (1992). *Mental health and the elderly: A social work perspective.* New York: The Free Press.

Warner, H. R., Butler, R. N., Sprott, R. L., & Schneider, E. L. (Eds.) (1987). *Modern biological theories of aging.* New York: Raven Press.

PERIODICALS

AFAR Newsletter. New York: American Federation for Aging Research.

Age and Ageing. British Geriatrics Society and British Society for Research on Ageing. Oxford, England: Oxford University Press.

Ageing International. Montreal, Canada: International Federation on Ageing.

Aging and Mental Health. Oxfordshire, UK, Cambridge, MA, and Cammeray, Australia: Carfax Publishing Company.

Aging Network News. McLean, VA: Hansan Group, Inc.

Aging and Work: A Journal on Age, Work and Retirement, 1978–1984 (formerly *Industrial Gerontology,* 1973–1977). Washington, DC: National Council on Aging.

Alzheimer's Disease and Associated Disorders. Philadelphia: Lippincott-Raven Press.

American Journal of Nursing. (American Nurses' Association) New York: American Journal of Nursing, Co.

American Journal of Public Health. Washington, DC: American Public Health Association.

Behavior, Health and Aging. New York: Springer.

Clinical Gerontologist: The Journal of Aging and Mental Health. Binghamton, NY: The Haworth Press.

Comprehensive Gerontology. Copenhagen: Munksgaard International Publishers. (ceased publication in 1989)

Currents. Washington, DC: American Association of Homes and Services for the Aging.

Contemporary Long Term Care. New York: Bill Communications.

Dementia. Basil, Switzerland: S. Karger AG.

Developmental Psychology. Washington, DC: American Psychological Association.

Educational Gerontology. Bristol, PA: Taylor & Francis.

Generations. San Francisco, CA: The American Society on Aging.

Geriatric Nursing: American Journal of Care for the Aging. St. Louis, MO: Mosby Year-Book.

Geriatrics. Cleveland, OH: Advanstar.

The Gerontologist. Washington, DC: Gerontological Society of America.

Gerontology and Geriatrics Education. Binghamton, NY: The Haworth Press.

Home Health Aide Digest. Kalamazoo, MI: Stonerock & Associates.

Home Health Care Services Quarterly. New York: The Haworth Press.

Human Development (formerly *Vita Humana*). Basel, Switzerland: S. Karger AG.

International Journal of Aging and Human Development. Amityville, NY: Baywood Journals.

International Journal of Geriatric Psychiatry. New York and W. Sussex, England: John Wiley & Sons.

International Journal of Geriatric Psychopharmacology. Hants, UK: Stockton Press.

International Psychogeriatrics. New York: Springer.

The Journal of Aging and Ethnicity. New York: Springer.

Journal of Aging Studies. Greenwich, CT and London, England: JAI Press Inc.

Journal of the American Geriatrics Society. Baltimore, MD: Williams & Wilkins.

Journal of Applied Gerontology. Thousand Oaks, CA: Sage.

Journal of Chronic Diseases. Oxford, England: Pergamon Press.

Journal of Elder Abuse and Neglect. Binghamton, NY: The Haworth Press.

Journal of Geriatric Psychiatry. Madison, CT: International Universities Press.

Journal of Gerontological Nursing. Thorofare, NJ: Slack.

Journal of Gerontological Social Work. Binghamton, NY: The Haworth Press.

Journal of Long-Term Care Administration. Alexandria, VA: American College of Nursing Home Administrators.

Journal of Nutrition for the Elderly. Binghamton, NY: The Haworth Press.

Journal of Women & Aging. Binghamton, NY: The Haworth Press.

Journals of Gerontology (Series A: Biological Sciences and Medical Sciences; Series B: Psychological Sciences and Social Sciences). Washington, DC: Gerontological Society.

Life-Span Development and Behavior. Mahwah, NJ: Lawrence Erlbaum Associates.

Loss, Grief & Care. Binghamton, NY: The Haworth Press.

Maturitas. New York: Elsevier Science.

McKnight's Long Term Care News. (formerly *Today's Nursing Home*) Northfield, IL: McKnight Medical Communications.

Modern Health Care. Chicago, IL: Crain Communications.

Modern Maturity. New York: American Association of Retired Persons.

NCEA Exchange (National Center on Elder Abuse). Newark, DE: College of Human Resources, University of Delaware.

NRTA (National Retired Teachers Association) Bulletin. Washington, DC: American Association of Retired Persons.

The Network. Washington, DC: The Gray Panthers.

Neurobiology of Aging. New York: Elsevier Science.

NSCL Washington Weekly. Washington, DC: National Senior Citizens Law Center.

Nursing Home Medicine. Plainsboro, NJ: MultiMedia HealthCare/Freedom, LLC.

Nursing Homes; Long Term Care Management. Cleveland, OH: Medquest Communications.

Nursing Outlook. (American Academy of Nursing). St. Louis, MO: Mosby Year-Book.

Omega: Journal of Death and Dying. Amityville, New York: Baywood Journals.

Perspective on Aging. Washington, DC: National Council on Aging.

Physical & Occupational Therapy in Geriatrics. Binghamton, NY: The Haworth Press.

Research on Aging: A Quarterly of Social Gerontology and Adult Development. Thousand Oaks, CA: Sage.

Retirement Life. Washington, DC: National Association of Retired Federal Employees.

Senior Citizens News. Silver Spring, MD: National Council of Senior Citizens.

Provider. Washington, DC: American Health Care Association.

Social Work. Washington, DC: National Association of Social Workers.

Women and Aging Letter. Waltham, MA: National Policy and Resource Center on Women and Aging, Brandeis University.

PAMPHLETS, BULLETINS, AND REPORTS

American Association of Retired Persons. *Age Line*—an on-line bibliographic data base available for a small fee.

National Center for Health Statistics. Reports.

National Institute on Aging. *Age Pages.*

Social Security Administration Bulletin.

U.S. Bureau of the Census. Reports.

U.S. Senate Special Committee on Aging. Hearings and Task Force reports.

ORGANIZATIONS PERTAINING
TO THE ELDERLY

GENERAL ORGANIZATIONS

ORGANIZATIONS CONCERNED
WITH OLDER WOMEN

LEGAL RESOURCES FOR THE ELDERLY

GENERAL ORGANIZATIONS

AFL-CIO Department of Employee Benefits*
815 16th St. NW
Washington, DC 20006

AFSCME Retiree Program*
1625 L St. NW
Washington, DC 20036

Aging Network Services
Suite 907
4400 East-West Highway
Bethesda, MD 20814
Nationwide for-profit network of private-practice geriatric social workers who serve as care managers for older parents who live at a distance.

Alliance for Aging Research*
2021 K St. NW
Suite 305
Washington, DC 20006

Alzheimer's Association*
919 N. Michigan Ave.
Suite 1000
Chicago, IL 60611-1676
Internet: http://www.alz.org
Information and Chapter Referral:
(800) 272-3900

Alzheimer's Disease Education and Referral Center
P.O. Box 8250
Silver Spring, MD 20907-8250
Internet:
http://www.alzheimers.org/adear/adcdir.html
Information: (800) 438-4380

American Aging Association (AGE)
2129 Providence Ave.
Chester, PA 19013-5506
Made up of scientists and others, mostly in the biomedical field, it promotes research in aging.

American Art Therapy Association
1202 Allanson Rd.
Mundelein, IL 60060
Internet:
http://www.louisville.edu/groups/aata-www/w/

American Academy of Physical Medicine and Rehabilitation
Suite 2500
One IBM Plaza
Chicago, IL 60611

American Association for Geriatric Psychiatry
7910 Woodmont Ave.
Suite 1350

Bethesda, MD 20814-3004
Internet: http://www.aagpgpa.org/

American Association for Marriage and Family
Therapy
1133 15th St. NW
Suite 300
Washington, DC 20005-2710
Internet: http://www.aamft.org

American Association for International Aging*
1900 L St. NW
Suite 510
Washington, DC 20036-5002

American Association of Homes and Services
for the Aging (AAHSA)*
901 E St. NW
Suite 500
Washington, DC 20004-2037
Internet: http://www.aahsa.org
AAHSA represents nonprofit homes and other
service providers for the aging—religious,
municipal, trust, fraternal.

American Association of Retired Persons
(AARP)*
601 E St. NW
Washington, DC 20049
Internet: http:www.aarp.org

American Association of Senior Physicians
(AASP)
American Medical Association (AMA)
515 North State St.
Chicago, IL 60610
Retired and non-retired physicians and
spouses aged 55 and older whose primary aim
is to advance the rights and benefits of senior
physicians.

American Cancer Society
1599 Clifton Rd. NE
Atlanta, GA 30329
Internet: http://www.cancer.org/
Cancer Response System: (800) ACS-2345

American College of Health Care Administrators
325 S. Patrick St.
Alexandria, VA 22314

American Counseling Association
Association for Adult Development and
Aging
5999 Stevenson Ave.
Alexandria, VA 22304
Internet: http://www.counseling.org/
Information: (800) 347-6647

American Dance Therapy Association (ADTA)
2000 Century Plaza
Suite 108
Columbia, MD 21044

American Diabetes Association
1660 Duke St.
Alexandria, VA 22314
Internet: http://www.diabetes.org

American Federation for Aging Research
(AFAR)
18th Floor
1414 Avenue of the Americas
New York, NY 10019
Internet: http://www.afar.org/

American Foundation for the Blind*
11 Pennsylvania Plaza
Suite 300
New York, NY 10001
Internet: http://www.afb.org/afb
Information: (800) AFB-LINE [232-5463]

American Geriatrics Society*
770 Lexington Ave.
Suite 300
New York, NY 10021
Internet: http://www.americangeriatrics.org
Made up of physicians and other health care
professionals.

American Health Care Association
1201 L St. NW
Washington, DC 20005
Represents nursing home, assisted living, and
subacute care facilities. Provides information
on long-term care.

American Heart Association
7272 Greenville Ave.
Dallas, TX 75231

Internet: http://www.amhrt.org
To find affiliate office:
(800) AHA-USA1 [242-8721]
Stroke Connection:
(800) 553-6321

American Horticultural Therapy Association
362 A Christopher Ave.
Gaithersburg, MD 20879-3660
Internet:
http://www.hort.vt.edu/human/ahta.html
Information: (800) 634-1603

American Legion
700 N. Pennsylvania St.
P.O. Box 1055
Indianapolis, IN 46206
Internet: http://www.legion.org/

American Nurses Association
Council for Community Primary and
Long-Term Care Nursing Practice
Suite 100 W
600 Maryland Ave. SW
Washington, DC 20024-2571
Internet: http://www.nursingworld.org/about.
Information: (800) 274-4262

American Occupational Therapy Association, Inc.
4720 Montgomery Lane
P.O. Box 31220
Bethesda, MD 20824-1220

American Optometric Association
243 N. Lindbergh Blvd.
St. Louis, MO 63141
Internet: http://www.webcom.com/aoanet/
welcome.html

American Osteopathic Association
142 E. Ontario St.
Chicago, IL 60611
Internet: http://www.am-osteo-assn.org/
Information: (800) 621-1773

American Parkinson's Disease Association
Suite 4B
1250 Hylan Blvd.
Staten Island, NY 10305
Information: (800) 223-2732

American Physical Therapy Association
Section on Geriatrics
1111 N. Fairfax St.
Alexandria, VA 22314
http:/www.geriatricpt.org/

American Podiatric Medical Association
9312 Old Georgetown Rd.
Bethesda, MD 20814
Internet: http://www.apma.org/
Foot Care Information Center: (800) FOOT-
CARE [366-8227]

American Psychiatric Association
1400 K St. NW
Washington, DC 20005
Internet: http://www.psych.org/

American Psychological Association
750 First St. NE
Washington, DC 20002
Internet: http:/www.apa.org
Information: (800) 336-5500

American Psychological Association
Division 20: Adult Development and Aging
Lisa C. McGuire Ph.D.
Allegheny College
Department of Psychology
Meadville, PA 16335
Internet:
http://www.iog.wayne.edu/apadiv20/apadiv20.
htm

American Public Health Association
Section of Gerontological Health
1015 15th St. NW
Suite 300
Washington, DC 20005
Internet: http://apha.org/

American Public Welfare Association
810 First St. NE
Suite 500
Washington, DC 20002-4267
Internet: http://apwa.org/

American Red Cross
430 17th St. NW
Washington, DC 20006

Internet: http://www.redcross.org
Local chapters' services are available to older persons without charge. Interesting volunteer opportunities.

American Society for Geriatric Dentistry
211 E. Chicago Ave.
Suite 948
Chicago, IL 60611

American Society on Aging*
833 Market St.
Suite 511
San Francisco, CA 94103
Internet:
http://www.housecall.com/sponsors/asa/asa/index.html

Arthritis Foundation
1314 Spring St. NW
Atlanta, GA 30309
Information: (800) 283-7800
Internet: http://www.arthritis.org

Asian and Pacific Coalition on Aging, Inc.
3100 W. Jefferson Blvd.
Los Angeles, CA 90018

Asociacion Nacional por Personas Mayores—
National Association for Hispanic Elderly
3325 Wilshire Blvd.
Suite 800
Los Angeles, CA 90010-1724
Project MAS (More Access to Services):
(800) 953-8553

Assisted Living Facilities Association
of America
10300 Eaton Pl.
Suite 400
Fairfax, VA 22031

Association for Gerontology Education in Social
Work (AGE-SW)
School of Social Work
University of Maryland at Baltimore
525 W. Redwood St.
Baltimore, MD 21201-1777
Internet: http://www.cs.umd.edu/users/conn

Association for Gerontology in Higher
Education*
1001 Connecticut Ave NW
Suite 410
Washington, DC 20036-5504
Internet: http://www.aghe.org/

Association for Gerontology and Human
Development in Historically Black Colleges and
Universities*
1424 K. St. NW
Suite 601
Washington, DC 20005

B'nai B'rith Center for Senior Housing
and Services*
1640 Rhode Island Ave, NW
Washington, DC 20036
Internet: http://www.bnaibrith.org/

Brookdale Center on Aging
425 E. 25th St.
New York, NY 10010
Internet: http://www.hunter.cuny.edu/health/htmls/bcoahp.html.
Information:
(800) 64-STAFF [647-8233]

Catholic Golden Age*
430 Penn Ave.
Scranton, PA 18503
Information: (800) 836-5699

Children of Aging Parents
Suite 302-A
1609 Woodbourne Rd.
Levittown, PA 19057
Information and Referral Service:
(800) 227-7294

Clearinghouse on Abuse and Neglect of the
Elderly (CANE)
College of Human Resources
University of Delaware
Newark, DE 19716

Council of Better Business Bureaus
4200 Wilson Blvd.
Suite 800

Arlington, VA 22203-1804
Internet: http:www.bbb.org

Disabled American Veterans
807 Maine Ave. SW
Washington, DC 20024
Internet: http://www.dav.org

Elder Craftsmen
921 Madison Ave.
New York, NY 10020

Eldercare America, Inc.*
1141 Loxford Terrace
Silver Spring, MD 20901

Elderhostel
80 Boylston St.
Suite 400
Boston, MA 02116
Internet: http://www.elderhostel.org/
This organization provides an international
educational program for people over 60 and a
unique vacation opportunity. Participants live
and eat on campus, and take advantage of
sports, social activities, and choose from
numerous interesting courses.

Episcopal Society for Ministry on Aging
323 Wyandotte St.
Bethlehem, PA 18015

Families USA Foundation (formerly Villers
Foundation)*
1334 G St. NW
Washington, DC 20005
Internet: http://epn.org/families.html

Family Caregiver Alliance
425 Bush St.
Suite 500
San Francisco, CA 94108
Internet: http://www.caregiver.org
Information, education, and services for adults
with cognitive disorders such as Alzheimer's,
stroke, head injury, Parkinson's, and
Huntington's diseases.

Family Services America
11700 W. Lake Park Dr.

Milwaukee, WI 53224
Agencies are located in nearly every state
and in most medium to large cities.
Programs include homemaker services
adapted to meet the needs of older people
and confidential casework to help solve
personal problems.

Foundation for Hospice and Home Care
513 C St. NE
Washington, DC 20002

French Foundation for Alzheimer Research
Suite 820
11620 Wilshire Blvd.
Los Angeles, CA 90025
Information: (800) 477-2243

Generations United
c/o CWLA
440 First St. NW
Suite 310
Washington, DC 20001-2086
Internet: http://www.gu.org

The Gerontological Society of America*
1275 K. St. NW
Suite 350
Washington, DC 20005-4006
Internet: http://www.geron.org
Professional society that promotes the
scientific study of aging in the biological,
medical, and social sciences.

Gray Panthers*
2025 Pennsylvania Ave. NW
Suite 821
Washington, DC 20006
Information: (800) 280-5462
Activist group of older people working for
social change.

Green Thumb, Inc.*
2000 N. 14th St.
Suite 800
Arlington, VA 22201
Promotes employment and training
opportunities for older people, particularly
providing essential community services.

Group for the Advancement of Psychiatry
P.O. Box 28218
Dallas, TX 75228

Homedco
3800 Annapolis Lane
Suite 195
Minneapolis, MN 55447
Provides respiratory and infusion therapy, and
rents and sells medical equipment.

Huntington's Disease Society of America
140 W. 22nd St.
6th Floor
New York, NY 10011-2420
Information: (800) 345-4372

Impotence World Association
Impotence Institute of America
Impotence World Services
(includes Impotents Anonymous and I-Anon)
10400 Little Patuxent Parkway
Suite 485
Columbia, MD 21044-3502
Information: (800) 660-1603

The Institute for Retired Professionals
The New School for Social Research
60 W. 12th St.
New York, NY 10011
This pioneering school led the way in
providing intellectual activities for retired
professional people.

The International Federation on Aging
380 St. Antoine St. SW
Suite 3200
Montreal, PQ, Canada H2Y 3X7
Confederation of aging organizations of
various nations.

International Institute on Ageing
(United Nations—Malta)
117 St. Paul St.
Valletta, Malta
Internet: http://www.inia.org.mt

International Hearing Society
20361 Middlebelt Rd.
Livonia, MI 48152

Information: (800) 521-5247
Society of hearing aid specialists.

International Longevity Center—U.S.
1216 Fifth Ave.
Room 552
New York, NY 10029

International Psychogeriatric Association
5700 Old Orchard Rd.
Skokie, IL 60077

International Senior Citizens Organization
255 S. Hill St.
Suite 409
Los Angeles, CA 90012

Mature Outlook
P.O. Box 10448
Des Moines, IA 50306
Information: (800) 336-6330
This for-profit organization for individuals
over 50 provides benefits, services, discounts
and information to members.

Medic Alert Foundation International
1735 N. Lynn St.
Suite 950
Arlington, VA 22209-2022

National Alliance of Senior Citizens
1700 18th St. NW
Suite 401
Washington, DC 20002
Lobbies state and federal legislatures.

National Asian Pacific Center on Aging*
Melbourne Tower, Suite 914
1511 3rd Ave.
Seattle, WA 98101

National Association for Continence (NAFC)
P.O. Box 8310
Spartanburg, SC 29305-8310
Information:
(800) BLADDER [252-3337]

National Association for Home Care*
228 7th St. SE
Washington, DC 20003
Internet: http://www.nahc.org/

National Association for Human Development
1424 16th St. NW
Suite 102
Washington, DC 20036
Information: (800) 424-5153

National Association for Independent Living
Independent Association
55 City Hall Plaza
Brockton, MA 12401

National Association for Music Therapy
1 Station Plaza
Ossining, NY 10562

National Association for Senior Living
Industries
184 Duke of Gloucester St.
Annapolis, MD 21404-2523
NASLI is a nonprofit association of
companies and organizations who provide
services to older persons. Its aim is to
improve the quality of living environments
available to older Americans through applied
research, counseling, training, and education
of the industry and the general public.

National Association of Activity Professionals
1401 I St. NW
Suite 900
Washington, DC 20005

National Association of Area Agencies on
Aging*
1112 16th St. NW
Suite 100
Washington, DC 20036-4823

National Association of Black Social
Workers, Inc.
8436 West McNichols
Detroit, MI 48221

National Association of Community
Health Centers
1330 New Hampshire Ave NW
Suite 122
Washington, DC 20036

National Association of Counties
Aging Program

440 1st St. NW
8th Floor
Washington, DC 20001
Internet: http://www.naco.org

National Association of Foster Grandparent
Program Directors*
Union/Snyder FGP
Laurelton Center
Box 300
Laurelton, PA 17835

National Association of Meal Programs*
1414 Prince St.
Suite 202
Alexandria, VA 22314

National Association of Nutrition and Aging
Services Programs*
2675 44th St. SW
Suite 305
Grand Rapids, MI 49509

The National Association of Professional
Geriatric Care Managers
1604 North Country Club Rd.
Tucson, AZ 85716

National Association of Retired Federal
Employees*
1533 New Hampshire Ave. NW
Washington, DC 20036
Internet: http://www.narfe.org/

National Association of Retired Senior Volunteer
Program Directors, Inc.*
Audobon Area RSVP
1650 W. 2nd St.
Owensboro, KY 42301

National Association of Senior Companion
Project Directors*
Senior Companion Program
Lutheran Social Service of Minnesota
2414 Park Ave.
Minneapolis, MN 55404

National Association of Social Workers
750 1st St. NE
Suite 700
Washington, DC 20002

National Association of State Units on Aging*
  1225 I St. NW
  Suite 725
  Washington, DC 20005
  Information: (800) 989-6537
  Eldercare Locator: (800) 677-1116
  Information resources on state policies on
  aging. Represents and lobbies for state
  agencies at the federal level.

National Association of the Deaf
  814 Thayer Ave.
  Silver Springs, MD 20910

National Caucus and Center on Black
Aged, Inc.*
  1424 K. St. NW
  Suite 500
  Washington, DC 20005
  Provides comprehensive program of
  coordination, information, and consultative
  services to meet the needs of older African
  Americans to improve their quality of life.

National Center for Vision and Aging
  The Lighthouse, Inc.
  111 E. 59th St.
  New York, NY 10022
  Information and Resource Service:
  (800) 334-5497

National Center on Elder Abuse
  810 1st St. NE
  Suite 500
  Washington, DC 20002-1267
  Internet: http://www.interinc.com/NCEA

National Citizens' Coalition for Nursing
Home Reform
  1424 16th St. NW
  Suite 202
  Washington, DC 20036-2211

National Committee for the Prevention of Elder
Abuse, Inc.
  Medical Center of Central Massachusetts
  Institute on Aging
  119 Belmont St.
  Worcester, MA 01605

National Committee to Preserve Social Security
and Medicare*
  2000 K St. NW
  Suite 800
  Washington, DC 20006
  Internet: http://ncpssm.org
  Senior Flash Hotline (800) 998-0180

National Conference of State Legislatures
  1560 Broadway
  Suite 700
  Denver, CO 80202
  Internet: http://www.ncsl.org

National Consumers League
  1701 K St. NW
  Suite 1200
  Washington, DC 20006
  National Fraud Information Center: (800)
  876-7060
  Internet://www.fraud.org

National Council of Senior Citizens*
  1331 F St. NW
  Washington, DC 20009
  Internet: http://www.ncscinc.org
  Represents and lobbies for the needs of older
  persons. Membership at any age.

The National Council on Aging, Inc.*
  409 3rd St. SW
  Second Floor
  Washington, DC 20024
  Research and service regarding older
  persons.

National Family Caregivers Association
  9621 E. Bexhill Dr.
  Kensington, MD 20895-3104
  Internet: http://www.nfcacares.org
  Information: (800) 896-3650

National Federation of Licensed Practical
Nurses
  1418 Aversboro Rd.
  Garner, NC 27529-4547

National Gerontological Nursing Association
  7250 Parkway Dr.

Suite 510
Hanover, MD 21076
Information: (800) 723-0560

National Hispanic Council on Aging*
2713 Ontario Rd. NW
Suite 200
Washington, DC 20009

National Hospice Organization
1901 N. Moore St.
Suite 901
Arlington, VA 22209
Internet: http://www.nho.org
Hospice Referral Line: (800) 658-8898

National Indian Council on Aging
City Centre
6400 Uptown Blvd. NE
Suite 510W
Albuquerque, NM 87110

National Institute of Senior Centers
c/o National Council on the Aging
409 3rd St. SW
2nd Floor
Washington, DC 20024

National Institute on Adult Daycare
c/o National Council on the Aging
409 3rd St. SW
2nd Floor
Washington, DC 20024

National Interfaith Coalition on Aging
National Council on the Aging
409 3rd St. SW
Suite 200
Washington, DC 20024
Coordinates the involvement of religious
groups in meeting the needs of the elderly.

National League for Nursing
350 Hudson St.
New York, NY 10014
Internet: http://www.nln.org
Information: (800) 669-1659

National Long Term Care Ombudsman
Resource Center

National Citizens' Coalition for Nursing
Home Reform
1424 16th St. NW
Suite 202
Washington, DC 20036-2211

National Mental Health Association
1021 Prince St.
Alexandria, VA 22314-2971
Internet: http://www.nmha.org
Information:
(800) 969-NMHA [969-6642]

National Osteoporosis Foundation*
1150 17th St. NW
Suite 500
Washington, DC 20036-4603
Internet: http://www.nof.org

National Policy Resource Center on Nutrition
and Aging
Florida International University
Department of Dietetics and Nutrition, OE200
Miami, FL 33199

National Resource Center on Long Term Care
National Association of State Units on Aging
1225 I St. NW
Suite 725
Washington, DC 20005

National Retired Teachers Association
Division of AARP
601 E St. NW
Washington, DC 20042
Members once active in an educational
system, public or private.

National Self-Help Clearinghouse
25 W. 43rd St.
Rm. 620
New York, NY 10036

National Senior Service Corps Directors
Associations*
4958 Butterworth Place NW
Washington, DC 20016

National Society to Prevent Blindness
500 E. Remington Rd.

Schaumberg, IL 60173
Center for Sight: (800) 331-2020
Through local societies in many states, it promotes and supports local glaucoma screening programs and provides consultation and information to individuals with eye problems.

National Stroke Association
8480 East Orchard Rd.
Suite 1000
Englewood, CO 80111-5015
Internet: http://www.stroke.org

National Therapeutic Recreation Society
2775 S. Quincy St.
Suite 300
Arlington, VA 22206

National Voluntary Organizations for Independent Living for the Aging (NVOILA)
National Council on Aging
409 3rd St. SW
Suite 200
Washington, DC 20024

North American Association of Jewish Homes and Housing for the Aging*
316 Pennsylvania Ave SE
Suite 402
Washington, DC 20003-1175

Retired Officers Association
201 N. Washington St.
Alexandria, VA 22314-2529
Internet: http://www.troa.org
Represents the needs of retired U.S. military officers.

The Salvation Army
National Headquarters
615 Slaters Ln.
Alexandria, VA 22313
Its services for older people include educational, cultural, recreational, and religious activities, in addition to camping and limited residence facilities.

Senior Action in a Gay Environment (SAGE)
208 W. 13th St.

New York, NY 10011
Serves the older gay community.

SeniorNet
One Kearney St.
3rd Floor
San Francisco, CA 94108
Internet: http://www.seniornet.org
Information: (800)747-6848
National nonprofit organization teaches older people computer skills, and maintains on-line network.

Sexuality Information and Education Council of the United States
130 W. 42nd St.
Suite 350
New York, NY 10036-7802
Internet://www.siecus.org
Part of its program is to provide sex information to older people.

Society for Neuroscience
11 Dupont Circle NW
Suite 500
Washington, DC 20036
Internet: http://www.sfa.org

United Auto Workers Retired Members Department*
8731 E. Jefferson Ave.
Detroit, MI 48214

United Seniors Health Cooperative
1331 H St. NW
Suite 500
Washington, DC 20005-4706
Internet: http://www.mgt.com/ushc

U.S. Conference of Mayors
1620 Eye St. NW
Washington, DC 20006
Internet: http://www.usmayors.org/uscm

* Denotes membership in the Leadership Council of Aging Organizations, 1997. The LCAO is a voluntary coalition of national organizations concerned with the well-being of the elderly and committed to representing the elderly and the elderly's interests in the federal policy arena. The coalition is chaired on a rotating basis by a different member organization each year.

ORGANIZATIONS CONCERNED WITH OLDER WOMEN

AARP Women's Initiative
American Association of Retired Persons
1909 K. St. NW
Washington, DC 20049

American College of Obstetricians and
Gynecologists
409 12th St. SW
Washington, DC 20024-2188
Internet: http://www.acog.com

International Menopause Society
Avenue de Broqueville 116
Boîte 9
B-1200 Brussels, Belgium

National Action Forum for Midlife and Older
Women
Box 816
Stony Brook, NY 11790-0609

National Black Women's Health Project
1237 Abernathy Blvd. SW
Atlanta, GA 30310

National Organization for Women
1000 16th St. NW
Suite 700
Washington, DC 20006
Internet: http://www.now.org

National Policy and Resource Center on Women
and Aging
Heller School MS 035
Brandeis University
P.O. Box 9110
Waltham, MA 02254-9110

National Women's Health Network
514 10th St. NW
Suite 400
Washington, DC 20004

National Women's Health Resource Center
2425 L. St. NW
Washington, DC 20037

The National Women's Political Caucus
1211 Connecticut Ave. NW
Suite 425
Washington, DC 20036
Internet: http://www.feminist.com/nwpc.html

North American Menopause Society
P.O. Box 94527
Cleveland, OH 44101
Internet: http://www.menopause.org

Older Women's League*
666 11th St. NW
Suite 700
Washington, DC 20001
Chapter Information:
(800) TAKE-OWL [825-3695]

Wider Opportunities for Women and the
National Commission on Working Women
815 15th St. NW
Suite 916
Washington, DC 20005

Women's Bureau
U.S. Dept. of Labor
200 Constitution Ave. NW
Room S-3002
Washington, DC 20210-0002
Internet: http://www.dol.gov/dol/wb
Information: (800) 827-5335

Women Work!
National Network for Women's Employment
1625 K. St. NW
Suite 300
Washington, DC 20006

LEGAL RESOURCES FOR THE ELDERLY

Black Elderly Legal Assistance Support Project
National Bar Association
1225 11th St. NW
Washington, DC 20001

The Center for Social Gerontology
2307 Shelby Ave.
Ann Arbor, MI 48103
Focus is on legal rights, guardianship and
alternative protective services, and delivery of
legal services.

Commission on the Legal Problems of the Elderly
American Bar Association
740 15th St. NW
Washington, DC 20005-1009
Internet:
http://www.abnet.org/elderly/home.html
A 15 member interdisciplinary commission which focuses on Social Security, housing, long-term care, age discrimination, and improving the availability of legal services.

Eldercare Initiative in Consumer Law
National Consumer Law Center, Inc.
18 Tremont St.
Suite 400
Boston, MA 02108

Legal Counsel for the Elderly, Inc.
American Association for Retired Persons
601 E St. NW
Washington, DC 20049

Legal Services for the Elderly
130 W. 42nd St.
17th Floor
New York, NY 10036

The National Academy of Elder Law Attorneys, Inc.
1604 N. Country Club Rd.
Tucson, AZ 85716
Internet:
http://www.primenet.com/~rbf/naela.html
Provides information, education, networking, and assistance to attorneys, bar organizations, and other individuals or groups advising elderly clients and their families.

National Clearinghouse for Legal Services, Inc.
205 W. Monroe St.
2nd Floor

Chicago, IL 60606-5013
Internet: http://nclsplp.com

National Eldercare Legal Assistance Project
National Senior Citizens Law Center
1815 H St. NW
Suite 700
Washington, DC 20006

National Senior Citizens Law Center*
1815 H St. NW
Suite 700
Washington, DC 20006
Internet: http://www.nsclc.org
A national support center, specializing in the legal problems of the older poor, funded by the Legal Services Corporation, the Administration on Aging, and the Community Services Administration. Its principal function is to provide support services to legal service attorneys and other publicly funded programs providing legal assistance to older persons.

Pension Rights Center
918 16th St. NW
Suite 704
Washington, DC 20006
Offers pension attorney referral service.

Selected Legal Reference Books

Arnason, S., Rosenzweig, E., & Koski, A. (1995). *The legal rights of the elderly.* New York: Practicing Law Institute.

Frolik, L. A., & Brown, M. C. (1992, supplemented semi-annually). *Advising the elderly client.* Boston: Warren, Gorham & Lamont.

Strauss, P. J., & Lederman, N. M. (1996). *The elder law handbook.* New York: Facts on File, Inc.

GOVERNMENT PROGRAMS FOR THE ELDERLY

VOLUNTEER AND EMPLOYMENT
PROGRAMS FOR OLDER PEOPLE

FEDERAL, CONGRESSIONAL, AND
EXECUTIVE OFFICES CONCERNED
WITH OLDER PEOPLE

STATE AND LOCAL GOVERNMENT OFFICES
CONCERNED WITH OLDER PEOPLE

VOLUNTEER AND EMPLOYMENT PROGRAMS FOR OLDER PEOPLE

VOLUNTEER EMPLOYMENT PROGRAM	SPONSOR	PURPOSE	ADDRESS
RSVP (Retired Senior Volunteer Program)	Corporation for National Service—National Senior Service Corps	Funds for volunteer programs in public and nonprofit institutions; volunteers reimbursed for expenses	RSVP, Corporation for National Service, 1201 New York Ave. NW, Washington, DC 20525; Internet: http://www.cns.gov; Information: (800) 424-8867
Foster Grandparent Program	Corporation for National Service—National Senior Service Corps	Foster grandparents serve 20 hours a week caring for mentally disabled, physically disabled, or troubled children and young people.	Foster Grandparent Program, Corporation for National Service, 1201 New York Ave. NW, Washington, DC 20525; Internet: http://www.cns.gov; Information: (800) 424-8867
Senior Companions Program	Corporation for National Service—National Senior Service Corps	Senior Companions serve 20 hours a week assisting seniors who have difficulty with daily living tasks.	Senior Companions Program, Corporation for National Service, 1201 New York Ave. NW, Washington, DC 20525;

(Continued)

VOLUNTEER EMPLOYMENT PROGRAM	SPONSOR	PURPOSE	ADDRESS
			Internet: http://www.cns.gov; Information: (800) 424-8867
AmeriCorps*VISTA (Volunteers in Service to America)	Corporation for National Service	Adult volunteers of all ages serve in disadvantaged communities in the United States.	AmeriCorps*VISTA, Corporation for National Service, 1201 New York Ave. NW, Washington, DC 20525; Internet: http://www.cns.gov; Information: (800) 942-2677
Peace Corps	Independent federal agency	Overseas service	Peace Corps, 1990 K St. NW, Washington, DC 10526; Internet: http://www.peacecorps.gov; Information (800) 424-8580.
Older American Act Programs	Administration on Aging	Volunteers augment paid staff at local aging agencies, help with senior meal programs, and/or deliver meals to homebound elderly.	Contact local Area Agency on Aging or call AoA's Eldercare Locator: (800) 677-1116.
SCORE (Service Corps of Retired Executives) Association	U.S. Department of Commerce, Small Business Administration	Retired businesspersons advise novices in business.	SCORE, 409 3rd St. SW, 4th Floor, Washington, DC 20024; Internet: http://www.sbaonline.sba.gov/SCORE/
Senior Community Service Employment Program (SCSEP)	U.S. Department of Labor (state and territorial governments and 10 national sponsors that administer this program, see below)	Part-time employment opportunities for low-income persons aged 55 and older, also promotes transition to unsubsidized employment.	Senior Community Service Employment Program, 200 Constitution Ave. NW, Room C4524, Washington, DC 20210
Senior Environmental Employment Program	Environmental Protection Agency and Administration on Aging	Provides funding for people aged 55 and older to work with EPA Pollution abatement and control programs.	Senior Environmental Employment Program, 401 M St. SW, 3711 Mall, Washington DC 20460.

VOLUNTEER EMPLOYMENT PROGRAM	SPONSOR	PURPOSE	ADDRESS
Volunteers in Parks	National Park Service	Volunteers in national parks	Volunteers in Parks, National Park Service, P.O. Box 37127, Washington, DC 20013-7127.
International Executive Service Corps (IESC)	Independent organization supported by government and nongovernment funds	Overseas service by executives	International Executive Service Corps (IESC), 333 Ludlow St., Stamford, CT 06902

SENIOR COMMUNITY SERVICE EMPLOYMENT PROGRAM (SCSEP) NATIONAL SPONSORS

1. Green Thumb, Inc., Senior Community Service Employment Program, 2000 North 14th St., Suite 800, Arlington, VA 22201
2. National Senior Citizen's Education and Research Center, Senior AIDES, 8403 Colesville Rd., Suite 1200, Silver Spring, MD 20910
3. National Council on the Aging, Inc., Senior Community Service Employment Program, 409 3rd St. SW, Suite 200, Washington, DC 20024
4. American Association of Retired Persons, Senior Community Service Employment Program, 601 E. St. NW, Washington, DC 20049
5. Asociacion Nacional por Personas Mayores, Senior Community Service Employment Program, 3325 Wilshire Blvd., Suite 800, Los Angeles, CA 90010
6. National Caucus/Center on Black Aged, Inc., Senior Community Service Employment Program, 1424 K. St. NW, Suite 500, Washington, DC 90010
7. National Indian Council on Aging, Inc., Senior Community Service Employment Program, 6400 Uptown Blvd. NE, City Center, Suite 510 West, Albuquerque, NM 87100
8. National Asian Pacific Center on Aging, Senior Community Service Employment Program, Melbourne Tower, 1511 3rd Ave., Suite 914, Seattle, WA 98101
9. National Urban League, Inc., Seniors in Community Service Program, 500 E. 82nd St., 11th Floor, New York, NY 10021
10. USDA—Forest Service, Senior Community Service Employment Program, Human Resource Programs, 1621 N. Kent St., Room 1010, RP-E, Rosslyn, VA 22209

FEDERAL, CONGRESSIONAL, AND EXECUTIVE OFFICES CONCERNED WITH OLDER PEOPLE

The following is a selected list of the many federal offices that deal with older people. For more information contact the Administration on Aging, or see the *Directory of Aging Resources,* published yearly by Business Publishers, Inc. in Silver Spring, MD. Information can also be obtained by contacting Federal Information Centers (FICs), part of the General Service Administration. If your local phone directory does not list a Federal Information Center, call (301) 722-9000, or reach their home page (http://www.gsa.gov/et/fic-firs/fichome.htm) for a list of local phone numbers. Several areas have toll-free numbers available.

Legislative Branch

1. U.S. Senate (http://www.senate.gov)

   a. U.S. Senate Special Committee on Aging
      G31 Dirksen Senate Office Building
      Washington, DC 20510
      Internet: http://www.senate.gov/~aging/

   b. U.S. Senate Committee of Labor and Human Resources Special Subcommittee on Aging
      615 Hart Senate Office Building
      Washington, DC 20510

   c. U.S. Senate Finance Committee Health Subcommittee
      219 Dirksen Senate Office Building
      Washington, DC 20510

   d. U.S. Senate Finance Committee Social Security and Family Policy Subcommittee
      219 Dirksen Senate Office Building
      Washington, DC 20510

   e. U.S. Senate Veterans' Affairs Committee
      412 Russell Senate Office Building
      Washington, DC 20510

   f. U.S. Senate Appropriations Committee Subcommittee on Labor, Health, Human Services, and Education
      184 Dirksen Senate Office Building
      Washington, DC 20510

2. U.S. House of Representatives (http://www.house.gov)

   a. Education and the Workforce Committee Early Childhood, Youth and Families Subcommittee (has jurisdiction over Older Americans Act programs)
      2181 Rayburn House Office Building
      Washington, DC 20515

   b. Appropriations Committee Subcommittee on Labor, Health, Human Services and Education
      2358 Rayburn House Office Building
      Washington, DC 20515

   c. Veteran's Affairs Committee
      335 Cannon House Office Building
      Washington, DC 20515-6335

   d. Ways and Means Committee

      I. Health Subcommittee
         1136 Longworth House Office Building
         Washington, DC 20515

      II. Human Resources Subcommittee
         B317 Rayburn House Office Building
         Washington, DC 20515

      III. Social Security Subcommittee
         B317 Rayburn House Office Building
         Washington, DC 20515

   e. House Older Americans Caucus

   f. House Congressional Social Security Caucus
      2407 Rayburn House Office Building
      Washington, DC 20515

Executive Branch

1. U.S. Department of Health and Human Services
   200 Independence Ave. SW

Washington, DC 20201
Internet: http://www.dhhs.gov

a. Administration on Aging
Department of Health and Human
Services
330 Independence Ave. SW
Washington, DC 20201
Internet: http://www.aoa.dhhs.gov
Eldercare Locator: (800) 677-1116

I. 10 AoA Regional Offices

II. 57 State Agencies (or Units) on
Aging (see below)

III. 660 Area Agencies on Aging

IV. Title VI Programs for Older
Indians, Alaska Natives, and Native
Hawaiians

V. AoA Supported Resource Centers

(1) National Resource Centers for
Long-Term Care
National Resource Center on
Long Term Care
National Association of State
Units on Aging
1225 I St. NW
Suite 725
Washington, DC 20005

(2) National Long-Term Care
Omsbudman Resource Center
National Citizens' Coalition for
Nursing Home Reform
1424 16th St. NW
Suite 202
Washington, DC 20036-2211

(3) National Center on Elder Abuse
810 1st St. NE
Suite 500
Washington, DC 20002-1267
Internet:
http://www.interinc.com/NCEA

(4) National Policy and Resource
Center on Nutrition and Aging
Florida International University
Department of Dietetics and

Nutrition, OE200
Miami, FL 33199

(5) National Policy and Resource
Center on Women and Aging
Heller School MS 035
Brandeis University
P.O. Box 9110
Waltham, MA 02254-9110

(6) National Minority Aging
Organizations

(7) National Resource Centers for
Older Indians, Alaska Natives,
and Native Hawaiians

VI. Legal Assistance for the Elderly
Support Centers

VII. National Aging Information Center
(NAIC)
Administration on Aging
330 Independence Ave. SW
Room 4656
Washington, DC 20201
Internet: http://www.ageinfo.org

b. Agency for Health Care Policy and
Research (AHCPR)
Department of Health and Human
Services
2101 E. Jefferson St.
Suite 600
Rockville, MD 20852
Internet: http://www.ahcpr.gov

c. Health Care Financing Administration
(HCFA) (Administers Medicare and
Medicaid)
P.O. Box 340
Columbia, MD 21045
Medicare Hotline: (800) 638-6833
Internet: http://www.hcfa.gov

d. National Institutes of Health
Division of Public Information
9000 Rockville Pike
Bethesda, MD 20892
Internet: http://www.nih.gov

I. National Institute on Aging (NIA)
Public Information Office

National Institutes of Health
9000 Rockville Pike
Building 31, Room 5C27
Bethesda, MD 20892-2292
Internet: http:www.nih.gov/nia
Information Clearinghouse: (800)
222-2225, TTY (800) 222-4225

II. National Institute of Mental Health
(NIMH)
Public Affairs
National Institutes of Health
5600 Fishers Lane
Room 7C-99
Rockville, MD 20857
Internet: http://www.nimh.nih.gov

III. National Cancer Institute
Office of Cancer Communications
Building 31, Room 10A07
31 Center Dr. MSC 2580
Bethesda, MD 20892-2580
Internet: http://www.nci.nih.gov
Cancer Information Service:
(800) 4-CANCER [422-6237]

IV. National Eye Institute
Information Office
900 Rockville Pike
Building 31, Room 6A32
Bethesda, MD 20892-2510
Internet: http://www.nei.nih.org

V. National Institute of Arthritis and
Musculoskeletal and Skin Diseases
31 Center Dr., MSC 2350
Building 31, Rm. 4C32
Bethesda, MD 20892-2350
Internet: http://www.nih.gov/niams

VI. National Institute on Deafness and
Other Communication Disorders
National Institutes of Health
31 Center Dr., MSC 2320
Bethesda, MD 20892
Internet: http://www.nih.gov/nidcd

e. Federal Council on Aging (Advises the
President, the Secretary of Health and
Human Services, the Assistant Secretary
on Aging, and Congress on matters

relating to the needs of older
Americans.)
Wilbur J. Cohen Building
330 Independence Ave., SW
Room 4661
Washington, DC 20210

f. Substance Abuse and Mental Health
Services Administration (SAMHSA)
Public Health Service
Parklawn Building
5600 Fishers Ln.
Room 12-105
Rockville, MD 20857
Internet: http://www.samhsa.gov

I. Center for Mental Health Services
Internet: http://www.samhsa.gov/
cmhs/cmhs.htm
National Mental Health Services
Knowledge Exchange Program
(KEN)
P.O. Box 424901
Washington, DC 20015
Information: (800) 789-2647
Internet: http://www.mentalhealth.org

II. Center for Substance Abuse
Prevention (CSAP)
Internet: http://www.samhsa.gov/
csap/csap.htm

III. Center for Substance Abuse
Treatment (CSAT)
Internet: http://www.samhsa.gov/
csat/csat.htm
National Drug and Alcohol
Treatment Routing Service:
(800) 662-HELP (4357)

IV. National Clearinghouse for Alcohol
and Drug Information (NCADI)
P.O. Box 2345
Rockville, MD 20847-2345
Internet: http://www.health.org
Information and Publications:
(800) 729-6686

V. National Resource Center for the
Prevention of Alcohol, Tobacco,
Other Drug Abuse and Mental

Illness in Women
Information: (800) 354-8824

g. Health Resources and Services
Administration
Public Health Service
Parklawn Building
5600 Fishers Ln.
Room 14-05
Rockville, MD 20857
Internet: http://www.hrsa.dhhs.gov

I. The Interdisciplinary, Geriatrics, and
Allied Health Branch (Supports
Geriatric Education Centers)
Division of Associated, Dental, and
Public Health Professions
Bureau of Health Professions
Health Resources and Services
Administration
5600 Fishers Lane—Room 8-103
Rockville, MD 20857

2. Department of Veterans Affairs
Internet: http://www.va.gov
Benefits Information: (800) 827-1000

a. Veterans Health Administration
810 Vermont Ave., NW
Washington, DC 20420

I. Office of Geriatrics and Extended
Care
Department of Veterans Affairs
810 Vermont Ave. NW
Mail Code 114
Washington, DC 20420

3. Social Security Administration
Office of Public Inquiries
6401 Security Blvd.
Room 4-C-5 Annex
Baltimore, MD 21235
Internet: http://www.ssa.gov
Information: (800) 772-1213

4. Pension Benefit Guaranty Corporation
1200 K St. NW
Washington, DC 20005
Internet: http://www.pbgc.gov
Information: (800) 400-7242
If a pension plan is terminated or about to

be terminated, information about payment
of benefits can be obtained here.

5. U.S. Department of Agriculture
14th St. and Independence Ave. SW
Washington, DC 20250
Internet: http://www.usda.gov

a. Nutrition Program for the Elderly
Food Distribution Division
Food and Consumer Services
Park Office Center
3101 Park Center Dr.
Room 503
Alexandria, VA 22302

b. Human Nutrition Research Center
on Aging
711 Washington St.
Room 911
Boston, MA 02111

c. Food Stamp Program
Food and Consumer Services
Park Office Center
3101 Park Center Dr.
Room 710
Alexandria, VA 22302

d. Child and Adult Care Food Program
Child Nutrition Division
Park Office Center
3101 Park Center Dr.
Room 1017
Alexandria, VA 22302

6. U.S. Department of Housing and Urban
Development
451 7th St. SW
Washington, DC 20401
Information: (800) 669-9777
Internet: http://www.hud.gov

a. Housing for the Elderly Program
(Section 202)
Housing for the Elderly and
Handicapped People Division
Elderly and Assisted Housing Office
Federal Housing Administration
451 7th St. SW
Room 6120
Washington, DC 20401

b. Section 8 Housing for Very Low-Income
Families
Moderate Rehabilitation Division
Elderly and Assisted Housing Office
Federal Housing Administration
470 L'Enfant Plaza East SW
Room 3201
Washington, DC 20024

7. Department of Commerce
14th St. and Constitution Ave. NW
Washington, DC 20230
Information: (800) 424-5197
Internet: http://www.doc.gov

a. U.S. Bureau of the Census
U.S. Department of Commerce
Washington, DC 20233
Internet: http://www.census.gov

8. Department of Education
440 Maryland Ave. SW
Washington, DC 20202
Internet: http://www.ed.gov

a. Adult Education and Literacy Division

9. Equal Employment Opportunity
Commission
1801 L St. NW
Washington, DC 20507

a. Age Discrimination in Employment Act
(ADEA) Division
1801 L St. NW
Suite 6017
Washington, DC 20507

10. U.S. Department of Justice
10th St. and Constitution Ave. NW
Washington, DC 20530
Information: (800) 546-3224
Internet: http://www.usdoj.gov

a. Civil Rights of Institutionalized Persons
Special Litigation Section
Civil Rights Division
P.O. Box 66400
Washington, DC 20035-6400

b. Protection of Voting Rights
Voting Section
Civil Rights Division

P.O. Box 66128
Washington, DC 20038-6128

11. U.S. Department of Labor
200 Constitution Ave. NW
Washington, DC 20210
Internet: http://www.dol.gov

a. Pension and Welfare Benefits
Administration (PWBA)
U.S. Dept. of Labor
200 Constitution Ave. NW
Room S-2524
Washington, DC 20210
Internet: http://www.dol.gov/dol/pwba

b. Senior Community Service Employment
Program
U.S. Dept. of Labor
200 Constitution Ave. NW
Room C-4524
Washington, DC 20210

c. Job Training Partnership Act Programs
U.S. Dept. of Labor
200 Constitution Ave. NW
Room N-4459
Washington, DC 20210

d. Women's Bureau
U.S. Dept. of Labor
200 Constitution Ave. NW
Room S-3002
Washington, DC 20210-0002
Internet: http://www.dol.gov/dol/wb
Information: (800) 827-5335

12. U.S. Department of the Treasury

a. Internal Revenue Service
Office of Public Affairs
1111 Constitution Ave. NW
Washington, DC 20224
Internet: www.irs.ustreas.gov

I. Tax Counseling for the Elderly
Taxpayer Services Branch
Internal Revenue Service
1111 Constitution Ave. NW
Washington, DC 20224
Free tax counseling and filing is
available for people aged 60 and older.

Contact local IRS office or call AARP toll-free at (888) 227-7669.

13. General Service Administration (GSA)

   a. Consumer Information Center
   P.O. Box 100
   Pueblo, CO 81009
   Internet: http://www.pueblo.gsa.gov/

14. Railroad Retirement Board
   844 N. Rush St.
   Chicago, IL 60611-2092
   Information: (800) 772-4258

15. Office of Personnel Management
   Retirement Operations Center
   Boyers, PA 16017
   Internet: http://www.opm.gov/retire

STATE AND LOCAL GOVERNMENT OFFICES CONCERNED WITH OLDER PEOPLE

1. National Association of Counties, Aging Program
   440 1st St. NW
   8th Floor
   Washington, DC 20001
   Internet: http://www.naco.org

2. U.S. Conference of Mayors
   1620 Eye St. NW
   Washington, DC 20006
   Internet: http://www.usmayors.org/uscm

3. National Association of State Units on Aging
   1225 I St. NW
   Suite 725
   Washington, DC 20005
   Information: (800) 989-6537

4. National Conference of State Legislatures
   1560 Broadway
   Suite 700
   Denver, CO 80202
   Internet: http://www.ncsl.org

5. State Agencies (or Units) on Aging
   All states have offices on aging that help coordinate services for older persons. The following is a list of the names and addresses of state agencies that should help in locating local Area Agencies on Aging.

Alabama
Alabama Commission on Aging
RSA Plaza, Suite 470
770 Washington Avenue
Montgomery, Al, 36130

Alaska
Alaska Commission on Aging
Division of Senior Services
Department of Administration
P.O. Box 110209
Juneau, AK 99811-0209

Arizona
Aging and Adult Administration
Department of Economic Security
1789 West Jefferson—950A Street
Phoenix, AZ 85007

Arkansas
Division of Aging and Adult Services
Arkansas Department of Human Services
P.O. Box 1437, Slot 1412
1417 Donaghey Plaza South
Little Rock, AR 72203-1437

California
California Department of Aging
1600 K Street
Sacramento, CA 95814

Colorado
Aging and Adult Services
Department of Social Services
110 16th St., Suite 200
Denver, CO 80202-4147

Connecticut
Community Services
Division of Elderly Services
25 Sigourney Street
Hartford, CT 06106-5033

Delaware
Delaware Department of Health
and Social Services
Division of Services for Aging and Adults
with Physical Disabilities
1901 North DuPont Highway
New Castle, DE 19720

District of Columbia
District of Columbia Office on Aging
441 4th St. NW, Suite 900 South
Washington DC 20001
(202) 724-5622

Florida
Department of Elder Affairs
4040 Esplanade Way
Tallahassee, FL 32399-7000

Georgia
Division of Aging Services
Department of Human Resources
2 Peachtree St. NE, 18th Floor
Atlanta, GA 30303

Guam
Division of Senior Citizens
Department of Public Health
& Social Services
P.O. Box 2816
Agana, Guam 96932

Hawaii
Hawaii Executive Office on Aging
335 Merchant Street, Room 241
Honolulu, HI 96813

Idaho
Idaho Commission on Aging
Room 108—Statehouse
Boise, ID 83720

Illinois
Illinois Department on Aging
421 East Capitol Ave., Suite 100
Springfield, IL
62701-1789

Indiana
Division of Disability, Aging and Rehabili-
tative Services
Family and Social Services Administration
Bureau of Aging and In-Home Services
402 W. Washington St.
Indianapolis, IN 46027-7083

Iowa
Department of Elder Affairs
Jewett Building—Suite 236
914 Grand Ave.
Des Moines, IA 50319

Kansas
Department on Aging
Docking State Office Building, Room 150
915 SW Harrison
Topeka, KS 66612-1505

Kentucky
Kentucky Division of Aging Services
Department of Social Services
275 East Main Street, 6 West
Frankfort, KY 40621

Louisiana
Governor's Office of Elderly Affairs
P.O. Box 80374
Baton Rouge, LA 70898-0374

Maine
Bureau of Elder and Adult Services
Department of Human Services
35 Anthony Ave.
State House—Station #11
Augusta, ME 04333

Maryland
Maryland Office on Aging
State Office Building, Room 1004
301 West Preston St.
Baltimore, MD 21201-2374

Massachusetts
Massachusetts Executive Office of Elder
Affairs

One Ashburton Place, 5th Floor
Boston, MA 02108

Michigan
Office of Services to the Aging
P.O. Box 30026
Lansing, MI 48909

Minnesota
Minnesota Board on Aging
444 Lafayette Road
St. Paul, MN 55155-3843

Mississippi
Division of Aging and Adult Services
750 State Street
Jackson, MS 39202

Missouri
Division on Aging
Department of Social Services
P.O. Box 1337
615 Howerton Court
Jefferson City, MO 65102-1337

Montana
Senior and Long Term Care Division
Department of Public Health and Human
Services
P.O. Box 4210
Helena, MT 59604

Nebraska
Office on Aging
P.O. Box 95044
301 Centennial Mall South
Lincoln, NE 68509-5044

Nevada
Nevada Division for Aging Services
Department of Human Resources
340 North 11th St., Suite 203
Las Vegas, NV 89101

New Hampshire
Division of Elderly and Adult Services
State Office Park South

115 Pleasant St., Annex Bldg. #1
Concord, NH 03301-6501

New Jersey
New Jersey Division on Aging
Department of Community Affairs
101 South Broad Street—CN 807
Trenton, New Jersey 08625-0807
1(800) 792-8820

New Mexico
State Agency on Aging
La Villa Rivera Building, Ground Floor
228 East Palace Avenue
Santa Fe, NM 87501

New York
New York State Office for the Aging
2 Empire State Plaza
Albany, NY 12223-1251
1(800) 342-9871

North Carolina
Division of Aging
CB 29531
693 Palmer Dr.
Raleigh, NC 27626-0531

North Dakota
Department of Human Services
Aging Services Division
600 South 2nd Street, Suite IC
Bismarck, ND 58504

North Mariana Islands
Office on Aging
Department of Community & Cultural
Affairs
Civic Center
Commonwealth of the Northern Mariana
Islands
Saipan, MP 96950

Ohio
Ohio Department of Aging
50 W. Broad St., 8th Floor
Columbus, OH 43266-0501

Oklahoma
Services for the Aging
Department of Human Services
P.O. Box 25352
Oklahoma City, OK 73125

Oregon
Senior and Disabled Services Division
500 Summer Street NE, 2nd Floor
Salem, OR 97310-1015

Palau
State Agency on Aging
Republic of Palau
Koror, PW 96940

Pennsylvania
Pennsylvania Department of Aging
Commonwealth of Pennsylvania
400 Market St., 6th Floor
Harrisburg, PA 17101-2301

Puerto Rico
Commonwealth of Puerto Rico
Governor's Office of Elderly Affairs
Call Box 50063
Old San Juan Station, PR 00902

Rhode Island
Department of Elderly Affairs
160 Pine Street
Providence, RI 02903-3708

American Samoa
Agency on Aging and Food and Nutrition
Services (AAFNS)
Government of American Samoa
Pago Pago, American Samoa 96799

South Carolina
South Carolina Division on Aging
202 Arbor Lake Drive, Suite 301
Columbia, SC 29223-4535

South Dakota
Office of Adult Services and Aging
Richard F. Kneip Building

700 Governors Drive
Pierre, SD 57501-2291

Tennessee
Commission on Aging
706 Church Street—Suite 201
Nashville, TN 37243-0860

Texas
Texas Department on Aging
P.O. Box 12786 Capitol Station
Austin, TX 78711

Utah
Division of Aging & Adult Services
Box 45500
120 North 200 West
Salt Lake City, UT 84145-0500

Vermont
Vermont Department of Aging
and Disabilities
Waterbury Complex
103 South Main St.
Waterbury, VT 05676

Virginia
Virginia Department for the Aging
700 East Franklin Street, 10th Floor
Richmond, VA 23219-2327

Virgin Islands
Virgin Islands Department of Human
Services
Knud Hansen Complex, Building A
1303 Hospital Ground
Charlotte Amalie, VI 00840

Washington
Aging and Adult Services Administration
Department of Social & Health Services
P.O. Box 45050
Olympia, WA 98504-5050

West Virginia
West Virginia Commission on Aging
Holly Grove—State Capitol

1900 Kanawha Boulevard East
Charleston, WV 25305-0160

Wisconsin
Bureau on Aging
Department of Health and Social Services
P.O. Box 7851
Madison, WI 53707

Wyoming
Department of Health
Division on Aging
117 Hathaway Building—Room 139
Cheyenne, WY 82002-0480

TRAINING AND EDUCATION
IN GERONTOLOGY AND GERIATRICS

EDUCATIONAL ASSOCIATIONS

SOURCES OF INFORMATION ON
CLINICAL GERIATRIC PSYCHIATRY
TRAINING OPPORTUNITIES

ACCREDITED PROGRAMS IN
GERIATRIC PSYCHIATRY

GERIATRIC EDUCATION CENTERS

ALZHEIMER'S DISEASE
RESEARCH CENTERS

GERIATRIC RESEARCH, EDUCATION,
AND CLINICAL CENTERS (GRECC)

EDUCATIONAL ASSOCIATIONS

Association for Gerontology Education
in Social Work (AGE-SW)
School of Social Work
University of Maryland at Baltimore
525 W. Redwood St.
Baltimore, MD 21201-1777
Internet:
http://www.cs.umd.edu/users/conn

Association for Gerontology in
Higher Education (AGHE)
1001 Connecticut Ave. NW
Suite 410
Washington, DC 20036-5504

For information on schools offering course work
in gerontology, see *The National Directory of
Educational Programs in Gerontology and Geriatrics* (contact AGHE for latest edition), or for
a small fee they will conduct a search of their
National Database on Gerontology in Higher
Education.

SOURCES OF INFORMATION
ON CLINICAL GERIATRIC PSYCHIATRY
TRAINING OPPORTUNITIES

American Board of Psychiatry and
Neurology, Inc.
Committee on Certification in Added
Qualification in Geriatric Psychiatry
500 Lake Cook Rd.
Suite 335
Deerfield, IL 60015

American Medical Students Association
Geriatric Health Task Force
1902 Association Drive
Reston, VA 22091
Internet: http://www.amsa.org

National Institute of Mental Health
Mental Disorders of the Aging Research Branch
5600 Fishers Lane
Rockville, MD 20857

Department of Veterans Affairs
Office of Geriatrics and Extended Care
810 Vermont Ave. NW

Mail Code 114
Washington, DC 20420

ACCREDITED PROGRAMS
IN GERIATRIC PSYCHIATRY

Alabama
University of Alabama Medical Center Geriatric
Psychiatry Program
University of Alabama at Birmingham
1713 6th Ave. South
CPM 253
Birmingham, AL 35233-0018
Participating Institutions:
University of Alabama School of Medicine
University of Alabama Hospital
Veterans Affairs Medical Center (Birmingham)

California
Stanford University Geriatric Psychiatry Program
Stanford University
101 Quarry Rd.
Stanford, CA 94305
Participating Institutions:
Stanford University School of Medicine
Stanford University Hospital

UCLA Medical Center Geriatric Psychiatry
Program
UCLA Neuropsychiatry Institute
760 Westwood Plaza
Los Angeles, CA 90024-1759
Participating Institutions:
UCLA School of Medicine
Veterans Affairs Medical Center
(West Los Angeles)
Veterans Affairs Medical Center (Sepulveda)
UCLA Neuropsychiatric Hospital

University of California (San Diego) Geriatric
Psychiatry Program
University of California, San Diego, School of
Medicine
9500 Gilman Drive, 9116A
La Jolla, CA 92093-9116

Participating Institutions:
University of California, San Diego, School of
Medicine
University of California, San Diego, Medical
Center
Veterans Affairs Medical Center (San Diego)

Florida
University of Florida Geriatric Psychiatry
Program
University of Florida Health Science Center
P.O. Box 100256
Gainesville, FL 32610
Participating Institutions:
University of Florida College of Medicine
Shands Hospital at the University of Florida
Veterans Affairs Medical Center (Gainesville)
University of Florida College of Medicine

University of Miami—Jackson Memorial
Medical Center Geriatric Psychiatry Program
University of Miami School of Medicine
1400 NW 10th Ave.
Suite 702
Miami, FL 33136
Participating Institutions:
University of Miami School of Medicine
Mount Sinai Medical Center of Greater Miami
University of Miami—Jackson Memorial
Medical Center
Miami Jewish Home and Hospital for the Aged

University of South Florida Geriatric Psychiatry
Program
TGH University Psychiatry Center
3515 E. Fletcher Ave.
Tampa, FL 33613
Participating Institutions:
University of South Florida College of Medicine
James A. Haley Veterans Hospital
TGH University Psychiatry Center

Georgia
Emory University Geriatric Psychiatry Program
The Emory Clinic at Wesley Woods

1841 Clifton Rd.
Atlanta, GA 30329
Participating Institutions:
Emory University School of Medicine
Emory University Hospital
Wesley Woods Geriatric Hospital

Hawaii
University of Hawaii Geriatric Psychiatry
Program
University of Hawaii
1356 Lusitana St.
4th Floor
Honolulu, HI 96813
Participating Institutions:
University of Hawaii at Manoa
Hawaii State Hospital
University of Hawaii John A. Burns School of
Medicine
VA Regional Office—Outpatient Clinic
(Honolulu)

Illinois
McGaw Medical Center of Northwestern
University Geriatric Psychiatry Program
McGaw Medical Center of Northwestern
University
446 E. Ontario
Suite 840
Chicago, IL 60611
Participating Institutions:
Northwestern University Medical School
Northwestern Memorial Hospital

Indiana
Indiana University School of Medicine Geriatric
Psychiatry Program
Indiana University School of Medicine
541 Clinical Dr.
Room 289
Indianapolis, IN 46202-5111
Participating Institutions:
Indiana University School of Medicine
William N. Wishard Memorial Hospital
Richard L. Boudebush Veterans Affairs Medical
Center
Clarian Indiana University Hospital

Kansas
University of Kansas (Wichita) Geriatric
Psychiatry Program
University of Kansas School of Medicine—
Wichita
1010 N. Kansas
Wichita, KS 67214-3199
Participating Institutions:
University of Kansas School of Medicine—
Wichita
Via Christi Regional Medical Center—St.
Francis
Via Christi Regional Medical Center—St. Joseph

Louisiana
Louisiana State University Geriatric Psychiatry
Program
Louisiana State University Medical Center
1542 Tulane Ave.
New Orleans, LA 70112
Participating Institutions:
LSU School of Medicine in New Orleans
Touro Infirmary
Louisiana State University School of Medicine

Maryland
Johns Hopkins University Geriatric Psychiatry
Program
John Hopkins Hospital
Meyer 279
600 N. Wolfe St.
Baltimore, MD 21287-7279
Participating Institutions:
John Hopkins University School of Medicine
John Hopkins Bayview Medical Center
John Hopkins Hospital

University of Maryland Geriatric Psychiatry
Program
Baltimore Veterans Administration
10 N. Greene St., 116A
Baltimore, MD 21201
Participating Institutions:
University of Maryland School of Medicine
University of Maryland Medical System
Veterans Affairs Medical Center
(Baltimore)

Massachusetts
McLean Hospital Geriatric Psychiatry Program
McLean Hospital
115 Mill St.
Belmont, MA 02178
Participating Institutions:
Harvard Medical School
McLean Hospital
Deaconess Hospital

Michigan
University of Michigan Geriatric Psychiatry
Program
University of Michigan
900 Wall St.
Ann Arbor, MI 48105
Participating Institutions:
University of Michigan Medical School
University Of Michigan Hospitals
Veterans Affairs Medical Center (Ann Arbor)

Wayne State University/LaFayette Clinic
Geriatric Psychiatry Program
Wayne State University
Walter P. Reuther Psychiatric Hospital
30901 Palmer
Westland, MI 48185
Participating Institutions:
Wayne State University School of Medicine
Walter P. Reuther Psychiatric Hospital

Minnesota
University of Minnesota Geriatric Psychiatry
Program
University of Minnesota
VA Medical Center
One Veterans Drive
Minneapolis, MN 55417
Participating Institutions:
University of Minnesota Medical School
Veterans Affairs Medical Center (Minneapolis)

Missouri
St. Louis University Group of Hospitals
Geriatric Psychiatry Program
St. Louis University Health Sciences Center
David P. Wohl Sr. Memorial Institute

1221 S. Grand Blvd.
St. Louis, MO 63104
Participating Institutions:
St. Louis University School of Medicine
St. Louis University Hospital

Nebraska
Creighton University/University of Nebraska
Geriatric Psychiatry Program
University of Nebraska Medical Center
600 S. 42nd St.
P.O. Box 98-5575
Omaha, NE 88198-5575
Participating Institutions:
University of Nebraska College of Medicine
University of Nebraska Medical Center

New Hampshire
Dartmouth Hitchcock Medical Center Geriatric
Psychiatry Program
Dartmouth Hitchcock Medical Center
1 Medical Center Drive
Lebanon, NH 03756-0001
Participating Institutions:
Dartmouth Medical School
New Hampshire Hospital
Mary Hitchcock Memorial Hospital

New Jersey
UMDNJ-Robert Wood Johnson Medical School
Geriatric Psychiatry Program
UMDNJ-CMHC at Piscataway
COPSA Institute for Alzheimer's Disease
667 Hoes Lane
P.O. Box 1392
Piscataway, NJ 08855-1392
Participating Institutions:
UMDNJ—Robert Wood Johnson Medical
School
Robert Wood Johnson University Hospital
Medical Center at Princeton

New York
Albert Einstein College of Medicine at Beth
Israel Medical Center Geriatric Psychiatry
Program
Beth Israel Medical Center

1st Ave. at 16th St.
New York, NY 10003
Participating Institutions:
Albert Einstein College of Medicine
Beth Israel Medical Center

Albert Einstein College of Medicine Geriatric
Psychiatry Program
Montefiore Medical Center
111 E. 210th St.
Bronx, NY 10457
Participating Institutions:
Albert Einstein College of Medicine
Bronx Psychiatric Center
Albert Einstein College of Medicine at Yeshiva
University

Albert Einstein College of Medicine at Long
Island Jewish Medical Center Geriatric
Psychiatry Program
Long Island Jewish Medical Center
Hillside Hospital Research Building
P.O. Box 38
Glen Oaks, NY 11004
Participating Institutions:
Albert Einstein College of Medicine
Long Island Jewish Medical Center
Central Islip Psychiatric Center
St. John's Episcopal Hospital—South Shore
Hillside Hospital (Long Island Jewish Medical
Center)

Columbia University (Binghampton) Geriatric
Psychiatry Program
Center for Geriatrics and Gerontology
100 Haven Ave.
#3-30F
New York, NY 10032
Participating Institutions:
Binghampton Psychiatric Center
Presbyterian Hospital in the City of New York
Tompkins Community Hospital
United Health Services Hospitals—
Binghampton

Mount Sinai School of Medicine Geriatric
Psychiatry Program
Mount Sinai Hospital
One Gustave L. Levy Place

Box 1230
New York, NY 10029
Participating Institutions:
Mount Sinai School of Medicine
Veterans Affairs Medical Center (Bronx)
Elmhurst Hospital Center—Mount Sinai Services

New York Hospital—Westchester
Division/Cornell Medical Center Geriatric
Psychiatry Program
Cornell University College of Medicine
21 Bloomingdale Rd.
White Plains, NY 10605
Participating Institutions:
Cornell University Medical College
New York Hospital
New York Hospital—Westchester Division

New York Medical Center at St. Vincent's
Hospital and Medical Center of New York
Geriatric Psychiatry Program
New York Medical College
153 W. 11th St.
New York, NY 10011
Participating Institutions:
New York Medical College
St. Vincent's Hospital and Medical Center of
New York

New York University Medical Center Geriatric
Psychiatry Program
New York University Medical Center
550 1st Ave.
New York, NY 10015
Participating Institutions:
New York University School of Medicine
Goldwater Memorial Hospital
Bellevue Hospital Center
Manhattan Psychiatric Center
New York University Medical Center

SUNY Health Science Center at Brooklyn
Geriatric Psychiatry Program
SUNY Health Science Center at Brooklyn
450 Clarkson Ave.
Brooklyn, NY 11203
Participating Institutions:
SUNY Health Science Center at Brooklyn
Kingsboro Psychiatric Center

St. John's Episcopal Hospital—South Shore University Hospital—SUNY Health Science Center at Brooklyn

University of Rochester Geriatric Psychiatry Program
University of Rochester Medical Center
300 Crittenden Blvd.
Rochester, NY 14642-8409
Participating Institutions:
University of Rochester School of Medicine
Rochester Psychiatric Center
Strong Medical Hospital of The University of Rochester

Ohio

University of Cincinnati Hospital Group Geriatric Psychiatry Program
University of Cincinnati College of Medicine
231 Bethesda Ave.
P.O. Box 670559
Cincinnati, OH 45267-0559
Participating Institutions:
University of Cincinnati College of Medicine
University of Cincinnati Hospital

Oregon

Oregon Health Sciences University Geriatric Psychiatry Program
Oregon Health Sciences University
Psychiatry Service (116A-P)
P.O. Box 1034
Portland, OR 97207-9823
Participating Institutions:
Oregon Health Sciences University School of Medicine
Oregon Health Sciences University Hospital
Oregon State Hospital
Veterans Affairs Medical Center (Portland)

Pennsylvania

Albert Einstein Medical Center Geriatric Psychiatry Program
Belmont Center for Comprehensive Treatment
4200 Monument Rd.
Philadelphia, PA 19131

Participating Institutions:
Temple University School of Medicine
Belmont Center for Comprehensive Treatment
Albert Einstein Medical Center

Milton S. Hershey Medical Center of Pennsylvania State University Geriatric Psychiatry Program
Milton S. Hershey Medical Center
PA State University
500 University Dr.
Hershey, PA 17033
Participating Institutions:
Pennsylvania State University College of Medicine
Penn State University Hospital—Milton S. Hershey Medical Center

University Health Center of Pittsburgh Program
University of Pittsburgh Medical Center
3811 O'Hara St.
Room 827
Pittsburgh, PA 15213-2593
Participating Institutions:
University of Pittsburgh School of Medicine
Western Psychiatric Institute and Clinic/UPMC
University Health Center of Pittsburgh

University of Pennsylvania Geriatric Psychiatry Program
Ralston-Penn Center
3615 Chestnut St.
Philadelphia, PA 19104-2676
Participating Institutions:
University of Pennsylvania School of Medicine
Hospital of the University of Pennsylvania

South Carolina

Medical University of South Carolina Geriatric Psychiatry Program
Medical University of South Carolina
Institute of Psychiatry PH141
171 Ashley Ave.
Charleston, SC 29425
Participating Institutions:
Medical University of South Carolina College of Medicine

Texas
University of Texas Southwestern Medical
School Geriatric Psychiatry Program
University of Texas Southwestern Medical
School at Dallas
5323 Harry Hines Blvd.
Dallas, TX 75235-9070
Participating Institutions:
University of Texas Southwestern Medical
School
Presbyterian Hospital of Dallas
Dallas County Mental Health and Mental
Retardation Center

Virginia
University of Virginia Geriatric Psychiatry
Program
Blue Ridge Hospital
Charlottesville, VA 22901
Participating Institutions:
University of Virginia School of Medicine
University of Virginia Medical Center
Western State Hospital

Washington
University of Washington Geriatric Psychiatry
Program
VA Medical Center
GREEC (182B)
1660 South Columbian Way
Seattle, WA 98108
Participating Institutions:
University of Washington School of Medicine
University of Washington Medical Center
Harborview Medical Center

Wisconsin
University of Wisconsin Geriatric Psychiatry
Program
William S. Middleton Memorial Hospital
Department of Psychiatry and Medicine
2500 Overlook Terrace
Madison, WI 53705
Participating Institutions:
University of Wisconsin Medical School

University of Wisconsin Hospital and Clinics
William S. Middleton Veterans Hospital
Mendota Mental Health Institute

GERIATRIC EDUCATION CENTERS

Geriatric Education Centers (GECs), funded by
U.S. Department of Health and Human Services
grants administered by the Bureau of Health Professions of the Health Resources and Services Administration, offer intensive geriatric education to
professionals in various health care disciplines
to enhance to quality and quantity of geriatric care.
Education functions include faculty and curriculum development, consultation and technical assistance, information collection and dissemination,
and continuing education.

The grants for Geriatric Education Centers are
currently under review. For an updated list of centers contact:

> The Interdisciplinary, Geriatrics, and Allied
> Health Branch
> Division of Associated, Dental, and Public
> Health Professions
> Bureau of Health Professions
> Health Resources and Services
> Administration
> 5600 Fishers Lane—Room 8-103
> Rockville, MD 20857

**ALZHEIMER'S DISEASE
RESEARCH CENTERS**

These centers are funded by the National Institute
on Aging in an effort to increase understanding
of the causes of the disease and what can be done
for its treatment. Research projects vary at individual institutions, with each center having its
own focus.

Alabama
Department of Neurology
University of Alabama at Birmingham
1720 7th Ave. South

Sparks Center 454
Birmingham, AL 35294-0017

California
Alzheimer's Disease Center
Alta Bates Medical Center
University of California, Davis
2001 Dwight Way
Berkeley, CA 94704

Department of Neurology and Psychiatry
University of California, Los Angeles
710 Westwood Plaza
Los Angeles, CA 90095-1769

Department of Neuroscience (0624)
University of California, San Diego School of
Medicine
9500 Gilman Dr.
La Jolla, CA 92093-0624

Division of Neurogerontology
Ethel Percy Andrus Gerontology Center
University Park, MC-0191
University of Southern California
3715 McClintock Ave.
Los Angeles, CA 90089-0191

Georgia
Department of Pathology and Laboratory
Medicine
Emory University School of Medicine
VA Medical Center (151)
1670 Clairmont Rd.
Decatur, GA 30033

Illinois
Cognitive Neurology and Alzheimer's Disease
Research Center
Northwestern University Medical School
320 E. Superior St.
Searle 11-450
Chicago, IL 60611

Rush Alzheimer's Disease Center
Rush-Presbyterian—St. Lukes Medical Center
1645 W. Jackson Blvd.

Suite 675
Chicago, IL 60612

Indiana
Indiana Alzheimer's Disease Center
Indiana University School of Medicine
635 Barnhill Dr.
Indianapolis, IN 46202-5120

Kansas
Department of Neurology
University of Kansas Medical Center
3901 Rainbow Blvd.
Kansas City, KS 66160-7314

Kentucky
Sanders-Brown Research Center on Aging
University of Kentucky
101 Sanders-Brown Building
800 South Lime
Lexington, KY 40536-0230

Maryland
The John Hopkins Medical Institutions
Department of Pathology
The John Hopkins University School of
Medicine
558 Ross Research Building
720 Rutland Ave.
Baltimore, MD 21205-2196

Massachusetts
Boston University Alzheimer's Disease Center
Geriatric Research, Education and Clinical
Center (182B)
Bedford VA Medical Center
200 Springs Rd.
Bedford, MA 10730

Massachusetts Alzheimer's Disease Research
Center
Department of Neurology
Massachusetts General Hospital
WAC 830
15 Parkman St.
Boston, MA 02114

Michigan
Michigan Alzheimer's Disease Research
Center
Department of Neurology
University of Michigan
1914 Taubman St.
Ann Arbor, MI 48109-0316

Minnesota
Department of Neurology
Mayo Clinic
200 1st St. SW
Rochester, MN 55905

Missouri
Alzheimer's Disease Research Center
Washington University Medical Center
4488 Forest Park Ave.
St. Louis, MO 63108-2881

New York
Alzheimer's Disease Research Center
Department of Pathology
Columbia University
630 W. 168th St.
New York, NY 10032

Department of Psychiatry
Mount Sinai School of Medicine
Mount Sinai Medical Center
1 Gustave Levy Place
Box #1230
New York, NY 10029-6574

Aging and Dementia Research Center
Department of Psychiatry (THN314)
New York University Medical Center
550 1st Ave.
New York, NY 10016

Alzheimer's Disease Center
Department of Neurobiology and Anatomy,
Box 603
University of Rochester Medical Center
601 Elmwood Ave.
Rochester, NY 14642

North Carolina
Joseph and Kathleen Bryan Alzheimer's Disease
Research Center (Duke University)
2200 Main St.
Suite A-230
Durham, NC 27705

Ohio
Alzheimer's Disease Research Center (Case
Western Reserve University)
University Hospitals of Cleveland
11100 Euclid Ave.
Cleveland, OH 44106

Oregon
Oregon Alzheimer's Disease Center (L226)
Oregon Health Sciences University
3181 SW Sam Jackson Park Rd.
Portland, OR 97201-3098

Pennsylvania
Pathology and Laboratory Medicine
University of Pennsylvania School of
Medicine
Room A009, Basement Maloney/HUP
36th and Spruce Streets
Philadelphia, PA 19104-4283

Alzheimer's Disease Research Center
University of Pittsburgh Medical Center
Montefiore University Hospital, 4 West
200 Lothrop St.
Pittsburgh, PA 15213

Texas
Alzheimer's Disease Research Center
Department of Neurology
Baylor College of Medicine
6501 Fannin, NB302
Houston, TX 77030-3498

Alzheimer's Disease Research Center
University of Texas
Southwestern Medical Center at Dallas
5323 Harry Hines Blvd.
Dallas, TX 75235-9036

Washington
Alzheimer's Disease Research Center
Department of Pathology
Box 357470, HSB K-543
University of Washington
1959 Pacific Ave.
Seattle, WA 98195-7470

GERIATRIC RESEARCH, EDUCATION, AND CLINICAL CENTERS (GRECC)

Geriatric research, education and clinical centers are located in VA medical centers throughout the United States. Their role is to develop the capability of the VA health care system to provide care to older veterans. GRECCs develop new knowledge regarding aging and geriatrics, disseminate information through education and training to health care professionals and students, and develop and evaluate alternative models of geriatric care.

Arkansas
John L. McClellan Memorial Hospital
4300 W. 7th St.
Little Rock, AR 72205-5484

California
VA Medical Center*
3801 Miranda Ave.
Palo Alto, CA 94304
Research Areas: Cognitive Function/Chronic Disease, Affective Disorders

VA Medical Center*
16111 Plummer St.
Sepulveda, CA 91343
Research Areas: Alzheimer's Disease

VA Medical Center
Wilshire & Sawtelle Blvds.
West Los Angeles, CA 90073

Florida
VA Medical Center*
1601 SW Archer Rd.

Gainesville, FL 32608-1197
Research Areas: Dementia

VA Medical Center
1201 NW 16th St.
Miami, FL 33125

Maryland
VA Medical Center
10 N. Green St.
Baltimore, MD 21201

Massachusetts
Boston GRECC—Bedford Division*
Edith Nourse Rogers Memorial Hospital
200 Springs Rd.
Bedford, MA 01730
Research Areas: Neuroscience/Cognitive Disorders, Management of Advanced Alzheimer's Disease and Other Dementias

Boston GRECC
VA Medical Center
1400 VFW Parkway
West Roxbury, MA 02132

Michigan
VA Medical Center
2215 Fuller Rd.
Ann Arbor, MI 48105

Minnesota
VA Medical Center*
One Veterans Dr.
Minneapolis, MN 55417
Research Areas: Aging Nervous System: Neurobiology, Neurology and Psychiatry, Behavioral Neurobiology, Alzheimer's Disease, Epedemiology of Dementia (has dementia department headed by a psychiatrist), Delirium, Psychopharmacology

Missouri
VA Medical Center
Jefferson Barracks Division

#1 Jefferson Barracks Dr.
St. Louis, MO 63125-4199

North Carolina
VA Medical Center
508 Fulton St.
Durham, NC 27705

Texas
Audie L. Murphy Memorial
VA Medical Center
7400 Merton Minter Blvd.
San Antonio, TX 78484

Utah
VA Medical Center
500 Foothill Dr.
Salt Lake City, UT 84148

Washington
VA Medical Center*
1660 Colombian Way
Seattle, WA 98108

American Lake VA Medical Center*
Tacoma, WA 98493
Research Area (Seattle and American Lakes
Divisions): Alzheimer's Disease, Dementia (has
dementia department headed by a psychiatrist),
Depression

Wisconsin
William S. Middleton Memorial Hospital
2500 Overlook Terrace
Madison, WI 33125

* These GRECC's conduct research related to mental
health. Other GRECC's, however, provide psychiatric
services.

APPENDIX E

STAFF INSERVICE EDUCATIONAL MATERIAL FOR WORK WITH OLDER PEOPLE

RECOMMENDED FICTION
LITERARY ANTHOLOGIES
PULITZER PRIZE–WINNING PLAYS
FEATURE FILMS
AUDIOVISUAL REVIEW SOURCES
AUDIOVISUAL RESOURCE GUIDES

SELECTED HISTORICAL REFERENCES
LIFE REVIEWS: ORAL HISTORY
PHOTOGRAPHY AND DRAWINGS OF OLD AGE
PHILOSOPHY

RECOMMENDED FICTION (CONCERNING LATER LIFE, MEMORY, TIME, AGING, DISEASE, AND DEATH)

In James Hilton's *Goodbye, Mr. Chips* (1934), the elderly protagonist reminisces in his room across from the school where he taught three generations of English boys.

Aldous Huxley's *After Many a Summer Dies the Swan* (1939) is a satirical novel. The hero is a California multimillionaire terrified of death. His physician is working on a theory of longevity. The novel ends in horror.

Georges Simenon's *The Bells of Bicetre* (English title: *The Patient*) portrays a powerful French newspaper owner who has a stroke that leaves him speechless and paralyzed. At first he is passive, with no wish to recover. His mind is clear; he views his wife, his doctor, and his own life with detachment. As his memories flow through his mind and he begins to recover his speech and movement, his mental attitude changes favorably.

In Muriel Spark's *Momento Mori* (1959), a woman's death and an anonymous phone caller who says "remember you must die" provoke a series of humorous adventures for a group of elderly English aristocrats.

Leo Tolstoy, in *The Death of Ivan Ilych* (1884), describes a Russian judge who learns that his wealth, status, and power are useless to him when he becomes ill. His painful disease and his death are merely inconveniences to his family and lifelong friends. A young peasant servant is his only comfort.

In John Updike's *The Poorhouse Fair* (1959), residents of an old folks' home put on their annual fair despite the well-intentioned mistakes of the new administrators and poor weather.

Adams, S. H. (1947). *Grandfather stories.* New York: Random House.
Albee, Edward. (1961). *The American dream.* New York: Coward, McCann and Geoghegan.
Ashton-Warner, S. (1961). *Spinster (1959).* New York: Bantam Books.

Balzac, Honore de. (1950). *Pere goriot.* New York: Modern Library.

Beckett, S. (1958). *Krapp's last tape* (1957). New York: Grove Press.

Bromfield, L. (1949). *Mrs. Parkington.* New York: Harper & Brothers.

Cary, J. (1942). *To be a pilgrim.* London: Michael Joseph.

Cervantes, M. (1957). *Don Quixote* (part 1, 1605; part II, 1615). New York: New American Library.

Chekov, A. (1958). *Uncle Vanya* in *Four great plays.* New York: Bantam Books.

Garcia Marquez, G. (1988). *Love in the time of cholera.* New York: Alfred A. Knopf.

Gardner, H. (1988). *I'm not Rappaport.* New York: Grove Press.

Hansberry, L. (1961). *A raisin in the sun.* New York: Random House.

Heinlein, Robert A. (1973). *Time enough for love.* New York: G. P. Putnam & Sons.

Hemingway, E. (1952). *The old man and the sea.* New York: Charles Scribner's Sons.

Ibsen, H. (1935). *The master builders.* In *Eleven plays of Henrik Ibsen,* New York: Random House.

James, H. (1945). "The beast in the jungle" (1903). In Fadiman, C., ed. *The short stories of Henry James.* New York: Random House, pp. 548–602.

Kaufman, G., & Hart, M. (1937). *You can't take it with you.* New York: Simon & Schuster.

Lampedusa, C. di. (1960). *The leopard.* New York: Pantheon Books.

Lessing, D. (1983). *The summer before dark.* New York: Random House.

Mann, Thomas. (1924). *Buddenbrooks.* New York: Random House.

Mann, T. (1954). *The black swan.* New York: Alfred A. Knopf.

Miller, A. (1949). *Death of a salesman.* New York: Viking Press.

Moliere, Jean. *The miser.* Available in various collections (in paperback and on record).

Paton, Alan. *Cry the beloved country.* Available in many editions.

Porter, K. A. (1930). "The jilting of Granny Weatherall." In *Flowering Judas.* New York: Harcourt, Brace & World.

Proust, M. (1934). *Remembrance of things past* (1913–1922). New York: Random House (two volumes).

Richter, C. (1960). *The waters of Kronos.* New York: Alfred A. Knopf.

Romains, J. (1961). *The death of a nobody* (1911). New York: Signet Book.

Shakespeare, W. (1960). *King Lear* (1608). Cambridge, England: Cambridge University Press.

Shaw, G. B. (1947). *Back to Methuselah.* Collection of five linked plays: *In the beginning; The gospel of the brothers Barnabas; The thing happens; The tragedy of an elderly gentleman;* and *As far as thought can reach.* New York: Oxford University Press.

Sophocles. *Oedipus at Colonus.* Available in various collections and in paperback.

Stegner, W. E. (1976). *The spectator bird.* Garden City, NJ: Doubleday.

Strindberg, J. August. (1964). *Storm.* In *Plays of Strindberg, Vol.1,* New York: Random House.

Trollope, A. (1882). *The fixed period.* Tauchnitz editions of English authors, Leipzig.

Turgenev, I. (1959). "A nest of gentlefolk." In *A nest of gentlefolk and other stories.* New York: Oxford University Press.

Uhry, A. (1988). *Driving Miss Daisy.* New York: Publishing Center for Cultural Resources.

Van Velde, J. (1960). *The big ward.* New York: Simon & Schuster.

Waugh, E. (1948). *The loved one.* Boston: Little, Brown & Co.

Wilde, O. (1956). *Picture of Dorian Gray* (1906). New York: Dell Books.

Williams, Tennessee. (1959). *Sweet bird of youth.* In *Three Plays.* New York: New Directions (paperback).

Yeats, W. B. (1957). "Underlying Love for Maud Sonne." In *The collected poems of William Butler Yeats.* New York: Macmillan.

LITERARY ANTHOLOGIES

Borenstein, Audrey. (1983). *Chimes of change and hours: Views of older women in twentieth century America.* London and Toronto: Associated University Presses.

Cole, T. R., & Winkler, M. G. (1994). *The Oxford book of aging.* New York: Oxford University Press.

Fowler, M., & McCutcheon, P. (1991). *Songs of experience: An anthology of literature and growing old.* New York: Ballantine Books.

Lyell, R. G. (Ed.) (1980). *Middle age, old age: Short stories, poems, plays and essays.* New York: Harcourt Brace Jovanovich.

Yahnke, R., & Eastman, R. M. (1996). *Literature and gerontology: A research guide.* Westport, CT: Greenwood Press.

PULITZER PRIZE–WINNING PLAYS

Coburn, D. L. *The gin game.*
Cristofer, M. *The shadow box.*
Uhry, A. *Driving Miss Daisy.*

FEATURE FILMS

The last laugh (1924), directed by F. W. Murnau. The story of an old doorman demoted to washroom attendant. 60 minutes.

Make way for tomorrow (1937), directed by Leo McCarey. An elderly couple are in financial difficulty and have to be parted because their children will not help. 92 minutes.

Goodbye, Mr. Chips (1939), directed by Sam Wood. Shy schoolmaster devotes his life to his students until a woman brings him out of his shell. 114 minutes.

Sunset boulevard (1950), directed by Billy Wilder. Faded silent-film star lives in the past. 110 minutes.

Ikiru (To live) (1952), directed by Akira Kurosawa. A bureaucrat discovers he has only six months to live and desperately struggles to accomplish something worthwhile. 143 minutes.

Umberto D. (1952), directed by Vittorio de Sica. Concerns an aging impoverished pensioner who considers suicide as he tries to keep his dignity while growing old in the squalor of postwar Italy. 89 minutes.

Tokyo story (1953), directed by Yasujiro Ozu. The story of an elderly couple's last visit to their children, its disappointments, its sadness. 134 minutes.

Wild strawberries (1957), directed by Ingmar Bergman. Concerns a 76-year-old physician who learns to love on the brink of eternity. 80 minutes.

The leopard (1965), directed by Luchino Visconti. Story of an aging Sicilian prince who realizes, "If one wants things to stay as they are, things have to change." 205 minutes.

The two of us (1968), directed by Claude Berri. About a 75-year-old man and a 9-year-old boy. 86 minutes.

The shameless old lady (1969), directed by Rene Allio. Story of a 70-year-old French widow who, having spent her life serving others, serves herself in the last 18 months of her life. 94 minutes.

I never sang for my father (1970), directed by Gilbert Cates. A sensitive son begins to lose patience with his cantankerous elderly father. 92 minutes.

Harold and Maude (1971), directed by Hal Ashby. A 19-year-old falls in love with a free-spirited septuagenarian. 92 minutes.

The autobiography of Miss Jane Pittman (1974), directed by John Forty. A 110-year-old slave remembers her life experiences, spanning the Civil War to the start of the civil rights movement. 110 minutes.

Harry and Tonto (1974), directed by Paul Mazursky. A retired schoolteacher travels cross-country with his faithful cat. 115 minutes.

Sendakan 8 (1975), directed by Kei Kumai.

Atlantic City (1981), directed by Louis Malle. The offbeat story of an aging gangster. 104 minutes.

On Golden Pond (1981), directed by Mark Rydell. A man struggles with the ravages of age. 109 minutes.

The twilight years (Kookotsu No Hito) (1984), directed by Sawako Ariyoshi.

Cocoon (1985), directed by Ron Howard. A fun piece of science fiction, where retirement villagers feel young again, thanks to visitors from another planet. 117 minutes.

Ran (1985), directed by Akira Kurosawa. Masterful Japanese adaptation of Shakespeare's *King Lear*. 161 minutes.

Whales of August (1988), directed by Lindsay Anderson. Story about the fates of two sisters who have spent over 60 summers together on a Maine island as they face the challenges of growing old. 90 minutes.

Driving Miss Daisy (1989), directed by Bruce Beresford. Chronicles the social changes occurring in the South between 1948 and 1973, while embracing the 25-year friendship between an elderly Jewish woman and her black chauffeur. 1989 Academy Award Winner. 99 minutes.

Near death (1989), directed by Frederick Wiseman. 350 minutes.

Avalon (1990), directed by Barry Levinson. Story of the transitions experienced by families over time. 126 minutes.

Dreams (1990), directed by Akira Kurosawa.

Strangers in good company (1991), directed by Cynthia Scott. Seven women ages 68–92, and one 31, (played by non-actors) get to know each other when their bus breaks down and strands them in the Canadian wilderness for three nights. 100 minutes.

Toto le heros (1991), directed by Jaco Van Dormeal. This Belgian film about an old man's life review revolves around the man's conviction that he was switched at birth with his neighbor. 90 minutes.

Fried green tomatoes (1991), directed by John Avnet. A younger woman befriends an older woman living in a nursing home and, through their relationship, both find meaning in their lives. 130 minutes.

Tatie Danielle (1991), directed by Etienne Chatilez. French black comedy about a mourning widow who wreaks havoc on people around her. 110 minutes.

I can't sleep (1995), directed by Claire Denis. Based on an actual serial murder case of old women in France. 110 minutes.

The line king (1996), directed by Susan Dryfoos. Biographical film about the artist Al Hirschfeld.

AUDIOVISUAL REVIEW SOURCES

National Institute on Human Resources and Aging
c/o Brookdale Center on Aging
425 E. 25th St.
New York, NY 10010-2590
Information: (800) 64-STAFF
Extensive filmographies and AV reviews are organized by topics and updated bi-monthly.

The Gerontologist (Washington, DC:
Gerontological Society of America)
Seven to ten audiovisuals produced within the last three years are reviewed in each bi-monthly issue.

AUDIOVISUAL RESOURCE GUIDES

Association of Gerontology in Higher Education. (1993). *Audiovisuals on aging.* Washington, DC: Association of Gerontology in Higher Education. A selective annotated bibliography of recommended AVs on a variety of topics.

Los Angeles Caregiver Resource Center. (1992). *Audiovisual guide: Resources in gerontology and geriatrics.* Los Angeles Caregiver Resource Center. USC Gerontology Center. 3715 McClintock Ave., Los Angeles, CA 90089-3191. A comprehensive, annotated bibliography of over 800 AV's under 75 subject headings.

National Council on the Aging. (1986). *An arts and aging media sourcebook.* Washington, DC: National Council on the Aging. AVs on the creative arts.

Yahnke, R. (1988). *The great circle of life: A resource guide to film on aging.* Baltimore, MD: Williams & Wilkins. Films, with synopses, previewing notes, group activities, scene summaries, discussion questions and worksheets, are categorized under 6 headings: Portraits of Aging, Documentaries, Symbolic Statements, Intergenerational Relationships, Relationships in Old Age, and Loss.

SELECTED HISTORICAL REFERENCES

Achenbaum, W. A. (1978). *Old age in the new land: The American experience since 1790.* Baltimore: The Johns Hopkins University Press.

Altmeyer, A. J. (1966). *The formative years of social security.* Madison, WI: University of Wisconsin Press.

Aries, P. (1962). *Centuries of childhood.* New York: Random House.

Charcot, J. M. (1881). *Clinical lectures on the diseases of old age* (*Lecons cliniques sur les maladies des vieillards et les maladies chroniques* [1867]). Hunt, L., translator. New York: William Wood.

Cicero, M. T. (1967). *De Senectute,* Copley, F. D., translator. Ann Arbor, MI: The University of Michigan Press.

Elder, G. (1975). *Children of the depression.* Chicago: The University of Chicago Press.

Emerson, R. W. (1862). Old age. *Atlantic Monthly.* 9:134–138.

Fischer, D. H. (1977). *Growing old in America.* New York: Oxford University Press.

Gruman, G. J. (1966). *A history of ideas about the prolongation of life: The evolution of prolongevity hypotheses to 1800.* Philadelphia: The American Philosophical Society.

Hall, G. S. (1922). *Senescence: The last half of life.* New York: D. Appleton.

Hareven, T. K. (1976). The last stage: Historical adulthood and old age. *Daedalus* 105: 20.

Metchnikoff, E. (1908). *The prolongation of life.* New York: G. P. Putnam's Sons.

Minot, C. S. (1885). Senility. In Buck, A. H., (Ed.), *Reference handbook of medical science,* vol. 6. New York: William Wood, p. 388.

Nascher, I. L. (1914). *Geriatrics.* Philadelphia: P. Blakiston's Son.

Rush, B. (1793). An account of the state of the mind and body in old age. In *Medical inquiries and observations,* 4 vol., (reprinted Philadelphia: Thomas Dobson, 1797).

Steams, P. N. (1976). *Old age in European society: The case in France.* New York: Holmes and Meier Publishers.

Stone, L. (1977, May 12). Walking over grandma. *New York Review of Books.*

Zeman, F. D. (1944–1947). Life's later years: Studies in the medical history of old age (series). *Journal of Mt. Sinai Hospital.*

LIFE REVIEWS: ORAL HISTORY

Blythe, R. (1979). *Akenfield: Portrait of an English village.* New York: Pantheon Books.

Hareven, T. K., & Langenbach, R. (1978). *Amoskeag: Life and work in an American factory city.* New York: Pantheon Books.

PHOTOGRAPHY AND DRAWINGS OF OLD AGE

Jacques, M. (1980). *Images of age.* Cambridge, MA: ABT Books.

Martine, F. (1980). *Le temps de vieillir.* Paris, France: Editions Filipacchi.

Miller, P. R., & Tupin, J. P. (1972). Multimedia teaching of introductory psychiatry. *American Journal of Psychiatry, 128,* 1219–1222.

PHILOSOPHY

McKee, P. L. (1982). *Philosophical foundations of gerontology.* New York: Human Sciences Press.

U.S. POLICY ON AGING: A HISTORICAL SUMMARY

1920: *The Civil Service Retirement Act* was enacted to provide a retirement system for many government employees, including members of the U. S. Congress and those in the uniformed and civil services.

1935: *The Social Security Act* was passed and signed into law by President Roosevelt "to provide protection as a matter of right for the American worker in retirement." Major provisions included "Old Age Assistance" and "Old Age Survivors Insurance."

1937: *The Railroad Retirement Act* was enacted to provide annuities (pensions) for retired railroad employees and their spouses.

1939: Benefits for dependents and survivors added to the Social Security Act.

1945: The State of Connecticut was among the first to establish a state agency on aging through its designation of a "State Commission on the Care and Treatment of the Chronically Ill, Aged and Infirm."

1950: The first national conference on aging convened in Washington, DC, sponsored by the Federal Security Agency.

1953: The Department of Health, Education, and Welfare (DHEW) was established in April to replace the former Federal Security Agency.

1956: A special staff on aging was assigned coordinative responsibilities for aging within the Office of the Secretary of DHEW.

1958: Representative John E. Fogarty introduced bill in Congress calling for a White House Conference on Aging.

1959: *The Housing Act* was enacted, authorizing a direct loan program of nonprofit rental projects for the elderly at low interest rates. Provisions also reduced the eligible age for public low-rent housing for low-income older persons to age 62 for women and age 50 for disabled individuals.

Creation of the U.S. Senate Special Committee on Aging.

1960: Social Security amendments made a number of changes in the law, including: (a) eliminating "age 50" as a minimum to qualify for disability benefits, and (b) liberalizing the retirement test and the requirement for fully insured status.

1961: First White House Conference on Aging convened in Washington, DC.

Social Security amendments lowered retirement age for men from age 65 to 62; increased minimum benefits paid; broadened program to include additional categories of retired persons; increased benefits to aged widows; and liberalized the retirement test.

1962: Legislation proposed by Senator McNamara and Representative Fogarty calling for the establishment of a permanent and independent three-member Commission on Aging attached to the presidency to serve as the focal point within federal government for developing national aging policy. More than 160 bills introduced in Congress related to the aged and aging—eight were enacted.

1965: Medicare health insurance program for the elderly was legislated. Financed through the Social Security system, the enactment culminated years of "extensive and comprehensive efforts at the Congressional level."

The Older Americans Act was passed and signed into law by President Johnson on July 14. Major provisions included establishment of the Administration on Aging within DHEW and grants to states for community planning, services and training. The Act also stipulated that state agencies on aging be established to administer the programs.

"Community Service and Continuing Education Programs" were authorized under the Higher Education Act of 1965. Emphasis was directed to solving community problems in urban and suburban areas and to expanding available learning opportunities for adults not adequately served by educational offerings in their communities.

Social Security amendments established Title XIX, "Grants to States for Medical Assistance."

1967:   Amendments to the Older Americans Act extended its provisions for two years and directed the Administration on Aging to undertake a study of personnel needs in the aging field.

Age Discrimination Act of 1967 was passed and signed into law by President Johnson.

The Administration on Aging was removed from the Office of the Secretary of DHEW and placed in a newly created Social and Rehabilitative Service Agency (SRS) within the Department.

1969:   Amendments to the Older Americans Act extended its provisions for three years and authorized the use of Title III funds to support area-wide model projects.

1971:   Second White House Conference on Aging convened in Washington, DC.

1972:   Supplemental Security Income program (SSI) created.

Automatic annual cost-of-living allowances were established for Social Security benefits.

The Nutrition Program for the Elderly Act was passed and signed into law by President Nixon (redesignated Title VII of the Older Americans Act, as amended in 1973).

The Federal Council on Aging and the House Select Committee on Aging were created.

1973:   The Older Americans Comprehensive Service Amendments established area agencies on aging under an expanded Title III authority. Amendments also authorized the use of Title III grants for model projects, senior centers and multidisciplinary centers of gerontology, added a new Title IX, "Older Americans Community Service Employment Act," authorized funding for Title VII nutrition projects, and extended the Act's provisions for two years.

The Domestic Volunteer Service Act was passed and signed into law by President Nixon on October 1. Major provisions included the RSVP and Foster Grandparent programs. Title VI of the Older Americans Act, as a result, was later repealed.

The Comprehensive Employment and Training Act (CETA) was enacted "to provide job training and employment opportunities for economically disadvantaged, unemployed or underemployed persons, including those facing barriers to employment commonly experienced by older workers."

1974:   Amendments to the Older Americans Act added a special transportation program under Title III "model projects."

The Housing and Community Development Act became law on August 22.

Major provisions included a directive to the Secretary of Housing and Urban Development (HUD) to consult with the Secretary of HEW to ensure the acceptable provision of low-income housing for the elderly or handicapped, pursuant to the U. S. Housing Act of 1937.

Social Security Amendments authorized Title XX, "Grants to States for Social Services." Among the programs which could be supported under this provision were: protective services; homemaker services; adult day care services; transportation services; training; employment opportunities; information and referral; nutrition assistance; and health support.

Congress authorized the establishment of the National Institute on Aging (NIA) on May 31 "to conduct and support biomedical, social and behavioral research and training related to the aging process and the diseases and other special problems and needs of the aging."

Title V, "Farm and Rural Housing" program of the National Housing Act of 1949 was expanded to include the rural elderly as a special target group.

1975: Amendments to the Older Americans Act added new language authorizing the Commissioner on Aging to make grants under Title III to Indian tribal organizations. For the first time, Priority Services were mandated (transportation, home care, legal services and home renovation/repair). Amendments also made minor changes in Title IX, "Community Service Employment for Older Americans."

The Age Discrimination Act of 1975 was passed and signed into law by President Nixon. It specifically excluded from its purview age discrimination in employment except as it related to participation in government-funded employment programs.

1977: Amendments to the Older Americans Act authorized changes in the Title VII nutrition services program, primarily related to the availability of surplus commodities through the U.S. Department of Agriculture.

1978: Comprehensive amendments to the Older Americans Act consolidated Titles III, V and VII (social services, multipurpose centers and nutrition services, respectively) into one Title III: redesignated the previous Title IX (Community Service Employment Act) as Title V; and added a new Title VI, "Grants for Indian Tribes."

The Congregate Housing Services Act was passed and signed into law on October 31. Major provisions authorized the Secretary of Housing and Urban Development (HUD) to enter into contracts with local public housing agencies and with nonprofit corporations to provide congregate services programs for the purpose of promoting and encouraging maximum independence within a home environment for individuals capable of self-care.

Amendments to the Age Discrimination in Employment Act were passed containing provisions reflective of the recommendations of the U. S. Civil Rights Commission which showed that the Age Discrimination Act of 1975 had been interpreted to allow discrimination in employment, which was clearly not the intent of Congress.

1980: The Department of Health and Human Services (DHHS) was created, replacing DHEW.

1981: Amendments to the Older Americans Act extended its program for three years through September 30, 1984.

The Third White House Conference on Aging convened in Washington, DC.

1984: Amendments to the Older Americans Act clarified the roles of state and area agencies on aging in coordinating community-based services and in maintaining accountability for the funding of national priority services (legal, access and in-home services); increased the flexibility in administering programs by providing for increased transfer authority between Parts B and C of Title III; a new Title VII was added providing for an Older Americans Personal Health Education and Training Program for funding grants to institutions of higher education and to develop standardized programs of health education and training for older persons to be operated in multipurpose senior center facilities; and the program was extended for three years, through September 30, 1987.

1985: *A Compendium of Papers Honoring the Twentieth Anniversary of the Older Americans Act* was compiled by the U.S. House of Representatives Select Committee on Aging, Subcommittee on Human Services, and published by the U. S. Government Printing Office, Washington, DC.

1987: Amendments to the Older Americans Act included the establishment of the Office for Native Hawaiian Programs within the Administration on Aging. It also authorized new initiatives on mental health, elder abuse, home health care for the frail elderly, and outreach to eligible SSI recipients.

1992: Amendments to the Older Americans Act included the addition of Title VII, the Vulnerable Elders Rights Protection Title, and funded efforts to increase education on how healthy lifestyles reduce the risk of chronic health problems in later life.

1995: The fourth White House Conference on Aging convened in Washington, DC.

1997: The Older Americans Act is up for reauthorization.

PERSONAL MENTAL HEALTH DATA FORM
FOR OLDER PERSONS

PERSONAL MENTAL HEALTH DATA FORM FOR OLDER PERSONS

Note to patients   **Confidential**

This Personal Data Form is an inventory, an overview of your past and present situation. For our purposes, it provides basic background data. For you, it is a way to begin reviewing your life, finding themes, in terms of both strengths and difficulties.

The material is confidential and will be treated with care. We do not share this material with **anyone** outside our office, unless specifically given permission by you. Thus candor and comprehensiveness, which add to the value, are encouraged. Some of the questions will be irrelevant, in which case simply leave blanks. If more writing space is needed, add an extra sheet.

You may be asked to write to other psychotherapists, doctors, and hospitals who have knowledge of you, giving them permission to send us extended summaries of their contacts with you. If you wish, we will furnish you with a copy of this form for your own use or for use with other health personnel such as your internist.

Thank you very much,

(signed by chief administrator)

This form was created by Myrna I. Lewis and Robert N. Butler, Mt. Sinai School of Medicine, New York. Revised 1997.

INFORMATION FOR OUR USE IN YOUR INSURANCE FORMS

TO BE COMPLETED BY PATIENT   Date: _____

Patient's name: _____

Social Security no.: _____   Medicare no.: _____

Medicaid no.: _____   Supplemental Security Income (SSI): _____

Date first seen at our office: _____

Approximate date symptoms appeared: _____

Health coverage *(indicate by a check mark)*

☐ None
☐ Blue Cross-Blue Shield:
☐ Aetna
☐ Kaiser Permanente
☐ Other Private Insurance (name): _____
☐ Champus
☐ Medicare: ☐ Part A   ☐ Part B
☐ Medicare Supplement
☐ Medicaid
☐ HMO/Managed Care (name): _____
☐ Veterans Administration
☐ Long Term Care Insurance Coverage
☐ Other *(name):* _____

Disability payments *(indicate by a check mark)*

☐ Private
☐ Social Security
☐ Veterans
☐ State

TO BE COMPLETED BY THERAPIST

Psychiatric diagnosis (NOTE TO PATIENTS: *We shall discuss any diagnosis with you before submitting it to your insurance company.*)

_____
_____

Nature of treatment *(indicate date treatment began)*

Consultation alone (diagnosis and evaluation): _____

Individual psychotherapy: _____

Group psychotherapy: _____

Couples (conjoint) therapy: _____

Family therapy: _____

Reminiscence or life review therapy: _____

Cognitive therapy: _____

Behavioral therapy: _____

Activities therapy (art, music, dance): _____

Drug therapy (specify drugs): _____

Referral for ECT: _____

Referral for hospitalization: _____

Case management/care coordination: _____

Emergency referral: _____

Other *(specify)*: _____

PERSONAL DATA FORM (LIFE REVIEW FORM)

I. BASIC BACKGROUND INFORMATION   Date: _____

A. Patient's full name: _____

Nickname(s): _____   Preferred first name: _____

Age: _____   Complete birth date: _____

Birthplace: _____

Present addresses: Residence: _____
                                  (Street)

                                  _____
                                  (City)   (State)   (Zip)

                                  _____
                                  (E-mail)

            Work: _____
                    (Street)

                    _____
                    (City)   (State)   (Zip)

                    _____
                    (E-mail)

Telephone numbers: Residence: _____   Fax: _____

                    Work: _____   Fax: _____

NOTE: *If you do not wish to be called at work except for emergencies, check here ☐.*
If you cannot be called at work at all, check here ☐.

REFERRAL SOURCE

Patient referred by: _____

IN CASE OF MEDICAL EMERGENCY: *Current doctor(s)*

1. Name: _____

Address: _____

Phone: _____   Specialty: _____

2. Name: _____

Address: _____

Phone: _____   Specialty: _____

3. Name: _____

Address: _____

Phone: _____   Specialty: _____

IN CASE OF EMERGENCY: *Nearest relatives and/or friends*

Name: _____

Address: _____   Phone: _____

Name: _____

Address: _____   Phone: _____

I. BASIC BACKGROUND INFORMATION—cont.

If you live alone, please give the name and phone number of a nearby neighbor or friend.

Name: _____   Phone: _____

B. Religion

Of family of origin: _____

Present religious affiliation, if any: _____

Are you active religiously? _____

Any religious conflict? _____

No religion: _____

C. Ethnic, racial, or cultural background: _____

Year of immigration to U.S.: _____

From where: _____

First language spoken: _____

Second language spoken: _____

D. Family status

Present marital status: ☐ Single

☐ Separated

☐ Widowed

☐ Married

☐ Divorced

☐ Living with someone

Most current marriage or living partner *(circle which)*

Full name of spouse or living partner: _____

Age difference: _____ (years older than you)

_____ (years younger than you)

Religion of spouse or living partner: _____

Place of birth of spouse or living partner: _____

Your courtship duration: _____

Date of marriage or when you began living together (month, day, year): _____

Closest anniversary attained: _____

Date of separation: _____

Date of divorce or widowhood (month, day, year): _____

Previous marriage or living partner *(circle which)*

Full name of spouse or living partner: _____

Age difference: _____ (years older than you)

_____ (years younger than you)

Religion of spouse or living partner: _____

Place of birth of spouse or living partner: _____

Your courtship duration: _____

Date of marriage or when you began living together (month, day, year): _____

Closest anniversary attained: _____

Date of separation: _____

Date of divorce or widowhood (month, day, year): _____

Other marriages or partnerships (describe): _____

_____

_____

Children:	Name	Sex	Age	City and state of residence	If deceased, date and cause of death
1.					
2.					
3.					
4.					
5.					
6.					

(Add an extra page for children if needed; include miscarriages, stillbirths, etc.)

Note: If any children are adopted, place an "A" after their name.
If any children are stepchildren, place an "S" after their name.

Your age when last child left home: _____

What are your feelings about being a parent? _____

_____

_____

Grandchildren:	Name	Sex	Age	City and state of residence	If deceased, date and cause of death
1.					
2.					
3.					
4.					
5.					
6.					

(Add an extra page for grandchildren if needed)

Note: If any grandchildren are adopted, place an "A" after their name.
If any grandchildren are step-grandchildren, place an "S" after their name.

Your age at birth of first grandchild: _____

What are your feelings about being a grandparent? _____

_____

_____

I. BASIC BACKGROUND INFORMATION—cont.

Great-Grandchildren:	Name	Sex	Age	City and state of residence	If deceased, date and cause of death
1.					
2.					
3.					
4.					
5.					
6.					

(Add an extra page for great-grandchildren if needed.)

Note: If any great-grandchildren are adopted, place an "A" after their name.
If any great-grandchildren are step-great-grandchildren, place an "S" after their name.

Your age at birth of first great-grandchild: _____

What are your feelings about being a great-grandparent? _____

_____

_____

Members of current household (include everyone who lives with you):

Name	Sex	Age	Relationship to you
1.			
2.			
3.			
4.			
5.			
6.			

E. Family history

Parents

Father's full name: _____

Occupation: _____

Year of birth: _____ Birthplace: _____

If dead: Year of death: _____ His age at death: _____

Cause of death: _____

Your age at his death: _____

Educational level he attained: _____

Brief description of his personality: _____

_____

_____

Mother's full name: _____

Occupation: _____

Year of birth: _____ Birthplace: _____

If dead: Year of death: _____ Her age at death: _____

Cause of death: _____

Your age at her death: _____

Educational level she attained: _____

Brief description of her personality: _____

_____

_____

With whom did you live up to age 21?: _____

Were you raised in a rural, small town, urban, or suburban setting? *(describe):* _____

_____

During childhood, who lived in your home other than immediate family? *(include relatives, nurses, maids, boarders, etc.):* _____

_____

Did anyone other than your parents help care for you? *(describe):* _____

_____

Siblings:	Name	Age	City and state of residence	If deceased, date and cause of death
1.				
2.				
3.				
4.				
5.				
6.				

(Add an extra page for siblings if needed.)

Note: If any siblings are step-siblings, place an "S" after their name.
If any siblings are half-siblings, place an "H" after their name.

Grandparents (amount and quality of contact with them)

Paternal: _____

_____

Maternal: _____

_____

Your socioeconomic conditions during childhood:

    Poor _____

    Average _____

    Wealthy _____

I. BASIC BACKGROUND INFORMATION—cont.

F. **Education (your years of schooling):** _____

Description of schools:	Name of school	Year of graduation	Degree

Grammar school: _____

High school: _____

Trade, technical, or vocational school: _____

College: _____

Graduate or professional school: _____

Later courses; other education: _____

Elderhostel: _____

Self-rating, as a student (check): ☐ Above average   ☐ Average   ☐ Below average

Any honors, awards, scholarships: _____

Who was the first person in your immediate or extended family to have a college education? ____

Would you like to obtain further education? *(describe):* _____

G. Work

Your occupation or profession: _____

Government Service (G.S.) level *(if applicable):* _____

Your second occupation or profession *(describe):* _____

Last three jobs and the durations of employment:

1. _____

2. _____

3. _____

How physically demanding has your work been (including physical labor, housework, etc.)?

☐ Mildly demanding: _____

☐ Moderately demanding: _____

☐ Severely demanding *(describe):* _____

Average number of hours a day that you work: _____

Occupation of spouse: _____

What are your major work interests? _____

Were you in military service? _____ Which branch? _____

Did you experience age, sex, racial, ethnic, or other discrimination at work? *(describe):* _____

How physically active was your work? _____

_____

Postretirement

Did you work after retirement? _____

If so, describe employment: _____

How many hours per week? _____

Employed or self-employed? _____

Did you experience any form of discrimination at work? *(describe:)* _____

_____

Are you currently employed? _____ If not, would you like to be? _____

H. Retirement

Your age at retirement: _____ Date of retirement: _____

Was it voluntary? _____ Welcomed? _____

Was it compulsory through company or union? _____

Was it forced because of illness? _____

Did you have preretirement preparation (seminars, etc.)? _____

Did you have postretirement counseling? _____

I. Economic status *(check all sources of income, not amount [s])*

☐ Employment   ☐ Public pension plan

☐ Social Security   ☐ Public assistance

☐ Veterans benefits   ☐ Insurance payments

☐ Disability benefits   ☐ Annuities

☐ Teachers' Insurance and Annuity Association   ☐ Savings

☐ College Retirement Equities Fund   ☐ IRA

☐ Railroad Retirement   ☐ Investments

☐ Private pension plan   ☐ Assistance from family

☐ Other: _____

Do you pay or receive alimony? _____

Do you pay child support? _____

Your annual family income:

☐ over $150,000   ☐ $90,000–$150,000   ☐ $60,000–$90,000

☐ $30,000–$60,000   ☐ $15,000–$30,000   ☐ $10,000–$15,000

☐ $5,000–$10,000   ☐ $3,000–$5,000   ☐ Less than $3,000

Do you have serious financial problems? *(describe):* _____

_____

_____

Has there been a recent income drop? _____

If so, what is the reason? _____

I. BASIC BACKGROUND INFORMATION—cont.

Have you given over power of attorney? _____

Durable? _____ To whom? _____

Have you established a guardianship? _____

Have you established a conservatorship? _____

Have you established any advance directives? (Check)

☐ Right to die with dignity card

☐ Instructions regarding "Do Not Resuscitate"

☐ Donation of body organs

☐ Other instructions (describe): _____

_____

J. Residence (check)

☐ House (☐ Owned   ☐ Rented)

☐ Condominium (☐ Owned   ☐ Rented)

☐ Apartment (☐ Owned   ☐ Rented)

☐ Hotel

☐ Rooming house

☐ Boarding house

☐ "Assisted living"

☐ Nursing home

☐ Home for aged

☐ Other (describe): _____

☐ Mental hospital

☐ Chronic disease hospital

☐ Personal care home

☐ Foster care

☐ Public housing

☐ Mobile home, trailer

☐ "202"

☐ No regular residence

Total monthly cost of housing: _____

Any problems with living situation? *(describe)*: _____

_____

_____

Is there an elevator? _____

If no elevator, how many flights of stairs? _____

Any problems in neighborhood? (describe): _____

_____

If you are temporarily not in your own home, is someone caring for your

☐ Possessions?   ☐ Plants?   ☐ Pets?

Have you moved since retirement? _____ From what kind of housing? _____

K. Transportation and mobility

Do you have a driver's license? _____

Do you own a car? _____

Do you have access to a car? _____

Do you regularly wear a seatbelt in cars? _____

How do you usually travel around? _____

Is public transportation available? _____

Do you use it? _____

Any physical disabilities that affect your mobility *(describe):* _____

_____

_____

Do you feel safe going out during the day? _____

Do you feel safe going out during the night? _____

Do you have a telephone? _____

L. Interests and pleasures *(describe)*

Avocations or hobbies: _____

_____

Sports: _____

Commercial recreation (movies, nightclubs, etc.): _____

Music: _____

Languages: _____

Travel (places and years): _____

_____

Vacation habits (what do you do and how often?): _____

_____

Gardening: _____

Collect anything: _____

Pet(s): _____

Use of community centers, senior centers, etc.: _____

_____

What is the *most* characteristic thing you do to relax and unwind? _____

_____

How many hours a day do you watch T.V.? _____

How many hours a day do you engage in your other interests and pleasures (excluding T.V.)? ____

_____

Are you satisfied with the balance between work and play in your life? _____

_____

M. Active community involvements *(describe)*

Memberships—organizations, clubs, etc.: _____

_____

Retiree or "senior citizens" groups: _____

_____

Political activity: _____

_____

477

I. BASIC BACKGROUND INFORMATION—cont.

Veterans organization: _____

_____

Voluntary work: _____

_____

Church work: _____

_____

Other: _____

N. Friendship patterns

Do you have someone to depend on in an emergency? _____

If so, who? _____

Are you lonely? _____

Is there someone you can talk to whenever you feel like it? _____

If so, who? _____

Who are the three closest living persons in your life?

Name	**How are they important?**
1. _____	_____
2. _____	_____
3. _____	_____

Describe contacts (list names, frequency of contact, and nature of contact; is the relationship a good one for you?)

1. Children: _____

_____

2. Grandchildren: _____

_____

3. Great-grandchildren: _____

_____

4. Siblings: _____

_____

5. Other relations: _____

_____

6. Friends: _____

_____

7. Neighbors: _____

_____

(Add an extra page for these descriptions if needed.)

O. Caregiving Responsibilities *(describe)*:

1. Are you caring for any children? *(describe):* _____

_____

2. Are you caring for any disabled person age 18–64? *(describe):* _____

_____

3. Are you caring for any elders? *(describe):* _____

_____

P. Prejudice (directed against you) *(describe)*

Age: _____

Sex (male or female): _____

Race: _____

Ethnic origin: _____

Religion: _____

Sexual preference: _____

II. MEDICAL INFORMATION

List significant doctors or medical specialists you see now or saw in the recent past:

Name	**Address**	**Phone**	**Problem**
1.			
2.			
3.			
4.			
5.			

Date of your last medical checkup: _____

How do you rate your general medical health? (check)

☐ Excellent   ☐ Good   ☐ Fair   ☐ Poor

History (any health problems)

When born: _____

When growing up: _____

Are there any physical or mental health conditions that seem to run in your family? *(describe):*

_____

_____

_____

_____

_____

Any heart disease? _____

Any cancer? _____

Any senile dementia? _____

II. MEDICAL INFORMATION—cont.

Blood type: _____

Transfusion: ☐ Yes   When? _____
               ☐ No

Have you ever had the following? *(list dates)*

1. Accidents, injuries, and falls

     Concussion or other head injury: _____

     Fracture: _____

     Hip injury: _____

     Other: _____

     Any operation as a result: _____

2. Operations:

Date	Type of operation	Name of hospital	City
1.			
2.			
3.			

3. Circulatory disorders

     Heart disease: _____

     History of rheumatic fever: _____

     High blood pressure: _____

     Transient ischemic attack (TIA): _____

     Stroke: _____

       Any residual: _____

     Leg cramps: _____

     Cholesterol levels: _____

     HDL level (high-density lipoprotein): _____

     LDL level (low-density lipoprotein): _____

     Triglycerides level: _____

4. Angina: _____

5. Heart attack: _____

6. Arthritis: _____

     Rheumatoid arthritis: _____

     Osteoarthritis: _____

     Gout: _____

7. Lung conditions (bronchitis, emphysema, tuberculosis): _____
_____

8. Osteoporosis: _____

     Bone pain? _____

Loss of height? _____

Fracture history *(describe):* _____

_____

9. Diabetes: _____

10. Cancer: _____

11. Thyroid problems (hyper- or hypo-): _____

12. Anemia: _____

13. Gastrointestinal problems: _____

Diverticulitis: _____

Constipation: _____

Diarrhea: _____

14. Bladder problems: _____

Decline in continence: _____

Nocturia (need for night time urination): _____

15. Kidney problems: _____

16. Prostate problems: _____

17. "Change of life" or menopausal problems: _____

18. Allergies (hay fever, drugs, etc.): _____

19. Foot problems: _____

20. Other symptoms

Malaise and fatigue: Nervousness, tension: _____

Frequent, severe headaches: _____

Other pain: _____

Difficulty in breathing (dyspnea): _____

Dizziness: _____

Fainting spells: _____

Fever: _____

Ringing or buzzing in ears: _____

Bleeding: _____

21. Psychosomatic disorders

Asthma: _____

Peptic ulcer: _____

Essential hypertension: _____

Ulcerative colitis: _____

Ileitis: _____

Other: _____

22. Epilepsy or seizures: _____

23. Parkinsonism: _____

Flu from the epidemic of 1918–1919: _____

II. MEDICAL INFORMATION—cont.

24. Venereal diseases: _____

25. AIDS: _____

26. Herpes Zoster (Shingles): _____

27. Other: _____

_____

_____

Do you have anything that you consider to be a significant handicap? *(describe):* _____

_____

_____

Do you have any chronic health problems? *(describe):* _____

_____

_____

Occupational Safety and Health:

Air pollution? *(describe):* _____

Significant asbestos exposure? _____

Vinyl chloride? _____

Benzene? _____

Cotton dust? _____

Coal dust? _____

Accidents? _____

Noise? _____

Other? *(describe):* _____

Do you have any of the following physical limitations?

☐ Hearing loss

    Do you wear a hearing aid? _____

    Do you have any problems with your hearing aid? _____

    Did you have occupational or other prolonged exposure to noise during your life? _____

    _____

☐ Vision loss

    Do you wear glasses? _____

    Macular Retinal Degeneration: _____

    Cataracts: _____

    Glaucoma: _____

    Diabetic Retinopathy: _____

    Other: _____

☐ Memory loss

    Mild? _____

    Moderate? _____

    Severe? _____

Do you wear dentures?   ☐ Partial   ☐ Complete

    Do you have any problems with your dentures? _____

Do you have any problems with manual dexterity (describe)? _____

_____

Do you use a cane? _____

    Wheelchair? _____

    Walker? _____

    Crutches? _____

Do you have a need for any other medical equipment or prosthetic devices? _____

_____

_____

Are you receiving any of the following therapies?

    ☐ Physical   ☐ Occupational   ☐ Speech   ☐ Inhalation   ☐ Recreational

    ☐ Other (specify): _____

Do you like physical massage? _____

Do you receive regular massage? How often? _____

Daily living habits

    Do you consider any of the following to be a serious personal problem?

       ☐ Overeating   ☐ Overdrinking   ☐ Smoking   ☐ Underactivity

    Alcohol consumption

    How many cocktails, highballs, etc. a day? _____

    How many glasses of beer a day? _____

    How many glasses of wine a day? _____

    Do you drink in the morning? _____

    How much before dinner? _____

    How much before bed? _____

    Water consumption: _____ (glasses a day)

    Caffeine consumption a day: Coffee _____ Tea _____ Cola _____

    Carbonated drink consumption a day: _____

    Do you smoke cigarettes, cigars, or a pipe? _____

       How much do you smoke a day? _____

       How long have you smoked? _____

       Have you had a heavy exposure to others smoking? (passive smoking) _____

_____

       Do you chew tobacco?_____

    Are you on a special diet? *(describe):* _____

_____

_____

    Type of diet:

       ☐ Diabetic   ☐ Low-salt   ☐ Low-fat   ☐ Low-cholesterol   ☐ Other: _____

II. MEDICAL INFORMATION—cont.

Is diet medically prescribed or self-prescribed? _____

How many meals a day do you eat? _____

Are you a vegetarian? _____

Do you take vitamin or mineral supplements? _____

    What kind?

        ☐ Vitamin B   ☐ Vitamin C   ☐ Vitamin D   ☐ Vitamin E

        ☐ Other *(specify):* _____

Do you drink milk? _____ How many glasses a day? _____

    Is it skim, low-fat, or regular? _____

Do you have lactose intolerance? _____

Do you take calcium supplements? *(describe):* _____

Do you have frequent sunlight exposure for Vitamin D? _____

Do you take iron? *(describe dosage):* _____

Current weight: _____

    Has there been recent loss or gain and how much? _____

    What has been your maximum and minimum weight?   Maximum: _____   Minimum: _____

Current height: _____   Any shrinkage in your original height? _____

Exercise

    Do you exercise regularly? _____

    What kind of exercise? (check)

        ☐ Aerobic (for the heart)

        ☐ Muscle strengthening

        ☐ Stretching (for flexibility)

        ☐ Other *(describe):* _____

How often each week? _____

How long each time? _____

Sleep

    Any difficulty falling asleep? _____

    Any difficulty staying asleep (sleep fragmentation)? _____

    Early awakening? _____

    Do you take naps? _____

    Average number hours of sleep a day: _____

    Have your sleeping patterns changed recently? _____

    Any sleep reversal with wakefulness at night and sleepiness in day? _____

    Do you take sleeping pills? _____   What kind? _____

    Do you snore? _____

Describe recurrent dreams (e.g., examination dreams, flight, falling, or chase dreams): _____

_____

_____

_____

_____

_____

Is there any dream that seems highly significant to you? _____

_____

_____

_____

_____

Drug usage *(dates drugs recently were or are now taken as well as schedule and amount of dosage)*

Prescription drugs *(describe)*

Sedatives: _____

Tranquilizers: _____

Antidepressants: _____

Lithium: _____

Stimulants: _____

Diuretics: _____

Digitalis: _____

Reserpine: _____

Antihypertensives other than reserpine: _____

Hormones: _____

Estrogen (specific type and dosage): _____

Progestin (specific type and dosage): _____

Thyroid replacements: _____

Nitroglycerin: _____

Other: _____

Over-the-counter drugs taken regularly:

Laxatives: _____

Aspirin (for headache, pain, etc.): _____

Baby aspirin (for stroke prevention): _____

Others: _____

_____

_____

Immunizations (dates)

Pneumonia vaccine: _____

Tetanus vaccine: _____

Annual flu shot: _____

Hepatitis A: _____

Hepatitis B: _____

II. MEDICAL INFORMATION—cont.

Sexual activity and concerns

Do you experience a desire for sexual activity? _____

Has there been a recent change in your sexual desire? *(describe):* _____

_____

Do you currently have sexual outlets? *(describe):* _____

_____

How frequently? _____

Are there any problems—emotional, physical, social—as far as you are concerned regarding sex? (describe): _____

_____

_____

Males: Any problems with potency? _____

Females: Any vaginal pain or irritation? _____

                 Any urine leakage problems? _____

                 Any uterine prolapse? _____

                 Do you do special (Kegel) exercises? _____

How important is sexual activity in your life?

☐ Very important   ☐ Moderately important   ☐ Unimportant

Are you satisfied with your current sex life? *(describe):* _____

_____

_____

III. PSYCHIATRIC INFORMATION

A. General

What brought you here (complaints, concerns, symptoms)? _____

_____

_____

_____

_____

_____

_____

_____

_____

How long have you had the above problems? _____

_____

Have you recently felt

☐ Depressed   ☐ Anxious   ☐ Lonely   ☐ Guilty   ☐ Angry

☐ Resentful   ☐ Fearful *(describe specific fears):* _____

Have you had recent losses of any kind (health, loved ones, job, etc.)? _____

_____

Previous psychiatric contact

Name(s) of therapist(s): _____

_____

Discipline (psychiatrist, psychologist, social worker, nurse, other): _____

_____

City where therapy was received: _____

When: _____

Describe general form of treatment (individual or group therapy, family therapy, couples therapy, parent and child therapy, sex counseling, other): _____

_____

_____

Have you had a specialized form of therapy or experience such as cognitive, Gestalt, encounter, EST, biofeedback, behavior modification, hypnosis, primal therapy, psychodrama, reevaluation counseling, feminist consciousness-raising, or other (identify)? _____

_____

_____

How long were you in treatment? _____

Were drugs given? _____   Which ones? _____

_____

Did you receive electroconvulsive (ECT) treatments? _____

Were you hospitalized and for how long? _____

_____

Outcome of treatment in your opinion: _____

_____

_____

_____

_____

Have you belonged to any self-help organizations such as Weight Watchers, Alcoholics Anonymous, Recovery, Inc., Parents without Partners, or others? _____

_____

_____

_____

When? _____

What was the outcome? _____

III. PSYCHIATRIC INFORMATION—cont.

Has your spouse or partner had psychiatric problems? _____

_____

Is there anyone in your current or previous family with psychiatric problems? _____

_____

Have you ever taken psychological tests? _____

    Which ones? _____

    Done by whom? _____

    For what purpose? _____

Briefly, what is your own theory as to why you are currently having difficulties? _____

_____

_____

_____

What "first-aid" techniques or home remedies have you found that make you feel or function better (e.g., "keeping busy," going to sleep, prayer, shopping, talking, sports)? _____

_____

_____

_____

How long does improvement last? _____

_____

Therapy goals

    What are the goals you wish to achieve in treatment?_____

    _____

    _____

    _____

    _____

    If married or living with someone, do you feel your partner would benefit from the following?

    ☐ Individual psychotherapy   ☐ Group psychotherapy   ☐ Couples therapy

    ☐ Brief consultation about your problem   ☐ Family therapy

B. Your attitudes toward aging and death

First experience with death *(describe):* _____

_____

Losses of loved ones (include relatives, friends; describe person and date)

    When you were a child (up to 10 years of age): _____

    _____

    From 10 to 21 years: _____

    _____

    From 21 to 60 years: _____

    _____

After age 60: _____

_____

What are your feelings about old age? _____

What are your feelings about death? _____

Do you worry much about illness? _____

Do you worry much about your own death? _____

Do you worry much about death of others? _____

Describe any arrangements you have already made concerning your death (funeral arrangements, a "living will," donation of your body for science and medicine, donation of various organs for transplant, etc.): _____

_____

_____

Are you a member of a memorial society? _____
Have you made a will? _____
Are there any further arrangements you still wish to make? _____
Describe the old age of your parents: _____

_____

_____

_____

Describe the old age of your grandparents: _____

_____

_____

Have you modeled your own later life after that of anyone else? _____
If so, who? _____

_____

C. **Self-view** *(use extra space as needed)*
Describe yourself (appearance, personality, personal assets, and liabilities): _____

_____

_____

_____

_____

_____

III. PSYCHIATRIC INFORMATION—cont.

_____

_____

_____

_____

How do you feel about your present status in life? _____

Do you feel you have much control over your own life? _____

Are you positive and optimistic? _____

Do you plan your days? _____

Do you have substantial goals or purpose in your life? _____

Do you feel you have much influence on others? _____

Have you been an independent person in the past? _____

Are you now an independent person? _____

Do you live alone? _____

Have you lived alone in the past and for how long? _____

What are your feelings about living alone? _____

Describe persons or things that have most influenced your life (friends, family, teachers, books, etc.): _____

_____

_____

_____

Do you tend to reminisce? _____

What is the most frequent subject matter? _____

What are your earliest memories? _____

_____

Who loved you most as a child? _____

Who disliked you most? _____

Who hurt you most? _____

Who disappointed you most? _____

Have you composed a diary? _____

    kept a photograph album? _____

    written an autobiography? _____

    saved letters, mementoes, souvenirs? _____

What are the two or three most traumatic events (and your approximate age at the time) in your life that specifically stand out in your memory (e.g., accidents, deaths, fires, moves, divorces, personal failures of any kind, illnesses, etc.)? _____

_____

_____

_____

_____

_____

What are the two or three happiest and most satisfying events that specifically stand out in your memory (and your approximate age at the time)? _____

_____

_____

_____

_____

_____

CONCLUSION

What have been your reactions to this review of your life? _____

_____

_____

_____

_____

_____

_____

_____

_____

_____

GLOSSARY

age cohort Groups of similar age moving through time; or all those who grew up in the same time period.

age grading Age used for the assignment of roles and opportunities for people in the society.

age norms Role expectations at various age levels.

ageism Aversion, hatred, and prejudice toward the aged and their manifestation in the form of discrimination on the basis of age.

androgen Any one of a number of male sex hormones.

arteriosclerosis The loss of elasticity or the hardening of the walls of the arteries.

atheroma A fatty plaque or deposit on the inner wall surface (intima) of blood vessels (usually arteries).

atherosclerosis A fibrous thickening of the inner walls (intima) of blood vessels, accompanied by the accumulation of soft, pasty, acellular fatty material.

autoimmunity Attack response by the immune system of the body to its own tissues as a result of the production of antibodies against such antigens.

cross-sectional study Research focusing on many different persons at the same period of time.

demography The statistical study of the incidence or distribution within populations of births, deaths, marriages, diseases, and so on.

dependency ratio The number of old (65 and over) plus the number of young (under 18) divided into the total working generation (those aged 18 to 65).

estrogen The generic term for the hormonal substance involved in the female monthly cycle or estrus; the female sex hormone.

geriatrics The practice of medicine concerned with the diseases associated with old age.

gerontocracy Governmental rule by older persons.

gerontology The branch of science concerned with aging.

gerontophilia Exalting and/or venerating the aged.

gerontophobia Fear and aversion of aging.

involution The return to a former, more primitive condition or previous form (for example, the involution of the uterus after giving birth); also, a degenerative change.

life expectancy The statistical prediction of how long an organism will live beyond a given initial age.

life span The maximum span of life of a specific species.

lipofuscin Brown pigment granules representing lipid-containing residues of lysosomal digestion, usually occurring with increased incidence with advancing age in certain tissues.

longitudinal study Research that focuses on the same persons over many years of time.

neuroplasticity The reestablishment of nerve connections in the central nervous system. Nerve receptors denervated because of death of neurons or brain cells may be reinervated by unaffected neurons. The terms "recircuitry" and "reactive symptogenesis" have been used.

osteoarthritis Inflammation of the articular extremities of bone resulting from structural changes in the cartilage and degeneration of the bones with osteophytic growths (bony outgrowths).

osteoporosis A gradual resorption of bone such that the tissue becomes unusually porous and fragile.

prolongevity Defined by Gruman in 1955 as "the belief that it is possible and desirable to extend significantly the length of life by human action." Another definition is "the significant extension of the length of life by human action."

social network Structural characteristics of a social group, such as the number of social ties, types of family members, and frequency of contact, which form the basis of a person's social support.

social support Social others who provide information, psychological and emotional support, material and economic aid, and assistance with activities and tasks. In terms of supporting the frail elderly, the term "care-giving" is often used.

AUTHOR INDEX

Note: Page numbers in italics locate entries in Endnotes or Suggested Readings.

SUBJECT INDEX

Abandonment, 31–36
Abnormal paired helical filaments (PHF), 134
Abuse, 173–174
Acalculia, 146
Activated Patient program, 369
Activities of daily living (ADL), 259, 269, 274–275
Activity, use of, 88–89
Activity theory, 63
Adaptation, 85–87, 89, 241
  historical factors in, 60
Administration on Aging (AOA), 158, 366–367
Adult children, 47
Adult day-care centers, 298
Advocacy, 372–373
Affective disorders. *See* Mood disorders
African Americans, 11, 12–13, 15, 17, 18
  community mental health centers and, 158–160
  improving mental health care for, 165–166, 238, 256
  institutional care and, 159–160
  outpatient care and, 159
Age
  awareness, 366
  composition, 5–11
  definition of, 5
Age-associated memory impairment, 131
"Aged and Community Mental Health, The," 208
Age Discrimination Act of 1975, 224, 366
Age Discrimination in Employment Act of 1976, 366, 372
Age-integrated, life-crisis group therapy, 362–363
Ageism, 208–209, 213
  institutionalized, 230
Age-related memory decline, 131
Aging
  emotional changes and, 57
  healthy and successful, 54–70
  historical factors in, 60
  intellectual changes and, 57–59
  myths about, 60–61
  physical changes and, 56–57
  psychosocial theories of, 62–64
  research and, 61–62
  social changes and, 59–60
Aging and Medical Education, 214
Aging Network Services, 281
Agitation, 112
Agnosia, 146
Agraphia, 146

AIDS, 185, 360
Al Anon, 178
Alateen, 178
Alcohol, 145, 400
Alcoholics Anonymous, 177, 178, 360
Alcoholism, 175–178
  chronic, 176
  criteria for, 176
  dipsomania and, 176
  as reversible cause of mental impairment, 145
Alienation. *See* Abandonment
Alinsky, Saul, 372
Aloneness, 75
Alprazolam, 396
Alzheimer's disease, 61, 83, 99–100, 133–139, 236, 237
  as brain pathology, 133–134, 135
  causes of, 137
  clinical symptoms of, 136–137
  course of illness of, 137
  dementia and, 126, 131, 132
  insomnia and, 398
  nomenclature, 126
  subtypes of, 136
  treatment of, 137–139
Alzheimer's Disease Association, 138–139, 369
Amatryptaline (Elavil), 390–391
American Academy of Family Practice, 282
American Association for Counseling and Development (AACD), 218
American Association for Geriatric Psychiatry (AAGP), 213
American Association of Homes and Services for the Aging (AAHSA), 296
American Association of Retired People (AARP), 256–257, 353, 368, 369, 374, 375, 389
American Bar Association, 373
American Board of Internal Medicine, 282
American Board of Neurology and Psychiatry, 214, 282
American Cancer Society, 369
American Counseling Association, 218
American Diabetes Association, 287, 369
American Foundation for the Blind, 183
American Geriatrics Society, 213
American Heart Association, 369
American Indians. *See* Native Americans
American Massage Therapy Association, 285
Americans for General Equity (AGE), 374

CEDAR MILL COMM LIBRARY
12505 NW CORNELL RD
CEDAR MILL COMM LIBRARY

Algorithms

by John Paul Mueller and Luca Massaron

for
dummies®
A Wiley Brand

Algorithms For Dummies®

Published by: **John Wiley & Sons, Inc.**, 111 River Street, Hoboken, NJ 07030-5774, www.wiley.com

Copyright © 2017 by John Wiley & Sons, Inc., Hoboken, New Jersey

Media and software compilation copyright © 2017 by John Wiley & Sons, Inc. All rights reserved.

Published simultaneously in Canada

No part of this publication may be reproduced, stored in a retrieval system or transmitted in any form or by any means, electronic, mechanical, photocopying, recording, scanning or otherwise, except as permitted under Sections 107 or 108 of the 1976 United States Copyright Act, without the prior written permission of the Publisher. Requests to the Publisher for permission should be addressed to the Permissions Department, John Wiley & Sons, Inc., 111 River Street, Hoboken, NJ 07030, (201) 748-6011, fax (201) 748-6008, or online at http://www.wiley.com/go/permissions.

Trademarks: Wiley, For Dummies, the Dummies Man logo, Dummies.com, Making Everything Easier, and related trade dress are trademarks or registered trademarks of John Wiley & Sons, Inc. and may not be used without written permission. All other trademarks are the property of their respective owners. John Wiley & Sons, Inc. is not associated with any product or vendor mentioned in this book.

LIMIT OF LIABILITY/DISCLAIMER OF WARRANTY: THE PUBLISHER AND THE AUTHOR MAKE NO REPRESENTATIONS OR WARRANTIES WITH RESPECT TO THE ACCURACY OR COMPLETENESS OF THE CONTENTS OF THIS WORK AND SPECIFICALLY DISCLAIM ALL WARRANTIES, INCLUDING WITHOUT LIMITATION WARRANTIES OF FITNESS FOR A PARTICULAR PURPOSE. NO WARRANTY MAY BE CREATED OR EXTENDED BY SALES OR PROMOTIONAL MATERIALS. THE ADVICE AND STRATEGIES CONTAINED HEREIN MAY NOT BE SUITABLE FOR EVERY SITUATION. THIS WORK IS SOLD WITH THE UNDERSTANDING THAT THE PUBLISHER IS NOT ENGAGED IN RENDERING LEGAL, ACCOUNTING, OR OTHER PROFESSIONAL SERVICES. IF PROFESSIONAL ASSISTANCE IS REQUIRED, THE SERVICES OF A COMPETENT PROFESSIONAL PERSON SHOULD BE SOUGHT. NEITHER THE PUBLISHER NOR THE AUTHOR SHALL BE LIABLE FOR DAMAGES ARISING HEREFROM. THE FACT THAT AN ORGANIZATION OR WEBSITE IS REFERRED TO IN THIS WORK AS A CITATION AND/OR A POTENTIAL SOURCE OF FURTHER INFORMATION DOES NOT MEAN THAT THE AUTHOR OR THE PUBLISHER ENDORSES THE INFORMATION THE ORGANIZATION OR WEBSITE MAY PROVIDE OR RECOMMENDATIONS IT MAY MAKE. FURTHER, READERS SHOULD BE AWARE THAT INTERNET WEBSITES LISTED IN THIS WORK MAY HAVE CHANGED OR DISAPPEARED BETWEEN WHEN THIS WORK WAS WRITTEN AND WHEN IT IS READ.

For general information on our other products and services, please contact our Customer Care Department within the U.S. at 877-762-2974, outside the U.S. at 317-572-3993, or fax 317-572-4002. For technical support, please visit https://hub.wiley.com/community/support/dummies.

Wiley publishes in a variety of print and electronic formats and by print-on-demand. Some material included with standard print versions of this book may not be included in e-books or in print-on-demand. If this book refers to media such as a CD or DVD that is not included in the version you purchased, you may download this material at http://booksupport.wiley.com. For more information about Wiley products, visit www.wiley.com.

Library of Congress Control Number: 2017936606

ISBN 978-1-119-33049-3 (pbk); ISBN 978-1-119-33053-0 (ebk); ISBN 978-1-119-33052-3 (ebk)

Manufactured in the United States of America

10 9 8 7 6 5 4 3 2 1

Contents at a Glance

Table of Contents

Introduction

You need to learn about algorithms for school or work. Yet, all the books you've tried on the subject end up being more along the lines of really good sleep-inducing aids rather than texts to teach you something. Assuming that you can get past the arcane symbols obviously written by a demented two-year-old with a penchant for squiggles, you end up having no idea of why you'd even want to know anything about them. Most math texts are boring! However, *Algorithms For Dummies* is different. The first thing you'll note is that this book has a definite lack of odd symbols (especially of the squiggly sort) floating about. Yes, you see a few (it is a math book, after all), but what you find instead are clear instructions for using algorithms that actually have names and a history behind them to perform useful tasks. You'll encounter simple coding techniques that perform amazing things that will intrigue your friends and certainly make them jealous as you perform amazing feats of math that they can't begin to understand. You get all this without having to strain your brain, even a little, and you won't even fall asleep (well, unless you really want to do so).

About This Book

Algorithms For Dummies is the math book that you wanted in college but didn't get. You discover, for example, that algorithms aren't new. After all, the Babylonians used algorithms to perform simple tasks as early as 1,600 BC. If the Babylonians could figure this stuff out, certainly you can, too! This book actually has three things that you won't find in most math books:

» Algorithms that have actual names and a historical basis so that you can remember the algorithm and know why someone took time to create it

» Simple explanations of how the algorithm performs amazing feats of data manipulation, data analysis, or probability prediction

» Code that shows how to use the algorithm without actually dealing with arcane symbols that no one without a math degree can understand

Part of the emphasis of this book is on using the right tools. This book uses Python to perform various tasks. Python has special features that make working with algorithms significantly easier. For example, Python provides access to a huge array of packages that let you do just about anything you can imagine, and more than a few that you can't. However, unlike many texts that use Python, this one doesn't bury you in packages. We use a select group of packages that provide great flexibility with a lot of functionality, but don't require you to pay anything. You can go through this entire book without forking over a cent of your hard-earned money.

You also discover some interesting techniques in this book. The most important is that you don't just see the algorithms used to perform tasks; you also get an explanation of how the algorithms work. Unlike many other books, *Algorithms For Dummies* enables you to fully understand what you're doing, but without requiring you to have a PhD in math. Every one of the examples shows the expected output and tells you why that output is important. You aren't left with the feeling that something is missing.

Of course, you might still be worried about the whole programming environment issue, and this book doesn't leave you in the dark there, either. At the beginning, you find complete installation instructions for Anaconda, which is the Python language Integrated Development Environment (IDE) used for this book. In addition, quick primers (with references) help you understand the basic Python programming that you need to perform. The emphasis is on getting you up and running as quickly as possible, and to make examples straightforward and simple so that the code doesn't become a stumbling block to learning.

To help you absorb the concepts, this book uses the following conventions:

>> Text that you're meant to type just as it appears in the book is in **bold**. The exception is when you're working through a step list: Because each step is bold, the text to type is not bold.

>> Words that we want you to type in that are also in *italics* are used as placeholders, which means that you need to replace them with something that works for you. For example, if you see "Type ***Your Name*** and press Enter," you need to replace *Your Name* with your actual name.

>> We also use *italics* for terms we define. This means that you don't have to rely on other sources to provide the definitions you need.

>> Web addresses and programming code appear in monofont. If you're reading a digital version of this book on a device connected to the Internet, you can click the live link to visit that website, like this: http://www.dummies.com.

>> When you need to click command sequences, you see them separated by a special arrow, like this: File ⇨ New File, which tells you to click File and then New File.

Foolish Assumptions

You might find it difficult to believe that we've assumed anything about you — after all, we haven't even met you yet! Although most assumptions are indeed foolish, we made certain assumptions to provide a starting point for the book.

The first assumption is that you're familiar with the platform you want to use, because the book doesn't provide any guidance in this regard. (Chapter 3 does, however, tell you how to install Anaconda; Chapter 4 provides a basic Python language overview; and Chapter 5 helps you understand how to perform the essential data manipulations using Python.) To give you the maximum information about Python with regard to algorithms, this book doesn't discuss any platform-specific issues. You really do need to know how to install applications, use applications, and generally work with your chosen platform before you begin working with this book.

This book isn't a math primer. Yes, you see lots of examples of complex math, but the emphasis is on helping you use Python to perform common tasks using algorithms rather than learning math theory. However, you do get explanations of many of the algorithms used in the book so that you can understand how the algorithms work. Chapters 1 and 2 guide you through a better understanding of precisely what you need to know in order to use this book successfully.

This book also assumes that you can access items on the Internet. Sprinkled throughout are numerous references to online material that will enhance your learning experience. However, these added sources are useful only if you actually find and use them.

Icons Used in This Book

As you read this book, you encounter icons in the margins that indicate material of interest (or not, as the case may be). Here's what the icons mean:

TIP

Tips are nice because they help you save time or perform some task without a lot of extra work. The tips in this book are time-saving techniques or pointers to resources that you should try so that you can get the maximum benefit from Python, or in performing algorithm-related or data analysis–related tasks.

WARNING

We don't want to sound like angry parents or some kind of maniacs, but you should avoid doing anything that's marked with a Warning icon. Otherwise, you might find that your application fails to work as expected, you get incorrect answers from seemingly bulletproof algorithms, or (in the worst-case scenario) you lose data.

TECHNICAL STUFF

Whenever you see this icon, think advanced tip or technique. You might find these tidbits of useful information just too boring for words, or they could contain the solution you need to get a program running. Skip these bits of information whenever you like.

REMEMBER

If you don't get anything else out of a particular chapter or section, remember the material marked by this icon. This text usually contains an essential process or a bit of information that you must know to work with Python, or to perform algorithm-related or data analysis–related tasks successfully.

Beyond the Book

This book isn't the end of your Python or algorithm learning experience — it's really just the beginning. We provide online content to make this book more flexible and better able to meet your needs. That way, as we receive email from you, we can address questions and tell you how updates to Python, or its associated add-ons affect book content. In fact, you gain access to all these cool additions:

>> **Cheat sheet:** You remember using crib notes in school to make a better mark on a test, don't you? You do? Well, a cheat sheet is sort of like that. It provides you with some special notes about tasks that you can do with Python, Anaconda, and algorithms that not every other person knows. To find the cheat sheet for this book, go to www.dummies.com and search for *Algorithms For Dummies Cheat Sheet*. It contains really neat information such as finding the algorithms that you commonly need to perform specific tasks.

>> **Updates:** Sometimes changes happen. For example, we might not have seen an upcoming change when we looked into our crystal ball during the writing of this book. In the past, this possibility simply meant that the book became outdated and less useful, but you can now find updates to the book at www.dummies.com/go/algorithmsfd.

In addition to these updates, check out the blog posts with answers to reader questions and demonstrations of useful book-related techniques at http://blog.johnmuellerbooks.com/.

>> **Companion files:** Hey! Who really wants to type all the code in the book and reconstruct all those plots manually? Most readers prefer to spend their time actually working with Python, performing tasks using algorithms, and seeing the interesting things they can do, rather than typing. Fortunately for you, the examples used in the book are available for download, so all you need to do is read the book to learn algorithm usage techniques. You can find these files at www.dummies.com/go/algorithmsfd.

Where to Go from Here

It's time to start your algorithm learning adventure! If you're completely new to algorithms, you should start with Chapter 1 and progress through the book at a pace that allows you to absorb as much of the material as possible. Make sure to read about Python because the book uses this language as needed for the examples.

If you're a novice who's in an absolute rush to get going with algorithms as quickly as possible, you can skip to Chapter 3 with the understanding that you may find some topics a bit confusing later. If you already have Anaconda installed, you can skim Chapter 3. To use this book, you must install Python version 3.4. The examples won't work with the 2.x version of Python because this version doesn't support some of the packages we use.

Readers who have some exposure to Python, and have the appropriate language versions installed, can save reading time by moving directly to Chapter 6. You can always go back to earlier chapters as necessary when you have questions. However, you do need to understand how each technique works before moving to the next one. Every technique, coding example, and procedure has important lessons for you, and you could miss vital content if you start skipping too much information.

1
Getting Started

IN THIS PART . . .

Discover how you can use algorithms to perform practical tasks.

Understand how algorithms are put together.

Install and configure Python to work with algorithms.

Use Python to work with algorithms.

Perform basic algorithm manipulations using Python.

Chapter **1**

Introducing Algorithms

I f you're in the majority of people, you're likely confused as you open this book and begin your adventure with algorithms because most texts never tell you what an algorithm is, much less why you'd want to use one. Most texts assume that you already know something about algorithms and that you are reading about them to refine and elevate your knowledge. Interestingly enough, some books actually provide a confusing definition for *algorithm* that doesn't really define it after all, and sometimes even equates it to some other form of abstract, numeric, or symbolic expression.

The first section of this chapter is dedicated to helping you understand precisely what the term *algorithm* means and why you benefit from knowing how to use algorithms. Far from being arcane, algorithms are actually used all over the place, and you have probably used or been helped by them for years without really knowing it. In truth, algorithms are becoming the spine that supports and regulates what is important in an increasingly complex and technological society like ours.

This chapter also discusses how you use computers to create solutions to problems using algorithms, how to distinguish between issues and solutions, and what you need to do to manipulate data to discover a solution. The goal of this chapter is to help you differentiate between algorithms and other tasks that people perform that they confuse with algorithms. In short, you discover why you really want to know about algorithms and how to apply them to data.

Describing Algorithms

Even though people have solved algorithms manually for literally thousands of years, doing so can consume huge amounts of time and require many numeric computations, depending on the complexity of the problem you want to solve. Algorithms are all about finding solutions, and the speedier and easier, the better. A huge gap exists between mathematical algorithms historically created by geniuses of their time, such as Euclid, Newton, or Gauss, and modern algorithms created in universities as well as private research and development laboratories. The main reason for this gap is the use of computers. Using computers to solve problems by employing the appropriate algorithm speeds up the task signifi-cantly, which is the reason that the development of new algorithms has pro-gressed so fast since the appearance of powerful computer systems. In fact, you may have noticed that more and more solutions to problems appear quickly today, in part, because computer power is both cheap and constantly increasing. Given their ability to solve problems using algorithms, computers (sometimes in the form of special hardware) are becoming ubiquitous.

When working with algorithms, you consider the inputs, desired outputs, and pro-cess (a sequence of actions) used to obtain a desired output from a given input. However, you can get the terminology wrong and view algorithms in the wrong way because you haven't really considered how they work in a real-world setting. The third section of the chapter discusses algorithms in a real-world manner, that is, by viewing the terminologies used to understand algorithms and to present algorithms in a way that shows that the real-world is often less than perfect. Understanding how to describe an algorithm in a realistic manner also makes it possible to temper expectations to reflect the realities of what an algorithm can actually do.

This book views algorithms in many ways. However, because it provides an over-view telling how algorithms are changing and enriching people's lives, the focus is on algorithms used to manipulate data with a computer providing the required processing. With this in mind, the algorithms you work with in this book require data input in a specific form, which sometimes means changing the data to match the algorithm's requirements. Data manipulation doesn't change the content of the data. What it does do is change the presentation and form of the data so that an algorithm can help you see new patterns that weren't apparent before (but were actually present in the data all along).

Sources of information about algorithms often present them in a way that proves confusing because they're too sophisticated or downright incorrect. Although you may find other definitions, this book uses the following definitions for terms that people often confuse with algorithms (but aren't):

>> **Equation:** Numbers and symbols that, when taken as a whole, equate to a specific value. An equation always contains an equals sign so that you know

that the numbers and symbols represent the specific value on the other side of the equals sign. Equations generally contain variable information presented as a symbol, but they're not required to use variables.

>> **Formula:** A combination of numbers and symbols used to express information or ideas. Formulas normally present mathematical or logical concepts, such as defining the Greatest Common Divisor (GCD) of two integers (the video at `https://www.khanacademy.org/math/in-sixth-grade-math/playing-numbers/highest-common-factor/v/greatest-common-divisor` tells how this works). Generally, they show the relationship between two or more variables. Most people see a formula as a special kind of equation.

REMEMBER

>> **Algorithm:** A sequence of steps used to solve a problem. The sequence presents a unique method of addressing an issue by providing a particular solution. An algorithm need not represent mathematical or logical concepts, even though the presentations in this book often do fall into that category because people most commonly use algorithms in this manner. Some special formulas are also algorithms, such as the quadratic formula. In order for a process to represent an algorithm, it must be

- **Finite:** The algorithm must eventually solve the problem. This book discusses problems with a known solution so that you can evaluate whether an algorithm solves the problem correctly.

- **Well-defined:** The series of steps must be precise and present steps that are understandable. Especially because computers are involved in algorithm use, the computer must be able to understand the steps to create a usable algorithm.

- **Effective:** An algorithm must solve all cases of the problem for which someone defined it. An algorithm should always solve the problem it has to solve. Even though you should anticipate some failures, the incidence of failure is rare and occurs only in situations that are acceptable for the intended algorithm use.

With these definitions in mind, the following sections help to clarify the precise nature of algorithms. The goal isn't to provide a precise definition for algorithms, but rather to help you understand how algorithms fit into the grand scheme of things so that you can develop your own understanding of what algorithms are and why they're so important.

Defining algorithm uses

An algorithm always presents a series of steps and doesn't necessarily perform these steps to solve a math formula. The scope of algorithms is incredibly large. You can find algorithms that solve problems in science, medicine, finance, industrial production and supply, and communication. Algorithms provide support for all parts of a person's daily life. Any time a sequence of actions achieving something in our life is finite, well-defined, and effective, you can view it as an algorithm. For example, you can turn even something as trivial and simple as making toast into an algorithm. In fact, the making toast procedure often appears in computer science classes, as discussed at http://brianaspinall.com/now-thats-how-you-make-toast-using-computer-algorithms/.

TIP

Unfortunately, the algorithm on the site is flawed. The instructor never removes the toast from the wrapper and never plugs the toaster in, so the result is damaged plain bread still in its wrapper stuffed into a nonfunctional toaster (see the discussion at http://blog.johnmuellerbooks.com/2013/03/04/procedures-in-technical-writing/ for details). Even so, the idea is the correct one, yet it requires some slight, but essential, adjustments to make the algorithm finite and effective.

One of the most common uses of algorithms is as a means of solving formulas. For example, when working with the GCD of two integer values, you can perform the task manually by listing each of the factors for the two integers and then selecting the greatest factor that is common to both. For example, GCD(20, 25) is 5 because 5 is the largest number that divides into both 20 and 25. However, processing every GCD manually (which is actually a kind of algorithm) is time consuming and error prone, so the Greek mathematician Euclid (https://en.wikipedia.org/wiki/Euclid) created an algorithm to perform the task. You can see the Euclidean method demonstrated at https://www.khanacademy.org/computing/computer-science/cryptography/modarithmetic/a/the-euclidean-algorithm.

However, a single formula, which is a presentation of symbols and numbers used to express information or ideas, can have multiple solutions, each of which is an algorithm. In the case of GCD, another common algorithm is one created by Lehmer (see https://www.imsc.res.in/~kapil/crypto/notes/node11.html and https://en.wikipedia.org/wiki/Lehmer%27s_GCD_algorithm for details). Because you can solve any formula multiple ways, people often spend a great deal of time comparing algorithms to determine which one works best in a given situation. (See a comparison of Euclid to Lehmer at http://citeseerx.ist.psu.edu/viewdoc/download?doi=10.1.1.31.693&rep=rep1&type=pdf.)

REMEMBER

Because our society and its accompanying technology are gaining momentum, running faster and faster, we need algorithms that can keep the pace. Scientific achievements such as sequencing the human genome were possible in our age because scientists found algorithms that run fast enough to complete the task. Measuring which algorithm is better in a given situation, or in an average usage situation, is really serious stuff and a topic of discussion among computer scientists.

When it comes to computer science, the same algorithm can see multiple presentations. For example, you can present the Euclidean algorithm in both a recursive and an iterative manner, as explained at http://cs.stackexchange.com/questions/1447/what-is-most-efficient-for-gcd. In short, algorithms present a method of solving formulas, but it would be a mistake to say that just one acceptable algorithm exists for any given formula or that there is only one acceptable presentation of an algorithm. Using algorithms to solve problems of various sorts has a long history — it isn't something that has just happened.

Even if you limit your gaze to computer science, data science, artificial intelligence, and other technical areas, you find many kinds of algorithms — too many for a single book. For example, *The Art of Computer Programming*, by Donald E. Knuth (Addison-Wesley), spans 3,168 pages in four volumes (see http://www.amazon.com/exec/obidos/ASIN/0321751043/datacservip0f-20/) and still doesn't manage to cover the topic (the author intended to write more volumes). However, here are some interesting uses for you to consider:

>> **Searching:** Locating information or verifying that the information you see is the information you want is an essential task. Without this ability, it wouldn't be possible to perform many tasks online, such as finding the website on the Internet selling the perfect coffee pot for your office.

>> **Sorting:** Determining which order to use to present information is important because most people today suffer from information overload, and putting information in order is one way to reduce the onrush of data. You likely learned as a child that when you place your toys in order, it's easier to find and play with a toy that interests you, compared to having toys scattered randomly everywhere. Imagine going to Amazon, finding that over a thousand coffee pots are for sale there, and yet not being able to sort them in order of price or most positive review. Moreover, many complex algorithms require data in the proper order to work dependably, therefore ordering is an important requisite for solving more problems.

>> **Transforming:** Converting one sort of data to another sort of data is critical to understanding and using the data effectively. For example, you might understand imperial weights just fine, but all your sources use the metric system. Converting between the two systems helps you understand the data. Likewise, the Fast Fourier Transform (FFT) converts signals between the time domain and the frequency domain so that it becomes possible to make things like your Wi-Fi router work.

>> **Scheduling:** Making the use of resources fair to all concerned is another way in which algorithms make their presence known in a big way. For example, timing lights at intersections are no longer simple devices that count down the seconds between light changes. Modern devices consider all sorts of issues, such as the time of day, weather conditions, and flow of traffic. Scheduling comes in many forms, however. For example, consider how your computer runs multiple tasks at the same time. Without a scheduling algorithm, the operating system might grab all the available resources and keep your application from doing any useful work.

- **Graph analysis:** Deciding on the shortest line between two points finds all sorts of uses. For example, in a routing problem, your GPS couldn't function without this particular algorithm because it could never direct you along city streets using the shortest route from point A to point B.

- **Cryptography:** Keeping data safe is an ongoing battle with hackers constantly attacking data sources. Algorithms make it possible to analyze data, put it into some other form, and then return it to its original form later.

- **Pseudorandom number generation:** Imagine playing games that never varied. You start at the same place; perform the same steps, in the same manner, every time you play. Without the capability to generate seemingly random numbers, many computer tasks become impossible.

REMEMBER

This list presents an incredibly short overview. People use algorithms for many different tasks and in many different ways, and constantly create new algorithms to solve both existing problems and new problems. The most important issue to consider when working with algorithms is that given a particular input, you should expect a specific output. Secondary issues include how many resources the algorithm requires to perform its task and how long it takes to complete the task. Depending on the kind of issue and the sort of algorithm used, you may also need to consider issues of accuracy and consistency.

Finding algorithms everywhere

The previous section mentions the toast algorithm for a specific reason. For some reason, making toast is probably the most popular algorithm ever created. Many grade-school children write their equivalent of the toast algorithm long before they can even solve the most basic math. It's not hard to imagine how many variations of the toast algorithm exist and what the precise output is of each of them. The results likely vary by individual and the level of creativity employed. In short, algorithms appear in great variety and often in unexpected places.

Every task you perform on a computer involves algorithms. Some algorithms appear as part of the computer hardware. (They are embedded, thus you hear of embedded microprocessors.) The very act of booting a computer involves the use of an algorithm. You also find algorithms in operating systems, applications, and every other piece of software. Even users rely on algorithms. Scripts help direct users to perform tasks in a specific way, but those same steps could appear as written instructions or as part of an organizational policy statement.

Daily routines often devolve into algorithms. Think about how you spend your day. If you're like most people, you perform essentially the same tasks every day in the same order, making your day an algorithm that solves the problem of how to live successfully while expending the least amount of energy possible. After all, that's what a routine does; it makes us efficient.

Emergency procedures often rely on algorithms. You take the emergency card out of the packet in front of you in the plane. On it are a series of pictographs showing how to open the emergency door and extend the slide. In some cases, you might not even see words, but the pictures convey the procedure required to perform the task and solve the problem of getting out of the plane in a hurry. Throughout this book, you see the same three elements for every algorithm:

1. Describe the problem.

2. Create a series of steps to solve the problem (well defined).

3. Perform the steps to obtain a desired result (finite and effective).

Using Computers to Solve Problems

The term *computer* sounds quite technical and possibly a bit overwhelming to some people, but people today are neck deep (possibly even deeper) in computers. You wear at least one computer, your smartphone, most of the time. If you have any sort of special device, such as a pacemaker, it also includes a computer. Your smart TV contains at least one computer, as does your smart appliance. A car can contain as many as 30 computers in the form of embedded microprocessors that regulate fuel consumption, engine combustion, transmission, steering, and stability (according to a *New York Times* article at `http://www.nytimes.com/2010/02/05/technology/05electronics.html`) and more lines of code than a jet fighter. The automated cars appearing in the car market will require even more embedded microprocessors and algorithms of greater complexity. A computer exists to solve problems quickly and with less effort than solving them manually. Consequently, it shouldn't surprise you that this book uses still more computers to help you understand algorithms better.

Computers vary in a number of ways. The computer in your watch is quite small; the one on your desktop quite large. Supercomputers are immense and contain many smaller computers all tasked to work together to solve complex issues, such as tomorrow's weather. The most complex algorithms rely on special computer functionality to obtain solutions to the issues people design them to solve. Yes, you could use lesser resources to perform the task, but the trade-off is waiting a lot longer for an answer or getting an answer that lacks sufficient accuracy to provide a useful solution. In some cases, you wait so long that the answer is no longer important. With the need for both speed and accuracy in mind, the following sections discuss some special computer features that can affect algorithms.

Leveraging modern CPUs and GPUs

General-purpose processors, CPUs, started out as a means to solve problems using algorithms. However, their general-purpose nature also means that a CPU can perform a great many other tasks, such as moving data around or interacting with external devices. A general-purpose processor does many things well, which means that it can perform the steps required to complete an algorithm, but not necessarily fast. In fact, owners of early general-purpose processors could add math coprocessors (special math-specific chips) to their systems to gain a speed advantage (see `http://www.computerhope.com/jargon/m/mathcopr.htm` for details). Today, general-purpose processors have the math coprocessor embedded into them, so when you get an Intel i7 processor, you actually get multiple processors in a single package.

TIP

Interestingly enough, Intel still markets specialty processor add-ons, such as the Xeon Phi processor used with the Xeon chips (see `http://www.intel.com/content/www/us/en/processors/xeon/xeon-phi-detail.html` and `https://en.wiki2.org/wiki/Intel_Xeon_Phi` for details). You use the Xeon Phi chip alongside a Xeon chip when performing compute-intensive tasks such as machine learning (see *Machine Learning For Dummies,* by John Mueller and Luca Massaron, for details on how machine learning uses algorithms to determine how to perform various tasks that help you use data to predict the unknown and to organize information meaningfully).

You may wonder why this section mentions Graphics Processing Units (GPUs). After all, GPUs are supposed to take data, manipulate it in a special way, and then display a pretty picture onscreen. Any computer hardware can serve more than one purpose. It turns out that GPUs are particularly adept at performing data transformations, which is a key task for solving algorithms in many cases. A GPU is a special-purpose processor, but one with capabilities that lend themselves to faster algorithm execution. It shouldn't surprise you to discover that people who create algorithms spend a lot of time thinking outside the box, which means that they often see methods of solving issues in nontraditional approaches.

The point is that CPUs and GPUs form the most commonly used chips for performing algorithm-related tasks. The first performs general-purpose tasks quite well, and the second specializes in providing support for math-intensive tasks, especially those that involve data transformations. Using multiple cores makes parallel processing (performing more than one algorithmic step at a time) possible. Adding multiple chips increases the number of cores available. Having more cores adds speed, but a number of factors keeps the speed gain to a minimum. Using two i7 chips won't produce double the speed of just one i7 chip.

Working with special-purpose chips

A math coprocessor and a GPU are two examples of common special-purpose chips in that you don't see them used to perform tasks such as booting the system. However, algorithms often require the use of uncommon special-purpose chips to solve problems. This isn't a hardware book, but spending a little time looking around can show you all sorts of interesting chips, such as the new artificial neurons that IBM is working on (see the story at http://www.computerworld.com/article/3103294/computer-processors/ibm-creates-artificial-neurons-from-phase-change-memory-for-cognitive-computing.html). Imagine performing algorithmic processing using memory that simulates the human brain. It would create an interesting environment for performing tasks that might not otherwise be possible today.

Neural networks, a technology that is used to simulate human thought and make deep learning techniques possible for machine learning scenarios, are now benefitting from the use of specialized chips, such as the Tesla P100 from NVidia (see the story at https://www.technologyreview.com/s/601195/a-2-billion-chip-to-accelerate-artificial-intelligence/ for details). These kinds of chips not only perform algorithmic processing extremely fast, but learn as they perform the tasks, making them faster still with each iteration. Learning computers will eventually power robots that can move (after a fashion) on their own, akin to the robots seen in the movie *I Robot* (see one such robot described at http://www.cbsnews.com/news/this-creepy-robot-is-powered-by-a-neural-network/). There are also special chips that perform tasks such as visual recognition (see https://www.technologyreview.com/s/537211/a-better-way-to-build-brain-inspired-chips/ for details).

REMEMBER

No matter how they work, specialized processors will eventually power all sorts of algorithms that will have real-world consequences. You can already find many of these real-world applications in a relatively simple form. For example, imagine the tasks that a pizza-making robot would have to solve — the variables it would have to consider on a real-time basis. This sort of robot already exists (this is just one example of the many industrial robots used to produce material goods by employing algorithms), and you can bet that it relies on algorithms to describe what to do, as well as on special chips to ensure that the tasks are done quickly (see the story at http://www.bloomberg.com/news/articles/2016-06-24/inside-silicon-valley-s-robot-pizzeria).

TECHNICAL
STUFF

Eventually, it might even be possible to use the human mind as a processor and output the information through a special interface. Some companies are now experimenting with putting processors directly into the human brain to enhance its ability to process information (see the story at https://www.washingtonpost.com/news/the-switch/wp/2016/08/15/putting-a-computer-in-your-brain-is-no-longer-science-fiction/ for details). Imagine a system in which humans can solve algorithms at the speed of computers, but with the creative "what if" potential of humans.

Leveraging networks

Unless you have unlimited funds, using some algorithms effectively may not be possible, even with specialized chips. In that case, you can network computers together. Using special software, one computer, a master, can use the processors of all slave computers running an *agent* (a kind of in-memory background application that makes the processor available). Using this approach, you can solve incredibly complex problems by offloading pieces of the problem to a number of slave computers. As each computer in the network solves its part of the problem, it sends the results back to the master, which puts the pieces together to create a consolidated answer, a technique called *cluster computing.*

Lest you think this is the stuff of science fiction, people are already using cluster computing techniques in all sorts of interesting ways. For example, the article at `http://www.zdnet.com/article/build-your-own-supercomputer-out-of-raspberry-pi-boards/` details how you can build your own supercomputer by combining multiple Raspberry Pi (`https://www.raspberrypi.org/`) boards into a single cluster.

Distributed computing, another version of cluster computing (but with a looser organization) is also popular. In fact, you can find a list of distributed computing projects at `http://www.distributedcomputing.info/projects.html`. The list of projects includes some major endeavors, such as Search for Extraterrestrial Intelligence (SETI). You can also donate your computer's extra processing power to work on a cure for cancer. The list of potential projects is amazing.

Networks also let you access other people's processing power in an unattached form. For example, Amazon Web Services (AWS) and other vendors provide the means to use their computers to perform your work. A network connection can make the remote computers feel as if they're part of your own network. The point is that you can use networking in all sorts of ways to create connections between computers to solve a variety of algorithms that would be too complicated to solve using just your system.

Leveraging available data

Part of solving an algorithm has nothing to do with processing power, creative thinking outside the box, or anything of a physical nature. To create a solution to most problems, you also need data on which to base a conclusion. For example, in the toast-making algorithm, you need to know about the availability of bread, a toaster, electricity to power the toaster, and so on before you can solve the problem of actually making toast. The data becomes important because you can't finish the algorithm when missing even one element of the required solution. Of course, you may need additional input data as well. For example, the person wanting the toast may not like rye. If this is the case and all you have is rye bread to use, the presence of bread still won't result in a successful result.

Data comes from all sorts of sources and in all kinds of forms. You can stream data from a source such as a real-time monitor, access a public data source, rely on private data in a database, scrape the data from websites, or get it in myriad other ways too numerous to mention here. The data may be static (unchanging) or dynamic (constantly changing). You may find that the data is complete or missing elements. The data may not appear in the right form (such as when you get imperial units and require metric units when solving a weight problem). The data may appear in a tabular format when you need it in some other form. It may reside in an unstructured way (for instance in a NoSQL database or just in a bunch of different data files) when you need the formal formatting of a relational database. In short, you need to know all sorts of things about the data used with your algorithm in order to solve problems with it.

REMEMBER

Because data comes in so many forms and you need to work with it in so many ways, this book pays a lot of attention to data. Starting in Chapter 6, you discover just how data structure comes into play. Moving on to Chapter 7, you begin looking at how to search through data to find what you need. Chapters 12 through 14 help you work with big data. However, you can find some sort of data-specific information in just about every chapter of the book because without data, an algorithm can't solve any problems.

Distinguishing between Issues and Solutions

This book discusses two parts of the algorithmic view of the real world. On the one hand, you have *issues,* which are problems that you need to solve. An issue can describe the desired output of an algorithm or it can describe a hurdle you must overcome to obtain the desired output. *Solutions* are the methods, or steps, used to address the issues. A solution can relate to just one step or many steps within the algorithm. In fact, the output of an algorithm, the response to the last step, is a solution. The following sections help you understand some of the important aspects of issues and solutions.

Being correct and efficient

Using algorithms is all about getting an acceptable answer. The reason you look for an acceptable answer is that some algorithms generate more than one answer in response to fuzzy input data. Life often makes precise answers impossible to get. Of course, getting a precise answer is always the goal, but often you end up with an acceptable answer instead.

Getting the most precise answer possible may take too much time. When you get a precise answer but that answer comes too late to use, the information becomes useless and you've wasted your time. Choosing between two algorithms that address the same issue may come down to a choice between speed and precision. A fast algorithm may not generate a precise answer, but the answer may still work well enough to provide useful output.

Wrong answers can be a problem. Creating a lot of wrong answers fast is just as bad as creating a lot of precisely correct answers slowly. Part of the focus of this book is helping you find the middle ground between too fast and too slow, and between inaccurate and too accurate. Even though your math teacher stressed the need for providing the correct answer in the way expressed by the book you used at the time, real-world math often involves weighing choices and making middle-ground decisions that affect you in ways you might not think possible.

Discovering there is no free lunch

You may have heard the common myth that you can have everything in the way of computer output without putting much effort into deriving the solution. Unfortunately, no absolute solution exists to any problem, and better answers are often quite costly. When working with algorithms, you quickly discover the need to provide additional resources when you require precise answers quickly. The size and complexity of the data sources you use greatly affect the solution resolution as well. As size and complexity increase, you find that the need to add resources increases as well.

Adapting the strategy to the problem

Part 5 of this book looks at strategies you can use to decrease the cost of working with algorithms. The best mathematicians use tricks to get more output from less computing. For example, you can create an ultimate algorithm to solve an issue, or you can use a host of simpler algorithms to solve the same issue, but using multiple processors. The host of simple algorithms will usually work faster and better than the single, complex algorithm, even though this approach seems counterintuitive.

Describing algorithms in a lingua franca

Algorithms do provide a basis for communication between people, even when those individuals have different perspectives and speak different languages. For example, Bayes' Theorem (the probability of an event occurring given certain premises; see `https://betterexplained.com/articles/an-intuitive-and-short-explanation-of-bayes-theorem/` for a quick explanation of this amazing theorem)

```
P(B|E) = P(E|B)*P(B)/P(E)
```

appears the same whether you speak English, Spanish, Chinese, German, French, or any other language. Regardless what language you speak, the algorithm looks the same and acts the same given the same data. Algorithms help cross all sorts of divides that serve to separate humans from each other by expressing ideas in a form that anyone can prove. As you go through this book, you discover the beauty and magic that algorithms can provide in communicating even subtle thoughts to others.

TIP

Apart from universal mathematical notations, algorithms take advantage of programming languages as a means for explaining and communicating the formulas they solve. You can find all the sorts of algorithms in C, C++, Java, Fortran, Python (as in this book), and other languages. Some writers rely on pseudocode to overcome the fact that an algorithm may be proposed in a programming language that you don't know. *Pseudocode* is a way to describe computer operations by using common English words.

Facing hard problems

An important consideration when working with algorithms is that you can use them to solve issues of any complexity. The algorithm doesn't think, have emotion, or care how you use it (or even abuse it). You can use algorithms in any way required to solve an issue. For example, the same group of algorithms used to perform facial recognition to act as an alternative to computer passwords (for security purposes) can find terrorists lurking in an airport or recognize a lost child wandering the streets. The same algorithm has different uses; how to use it depends on the interests of the user. Part of the reason you want to read this book carefully is to help you solve those hard problems that may require only a simple algorithm to address.

Structuring Data to Obtain a Solution

Humans think about data in nonspecific ways and apply various rules to the same data to understand it in ways that computers never can. A computer's view of data is structured, simple, uncompromising, and most definitely not creative. When humans prepare data for a computer to use, the data often interacts with the algorithms in unexpected ways and produces undesirable output. The problem is one in which the human fails to appreciate the limited view of data that a computer has. The following sections describe two aspects of data that you see illustrated in many of the chapters to follow.

Understanding a computer's point of view

A computer has a simple view of data, but it's also a view that humans typically don't understand. For one thing, everything is a number to a computer because computers aren't designed to work with any other kind of data. Humans see characters on the computer display and assume that the computer interacts with the data in that manner, but the computer doesn't understand the data or its implications. The letter A is simply the number 65 to the computer. In fact, it's not truly even the number 65. The computer sees a series of electrical impulses that equate to a binary value of 0100 0001.

Computers also don't understand the whole concept of uppercase and lowercase. To a human, the lowercase *a* is simply another form of the uppercase *A*, but to a computer they're two different letters. A lowercase *a* appears as the number 97 to the computer (a binary value of 0110 0001).

If these simple sorts of single letter comparisons could cause such problems between humans and computers, it isn't hard to imagine what happens when humans start assuming too much about other kinds of data. For example, a computer can't hear or appreciate music. Yet, music comes out of the computer speakers. The same holds true for graphics. A computer sees a series of 0s and 1s, not a graphic containing a pretty scene of the countryside.

REMEMBER

It's important to consider data from the computer's perspective when using algorithms. The computer sees only 0s and 1s, nothing else. Consequently, when you start working through the needs of the algorithm, you must view the data in that manner. You may actually find it beneficial to know that the computer's view of data makes some solutions easier to find, not harder. You discover more about this oddity in viewing data as the book progresses.

Arranging data makes the difference

Computers also have a strict idea about the form and structure of data. When you begin working with algorithms, you find that a large part of the job involves making the data appear in a form that the computer can use when using the algorithm to find a solution to an issue. Although a human can mentally see patterns in data that isn't arranged precisely right, computers really do need the precision to find the same pattern. The benefit of this precision is that computers can often make new patterns visible. In fact, that's one of the main reasons to use algorithms with computers — to help locate new patterns and then use those patterns to perform other tasks. For example, a computer may recognize a customer's spending pattern so that you can use the information to generate more sales automatically.

Chapter **2**

Considering Algorithm Design

A s stated in Chapter 1, an algorithm consists of a series of steps used to solve a problem. In most cases, input data provides the basis of solving the problem and sometimes offers constraints that any solution must consider before anyone will see the algorithm as being effective. The first section of this chapter helps you consider the *problem solution* (the solution to the problem you're trying to solve). It helps you understand the need to create algorithms that are both flexible (in that they can handle a wide range of data inputs) and effective (in that they yield the desired output).

Some problems are quite complex. In fact, you look at them at first and may decide that they're too complicated to solve. Feeling overwhelmed by a problem is common. The most common way to solve the issue is to divide the problem into smaller pieces, each of which is manageable on its own. The divide-and-conquer approach to problem solving, discussed in this chapter's second section, originally referred to warfare (see `http://classroom.synonym.com/civilization-invented-divide-conquer-strategy-12746.html` for a history of this approach). However, people use the same ideas to cut problems of all sorts down to size.

REMEMBER

The third section of the chapter refers to the greedy approach to problem solving. Greed normally has a negative connotation, but not in this case. A *greedy algorithm* is one that makes an optimal choice at each problem-solving stage. By doing so, it hopes to obtain an overall optimal solution to solve the problem. Unfortunately, this strategy doesn't always work, but it's always worth a try. It often yields a *good enough* solution, making it a good baseline.

No matter what problem-solving approach you choose, every algorithm comes with costs. Being good shoppers, people who rely heavily on algorithms want the best possible deal, which means performing a cost/benefit analysis. Of course, getting the best deal also assumes that a person using the algorithm has some idea of what sort of solution is good enough. Getting a solution that is too precise or one that offers too much in the way of output is often wasteful, so part of keeping costs under control is getting what you need as output and nothing more.

To know what you have with an algorithm, you need to know how to measure it in various ways. Measurements create a picture of usability, size, resource usage, and cost in your mind. More important, measurements offer the means of making comparisons. You can't compare algorithms without measurements. Until you can compare the algorithms, you can't choose the best one for a task.

Starting to Solve a Problem

Before you can solve any problem, you must understand it. It isn't just a matter of sizing up the problem, either. Knowing that you have certain inputs and require certain outputs is a start, but that's not really enough to create a solution. Part of the solution process is to

>> Discover how other people have created new problem solutions

>> Know what resources you have on hand

>> Determine the sorts of solutions that worked for similar problems in the past

>> Consider what sorts of solutions haven't produced a desirable result

The following sections help you understand these phases of solving a problem. Realize that you won't necessarily perform these phases in order and that sometimes you revisit a phase after getting more information. The process of starting a problem solution is iterative; you keep at it until you have a good understanding of the problem at hand.

Modeling real-world problems

Real-world problems differ from those found in textbooks. When creating a textbook, the author often creates a simple example to help the reader understand the basic principles at work. The example models just one aspect of a more complex problem. A real-world problem may require that you combine several techniques to create a complete solution. For example, to locate the best answer to a problem, you may:

1. Need to sort the answer set by a specific criterion.

2. Perform some sort of filtering and transformation.

3. Search the result.

Without this sequence of steps, comparing each of the answers adequately may prove impossible, and you end up with a less-than-optimal result. A series of algorithms used together to create a desired result is an *ensemble*. You can read about their use in machine learning in *Machine Learning For Dummies*, by John Paul Mueller and Luca Massaron (Wiley). The article at https://www.toptal.com/machine-learning/ensemble-methods-machine-learning gives you a quick overview of how ensembles work.

However, real-world problems are even more complex than simply looking at static data or iterating that data only once. For example, anything that moves, such as a car, airplane, or robot, receives constant input. Each updated input includes error information that a real-world solution will need to incorporate into the result in order to keep these machines working properly. In addition to other algorithms, the constant calculations require the proportional integral derivative (PID) algorithm (see http://www.ni.com/white-paper/3782/en/ for a detailed explanation of this algorithm) to control the machine using a feedback loop. Every calculation brings the solution used to control the machine into better focus, which is why machines often go through a settling stage when you first turn them on. (If you work with computers regularly, you might be used to the idea of iterations. PIDs are for continuous systems; therefore, there are no iterations.) Finding the right solution is called *settling time* — the time during which the algorithm controlling the machine hasn't yet found the right answer.

When modeling a real-world problem, you must also consider non-obvious issues that crop up. An obvious solution, even one based on significant mathematical input and solid theory, may not work. For example, during WWII, the allies had a serious problem with bomber losses. Therefore, the engineers analyzed every bullet hole in every plane that came back. After the analysis, the engineers used their solution to armor the allied planes more heavily to ensure that more of them would come back. It didn't work. Enter Abraham Wald. This mathematician suggested a non-obvious solution: Put armor plating in all the places that lacked bullet holes (because the areas with bullet holes are already strong enough;

otherwise the plane wouldn't have returned). The resulting solution did work and is now used as the basis for *survivor bias* (the fact that the survivors of an incident often don't show what actually caused a loss) in working with algorithms. You can read more about this fascinating bit of history at `http://www.macgetit.com/solving-problems-of-wwii-bombers/`. The point is that biases and other problems in modeling problems can create solutions that don't work.

Real-world modeling may also include the addition of what scientists normally consider undesirable traits. For example, scientists often consider noise undesirable because it hides the underlying data. Consider a hearing aid, which removes noise to enable someone to hear better (see the discussion at `http://www.ncbi.nlm.nih.gov/pmc/articles/PMC4111515/` for details). Many methods exist for removing noise, some of which you can find in this book starting with Chapter 9 as part of other topic discussions. However, as counterintuitive as it might seem, adding noise also requires an algorithm that provides useful output. For example, Ken Perlin wanted to get rid of the machine-like look of computer-generated graphics in 1983 and created an algorithm to do so. The result is Perlin noise (see `http://paulbourke.net/texture_colour/perlin/` for details). The effect is so useful that Ken won an Academy Award for his work (see `http://mrl.nyu.edu/~perlin/doc/oscar.html` for details). Other people, such as Steven Worley, have created other sorts of noise that affect graphics in other ways (see the discussion at `http://procworld.blogspot.com/2011/05/hello-worley.html`, which compares Perlin noise to Worley noise). The point is that whether you need to remove or add noise depends on the problem domain you want to solve. A real-world scenario often requires choices that may not be obvious when working in the lab or during the learning process.

REMEMBER

The main gist of this section is that solutions often require several iterations to create, you may have to spend a lot of time refining them, and obvious solutions may not work at all. When modeling a real-world problem, you do begin with the solutions found in textbooks, but then you must move beyond theory to find the actual solution to your problem. As this book progresses, you're exposed to a wide variety of algorithms — all of which help you find solutions. The important thing to remember is that you may need to combine these examples in various ways and discover methods for interacting with data so that it lends itself to finding patterns that match the output you require.

Finding solutions and counterexamples

The previous section introduces you to the vagaries of discovering real-world solutions that consider issues that solutions found in the lab can't consider. However, just finding a solution — even a good one — isn't sufficient because even good solutions fail on occasion. Playing the devil's advocate by locating counterexamples is an important part of starting to solve a problem. The purpose of counterexamples is to

» Potentially disprove the solution

» Provide boundaries that define the solution better

» Consider situations in which the hypothesis used as a basis for the solution remains untested

» Help you understand the limits of the solution

A common scenario that illustrates a solution and counterexample is the statement that all prime numbers are odd. (*Prime numbers* are integers that can be divided only by themselves and 1 to produce an integer result.) Of course, the number 2 is prime, but it's also even, which makes the original statement false. Someone making the statement could then qualify it by saying that all prime numbers are odd except 2. The partial solution to the problem of finding all the prime numbers is that you need to find odd numbers, except in the case of 2, which is even. In this second case, disproving the solution is no longer possible, but adding to the original statement provides a boundary.

By casting doubt on the original assertion, you can also consider situations in which the hypothesis, all prime numbers except 2 are odd, may not hold true. For example, 1 is an odd number but isn't considered prime (see the discussion at `https://primes.utm.edu/notes/faq/one.html` for details). So now the original statement has two boundaries, and you must restate it as follows: Prime numbers are greater than 1 and usually odd, except for 2, which is even. The boundaries for prime numbers are better defined by locating and considering counterexamples. Just in case you're wondering, 0 is also not considered a prime number, for the reasons discussed at `http://math.stackexchange.com/questions/539174/is-zero-a-prime-number`.

TIP

As the complexity of a problem grows, the potential for finding counterexamples grows as well. An essential rule to consider is that, as with reliability, having more failure points means greater potential for a failure to occur. Thinking of algorithms in this way is important. Ensembles of simple algorithms can produce better results with fewer potential counterexamples than a single complex algorithm.

Standing on the shoulders of giants

A myth that defies explanation is that the techniques currently used to process huge quantities of data are somehow new. Yes, new algorithms do appear all the time, but the basis for these algorithms is all of the algorithms that have gone before. In fact, when you think about Sir Isaac Newton, you might think of someone who invented something new, yet even he stated (using correct spelling for his time), "If I have seen further it is by standing on the sholders of Giants" (see `https://en.wikiquote.org/wiki/Isaac_Newton` for additional quotes and insights).

The fact is that the algorithms you use today weren't even new in the days of Aristotle (see `http://plato.stanford.edu/entries/aristotle-mathematics/` for a discussion of how Aristotle used math) and Plato (see `http://www.story ofmathematics.com/greek_plato.html` for a discussion of how Plato used math). The origins of algorithms in use today are so hidden in history that the best that anyone can say is that math relies on adaptations of knowledge from ancient times. The use of algorithms since antiquity should give you a certain feeling of comfort because the algorithms in use today are based on knowledge tested for thousands of years.

This isn't to say that some mathematicians haven't overturned the apple cart over the years. For example, John Nash's theory, Nash Equilibrium, significantly changed how economics are considered today (see `https://www.khanacademy. org/economics-finance-domain/microeconomics/nash-equilibrium-tutorial` for a basic tutorial on this theory). Of course, recognition for such work comes slowly (and sometimes not at all). Nash had to wait for a long time before he received much in the way of professional recognition (see the story at `https://www.princeton.edu/main/news/archive/S42/72/29C63/index.xml`) despite having won a Nobel Prize in economics for his contributions. Just in case you're interested, John Nash's story is depicted in the movie *A Beautiful Mind,* which contains some much-debated scenes, including one containing a claim that the Nash Equilibrium somehow overturns some of the work of Adam Smith, another contributor to economic theories. (See one such discussion at `https://www.quora.com/Was-Adam-Smith-wrong-as-claimed-by-John-Nash-in-the-movie-A-Beautiful-Mind.`)

Dividing and Conquering

If solving problems were easy, everyone would do it. However, the world is still filled with unsolved problems and the condition isn't likely to change anytime soon, for one simple reason: Problems often appear so large that no solution is imaginable. Ancient warriors faced a similar problem. An opposing army would seem so large and their forces so small as to make the problem of winning a war unimaginably hard, perhaps impossible. Yet, by dividing the opposing army into small pieces and attacking it a little at a time, a small army could potentially defeat a much larger opponent. (The ancient Greeks, Romans, and Napoleon Bonaparte were all great users of the divide-and-conquer strategy; see *Napoleon For Dummies,* by J. David Markham [Wiley], for details.)

You face the same problem as those ancient warriors. Often, the resources at your disposal seem quite small and inadequate. However, by dividing a huge problem into small pieces so that you can understand each piece, you can eventually create a solution that works for the problem as a whole. Algorithms have this premise at their core: to use steps to solve problems one small piece at a time. The following sections help you understand the divide-and-conquer approach to problem solving in more detail.

Avoiding brute-force solutions

A *brute-force solution* is one in which you try each possible answer, one at a time, to locate the best possible answer. It's thorough, this much is certain, but it also wastes time and resources in most cases. Testing every answer, even when it's easy to prove that a particular answer has no chance of success, wastes time that an algorithm can use on answers that have a better chance of success. In addition, testing the various answers using this approach generally wastes resources, such as memory. Think of it this way: You want to break the combination for a lock, so you begin at 0, 0, 0, even though you know that this particular combination has no chance of success given the physical characteristics of combination locks. A brute-force solution would proceed with testing 0, 0, 0 anyway and then move on to the equally ridiculous 0, 0, 1.

REMEMBER

It's important to understand that every solution type does come with advantages, sometimes quite small. A brute-force solution has one such advantage. Because you test every answer anyway, you don't need to perform any sort of preprocessing when working with a brute-force solution. The time saved in skipping the preprocessing, though, is unlikely to ever pay back the time lost in trying every answer. However, you may find occasion to use a brute-force solution when

» Finding a solution, if one exists, is essential.

» The problem size is limited.

» You can use heuristics to reduce the size of the solution set.

» Simplicity of implementation is more important than speed.

Starting by making it simpler

The brute-force solution has a serious drawback. It looks at the entire problem at one time. It's sort of like going into a package and hunting book by book through the shelves without ever considering any method of making your search simpler. The divide-and-conquer approach to package searches is different. In this case, you begin by dividing the package into children's and adults' sections. After that, you divide the adults' section into categories. Finally, you search just the part of the category that contains the book of interest. This is the purpose of classification systems such as the Dewey Decimal System (see https://en.wikipedia.org/wiki/List_of_Dewey_Decimal_classes for a list of classes, hierarchical divisions, and sections). The point is that divide and conquer simplifies the problem. You make things faster and easier by reducing the number of book candidates.

The divide part of divide and conquer is an essential way to understand a problem better as well. Trying to understand the layout of an entire package could prove difficult. However, knowing that the book on comparative psychology you want to find appears as part of Class 100 in Division 150 of Section 156 makes your job easier. You can understand this smaller problem because you know that every Section 156 book will contain something about the topic you wish to know about. Algorithms work the same way. By making the problem simpler, you can create a set of simpler steps to finding a problem solution, which reduces the time to find the solution, reduces the number of resources used, and improves your chances of finding precisely the solution you need.

Breaking down a problem is usually better

After you have divided a problem into manageable pieces, you need to conquer the piece in question. This means creating a precise problem definition. You don't want just any book on comparative psychology; you want one written by George Romanes. Knowing that the book you want appears in Section 156 of the Dewey Decimal System is a good start, but it doesn't solve the problem. Now you need a process for reviewing every book in Section 156 for the specific book you need. The process might go further still and look for books with specific content. To make this process viable, you must break the problem down completely, define precisely what you need, and then, after you understand the problem thoroughly, use the correct set of steps (algorithm) to find what you need.

ALGORITHMS HAVE NO ABSOLUTES

You may think that you can create a scenario in which you can say that you always use a particular kind of algorithm to solve a particular kind of problem. However, this isn't the case. For example, you can find discussions of the relative merits of using brute-force techniques against certain problems as compared to divide and conquer. It shouldn't surprise you to discover that divide and conquer doesn't win in every situation. For example, when looking for the maximum value in an array, a brute-force approach can win the day when the array isn't sorted. You can read a discussion of this particular topic at http://stackoverflow.com/questions/11043226/why-do-divide-and-conquer-algorithms-often-run-faster-than-brute-force. The interesting thing is that the brute-force approach also uses fewer resources in this particular case. Always remember that rules have exceptions and knowing the exceptions can save you time and effort later.

Learning that Greed Can Be Good

In some cases, you can't see the end of a solution process or even know whether you're winning the war. The only thing you can really do is to ensure that you win the individual battles to create a problem solution in hopes of also winning the war. A greedy method to problem solving uses this approach. It looks for an overall solution such that it chooses the best possible outcome at each problem solution stage.

REMEMBER

It seems that winning each battle would necessarily mean winning the war as well, but sometimes the real world doesn't work that way. A *Pyrrhic victory* is one in which someone wins every battle but ends up losing the war because the cost of the victory exceeds the gains of winning by such a large margin. You can read about five Pyrrhic victories at http://www.history.com/news/history-lists/ 5-famous-Pyrrhic-victories. The important lesson from these histories is that a greedy algorithm often does work, but not always, so you need to consider the best overall solution to a problem rather than become blinded by interim wins. The following sections describe how to avoid the Pyrrhic victory when working with algorithms.

Applying greedy reasoning

Greedy reasoning is often used as part of an optimization process. The algorithm views the problem one step at a time and focuses just on the step at hand. Every greedy algorithm makes two assumptions:

>> You can make a single optimal choice at a given step.

>> By choosing the optimal selection at each step, you can find an optimal solution for the overall problem.

You can find many greedy algorithms, each optimized to perform particular tasks. Here are some common examples of greedy algorithms used for graph analysis (see Chapter 9 for more about graphs) and data compression (see Chapter 14 for more about data compression) and the reason you might want to use them:

>> **Kruskal's Minimum Spanning Tree (MST):** This algorithm actually demonstrates one of the principles of greedy algorithms that people might not think about immediately. In this case, the algorithm chooses the edge between two nodes with the smallest value, not the greatest value as the word *greedy* might initially convey. This sort of algorithm might help you find the shortest path between two locations on a map or perform other graph-related tasks.

>> **Prim's MST:** This algorithm splits an undirected graph (one in which direction isn't considered) in half. It then selects the edge that connects the two halves such that the total weight of the two halves is the smallest that it can be. You

might find this algorithm used in a maze game to locate the shortest distance between the start and the finish of the maze.

>> **Huffman Encoding:** This algorithm is quite famous in computers because it forms the basis for many data-compression techniques. The algorithm assigns a code to every unique data entry in a stream of entries, such that the most commonly used data entry receives the shortest code. For example, the letter *E* would normally receive the shortest code when compressing English text, because you use it more often than any other letter in the alphabet. By changing the encoding technique, you can compress the text and make it considerably smaller, reducing transmission time.

Reaching a good solution

Scientists and mathematicians use greedy algorithms so often that Chapter 15 covers them in depth. However, it's important to realize that what you really want is a good solution, not just a particular solution. In most cases, a good solution provides optimal results of the sort you can measure, but the word *good* can include many meanings, depending on the problem domain. You must ask what problem you want to solve and which solution solves the problem in a manner that best meets your needs. For example, when working in engineering, you might need to weigh solutions that consider weight, size, cost, or other considerations, or perhaps some combination of all these outputs that meet a specific requirement.

To put this issue into context, say that you build a coin machine that creates change for particular monetary amounts using the fewest coins possible (perhaps as part of an automatic checkout at a store). The reason to use the fewest coins possible is to reduce equipment wear, the weight of coins needed, and the time required to make change (your customers are always in a hurry, after all). A greedy solution solves the problem by using the largest coins possible. For example, to output $0.16 in change, you use a dime ($0.10), a nickel ($0.05), and a penny ($0.01).

REMEMBER

A problem occurs when you're unable to use every coin type in creating a solution. The change machine might be out of nickels, for example. To provide $0.40 in change, a greedy solution would start with a quarter ($0.25) and a dime ($0.10). Unfortunately, there are no nickels, so the coin machine then outputs five pennies (5 × $0.01) for a total of seven coins. The optimal solution in this case is to use four dimes instead (4 × $0.10). As a result, the greedy algorithm provides a particular solution, but not a good (optimal) solution in this case. The change-making problem receives considerable attention because it's so hard to solve. You can find additional information in discussions such as "Combinatorics of the Change-Making Problem," by Anna Adamaszeka and Michal Adamaszek (see http://www.sciencedirect.com/science/article/pii/S0195669809001292 for details).

Computing Costs and Following Heuristics

Even when you find a good solution, one that is both efficient and effective, you still need to know precisely what the solution costs. You may find that the cost of using a particular solution is still too high, even when everything else is considered. Perhaps the answer comes almost, but not quite, on time or it uses too many computing resources. The search for a good solution involves creating an environment in which you can fully test the algorithm, the states it creates, the operators it uses to change those states, and the time required to derive a solution.

Often, you find that a *heuristic approach,* one that relies on self-discovery and produces sufficiently useful results (not necessarily optimal, but good enough) is the method you actually need to solve a problem. Getting the algorithm to perform some of the required work for you saves time and effort because you can create algorithms that see patterns better than humans do. Consequently, self-discovery is the process of allowing the algorithm to show you a potentially useful path to a solution (but you must still count on human intuition and understanding to know whether the solution is the right one). The following sections describe techniques you can use to compute the cost of an algorithm using heuristics as a method of discovering the actual usefulness of any given solution.

Representing the problem as a space

A *problem space* is an environment in which a search for a solution takes place. A set of states and the operators used to change those states represent the problem space. For example, consider a tile game that has eight tiles in a 3-x-3 frame. Each tile shows one part of a picture, and the tiles start in some random order so that the picture is scrambled. The goal is to move one tile at a time to place all the tiles in the right order and reveal the picture. You can see an example of this sort of puzzle at `http://mypuzzle.org/sliding`.

The combination of the start state, the randomized tiles, and the goal state — the tiles in a particular order — is the *problem instance.* You could represent the puzzle graphically using a *problem space graph.* Each node of the problem space graph presents a state (the eight tiles in a particular position). The edges represent operations, such as to move tile number eight up. When you move tile eight up, the picture changes — it moves to another state.

Winning the game by moving from the start state to the goal state isn't the only consideration. To solve the game efficiently, you need to perform the task in the least number of moves possible, which means using the smallest number of operators. The minimum number of moves used to solve the puzzle is the *problem depth.*

You must consider several factors when representing a problem as a space. For example, you must consider the maximum number of nodes that will fit in memory, which represents the *space complexity*. When you can't fit all the nodes in memory at one time, the computer must store some nodes in other locations, such as the hard drive, which can slow the algorithm considerably. To determine whether the nodes will fit in memory, you must consider the *time complexity*, which is the maximum number of nodes created to solve the problem. In addition, it's important to consider the *branching factor*, which is the average number of nodes created in the problem space graph to solve a problem.

Going random and being blessed by luck

Solving a search problem using brute-force techniques (described in "Avoiding brute-force techniques," earlier in this chapter) is possible. The advantage of this approach is that you don't need any domain-specific knowledge to use one of these algorithms. A brute-force algorithm tends to use the simplest possible approach to solving the problem. The disadvantage is that a brute-force approach works well only for a small number of nodes. Here are some of the common brute-force search algorithms:

>> **Breadth-first search:** This technique begins at the root node, explores each of the child nodes first, and only then moves down to the next level. It progresses level by level until it finds a solution. The disadvantage of this algorithm is that it must store every node in memory, which means that it uses a considerable amount of memory for a large number of nodes. This technique can check for duplicate nodes, which saves time, and it always comes up with a solution.

>> **Depth-first search:** This technique begins at the root node and explores a set of connected child nodes until it reaches a leaf node. It progresses branch by branch until it finds a solution. The disadvantage of this algorithm is that it can't check for duplicate nodes, which means that it might traverse the same node paths more than once. In fact, this algorithm may not find a solution at all, which means that you must define a cutoff point to keep the algorithm from searching infinitely. An advantage of this approach is that it's memory efficient.

>> **Bidirectional search:** This technique searches simultaneously from the root node and the goal node until the two search paths meet in the middle. An advantage of this approach is that it's time efficient because it finds the solution faster than many other brute-force solutions. In addition, it uses memory more efficiently than other approaches and always finds a solution. The main disadvantage is complexity of implementation, translating into a longer development cycle.

Using a heuristic and a cost function

For some people, the word *heuristic* just sounds complicated. It would be just as easy to say that the algorithm makes an educated guess and then tries again when it fails. Unlike brute-force methods, heuristic algorithms learn. They also use cost functions to make better choices. Consequently, heuristic algorithms are more complex, but they have a distinct advantage in solving complex problems. As with brute-force algorithms, there are many heuristic algorithms and each comes with its own set of advantages, disadvantages, and special requirements. The following list describes a few of the most common heuristic algorithms:

>> **Pure heuristic search:** The algorithm expands nodes in order of their cost. It maintains two lists. The closed list contains the nodes it has already explored; the open list contains the nodes it must yet explore. In each iteration, the algorithm expands the node with the lowest possible cost. All its child nodes are placed in the closed list and the individual child node costs are calculated. The algorithm sends the child nodes with a low cost back to the open list and deletes the child nodes with a high cost. Consequently, the algorithm performs an intelligent, cost-based search for the solution.

>> **A * search:** The algorithm tracks the cost of nodes as it explores them using the equation: $f(n) = g(n) + h(n)$, where

- n is the node identifier.

- g(n) is the cost of reaching the node so far.

- h(n) is the estimated cost to reach the goal from the node.

- f(n) is the estimated cost of the path from n to the goal.

The idea is to search the most promising paths first and avoid expensive paths.

>> **Greedy best-first search:** The algorithm always chooses the path that is closest to the goal using the equation: $f(n) = h(n)$. This particular algorithm can find solutions quite quickly, but it can also get stuck in loops, so many people don't consider it an optimal approach to finding a solution.

Evaluating Algorithms

Gaining insights into precisely how algorithms work is important because otherwise you can't determine whether an algorithm actually performs in the way you need it to. In addition, without good measurements, you can't perform accurate comparisons to know whether you really do need to discover a new method of solving a problem when an older solution works too slowly or uses too many resources. The reality is that you'll use algorithms made by others most of the time, potentially devising a few of your own. Knowing the basis to use to compare different solutions and deciding between them is an essential skill when dealing with algorithms.

The issue of efficiency has been part of discovering and designing new algorithms since the concept of algorithms first came into being, which is why you see so many different algorithms competing to solve the same problem (sometimes a real embarrassment of riches). The concept of measuring the size of the functions within an algorithm and analyzing how the algorithm works isn't new; both Ada Lovelace and Charles Babbage considered the problems of algorithm efficiency in reference to computers as early as 1843 (see a short history of the Babbage engine at `http://www.computerhistory.org/babbage/adalovelace/`).

Donald Knuth (`http://www-cs-faculty.stanford.edu/~uno/`), computer scientist, mathematician, professor emeritus at Stanford University, and author of the milestone, multivolume book *The Art of Computer Programming* (Addison-Wesley), devoted much of his research and studies to comparing algorithms. He strived to formalize how to estimate the resource needs of algorithms in a mathematical way and to allow a correct comparison between alternative solutions. He coined the term *analysis of algorithms,* which is the branch of computer science devoted to understanding how algorithms work in a formal way. The analysis measures resources required in terms of the number of operations an algorithm requires to reach a solution or by its occupied space (such as the storage an algorithm requires in computer memory).

Analysis of algorithms requires some mathematical understanding and some computations, but it's extremely beneficial in your journey to discover, appreciate, and effectively use algorithms. This topic is considerably more abstract than other topics in this book. To make the discussion less theoretical, later chapters present more practicalities of such measurement by examining algorithms together in detail. The following sections provide you with the basics.

Simulating using abstract machines

The more operations an algorithm requires, the more complex it is. Complexity is a measure of algorithm efficiency in terms of time usage because each operation takes some time. Given the same problem, complex algorithms are generally less favorable than simple algorithms because complex algorithms require more time. Think about those times when speed of execution makes the difference, such as in the medical or financial sector, or when flying on automatic pilot on an airplane or space rocket. Measuring algorithm complexity is a challenging task, though a necessary one if you want to employ the right solution. The first measurement technique uses abstract machines like the Random Access Machine (RAM).

REMEMBER

RAM also stands for Random-Access Memory, which is the internal memory that your computer uses when running programs. Even though it uses the same acronym, a Random-Access Machine is something completely different.

Abstract machines aren't real computers, but theoretical ones, computers that are imagined in their functioning. You use abstract machines to consider how well an algorithm would work on a computer without testing it on the real thing, yet bound by the type of hardware you'd use. A RAM computer performs basic arithmetic operations and interacts with information in memory, that's all. Every time a RAM computer does anything, it takes a time step (a time unit). When you evaluate an algorithm in a RAM simulation, you count time steps using the following procedure:

1. Count each simple operation (arithmetic ones) as a time step.

2. Break complex operations into simple arithmetic operations and count time steps as defined in Step 1.

3. Count every data access from memory as one time step.

To perform this accounting, you write a pseudocode version of your algorithm (as mentioned in Chapter 1) and perform these steps using paper and pencil. In the end, it's a simple approach based on a basic idea of how computers work, a useful approximation that you can use to compare solutions regardless of the power and speed of your hardware or the programming language you use.

REMEMBER

Using a simulation is different from running the algorithm on a computer because you use a standard and predefined input. Real computer measurements require that you run the code and verify the time required to run it. Running code on a computer is actually a *benchmark,* another form of efficiency measurement, in which you also account for the application environment (such as the type of hardware used and the software implementation). A benchmark is useful but lacks generalization. Consider, for instance, how newer hardware can quickly execute an algorithm that took ages on your previous computer.

Getting even more abstract

Measuring a series of steps devised to achieve a solution to a problem poses quite a few challenges. The previous section discusses counting time steps (number of operations), but sometimes you also need to compute space (such as the memory an algorithm consumes). You consider space when your problem is greedy for resources. Depending on the problem, you may consider an algorithm better when it works efficiently with regard to one of these resource consumption aspects:

>> Running time

>> Computer memory requirements

>> Hard-disk usage

>> Power consumption

>> Data-transmission speed in a network

Some of these aspects relate to others in an inverse manner, so if, for instance, you want speedier execution time, you can increase memory or power consumption to get it. Not only can you have different efficiency configurations when running an algorithm, you can also change the hardware characteristics and software implementation to accomplish your goals. In terms of hardware, using a supercomputer or a general-purpose computer does matter, and the software, or language used to write the algorithm, is definitely a game changer. In addition, the quantity and kind of data you feed the algorithm could result in better or worse performance measurements.

RAM simulations count time because when you can employ a solution in so many environments and its resource usage depends on so many factors, you have to find a way to simplify comparisons so that they become standard. Otherwise, you can't compare possible alternatives. The solution is, as so often happens with many other problems, to use a single measure and say that one size fits all. In this case, the measure is time, which you make equal to the number of operations, that is, the complexity of the algorithm.

A RAM simulation places the algorithm in a situation that's both language and machine agnostic (it's independent of programming language and computer type). However, explaining how a RAM simulation works to others requires quite an effort. The analysis of algorithms proposes to use the number of operations you get from a RAM simulation and turn them into a mathematical function expressing how your algorithm behaves in terms of time, which is a quantification of the steps or operations required when the number of data inputs grows. For instance, if your algorithm sorts objects, you can express complexity using a function that reports how many operations it needs depending on the number of objects it receives.

Working with functions

A function in mathematics is simply a way to map some inputs to a response. Expressed in a different way, a *function* is a transformation (based on math operations) that transforms (maps) your input to an answer. For certain values of input (usually denoted by the letters *x* or *n*), you have a corresponding answer using the math that defines the function. For instance, a function like $f(n) = 2n$ tells you that when your input is a number *n*, your answer is the number *n* multiplied by 2.

Using the size of the input does make sense given that this is a time-critical age and people's lives are crammed with a growing quantity of data. Making everything a mathematical function is a little less intuitive, but a function describing how an algorithm relates its solution to the quantity of data it receives is something you can analyze without specific hardware or software support. It's also easy to compare with other solutions, given the size of your problem. Analysis of algorithms is really a mind-blowing concept because it reduces a complex series of steps into a mathematical formula.

Moreover, most of the time, an analysis of algorithms isn't even interested in defining the function exactly. What you really want to do is compare a target function with another function. These comparison functions appear within a set of proposed functions that perform poorly when contrasted to the target algorithm. In this way, you don't have to plug numbers into functions of greater or lesser complexity; instead, you deal with simple, premade, and well-known functions. It may sound rough, but it's more effective and is similar to classifying the performance of algorithms into categories, rather than obtaining an exact performance measurement.

The set of generalized functions is called *Big O* notation, and in this book, you often encounter this small set of functions (put into parentheses and preceded by a capital O) used to represent the performance of algorithms. Figure 2-1 shows the analysis of an algorithm. A Cartesian coordinate system can represent its function as measured by RAM simulation, where the *abscissa* (the x coordinate) is the size of the input and the *ordinate* (the y coordinate) is its resulting number of operations. You can see three curves represented. Input size matters. However, quality also matters (for instance, when ordering problems, it's faster to order an input which is already almost ordered). Consequently, the analysis shows a worst case, $f_1(n)$, an average case, $f_2(n)$, and a best case, $f_3(n)$. Even though the average case might give you a general idea, what you really care about is the worst case, because problems may arise when your algorithm struggles to reach a solution. The Big O function is the one that, after a certain n_0 value (the threshold for considering an input big), always results in a larger number of operations given the same input than the worst-case function f_1. Thus, the Big O function is even more pessimistic than the one representing your algorithm, so that no matter the quality of input, you can be sure that things cannot get worse than that.

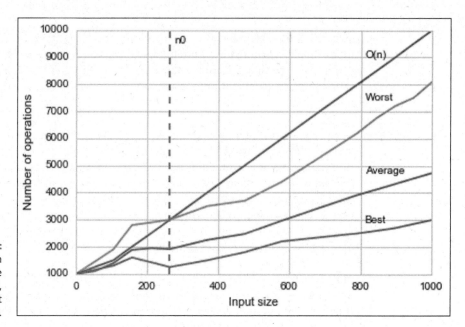

FIGURE 2-1:
Complexity of an algorithm in case of best, average, and worst input case.

Many possible functions can result in worse results, but the choice of functions offered by the Big O notation that you can use is restricted because its purpose is to simplify complexity measurement by proposing a standard. Consequently, this section contains just the few functions that are part of the Big O notation. The following list describes them in growing order of complexity:

» **Constant complexity O(1):** The same time, no matter how much input you provide. In the end, it is a constant number of operations, no matter how long the input data is. This level of complexity is quite rare in practice.

» **Logarithmic complexity O(log n):** The number of operations grows at a slower rate than the input, making the algorithm less efficient with small inputs and more efficient with larger ones. A typical algorithm of this class is the binary search, as described in Chapter 7 on arranging and searching data.

» **Linear complexity O(n):** Operations grow with the input in a 1:1 ratio. A typical algorithm is iteration, which is when you scan input once and apply an operation to each element of it. Chapter 5 discusses iterations.

» **Linearithmic complexity O(n log n):** Complexity is a mix between logarithmic and linear complexity. It is typical of some smart algorithms used to order data, such as Mergesort, Heapsort, and Quicksort. Chapter 7 tells you about most of them.

» **Quadratic complexity $O(n^2)$:** Operations grow as a square of the number of inputs. When you have one iteration inside another iteration (nested iterations, in computer science), you have quadratic complexity. For instance, you have a list of names and, in order to find the most similar ones, you compare each name against all the other names. Some less efficient ordering algorithms present such complexity: bubble sort, selection sort, and insertion sort. This level of complexity means that your algorithms may run for hours or even days before reaching a solution.

» **Cubic complexity $O(n^3)$:** Operations grow even faster than quadratic complexity because now you have multiple nested iterations. When an algorithm has this order of complexity and you need to process a modest amount of data (100,000 elements), your algorithm may run for years. When you have a number of operations that is a power of the input, it is common to refer to the algorithm as *running in polynomial time.*

» **Exponential complexity $O(2^n)$:** The algorithm takes twice the number of previous operations for every new element added. When an algorithm has this complexity, even small problems may take forever. Many algorithms doing exhaustive searches have exponential complexity. However, the classic example for this level of complexity is the calculation of Fibonacci numbers (which, being a recursive algorithm, is dealt with in Chapter 5).

» **Factorial complexity $O(n!)$:** A real nightmare of complexity because of the large number of possible combinations between the elements. Just imagine: If your input is 100 objects and an operation on your computer takes 10^{-6} seconds (a reasonable speed for every computer, nowadays), you will need about 10^{140} years to complete the task successfully (an impossible amount of time since the age of the universe is estimated as being 10^{14} years). A famous factorial complexity problem is the traveling salesman problem, in which a salesman has to find the shortest route for visiting many cities and coming back to the starting city (presented in Chapter 18).

Chapter **3**

Using Python to Work with Algorithms

You have many good choices when it comes to using computer assistance to discover the wonders of algorithms. For example, apart from Python, many people rely on MATLAB and many others use R. In fact, some people use all three and then compare the sorts of outputs they get (see one such comparison at `https://www.r-bloggers.com/evaluating-optimization-algorithms-in-matlab-python-and-r/`). If you just had the three choices, you'd still need to think about them for a while and might choose to learn more than one language, but you actually have more than three choices, and this book can't begin to cover them all. If you get deep into the world of algorithms, you discover that you can use all programming languages to write algorithms and that some are appreciated because they boil everything down to simple operations, such as the RAM simulation described in Chapter 2. For instance, Donald Knuth, winner of the Turing Award, wrote examples in Assembly language in his book *The Art of Computer Programming* (Addison-Wesley). Assembly language is a programming language that resembles machine code, the language used natively by computers (but not understandable by most humans).

This book uses Python for a number of good reasons, including the community support it enjoys and the fact that it's full featured, yet easy to learn. Python is also a verbose language, resembling how a human creates instructions rather than how a computer interprets them. The first section of this chapter fills in the details of why this book uses Python for the examples, but also tells you why other options are useful and why you may need to consider them as your journey continues.

When you speak a human language, you add nuances of meaning by employing specific word combinations that others in your community understand. The use of nuanced meaning comes naturally and represents a dialect. In some cases, dialects also form because one group wants to demonstrate a difference with another group. For example, Noah Webster wrote and published *A Grammatical Institute of the English Language,* in part to remove the influence of the British aristocracy from the American public (see http://connecticuthistory.org/noah-webster-and-the-dream-of-a-common-language/ for details). Likewise, computer languages often come with flavors, and vendors purposely add extensions that make their product unique to provide a reason to buy their product over another offering.

The second section of the chapter introduces you to various Python distributions, each of which provides a Python dialect. This book uses Analytics Anaconda, which is the product you should use to obtain the best results from your learning experience. Using another product, essentially another dialect, can cause problems in making the examples work — the same sort of thing that happens sometimes when someone who speaks British English talks to someone who speaks American English. However, knowing about other distributions can be helpful when you need to obtain access to features that Anaconda may not provide.

The next three sections of this chapter help you install Anaconda on your platform. The examples in this book are tested on the Linux, Mac OS X, and Windows platforms. They may also work with other platforms, but the examples aren't tested on these platforms, so you have no guarantee that they'll work. By installing Anaconda using the procedures found in this chapter, you reduce the chance of getting an installation that won't work with the example code. To use the examples in this book, you must install Anaconda 4.2.0 with support for Python 3.5. Other versions of Anaconda and Python may not work with the example code because, as with human language dialects, they could misunderstand the instructions that the code provides.

Algorithms work with data in specific ways. To see particular output from an algorithm, you need consistent data. Fortunately, the Python community is busy creating datasets that anyone can use for testing purposes. This allows the community to repeat results that others get without having to download custom datasets from an unknown source. The final section of this chapter helps you get and install the datasets needed for the examples.

Considering the Benefits of Python

To work with algorithms on a computer, you need some means of communicating with the computer. If this were *Star Trek,* you could probably just tell the computer what you want and it would dutifully perform the task for you. In fact, Scotty seems quite confused about the lack of a voice computer interface in *Star Trek IV* (see `http://www.davidalison.com/2008/07/keyboard-vs-mouse.html` for details). The point is that you still need to use the mouse and keyboard, along with a special language, to communicate your ideas to the computer because the computer isn't going to make an effort to communicate with you. Python is one of a number of languages that is especially adept at making it easy for nondevelopers to communicate ideas to the computer, but it isn't the only choice. The following paragraphs help you understand why this book uses Python and what your other choices are.

Understanding why this book uses Python

Every computer language available today translates algorithms into a form that the computer can process. In fact, languages like ALGOL (ALGOrithmic Language) and FORTRAN (FORmula TRANslation) make this focus clear. Remember the definition of an algorithm from Chapter 1 as being a sequence of steps used to solve a problem. The method used to perform this translation differs by language, and the techniques used by some languages are quite arcane, requiring specialized knowledge even to make an attempt.

REMEMBER

Computers speak only one language, *machine code* (the 0s and 1s that a computer interprets to perform tasks), which is so incredibly hard for humans to speak that early developers created a huge array of alternatives. Computer languages exist to make human communication with computers easier. Consequently, if you find yourself struggling to make anything work, perhaps you have the wrong language. It's always best to have more than one language at your fingertips so that you can perform computer communications with ease. Python happens to be one of the languages that works exceptionally well for people who work in disciplines outside application development.

Python is the vision of a single person, Guido van Rossum (see his home page at `https://gvanrossum.github.io/`). You might be surprised to learn that Python has been around for a long time — Guido started the language in December 1989 as a replacement for the ABC language. Not much information is available as to the precise goals for Python, but it does retain ABC's capability to create applications using less code. However, it far exceeds the capability of ABC to create applications of all types, and in contrast to ABC, boasts four programming styles. In short, Guido took ABC as a starting point, found it limited, and created a new language without those limitations. It's an example of creating a new language that really is better than its predecessor.

Python has gone through a number of iterations and currently has two development paths. The 2.*x* path is backward compatible with previous versions of Python; the 3.*x* path isn't. The compatibility issue is one that figures into how you use Python to perform algorithm-related tasks because at least some of the packages won't work with 3.*x*. In addition, some versions use different licensing because Guido was working at various companies during Python's development. You can see a listing of the versions and their respective licenses at `https://docs.python.org/3/license.html`. The Python Software Foundation (PSF) owns all current versions of Python, so unless you use an older version, you really don't need to worry about the licensing issue.

TECHNICAL STUFF

Guido actually started Python as a *skunkworks project* (a project developed by a small and loosely structured group of people). The core concept was to create Python as quickly as possible, yet create a language that is flexible, runs on any platform, and provides significant potential for extension. Python provides all these features and many more. Of course, there are always bumps in the road, such as figuring out just how much of the underlying system to expose. You can read more about the Python design philosophy at `http://python-history.blogspot.com/2009/01/pythons-design-philosophy.html`. The history of Python at `http://python-history.blogspot.com/2009/01/introduction-and-overview.html` also provides some useful information.

The original development (or design) goals for Python don't quite match what has happened to the language since that time. Guido originally intended Python as a second language for developers who needed to create one-off code but who couldn't quite achieve their goals using a scripting language. The original target audience for Python was the C developer. You can read about these original goals in the interview at `http://www.artima.com/intv/pyscale.html`.

You can find a number of applications written in Python today, so the idea of using it solely for scripting didn't come to fruition. In fact, you can find listings of Python applications at `https://www.python.org/about/apps/` and `https://www.python.org/about/success/`.

Naturally, with all these success stories to go on, people are enthusiastic about adding to Python. You can find lists of Python Enhancement Proposals (PEPs) at `http://legacy.python.org/dev/peps/`. These PEPs may or may not see the light of day, but they prove that Python is a living, growing language that will continue to provide features that developers truly need to create great applications of all types.

Working with MATLAB

Python has advantages over many other languages by offering multiple coding styles, fantastic flexibility, and great extensibility, but it's still a programming language. If you honestly don't want to use a programming language, you do have other options, such as MATLAB (`https://www.mathworks.com/products/matlab/`), which focuses more on algorithms. MATLAB is still a scripting language of a sort, and to perform any significant tasks with it, you still need to know a little about coding, but not as much as with Python.

One of the major issues with using MATLAB is the price you pay. Unlike Python, MATLAB requires a monetary investment on your part (see `https://www.mathworks.com/pricing-licensing/` for licensing costs). The environment is indeed easier to use, but as with most things, there is no free lunch, and you must consider the cost differential as part of determining which product to use.

Many people are curious about MATLAB, that is, its strengths and weaknesses when compared to Python. This book doesn't have room to provide a full comparison, but you can find a great overview at `http://www.pyzo.org/python_vs_matlab.html`. In addition, you can call Python packages from MATLAB using the techniques found at `https://www.mathworks.com/help/matlab/call-python-libraries.html`. In fact, MATLAB also works with the following:

» MEX (`https://www.mathworks.com/help/matlab/call-mex-file-functions.html`)

» C (`https://www.mathworks.com/help/matlab/using-c-shared-library-functions-in-matlab-.html`)

» Java (`https://www.mathworks.com/help/matlab/using-java-libraries-in-matlab.html`)

» .NET (`https://www.mathworks.com/help/matlab/using-net-libraries-in-matlab.html`)

» COM (`https://www.mathworks.com/help/matlab/using-com-objects-in-matlab.html`)

Therefore, you don't necessarily have to choose between MATLAB and Python (or other language), but the more Python features you use, the easier it becomes to simply work with Python and skip MATLAB. You can discover more about MATLAB in *MATLAB For Dummies,* by Jim Sizemore and John Paul Mueller (Wiley).

Considering other algorithm testing environments

A third major contender for algorithm-related work is R. The R programming language, like Python, is free of charge. It also supports a large number of packages and offers great flexibility. Some of the programming constructs are different, however, and some people find R harder to use than Python. Most people view R as the winner when it comes to performing statistics, but they see the general-purpose nature of Python as having major benefits (see the articles at `https://www.datacamp.com/community/tutorials/r-or-python-for-data-analysis` and `http://www.kdnuggets.com/2015/05/r-vs-python-data-science.html`). The stronger community support for Python is also a major advantage.

As previously mentioned, you can use any computer programming language to perform algorithm-related work, but most languages have a specific purpose in mind. For example, you can perform algorithm-related tasks using a language such as Structured Query Language (SQL), but this language focuses on data management, so some algorithm-related tasks might become convoluted and difficult to perform. A significant lack in SQL is the ability to plot data with ease and to perform some of the translations and transformations that algorithm-specific work requires. In short, you need to consider what you plan to do when choosing a language. This book uses Python because it truly is the best overall language to perform the tasks at hand, but it's important to realize that you may need another language at some point.

Looking at the Python Distributions

You can quite possibly obtain a generic copy of Python and add all the packages required to work with algorithms to it. The process can be difficult because you need to ensure that you have all the required packages in the correct versions to guarantee success. In addition, you need to perform the configuration required to make sure that the packages are accessible when you need them. Fortunately, going through the required work is not necessary because numerous Python products that work well with algorithms are available for you to use. These products provide everything needed to get started with algorithm-related projects.

REMEMBER

You can use any of the packages mentioned in the following sections to work with the examples in this book. However, the book's source code and downloadable source code rely on Continuum Analytics Anaconda 4.2.0 because this particular package works on every platform this book supports: Linux, Mac OS X, and Windows. The book doesn't mention a specific package in the chapters that follow, but any screenshots reflect how things look when using Anaconda on Windows. You may need to tweak the code to use another package, and the screens will look different if you use Anaconda on some other platform.

WARNING

Windows 10 presents some serious installation issues when working with Python. You can read about these issues on my (John's) blog at `http://blog.john muellerbooks.com/2015/10/30/python-and-windows-10/`. Given that so many readers of my other Python books have sent feedback saying that Windows 10 doesn't provide a good environment, I can't recommend Windows 10 as a Python platform for this book. If you're working with Windows 10, simply be aware that your road to a Python installation will be a rocky one.

Obtaining Analytics Anaconda

The basic Anaconda package is a free download that you obtain at `https://store.continuum.io/cshop/anaconda/`. Simply click Download Anaconda to obtain access to the free product. You do need to provide an email address to get a copy of Anaconda. After you provide your email address, you go to another page, where you can choose your platform and the installer for that platform. Anaconda supports the following platforms:

» Windows 32-bit and 64-bit (the installer may offer you only the 64-bit or 32-bit version, depending on which version of Windows it detects)

» Linux 32-bit and 64-bit

» Mac OS X 64-bit

Because package support for Python 3.5 has gotten better than previous 3.*x* versions, you see both Python 3.*x* and 2.*x* equally supported on the Analytics site. This book uses Python 3.5 because the package support is now substantial enough and stable enough to support all the programming examples, and because Python 3.*x* represents the future direction of Python.

TIP

You can obtain Anaconda with older versions of Python. If you want to use an older version of Python, click the installer archive link near the bottom of the page. You should use an older version of Python only when you have a pressing need to do so.

The Miniconda installer can potentially save time by limiting the number of features you install. However, trying to figure out precisely which packages you do need is an error-prone and time-consuming process. In general, you want to perform a full installation to ensure that you have everything needed for your projects. Even a full install doesn't require much time or effort to download and install on most systems.

The free product is all you need for this book. However, when you look on the site, you see that many other add-on products are available. These products can help you create robust applications. For example, when you add Accelerate to the mix, you obtain the capability to perform multicore and GPU-enabled operations. The use of these add-on products is outside the scope of this book, but the Anaconda site provides details on using them.

Considering Enthought Canopy Express

Enthought Canopy Express is a free product for producing both technical and scientific applications using Python. You can obtain it at `https://www.enthought.com/canopy-express/`. Click Download Free on the main page to see a listing of the versions that you can download. Only Canopy Express is free; the full Canopy product comes at a cost. However, you can use Canopy Express to work with the examples in this book. Canopy Express supports the following platforms:

» Windows 32-bit and 64-bit

» Linux 32-bit and 64-bit

» Mac OS X 32-bit and 64-bit

Choose the platform and version you want to download. When you click Download Canopy Express, you see an optional form for providing information about yourself. The download starts automatically, even if you don't provide personal information to the company.

One of the advantages of Canopy Express is that Enthought is heavily involved in providing support for both students and teachers. People also can take classes, including online classes, that teach the use of Canopy Express in various ways (see `https://training.enthought.com/courses`).

Considering pythonxy

The pythonxy Integrated Development Environment (IDE) is a community project hosted on Google at `http://python-xy.github.io/`. It's a Windows-only product, so you can't easily use it for cross-platform needs. (In fact, it supports only

Windows Vista, Windows 7, and Windows 8.) However, it does come with a full set of packages, and you can easily use it for this book if you want.

Because pythonxy uses the GNU General Public License (GPL) v3 (see http://www.gnu.org/licenses/gpl.html), you have no add-ons, training, or other paid features to worry about. No one will come calling at your door hoping to sell you something. In addition, you have access to all the source code for pythonxy, so you can make modifications if you want.

Considering WinPython

The name tells you that WinPython is a Windows-only product that you can find at http://winpython.sourceforge.net/. This product is actually a spin-off of pythonxy and isn't meant to replace it. Quite the contrary: WinPython is simply a more flexible way to work with pythonxy. You can read about the motivation for creating WinPython at http://sourceforge.net/p/winpython/wiki/Roadmap/.

The bottom line for this product is that you gain flexibility at the cost of friendliness and a little platform integration. However, for developers who need to maintain multiple versions of an IDE, WinPython may make a significant difference. When using WinPython with this book, make sure to pay particular attention to configuration issues or you'll find that even the downloadable code has little chance of working.

Installing Python on Linux

You use the command line to install Anaconda on Linux — you're given no graphical installation option. Before you can perform the install, you must download a copy of the Linux software from the Continuum Analytics site. You can find the required download information in the "Obtaining Analytics Anaconda" section, earlier in this chapter. The following procedure should work fine on any Linux system, whether you use the 32-bit or 64-bit version of Anaconda:

1. **Open a copy of Terminal.**

   The Terminal window appears.

2. **Change directories to the downloaded copy of Anaconda on your system.**

   The name of this file varies, but normally it appears as Anaconda3-4.2.0-Linux-x86.sh for 32-bit systems and Anaconda3-4.2.0-Linux-x86_64.sh for 64-bit systems. The version number is embedded as part of the filename. In this case, the filename refers to version 4.2.0, which is the version used for this book. If you use some other version, you may experience problems with the source code and need to make adjustments when working with it.

3. **Type** bash Anaconda3-4.2.0-Linux-x86.sh **(for the 32-bit version) or** bash Anaconda3-4.2.0-Linux-x86_64.sh **(for the 64-bit version) and press Enter.**

   An installation wizard starts that asks you to accept the licensing terms for using Anaconda.

4. **Read the licensing agreement and accept the terms using the method required for your version of Linux.**

   The wizard asks you to provide an installation location for Anaconda. The book assumes that you use the default location of ~/anaconda. If you choose some other location, you may have to modify some procedures later in the book to work with your setup.

5. **Provide an installation location (if necessary) and press Enter (or click Next).**

   The application extraction process begins. After the extraction is complete, you see a completion message.

6. **Add the installation path to your** PATH **statement using the method required for your version of Linux.**

   You're ready to begin using Anaconda.

Installing Python on MacOS

The Mac OS X installation comes in only one form: 64-bit. Before you can perform the install, you must download a copy of the Mac software from the Continuum Analytics site. You can find the required download information in the "Obtaining Analytics Anaconda" section, earlier in this chapter.

The installation files come in two forms. The first depends on a graphical installer; the second relies on the command line. The command-line version works much like the Linux version described in the "Installing Python on Linux" section of this chapter. The following steps help you install Anaconda 64-bit on a Mac system using the graphical installer:

1. **Locate the downloaded copy of Anaconda on your system.**

   The name of this file varies, but normally it appears as Anaconda3-4.2.0-MacOSX-x86_64.pkg. The version number is embedded as part of the filename. In this case, the filename refers to version 4.2.0, which is the version used for this book. If you use some other version, you may experience problems with the source code and need to make adjustments when working with it.

2. **Double-click the installation file.**

An introduction dialog box appears.

3. **Click Continue.**

The wizard asks whether you want to review the Read Me materials. You can read these materials later. For now, you can safely skip the information.

4. **Click Continue.**

The wizard displays a licensing agreement. Be sure to read through the licensing agreement so that you know the terms of usage.

5. **Click I Agree if you agree to the licensing agreement.**

The wizard asks you to provide a destination for the installation. The destination controls whether the installation is for an individual user or a group.

WARNING

You may see an error message stating that you can't install Anaconda on the system. The error message occurs because of a bug in the installer and has nothing to do with your system. To get rid of the error message, choose the Install Only for Me option. You can't install Anaconda for a group of users on a Mac system.

6. **Click Continue.**

The installer displays a dialog box containing options for changing the installation type. Click Change Install Location if you want to modify where Anaconda is installed on your system. (The book assumes that you use the default path of ~/anaconda.) Click Customize if you want to modify how the installer works. For example, you can choose not to add Anaconda to your PATH statement. However, the book assumes that you have chosen the default install options, and no good reason exists to change them unless you have another copy of Python 3.5 installed somewhere else.

7. **Click Install.**

The installation begins. A progress bar tells you how the installation process is progressing. When the installation is complete, you see a completion dialog box.

8. **Click Continue.**

You're ready to begin using Anaconda.

Installing Python on Windows

Anaconda comes with a graphical installation application for Windows, so getting a good install means using a wizard, as you would for any other installation. Of course, you need a copy of the installation file before you begin, and you can find the required download information in the "Obtaining Analytics Anaconda" section, earlier in this chapter. The following procedure should work fine on any Windows system, whether you use the 32-bit or the 64-bit version of Anaconda:

1. **Locate the downloaded copy of Anaconda on your system.**

    The name of this file varies, but normally it appears as Anaconda3-4.2.0-Windows-x86.exe for 32-bit systems and Anaconda3-4.2.0-Windows-x86_64.exe for 64-bit systems. The version number is embedded as part of the filename. In this case, the filename refers to version 4.2.0, which is the version used for this book. If you use some other version, you may experience problems with the source code and need to make adjustments when working with it.

2. **Double-click the installation file.**

    (You may see an Open File – Security Warning dialog box that asks whether you want to run this file. Click Run if you see this dialog box pop up.) You see an Anaconda 4.2.0 Setup dialog box similar to the one shown in Figure 3-1. The exact dialog box that you see depends on which version of the Anaconda installation program you download. If you have a 64-bit operating system, using the 64-bit version of Anaconda is always best so that you obtain the best possible performance. This first dialog box tells you when you have the 64-bit version of the product.

3. **Click Next.**

    The wizard displays a licensing agreement. Be sure to read through the licensing agreement so that you know the terms of usage.

4. **Click I Agree if you agree to the licensing agreement.**

    You're asked what sort of installation type to perform, as shown in Figure 3-2. In most cases, you want to install the product just for yourself. The exception is if you have multiple people using your system and they all need access to Anaconda.

5. **Choose one of the installation types and then click Next.**

    The wizard asks where to install Anaconda on disk, as shown in Figure 3-3. The book assumes that you use the default location. If you choose some other location, you may have to modify some procedures later in the book to work with your setup.

FIGURE 3-1:
The setup process begins by telling you whether you have the 64-bit version.

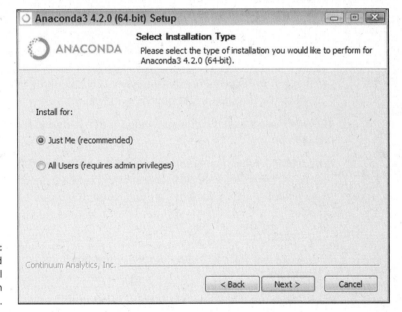

FIGURE 3-2:
Tell the wizard how to install Anaconda on your system.

FIGURE 3-3:
Specify an
installation
location.

6. **Choose an installation location (if necessary) and then click Next.**

You see the Advanced Installation Options, shown in Figure 3-4. These options are selected by default, and no good reason exists to change them in most cases. You might need to change them if Anaconda won't provide your default Python 3.5 (or Python 2.7) setup. However, the book assumes that you've set up Anaconda using the default options.

7. **Change the advanced installation options (if necessary) and then click Install.**

You see an Installing dialog box with a progress bar. The installation process can take a few minutes, so get yourself a cup of coffee and read the comics for a while. When the installation process is over, you see a Next button enabled.

8. **Click Next.**

The wizard tells you that the installation is complete.

9. **Click Finish.**

You're ready to begin using Anaconda.

FIGURE 3-4:
Configure the advanced installation options.

A WORD ABOUT THE SCREENSHOTS

As you work your way through the book, you use an IDE of your choice to open the Python and Jupyter Notebook files containing the book's source code. Every screenshot that contains IDE-specific information relies on Anaconda because Anaconda runs on all three platforms supported by the book. The use of Anaconda doesn't imply that it's the best IDE or that the authors are making any sort of recommendation for it; Anaconda simply works well as a demonstration product.

When you work with Anaconda, the name of the graphical (GUI) environment, Jupyter Notebook, is precisely the same across all three platforms, and you won't even see any significant difference in the presentation. (Jupyter Notebook is an evolution of IPython, so you may see online resources refer to IPython Notebook.) The differences that you do see are minor, and you should ignore them as you work through the book. With this in mind, the book does rely heavily on Windows 7 screenshots. When working on a Linux, Mac OS X, or other Windows version platform, you should expect to see some differences in presentation, but these differences shouldn't reduce your ability to work with the examples.

Downloading the Datasets and Example Code

This book is about using Python to perform machine learning tasks. Of course, you can spend all your time creating the example code from scratch, debugging it, and only then discovering how it relates to machine learning, or you can take the easy way and download the prewritten code from the Dummies site (see the Introduction of this book for details) so that you can get right to work. Likewise, creating datasets large enough for algorithm learning purposes would take quite a while. Fortunately, you can access standardized, precreated data sets quite easily by using features provided in some of the data science packages (which also work just fine for all sorts of purposes, including learning to work with algorithms). The following sections help you download and use the example code and datasets so that you can save time and get right to work with algorithm-specific tasks.

Using Jupyter Notebook

To make working with the relatively complex code in this book easier, you use Jupyter Notebook. This interface lets you easily create Python notebook files that can contain any number of examples, each of which can run individually. The program runs in your browser, so which platform you use for development doesn't matter; as long as it has a browser, you should be okay.

Starting Jupyter Notebook

Most platforms provide an icon to access Jupyter Notebook. Just click this icon to access Jupyter Notebook. For example, on a Windows system, you choose Start ⇨ All Programs ⇨ Anaconda 3 ⇨ Jupyter Notebook. Figure 3-5 shows how the interface looks when viewed in a Firefox browser. The precise appearance on your system depends on the browser you use and the kind of platform you have installed.

If you have a platform that doesn't offer easy access through an icon, you can use these steps to access Jupyter Notebook:

1. **Open a Command Prompt or Terminal Window on your system.**

   The window opens so that you can type commands.

2. **Change directories to the `\Anaconda3\Scripts` directory on your machine.**

   Most systems let you use the CD command for this task.

3. **Type** python jupyter-notebook-script.py **and press Enter.**

   The Jupyter Notebook page opens in your browser.

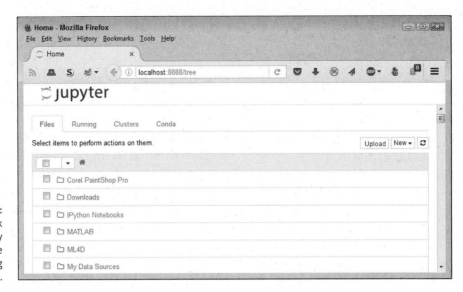

FIGURE 3-5:
Jupyter Notebook
provides an easy
method to create
machine learning
examples.

Stopping the Jupyter Notebook server

No matter how you start Jupyter Notebook (or just Notebook, as it appears in the remainder of the book), the system generally opens a command prompt or terminal window to host Jupyter Notebook. This window contains a server that makes the application work. After you close the browser window when a session is complete, select the server window and press Ctrl+C or Ctrl+Break to stop the server.

Defining the code repository

The code you create and use in this book will reside in a repository on your hard drive. Think of a *repository* as a kind of filing cabinet where you put your code. Notebook opens a drawer, takes out the folder, and shows the code to you. You can modify it, run individual examples within the folder, add new examples, and simply interact with your code in a natural manner. The following sections get you started with Notebook so that you can see how this whole repository concept works.

Defining the book's folder

It pays to organize your files so that you can access them easier later. This book keeps its files in the A4D (*Algorithms For Dummies*) folder. Use these steps within Notebook to create a new folder.

1. Choose New ⇨ Folder.

Notebook creates a new folder named Untitled Folder, as shown in Figure 3-6. The file appears in alphanumeric order, so you may not initially see it. You must scroll down to the correct location.

FIGURE 3-6:
New folders appear with a name of Untitled Folder.

2. Select the box next to the Untitled Folder entry.

3. Click Rename at the top of the page.

You see a Rename Directory dialog box like the one shown in Figure 3-7.

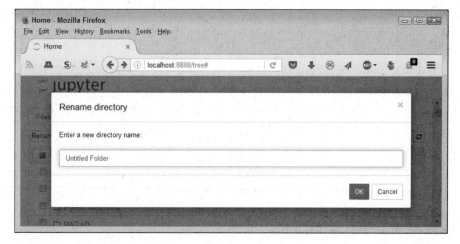

FIGURE 3-7:
Rename the folder so that you remember the kinds of entries it contains.

4. Type A4D and click OK.

Notebook changes the name of the folder for you.

5. Click the new A4D entry in the list.

Notebook changes the location to the A4D folder in which you perform tasks related to the exercises in this book.

Creating a new notebook

Every new notebook is like a file folder. You can place individual examples within the file folder, just as you would sheets of paper into a physical file folder. Each example appears in a cell. You can put other sorts of things in the file folder, too, but you see how these things work as the book progresses. Use these steps to create a new notebook:

1. **Click New ⇨ Python (default).**

   A new tab opens in the browser with the new notebook, as shown in Figure 3-8. Notice that the notebook contains a cell and that Notebook has highlighted the cell so that you can begin typing code in it. The title of the notebook is Untitled right now. That's not a particularly helpful title, so you need to change it.

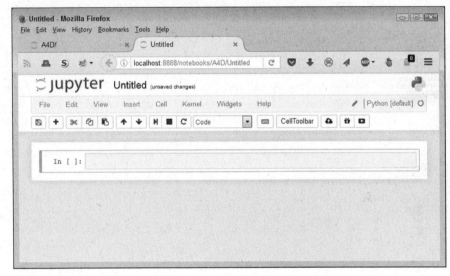

FIGURE 3-8:
A notebook contains cells that you use to hold code.

2. **Click Untitled on the page.**

   Notebook asks what you want to use as a new name, as shown in Figure 3-9.

3. **Type A4D; 03; Sample and press Enter.**

   The new name tells you that this is a file for *Algorithms For Dummies,* Chapter 3, Sample.ipynb. Using this naming convention lets you easily differentiate these files from other files in your repository.

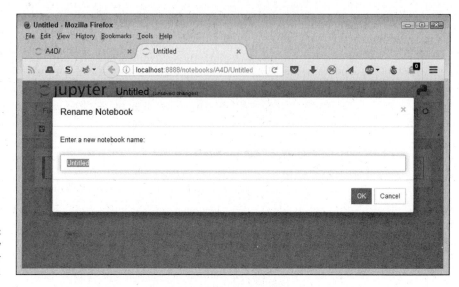

FIGURE 3-9:
Provide a new
name for your
notebook.

Of course, the Sample notebook doesn't contain anything just yet. Place the cursor
in the cell, type **print('Python is really cool!')**, and then click the Run button (the
button with the right-pointing arrow on the toolbar). You see the output shown in
Figure 3-10. The output is part of the same cell as the code. (The code resides in a
square box and the output resides outside that square box, but both are within the
cell.) However, Notebook visually separates the output from the code so that you
can tell them apart. Notebook automatically creates a new cell for you.

FIGURE 3-10:
Notebook uses
cells to store
your code.

When you finish working with a notebook, shutting it down is important. To close a notebook, choose File ⇨ Close and Halt. You return to the Home page, where you can see that the notebook you just created is added to the list, as shown in Figure 3-11.

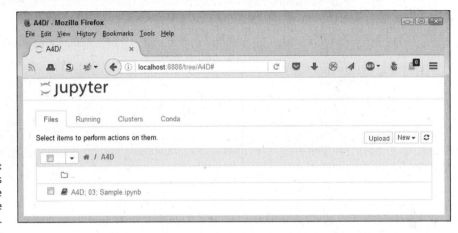

FIGURE 3-11:
Any notebooks you create appear in the repository list.

Exporting a notebook

Creating notebooks and keeping them all to yourself isn't much fun. At some point, you want to share them with other people. To perform this task, you must export your notebook from the repository to a file. You can then send the file to someone else, who will import it into his or her repository.

The previous section shows how to create a notebook named A4D; 03; Sample. You can open this notebook by clicking its entry in the repository list. The file reopens so that you can see your code again. To export this code, choose File ⇨ Download As ⇨ Notebook (.ipynb). What you see next depends on your browser, but you generally see some sort of dialog box for saving the notebook as a file. Use the same method for saving the IPython Notebook file as you use for any other file you save using your browser.

Removing a notebook

Sometimes notebooks get outdated or you simply don't need to work with them any longer. Rather than allow your repository to get clogged with files you don't need, you can remove these unwanted notebooks from the list. Use these steps to remove the file:

1. **Select the box next to the A4D; 03; Sample.ipynb entry.**

2. **Click the trash can icon (Delete) at the top of the page.**

   You see a Delete notebook warning message like the one shown in Figure 3-12.

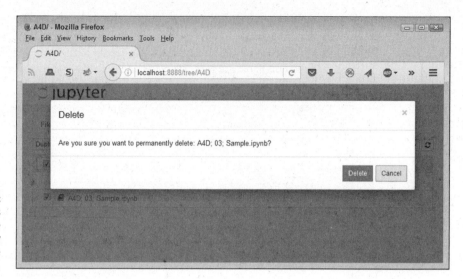

FIGURE 3-12:
Notebook warns
you before
removing any
files from the
repository.

3. **Click Delete.**

The file gets removed from the list.

Importing a notebook

To use the source code from this book, you must import the downloaded files into your repository. The source code comes in an archive file that you extract to a location on your hard drive. The archive contains a list of .ipynb (IPython Notebook) files containing the source code for this book (see the Introduction for details on downloading the source code). The following steps tell how to import these files into your repository:

1. **Click Upload at the top of the page.**

What you see depends on your browser. In most cases, you see some type of File Upload dialog box that provides access to the files on your hard drive.

2. **Navigate to the directory containing the files that you want to import into Notebook.**

3. **Highlight one or more files to import and click the Open (or other, similar) button to begin the upload process.**

You see the file added to an upload list, as shown in Figure 3-13. The file isn't part of the repository yet — you've simply selected it for upload.

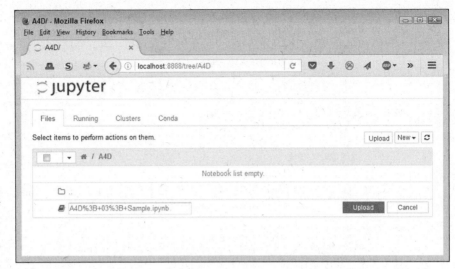

FIGURE 3-13:
The files that you want to add to the repository appear as part of an upload list consisting of one or more filenames.

TIP

When you export a file, Notebook converts any special characters to a form that your system will accept with greater ease. Figure 3-13 shows this conversion in action. The semicolons appear as %3B, and spaces appear as a + (plus sign). You must change these characters to their Notebook form to see the title as you expect it.

4. **Click Upload.**

Notebook places the file in the repository so that you can begin using it.

Understanding the datasets used in this book

This book uses a number of datasets, all of which appear in the scikit-learn package. These datasets demonstrate various ways in which you can interact with data, and you use them in the examples to perform a variety of tasks. The following list provides a quick overview of the function used to import each of the datasets into your Python code:

» `load_boston()`: Regression analysis with the Boston house-prices dataset

» `load_iris()`: Classification with the iris dataset

» `load_diabetes()`: Regression with the diabetes dataset

» `load_digits([n_class])`: Classification with the digits dataset

» `fetch_20newsgroups(subset='train')`: Data from 20 newsgroups

» `fetch_olivetti_faces()`:Olivetti faces dataset from AT&T

The technique for loading each of these datasets is the same across examples. The following example shows how to load the Boston house-prices dataset. You can find the code in the A4D; 03; Dataset Load.ipynb notebook.

```
from sklearn.datasets import load_boston
Boston = load_boston()
print(Boston.data.shape)

(506, 13)
```

To see how the code works, click Run Cell. The output from the print() call is (506, 13). You can see the output shown in Figure 3-14.

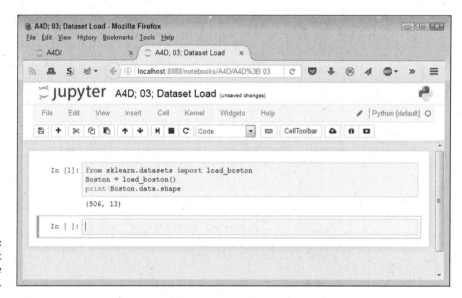

FIGURE 3-14:
The Boston object contains the loaded dataset.

» **Working with strings**

» **Performing tasks with dates**

» **Packaging code by using functions**

» **Making decisions and repeating steps**

» **Managing data in memory**

» **Reading data in storage objects**

» **Finding data faster by using dictionaries**

Chapter **4**

Introducing Python for Algorithm Programming

recipe is a kind of algorithm because it helps you cook tasty food by using a series of steps (and thereby get rid of your hunger). You can devise many ways to create a sequence of steps that solve a problem. Procedures of every variety and description abound, all of which describe a sequence of steps used to solve a problem. Not every sequence of steps is concrete. Mathematical notations present a series of steps to solve a numeric problem, but many people view them as so many oddly shaped symbols in an arcane language that few can understand. A computer language can turn the arcane language into a concrete form of English-like statements that solve the problem in a manner that works for most humans.

The previous chapter in this book, Chapter 3, helps you install a copy of Python to work with the examples in this book. You use Python throughout the book to solve numeric problems using algorithms that you can also express in mathematical notation. The reason that this book uses a programming language is to turn those oddly shaped abstract symbols into something that most people can understand and use to solve real-world problems.

Before you can use Python to perform tasks with algorithms, you need at least a passing knowledge of how Python works. This chapter isn't designed to make you a Python expert. However, it does provide you with enough information to make sense of the example code with the commentary provided. The various sections help you understand how Python performs tasks in a concrete manner. For example, you need to know how Python works with various kinds of data in order to determine what the example code is doing with that data. You find the essentials of working with numeric, logical, string, and date data in the first three sections.

Imagine a cookbook, or any book for that matter, that provided steps for performing every task that the book tells you how to perform as one long narrative without any breaks. Trying to find a specific recipe (or other procedure) would become impossible and the book would be useless. In fact, no one would write such a book. The fourth section of the chapter discusses functions, which are akin to the individual recipes in a cookbook. You can combine functions to create an entire program, much as you would combine recipes to create an entire dinner.

The next four sections discuss various ways to manage data, which means reading, writing, modifying, and erasing it as needed. You also need to know how to make decisions and what to do when you need to perform the same set of steps more than one time. Data is a resource, just as flour, sugar, and other ingredients are resources you use when working with a recipe. The different kinds of data require different techniques to make them into an application that solves the problem proposed by an algorithm. These sections tell you about the various ways to manipulate data and work with it to solve problems.

Working with Numbers and Logic

Interacting with algorithms involves working with data of various sorts, but much of the work involves numbers. In addition, you use logical values to make decisions about the data you use. For example, you might need to know whether two values are equal or whether one value is greater than another value. Python supports these number and logic value types:

>> Any whole number is an *integer*. For example, the value 1 is a whole number, so it's an integer. On the other hand, 1.0 isn't a whole number; it has a decimal part to it, so it's not an integer. Integers are represented by the `int` data type. On most platforms, you can store numbers between –9,223,372,036,854,775,808

and 9,223,372,036,854,775,807 within an `int` (which is the maximum value that fits in a 64-bit variable).

» Any number that includes a decimal portion is a *floating-point* value. For example, 1.0 has a decimal part, so it's a floating-point value. Many people get confused about whole numbers and floating-point numbers, but the difference is easy to remember. If you see a decimal in the number, it's a floating-point value. Python stores floating-point values in the `float` data type. The maximum value that a floating point variable can contain is $\pm 1.7976931348623157 \times 10^{308}$ and the minimum value that a floating point variable can contain is $\pm 2.2250738585072014 \times 10^{-308}$ on most platforms.

» A *complex number* consists of a real number and an imaginary number that are paired together. In case you've completely forgotten about complex numbers, you can read about them at http://www.mathsisfun.com/numbers/complex-numbers.html. The imaginary part of a complex number always appears with a *j* after it. So if you want to create a complex number with 3 as the real part and 4 as the imaginary part, you make an assignment like this: `myComplex = 3 + 4j`.

» Logical arguments require Boolean values, which are named after George Bool. When using a Boolean value in Python, you rely on the `bool` type. A variable of this type can contain only two values: `True` or `False`. You can assign a value by using the `True` or `False` keywords, or you can create an expression that defines a logical idea that equates to true or false. For example, you could say `myBool = 1 > 2`, which would equate to False because 1 is most definitely not greater than 2.

Now that you have the basics down, it's time to see the data types in action. The following paragraphs provide a quick overview of how you can work with both numeric and logical data in Python.

Performing variable assignments

When working with applications, you store information in *variables*. A variable is a kind of storage box. Whenever you want to work with the information, you access it using the variable. If you have new information that you want to store, you put it in a variable. Changing information means accessing the variable first and then storing the new value in the variable. Just as you store things in boxes in the real world, so you store things in variables (a kind of storage box) when working with applications. To store data in a variable, you *assign* the data to it using any of a number of *assignment operators* (special symbols that tell how to store the data). Table 4-1 shows the assignment operators that Python supports.

TABLE 4-1   ## Python Assignment Operators

Operator	Description	Example
=	Assigns the value found in the right operand to the left operand	MyVar = 5 results in MyVar containing 5
+=	Adds the value found in the right operand to the value found in the left operand and places the result in the left operand	MyVar += 2 results in MyVar containing 7
-=	Subtracts the value found in the right operand from the value found in the left operand and places the result in the left operand	MyVar -= 2 results in MyVar containing 3
*=	Multiplies the value found in the right operand by the value found in the left operand and places the result in the left operand	MyVar *= 2 results in MyVar containing 10
/=	Divides the value found in the left operand by the value found in the right operand and places the result in the left operand	MyVar /= 2 results in MyVar containing 2.5
%=	Divides the value found in the left operand by the value found in the right operand and places the remainder in the left operand	MyVar %= 2 results in MyVar containing 1
**=	Determines the exponential value found in the left operand when raised to the power of the value found in the right operand and places the result in the left operand	MyVar ** 2 results in MyVar containing 25
//=	Divides the value found in the left operand by the value found in the right operand and places the integer (whole number) result in the left operand	MyVar //= 2 results in MyVar containing 2

Doing arithmetic

Storing information in variables makes it easily accessible. However, to perform any useful work with the variable, you usually perform some type of arithmetic operation on it. Python supports the common arithmetic operators you use to perform tasks by hand. They appear in Table 4-2.

TABLE 4-2   ## Python Arithmetic Operators

Operator	Description	Example
+	Adds two values together	5 + 2 = 7
-	Subtracts the right operand from the left operand	5 – 2 = 3
*	Multiplies the right operand by the left operand	5 * 2 = 10
/	Divides the left operand by the right operand	5 / 2 = 2.5
%	Divides the left operand by the right operand and returns the remainder	5 % 2 = 1
**	Calculates the exponential value of the right operand by the left operand	5 ** 2 = 25
//	Performs integer division, in which the left operand is divided by the right operand and only the whole number is returned (also called floor division)	5 // 2 = 2

Sometimes you need to interact with just one variable. Python supports a number of *unary operators*, those that work with just one variable, as shown in Table 4-3.

TABLE 4-3 **Python Unary Operators**

Operator	Description	Example
~	Inverts the bits in a number so that all the 0 bits become 1 bits and vice versa	~4 results in a value of –5
-	Negates the original value so that positive becomes negative and vice versa	–(–4) results in 4 and –4 results in –4
+	Is provided purely for the sake of completeness; returns the same value that you provide as input	+4 results in a value of 4

Computers can perform other sorts of math tasks because of the way in which the processor works. It's important to remember that computers store data as a series of individual bits. Python lets you access these individual bits by using *bitwise operators*, as shown in Table 4-4.

TABLE 4-4 **Python Bitwise Operators**

Operator	Description	Example
& (And)	Determines whether both individual bits within two operators are true and sets the resulting bit to true when they are.	0b1100 & 0b0110 = 0b0100
| (Or)	Determines whether either of the individual bits within two operators are true and sets the resulting bit to true when they are.	0b1100 | 0b0110 = 0b1110
^ (Exclusive or)	Determines whether just one of the individual bits within two operators is true and sets the resulting bit to true when one is. When both bits are true or both bits are false, the result is false.	0b1100 ^ 0b0110 = 0b1010
~ (One's complement)	Calculates the one's complement value of a number.	~0b1100 = –0b1101 ~0b0110 = –0b0111
<< (Left shift)	Shifts the bits in the left operand left by the value of the right operand. All new bits are set to 0 and all bits that flow off the end are lost.	0b00110011 << 2 = 0b11001100
>> (Right shift)	Shifts the bits in the left operand right by the value of the right operand. All new bits are set to 0 and all bits that flow off the end are lost.	0b00110011 >> 2 = 0b00001100

Comparing data by using Boolean expressions

Using arithmetic to modify the content of variables is a kind of data manipulation. To determine the effect of data manipulation, a computer must compare the current state of the variable against its original state or the state of a known value. In some cases, detecting the status of one input against another is also necessary. All these operations check the relationship between two variables, so the resulting operators are relational operators, as shown in Table 4-5.

TABLE 4-5   **Python Relational Operators**

Operator	Description	Example
==	Determines whether two values are equal. Notice that the relational operator uses two equals signs. A mistake many developers make is using just one equals sign, which results in one value being assigned to another.	1 == 2 is False
!=	Determines whether two values are not equal. Some older versions of Python allowed you to use the <> operator in place of the != operator. Using the <> operator results in an error in current versions of Python.	1 != 2 is True
>	Verifies that the left operand value is greater than the right operand value.	1 > 2 is False
<	Verifies that the left operand value is less than the right operand value.	1 < 2 is True
>=	Verifies that the left operand value is greater than or equal to the right operand value.	1 >= 2 is False
<=	Verifies that the left operand value is less than or equal to the right operand value.	1 <= 2 is True

Sometimes a relational operator can't tell the whole story of the comparison of two values. For example, you might need to check a condition in which two separate comparisons are needed, such as `MyAge > 40` and `MyHeight < 74`. The need to add conditions to the comparison requires a logical operator of the sort shown in Table 4-6.

TABLE 4-6 **Python Logical Operators**

Operator	Description	Example
and	Determines whether both operands are true.	True and True is True
		True and False is False
		False and True is False
		False and False is False
or	Determines when one of two operands is true.	True or True is True
		True or False is True
		False or True is True
		False or False is False
not	Negates the truth value of a single operand. A true value becomes false and a false value becomes true.	not True is False
		not False is True

Computers provide order to comparisons by making some operators more significant than others. The ordering of operators is *operator precedence.* Table 4-7 shows the operator precedence of all the common Python operators, including a few you haven't seen as part of a discussion yet. When making comparisons, always consider operator precedence because otherwise, the assumptions you make about a comparison outcome will likely be wrong.

TABLE 4-7 **Python Operator Precedence**

Operator	Description
()	You use parentheses to group expressions and to override the default precedence so that you can force an operation of lower precedence (such as addition) to take precedence over an operation of higher precedence (such as multiplication).
**	Exponentiation raises the value of the left operand to the power of the right operand.
~ + -	Unary operators interact with a single variable or expression.
* / % //	Multiply, divide, modulo, and floor division.
+ -	Addition and subtraction.
>> <<	Right and left bitwise shift.
&	Bitwise AND.
^ |	Bitwise exclusive OR and standard OR.
<= < > >=	Comparison operators.

(continued)

TABLE 4-7 *(continued)*

Operator	Description
== !=	Equality operators.
= %= /= //= -= += *= **=	Assignment operators.
is is not	Identity operators.
in not in	Membership operators.
not or and	Logical operators.

Creating and Using Strings

Of all the data types, strings are the most easily understood by humans and not understood at all by computers. A *string* is simply any grouping of characters you place within double quotation marks. For example, `myString = "Python is a great language."` assigns a string of characters to `myString`.

REMEMBER

The main reason to use strings when working with algorithms is to provide user interaction — either as requests for input or as a means of making output easier to understand. You can also perform analysis of string data as part of working with algorithms, but the computer doesn't actually require strings as part of its sequence of steps to obtain a solution to a problem. In fact, the computer doesn't see letters at all. Every letter you use is represented by a number in memory. For example, the letter *A* is actually the number 65. To see this for yourself, type **ord("A")** at the Python prompt and press Enter. You see 65 as output. You can convert any single letter to its numeric equivalent using the `ord()` command.

STARTING IPython

Most of the book relies on Jupyter Notebook (see Chapter 3) because it provides methods for creating, managing, and interacting with complex coding examples. However, sometimes you need a simple interactive environment to use for quick tests, which is the route this chapter uses. Anaconda comes with two such environments, IPython and Jupyter QT Console. Of the two, IPython is the simplest to use, but both environments provide similar functionality. To start IPython, simply click its entry in the Anaconda3 folder on your system. For example, when working with Windows, you choose Start ➪ All Programs ➪ Anaconda3 ➪ IPython. You can also start IPython in a console or terminal window by typing **IPython** and pressing Enter.

Because the computer doesn't really understand strings, but strings are so useful in writing applications, you sometimes need to convert a string to a number. You can use the int() and float() commands to perform this conversion. For example, if you type **myInt = int("123")** and press Enter at the Python prompt, you create an int named myInt that contains the value 123.

REMEMBER

You can convert numbers to a string as well by using the str() command. For example, if you type **myStr = str(1234.56)** and press Enter, you create a string containing the value "1234.56" and assign it to myStr. The point is that you can go back and forth between strings and numbers with great ease. Later chapters demonstrate how these conversions make many seemingly impossible tasks quite doable.

As with numbers, you can use some special operators with strings (and many objects). The *member operators* enable you to determine when a string contains specific content. Table 4-8 shows these operators.

TABLE 4-8   **Python Membership Operators**

Operator	Description	Example
in	Determines whether the value in the left operand appears in the sequence found in the right operand	"Hello" in "Hello Goodbye" is True
not in	Determines whether the value in the left operand is missing from the sequence found in the right operand	"Hello" not in "Hello Goodbye" is False

The discussion in this section also makes it obvious that you need to know the kind of data that variables contain. You use the *identity operators* to perform this task, as shown in Table 4-9.

TABLE 4-9   **Python Identity Operators**

Operator	Description	Example
is	Evaluates to true when the type of the value or expression in the right operand points to the same type in the left operand	type(2) is int is True
is not	Evaluates to true when the type of the value or expression in the right operand points to a different type than the value or expression in the left operand	type(2) is not int is False

Interacting with Dates

Dates and times are items that most people work with quite a bit. Society bases almost everything on the date and time that a task needs to be or was completed. We make appointments and plan events for specific dates and times. Most of our day revolves around the clock. When working with algorithms, the date or time at which a particular step in a sequence occurs can be just as important as how the step occurs and what happens as a result of performing the step. Algorithms rely on date and time to organize data so that humans can better understand the data and the resulting output of the algorithm.

Because of the time-oriented nature of humans, it's a good idea to look at how Python deals with interacting with date and time (especially storing these values for later use). As with everything else, computers understand only numbers — date and time don't really exist. The algorithm, not the computer, relies on date and time to help organize the series of steps performed to solve a problem.

REMEMBER

To work with dates and times, you must issue a special `import datetime` command. Technically, this act is called *importing a module.* Don't worry about how the command works right now — just use it whenever you want to do something with date and time.

Computers do have clocks inside them, but the clocks are for the humans using the computer. Yes, some software also depends on the clock, but again, the emphasis is on human needs rather than anything the computer might require. To get the current time, you can simply type **datetime.datetime.now()** and press Enter. You see the full date and time information as found on your computer's clock, such as `datetime.datetime(2016, 12, 20, 10, 37, 24, 460099)`.

You may have noticed that the date and time are a little hard to read in the existing format. Say that you want to get just the current date, and in a readable format. To accomplish this task, you access just the date portion of the output and convert it into a string. Type **str(datetime.datetime.now().date())** and press Enter. You now have something a little more usable, such as `'2016-12-20'`.

Interestingly enough, Python also has a `time()` command, which you can use to obtain the current time. You can obtain separate values for each of the components that make up date and time using the `day`, `month`, `year`, `hour`, `minute`, `second`, and `microsecond` values. Later chapters help you understand how to use these various date and time features to make working with algorithms easier.

Creating and Using Functions

Every step in an algorithm normally requires a single line of Python code — an English-like instruction that tells the computer how to move the problem solution one step closer to completion. You combine these lines of code to achieve a desired result. Sometimes you need to repeat the instructions with different data, and in some cases your code becomes so long that it's hard to keep track of what each part does. Functions serve as organization tools that keep your code neat and tidy. In addition, functions make it easy to reuse the instructions you've created as needed with different data. This section of the chapter tells you all about functions. More important, in this section you start creating your first serious applications in the same way that professional developers do.

Creating reusable functions

You go to your closet, take out pants and shirt, remove the labels, and put them on. At the end of the day, you take everything off and throw it in the trash. Hmmm . . . that really isn't what most people do. Most people take the clothes off, wash them, and then put them back into the closet for reuse. Functions are reusable, too. No one wants to keep repeating the same task; it becomes monotonous and boring. When you create a function, you define a package of code that you can use over and over to perform the same task. All you need to do is tell the computer to perform a specific task by telling it which function to use. The computer faithfully executes each instruction in the function absolutely every time you ask it to do so.

REMEMBER

When you work with functions, the code that needs services from the function is named the *caller,* and it calls upon the function to perform tasks for it. Much of the information you see about functions refers to the caller. The caller must supply information to the function, and the function returns information to the caller.

At one time, computer programs didn't include the concept of code reusability. As a result, developers had to keep reinventing the same code. It didn't take long for someone to come up with the idea of functions, though, and the concept has evolved over the years until functions have become quite flexible. You can make functions do anything you want. Code reusability is a necessary part of applications to

>> Reduce development time

>> Reduce programmer error

>> Increase application reliability

>> Allow entire groups to benefit from the work of one programmer

>> Make code easier to understand

>> Improve application efficiency

In fact, functions do a whole list of things for applications in the form of reusability. As you work through the examples in this book, you see how reusability makes your life significantly easier. If not for reusability, you'd still be programming by plugging 0s and 1s into the computer by hand.

Creating a function doesn't require much work. To see how functions work, open a copy of IPython and type in the following code (pressing Enter at the end of each line):

```
def SayHello():
    print('Hello There!')
```

To end the function, you press Enter a second time after the last line. A function begins with the keyword def (for define). You provide a function name, parentheses that can contain function *arguments* (data used in the function), and a colon. The editor automatically indents the next line for you. Python relies on whitespace to define *code blocks* (statements that are associated with each other in a function).

You can now use the function. Simply type **SayHello()** and press Enter. The parentheses after the function name are important because they tell Python to execute the function rather than tell you that you are accessing a function as an object (to determine what it is). You see Hello There! as the output.

Calling functions

Functions can accept arguments (additional bits of data) and return values. The capability to exchange data makes functions far more useful than they otherwise might be. The following sections describe how to call functions in a variety of ways to both send and receive data.

Sending requirement arguments

A function can require the caller to provide arguments to it. A required argument is a variable that must contain data for the function to work. Open a copy of IPython and type the following code:

```
def DoSum(Value1, Value2):
    return Value1 + Value2
```

You have a new function, DoSum(). This function requires that you provide two arguments to use it. At least, that's what you've heard so far. Type **DoSum()** and press Enter. You see an error message like this one:

```
TypeError
    Traceback (most recent call last)
<ipython-input-2-a37c1b30cd89> in <module>()
----> 1 DoSum()

TypeError: DoSum() missing 2 required positional
    arguments: 'Value1' and 'Value2'
```

Trying DoSum() with just one argument would result in another error message. To use DoSum(), you must provide two arguments. To see how this works, type **DoSum(1, 2)** and press Enter. You see the expected result of 3.

TIP

Notice that DoSum() provides an output value of 3 when you supply 1 and 2 as inputs. The return statement provides the output value. Whenever you see return in a function, you know that the function provides an output value.

Sending arguments by keyword

As your functions become more complex and the methods to use them do as well, you may want to provide a little more control over precisely how you call the function and provide arguments to it. Until now, you have *positional arguments,* which means that you have supplied values in the order in which they appear in the argument list for the function definition. However, Python also has a method for sending arguments by keyword. In this case, you supply the name of the argument followed by an equals sign (=) and the argument value. To see how this works, open a copy of IPython and type the following code:

```
def DisplaySum(Value1, Value2):
    print(str(Value1) + ' + ' + str(Value2) + ' = ' +
    str((Value1 + Value2)))
```

REMEMBER

Notice that the print() function argument includes a list of items to print and that those items are separated by plus signs (+). In addition, the arguments are of different types, so you must convert them using the str() function. Python makes it easy to mix and match arguments in this manner. This function also introduces the concept of automatic line continuation. The print() function actually appears on two lines, and Python automatically continues the function from the first line to the second.

Next, it's time to test `DisplaySum()`. Of course, you want to try the function using positional arguments first, so type **DisplaySum(2, 3)** and press Enter. You see the expected output of 2 + 3 = 5. Now type **DisplaySum(Value2 = 3, Value1 = 2)** and press Enter. Again, you receive the output 2 + 3 = 5 even though the position of the arguments has been reversed.

Giving function arguments a default value

Whether you make the call using positional arguments or keyword arguments, the functions to this point have required that you supply a value. Sometimes a function can use default values when a common value is available. Default values make the function easier to use and less likely to cause errors when a developer doesn't provide an input. To create a default value, you simply follow the argument name with an equals sign and the default value. To see how this works, open a copy of IPython and type the following code:

```
def SayHello(Greeting = "No Value Supplied"):
    print(Greeting)
```

The `SayHello()` function provides an automatic value for Greeting when a caller doesn't provide one. When someone tries to call `SayHello()` without an argument, it doesn't raise an error. Type **SayHello()** and press Enter to see for yourself — you see the default message. Type **SayHello("Howdy!")** to see a normal response.

Creating functions with a variable number of arguments

In most cases, you know precisely how many arguments to provide with your function. It pays to work toward this goal whenever you can because functions with a fixed number of arguments are easier to troubleshoot later. However, sometimes you simply can't determine how many arguments the function will receive at the outset. For example, when you create a Python application that works at the command line, the user might provide no arguments, the maximum number of arguments (assuming there is one), or any number of arguments in between.

Fortunately, Python provides a technique for sending a variable number of arguments to a function. You simply create an argument that has an asterisk in front of it, such as *VarArgs. The usual technique is to provide a second argument that contains the number of arguments passed as an input. To see how this works, open a copy of IPython and type the following code:

```
def DisplayMulti(ArgCount = 0, *VarArgs):
    print('You passed ' + str(ArgCount) + ' arguments.',
    VarArgs)
```

Notice that the `print()` function displays a string and then the list of arguments. Because of the way this function is designed, you can type **DisplayMulti()** and press Enter to see that you can pass zero arguments. To see multiple arguments at work, type **DisplayMulti(3, 'Hello', 1, True)** and press Enter. The output of (`'You passed 3 arguments.'`, (`'Hello'`, `1`, `True`)) shows that you need not pass values of any particular type.

Using Conditional and Loop Statements

Algorithms often require steps that make decisions or perform some steps more than one time. For example, you might need to throw out a value that doesn't fit with the rest of the data, which requires making a decision, or you might need to process the data more than once to obtain a desired result, such as when you filter the data. Python accommodates this need by providing special statements that make decisions or let you perform steps more than once, as described in the sections that follow.

Making decisions using the if statement

You use if statements regularly in everyday life. For example, you may say to yourself, "If it's Wednesday, I'll eat tuna salad for lunch." The Python `if` statement is a little less verbose, but it follows precisely the same pattern. To see how this works, open a copy of IPython and type the following code:

```
def TestValue(Value):
    if Value == 5:
        print('Value equals 5!')
    elif Value == 6:
        print('Value equals 6!')
    else:
        print('Value is something else.')
        print('It equals ' + str(Value))
```

Every Python `if` statement begins, oddly enough, with the word *if*. When Python sees `if`, it knows that you want it to make a decision. After the word *if* comes a condition. A *condition* simply states what sort of comparison you want Python to make. In this case, you want Python to determine whether `Value` contains the value 5.

WARNING

Notice that the condition uses the relational equality operator, ==, and not the assignment operator, =. A common mistake that developers make is to use the assignment operator rather than the equality operator. Using the assignment operator in place of the equality operator will cause your code to malfunction.

The condition always ends with a colon (:). If you don't provide a colon, Python doesn't know that the condition has ended and will continue to look for additional conditions on which to base its decision. After the colon comes any tasks you want Python to perform.

You may need to perform multiple tasks using a single if statement. The elif clause makes it possible to add an additional condition and associated tasks. A *clause* is an addendum to a previous condition, which is an if statement in this case. The elif clause always provides a condition, just as the if statement does, and it has its own associated set of tasks to perform.

Sometimes you need to do something no matter what the condition might be. In this case, you add the else clause. The else clause tells Python to do something in particular when the conditions of the if statement aren't met.

REMEMBER

Notice how indenting is becoming more important as the functions become more complex. The function contains an if statement. The if statement contains just one print() statement. The else clause contains two print() statements.

To see this function in action, type **TestValue(1)** and press Enter. You see the output from the else clause. Type **TestValue(5)** and press Enter. The output now reflects the if statement output. Type **TestValue(6)** and press Enter. The output now shows the results of the elif clause. The result is that this function is more flexible than previous functions in the chapter because it can make decisions.

Choosing between multiple options using nested decisions

Nesting is the process of placing a subordinate statement within another statement. You can nest any statement within any other statement, in most cases. To see how this works, open a copy of IPython and type the following code:

```
def SecretNumber():
    One = int(input("Type a number between 1 and 10: "))
    Two = int(input("Type a number between 1 and 10: "))

    if (One >= 1) and (One <= 10):
        if (Two >= 1) and (Two <= 10):
```

```
            print('Your secret number is: ' + str(One * Two))
        else:
            print("Incorrect second value!")
    else:
        print("Incorrect first value!")
```

In this case, SecretNumber() asks you to provide two inputs. Yes, you can get inputs from a user when needed by using the input() function. The int() function converts the inputs to a number.

There are two levels of if statement this time. The first level checks for the validity of the number in One. The second level checks for the validity of the number in Two. When both One and Two have values between 1 and 10, .SecretNumber() outputs a secret number for the user.

To see SecretNumber() in action, type **SecretNumber()** and press Enter. Type **20** and press Enter when asked for the first input value, and type 10 and press Enter when asked for the second. You see an error message telling you that the first value is incorrect. Type **SecretNumber()** and press Enter again. This time, use values of 10 and 20. The function will tell you that the second input is incorrect. Try the same sequence again using input values of 10 and 10.

Performing repetitive tasks using the for loop

Sometimes you need to perform a task more than one time. You use the for loop statement when you need to perform a task a specific number of times. The for loop has a definite beginning and a definite end. The number of times that this loop executes depends on the number of elements in the variable you provide. To see how this works, open a copy of IPython and type the following code:

```
def DisplayMulti(*VarArgs):
    for Arg in VarArgs:
        if Arg.upper() == 'CONT':
            continue
            print('Continue Argument: ' + Arg)
        elif Arg.upper() == 'BREAK':
            break
            print('Break Argument: ' + Arg)
        print('Good Argument: ' + Arg)
```

In this case, the for loop attempts to process each element in VarArgs. Notice that there is a nested if statement in the loop and it tests for two ending conditions.

In most cases, the code skips the if statement and simply prints the argument. However, when the if statement finds the words CONT or BREAK in the input values, it performs one of these two tasks:

>> continue: Forces the loop to continue from the current point of execution with the next entry in VarArgs.

>> break: Stops the loop from executing.

TIP

The keywords can appear using any combination of uppercase and lowercase letters, such as ConT, because the upper() function converts them to uppercase. The DisplayMulti() function can process any number of input strings. To see it in action, type **DisplayMulti('Hello', 'Goodbye', 'First', 'Last')** and press Enter. You see each of the input strings presented on a separate line in the output. Now type **DisplayMulti('Hello', 'Cont', 'Goodbye', 'Break', 'Last')** and press Enter. Notice that the words Cont and Break don't appear in the output because they're keywords. In addition, the word Last doesn't appear in the output because the for loop ends before this word is processed.

Using the while statement

The while loop statement continues to perform tasks until such time that a condition is no longer true. As with the for statement, the while statement supports both the continue and break keywords for ending the loop prematurely. To see how this works, open a copy of IPython and type the following code:

```
def SecretNumber():
    GotIt = False
    while GotIt == False:
        One = int(input("Type a number between 1 and 10: "))
        Two = int(input("Type a number between 1 and 10: "))

        if (One >= 1) and (One <= 10):
            if (Two >= 1) and (Two <= 10):
                print('Secret number is: ' + str(One * Two))
                GotIt = True
                continue
            else:
                print("Incorrect second value!")
        else:
            print("Incorrect first value!")
        print("Try again!")
```

This is an expansion of the SecretNumber() function first described in the "Choosing between multiple options using nested decisions" section, earlier in this chapter. However, in this case, the addition of a while loop statement means that the function continues to ask for input until it receives a valid response.

To see how the while statement works, type **SecretNumber()** and press Enter. Type **20** and press Enter for the first prompt. Type **10** and press Enter for the second prompt. The example tells you that the first number is wrong and then tells you to try again. Try a second time using values of 10 and 20. This time, the second number is wrong and you still need to try again. On the third try, use values of 10 and 10. This time, you get a secret number. Notice that the use of a continue clause means that the application doesn't tell you to try again.

Storing Data Using Sets, Lists, and Tuples

When working with algorithms, it's all about the data. Python provides a host of methods for storing data in memory. Each method has advantages and disadvantages. Choosing the most appropriate method for your particular need is important. The following sections discuss three common techniques used for storing data for data science needs.

Creating sets

Most people have used sets at one time or another in school to create lists of items that belong together. These lists then became the topic of manipulation using math operations such as intersection, union, difference, and symmetric difference. Sets are the best option to choose when you need to perform membership testing and remove duplicates from a list. You can't perform sequence-related tasks using sets, such as indexing or slicing. To see how you can work with sets, start a copy of IPython and type the following code:

```
SetA = set(['Red', 'Blue', 'Green', 'Black'])
SetB = set(['Black', 'Green', 'Yellow', 'Orange'])
SetX = SetA.union(SetB)
SetY = SetA.intersection(SetB)
SetZ = SetA.difference(SetB)
```

You now have five different sets to play with, each of which has some common elements. To see the results of each math operation, type **print('{0}\n{1}\n{2}'**.

format(SetX, SetY, SetZ)) and press Enter. You see one set printed on each line, like this:

```
{'Blue', 'Orange', 'Red', 'Green', 'Black', 'Yellow'}
{'Green', 'Black'}
{'Blue', 'Red'}
```

TIP

The outputs show the results of the math operations: `union()`, `intersection()`, and `difference()`. Python's fancier print formatting can be useful in working with collections such as sets. The `format()` function tells Python which objects to place within each of the placeholders in the string. A *placeholder* is a set of curly brackets ({}) with an optional number in it. The *escape character* (essentially a kind of control or special character), /n, provides a newline character between entries. You can read more about fancy formatting at `https://docs.python.org/3/tutorial/inputoutput.html`.

You can also test relationships between the various sets. For example, type **SetA.issuperset(SetY)** and press Enter. The output value of `True` tells you that `SetA` is a superset of `SetY`. Likewise, if you type **SetA.issubset(SetX)** and press Enter, you find that `SetA` is a subset of `SetX`.

It's important to understand that sets are either mutable or immutable. All the sets in this example are mutable, which means that you can add or remove elements from them. For example, if you type **SetA.add('Purple')** and press Enter, `SetA` receives a new element. If you type **SetA.issubset(SetX)** and press Enter now, you find that `SetA` is no longer a subset of `SetX` because `SetA` has the `'Purple'` element in it.

Creating lists

The Python specification defines a list as a kind of sequence. *Sequences* simply provide some means of allowing multiple data items to exist together in a single storage unit, but as separate entities. Think about one of those large mail holders you see in apartment buildings. A single mail holder contains a number of small mailboxes, each of which can contain mail. Python supports other kinds of sequences as well:

>> **Tuples:** A tuple is a collection that's used to create complex, list-like sequences. An advantage of tuples is that you can nest the content of a tuple. This feature lets you create structures that can hold employee records or x-y coordinate pairs.

>> **Dictionaries:** As with the real dictionaries, you create key/value pairs when using the dictionary collection (think of a word and its associated definition).

A dictionary provides incredibly fast search times and makes ordering data significantly easier.

>> **Stacks:** Most programming languages support stacks directly. However, Python doesn't support the stack, although a workaround exists for that. A stack is a last in/first out (LIFO) sequence. Think of a pile of pancakes: You can add new pancakes to the top and also take them off the top. A stack is an important collection that you can simulate in Python by using a list.

>> **Queues:** A queue is a first in/first out (FIFO) collection. You use it to track items that need to be processed in some way. Think of a queue as a line at the bank. You go into the line, wait your turn, and are eventually called to talk with a teller.

>> **Deques:** A double-ended queue (deque) is a queue-like structure that lets you add or remove items from either end, but not from the middle. You can use a deque as a queue or a stack or any other kind of collection to which you're adding and from which you're removing items in an orderly manner (in contrast to lists, tuples, and dictionaries, which allow randomized access and management).

Of all the sequences, lists are the easiest to understand and are the most directly related to a real-world object. Working with lists helps you become better able to work with other kinds of sequences that provide greater functionality and improved flexibility. The point is that the data is stored in a list much as you would write it on a piece of paper: One item comes after another. The list has a beginning, a middle, and an end. Python numbers the items in the list. (Even if you might not normally number the list items in real life, using a numbered list makes the items easy to access.) To see how you can work with lists, start a copy of IPython and type the following code:

```
ListA = [0, 1, 2, 3]
ListB = [4, 5, 6, 7]
ListA.extend(ListB)
ListA
```

When you type the last line of code, you see the output of [0, 1, 2, 3, 4, 5, 6, 7]. The extend() function adds the members of ListB to ListA. Besides extending lists, you can also add to them by using the append() function. Type **ListA.append(-5)** and press Enter. When you type **ListA** and press Enter again, you see that Python has added −5 to the end of the list. You may find that you need to remove items again, and you do that by using the remove() function. For example, type **ListA.remove(-5)** and press Enter. When you list ListA again by typing **ListA** and pressing Enter, you see that the added entry is gone.

REMEMBER

Lists also support *concatenation* by using the plus (+) sign to add one list to another. For example, if you type **ListX = ListA + ListB** and press Enter, you find that the newly created ListX contains both ListA and ListB in it, with the elements of ListA coming first.

Creating and using tuples

A tuple is a collection used to create complex lists, in which you can embed one tuple within another. This embedding lets you create hierarchies with tuples. A hierarchy can be something as simple as the directory listing of your hard drive or an organizational chart for your company. The idea is that you can create complex data structures using a tuple.

REMEMBER

Tuples are *immutable,* which means that you can't change them. You can create a new tuple with the same name and modify it in some way, but you can't modify an existing tuple. Lists are mutable, which means that you can change them. So a tuple can seem at first to be at a disadvantage, but immutability has all sorts of advantages, such as being more secure as well as faster. In addition, immutable objects are easier to use with multiple processors. To see how you can work with tuples, start a copy of IPython and type the following code:

```
MyTuple = (1, 2, 3, (4, 5, 6, (7, 8, 9)))
```

MyTuple is nested three levels deep. The first level consists of the values 1, 2, 3, and a tuple. The second level consists of the values 4, 5, 6, and yet another tuple. The third level consists of the values 7, 8, and 9. To see how this works, type the following code into IPython:

```
for Value1 in MyTuple:
    if type(Value1) == int:
        print(Value1)
    else:
        for Value2 in Value1:
            if type(Value2) == int:
                print("\t", Value2)
            else:
                for Value3 in Value2:
                    print("\t\t", Value3)
```

When you run this code, you find that the values really are at three different levels. You can see the indentations showing the level:

```
1
2
3
        4
        5
        6
            7
            8
            9
```

TIP

It is possible to perform tasks such as adding new values, but you must do it by adding the original entries and the new values to a new tuple. In addition, you can add tuples to an existing tuple only. To see how this works, type **MyNewTuple = MyTuple.__add__((10, 11, 12, (13, 14, 15)))** and press Enter. MyNewTuple contains new entries at both the first and second levels, like this: (1, 2, 3, (4, 5, 6, (7, 8, 9)), 10, 11, 12, (13, 14, 15)).

Defining Useful Iterators

The chapters that follow use all kinds of techniques to access individual values in various types of data structures. For this section, you use two simple lists, defined as the following:

```
ListA = ['Orange', 'Yellow', 'Green', 'Brown']
ListB = [1, 2, 3, 4]
```

The simplest method of accessing a particular value is to use an index. For example, if you type **ListA[1]** and press Enter, you see 'Yellow' as the output. All indexes in Python are zero based, which means that the first entry is 0, not 1.

Ranges present another simple method of accessing values. For example, if you type **ListB[1:3]** and press Enter, the output is [2, 3]. You could use the range as input to a for loop, such as

```
for Value in ListB[1:3]:
    print(Value)
```

Instead of the entire list, you see just 2 and 3 as outputs, printed on separate lines. The range has two values separated by a colon. However, the values are optional. For example, ListB[:3] would output [1, 2, 3]. When you leave out a value, the range starts at the beginning or the end of the list, as appropriate.

Sometimes you need to process two lists in parallel. The simplest method of doing this is to use the zip() function. Here's an example of the zip() function in action:

```
for Value1, Value2 in zip(ListA, ListB):
    print(Value1, '\t', Value2)
```

This code processes both ListA and ListB at the same time. The processing ends when the for loop reaches the shortest of the two lists. In this case, you see the following:

```
Orange  1
Yellow  2
Green   3
Brown   4
```

REMEMBER

This is the tip of the iceberg. You see a host of iterator types used throughout the book. The idea is to enable you to list just the items you want, rather than all the items in a list or other data structure. Some of the iterators used in upcoming chapters are a little more complicated than what you see here, but this is an important start.

Indexing Data Using Dictionaries

A dictionary is a special kind of sequence that uses a name and value pair. The use of a name makes it easy to access particular values with something other than a numeric index. To create a dictionary, you enclose name and value pairs in curly brackets. Create a test dictionary by typing **MyDict = {'Orange':1, 'Blue':2, 'Pink':3}** and pressing Enter.

To access a particular value, you use the name as an index. For example, type **MyDict['Pink']** and press Enter to see the output value of 3. The use of dictionaries as data structures makes it easy to access incredibly complex data sets using terms that everyone can understand. In many other respects, working with a dictionary is the same as working with any other sequence.

Dictionaries do have some special features. For example, type **MyDict.keys()** and press Enter to see a list of the keys. You can use the values() function to see the list of values in the dictionary.

Chapter **5**

Performing Essential Data Manipulations Using Python

Chapter 4 discusses the use of Python as a means for expressing in concrete terms those arcane symbols often used in mathematical representations of algorithms. In that chapter, you discover the various language constructs used to perform tasks in Python. However, simply knowing how to control a language by using its constructs to perform tasks isn't enough. The goal of mathematical algorithms is to turn one kind of data into another kind of data. *Manipulating data* means taking raw input and doing something with it to achieve a desired result. (As with data science, this is a topic covered in *Python for Data Science For Dummies*, by John Paul Mueller and Luca Massaron [Wiley].) For example, until you do something with traffic data, you can't see the patterns that emerge that tell you where to spend additional money in improvements. The traffic data in its raw form does nothing to inform you — you must manipulate it to see the pattern in a useful manner. Therefore, those arcane symbols are useful after all. You use them as a sort of machine to turn raw data into something helpful, which is what you discover in this chapter.

In times past, people actually had to perform the various manipulations to make data useful by hand, which required advanced knowledge of math. Fortunately, you can find Python packages to perform most of these manipulations using a little code. You don't have to memorize arcane manipulations anymore — just know which Python features to use. That's what this chapter helps you achieve. You discover the means to perform various kinds of data manipulations using easily accessed Python packages designed especially for the purpose. The chapter begins with vector and matrix manipulations. Later sections discuss techniques such as recursion that can make the tasks even simpler and perform some tasks that are nearly impossible using other means. You also discover how to speed up the calculations so that you spend less time manipulating the data and more time doing something really interesting with it, such as discovering just how to keep quite so many traffic jams from occurring.

Performing Calculations Using Vectors and Matrixes

To perform useful work with Python, you often need to work with larger amounts of data that comes in specific forms. These forms have odd-sounding names, but the names are quite important. The three terms you need to know for this chapter are as follows:

>> **Scalar:** A single base data item. For example, the number 2 shown by itself is a scalar.

>> **Vector:** A one-dimensional array (essentially a list) of data items. For example, an array containing the numbers 2, 3, 4, and 5 would be a vector. You access items in a vector using a zero-based *index*, a pointer to the item you want. The item at index 0 is the first item in the vector, which is 2 in this case.

>> **Matrix:** A two-or-more-dimensional array (essentially a table) of data items. For example, an array containing the numbers 2, 3, 4, and 5 in the first row and 6, 7, 8, and 9 in the second row is a matrix. You access items in a matrix using a zero-based row-and-column index. The item at row 0, column 0 is the first item in the matrix, which is 2 in this case.

Python provides an interesting assortment of features on its own, as described in Chapter 4, but you'd still need to do a lot of work to perform some tasks. To reduce the amount of work you do, you can rely on code written by other people and found in packages. The following sections describe how to use the NumPy package to perform various tasks on scalars, vectors, and matrixes.

Understanding scalar and vector operations

The NumPy package provides essential functionality for scientific computing in Python. To use numpy, you import it using a command such as import numpy as np. Now you can access numpy using the common two-letter abbreviation np.

REMEMBER

Python provides access to just one data type in any particular category. For example, if you need to create a variable that represents a number without a decimal portion, you use the integer data type. Using a generic designation like this is useful because it simplifies code and gives the developer a lot less to worry about. However, in scientific calculations, you often need better control over how data appears in memory, which means having more data types, something that numpy provides for you. For example, you might need to define a particular scalar as a short (a value that is 16 bits long). Using numpy, you could define it as myShort = np.short(15). You could define a variable of precisely the same size using the np.int16 function. The NumPy package provides access to a side assortment of data types described at https://docs.scipy.org/doc/numpy/reference/arrays.scalars.html.

Use the numpy array function to create a vector. For example, myVect = np.array([1, 2, 3, 4]) creates a vector with four elements. In this case, the vector contains standard Python integers. You can also use the arange function to produce vectors, such as myVect = np.arange(1, 10, 2), which fills myVect with array([1, 3, 5, 7, 9]). The first input tells the starting point, the second the stopping point, and the third the step between each number. A fourth argument lets you define the data type for the vector. You can also create a vector with a specific data type. All you need to do is specify the data type like this: myVect = np.array(np.int16([1, 2, 3, 4])) to fill myVect with a vector like this: array([1, 2, 3, 4], dtype=int16).

In some cases, you need special numpy functions to create a vector (or a matrix) of a specific type. For example, some math tasks require that you fill the vector with ones. In this case, you use the ones function like this: myVect = np.ones(4, dtype=np.int16) to fill myVect with ones of specific data types like this: array([1, 1, 1, 1], dtype=int16). You can also use a zeros function to fill a vector with zeros.

TIP

You can perform basic math functions on vectors as a whole, which makes this incredibly useful and less prone to errors that can occur when using programming constructs such as loops to perform the same task. For example, myVect + 1 produces an output of array([2, 3, 4, 5]) when working with standard Python integers. If you choose to work with the numpy int16 data type, myVect + 1 produces array([2, 3, 4, 5], dtype=int16). Note that the output tells you specifically which data type is in use. As you might expect, myVect - 1 produces an output of `array([0, 1, 2, 3])`. You can even use vectors in more complex math scenarios, such as `2 ** myVect`, where the output is `array([ 2, 4, 8, 16], dtype=int32)`. When used in this manner, however, `numpy` often assigns a specific type to the output, even when you define a vector using standard Python integers.

As a final thought on scalar and vector operations, you can also perform both logical and comparison tasks. For example, the following code performs comparison operations on two arrays:

```
a = np.array([1, 2, 3, 4])
b = np.array([2, 2, 4, 4])

a == b
array([False,  True, False,  True], dtype=bool)


a < b
array([ True, False,  True, False], dtype=bool)
```

Starting with two vectors, `a` and `b`, the code checks whether the individual elements in a equal those in b. In this case, `a[0]` doesn't equal `b[0]`. However, `a[1]` does equal `b[1]`. The output is a vector of type `bool` that contains true or false values based on the individual comparisons. Likewise, you can check for instances when `a < b` and produce another vector containing the truth-values in this instance.

Logical operations rely on special functions. You check the logical output of the Boolean operators AND, OR, XOR, and NOT. Here is an example of the logical functions:

```
a = np.array([True, False, True, False])
b = np.array([True, True, False, False])

np.logical_or(a, b)
array([ True,  True,  True, False], dtype=bool)


np.logical_and(a, b)
array([ True, False, False, False], dtype=bool)


np.logical_not(a)
array([False,  True, False,  True], dtype=bool)


np.logical_xor(a, b)
array([False,  True,  True, False], dtype=bool)
```

You can also use numeric input to these functions. When using numeric input, a 0 is false and a 1 is true. As with comparisons, the functions work on an element-by-element basis even though you make just one call. You can read more about the logic functions at `https://docs.scipy.org/doc/numpy-1.10.0/reference/routines.logic.html`.

Performing vector multiplication

Adding, subtracting, or dividing vectors occurs on an element-by-element basis, as described in the previous section. However, when it comes to multiplication, things get a little odd. In fact, depending on what you really want to do, things can become quite odd indeed. Consider the sort of multiplication discussed in the previous section. Both `myVect * myVect` and `np.multiply(myVect, myVect)` produce an element-by-element output of `array([ 1,  4,  9, 16])`.

WARNING

Unfortunately, an element-by-element multiplication can produce incorrect results when working with algorithms. In many cases, what you really need is a *dot product*, which is the sum of the products of two number sequences. When working with vectors, the dot product is always the sum of the individual element-by-element multiplications and results in a single number. For example, `myVect.dot(myVect)` results in an output of 30. If you sum the values from the element-by-element multiplication, you find that they do indeed add up to 30. The discussion at `https://www.mathsisfun.com/algebra/vectors-dot-product.html` tells you about dot products and helps you understand where they might fit in with algorithms. You can learn more about the linear algebra manipulation functions for `numpy` at `https://docs.scipy.org/doc/numpy/reference/routines.linalg.html`.

Creating a matrix is the right way to start

Many of the same techniques you use with vectors also work with matrixes. To create a basic matrix, you simply use the `array` function as you would with a vector, but you define additional dimensions. A *dimension* is a direction in the matrix. For example, a two-dimensional matrix contains rows (one direction) and columns (a second direction). The array call `myMatrix = np.array([[1,2,3], [4,5,6], [7,8,9]])` produces a matrix containing three rows and three columns, like this:

```
array([[1, 2, 3],
       [4, 5, 6],
       [7, 8, 9]])
```

Note how you embed three lists within a container list to create the two dimensions. To access a particular array element, you provide a row and column index value, such as `myMatrix[0, 0]` to access the first value of 1. You can produce matrixes with any number of dimensions using a similar technique. For example, `myMatrix = np.array([[[1,2], [3,4]], [[5,6], [7,8]]])` produces a three-dimensional matrix with an x, y, and z axis that looks like this:

```
array([[[1, 2],
        [3, 4]],

       [[5, 6],
        [7, 8]]])
```

In this case, you embed two lists, within two container lists, within a single container list that holds everything together. In this case, you must provide an x, y, and z index value to access a particular value. For example, `myMatrix[0, 1, 1]` accesses the value 4.

TIP

In some cases, you need to create a matrix that has certain start values. For example, if you need a matrix filled with ones at the outset, you can use the `ones` function. The call to `myMatrix = np.ones([4,4], dtype=np.int32)` produces a matrix containing four rows and four columns filled with `int32` values, like this:

```
array([[1, 1, 1, 1],
       [1, 1, 1, 1],
       [1, 1, 1, 1],
       [1, 1, 1, 1]])
```

Likewise, a call to `myMatrix = np.ones([4,4,4], dtype=np.bool)` will create a three-dimensional array. This time, the matrix will contain Boolean values of `True`. There are also functions for creating a matrix filled with zeros, the identity matrix, and for meeting other needs. You can find a full listing of vector and matrix array-creation functions at https://docs.scipy.org/doc/numpy/reference/routines.array-creation.html.

REMEMBER

The NumPy package supports an actual `matrix` class. The `matrix` class supports special features that make it easier to perform matrix-specific tasks. You discover these features later in the chapter. For now, all you really need to know is how to create a matrix of the `matrix` data type. The easiest method is to make a call similar to the one you use for the `array` function, but using the `mat` function instead, such as `myMatrix = np.mat([[1,2,3], [4,5,6], [7,8,9]])`, which produces the following matrix:

```
matrix([[1, 2, 3],
        [4, 5, 6],
        [7, 8, 9]])
```

You can also convert an existing array to a matrix using the asmatrix function. Use the asarray function to convert a matrix object back to an array form.

WARNING

The only problem with the matrix class is that it works on only two-dimensional matrixes. If you attempt to convert a three-dimensional matrix to the matrix class, you see an error message telling you that the shape is too large to be a matrix.

Multiplying matrixes

Multiplying two matrixes involves the same concerns as multiplying two vectors (as discussed in the "Performing vector multiplication" section, earlier in this chapter). The following code produces an element-by-element multiplication of two matrixes.

```
a = np.array([[1,2,3],[4,5,6]])
b = np.array([[1,2,3],[4,5,6]])

a*b
array([[ 1,  4,  9],
       [16, 25, 36]])
```

WARNING

Note that a and b are the same shape, two rows and three columns. To perform an element-by-element multiplication, the two matrixes must be the same shape. Otherwise, you see an error message telling you that the shapes are wrong. As with vectors, the multiply function also produces an element-by-element result.

Dot products work completely differently with matrixes. In this case, the number of columns in matrix a must match the number of rows in matrix b. However, the number of rows in matrix a can be any number, and the number of columns in matrix b can be any number as long as you multiply a by b. For example, the following code produces a correct dot product:

```
a = np.array([[1,2,3],[4,5,6]])
b = np.array([[1,2,3],[3,4,5],[5,6,7]])

a.dot(b)
array([[22, 28, 34],
       [49, 64, 79]])
```

Note that the output contains the number of rows found in matrix a and the number of columns found in matrix b. So how does this all work? To obtain the value found in the output array at index [0,0] of 22, you sum the values of a[0,0]*b[0,0] (which is 1), a[0,1]*b[1,0] (which is 6), and a[0,2]*b[2,0] (which is 15) to obtain the value of 22. The other entries work precisely the same way.

TIP

An advantage of using the NumPy matrix class is that some tasks become more straightforward. For example, multiplication works precisely as you expect it should. The following code produces a dot product using the matrix class:

```
a = np.mat([[1,2,3],[4,5,6]])
b = np.mat([[1,2,3],[3,4,5],[5,6,7]])

a*b
matrix([[22, 28, 34],
        [49, 64, 79]])
```

The output with the * operator is the same as using the dot function with an array. This example also points out that you must know whether you're using an array or a matrix object when performing tasks such as multiplying two matrixes.

TIP

To perform an element-by-element multiplication using two matrix objects, you must use the numpy multiply function.

Defining advanced matrix operations

This book takes you through all sorts of interesting matrix operations, but you use some of them commonly, which is why they appear in this chapter. When working with arrays, you sometimes get data in a shape that doesn't work with the algorithm. Fortunately, numpy comes with a special reshape function that lets you put the data into any shape needed. In fact, you can use it to reshape a vector into a matrix, as shown in the following code:

```
changeIt = np.array([1,2,3,4,5,6,7,8])

changeIt
array([1, 2, 3, 4, 5, 6, 7, 8])

changeIt.reshape(2,4)
array([[1, 2, 3, 4],
       [5, 6, 7, 8]])
```

```
changeIt.reshape(2,2,2)
array([[[1, 2],
        [3, 4]],

       [[5, 6],
        [7, 8]]])
```

REMEMBER

The starting shape of changeIt is a vector, but using the reshape function turns it into a matrix. In addition, you can shape the matrix into any number of dimensions that work with the data. However, you must provide a shape that fits with the required number of elements. For example, calling changeIt.reshape(2,3,2) will fail because there aren't enough elements to provide a matrix of that size.

You may encounter two important matrix operations in some algorithm formulations. They are the transpose and inverse of a matrix. *Transposition* occurs when a matrix of shape n x m is transformed into a matrix m x n by exchanging the rows with the columns. Most texts indicate this operation by using the superscript T, as in A^T. You see this operation used most often for multiplication in order to obtain the right dimensions. When working with numpy, you use the transpose function to perform the required work. For example, when starting with a matrix that has two rows and four columns, you can transpose it to contain four rows with two columns each, as shown in this example:

```
changeIt
array([[1, 2, 3, 4],
       [5, 6, 7, 8]])

np.transpose(changeIt)
array([[1, 5],
       [2, 6],
       [3, 7],
       [4, 8]])
```

You apply *matrix inversion* to matrixes of shape m x m, which are square matrixes that have the same number of rows and columns. This operation is quite important because it allows the immediate resolution of equations involving matrix multiplication, such as y=bX, where you have to discover the values in the vector b. Because most scalar numbers (exceptions include zero) have a number whose multiplication results in a value of 1, the idea is to find a matrix inverse whose multiplication will result in a special matrix called the *identity matrix*. To see an identity matrix in numpy, use the identity function like this:

```
np.identity(4)
array([[ 1.,  0.,  0.,  0.],
```

```
       [ 0.,   1.,   0.,   0.],
       [ 0.,   0.,   1.,   0.],
       [ 0.,   0.,   0.,   1.]])
```

Note that an identity matrix contains all ones on the diagonal. Finding the inverse of a scalar is quite easy (the scalar number n has an inverse of n^{-1} that is 1/n). It's a different story for a matrix. Matrix inversion involves quite a large number of computations. The inverse of a matrix A is indicated as A^{-1}. When working with numpy, you use the linalg.inv function to create an inverse. The following example shows how to create an inverse, use it to obtain a dot product, and then compare that dot product to the identity matrix by using the allclose function.

```
a = np.array([[1,2], [3,4]])
b = np.linalg.inv(a)

np.allclose(np.dot(a,b), np.identity(2))
True
```

REMEMBER

Sometimes, finding the inverse of a matrix is impossible. When a matrix cannot be inverted, it is referred to as a *singular matrix* or a *degenerate matrix*. Singular matrixes aren't the norm; they're quite rare.

Creating Combinations the Right Way

Shaping data often involves viewing the data in multiple ways. Data isn't simply a sequence of numbers — it presents a meaningful sequence that, when ordered the proper way, conveys information to the viewer. Creating the right data combinations by manipulating data sequences is an essential part of making algorithms do what you want them to do. The following sections look at three data-shaping techniques: permutations, combinations, and repetitions.

Distinguishing permutations

When you receive raw data, it appears in a specific order. The order can represent just about anything, such as the log of a data input device that monitors something like a production line. Perhaps the data is a series of numbers representing the number of products made at any particular moment in time. The reason that you receive the data in a particular order is important, but perhaps that order doesn't lend itself to obtaining the output you need from an algorithm. Perhaps creating a data *permutation*, a reordering of the data so that it presents a different view, will help achieve a desired result.

You can view permutations in a number of ways. One method of viewing a permutation is as a random presentation of the sequence order. In this case, you can use the `numpy random.permutation` function, as shown here:

```
a = np.array([1,2,3])
np.random.permutation(a)
array([2, 3, 1])
```

The output on your system will likely vary from the output shown. Each time you run this code, you receive a different random ordering of the data sequence, which comes in handy with algorithms that require you to randomize the dataset to obtain the desired results. For example, sampling is an essential part of data analytics, and the technique shown is an efficient way to perform this task.

Another way to view the issue is the need to obtain all the permutations for a dataset so that you can try each one in turn. To perform this task, you need to import the `itertools` package. The following code shows a technique you can use to obtain a list of all the permutations of a particular vector:

```
from itertools import permutations

a = np.array([1,2,3])

for p in permutations(a):
    print(p)

(1, 2, 3)
(1, 3, 2)
(2, 1, 3)
(2, 3, 1)
(3, 1, 2)
(3, 2, 1)
```

TIP

To save the list of sets, you could always create a blank list and rely on the `append` function to add each set to the list instead of printing the items one at a time, as shown in the code. The resulting list could serve as input to an algorithm designed to work with multiple sets. You can read more about `itertools` at `https://docs.python.org/3/library/itertools.html`.

Shuffling combinations

In some cases, you don't need an entire dataset; all you really need are a few of the members in combinations of a specific length. For example, you might have a dataset containing four numbers and want only two number combinations from it.

(The ability to obtain parts of a dataset is a key function for generating a fully connected graph, which is described in Part 3 of the book.) The following code shows how to obtain such combinations:

```
from itertools import combinations

a = np.array([1,2,3,4])

for comb in combinations(a, 2):
    print(comb)

(1, 2)
(1, 3)
(1, 4)
(2, 3)
(2, 4)
(3, 4)
```

The output contains all the possible two-number combinations of a. Note that this example uses the `itertools combinations` function (the `permutations` function appears in the previous section). Of course, you might not need all those combinations; perhaps a random subset of them would work better. In this case, you can rely on the `random.sample` function to come to your aid, as shown here:

```
pool = []

for comb in combinations(a, 2):
    pool.append(comb)


random.sample(pool, 3)
[(1, 4), (3, 4), (1, 2)]
```

The precise combinations you see as output will vary. However, the idea is that you've limited your dataset in two ways. First, you're not using all the data elements all the time, and second, you're not using all the possible combinations of those data elements. The effect is to create a relatively random-looking set of data elements that you can use as input to an algorithm.

TIP

Another variation of this theme is to create a complete list but randomize the order of the elements. The act of randomizing the list order is shuffling, and you use the `random.shuffle` function to do it. In fact, Python provides a whole host of randomizing methods that you can see at https://docs.python.org/3/library/random.html. Many of the later examples in this book also rely on randomization to help obtain the correct output from algorithms.

Facing repetitions

Repeated data can unfairly weight the output of an algorithm so that you get inaccurate results. Sometimes you need unique values to determine the outcome of a data manipulation. Fortunately, Python makes it easy to remove certain types of repeated data. Consider this example:

```
a = np.array([1,2,3,4,5,6,6,7,7,1,2,3])
b = np.array(list(set(a)))

b
array([1, 2, 3, 4, 5, 6, 7])
```

REMEMBER

In this case, a begins with an assortment of numbers in no particular order and with plenty of repetitions. In Python, a set never contains repeated data. Consequently, by converting the list in a to a set and then back to a list, and then placing that list in an array, you obtain a vector that has no repeats.

Getting the Desired Results Using Recursion

Recursion is an elegant method of solving many computer problems that relies on the capability of a function to continue calling itself until it satisfies a particular condition. The term *recursion* actually comes from the Latin verb *recurrere*, which means to run back.

When you use recursion, you solve a problem by calling the same function multiple times but modifying the terms under which you call it. The main reason for using recursion is that it provides an easier way to solve problems when working with some algorithms because it mimics the way a human would solve it. Unfortunately, recursion is not an easy tool because it requires some effort to understand how to build a recursive routine and it can cause out-of-memory problems on your computer if you don't set some memory settings. The following sections detail how recursion works and give you an example of how recursion works in Python.

Explaining recursion

Many people have a problem using recursion because they can't easily visualize how it works. In most cases, you call a Python function, it does something, and then it stops. However, in recursion, you call a Python function, it does something, and then it calls itself repeatedly until the task reaches a specific condition — but all those previous calls are still active. The calls unwind themselves one at a time until the first call finally ends with the correct answer, and this unwinding process is where most people encounter a problem. Figure 5-1 shows how recursion looks when using a flow chart.

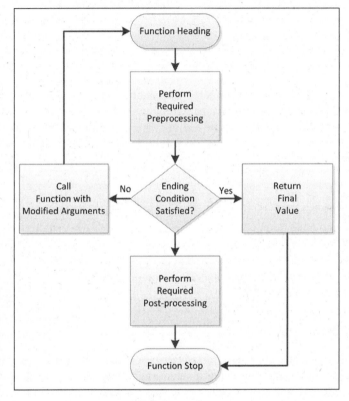

FIGURE 5-1:
In the recursion process, a function continuously calls itself until it meets a condition.

Notice the conditional in the center. To make recursion work, the function must have such a conditional or it could become an endless loop. The conditional determines one of two things:

>> The conditions for ending recursion haven't been met, so the function must call itself again.

>> The conditions for ending recursion have been met, so the function returns a final value that is used to calculate the ending result.

REMEMBER

When a function calls itself, it doesn't use the same arguments that were passed to it. If it continuously used the same arguments, the condition would never change and the recursion would never end. Consequently, recursion requires that subsequent calls to the function must change the call arguments in order to bring the function closer to an ending solution.

One of the most common examples of recursion for all programming languages is the calculation of a factorial. A *factorial* is the multiplication of a series of numbers between a starting point and an ending point in which each number in the series is one less than the number before it. For example, to calculate 5! (read as five factorial) you multiple 5 * 4 * 3 * 2 * 1. The calculation represents a perfect and simple example of recursion. Here's the Python code you can use to perform the calculation. (You can find this code in the A4D; 05; Recursion.ipynb file on the Dummies site as part of the downloadable code; see the Introduction for details.)

```
def factorial(n):
    print("factorial called with n = ", str(n))
    if n == 1 or n == 0:
        print("Ending condition met.")
        return 1
    else:
        return n * factorial(n-1)

print(factorial(5))

factorial called with n =  5
factorial called with n =  4
factorial called with n =  3
factorial called with n =  2
factorial called with n =  1
Ending condition met.
120
```

The code meets the ending condition when n == 1. Each successive call to factorial uses factorial(n-1), which reduces the starting argument by 1. The output shows each successive call to factorial and the meeting of the final condition. The result, 120, equals 5! (five factorial).

It's important to realize that there isn't just one method for using recursion to solve a problem. As with any other programming technique, you can find all sorts of ways to accomplish the same thing. For example, here's another version of the factorial recursion that uses fewer lines of code but effectively performs the same task:

```
def factorial(n):
    print("factorial called with n = ", str(n))
```

```
    if n > 1:
        return n * factorial(n-1)
    print("Ending condition met.")
    return 1

print(factorial(5))

factorial called with n =  5
factorial called with n =  4
factorial called with n =  3
factorial called with n =  2
factorial called with n =  1
Ending condition met.
120
```

REMEMBER

Note the difference. Instead of checking the ending condition, this version checks the continuation condition. As long as n is greater than 1, the code will continue to make recursive calls. Even though this code is shorter than the previous version, it's also less clear because now you must think about what condition will end the recursion.

Eliminating tail call recursion

Many forms of recursion rely on a tail call. In fact, the example in the previous section does. A *tail call* occurs any time the recursion makes a call to the function as the last thing before it returns. In the previous section, the line return n * factorial(n-1) is the tail call.

Tail calls aren't necessarily bad, and they represent the manner in which most people write recursive routines. However, using a tail call forces Python to keep track of the individual call values until the recursion rewinds. Each call consumes memory. At some point, the system will run out of memory and the call will fail, causing your algorithm to fail as well. Given the complexity and huge datasets used by some algorithms today, tail calls can cause considerable woe to anyone using them.

With a little fancy programming, you can potentially eliminate tail calls from your recursive routines. You can find a host of truly amazing techniques online, such as the use of a trampoline, as explained at http://blog.moertel.com/posts/2013-06-12-recursion-to-iteration-4-trampolines.html. However, the simplest approach to take when you want to eliminate recursion is to create an iterative alternative that performs the same task. For example, here is a factorial function that uses iteration instead of recursion to eliminate the potential for memory issues:

```
def factorial(n):
    print("factorial called with n = ", str(n))
    result = 1
    while n > 1:
        result = result * n
        n = n - 1
        print("Current value of n is ", str(n))
    print("Ending condition met.")
    return result

print(factorial(5))

factorial called with n =  5
Current value of n is  4
Current value of n is  3
Current value of n is  2
Current value of n is  1
Ending condition met.
120
```

The basic flow of this function is the same as the recursive function. A while loop replaces the recursive call, but you still need to check for the same condition and continue looping until the data meets the condition. The result is the same. However, replacing recursion with iteration is nontrivial in some cases, as explored in the example at http://blog.moertel.com/posts/2013-06-03-recursion-to-iteration-3.html.

Performing Tasks More Quickly

Obviously, getting tasks done as quickly as possible is always ideal. However, you always need to carefully weigh the techniques you use to achieve this. Trading a little memory to perform a task faster is great as long as you have the memory to spare. Later chapters in the book explore all sorts of ways to perform tasks faster, but you can try some essential techniques no matter what sort of algorithm you're working with at any given time. The following sections explore some of these techniques.

Considering divide and conquer

Some problems look overwhelming when you start them. Take, for example, writing a book. If you consider the entire book, writing it is an overwhelming task. However, if you break the book into chapters and consider just one chapter, the problem seems a little more doable. Of course, an entire chapter can seem a bit daunting, too, so you break the task down into first-level headings, which seems even more doable, but still not quite doable enough. The first-level headings could contain second-level headings and so on until you have broken down the problem of writing about a topic into short articles as much as you can. Even a short article can seem too hard, so you break it down into paragraphs, then into sentences, and finally into individual words. Writing a single word isn't too hard. So, writing a book comes down to writing individuals words —lots of them. This is how divide and conquer works. You break a problem down into smaller problems until you find a problem that you can solve without too much trouble.

Computers can use the divide-and-conquer approach as well. Trying to solve a huge problem with an enormous dataset could take days — assuming that the task is even doable. However, by breaking the big problem down into smaller pieces, you can solve the problem much faster and with fewer resources. For example, when searching for an entry in a database, searching the entire database isn't necessary if you use a sorted database. Say that you're looking for the word *Hello* in the database. You can begin by splitting the database in half (letters *A* through *M* and letters *N* through *Z*). The numeric value of the *H* in *Hello* (a value of 72 when using a standard ASCII table) is less than *M* (a value of 77) in the alphabet, so you look at the first half of the database rather than the second. Splitting the remaining half again (letters *A* through *G* and letters *H* through *M*), you now find that you need the second half of the remainder, which is now only a quarter of the database. Further splits eventually help you find precisely what you want by searching only a small fraction of the entire database. You call this search approach a *binary search.* The problem becomes one of following these steps:

1. Split the content in question in half.

2. Compare the keys for the content with the search term.

3. Choose the half that contains the key.

4. Repeat Steps 1 through 3 until you find the key.

REMEMBER

Most divide-and-conquer problems follow a similar approach, even though some of these approaches become quite convoluted. For example, instead of just splitting the database in half, you might split it into thirds in some cases. However, the goal is the same in all cases: Divide the problem into a smaller piece and determine whether you can solve the problem using just that piece as a generalized case. After you find the generalized case that you know how to solve, you can use that piece to solve any other piece as well. The following code shows an extremely simple version of a binary search that assumes that you have the list sorted. (You can find this code in the A4D; 05; `Binary Search.ipynb` file on the Dummies site as part of the downloadable code; see the Introduction for details.)

```
def search(searchList, key):
    mid = int(len(searchList) / 2)
    print("Searching midpoint at ", str(searchList[mid]))

    if mid == 0:
        print("Key Not Found!")
        return key

    elif key == searchList[mid]:
        print("Key Found!")
        return searchList[mid]

    elif key > searchList[mid]:
        print("searchList now contains ",
              searchList[mid:len(searchList)])
        search(searchList[mid:len(searchList)], key)

    else:
        print("searchList now contains ",
              searchList[0:mid])
        search(searchList[0:mid], key)

aList = list(range(1, 21))
search(aList, 5)

Searching midpoint at  11
searchList now contains  [1, 2, 3, 4, 5, 6, 7, 8, 9, 10]
Searching midpoint at  6
searchList now contains  [1, 2, 3, 4, 5]
Searching midpoint at  3
searchList now contains  [3, 4, 5]
Searching midpoint at  4
searchList now contains  [4, 5]
Searching midpoint at  5
Key Found!
```

This recursive approach to the binary search begins with aList containing the numbers 1 through 20. It searches for a value of 5 in aList. Each iteration of the recursion begins by looking for the list's midpoint, mid, and then using that midpoint to determine the next step. When the key matches the midpoint, the value is found in the list and the recursion ends.

REMEMBER

Note that this example makes one of two recursive calls. When `key` is greater than the midpoint value of the existing list, `searchList[mid]`, the code calls `search` again with just the right side of the remaining list. In other words, every call to `search` uses just half the list found in the previous call. When `key` is less than or equal to `searchList[mid]`, search receives the left half of the existing list.

WARNING

The list may not contain a search value, so you must always provide an escape method for the recursion or the stack will fill, resulting in an error message. In this case, the escape occurs when `mid == 0`, which means that there is no more `searchList` to search. For example, if you change `search(aList, 5)` to `search(aList, 22)`, you obtain the following output instead:

```
Searching midpoint at  11
searchList now contains  [11, 12, 13, 14, 15, 16, 17, 18,
 19, 20]
Searching midpoint at  16
searchList now contains  [16, 17, 18, 19, 20]
Searching midpoint at  18
searchList now contains  [18, 19, 20]
Searching midpoint at  19
searchList now contains  [19, 20]
Searching midpoint at  20
searchList now contains  [20]
Searching midpoint at  20
Key Not Found!
```

Note also that the code looks for the escape condition before performing any other work to ensure that the code doesn't inadvertently cause an error because of the lack of `searchList` content. When working with recursion, you must remain proactive or endure the consequences later.

Distinguishing between different possible solutions

Recursion is part of many different algorithmic programming solutions, as you see in the upcoming chapters. In fact, it's hard to get away from recursion in many cases because an iterative approach proves nonintuitive, cumbersome, and time consuming. However, you can create a number of different versions of the same solution, each of which has its own characteristics, flaws, and virtues.

The solution that this chapter doesn't consider is sequential search, because a sequential search generally takes longer than any other solution you can employ. In a best-case scenario, a sequential search requires just one comparison to complete the search, but in a worst-case scenario, you find the item you want as the last check. As an average, sequential search requires $(n+1)/2$ checks or $O(n)$ time to complete.

The binary search in the previous section does a much better job than a sequential search does. It works on logarithmic time or $O(\log n)$. In a best-case scenario, it takes only one check, as with a sequential search, but the output from the example shows that even a worst-case scenario, where the value doesn't even appear in the list, takes only six checks rather than the 21 checks that a sequential search would require.

TIP

This book covers a wide variety of search and sort algorithms because searching and sorting represent two major categories of computer processing. Think about how much time you spend Googling data each day. In theory, you might spend entire days doing nothing but searching for data. Search routines work best with sorted data, so you see the need for efficient search and sort routines. Fortunately, you don't have to spend hours trying to figure out which search and sort routines work best. Sites such as Big-O Cheat Sheet, `http://bigocheatsheet.com/`, provide you with the data needed to determine which solution performs best.

WARNING

If you look at performance times alone, however, the data you receive can mislead you into thinking that a particular solution will work incredibly well for your application when in fact it won't. You must also consider the kind of data you work with, the complexity of creating the solution, and a host of other factors. That's why later examples in this book also consider the pros and cons of each approach — the hidden dangers of choosing a solution that seems to have potential and then fails to produce the desired result.

2

Understanding the Need to Sort and Search

Use various Python data structures.

Work with trees and graphs.

Sort data to make algorithms work faster.

Search data to locate precisely the right information quickly.

Employ hashing techniques to create smaller data indexes.

Chapter **6**

Structuring Data

Raw data is just that: raw. It's not structured or cleaned in any way. You might find some parts of it missing or damaged in some way, or simply that it won't work for your problem. In fact, you're not entirely sure just what you're getting because it's raw.

Before you can do anything with most data, you must structure it in some manner so that you can begin to see what the data contains (and, sometimes, what it doesn't). Structuring data entails organizing it in some way so that all the data has the same attributes, appearance, and components. For example, you might get data from one source that contains dates in string form and another source that uses date objects. To use the information, you must make the kinds of data match. Data sources might also structure the data differently. One source might have the last and first name in a single field; another source might use individual fields for the same information. An important part of structuring data is organization. You aren't changing the data in any way — simply making the data more useful. (Structuring data contrasts with remediating or shaping the data where you sometimes do change values to convert one data type to another or experience a loss of accuracy, such as with dates, when moving between data sources.)

Python provides access to a number of organizational structures for data. The book uses these structures, especially stacks, queues, and dictionaries, for many of the examples. Each data structure provides a different means of working with the data and a different set of tools for performing tasks such as sorting the data into a particular order. This chapter presents you with the most common organizational methods, including both trees and graphs (both of which are so important that they appear in their own sections).

Determining the Need for Structure

Structure is an essential element in making algorithms work. As shown in the binary search example in Chapter 5, implementing an algorithm using structured data is much easier than trying to figure out how to interpret the data in code. For example, the binary search example relies on having the data in sorted order. Trying to perform the required comparisons with unsorted data would require a lot more effort and potentially prove impossible to implement. With all this in mind, you need to consider the structural requirements for the data you use with your algorithms, as discussed in the following sections.

Making it easier to see the content

An essential need to meet as part of working with data is to understand the data content. A search algorithm works only when you understand the dataset so that you know what to search for using the algorithm. Looking for words when the dataset contains numbers is an impossible task that always results in errors. Yet, search errors due to a lack of understanding of dataset content are a common occurrence even with the best search engines. Humans make assumptions about dataset content that cause algorithms to fail. Consequently, the better you can see and understand the content through structured formatting, the easier it becomes to perform algorithm-based tasks successfully.

However, even looking at the content is often error prone when dealing with humans and computers. For example, if you attempt to search for a number formatted as a string when the dataset contains the numbers formatted as integers, the search will fail. Computers don't automatically translate between strings and integers as humans do. In fact, computers see everything as numbers, and strings are only an interpretation imposed on the numbers by a programmer. Therefore, when searching for "1" (the string), the computer sees it as a request for the number 49 when using ASCII characters. To find the numeric value 1, you must search for a 1 as an integer value.

REMEMBER

Structure also enables you to discover nuanced data details. For example, a telephone number can appear in the form (555)555-1212. If you perform a search or other algorithm task using the form 1(555)555-1212, the search might fail because of the addition of a 1 at the beginning of the search term. These sorts of issues cause significant problems because most people see the two forms as equal, but the computer doesn't. The computer sees two completely different forms and even sees them as being two different lengths. Trying to impose form on humans rarely works and generally results in frustration that makes using the algorithm even harder, so structure imposed through data manipulation becomes even more important.

Matching data from various sources

Interacting with data from a single source is one problem; interacting with data from several sources is quite another. However, datasets today generally come from more than one source, so you need to understand the complications that using multiple data sources can cause. When working with multiple data sources, you must do the following:

» Determine whether both datasets contain all the required data. Two designers are unlikely to create datasets that contain precisely the same data, in the same format, of the same type, and in the same order. Consequently, you need to consider whether the datasets provide the data you need or whether you need to remediate the data in some way to obtain the desired result, as discussed in the next section.

» Check both datasets for data type issues. One dataset could have dates input as strings, and another could have the dates input as actual date objects. Inconsistencies between data types will cause problems for an algorithm that expects data in one form and receives it in another.

» Ensure that all datasets place the same meaning on data elements. Data created by one source might have a different meaning than data created by another source. For example, the size of an integer can vary across sources, so you might see a 16-bit integer from one source and a 32-bit integer from another. Lower values have the same meaning, but the 32-bit integer can contain larger values, which can cause problems with the algorithm. Dates can also cause problems because they often rely on storing so many milliseconds since a given date (such as JavaScript, which stores the number of milliseconds since 01 January, 1970 UTC). The computer sees only numbers; humans add meaning to these numbers so that applications interpret them in specific ways.

» Verify the data attributes. Data items have specific attributes, which is why Chapter 4 tells you all about how Python interprets various data types. Chapter 5 points out that this interpretation can change when using numpy. In fact, you find that data attributes change between environments, and developers can change them even more by creating custom data types. To combine data from various sources, you must understand these attributes to ensure that you interpret the data correctly.

REMEMBER

The more time you spend verifying the compatibility of data from each of the sources you want to use for a dataset, the less likely you are to encounter problems when working with an algorithm. Data incompatibility issues don't always appear as outright errors. In some cases, an incompatibility can cause other issues, such as errant results that look correct but provide misleading information.

Combining data from multiple sources may not always mean creating a new dataset that looks precisely like the source datasets, either. In some cases, you create data aggregates or perform other forms of manipulation to create new data from the existing data. Analysis takes all sorts of forms, and some of the more exotic forms can produce terrible errors when used incorrectly. For example, one data source could provide general customer information and a second data source could provide customer-buying habits. Mismatches between the two sources might match customers with incorrect buying habit information and cause problems when you try to market new products to these customers. As an extreme example, consider what would happen when combining patient information from several sources and creating combined patient entries in a new data source with all sorts of mismatches. A patient without a history of a particular disease could end up with records showing diagnosis and care of the disease.

Considering the need for remediation

After you find problems with your dataset, you need to remediate it so that the dataset works properly with the algorithms you use. For example, when working with conflicting data types, you must change the data types of each data source so that they match and then create the single data source used with the algorithm. Most of this remediation, although time consuming, is straightforward. You simply need to ensure that you understand the data before making changes, which means being able to see the content in the context of what you plan to do with it. However, you need to consider what to do in two special cases: data duplication and missing data. The following sections show how to deal with these issues.

Dealing with data duplication

Duplicated data occurs for a number of reasons. Some of them are obvious. A user could enter the same data more than once. Distractions cause people to lose their place in a list or sometimes two users enter the same record. Some of the sources are less obvious. Combining two or more datasets could create multiple records when the data appears in more than one location. You could also create data duplications when using various data-shaping techniques to create new data from existing data sources. Fortunately, packages such as Pandas let you remove duplicate data, as shown in the following example. (You can find this code in the A4D; 06; Remediation.ipynb file on the Dummies site as part of the downloadable code; see the Introduction for details.)

```
import pandas as pd

df = pd.DataFrame({'A': [0,0,0,0,0,1,0],
                   'B': [0,2,3,5,0,2,0],
                   'C': [0,3,4,1,0,2,0]})
```

```
print(df, "\n")

df = df.drop_duplicates()
print(df)

   A  B  C
0  0  0  0
1  0  2  3
2  0  3  4
3  0  5  1
4  0  0  0
5  1  2  2
6  0  0  0

   A  B  C
0  0  0  0
1  0  2  3
2  0  3  4
3  0  5  1
5  1  2  2
```

The drop_duplicates function removes the duplicate records found in rows 4 and 6 in this example. By reading your data from a source into a pandas DataFrame, you can quickly remove the extra entries so that the duplicates don't unfairly weight the output of any algorithms you use.

Dealing with missing values

Missing values can also skew the results of an algorithm's output. In fact, they can cause some algorithms to react oddly or even raise an error. The point is that missing values cause problems with your data, so you need to remove them. You do have many options when working with missing values. For example, you could simply set them to a standard value, such as 0 for integers. Of course, using a standard setting could also skew the results. Another approach is to use the mean of all the values, which tends to make the missing values not count. Using a mean is the approach taken in the following example

```
import pandas as pd
import numpy as np

df = pd.DataFrame({'A': [0,0,1,None],
                   'B': [1,2,3,4],
                   'C': [np.NAN,3,4,1]},
                  dtype=int)
```

```
print(df, "\n")

values = pd.Series(df.mean(), dtype=int)
print(values, "\n")

df = df.fillna(values)
print(df)

      A  B   C
0     0  1  NaN
1     0  2   3
2     1  3   4
3  None  4   1

A  0
B  2
C  2
dtype: int32

   A  B  C
0  0  1  2
1  0  2  3
2  1  3  4
3  0  4  1
```

The fillna function enables you to get rid of the missing values whether they're not a number (NAN) or simply missing (None). You can supply the missing data values in a number of forms. This example relies on a series that contains the mean for each separate column of data (much as you would do when working with a database).

REMEMBER

Note that the code is careful not to introduce errors into the output by ensuring that values is of the right data type. Normally, the mean function outputs floating-point values, but you can force the series it fills into the right type. Consequently, the output not only lacks missing values but also does contain values of the correct type.

Understanding other remediation issues

Remediation can take a number of other forms. Sometimes a user provides inconsistent or incorrect input. Applications don't always enforce data input rules, so users can enter incorrect state or region names. Misspellings also occur. Sometimes values are out of range or are simply impossible in a given situation. You may not always be able to clean your data completely on the first try. Often, you become aware of a problem by running the algorithm and noting that the results are skewed in some way or that the algorithm doesn't work at all (even if it did work on a subset of the data). When in doubt, check your data for potential remediation needs.

Stacking and Piling Data in Order

Python provides a number of storage methodologies, as discussed in Chapter 4. As you've already seen in Chapter 5, and this chapter, packages often offer additional storage methods. Both NumPy and Pandas provide storage alternatives that you might consider when working through various data structuring problems.

REMEMBER

A common problem of data storage isn't just the fact that you need to store the data, but that you must store it in a particular order so that you can access it when necessary. For example, you may want to ensure that the first item you place on a stack of items to process is also the first item you actually do process. With this data-ordering issue in mind, the following sections describe the standard Python methods for ensuring orderly data storage that let you have a specific processing arrangement.

Ordering in stacks

A stack provides last in/first out (LIFO) data storage. The NumPy package provides an actual stack implementation. In addition, Pandas associates stacks with objects such as the DataFrame. However, both packages hide the stack implementation details, and seeing how a stack works really does help. Consequently, the following example implements a stack using a standard Python list. (You can find this code in the A4D; 06; Stacks, Queues, and Dictionaries.ipynb file on the Dummies site as part of the downloadable code; see the Introduction for details.)

```
MyStack = []
StackSize = 3

def DisplayStack():
    print("Stack currently contains:")
    for Item in MyStack:
        print(Item)

def Push(Value):
    if len(MyStack) < StackSize:
        MyStack.append(Value)
```

```
        else:
            print("Stack is full!")

def Pop():
    if len(MyStack) > 0:
        print("Popping: ", MyStack.pop())
    else:
        print("Stack is empty.")

Push(1)
Push(2)
Push(3)
DisplayStack()

Push(4)

Pop()
DisplayStack()

Pop()
Pop()
Pop()

Stack currently contains:
1
2
3
Stack is full!
Popping:  3
Stack currently contains:
1
2
Popping:  2
Popping:  1
Stack is empty.
```

The example ensures that the stack maintains the integrity of the data and works with it in the order you expect. The code relies on simple `list` manipulation, but it's effective in providing a stack representation that you can use for any need.

TIP

Python lists are ordered lists of data values that are easy and intuitive to use. From an algorithm perspective, they often don't perform well because they store the list elements in computer memory and access them using an index and *memory pointers* (a number that provides the memory address of the data). They work exactly the way a book index or a package does. Lists don't have knowledge of their content.

When your application makes a data request, the list scans through all its items, which is even slower. When data is scattered across your computer's memory, lists must gather the data from each location individually and slowing access more.

Using queues

Unlike stacks, queues are first in/first out (FIFO) data structures. As with stacks, you can find predefined implementations in many packages, including both NumPy and Pandas. Fortunately, you can also find a specific queue implementation in Python, which you find demonstrated in the following code:

```
import queue

MyQueue = queue.Queue(3)

print("Queue empty: ", MyQueue.empty())

MyQueue.put(1)
MyQueue.put(2)
MyQueue.put(3)
print("Queue full: ", MyQueue.full())

print("Popping: ", MyQueue.get())
print("Queue full: ", MyQueue.full())

print("Popping: ", MyQueue.get())
print("Popping: ", MyQueue.get())
print("Queue empty: ", MyQueue.empty())

Queue empty:    True
Queue full:    True
Popping:  1
Queue full:    False
Popping:  2
Popping:  3
Queue empty:    True
```

Using the built-in queue requires a lot less code than building a stack from scratch using a list, but notice how the two differ in output. The stack example pushes 1, 2, and 3 onto the stack, so the first value popped from the stack is 3. However, in this example, pushing 1, 2, and 3 onto the queue results in a first popped value of 1.

Finding data using dictionaries

Creating and using a dictionary is much like working with a list except that you must now define a key and value pair. The great advantage of this data structure is that dictionaries can quickly provide access to specific data items using the key. There are limits to the kinds of keys you can use. Here are the special rules for creating a key:

>> **The key must be unique.** When you enter a duplicate key, the information found in the second entry wins; the first entry replaces the second.

>> **The key must be immutable.** This rule means that you can use strings, numbers, or tuples for the key. You can't, however, use a list for a key.

REMEMBER

The difference between mutable and immutable values is that immutable values can't change. To change the value of a string, for example, Python actually creates a new string that contains the new value and gives the new string the same name as the old one. It then destroys the old string.

TIP

Python dictionaries are the software implementation of a data structure called a *hash table*, an array that maps keys to values. Chapter 7 explains hashes in detail and how using hashes can help dictionaries perform faster. You have no restrictions on the values you provide. A value can be any Python object, so you can use a dictionary to access an employee record or other complex data. The following example helps you understand how to use dictionaries better:

```python
Colors = {"Sam": "Blue", "Amy": "Red", "Sarah": "Yellow"}

print(Colors["Sarah"])
print(Colors.keys())

for Item in Colors.keys():
    print("{0} likes the color {1}."
        .format(Item, Colors[Item]))

Colors["Sarah"] = "Purple"
Colors.update({"Harry": "Orange"})
del Colors["Sam"]

print(Colors)

Yellow
dict_keys(['Sarah', 'Amy', 'Sam'])
Sarah likes the color Yellow.
Amy likes the color Red.
```

```
Sam likes the color Blue.
{'Harry': 'Orange', 'Sarah': 'Purple', 'Amy': 'Red'}
```

As you can see, a dictionary always has a key and value pair separated from each other by a colon (:). Instead of using an index to access individual values, you use the key. The special `keys` function lets you obtain a list of keys that you can manipulate in various ways. For example, you can use the keys to perform iterative processing of the data values that the dictionary contains.

TIP

Dictionaries are a bit like individual tables within a database. You can update, add, and delete records to a dictionary as shown. The `update` function can overwrite or add new entries to the dictionary.

Working with Trees

A tree structure looks much like the physical object in the natural world. Using trees helps you organize data quickly and find it in a shorter time than using other data-storage techniques. You commonly find trees used for search and sort routines, but they have many other purposes as well. The following sections help you understand trees at a basic level. You find trees used in many of the examples in upcoming chapters.

Understanding the basics of trees

Building a tree works much like building a tree in the physical world. Each item you add to the tree is a *node*. Nodes connect to each other using *links*. The combination of nodes and links forms a structure that looks much like a tree, as shown in Figure 6-1.

REMEMBER

Note that the tree has just one root node— just as with a physical tree. The *root node* provides the starting point for the various kinds of processing you perform. Connected to the root node are either branches or leaves. A *leaf node* is always an ending point for the tree. *Branch nodes* support either other branches or leaves. The type of tree shown in Figure 6-1 is a binary tree because each node has, at most, two connections.

In looking at the tree, Branch B is the child of the Root node. That's because the Root node appears first in the list. Leaf E and Leaf F are both children of Branch B, making Branch B the parent of Leaf E and Leaf F. The relationship between nodes is important because discussions about trees often consider the child/parent relationship between nodes. Without these terms, discussions of trees could become quite confusing.

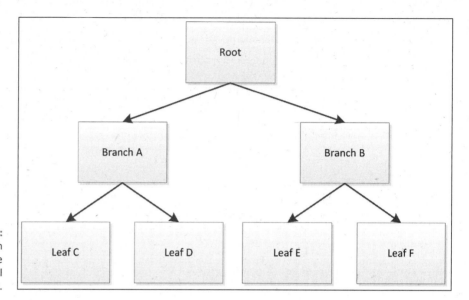

FIGURE 6-1:
A tree in Python looks much like the physical alternative.

Building a tree

Python doesn't come with a built-in tree object. You must either create your own implementation or use a tree supplied with a package. A basic tree implementation requires that you create a class to hold the tree data object. The following code shows how you can create a basic tree class. (You can find this code in the A4D; 06; Trees.ipynb file on the Dummies site as part of the downloadable code; see the Introduction for details.)

```
class binaryTree:
    def __init__(self, nodeData, left=None, right=None):
        self.nodeData = nodeData
        self.left  = left
        self.right = right

    def __str__(self):
        return str(self.nodeData)
```

All this code does is create a basic tree object that defines the three elements that a node must include: data storage, left connection, and right connection. Because leaf nodes have no connection, the default value for left and right is None. The class also includes a method for printing the content of nodeData so that you can see what data the node stores.

Using this simple tree requires that you not try to store anything in left or right other than a reference to another node. Otherwise, the code will fail because there isn't any error trapping. The nodeData entry can contain any value. The following code shows how to use the binaryTree class to build the tree shown in Figure 6-1:

```
tree = binaryTree("Root")
BranchA = binaryTree("Branch A")
BranchB = binaryTree("Branch B")
tree.left = BranchA
tree.right = BranchB

LeafC = binaryTree("Leaf C")
LeafD = binaryTree("Leaf D")
LeafE = binaryTree("Leaf E")
LeafF = binaryTree("Leaf F")
BranchA.left = LeafC
BranchA.right = LeafD
BranchB.left = LeafE
BranchB.right = LeafF
```

You have many options when building a tree, but building it from the top down (as shown in this code) or the bottom up (in which you build the leaves first) are two common methods. Of course, you don't really know whether the tree actually works at this point. *Traversing the tree* means checking the links and verifying that they actually do connect as you think they should. The following code shows how to use recursion (as described in Chapter 5) to traverse the tree you just built.

```
def traverse(tree):
    if tree.left != None:
        traverse(tree.left)
    if tree.right != None:
        traverse(tree.right)
    print(tree.nodeData)

traverse(tree)

Leaf C
Leaf D
Branch A
Leaf E
Leaf F
Branch B
Root
```

As the output shows, the `traverse` function doesn't print anything until it gets to the first leaf. It then prints both leaves and the parent of those leaves. The traversal follows the left branch first, and then the right branch. The root node comes last.

TECHNICAL
STUFF

There are different kinds of data storage structures. Here is a quick list of the kinds of structures you commonly find:

>> **Balanced trees:** A kind of tree that maintains a balanced structure through reorganization so that it can provide reduced access times. The number of elements on the left size differs from the number on the right side by at most one.

>> **Unbalanced trees:** A tree that places new data items wherever necessary in the tree without regard to balance. This method of adding items makes building the tree faster but reduces access speed when searching or sorting.

>> **Heaps:** A sophisticated tree that allows data insertions into the tree structure. The use of data insertion makes sorting faster. You can further classify these trees as max heaps and min heaps, depending on the tree's capability to immediately provide the maximum or minimum value present in the tree.

Later in the book, you find algorithms that use balanced trees, unbalanced trees, and heaps. For instance, Chapter 9 discusses the Dijkstra algorithm and Chapter 14 discusses Huffman encoding. As part of these discussions, the book provides pictures and code to explain how each data structure functions and its role in making the algorithm work.

Representing Relations in a Graph

Graphs are another form of common data structure used in algorithms. You see graphs used in places like maps for GPS and all sorts of other places where the top down approach of a tree won't work. The following sections describe graphs in more detail.

Going beyond trees

A graph is a sort of a tree extension. As with trees, you have nodes that connect to each other to create relationships. However, unlike binary trees, a graph can have more than one or two connections. In fact, graph nodes often have a multitude of connections. To keep things simple, though, consider the graph shown in Figure 6-2.

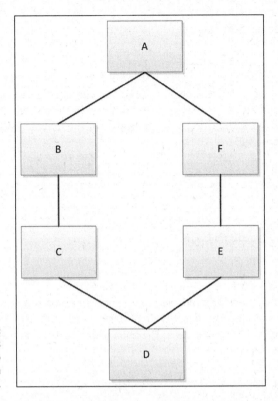

FIGURE 6-2:
Graph nodes
can connect to
each other in
myriad ways.

In this case, the graph creates a ring where A connects to both B and F. However, it need not be that way. A could be a disconnected node or could also connect to C. A graph shows connectivity between nodes in a way that is useful for defining complex relationships.

Graphs also add a few new twists that you might not have thought about before. For example, a graph can include the concept of directionality. Unlike a tree, which has parent/child relationships, a graph node can connect to any other node with a specific direction in mind. Think about streets in a city. Most streets are bidirectional, but some are one-way streets that allow movement in only one direction.

The presentation of a graph connection might not actually reflect the realities of the graph. A graph can designate a weight to a particular connection. The weight could define the distance between two points, define the time required to traverse the route, or provide other sorts of information.

Building graphs

Most developers use dictionaries (or sometimes lists) to build graphs. Using a dictionary makes building the graph easy because the key is the node name and the values are the connections for that node. For example, here is a dictionary that creates the graph shown in Figure 6-2. (You can find this code in the A4D; 06; Graphs.ipynb file on the Dummies site as part of the downloadable code; see the Introduction for details.)

```
graph = {'A': ['B', 'F'],
         'B': ['A', 'C'],
         'C': ['B', 'D'],
         'D': ['C', 'E'],
         'E': ['D', 'F'],
         'F': ['E', 'A']}
```

This dictionary reflects the bidirectional nature of the graph in Figure 6-2. It could just as easily define unidirectional connections or provide nodes without any connections at all. However, the dictionary works quite well for this purpose, and you see it used in other areas of the book. Now it's time to traverse the graph using the following code:

```
def find_path(graph, start, end, path=[]):
        path = path + [start]

        if start == end:
            print("Ending")
            return path

        for node in graph[start]:
            print("Checking Node ", node)

            if node not in path:
                print("Path so far ", path)

                newp = find_path(graph, node, end, path)
                if newp:
                    return newp

find_path(graph, 'B', 'E')

Checking Node  A
Path so far  ['B']
Checking Node  B
```

```
Checking Node  F
Path so far  ['B', 'A']
Checking Node  E
Path so far  ['B', 'A', 'F']
Ending

['B', 'A', 'F', 'E']
```

Later chapters discuss how to find the shortest path. For now, the code finds only a path. It begins by building the path node by node. As with all recursive routines, this one requires an exit strategy, which is that when the start value matches the end value, the path ends.

Because each node in the graph can connect to multiple nodes, you need a for loop to check each of the potential connections. When the node in question already appears in the path, the code skips it. Otherwise, the code tracks the current path and recursively calls find_path to locate the next node in the path.

Chapter 7

Arranging and Searching Data

D ata surrounds you all the time. In fact, you really can't get away from it. Everything from the data needed to make business work to the nutritional guide on the side of your box of cereal relies on data. The four data operations are create, read, update, and delete (CRUD), which focus on the need to access the data you need to perform just about every task in life quickly and easily. That's why having the means to arrange and search data in a number of ways is essential. Unless you can access the data when you want in the manner you want, the CRUD required to make your business work will become quite cruddy indeed. Consequently, this is an especially important chapter for everyone who wants to make an application shine.

The first section of this chapter focuses on sorting data. Placing data in an order that makes it easy to perform CRUD operations is important because the less code you need to make data access work, the better. In addition, even though sorting data might not seem particularly important, sorted data makes searches considerably faster, as long as the sort matches the search. Sorting and searching go together: You sort the data in a way that makes searching faster.

The second section of the chapter discusses searching. You won't be surprised to learn that many different ways are available to search for data. Some of these techniques are slower than others; some have attributes that make them attractive to developers. The fact is that no perfect search strategy exists, but the exploration for such a method continues.

The final section of the chapter looks at hashing and dictionaries. The use of indexing makes sorting and searching significantly faster but also comes with trade-offs that you need to consider (such as the use of additional resources). An *index* is a kind of pointer or an address. It's not the data, but it points to the data, much as your address points to your home. A block-by-block manual search for your home in the city would be time consuming because the person looking for you would need to ask each person at each address whether you're there, but finding your address in the phone book and then using that address to locate your home is much faster.

Sorting Data Using Mergesort and Quicksort

Sorting is one of the essentials of working with data. Consequently, a lot of people have come up with a lot of different ways in which to sort data over the years. All these techniques result in ordered data, but some work better than others do, and some work exceptionally well for specific tasks. The following sections help you understand the need for searching as well as consider the various search options.

Defining why sorting data is important

A case can be made for not sorting data. After all, the data is still accessible, even if you don't sort it — and sorting takes time. Of course, the problem with unsorted data is the same problem as that junk drawer in your kitchen (or wherever you have your junk drawer — assuming that you can find it at all). Looking for anything in the junk drawer is time consuming because you can't even begin to guess where to find something. Rather than just reach in and take what you want, you must take out myriad other items that you don't want in an effort to find the one item you need. Unfortunately, the item you need might not be in the junk drawer in the first place—you might have thrown it out or put it in a different drawer.

The junk drawer in your home is just like unsorted data on your system. When the data is unsorted, you need to search one item at a time, and you don't even know whether you'll find what you need without searching every item in the dataset first. It's a frustrating way to work with data. The binary search example in the "Considering divide and conquer" section of Chapter 5 points out the need for sorting quite well. Imagine trying to find an item in a list without sorting it first. Every search becomes a time-consuming sequential search.

REMEMBER

Of course, simply sorting the data isn't enough. If you have an employee database sorted by last name, yet need to look up an employee by birth date, the sorting isn't useful. (Say you want to find all of the employees who have a birthday on a certain day.) To find the birth date you need, you must still search the entire dataset one item at a time. Consequently, sorting must focus on a particular need. Yes, you needed the employee database sorted by department at one point and by last name at another time, but now you need it sorted by birth date in order to use the dataset effectively.

The need to maintain several sorted orders for the same data is the reason that developers created indexes. Sorting a small index is faster than sorting the entire dataset. The index maintains a specific data order and points to the full dataset so that you can find what you need extremely fast. By maintaining an index for each sort requirement, you can effectively cut data access time and allow several people to access the data at the same time in the order in which they need to access it. The "Relying on Hashing" section, later in this chapter, gives you an idea of how indexing works and why you really need it in some cases, despite the additional time and resources needed to maintain the indexes.

TECHNICAL
STUFF

Many ways are available to categorize sorting algorithms. One of these ways is the speed of the sort. When considering how effective a particular sort algorithm is at arranging the data, timing benchmarks typically look at two factors:

>> **Comparisons:** To move data from one location in a dataset to another, you need to know where to move it, which means comparing the target data to other data in the dataset. Having fewer comparisons means better performance.

>> **Exchanges:** Depending on how you write an algorithm, the data may not get to its final location in the dataset on the first try. The data might actually move several times. The number of exchanges affects speed considerably because now you're actually moving data from one location to another in memory. Fewer and smaller exchanges (such as when using indexes) means better performance.

Ordering data naïvely

Ordering data naively means to order it using brute-force methods — without any regard whatsoever to making any kind of guess as to where the data should appear in the list. In addition, these techniques tend to work with the entire dataset instead of applying approaches that would likely reduce sorting time (such as the divide and conquer technique described in Chapter 5). However, these searches are also relatively easy to understand, and they use resources efficiently. Consequently, you shouldn't rule them out completely. Even though many searches fall into this category, the following sections look at the two most popular approaches.

Using a selection sort

The selection sort replaced a predecessor, the bubble sort, because it tends to provide better performance than the bubble sort. Even though both sorts have a worst-case sort speed of O(n²), the selection sort performs fewer exchanges. A selection sort works in one of two ways: It either looks for the smallest item in the list and places it in the front of the list (ensuring that the item is in its correct location) or looks for the largest item and places it in the back of the list. Either way, the sort is exceptionally easy to implement and guarantees that items immediately appear in the final location once moved (which is why some people call it an in-place comparison sort). Here's an example of a selection sort. (You can find this code in the A4D; 07; Sorting Techniques.ipynb file on the Dummies site as part of the downloadable code; see the Introduction for details.)

```
data = [9, 5, 7, 4, 2, 8, 1, 10, 6, 3]

for scanIndex in range(0, len(data)):
    minIndex = scanIndex

    for compIndex in range(scanIndex + 1, len(data)):
        if data[compIndex] < data[minIndex]:
            minIndex = compIndex

    if minIndex != scanIndex:
        data[scanIndex], data[minIndex] = \
            data[minIndex], data[scanIndex]
        print(data)

[1, 5, 7, 4, 2, 8, 9, 10, 6, 3]
[1, 2, 7, 4, 5, 8, 9, 10, 6, 3]
[1, 2, 3, 4, 5, 8, 9, 10, 6, 7]
[1, 2, 3, 4, 5, 6, 9, 10, 8, 7]
[1, 2, 3, 4, 5, 6, 7, 10, 8, 9]
[1, 2, 3, 4, 5, 6, 7, 8, 10, 9]
[1, 2, 3, 4, 5, 6, 7, 8, 9, 10]
```

Switching to an insertion sort

An insertion sort works by using a single item as a starting point and adding items to the left or right of it based on whether these items are less than or greater than the selected item. As the number of sorted items builds, the algorithm checks new items against the sorted items and inserts the new item into the right position in the list. An insertion sort has a best-case sort speed of O(n) and a worst case sort speed of O(n²).

**TECHNICAL
STUFF**

An example of best-case sort speed is when the entire dataset is already sorted because the insertion sort won't have to move any values. An example of the worst-case sort speed is when the entire dataset is sorted in reverse order because every insertion will require moving every value that already appears in the output. You can read more about the math involved in this sort at `https://www.khanacademy.org/computing/computer-science/algorithms/insertion-sort/a/analysis-of-insertion-sort`.

The insertion sort is still a brute-force method of sorting items, but it can require fewer comparisons than a selection sort. Here's an example of an insertion sort:

```python
data = [9, 5, 7, 4, 2, 8, 1, 10, 6, 3]

for scanIndex in range(1, len(data)):
    temp = data[scanIndex]

    minIndex = scanIndex

    while minIndex > 0 and temp < data[minIndex - 1]:
        data[minIndex] = data[minIndex - 1]
        minIndex -= 1

    data[minIndex] = temp
    print(data)

[5, 9, 7, 4, 2, 8, 1, 10, 6, 3]
[5, 7, 9, 4, 2, 8, 1, 10, 6, 3]
[4, 5, 7, 9, 2, 8, 1, 10, 6, 3]
[2, 4, 5, 7, 9, 8, 1, 10, 6, 3]
[2, 4, 5, 7, 8, 9, 1, 10, 6, 3]
[1, 2, 4, 5, 7, 8, 9, 10, 6, 3]
[1, 2, 4, 5, 7, 8, 9, 10, 6, 3]
[1, 2, 4, 5, 6, 7, 8, 9, 10, 3]
[1, 2, 3, 4, 5, 6, 7, 8, 9, 10]
```

Employing better sort techniques

As sort technology improves, the sort algorithms begin taking a more intelligent approach to getting data into the right order. The idea is to make the problem smaller and easier to manage. Rather than work with an entire dataset, smart sorting algorithms work with individual items, reducing the work required to perform the task. The following sections discuss two such smart sorting techniques.

Rearranging data with Mergesort

A Mergesort works by applying the divide and conquer approach. The sort begins by breaking the dataset into individual pieces and sorting the pieces. It then merges the pieces in a manner that ensures that it has sorted the merged piece. The sorting and merging continues until the entire dataset is again a single piece. The worst-case sort speed of the Mergesort is O(n log n), which makes it considerably faster than the techniques used in the previous section (because log n is always smaller than n). This sort actually requires the use of two functions. The first function works recursively to split the pieces apart and put them back together again.

```
data = [9, 5, 7, 4, 2, 8, 1, 10, 6, 3]

def mergeSort(list):
    # Determine whether the list is broken into
    # individual pieces.
    if len(list) < 2:
        return list

    # Find the middle of the list.
    middle = len(list)//2

    # Break the list into two pieces.
    left = mergeSort(list[:middle])
    right = mergeSort(list[middle:])

    # Merge the two sorted pieces into a larger piece.
    print("Left side: ", left)
    print("Right side: ", right)
    merged = merge(left, right)
    print("Merged ", merged)
    return merged
```

The second function performs the actual task of merging the two sides using an iterative process. Here's the code used to merge the two pieces:

```
def merge(left, right):
    # When the left side or the right side is empty,
    # it means that this is an individual item and is
    # already sorted.
    if not len(left):
        return left
    if not len(right):
        return right
```

```
    # Define variables used to merge the two pieces.
    result = []
    leftIndex = 0
    rightIndex = 0
    totalLen = len(left) + len(right)

    # Keep working until all of the items are merged.
    while (len(result) < totalLen):

        # Perform the required comparisons and merge
        # the pieces according to value.
        if left[leftIndex] < right[rightIndex]:
            result.append(left[leftIndex])
            leftIndex+= 1
        else:
            result.append(right[rightIndex])
            rightIndex+= 1

        # When the left side or the right side is longer,
        # add the remaining elements to the result.
        if leftIndex == len(left) or \
            rightIndex == len(right):
                result.extend(left[leftIndex:]
                            or right[rightIndex:])
                break

    return result

mergeSort(data)
```

The print statements in the code help you see how the merging process works. Even though the process seems quite complex, it really is relatively straight-forward when you work through the merging process shown here.

```
Left side:   [9]
Right side:  [5]
Merged  [5, 9]
Left side:   [4]
Right side:  [2]
Merged  [2, 4]
Left side:   [7]
Right side:  [2, 4]
Merged  [2, 4, 7]
Left side:   [5, 9]
```

```
Right side:  [2, 4, 7]
Merged  [2, 4, 5, 7, 9]
Left side:  [8]
Right side:  [1]
Merged  [1, 8]
Left side:  [6]
Right side:  [3]
Merged  [3, 6]
Left side:  [10]
Right side:  [3, 6]
Merged  [3, 6, 10]
Left side:  [1, 8]
Right side:  [3, 6, 10]
Merged  [1, 3, 6, 8, 10]
Left side:  [2, 4, 5, 7, 9]
Right side:  [1, 3, 6, 8, 10]
Merged  [1, 2, 3, 4, 5, 6, 7, 8, 9, 10]
```

Solving sorting issues the best way using Quicksort

The Quicksort is one of the fastest methods of sorting data. In reading about Mergesort and Quicksort online, you find that some people prefer to use one over the other in a given situation. For example, most people feel that a Quicksort works best for sorting arrays, and Mergesort works best for sorting linked lists (see the discussion at http://www.geeksforgeeks.org/why-quick-sort-preferred-for-arrays-and-merge-sort-for-linked-lists/). Tony Hoare wrote the first version of Quicksort in 1959, but since that time, developers have written many other versions of Quicksort. The average sort time of a Quicksort is O(n log n), but the worst-case sort time is O(n²).

The first part of the task is to partition the data. The code chooses a pivot point that determines the left and right side of the sort. Here is the partitioning code for this example:

```
data = [9, 5, 7, 4, 2, 8, 1, 10, 6, 3]

def partition(data, left, right):
    pivot = data[left]
    lIndex = left + 1
    rIndex = right
```

```
while True:
    while lIndex <= rIndex and data[lIndex] <= pivot:
        lIndex += 1
    while rIndex >= lIndex and data[rIndex] >= pivot:
        rIndex -= 1
    if rIndex <= lIndex:
        break
    data[lIndex], data[rIndex] = \
        data[rIndex], data[lIndex]
    print(data)

data[left], data[rIndex] = data[rIndex], data[left]
print(data)
return rIndex
```

UNDERSTANDING QUICKSORT WORST-CASE PERFORMANCE

TECHNICAL STUFF

Quicksort seldom incurs the worst-case sort time. However, even modified versions of the Quicksort can have a worst-case sort time of $O(n^2)$ when one of these events occurs:

- The dataset is already sorted in the desired order.

- The dataset is sorted in reverse order.

- All the elements in the dataset are the same.

All these problems occur because of the pivot point that a less intelligent sort function uses. Fortunately, using the right programming technique can mitigate these problems by defining something other than the leftmost or rightmost index as the pivot point. The techniques that modern Quicksort versions rely on include:

- Choosing a random index

- Choosing the middle index of the partition

- Choosing the median of the first, middle, and last element of the partition for the pivot (especially for longer partitions)

The inner loop of this example continuously searches for elements that are in the wrong place and swaps them. When the code can no longer swap items, it breaks out of the loop and sets a new pivot point, which it returns to the caller. This is the iterative part of the process. The recursive part of the process handles the left and right side of the dataset, as shown here:

```
def quickSort(data, left, right):
    if right <= left:
        return
    else:
        pivot = partition(data, left, right)
        quickSort(data, left, pivot-1)
        quickSort(data, pivot+1, right)

    return data

quickSort(data, 0, len(data)-1)
```

The amount of comparisons and exchanges for this example are relatively small compared to the other examples. Here is the output from this example:

```
[9, 5, 7, 4, 2, 8, 1, 3, 6, 10]
[6, 5, 7, 4, 2, 8, 1, 3, 9, 10]
[6, 5, 3, 4, 2, 8, 1, 7, 9, 10]
[6, 5, 3, 4, 2, 1, 8, 7, 9, 10]
[1, 5, 3, 4, 2, 6, 8, 7, 9, 10]
[1, 5, 3, 4, 2, 6, 8, 7, 9, 10]
[1, 2, 3, 4, 5, 6, 8, 7, 9, 10]
[1, 2, 3, 4, 5, 6, 8, 7, 9, 10]
[1, 2, 3, 4, 5, 6, 8, 7, 9, 10]
[1, 2, 3, 4, 5, 6, 7, 8, 9, 10]
```

Using Search Trees and the Heap

Search trees enable you to look for data quickly. Chapter 5 introduces you to the idea of a binary search, and the "Working with Trees" section of Chapter 6 helps you understand trees to some extent. Obtaining data items, placing them in sorted order in a tree, and then searching that tree is one of the faster ways to find information.

A special kind of tree structure is the *binary heap*, which places each of the node elements in a special order. The root node always contains the smallest value. When viewing the branches, you see that upper-level branches are always a smaller value than lower-level branches and leaves. The effect is to keep the tree balanced and in a predictable order so that searching becomes extremely efficient. The cost is in keeping the tree balanced. The following sections describe how search trees and the heap work in detail.

Considering the need to search effectively

Of all the tasks that applications do, searching is the more time consuming and also the one required most. Even though adding data (and sorting it later) does require some amount of time, the benefit to creating and maintaining a dataset comes from using it to perform useful work, which means searching it for important information. Consequently, you can sometimes get by with less efficient CRUD functionality and even a less-than-optimal sort routine, but searches must proceed as efficiently as possible. The only problem is that no one search performs every task with absolute efficiency, so you must weigh your options based on what you expect to do as part of the search routines.

Two of the more efficient methods of searching involve the use of the binary search tree (BST) and binary heap. Both of the search techniques rely on a tree-like structure to hold the keys used to access data elements. However, the arrangement of the two methods is different, which is why one has advantages over the other when performing certain tasks. Figure 7-1 shows the arrangement for a BST.

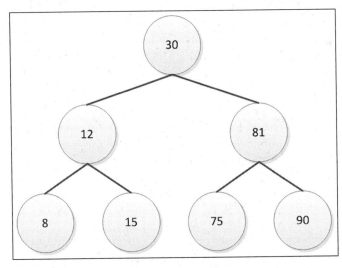

FIGURE 7-1:
The arrangement
of keys when
using a BST.

Note how the keys follow an order in which lesser numbers appear to the left and greater numbers appear to the right. The root node contains a value that is in the middle of the range of keys, giving the BST an easily understood balanced approach to storing the keys. Contrast this arrangement to the binary heap shown in Figure 7-2.

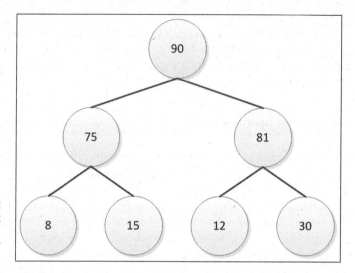

FIGURE 7-2:
The arrangement
of keys when
using a binary
heap.

Each level contains values that are less than the previous level, and the root contains the maximum key value for the tree. In addition, in this particular case, the lesser values appear on the left and the greater on the right (although this order isn't strictly enforced). The figure actually depicts a *binary max heap*. You can also create a *binary min heap* in which the root contains the lowest key value and each level builds to higher values, with the highest values appearing as part of the leaves.

REMEMBER

As previously noted, BST has some advantages over binary heap when used to perform a search. The following list provides some of the highlights of these advantages:

» Searching for an element requires O(log n) time, contrasted to O(n) time for a binary heap.

» Printing the elements in order requires only O(log n) time, contrasted to O(n log n) time for a binary heap.

» Finding the floor and ceiling requires O(log n) time.

» Locating Kth smallest/largest element requires O(log n) time when the tree is properly configured.

Whether these times are important depends on your application. BST tends to work best in situations in which you spend more time searching and less time building the tree. A binary heap tends to work best in dynamic situations in which keys change regularly. The binary heap also offers advantages, as described in the following list:

» Creating the required structures requires fewer resources because binary heaps rely on arrays, making them cache friendlier as well.

» Building a binary heap requires O(n) time, contrasted to BST, which requires O(n log n) time.

» Using pointers to implement the tree isn't necessary.

» Relying on binary heap variations (for example, the Fibonacci Heap) offers advantages such as increase and decrease key times of O(1) time.

Building a binary search tree

You can build a BST using a variety of methods. Some people simply use a dictionary; others use custom code (see the article at https://interactivepython.org/courselib/static/pythonds/Trees/SearchTreeImplementation.html and http://code.activestate.com/recipes/577540-python-binary-search-tree/ as examples). However, most developers don't want to reinvent the wheel when it comes to BST. With this in mind, you need a package, such as bintrees, which provides all the required functionality to create and interact with BST using a minimum of code. To download and install bintrees, open a command prompt, type **pip install bintrees**, and press Enter. You see bintrees installed on your system. The documentation for this package appears at https://pypi.python.org/pypi/bintrees/2.0.6.

You can use bintrees for all sorts of needs, but the example in this section looks specifically at a BST. In this case, the tree is unbalanced. The following code shows how to build and display a BST using bintrees. (You can find this code in the A4D; 07; Search Techniques.ipynb file on the Dummies site as part of the downloadable code; see the Introduction for details.)

```
from bintrees import BinaryTree

data = {3:'White', 2:'Red', 1:'Green', 5:'Orange',
        4:'Yellow', 7:'Purple', 0:'Magenta'}

tree = BinaryTree(data)
tree.update({6:'Teal'})

def displayKeyValue(key, value):
    print('Key: ', key, 'Value: ', value)

tree.foreach(displayKeyValue)
print('Item 3 contains: ', tree.get(3))
print('The maximum item is: ', tree.max_item())
```

```
Key:    0 Value:    Magenta
Key:    1 Value:    Green
Key:    2 Value:    Red
Key:    3 Value:    White
Key:    4 Value:    Yellow
Key:    5 Value:    Orange
Key:    6 Value:    Teal
Key:    7 Value:    Purple
Item 3 contains:  White
The maximum item is:  (7, 'Purple')
```

To create a binary tree, you must supply key and value pairs. One way to perform this task is to create a dictionary as shown. After you create the tree, you can use the update function to add new entries. The entries must include a key and value pair as shown.

TIP

This example uses a function to perform a task with the data in tree. In this case, the function merely prints the key and value pairs, but you could use the tree as input to an algorithm for analysis (among other tasks). The function, display KeyValue, acts as input to the foreach function, which displays the key and value pairs as output. You also have access to myriad other features, such as using get to obtain a single item or max_item to obtain the maximum item stored in tree.

Performing specialized searches using a binary heap

As with BST, you have many ways to implement a binary heap. Writing one by hand or using a dictionary does work well, but relying on a package makes things considerably faster and more reliable. The heapq package comes with Python, so you don't even need to install it. You can find the documentation for this package at https://docs.python.org/3/library/heapq.html. The following example shows how to build and search a binary heap using heapq:

```
import heapq

data = {3:'White', 2:'Red', 1:'Green', 5:'Orange',
        4:'Yellow', 7:'Purple', 0:'Magenta'}

heap = []
for key, value in data.items():
    heapq.heappush(heap, (key, value))
heapq.heappush(heap, (6, 'Teal'))
heap.sort()
```

```
for item in heap:
    print('Key: ', item[0], 'Value: ', item[1])
print('Item 3 contains: ', heap[3][1])
print('The maximum item is: ', heapq.nlargest(1, heap))

Key:  0 Value:  Magenta
Key:  1 Value:  Green
Key:  2 Value:  Red
Key:  3 Value:  White
Key:  4 Value:  Yellow
Key:  5 Value:  Orange
Key:  6 Value:  Teal
Key:  7 Value:  Purple
Item 3 contains:  White
The maximum item is:  [(7, 'Purple')]
```

The example code performs the same tasks and provides the same output as the example in the previous section, except that it relies on a binary heap in this case. The dataset is the same as before. However, note the difference in the way you add the data to the heap using heappush. In addition, after adding a new item, you must call sort to ensure that the items appear in sorted order. Manipulating the data is much like manipulating a list, as contrasted to the dictionary approach used for bintrees. Whichever approach you use, it pays to choose an option that works well with the application you want to create and provides the fastest possible search times for the tasks you perform.

Relying on Hashing

A major problem with most sort routines is that they sort all the data in a dataset. When the dataset is small, you hardly notice the amount of data that the sort routine attempts to move. However, as the dataset gets larger, the data movement becomes noticeable as you sit staring at the screen for hours on end. A way around this problem is to sort just the key information. A *key* is the identifying data for a particular data record. When you interact with an employee record, the employee name or number usually serves as a key for accessing all the other information you have about the employee. It's senseless to sort all the employee information when you really need only the keys sorted, which is what using hashing is all about. When working with these data structures, you gain a major speed advantage by sorting the smaller amount of data presented by the keys, rather than the records as a whole.

Putting everything into buckets

Until now, the search and sort routines in the book work by performing a series of comparisons until the algorithm finds the correct value. The act of performing comparisons slows the algorithms because each comparison takes some amount of time to complete.

A smarter way to perform the task involves predicting the location of a particular data item in the data structure (whatever that structure might be) before actually looking for it. That's what a *hash table* does —provides the means to create an index of keys that points to individual items in a data structure so that an algorithm can easily predict the location of the data. Placing keys into the index involves using a *hash function* that turns the key into a numeric value. The numeric value acts as an index into the hash table, and the hash table provides a pointer to the full record in the dataset. Because the hash function produces repeatable results, you can predict the location of the required data. In many cases, a hash table provides a search time of $O(1)$. In other words, you need only one comparison to find the data.

REMEMBER

A hash table contains a specific number of *slots* that you can view as buckets for holding data. Each slot can hold one data item. The number of filled slots when compared to the number of available slots is the *load factor*. When the load factor is high, the potential for *collisions* (where two data entries have the same hash value) becomes greater as well. The next section of the chapter discusses how to avoid collisions, but all you really need to know for now is that they can occur.

One of the more typical methods for calculating the hash value for an input is to obtain the modulus of the value divided by the number of slots. For example, if you want to store the number 54 into a hash table containing 15 slots, the hash value is 9. Consequently, the value 54 goes into slot 9 of the hash table when the slots are numbers from 0 through 14 (given that the table has 15 slots). A real hash table will contain a considerably greater number of slots, but 15 works fine for the purposes of this section. After placing the item into the hash slot, you can use the hash function a second time to find its location.

TIP

Theoretically, if you have a perfect hash function and an infinite number of slots, every value you present to the hash function will produce a unique value. In some cases, the hash calculation can become quite complex to ensure unique values most of the time. However, the more complex the hash calculation, the less benefit you receive from hashing, so keeping things simple is the best way to go.

Hashing can work with all sorts of data structures. However, for the purposes of demonstration, the following example uses a simple list to hold the original data and a second list to hold the resulting hash. (You can find this code in the A4D; 07; Hashing.ipynb file on the Dummies site as part of the downloadable code; see the Introduction for details.)

```
data = [22, 40, 102, 105, 23, 31, 6, 5]
hash_table = [None] * 15
tblLen = len(hash_table)

def hash_function(value, table_size):
    return value % table_size

for value in data:
    hash_table[hash_function(value, tblLen)] = value

print(hash_table)

[105, 31, None, None, None, 5, 6, 22, 23, None, 40, None,
 102, None, None]
```

To find a particular value again, you just run it through hash_function. For example, print(hash_table[hash_function(102, tblLen)]) displays 102 as output after locating its entry in hash_table. Because the hash values are unique in this particular case, hash_function can locate the needed data every time.

Avoiding collisions

A problem occurs when two data entries have the same hash value. If you simply write the value into the hash table, the second entry will overwrite the first, resulting in a loss of data. *Collisions,* the use of the same hash value by two values, require you to have some sort of strategy in mind for handling them. Of course, the best strategy is to avoid the collision in the first place.

One of the methods for avoiding collisions is to ensure that you have a large enough hash table. Keeping the load factor low is your first line of defense against having to become creative in the use of your hash table. However, even with a large table, you can't always avoid collisions. Sometimes the potential dataset is so large, but the used dataset is so small, that avoiding the problem becomes impossible. For example, if you have a school with 400 children and rely on their social security number for identification, collisions are inevitable because no one is going to create a hash table with a billion entries for that many children. The waste of memory would be enormous. Consequently, a hash function may have to use more than just a simple modulus output to create the hash value. Here are some techniques you can use to avoid collisions:

>> **Partial values:** When working with some types of information, part of that information repeats, which can create collisions. For example, the first three digits of a telephone number can repeat for a given area, so removing those numbers and using just the remaining four may help solve a collision problem.

>> **Folding:** Creating a unique number might be as easy as dividing the original number into pieces, adding the pieces together, and using the result for the hash value. For example, using the telephone number 555-1234, the hash could begin by breaking it into pieces: 55 51 234, and then adding the result together to obtain 340 as the number used to generate the hash.

>> **Mid-square:** The hash squares the value in question, uses some number of digits from the center of the resulting number, and discards the rest of those digits. For example, consider the value 120. When squared, you get 14,400. The hash could use 440 to generate the hash value and discard the 1 from the left and the 0 from the right.

Obviously, there are as many ways to generate the hash as someone has imagination to create them. Unfortunately, no amount of creativity is going to solve every collision problem, and collisions are still likely to occur. Therefore, you need another plan. When a collision does occur, you can use one of the following methods to address it:

>> **Open addressing:** The code stores the value in the next open slot by looking through the slots sequentially until it finds an open slot to use. The problem with this approach is that it assumes an open slot for each potential value, which may not be the case. In addition, open addressing means that the search slows considerably after the load factor increases. You can no longer find the needed value on the first comparison.

>> **Rehashing:** The code hashes the hash value plus a constant. For example, consider the value 1,020 when working with a hash table containing 30 slots and a constant of 100. The hash value in this case is 22. However, if slot 22 already contains a value, rehashing ((22 + 100) % 30) produces a new hash value of 2. In this case, you don't need to search the hash table sequentially for a value. When implemented correctly, a search might still include a low number of comparisons to find the target value.

>> **Chaining:** Each slot in the hash table can hold multiple values. You can implement this approach by using a list within a list. Every time a collision occurs, the code simply appends the value to the list in the target slot. This approach offers the benefit of knowing that the hash will always produce the correct slot, but the list within that slot will still require some sort of sequential (or other) search to find the specific value.

Creating your own hash function

You may at times need to create custom hash functions in order to meet the needs of the algorithm you use or to improve its performance. Apart from cryptographic uses (which deserve a book alone), Chapter 12 presents common algorithms that leverage different hash functions, such as the *Bloom Filter*, the *HyperLogLog*, and the *Count-Min Sketch*, that leverage the properties of custom hash functions to extract information from huge amounts of data.

You can find many examples of different hash functions in the Python `hashlib` package. The `hashlib` package contains algorithms such as these:

>> **Secure Hash Algorithms (SHA):** These algorithms include SHA1, SHA224, SHA256, SHA384, and SHA512. Released by the National Institute of Standards and Technology (NIST) as a U.S. Federal Information Processing Standard (FIPS), SHA algorithms provide support for security applications and protocols.

>> **RSA's MD5 algorithm:** Initially designed for security applications, this hash turned into a popular way to checksum files. Checksums reduce files to a single number that enables you to determine whether the file was modified since hash creation (it lets you determine whether the file you downloaded wasn't corrupted and hasn't been altered by a hacker). To ensure file integrity, just check whether the MD5 checksum of your copy corresponds to the original one communicated by the author of the file.

TIP

If `hashlib` isn't available on your Python installation, you can install the package using the `pip install hashlib` command from a command shell. The algorithms in `hashlib` work well for simple applications when used alone.

DISCOVERING UNEXPECTED USES OF HASHES

Apart from the algorithms detailed in this book, other important algorithms are based on hashes. For instance, the *Locality-sensitive Hashing* (LSH) algorithm relies on a large number of hash functions to stitch apparently separated information together. If you wonder how marketing companies and intelligence services put different chunks of information together based on names and addresses that aren't identical (for example, guessing that "Los Angels," "Los Angles," and "Los Angleles" all refer to Los Angeles) the answer is LSH. LSH chunks the information to check into parts and digests it using many hash functions, resulting in the production of a special hash result, which is an address for a bucket used to hold similar words. LSH is quite complex in its implementation, but check out this material from the Massachusetts Institute of Technology (MIT): `http://www.mit.edu/~andoni/LSH/`.

However, you can combine the output of multiple hash functions when working with complex applications that rely on a large dataset. Simply sum the results of the various outputs after having done a multiplication on one or more of them. The sum of two hash functions treated in this way retains the qualities of the original hash functions even though the result is different and impossible to recover as the original elements of the sum. Using this approach means that you have a brand-new hash function to use as your secret hash recipe for algorithms and applications.

The following code snippet relies on the hashlib package and the md5 and sha1 hash algorithms. You just provide a number to use for the multiplication inside the hash sum. (Because numbers are infinite, you have a function that can produce infinite hashes.)

```
from hashlib import md5, sha1

def hash_f(element, i, length):
    """ Function to create many hash functions """
    h1 = int(md5(element.encode('ascii')).hexdigest(),16)
    h2 = int(sha1(element.encode('ascii')).hexdigest(),16)
    return (h1 + i*h2) % length

print (hash_f("CAT", 1, 10**5))
64018

print (hash_f("CAT", 2, 10**5))
43738
```

REMEMBER

If you wonder where to find other uses of hash tables around you, check out Python's dictionaries. Dictionaries are, in fact, hash tables, even though they have a smart way to deal with collisions and you won't lose your data because two hashed keys casually have the same result. The fact that the dictionary index uses a hash is also the reason for its speed in checking whether a key is present. In addition, the use of a hash explains why you can't use every data type as a key. The key you choose must be something that Python can turn into a hash result. Lists, for instance, are unhashable because they are mutable; you can change them by adding or removing elements. Nevertheless, if you transform your list into a string, you can use it as a key for a dictionary in Python.

3

Exploring the World of Graphs

IN THIS PART . . .

Discover graph essentials that help you draw, measure, and analyze graphs.

Interact with graphs to locate nodes, sort graph elements, and find the shortest path.

Work with social media in graph form.

Explore graphs to find patterns and make decisions based on those patterns.

Use the PageRank algorithm to rate web pages.

Chapter **8**

Understanding Graph Basics

G raphs are structures that present a number of nodes (or vertexes) connected by a number of edges or arcs (depending on the representation). When you think about a graph, think about a structure like a map, where each location on the map is a node and the streets are the edges. This presentation differs from a tree where each path ends up in a leaf node. Remember from Chapter 7 that a tree could look like an organizational chart or a family hierarchy. Most important, tree structures actually do look like trees and have a definite start and a definite end. This chapter begins by helping you understand the importance of networks, which are a kind of graph commonly used for all sorts of purposes.

REMEMBER

You can represent graphs in all sorts of ways, most of them abstract. Unless you're really good at visualizing things in your mind (most people aren't), you need to know how to draw a graph so you can actually see it. People rely on their vision to understand how things work. The act of turning the numbers that represent a graph into a graphic visualization is *plotting*. Languages like Python excel at plotting because it's such an incredibly important feature. In fact, it's one of the reasons that this book uses Python rather than another language, such as C (which is good at performing a completely different set of tasks).

After you can visualize a graph, it's important to know what to do with the graphic representation. This chapter starts you off by measuring graph functionality.

You do things like count the edges and vertexes to determine things like graph complexity. Seeing a graph also enables you to perform tasks like computing centrality with greater ease. Of course, you build on what you discover in this chapter in Chapter 9.

The numeric presentation of a graph is important, even if it makes understanding the graph hard. The plot is for you, but the computer doesn't really understand the plot (despite having drawn it for you). Think of the computer as more of an abstract thinker. With the need to present a graph in a form that the computer can understand in mind, this chapter discusses three techniques for putting a graph into numeric format: matrixes, sparse representations, and lists. All these techniques have advantages and disadvantages, and you use them in specific ways in future chapters (beginning with Chapter 9). Other ways are also available to put a graph in numeric format, but these three methods will serve you well in communicating with the computer.

Explaining the Importance of Networks

A *network* is a kind of graph that associates names with the vertexes (nodes or points), edges (arcs or lines), or both. Associating names with the graph features reduces the level of abstraction and makes understanding the graph easier. The data that the graph models becomes real in the mind of the person viewing it, even though the graph truly is an abstraction of the real world put into a form that both humans and computers can understand in different ways. The following sections help you understand the importance of networks better so that you can see how their use in this book simplifies the task of discovering how algorithms work and how you can benefit from their use.

Considering the essence of a graph

Graphs appear as ordered pairs in the form G = (V,E), where G is the graph, V is a list of vertexes, and E is a list of edges that connect the vertexes. An edge is actually a numeric pair that expresses the two vertexes that it connects. Consequently, if you have two vertexes that represent cities, Houston (which equals 1) and Dallas (which equals 2), and you want to connect them with a road, then you create an edge, `Highway`, that contains a pair of vertex references, `Highway = [Houston, Dallas]`. The graph would appear as G = [(Houston, Dallas)], which simply says that there is a first vertex, Houston, with a connection to Dallas, the second vertex. Using the order of presentation of the vertexes, Houston is adjacent to Dallas; in other words, a car would leave Houston and enter Dallas.

Graphs come in several forms. An *undirected graph* (as shown in Figure 8-1) is one in which the order of the edge entries doesn't matter. A road map would represent an undirected graph in most cases because traffic can travel along the road in both directions.

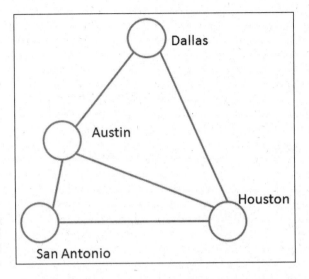

FIGURE 8-1:
Presenting a
simple undirected
graph.

A *directed graph*, like the one shown in Figure 8-2, is one in which the order of the edge entries does matter because the flow is from the first entry to the second. In this case, most people call the edges *arcs* to differentiate them from undirected entries. Consider a graph representation of a traffic light sequence where Red equals 1, Yellow equals 2, and Green equals 3. The three arcs required to express the sequence are: Go = [Red, Green], Caution = [Green, Yellow], and Stop = [Yellow, Red]. The order of the entries is important because the flow from Go, to Caution, to Stop is important. Imagine the chaos that would result if the signal light chose to ignore the directed graph nature of the sequence.

A third essential kind of graph that you must consider is the mixed graph. Think about the road map again. It isn't always true that traffic flows both ways on all roads. When creating some maps, you must consider the presence of one-way streets. Consequently, you need both undirected and directed subgraphs in the same graph, which is what you get with a *mixed graph*.

Another graph type for your consideration is the *weighted graph* (shown in Figure 8-3), which is a graph that has values assigned to each of the edges or arcs. Think about the road map again. Some people want to know more than simply the direction to travel; they also want to know how far away the next destination is or how much time to allocate for getting there. A weighted graph provides this sort of information, and you use the weights in many different ways when performing calculations using graphs.

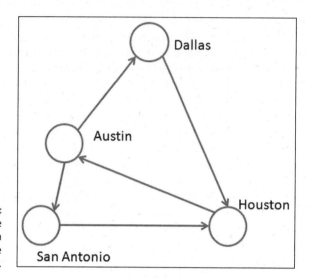

FIGURE 8-2:
Creating the
directed version
of the same
graph.

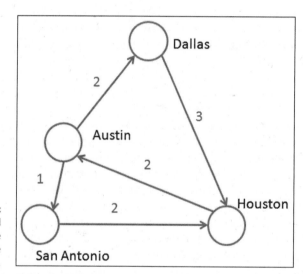

FIGURE 8-3:
Using a weighted
graph to make
things more
realistic.

Along with the weighted graph, you might also need a vertex-labeled graph when creating a road map. When working with a *vertex-labeled graph*, each vertex has a name associated with it. Consider looking at a road map where the mapmaker hasn't labeled the towns. Yes, you can see the towns, but you don't know which one is which without labels. You can find additional graph types described at http://web.cecs.pdx.edu/~sheard/course/Cs163/Doc/Graphs.html.

Finding graphs everywhere

Graphs might seem like one of those esoteric math features that you found boring in school, but graphs are actually quite exciting because you use them all the time without really thinking about it. Of course, it helps to know that you won't normally deal with the numbers behind the graphs. Think about a map. What you see is a graph, but you see it in graphic format, with cities, roads, and all sorts of other features. The thing is, when you see a map, you think about a map, not a graph (but your GPS does see a graph, which is why it can always suggest the shortest route to your destination). If you were to start looking around, you'd find many common items that are graphs but are called something else.

REMEMBER

Some graphs aren't visual in nature, but you still don't see them as graphs. For example, telephone menu systems are a form of directional graph. In fact, for their seeming simplicity, telephone graphs are actually somewhat complex. They can include loops and all sorts of other interesting structures. Something you might try is to map out the graph for a menu system at some point. You might be surprised at just how complex some of them can be.

Another form of menu system appears as part of applications. To perform tasks, most applications take you through a series of steps in a special kind of subapplication called a wizard. The use of wizards make seemingly complex applications much easier to use, but to make the wizards work, the application developer must create a graph depicting the series of steps.

It may surprise you to find that even recipes in cookbooks are a kind of graph (and creating a pictorial representation of the relationships between ingredients can prove interesting). Each ingredient in the recipe is a node. The nodes connect using the edges created by the instructions for mixing the ingredients. Of course, a recipe is just a kind of chemistry, and chemical graphics show the relationship between elements in a molecule. (Yes, people actually are having this discussion; you can see one such thread at http://stackoverflow.com/questions/7749073/representing-a-cooking-recipe-in-a-graph-database.)

REMEMBER

The point is that you see these graphs all the time, but you don't see them as graphs — you see them as something else, such as a recipe or a chemical formula. Graphs can represent many kinds of relationships between objects, implying an order sequence, time dependence, or causality.

Showing the social side of graphs

Graphs have social implications because they often reflect relationships between people in various settings. One of the most obvious uses of graphs is the organizational chart. Think about it. Each node is a different person in the organization, with edges connecting the nodes to show the various relationships between individuals. The same holds true for all sorts of graphs, such as those that show family history. However, in the first case, the graph is undirected because communication flows both ways between managers and subordinates (although the nature of the conversation differs based on direction). In the second case, the graph is directed because two parents bear children. The flow shows the direction of heredity from a founding member to the current children.

Social media benefits from the use of graphs as well. For example, a whole industry exists for analyzing the relationships between tweets on Twitter (see `http://twittertoolsbook.com/10-awesome-twitter-analytics-visualization-tools/` for an example of just some of these tools). The analysis relies on the use of graphs to discover the relationships between individual tweets.

However, you don't have to look at anything more arcane than email to see graphs used for social needs. The Enron corpus includes the 200,399 email messages of 158 senior executives, dumped onto the Internet by the Federal Energy Regulatory Commission (FERC). Scientists and scholars have used this corpus to create many social graphs to disclose how the seventh largest company in the United States needed to file bankruptcy in 2001 (see `https://www.technologyreview.com/s/515801/the-immortal-life-of-the-enron-e-mails/` to learn how this corpus has helped and is actually helping advance the analysis of complex graphs).

Even your computer has social graphs on it. No matter which email application you use, you can group emails in various ways, and these grouping methods normally rely on graphs to provide a structure. After all, trying to follow the flow of discussion without knowing which messages are responses to other messages is a lost cause. Yes, you could do it, but as the number of messages increases, the effort requires more and more time until it's wasted because of time constraints most people have.

Understanding subgraphs

Relationships depicted by graphs can become quite complex. For example, when depicting city streets, most streets allow traffic in both directions, making an undirected graph perfect for representation purposes. However, some streets allow traffic in only one direction, which means that you need a directed graph in this case. The combination of two-way and one-way streets makes representation using a single graph type impossible (or at least inconvenient). Mixing undirected and directed graphs in a single graph means that you must create subgraphs to depict each graph type and then connect the subgraphs in a larger graph. Some graphs that contain subgraphs are so common that they have specific names, which is a mixed graph in this case.

Subgraphs are useful for other purposes as well. For example, you might want to analyze a loop within a graph, which means describing that loop as a subgraph. You don't need the entire graph, just the nodes and edges required to perform the analysis. All sorts of disciplines use this approach. Yes, developers use it to ensure that parts of an application work as expected, but city engineers also use it to understand the nature of traffic flow in a particularly busy section of the city.

Medical professionals also use subgraphs to understand the flow of blood or other liquids between organs in the body. The organs are the nodes and the blood vessels are the edges. In fact, many of these graphs are weighted — it's essential to know how much blood is flowing, not just that it's flowing.

Complex graphs can also hide patterns that you need to know about. For example, the same cycle can appear in multiple parts of the graph, or you might see the same cycle within different graphs. By creating a subgraph from the cycle, you can easily perform comparisons within the same graph or between graphs to see how they compare. For example, a biologist might want to compare the cycle of mutation for one animal against the cycle of mutation for another animal. To make this comparison, the biologist would need to create the representation as a subgraph of the processes for the entire animal. (You can see an interesting view of this particular use of graphs at `http://www.sciencedirect.com/science/article/pii/S1359027896000569`.). The graph appears near the beginning of the article as Figure 1.

Defining How to Draw a Graph

A few people can visualize data directly in their minds. However, most people really do need a graphic presentation of the data in order to understand it. This point is made clear by the use of graphics in business presentations. You could tell others about last year's sales by presenting tables of numbers. After a while, most of your audience would nod off and you'd never get your point across. The reason is simple: The tables of numbers are precise and present a lot of information, but they don't do it in a way that people understand.

REMEMBER

Plotting the data and showing the sales numbers as a bar chart helps people see the relationships between the numbers with greater ease. If you want to point out that sales are increasing each year, a bar chart with bars of increasing length makes this point quickly. Interestingly enough, using the plot actually presents the data in a less accurate way. Trying to see that the company made $3,400,026.15 last year and $3,552,215.82 this year when looking at a bar chart is nearly impossible. Yes, the table would show this information, but people don't really need to know that level of detail — they simply need to see the annual increase, the contrast in earnings from year to year. However, your computer is interested in details, which is why plots are for humans and matrixes are for computers.

The following sections help you discover the wonders of plotting. You get a quick overview of how plots work with Python. Of course, these principles appear in later chapters in a more detailed form. These sections provide a start so that you can more easily understand the plots presented later.

Distinguishing the key attributes

Before you can draw a graph, you need to know about graph attributes. As previously mentioned, graphs consist of nodes (or vertexes) and either edges (for undirected graphs) or arcs (for directed graphs). Any graph that you want to draw will contain these elements. However, how you represent these elements depends partly upon the package you choose to use. For the sake of simplicity, the book relies on a combination of two packages:

>> **NetworkX** (https://networkx.github.io/): Contains code for drawing graphs.

>> **matplotlib** (http://matplotlib.org/): Provides access to all sorts of drawing routines, some of which can display graphs created by NetworkX.

REMEMBER

To use packages in Python, you must import them. When you need to use external packages, you must add special code, such as the following lines of code that provide access to matplotlib and networkx. (You can find this code in the A4D; 08; Draw Graph.ipynb file on the Dummies site as part of the downloadable code; see the Introduction for details.)

```
import networkx as nx
import matplotlib.pyplot as plt
%matplotlib inline
```

TIP

The special %matplotlib inline entry lets you see your plots directly in the Notebook rather than as an external graphic. Using this entry means that you can create a Notebook with graphics already included so that you don't have to run the code again to see the results you received in the past.

Now that you have access to the packages, you create a graph. In this case, a graph is a sort of container that holds the key attributes that define the graph. Creating a container lets you draw the graph so that you can see it later. The following code creates a NetworkX Graph object.

```
AGraph = nx.Graph()
```

Adding the key attributes to AGraph comes next. You must add both nodes and edges using the following code.

```
Nodes = range(1,5)
Edges = [(1,2), (2,3), (3,4), (4,5), (1,3), (1,5)]
```

As previously mentioned, Edges describe connections between Nodes. In this case, Nodes contains values from 1 through 5, so Edges contains connections between those values.

Of course, the Nodes and Edges are just sitting there now and won't appear as part of AGraph. You must put them into the container to see them. Use the following code to add the Nodes and Edges to AGraph.

```
AGraph.add_nodes_from(Nodes)
AGraph.add_edges_from(Edges)
```

The NetworkX package contains all sorts of functions you can use to interact with individual nodes and edges, but the approach shown here is the fastest way to do things. Even so, you might find that you want to add additional edges later. For example, you might want to add an edge between 2 and 4, in which case you would call the AGraph.add_edge(2, 4) function.

Drawing the graph

You can interact in all sorts of ways with the AGraph container object that you created in the previous section, but many of those ways to interact are abstract and not very satisfying if you're a visually oriented person. Sometimes it's just nice to see what an object contains by looking at it. The following code displays the graph contained in AGraph:

```
nx.draw(AGraph, with_labels=True)
```

The draw() function provides various arguments that you can use to dress up the display, such as modifying the node color using the node_color argument and the edge color using the edge_color argument. Figure 8-4 shows the graph contained in AGraph.

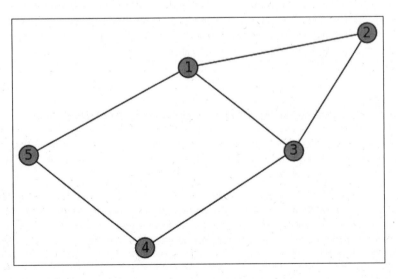

FIGURE 8-4:
Seeing what a graph contains makes it easier to understand.

DIFFERENCES IN FIGURE OUTPUT

Figure 8-4 shows typical output. However, your graph might appear to be slightly different from the one shown. For example, the triangle could appear at the bottom instead of the top, or the angles between the nodes could vary. The connections between the nodes matter most, so slight differences in actual appearance aren't important. Running the code several times would demonstrate that the orientation of the graph changes, along with the angles between edges. You see this same difference in other screenshots in the book. Always view the image with node connections in mind, rather than expecting a precise match between your output and the book's output.

Measuring Graph Functionality

After you can visualize and understand a graph, you need to consider the question of which parts of the graph are important. After all, you don't want to spend your time performing analysis on data that doesn't really matter in the grand scheme of things. Think about someone who is analyzing traffic flow to improve the street system. The intersections represent vertexes and the streets represent edges along which the traffic flows. By knowing how the traffic flows, that is, which vertexes and edges see the most traffic, you can start thinking about which roads to widen and which need more repair because more traffic uses them.

However, just looking at individual streets isn't enough. A new skyscraper may bring with it a lot of traffic that affects an entire area. The skyscraper represents a central point around which traffic flow becomes more important. The most important vertexes are those central to the new skyscraper. Calculating *centrality*, the most important vertexes in a graph, can help you understand which parts of the graph require more attention. The following sections discuss the basic issues you must consider when measuring *graph functionality*, which is the capability of the graph to model a specific problem.

Counting edges and vertexes

As graphs become more complex, they convey more information, but they also become harder to understand and manipulate. The number of edges and vertexes in a graph determines graph complexity. However, you use the combination of edges and vertexes to tell the full story. For example, you can have a node that isn't connected to the other nodes in any way. It's legal to create such a node in a graph to represent a value that lacks connections to the others. Using the following code, you can easily determine that node 6 has no connections to the others because it lacks any edge information. (You can find this code in the A4D; 08; Graph Measurements.ipynb file.)

```
import networkx as nx
import matplotlib.pyplot as plt
%matplotlib inline

AGraph = nx.Graph()

Nodes = range(1,5)
Edges = [(1,2), (2,3), (3,4), (4,5), (1,3), (1,5)]

AGraph.add_nodes_from(Nodes)
AGraph.add_edges_from(Edges)

AGraph.add_node(6)
sorted(nx.connected_components(AGraph))

[{1, 2, 3, 4, 5}, {6}]
```

The output from this code shows that nodes 1 through 5 are connected and that node 6 lacks a connection. Of course, you can remedy this situation by adding another edge by using the following code and then checking again:

```
AGraph.add_edge(1,6)
sorted(nx.connected_components(AGraph))

[{1, 2, 3, 4, 5, 6}]
```

The output now shows that every one of the nodes connects to at least one other node. However, you don't know which nodes have the most connections. The count of edges to a particular node is the *degree*. The higher the degree, the more complex the node becomes. By knowing the degree, you can develop an idea of which nodes are most important. The following code shows how to obtain the degree for the example graph.

```
nx.degree(AGraph).values()

dict_values([4, 2, 3, 2, 2, 1])
```

The degree values appear in node order, so node 1 has four connections and node 6 has only one connection. Consequently, node 1 is the most important, followed by node 3, which has three connections.

USE OF WHITESPACE IN OUTPUT

The output for this example appears on two lines in the book, even though it appears on just one line in Jupyter Notebook. The addition of whitespace helps the output appear in a readable size on the page — it doesn't affect the actual information. Other examples in the book also show output on multiple lines, even when it appears on a single line in Jupyter Notebook.

When modeling real-world data, such as the tweets about a particular topic, the nodes also tend to cluster. You might think of this tendency as a kind of trending — what people feel is important now. The fancy math term for this tendency is *clustering*, and measuring this tendency helps you understand which group of nodes is most important in a graph. Here is the code you use to measure clustering for the example graph:

```
nx.clustering(AGraph)

{1: 0.16666666666666666, 2: 1.0, 3: 0.3333333333333333,
 4: 0.0, 5: 0.0, 6: 0.0}
```

The output shows that the nodes are most likely to cluster around node 2 even though node 1 has the highest degree. That's because both nodes 1 and 3 have high degrees and node 2 is between them.

REMEMBER

Clustering graphs helps aid understanding data. The technique helps show that there are nodes in the graph that are better connected and nodes that risk isolation. When you understand how elements connect in a graph, you can determine how to strengthen its structure or, on the contrary, destroy it. During the Cold war, military scientists from both the United States and the Soviet bloc studied graph clustering to better understand how to disrupt the other side's supply chain in case of a conflict.

Computing centrality

Centrality comes in a number of different forms because importance often depends on different factors. The important elements of a graph when analyzing tweets will differ from the important elements when analyzing traffic flow. Fortunately, NetworkX provides you with a number of methods for calculating centrality. For example, you can calculate centrality based on node degrees. The following code uses the modified graph from the previous section of the chapter. (You can find this code in the A4D; 08; Graph Centrality.ipynb file.)

```
import networkx as nx
import matplotlib.pyplot as plt
%matplotlib inline

AGraph = nx.Graph()

Nodes = range(1,6)
Edges = [(1,2), (2,3), (3,4), (4,5), (1,3), (1,5), (1,6)]

AGraph.add_nodes_from(Nodes)
AGraph.add_edges_from(Edges)

nx.degree_centrality(AGraph)

{1: 0.8, 2: 0.4, 3: 0.6000000000000001, 4: 0.4, 5: 0.4,
 6: 0.2}
```

The values differ by the number of connections for each node. Because node 1 has four connections (it has the highest degree), it also has the highest centrality. You can see how this works by plotting the graph using a call to nx.draw(AGraph, with_labels=True), as shown in Figure 8-5.

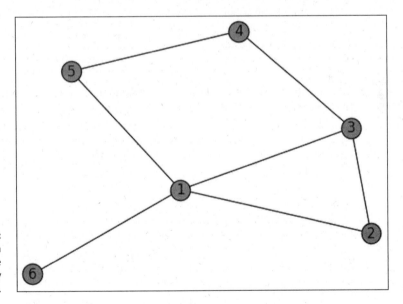

FIGURE 8-5:
Plotting the graph can help you see degree centrality with greater ease.

Node 1 is indeed in the center of the graph with the most connections. The node 1 degree ensures that it's the most important based on the number of connections. When working with directed graphs, you can also use the `in_degree_centrality()` and `out_degree_centrality()` functions to determine degree centrality based on connection type rather than just the number of connections.

When working with traffic analysis, you might need to determine which locations are central based on their distance to other nodes. Even though a shopping center in the suburbs may have all sorts of connections to it, the fact that it is in the suburbs may reduce its impact on traffic. Yet, a supermarket in the center of the city with few connections might have a great impact on traffic because it's close to so many other nodes. To see how this works, add another node, 7, that is disconnected to the graph. The centrality of that node is infinite because no other node can reach it. The following code shows how to calculate the closeness centrality for the various nodes in the example graph:

```
AGraph.add_node(7)
nx.closeness_centrality(AGraph)

{1: 0.6944444444444445,
 2: 0.5208333333333334,
 3: 0.5952380952380952,
 4: 0.462962962962963,
 5: 0.5208333333333334,
 6: 0.4166666666666667,
 7: 0.0}
```

The output shows the centrality of each node in the graph based on its closeness to every other node. Notice that node 7 has a value of 0, which means that it's an infinite distance to every other node. On the other hand, node 1 has a high value because it's close to every node to which it has a connection. By calculating the closeness centrality, you can determine which nodes are the most important based on their location.

Another form of distance centrality is betweenness. Say that you're running a company that transfers goods throughout the city. You'd like to know which nodes have the greatest effect on these transfers. Perhaps you can route some traffic around this node to make your operation more specific. When calculating betweenness centrality, you determine the node that has the highest number of short paths coming to it. Here's the code used to perform this calculation (with the disconnected node 7 still in place):

```
nx.betweenness_centrality(AGraph)

{1: 0.36666666666666664,
```

```
2: 0.0,
3: 0.13333333333333333,
4: 0.03333333333333333,
5: 0.06666666666666667,
6: 0.0,
7: 0.0}
```

As you might expect, node 7 has no effect on transfer between other nodes because it has no connections to the other nodes. Likewise, because node 6 is a leaf node with only one connection to another node, it has no effect on transfers. Look again at Figure 8-5. The subgraph consisting of nodes 1, 3, 4, and 5 have the greatest effect on the transfer of items in this case. No connection exists between nodes 1 and 4, so nodes 3 and 5 act as intermediaries. In this case, node 2 acts like a leaf node.

TIP

NetworkX provides you with a number of other centrality functions. You find a complete list of these functions at http://networkx.readthedocs.io/en/stable/reference/algorithms.centrality.html. The important consideration is determining how you want to calculate importance. Considering centrality in light of the kind of importance you want to attach to the vertexes and edges in a graph is essential.

Putting a Graph in Numeric Format

Precision is an important part of using algorithms. Even though too much precision hides the overall pictures from humans, computers thrive on detail. Often, the more detail you can provide, the better the results you receive. However, the form of that detail is important. To use certain algorithms, the data you provide must appear in certain forms or the result you receive won't make sense (it will contain errors or have other issues).

Fortunately, NetworkX provides a number of functions to convert your graph into forms that other packages and environments can use. These functions appear at http://networkx.readthedocs.io/en/stable/reference/convert.html. The following sections show how to present graph data as a NumPy (http://www.numpy.org/) matrix, SciPy (https://www.scipy.org/) sparse representation, and a standard Python list. You use these presentations as the book progresses to work with the various algorithms. (The code in the following sections appears in the A4D; 08; Graph Conversion.ipynb file and relies on the graph you created in the "Counting edges and vertexes" section of the chapter.)

Adding a graph to a matrix

Using NetworkX, you can easily move your graph to a NumPy matrix and back again as needed to perform various tasks. You use NumPy to perform all sorts of data manipulation tasks. By analyzing the data in a graph, you might see patterns that wouldn't ordinarily be visible. Here's the code used to convert the graph into a matrix that NumPy can understand:

```
import networkx as nx
import matplotlib.pyplot as plt
%matplotlib inline

AGraph = nx.Graph()

Nodes = range(1,6)
Edges = [(1,2), (2,3), (3,4), (4,5), (1,3), (1,5), (1,6)]

AGraph.add_nodes_from(Nodes)
AGraph.add_edges_from(Edges)

nx.to_numpy_matrix(AGraph)

matrix([[ 0.,  1.,  1.,  0.,  1.,  1.],
        [ 1.,  0.,  1.,  0.,  0.,  0.],
        [ 1.,  1.,  0.,  1.,  0.,  0.],
        [ 0.,  0.,  1.,  0.,  1.,  0.],
        [ 1.,  0.,  0.,  1.,  0.,  0.],
        [ 1.,  0.,  0.,  0.,  0.,  0.]])
```

The resulting rows and columns show where connections exist. For example, there is no connection between node 1 and itself, so row 1, column 1, has a 0 in it. However, there is a connection between node 1 and node 2, so you see a 1 in row 1, column 2, and row 2, column 1 (which means that the connection goes both ways as an undirected connection).

The size of this matrix is affected by the number of nodes (the marix has as many rows and columns as nodes), and when it grows huge, it has many nodes to represent because the total number of cells is the square of the number of nodes. For instance, you can't represent the Internet using such a matrix because a conservative estimate calculates that at 10^{10} websites, you'd need a matrix with 10^{20} cells to store its structure, something impossible with the present computing capacity.

In addition, the number of nodes affects its content. If n is number of nodes, you find a minimum of (n–1) ones and a maximum of n(n–1) ones. The fact that the number of ones is few or large makes the graph dense or sparse, and that's relevant because if the connection between nodes are few, such as in the case of websites, more efficient solutions exist for storing graph data.

Using sparse representations

The SciPy package also performs various math, scientific, and engineering tasks. When using this package, you can rely on a sparse matrix to hold the data. A sparse matrix is one in which only the actual connections appear in the matrix; all other entries don't exist. Using a sparse matrix saves resources because the memory requirements for a sparse matrix are small. Here is the code you use to create a SciPy sparse matrix from a NetworkX graph:

```
print(nx.to_scipy_sparse_matrix(AGraph))

  (0, 1)    1
  (0, 2)    1
  (0, 4)    1
  (0, 5)    1
  (1, 0)    1
  (1, 2)    1
  (2, 0)    1
  (2, 1)    1
  (2, 3)    1
  (3, 2)    1
  (3, 4)    1
  (4, 0)    1
  (4, 3)    1
  (5, 0)    1
```

As you can see, the entries show the various edge coordinates. Each active coordinate has a 1 associated with it. The coordinates are 0 based. This means that (0, 1) actually refers to a connection between nodes 1 and 2.

Using a list to hold a graph

Depending on your needs, you might find that you also require the ability to create a dictionary of lists. Many developers use this approach to create code that performs various analysis tasks on graphs. You can see one such example at https://www.python.org/doc/essays/graphs/. The following code shows how to create a dictionary of lists for the example graph:

```
nx.to_dict_of_lists(AGraph)

{1: [2, 3, 5, 6], 2: [1, 3], 3: [1, 2, 4], 4: [3, 5],
 5: [1, 4], 6: [1]}
```

Notice that each node represents a dictionary entry, followed by a list of the nodes to which it connects. For example, node 1 connects to nodes 2, 3, 5, and 6.

Chapter **9**

Reconnecting the Dots

This chapter is about working with graphs. You use graphs every day to perform a range of tasks. A *graph* is simply a set of vertexes, nodes, or points connected by edges, arcs, or lines. Putting this definition in simpler terms, every time you use a map, you use a graph. The starting point, intermediate points, and destination are all nodes. These nodes connect to each other with streets, which represent the lines. Using graphs enables you to describe relationships of various sorts. The reason that Global Positioning System (GPS) setups work is that you can use math to describe the relationships between points on the map and the streets that connect them. In fact, by the time you finish this chapter, you understand the basis used to create a GPS (but not necessarily the mechanics of making it happen). Of course, the fundamental requirement for using a graph to create a GPS is the capability to search for connections between points on the map, as discussed in the first section of the chapter.

To make sense of a graph, you need to sort the nodes, as described in the second section of the chapter, to create a specific organization. Without organization, making any sort of decision becomes impossible. An algorithm might end up going in circles or giving inconvenient output. For example, some early GPS setups didn't correctly find the shortest distance between two points, or sometimes ended up sending someone to the wrong place. Part of the reason for these problems is the need to sort the data so that you can view it in the same manner each time the algorithm traverses the nodes (providing you with a route between your home and your business).

When you view a map, you don't look at the information in the lower-right corner when you actually need to work with locations and roads in the upper-left corner.

A computer doesn't know that it needs to look in a specific place until you tell it to do so. To focus attention in a specific location, you need to reduce the graph size, as described in the third section of the chapter.

Now that the problem is simplified, an algorithm can find the shortest route between two points, as described in the fourth section of the chapter. After all, you don't want to spend any more time than is necessary in traffic fighting your way from home to the office (and back again). The concept of finding the shortest route is a bit more convoluted than you might think, so the fourth section looks at some of the specific requirements for performing routing tasks in detail.

Traversing a Graph Efficiently

Traversing a graph means to search (visit) each vertex (node) in a specific order. The process of visiting a vertex can include both reading and updating it. As you traverse a graph, an unvisited vertex is *undiscovered.* After a visit, the vertex becomes *discovered* (because you just visited it) or *processed* (because the algorithm tried all the edges departing from it). The order of the search determines the kind of search performed, and many algorithms are available to perform this task. The following sections discuss two such algorithms.

CONSIDERING REDUNDANCY

When traversing a tree, every path ends in a leaf node so that you know that you have reached the end of that path. However, when working with a graph, the nodes interconnect such that you might have to traverse some nodes more than once to explore the entire graph. As the graph becomes denser, the possibility of visiting the same node more than once increases. Dense graphs can greatly increase both computational and storage requirements.

To reduce the negative effects of visiting a node more than once, it's common to mark each visited node in some manner to show that the algorithm has visited it. When the algorithm detects that it has visited a particular node, it can simply skip that node and move onto the next node in the path. Marking visited nodes decreases the performance penalties inherent in redundancy.

Marking visited nodes also enables verification that the search is complete. Otherwise, an algorithm can end up in a loop and continue to make the rounds through the graph indefinitely.

Creating the graph

To see how traversing a graph might work, you need a graph. The examples in this section rely on a common graph so that you can see how the two techniques work. The following code shows the adjacency list found at the end of Chapter 8. (You can find this code in the A4D; 09; Graph Traversing.ipynb file on the Dummies site as part of the downloadable code; see the Introduction for details.)

```
graph = {'A': ['B', 'C'],
         'B': ['A', 'C', 'D'],
         'C': ['A', 'B', 'D', 'E'],
         'D': ['B', 'C', 'E', 'F'],
         'E': ['C', 'D', 'F'],
         'F': ['D', 'E']}
```

The graph features a bidirectional path that goes from A, B, D, and F on one side (starting at the root) and A, C, E, and F along the second side (again, starting at the root). There are also connections (that act as possible shortcuts) going from B to C, from C to D, and from D to E. Using the NetworkX package presented in Chapter 8 lets you display the adjacency as a picture so that you can see how the vertexes and edges appear (see Figure 9-1) by using the following code:

```
import numpy as np
import networkx as nx
import matplotlib.pyplot as plt
%matplotlib inline

Graph = nx.Graph()
for node in graph:
    Graph.add_nodes_from(node)
    for edge in graph[node]:
        Graph.add_edge(node,edge)

pos = { 'A': [0.00, 0.50], 'B': [0.25, 0.75],
        'C': [0.25, 0.25], 'D': [0.75, 0.75],
        'E': [0.75, 0.25], 'F': [1.00, 0.50]}

nx.draw(Graph, pos, with_labels=True)
nx.draw_networkx(Graph, pos)
plt.show()
```

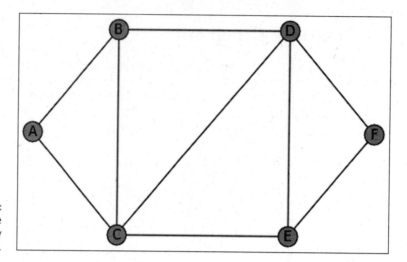

FIGURE 9-1:
Representing the
example graph by
NetworkX.

Applying breadth-first search

A breadth-first search (BFS) begins at the graph root and explores every node that attaches to the root. It then searches the next level — exploring each level in turn until it reaches the end. Consequently, in the example graph, the search explores from A to B and C before it moves on to explore D. BFS explores the graph in a systematic way, exploring vertexes all around the starting vertex in a circular fashion. It begins by visiting all the vertexes a single step from the starting vertex; it then moves two steps out, then three steps out, and so on. The following code demonstrates how to perform a breadth-first search.

```
def bfs(graph, start):
    queue = [start]
    queued = list()
    path = list()
    while queue:
        print ('Queue is: %s' % queue)
        vertex = queue.pop(0)
        print ('Processing %s' % vertex)
        for candidate in graph[vertex]:
            if candidate not in queued:
                queued.append(candidate)
                queue.append(candidate)
                path.append(vertex+'>'+candidate)
                print ('Adding %s to the queue'
                        % candidate)
    return path
```

```
steps = bfs(graph, 'A')
print ('\nBFS:', steps)

Queue is: ['A']
Processing A
Adding B to the queue
Adding C to the queue
Queue is: ['B', 'C']
Processing B
Adding A to the queue
Adding D to the queue
Queue is: ['C', 'A', 'D']
Processing C
Adding E to the queue
Queue is: ['A', 'D', 'E']
Processing A
Queue is: ['D', 'E']
Processing D
Adding F to the queue
Queue is: ['E', 'F']
Processing E
Queue is: ['F']
Processing F

BFS: ['A>B', 'A>C', 'B>A', 'B>D', 'C>E', 'D>F']
```

REMEMBER

The output shows how the algorithm searches. It's in the order that you expect — one level at a time. The biggest advantage of using BFS is that it's guaranteed to return the shortest path between two points as the first output when used to find paths.

TIP

The example code uses a simple list as a queue. As described in Chapter 4, a queue is a first in/first out (FIFO) data structure that works like a line at a bank, where the first item put into the queue is also the first item that comes out. For this purpose, Python provides an even better data structure called a deque (pronounced deck). You create it using the deque function from the collections package. It performs insertions and extractions in linear time, and you can use it as both a queue and a stack. You can discover more about the deque function at https://pymotw.com/2/collections/deque.html.

Applying depth-first search

In addition to BFS, you can use a depth-first search (DFS) to discover the vertexes in a graph. When performing a DFS, the algorithm begins at the graph root and then explores every node from that root down a single path to the end. It then backtracks and begins exploring the paths not taken in the current search path until it reaches the root again. At that point, if other paths to take from the root are available, the algorithm chooses one and begins the same search again. The idea is to explore each path completely before exploring any other path. To make this search technique work, the algorithm must mark each vertex it visits. In this way, it knows which vertexes require a visit and can determine which path to take next. Using BFS or DFS can make a difference according to the way in which you need to traverse a graph. From a programming point of view, the difference between the two algorithms is how each one stores the vertexes to explore the following:

>> A queue for BFS, a list that works according to the FIFO principle. Newly discovered vertexes don't wait long for processing.

>> A stack for DFS, a list that works according to the last in/first out (LIFO) principle.

The following code shows how to create a DFS:

```
def dfs(graph, start):
    stack = [start]
    parents = {start: start}
    path = list()
    while stack:
        print ('Stack is: %s' % stack)
        vertex = stack.pop(-1)
        print ('Processing %s' % vertex)
        for candidate in graph[vertex]:
            if candidate not in parents:
                parents[candidate] = vertex
                stack.append(candidate)
                print ('Adding %s to the stack'
                        % candidate)
        path.append(parents[vertex]+'>'+vertex)
    return path[1:]

steps = dfs(graph, 'A')
print ('\nDFS:', steps)

Stack is: ['A']
Processing A
Adding B to the stack
Adding C to the stack
```

```
Stack is: ['B', 'C']
Processing C
Adding D to the stack
Adding E to the stack
Stack is: ['B', 'D', 'E']
Processing E
Adding F to the stack
Stack is: ['B', 'D', 'F']
Processing F
Stack is: ['B', 'D']
Processing D
Stack is: ['B']
Processing B

DFS: ['A>C', 'C>E', 'E>F', 'C>D', 'A>B']
```

The first line of output shows the actual search order. Note that the search begins at the root, as expected, but then follows down the left side of the graph around to the beginning. The final step is to search the only branch off the loop that creates the graph in this case, which is D.

Note that the output is not the same as for the BFS. In this case, the processing route begins with node A and moves to the opposite side of the graph, to node F. The code then retraces back to look for overlooked paths. As discussed, this behavior depends on the use of a stack structure in place of a queue. Reliance on a stack means that you could also implement this kind of search using recursion. The use of recursion would make the algorithm faster, so you could obtain results faster than when using a BFS. The trade-off is that you use more memory when using recursion.

TIP

When your algorithm uses a stack, it's using the last result available (as contrasted to a queue, where it would use the first result placed in the queue). Recursive functions produce a result and then apply themselves using that same result. A stack does exactly the same thing in an iteration: The algorithm produces a result, the result is put on a stack, and then the result is immediately taken from the stack and processed again.

Determining which application to use

The choice between BFS and DFS depends on how you plan to apply the output from the search. Developers often employ BFS to locate the shortest route between two points as quickly as possible. This means that you commonly find BFS used in applications such as GPS, where finding the shortest route is paramount. For the purposes of this book, you also see BFS used for spanning tree, shortest path, and many other minimization algorithms.

A DFS focuses on finding an entire path before exploring any other path. You use it when you need to search in detail, rather than generally. For this reason, you often see DFS used in games, where finding a complete path is important. It's also an optimal approach to perform tasks such as finding a solution to a maze.

REMEMBER

Sometimes you have to decide between BFS and DFS based on the limitations of each technique. BFS needs lots of memory because it systematically stores all the paths before finding a solution. On the other hand, DFS needs less memory, but you have no guarantee that it'll find the shortest and most direct solution.

Sorting the Graph Elements

The ability to search graphs efficiently relies on sorting. After all, imagine going to a library and finding the books placed in any order the library felt like putting them on the shelves. Locating a single book would take hours. A library works because the individual books appear in specific locations that make them easy to find.

Libraries also exhibit another property that's important when working with certain kinds of graphs. When performing a book search, you begin with a specific category, then a row of books, then a shelf in that row, and finally the book. You move from less specific to more specific when performing the search, which means that you don't revisit the previous levels. Therefore, you don't end up in odd parts of the library that have nothing to do with the topic at hand.

GRAPHS WITH LOOPS

Sometimes you need to express a process in such a manner that a set of steps repeats. For example, when washing your car, you rinse, soap down, and then rinse again. However, you find a dirty spot, an area that the soap didn't clean the first time. To clean that spot, you soap it again and rinse it again to verify that the spot is gone. Unfortunately, it's a really stubborn spot, so you repeat the process again. In fact, you repeat the soap and rinse steps until the spot is clean. That's what a loop does; it creates a situation in which a set of steps repeats in one of two ways:

- **Meets a specific condition:** The spot on the car is gone.

- **Performs a specific number of times:** This is the number of repetitions you perform during the exercise.

The following sections review *Directed Acyclic Graphs (DAGs)*, which are finite directed graphs that don't have any loops in them. In other words, you start from a particular location and follow a specific route to an ending location without ever going back to the starting location. When using topological sorting, a DAG always directs earlier vertexes to later vertexes. This kind of graph has all sorts of practical uses, such as schedules, with each milestone representing a particular milestone.

Working on Directed Acyclic Graphs (DAGs)

DAGs are one of the most important kinds of graphs because they see so many practical uses. The basic principles of DAGs are that they

> » Follow a particular order so that you can't get from one vertex to another and back to the beginning vertex using any route.

> » Provide a specific path from one vertex to another so that you can create a predictable set of routes.

You see DAGs used for many organizational needs. For example, a family tree is an example of a DAG. Even when the activity doesn't follow a chronological or other overriding order, the DAG enables you to create predictable routes, which makes DAGs easier to process than many other kinds of graphs you work with.

However, DAGs can use optional routes. Imagine that you're building a burger. The menu system starts with a bun bottom. You can optionally add condiments to the bun bottom, or you can move directly to the burger on the bun. The route always ends up with a burger, but you have multiple paths for getting to the burger. After you have the burger in place, you can choose to add cheese or bacon before adding the bun top. The point is that you take a specific path, but each path can connect to the next level in several different ways.

REMEMBER

So far, the chapter has shown you a few different kinds of graph configurations, some of which can appear in combination, such as a directed, weighted, dense graph:

> » **Directed:** Edges have a single direction and can have these additional properties:
>
> • **Cyclic:** The edges form a cycle that take you back to the initial vertex after having visited the intermediary vertexes.
>
> • **A-cyclic:** This graph lacks cycles.

> » **Undirected:** Edges connect vertexes in both directions.

- » **Weighted:** Each edge has a cost associated with it, such as time, money, or energy, which you must pay to pass through it.

- » **Unweighted:** All the edges have no cost or the same cost.

- » **Dense:** A graph that has a large number of edges when compared to the number of vertexes.

- » **Sparse:** A graph that has a small number of edges when compared to the number of vertexes.

Relying on topological sorting

An important element of DAGs is that you can represent a myriad of activities using them. However, some activities require that you approach tasks in a specific order. This is where topological sorting comes into play. *Topological sorting* orders all the vertexes of a graph on a line with the direct edges pointing from left to right. Arranged in such a fashion, the code can easily traverse the graph and process the vertexes one after the other, in order.

When you use topological sorting, you organize the graph so that every graph vertex leads to a later vertex in the sequence. For example, when creating a schedule for building a skyscraper, you don't start at the top and work your way down. You begin with the foundation and work your way up. Each floor can represent a milestone. When you complete the second floor, you don't go to the third and then redo the second floor. Instead, you move on from the third floor to the fourth floor, and so on. Any sort of scheduling that requires you to move from a specific starting point to a specific ending point can rely on a DAG with topological sorting.

Topological sorting can help you determine that your graph has no cycles (because otherwise, you can't order the edges connecting the vertexes from left to right; at least one node will refer to a previous node). In addition, topological sorting also proves helpful in algorithms that process complex graphs because it shows the best order for processing them.

You can obtain topological sorting using the DFS traversal algorithm. Simply note the processing order of the vertexes by the algorithm. In the previous example, the output appears in this order: A, C, E, F, D, and B. Follow the sequence in Figure 9-1 and you notice that the topological sorting follows the edges on the external perimeter of graph. It then makes a complete tour: After reaching the last node of the topological sort, you're just a step away from A, the start of the sequence.

Reducing to a Minimum Spanning Tree

Many problems that algorithms solve rely on defining a minimum of resources to use, such as defining an economical way to reach all the points on a map. This problem was paramount in the late nineteenth and early twentieth centuries when railway and electricity networks started appearing in many countries, revolutionizing transportation and ways of living. Using private companies to build such networks was expensive (it took a lot of time and workers). Using less material and a smaller workforce offered savings by reducing redundant connections.

REMEMBER

Some redundancy is desirable in critical transportation or energy networks even when striving for economical solutions. Otherwise, if only one method connects the network, it's easily disrupted accidentally or by a voluntary act (such as an act of war), interrupting services to many customers.

In Moravia, the eastern part of Czech Republic, the Czech mathematician Otakar Borůvka found a solution in 1926 that allows constructing an electrical network using the least amount of wire possible. His solution is quite efficient because it not only allows finding a way to connect all the towns in Moravia in the most economical way possible, but it had a time complexity of $O(m*\log n)$, where m is the number of edges (the electrical cable) and n the number of vertexes (the towns). Others have improved Borůvka's solution since then. (In fact, algorithm experts partially forgot and then rediscovered it.) Even though the algorithms you find in books are better designed and easier to grasp (those from Prim and Kruskal), they don't achieve better results in terms of time complexity.

A minimal spanning tree defines the problem of finding the most economical way to accomplish a task. A *spanning tree* is the list of edges required to connect all the vertexes in an undirected graph. A single graph could contain multiple spanning trees, depending on the graph arrangement, and determining how many trees it contains is a complex issue. Each path you can take from start to completion in a graph is another spanning tree. The spanning tree visits each vertex only once; it doesn't loop or do anything to repeat path elements.

When you work on an unweighted graph, the spanning trees are the same length. In unweighted graphs, all edges have the same length, and the order you visit them in doesn't matter because the run path is always the same. All possible spanning trees have the same number of edges, n–1 edges (n is the number of vertexes), of the same exact length. Moreover, any graph traversal algorithm, such as BFS or DFS, suffices to find one of the possible spanning trees.

Things become tricky when working with a weighted graph with edges of different lengths. In this case, of the many possible spanning trees, a few, or just one, have the minimum length possible. A *minimum spanning tree* is the one spanning tree that guarantees a path with the least possible edge weight. An undirected graph generally contains just one minimum spanning tree, but, again, it depends on the configuration. Think about minimum spanning trees this way: When looking at a map, you see a number of paths to get from point A to point B. Each path has places where you must turn or change roads, and each of these junctions is a vertex. The distance between vertexes represents the edge weight. Generally, one path between point A and point B provides the shortest route.

However, minimum spanning trees need not always consider the obvious. For example, when considering maps, you might not be interested in distance; you might instead want to consider time, fuel consumption, or myriad other needs. Each of these needs could have a completely different minimum spanning tree. With this in mind, the following sections help you understand minimum spanning trees better and demonstrate how to solve the problem of figuring out the smallest edge weight for any given problem. To demonstrate a minimum spanning tree solution using Python, the following code updates the previous graph by adding edge weights. (You can find this code in the A4D; 09; Minimum Spanning Tree. ipynb file on the Dummies site as part of the downloadable code; see the Introduction for details.)

```python
import numpy as np
import networkx as nx
import matplotlib.pyplot as plt
%matplotlib inline

graph = {'A': {'B':2, 'C':3},
         'B': {'A':2, 'C':2, 'D':2},
         'C': {'A':3, 'B':2, 'D':3, 'E':2},
         'D': {'B':2, 'C':3, 'E':1, 'F':3},
         'E': {'C':2, 'D':1, 'F':1},
         'F': {'D':3, 'E':1}}

Graph = nx.Graph()
for node in graph:
    Graph.add_nodes_from(node)
    for edge, weight in graph[node].items():
        Graph.add_edge(node,edge, weight=weight)

pos = { 'A': [0.00, 0.50], 'B': [0.25, 0.75],
        'C': [0.25, 0.25], 'D': [0.75, 0.75],
        'E': [0.75, 0.25], 'F': [1.00, 0.50]}

labels = nx.get_edge_attributes(Graph,'weight')
nx.draw(Graph, pos, with_labels=True)
```

```
nx.draw_networkx_edge_labels(Graph, pos,
                             edge_labels=labels)
nx.draw_networkx(Graph,pos)
plt.show()
```

Figure 9-2 shows that all edges have a value now. This value can represent something like time, fuel, or money. Weighted graphs can represent many possible optimization problems that occur in geographical space (such as movement between cities) because they represent situations in which you can come and go from a vertex.

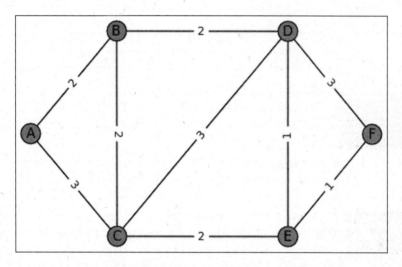

FIGURE 9-2:
The example
graph becomes
weighted.

Interestingly, all edges have positive weights in this example. However, weighted graphs can have negative weights on some edges. Many situations take advantage of negative edges. For instance, they're useful when you can both gain and lose from moving between vertexes, such as gaining or losing money when transporting or trading goods, or releasing energy in a chemical process.

Not all algorithms are well suited for handling negative edges. It's important to note those that can work with only positive weights.

REMEMBER

Discovering the correct algorithms to use

You can find many different algorithms to use to create a minimum spanning tree. The most common are greedy algorithms, which run in polynomial time. *Polynomial time* is a power of the number of edges, such as O(n²) or O(n³) (see Part 5 for additional information about polynomial time). The major factors that affect the running speed of such algorithms involve the decision-making process — that is, whether a particular edge belongs in the minimum spanning tree or whether the minimum total weight of the resulting tree exceeds a certain value. With this in mind, here are some of the algorithms available for solving a minimum spanning tree:

>> **Borůvka's:** Invented by Otakar Borůvka in 1926 to solve the problem of finding the optimal way to supply electricity in Moravia. The algorithm relies on a series of stages in which it identifies the edges with the smallest weight in each stage. The calculations begin by looking at individual vertexes, finding the smallest weight for that vertex, and then combining paths to form forests of individual trees until it creates a path that combines all the forests with the smallest weight.

>> **Prim's:** Originally invented by Jarnik in 1930, Prim rediscovered it in 1957. This algorithm starts with an arbitrary vertex and grows the minimum spanning tree one edge at a time by always choosing the edge with the least weight.

>> **Kruskal's:** Developed by Joseph Kruskal in 1956, it uses an approach that combines Borůvka's algorithm (creating forests of individual trees) and Prim's algorithm (looking for the minimum edge for each vertex and building the forests one edge at a time).

>> **Reverse-delete:** This is actually a reversal of Kruskal's algorithm. It isn't commonly used.

TIP

These algorithms use a greedy approach. Greedy algorithms appear in Chapter 2 among the families of algorithms, and you see them in detail in Chapter 15. In a *greedy approach*, the algorithm gradually arrives at a solution by taking, in an irreversible way, the best decision available at each step. For instance, if you need the shortest path between many vertexes, a greedy algorithm takes the shortest edges among those available between all vertexes.

Introducing priority queues

Later in this chapter, you see how to implement Prim's and Kruskal's algorithm for a minimum spanning tree, and Dijkstra's algorithm for the shortest path in a graph using Python. However, before you can do that, you need a method to find the edges with the minimum weight among a set of edges. Such an operation implies ordering, and ordering elements costs time. It's a complex operation, as described in Chapter 7. Because the examples repeatedly reorder edges, a data structure called the *priority queue* comes in handy.

Priority queues rely on heap tree-based data structures that allow fast element ordering when you insert them inside the heap. Like the magician's magic hat, priority heaps store edges with their weights and are immediately ready to provide you with the inserted edge whose weight is the minimum among those stores.

This example uses a class that allows it to perform priority-queue comparisons that determine whether the queue contains elements and when those elements contain a certain edge (avoiding double insertions). The priority queue has another useful characteristic (whose usefulness is explained when working on Dijkstra's algorithm): If you insert an edge with a different weight than previously stored, the code updates the edge weight and rearranges the edge position in the heap.

```
from heapq import heapify, heappop, heappush

class priority_queue():
    def __init__(self):
        self.queue = list()
        heapify(self.queue)
        self.index = dict()
    def push(self, priority, label):
        if label in self.index:
            self.queue = [(w,l)
                for w,l in self.queue if l!=label]
            heapify(self.queue)
        heappush(self.queue, (priority, label))
        self.index[label] = priority
    def pop(self):
        if self.queue:
            return heappop(self.queue)
    def __contains__(self, label):
        return label in self.index
    def __len__(self):
        return len(self.queue)
```

Leveraging Prim's algorithm

Prim's algorithm generates the minimum spanning tree for a graph by traversing the graph vertex by vertex. Starting from any chosen vertex, the algorithm adds edges using a constraint in which, if one vertex is currently part of the spanning tree and the second vertex isn't part of it, the edge weight between the two must be the least possible among those available. By proceeding in this fashion, creating cycles in the spanning tree is impossible (it could happen only if you add an edge whose vertexes are already both in the spanning tree) and you're guaranteed to obtain a minimal tree because you add the edges with the least weight. In terms of steps, the algorithm includes these three phases, with the last one being iterative:

1. Track both the edges of the minimum spanning tree and the used vertexes as they become part of the solution.

2. Start from any vertex in the graph and place it into the solution.

3. Determine whether there are still vertexes that aren't part of the solution:

- Enumerate the edges that touch the vertexes in the solution.

- Insert the edge with the minimum weight into the spanning tree. (This is the greedy principle at work in the algorithm: Always choose the minimum at each step to obtain an overall minimum result.)

By translating these steps into Python code, you can test the algorithm on the example weighted graph using the following code:

```
def prim(graph, start):
    treepath = {}
    total = 0
    queue = priority_queue()
    queue.push(0 , (start, start))
    while queue:
        weight, (node_start, node_end) = queue.pop()
        if node_end not in treepath:
            treepath[node_end] = node_start
            if weight:
                print("Added edge from %s" \
                      " to %s weighting %i"
                      % (node_start, node_end, weight))
                total += weight
            for next_node, weight \
            in graph[node_end].items():
                queue.push(weight , (node_end, next_node))
    print ("Total spanning tree length: %i" % total)
    return treepath

treepath = prim(graph, 'A')

Added edge from A to B weighting 2
Added edge from B to C weighting 2
Added edge from B to D weighting 2
Added edge from D to E weighting 1
Added edge from E to F weighting 1
Total spanning tree length: 8
```

The algorithm prints the processing steps, showing the edge it adds at each stage and the weight the edge adds to the total. The example displays the total sum of weights and the algorithm returns a Python dictionary containing the ending vertex as key and the starting vertex as value for each edge of the resulting spanning tree. Another function, `represent_tree`, turns the key and value pairs of the dictionary into a tuple and then sorts each of the resulting tuples for better readability of the tree path:

```
def represent_tree(treepath):
    progression = list()
    for node in treepath:
        if node != treepath[node]:
            progression.append((treepath[node], node))
    return sorted(progression, key=lambda x:x[0])


print (represent_tree(treepath))

[('A','B'), ('B','C'), ('B','D'), ('D','E'), ('E','F')]
```

REMEMBER

The `represent_tree` function reorders the output of Prim's algorithm for better readability. However, the algorithm works on an undirected graph, which means that you can traverse the edges in both directions. The algorithm incorporates this assumption because there is no edge directionality check to add to the priority queue for later processing.

Testing Kruskal's algorithm

Kruskal's algorithm uses a greedy strategy, just as Prim's does, but it picks the shortest edges from a global pool containing all the edges (whereas Prim's evaluates the edges according to the vertexes in the spanning tree). To determine whether an edge is a suitable part of the solution, the algorithm relies on an aggregative process in which it gathers vertexes together. When an edge involves vertexes already in the solution, the algorithm discards it to avoid creating a cycle. The algorithm proceeds in the following fashion:

1. Put all the edges into a heap and sort them so that the shortest edges are on top.

2. Create a set of trees, each one containing only one vertex (so that the number of trees is the same number as the vertexes). You connect trees as an aggregate until the trees converge into a unique tree of minimal length that spans all the vertexes.

3. Repeat the following operations until the solution doesn't contain as many edges as the number of vertexes in the graph:

   a. Choose the shortest edge from the heap.

   b. Determine whether the two vertexes connected by the edge appear in different trees from among the set of connected trees.

c. When the trees differ, connect the trees using the edge (defining an aggregation).

d. When the vertexes appear in the same tree, discard the edge.

e. Repeat steps a through d for the remaining edges on the heap.

The following example demonstrates how to turn these steps into Python code:

```python
def kruskal(graph):
    priority = priority_queue()
    print ("Pushing all edges into the priority queue")
    treepath = list()
    connected = dict()
    for node in graph:
        connected[node] = [node]
        for dest, weight in graph[node].items():
            priority.push(weight, (node,dest))
    print ("Totally %i edges" % len(priority))
    print ("Connected components: %s"
            % connected.values())

    total = 0
    while len(treepath) < (len(graph)-1):
        (weight, (start, end)) = priority.pop()
        if end not in connected[start]:
            treepath.append((start, end))
            print ("Summing %s and %s components:"
                    % (connected[start],connected[end]))
            print ("\tadded edge from %s " \
                "to %s weighting %i"
                % (start, end, weight))
            total += weight
            connected[start] += connected[end][:]
            for element in connected[end]:
                connected[element]= connected[start]
    print ("Total spanning tree length: %i" % total)
    return sorted(treepath, key=lambda x:x[0])

print ('\nMinimum spanning tree: %s' % kruskal(graph))

Pushing all edges into the priority queue
Totally 9 edges
Connected components: dict_values([['A'], ['E'], ['F'],
                                    ['B'], ['D'], ['C']])
```

```
Summing ['E'] and ['D'] components:
        added edge from E to D weighting 1
Summing ['E', 'D'] and ['F'] components:
        added edge from E to F weighting 1
Summing ['A'] and ['B'] components:
        added edge from A to B weighting 2
Summing ['A', 'B'] and ['C'] components:
        added edge from B to C weighting 2
Summing ['A', 'B', 'C'] and ['E', 'D', 'F'] components:
        added edge from B to D weighting 2
Total spanning tree length: 8

Minimum spanning tree:
[('A','B'), ('B','C'), ('B','D'), ('E','D'), ('E','F')]
```

TIP

Kruskal's algorithm offers a solution that's similar to the one proposed by Prim's algorithm. However, different graphs may provide different solutions for the minimum spanning tree when using Prim's and Kruskal's algorithms because each algorithm proceeds in different ways to reach its conclusions. Different approaches often imply different minimal spanning trees as output.

Determining which algorithm works best

Both Prim's and Kruskal's algorithms output a single connected component, joining all the vertexes in the graph by using the least (or one of the least) long sequences of edges (a minimum spanning tree). By summing the edge weights, you can determine the length of the resulting spanning tree. Because both algorithms always provide you with a working solution, you must rely on running time and decide whether they can take on any kind of weighted graph to determine which is best.

As for running time, both algorithms provide similar results with Big-O complexity rating of $O(E*log(V))$, where E is the number of edges and V the number of vertexes. However, you must account for how they solve the problem because there are differences in the average expected running time.

Prim's algorithm incrementally builds a single solution by adding edges, whereas Kruskal's algorithm creates an ensemble of partial solutions and aggregates them. In creating its solution, Prim's algorithm relies on data structures that are more complex than Kruskal's because it continuously adds potential edges as candidates and keeps picking the shortest edge to proceed toward its solution. When operating on a dense graph, Prim's algorithm is preferred over Kruskal's because its priority queue based on heaps does all the sorting jobs quickly and efficiently.

REMEMBER

The example uses a priority queue based on a binary heap for the heavy job of picking up the shortest edges, but there are even faster data structures, such as the *Fibonacci heap*, which can produce faster results when the heap contains many edges. Using a Fibonacci heap, the running complexity of Prim's algorithm can mutate to $O(E + V*\log(V))$, which is clearly advantageous if you have a lot of edges (the E component is now summed instead of multiplied) compared to the previous reported running time $O(E*\log(V))$.

Kruskal's algorithm doesn't much need a priority queue (even though one of the examples uses one) because the enumeration and sorting of edges happens just once at the beginning of the process. Being based on simpler data structures that work through the sorted edges, it's the ideal candidate for regular, sparse graphs with fewer edges.

Finding the Shortest Route

The shortest route between two points isn't necessarily a straight line, especially when a straight line doesn't exist in your graph. Say that you need to run electrical lines in a community. The shortest route would involve running the lines as needed between each location without regard to where those lines go. However, real life tends not to allow a simple solution. You may need to run the cables beside roads and not across private property, which means finding routes that reduce the distances as much as possible.

Defining what it means to find the shortest path

Many applications exist for shortest-route algorithms. The idea is to find the path that offers the smallest distance between point A and point B. Finding the shortest path is useful for both transportation (how to arrive at a destination consuming the least fuel) and communication (how to route information to allow it to arrive earlier). Nevertheless, unexpected applications of the shortest-path problem may also arise in image processing (for separating contours of images), gaming (how to achieve certain game goals using the fewest moves), and many other fields in which you can reduce the problem to an undirected or directed weighted graph.

The Dijkstra algorithm can solve the shortest-path problem and has found the most uses. Edsger W. Dijkstra, a Dutch computer scientist, devised the algorithm as a demonstration of the processing power of a new computer called ARMAC (http://www-set.win.tue.nl/UnsungHeroes/machines/armac.html) in 1959. The algorithm initially solved the shortest distance between 64 cities in the Netherlands based on a simple graph map.

REMEMBER

Other algorithms can solve the shortest-path problem. The Bellman-Ford and Floyd-Warshall are more complex but can handle graphs with negative weights. (Negative weights can represent some problems better.) Both algorithms are beyond the scope of this book, but the site at https://www.hackerearth.com/ja/practice/algorithms/graphs/shortest-path-algorithms/tutorial/ provides additional information about them. Because the shortest-path problem involves graphs that are both weighted and directed, the example graph requires another update before proceeding (you can see the result in Figure 9-3). (You can find this code in the A4D; 09; Shortest Path.ipynb file on the Dummies site as part of the downloadable code; see the Introduction for details.)

```
import numpy as np
import networkx as nx
import matplotlib.pyplot as plt
%matplotlib inline

graph = {'A': {'B':2, 'C':3},
         'B': {'C':2, 'D':2},
         'C': {'D':3, 'E':2},
         'D': {'F':3},
         'E': {'D':1,'F':1},
         'F': {}}

Graph = nx.DiGraph()
for node in graph:
    Graph.add_nodes_from(node)
    for edge, weight in graph[node].items():
        Graph.add_edge(node,edge, weight=weight)

pos = { 'A': [0.00, 0.50], 'B': [0.25, 0.75],
        'C': [0.25, 0.25], 'D': [0.75, 0.75],
        'E': [0.75, 0.25], 'F': [1.00, 0.50]}

labels = nx.get_edge_attributes(Graph,'weight')
nx.draw(Graph, pos, with_labels=True)
nx.draw_networkx_edge_labels(Graph, pos,
                              edge_labels=labels)
nx.draw_networkx(Graph,pos)
plt.show()
```

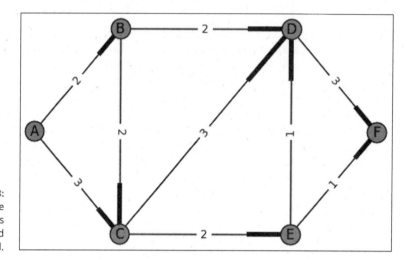

FIGURE 9-3:
The example graph becomes weighted and directed.

Explaining Dijkstra's algorithm

Dijkstra's algorithm requires a starting and (optionally) ending vertex as input. If you don't provide an ending vertex, the algorithm computes the shortest distance between the starting vertex and any other vertexes in the graph. When you define an ending vertex, the algorithm stops upon reading that vertex and returns the result up to that point, no matter how much of the graph remains unexplored.

The algorithm starts by estimating the distance of the other vertexes from the starting point. This is the starting belief it records in the priority queue and is set to infinity by convention. Then the algorithm proceeds to explore the neighboring nodes, similar to a BFS. This allows the algorithm to determine which nodes are near and that their distance is the weight of the connecting edges. It stores this information in the priority queue by an appropriate weight update.

REMEMBER

Naturally, the algorithm explores the neighbors because a directed edge connects them with the starting vertex. Dijkstra's algorithm accounts for the edge direction.

At this point, the algorithm moves to the nearest vertex on the graph based on the shortest edge in the priority queue. Technically, the algorithm *visits* a new vertex. It starts exploring the neighboring vertexes, excluding the vertexes that it has already visited, determines how much it costs to visit each of the unvisited vertexes, and evaluates whether the distance to visit them is less than the distance it recorded in the priority queue.

When the distance in the priority queue is infinite, this means that it's the algorithm's first visit to that vertex, and the algorithm records the shorter distance.

When the distance recorded in the priority queue isn't infinite, but it's more than the distance that the algorithm has just calculated, it means that the algorithm has found a *shortcut*, a shorter way to reach that vertex from the starting point, and it stores the information in the priority queue. Of course, if the distance recorded in the priority queue is shorter than the one just evaluated by the algorithm, the algorithm discards the information because the new route is longer. After updating all the distances to the neighboring vertexes, the algorithm determines whether it has reached the end vertex. If not, it picks the shortest edge present in the priority queue, visits it, and starts evaluating the distance to the new neighboring vertexes.

REMEMBER

As the narrative of the algorithm explained, Dijikstra's algorithm keeps a precise accounting of the cost to reach every vertex that it encounters, and it updates its information only when it finds a shorter way. The running complexity of the algorithm in Big-O notation is O(E*log(V)), where E is the number of edges and V the number of vertexes in the graph. The following code shows how to implement Dijikstra's algorithm using Python:

```python
def dijkstra(graph, start, end):
    inf = float('inf')
    known = set()
    priority = priority_queue()
    path = {start: start}

    for vertex in graph:
        if vertex == start:
            priority.push(0, vertex)
        else:
            priority.push(inf, vertex)
    last = start

    while last != end:
        (weight, actual_node) = priority.pop()
        if actual_node not in known:
            for next_node in graph[actual_node]:
                upto_actual = priority.index[actual_node]
                upto_next = priority.index[next_node]
                to_next = upto_actual + \
                graph[actual_node][next_node]
                if to_next < upto_next:
                    priority.push(to_next, next_node)
                    print("Found shortcut from %s to %s"
                            % (actual_node, next_node))
                    print ("\tTotal length up so far: %i"
```

```
                        % to_next)
                    path[next_node] = actual_node

            last = actual_node
            known.add(actual_node)

    return priority.index, path

dist, path = dijkstra(graph, 'A', 'F')

Found shortcut from A to C
   Total length up so far: 3
Found shortcut from A to B
   Total length up so far: 2
Found shortcut from B to D
   Total length up so far: 4
Found shortcut from C to E
   Total length up so far: 5
Found shortcut from D to F
   Total length up so far: 7
Found shortcut from E to F
   Total length up so far: 6
```

The algorithm returns a couple of useful pieces of information: the shortest path to destination and the minimum recorded distances for the visited vertexes. To visualize the shortest path, you need a `reverse_path` function that rearranges the path to make it readable:

```
def reverse_path(path, start, end):
    progression = [end]
    while progression[-1] != start:
        progression.append(path[progression[-1]])
    return progression[::-1]

print (reverse_path(path, 'A', 'F'))

['A', 'C', 'E', 'F']
```

You can also know the shortest distance to every node encountered by querying the `dist` dictionary:

```
print (dist)

{'D': 4, 'A': 0, 'B': 2, 'F': 6, 'C': 3, 'E': 5}
```

Chapter **10**

Discovering Graph Secrets

Chapter 8 helps you understand the foundations of graphs as they apply to mathematics. Chapter 9 increases your knowledge by helping you see the relationship of graphs to algorithms. This chapter helps you focus on applying the theories of these previous two chapters to interact with graphs in practical ways.

The first section conveys the character of social networks by using graphs. Considering the connections created by social networks is important. For example, conversation analysis can reveal patterns that help you understand the underlying topic better than simply reading the conversations would do. A particular conversation branch might attract greater attention because it's more important than another conversation branch. Of course, you must perform this analysis while dealing with issues such as spam. Analysis of this sort can lead to all sorts of interesting conclusions, such as where to spend more advertising money in order to attract the most attention and, therefore, sales.

The second section looks at navigating graphs to achieve specific results. For example, when driving, you might need to know the best route to take between two points given that, even though one route is shorter, it also has construction that makes a second route better. Sometimes you need to randomize your search to discover a best route or a best conclusion. This section of the chapter also discusses that issue.

Envisioning Social Networks as Graphs

Every social interaction necessarily connects with every other social interaction of the same type. For example, consider a social network such as Facebook. The links on your page connect with family members, but they also connect with outside sources that in turn connect with other outside sources. Each of your family members also has external links. Direct and indirect connections between various pages eventually link every other page together, even though the process of getting from one page to another may require the use of myriad links. Connectivity occurs in all sorts of other ways as well. The point is that studying social networks simply by viewing a Facebook page or other source of information is hard. *Social Network Analysis (SNA)* is the process of studying the interactions in social networks using graphs called *sociograms,* in which nodes (such as a Facebook page) appear as points, and ties (such as external page links) appear as lines. The following sections discuss some of the issues surrounding the study of social networks as graphs.

Clustering networks in groups

People tend to form communities — clusters of other people who have like ideas and sentiments. By studying these clusters, attributing certain behaviors to the group as a whole becomes easier (although attributing the behavior to an individual is both dangerous and unreliable). The idea behind the study of clusters is that if a connection exists between people, they often have a common set of ideas and goals. By finding clusters, you can determine these ideas by inspecting group membership. For instance, it's common to try to find clusters of people in insurance fraud detection and tax inspection. Unexpected groups of people might raise suspicion that they're part of a group of fraudsters or tax evaders because they lack the usual reasons for people to gather in such circumstances.

Friendship graphs can represent how people connect with each other. The vertexes represent individuals and the edges represent their connections, such as family relationships, business contacts, or friendship ties. Typically, friendship graphs are undirected because they represent mutual relationships, and sometimes they're weighted to represent the strength of the bond between two persons.

TIP

Many studies focus on undirected graphs that concentrate solely on associations. You can also use directed graphs to show that Person A knows about Person B, but Person B doesn't even know that Person A exists. In this case, you actually have 16 different kinds of triads to consider. For the sake of simplicity, this chapter focuses solely on these four types: closed, open, connected pair, and unconnected.

When looking for clusters in a friendship graph, the connections between nodes in these clusters depend on triads — essentially, special kinds of triangles. Connections between three people can fall into these categories:

>> **Closed:** All three people know each other. Think about a family setting in this case, in which everyone knows everyone else.

>> **Open:** One person knows two other people, but the two other people don't know each other. Think about a person who knows an individual at work and another individual at home, but the individual at work doesn't know anything about the individual at home.

>> **Connected pair:** One person knows one of the other people in a triad but doesn't know the third person. This situation involves two people who know something about each other meeting someone new — someone who potentially wants to be part of the group.

>> **Unconnected:** The triad forms a group, but no one in the group knows each other. This last one might seem a bit odd, but think about a convention or seminar. The people at these events form a group, but they may not know anything about each other. However, because they have similar interests, you can use clustering to understand the behavior of the group.

Triads occur naturally in relationships, and many Internet social networks have leveraged this idea to accelerate the connections between participants. The density of connections is important for any kind of social network because a connected network can spread information and share content more easily. For instance, when LinkedIn, the professional social network (`https://www.linkedin.com/`), decided to increase the connection density of its network, it started by looking for open triads and trying to close them by inviting people to connect. Closing triads is at the foundation of LinkedIn's *Connection Suggestion algorithm.* You can discover more about how it works by reading the Quora's answer at: `https://www.quora.com/How-does-LinkedIns-People-You-May-Know-work`.

The example in this section relies on the Zachary's Karate Club sample graph described at `https://networkdata.ics.uci.edu/data.php?id=105`. It's a small graph that lets you see how networks work without spending a lot of time loading a large dataset. Fortunately, this dataset appears as part of the `networkx` package introduced in Chapter 8. The Zachary's Karate Club network represents the friendship relationships between 34 members of a karate club from 1970 to 1972. Sociologist Wayne W. Zachary used it as a topic of study. He wrote a paper on it entitled "An Information Flow Model for Conflict and Fission in Small Groups." The interesting fact about this graph and its paper is that in those years, a conflict arose in the club between one of the karate instructors (node number 0) and the president of the club (node number 33). By clustering the graph, you can almost perfectly predict the split of the club into two groups shortly after the occurrence.

Because this example also draws a graph showing the groups (so that you can visualize them easier), you also need to use the `matplotlib` package. The following code shows how to graph the nodes and edges of the dataset. (You can find this code in the A4D; 10; Social Networks.ipynb file on the Dummies site as part of the downloadable code; see the Introduction for details.)

```
import networkx as nx
import matplotlib.pyplot as plt
%matplotlib inline

graph = nx.karate_club_graph()

pos=nx.spring_layout(graph)
nx.draw(graph, pos, with_labels=True)
plt.show()
```

To display the graphic onscreen, you also need to provide a layout that determines how to position the nodes onscreen. This example uses the Fruchterman-Reingold force-directed algorithm (the call to nx.spring_layout). However, you can choose one of the other layouts described in the Graph Layout section at https://networkx.github.io/documentation/networkx-1.9/reference/drawing.html. Figure 10-1 shows the output from the example. (Your output may look slightly different.)

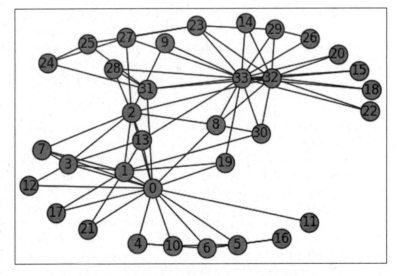

FIGURE 10-1:
A graph showing the network clusters of relationships between friends.

REMEMBER

The Fruchterman-Reingold force-directed algorithm for generating automatic layouts of graphs creates understandable layouts with separated nodes and edges that tend not to cross by mimicking what happens in physics between electrically charged particles or magnets bearing the same sign. In looking at the graph output, you can see that some nodes have just one connection, some two, and some more than two. The edges form triads, as previously mentioned. However, the most important consideration is that Figure 10-1 clearly shows the clustering that occurs in a social network.

Discovering communities

A group of tightly associated people often defines a community. In fact, the term *clique* applies to a group whose membership to the group is exclusive and everyone knows everyone else quite well. Most people have childhood memories of a tight group of friends at school or in the neighborhood who always spent their time together. That's a clique.

REMEMBER

You can find cliques in undirected graphs. Directed graphs distinguish strongly between connected components when a direct connection exists between all the node pairs in the component itself. A city is an example of a strongly connected component because you can reach any destination from any starting point by following one-way and two-way streets.

Mathematically, a clique is even more rigorous because it implies a *subgraph* (a part of a network graph that you can separate from other parts as a complete element in its own right) that has maximum connectivity. In looking at various kinds of social networks, picking out the clusters is easy, but what can prove difficult is finding the cliques — the groups with maximum connectivity — within the clusters. By knowing where cliques exist, you can begin to understand the cohesive nature of a community better. In addition, the exclusive nature of cliques tends to create a group that has its own rules outside of those that might exist in the social network as a whole. The following example shows how to extract cliques and communities from the karate club graph used in the previous section:

```
graph = nx.karate_club_graph()
# Finding and printing all cliques of four
cliques = nx.find_cliques(graph)
print ('All cliques of four: %s'
        % [c for c in cliques if len(c)>=4])

# Joining cliques of four into communities
communities = nx.k_clique_communities(graph, k=4)
communities_list = [list(c) for c in communities]
nodes_list = [node for community in communities_list for
              node in community]
print ('Found these communities: %s' % communities_list)
```

```
# Printing the subgraph of communities
subgraph = graph.subgraph(nodes_list)
nx.draw(subgraph, with_labels=True)
plt.show()

All cliques of four: [[0, 1, 2, 3, 13], [0, 1, 2, 3, 7],
                      [33, 32, 8, 30], [33, 32, 23, 29]]
Found these communities: [[0, 1, 2, 3, 7, 13],
                          [32, 33, 29, 23], [32, 33, 8, 30]]
```

The example begins by extracting just the nodes in the karate club dataset that have four or more connections, and then prints the cliques with a minimum size of four. Of course, you can set any level of connections needed to obtain the desired resource. Perhaps you consider a clique a community in which each node has twenty connections, but other people might see a clique as a community where each node has just three connections.

The list of cliques doesn't really help you much, though, if you want to see the communities. To see them, you need to rely on specialized and complex algorithms to merge overlapping cliques and find clusters, such as the clique percolation method described at https://gaplogs.net/2012/04/01/simple-community-detection-algorithms/. The NetworkX package offers k_clique_communities, an implementation of the clique percolation algorithm, which results in the union of all the cliques of a certain size (the k parameter). These cliques of a certain size share k-1 elements (that is, they differ by just one component, a truly strict rule).

Clique percolation provides you with a list of all the communities found. In this example, one clique revolves around the karate instructor and another revolves around the president of the club. In addition, you can extract all the nodes that are part of a community into a single set, which helps you create a subgraph made of just communities.

Finally, you can draw the subgraph and display it. Figure 10-2 shows the output of this example, which displays the ensemble of cliques with four or more connections.

Finding cliques in graphs is a complex problem requiring many computations (it's a difficult problem) that an algorithm solves using a brute-force search, which means trying all possible subsets of vertexes to determine whether they're cliques. With some luck, because some randomization is needed for the algorithm to succeed, you can find a large clique using a simple approach whose complexity is $O(n+m)$, where n is the number of vertexes and m the edges. The following steps describe this process.

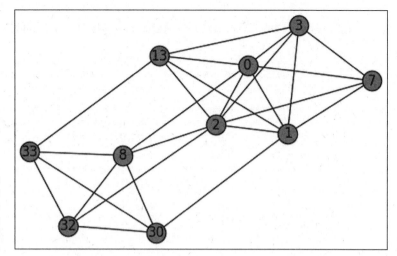

FIGURE 10-2:
FIGURE 10-2:
Communities
often contain
cliques that can
prove useful
for SNA.

1. Sort the vertexes by degree (which is the number of vertex connections), from the highest to the lowest.

2. Place the vertex with the highest degree into the clique (or as an alternative, randomly choose from one of the highest-degree vertexes).

3. Repeat Steps 1 and 2 until you have no more vertexes to test.

4. Verify the next vertex as being part of the clique:

   - If it's part of the clique, add it to the clique.

   - If it isn't part of the clique, repeat the test on the remaining vertexes.

At the end, after a few algorithm trials, you should have a list of vertexes that constitutes the largest clique present in the graph.

Navigating a Graph

Navigating or *traversing* a graph means visiting each of the graph nodes. The purpose of navigating a graph can include determining node content or updating it as needed. When navigating a graph, it's entirely possible that you visit particular nodes more than once because of the connectivity that graphs provide. Consequently, you also need to consider marking nodes as visited after you see their content. The act of navigating a graph is important in determining how the nodes connect so that you can perform various tasks. Previous chapters discuss basic graph navigation techniques. The following sections help you understand a few of the more advanced graph navigation techniques.

Counting the degrees of separation

The term *degrees of separation* defines the distance between nodes in a graph. When working with an undirected graph without weighted edges, each edge counts for a value of one degree of separation. However, when working with other sorts of graphs, such as maps, where each edge can represent a distance or time value, the degrees of separation can become quite different. The point is that degrees of separation indicate some sort of distance. The example in this section (and the one that follows) relies on the following graph data. (You can find this code in the A4D; 10; Graph Navigation.ipynb file on the Dummies site as part of the downloadable code; see the Introduction for details.)

```
import networkx as nx
import matplotlib.pyplot as plt
%matplotlib inline

data = {'A': ['B', 'F', 'H'],
        'B': ['A', 'C'],
        'C': ['B', 'D'],
        'D': ['C', 'E'],
        'E': ['D', 'F', 'G'],
        'F': ['E', 'A'],
        'G': ['E', 'H'],
        'H': ['G', 'A']}

graph = nx.DiGraph(data)
pos=nx.spring_layout(graph)
nx.draw_networkx_labels(graph, pos)
nx.draw_networkx_nodes(graph, pos)
nx.draw_networkx_edges(graph, pos)
plt.show()
```

This is an expansion of the graph used in Chapter 6. Figure 10-3 shows how this graph appears so that you can visualize what the function call is doing. Note that this is a directed graph (networkx DiGraph) because using a directed graph has certain advantages when determining degrees of separation (and performing a wealth of other calculations).

To discover the degrees of separation between two items, you must have a starting point. For the purpose of this example, you can use node 'A'. The following code shows the required networkx package function call and output:

```
nx.shortest_path_length(graph, 'A')

{'A': 0, 'B': 1, 'C': 2, 'D': 3, 'E': 2, 'F': 1, 'G': 2,
 'H': 1}
```

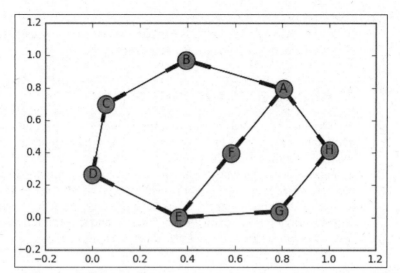

FIGURE 10-3:
A sample graph
used for
navigation
purposes.

The distance between node A and node A is 0, of course. The greatest degree of separation comes from node A to node D, which is 3. You can use this kind of information to determine which route to take or to perform an analysis of the cost in gas versus the cost in time of various paths. The point is that knowing the shortest distance between two points can be quite important. The networkx package used for this example comes in a wide array of distance-measuring algorithms, as described at https://networkx.github.io/documentation/development/reference/algorithms.shortest_paths.html.

TECHNICAL STUFF

To see how using a directed graph can make a big difference when performing degrees-of-separation calculations, try removing the connection between nodes A and F. Change the data so that it looks like this:

```
data = {'A': ['B', 'H'],
        'B': ['A', 'C'],
        'C': ['B', 'D'],
        'D': ['C', 'E'],
        'E': ['D', 'F', 'G'],
        'F': ['E', 'A'],
        'G': ['E', 'H'],
        'H': ['G', 'A']}
```

When you perform the call to nx.shortest_path_length this time, the output becomes quite different because you can no longer go from A to F directly. Here's the new output from the call:

```
{'A': 0, 'B': 1, 'C': 2, 'D': 3, 'E': 3, 'F': 4, 'G': 2,
 'H': 1}
```

Notice that the loss of the path has changed some of the degrees of separation. The distance to node F is now the longest at 4.

Walking a graph randomly

You might find a need to walk a graph randomly. The act of walking the graph randomly, rather than look for a specific path, can simulate natural activities, such as an animal foraging for food. It also plays in to all sorts of other interesting activities, such as playing games. However, random graph walking can have practical aspects. For example, a car is held up in traffic because of an accident, so the shortest path is no longer available. In some cases, choosing a random alternative might work best because traffic along the second shortest route could be heavy as a result of the traffic jam along the shortest route.

REMEMBER

The networkx package doesn't provide the means for obtaining a random path directly. However, it does provide the means for finding all available paths, after which you can select a path from the list randomly. The following code shows how this process might work using the graph from the previous section.

```
import random
random.seed(0)

paths = nx.all_simple_paths(graph, 'A', 'H')

path_list = []
for path in paths:
    path_list.append(path)
    print("Path Candidate: ", path)

sel_path = random.randint(0, len(path_list) - 1)

print("The selected path is: ", path_list[sel_path])

Path Candidate:  ['A', 'B', 'C', 'D', 'E', 'G', 'H']
Path Candidate:  ['A', 'H']
Path Candidate:  ['A', 'F', 'E', 'G', 'H']
The selected path is:  ['A', 'H']
```

The code sets the seed to a specific value to ensure that you get the same result every time. However, by changing the seed value, you can see different results from the example code. The point is that even the simple graph shown in Figure 10-3 offers three ways to get from node A to node H (two of which are definitely longer than the selected path in this case). Choosing just one of them ensures that you get from one node to the other, albeit by a potentially round-about way.

Chapter **11**

Getting the Right Web page

The last few chapters review graphs at length. The web is one of the most interesting examples because of its extent and complexity. After providing an understanding of the basic algorithms that allow graph traversal and extraction of useful structures (such as the presence of clusters or communities), this chapter concludes the discussion of graphs by presenting the PageRank algorithm that has revolutionized people's lives as much as the web and Internet did because it makes the web usable. PageRank isn't only the engine behind Google and many other search engines, but it's also a smart way to derive latent information, such as relevance, importance, and reputation, from a graph structure.

Libraries rely on catalogues and librarians to offer an easy way to find particular texts or explore certain subjects. Books aren't all the same: Some are good at presenting certain kinds of information; some are better. Scholar recommendations make a book an authoritative source because these recommendations often appear in other books as quotes and citations. This sort of cross-reference didn't exist on the web initially. The presence of certain words in the title or in the text of the body recommended a particular web page. This approach is practically like judging a book by its title and the number of words it contains.

The PageRank algorithm changes all that by transforming the presence of the links on pages and turning them into recommendations, akin to the input of expert scholars. The growing scale of the web also plays a role in the success of the algorithm. Good signals are easy to find and distinguished from noise because they appear regularly. Noise, though confounding, is naturally casual. The larger the web, the more likely you are to get good signals for a smart algorithm like PageRank.

Finding the World in a Search Engine

For many people, their personal and professional lives are unthinkable without the Internet and the web. The Internet network is composed of interconnected pages (among other things). The web is composed of sites that are reachable by domains, each one composed of pages and hyperlinks that connect sites internally and with other sites externally. Service and knowledge resources are available through the web if you know exactly where to look. Accessing the web is unthinkable without search engines, those sites that allow you to find anything on the web using a simple query.

Searching the Internet for data

With an estimated size of almost 50 billion pages (http://www.worldwide websize.com/), the web isn't easy to represent. Studies describe the web as a bowtie shaped graph (see http://www.immorlica.com/socNet/broder.pdf and http://vigna.di.unimi.it/ftp/papers/GraphStructureRevisited.pdf). The web mainly consists of an interconnected core and other parts that link to that core. However, some parts are completely unreachable. By taking any road in the real world, you can go anywhere (you may have to cross the oceans to do it). On the web, you can't touch all the sites just by following its structure; some parts aren't easily accessible (they are disconnected or you're on the wrong side to reach them). If you want to find something on the web, even when time isn't a problem, you still need an index.

Considering how to find the right data

Finding the right data has been a problem since the early years of the web, but the first search engines didn't appear until the 1990s. Search engines weren't thought of earlier because other solutions, such as simple domain listings or specialized site catalogues, worked fine. Only when these solutions stopped scaling well because of the rapidly growing size of the web did search engines such as Lycos, Magellan, Yahoo, Excite, Inktomi, and Altavista appear.

URLs WITH .PDF EXTENSIONS

Many of the resource URLs found in this book have a .pdf extension. When you attempt to open the link, you may see a warning from your browser indicating that the .pdf file could contain a virus. It's entirely possible for a .pdf file to contain a virus (see `http://security.stackexchange.com/questions/64052/can-a-pdf-file-contain-a-virus` for a discussion of the topic). However, the research .pdf file links provided in this book are unlikely to contain viruses, so you can download them safely and then use a scanner to verify the content. As with any online content, you're always better off to be safe than sorry when it comes to files. Please do let us know if any of the .pdfs referenced in the book actually do contain viruses by writing to `John@JohnMuellerBooks.com`. In addition, please contact the webmaster for the site hosting the file.

All these search engines worked by having specialized software autonomously visit the web, using domain lists and testing hyperlinks found on the visited pages. These *spiders* explored each new link in a process called *crawling*. Spiders are pieces of software that read the pages as plain text (they can't understand images or other nontextual content).

Early search engines worked by crawling the web, collecting the information from spiders, and processing it in order to create inverted indexes. The indexes allowed retracing pages based on the words they contained. When you made a query, such inverted indexes reported all the pages containing the terms and helped score the pages, thus creating a ranking that turned into a search result (a list of ordered pages, ranging from the anticipated most useful page to the least useful page).

The scoring was quite naive because it often counted how frequently the keywords appeared on pages or whether they appeared in the titles or in the header of the page itself. Sometimes keywords were even scored more if they mixed or clustered together. Clearly, such simple indexing and scoring techniques allowed some web users to take advantage by using various tricks:

>> **Web spammers:** Used their ability to fill the search results with pages containing poor content and a lot of advertising.

>> **Black Hat search engine optimization (Black Hat SEO):** Used by people who employ their knowledge of search engines to make the search engine ranking higher for pages they manipulated despite their poor quality. Unfortunately, these issues still persist because every search engine, even the most evolved ones, aren't immune to people who want to game the system to obtain a higher search engine ranking. The PageRank algorithm may eliminate many of the older spammers and Black Hat SEO people, but it's not a panacea.

REMEMBER

It's essential to distinguish Black Hat SEO from White Hat SEO (usually simply SEO). People who use *White Hat SEO* are professionals who employ their knowledge of search engines to better promote valid and useful pages in a legal and ethical way.

The emergence of such actors and the possibility of manipulating search engines' results created the need for better ranking algorithms in search engines. One such result is the PageRank algorithm.

Explaining the PageRank Algorithm

The PageRank algorithm is named after Google cofounder Larry Page. It made its first public appearance in a 1998 paper entitled "The Anatomy of a LargeScale Hypertextual Web Search Engine," by Sergey Brin and Larry Page, published by the journal *Computer Networks and ISDN Systems* (`http://ilpubs.stanford.edu:8090/361/1/1998-8.pdf`). At that time, both Brin and Page were PhD candidates, and the algorithm, the very foundation of Google's search technology, was initially a research project at Stanford University.

Simply stated, *PageRank* scores the importance of each node in a graph in such a way that the higher the score the more important the node in a graph. Determining the node importance in a graph like the web means computing whether a page is relevant as part of a query's results, thus better servicing users looking for good web content.

A page is a good response to a query when it matches the query's criteria and has prominence in the system of hyperlinks that ties pages together. The logic behind prominence is that because users build the web, a page has importance in the network for good reason (the quality and authority of the page's content is assessed by its importance in the web's network of hyperlinks).

Understanding the reasoning behind the PageRank algorithm

In 1998, when both Brin and Page were still students at Stanford, the quality of search results was an issue for anyone using the web. Mainstream search engines of the time struggled both with an ever-growing web structure (the next part of the book discusses algorithm scaling issues and how to make them work with big data) and with a myriad of spammers.

REMEMBER

The use of spammers in this case doesn't refer to email spammers (those spammers who send unrequested emails to your Inbox) but rather to web spammers (those who know the economic importance of having pages at the top of search results). This group devised sophisticated and malicious tricks in order to fool search results. Popular hacks by web spammers of the day include:

>> **Keyword stuffing:** Implies overusing particular keywords in a page to trick the search engine into thinking the page seriously discusses the keyword topic.

>> **Invisible text:** Requires copying the content of a page result on top of a query into a different page using the same color for both characters and background. The copied content is invisible to users but not to the search engine's spiders (which were, and still are, just scanning textual data) and to its algorithms. The trick ranks the page with invisible text as high as the originating page in a search.

>> **Cloaking:** Defines a more sophisticated variant of invisible text where, instead of text, scripts or images provide different content to search engine spiders than users actually see.

Web spammers use such tricks to trick search engines to rank pages highly, even though the page content is poor and, at best, misleading. These tricks have consequences. For instance, a user might look for information relating to university research and instead be exposed to commercial advertising or inappropriate content. Users became disappointed because they often ended up at pages unrelated to their needs, requiring them to restate their queries and to spend time digging for useful information among pages of results, wasting energy in distinguishing good references from bad ones. Scholars and experts, noting the need to cope with spam results and fearing that the development of the web could halt because users had difficulties finding what they really wanted, started working on possible solutions.

As Brin and Page worked on their solving algorithm, other ideas were drafted and publicized, or developed in parallel. One such idea is Hyper Search, by Massimo Marchiori, who first pointed out the importance of web links in determining the prominence of a web page as a factor to consider during a search: `https://www.w3.org/People/Massimo/papers/WWW6/`). Another interesting solution is a web search engine project called HITS (Hypertext-Induced Topic Search), also based on the web links structure and developed by Jon Kleinberg, a young scientist working at IBM Almaden in Silicon Valley. The interesting fact about HITS is that it classifies pages into *hubs* (a page with many links to authoritative pages) and *authorities* (pages considered authoritative by many links from hubs), something that PageRank doesn't do explicitly (but implicitly does in computations) (`http://www.math.cornell.edu/~mec/Winter2009/RalucaRemus/Lecture4/lecture4.html`).

REMEMBER

When the time is ripe, the same idea or something similar often sprouts in different places. Sometimes sharing of basic ideas occurs between researchers and scientists; sometimes ideas are developed in a completely independent way (see the history of Japanese mathematician Takakazu Seki `http://www-history.mcs.st-andrews.ac.uk/history/Biographies/Seki.html`, who independently discovered many of the same things as European mathematicians such as Newton, Leibniz, and Bernoulli did around the same period). In 1998, only Brin and Page took steps to create a search engine company based on their algorithm by taking a leave from Stanford University and their doctoral studies to focus on making their algorithm work with more than a billion web pages.

Explaining the nuts and bolts of PageRank

The innovation brought about by PageRank is that an inverted index of terms isn't enough to determine whether a page matches a user's information query. Matching words (or meaning, the semantic query match discussed at the end of the chapter) between a query and the page text is a prerequisite, but it isn't sufficient because hyperlinks are necessary to assess whether the page offers quality content and is authoritative.

When discussing sites, distinguishing between inbound and outbound links is important, and you shouldn't consider internal links that connect within the same site. The links you see on a page are *outbound* when they lead to another page on another site. The links that bring someone to your page from another page on another site are *inbound* links (backlinks). As the page creator, you use outbound links to provide additional information to the page content. You presumably won't use random links on your page (or links pointing to useless or bad content) because that would spoil the page quality. As you point to good content using links, other page creators use links on their pages to point to your page when your page is interesting and of high quality.

It's a chain of trust. Hyperlinks are like endorsements or recommendations for pages. Inbound links show that other page creators trust you, and you share part of that trust by adding outbound links on your pages to point to other pages.

Implementing PageRank

Representing this chain of trust mathematically requires simultaneously determining how much authority your page has, as measured by inbound links, and how much it donates to other pages by outbound links. You can achieve such computations in two ways:

>> **Simulation:** Uses the behavior of a web surfer who browses randomly on the web (a *random surfer*). This approach requires that you recreate the web structure and run the simulation.

>> **Matrix computation:** Replicates the behavior of a random surfer using a *sparse matrix* (a matrix in which most data is zero) replicating the web structure. This approach requires some matrix operations, as explained in Chapter 5, and a series of computations that reach a result by successive approximation.

Even though it's more abstract, using the matrix computation for PageRank requires fewer programming instructions, and you can easily implement it using Python. (You can try the PageRank algorithm on real-world sites using an automatic PageRank checker, such as http://checkpagerank.net/index.php. Unfortunately, the program may produce inaccurate results for newer sites because they haven't been crawled properly yet, it can give you an idea of what PageRank is like in practice.)

Implementing a Python script

PageRank is a function that scores the nodes in a graph with a number (the higher the number, the more important the node). When scoring a web page, the number could represent the probability of a random surfer visit. You express probabilities using a number from 0.0 to a maximum 1.0 and, ideally, when representing the probability of being on a particular site among all available sites, the sum of all the probabilities of the pages on the web should equal 1.0.

REMEMBER

Many versions of PageRank exist, each one changing its recipe a little to fit the kind of graph it has to score. The example in this section presents you with the original version for the web presented in the previously mentioned paper by Brin and Page and in the paper "PageRank: Bringing Order to the Web" (http://ilpubs.stanford.edu:8090/422/1/1999-66.pdf).

The example creates three different web networks made of six nodes (web pages). The first one is a good working network, and the other two demonstrate problems that a random surfer may encounter because of the web structure or a web spammer's actions. This example also uses the NetworkX commands discussed in Chapter 8. (You can find this code in the A4D; 11; PageRank.ipynb file on the Dummies site as part of the downloadable code; see the Introduction for details.)

```
import numpy as np
import networkx as nx
import matplotlib.pyplot as plt
%matplotlib inline
```

```
Graph_A = nx.DiGraph()
Graph_B = nx.DiGraph()
Graph_C = nx.DiGraph()
Nodes = range(1,6)
Edges_OK = [(1,2),(1,3),(2,3),(3,1),(3,2),(3,4),(4,5),
            (4,6),(5,4),(5,6),(6,5),(6,1)]
Edges_dead_end = [(1,2),(1,3),(3,1),(3,2),(3,4),(4,5),
                  (4,6),(5,4),(5,6),(6,5),(6,1)]
Edges_trap = [(1,2),(1,3),(2,3),(3,1),(3,2),(3,4),(4,5),
              (4,6),(5,4),(5,6),(6,5)]
Graph_A.add_nodes_from(Nodes)
Graph_A.add_edges_from(Edges_OK)
Graph_B.add_nodes_from(Nodes)
Graph_B.add_edges_from(Edges_dead_end)
Graph_C.add_nodes_from(Nodes)
Graph_C.add_edges_from(Edges_trap)
```

This code displays the first network, the good one, as shown in Figure 11-1.

```
np.random.seed(2)
pos=nx.shell_layout(Graph_A)
nx.draw(Graph_A, pos, arrows=True, with_labels=True)
plt.show()
```

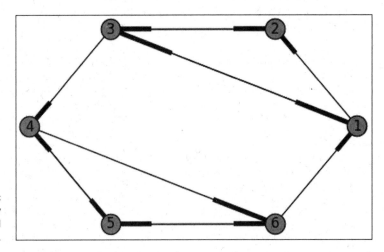

FIGURE 11-1:
A strongly
connected
network.

TIP

All nodes connect with each other. This is an example of a strongly connected graph, which contains no isolated nodes or single nodes and enclaves that act as dead ends. A random surfer can freely run through it and never stop, and any node can reach any other node. In the NetworkX representation of a directed graph, there are no arrows, but the direction of an edge is represented by a thicker line entering a node. For example, a surfer can go from node 4 to node 6 because there is a thick line entering node 6 from node 4. However, the surfer can't go from node 6 to node 4 because the line entering node 4 from node 6 is thin.

The second graph isn't strongly connected. It presents a trap for a random surfer because the second node has no outbound links, and a user visiting the page could stop there and find no way out. This isn't an unusual event considering the structure of the web, but it could also show a spammer artifact, such that the spammer created a spam factory with many links that direct to a dead end site in order to trap web surfers. Figure 11-2 shows the output of the following code, which was used to display this graph.

```
np.random.seed(2)
pos=nx.shell_layout(Graph_B)
nx.draw(Graph_B, pos, arrows=True, with_labels=True)
plt.show()
```

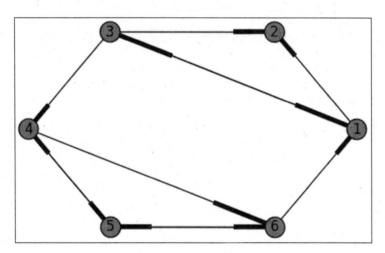

FIGURE 11-2:
A dead end.

Another situation that may be natural or the result of a spammer's action is a spider trap. It's another dead end for a surfer, this time not on a single page but on a closed site that lacks links to an outside network of pages. Figure 11-3 shows the output of the following code, which was used to display this graph.

```
np.random.seed(2)
pos=nx.shell_layout(Graph_C)
nx.draw(Graph_C, pos, arrows=True, with_labels=True)
plt.show()
```

FIGURE 11-3:
A spider trap.

REMEMBER

It's called a *spider trap* because spammers devised it as a way to catch search engine software spiders in a loop and let them believe that the only websites were the ones inside the closed network.

Struggling with a naive implementation

Given a graph made by using Python and NetworkX, you can extract its structure and render it as a *transition matrix*, a matrix that represents nodes in columns and rows:

>> **Columns:** Contain the node a web surfer is on

>> **Rows:** Contain the probability that the surfer will visit other nodes because of outbound links

In the real web, the transition matrix that feeds the PageRank algorithm is built by spiders' continuous exploration of links.

```
def initialize_PageRank(graph):
    nodes = len(graph)
    M = nx.to_numpy_matrix(graph)
    outbound = np.squeeze(np.asarray(np.sum(M, axis=1)))
    prob_outbound = np.array(
        [1.0/count
            if count>0 else 0.0 for count in outbound])
    G = np.asarray(np.multiply(M.T, prob_outbound))
    p = np.ones(nodes) / float(nodes)
    if np.min(np.sum(G,axis=0)) < 1.0:
        print ('Warning: G is substochastic')
    return G, p
```

The Python code creates the function `initialize_PageRank` that extracts both the transition matrix and the initial vector of default PageRank scores.

```
G, p = initialize_PageRank(Graph_A)
print (G)

[[ 0.       0.       0.33333333 0.       0.       0.5 ]
 [ 0.5      0.       0.33333333 0.       0.       0.  ]
 [ 0.5      1.       0.         0.       0.       0.  ]
 [ 0.       0.       0.33333333 0.       0.5      0.  ]
 [ 0.       0.       0.         0.5      0.       0.5 ]
 [ 0.       0.       0.         0.5      0.5      0.  ]]
```

The printed transition matrix G represents the transition matrix of the network described in Figure 11-1. Each column represents a node in the sequence 1 through 6. For instance, the third column represents node 3. Each row in the column shows the connections with other nodes (outbound links toward nodes 1, 2, and 4) and values that define the probability of a random surfer using any of the outbound links (that is, 1/3, 1/3, 1/3).

TIP

The diagonal of the matrix is always zero unless a page has an outbound link toward itself (it is a possibility).

The matrix contains more zeros than values. This is also true in reality because estimates show that each site has only ten outbound links on average. Because billions of sites exist, the nonzero values in a transition matrix representing the web are minimal. In this case, it's helpful to use a data structure such as an adjacency list (explained in Chapter 8) to represent data without wasting disk or memory space with zero values:

```
from scipy import sparse
sG = sparse.csr_matrix(G)
print (sG)

  (0, 2)    0.333333333333
  (0, 5)    0.5
  (1, 0)    0.5
  (1, 2)    0.333333333333
  (2, 0)    0.5
  (2, 1)    1.0
  (3, 2)    0.333333333333
  (3, 4)    0.5
  (4, 3)    0.5
  (4, 5)    0.5
  (5, 3)    0.5
  (5, 4)    0.5
```

This example has just 12 links out of 30 possible (without counting links to *self*, which is the current site). Another particular aspect of the transition matrix to note is that if you sum the columns, the result should be 1.0. If it is a value less than 1.0, the matrix is *substochastic* (which means that the matrix data isn't representing probabilities properly because probabilities should sum to 1.0) and cannot work perfectly with PageRank estimations.

Accompanying G is a vector p, the initial estimate of the total PageRank score, equally distributed among the nodes. In this example, because the total PageRank is 1.0 (the probability of a random surfer being in the network, which is 100 percent), it's distributed as 1/6 among the six nodes:

```
print(p)

[ 0.16666667  0.16666667  0.16666667  0.16666667
  0.16666667  0.16666667]
```

To estimate the PageRank, take the initial estimate for a node in the vector p, multiply it by the corresponding column in the transition matrix, and determine how much of its PageRank (its authority) transfers to other nodes. Repeat for all nodes and you'll know how PageRank transfers between nodes because of the network structure. You can achieve this computation using a matrix-vector multiplication:

```
print(np.dot(G,p))

[ 0.13888889  0.13888889  0.25        0.13888889
  0.16666667  0.16666667]
```

After the first matrix-vector multiplication, you obtain another estimate of PageRank that you use for redistribution among the nodes. By redistributing multiple times, the PageRank estimate stabilizes (results won't change), and you'll have the score you need. Using a transition matrix containing probabilities and estimation by successive approximation using matrix-vector multiplication obtains the same results as a computer simulation with a random surfer:

```
def PageRank_naive(graph, iters = 50):
    G, p = initialize_PageRank(graph)
    for i in range(iters):
        p = np.dot(G,p)
    return np.round(p,3)

print(PageRank_naive(Graph_A))

[ 0.154  0.154  0.231  0.154  0.154  0.154]
```

The new function `PageRank_naive` wraps all the previously described operations and emits a vector of probabilities (the PageRank score) for each node in the network. The third node emerges as the one with most importance. Unfortunately, the same function doesn't work with the other two networks:

```
print(PageRank_naive(Graph_B))
Warning: G is substochastic
[ 0.  0.  0.  0.  0.  0.]

print(PageRank_naive(Graph_C))
[ 0.      0.      0.      0.222  0.444  0.333]
```

In the first case, the probabilities seem to drain out of the network — the effect of a dead-end website and the resulting substochastic transition matrix. In the second case, the bottom half of the network unfairly gets all the importance, leaving the top part as insignificant.

Introducing boredom and teleporting

Both dead ends (*rank sinks*) and spider traps (*cycles*) are common situations on the web because of users' choices and spammers' actions. The problem, however, is easily solved by making the random surfer randomly jump to another network node (*teleporting*, as in the sci-fi devices that take you instantaneously from one place to another). The theory is that a surfer will get bored at one point or another and move away from deadlocking situations. Mathematically, you define an alpha value representing the probability of continuing the random journey on the graph by the surfer. The alpha value redistributes the probability of being on a node independently of the transition matrix.

TIP

The value originally suggested by Brin and Page for alpha (also called the damping factor) is 0.85, but you can change it according to your needs. For the web, it works the best between 0.8 and 0.9 and you can read why this is the best value range at `https://www.cise.ufl.edu/~adobra/DaMn/talks/damn05-santini.pdf`. The smaller the alpha value, the shorter the trip of the surfer on the network, on average, before restarting somewhere else.

```
def PageRank_teleporting(graph, iters = 50, alpha=0.85,
                         rounding=3):
    G, p = initialize_PageRank(graph)
    u = np.ones(len(p)) / float(len(p))
    for i in range(iters):
        p = alpha * np.dot(G,p) + (1.0 - alpha) * u
    return np.round(p / np.sum(p), rounding)
```

```
print('Graph A:', PageRank_teleporting(Graph_A,
                                        rounding=8))
print('Graph B:', PageRank_teleporting(Graph_B,
                                        rounding=8))
print('Graph C:', PageRank_teleporting(Graph_C,
                                        rounding=8))

Graph A: [ 0.15477863   0.15346061   0.22122243   0.15477863
           0.15787985   0.15787985]
Warning: G is substochastic
Graph B: [ 0.16502904   0.14922238   0.11627717   0.16502904
           0.20222118   0.20222118]
Graph C: [ 0.0598128    0.08523323   0.12286869   0.18996342
           0.30623677   0.23588508]
```

After applying the modifications to a new function, `PageRank_teleporting`, you can get similar estimates for the first graph and much more realistic (and useful) estimates for both the second and third graphs, without falling into the traps of dead ends or rank sinks. Interestingly, the function is equivalent to the one provided by NetworkX: `http://networkx.readthedocs.io/en/networkx-1.11/ reference/generated/networkx.algorithms.link_analysis.pagerank_alg. pagerank.html`.

```
nx.pagerank(Graph_A, alpha=0.85)

{1: 0.15477892494151968,
 2: 0.1534602056628941,
 3: 0.2212224378270561,
 4: 0.15477892494151968,
 5: 0.1578797533135051,
 6: 0.15787975331350507}
```

Looking inside the life of a search engine

Though it only reports on the web hyperlink structure, PageRank reveals how authoritative a page can become. However, Google isn't composed only of PageRank. The algorithm provides solid foundations for any query, and it initially bootstrapped Google's fame as a reliable search engine. Today, PageRank is just one of the many ranking factors that intervene when processing a query.

Specialized sources in SEO knowledge quote more than 200 factors as contributing to the results that Google provides. To see what other sorts of ranking factors Google considers, consult the list at `https://moz.com/search-ranking-factors`

(made by MOZ, a U.S. company). You can also download the yearly reports from `http://www.searchmetrics.com/knowledge-base/ranking-factors/`, by Searchmetrics, a German company from Berlin specializing in SEO software.

You must also consider that the Google algorithm has received many updates, and at this point, it's more of an ensemble of different algorithms, each one named with a fantasy name (Caffeine, Panda, Penguin, Hummingbird, Pigeon, Mobile Update). Many of these updates have caused shake-ups of previous search rankings and were motivated by the need to fix spamming techniques or make the surfing the web more useful for users (for instance, the Mobile Update induced many sites to render their interfaces mobile-phone friendly).

Considering other uses of PageRank

Although PageRank provides better search results, its applicability isn't limited to Google or search engines. You can use PageRank anywhere you can reduce your problem to a graph. Just modify and tune the algorithm to your needs. Cornell University has enumerated some other potential uses of PageRank in different sectors (`https://blogs.cornell.edu/info2040/2014/11/03/more-than-just-a-web-search-algorithm-googles-pagerank-in-non-internet-contexts/`), and surprising reports have emerged of the algorithm being successfully used in computational biology (`https://www.wired.com/2009/09/googlefoodwebs/`). By creating a teleportation tied to specific nodes that you want to explore, you see the algorithm shining at diverse applications such as the following:

>> **Fraud detection:** Revealing how certain persons and facts are related in unexpected ways

>> **Product recommendation:** Suggesting products that a person with a certain affinity might like

Going Beyond the PageRank Paradigm

In recent years, Google has done more than introduce more ranking factors that modify the original PageRank algorithm. It has introduced some radical changes that leverage page content better (to avoid being fooled by the presence of certain keywords) and has adopted AI algorithms that rank the relevance of a page in a search result autonomously. These changes have led some search experts to declare that PageRank doesn't determine the position of a page in a search any longer (see `https://www.entrepreneur.com/article/269574`). They still debate the question, but it's most likely safe to assume that PageRank is still powering the Google engine as a ranking factor, albeit not sufficiently to enlist a page into the best results after a query.

Introducing semantic queries

If you currently try to pose questions, not just chains of keywords, to Google, you'll notice that it tends to answer smartly and gets the sense of question. Since 2012, Google became better able to understand synonyms and concepts. However, after August 2013, with the Hummingbird update (http://searchengineland. com/google-hummingbird-172816), the search engine became capable of understanding conversational searches (queries in which you ask something as you would say it to another person) as well as the semantics behind queries and a page's contents.

Since this update, the Google algorithm works by disambiguating both users' intentions and the meanings expressed by pages, not just by the keywords. Now, the search engine works more in a semantic way, which means understanding what words imply on both sides: the query and resulting web pages. In this sense, it can't be tricked anymore by playing with keywords. Even without much support from PageRank, it can look at how a page is written and get a sense of whether the page contains good enough content for inclusion in the results of a query.

Using AI for ranking search results

PageRank is still at the core, but the results have less weight because of the introduction of machine learning technology into ranking, the so-called RankBrain. According to some sources (see https://www.bloomberg.com/news/articles/ 2015-10-26/google-turning-its-lucrative-web-search-over-to-ai- machines), the machine learning algorithm now examines all Google queries and directly handles 15 percent of the volume of search queries it receives every day, specializing in

>> Ambiguous and unclear search queries

>> Queries expressed in slang or colloquial terms

>> Queries expressed as though they were occurring in a conversation with the search engine

Even though RankBrain is still cloaked in secrecy, the algorithm seems to be capable of guessing, with much higher accuracy than performed by a human being, whether the contents of a page can appear in search results. It replaces all other ranking factors in cases that are difficult to judge. This is another example of an additional algorithm that limits the role played by the original PageRank algorithm.

4

Struggling with Big Data

Interact with large datasets.

Work with streamed data to use even larger datasets.

Perform tasks in parallel to perform management and analysis tasks faster.

Encode data to reduce redundancies and to keep data safe.

Compress and decompress data using the LZW algorithm.

Chapter **12**

Managing Big Data

M ore than a buzzword used by vendors to propose innovative ways to store data and analyze it, big data is a reality and a driving force of our times. You may have heard it mentioned in many specialized scientific and business publications and even wondered what big data really means. From a technical point of view, big data refers to large and complex amounts of computer data, so large (as the name implies) and intricate that the data cannot be dealt with by making more storage available on your computers or by making new computers more powerful and faster in their computations. Big data implies a revolution in the way you store and deal with data.

However, this copious and sophisticated store of data didn't appear suddenly. It took time to develop the technology to store this amount of data. In addition, it took time to spread the technology that generates and delivers data, namely computers, sensors, smart mobile phones, the Internet, and its World Wide Web services. This chapter discusses what drives this huge data production.

Even though it took time to build this much data, technology changes in recent years have finally helped people realize the potential game changer that having huge amounts of data (of any nature) at hand represents. For centuries, humans have emphasized the power of the human intellect in determining the causes and forces driving the natural world using a few accurate observations (small data).

Humans also developed a method, the scientific method, that is at the foundation of our modern world based on scientific discovery. Suddenly people have found (with a certain surprise) that they can solve problems earlier and more successfully by learning the solution from large amounts of data rather than spending long years developing and elaborating theories using well-designed tests and experiments.

Simply having data won't find solutions to the many problems still afflicting civilization. However, having enough data, which actually equates to incredible amounts of it, and the right algorithm enables people to connect the dots between thousands and thousands of hints. Big data and algorithms enable access to wondrous new scientific (but also practical and business) discoveries.

Transforming Power into Data

In 1965, Gordon Moore, cofounder of Intel and Fairchild Semiconductor (two giant companies that produce electronic components for electronics and computers), stated in an *Electronics* magazine paper entitled "Cramming More Components Onto Integrated Circuits" that the number of components found in integrated circuits would double every year for the next decade. At that time, transistors dominated electronics. Being able to stuff more transistors into a circuit using a single electronic component that gathered the functionalities of many of them (an integrated circuit), meant being able to make electronic devices more capable and useful. This process is *integration* and implies a strong process of electronics miniaturization (making the same circuit much smaller, which makes sense because the same volume should contain double the circuitry as the previous year).

As miniaturization proceeds, electronic devices, the final product of the process, become smaller or simply more powerful. For instance, today's computers aren't all that much smaller than computers of a decade ago, yet they are decisively more powerful. The same goes for mobile phones. Even though they're the same size as their predecessors, they have become able to perform more tasks. Other devices, such as sensors, are simply smaller, which means that you can put them everywhere.

Understanding Moore's implications

What Moore stated in that article actually proved true for many years, and the semiconductor industry calls it Moore's Law (see http://www.mooreslaw.org/ for details). Doubling did occur for the first ten years, as predicted. In 1975, Moore corrected his statement, forecasting a doubling every two years. Figure 12-1 shows the effects of this doubling. This rate of doubling is still valid, although now it's common opinion that it won't hold longer than the end of the present decade (up to about 2020). Starting in 2012, a mismatch occurs between the expectation of cramming more transistors into a component to make it faster and what semiconductor companies can achieve with regard to miniaturization. In truth, physical barriers exist to integrating more circuitry into an integrated circuit using the present silica components. (However, innovation will continue; you can read the article at http://www.nature.com/news/the-chips-are-down-for-moore-s-law-1.19338 for more details.) In addition, Moore's Law isn't actually a law. Physical laws, such as the law of universal gravitation (which explains why things are attracted to the ground as discovered by Newton), are based on proofs of various sorts that have received peer review for their accuracy. Moore's Law isn't anything more than mere observation, or even a tentative goal for the industry to strive to achieve (a self-fulfilling prophecy, in a certain sense).

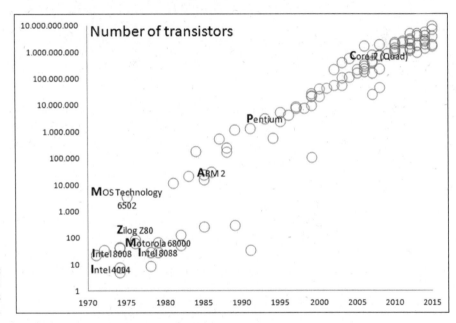

FIGURE 12-1:
Stuffing more and more transistors into a CPU.

In the future, Moore's Law may not apply anymore because industry will switch to new technology (such as making components by using optical lasers instead of transistors; see the article at http://www.extremetech.com/extreme/187746-by-2020-you-could-have-an-exascale-speed-of-light-optical-computer-on-your-desk for details about optical computing). What matters is that since 1965, about every two years the computer industry experienced great advancements in digital electronics that had consequences.

CONSIDERING THE POLITICAL ASPECTS OF VARIOUS LAWS

Depending on whom you talk with, the whole issue of whether a law will stand the test of time can look different because that person will have a different perspective. This book isn't here to convince you of one point of view or another, but simply reports the prevalent view. For example, it's possible to argue that Moore's Law is every bit proven as the laws of thermodynamics. If you look into conventional physics more, you can find many discrepancies with its laws and many of its assumptions. It's not a matter of devaluing science in any way — just pinpointing the fact that everything in science, including its laws, is a work in progress.

As to whether Moore's Law will cease to exist, generally speaking, laws don't stop applying; scientists refurbish them so that they are more general. Moore's Law may undergo the same transformation. Linear or overly simplistic laws rarely apply in a general sense because there are no straight lines anywhere in nature, including its temporal models. Therefore, the most likely scenario is that Moore's Law will change into a more sigmoidal function in an attempt to adhere to reality.

REMEMBER

Some advocate that Moore's Law already no longer holds. The chip industry has kept up the promise so far, but now it's lowering expectations. Intel has already increased the time between its generations of CPUs, saying that in five years, chip miniaturization will hit a wall. You can read this interesting story on the MIT Technology Review at https://www.technologyreview.com/s/601441/moores-law-is-dead-now-what/.

Moore's Law has a direct effect on data. It begins with smarter devices. The smarter the devices, the more diffusion (electronics are everywhere in our day and age). The greater the diffusion, the lower the price becomes, creating an endless loop that drove and is driving the use of powerful computing machines and small sensors everywhere. With large amounts of computer memory available and larger storage disks for data, the consequences are an expansion of the availability of data, such as websites, transaction records, a host of various measurements, digital images, and other sorts of data flooding from everywhere.

Finding data everywhere

Scientists began fighting against impressive amounts of data for years before anyone coined the term *big data*. At this point, the Internet didn't produce the vast sums for data that it does today. It's useful to remember that big data is not just simply a fad created by software and hardware vendors but has a basis in many of the following fields:

» **Astronomy:** Consider the data received from spacecraft on a mission (such as Voyager or Galileo) and all the data received from radio telescopes, which are specialized antennas used to receive radio waves from astronomical bodies. A common example is the Search for Extraterrestrial Intelligence (SETI) project (http://www.seti.org/), which looks for extraterrestrial signals by observing radio frequencies arriving from space. The amount of data received and the computer power used to analyze a portion of the sky for a single hour is impressive (http://www.setileague.org/askdr/howmuch.htm). If aliens are out there, it's very hard to spot them. (The movie *Contact* https://www.amazon.com/exec/obidos/ASIN/B002GHHHKQ/datacservip0f-20/ explores what could happen should humans actually intercept a signal.)

» **Meteorology:** Think about trying to predict weather for the near term given the large number of required measures, such as temperature, atmospheric pressure, humidity, winds, and precipitation at different times, locations, and altitudes. Weather forecasting is really one of the first problems in big data and quite a relevant one. According to Weather Analytics, a company that provides climate data, more than 33 percent of Worldwide Gross Domestic Product (GDP) is determined by how weather conditions affect agriculture, fishing, tourism, and transportation, just to name a few. Dating back to the 1950s, the first supercomputers of the time were used to crunch as much data as possible because, in meteorology, the more data, the more accurate the forecast. That's the reason everyone is amassing more storage and processing capacity, as you can read in this story regarding the Korean Meteorological Association https://www.wired.com/insights/2013/02/how-big-data-can-boost-weather-forecasting/ for weather forecasting and studying climate change.

» **Physics:** Consider the large amounts of data produced by experiments using particle accelerators in an attempt to determine the structure of matter, space, and time. For example, the Large Hadron Collider (https://home.cern/topics/large-hadron-collider), the largest particle accelerator ever created, produces 15PB (petabytes) of data every year as a result of particle collisions (http://home.web.cern.ch/about/computing).

» **Genomics:** Sequencing a single DNA strand, which means determining the precise order of the many combinations of the four bases — adenine, guanine, cytosine, and thymine — that constitute the structure of the molecule, requires quite a lot of data. For instance, a single chromosome, a structure containing the DNA in the cell, may require from 50MB to 300MB. A human being has 46 chromosomes, and the DNA data for just one person consumes an entire DVD. Just imagine the massive storage required to document the DNA data of a large number of people or to sequence other life forms on earth (https://www.wired.com/2013/10/big-data-biology/).

>> **Oceanography:** Because of the many sensors placed in the oceans to measure temperature, currents, and, using hydrophones, even sounds for acoustic monitoring for scientific purposes (discovering about fish, whales, and plankton) and military defense purposes (finding sneaky submarines from other countries). You can have a sneak peek at this old surveillance problem, which is turning more complex and digital, by reading this article: `http://www.theatlantic.com/technology/archive/2014/08/listening-in-the-navy-is-tracking-ocean-sounds-collected-by-scientists/378630/`.

>> **Satellites:** Recording images from the entire globe and sending them back to earth in order to monitor the Earth's surface and its atmosphere isn't a new business (TIROS 1, the first satellite to send back images and data, dates back to 1960). Over the years, however, the world has launched more than 1,400 active satellites that provide earth observation. The amount of data arriving on earth is astonishing and serves both military (surveillance) and civilian purposes, such as tracking economic development, monitoring agriculture, and monitoring changes and risks. A single European Space Agency's satellite, Sentinel 1A, generates 5PB of data during two years of operation, as you can read at `https://spaceflightnow.com/2016/04/28/europes-sentinel-satellites-generating-huge-big-data-archive/`).

Accompanying these older data trends, new amounts of data are now generated or carried about by the Internet, creating new issues and requiring solutions in terms of both data storage and algorithms for processing:

>> As reported by the National Security Agency (NSA), the amount of information flowing through the Internet every day from all over the world amounted to 1,826PB of data in 2013, and 1.6 percent of it consisted of e-mails and telephone calls. To assure national security, the NSA must verify the content of at least 0.025 percent of all emails and phone calls (looking for key words that could signal something like a terrorist plot). That still amounts to 25PB per year, which equates to 37,500 CD-ROMs every year of data stored and analyzed (and that's growing). You can read the full story at `http://www.business-standard.com/article/news-ani/nsa-claims-analysts-look-at-only-0-00004-of-world-s-internet-traffic-for-surveillance-113081100075_1.html`.

>> The Internet of Things (IoT) is becoming a reality. You may have heard the term many times in the last 15 years, but now the growth of the stuff connected to the Internet is going to explode. The idea is to put sensors and transmitters on everything and use the data to both better control what happens in the world and to make objects smarter. Transmitting devices are getting tinier, cheaper and less power demanding; some are already so small that they can be put everywhere. (Just look at the ant-sized radio developed by

Stanford engineers at `http://news.stanford.edu/news/2014/september/ant-radio-arbabian-090914.html`.) Experts estimate that by 2020, there will be six times as many connected things on earth as there will be people, but many research companies and think tanks are already revisiting those figures (`http://www.gartner.com/newsroom/id/3165317`).

Getting algorithms into business

The human race is now at an incredible intersection of unprecedented volumes of data, generated by increasingly smaller and powerful hardware, and analyzed by algorithms that this same process helped develop. It's not simply a matter of volume, which by itself is a difficult challenge. As formalized by the research company Gartner in 2001 and then reprised and expanded by other companies, such as IBM, big data can be summarized by four Vs representing its key characteristics (you can read more on this topic at `http://www.ibmbigdatahub.com/infographic/four-vs-big-data`):

>> **Volume:** The amount of data

>> **Velocity:** The speed of data generation

>> **Variety:** The number and types of data sources

>> **Veracity:** The quality and authoritative voice of the data (quantifying errors, bad data, and noise mixed with signals), a measure of the uncertainty of the data

TIP

Each big data characteristic offers a challenge and an opportunity. For instance, volume considers the amount of useful data. What one organization considers big data could be small data for another one. The inability to process the data on a single machine doesn't make the data big. What differentiates big data from the business-as-usual data is that it forces an organization to revise its prevalent methods and solutions, and pushes present technologies and algorithms to look ahead.

Variety enables the use of big data to challenge the scientific method, as explained by this milestone and much discussed article written by Chris Anderson, *Wired*'s editor-in-chief at the time, on how large amounts of data can help scientific discoveries outside the scientific method: `https://www.wired.com/2008/06/pb-theory/`. The author relies on the example of Google in the advertising and translation business sectors, where the company could achieve prominence without using specific models or theories, but by applying algorithms to learn from data. As in advertising, science (physics, biology) data can support innovation that allows scientists to approach problems without hypotheses but by considering the variations found in large amounts of data and by discovery algorithms.

The veracity characteristic helps the democratization of data itself. In the past, organizations hoarded data because it was precious and difficult to obtain. At this point, various sources create data in such growing amounts that hoarding it is meaningless (90 percent of the world's data has been created in the last two years), so there is no reason to limit access. Data is turning into such a commodity that there are many open data programs going all around the world. (The United States has a long tradition of open access; the first open data programs date back to the 1970s when the National Oceanic and Atmospheric Administration, NOAA, started releasing weather data freely to the public.) However, because data has become a commodity, the uncertainty of that data has become an issue. You no longer know whether the data is completely true because you may not even know its source.

REMEMBER

Data has become so ubiquitous that its value is no longer in the actual information (such as data stored in a firm's database). The value of data exists in how you use it. Here algorithms come into play and change the game. A company like Google feeds itself from freely available data, such as the content of websites or the text found in publicly available texts and books. Yet, the value Google extracts from the data mostly derives from its algorithms. As an example, data value resides in the PageRank algorithm (illustrated in Chapter 11), which is the very foundation of Google's business. The value of algorithms is true for other companies as well. Amazon's recommendation engine contributes a significant part of the company's revenues. Many financial firms use algorithmic trading and robo-advice, leveraging freely available stock data and economic information for investments.

Streaming Flows of Data

When data flows in huge amounts, storing it all may be difficult or even impossible. In fact, storing it all might not even be useful. Here are some figures of just some of what you can expect to happen within a single minute on the Internet:

>> 150 million e-mails sent

>> 350,000 new tweets sent on Twitter

>> 2.4 million queries requested on Google

>> 700,000 people logged in to their account on Facebook

Given such volumes, accumulating the data all day for incremental analysis might not seem efficient. You simply store it away somewhere and analyze it on the following or on a later day (which is the widespread archival strategy that's typical of databases and data warehouses). However, useful data queries tend to ask about the most recent data in the stream, and data becomes less useful when it ages (in some sectors, such as financial, a day can be a lot of time).

Moreover, you can expect even more data to arrive tomorrow (the amount of data increases daily) and that makes it difficult, if not impossible, to pull data from repositories as you push new data in. Pulling old data from repositories as fresh data pours in is akin to the punishment of Sisyphus. Sisyphus, as a Greek myth narrates, received a terrible punishment from the god Zeus: Being forced to eternally roll an immense boulder up on the top of a hill, only to watch it roll back down each time (see `http://www.mythweb.com/encyc/entries/sisyphus.html` for additional details).

Sometimes, rendering things even more impossible to handle, data can arrive so fast and in such large quantities that writing it to disk is impossible: New information arrives faster than the time required to write it to the hard disk. This is a problem typical of particle experiments with particle accelerators such as the Large Hadron Collider, requiring scientists to decide what data to keep (`http://home.cern/about/computing/processing-what-record`). Of course, you may queue data for some time, but not for too long, because the queue will quickly grow and become impossible to maintain. For instance, if kept in memory, queue data will soon lead to an out-of-memory error.

Because new data flows may render the previous processing on old data obsolete, and procrastination is not a solution, people have devised multiple strategies to deal instantaneously with massive and changeable data amounts. People use three ways to deal with large amounts of data:

>> **Stored:** Some data is stored because it may help answer unclear questions later. This method relies on techniques to store it immediately and analyze it later very fast, no matter how massive it is.

>> **Summarized:** Some data is summarized because keeping it all as it is makes no sense; only the important data is kept.

>> **Consumed:** The remaining data is consumed because its usage is predetermined. Algorithms can instantly read, digest, and turn the data into information. After that, the system forgets the data forever.

The book deals with the first point in Chapter 13, which is about distributing data among multiple computers and understanding the algorithms used to deal with it (a divide-and-conquer strategy). The following sections address the second and third points, applying them to data that streams in systems.

TIP

When talking of massive data arriving into a computer system, you will often hear it compared to water: streaming data, data streams, data fire hose.

You discover how data streams is like consuming tap water: Opening the tap lets you store the water in cups or drinking bottles, or you can use it for cooking, scrubbing food, cleaning plates, or washing hands. In any case, most or all of the water is gone, yet it proves very useful and indeed vital.

Analyzing streams with the right recipe

Streaming data needs streaming algorithms, and the key thing to know about streaming algorithms is that, apart a few measures that it can compute exactly, a streaming algorithm necessarily provides approximate results. The algorithm output is almost correct, guessing not the precisely right answer, but close to it.

When dealing with streams, you clearly have to concentrate only on the measures of interest and leave out many details. You could be interested in a statistical measurement, such as mean, minimum, or maximum. Moreover, you could want to count elements in the stream or distinguish old information from new. There are many algorithms to use, depending on the problem, yet the recipes always use the same ingredients. The trick of cooking the perfect stream is to use one or all of these algorithmic tools as ingredients:

>> **Sampling:** Reduce your stream to a more manageable data size; represent the entire stream or the most recent observations using a shifting data window.

>> **Hashing:** Reduce infinite stream variety to a limited set of simple integer numbers (as seen in the "Relying on Hashing" section of Chapter 7).

>> **Sketching:** Create a short summary of the measure you need, removing the less useful details. This approach lets you leverage a simple working storage, which can be your computer's main memory or its hard disk.

Another characteristic to keep in mind about algorithms operating on streams is their simplicity and low computational complexity. Data streams can be quite fast. Algorithms that require too many calculations can miss essential data, which means that the data is gone forever. When you view the situation in this light, you can appreciate how hash functions prove useful because they're prompt in transforming inputs into something easier to handle and search because for both operations, complexity is $O(1)$. You can also appreciate the sketching and sampling techniques, which bring about the idea of *lossy compression* (more on compression in Chapter 14). Lossy compression enables you to represent something complex by using a simpler form. You lose some detail but save a great deal of computer time and storage.

Sampling means drawing a limited set of examples from your stream and treating them as if they represented the entire stream. It is a well-known tool in statistics through which you can make inferences on a larger context (technically called the *universe* or the *population*) by using a small part of it.

Reserving the right data

Statistics was born in a time when obtaining a census was impossible. A *census* is a systematic investigation on a population, counting it, and acquiring useful data from it. The government asks all the people in a country about where they live, their family, their daily life, and their work. The census has its origins in ancient times. In the Bible, a census occurs in the book of Numbers; the Israelite population is counted after the exodus from Egypt. For tax purposes, the ancient Romans periodically held a census to count the population of their large empire. Historical documents provide accounts of similar census activities in ancient Egypt, Greece, India, and China.

Statistics, in particular the branch of statistics called inferential statistics, can achieve the same outcome as a census, with an acceptable margin of error, by interrogating a smaller number of individuals (called a *sample*). Thus, by querying a few people, pollsters can determine the general opinion of a larger population on a variety of issues, such as who will win an election. In the United States, for instance, the statistician Nate Silver made news by predicting the winner of the 2012 presidential election in all 50 states, using data from samples (https://www.cnet.com/news/obamas-win-a-big-vindication-for-nate-silver-king-of-the-quants/).

Clearly, holding a census implies huge costs (the larger the population, the greater the costs) and requires a lot of organization (which is why censuses are infrequent), whereas a statistical sample is faster and cheaper. Reduced costs and lower organizational requirements also make statistics ideal for big data streaming: Users of big data streaming don't need every scrap of information and they can summarize the data's complexity.

However, there's a problem with using statistical samples. At the core of statistics is sampling, and sampling requires randomly picking a few examples from the pool of the entire population. The key element of the recipe is that every element from the population has exactly the same probability of being part of the sample. If a population consists of a million people and your sample size is one, each person's probability of being part of the sample is one out of a million. In mathematical terms, if you represent the population using the variable N and the sample size is n, the probability of being part of a sample is n/N, as shown in Figure 12-2. The represented sample is a *simple random sample*. (Other sample types have greater complexity; this is the simplest sample type and all the others build upon it.)

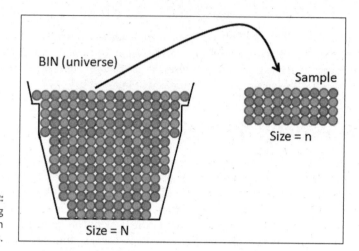

FIGURE 12-2:
How sampling from an urn works.

Using a simple random sample is just like playing the lottery, but you need to have all the numbers inside an urn in order to extract a few to represent the whole. You can't easily put data streams into a repository from which you can extract a sample; instead, you have to extract your sample on the fly. What you really need is another sample type named *reservoir sampling.* Just as a reservoir retains water for later use, yet its water isn't still because some enters and some leaves, so this algorithm works by randomly choosing elements to keep as samples until other elements arrive to replace them.

The reservoir sampling algorithm is more sophisticated than another algorithmic strategy, called *windowing,* in which you create a queue and let new elements enter the queue (see Figure 12-3). Older elements leave the queue based on a trigger. This method applies when you want reports from the stream at exact time intervals. For instance, you may want to know how many pages users request from an Internet server each minute. Using windowing, you start queuing page requests a minute of time, count the elements in the queue, report the number, discard the content of the queue, and start queuing again.

Another motivation for using windowing is to have a fixed amount of the most recent data. In that case, every time you insert an element into the queue, the oldest element leaves. A queue is a First In, First Out (FIFO) structure discussed in Chapter 6.

Windowing looks at samples using a sliding window — it shows the elements under the window, which represent a certain time slice or a certain segment of the stream. Reservoir sampling represents the entire stream scope instead by offering a manageable amount of data, which is a statistical sample of the stream.

FIGURE 12-3:
An example of
windowing
a stream of
DNA data.

Here is how reservoir sample works: Given a stream of data, containing many elements, you initialize the reservoir sample with elements taken from the stream until the sample is complete. For instance, if the sample contains 1,000 elements, a number that usually fits in the computer's internal memory, you start by picking the first 1,000 stream elements. The number of elements you want in the sample is k, and k implies a sample that fits into the computer's memory. At the point when you reserve the first k stream elements, the algorithm starts making its selections:

1. From the beginning of the stream, the algorithm counts every new element that arrives. It tracks the counting using the variable named as n. When the algorithm gets into action, the value of n is equivalent to k.

2. Now, new elements arrive, and they increment the value of n. A new element arriving from the stream has a probability of being inserted into the reservoir sample of k/n and probability of not being inserted equal to (1 – k/n).

3. The probability is verified for each new element arriving. It's like a lottery: If the probability is verified, the new element is inserted. On the other hand, if it isn't inserted, the new element is discarded. If it's inserted, the algorithm discards an old element in the sample according to some rule (the easiest being to pick an old element at random) and replaces it with the new element.

The following code shows a simple example in Python so that you can see this algorithm in action. The example relies on a sequence of alphabet letters (pretend that they are a data stream) and creates a sample of five elements. (You can find this code in the A4D; 12; Managing Big Data.ipynb file on the Dummies site as part of the downloadable code; see the Introduction for details.)

```
import string
datastream = list(string.ascii_uppercase) + list(
    string.ascii_lowercase)
print(datastream)
```

```
['A', 'B', 'C', 'D', 'E', 'F', 'G', 'H', 'I', 'J', 'K', 'L',
 'M', 'N', 'O', 'P', 'Q', 'R', 'S', 'T', 'U', 'V', 'W', 'X',
 'Y', 'Z', 'a', 'b', 'c', 'd', 'e', 'f', 'g', 'h', 'i', 'j',
 'k', 'l', 'm', 'n', 'o', 'p', 'q', 'r', 's', 't', 'u', 'v',
 'w', 'x', 'y', 'z']
```

Apart from strings, the example uses functions from the random package to create a seed (for stable and replicable solutions) and, drawing a random integer number, it checks whether it needs to change an element in the reservoir. Apart from the seed value, you can experiment with modifying the sample size or even feeding the algorithm a different stream (it should be in a Python list for the example to work correctly).

```
from random import seed, randint
seed(9) # change this value for different results
sample_size = 5
sample = []

for index, element in enumerate(datastream):
        # Until the reservoir is filled, we add elements
        if index < sample_size:
                sample.append(element)
        else:
                # Having filled the reservoir, we test a
                # random replacement based on the elements
                # seen in the data stream
                drawn = randint(0, index)
                # If the drawn number is less or equal the
                # sample size, we replace a previous
                # element with the one arriving from the
                # stream
                if drawn < sample_size:
                        sample[drawn] = element

print (sample)

['y', 'e', 'v', 'F', 'i']
```

This procedure assures you that, at any time, your reservoir sample is a good sample representing the overall data stream. In this implementation, the variable index plays the role of n and the variable sample_size acts as k. Note two particular aspects of this algorithm:

>> As the variable `index` grows, because the stream floods with data, the probability of being part of the sample decreases. Consequently, at the beginning of the stream, many elements enter and leave the sample, but the rate of change decreases as the stream continues to flow.

>> If you check the probability at which each element present in the sample enters, and you average them all, the average will approximate the probability of an element of a population's being picked into a sample, which is k/n.

Sketching an Answer from Stream Data

Sampling is an excellent strategy for dealing with streams but it doesn't answer all the questions you may have from your data stream. For instance, a sample can't tell you when you've already seen a stream element because the sample doesn't contain all the stream information. The same holds true for problems such as counting the distinct number of elements in a stream or computing element frequency.

To achieve such results, you need hash functions (as seen in Chapter 7) and sketches, which are simple and approximate data summaries. The following sections start with hashes, and you discover how to be correct in finding when an arriving stream element has appeared before, even if your stream is infinite and you cannot keep exact memory of everything that flowed before.

Filtering stream elements by heart

At the heart of many streaming algorithms are Bloom filters. Created almost 50 years ago by Burton H. Bloom, at a time when computer science was still quite young, the original intent of this algorithm's creator was to trade space (memory) and/or time (complexity) against what he called *allowable errors.* His original paper is entitled *Space/Time Trade-offs in Hash Coding with Allowable Errors* (see: `http://citeseerx.ist.psu.edu/viewdoc/summary?doi=10.1.1.20.2080&rank=2` for details).

You may wonder about the space and time that Bloom considers motivators for his algorithm. Imagine that you need to determine whether an element has already appeared in a stream using some previously discussed data structure. Finding something in a stream implies recording and searching are fast, thus a hash table seems an ideal choice. *Hash tables,* as discussed in Chapter 7, simply require adding the elements that you want to record and storing them. Recovering an element from a hash table is fast because the hash table uses easily manipulated values to represent the element, rather than the element itself (which could be quite complex). Yet, storing both elements and an index to those elements has limitations. If a hash table faces more elements than it can handle, such as the elements in a continuous and potentially infinite stream, you'll end up incurring memory problems at some point.

REMEMBER

An essential consideration for Bloom filters is that false positives can occur, but false negatives can't. For example, a data stream might contain real-time monitoring data for a power plant. When using a Bloom filter, the analysis of the data stream would show that expected readings are probably part of the set of allowed readings, with some errors allowed. However, when an error occurs in the system, the same analysis shows that the readings aren't part of the set of allowed readings. The false positives are unlikely to cause problems, but the absence of false negatives means that everyone remains safe. Because of the potential for false positives, filters such as the Bloom filter are probabilistic data structures — they don't provide a certain answer but a probable one.

REMEMBER

Hashes, the individual entries in a hash table, are fast because they act like the index of a book. You use a *hash function* to produce the hash; the input is an element containing complex data, and the output is a simple number that acts as an index to that element. A hash function is deterministic because it produces the same number every time you feed it a specific data input. You use the hash to locate the complex information you need. Bloom filters are helpful because they are a frugal way to record traces of many elements without having to store them away as a hash table does. They work in a simple way and use the following as main ingredients:

>> **A bit vector:** A list of bit elements, where each bit in the element can have a value of 0 or 1. The list is a long number of bits called m. The greater m is, the better, though there are ways of optimally defining its size.

>> **A series of hash functions:** Each hash function represents a different value. The hash functions can quickly crunch data and produce uniformly distributed results, which are results equally ranging from the minimum to the maximum output values of the hash.

Adding elements to Bloom filters

Generally, you create Bloom filters of a fixed size (recently developed versions allow you to resize the filter). You operate them by adding new elements to the filter and looking them up when already present. It's not possible to remove an element from the filter after adding it (the filter has an indelible memory). When adding an element to a bit vector, the bit vector has some bits set to 1, as shown in Figure 12-4. In this case, the Bloom filter adds X to the bit vector.

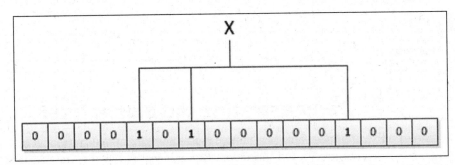

FIGURE 12-4:
Adding a single element to a bit vector.

You can add as many elements as is necessary to the bit vector. For example, Figure 12-5 shows what happens when adding another element, Y, to the bit vector. Note that bit 7 is the same for both X and Y. Consequently, bit 7 represents a collision between X and Y. These collisions are the source of the potential false positives; because of them, the algorithm could say that an element is already added to the bit vector when it isn't. Using a larger bit vector makes collisions less likely and improves the performance of the Bloom filter, but does so at the cost of both space and time.

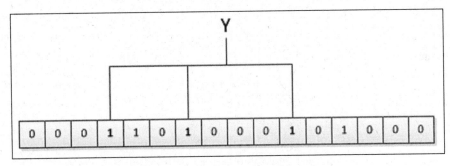

FIGURE 12-5:
Adding a second element can cause collisions.

Searching a Bloom filter for an element

Searching a Bloom filter lets you determine whether a particular element appears in the bit vector. During the search process, the algorithm looks for the presence of a 0 in the bit vector. For example, the previous section added elements X and Y to the bit vector. In searching for element Z, the algorithm finds a 0 in the second bit, as shown in Figure 12-6. The presence of a 0 means that Z isn't part of the bit vector.

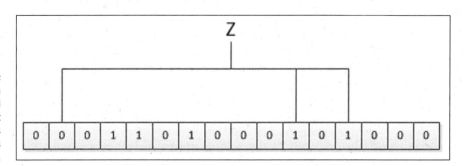

FIGURE 12-6:
Locating an
element and
determining that
it exists means
searching for 0s
in the bit vector.

Demonstrating the Bloom filter

This example uses Python to demonstrate a Bloom filter and shows the result with
a graphical visualization. Say that you're using a crawler, which is specialized
software that journeys the web to check whether something has changed in the
monitored websites (which may imply copying part of the website's data, an
activity known as *scraping*). The example uses a short bit vector and three hash
functions, which isn't the best setting for handling a large number of elements
(the bit vector will get filled quickly), but enough for a working example.

```python
hash_functions = 3
bit_vector_length = 10
bit_vector = [0] * bit_vector_length

from hashlib import md5, sha1

def hash_f(element, i, length):
    """ This is a magic function """
    h1 = int(md5(element.encode('ascii')).hexdigest(),16)
    h2 = int(sha1(element.encode('ascii')).hexdigest(),16)
    return (h1 + i*h2) % length

def insert_filter(website):
    result = list()
    for hash_number in range(hash_functions):
        position = hash_f(website, hash_number,
                          bit_vector_length)
        result.append(position)
        bit_vector[position] = 1
    print ('Inserted in positions: %s' % result)

def check_filter(website):
    result = list()
    for hash_number in range(hash_functions):
```

```
        position = hash_f(website, hash_number,
                          bit_vector_length)
        result.append((position,bit_vector[position]))
    print ('Bytes in positions: %s' % result)
```

The code begins by creating a bit vector and some functions that can do the following:

>> Generate multiple hash functions (using the double hash trick mentioned in Chapter 7) based on the md5 and sha1 hashing algorithms

>> Insert an object into the bit vector

>> Check whether the bytes relative to an object in the bit vector are turned on

All these elements together constitute a Bloom filter (though the bit vector is the key part of it). This example has the crawler first visiting the website wikipedia. org to take some information from a few pages:

```
insert_filter('wikipedia.org')
print (bit_vector)

Inserted in positions: [0, 8, 6]
[1, 0, 0, 1, 0, 0, 1, 1, 1, 0]
```

That activity turns on the bits in positions 0, 6, and 8 of the bit vector. The example now crawls the youtube.com website (which has some new videos of kittens) and so it inserts the information of the visit into the Bloom filter:

```
insert_filter('youtube.com')
print (bit_vector)

Inserted in positions: [3, 0, 7]
[1, 0, 0, 1, 0, 0, 1, 1, 1, 0]
```

Here the Bloom filter is activated on positions 0, 3, and 7. Given the short length of the bit vector, there is already a collision on position 0, but positions 3 and 7 are completely new. At this point, because the algorithm can't remember what it visited before (but visited sites can be verified using the Bloom filter), the example verifies that it hasn't visited yahoo.com in order to avoid redoing things, as shown in Figure 12-7:

```
check_filter('yahoo.com')

Bytes in positions: [(7, 1), (5, 0), (3, 1)]
```

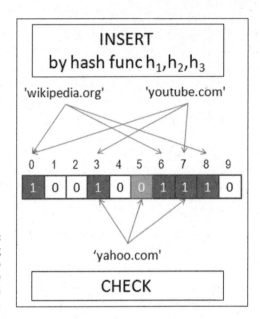

FIGURE 12-7:
Testing
membership
of a website
using a
Bloom filter.

As graphically represented, in this case you can be sure that the example never visited yahoo.com because the Bloom filter reports at least one position, position 5, whose bit was never set on.

TIP

A crawler is often concerned with getting new content from websites and not copying data that it has already recorded and transmitted. Instead of hashing the domain or the address of a single page, you can directly populate a Bloom filter using part of the website content, and you can use it to check the same website for changes later.

There is a simple and straightforward way of decreasing the probability of having a false positive. You just increase the size of the bit vector that is the core of a Bloom filter. More addresses equate fewer chances for a collision by the hash functions' results. Ideally, the size m of the bit vector can be calculated estimating n, the number of distinct objects that you expect to add by keeping m much larger than n. The ideal number k of hash functions to use to minimize collisions can then be estimated using the following formula (ln is the natural logarithm):

$$k = (m/n)*\ln(2)$$

After you have m, n, and k defined, this second formula helps you estimate the probability of a collision (a false positive rate) using a Bloom filter:

$$\text{false positive rate} = (1-\exp(-kn/m))^k$$

If you can't determine n due to the variety of the data in the stream, you have to change m, the bit vector size (which equates to memory space), or k, the number of hash functions (which equates to time), to adjust the false positive rate. The trade-off reflects the relationships that Bloom considers in the original paper between space, time, and probability of an error.

Finding the number of distinct elements

Even though a Bloom filter can track objects arriving from a stream, it can't tell how many objects are there. A bit vector filled by ones can (depending on the number of hashes and the probability of collision) hide the true number of objects being hashed at the same address.

Knowing the distinct number of objects is useful in various situations, such as when you want to know how many distinct users have seen a certain website page or the number of distinct search engine queries. Storing all the elements and finding the duplicates among them can't work with millions of elements, especially coming from a stream. When you want to know the number of distinct objects in a stream, you still have to rely on a hash function, but the approach involves taking a numeric sketch.

Sketching means taking an approximation, that is an inexact yet not completely wrong value as an answer. Approximation is acceptable because the real value is not too far from it. In this smart algorithm, *HyperLogLog*, which is based on probability and approximation, you observe the characteristics of numbers generated from the stream. HyperLogLog derives from the studies of computer scientists Nigel Martin and Philippe Flajolet. Flajolet improved their initial algorithm, *Flajolet–Martin* (or the LogLog algorithm), into the more robust HyperLogLog version, which works like this:

1. A hash converts every element received from the stream into a number.

2. The algorithm converts the number into binary, the base 2 numeric standard that computers use.

3. The algorithm counts the number of initial zeros in the binary number and tracks of the maximum number it sees, which is n.

4. The algorithm estimates the number of distinct elements passed in the stream using n. The number of distinct elements is 2^n.

For instance, the first element in the string is the word *dog*. The algorithm hashes it into an integer value and converts it to binary, with a result of 01101010. Only one zero appears at the beginning of the number, so the algorithm records it as the maximum number of trailing zeros seen. The algorithm then sees the words *parrot* and *wolf*, whose binary equivalents are 11101011 and 01101110, leaving n unchanged. However, when the word *cat* passes, the output is 00101110, so n becomes 2. To estimate the number of distinct elements, the algorithm computes 2^n, that is, 2^2=4. Figure 12-8 shows this process.

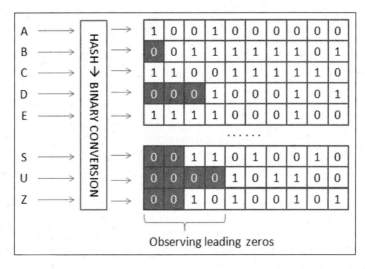

FIGURE 12-8: Counting only leading zeros.

The trick of the algorithm is that if your hash is producing random results, equally distributed (as in a Bloom filter), by looking at the binary representation, you can calculate the probability that a sequence of zeros appeared. Because the probability of a single binary number to be 0 is one in two, for calculating the probability of sequences of zeros, you just multiply that 1/2 probability as many times as the length of the sequence of zeros:

» 50 percent (1/2) probability for numbers starting with 0

» 25 percent (1/2 * 1/2) probability for numbers starting with 00

» 12.5 percent (1/2 * 1/2 * 1/2) probability for numbers starting with 000

» (1/2)^k probability for numbers starting with k zeros (you use powers for faster calculations of many multiplications of the same number)

TIP

The fewer the numbers that HyperLogLog sees, the greater the imprecision. Accuracy increases when you use the HyperLogLog calculation many times using different hash functions and average together the answers from each calculation, but hashing many times takes time, and streams are fast. As an alternative, you can use the same hash but divide the stream into groups (such as by separating the elements into groups as they arrive based on their arrival order) and for each group, you keep track of the maximum number of trailing zeros. In the end, you compute the distinct element estimate for each group and compute the arithmetic average of all the estimates. This approach is *stochastic averaging* and provides more precise estimates than applying the algorithm to the entire stream.

Learning to count objects in a stream

This last algorithm in the chapter also leverages hash functions and approximate sketches. It does so after filtering duplicated objects and counting distinct elements that have appeared in the data stream. Learning to count objects in a stream can help you find the most frequent items or rank usual and unusual events. You use this technique to solve problems like finding the most frequent queries in a search engine, the bestselling items from an online retailer, the highly popular pages in a website, or the most volatile stocks (by counting the times a stock is sold and bought).

You apply the solution to this problem, *Count-Min Sketch*, to a data stream. It requires just one data pass and stores as little information as possible. This algorithm is applied in many real-world situations (such as analyzing network traffic or managing distributed data flows). The recipe requires using a bunch of hash functions, each one associated with a bit vector, in a way that resembles a Bloom filter, as shown in Figure 12-9:

1. Initialize all the bit vectors to zeroes in all positions.

2. Apply the hash function for each bit vector when receiving an object from a stream. Use the resulting numeric address to increment the value at that position.

3. Apply the hash function to an object and retrieve the value at the associated position when asked to estimate the frequency of an object. Of all the values received from the bit vectors, you take the smallest as the frequency of the stream.

FIGURE 12-9:
How values are
updated in a
Count-Min
Sketch.

REMEMBER

Because collisions are always possible when using a hash function, especially if the associated bit vector has few slots, having multiple bit vectors at hand assures you that at least one of them keeps the correct value. The value of choice should be the smallest because it isn't mixed with false positive counts due to collisions.

Chapter **13**

Parallelizing Operations

anaging immense amounts of data using streaming or sampling strategies has clear advantages (as discussed in Chapter 12) when you have to deal with massive data processing. Using streaming and sampling algorithms helps you obtain a result even when your computational power is limited (for instance, when using your own computer). However, some costs are associated with these approaches:

» **Streaming:** Handles infinite amounts of data. Yet your algorithms perform at low speed because they process individual pieces of data and the stream speed rules the pace.

» **Sampling:** Applies any algorithms on any machine. Yet the obtained result is imprecise because you have only a probability, not a certainty, of getting the right answer. Most often, you just get something plausible.

Some problems require that you handle great amounts of data in a both precise and timely fashion. Examples abound in the digital world, such as making a keyword query among billions of websites or processing multiple pieces of information (searching for an image in a video repository or a match in multiple DNA sequences). Doing such calculations sequentially would take a lifetime.

The solution is using *distributed computing*, which means interconnecting many computers in a network and using their computational capabilities together, combined with algorithms running on them in an independent, parallel manner.

Managing Immense Amounts of Data

The use of the Internet to perform a wide range of tasks and the increase in popularity of its most successful applications, such as search engines or social networking, has required professionals in many fields to rethink how to apply algorithms and software solutions to cope with a deluge of data. Searching for topics and connecting people drive this revolution.

Just imagine the progression, in terms of available websites and pages, that has occurred in the last 15 years. Even if you use a smart algorithm, such as PageRank (discussed and explored in Chapter 11), coping with ever larger and changeable data is still hard. The same goes for social networking services offered by companies such as Facebook, Twitter, Pinterest, LinkedIn, and so on. As the number of users increases and their reciprocal relationships unfold, the underlying graph connecting them turns massive in scale. With large scale, handling nodes and links to find groups and connections becomes incredibly difficult. (Part 3 of the book discusses graphs in detail.)

In addition to communication-based data, consider online retailers that provide virtual warehouses of thousands and thousands of products and services (books, films, games, and so on). Even though you understand why you bought something, the retailer sees the items in your basket as small pieces of a purchase decision-making puzzle to solve to understand buying preferences. Solving the puzzle enables a retailer to suggest and sell alternative or supplementary products.

Understanding the parallel paradigm

CPU makers found a simple solution when challenged to stuff more computing power into microprocessors (as forecasted and partially prescribed by Moore's law, discussed in Chapter 12). Yet, bigger, larger, and faster isn't always the right solution. When they found that power absorption and heat generation limited the addition of more CPUs to a single chip, engineers compromised by creating *multicore processing units,* which are CPUs made by stacking two or more CPUs together. The use of multicore technology gave raise to parallel computing to a larger audience.

Parallel computing has existed for a long time, but it mainly appeared in high-performance computers, such as the Cray super-computers created by Seymour Cray at Control Data Corporation (CDC) starting in the 1960s. Simply stated, the associative and commutative properties in math express the core idea of parallelism. In a math addition, for instance, you can group part of the sums together or you can add the parts in a different order than the one shown by the formulas:

```
Associative property
2 + (3 + 4) = (2 + 3) + 4

Commutative property
2 + 3 + 4 = 4 + 3 + 2
```

The same concepts apply to computing algorithms, regardless of whether you have a series of operations or a mathematical function. Most often, you can reduce the algorithm to a simpler form when you apply associative and commutative properties, as shown in Figure 13-1. Then you can split the parts and have different units perform atomic operations separately, summing the result at the end.

FIGURE 13-1: Associative and commutative properties allow parallelism.

In this example, two CPUs split a simple function with three inputs (x, y, and z) by leveraging both associative and commutative properties. The equation solution requires sharing common data (CPU1 needs x and y values; CPU2 needs y and z values instead), but the processing proceeds in parallel until the two CPUs emit their results, which are summed to obtain the answer.

Parallelism allows processing of large numbers of calculations simultaneously. The more processes, the higher the speed of computation execution, although the time spent is not linearly proportional to the number of parallel executors. (It is not completely true that two CPUs imply double speed, three CPUs imply three times the speed, and so on.) In fact, you can't expect the associative or commutative properties to work on every part of your algorithm or computer instructions. The algorithm simply can't make some parts parallel as stated by Amdahl's law, which helps determine the parallelism speed advantage of your computation (for details, see `http://home.wlu.edu/~whaleyt/classes/parallel/topics/amdahl.html`). In addition, other aspects can dampen the positive effect of parallelism:

>> **Overhead:** You can't sum the results in parallel.

>> **Housekeeping:** The underlying conversion from a human-readable language to machine language requires time. Keeping the processors working together increases the conversion costs, making it impossible to see a doubling effect from two processors even if you can perform every part of the task in parallel.

>> **Asynchronous Outputs:** Because parallel executors don't perform tasks at the same exact speed, the overall speed is bound to the slowest one. (As with a fleet, the speed of the fleet is determined by the slowest boat.)

Even if not always as beneficial as expected, parallelism can potentially address the problem of handling a massive number of operations faster than using a single processor (if a massive number of executors can process them in parallel). Yet, parallelism can't address the massive amounts of data behind the computations without another solution: distributed computing on distributed systems.

REMEMBER

When you buy a new computer, the seller likely tells you about cores and threads. *Cores* are the CPUs that are stacked inside the single CPU chip and that work in a parallel fashion using multiprocessing. Because each core is independent, the tasks occur simultaneously. *Threads* refer instead to the capability of a single core to split its activity between multiple processes, in an almost parallel way. However, in this case, each thread takes its turn with the processor, so the tasks don't occur simultaneously. This is called *multithreading*.

Distributing files and operations

Large graphs, huge amounts of text files, images, and videos, and immense adjacency relation matrices call forth the parallel approach. Fortunately, you no longer need a supercomputer to deal with them, but can instead rely on parallelism by a bunch of much less powerful computers. The fact that these large data sources keep growing means that you need a different approach than using a single computer specially designed to handle them. The data grows so fast that when you finish designing and producing a supercomputer for crunching the data, it may well no longer be suitable because the data has already grown too large.

The solution starts with an online service such as Google, Microsoft Azure, or Amazon Web Services (AWS). The first step to solve the problem is deciding where to put the data. The second step is to decide how to compute efficiently without moving the data around too much (because large data transfers take a lot of time to transit from one computer to another over a network or the Internet).

Most of these services work in a similar fashion. Engineers put many existing technological ideas together and create a Distributed File System (DFS) of some sort. When using a DFS, data isn't stored in a single powerful computer with a giant hard disk; instead, the DFS spreads it among multiple smaller computers, similar to a personal computer. The engineers arrange the computers into a *cluster,* a physical system of racks and cable connections. Racks are the true backbone of the network, in which multiple computers are stored next to each other. In a single rack of the network, you may find a variable number of computers, from eight to 64, each one connected to the other. Each rack connects to other racks by means of a cable network, created by interconnecting the racks not directly between themselves, but to various layers of *switches,* which are computer-networking devices able to efficiently handle and manage the data exchange between racks, as shown in Figure 13-2.

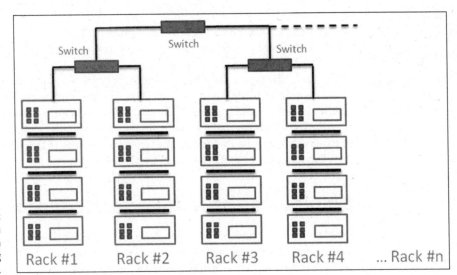

FIGURE 13-2:
A schema representing a computing cluster.

You can find all this hardware at any computer store, yet it's exactly what makes the DFS infrastructure viable. Theoretically, you could find a million or more computers interconnected in a network. (You can read about the Google version of this setup at `http://www.datacenterknowledge.com/archives/2011/08/01/report-google-uses-about-900000-servers/`.) The interesting point is that these services increase computational power when needed by adding more computers, not by creating new networks.

In this system, as data arrives, the DFS splits it into chunks (each one up to 64MB in size). The DFS copies the chunks into multiple duplicates and then distributes each copy to a computer part on the network. The action of splitting data into chunks, duplicating it, and distributing it is quite fast, no matter how the data is structured (tidy and ordered information or messy ensemble). The only requirement pertains to the recording of the chunks' address in the DFS, which is achieved by an index for each file (itself replicated and distributed), called the master node. The DFS execution speed is due to how the DFS handles the data. Contrary to previous storage techniques (such as data warehouses), a DFS doesn't require any particular sorting, ordering, or cleaning operation on the data itself; on the contrary, it does the following:

>> Handles data of any size because the data is split into manageable chunks

>> Stores new data by piling it next to the old data; a DFS never updates any previously received data

>> Replicates data redundantly so that you don't need to back it up; duplication is in itself a backup

REMEMBER

Computers fail in a number of ways: hard disk, CPU, power system, or some other component. Statistically, you can expect a computer serving in a network to work for about 1,000 days (about three years). Consequently, a service with a million computers, can expect 1,000 of its computers to fail every day. That is why the DFS spreads three or more copies of your data inside multiple computers in the network. Replication reduces the likelihood of losing data because of a failure. The probability of having a failure that involves only computers where the same chunk of data is stored is about one out of a billion (assuming that the DFS replicates the data three times), making this a tiny, acceptable risk.

Employing the MapReduce solution

Even though distributed systems store data quickly, retrieving data is much slower, especially when performing analysis and applying algorithms. The same sort of problem occurs when you break a jigsaw puzzle into pieces and scatter the pieces around (easy). You must then pick the pieces up and recreate the original image (hard and time consuming). When working with data in a DFS:

USING A PACKAGE SOLUTION FOR MAPREDUCE

Even though the book demonstrates how to create a MapReduce solution from scratch, you don't need to reinvent the wheel every time you want to perform this task. Packages such as MrJob (https://pythonhosted.org/mrjob/) enable you to perform MapReduce tasks quickly and easily. In addition, by using a package, you can make it easy to execute the task using cloud-based resources, such as Amazon Web Services using Elastic MapReduce (EMR) (https://aws.amazon.com/emr/) or with Hadoop (http://hadoop.apache.org/). The point is that you do need to know how the algorithm works, which is the point of this book, but having to write all the required code may be unnecessary in the right situation.

1. Get the master node and read it to determine the location of the file parts.

2. Dispatch a fetch order to the computers in the network to obtain the previously stored data chunks.

3. Gather the data chunks stored on multiple computers onto a single computer (if doing so is possible; some files may be too large to store on a single machine).

Obviously, this process can become complex, so web service engineers have decided that it's better not to recompose files before processing them. A smarter solution is to leave them in chunks on the source computer and let the hosting computer process them. Only a reduce version, which is already almost completely processed, would have to move across the network, limiting the data transmission. MapReduce is the solution that provides the means to process algorithms in parallel in a data–distributed system. As an algorithm itself, MapReduce consists of just two parts, map and reduce.

Explaining map

The first phase of the MapReduce algorithm is the map part, a function found in many *functional programming languages* (a style of programming that treats computing as a mathematical function). map is straightforward: You begin with a one-dimensional array (which, in Python, could be a list) and a function. By applying the function on each array element, you obtain an identically shaped array whose values are transformed. The following example contains a list of ten numbers that the function transforms into their power equivalent:

```
L = [0, 1, 2, 3, 4, 5, 6, 7, 8, 9]
m = list(map(lambda x: x**2, L))
```

```
print(m)

[0, 1, 4, 9, 16, 25, 36, 49, 64, 81]
```

The map function applies the Python lambda function (a *lambda* function is a function defined on the fly) to transform each element in the initial list into a resulting element. Figure 13-3 shows the result of this mapping process.

FIGURE 13-3:
Mapping a list of
numbers by a
square function.

Note that each list element transformation is independent of the others. You can apply the function to the list elements in any order. (However, you must store the result in the right position in the final array.) The capability to process the list elements in any order creates a scenario that is naturally parallelized without any particular effort.

REMEMBER

Not all problems are naturally parallel, and some will never be. However, sometimes you can rethink or redefine your problem in order to achieve a set of computations that the computer can deal with in a parallel way.

Explaining reduce

The second phase of the MapReduce algorithm is the reduce part (there is also an intermediate step, Shuffle and Sort, explained later but not important for now). When given a list, reduce applies a function in a sequence that cumulates the results. Thus, when using a summation function, reduce applies the summation to all the input list elements. reduce takes the first two array elements and combines them. Then it combines this partial result with the next array element and so on until it completes the array.

TIP

You can also supply a starting number. When you supply a starting number, reduce starts by combining the starting number with the first list element to obtain the first partial result. The following example uses the result from the mapping phase and reduces it using a summation function (as displayed in Figure 13-4):

```
from functools import reduce
L = [0, 1, 2, 3, 4, 5, 6, 7, 8, 9]
m = list(map(lambda x: x**2, L))
r = reduce(lambda x, y: x+y, m)
print(r)

285
```

FIGURE 13-4:
Reducing a list
of numbers to
its sum.

REMEMBER

The reduce function operates on the input array as if it were a data stream (as discussed in Chapter 12). It usually works with one element at a time and tracks the intermediate results.

Distributing operations

Between the map and reduce phases is an intermediate phase, shuffling and sorting. As soon as a map task completes, the host redirects the resulting tuples of key and value pairs to the right computer on the network to apply the reduce phase. This is typically done by grouping matching key pairs into a single list and using a hash function on the key in a manner similar to Bloom filters (see Chapter 12). The output is an address in the computing cluster for transferring the lists.

On the other end of the transmission, the computer performing the reduce phase starts receiving lists of tuples of one or multiple keys. Multiple keys occur when a hash collision occurs, which happens when different keys result in the same hashed value, so they end up to the same computer. The computer performing the reduce phase sorts them into lists containing the same key before feeding each list into the reduce phase, as shown in Figure 13-5.

As shown in the figure, MapReduce takes multiple inputs at each computer in the computing cluster where they are stored, maps the data, and transforms it into tuples of key and value pairs. Arranged into lists, the host transmits these tuples to other computers over the network, where the receiving computers operate sort and reduce operations that lead to a result.

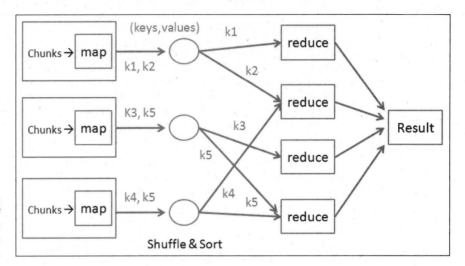

FIGURE 13-5:
An overview of
the complete
MapReduce
computation.

Working Out Algorithms for MapReduce

Contrary to other examples in this book, you can think of MapReduce as more of a style of computing or a Big Data framework than an algorithm. As a framework, it enables you to combine different distributed algorithms (parallel algorithms that spread computations across different computers) and allow them to work efficiently and successfully with large amounts of data. You can find MapReduce algorithms in many applications, and you can read about them at the Apache wiki regarding Hadoop, detailing the company that uses it, how it is used, and on what kind of computing cluster: http://wiki.apache.org/hadoop/PoweredBy. Even though possibilities are many, you most often find MapReduce used to perform these tasks:

>> Text algorithms for splitting the text into elements (tokens), creating indexes, and searching for relevant words and phrases

>> Graph creation and graph algorithms

>> Data mining and learning new algorithms from data (machine learning)

One of the most common MapReduce algorithm uses is to process text. The example in this section demonstrates how to solve a simple task, counting certain words in a text passage using a map and reduce approach, and leveraging multithreading or multiprocessing (depending on the operating system installed on your computer).

TECHNICAL STUFF

The Python programming language is not the ideal computer language for parallel operations. Technically, because of synchronization and shared memory access problems, the Python interpreter isn't thread safe, which means that it can experience errors when executing applications using multiple processes or threads on multiple cores. Consequently, Python limits multithreading to a single thread (code is distributed but no performance increase occurs) and multicore parallelism by multiple processes is indeed tricky to achieve, especially on computers running on Windows. You can learn more about the difference in threads and processes by reading the Microsoft article at https://msdn.microsoft.com/en-us/library/windows/desktop/ms681917(v=vs.85).aspx.

Setting up a MapReduce simulation

This example processes text that is in the public domain, obtained from the non-profit Project Gutenberg organization (https://www.gutenberg.org/) site. The first text processed is the novel *War and Peace*, by Leo Tolstoy (who is also known by other names in other languages, such as Lev Tolstoj). The following code loads the data into memory:

```
import urllib.request
url = 'http://gutenberg.readingroo.ms/2/6/0/2600/2600.txt'
response = urllib.request.urlopen(url)
data = response.read()
text = data.decode('utf-8')[627:]

print (text[:37])

WAR AND PEACE

By Leo Tolstoy/Tolstoi
```

Be patient! Loading the book takes time (just try reading it in as short a time as the computer does). When complete, the code displays the first few lines with the title. The code stores the data in the text variable. Part of the process splits the text into words and stores them in a list, as shown in the following code:

```
words = text.split()
print ('Number of words: %i' % len(words))

Number of words: 566218
```

The words variable now contains individual words from the book. It's time to import the necessary Python packages and the functions for the example using the following code:

```python
import os
if os.name == "nt":
    #Safer multithreading on Windows
    from multiprocessing.dummy import Pool
else:
    #Multiprocessing on Linux,Mac
    from multiprocessing import Pool

from multiprocessing import cpu_count
from functools import partial
```

Depending on your operating system, the example relies on multiprocessing or multithreading. Windows uses multithreading, which splits the task into multiple threads processed at the same time by the same core. On Linux and Mac systems, the code executes in parallel instead, and each operation is taken care of by a different computer core.

The code that comes next counts words from a list that corresponds to a set of keywords. After removing any punctuation, the code compares words, and if it finds any match with a keyword, the function returns a tuple consisting of a key, the matched keyword, and a unit value, which is a count. This output represents the core of the MapReduce map:

```python
def remove_punctuation(text):
    return ''.join([l for l in text if l not in ['.',
            ',', '!', '?', '"']])

def count_words(list_of_words, keywords):
    results = list()
    for word in list_of_words:
        for keyword in keywords:
            if keyword == remove_punctuation(
                        word.upper()):
                results.append((keyword,1))
    return results
```

The functions that follow partition the data. This approach is similar to the way in which a distributed system partitions the data. The code distributes the computation and gathers the results:

```
def Partition(data, size):
    return [data[x:x+size] for x in range(0, len(data),
                                           size)]


def Distribute(function, data, cores):
    pool = Pool(cores)
    results = pool.map(function, data)
    pool.close()
    return results
```

Finally, the following functions shuffle and order the data to reduce the results. This step represents the last two phases of a MapReduce job:

```
def Shuffle_Sort(L):
    # Shuffle
    Mapping = dict()
    for sublist in L:
        for key_pair in sublist:
            key, value = key_pair
            if key in Mapping:
                Mapping[key].append(key_pair)
            else:
                Mapping[key] = [key_pair]
    return [Mapping[key] for key in Mapping]


def Reduce(Mapping):
  return (Mapping[0][0], sum([value for (key, value
                             ) in Mapping]))
```

Inquiring by mapping

The following code simulates a distributed environment using multiple processor cores. It begins by requesting the number of available cores from the operating system. The number of cores you see will vary by the number of cores available in your computer. Most modern computers provide four or eight cores.

```
n = cpu_count()
print ('You have %i cores available for MapReduce' % n)

You have 4 cores available for MapReduce
```

REMEMBER

If you're running the code on Windows, for technical reasons you work with a single core, so you won't take advantage of the total number of available cores. The simulation still appears to work, but you won't see any increase in speed.

In order to start, the code first defines the map operation. It then distributes the map function to threads, each of which processes a partition of the initial data (the list containing the words from *War and Peace*). The map operation finds the words *peace, war* (is there more war or peace in *War and Peace?*), *Napoleon,* and *Russia:*

```
Map = partial(count_words,
            keywords=['WAR', 'PEACE', 'RUSSIA',
                      'NAPOLEON'])
map_result = Distribute(Map,
                        Partition(
        words,len(words)//n+1), n)
print ('map_result is a list made of %i elements' %
        len(map_result))
print ('Preview of one element: %s]'% map_result[0][:5])

Map is a list made of 4 elements
Preview of one element: [('WAR', 1), ('PEACE', 1), ('WAR', 1),
        ('WAR', 1), ('RUSSIA', 1)]]
```

After a while, the code prints the results. In this case, the resulting list contains four elements because the host system has four cores (you may see greater or fewer elements, depending on the number of cores on your machine). Each element in the list is another list containing the results of the mapping on that part of the word data. By previewing one of these lists, you can see that it's a sequence of coupled keys (depending on the keyword found) and unit values. The keys aren't in order; they appear in the order in which the code generated them. Consequently, before passing the lists to the reduce phase for summing the total results, the code arranges the keys in order and sends them to the appropriate core for reducing:

```
Shuffled = Shuffle_Sort(map_result)
print ('Shuffled is a list made of %i elements' %
        len(Shuffled))
print ('Preview of first element: %s]'% Shuffled[0][:5])
print ('Preview of second element: %s]'% Shuffled[1][:5])
```

```
Shuffled is a list made of 4 elements
Preview of first element: [('RUSSIA', 1), ('RUSSIA', 1),
 ('RUSSIA', 1), ('RUSSIA', 1), ('RUSSIA', 1)]]
Preview of second element: [('NAPOLEON', 1), ('NAPOLEON',
 1), ('NAPOLEON', 1), ('NAPOLEON', 1), ('NAPOLEON', 1)]]
```

As shown in the example, the Shuffle_Sort function creates a list of four lists, each one containing tuples featuring one of the four keywords. In a cluster setting, this processing equates to having each mapping node pass through the emitted results, and, by using some kind of addressing (for instance, using a hash function, as seen in the bit vector of a Bloom filter Chapter 12), they send (shuffle phase) the tuple data to the appropriate reducing node. The receiving node places each key in the appropriate list (order phase):

```
result = Distribute(Reduce, Shuffled, n)
print ('Emitted results are: %s' % result)

Emitted results are: [('RUSSIA', 156), ('NAPOLEON', 469),
   ('WAR', 288), ('PEACE', 111)]
```

The reduce phase sums the distributed and ordered tuples and reports the total summation for each key, as seen in the result printed by the code that replicates a MapReduce. Reading the results, you can see that Tolstoy mentions war more than peace in *War and Peace*, but he mentions Napoleon even more often.

You can easily repeat the experiment on other texts or, even hack the map function in order to apply a different function to the text. For instance, you could choose to analyze some of the most famous novels by Sir Arthur Conan Doyle and try to discover how many times Sherlock Holmes used the phrase "Elementary, Watson":

```
import urllib.request
url = "http://gutenberg.pglaf.org/1/6/6/1661/1661.txt"
text = urllib.request.urlopen(url).read().decode(
                                    'utf-8')[723:]
words = text.split()

print (text[:65])
print ('\nTotal words are %i' % len(words))
```

```
Map = partial(count_words,
              keywords=['WATSON', 'ELEMENTARY'])
result = Distribute(Reduce,
                    Shuffle_Sort(Distribute(Map,
                    Partition(words,len(words)//n), n)),
                    1)
print ('Emitted results are: %s' % result)


THE ADVENTURES OF SHERLOCK HOLMES
by
SIR ARTHUR CONAN DOYLE

Total words are 107431
Emitted results are: [('WATSON', 81), ('ELEMENTARY', 1)]
```

The result may be surprising! You never actually find that phrase in the novels; it's a catchphrase that authors inserted later into the film screenplays: http:// www.phrases.org.uk/meanings/elementary-my-dear-watson.html.

Chapter **14**

Compressing Data

The last decade has seen the world flooded by data. In fact, data is the new oil, and specialists of all sorts hope to extract new knowledge and richness from it. As a result, you find data piled everywhere and often archived as soon as it arrives. The sometimes careless storage of data comes from an increased capacity to store information; it has become cheap to buy larger drives to store everything, useful or not. Chapters 12 and 13 discuss the drivers behind this data deluge, how to deal with massive data streams, methods used to distribute it over clusters of connected computers, and techniques you can use to process data rapidly and efficiently.

Data hasn't always been readily available, however. In previous decades, storing data required large investments in expensive mass-storage devices (hard disk, tapes, floppy disks, CDs) that couldn't store much data. Storing data required a certain efficiency (saving disk space meant saving money), and data compression algorithms offered the solution of compacting data to store more of it on a single device at the cost of computer processing time. Trading disk space for computer time reduced costs.

Compression algorithms have long been a topic of study and are now considered classics in computer knowledge. Even though storage disks are larger and cheaper today, these algorithms still play a role in mobile data transmission and see use anywhere there is a data stream bottleneck or high memory costs. Compression is also handy in situations in which data infrastructure growth doesn't match data growth, which is especially true of both wireless and mobile bandwidth in developing countries. In addition, compression helps deliver complex web pages faster, stream videos efficiently, store data on a mobile device, or reduce mobile phone data transmission costs. This chapter helps you understand how data compression works and when you need to use it.

Making Data Smaller

Computer data is made of bits — sequences of zeros and ones. This chapter explains the use of zeros and ones to create data in more depth than previous chapters because compression leverages these zeros and ones in multiple ways. To understand compression, you must know how a computer creates and stores binary numbers. The following sections discuss the use of binary numbers in computers.

Understanding encoding

Zeros and ones are the only numbers in the binary system. They represent the two possible states in an electric circuit: absence and presence of electricity. Computers started as simple circuits made of tubes or transistors; using the binary system instead of the human decimal system made things easier. Humans use ten fingers to count numbers from 0 to 9. When they have to count more, they add a unit number to the left. You may never have thought about it, but you can express counting by using powers of ten. Therefore a number such as 199 can be expressed as $10^2*1 + 10^1*9 + 10^0*9 = 199$; that is, you can separate hundreds from tens and units by multiplying each figure by the power of ten relative to its position: 10^0 for units, 10^1 for tens, 10^2 for hundreds, and so on.

REMEMBER

Knowing this information helps you understand binary numbers better because they actually work in exactly the same way. However, binary numbers use powers of two rather than powers of ten. For instance, the number 11000111 is simply

```
2⁷*1+2⁶*1+2⁵*0+2⁴*0+2³*0+2²*1+2¹*1+2⁰*1 =
128*1+64*1+32*0+16*0+8*0+4*1+2*1+1*1 =
128+64+4+2+1 = 199
```

You can represent any number as a binary value in a computer. A value occupies the memory space required by its total length. For example, binary 199 is 8 figures, each figure is a bit, and 8 bits are called a byte. The computer hardware knows data only as bits because it has only circuitry to store bits. However, from a higher point of view, computer software can interpret bits as letters, ideograms, pictures, films, and sounds, which is where encoding comes into play.

Encoding uses a sequence of bits to represent something other than the number expressed by the sequence itself. For instance, you can represent a letter using a particular sequence of bits. Computer software commonly represents the letter A using the number 65, or binary 01000001 when working with the American Standard Code for Information Interchange (ASCII) encoding standard. You can see sequences used by ASCII system at `http://www.asciitable.com/`. ASCII uses just 7 bits for its encoding (8 bits, or a byte, in the extended version), which means that you can represent 128 different characters (the extended version has 256 characters). Python can represent the string "Hello World" using bytes:

```
print ('' .join(['{0:08b}' .format(ord(l))
                  for l in "Hello World"]))

0100100001100101011011000110110001101111001000000101011101
0111101110010011011000011000100
```

When using extended ASCII, a computer knows that a sequence of exactly 8 bits represent a character. It can separate each sequence into 8-bit bytes and, using a conversion table called a *symbolic table*, it can turn these bytes into characters.

REMEMBER

ASCII encoding can represent the standard Western alphabet, but it doesn't support the variety of accented European characters or the richness of non-European alphabets, such as the ideograms used by the Chinese and Japanese languages. Chances are that you're using a robust encoding system such as UTF-8 or another form of Unicode encoding (see `http://unicode.org/` for more information). Unicode encoding is the default encoding in Python 3.

Using a complex encoding system requires that you use longer sequences than those required by ASCII. Depending on the encoding you choose, defining a character may require up to 4 bytes (32 bits). When representing textual information, a computer creates long bit sequences. It decodes each letter easily because encoding uses fixed-length sequences in a single file. Encoding strategies, such as Unicode Transformation Format 8 (UTF-8), can use variable numbers of bytes (1 to 4 in this case). You can read more about how UTF-8 works at `http://www.fileformat.info/info/unicode/utf8.htm`.

Considering the effects of compression

The use of fixed-sized character sequences leaves a lot of room for improvement. You may not use all the letters in an alphabet, or you use some letters more than others. This is where compression comes into play. By using variable-length character sequences, you can greatly reduce the size of a file. However, the file also requires additional processing to turn it back into an uncompressed format that applications understand. Compression removes space in an organized and methodical manner; decompression adds the space back into the character strings. When it's possible to compress and decompress data in a manner that doesn't result in any data loss, you're using *lossless* compression.

The same idea behind compression goes for images and sounds that involve framing sequences of bits of a certain size in order to represent video details or to reproduce a second of a sound using the computer's speakers. Videos are simply sequences of bits, and each bit sequence is a *pixel*, which is composed of small points that constitute an image. Likewise, audio is composed of sequences of bits that represent an individual sample. Audio files store a certain number of samples per second to recreate a sound. The discussion at `http://kias.dyndns.org/comath/44.html` provides more information about both video and audio storage. Computers store data in many predefined formats of long sequences of bits (commonly called *bit streams*). Compression algorithms can exploit the way each format works to obtain the same result using a shorter, custom format.

You can compress data that represents images and sounds further by eliminating details that you can't process. Humans have both visual and aural limits, so they aren't likely to notice the loss of detail imposed by compressing the data in specific ways. You may have heard of MP3 compression that allows you to store entire collections of CDs on your computer or on a portable reader. The MP3 file format simplifies the original cumbersome WAV format used by computers. WAV files contain all the sound waves received by the computer, but MP3 saves space by removing and compacting waves that you can't hear. (For more more about MP3, see the article at `http://arstechnica.com/features/2007/10/the-audiofile-understanding-mp3-compression/`).

TIP

Removing details from data creates *lossy* compression. JPEG, DjVu, MPEG, MP3, and WMA are all lossy compression algorithms specialized in a particular kind of media data (images, video, sound), and there are many others. Lossy compression is fine for data meant for human input; however, by removing the details, you can't revert to the original data structure. Thus, you can get good digital photo compression and represent it in a useful way on a computer's screen. Yet when you print the compressed photo on paper, you may notice that the quality, though acceptable, is not as good as the original picture. The display provides output at 96 dots per inch (dpi), but a printer typically provides output at 300 to 1200 dpi (or higher). The effects of lossy compression become obvious because a printer is able to display them in a manner that humans can see.

AN EXAMPLE OF LOSSY COMPRESSION BENEFITS

An example of the difference that lossy compression can make is in photography. A raw formatted picture file contains all the information originally provided by the camera's sensor, so it doesn't include any sort of compression. When working with a certain camera, you might find that this file consumes 29.8MB of hard drive space. A raw file often uses the .raw file extension to show that no processing has occurred. Opening the file and saving it as a lossy .jpeg might result in a file size of only 3.7 MB, but with a corresponding loss of detail. To save some of the detail but obtain some savings in file size as well, you might choose to use the .jpeg file format. In this case, the file size might be 12.4MB, which represents a good compromise in file size savings to loss of image data.

REMEMBER

Choosing between lossless and lossy compression is important. Discarding details is a good strategy for media, but it doesn't work so well with text, because losing words or letters may change the meaning of the text. (Discarding details doesn't work for programming languages or computer instructions for the same reason.) Even though lossy compression is an effective compression solution when details aren't as important, it doesn't work in situations in which precise meaning must be retained.

Choosing a particular kind of compression

Lossless algorithms simply compress data to reduce its size and decompress it to its original state. Lossless algorithms have more general applications than lossy compression because you can use them for any data problem. (Even when using lossy compression, you remove some detail and further compress what remains using lossless compression.) Just as you can find many lossy algorithms that are specialized for use with different media, so can you find many lossless algorithms, each one adept at exploiting some data characteristics. (To get an idea of how large the lossless algorithm family is, read more details at `http://ethw.org/History_of_Lossless_Data_Compression_Algorithms`).

REMEMBER

It's essential to remember that the goal of both lossy and lossless compression is to reduce the redundancy contained in data. The more redundancies the data contains, the more effective the compression.

Chances are that you have many lossless data compression programs installed on your computer that output files such as ZIP, LHA, 7-Zip, and RAR, and you aren't sure which one is better. A "best" option may not exist, because you can use bit sequences in many different ways to represent information on a computer; also, different compression strategies work better with different bit sequences. This is the no-free-lunch problem discussed in Chapter 1. The option you choose depends on the data content you need to compress.

To see how compression varies by the sample you provide, you should try various text samples using the same algorithm. The following Python example uses the ZIP algorithm to compress the text of *The Adventures of Sherlock Holmes,* by Arthur Conan Doyle, and then to reduce the size of a randomly generated sequence of letters. (You can find the complete code for this example in the Compression Performances section of the A4D; 14; Compression.ipynb file of the downloadable source code for this book; see the Introduction for details).

```
import urllib.request
import zlib
from random import randint
url = "http://gutenberg.pglaf.org/1/6/6/1661/1661.txt"
sh = urllib.request.urlopen(url).read().decode('utf-8')
sh_length = len(sh)
rnd = ''.join([chr(randint(0,126)) for k in
               range(sh_length)])

def zipped(text):
    return len(zlib.compress(text.encode("ascii")))

print ("Original size for both texts: %s characters" %
       sh_length)
print ("The Adventures of Sherlock Holmes to %s" %
       zipped(sh))
print ("Random file to %s " % zipped(rnd))

Original size for both texts: 594941 characters
The Adventures of Sherlock Holmes to 226824
Random file to 521448
```

The output of the example is enlightening. Even though the example application can reduce the size of the short story to less than half of its original size, the size reduction for the random text is much less (both texts have the same original length). The output implies that the ZIP algorithm leverages the characteristics of the written text but doesn't do as well on random text that lacks a predictable structure.

TIP

When performing data compression, you can measure performance by calculating the compression ratio: Just divide the new compressed size of the file by the original size of the file. The compression ratio can tell you about algorithm efficiency in saving space, but high-performance algorithms also require time to perform the task. In case time is your concern, most algorithms let you trade some compression ratio for speedier compression and decompression. In the preceding example for the *Sherlock Holmes* text, the compression ratio is 226824 / 594941, that is, about 0.381. The compress method found in the example has a second optional parameter, level, which controls the level of compression. Changing this parameter controls the ratio between the time to perform the task and the amount of compression achieved.

Choosing your encoding wisely

The example in the preceding section shows what happens when you apply the ZIP algorithm to random text. The results help you understand why compression works. Boiling down all the available compression algorithms, you discover four main reasons:

>> **Shrinking character encoding:** Compression forces characters to use fewer bits by coding them according to some feature, such as commonality of use. For example, if you use only some of the characters in a character set, you can reduce the number of bits to reflect that level of usage. It's the same difference that occurs between ASCII, which uses 7 bits, and extended ASCII, which uses 8 bits. This solution is particularly effective with problems like DNA encoding, in which you can devise a better encoding than the standard one.

>> **Shrinking long sequences of identical bits:** Compression uses a special code to identify multiple copies of the same bits and replaces those copies with just one copy, along with the number of times to repeat it. This option is very effective with images (it works fine with fax black and white images) or with any data that you can rearrange in order to group similar characters together (DNA data is one of this kind).

>> **Leveraging statistics:** Compression encodes frequently used characters in a shorter way. For example, the letter *E* appears commonly in English, so if the letter *E* uses only 3 bits, rather than a full 8 bits, you save considerable space. This is the strategy used by Huffman encoding, in which you recreate the symbolic table and save space, on average, because common characters are shorter.

>> **Encoding frequent long sequences of characters efficiently:** This is similar to shrinking long sequences of identical bits, but it works with character sequences rather than single characters. This is the strategy used by LZW, which learns data patterns on the fly and creates a short encoding for long sequences of characters.

To understand how rethinking encoding can help in compression, start with the first reason. Scientists working on the Genome Project around 2008 (https://www.genome.gov/10001772/all-about-the--human-genome-project-hgp/) managed to drastically reduce the size of their data using a simple encoding trick. Using this trick made the task of mapping the entire human DNA simpler, helping the scientists understand more about the life, disease, and death scripted into our body cells.

Scientists describe DNA using sequences of the letters A, C, T, and G (representing the four nucleotides present in all living beings). The human genome contains six billion nucleotides (you find them associated in couples, called bases) that add up to more than 50GB using ASCII encoding. In fact, you can represent A, C, T, and G in ASCII encoding as follows:

```
print (' '.join(['{0:08b}'.format(ord(l))
                  for l in "ACTG"]))

01000001 01000011 01010100 01000111
```

The sum of the preceding line is 32 bits, but because DNA maps just four characters, you can use 2 bits each, saving 75 percent of the previously used bits:

```
00 01 10 11
```

REMEMBER

Such a gain demonstrates the reason to choose the right encoding. The encoding works fine in this case because the DNA alphabet is made of four letters, and using a full ASCII table based on 8 bits is overkill. If a problem requires that you use the complete ASCII alphabet, you can't compress the data by redefining the encoding used. Instead, you have to approach the problem using Huffman compression.

If you can't shrink the character encoding (or you have already done it), you can still shrink long sequences, reducing them to a simpler encoding. Observe how binary data can repeat long sequences of ones and zeros:

```
00000000 00000000 01111111 11111111 10000011 11111111
```

In this case, the sequence starts from zero. You can therefore count the number of zeros, and then count the number of ones that follow, and then repeat with the next count of zeros, and so on. Because the sequence has only zeros and ones, you can count them and obtain sequence of counts to compress the data. In this case, the data compresses into values of 17 15 5 10. Translating these counts into bytes shortens the initial data in an easily reversible way:

```
00010001 00001111 00000101 00001010
```

Instead of using 6 bytes to represent the data, you now need only 4 bytes. To use this approach, you limit the maximum count to 255 consecutive values, which means:

>> You can encode each sequence in a byte.

>> The first value is a zero when the sequence starts from 1 instead of 0.

>> When a block of values is longer than 255 elements, you insert a 0 value (so the decoder switches to the other value for 0 counts and then starts counting the first value again).

This algorithm, *run-length encoding* (RLE), is very effective if your data has many long repetitions. This algorithm enjoyed great success in the 1980s because it could reduce fax transmission times. Fax machines worked on just black-and-white images, and by land-line telephone, shrinking the long sequences of zeros and ones that made up images and text proved to be convenient. Though businesses seldom use fax machines now, scientists still use RLE for DNA compression in combination with the Burrows-Wheeler Transform (an advanced algorithm that you can read about at `http://marknelson.us/1996/09/01/bwt/`), which rearranges (in a reversible way) the genome sequence in long runs of the same nucleotide. You also find RLE used for compression of other data formats, such as JPEG and MPEG (see `http://motorscript.com/mpeg-jpeg-compression/` for additional details).

TIP

Data characteristics rule the success of a compression algorithm. By knowing how algorithms work and exploring your data characteristics, you can choose the best-performing algorithm or combine more algorithms in an effective way. Using multiple algorithms together creates an *ensemble of algorithms.*

Encoding using Huffman compression

Redefining an encoding, such as when mapping nucleotides in DNA, is a smart move that works only when you use a part of the alphabet that the encoding represents. When you use all the symbols in the encoding, you can't use this solution. David A. Huffman discovered another way to encode letters, numbers, and symbols efficiently even when using all of them. He achieved this accomplishment when he was a student at MIT in 1952 as part of a term paper required by his professor, Prof. Robert M. Fano. His professor and another famous scientist, Claude Shannon (the father of information theory), had struggled with the same problem.

In his paper, "A Method for the Construction of Minimum-Redundancy Codes," Huffman describes in just three pages his mind-blowing encoding method.

It changed the way we stored data until the end of 1990s. You can read the details about this incredible algorithm in a September 1991 *Scientific American* article at `http://www.huffmancoding.com/my-uncle/scientific-american`. Huffman codes have three key ideas:

>> **Encode frequent symbols with shorter sequences of bits.** For instance, if your text uses the letter *a* often, but rarely uses the letter *z*, you can encode *a* using a couple of bits and reserve an entire byte (or more) for *z*. Using shorter sequences for common letters means that overall your text requires fewer bytes than when you rely on ASCII encoding.

>> **Encode shorter sequences using a unique series of bits.** When using variable length bit sequences, you have to ensure that you can't misinterpret a shorter sequence in place of a longer one because they are similar. For instance, if the letter *a* in binary is 110 and *z* is 110110, you could misinterpret the letter *z* as a series of two-letter *a* characters. Huffman encoding avoids this problem by using prefix-free codes: The algorithm never reuses shorter sequences as initial parts of longer sequences. For example, if *a* is 110, then *z* will be 101110 and not 110110.

>> **Manage prefix-free coding using a specific strategy.** Huffman encoding manages prefix-free codes by using binary trees in a smart way. Binary trees are a data structure discussed in Chapters 6 and 7. The Huffman algorithm uses binary trees (called Huffman trees) in an advanced fashion. You can read more about the internals of the algorithm in the tutorial at `https://www.siggraph. org/education/materials/HyperGraph/video/mpeg/mpegfaq/huffman_ tutorial.html`.

TECHNICAL
STUFF

The algorithm used to perform Huffman encoding uses an iterative process that relies on *heaps*, which are specialized tree-based data structures (mentioned in Chapter 6). A heap is a complex data structure. Because of the manner in which you use a heap to arrange data, it's useful for achieving a *greedy* strategy. In the next chapter, which is devoted to greedy algorithms, you test Huffman encoding yourself, using the working examples in the downloadable code accompanying the book (the Huffman Compression example in the `A4D; 15; Greedy Algorithms. ipynb` file; see the Introduction for details).

For the moment, as an example of a Huffman encoding output, Figure 14-1 shows the Huffman encoding binary tree used to encode a long sequence of *ABCDE* letters distributed in a way that *A* is more frequent than *B*, *B* more than *C*, *C* more than *D*, and *D* more than *E*.

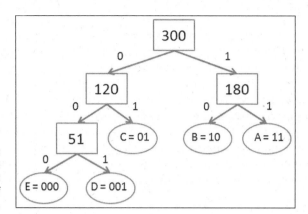

FIGURE 14-1:
A Huffman tree and its symbolic table of conversion.

The square nodes represent *branch nodes,* where the algorithm places the number of the remaining letters it distributes to the *child nodes* (those that are below the branch nodes in the hierarchy). The round nodes represent *leaf nodes,* where you find the successfully encoded letters. The tree starts at the *root* with 300 letters left to distribute (the length of the text). It distributes the letters by branching the 0 and 1 bits, respectively, on the left and on the right branches until it reaches all the leaves necessary for encoding. By reading from the top of the sequence of branches to a specific letter, you determine the binary sequence representing that letter. Less frequent letters (*D* and *E*) get the longest binary sequences.

TIP

Following the Huffman tree from bottom to top lets you compress a symbol into a binary sequence. By following the tree from top to bottom, you can decompress a binary sequence into a symbol (as represented by the first leaf node you encounter).

REMEMBER

For decompression, you need to store both the compressed binary sequence and the Huffman tree that made the compression possible. When your text or data is too short, the Huffman tree could require more space than the compressed data, thus making compression ineffective. Huffman code works best on larger data files.

Remembering sequences with LZW

Huffman encoding takes advantage of the most frequent characters, numbers, or symbols in data and shortens their encoding. The LZW algorithm performs a similar task but extends the encoding process to the most frequent sequences of characters. The LZW algorithm dates to 1984 and was created by Abraham Lempel, Jacob Ziv, and Terry Welch based on an earlier LZ78 algorithm (developed in 1978 by Lempel and Ziv alone). Both Unix compression and the GIF image format rely on this algorithm. LZW leverages repetitions, so it's also ideal for document and book text compression because humans often use the same words when writing. In addition, LZW can operate on streaming data, but Huffman can't; Huffman needs the full dataset to build its mapping table.

As the algorithm skims through the data-bit stream, it learns sequences of characters from it and assigns each sequence to a short code. Thus, when later reencountering the same series of characters, LZW can compress them using a simpler encoding. The interesting aspect of this algorithm is that it starts from a symbolic table made of single characters (usually the ASCII table) and then it enlarges that table using the character sequences it learns from the data it compresses.

Moreover, LZW doesn't need to store the learned sequences in a table for decompression; it can rebuild them easily by reading the compressed data. LZW can reconstruct the steps it took when compressing the original data and the sequences it encoded. This capability comes at a price; LZW isn't efficient at first. It works best with large pieces of data or text (a characteristic common to other compression algorithms).

LZW isn't a complex algorithm, but you need to see a number of examples to understand it fully. You can find quite a few good tutorials at http://marknelson. us/2011/11/08/lzw-revisited/ and http://www.matthewflickinger.com/lab/ whatsinagif/lzw_image_data.asp. The second tutorial explains how to use LZW to compress images. The following example shows a Python implementation. (You can find the complete code for this example in the LZW section of the A4D; 14; Compression.ipynb file of the downloadable source code for this book; see the Introduction for details).

```python
def lzw_compress(text):
    dictionary = {chr(k): k for k in range(256)}
    encoded = list()
    s = text[0]
    for c in text[1:]:
        if s+c in dictionary:
            s = s+c
        else:
            print ('> %s' %s)
            encoded.append(dictionary[s])
            print ('found: %s compressed as %s' %
                    (s,dictionary[s]))
            dictionary[s+c] = max(dictionary.values()) + 1
            print ('New sequence %s indexed as %s' %
                    (s+c, dictionary[s+c]))
            s = c
```

```
        encoded.append(dictionary[s])
        print ('found: %s compressed as %s'
               %(s,dictionary[s]))
        return encoded
```

In this example, the algorithm scans the text by checking the text a character at a time. It begins by encoding characters using the initial symbolic table, which is actually the ASCII table in this case. The best way to see how this code works is to see a series of output messages and then analyze what has taken place, as shown here:

```
text = "ABABCABCABC"
compressed = lzw_compress(text)
print('\nCompressed: %s \n' % compressed)

> A
found: A compressed as 65
New sequence AB indexed as 256
> B
found: B compressed as 66
New sequence BA indexed as 257
> AB
found: AB compressed as 256
New sequence ABC indexed as 258
> C
found: C compressed as 67
New sequence CA indexed as 259
> ABC
found: ABC compressed as 258
New sequence ABCA indexed as 260
found: ABC compressed as 258
```

Here is a quick synopsis of what these output messages mean:

1. The first letter, A, appears in the initial symbolic table, so the algorithm encodes it as 65.

2. The second letter, B, is different from A but also appears in the initial symbolic table, so the algorithm encodes it as 66.

3. The third letter is another A, so the algorithm reads the next letter, which is a B, and encodes the two-letter combination, AB, as 256.

4. The fourth letter, a C, is different from any of the previous letters and also appears in the initial symbolic table, so the algorithm encodes it as 67.

5. The next letter has already appeared before; it's an *A*. The next letter is a *B*, which makes the *AB* letter combination; this also appears in the symbolic table. However, the next letter is a *C*, which makes a new sequence and which the algorithm now encodes as 258.

6. The final three letters are another set of *ABC*, so the code for them is 258 again. Consequently, the encoded output for *ABABCABCABC* is

```
Compressed: [65, 66, 256, 67, 258, 258]
```

All the learning and encoding operations translated into final compression data consisting of just six numeric codes (costing 8 bits each) against the initial 11 test letters. The encoding results in a good compression ratio of about half the initial data: 6/11 = 0.55.

Retrieving the original text from the compressed data requires a different, inverse procedure, which accounts for the only situation when LZW decoding may fail to reconstruct the symbolic table when a sequence starts and ends with the same character. This particular case is taken care of by Python using an if-then-else command block, so you can safely use the algorithm to encode and decode anything:

```python
def lzw_decompress(encoded):
    reverse_dictionary = {k:chr(k) for k in range(256)}
    current = encoded[0]
    output = reverse_dictionary[current]
    print ('Decompressed %s ' % output)
    print ('>%s' % output)
    for element in encoded[1:]:
        previous = current
        current = element
        if current in reverse_dictionary:
            s = reverse_dictionary[current]
            print ('Decompressed %s ' % s)
            output += s
            print ('>%s' % output)
            new_index = max(reverse_dictionary.keys()) + 1
            reverse_dictionary[new_index
            ] = reverse_dictionary[previous] + s[0]
            print ('New dictionary entry %s at index %s' %
                    (reverse_dictionary[previous] + s[0],
                    new_index))
```

```
        else:
            print ('Not found:',current,'Output:',
                   reverse_dictionary[previous
                   ] + reverse_dictionary[previous][0])
            s = reverse_dictionary[previous
                ] + reverse_dictionary[previous][0]
            print ('New dictionary entry %s at index %s' %
                   (s, max(reverse_dictionary.keys())+1))
            reverse_dictionary[
                max(reverse_dictionary.keys())+1] = s
            print ('Decompressed %s' % s)
        output += s
        print ('>%s' % output)
    return output
```

Running the function on the previously compressed sequence recovers the original information by scanning through the symbolic table, as shown here:

```
print ('\ndecompressed string : %s' %
       lzw_decompress(compressed))
print ('original string was : %s' % text)

Decompressed A
> A
Decompressed B
> AB
New dictionary entry AB at index 256
Decompressed AB
> ABAB
New dictionary entry BA at index 257
Decompressed C
> ABABC
New dictionary entry ABC at index 258
Decompressed ABC
> ABABCABC
New dictionary entry CA at index 259
Decompressed ABC
> ABABCABCABC
New dictionary entry ABCA at index 260

decompressed string : ABABCABCABC
original string was : ABABCABCABC
```

5

Challenging Difficult Problems

Use greedy programming techniques to obtain results faster.

Perform dynamic programming to perform tasks using a smart approach.

Randomize your results to solve problems where a straightforward approach doesn't work well.

Search locally to final solutions that are good enough in a short time.

Use linear programming techniques to perform scheduling and planning tasks.

Employ heuristics and interact with robots.

Chapter **15**

Working with Greedy Algorithms

After taking your first steps into the world of algorithms by presenting what algorithms are and discussing ordering, searching, graphs, and big data, it's time to enter a more general part of the book. In this latter part of the book, you deal with some difficult examples and see general algorithmic approaches that you can use under different circumstances when solving real-world problems.

By taking new routes and approaches, this chapter goes well beyond the divide-and-conquer recursion approach that dominates in most sorting problems. Some of the discussed solutions aren't completely new; you've seen them in previous chapters. However, this chapter discusses those previous algorithms in greater depth, under the new *paradigms* (a consideration of application rules and conditions, general approach and steps to the solution of a problem, and analysis of problem complexity, limitations, and caveats) that the chapter illustrates.

Making some solutions general and describing them as widely applicable paradigms is a way to offer hints to solve new practical problems and is part of the analysis and design of algorithms. The remainder of this book discusses the following general approaches:

>> Greedy algorithms (explained in this chapter)

>> Dynamic programming

>> Randomization, local search, and farsighted heuristics

>> Linear programming and optimization problems

Deciding When It Is Better to Be Greedy

When faced with difficult problems, you quickly discover that no magic potion exists for making wishes come true or silver bullets to dispel bad things. Similarly, no algorithmic technique saves the day every time. That's the *no-free-lunch* principle often quoted in the book. The good news is, you can arm yourself with different general techniques and test them all on your problem, because you have a good chance that something will work well.

Greedy algorithms come in handy for solving a wide array of problems, especially when drafting a global solution is difficult. Sometimes, it's worth giving up complicated plans and simply start looking for low-hanging fruit that resembles the solution you need. In algorithms, you can describe a shortsighted approach like this as *greedy*. Looking for easy-to-grasp solutions constitutes the core distinguishing characteristic of greedy algorithms. A greedy algorithm reaches a problem solution using sequential steps where, at each step, it makes a decision based on the best solution at that time, without considering future consequences or implications.

REMEMBER

Two elements are essential for distinguishing a greedy algorithm:

>> At each turn, you always make the best decision you can at that particular instant.

>> You hope that making a series of best decisions results in the best final solution.

Greedy algorithms are simple, intuitive, small, and fast because they usually run in *linear time* (the running time is proportional to the number of inputs provided). Unfortunately, they don't offer the best solution for all problems, but when they do, they provide the best results quickly. Even when they don't offer the top answers, they can give a nonoptimal solution that may suffice or that you can use as a starting point for further refinement by another algorithmic strategy.

Interestingly, greedy algorithms resemble how humans solve many simple problems without using much brainpower or with limited information. For instance, when working as cashiers and making change, a human naturally uses a greedy approach. You can state the *make-change* problem as paying a given amount (the change) using the least number of bills and coins among the available denominations. The following Python example demonstrates the make-change problem is solvable by a greedy approach. It uses the 1, 5, 10, 20, 50, and 100 USD bills, but no coins.

```
def change(to_be_changed, denomination):
    resulting_change = list()
    for bill in denomination:
        while to_be_changed >= bill:
            resulting_change.append(bill)
            to_be_changed = to_be_changed - bill
    return resulting_change, len(resulting_change)

currency = [100, 50, 20, 10, 5, 1]
amount = 367
print ('Change: %s (using %i bills)'
       % (change(amount, currency)))

Change: [100, 100, 100, 50, 10, 5, 1, 1] (using 8 bills)
```

The algorithm, encapsulated in the change() function, scans the denominations available, from the largest to the smallest. It uses the largest available currency to make change until the amount due is less than the denomination. It then moves to the next denomination and performs the same task until it finally reaches the lowest denomination. In this way, change() always provides the largest bill possible given an amount to deliver. (This is the greedy principle in action.)

Greedy algorithms are particularly appreciated for scheduling problems, optimal caching, and compression using Huffman coding. They also work fine for some graph problems. For instance, Kruskal's and Prim's algorithms for finding a minimum-cost spanning tree and Dijkstra's shortest-path algorithm are all greedy ones (see Chapter 9 for details). A greedy approach can also offer a nonoptimal, yet an acceptable first approximation, solution to the traveling salesman problem (TSP) and solve the knapsack problem when quantities aren't discrete. (Chapter 16 discusses both problems.)

Understanding why greedy is good

It shouldn't surprise you that a greedy strategy works so well in the make-change problem. In fact, some problems don't require farsighted strategies: The solution is built using intermediate results (a sequence of decisions), and at every step the right decision is always the best one according to an initially chosen criteria.

Acting greedy is also a very human (and effective) approach to solving economic problems. In the 1987 film *Wall Street*, Gordon Gecko, the protagonist, declares that "Greed, for lack of a better word, is good" and celebrates greediness as a positive act in economics. Greediness (not in the moral sense, but in the sense of acting to maximize singular objectives, as in a greedy algorithm) is at the core of the neoclassical economy. Economists such as Adam Smith, in the eighteenth century, theorized that the individual's pursuit of self-interest (without a global vision or purpose) benefits society as a whole greatly and renders it prosperous in economy (it's the theory of the invisible hand: `https://plus.maths.org/ content/adam-smith-and-invisible-hand`).

Detailing how a greedy algorithm works (and under what conditions it can work correctly) is straightforward, as explained in the following four steps:

1. You can divide the problem into partial problems. The sum (or other combination) of these partial problems provides the right solution. In this sense, a greedy algorithm isn't much different from a divide-and-conquer algorithm (like Quicksort or Mergesort, both of which appear in Chapter 7).

2. The successful execution of the algorithm depends on the successful execution of every partial step. This is the *optimal substructure characteristic* because an optimal solution is made only of optimal subsolutions.

3. To achieve success at each step, the algorithm considers the input data only at that step. That is, situation status (previous decisions) determines the decision the algorithm makes, but the algorithm doesn't consider consequences. This complete lack of a global strategy is the *greedy choice property* because being greedy at every phase is enough to offer ultimate success. As an analogy, it's akin to playing the game of chess by not looking ahead more than one move, and yet winning the game.

4. Because the greedy choice property provides hope for success, a greedy algorithm lacks a complex decision rule because it needs, at worst, to consider all the available input elements at each phase. There is no need to compute possible decision implications; consequently, the computational complexity is at worst linear $O(n)$. Greedy algorithms shine because they take the simple route to solving highly complex problems that other algorithms take forever to compute because they look too deep.

Keeping greedy algorithms under control

When faced with a new difficult problem, it's not hard to come up with a greedy solution using the four steps described in the previous section. All you have to do is divide your problems into phases and determine which greedy rule to apply at each step. That is, you do the following:

>> Choose how to make your decision (determine which approach is the simplest, most intuitive, smallest, and fastest)

>> Start solving the problem by applying your decision rule

>> Record the result of your decision (if needed) and determine the status of your problem

>> Repeatedly apply the same approach at every step until reaching the problem conclusion

No matter how you apply the previous steps, you must determine whether you're accomplishing your goal by relying on a series of myopic decisions. The greedy approach works for some problems and sometimes for specific cases of some problems, but it doesn't work for every problem. For instance, the make-change problem works perfectly with U.S. currency but produces less-than-optimal results with other currencies. For example, using a fictional currency (call it *credits*, using a term in many sci-fi games and fiction) with denominations of 1, 15, and 25 credits, the previous algorithm fails to deliver the optimal change for a due sum of 30 credits:

```
print ('Change: %s (using %i bills)'
       % (change(30, [25, 15, 1])))

Change: [25, 1, 1, 1, 1, 1] (using 6 bills)
```

Clearly, the optimal solution is to return two 15 credit bills, but the algorithm, being shortsighted, started with the highest denomination available (25 credits) and then used five 1 credit bills to make up the residual 5 credits.

TECHNICAL STUFF

Some complex mathematical frameworks called *matroids* (read the article at https://jeremykun.com/2014/08/26/when-greedy-algorithms-are-perfect-the-matroid/ for details) can help verify whether you can use a greedy solution to optimally solve a particular problem. If phrasing a problem using a matroid framework is possible, a greedy solution will provide an optimal result. Yet there are problems that have optimal greedy solutions that don't abide by the matroid framework. (You can read about matroid structures being sufficient, but not necessary for an optimal greedy solution in the article found at http://cstheory.stackexchange.com/questions/21367/does-every-greedy-algorithm-have-matroid-structure.)

The greedy algorithms user should know that greedy algorithms do perform well but don't always provide the best possible results. When they do, it's because the problem consists of known examples or because the problem is compatible with matroid mathematical framework. Even when a greedy algorithm works best in one setting, changing the setting may *break the toy* and generate just good or acceptable solutions. In fact, the cases of just good or acceptable results are many, because greedy algorithms don't often outperform other solutions, as shown by

>> The make-change problem solutions demonstrated earlier in this chapter show how a change in setting can cause a greedy algorithm to stop working.

>> The scheduling problem (described in the "Finding Out How Greedy Can Be Useful" section, later in this chapter) illustrates how a greedy solution works perfectly with one worker, but don't expect it to work with more than one.

>> The Dijkstra shortest-path algorithm works only with edges having positive weights. (Negative weights will cause the algorithm to loop around some nodes indefinitely.)

Demonstrating that a greedy algorithm works the best is a hard task, requiring a solid knowledge of mathematics. Otherwise, you can devise a proof in a more empirical way by testing the greedy solution against one of the following:

>> Against a known optimal solution, when the greedy algorithm produces the optimal solution or you can change such a solution by exchanging its elements into an equivalent best solution (without any loss of performance or success). When a greedy solution matches the result of an optimal solution, you know that the greedy solution is equivalent and that it works best (this is the *exchange* proof).

>> Against another algorithm when, as you see the greedy solution unfolding, you notice that the greedy solution *stays ahead* of the other algorithm; that is, the greedy solution always provides a better solution at every step than is provided by another algorithm.

TIP

Even considering that it's more the exception than a rule that a successful greedy approach will determine the top solution, greedy solutions often outperform other tentative solutions. You may not always get the top solution, but the solution will provide results that are good enough to act as a starting point (as a minimum), which is why you should start by trying greedy solutions first on new problems.

Considering NP complete problems

Usually you think of a greedy algorithm because other choices don't compute the solution you need in a feasible time. The greedy approach suits problems for which you have many choices and have to combine them. As the number of possible combinations increases, complexity explodes and even the most powerful computer available fails to provide an answer in a reasonable time. For example, when attempting to solve a puzzle, you could try to solve it by determining all the possible ways you can fit the available pieces together. A more reasonable way is to start solving the problem by choosing a single location and then finding the best-fitting piece for it. Solving the puzzle this way means using time to find the best fitting piece, but you don't have to consider that location again, reducing the total number of pieces for each iteration.

Puzzle problems, in which the number of possible decisions can become huge, are more frequent than you expect. Some problems of this type have already been solved, but many others aren't, and we can't even transform them (yet) into versions we know how to solve. Until someone is smart enough to find a generic solution for these problems, a greedy approach may be the easiest way to approach them, provided that you accept that you won't always be getting the best solution but a roughly acceptable one instead (in many cases).

These difficult problems vary in characteristics and problem domain. Different examples of difficult problems are protein unfolding (which can help cure cancer) or breaking strong password encryption, such as the popular RSA cryptosystem (http://blogs.ams.org/mathgradblog/2014/03/30/rsa/). In the 1960s, researchers found a common pattern for all of them: They are all equally difficult to solve. This pattern is called the NP-completeness theory (NP stands for nondeterministic polynomial). In a sense, these problems distinguish themselves from others because it's not yet possible to find a solution in a reasonable time —that is, in polynomial time.

Polynomial time means that an algorithm runs in powers of the number of inputs (known as P problems). Linear time is polynomial time because it runs $O(n^1)$. Also quadratic $O(n^2)$ and cubic $O(n^3)$ complexities are polynomial time, and though they grow quite fast, they don't compare to NP-complete complexity, which is usually exponential time, that is, $O(c^n)$. *Exponential time* complexity makes it impossible to find a reasonable solution for any of these problems using brute force. In fact if *n* is large enough, you may easily have to try a number of solutions larger than the number of atoms present in the known universe. The hope of algorithm experts is that someone will find a way to solve any of these problems in the future, thus opening the door to solving all the NP-complete problems at one time. Solving NP-complete problems is one of the "Millennium Prize Problems" proposed by the Clay Mathematics Institute, which offers an award of one million USD to anyone who can devise a solution (http://www.claymath.org/millennium-problems/p-vs-np-problem).

REMEMBER

NP is a broad class of algorithmic problems that comprises both P and NP-complete problems. Generally, NP problems are difficult (the ones that require you to devise a smart algorithm). P problems are solvable in polynomial time; NP-complete problems are so hard to solve that the associated algorithms run in exponential time. Fortunately, if you have a solution for an NP-complete problem, you can easily check its validity.

TIP

Maybe you won't solve any NP-complete problem using an algorithm specifically designed to find an optimal solution. However, you can still find a reasonable solution using greedy algorithms.

Finding Out How Greedy Can Be Useful

After discussing greedy algorithms generally, it's illuminating to describe some of them in detail, understanding how they work and determine how to reuse their strategies for solving other problems. The following sections review the Huffman coding algorithm to provide more insight on the way it works to create new efficient encoding systems. These sections also describe how a *computer cache* (an algorithm always found under the hood of any computer) works. In addition, you discover how to schedule tasks correctly to achieve deadlines and priorities. Production of material goods strongly relies on greedy algorithms to schedule resources and activities. Usually, activity algorithms appear at the core of Material Requirements Planning (MRP) software, and they help run a factory efficiently (http://searchmanufacturingerp.techtarget.com/definition/Material-requirements-planning-MRP).

Arranging cached computer data

Computers are often processing the same data multiple times. Obtaining data from disk or the Internet requires times and costs computational time. Consequently, it's useful to store often-used data in local storage where it's easier to access (and maybe already preprocessed). A *cache,* which is usually a series of memory slots or space on disk reserved for that need, fulfills the purpose.

For instance, when reviewing your web browser's history, you likely notice that only a part of traffic is made of new websites, whereas you spend a large amount of time and page requests on sites you know well. Storing in cache some parts of commonly seen websites (such as the header, background, some pictures, and some pages that seldom change) can really improve your web experience because it reduces the need to download data again. All you need is the new data from the Internet because most of what you want to see is already somewhere in your computer. (The cache of a web browser is a disk directory.)

The problem isn't new. In the 1960s, László Bélády, a Hungarian computer scientist working at IBM Research, hypothesized that the best way to store information in a computer for prompt reuse is to know what data is needed in the future and for how long. It isn't possible to implement such forecasting in practice because computer usage can be unpredictable and not predetermined.

Yet, as a principle, the idea of anticipating the future can inspire an *optimal replacement strategy*, a greedy choice based on the idea of keeping the pages that you expect to use soon based on previous requests to the cache. Bélády's optimal page replacement policy (also known as the *clairvoyant replacement algorithm*) works on a greedy principle: to discard data from the cache whose next use will likely occur farthest in the future in order to minimize the chance of discarding something you need soon. To implement this idea, the algorithm follows these steps:

1. Fill the computer cache by recording data from every request made. Only when the cache is full do you start discarding past stuff to make room for new data.

2. Define a method for determining recent usage. This algorithm can use file date stamps or a system of memory flags (which flags recently used pages and clears all the flags after a certain time) to make the determination.

3. When you have to fit new data, you discard data that hasn't been used recently from the cache. The algorithm picks one piece of data randomly among the ones not used.

For instance, if your cache has only four memory slots, and it is filled by four alphabet letters that arrive in the following order:

A	B	C	D

when a new letter is processed, such as the letter E, the computer makes space for it by removing one of the letters that are less likely to be requested at this point. In this example, good candidates are A, B, or C (D is the most recent addition). The algorithm will pick one slot randomly and evict its data from the cache in order to let E in.

Competing for resources

When you want to achieve an objective, such as to create a service or produce a material object, a common problem is scheduling several competing activities that require exclusive access to resources. Resources can include time or a production machine. Examples of such situations abound in the real world, ranging from scheduling your attendance at university courses to arranging the supplies of an army, or from assembling a complex product such as a car to organizing a computational job sequence in a data center. Invariably, common goals in such situations are to

- » Achieve getting the most jobs done in a certain amount of time
- » Manage jobs as quickly as possible, on average
- » Respect some strict priorities (hard deadlines)
- » Respect some priority indications (soft deadlines)

Job scheduling falls into two categories:

- » Jobs that are hard to solve properly and require advanced algorithms to solve
- » Jobs that are easier to deal with and that can be solved by simple greedy algorithms

Most of the scheduling you perform actually falls among those solvable by greedy algorithms. For instance, managing jobs as quickly as possible is a common requirement for industrial production or the service industry when each job serves the needs of a client and you want to do your best for all your clients. Here's how you can determine a context for such an algorithm:

- » You have a single machine (or worker) that can work out orders.
- » Orders arrive in batches, so you have many to choose from at a time.
- » Orders differ in length, each requiring a different execution time.

For instance, you receive four jobs from four business customers requiring eight, four, 12, and three hours, respectively, to execute. Even though the total execution time remains the same, changing the job-execution order changes the time when you complete the jobs and dictates how long each business customer has to wait before having its job done. The following sections consider different methods for meeting business customer needs given specific goals.

Addressing customer satisfaction

Business is about keeping customers happy. If you execute the jobs in the order presented, the work takes 8+4+12+3=27 hours to execute completely. Yet, the first customer will receive its job after eight hours, the last one after 27 hours. In fact, the first job completes in eight hours, the second in 8+4=12 hours, the third in 8+4+12=24 hours, the last in 8+4+12+3=27 hours.

If you aim at having all your customers happy and satisfied, you should strive to minimize the average waiting time for each of them. This measure is given by the average of the delivery times: (8+12+24+27)/4=17.75 hours on average to wait for a job. To reduce the average wait time, you could start simulating all the possible combinations of order execution and recalculate the estimate. This is feasible for a few jobs on a single machine, but if you have hundreds of them on multiple machines, that becomes a very heavy computational problem. A greedy algorithm can save the day without much planning: just execute the shortest first. The resulting average will be the smallest possible: $(3+(3+4)+(3+4+8)+(3+4+8+12))/4=$ 13 hours on average.

REMEMBER

To obtain the average wait time, you take the average of the cumulated sums of runtimes. If you instead take the average of raw times, you obtain the average length of a task, which doesn't represent the customer's waiting time.

The greedy principle is simple: Because you sum cumulative times, if you start by running the longest tasks, you extend the longest run to all successive execution times (because it is a cumulative sum). If instead you start with the shortest jobs, you draw the smallest times first, positively affecting the average (and your customers' level of satisfaction).

Meeting deadlines

Sometimes, more than just wanting to make your customers wait less time, you also have to respect their time requirements, meaning that you have deadlines. When you have deadlines, the greedy mechanism changes. Now you don't start from the shortest task but with the task that you must deliver the earliest, according to the principle *the earliest, the better*. This is the problem of hard deadlines, and it's a problem you can actually fail to solve. (Some deadlines are simply impossible to meet.)

TIP

If you try a greedy strategy and can't solve the problem, you can acknowledge that no solution to the required deadline exists. When hard deadlines can't work, you can try to solve the problem using soft deadlines instead, meaning that you have to respect a priority (executing certain tasks first).

In this example, you have both the lengths of the tasks, as discussed in the previous section, and you have a value (a *weight*) that defines the task importance (larger weights, higher priority). It's the same problem, but this time you must minimize the weighted average completion time. To achieve this goal, you create a priority score by dividing the time lengths by the weights, and you start with the tasks that have the lowest score. If a task has the lowest score, it's because it is high priority or very short.

For instance, reprising the previous example, you now have tuples of both weights and lengths: (40,8), (30,4), (20,12), (10,3), where 40 in the first tuple is a weight and 8 is a length. Divide each length by the weight and you get priority scores of: 0.20, 0.13, 0.60, and 0.30. Start from the lowest-priority score and, adding the lowest left priority score, you obtain a best schedule that assures that you both minimize times and respect priorities: (30,4), (40,8), (10,3), (20,12).

Revisiting Huffman coding

As seen in the previous chapter, Huffman coding can represent data content in a more compact form by exploiting the fact that some data (for instance certain characters of the alphabet) appear more frequently in a data stream. By using encodings of different length (shorter for the most frequent characters, longer for the least frequent ones), the data consumes less space. Prof. Robert M. Fano (Huffman's professor) and Claude Shannon already envisioned such a compression strategy but couldn't find an efficient way to determine an encoding arrangement that would make it impossible to mistake one character for another.

REMEMBER

Prefix-free codes are necessary in order to avoid errors when decoding the message. It means that no previously used bit encoding should be used as the starting point of another bit encoding. Huffman found a simple and workable solution for implementing prefix-free codes using a greedy algorithm. The solution to the prefix-free problem found by Huffman is to transform the originally balanced tree (a data structure discussed in Chapter 6) containing the fixed-length encoding into an unbalanced tree, as shown in Figure 15-1.

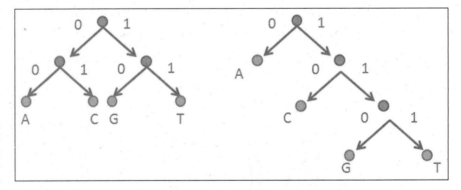

FIGURE 15-1:
From a balanced tree (left) to an unbalanced tree (right).

An unbalanced tree has a special characteristic that each node has only one branch that keeps on developing in other nodes and branches, whereas the other branch terminates with an encoded character. This characteristic assures that no previously used encoding sequence can start a new sequence (graphically, a branch terminating with an encoded character is a dead end).

Apart from graphically drafting the unbalanced structure, a greedy algorithm can also construct an unbalanced tree. The idea is to build the structure up from the root, starting with the least frequently used characters. The algorithm creates the upper levels of the tree by aggregating less frequent characters in sequence until there are no more characters and you reach the top.

To demonstrate the greedy recipe behind the algorithm, this section provides a Python code example based on DNA. DNA is represented as a sequence of the letters A, C, T, and G (the four nucleotides present in all living beings). A good trick is to use just two bits in order to represent each of the four letters, which is already a good memory-saving strategy when compared to using a full ASCII encoding (which is at least 7 bits).

The nucleotides aren't uniformly distributed. The distribution varies depending on what genes you study. The following table shows a gene with an uneven distribution, allowing for a predominance of A and C nucleotides.

Nucleotides	Percentage	Fixed Encoding	Huffman Encoding
A	40.5%	00	0
C	29.2%	01	10
G	14.5%	10	110
T	15.8%	11	111
Weighted bit average		2.00	1.90

By multiplying the number of bits of the two encodings by their percentage and summing everything, you obtain the weighted average of bits used by each of them. In this case, the result is 1.9 for the Huffman encoding versus 2.0 for the fixed encoding. It means that you obtain a five percent bit saving in this example. You could save even more space when having genes with an even more unbalanced distribution in favor of some nucleotide.

The following example generates a random DNA sequence and shows how the code systematically generates the encoding. (If you change the seed value, the random generation of the DNA sequences may lead to a different result, both in the distribution of nucleotides and Huffman encoding.)

```
from heapq import heappush, heappop, heapify
from collections import defaultdict, Counter
from random import shuffle, seed
```

```
generator = ["A"]*6+["C"]*4+["G"]*2+["T"]*2
text = ""
seed(4)
for i in range(1000):
    shuffle(generator)
    text += generator[0]

print(text)
frequencies = Counter(list(text))
print(frequencies)

CAACCCCGACACGCCTCCATAGCCACAACAAGCAAAAAAGGC ...
Counter({'A': 405, 'C': 292, 'T': 158, 'G': 145})
```

After making the data inputs ready to compress, the code prepares a heap data structure (see the "Performing specialized searches using a binary heap" section of Chapter 7 for details) to arrange the results efficiently along the steps the algorithm takes. The elements in the heap contain the frequency number of nucleotides, the nucleotide characters, and its encoding. With a log-linear time complexity, $O(n*log(n))$, a heap is the right structure to use to order the results and allow the algorithm to draw the two smallest elements quickly.

```
heap = ([[freq, [char, ""]] for char, freq in
            frequencies.items()])
heapify(heap)
print(heap)

[[145, ['G', '']], [158, ['T', '']], [405, ['A', '']],
   [292, ['C', '']]]
```

When you run the algorithm, it picks the nucleotides with fewer frequencies from the heap (the greedy choice). It aggregates these nucleotides into a new element, replacing the previous two. The process continues until the last aggregation reduces the number of elements in the heap to one.

```
iteration = 0
while len(heap) > 1:
    iteration += 1
    lo = heappop(heap)
    hi = heappop(heap)
    print ('Step %i 1st:%s 2nd:%s' % (iteration, lo,hi))
    for pair in lo[1:]:
        pair[1] = '0' + pair[1]
    for pair in hi[1:]:
```

```
        pair[1] = '1' + pair[1]
    heappush(heap, [lo[0] + hi[0]] + lo[1:] + hi[1:])

Step 1 1st:[145, ['G', '']] 2nd:[158, ['T', '']]
Step 2 1st:[292, ['C', '']] 2nd:[303, ['G', '0'],
 ['T', '1']]
Step 3 1st:[405, ['A', '']] 2nd:[595, ['C', '0'],
 ['G', '10'], ['T', '11']]
```

As the aggregations put the nucleotides together, which constitutes different levels of the unbalanced tree, their Huffman encoding is systematically modified; adding a zero in front of the encoding of the lowest frequent aggregate and adding one to the second-lowest frequent one. In this way, the algorithm efficiently replicates the unbalanced tree structure previously illustrated.

```
tree = sorted(heappop(heap)[1:], key=lambda p: (len(p[-
        1]), p))
print ("Symbol\tWeight\tCode")
for e in tree:
    print ("%s\t%s\t%s" % (e[0], frequencies[e[0]], e[1]))

Symbol    Weight    Code
A         405       0
C         292       10
G         145       110
T         158       111
```

The final step is to print the result, sorting it by the bit encoding and showing the final symbol table generated.

» Using memoization effectively for dynamic programming

» Discovering how the knapsack problem can be useful for optimization

» Working with the NP-complete traveling salesman problem

Chapter **16**

Relying on Dynamic Programming

I nstead of using brute force, which implies trying all possible solutions to a problem, greedy algorithms provide an answer that is quick and often satisfying. In fact, a greedy algorithm can potentially solve the problem fully. Yet, greedy algorithms are also limited because they make decisions that don't consider the consequences of their choices. Chapter 15 shows that you can't always solve a problem using a greedy algorithm. Therefore, an algorithm may make an apparently optimal decision at a certain stage, which later appears limiting and suboptimal for achieving the best solution. A better algorithm, one that doesn't rely on the greedy approach, can revise past decisions or anticipate that an apparently good decision is not as promising as it might seem. This is the approach that dynamic programming takes.

Dynamic programming is an algorithm approach devised in the 1950s by Richard Ernest Bellman (an applied mathematician also known for other discoveries in the field of mathematics and algorithms, you can read more at https://en.wikipedia.org/wiki/Richard_E._Bellman) that tests more solutions than a corresponding greedy approach. Testing more solutions provides the ability to rethink and ponder the consequences of decisions. Dynamic programming avoids performing heavy computations thanks to a smart caching system (a *cache* is a storage system collecting data or information) called *memoization,* a term defined later in the chapter.

This chapter offers you more than a simple definition of dynamic programming. It also explains why dynamic programming has such a complicated name and how to transform any algorithm (especially recursive ones) into dynamic programming using Python and its function decorators (powerful tools in Python that allow changing an existing function without rewriting its code). In addition, you discover applications of dynamic programming to optimize resources and returns, creating short tours between places and comparing strings in an approximate way. Dynamic programming provides a natural approach to dealing with many problems you encounter while journeying through the world of algorithms.

Explaining Dynamic Programming

Dynamic programming is as effective as an exhaustive algorithm (thus providing correct solutions), yet it is often as efficient as an approximate solution (the computational time of many dynamic programming algorithms is polynomial). It seems to work like magic because the solution you need often requires the algorithm to perform the same calculations many times. By modifying the algorithm and making it dynamic, you can record the computation results and reuse them when needed. Reusing takes little time when compared to recalculating, thus the algorithm finishes the steps quickly. The following sections discuss what dynamic programming involves in more detail.

Obtaining a historical basis

You can boil *dynamic programming* down to having an algorithm remember the previous problem results where you'd otherwise have to perform the same calculation repeatedly. Even though dynamic programming might appear to be quite complex, the implementation is actually straightforward. However, it does have some interesting historical origins.

Bellman described the name as the result of necessity and convenience in his autobiography, *In the Eye of the Hurricane.* He writes that the name choice was a way to hide the true nature of his research at the RAND Corporation (a research and development institution funded by both the U.S. government and private financers) from Charles Erwin Wilson, the Secretary of Defense under the Eisenhower presidency. Cloaking the true nature of his research helped Bellman remain employed at the RAND Corporation. You can read his explanation in more detail in the excerpt at: http://smo.sogang.ac.kr/doc/dy_birth.pdf. Some researchers don't agree about the name source. For example, Stuart Russell and Peter Norvig, in their book *Artificial Intelligence: A Modern Approach,* argue that Bellman actually used the term *dynamic programming* in a paper dating 1952, which is before Wilson became Secretary in 1953 (and Wilson himself was CEO of General Motors before becoming an engineer involved in research and development).

Computer programming languages weren't widespread during the time that Bellman worked in operations research, a discipline that applies mathematics to make better decisions when approaching mainly production or logistic problems (but is also used for other practical problems). Computing was at the early stages and used mostly for planning. The basic approach of dynamic programming is the same as *linear programming,* another algorithmic technique (see Chapter 19) defined in those years when programming meant planning a specific process to find an optimal solution. The term *dynamic* reminds you that the algorithm moves and stores partial solutions. Dynamic programming is a complex name for a smart and effective technique to improve algorithm running times.

Making problems dynamic

Because dynamic programming takes advantage of repeated operations, it operates well on problems that have solutions built around solving subproblems that the algorithm later assembles to provide a complete answer. In order to work effectively, a dynamic programming approach uses subproblems nested in other subproblems. (This approach is akin to greedy algorithms, which also require an optimal substructure, as explained in Chapter 15.) Only when you can break down a problem into nested subproblems can dynamic programming beat brute-force approaches that repeatedly rework the same subproblems.

REMEMBER

As a concept, dynamic programming is a huge umbrella covering many different applications because it isn't really a specific algorithm for solving a specific problem. Rather, it's a general technique that supports problem solving.

You can trace dynamic programming to two large families of solutions:

>> **Bottom-up:** Builds an array of partial results that aggregate into a complete solution

>> **Top-down:** Splits the problem into subproblems, starting from the complete solution (this approach is typical of recursive algorithms) and using memoization (defined in the next section) to avoid repeating computations more than once

Typically, the top-down approach is more computationally efficient because it generates only the subproblems necessary for the complete solution. The bottom-up approach is more explorative and, using trial and error, often obtains partial results that you won't use later. On the other hand, bottom-up approaches better reflect the approach that you'd take in everyday life when facing a problem (thinking recursively, instead, needs abstraction and training before application). Both top-down and bottom-up approaches aren't all that easy to understand at times. That's because using dynamic programming transforms the way you solve problems, as detailed in these steps:

1. Create a working solution using brute-force or recursion. The solution works but it takes a long time or won't finish at all.

2. Store the results of subproblems to speed your computations and reach a solution in a reasonable time.

3. Change the way you approach the problem and gain even more speed.

4. Redefine the problem approach, in a less intuitive but more efficient way to obtain the greatest advantage from dynamic programming.

Transforming algorithms using dynamic programming to make them work efficiently makes them harder to understand. In fact, you might look at the solutions and think they work by magic. Becoming proficient in dynamic programming requires repeated observations of existing solutions and some practical exercise. This proficiency is worth the effort, however, because dynamic programming can help you solve problems for which you have to systematically compare or compute solutions.

TIP

Dynamic programming is especially known for helping solve (or at least make less time demanding) combinatorial optimization problems, which are problems that require obtaining combinations of input elements as a solution. Examples of such problems solved by dynamic programming are the traveling salesman and the knapsack problems, described later in the chapter.

Casting recursion dynamically

The basis of dynamic programming is to achieve something as effective as brute-force searching without actually spending all the time doing the computations required by a brute-force approach. You achieve the result by trading time for disk space or memory, which is usually done by creating a data structure (a hash table, an array, or a data matrix) to store previous results. Using lookup tables allows you to access results without having to perform a calculation a second time.

REMEMBER

The technique of storing previous function results and using them instead of the function is *memoization,* a term you shouldn't confuse with memorization. Memoization derives from *memorandum,* the Latin word for "to be remembered."

REMEMBER

Caching is another term that you find used when talking about memoization. *Caching* refers to using a special area of computer memory to serve data faster when required, which has more general uses than memoization.

To be effective, dynamic programming needs problems that repeat or retrace previous steps. A good example of a similar situation is using recursion, and the landmark of recursion is calculating Fibonacci numbers. The Fibonacci sequence is simply a sequence of numbers in which the next number is the sum of the previous two. The sequence starts with 0 followed by 1. After defining the first two elements, every following number in the sequence is the sum of the previous ones. Here are the first eleven numbers:

```
[0, 1, 1, 2, 3, 5, 8, 13, 21, 34, 55]
```

As with indexing in Python, counting starts from the zero position, and the last number in the sequence is the tenth position. The inventor of the sequence, the Italian mathematician Leonardo Pisano, known as Fibonacci, lived in 1200. Fibonacci thought that the fact that each number is the sum of the previous two should have made the numbers suitable for representing the growth patterns of a group of rabbits. The sequence didn't work great for rabbit demographics, but it offered unexpected insights into both mathematics and nature itself because the numbers appear in botany and zoology. For instance, you see this progression in the branching of trees, in the arrangements of leaves in a stem, and of seeds in a sunflower (you can read about this arrangement at https://www.goldennumber.net/spirals/).

REMEMBER

Fibonacci was also the mathematician who introduced Hindu-Arabic numerals to Europe, the system we daily use today. He described both the numbers and the sequence in his masterpiece, the *Liber Abaci*, in 1202.

You can calculate a Fibonacci number sequence using recursion. When you input a number, the recursion splits the number into the sum of the previous two Fibonacci numbers in the sequence. After the first split, the recursion proceeds by performing the same task for each element of the split, splitting each of the two numbers into the previous two Fibonacci numbers. The recursion continues splitting numbers into their sums, until it finally finds the roots of the sequence, the numbers 0 and 1. Reviewing the two types of dynamic programming algorithm described in the previous paragraph, this solution uses a top-down approach. The following code shows the recursive approach in Python. (You can find this code in the A4D; 16; Fibonacci.ipynb file on the Dummies site as part of the downloadable code; see the Introduction for details.)

```
def fib(n, tab=0):
    if n==0:
        return 0
```

```
    elif n == 1:
        return 1
    else:
        print ("lvl %i, Summing fib(%i) and fib(%i)" %
            (tab, n-1, n-2))
        return fib(n-1,tab+1) + fib(n-2,tab+1)
```

The code prints the splits generated by each recursion level. The following output shows what happens when you call fib() with an input value of 7:

```
fib(7)

lvl 0, Summing fib(6) and fib(5)
lvl 1, Summing fib(5) and fib(4)
lvl 2, Summing fib(4) and fib(3)
lvl 3, Summing fib(3) and fib(2)
lvl 4, Summing fib(2) and fib(1)
lvl 5, Summing fib(1) and fib(0)
lvl 4, Summing fib(1) and fib(0)
lvl 3, Summing fib(2) and fib(1)
lvl 4, Summing fib(1) and fib(0)
lvl 2, Summing fib(3) and fib(2)
lvl 3, Summing fib(2) and fib(1)
lvl 4, Summing fib(1) and fib(0)
lvl 3, Summing fib(1) and fib(0)
lvl 1, Summing fib(4) and fib(3)
lvl 2, Summing fib(3) and fib(2)
lvl 3, Summing fib(2) and fib(1)
lvl 4, Summing fib(1) and fib(0)
lvl 3, Summing fib(1) and fib(0)
lvl 2, Summing fib(2) and fib(1)
lvl 3, Summing fib(1) and fib(0)

13
```

The output shows 20 splits. Some numbers appear more than once as part of the splits. It seems like an ideal case for applying dynamic programming. The following code adds a dictionary, called memo, which stores previous results. After the recursion splits a number, it checks whether the result already appears in the dictionary before starting the next recursive branch. If it finds the result, the code uses the precomputed result, as shown here:

```
memo = dict()
def fib_mem(n, tab=0):
```

```
    if n==0:
        return 0
    elif n == 1:
        return 1
    else:
        if (n-1, n-2) not in memo:
            print ("lvl %i, Summing fib(%i) and fib(%i)" %
                    (tab, n-1, n-2))
            memo[(n-1,n-2)] = fib_mem(n-1,tab+1
                            ) + fib_mem(n-2,tab+1)
        return memo[(n-1,n-2)]
```

Using memoization, the recursive function doesn't compute 20 additions but rather uses just six, the essential ones used as building blocks to solve the initial requirement for computing a certain number in the sequence:

```
fib_mem(7)

lvl 0, Summing fib(6) and fib(5)
lvl 1, Summing fib(5) and fib(4)
lvl 2, Summing fib(4) and fib(3)
lvl 3, Summing fib(3) and fib(2)
lvl 4, Summing fib(2) and fib(1)
lvl 5, Summing fib(1) and fib(0)

13
```

Looking inside the memo dictionary, you can find the sequence of sums that define the Fibonacci sequence starting from 1:

```
memo
{(1, 0): 1, (2, 1): 2, (3, 2): 3, (4, 3): 5, (5, 4): 8,
 (6, 5): 13}
```

Leveraging memoization

Memoization is the essence of dynamic programming. You often find the need to use it when scripting an algorithm yourself. When creating a function, whether recursive or not, you can easily transform it using a simple command, a *decorator*, which is a special Python function that transforms functions. To see how to work with a decorator, start with a recursive function, stripped of any print statement:

```
def fib(n):
    if n==0:
        return 0
    elif n == 1:
        return 1
    else:
        return fib(n-1) + fib(n-2)
```

When using Jupyter, you use IPython built-in magic commands, such as timeit, to measure the execution time of a command on your computer:

```
%timeit -n 1 -r 1 print(fib(36))

14930352
1 loop, best of 1: 15.5 s per loop
```

The output shows that the function requires about 15 seconds to execute. However, depending on your machine, function execution may require more or less time. No matter the speed of your computer, it will certainly take a few seconds to complete, because the Fibonacci number for 36 is quite huge: 14930352. Testing the same function for higher Fibonacci numbers takes even longer.

Now it's time to see the effect of decorating the function. Using the lru_cache function from the functools package can radically reduce execution time. This function is available only when using Python3. It transforms a function by automatically adding a cache to hold its results. You can also set the cache size by using the maxsize parameter (lru_cache uses a cache with an optimal replacement strategy, as explained in the Chapter 15). If you set maxsize=None, the cache uses all the available memory, without limits.

```
from functools import lru_cache

@lru_cache(maxsize=None)
def fib(n):
    if n==0:
        return 0
    elif n == 1:
        return 1
    else:
        return fib(n-1) + fib(n-2)
```

Note that the function is the same as before. The only addition is the imported lru_cache (https://docs.python.org/3.5/library/functools.html), which you call by putting an @ symbol in front of it. Any call with the @ symbol in front is an *annotation* and calls the lru_cache function as a decorator of the following function.

TECHNICAL STUFF

Using decorators is an advanced technique in Python. Decorators don't need to be explained in detail in this book, but you can still take advantage of them because they are so easy to use. (You can find additional information about decorators at http://simeonfranklin.com/blog/2012/jul/1/python-decorators-in-12-steps/ and https://www.learnpython.org/en/Decorators.) Just remember that you call them using annotations (@ + *decorator function's name*) and that you put them in front of the function you want to transform. The original function is fed into the decorator and comes out transformed. In this example of a simple recursive function, the decorator outputs a recursion function enriched by memoization.

It's time to test the function speed, as before:

```
%timeit -n 1 -r 1 print(fib(36))

14930352
1 loop, best of 1: 60.6 µs per loop
```

Even if your execution time is different, it should decrease from seconds to milliseconds. Such is the power of memoization. You can also explore how your function uses its cache by calling the cache_info method from the decorated function:

```
fib.cache_info()

CacheInfo(hits=34, misses=37, maxsize=None, currsize=37)
```

The output tells you that there are 37 function calls that don't find an answer in the cache. However, 34 other calls did find a useful answer in the cache.

TIP

Just by importing lru_cache from functools and using it in annotations in front of your heavy-duty algorithms in Python, you will experience a great increase in performance (unless they are greedy algorithms).

Discovering the Best Dynamic Recipes

Even dynamic programming has limitations. The biggest limitation of all relates to its main strength: If you keep track of too many partial solutions to improve running time, you may run out of memory. You may have too many partial solutions in store because the problem is complex, or simply because the order you use to produce partial solutions is not an optimal one and too many of the solutions don't fit the problem requirements.

The order used to solve subproblems is something you must track. The order you choose should make sense for the efficient progression of the algorithm (you solve something that you're going to reuse immediately) because the trick is in smart reuse of previously built building blocks. Therefore, using memoization may not provide enough benefit. Rearranging your problems in the right order can improve the results. You can learn how to correctly order your subproblems by learning directly from the best dynamic programming recipes available: knapsack, traveling salesman, and approximate string search, as described in the sections that follow.

Looking inside the knapsack

The knapsack problem has been around since at least 1897 and is likely the work of Tobias Dantzig (https://www.britannica.com/biography/Tobias-Dantzig). In this case, you have to pack up your knapsack with as many items as possible. Each item has a value, so you want maximize the total value of the items you carry. The knapsack has a threshold capacity or you have a limit of weight you can carry, so you can't carry all the items.

The general situation fits any problem that involves a budget and resources, and you want to allocate them in the smartest way possible. This problem setting is so common that many people consider the knapsack problem to be one of the most popular algorithmic problems. The knapsack problem finds applications in computer science, manufacturing, finance, logistics, and cryptography. For instance, real-world applications of the knapsack problem are how to best load a cargo ship with goods or how to optimally cut raw materials, thus creating the least waste possible.

REMEMBER

Even though it's such a popular problem, this book doesn't explore the knapsack problem again because the dynamic approach is incontestably one of the best solving approaches. It's important to remember, though, that in specific cases, for such as when the items are quantities, other approaches, such as using greedy algorithms, may work equally well (or even better).

This section shows how to solve the *1-0 knapsack problem*. In this case, you have a finite number of items and can put each of them into the knapsack (the one status) or not (the zero status). It's useful to know there are other possible variants of the problem:

>> **Fractional knapsack problem:** Deals with quantities. For example, an item could be kilograms of flour, and you must pick the best quantity. You can solve this version using a greedy algorithm.

>> **Bounded knapsack problem:** Puts one or more copies of the same item into the knapsack. In this case, you must deal with minimum and maximum number requirements for each item you pick.

>> **Unbounded knapsack problem:** Puts one or more copies of the same item into the knapsack without constraints. The only limit is that you can't put a negative number of items into the knapsack.

The 1-0 knapsack problem relies on a dynamic programming solution and runs in pseudo-polynomial time (which is worse than just polynomial time) because the running time depends on the number of items (n) multiplied by the number of fractions of the knapsack capacity (W) that you use on building your partial solution. When using big-O notation, you can say that the running time is $O(nW)$. The brute-force version of the algorithm instead runs in $O(2^n)$. The algorithm works like this:

1. Given the knapsack capacity, test a range of smaller knapsacks (subproblems). In this case, given a knapsack capable of carrying 20 kilograms, the algorithm tests a range of knapsacks carrying from 0 kilograms to 20 kilograms.

2. For each item, test how it fits in each of the knapsacks, from the smallest knapsack to the largest. At each test, if the item can fit, choose the best value from the following:

   a. The solution offered by the previous smaller knapsack

   b. The test item, plus you fill the residual space with the best valued solution previously that filled that space

The code runs the knapsack algorithm and solves the problem with a set of six items of different weight and value combinations as well as a 20-kg knapsack:

Item	1	2	3	4	5	6
Weight in kg	2	3	4	4	5	9
Profit in 100 USD	3	4	3	5	8	10

Here is the code to execute the dynamic programming procedure described. (You can find this code in the A4D; 16; Knapsack.ipynb file on the Dummies site as part of the downloadable code; see the Introduction for details.)

```python
import numpy as np

values = np.array([3,4,3,5,8,10])
weights = np.array([2,3,4,4,5,9])
items = len(weights)
capacity = 20

memo = dict()
for size in range(0, capacity+1, 1):
    memo[(-1, size)] = ([], 0)

for item in range(items):
    for size in range(0, capacity+1, 1):
        # if the object doesn't fit in the knapsack
        if weights[item] > size:
            memo[item, size] = memo[item-1, size]
        else:
            # if the objcts fits, we check what can best fit
            # in the residual space
            previous_row, previous_row_value = memo[
                    item-1, size-weights[item]]
            if memo[item-1, size][1] > values[item
                    ] + previous_row_value:
                memo[item, size] = memo[item-1, size]
            else:
                memo[item, size] = (previous_row + [item
                    ], previous_row_value + values[item])
```

The best solution is the cached result when the code tests inserting the last item with the full capacity (20 kg) knapsack:

```python
best_set, score = memo[items-1, capacity]
print ('The best set %s weights %i and values %i'
        % (best_set, np.sum((weights[best_set])), score))

The best set [0, 3, 4, 5] weights 20 and values 26
```

You may be curious to know what happened inside the memoization dictionary:

```
print (len(memo))

147

print (memo[2, 10])

([0, 1, 2], 10)
```

It contains 147 subproblems. In fact, six items multiplied by 21 knapsacks is 126 solutions, but you have to add another 21 naive solutions to allow the algorithm to work properly (*naive* means leaving the knapsack empty), which increases the number of subproblems to 147.

You may find solving 147 subproblems daunting (even though they're blazingly fast to solve). Using brute force alone to solve the problem means solving fewer subproblems in this particular case. Solving fewer subproblems requires less time, a fact you can test by solving the accounts using Python and the comb function:

```
from scipy.misc import comb
objects = 6
np.sum([comb(objects,k+1) for k in range(objects)])
```

It takes testing 63 combinations to solve this problem. However, if you try using more objects, say, 20, running times look much different because there are now 1,048,575 combinations to test. Contrast this huge number with dynamic programming, which requires solving just 20*21+21 = 441 subproblems.

REMEMBER

This is the difference between quasi-polynomial and exponential time. (As a reminder, the book discusses exponential complexity in Chapter 2 when illustrating the Big O Notation. In Chapter 15, you discover polynomial time as part of the discussion about NP complete problems.) Using dynamic programming becomes fruitful when your problems are complex. Toy problems are good for learning but they can't demonstrate the full extent of employing smart algorithm techniques such as dynamic programming. Each solution tests what happens after adding a certain item when the knapsack has a certain size. The preceding example adds item 2 (weight=4, value=3) and outputs a solution that puts items 0, 1, and 2 into the knapsack (total weight 9 kg) for a value of 10. This intermediate solution leverages previous solutions and is the basis for many of the following solutions before the algorithm reaches its end.

TIP

You may wonder whether the result offered by the script is really the best one achievable. Unfortunately, the only way to be sure is to know the right answer, which means running a brute-force algorithm (when feasible in terms of running time on your computer). This chapter doesn't use brute force for the knapsack problem but you'll see a brute-force approach used in the traveling salesman problem that follows.

Touring around cities

The traveling salesman problem (TSP for short) is at least as widely known as the knapsack problem. You use it mostly in logistics and transportation (such as the derivative Vehicle Routing Problem shown at http://neo.lcc.uma.es/vrp/vehicle-routing-problem/), so it doesn't see as much use as the knapsack problem. The TSP problem asks a traveling salesperson to visit a certain number of cities and then come back to the initial starting city (because it's circular, it's called a tour) using the shortest path possible.

TSP is similar to graph problems, but without the edges because the cities are all interconnected. For this reason, TSP usually relies on a distance matrix as input, which is a table listing the cities on both rows and columns. The intersections contain the distance from a row city to a column city. TSP problem variants may provide a matrix containing time or fuel consumption instead of distances.

TSP is an NP-hard problem, but you can solve the problem using various approaches, some approximate (heuristic) and some exact (dynamic programming). The problem, as with any other NP-hard problem, is the running time. Although you can count on solutions that you presume optimally solve the problem (you can't be certain except when solving short tours), you can't know for sure with problems as complex as touring the world: http://www.math.uwaterloo.ca/tsp/world/. The following example tests various algorithms, such as brute force, greedy, and dynamic programming, on a simple tour of six cities, represented as a weighted graph (see Figure 16-1). (You can find this code in the A4D; 16; TSP.ipynb file on the Dummies site as part of the downloadable code; see the Introduction for details.)

```
import numpy as np
import networkx as nx
import matplotlib.pyplot as plt
%matplotlib inline

D = np.array([[0,20,16,25,24],[20,0,12,12,27],
              [16,12,0,10,14],[25,12,10,0,20],
              [24,27,14,20,0]])
```

```
Graph = nx.Graph()
Graph.add_nodes_from(range(D.shape[0]))
for i in range(D.shape[0]):
    for j in range(D.shape[0]):
        Graph.add_edge(i,j,weight=D[i,j])

np.random.seed(2)
pos=nx.shell_layout(Graph)
nx.draw(Graph, pos, with_labels=True)
labels = nx.get_edge_attributes(Graph,'weight')
nx.draw_networkx_edge_labels(Graph,pos,
                    edge_labels=labels)
plt.show()
```

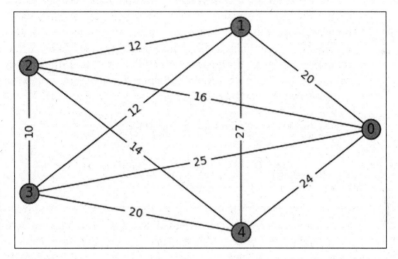

FIGURE 16-1:
Cities represented as nodes in a weighted graph.

After defining the D (distance) matrix, the example tests the first, simplest solution to determine the shortest tour starting and ending from city zero. This solution relies on brute force, which generates all the possible order permutations between the cities, leaving out zero. The distance from zero to the first city and from the last city of the tour to zero is added after the total distance of each solution is calculated. When all the solutions are available, you simply choose the shortest.

```
from itertools import permutations
best_solution = [None, np.sum(D)]
for solution in list(permutations(range(1,D.shape[0]))):
```

```
    start, distance = (0,0)
    for next_one in solution:
        distance += D[start, next_one]
        start = next_one
    distance += D[start,0]
    if distance <= best_solution[1]:
        best_solution = [[0]+list(solution)+[0], distance]
        print ('Best solution so far: %s kms' %
                str(best_solution)[1:-1])


Best solution so far: [0, 1, 2, 3, 4, 0], 86 kms
Best solution so far: [0, 1, 3, 2, 4, 0], 80 kms
Best solution so far: [0, 4, 2, 3, 1, 0], 80 kms
```

The brute-force algorithm quickly determines the best solution and its symmetric path. However, as a result of the small problem size, you obtain a prompt answer because, given four cities, just 24 possible solutions exist. As the number of cities increases, the number of permutations to test becomes intractable, even after removing the symmetric paths (which halves the permutations) and using a fast computer. For example, consider the number of computations when working with 13 cities plus the starting/ending point:

```
from scipy.special import perm
print (perm(13,13)/2)

3113510400.0
```

Dynamic programming can simplify the running time. The Held–Karp algorithm (also known as the Bellman–Held–Karp algorithm because Bellman published it in 1962, the same year as Michael Held and Richard Karp) can cut time complexity to $O(2^n n^2)$. It's still exponential complexity, yet it requires less time than applying the exhaustive enumeration of all tours by brute force.

TIP

Approximate and heuristic algorithms can provide fast and useful results (even though the result may not always reflect the optimal solution, it's usually good enough). You see TSP again later in the book (see Chapters 18 and 20), when dealing with local search and heuristics.

To find the best TSP solution for n cities, starting and ending from city 0, the algorithm proceeds from city 0 and keeps records of the shortest path possible, considering different settings. It always uses a different ending city and touches only a city subset. As the subsets become larger, the algorithm learns how to solve the problem efficiently. Therefore, when solving TSP for five cities, the algorithm first considers solutions involving two cities, then three cities, then four, and finally five (sets have dimensions 1 to *n*). Here are the steps the algorithm uses:

1. Initialize a table to track the distances from city 0 to all other cities. These sets contain only the initial city and a destination city because they represent the initial step.

2. Consider every possible set size, from two to the number of tour cities. This is a first iteration, the outer loop.

3. Inside the outer loop, for each set size, consider every possible combination of cities of that size, not containing the initial city. This is an inner iteration.

4. Inside the inner iteration (Step 3), for every available combination, consider each city inside the combination as the ending city. This is another inner iteration.

5. Inside the inner iteration (Step 4), given a different destination city, determine the shortest path connecting the cities in the set from the city that starts the tour (city 0). In finding the shortest path, use any useful, previously stored information, thus applying dynamic programming. This step saves computations and provides the rationale for working by growing subsets of cities. Reusing previously solved subproblems, you find the shorter tours by adding to a previous shortest path the distance necessary to reach the destination city. Given a certain set of cities, a specific initial city, and a specific destination city, the algorithm stores the best path and its length.

6. When all the iterations end, you have as many different shortest solutions as *n*–1 cities, with each solution covering all the cities but ending at a different city. Add a closing point, the city 0, to each one to conclude the tour.

7. Determine the shortest solution and output it as the result.

TECHNICAL STUFF

The Python implementation of this algorithm isn't very simple because it involves some iterations and manipulating sets. It's an exhaustive search reinforced by dynamic programming and relies on an iterative approach with subsets of cities and with candidates to add to them. The following commented Python example explores how this solution works. You can use it to calculate customized tours (possibly using cities in your region or county as entries in the distance matrix). The script uses advanced commands such as frozenset (a command that makes a set usable as a dictionary key) and operators for sets in order to achieve the solution.

```
from itertools import combinations

memo = {(frozenset([0, idx+1]), idx+1): (dist, [0,idx+1])
```

```
        for idx,dist in enumerate(D[0][1:])}
cities = D.shape[0]
for subset_size in range(2, cities):
    # Here we define the size of the subset of cities
    new_memo = dict()
    for subset in [frozenset(comb) | {0} for comb in
                    combinations(range(1, cities),
                                    subset_size)]:
        # We enumerate the subsets having a certain subset
        # size
        for ending in subset - {0}:
            # We consider every ending point in the subset
            all_paths = list()
            for k in subset:
                # We check the shortest path for every
                # element in the subset
                if k != 0 and k!=ending:
                    length = memo[(subset-{ending},k)][0
                                        ] + D[k][ending]
                    index  = memo[(subset-{ending},k)][1
                                        ] + [ending]
                    all_paths.append((length, index))
            new_memo[(subset, ending)] = min(all_paths)
    # In order to save memory, we just record the previous
    # subsets since we won't use shorter ones anymore
    memo = new_memo
# Now we close the cycle and get back to the start of the
# tour, city zero
tours = list()
for distance, path in memo.values():
    distance += D[path[-1],0]
    tours.append((distance, path+[0]))
# We can now declare the shortest tour
distance, path = min(tours)
print ('Shortest dynamic programming tour is: %s, %i kms'
        % (path, distance))
Shortest dynamic programming tour is:
 [0, 1, 3, 2, 4, 0], 80 kms
```

Approximating string search

Determining when one word is similar to another isn't always simple. Words may differ slightly because of misspelling or different ways of writing the word itself, thus rendering any exact match impossible. This isn't just a problem that raises interesting issues during a spell check, though. For example, putting similar text strings together (such as names, addresses, or code identifiers) that refer to the same person may help create a one-customer view of a firm's customer base or help a national security agency locate a dangerous criminal.

REMEMBER

Approximating string searches has many applications in machine translation, speech recognition, spell checking and text processing, computational biology, and information retrieval. Thinking about the manner in which sources input data into databases, you know there are many mismatches between data fields that a smart algorithm must solve. Matching a similar, but not precisely equal, series of letters is an ability that finds uses in fields such as genetics when comparing DNA sequences (expressed by letters representing nucleotides G,A,T, and C) to determine whether two sequences are similar and how they resemble each other.

Vladimir Levenshtein, a Russian scientist expert in information theory (see http://ethw.org/Vladimir_I._Levenshtein for details), devised a simple measure (named after him) in 1965 that computes the grade of similarity between two strings by counting how many transformations it takes to change the first string into the second. The Levenshtein distance (also known as edit distance) counts how many changes are necessary in a word:

>> **Deletion:** Removing a letter from a word

>> **Insertion:** Inserting a letter into a word and obtaining another word

>> **Substitution:** Replacing one letter with another, such as changing the *p* letter into an *f* letter and obtaining *fan* from *pan*

TIP

Each edit has a cost, which Levenshtein defines as 1 for each transformation. However, depending on how you apply the algorithm, you could set the cost differently for deletion, insertion, and substitution. For example, when searching for similar street names, misspellings are more common than outright differences in lettering, so substitution might incur only a cost of 1, and deletion or insertion might incur a cost of 2. On the other hand, when looking for monetary amounts, similar values quite possibly will have different numbers of numbers. Someone could enter $123 or $123.00 into the database. The numbers are the same, but the number of numbers is different, so insertion and deletion might cost less than substitution (a value of $124 is not quite the same as a value of $123, so substituting 3 for 4 should cost more).

You can render the counting algorithm as a recursion or an iteration. However, it works much faster using a bottom-up dynamic programming solution, as described in the 1974 paper "The String-to-string Correction Problem," by Robert A. Wagner and Michael J. Fischer (http://www.inrg.csie.ntu.edu.tw/algorithm2014/homework/Wagner-74.pdf). The time complexity of this solution is $O(mn)$, where n and m are the lengths in letter of the two words being compared. The following code computes the number of changes required to turn the word *Saturday* into *Sunday* by using dynamic programming with a matrix (see Figure 16-2) to store previous results (the bottom-up approach). (You can find this code in the A4D; 16; Levenshtein.ipynb file on the Dummies site as part of the downloadable code; see the Introduction for details.)

```
import numpy as np
import pandas as pd


s1 = 'Saturday'
s2 = 'Sunday'
m = len(s1)
n = len(s2)
D = np.zeros((m+1,n+1))
D[0,:] = list(range(n+1))
D[:,0] = list(range(m+1))


for j in range(1, n+1):
    for i in range(1, m+1):
        if s1[i-1] == s2[j-1]:
            D[i, j] = D[i-1, j-1]
        else:
            D[i, j] = np.min([
            D[i-1, j]   + 1,   # a deletion
            D[i, j-1]   + 1,   # an insertion
            D[i-1, j-1] + 1    # a substitution
            ])
print ('Levenshtein distance is %i' % D[-1,-1])

Levenshtein distance is 3
```

You can plot or print the result using the following command:

```
pd.DataFrame(D, index=list(' '+s1), columns=list(' '+s2))
```

The algorithm builds the matrix, placing the best solution in the last cell. After building the matrix using the letters of the first string as rows and the letters of the second one as columns, it proceeds by columns, computing the differences between each letter in the rows compared to those in the columns. In this way, the algorithm makes a number of comparisons equivalent to the multiplication of the number of the letters in the two strings. As the algorithm continues, it accounts for the result of previous comparisons by looking at the solutions present in the previous matrix cells and choosing the solution with the least number of edits.

		S	u	n	d	a	y
	0.0	1.0	2.0	3.0	4.0	5.0	6.0
S	1.0	0.0	1.0	2.0	3.0	4.0	5.0
a	2.0	1.0	1.0	2.0	3.0	3.0	4.0
t	3.0	2.0	2.0	2.0	3.0	4.0	4.0
u	4.0	3.0	2.0	3.0	3.0	4.0	5.0
r	5.0	4.0	3.0	3.0	4.0	4.0	5.0
d	6.0	5.0	4.0	4.0	3.0	4.0	5.0
a	7.0	6.0	5.0	5.0	4.0	3.0	4.0
y	8.0	7.0	6.0	6.0	5.0	4.0	3.0

FIGURE 16-2: Transforming Sunday into Saturday.

When the matrix iteration completes, the resulting number represents the minimum number of edits necessary for the transformation to occur — the smaller the number, the more similar the two strings. Retracing from the last cell to the first one by moving to the previous cell with the least value (if more directions are available, it prefers to move diagonally) hints at what transformations to execute (see Figure 16-3):

>> A diagonal backward movement hints at a substitution in the first string if the letters on the row and column differ (otherwise, no edit needs to be done)

>> An upward movement dictates a deletion of a letter in the first string

>> A left backward move indicates that an insertion of a new letter should be done on the first string

In this example, the backtracking points out the following transformations (two deletions and one substitution):

Saturday => Sturday => Surday => Sunday

		S	u	n	d	a	y
	0.0	1.0	2.0	3.0	4.0	5.0	6.0
s	1.0	0.0	1.0	2.0	3.0	4.0	5.0
a	2.0	1.0	1.0	2.0	3.0	3.0	4.0
t	3.0	2.0	2.0	2.0	3.0	4.0	4.0
u	4.0	3.0	2.0	3.0	3.0	4.0	5.0
r	5.0	4.0	3.0	3.0	4.0	4.0	5.0
d	6.0	5.0	4.0	4.0	3.0	4.0	5.0
a	7.0	6.0	5.0	5.0	4.0	3.0	4.0
y	8.0	7.0	6.0	6.0	5.0	4.0	3.0

FIGURE 16-3:
Highlighting what transformations are applied.

Chapter **17**

Using Randomized Algorithms

R andom number generators are a key function in computing and play an important role in the algorithmic techniques discussed in this part of the book. Randomization isn't just for gaming or for gambling, but people employ it to solve a large variety of problems. Randomization sometimes proves more effective during optimization than other techniques and in obtaining the right solution than more reasoned ways. It helps different techniques work better, from local search and simulated annealing to heuristics, cryptography, and distributed computing (with cryptography for concealing information being the most critical).

You can find randomization embedded into unexpected everyday tools. The robot vacuum cleaner Roomba (designed by a company founded by the Massachusetts Institute of Technology [MIT]) cleans rooms without having a precise plan and a blueprint of the place. The tool works most of the time by wandering randomly around the room and, according to the original patent, after hitting an obstacle, it turns a random number of degrees and starts in a new direction. Yet Roomba always completes its cleaning chores. (If you are curious about how it operates, you can consult http://www.explainthatstuff.com/how-roomba-works.html.)

From a historical perspective, randomized algorithms are a recent innovation, because the first algorithm of this kind, the closest-pair algorithm (which determines the pair of points, among many on a geometric plane, with the smallest distance between the points without having to compare them all) was developed by Michael Rabin in 1976. That first algorithm was followed the next year by the randomized primality test (an algorithm for determining whether a number is a composite or a probable prime number), by Robert M. Solovay and Volker Strassen. Soon after, applications in cryptography and distributed computing made randomization more popular and the subject of intense research, although the field is still new and uncharted.

Randomization makes finding a solution simpler, trading time against complexity. Simplifying tasks isn't its only advantage: Randomization saves resources and operates in a distributed way with a reduced need for communication and coordination. This chapter introduces you to the information needed to understand how enriching your algorithms with randomness can help solve problems (the chapter uses the term *injecting randomness,* as if it were a cure). Even more applications wait in the following chapters, so this chapter also discusses key topics such as probability basics, probability distributions, and Monte Carlo simulations.

Defining How Randomization Works

Randomization relies on the capability by your computer to generate random numbers, which means creating the number without a plan. Therefore, a random number is unpredictable, and as you generate subsequent random numbers, they shouldn't relate to each other.

REMEMBER

However, randomness is hard to achieve. Even when you throw dice, the result can't be completely unexpected because of the way you hold the dice, the way you throw them, and the fact that the dice aren't perfectly shaped. Computers aren't good at creating random numbers, either. They generate randomness by using algorithms or pseudorandom tables (which work by using a *seed* value as a starting point, a number equivalent to an index) because a computer can't create a truly random number. Computers are deterministic machines; everything inside them responds to a well-defined response pattern, which means that it imitates randomness in some way.

Considering why randomization is needed

Even if a computer can't create true randomness, streams of pseudorandom numbers (numbers that appear as random but that are somehow predetermined) can still make the difference in many computer science problems. Any algorithm that employs randomness in its logic can appear as a randomized algorithm, no matter whether randomness determines its results, improves performance, or mitigates the risk of failing by providing a solution in certain cases.

Usually you find randomness employed in selecting input data, the start point of the optimization, or the number and kind of operations to apply to the data. When randomness is a core part of the algorithm logic and not just an aid to its performance, the expected running time of the algorithm and even its results may become uncertain and subject to randomness, too; for instance, an algorithm may provide different, though equally good, results during each run. It's therefore useful to distinguish between kinds of randomized solutions, each one named after iconic gambling locations:

>> **Las Vegas:** These algorithms are notable for using random inputs or resources to provide the correct problem answer every time. Obtaining a result may take an uncertain amount of time because of its random procedures. An example is the Quicksort algorithm.

>> **Monte Carlo:** Because of their use of randomness, Monte Carlo algorithms may not provide a correct answer or even an answer at all, although these outcomes seldom happen. Because the result is uncertain, a maximum number of trials in their running time may bind them. Monte Carlo algorithms demonstrate that algorithms do not necessarily always successfully solve the problems they are supposed to. An example is the Solovay–Strassen primality test.

>> **Atlantic City:** These algorithms run in polynomial time, providing a correct problem answer at least 75 percent of the time. Monte Carlo algorithms are always fast but not always correct, and Las Vegas algorithms are always correct but not always fast. People therefore think of Atlantic City algorithms as halfway between the two because they are usually both fast and correct. This class of algorithms was introduced in 1982 by J. Finn in an unpublished manuscript entitled *Comparison of Probabilistic Test for Primality.* Created for theoretical reasons to test for prime numbers, this class comprises hard-to-design solutions, thus very few of them exist today.

Understanding how probability works

Probability tells you the likelihood of an event, which you normally express as a number. In this book, and generally in the field of probabilistic studies, the probability of an event is measured in the range between 0 (no probability that an event will occur) and 1 (certainty that an event will occur). Intermediate values, such as 0.25 or 0.75, indicate that the event will happen with a certain frequency under conditions that should lead to that event (referred to as *trials*). Even if a numeric range from 0 to 1 doesn't seem intuitive at first, working with probability over time makes the reason for using such a range easier to understand. When an event occurs with probability 0.25, you know that out of 100 trials, the event will happen 0.25 * 100 = 25 times.

For instance, when the probability of your favorite sports team winning is 0.75, you can use the number to determine the chances of success when your team plays a game against another team. You can even get more specific information, such as the probability of winning a certain tournament (your team has a 0.65 probability of winning a match in this tournament) or conditioned by another event (when a visitor, the probability of winning for your team decreases to 0.60).

Probabilities can tell you a lot about an event, and they're helpful for algorithms, too. In a randomized algorithmic approach, you may wonder when to stop an algorithm because it should have reached a solution. It's good to know how long to look for a solution before giving up. Probabilities can help you determine how many iterations you may need. The discussion of the 2-satisfiability (o 2-SAT) algorithm in Chapter 18 provides a working example of using probabilities as stopping rules for an algorithm.

REMEMBER

You commonly hear about probabilities as percentages in sports and economics, telling you that an event occurs a certain number of times after 100 trials. It's exactly the same probability no matter whether you express it as 0.25 or 25 percent. That's just a matter of conventions. In gambling, you even hear about odds, which is another way of expressing probability, where you compare the likelihood of an event (for example, having a certain horse win the race) against not having the event happen at all. In this case, you express 0.25 as 25 against 75 or in any other way resulting in the same ratio.

You can multiply a probability for a number of trials and get an estimated number of occurrences of the event, but by doing the inverse, you can empirically estimate a probability. Perform a certain number of trials, observe each of them, and count the number of times an event occurs. The ratio between the number of occurrences and the number of trials is your probability estimate. For instance, the probability 0.25 is the probability of picking a certain suit when choosing a card randomly from a deck of cards. French playing cards (the most widely used deck; it also appears in America and Britain) provide a classic example for explaining probabilities. (The Italians, Germans, and Swiss, for example, use decks with different suits, which you can read about at `http://healthy.uwaterloo.ca/museum/VirtualExhibits/Playing%20Cards/decks/index.html`.) The deck contains 52 cards equally distributed into four suits: clubs and spades, which are black, and diamonds and hearts, which are red. If you want to determine the probability of picking an ace, you must consider that, by picking cards from a deck, you will observe four aces. Your trials at picking the cards are 52 (the number of cards), therefore the answer in terms of probability is 4/52 = 0.077.

TIP

You can get a more reliable estimate of an empirical probability by using a larger number of trials. When using a few trials, you may not get a correct estimate of the event probability because of the influence of chance. As the number of trials grows, event observations will get nearer to the true probability of the event itself. The principle there is a generating process behind events. To understand how the generating process works, you need many trials. Using trials in such a way is also known as *sampling* from a probabilistic distribution.

Understanding distributions

Probability distribution is another idea that is important for working out better algorithms. A *distribution* is a table of values or a mathematical function that links every possible value of an input to the probability that such values could occur. Probability distributions are usually (but not solely) represented in charts whose abscissa axis represents the possible values of an input and whose ordinal axis represents the probability of occurrence. Most statistical models rely on the normal distributions, a distribution which is symmetric and has a characteristic bell shape. Representing a normal distribution in Python (as shown in Figure 17-1) requires a few lines of code. (You can find this code in the A4D; 17; Probability. ipynb file on the Dummies site as part of the downloadable code; see the Introduction for details.)

```
import numpy as np
from numpy.random import normal, uniform
import matplotlib.pyplot as plt
%matplotlib inline

normal_distribution = normal(size=10000) * 25 + 100
weights = np.ones_like(normal_distribution
                      ) / len(normal_distribution)
plt.hist(normal_distribution, bins=20, weights=weights)
plt.xlabel("Value")
plt.ylabel("Probability")
plt.show()
```

The plotted distribution represents an input of 10,000 numbers whose average is about 100. Each bar in the histogram represents the probability that a certain range of values will appear in the input. If you sum all the bars, you obtain the value of 1, which comprises all the probabilities expressed by the distribution.

FIGURE 17-1:
A histogram
of a normal
distribution.

In a normal distribution, most of the values are around the mean value. Therefore, if you pick a random number from the input, you most likely get a number around the center of the distribution. However; though less likely, you may also draw a number far from the center. If your algorithm works better by using the mean than it does with any other number, picking a number at random makes sense and may be less trouble than devising a smarter way to draw values from your input.

Another important distribution mentioned in this chapter is the uniform distribution. You can represent it using some Python code (the output appears in Figure 17-2), too:

```python
uniform_distribution = uniform(size=10000) * 100
weights = np.ones_like(uniform_distribution
                      ) / len(uniform_distribution)
plt.hist(uniform_distribution, bins=20, weights=weights)
plt.xlabel("Value")
plt.ylabel("Probability")
plt.show()
```

The uniform distribution is noticeably different from the normal distribution because each number has the same probability of being in the input as any other. Consequently, the histogram bars are all roughly of the same size, and picking a number in a uniform distribution means giving all the numbers the same chance to appear. It's a way to avoid systematically picking the same groups of numbers when your algorithm works better with varied inputs. For instance, uniform distributions work well when your algorithm works fine with certain numbers, so-so with most, and badly with a few others, and you prefer to pick numbers randomly to avoid picking a series of bad numbers. This is the strategy used by the Quickselect and randomized Quicksort algorithms, described later in the chapter.

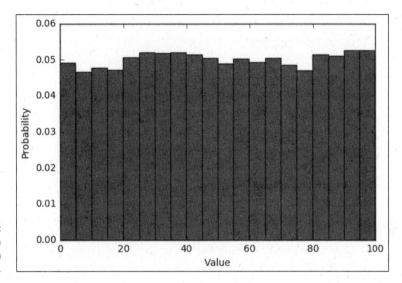

FIGURE 17-2:
A histogram
of a uniform
distribution.

Because algorithms need numeric inputs, knowing their distribution can help make them work smarter. It's not just the initial distribution that counts. You can also take advantage of how data distribution changes as the algorithm proceeds. As an example of how a changing distribution can improve your algorithm, the following code shows how to guess a card in a French deck by random choice:

```
numbers = ['Ace','2','3','4','5','6','7','8','9','10',
                           'Jack','Queen','King']
seeds = ['Clubs','Spades','Diamonds','Hearts']
deck = [s+'_'+n for n in numbers for s in seeds]

from random import choice
my_cards = deck.copy()
guessed = 0
for card in deck:
    if card == choice(my_cards):
        guessed += 1
print ('Guessed %i card(s)' % guessed)

Guessed 1 card(s)
```

This strategy brings few results, and on average, you'll guess a single card in all 52 trials. In fact, for each trial, you have a 1/52 probability of guessing the correct card, which amounts to 1 after picking all the cards: (1/52) * 52 = 1. Instead, you can change this simple random algorithm by discarding the cards that you've seen from your possible choices:

```
from random import choice
my_cards = deck.copy()
guessed = 0
for card in deck:
    if card == choice(my_cards):
        guessed += 1
    else:
        my_cards.pop(my_cards.index(card))
print ('Guessed %i card(s)' % guessed)

Guessed 1 card(s)
```

Now, on average, you'll guess the right card more often because as the deck decreases, your chances of guessing increases and you'll likely guess correctly more often when nearing the end of the game. (Your chances are 1 divided by the number of cards left in the deck).

TIP

Counting cards can provide an advantage in card games. A team of MIT students used card counting and probability estimates to win huge amounts in Las Vegas until the practice was banned from Casinos. The story even inspired a 2008 film entitled 21, starring Kevin Spacey. You can read more about the story at: http://www.bbc.com/news/magazine-27519748.

Simulating the use of the Monte Carlo method

Calculating probabilities, apart from the operations discussed earlier in this chapter, is beyond the scope of this book. Understanding how an algorithm incorporating randomness works is not an easy task, even when you know how to compute probabilities because it may be the result of blending many different probability distributions. However, a discussion of the Monte Carlo method casts light on the results of the most complex algorithms and helps you understand how they work. This method sees use in both mathematics and physics to solve many problems. For instance, scientists such as Enrico Fermi and Edward Teller used Monte Carlo simulations on specially devised supercomputers during the Manhattan project (which developed the atomic bomb during World War II) to accelerate their experiments. You can read more about this use at http://www.atomicheritage.org/history/computing-and-manhattan-project.

REMEMBER

Don't confuse the Monte Carlo method with the Monte Carlo algorithm. The Monte Carlo method is a way to understand how a probability distribution affects a problem, whereas, as discussed previously, the Monte Carlo algorithm is a randomized algorithm that isn't guaranteed to reach a solution.

In a Monte Carlo simulation, you repeatedly sample the algorithm results. You store a certain number of results and then calculate statistics, such as the mean, and visualize them as a distribution. For instance, if you want to understand better how reducing the size of the deck you're drawing from can help you achieve better results (as in the previous Python script), you iterate the algorithm a few times and record the success rate:

```
import numpy as np
samples = list()
for trial in range(1000):
    my_cards = deck.copy()
    guessed = 0
    for card in deck:
        if card == choice(my_cards):
            guessed += 1
        else:
            my_cards.pop(my_cards.index(card))
    samples.append(guessed)
```

Running a Monte Carlo simulation may take a few seconds. The time required depends on the speed of the algorithm, the size of the problem, and the number of trials. However, when sampling from distributions, the more trials you make, the more stable the result. This example performs 1,000 trials. You can both estimate and visualize the expected result (see Figure 17-3) using the following code:

```
plt.hist(samples, bins=8)
plt.xlabel("Guesses")
plt.ylabel("Frequency")
plt.show()
print ('On average you can expect %0.2f guesses each run'
       % np.mean(samples))

On average you can expect 3.15 guesses each run
```

Observing the resulting histogram, you can determine that you get a result of three in about 300 runs out of the 1,000 trials, which gives three the highest probability of happening. Interestingly you never got a result of zero, but it is also rare to score seven or more hits. Later examples in the chapter use Monte Carlo simulations to understand how more sophisticated randomized algorithms work.

FIGURE 17-3:
Displaying the
results of a
Monte Carlo
simulation.

Putting Randomness into your Logic

Here are some of many reasons to include randomness in the logic of your algorithm:

>> It makes algorithms work better and provide smarter solutions.

>> It requires fewer resources, in terms of memory and computations.

>> It creates algorithms that have a distributed output with little or no supervision.

In the next chapter, which is dedicated to local search, you see how randomization and probability can prove helpful when it's difficult to determine what direction your algorithm should take. The examples in the sections that follow demonstrate how randomization helps to quickly find values in a certain position in your data input and how relying on randomness can speed up sorting.

Calculating a median using Quickselect

Calculating a statistical measure, the median, can prove challenging when you work on unsorted input lists. In fact, a median relies on the position of your data when it is ordered:

>> If the data inputs have an odd number of elements, the median is exactly the middle value.

>> If the data inputs have an even number of elements, the median is the average of the pair of middle numbers in the ordered input list.

REMEMBER

A median is like a mean, a single value that can represent a distribution of values. The median, based on the input vector element order, isn't influenced much by the values present in your list. It's simply the middle value. Instead, the values present at the head and tail of the input can influence the mean when they're extremely small or large. This robustness makes the median very helpful in many situations when using statistics. A simple example of a median calculation using Python functions helps you understand this measure. (You can find this code in the A4D; 17; Quickselect.ipynb file on the Dummies site as part of the downloadable code; see the Introduction for details.)

```
from random import randint, random, choice
import numpy as np
import sys
sys.setrecursionlimit(1500)

n = 501
series = [randint(1,25) for i in range(n)]
print ('Median is %0.1f' % np.median(series))

Median is 14.0
```

The code creates a list of 501 elements and obtains the list median using the median function from the NumPy package. The reported median is actually the middle point of the ordered list, which is the 251st element:

```
print ('251st element of the ordered series is %0.1f' %
       sorted(series)[250])

251st element of the ordered series is 14.0
```

Ordering the list and extracting the necessary element demonstrates how median works. Because ordering is involved in calculating a median, you can expect a best running time of $O(n*\log(n))$. By using randomization provided by the Quickselect algorithm, you can get an even better result, a running time of $O(n)$. Quickselect works recursively, which is why you must set a higher recursion limit in Python, given a list and the position of the value needed from an ordered list.

The value index is called *k*, and the algorithm is also known as the largest *kth value algorithm*. It uses the following steps to obtain a result:

1. Determine a pivot number in the data list and split the list into two parts, a left list whose numbers are less than the pivot number, and a right list whose numbers are higher.

2. Determine the length of each list. When the length of the left list is larger than the kth position, the median value is inside the left part. The algorithm applies itself recursively to just that list.

3. Compute the number of pivot number duplicates in the list (subtract from the length of the list the length of the left and right sides).

4. Determine whether the number of duplicates is more than k.

   a. When this condition is true, it means that the algorithm has found the solution because the kth position is contained in the duplicates (it's the pivot number).

   b. When this condition isn't true, remove the number of duplicates from k and apply the result recursively to the right side, which must contain the value of the kth position.

Now that you understand the process, you can look at some code. The following example shows how to implement a Quickselect algorithm.

```
def quickselect(series, k):
    pivot = choice(series)

    left, right = list(),list()
    for item in series:
        if item < pivot:
            left.append(item)
        if item > pivot:
            right.append(item)

    length_left = len(left)
    if length_left > k:
        return quickselect(left, k)
    k -= length_left

    duplicates = len(series) - (length_left + len(right))
    if duplicates > k:
        return float(pivot)
    k -= duplicates
```

```
    return quickselect(right, k)

quickselect(series, 250)

14.0
```

The algorithm works well because it keeps reducing the problem size. It works best when the random pivot number is drawn nearer to the kth position (the stopping rule is that the pivot number is the value in the kth position). Unfortunately, because you can't know the kth position in the unordered list, drawing randomly by using a uniform distribution (each element in the list has the same chance of being chosen) is the best solution because the algorithm eventually finds the right solution. Even when random chance doesn't work in the algorithm's favor, the algorithm keeps on reducing the problem, thus getting more chances to find the solution, as demonstrated earlier in the chapter when guessing the cards randomly picked from a deck. As the deck gets smaller, guessing the answer gets easier. The following code shows how to use Quickselect to determine the median of a list of numbers:

```
def median(series):
    if len(series) % 2 != 0:
        return quickselect(series, len(series)//2)
    else:
        left  = quickselect(series, (len(series)-1) // 2)
        right = quickselect(series, (len(series)+1) // 2)
        return (left + right) / 2

median(series)

14.0
```

Doing simulations using Monte Carlo

As part of understanding the Quickselect algorithm, it pays to know how it works internally. By setting a counter inside the `quickselect` function, you can check performance under different conditions using a Monte Carlo simulation:

```
def quickselect(series, k, counter=0):
    pivot = choice(series)

    left, right = list(),list()
    for item in series:
        if item < pivot:
```

```
                left.append(item)
            if item > pivot:
                right.append(item)

    counter += len(series)

    length_left = len(left)
    if length_left > k:
        return quickselect(left, k, counter)
    k -= length_left

    duplicates = series.count(pivot)
    if duplicates > k:
        return float(pivot), counter
    k -= duplicates

    return quickselect(right, k, counter)
```

The first experiment tries to determine how many operations the algorithm needs, on average, to find the median of an input list of 1001 numbers:

```
results = list()
for run in range(1000):
    n = 1001
    series = [randint(1,25) for i in range(n)]
    median,count = quickselect(series, n//2)
    assert(median==np.median(series))
    results.append(count)

print ("Mean operations: %i" % np.mean(results))

Mean operations: 2764
```

Displaying the results on a histogram (see Figure 17-4) reveals that the algorithm computes from two to four times the size of the input, with three times being the most likely number of processed computations.

```
import matplotlib.pyplot as plt

%matplotlib inline

plt.hist(results, bins='auto')
plt.xlabel("Computations")
plt.ylabel("Frequency")
plt.show()
```

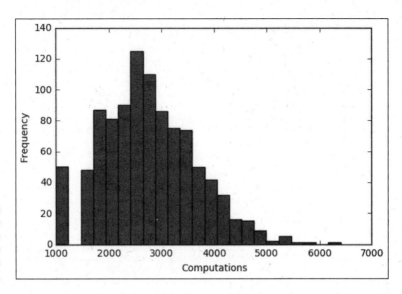

FIGURE 17-4:
Displaying the results of a Monte Carlo simulation on Quickselect.

If on average it takes about three times the size of the input, Quickselect is providing good performance. However, you may wonder whether the proportion between inputs and computations will hold when the input size grows. As seen when studying NP-complete problems, many problems explode when the input size grows. You can prove this theory by using another Monte Carlo simulation on top of the previous one and plotting the output, as shown in Figure 17-5.

```
input_size = [501, 1001, 5001, 10001, 20001, 50001]
computations = list()
for n in input_size:
    results = list()
    for run in range(1000):
        series = [randint(1, 25) for i in range(n)]
        median,count = quickselect(series, n//2)
        assert(median==np.median(series))
        results.append(count)
    computations.append(np.mean(results))

plt.plot(input_size, computations, '-o')
plt.xlabel("Input size")
plt.ylabel("Number of computations")
plt.show()
```

WARNING

Completing the computations from this example may take up to ten minutes (some Monte Carlo simulations may be quite time consuming), but the result helps you visualize what it means to work with an algorithm that works with linear time. As the input grows (represented in abscissa), the computations (represented on the ordinal axis) grow proportionally, making the growth curve a perfect line.

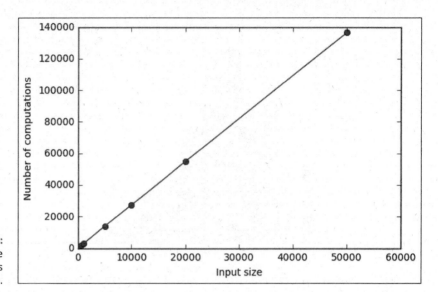

FIGURE 17-5:
Displaying Monte
Carlo simulations
as input grows.

Ordering faster with Quicksort

Chapter 7 explains ordering algorithms, the true foundations of all the modern computer-based algorithmic knowledge. The Quicksort algorithm, which can run in logarithmic time but sometimes fails and produces results in quadratic time under ill-conditioned inputs, will surely amaze you. This section explores the reasons why this algorithm may fail and provides an effective solution by injecting randomness into it. You start by examining the following code:

```
def quicksort(series, get):

    try:
        global operations
        operations += len(series)
    except:pass

    if len(series) <= 3:
        return sorted(series)

    pivot = get(series)
    duplicates = series.count(pivot)

    left, right = list(),list()
    for item in series:
        if item < pivot:
            left.append(item)
```

```
        if item > pivot:
            right.append(item)

    return quicksort(left, get) + [pivot
            ] * duplicates + quicksort(right, get)
```

This is another implementation of the algorithm from Chapter 7. However, this time the code extracts the function that decides the pivot the algorithm uses to recursively split the initial list. The algorithm decides the split by taking the first list value. It also tracks how many operations it takes to complete the ordering using the operations global variable, which is defined, reset, and accessed as a counter outside the function. The following code tests the algorithm, under unusual conditions, requiring it to process an already ordered list. Note its performance:

```
series = list(range(25))
operations = 0
sorted_list = quicksort(series, choose_leftmost)
print ("Operations: %i" % operations)

Operations: 322
```

In this case, the algorithm takes 322 operations to order a list of 25 elements, which is horrid performance. Using an already ordered list causes the problem because the algorithm splits the list into two lists: an empty one and another one with the residual values. It has to repeat this unhelpful split for all the unique values present in the list. Usually the Quicksort algorithm works fine because it works with unordered lists, and picking the leftmost element is equivalent to randomly drawing a number as the pivot. To avoid this problem, you can use a variation of the algorithm that provides a true random draw of the pivot value.

```
def choose_random(l): return choice(l)

series = [randint(1,25) for i in range(25)]
operations = 0
sorted_list = quicksort(series, choose_random)
print ("Operations: %i" % operations)

Operations: 81
```

Now the algorithm performs its task using a lower number of operations, which is exactly the running time $n * \log(n)$ that is $25 * \log(25) = 80.5$.

Chapter **18**

Performing Local Search

When dealing with an NP–hard problem, a problem for which no known solution has a running complexity less than exponential (see the NP–completeness theory discussion in Chapter 15), you have a few alternatives worth trying. Based on the idea that NP–class problems require some compromise (such as accepting partial or nonoptimal results), the following options offer a solution to this otherwise intractable problem:

» Identify special cases under which you can solve the problem efficiently in polynomial time using an exact method or a greedy algorithm. This approach simplifies the problem and limits the number of solution combinations to try.

» Employ dynamic programming techniques (described in Chapter 16) that improve on brute-force search and reduce the complexity of the problem.

» Compromise and sketch an approximate algorithm that finds a *partial,* close-to-optimal solution. When you're satisfied with a partial solution, you cut the algorithm's running time short. Approximate algorithms can be

   • Greedy algorithms (as discussed in Chapter 15)

   • Local search using randomization or some other heuristic technique (the topic of the present chapter)

   • Linear programming (the topic of Chapter 19)

>> Choose a heuristic or a *meta-heuristic* (a heuristic that helps you determine which heuristic to use) that works well for your problem in practice. However, it has no theoretical guarantee and tends to be empiric.

Understanding Local Search

Local search is a general approach to solving problems that comprises a large range of algorithms, which will help you escape the exponential complexities of many NP problems. A local search starts from an imperfect problem solution and moves away from it, a step at a time. It determines the viability of nearby solutions, potentially leading to a perfect solution, based on random choice or an astute heuristic (no exact method is involved).

REMEMBER

A *heuristic* is an educated guess about a solution, such as a rule of thumb that points to the direction of a desired outcome but can't tell exactly how to reach it. It's like being lost in an unknown city and having people tell you to go a certain way to reach your hotel (but without precise instructions) or just how far you are from it. Some local search solutions use heuristics, so you find them in this chapter. Chapter 20 delves into the full details of using heuristics to perform practical tasks.

You have no guarantee that a local search will arrive at a problem solution, but your chances do improve from the starting point when you provide enough time for the search to run its computations. It stops only after it can't find any further way to improve the solution it has reached.

Knowing the neighborhood

Local search algorithms iteratively improve from a starting solution, moving one step at a time through neighboring solutions until they can't improve the solution any further. Because local search algorithms are as simple and intuitive as greedy algorithms, designing a local search approach to an algorithmic problem is not difficult. The key is defining the correct procedure:

1. Start with an existing solution (usually a random solution or a solution from another algorithm).

2. Search for a set of possible new solutions within the current solution's neighborhood, which constitutes the *candidates' list*.

3. Determine which solution to use in place of the current solution based on the output of a heuristic that accepts the candidates' list as input.

4. Continue performing Steps 2 and 3 until you see no further improvement on the solution, which means that you have the best solution available.

REMEMBER

Although easy to design, local search solutions may not find a solution in a reasonable time (you can stop the process and use the current solution) or produce a minimum quality solution. You can employ some tricks of the trade to ensure that you get the most out of this approach.

At the start of the local search, you pick an initial solution. If you decide on a random solution, it's helpful to wrap the search in repeated iterations in which you generate different random start solutions. Sometimes, arriving at a good final solution depends on the starting point. If you start from an existing solution to be refined, plugging the solution into a greedy algorithm may prove to be a good compromise in fitting a solution that doesn't take too long to produce.

After choosing a starting point, define the neighborhood and determine its size. Defining a neighborhood requires figuring the smallest change you can impose on your solution. If a solution is a set of elements, all the neighboring solutions are the sets in which one of the elements mutates. For instance, in the traveling salesman problem (TSP), neighboring solutions could involve changing the ending cities of two (or more) trips, as shown in Figure 18-1.

FIGURE 18-1: Switching ending trips in a TSP problem may bring better results.

Based on how you create the neighborhood, you may have a smaller or a larger candidates' list. Larger lists require more time and computations but, contrary to short lists, may offer more opportunities for the process to end earlier and better.

List length involves a trade-off that you refine by using experimentation after each test to determine whether enlarging or shrinking the candidate list brings an advantage or a disadvantage in terms of time to complete and solution quality.

Base the choice of the new solution on a heuristic and, given the problem, decide on the best solution. For instance, in the TSP problem, use the trip switches that shorten the total tour length the most. In certain cases, you can use a random solution in place of a heuristic (as you discover in the SAT-2 problem in this chapter). Even when you have a clear heuristic, the algorithm could find multiple best solutions. Injecting some randomness could make your local search more efficient. When faced with many solutions, you can safely choose one randomly.

TIP

Ideally, in a local search, you get the best results when you run multiple searches, injecting randomness as much as you can into the start solution and along the way as you decide the next process step. Let the heuristic decide only when you see a clear advantage to doing so. Local search and randomness are good friends.

Your search has to stop at a certain point, so you need to choose stopping rules for the local search. When your heuristic can't find good neighbors anymore or it can't improve solution quality (for instance, computing a cost function, as it happens in TSP, by measuring the total length of the tour). Depending on the problem, if you don't create a stopping rule, your search may go on forever or take an unacceptably long time. In case you can't define a stopping, just limit the time spent looking for solutions or count the number of trials. When counting trials, you can decide that it's not worth going on because you calculate the probability of success and at a certain point, the probability of success becomes too small.

Presenting local search tricks

Local search tracks the current solution and moves to neighboring solutions one at a time until it finds a solution (or can't improve on the present solution). It presents some key advantages when working on NP-hard problems because it

>> Is simple to devise and execute

>> Uses little memory and computer resources (but searches require running time)

>> Finds acceptable or even good problem solutions when starting from a less-than-perfect solution (neighboring solutions should create a path to the final solution)

TIP

You can see the problems that a local search can solve as a graph of interconnected solutions. The algorithm traverses the graph, moving from node to node looking for the node that satisfies the task requirements. Using this perspective, a local search takes advantage of graph exploration algorithms such as depth-first search (DFS) or breadth-first search (BFS), both discussed in Chapter 9.

Local search provides a viable way to find acceptable solutions to NP-hard problems. However, it can't work properly without the right heuristic. Randomization can provide a good match with local search, and it helps by using

>> **Random sampling:** Generating solutions to start

>> **Random walk:** Picking a random solution that neighbors the current one. (You find more on random walks in the "Solving 2-SAT using randomization" section, later in this chapter.)

Randomization isn't the only heuristic available. A local search can rely on a more reasoned exploration of solutions using an objective function to get directions (as in *hill-climbing* optimization) and avoid the trap of so-so solutions (as in *simulated annealing* and *Tabu Search*). An *objective function* is a computation that can assess the quality of your solution by outputting a score number. If you need higher scores in hill climbing, you have a maximization problem; if you are looking for smaller score numbers, you have a problem of minimization.

Explaining hill climbing with n-queens

You can easily find analogies of the techniques employed by local search because many phenomena imply a gradual transition from one situation to another. Local search isn't just a technique devised by experts on algorithms but is actually a process that you see in both nature and human society. In society and science, for instance, you can view innovation as a local search of the next step among the currently available technologies: https://www.technologyreview.com/s/603366/mathematical-model-reveals-the-patterns-of-how-innovations-arise/. Many heuristics derive from the physical world, taking inspiration from the force of gravity, the fusion of metals, the evolution of DNA in animals, and the behavior of swarms of ants, bees, and fireflies (the paper at https://arxiv.org/pdf/1003.1464.pdf explains the Lévy-Flight Firefly algorithm).

Hill climbing takes inspiration from the force of gravity. It relies on the observation that as a ball rolls down a valley, it takes the steepest descent, and when it climbs a hill, it tends to take the most direct upward direction to reach the top. Gradually, one step after the other, no matter whether it's climbing up or down, the ball arrives at its destination, where proceeding higher or lower isn't possible.

In local search, you can mimic the same procedure successfully using an *objective function*, a measurement that evaluates the neighboring solutions and determines which one improves on the current one. Using the hill-climbing analogy, having an objective function is like feeling the inclination of the terrain and determining the next best move. From the current position, a hiker evaluates each direction to determine the terrain's slope. When the goal is to reach the top, the hiker chooses the direction with the greatest upward slope to reach the top. However, that's just the ideal situation; hikers often encounter problems during a climb and must use other solutions to circumnavigate them.

An objective function is similar to a greedy criterion (see Chapter 5). It's blind with respect to its final destination, so it can determine direction but not detect obstacles. Think about the effect of blindness when climbing the mountains — it's difficult to say when a hiker reaches the top. Flat terrain that lacks any opportunities for upward movement could indicate that the hiker reached the top. Unfortunately, a flat spot can also be a plain, an elbow, or even a hole the hiker happened to fall into. You can't be sure because the hiker can't see.

The same problem happens when using a local search guided by a hill-climbing heuristic: It pursues progressively better neighbor solutions until it can't find a better solution by checking the solutions that exist around the current one. At this point, the algorithm declares it found the solution. It also says that it has found a global solution, even though, as illustrated in Figure 18-2, it may have simply found a local *maximum*, a solution that's the best around because it's surrounded by worse solutions. It's still possible to find a better solution through further exploration.

FIGURE 18-2: Local search explores the landscape by hill climbing.

An example of hill climbing in action (and of the risks of getting stuck in a local maximum or in a local minimum when you're descending, as in this example) is the n-queens puzzle, first created by the chess expert Max Bezzel, in 1848, as a challenge for chess lovers. In this problem, you have a number of queens (this number is *n*) to place on a chessboard of *n* x *n* dimensions. You must place them so that no queen is threatened by any other. (In chess, a queen can attack by any direction by row, column, or diagonal.)

TIP

This is really a NP-hard problem. If you have eight queens to place on a 8 x 8 chessboard, there are 4,426,165,368 different ways to place them but only 92 configurations solve the problem. Clearly, you can't solve this problem using brute force or luck alone. Local search solves this problem in a very simple way using hill climbing:

1. Place the *n* queens randomly on the chessboard so that each one is on a different column (no two queens on the same column).

2. Evaluate the next set of solutions by moving each queen one square up or down in its column. This step requires 2*n* moves.

3. Determine how many queens are attacking each other after each move.

4. Determine which solution has the fewest queens attacking each other and use that solution for the next iteration.

5. Perform Steps 4 and 5 until you find a solution.

Unfortunately, this approach works only about 14 percent of the time because it gets stuck in a chessboard configuration that won't allow any further improvement 86 percent of the time. (The number of queens under attack won't diminish for all 2*n* moves available as next solutions.) The only way you get away from such a block is to restart the local search from scratch by choosing another random starting configuration of the queens on the chessboard. Figure 18-3 shows a successful solution.

In spite of this weakness, hill-climbing algorithms are used everywhere, especially in artificial intelligence and machine learning. Neural networks that recognize sounds or images, power mobile phones, and motivate self-driving cars mostly rely on a hill-climbing optimization called *gradient descent*. Randomized starts and random injections in the hill-climbing procedure make it possible to escape any local solution and reach the global maximum. Both simulated annealing and Tabu Search are smart ways to use random decisions in hill climbing.

FIGURE 18-3:
An 8-queen puzzle solved.

Discovering simulated annealing

At a certain point in the search, if your objective function stops giving you the right indications, you can use another heuristic to control the situation and try to find a better path to a better task solution. This is how both simulated annealing and Tabu Search work: They provide you with an emergency exit when needed.

Simulated annealing take its name from a technique in metallurgy, which heats the metal to a high temperature and then slowly cools it to soften the metal for cold working and to remove internal crystalline defects (see http://www.brighthubengineering.com/manufacturing-technology/30476-what-is-heat-treatment/ for details on this metal-working process). Local search replicates this idea by viewing the solution search as an atomic structure that changes to improve its workability. The temperature is the game changer in the optimization process. Just as high temperatures make the structure of a material relax (solids melt and liquid evaporate at high temperatures), so high temperatures in a local search algorithm induce relaxation of the objective function, allowing it to prefer worse solutions to better ones. Simulated annealing modifies the hill-climbing procedure, keeping the objective function for neighbor solution evaluation but allowing it to determine the search solution choice in a different way:

1. Obtain a temperature expressed as probability. (The Gibbs-Boltzmann physics function is a formula that converts temperature to probability. An explanation of this function is beyond the scope of this book, but you can explore it at: http://www.iue.tuwien.ac.at/phd/binder/node87.html.)

2. Set a temperature schedule. The temperature decreases at a certain rate as time passes and the search runs.

3. Define a starting solution (using random sampling or another algorithm) and start a loop. As the loop proceeds, the temperature decreases.

4. Stop the optimization when the temperature is zero.

5. Propose the current result as the solution.

At this point, you must iterate the search for solutions. For each step in the previous iteration, between the preceding Steps 3 and 4, do the following:

1. List the neighboring solutions and choose one at random.

2. Set the neighboring solution as the current solution when the neighboring solution is better than the current one.

3. Otherwise, pick a random number between 0 and 1 based on a threshold probability associated with the actual temperature and determine whether it's less than the threshold probability:

   - If it's less, set the neighboring solution as the current solution (even if it's worse than the current solution, according to the objective function).

   - If it's more, keep the current solution.

Simulated annealing is a smart way to improve hill climbing because it avoids having the search stopped at a local solution. When the temperature is high enough, the search might use a random solution and find another way to a better optimization. Because the temperature is higher at the beginning of the search, the algorithm has a chance of injecting randomness into the optimization. As the temperature cools to zero, less and less chance exists for picking a random solution, and the local search proceeds as in hill climbing. In TSP, for instance, the algorithm achieves simulated annealing by challenging the present solution at high temperatures by

>> Choosing a segment of the tour randomly and traversing it in the opposite direction

>> Visiting a city earlier or afterward in the tour, leaving the order of visit to the other cities the same

If the resulting adjustments worsen the tour's length, the algorithm keeps or rejects them according to the temperature in the simulated annealing process.

Avoiding repeats using Tabu Search

Tabu is an ancient word from Polynesian Tongan that says certain things can't be touched because they're sacred. The word *tabu* (which is spelled as taboo in

English) passed from anthropological studies to the everyday language to indicate something that is prohibited. In local search optimization, it's common to become stuck in a neighborhood of solutions that don't offer any improvement; that is, it's a local solution that appears as the best solution but is far from being the solution you want. Tabu search relaxes some rules and enforces others to offer a way out of local minima and help you reach better solutions.

The Tabu Search heuristics wraps objective functions and works its way along many neighboring solutions. It intervenes when you can't proceed because the next solutions don't improve on your objective. When such happens, Tabu Search does the following:

>> Allows use of a pejorative solution for a few times to see whether moving away from the local solution can help the search find a better path to the best solution.

>> Remembers the solutions that the search tries and forbids it from using them anymore, thus assuring that the search doesn't loop between the same solutions around the local solution without finding an escape route.

>> Creates a long-term or short-term memory of Tabu solutions by modifying the length of the queue used to store past solutions. When the queue is full, the heuristic drops the oldest Tabu to make space for the new one.

You can relate Tabu Search to caching and memoization (see Chapter 16) because it requires the algorithm to track its steps to save time and avoid retracing previously used solutions. In the TSP, it can help when you try optimizing your solution by swapping the visit order of two or more cities by avoiding repeat solution sets.

Solving satisfiability of Boolean circuits

As a practical view of how a local search works, this example delves into circuit satisfiability, a classical NP-complete problem. It uses a randomization and Monte Carlo algorithm approach. As seen in Chapter 17, a Monte Carlo algorithm relies on random choices during its optimization process and isn't guaranteed to succeed in its task, although it has a high likelihood of completing the task successfully. The problem isn't merely theoretical, though, because it tests how electronic circuits work, optimizing them by removing circuits that can't transport electric signals. Moreover, the solving algorithm sees use in other applications: automatic labeling on maps and charts, discrete tomography, scheduling with constraints, data clustering into groups, and other problems for which you have to make conflicting choices.

Computer circuits are composed of a series of connected components, each one opening or closing a circuit based on its inputs. Such elements are called *logic gates* (physically, their role is played by transistors) and if you build a circuit with many logic gates, you need to understand whether electricity can pass through it and under what circumstances.

Chapter 14 discusses the internal representation of a computer, based on zeros (absence of electricity in the circuit) or ones (presence of electricity). You can render this 0/1 representation from a logical perspective, turning signals into False (there isn't electricity in the circuit) or True (there is indeed electricity) conditions. Chapter 4 examines the Boolean operators (AND, OR, and NOT), as shown in Figure 18-4, which work on True and False conditions as inputs and transform them into a different output. All these concepts help you represent a physical electric circuit as a sequence of Boolean operators defining logic gates. The combination of all their conditions determines whether the circuit can carry electricity.

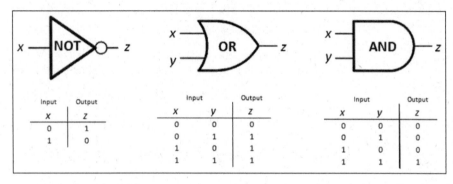

FIGURE 18-4: Symbols and truth tables of logic operators AND, OR, and NOT.

| Input | Output |
X	Z
0	1
1	0

| Input | | Output |
X	y	Z
0	0	0
0	1	1
1	0	1
1	1	1

| Input | | Output |
X	y	Z
0	0	0
0	1	0
1	0	0
1	1	1

This logic representation is a *Boolean combinational circuit,* and the test to verify its functionality is the *circuit satisfiability.* In the easiest scenario, the circuit consists of only NOT conditions (called *inverters*) that accept one wire input, and OR conditions that accept two wires as inputs. This is a satisfiability-two (2-SAT) scenario, and if the algorithm were to go through it using an exhaustive search, it would take at worst 2^k trials (having k as the number of input wires) to find a set of conditions that makes electricity pass through the whole circuit. There are even more complex versions of the problem, accepting more inputs for each OR logic gate and using AND gates, but they are beyond the scope of this book.

Solving 2-SAT using randomization

No matter the electronic circuit you have to test using a Boolean representation, you can render it as a vector of Boolean variables. You can also create another vector to contain the *clauses,* the set of conditions the circuit needs to satisfy (for example, that wire A and wire B should both be True). This isn't the only way to represent the problem; in fact, there are other solutions involving the use of graphs. However, for this example, these two vectors are enough.

You solve the problem using a randomized local search in polynomial time. Professor Christos H. Papadimitriou, teaching at the University of California at Berkeley (https://people.eecs.berkeley.edu/~christos/), devised this algorithm, called *RandomWalkSAT.* He presented it in his paper "On Selecting a Satisfying Truth Assignment," published in 1991 on the Proceedings of the 32nd IEEE Symposium on the Foundations of Computer Science. The algorithm is competitive when compared to more reasoned ways, and it is an exemplary local search approach because it makes just one change at a time on the current solution. It uses two nested loops, one for trying the starting solution multiple times and one for randomly amending the initial random solution. Repeat the outer loop $\log_2(k)$ times (where k is the number of wires). The inner loop uses the following steps:

1. Pick a random problem solution.

2. Repeat the following steps $2*k^2$ times:

   a. Determine whether the current solution is the right one. When it is the correct solution, break free of all the loops and report the solution.

   b. Pick an unsatisfied clause at random. Choose one of the conditions in it at random and amend it.

Implementing the Python code

To solve the 2-SAT problem using Python and the RandomWalkSAT algorithm, you need to set a few helpful functions. The create_clauses and signed functions help generate a circuit problem to solve by handling the OR and NOT gates, respectively. Using these functions, you specify the number of OR gates and provide a seed number that guarantees that you can recreate the resulting problem later (allowing you to try the problem multiple times and on different computers).

The create_random_solutions function provides a cold problem start by providing a random solution that sets the inputs. The chances of finding the right solution using random luck is slim (one out of the power of two to the number of gates), but on average, you can expect that three quarters of the gates are correctly set (because, as seen using the truth table for the OR function, three inputs out of four possible are True). The check_solution function determines when the circuit is satisfied (indicating a correct solution). Otherwise, it outputs what conditions aren't satisfied. (You can find this code in the A4D; 18; Local Search.ipynb file on the Dummies site as part of the downloadable code; see the Introduction for details.)

```
import numpy as np
import random
from math import log2

import matplotlib.pyplot as plt
% matplotlib inline

def signed(v):
    return v if np.random.random()<0.5 else -v

def create_clauses(i, seed=1):
    np.random.seed(seed)
    return [(signed(np.random.randint(i)), signed(
                np.random.randint(i))) for j in range(i)]

def create_random_solution(i, *kwargs):
    return {j:signed(1)==1 for j in range(i)}

def check_solution(solution, clauses):
    violations = list()
    for k,(a,b) in enumerate(clauses):
        if not (((solution[abs(a)]) == (a>0)) |
                ((solution[abs(b)]) == (b>0))):
            violations.append(k)
    return violations
```

After setting these functions, you have all the building blocks for a sat2 function to solve the problem. This solution uses two nested iterations: The first replicates many starts; the second picks unsatisfied conditions at random and makes them true. The solution runs in polynomial time. The function isn't guaranteed to find a solution, if one exists, but chances are, it will provide a solution when one exists. In fact, the internal iteration loop makes $2*k^2$ random attempts to solve the circuit, which usually proves enough for a random walk on a line to reach its destination.

REMEMBER

A random walk is a series of computations representing an object that moves away from its initial position by taking a random direction at every step. You might imagine a random walk as the journey of a drunken person from one light pole to the next. Random walks are useful for representing a mathematical model of many real-world aspects. They find applications in biology, physics, chemistry, computer science, and economics, especially in stock market analysis. If you want to know more about random walks, go to http://www.mit.edu/~kardar/ teaching/projects/chemotaxis(AndreaSchmidt)/random.htm.

A random walk on a line is the easiest example of a random walk. On average, k^2 steps of a random walk are required to arrive at a k distance from the starting point. This expected effort explains why RandomWalkSAT requires $2*k^2$ random chances to amend the starting solution. The number of chances provides a high probability that the algorithm will fix the k clauses. Moreover, it works as the random card guessing game discussed in the previous chapter. As the algorithm proceeds, choosing the right answer becomes easier. The external replications guarantee an escape from unfortunate internal-loop random choices that may stop the process in a local solution.

```python
def sat2(clauses, n, start=create_random_solution):
    for external_loop in range(round(log2(n))):
        solution = start(n, clauses)
        history = list()
        for internal_loop in range(2*n**2):
            response = check_solution(solution, clauses)
            unsatisfied = len(response)
            history.append(unsatisfied)
            if unsatisfied==0:
                print ("Solution in %i external loops," %
                        (external_loop+1), end=" ")
                print ("%i internal loops" %
                        (internal_loop+1))
                break
            else:
                r1 = random.choice(response)
                r2 = np.random.randint(2)
                clause_to_fix = clauses[r1][r2]
                solution[abs(clause_to_fix)] = (
                  clause_to_fix>0)
        else:
            continue
        break
    return history, solution
```

Now that all the functions are correctly set, you can run the code to solve a problem. Here's the first example, which tries the circuit created by seed 0 and uses 1,000 logic gates.

```
n = 1000
# Solvable seeds with n=1000 : 0,1,2,3,4,5,6,9,10
# Unsolvable seeds with n=1000 : 8
clauses = create_clauses(n, seed=0)
history, solution = sat2(clauses, n,
        start=create_random_solution)

Found solution in 1 external loops, 1360 internal loops
```

Plotting the solution, as a chart representing the number of steps on the abscissa (random emendations of the solution) and the clauses left to fix on the ordinal axis, you can verify that the algorithm tends to find the correct solution in the long run, as shown in Figure 18-5.

```
plt.plot(np.array(history), 'b-')
plt.xlabel("Random adjustments")
plt.ylabel("Unsatisfied clauses")
plt.grid(True)
plt.show()
```

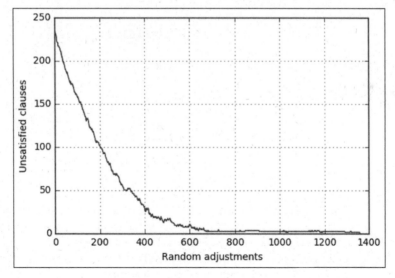

FIGURE 18-5: The number of unsatisfiable clauses decreases after random adjustments.

If you try the circuit with 1,000 gates and seed equal to 8, you will notice that it seems to never end. This is because the circuit is not solvable, and making all the random choices and attempts takes a long time. In the end, the algorithm won't provide you with any solution.

Realizing that the starting point is important

Even though the `RandomWalkSAT` algorithm has a runtime complexity of $O(\log_2 k * k^2)$ at worst, with k the number of inputs, you can speed it up by hacking the starting point. In fact, even though starting with a random configuration means that a quarter of the clauses remains unsatisfied at the start on average, you can fix many of them using a pass over the data.

The problem with clauses is that many require a true input, and simultaneously, many others require a false input. When all clauses require an input to be true or false, you can set it to the required condition, which satisfies a large number of clauses and makes solving the residual ones easier. The following new `RandomWalkSAT` implementation includes a start phase that immediately solves the situations in which an input requires a specific true or false setting by all the clauses they interact with:

```python
def better_start(n, clauses):
    clause_dict = dict()
    for pair in clauses:
        for clause in pair:
            if abs(clause) in clause_dict:
                clause_dict[abs(clause)].add(clause)
            else:
                clause_dict[abs(clause)] = {clause}

    solution = create_random_solution(n)

    for clause, value in clause_dict.items():
        if len(value)==1:
            solution[clause] = value.pop() > 0
    return solution
```

The code defines a new function for the cold start where, after generating a random solution, it scans through the solution and finds all the inputs associated with a single state (true or false). By setting them immediately to the required state, you can reduce the number of clauses requiring amendment, and have the local search do less work and complete earlier.

```python
n = 1000
# Solvable seeds = 0,1,2,3,4,5,6,9,10
# Unsolvable seeds = 8
clauses = create_clauses(n, seed=0)
```

```
history, solution = sat2(clauses, n, start=better_start)

Found solution in 1 external loops, 393 internal loops
```

By providing this new, simplified starting point, after charting the results you can immediately see an improvement because on average, fewer operations are needed to complete the task.

TIP

In a local search, always consider that the starting point is important to allow the algorithm to complete earlier and more successfully, as shown in Figure 18-6. In sum, try to provide the best-quality start for your search as possible.

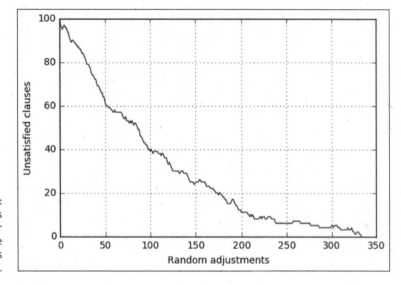

FIGURE 18-6:
Execution is speedier because the starting point is better.

Chapter **19**

Employing Linear Programming

L inear programming made a first appearance during World War II when logistics proved critical in maneuvering armies of millions of soldiers, weapons, and supplies across geographically variegated battlefields. Tanks and airplanes needed to refuel and rearm, which required a massive organizational effort to succeed in spite of limitations in time, resources, and actions from the enemy.

You can express most of these military problems in mathematical form. Mathematician George Bernard Dantzig, who was employed in the U.S. Air Force Office of Statistical Control, devised a smart way to solve these problems using the *simplex* algorithm. Simplex is the core idea that created interest in numerical optimization after the war and gave birth to the promising field of linear programming. The availability of the first performing computers of the time also increased interest, rendering complex computations solvable in a new and fast way. You can view the early history of computing in the 1950s and 1960s as a quest to optimize logistical problems using the simplex method and applying both high-speed computers and specialized programming languages.

Dantzig died in 2005, and the field he inaugurated is still under constant development. In the recent years, fresh ideas and methods related to linear programming continue to make successful appearances, such as the following:

>> **Constrain programming:** Expresses the relationships between the variables in a computer program as constraints in linear programming.

>> **Genetic algorithms:** Considers the idea that math formulas can replicate and mutate in order to solve problems in the same manner as DNA does in nature by evolution. Genetic algorithms also appear in Chapter 20 because of their heuristic approach to optimization.

This chapter helps you understand linear programming. In addition, you see how to apply linear programming to real-world problems by using Python as the tool to express those problems in code.

Using Linear Functions as a Tool

This section shows how to address a problem where someone transforms the *objective* (the representation of cost, profit, or some other quantity to maximize or minimize subject to the constraints) and *constraints* (linear inequalities derived from the application, such as the limit of a 40-hour work week) of that problem into linear functions. The purpose of linear programming is to provide an optimum numeric solution, which could be a maximum or a minimum value, and the set of conditions to obtain it.

This definition may sound a little bit tricky because both math and some abstraction is involved (objective and constraints as linear functions), but things become clearer after considering what a function is and when we can determine whether a function is linear or not. Beyond the math jargon, linear programming is just a different point of view when dealing with algorithmic problems, where you trade operations and manipulations of data inputs with mathematical functions and you perform calculations using a software program called an *optimizer*.

You can't use linear programming to solve all problems, but a large number of them fit linear programming requirements, especially problems requiring optimization using previously defined limits. Previous chapters discuss how dynamic programming is the best approach when you need to optimize problems subject to constraints. Dynamic programming works with problems that are discrete, that is the numbers you work with are whole numbers. Linear programming mainly works with decimal numbers, although special optimization algorithms are available that provide solutions as integer numbers (for instance you can solve the traveling salesman problem using integer linear programming). Linear programming has a wider scope, because it can cope with almost any polynomial time problem.

Linear programming sees use for needs such as manufacturing, logistics, transportation (especially for airlines, for defining routes, timetables, and the cost of tickets), marketing, finance, and telecommunications. All these applications require that you obtain a maximum economic result and minimum cost while optimizing available resource allocation and satisfying all constraints and limitations. In addition, you can apply linear programming to common applications such as video games and computer visualization, because games require dealing with bidimensional and tridimensional complex shapes, and you need to determine whether any shapes collide as well as ensure that they respect the rules of the game. You achieve these aims via the convex hull algorithm powered by linear programming (see `http://www.tcs.fudan.edu.cn/rudolf/Courses/Algorithms/Alg_ss_07w/Webprojects/Chen_hull/applications.htm`). Finally, linear programming is at work in search engines for document-retrieval problems; you can transform words, phrases, and documents into functions and determine how to maximize your search result (getting the documents you need in order to answer your query) when you look for documents with certain mathematical characteristics.

Grasping the basic math you need

In computer programming, functions provide the means for packaging code that you intend to use more than once. Functions turn code into a black box, an entity to which you provide inputs and expect certain outputs. Chapter 4 discusses how to create functions in Python. Mathematics uses functions in a similar manner to programming; they are set of mathematical operations that transform some input into an output. The input can include one or more variables, resulting in a unique output based on the input. Usually a function has this form:

```
f (x) = x*2
```

- **f:** Determines the function name. It can be anything; you can use any letter of the alphabet or even a word.

- **(x):** Specifies the input. In this example, the input is the variable x, but you can use more inputs and of any complexity, including multiple variables or matrices.

- **x*2:** Defines the set of operations that the function performs after receiving the input. The result is the function output in the form of a number.

If you plug the input 2 as x in this example, you obtain:

```
f(2) = 4
```

In math terms, by calling this function, you mapped the input 2 to the output 4.

REMEMBER

Functions can be simple or complex, but every function has one and only one result for every set of inputs that you provide (even when the input is made of multiple variables).

Linear programming leverages functions to render the objectives it has to reach in a mathematical way to solve the problem at hand. When you turn objectives into a math function, the problem translates into determining the input to the function that maps the maximum output (or the minimum, depending on what you want to achieve). The function representing the optimization objective is the *objective function.* In addition, linear programming uses functions and inequalities to express constraints or bounds that keep you from plugging just any input you want into the objective function. For instance, inequalities are

```
0 <= x <= 4
y + x < 10
```

The first of these inequalities translates into limiting the input of the objective function to values between 0 and 4. Inequalities can involve more input variables at a time. The second of these inequalities ties the values of an input to other values because their sum can't exceed 10.

REMEMBER

Bounds imply an input limitation between values, as in the first example. *Constraints* always involve a math expression comprising more than one variable, as in the second example.

The final linear programming requirement is for both the objective function and the inequalities to be linear expressions. This means that the objective function and inequalities can't contain variables that multiply each other, or contain variables raised to a power (squared or cubed, for instance).

TECHNICAL STUFF

All the functions in an optimization should be linear expressions because the procedure represents them as lines in a Cartesian space. (If you need to review the concept of a Cartesian space, you can find useful information at http://www.mathsisfun.com/data/cartesian-coordinates.html.) As explained in the "Using Linear Programming in Practice" section, later in this chapter, you can imagine working with linear programming more as solving a geometric problem than a mathematical one.

Learning to simplify when planning

The problems that the original simplex algorithm solved were all of the kind that you usually read as math problems in a textbook. In such problems, all the data, information, and limitations are stated clearly, there is no irrelevant or redundant information, and you clearly have to apply a math formula (and most likely the one you just studied) to solve the problem.

In the real world, solutions to problems are never so nicely hinted at. Instead, they often appear in a confused way, and any necessary information isn't readily available for you to process. Yet, you can analyze the problem and locate required data and other information. In addition, you can discover limitations such as money, time, or some rule or order that you must consider. When solving the problem, you gather the information and devise the means to simplify it.

Simplification implies some loss of realism but renders things simpler, which can highlight the underlying processes that make things move, thereby helping you decide what happens. A simpler problem allows you to develop a model representing the reality. A model can approximate what happens in reality, and you can use it for both managing simulations and linear programming.

For instance, if you work in a factory and have to plan a production schedule, you know that the more people you add, the speedier production will be. However, you won't always obtain the same gain with the same addition of people. For example, the skills of the operators you add to the job affects results. In addition, you may find that adding more people to the job brings decreasing results when those people spend more time communicating and coordinating between themselves than performing useful work. Yet, you can make the model easier by pretending that every person you add to the task will produce a certain amount of final or intermediate goods.

Working with geometry using simplex

Classic examples of linear programming problems imply production of goods using limited resources (time, workers, or materials). As an example for depicting how linear programming approaches such challenges, imagine a factory that assembles two or more products that it must deliver in a certain time. The factory workers produce two products, x and y, during an eight-hour shift. For each product, they get a different profit (that you compute by subtracting costs from revenue), different hourly production rates, and different daily demands from the market:

>> **Revenue in USD for each product:** x=15, y=25

>> **Production rate per hour:** x=50, y=40

>> **Daily demand per product:** x=300, y=200

In essence, the business problem is to decide whether to produce more x, which is easier to assemble but pays less, or y, which guarantees more revenue but less production. To solve the problem, first determine the objective function. Express it as the sum of the quantities of the two products, multiplied by their expected unit revenue, which you know you have to maximize (only if the problem is about costs do you have to minimize the objective function):

```
f(x,y) = 15 * x + 25 * y
```

This problem has inequalities, which are bounded by x and y values that have to hold true to obtain a valid result from the optimization:

```
0 <= x <= 300
0 <= y <= 200
```

In fact, you can't produce a negative number of products, nor does it make sense to produce more products than the market demands. Another important limitation is available time, because you can't exceed eight hours for each work shift. This means calculating the time to produce both x and y products and constraining the total time to less than or equal to eight hours.

```
x/40 + y/50 <= 8
```

You can represent functions on a Cartesian plane. (For a refresher on plotting functions, consult http://www.mathplanet.com/education/pre-algebra/graphing-and-functions/linear-equations-in-the-coordinate-plane.) Because you can express everything using functions in this problem, you can also solve the linear programming problems as geometry problems on a Cartesian coordinate space. If the problem doesn't involve more than two variables, you can plot the two functions and their constraints as lines on a plane, and determine how they delimit a geometric shape. You'll discover that the lines delimit an area, shaped as a polygon, called the *feasible region*. This region is where you find the solution, which contains all the valid (according to constraints) inputs for the problem.

REMEMBER

When the problem deals with more than two variables, you can still imagine it using lines intersecting in a space, but you can't represent this visually because each input variable needs a dimension in the graph, and graphs are bound to the three dimensions of the world we live in.

At this point, the linear programming algorithm explores the delimited feasible region in a smart way and reports back with the solution. In fact, you don't need to check every point in the delimited area to determine the best problem solution. Imagine the objective function as another line that you represent on the plane (after all, even the objective function is a linear function). You can see that the solution you are looking for is the coordinate points where the feasible area and the objective function line first touch each other (see Figure 19-1). When the objective function line descends from above (arriving from outside the feasible region, where results occur that you can't accept because of the constraints), at a certain point it will touch the area. This contact point is usually a vertex of the area, but it could be an entire side of the polygon (in which case each point on that side is an optimal solution).

FIGURE 19-1:
Looking where the objective function is going to touch the feasible area.

As a practical matter, the simplex algorithm can't make lines visually descend, as in this example. Instead, it walks along the border of the feasible area (by enumerating the vertexes) and tests the resulting objective function values at each vertex until it finds the solution. Consequently, the effective running time depends on the number of vertexes, which for its part depends on the number of constraints and variables involved in the solution. (More variables mean more dimensions and more vertexes.)

Understanding the limitations

As you gain more confidence with linear programming and the problems become more challenging, you require more complex approaches than the basic simplex algorithm presented in this chapter. In fact, the simplex isn't used anymore because more sophisticated algorithms have replaced it —algorithms that geometrically cut through the interior of the feasible region instead of walking along it. These newer algorithms take a shortcut when the algorithm is clearly looking for the solution at the wrong side of the region.

You can also find working with floating-point numbers limiting because many problems require a binary (1/0) or integer answer. Moreover, other problems may require using curves, not lines, to represent the problem space and feasible region correctly. You find integer linear programming and nonlinear programming algorithms implemented in commercial software. Just be aware that both integer and nonlinear programming are NP-complete problems and may require as much, if not more, time than other algorithms you know.

Using Linear Programming in Practice

The best way to start in linear programming is to use predefined solutions, rather than create custom applications on your own. The first section that follows helps you install a predefined solution used for the examples that follow.

WARNING

When working with a software product, you may find significant differences between open source software and commercial packages. Although open source software offers a wide spectrum of algorithms, performance could be disappointing on large and complex problems. Much art is still involved in implementing linear programming algorithms as part of working software, and you can't expect open source software to run as fast and smoothly as commercial offerings.

Even so, open source provides some nice options for learning linear program. The following sections use an open source Python solution named PuLP that allows you to create linear programming optimizations after defining a cost function and constraints as Python functions. It's mostly a didactical solution, suitable to help you test how linear programming works on some problems and get insight on formulating problems in math terms.

TECHNICAL STUFF

PuLP provides an interface to the underlying solver programs. Python comes with a default, open source, solver program that PuLP helps you access. The performance (speed, accuracy, and scalability) that PuLP provides depends almost entirely on the solver and optimizer that the user chooses. The best solvers are commercial products, such as CPLEX (https://en.wikipedia.org/wiki/CPLEX), XPRESS (https://en.wikipedia.org/wiki/FICO_Xpress), and GuRoBi (https://en.wikipedia.org/wiki/Gurobi), which provide a huge speed advantage when compared to open source solvers.

Setting up PuLP at home

PuLP is a Python open source project created by Jean-Sebastien Roy, later modified and maintained by Stuart Antony Mitchell. The PuLP package helps you define linear programming problems and solve them using the internal solver (which relies on the simplex algorithm). You can also use other solvers that are available on public domain repositories or by paying for a license. The project repository (containing all the source code and many examples) is at https:// github.com/coin-or/pulp . The complete documentation is located at https:// pythonhosted.org/PuLP/.

PuLP isn't readily available as part of the Anaconda distribution, thus you have to install it yourself. You must use the Anaconda3 (or above) command prompt to install PuLP because the older versions of the Anaconda command prompt won't work. Open a command-line shell, type **pip install pulp** and press Enter. If you have Internet access, the pip command downloads the PuLP package and installs it in Python. (The version used by the examples in this chapter is PuLP 1.6.1, but later versions should provide the same functionality.)

Optimizing production and revenue

The problem in this section is another optimization related to production. You work with two products (because this implies just two variables that you can represent on a bidimensional chart), product A and B, which have to undergo a series of transformations through three stages. Each stage requires a number of operators (the value n), which could be workers or robots, and each stage is operative at most for a number of days in the month (represented by the value t). Each stage operates differently on each product, requiring a different number of days before completion. For instance, a worker in the first stage (called 'res_1') takes two days to finish product A but three days for product B. Finally, each product has a different profit: product A brings $3,000 USD each and product B $2,500 USD each. The following table summarizes the problem:

Production Stage	Time for Product A per Worker (Days)	Time for Product B per Worker (Days)	Uptime (Days)	Workers
res_1	2	3	30	2
res_2	3	2	30	2
res_3	3	3	22	3

To find the objective function, compute the sum of each product quantity multiplied by its profit. It has to be maximized. Although not stated explicitly by the problem, some constraints exist. First is the fact that uptime limits productivity at each stage. Second is the number of workers. Third is productivity relative to the processed product type. You can restate the problem as the sum of the time used to process each product at each stage, which can't exceed the uptime multiplied by the number of workers available. The number of workers multiplied by number of working days provides you the time resources you can use. These resources can't be less than the time it takes to produce all the products you plan to deliver. Here are the resulting formulations with constraints for each stage:

```
objective = 3000 * qty_A + 2500 * qty_B
    production_rate_A * qty_A + production_rate_B * qty_B
      <= uptime_days * workers
```

You can express each constraint using the quantity of one product to determine the other (in fact, if you produce A, you can't produce B when A's production leaves no time):

```
qty_B <= ((uptime_days * workers) -
    (production_rate_A * qty_A) ) / production_rate_B
```

You can record all the values relative to each stage for `production_rate_A`, `production_rate_B`, `uptime_days`, and `workers` for easier access into a Python dictionary. Keep profits in variables instead. (You can find this code in the A4D; 19; Linear Programming.ipynb file on the Dummies site as part of the downloadable code; see the Introduction for details.)

```
import numpy as np
import matplotlib.pyplot as plt
import pulp

%matplotlib inline

res_1 = {'A':2, 'B':3, 't':30, 'n':2}
res_2 = {'A':3, 'B':2, 't':30, 'n':2}
res_3 = {'A':3, 'B':3, 't':22, 'n':3}
res = {'res_1':res_1, 'res_2':res_2, 'res_3':res_3}
profit_A = 3000
profit_B = 2500
```

Having framed the problem in a suitable data structure, try to visualize it using the Python plotting functions. Set product A as the abscissa and, because you don't know the solution, represent the production of product A as a vector of quantities ranging from 0 to 30 (quantities can't be negative). As for product B (as seen in the formulations above), derive it from the production remaining after A is done. Formulate three functions, one for each stage, so that as you decide the quantity for A, you get the consequent quantity of B — considering the constraints.

```
a = np.linspace(0, 30, 30)
c1 = ((res['res_1']['t'] * res['res_1']['n'])-
      res['res_1']['A']*a) / res['res_1']['B']
c2 = ((res['res_2']['t'] * res['res_2']['n'])-
      res['res_2']['A']*a) / res['res_2']['B']
c3 = ((res['res_3']['t'] * res['res_3']['n'])-
      res['res_3']['A']*a) / res['res_3']['B']

plt.plot(a, c1, label='constrain #1')
plt.plot(a, c2, label='constrain #2')
plt.plot(a, c3, label='constrain #3')

axes = plt.gca()
axes.set_xlim([0,30])
axes.set_ylim([0,30])
plt.xlabel('qty model A')
plt.ylabel('qty model B')

border = np.array((c1,c2,c3)).min(axis=0)

plt.fill_between(a, border, color='yellow', alpha=0.5)
plt.scatter(*zip(*[(0,0), (20,0),
                   (0,20), (16,6), (6,16)]))
plt.legend()
plt.show()
```

The constraints turn into three lines on a chart, as shown in Figure 19-2. The lines intersect among themselves, showing the feasible area. This is the area delimited by the three lines whose A and B values are always inferior or equal compared to the values on any of the constraint lines. (The constraints represent a frontier; you can't have A or B values beyond them.)

According to the simplex method, the optimal solution is one of the five vertexes of the polygon (which are (0,0), (20,0), (0,20), (16,6), and (6,16)). You can discover which one is the solution by setting the necessary functions from the PuLP package. First, define the problem and call it *model*. By doing so, you determine that it's a maximization problem and that both A and B should be positive.

```
model = pulp.LpProblem("Max profit", pulp.LpMaximize)
A = pulp.LpVariable('A', lowBound=0)
B = pulp.LpVariable('B', lowBound=0)
```

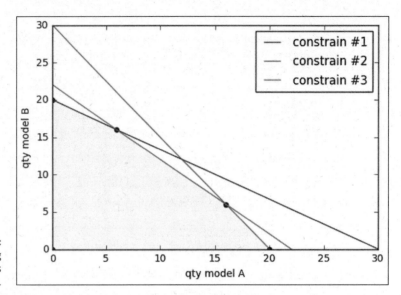

FIGURE 19-2:
Wondering
which vertex is
the right one.

TIP

The PuLP solver can also look for integer solutions, something the original simplex can't do. Just add `cat='Integer'` as a parameter when defining a variable: `A = pulp.LpVariable('A', lowBound=0, cat='Integer')`, and you get only whole numbers as a solution. Be aware that in certain problems, integer number results may prove less optimal than the decimal number results; therefore, use an integer solution only if it makes sense for your problem (for instance, you can't produce a fraction of a product).

Next, add the objective function by summing the sum of the two variables defined by `pulp.LpVariable` and representing the ideal quantities of products A and B, multiplied by each unit profit value.

```
model += profit_A * A + profit_B * B
```

Finally, add the constraints, in exactly the same way as the objective function. You create the formulation by using the appropriate values (taken from the data dictionary) and the predefined A and B variables.

```
model += res['res_1']['A'] * A + res['res_1']['B'
        ] * B <= res['res_1']['t'] * res['res_1']['n']
model += res['res_2']['A'] * A + res['res_2']['B'
        ] * B <= res['res_2']['t'] * res['res_2']['n']
model += res['res_3']['A'] * A + res['res_3']['B'
        ] * B <= res['res_3']['t'] * res['res_3']['n']
```

The model is ready to optimize (it has ingested both the objective function and the constraints). Call the `solve` method and then check its status. (Sometimes a solution may prove impossible to find or may not be optimal.)

```
model.solve()
print ('Completion status: %s'
       % pulp.LpStatus[model.status])

Completion status: Optimal
```

Having received confirmation that the optimizer found the optimal solution, you print the related quantities of product A and B.

```
print ("Production of model A = %0.1f" % A.varValue)
print ("Production of model B = %0.1f" % B.varValue)

Production of model A = 16.0
Production of model B = 6.0
```

In addition, you print the resulting total profit achievable by this solution.

```
print ('Maximum profit achieved: %0.1f'
       % pulp.value(model.objective))

Maximum profit achieved: 63000.0
```

IN THIS CHAPTER

» **Understanding when heuristics are useful to algorithms**

» **Discovering how pathfinding can be difficult for a robot**

» **Getting a fast start using the Best-first search**

» **Improving on Dijkstra's algorithm and taking the best heuristic route using A***

Chapter **20**

Considering Heuristics

A s a concluding topic, this chapter completes the overview of heuristics started in Chapter 18 that describes heuristics as an effective means of using a local search to navigate neighboring solutions. Chapter 18 defines heuristics as educated guesses about a solution — that is, they are sets of rules of thumb pointing to the desired outcome, thus helping algorithms take the right steps toward it; however, heuristics alone can't tell you exactly how to reach the solution.

There are shades of heuristics, just as there can be shades to the truth. Heuristics touch the fringes of algorithm development today. The AI revolution builds on the algorithms presented so far in the book that order, arrange, search, and manipulate data inputs. At the top of the hierarchy are heuristic algorithms that power optimization, as well as searches that determine how machines learn from data and become capable of solving problems autonomously from direct intervention.

Heuristics aren't silver bullets; no solution solves every problem. Heuristic algorithms have serious drawbacks, and you need to know when to use them. In addition, heuristics can lead to wrong conclusions, both for computers and humans. As for humans, biases that save time when evaluating a person or situation can often prove wrong, and even rules of conduct taken from experience obtain the right solution only under certain circumstances. For instance, consider the habit of hitting electric appliances when they don't work. If the problem is a loose connection, hitting the appliance may prove beneficial by reestablishing the electric connection, but you can't make it a general heuristic because in other cases, that "solution" may prove ineffective or even cause serious damage to the appliance.

Differentiating Heuristics

The word *heuristic* comes from the ancient Greek *heuriskein*, which meant to invent or discover. Its original meaning underlines the fact that employing heuristics is a practical means of finding a solution that isn't well defined, but that is found through exploration and an intuitive grasp of the general direction to take. Heuristics rely on the lucky guess or a trial-and-error approach of trying different solutions. A *heuristic algorithm*, which is an algorithm powered by heuristics, solves a problem faster and more efficiently in terms of computational resources by sacrificing solution precision and completeness, in contrast to most algorithms, which have certain output guarantees. When a problem becomes too complex, a heuristic algorithm can represent the only way to obtain a solution.

Considering the goals of heuristics

Heuristics can speed the long, exhaustive searches performed by other solutions, especially with NP-hard problems that require an exponential number of attempts based on the number of their inputs. For example, consider the traveling salesman problem or variants of the SAT problem, such as the MAX-3SAT (both problems appear in Chapter 18). Heuristics determine the search direction using an estimation, which eliminates a large number of the combinations it would have to test otherwise.

Because a heuristic is an estimate or a guess, it can lead the algorithm that relies on it to a wrong conclusion, which could be an inexact solution or just a suboptimal solution, which is a solution that works but is far from being the best possible. For example, in a numerical estimation, a heuristic might answer that the solution is 41 instead of 42. Other problems often associated with heuristics are the impossibility of finding all best solutions and the variability of time and computations required to reach a solution.

A heuristic provides a perfect match when working with algorithms that would otherwise incur a higher cost when running using other algorithmic techniques. For instance, you can't solve certain problems without heuristics because of the poor quality and overwhelming number of data inputs. The traveling salesman problem (TSP) is one of these: If you have to tour a large number of cities, you cannot use any exact method. TSP and other problems exclude any exact solution. AI applications fall into this category because many AI problems, such as recognizing spoken words or the content of an image, aren't solvable in an exact sequence of steps and rules.

Going from genetic to AI

The Chapter 18 local search discussion presents heuristics such as simulated annealing and tabu search, which helps with hill–climbing optimization (not getting stuck with solutions that are less than ideal). Apart from these, the family of heuristics comprises many different applications, among which are the following:

>> **Swarm intelligence:** A set of heuristics based on the study of the behavior of insect swarms (such as bees, ants, or fireflies) or particles. The method uses multiple attempts to find a solution using agents (such as running several instances of the same algorithm) that interact cooperatively between themselves and the problem setting. Professor Marco Dorigo, one of the top experts and contributors on the study of swarm intelligence algorithms, provides more information on this topic at http://www.aco-metaheuristic.org/.

>> **Metaheuristics:** Heuristics that help you determine (or even generate) the right heuristic for your problem. Among metaheuristics, the most widely known are *genetic algorithms,* inspired by natural evolution. Genetic algorithms start with a pool of possible problem solutions and then generate new solutions using mutation (they add or remove something in the solution) and cross-over (they mix parts of different solutions when a solution is divisible). For instance, in the n-Queen problem (Chapter 18), you see that you can split a checkerboard vertically into parts because the Queens do not move horizontally, making it a problem suitable for cross-over. When the pool is enough large, genetic algorithms select the surviving solutions by ruling out those that don't work or lack promise. The selected pool then undergoes another iteration of mutation, cross-over, and selection. After enough time and iterations, genetic algorithms can find solutions that perform better and are completely different from the initial ones.

>> **Machine learning:** Approaches such as neuro-fuzzy systems, support vector machines, and neural networks, which are the foundation of how a computer learns to estimate and classify from training examples that are provided as part of datasets of data. Similar to how a child learns by experience, machine learning algorithms determine how to deliver the most plausible answer without using precise rules and detailed rules of conduct. (See *Machine Learning For Dummies,* by John Paul Mueller and Luca Massaron [Wiley], for details on how machine learning works.)

>> **Heuristic routing:** A set of heuristics that helps robots (but also found in network telecommunications and logistic transportations) to choose the best path to avoid obstacles when moving around.

Routing Robots Using Heuristics

Guiding a robot in an unknown environment means avoiding obstacles and reaching a specific target. It's both a fundamental and challenging task in artificial intelligence. Robots can rely on *laser rangefinder, lidar* (devices that allow you to determine the distance to an object by means of a laser ray), or *sonar arrays* (devices that use sounds to see their environment) to navigate their surroundings. Yet, no matter the sophisticated hardware they are equipped with, robots still need proper algorithms to

>> Find the shortest path to a destination (or at least a reasonably short one)

>> Avoid obstacles on the way

>> Perform custom behaviors such as minimizing turning or braking

A *pathfinding* (also called *path planning* or simply *pathing*) algorithm helps a robot start in one location and reach a goal using the shortest path between the two, anticipating and avoiding obstacles along the way (it isn't enough to react after hitting a wall). Pathfinding is also useful when moving any other device to a target in space, even a virtual one, such as in a video game or the pages in the World Wide Web.

REMEMBER

Routing autonomously is a key capability of self-driving cars (SDC), vehicles that can sense the road environment and drive to the destination without any human intervention. (You still need to tell the car where to go; it can't read minds.) This recent article from the *Guardian* newspaper provides a good overview about the developments and expectations for self-driving cars: https://www.theguardian.com/technology/2015/sep/13/self-driving-cars-bmw-google-2020-driving.

Scouting in unknown territories

Pathfinding algorithms achieve all the previously discussed tasks to achieve shortest routing, obstacle avoidance, and other desired behaviors. Algorithms work by using basic schematic maps of their surroundings. These maps are of two kinds:

>> **Topological maps:** Simplified diagrams that remove every unnecessary detail. The maps retain key landmarks, correct directions, and some scale proportions for distances. Real-life examples of topological maps include subway maps of Tokyo (http://www.tokyometro.jp/en/subwaymap/) and London (https://tfl.gov.uk/maps/track/tube).

>> **Occupancy grid maps:** These maps divide the surroundings into small, empty squares or hexagons, filling them in when the robot's sensors find an obstacle on the spot they represent. You can see an example of such a map at the Czech Technical University in Prague: http://cmp.felk.cvut.cz/cmp/demos/Omni/mobil/. In addition, check out the videos showing how a robot builds and visualizes such a map at https://www.youtube.com/watch?v=zjl7NmutMIc and https://www.youtube.com/watch?v=RhPlzIyTT58.

You can visualize both topological and occupancy grid maps as graphic diagrams. However, they're best understood by algorithms when rendered into an appropriate data structure. The best data structure for this purpose is the graph because vertexes can easily represent squares, hexagons, landmarks, and waypoints. Edges can connect vertexes in the same way that road, passages, and paths do.

REMEMBER

Your GPS navigation device operates using graphs. Underlying the continuous, detailed, colorful map that the device displays on screen, road maps are elaborated behind the scenes as sets of vertexes and edges traversed by algorithms helping you find the way while avoiding traffic jams.

Representing the robot's territory as a graph re-introduces problems discussed in Chapter 9, which examines how to travel from one vertex to another using the shortest path. The shortest path can be the path that touches the fewest vertexes or the path that costs less (given the sum of the cost of the crossed edge weights, which may represent the length of the edge or some other cost). As when driving your car, you decide not only on the distance driven to reach your destination but also on traffic (roads crowded with traffic or blocked by traffic jams), road conditions, and speed limits that may influence the quality of your journey.

When finding the shortest path to a destination in a graph, the simplest and most basic algorithms in graph theory are depth-first search and Dijkstra's algorithm (described in Chapter 9). Depth-first search explores the graph by going as far as possible from the start and then retracing its steps to explore other paths until it finds the destination. Dijkstra's algorithm explores the graph in a smart and greedy way, considering only the shortest paths. Despite their simplicity, both algorithms are extremely effective when evaluating a simple graph, as in a bird's-eye view, with complete knowledge of the directions you must take to reach the destination and little cost in evaluating the various possible paths.

The situation with a robot is slightly different because it can't perceive all the possible paths at one time, being limited in both visibility and range of sight (obstacles may hide the path or the target may be too far). A robot discovers its environment as it moves and, at best, can assess the distance and direction of its final destination. It's like solving a maze, though not as when playing in a puzzle maze but more akin to immersion in a hedge maze, where you can feel the direction you are taking or you can spot the destination in the distance.

TIP

Hedges are found everywhere in the world. Some of the most famous were built in Europe from the mid-sixteenth century to eighteenth century. In a hedge maze, you can't see where you're going because the hedges are too high. You can perceive direction (if you can see the sun) and even spot the target (see https://www. venetoinside.com/hidden-treasures/post/maze-of-villa-pisani-in-stra-venice/ as an example). There are also famous hedge mazes in films such as *The Shining* by Stanley Kubrick and in *Harry Potter and the Goblet of Fire*.

Using distance measures as heuristics

When you can't solve real-life problems in a precise algorithmic way because their input is confused, missing, or unstable, using heuristics can help. When performing path finding using coordinates in a Cartesian plane (flat maps that rely on a set of horizontal and vertical coordinates), two simple measures can provide the distances between two points in that plane: the Euclidean distance and the Manhattan distance.

People commonly use the Euclidean distance because it derives from the Pythagorean Theorem on triangles. If you want to know the distance in line of sight between two points in a plane, say, A and B, and you know their coordinates, you can pretend they're the extremes of the hypotenuse (the longest side in a triangle). As depicted in Figure 20-1, you calculate distance based on the length of the other two sides by creating a third point, C, whose horizontal coordinate is derived from B and whose vertical coordinate is from A.

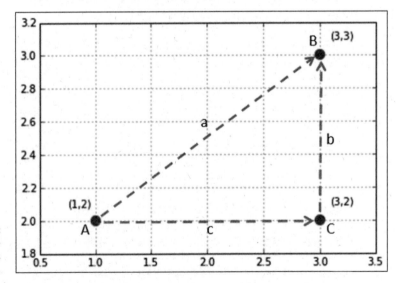

FIGURE 20-1:
A and B are points on a map's coordinates.

This process translates into taking the difference between the horizontal and vertical coordinates of your two points, squaring both the differences (so that they both become positive), sum them, and finally taking the square root of the result. In this example, going from A to B uses coordinates of (1,2) and (3,3):

```
sqrt((1-3)² + (2-3)²) = sqrt(2²+1²) = sqrt(5) = 2.236
```

The Manhattan distance works differently. You begin by summing the lengths of the sides B and C, which equates summing the absolute value of the differences between the horizontal and vertical coordinates of the points A and B.

```
|(1-3)| + |(2-3)| = 2 + 1 = 3
```

The Euclidean distance marks the shortest route, and the Manhattan distance provides the longest yet most plausible route if you expect obstacles when taking a direct route. In fact, the movement represents the trajectory of a taxi in Manhattan (hence the name), moving along a city block to reach its destination (taking the short route through buildings would never work). Other names for this approach are the city block distance or the taxicab distance. Consequently, if you have to move from A to B but you don't know whether you'll find obstacles between them, taking a detour through point C is a good heuristic because that's the distance you expect at worst.

Explaining Path Finding Algorithms

This last part of the chapter concentrates on explaining two algorithms, best-first search and A* (read as "A star"), both based on heuristics. The following sections demonstrate that both these algorithms provide a fast solution to a maze problem representing a topological or occupancy grid map that's represented as a graph. Both algorithms are widely used in robotics and video gaming.

Creating a maze

A topological or occupancy grid map resembles a hedge maze, as mentioned previously, especially if obstacles exist between the start and the end of the route. There are specialized algorithms for both creating and processing mazes, most notably the Wall Follower (known since antiquity: You place your hand on a wall and never pull it away until you get out of the maze) or the Pledge algorithm (read more about the seven maze classifications at http://www.astrolog.org/labyrnth/algrithm.htm). However, pathfinding is fundamentally different from maze solving because in pathfinding, you know where the target should be, whereas maze-solving algorithms try to solve the problem in complete ignorance of where the exit is.

Consequently, the procedure for simulating a maze of obstacles that a robot has to navigate takes a different and simpler approach. Instead of creating a riddle of obstacles, you create a graph of vertexes arranged in a grid (resembling a map) and randomly remove connections to simulate the presence of obstacles. The graph is undirected (you can traverse each edge in both directions) and weighted because it takes time to move from one vertex to another. In particular, it takes longer to move diagonally than to move upward/downward or left/right.

The first step is to import the necessary Python packages. The code defines the Euclidean and the Manhattan distance functions next. (You can find this code in the A4D; 20; Heuristic Algorithms.ipynb file on the Dummies site as part of the downloadable code; see the Introduction for details.)

```python
import numpy as np
import string
import networkx as nx
import matplotlib.pyplot as plt
%matplotlib inline

def euclidean_dist(a, b, coord):
    (x1, y1) = coord[a]
    (x2, y2) = coord[b]
    return np.sqrt((x1-x2)**2+(y1-y2)**2)

def manhattan_dist(a, b, coord):
    (x1, y1) = coord[a]
    (x2, y2) = coord[b]
    return abs(x1 - x2) + abs(y1 - y2)

def non_informative(a,b):
    return 0
```

The next step creates a function to generate random mazes. It's based on an integer number seed of your choice that allows you to recreate the same maze every time you provide the same number. Otherwise, maze generation is completely random.

```python
def create_maze(seed=2, drawing=True):
    np.random.seed(seed)
    letters = [l for l in string.ascii_uppercase[:25]]
    checkboard = np.array(letters[:25]).reshape((5,5))
```

```
Graph = nx.Graph()
for j, node in enumerate(letters):
    Graph.add_nodes_from(node)
    x, y = j // 5, j % 5
    x_min = max(0, x-1)
    x_max = min(4, x+1)+1
    y_min = max(0, y-1)
    y_max = min(4, y+1)+1
    adjacent_nodes = np.ravel(
        checkboard[x_min:x_max,y_min:y_max])
    exits = np.random.choice(adjacent_nodes,
        size=np.random.randint(1,4), replace=False)
    for exit in exits:
        if exit not in Graph.edge[node]:
            Graph.add_edge(node, exit)
spacing = np.arange(0.0, 1.0, 0.2)
coordinates = [[x,y] for x in spacing \
            for y in spacing]
position  = {l:c for l,c in zip(letters, coordinates)}

for node in Graph.edge:
    for exit in Graph.edge[node]:
        length = int(round(
                euclidean_dist(
                    node, exit, position)*10,0))
        Graph.add_edge(node,exit,weight=length)

if drawing:
    nx.draw(Graph, position, with_labels=True)
    labels = nx.get_edge_attributes(Graph,'weight')
    nx.draw_networkx_edge_labels(Graph, position,
                            edge_labels=labels)
    plt.show()

return Graph, position
```

The functions return a NetworkX graph (Graph), a favorite data structure for representing graphs, which contains 25 vertexes (or nodes, if you prefer) and a Cartesian map of points (position). The vertexes are placed on a 5 x 5 grid, as shown in Figure 20-2. The output also applies distance functions and calculates the position of vertexes.

```
graph, coordinates = create_maze(seed=3)
```

TIP

FIGURE 20-2:
A maze
representing a
topological map
with obstacles.

In the maze generated by a seed value of 2, every vertex connects with the others. Because the generation process is random, some maps may contain disconnected vertexes, which precludes going between the disconnected vertexes. To see how this works, try a seed value of 13. This actually happens in reality; for example, sometimes a robot can't reach a particular destination.

Looking for a quick best-first route

The depth-first search algorithm explores the graph by moving from vertex to vertex and adding directions to a stack data structure. When it's time to move, the algorithm moves to the first direction found on the stack. It's like moving through a maze of rooms by taking the first exit you see. Most probably, you arrive at a dead end, which isn't your destination. You then retrace your steps to the previously visited rooms to see whether you encounter another exit, but it takes a long time when you're far from your target.

Heuristics can greatly help with the repetition created by a depth-first search strategy. Using heuristics can tell you whether you're getting nearer or farther from your target. This combination is called the *best-first search* algorithm (BFS). In this case, the *best* in the name hints at the fact that, as you explore the graph, you don't take the first edge in sight, but rather evaluate which edge to take and choose the one that, based on the heuristic, should take you closer to your desired outcome. This behavior resembles greedy optimization (the best first), and some people also call this algorithm *greedy best-first search*. BFS will probably miss the target at first, but because of heuristics, it won't end up far from target and will retrace less than it would if using depth-first search alone.

REMEMBER

You use the BFS algorithm principally in web crawlers that look for certain information on the web. In fact, BFS allows a software agent to move in a mostly unknown graph, using heuristics to detect how closely the content of the next page resembles the initial one (to explore for better content). The algorithm is also widely used in video games, helping characters controlled by the computer move in search of enemies and bounties, thereby resembling a greedy, target-oriented behavior.

Demonstrating BFS in Python using the previously built maze illustrates how a robot can move in a space by seeing it as a graph. The following code shows some general functions, which are also used for the next algorithm in this section. These two functions provide the directions to take from a vertex (node_neighbors) and determines the cost of going from one vertex to another (graph_weight). Weight represents distance or time.

```python
def graph_weight(graph, a, b):
    return graph.edge[a][b]['weight']

def node_neighbors(graph, node):
    return graph.edge[node]
```

The path-planning algorithm simulates robot movement in a graph. When it found a solution, the plan translates into movement. Therefore, path-planning algorithms provide an output telling you how to best move from one vertex to another, you still need a function to translate the information and determine the route to take and calculate trip length. The functions reconstruct_path and compute_path provide the plan in terms of steps and expected cost when provided with the result from the path-planning algorithm.

```python
def reconstruct_path(connections, start, goal):
    if goal in connections:
        current = goal
        path = [current]
        while current != start:
            current = connections[current]
            path.append(current)
        return path[::-1]

def compute_path_dist(path, graph):
    if path:
        run = 0
        for step in range(len(path)-1):
            A = path[step]
            B = path[step+1]
```

```
        run += graph_weight(graph, A, B)
    return run
else:
    return 0
```

Having prepared all the basic functions, the example creates a maze using a seed value of 30. This maze presents two main routes going from vertex A to vertex Y because there are some obstacles in the middle of the map (as shown in Figure 20-3). There are also some dead ends on the way (such as vertexes E and O).

```
graph, coordinates = create_maze(seed=30)
start = 'A'
goal  = 'Y'
scoring=manhattan_dist
```

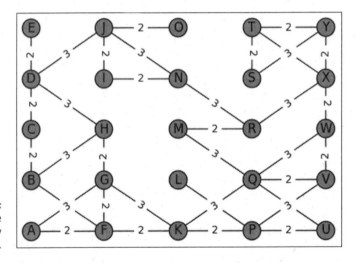

FIGURE 20-3:
An intricate maze to be solved by heuristics.

The BFS implementation is a bit more complex than the depth-first search code found in Chapter 9. It uses two lists: one to hold the never-visited vertexes (called open_list), and another to hold the visited ones (closed_list). The open_list list acts as a priority queue, one in which a priority determines the first element to extract. In this case, the heuristic provides the priority, thus the priority queue provides a direction that's closer to the target. The Manhattan distance heuristic works best because of the obstacles obstructing the way to the destination:

```
# Best-first search
path = {}
open_list = set(graph.nodes())
```

```python
closed_list = {start: manhattan_dist(start, goal,
                                      coordinates)}

while open_list:

    candidates = open_list&closed_list.keys()
    if len(candidates)==0:
        print ("Cannot find a way to the goal %s" % goal)
        break
    frontier = [(closed_list[node],
                 node) for node in candidates]
    score, min_node =sorted(frontier)[0]

    if min_node==goal:
        print ("Arrived at final vertex %s" % goal)
        print ('Unvisited vertices: %i' % (len(
                    open_list)-1))
        break
    else:
        print("Processing vertex %s, " % min_node, end="")

    open_list = open_list.difference(min_node)
    neighbors = node_neighbors(graph, min_node)
    to_be_visited = list(neighbors-closed_list.keys())

    if len(to_be_visited) == 0:
        print ("found no exit, retracing to %s"
                % path[min_node])
    else:
        print ("discovered %s" % str(to_be_visited))

    for node in neighbors:
        if node not in closed_list:
            closed_list[node] = scoring(node, goal,
                                        coordinates)
            path[node] = min_node

print ('\nBest path is:', reconstruct_path(
        path, start, goal))
print ('Length of path: %i' % compute_path_dist(
        reconstruct_path(path, start, goal), graph))
```

```
Processing vertex A, discovered ['F', 'G']
Processing vertex G, discovered ['K', 'H']
Processing vertex H, discovered ['B', 'D']
Processing vertex D, discovered ['E', 'J', 'C']
Processing vertex J, discovered ['O', 'I', 'N']
Processing vertex O, found no exit, retracing to J
Processing vertex N, discovered ['R']
Processing vertex R, discovered ['M', 'X']
Processing vertex X, discovered ['T', 'W', 'Y']
Arrived at final vertex Y
Unvisited vertices: 15

Best path is: ['A', 'G', 'H', 'D', 'J', 'N', 'R', 'X',
 'Y']
Length of path: 22
```

The verbose output from the example tells you how the algorithm works. BFS keeps moving until it runs out of vertexes to explore. When it exhausts the vertexes without reaching the target, the code tells you that it can't reach the target and the robot won't budge. When the code does find the destination, it stops processing vertexes, even if open_list still contains vertexes, which saves time.

Finding a dead end, such as ending up in vertex O, means looking for a previously unused route. The best alternative immediately pops up thanks to the priority queue, and the algorithm takes it. In this example, BFS efficiently ignores 15 vertexes and takes the upward route in the map, completing its journey from A to Y in 22 steps.

TIP

You can test other mazes by setting a different seed number and comparing the BFS results with the A* algorithm described in the next section. You'll find that sometimes BFS is both fast and accurate in choosing the best way, sometimes not. If you need a robot that searches quickly, BFS is the best choice.

Going heuristically around by A*

The A* algorithm speedily produces best shortest paths in a graph by combining the Dijikstra greedy search discussed in Chapter 9 with an early stop (the algorithm stops when it reaches its destination vertex) and a heuristic estimate (usually based on the Manhattan distance) that hints at the graph area to explore first. A* was developed at the Artificial Intelligence Center of Stanford Research Institute (now called SRI International) in 1968 as part of the Shakey the robot project. Shakey was the first mobile robot to autonomously decide how to go somewhere (although it was limited to wandering around a few rooms in the labs). To render

Shakey fully autonomous, its developers came up with the A* algorithm, the Hough transform (an image-processing transformation to detect the edges of an object), and the visibility graph method (a way to represent a path as a graph). The article at `http://www.ai.sri.com/shakey/` describes Shakey in more detail and even shows it in action. It is still surprising watching what Shakey was capable of doing; go to `https://www.youtube.com/watch?v=qXdn6ynwpiI` to take a look. The A* algorithm is currently the best available algorithm when you're looking for the shortest route in a graph and you must deal with partial information and expectations (as captured by the heuristic function guiding the search). A* is able to

>> **Find the shortest path solution every time:** The algorithm can do this if such a path exists and if A* is properly informed by the heuristic estimate. A* is powered by the Dijkstra algorithm, which guarantees always finding the best solution.

>> **Find the solution faster than any other algorithm:** A* can do this if given access to a fair heuristic — one that provides the right directions to reach the target proximity in a similar, though even smarter, way as BFS.

>> **Computes weights when traversing edges:** Weights account for the cost of moving in a certain direction. For example, turning may take longer than going straight, as in the case of Shakey the robot.

REMEMBER

A proper, fair, *admissible* heuristic provides useful information to A* about the distance to the target by never overestimating the cost of reaching it. Moreover, A* makes greater use of its heuristic than BFS, therefore the heuristic must perform calculations quickly or the overall processing time will be too long.

The Python implementation in this example uses the same code and data structures used for BFS, but there are differences between them. The main differences are that as the algorithm proceeds, it updates the cost of reaching from the start vertex to each of the explored vertexes. In addition, when it decides on a route, A* considers the shortest path from the start to the target, passing by the current vertex, because it sums the estimate from the heuristic with the cost of the path computed to the current vertex. This process allows the algorithm to perform more computations than BFS when the heuristic is a proper estimate and to determine the best path possible.

TIP

Finding the shortest path possible in cost terms is the core Dijkstra algorithm function. A* is simply a Dijkstra algorithm in which the cost of reaching a vertex is enhanced by the heuristic of the expected distance to the target. Chapter 9 describes the Dijkstra algorithm in detail. Revisiting the Chapter 9 discussion will help you better understand how A* operates in leveraging heuristics.

```
# A*
open_list = set(graph.nodes())
closed_list = {start: manhattan_dist(
        start, goal, coordinates)}
visited = {start: 0}
path = {}

while open_list:

    candidates = open_list&closed_list.keys()
    if len(candidates)==0:
        print ("Cannot find a way to the goal %s" % goal)
        break
    frontier = [(closed_list[node],
                 node) for node in candidates]
    score, min_node =sorted(frontier)[0]

    if min_node==goal:
        print ("Arrived at final vertex %s" % goal)
        print ('Unvisited vertices: %i' % (len(
                open_list)-1))
        break
    else:
        print("Processing vertex %s, " % min_node, end="")

    open_list = open_list.difference(min_node)
    current_weight = visited[min_node]
    neighbors = node_neighbors(graph, min_node)
    to_be_visited = list(neighbors-visited.keys())

    for node in neighbors:
        new_weight = current_weight + graph_weight(
                     graph, min_node, node)
        if node not in visited or \
         new_weight < visited[node]:
            visited[node] = new_weight
            closed_list[node] = manhattan_dist(node, goal,
                     coordinates) + new_weight
            path[node] = min_node

    if to_be_visited:
        print ("discovered %s" % to_be_visited)
    else:
        print ("getting back to open list")
```

```
print ('\nBest path is:', reconstruct_path(
        path, start, goal))
print ('Length of path: %i' % compute_path_dist(
        reconstruct_path(path, start, goal), graph))

Processing vertex A, discovered ['F', 'G']
Processing vertex F, discovered ['B', 'K']
Processing vertex G, discovered  ['H']
Processing vertex K, discovered  ['Q', 'P']
Processing vertex H, discovered  ['D']
Processing vertex B, discovered  ['C']
Processing vertex P, discovered  ['L', 'U', 'V']
Processing vertex Q, discovered  ['M', 'W']
Processing vertex C, getting back to open list
Processing vertex U, getting back to open list
Processing vertex D, discovered  ['E', 'J']
Processing vertex V, getting back to open list
Processing vertex L, getting back to open list
Processing vertex W, discovered  ['X']
Processing vertex E, getting back to open list
Processing vertex M, discovered  ['R']
Processing vertex J, discovered  ['O', 'I', 'N']
Processing vertex X, discovered ['T', 'Y']
Processing vertex R, getting back to open list
Processing vertex O, getting back to open list
Processing vertex I, getting back to open list
Arrived at final vertex Y
Unvisited vertices: 3

Best path is: ['A', 'F', 'K', 'Q', 'W', 'X', 'Y']
Length of path: 14
```

When the A* has completed analyzing the maze, it outputs a best path that's much shorter than the BFS solution. This solution comes at a cost: A* explores almost all the present vertexes, leaving just three vertexes unconsidered. As with Dijkstra, its worst running time is $O(v^2)$, where v is the number of vertexes in the graph; or $O(e + v*\log(v))$, where e is the number of edges, when using min-priority queues, an efficient data structure when you need to obtain the minimum value for a long list. The A* algorithm is not different in its worst running time than Dijkstra's, though on average, it performs better on large graphs because it first finds the target vertex when correctly guided by the heuristic measurement (in the case of a routing robot, the Manhattan distance).

6

The Part of Tens

Chapter **21**

Ten Algorithms That Are Changing the World

I t's hard to imagine an algorithm doing much of anything, much less changing the world. However, algorithms today appear everywhere, and you might not even realize just how much effect they have on your life.

Most people realize that online stores and other sales venues rely on algorithms to determine which add-on products to suggest based on previous purchases. However, most people are unaware of the uses of algorithms in medicine, many of which help a doctor decide what diagnosis to provide.

Algorithms appear in the oddest places. The timing of traffic lights often depends on the calculations of algorithms. Algorithms will help your smartphone talk to you today, and you see algorithms at work in making your television do more than any television has done in the past. Consequently, it's not all that impossible to believe that algorithms are poised to change the world. This chapter highlights ten of them.

REMEMBER

For algorithm purists, you can say that the algorithm has changed the world throughout the centuries, so nothing has really changed for thousands of years. The Babylonians used algorithms to perform factorization and find square roots as early as 1600 BC. Al-Khawarizmi described algorithms to solve both linear and quadratic equations around 820. This chapter focuses on computer-based algorithms, but algorithms have been around for a long time.

Using Sort Routines

Without ordered data, most of the world would come to a stop. To use data, you must be able to find it. You can find hundreds of sort algorithms explained on sites such as `https://betterexplained.com/articles/sorting-algorithms/` and as part of this book (see Chapter 7).

However, the three most common sort routines are Mergesort, Quicksort, and Heapsort because of the superior speed they provide (see the time comparisons at `http://www.cprogramming.com/tutorial/computersciencetheory/sortcomp.html`). The sort routine that works best for your application depends on the following:

>> What you expect the application to do

>> The kind of data you work with

>> The computing resources you have available

The point is that the capability to sort data into whatever form an application needs to accomplish a task makes the world run, and this capability is changing how the world works.

Some businesses today thrive as a result of the sort algorithm. For example, consider the fact that Google exists because it helps people find things, and this ability resides substantially in the capability to sort data to make it readily accessible. Consider just how hard it would be to find an item on Amazon without the sort routine. Even that recipe application on your computer at home relies heavily on sort routines to keep the data it contains in order. In fact, it probably wouldn't be too much of a stretch to say that any substantial application relies heavily on sort routines.

Looking for Things with Search Routines

As with sort routines, search routines appear in nearly every application of any size today. The applications appear everywhere, even in places that you might not think too much about, such as your car. Finding information quickly is an essential part of daily life. For example, imagine being late for an appointment and suddenly discovering that your GPS can't find the address you need. As with sort routines, search routines come in all shapes and sizes, and you can find them described on sites such as https://tekmarathon.com/2012/10/05/best-searching-algorithm-2/ and http://research.cs.queensu.ca/home/cisc121/2006s/webnotes/search.html. In fact, if anything, there are more search routines than sort routines because search requirements are often more strenuous and complex. You find a lot of search routines discussed in this book as well (see Chapter 7).

Shaking Things Up with Random Numbers

All sorts of things would be a lot less fun without randomness. For example, imagine starting Solitaire and seeing precisely the same game every time you start it. No one would play such a game. Consequently, random number generation is an essential part of the gaming experience. In fact, as expressed in a number of chapters in this book, some algorithms actually require some level of randomness to work properly (see the "Arranging caching computer data" section of Chapter 15 as an example). You also find that testing works better when using random values in some cases (see the "Choosing a particular kind of compression" section of Chapter 14 as an example).

REMEMBER

The numbers that you obtain from an algorithm are actually pseudo-random, which means that you can potentially predict the next number in a series by knowing the algorithm and the seed value used to generate the number. That's why this information is so closely guarded.

TECHNICAL STUFF

Not all applications and not all computers rely on pseudo-random numbers generated by algorithms (the vast majority do, however). Computer hardware-based methods of creating random numbers exist, such as relying on atmospheric noise or temperature changes (see http://engineering.mit.edu/ask/can-computer-generate-truly-random-number for details). In fact, you can get a hardware-based random number solution, such as ChaosKey (http://altusmetrum.org/ChaosKey/) and plug it into your USB slot to generate what likely are true random numbers. The interesting thing about the ChaosKey site is that it provides you with a schematic to show how it collects random noise and changes it into a random number.

Performing Data Compression

Chapter 14 discusses data compression techniques and uses the kind of compression that you normally find used for files. However, data compression affects every aspect of computing today. For example, most graphics, video, and audio files rely on data compression. Without data compression, you couldn't possibly obtain the required level of throughput to make tasks such as streamed movies work.

However, data compression finds even more uses than you might expect. Just about every Database Management System (DBMS) relies on data compression to make data fit in a reasonable amount of space on disk. Cloud computing wouldn't work without data compression because it downloading items from the cloud to local machines would take too long. Even web pages often rely on data compression to get information from one place to another.

Keeping Data Secret

The concept of keeping data secret isn't new. In fact, it's one of the oldest reasons to use an algorithm of some sort. The word cryptography actually comes from two Greek words: *kryptós* (hidden or secret) and *graphein* (writing). In fact, the Greeks were probably the first users of cryptography, and ancient texts report that Julius Caesar used encrypted missives to communicate with his generals. The point is, keeping data secret is one of the longest running battles in history. The moment one party finds a way to keep a secret, someone else finds a way to make the secret public by breaking the cryptography. General uses for computer-driven cryptography today include:

>> **Confidentiality:** Ensuring that no one can see information exchanged between two parties.

>> **Data integrity:** Reducing the likelihood that someone or something can change the content of data passed between two parties.

>> **Authentication:** Determining the identity of one or more parties.

>> **Nonrepudiation:** Reducing the ability of a party to say he or she didn't commit a particular act.

TIP

Because keeping a secret when using computers, the history of computer-based cryptographic algorithms is long and interesting. You can find a list of commonly used algorithms (both present and historical) at http://www.cryptographyworld. com/algo.htm and https://www.dwheeler.com/secure-programs/Secure-Programs-HOWTO/crypto.html. The guide at https://www.owasp.org/index. php/Guide_to_Cryptography provides additional details on how cryptography works.

Changing the Data Domain

The Fourier Transform and Fast Fourier Transform (FFT) make a huge difference in how applications perceive data. These two algorithms transform data from the frequency domain (how fast a signal oscillates) to the time domain (the time differential between signal changes). In fact, it's impossible to get any sort of computer hardware degree without having spent time working with these two algorithms extensively. Timing is everything.

REMEMBER

By knowing how often something changes, you can figure out the time interval between changes and therefore know how long you have to perform a task before a change in state requires that you do something else. These algorithms commonly see use in filters of all sorts. Without the filtering effects of these algorithms, reproducing video and audio faithfully through a streamed connection would be impossible. All these applications sound rather advanced, and they are, but some amazing tutorials give you a better sense of how these algorithms work (see the tutorial at http://w.astro.berkeley.edu/~jrg/ngst/fft/fft.html as an example). The tutorial at https://betterexplained.com/articles/an-interactive-guide-to-the-fourier-transform/ is possibly the most interesting and especially entertaining if you like smoothies.

Analyzing Links

The capability to analyze relationships is something that has made modern computing unique. In fact, the capability to first create a representation of these relationships and then analyze them is the subject of Part III of this book. The whole idea of the web, in fact, is to create connections, and connectivity was a consideration at the start of what has become a worldwide phenomenon. Without the capability to analyze and utilize links, applications such as databases and e-mail wouldn't work. You couldn't communicate well with friends on Facebook.

As the web has matured and people have become more in tune with devices that make connectivity both simpler and ubiquitous, applications such as Facebook and sales sites such as Amazon have made greater use of link analysis to do things like sell you more products. Of course, some of this connectivity has a negative outcome (see `http://www.pcmag.com/commentary/351623/facebook-a-tool-for-evil` as an example), but for the most part, link analysis does make it possible for people to remain better informed and in better contact with the world around them.

Of course, link analysis does more than inform in a connected sort of way. Consider the use of link analysis to provide driving directions or to find casual links between human activity and disease. Link analysis enables you to see the connection between things that you might not ordinarily consider but that do have an impact on your daily live. Because of link analysis, you might live longer because a doctor can advise you on which habits to change to correct issues that could become problems later. The point is that connections exist everywhere, and link analysis offers a method to determine where these connections exist and whether they're actually important.

Spotting Data Patterns

Data doesn't exist in a vacuum. All sorts of factors affect data, including biases that color how humans perceive data. Chapter 10 starts a discussion of how data tends to cluster in certain environments and how analysis of these clusters can tell you all sorts of things about the data.

TIP

Pattern analysis is at the forefront of some of the more amazing uses of computers today. For example, the Viola–Jones object detection framework makes real-time facial recognition possible. This algorithm could enable people to create better security in places like airports where nefarious individuals currently ply their trade. Similar algorithms could help your doctor detect cancers of various sorts long before the cancer is actually visible to the human eye. Earlier detection makes a full recovery a higher probability. The same holds true for all sorts of other medical problems (such as finding bone fractures that are currently too small to see but cause pain nonetheless).

You also find pattern recognition used for more mundane purposes. For example, pattern analysis lets people detect potential traffic problems before they occur. It's also possible to use pattern analysis to help farmers grow more food at a lower cost by applying water and fertilizer only when necessary. The use of pattern recognition can also help move drones around fields so that the farmer becomes more time efficient and can work more land at a lower cost. Without algorithms, these sorts of patterns, which have such a high impact on daily life, can't be recognized.

Dealing with Automation and Automatic Responses

The proportional integral derivative algorithm is quite a mouthful. Just try saying it three times fast! However, it's one of the most important secret algorithms you've never heard about, yet rely on every day. This particular algorithm relies on a control loop feedback mechanism to minimize the error between the desired output signal and the real output signal. You see it used all over the place to control automation and automatic responses. For example, when your car goes into a skid because you break too hard, this algorithm helps ensure that the Automatic Breaking System (ABS) actually works as intended. Otherwise, the ABS could overcompensate and make matters worse.

Just about every form of machinery today uses the proportional integral derivative algorithm. In fact, robotics wouldn't be possible without it. Imagine what would happen to a factory if all of the robots constantly overcompensated for every activity in which they engaged. The resulting chaos would quickly convince owners to stop using machines for any purpose whatsoever.

Creating Unique Identifiers

It seems as if we're all just a number. Actually, not just one number — lots and lots of numbers. Each of our credit cards has a number, as does our driver license, as does our government identifier, as do all sorts of other businesses and organizations. People actually have to keep lists of all of the numbers because they simply have too many to track. Yet, each of these numbers must identify the person uniquely to some party. Behind all of this uniqueness are various kinds of algorithms.

Chapter 7 discusses hashes, which are one way to ensure uniqueness. Underlying both hashes and cryptography is integer factorization, a kind of algorithm that breaks really large numbers into prime numbers. In fact, integer factorization is one of the hardest kinds of problems to solve with algorithms, but people are working on the problem all the time. So much of society today depends on your ability to identify yourself uniquely that the hidden secrets of creating these identifiers is an essential part of a modern world.

Chapter **22**

Ten Algorithmic Problems Yet to Solve

lgorithms have indeed been around for centuries, so you'd think that scientists would have discovered and solved every algorithm by now. Unfortunately, the opposite is true. Solving a particular algorithm often presents a few more questions that the algorithm doesn't solve and that didn't seem apparent until someone did come up with the solution. In addition, changes in technologies and lifestyle often present new challenges that call for yet more algorithms. For example, the connected nature of society and the use of robots have both increased the need for new algorithms.

As presented in Chapter 1, algorithms are a series of steps used to solve a problem, and you shouldn't confuse them with other entities, such as equations. An algorithm is never a solution in search of a problem. No one would create a series of steps to solve a problem that doesn't yet exist (or may never exist). In addition, many problems are interesting but have no pressing need for a solution. Consequently, even though everyone knows about the problem and understands that someone might want a solution for it, no one is in a hurry to create the solution.

This chapter is about algorithmic problems that would serve a purpose should someone find a solution for them. In short, the reason you need to care about this chapter is that you might find a problem that you'd really like to solve and might even decide to become part of the team that solves it.

Dealing with Text Searches

Many text searches involve the use of regular expressions — a sort of shorthand that tells the computer what to find. The grammar used for the regular expression depends on the language or application, but you find regular expressions used in a number of places, including word processors, email applications, search dialogs, and in all sorts of other places where you need to provide precise search terms for a range of text items. You can read more about regular expressions at http://www.regular-expressions.info/.

REMEMBER

One of the current problems with regular expressions is that it seems as if every application environment has a similar set of rules, but with just enough differences to make creating a search term hard. The generalized star-height problem seeks to discover whether a generalized regular expression syntax exists. If so, the resulting algorithm would make it possible for someone to learn just one method of creating regular expressions to perform searches. You can read more about this problem at https://www.irif.fr/~jep/Problemes/starheight.html.

Differentiating Words

When working with characters, a computer sees numbers, not letters. The numbers are actually just a series of 0s and 1s to the computer and don't actually have any meaning. Combining characters into strings just makes the series of 0s and 1s longer. Consequently, comparing two strings, something that a human can do at a glance, can take time within a computer, and confusion is likely between conjugates. For example, unless you're careful in constructing the algorithm, a computer could confuse *enlist* and *listen*. More important, the computer would require time to discern the difference between the two. The separating words problem seeks to find the smallest (and fastest) possible algorithm (a deterministic finite automaton, DFN, in this case) to perform word separation. The goal is to accept one word and reject another, given two words of a particular length.

Determining Whether an Application Will End

One of the problems that Alan Turing proposed in 1936 is the issue of whether an algorithm, given a description of a program and an input, could determine whether the program would eventually halt (the *halting problem*). When working with a simple application, it's easy to determine in many cases whether the program will halt or continue running in an endless loop. However, as program complexity increases, determining the result of running the program with any given input becomes harder. A Turing machine can't make this determination; the result is buggy code with infinite loops. No amount of testing that uses current technology can solve this issue.

REMEMBER

A *hypercomputer* is a computing model that goes beyond the Turing machine to solve problems such as the halting problem. However, such machines aren't possible using current technology. If they were possible, you would be able to ask them all kinds of imponderables that computers can't currently answer. The article at https://www.newscientist.com/article/mg22329781-500-what-will-hypercomputers-let-us-do-good-question/ provides you with a good idea of what would happen if someone were able to solve this problem.

Creating and Using One-Way Functions

A one-way function is a function that is easy to use to obtain an answer in one direction, but nearly impossible to use with the inverse of that answer. In other words, you use a one-way function to create something like a hash that would appear as part of a solution for cryptography, personal identification, authentication, or other data security needs.

REMEMBER

The existence of a one-way function is less mystery and more a matter of proof. Many telecommunications, e-commerce, and e-banking systems currently rely on functions that are purportedly one way, but no one truly knows whether they really are one way. The existence of a one-way function is currently a hypothesis, not a theory (see an explanation of the difference between the two at http://www.diffen.com/difference/Hypothesis_vs_Theory). If someone were able to prove that a one-way function exists, data security issues would be easier to solve from a programming perspective.

Multiplying Really Large Numbers

Really large numbers exist in many places. For example, consider performing the calculations involving distances to Mars, or perhaps Pluto. Methods currently do exist for performing multiplication on really large numbers, but they tend to be slow because they require multiple operations to complete. The problem occurs when the numbers are too large to fit in the processor's registers. At that point, the multiplication must occur in more than one step, which slows things considerably. The current solutions include:

>> Gauss's complex multiplication algorithm

>> Karatsuba multiplication

>> Toom-Cook

>> Fourier transform methods

Even though many of the methods currently available produce acceptable results, they all take time, and when you have a lot of calculations to perform, the time problem can become critical. Consequently, large number multiplication is one of those problems that requires a better solution than those available today.

Dividing a Resource Equally

Dividing resources equally may not seem hard, but humans, being the envious sort, might see the resource as being unequally divided unless you can find a way to assure everyone that the division is indeed fair. This is the envy-free cake-cutting problem. Of course, when you cut a cake, no matter how fairly you attempt to do it, there is always the perception that the division is unfair. Creating a fair division of resources is important in daily life to minimize strife between stakeholders in any organization, making everyone more efficient.

TIP

Two solutions already exist for the envy-free cake-cutting problem with a specific number of people, but no general solution exists. When there are two people involved, the first cuts the cake and the second chooses the first piece. In this way, both parties are assured of an equal division. The problem becomes harder with three people, but you can find the Selfridge-Conway solution for the problem at https://ochronus.com/cutting-the-pie (even though the site discusses pie, the process is the same). However, after you get to four people, no solution exists.

Reducing Edit Distance Calculation Time

The *edit distance* between two strings is the number of operations required to transform one string into the other string. The distance calculation revolves around the Levenshtein distance operations, which are the removal, insertion, or substitution of a character in the string. This particular technique sees use in natural language interfaces, DNA sequence quantification, and all sorts of other places where you can have two similar strings that require some sort of comparison or modification.

A number of solutions for this problem currently exist, all of them quite slow. In fact, most of them take exponential time, so the time required to perform a transformation quickly adds up to the point where humans can see pauses in the processing of input. The pause isn't quite so bad when using a word processor that performs automatic word checks and changes a misspelled word into the correct one. However, when using voice interfaces, the pause can become quite noticeable and cause the human operator to make mistakes. The current goal is to allow edit distance calculation in subquadratic time: $O(n^{2-c})$.

Solving Problems Quickly

As machine learning takes off and we count more and more on computers to solve problems, the issue of how quickly a computer can solve a problem becomes critical. The P versus NP problem simply asks whether a computer can solve a problem quickly when it can verify the solution to the problem quickly. In other words, if the computer can reasonably ascertain that a human response to a problem is correct in polynomial time or less, can it also solve the problem itself in polynomial time or less?

This question was originally discussed in the 1950s by John Nash in letters to the National Security Agency (NSA) and again in letters between Kurt Gödel and John von Neumann. In addition to machine learning (and AI in general), this particular problem is a concern to many other fields, including mathematics, cryptography, algorithm research, game theory, multimedia processing, philosophy, and economics.

Playing the Parity Game

At first, solving a game might not seem all that useful in real life. Yes, games are fun and interesting, but they don't really provide a background for doing anything useful — at least, that's the general theory. However, game theory does come into play in a large number of real-life scenarios, many of which involve complex processes that someone can understand more easily as games than as actual processes. In this case, the game helps people understand automated verification and controller synthesis, among other things. You can read more about the parity game at `http://www.sciencedirect.com/science/article/pii/S0890540115 000723`. In fact, you can play it if you'd like at `https://www.abefehr.com/ parity/`.

Understanding Spatial Issues

To put this particular problem into context, think about moving boxes around in a warehouse or some other situations in which you need to consider the space in which things move. Obviously, if you have many boxes in a big warehouse and they all require a forklift to pick up, you don't want to try to figure out how to store them optimally by physically rearranging them. This is where you need to work through the problem by visualizing a solution.

However, the question is whether all spatial problems have a solution. In this case, think about one of those kids' puzzles that has you putting a picture together by sliding the little tiles around. It seems as if a solution should exist in all cases, but in some situations, a bad starting point can result in a situation that has no solution. You can find a discussion of such a problem at `http://math.stack exchange.com/questions/754827/does-a-15-puzzle-always-have-a-solution`.

TIP

Mathematicians such as Sam Loyd (see `https://www.mathsisfun.com/puzzles/ sam-loyd-puzzles-index.html`) often use puzzles to demonstrate complex math problems, some of which have no solution today. Visiting these sites is fun because you not only get some free entertainment but also, food for thought. The issues that these puzzles raise do have practical applications, but they're presented in a fun way.

Index

A

A* algorithm, 35, 384–387
abscissa, 39
abstract machines, simulating using, 36–37
a-cyclic graph, 181
Adamszek, Anna and Michal (authors)
  "Combinatorics of the Change-Making Problem," 32
advanced matrix operations, 98–100
ALGOrithmic Language (ALGOL), 45
algorithms. *See also specific algorithms; specific topics*
  about, 9–11
  evaluating, 35–41
  finding, 14–15
  uses of, 11–14
  world-changing, 391–397
allclose function, 100
allowable errors, 239
Amazon Web Services (AWS), 18
Anaconda, 44
analysis of algorithms, 36
"The Anatomy of a LargeScale Hypertextual Web
  Search Engine" (Brin and Page), 210
Anderson, Chris (editor-in-chief), 231
annotation, 307
append( ) function, 87
approximating string search, 317–320
arcs, 157
arguments, 78–81
Aristotle (philosopher), 28
arithmetic operators, 70–71
ARMAC, 192
array function, 95
Artificial Intelligence: A Modern Approach (Russell and
  Norvig), 301
artificial neurons, 17
The Art of Computer Programming (Knuth), 13, 36, 43
asarray function, 97
ASCII system, 267
asmatrix function, 97

assignment operators, 69–70, 82
astronomy, big data and, 229
asynchronous outputs, parallelism and, 252
Atlantic City algorithms, 323
authorities, 211
automatic responses, 397
automation, 397
available data, leveraging, 18–19
AWS (Amazon Web Services), 18

B

Babbage, Charles (mathematician), 36
balanced trees, 128
Bayes' Theorem, 20–21
Bélády, László (computer scientist), 290–291
Bellman, Richard Ernest (mathematician), 299, 300
Bellman-Ford algorithm, 193
best-first search (BFS), 380
Bezzel, Max (chess expert), 345
BFS (best-first search), 380
BFS (breadth-first search), 34, 176–177, 343
bidirectional search, 34
big data
  about, 225–226
  characteristics of, 231
  streaming flows of, 232–248
  transforming power into, 226–232
Big O notation, 39–41, 111
binary heaps, 142–143, 146–147
binary max heap, 144
binary min heap, 144
binary search tree (BST), 143
binary search trees, building, 145–146
binary trees, creating, 146
binaryTree class, 127
bintrees, 145–146
bit streams, 268
bit vector, 240

convex hull algorithm, 359

cores, 252

costs, computing, 33–35

counterexamples, finding, 26–27

Count-Min Sketch algorithm, 151, 247–248

CPLEX, 364

CPUs, leveraging, 16

crawling, 209

Cray, Seymour (computer scientist), 251

create, read, update, and delete (CRUD), 133

create_random_solutions function, 350

CRUD (create, read, update, and delete), 133

cryptography, 14, 394–395

cubic complexity $O(n^3)$, 41

curly brackets ({}), 86

customer satisfaction, 292–293

cycles, 219

cyclic graph, 181

D

DAGs (Directed Acyclic Graphs), 181–182

damping factor, 219

Dantzig, George Bernard (mathematician), 357

Dantzig, Tobias (mathematician), 308

data. *See also* big data; compressing data; manipulating data

arranging, 133–152

comparing using Boolean expressions, 72–74

finding, 124–125, 208–210

finding using dictionaries, 124–125

indexing using dictionaries, 90

managing large amounts of, 250–258

matching, 117–118

patterns in, 396–397

searching, 133–152

sorting, 134–142, 392

storing using sets, lists, and tuples, 85–89

data duplication, 118–119

data structuring

about, 21–22, 115

determining need for, 116–121

graphing, 128–131

piling in order, 121–125

stacking in order, 121–125

trees, 125–128

datasets

downloading, 58–66

used in this book, 65–66

dates, interacting with, 76

dead ends, 219

deadlines, meeting, 293–294

decompression, 275

decorator, 305–306

default value, giving function arguments a, 80

degenerate matrix, 100

degree, 165

degrees of separation, 204–206

deletion, 317

dense graph, 182

depth-first search (DFS), 34, 177–179, 343, 380

deque function, 177

deques, 87

design

about, 23–24

computing costs, 33–35

dividing problems into small pieces, 28–30

evaluating algorithms, 35–41

finding solutions and counterexamples, 26–28

greedy algorithms, 31–32

heuristic approach, 33–35

modeling real-world problems, 25–26

Dewey Decimal System, 29–30

DFS (depth-first search), 34, 177–179, 343, 380

DFS (Distributed File System), 253

dictionaries, 86–87, 90, 124–125

difference( ), 86

Dijkstra algorithm, 194–196, 385

dimension, 95

Directed Acyclic Graphs (DAGs), 181–182

directed graph, 157, 181

discovered vertex, 174

display KeyValue function, 146

DisplayMulti( ) function, 84

DisplaySum( ) function, 80

distance measures, using as heuristics, 376–377

About the Authors

John Mueller is a freelance author and technical editor. He has writing in his blood, having produced 102 books and more than 600 articles to date. The topics range from networking to artificial intelligence and from database management to heads-down programming. Some of his current books include a book on Python for beginners, Python for data science, and a book about MATLAB. He has also written books about Amazon Web Services for Administrators, web application security, HTML5 development with JavaScript, and CSS3. His technical editing skills have helped more than 63 authors refine the content of their manuscripts. John has provided technical editing services to various technical magazines as well. It was during his time with *Data Based Advisor* that John was first exposed to MATLAB, and he has continued to follow the progress in MATLAB development ever since. During his time at Cubic Corporation, John was exposed to reliability engineering and has continued his interest in probability. Be sure to read John's blog at http://blog.johnmuellerbooks.com/.

When John isn't working at the computer, you can find him outside in the garden, cutting wood, or generally enjoying nature. John also likes making wine, baking cookies, and knitting. You can reach John on the Internet at John@JohnMueller Books.com. John is also setting up a website at http://www.johnmuellerbooks.com/. Feel free to take a look and make suggestions on how he can improve it.

Luca Massaron is a data scientist and marketing research director who is specialized in multivariate statistical analysis, machine learning, and customer insight, with more than a decade of experience in solving real-world problems and generating value for stakeholders by applying reasoning, statistics, data mining, and algorithms. Passionate about everything regarding data and analysis and about demonstrating the potentiality of data-driven knowledge discovery to both experts and non-experts, Luca is the coauthor of *Python for Data Science For Dummies* and *Machine Learning For Dummies.* Favoring simplicity over unnecessary sophistication, he believes that a lot can be achieved by understanding in simple terms and practicing the essentials of any discipline.

John's Dedication

This book is dedicated to Julie Thrond, a friend who is both faithful and kind. May she always win out against the struggles in life.

Luca's Dedication

I dedicate this book to my wife, Yukiko, whom I always find curious and ready to marvel at the wonders of this amazing and baffling world. Stay curious. Enjoy the surprise of both little and great things alike. Do not have fear of anything or let foolish details bother you. Stay young at heart forever. With love.

John's Acknowledgments

Thanks to my wife, Rebecca. Even though she is gone now, her spirit is in every book I write, in every word that appears on the page. She believed in me when no one else would.

Russ Mullen deserves thanks for his technical edit of this book. He greatly added to the accuracy and depth of the material you see here. Russ worked exceptionally hard helping with the research for this book by locating hard-to-find URLs and also offering a lot of suggestions. Matt Wagner, my agent, deserves credit for helping me get the contract in the first place and taking care of all the details that most authors don't really consider. I always appreciate his assistance. It's good to know that someone wants to help.

A number of people read all or part of this book to help me refine the approach, test scripts, and generally provide input that all readers wish they could have. These unpaid volunteers helped in ways too numerous to mention here. I especially appreciate the efforts of Eva Beattie, Glenn A. Russell, Alberto Boschetti, Cristian Mastrofrancesco, Diego Paladini, Dimitris Papadopoulos, Matteo Malosetti, Sebastiano Di Paola, Warren B, and Zacharias Voulgaris, who provided general input, read the entire book, and selflessly devoted themselves to this project.

Finally, I would like to thank Katie Mohr, Susan Christophersen, and the rest of the Wiley editorial and production staff for their unparalleled support of this writing effort.

Luca's Acknowledgments

My first greatest thanks to my family, Yukiko and Amelia, for their support, sacrifices, and loving patience during the long days/nights, weeks, and months I've been involved in working on this book.

I thank all the editorial and production staff at Wiley, in particular Katie Mohr and Susan Christophersen, for their great professionalism and support in all the phases of writing this book of the *For Dummies* series.

Publisher's Acknowledgments

Acquisitions Editor: Katie Mohr

Project and Copy Editor: Susan Christophersen

Technical Editor: Russ Mullen

Editorial Assistant: Serena Novosel

Sr. Editorial Assistant: Cherie Case

Production Editor: Selvakumaran Rajendiran

Cover Image: © Nobi_Prizue/iStockphoto